Routing TCP/IP, Volume II

CCIE Professional Development, Second Edition

Jeff Doyle

Cisco Press

800 East 96th Street

Indianapolis, IN 46240

Routing TCP/IP, Volume II

CCIE Professional Development, Second Edition

Jeff Doyle

Copyright© 2017 Cisco Systems, Inc.

Published by:
Cisco Press
800 East 96th Street
Indianapolis, IN 46240 USA

Printed in the United States of America

1   16

Library of Congress Control Number: 2016936742

ISBN-13: 978-1-58705-470-9
ISBN-10: 1-58705-470-1

Warning and Disclaimer

This book is designed to provide information about routing TCP/IP. Every effort has been made to make this book as complete and as accurate as possible, but no warranty or fitness is implied.

The information is provided on an "as is" basis. The authors, Cisco Press, and Cisco Systems, Inc. shall have neither liability nor responsibility to any person or entity with respect to any loss or damages arising from the information contained in this book or from the use of the discs or programs that may accompany it.

The opinions expressed in this book belong to the author and are not necessarily those of Cisco Systems, Inc.

Trademark Acknowledgments

All terms mentioned in this book that are known to be trademarks or service marks have been appropriately capitalized. Cisco Press or Cisco Systems, Inc., cannot attest to the accuracy of this information. Use of a term in this book should not be regarded as affecting the validity of any trademark or service mark.

Special Sales

For information about buying this title in bulk quantities, or for special sales opportunities (which may include electronic versions; custom cover designs; and content particular to your business, training goals, marketing focus, or branding interests), please contact our corporate sales department at corpsales@pearsoned.com or (800) 382-3419.

For government sales inquiries, please contact governmentsales@pearsoned.com.

For questions about sales outside the U.S., please contact intlcs@pearson.com.

Feedback Information

At Cisco Press, our goal is to create in-depth technical books of the highest quality and value. Each book is crafted with care and precision, undergoing rigorous development that involves the unique expertise of members from the professional technical community.

Readers' feedback is a natural continuation of this process. If you have any comments regarding how we could improve the quality of this book, or otherwise alter it to better suit your needs, you can contact us through email at feedback@ciscopress.com. Please make sure to include the book title and ISBN in your message.

We greatly appreciate your assistance.

Editor-in-Chief: Mark Taub

Product Line Manager: Brett Bartow

Alliances Manager, Cisco Press: Ron Fligge

Managing Editor: Sandra Schroeder

Development Editor: Christopher Cleveland

Project Editor: Deadline Driven Publishing

Copy Editor: Deadline Driven Publishing

Technical Editors: Darien Hirotsu, Pete Moyer

Editorial Assistant: Vanessa Evans

Cover Designer: Chuti Prasertsith

Composition: Patricia Ratcliff

Indexer: Angie Martin

Proofreader: Deadline Driven Publishing

CISCO

Americas Headquarters	Asia Pacific Headquarters	Europe Headquarters
Cisco Systems, Inc.	Cisco Systems (USA) Pte. Ltd.	Cisco Systems International BV
San Jose, CA	Singapore	Amsterdam, The Netherlands

Cisco has more than 200 offices worldwide. Addresses, phone numbers, and fax numbers are listed on the Cisco Website at **www.cisco.com/go/offices**.

CCDE, CCENT, Cisco Eos, Cisco HealthPresence, the Cisco logo, Cisco Lumin, Cisco Nexus, Cisco StadiumVision, Cisco TelePresence, Cisco WebEx, DCE, and Welcome to the Human Network are trademarks; Changing the Way We Work, Live, Play, and Learn and Cisco Store are service marks; and Access Registrar, Aironet, AsyncOS, Bringing the Meeting To You, Catalyst, CCDA, CCDP, CCIE, CCIP, CCNA, CCNP, CCSP, CCVP, Cisco, the Cisco Certified Internetwork Expert logo, Cisco IOS, Cisco Press, Cisco Systems, Cisco Systems Capital, the Cisco Systems logo, Cisco Unity, Collaboration Without Limitation, EtherFast, EtherSwitch, Event Center, Fast Step, Follow Me Browsing, FormShare, GigaDrive, HomeLink, Internet Quotient, IOS, iPhone, iQuick Study, IronPort, the IronPort logo, LightStream, Linksys, MediaTone, MeetingPlace, MeetingPlace Chime Sound, MGX, Networkers, Networking Academy, Network Registrar, PCNow, PIX, PowerPanels, ProConnect, ScriptShare, SenderBase, SMARTnet, Spectrum Expert, StackWise, The Fastest Way to Increase Your Internet Quotient, TransPath, WebEx, and the WebEx logo are registered trademarks of Cisco Systems, Inc. and/or its affiliates in the United States and certain other countries.

All other trademarks mentioned in this document or website are the property of their respective owners. The use of the word partner does not imply a partnership relationship between Cisco and any other company. (0812R)

About the Author

Jeff Doyle, CCIE No. 1919, is vice president of research at Fishtech Labs. Specializing in IP routing protocols, SDN/NFV, data center fabrics, MPLS, and IPv6, Jeff has designed or assisted in the design of large-scale IP service provider and enterprise networks in 26 countries over 6 continents. He worked with early IPv6 adopters in Japan, China, and South Korea, and has advised service providers, government agencies, military contractors, equipment manufacturers, and large enterprises on best-practice IPv6 deployment. He now advises large enterprises on evolving data center infrastructures, SDN, and SD-WAN.

Jeff is the author of *CCIE Professional Development: Routing TCP/IP*, Volumes I and II and *OSPF and IS-IS: Choosing an IGP for Large-Scale Networks*; a co-author of *Software Defined Networking: Anatomy of OpenFlow*; and an editor and contributing author of *Juniper Networks Routers: The Complete Reference*. He also writes for *Forbes* and blogs for both *Network World* and *Network Computing*. Jeff is one of the founders of the Rocky Mountain IPv6 Task Force, is an IPv6 Forum Fellow, and serves on the executive board of the Colorado chapter of the Internet Society (ISOC).

Jeff lives in Westminster, Colorado, with his wife Sara and a Sheltie named Max, the Forrest Gump of the dog world. Jeff and Sara count themselves especially fortunate that their four grown children and a growing herd of grandchildren all live within a few miles.

About the Contributing Authors

Khaled W. Abuelenain, CCIE No. 27401, is currently the consulting director for Acuative, a Cisco Certified Managed Services Master Partner, at the company's EMEA office in Saudi Arabia. He is a certified double CCIE (R&S, SP), holds a B.Sc. degree in electronics and communication engineering from Ain Shams University, Egypt, and is an IEEE member since 1997. Khaled has been designing, operating, or optimizing large-scale networks for more than 14 years throughout the Middle East, typically for service providers and mobile operators with multinational presence, banks, and government agencies. He has extensive experience in routing, BGP, MPLS, and IPv6. Khaled is also an expert on data center technologies and network programmability, with a special interest in Python programming for SDN solutions. He is an active member of both the Cloud Computing and SDN IEEE societies.

Nicolas Michel, dual CCIE No. 29410 R/S and DC, is a network architect with 10 years of experience in several fields: routing switching, data center, and unified communications. Nicolas is a former Sergeant in the French Air Force and started to work as a network engineer during the time he was serving. He has worked on several NATO-related projects.

He decided to move to Switzerland in 2011, to work for the local leading networking consulting company.

He was the principal UC architect for the UEFA EURO 2016 football tournament.

Nicolas is also an eager reader about emerging network technologies (SDN, Automation/Network programmability). He blogs at http://vpackets.net and is also a president for a nongovernmental organization that helps children with autism.

He participates in an open source network simulation project: http://www.unetlab.com/.

Nicolas is actually trying to relocate to the United States.

From Nicolas: I would like to dedicate the work I have done on this book to my wonderful wife who has supported me throughout my career and helps me become a better engineer and a better man. I wouldn't be the same man without her.

Also I would like to dedicate this work to my kids and my parents, who taught me to never give up and to enjoy every moment.

Finally, I would express my heartfelt thanks to Jeff Doyle for giving me the opportunity to work on this project. I learned so many things and I still can't believe how lucky I was.

About the Technical Reviewers

Darien Hirotsu is a networking professional who has been in the industry for nearly a decade working on service provider, data center, and enterprise networks. He earned a master's degree in network engineering from UC Santa Cruz and a bachelor's degree in electrical engineering from Cal Poly San Luis Obispo. He also holds multiple expert level certifications, and is equally passionate about both the software and networking parts of SDN.

Darien would like to send extra special thanks to his fiancé Rebecca Nguyen. Editing this book was both rewarding and time consuming. During the whole process and through the long weekends, Rebecca's love, support, and patience never wavered, and for that, he will always be grateful. Thank you for everything you do, Rebecca!

Pete Moyer is an old-timer IP/MPLS consulting engineer who has turned his focus toward SDN in recent years. He has multivendor experience in IP networking, having earned the first awarded JNCIE in the early 2000s and his CCIE in the late 1990s. He is a co-author and technical editor of several networking books on IP and SDN and has authored many articles and blogs on various networking topics. His current focus is on large-scale data center and service provider networks, including the Research & Education Network (REN) market. He also holds a B.S. degree in CMIS from the University of Maryland.

Dedications

This book is dedicated to my wife Sara; my children, Anna, Carol, James, and Katherine; and my grandchildren, Claire, Caroline, and Sam. They are my refuge, and they keep me sane, humble, and happy.

Acknowledgments

An author of a technical book is just a front for a small army of brilliant, dedicated people. This book is no exception. At the risk of sounding like I'm making an Academy Award acceptance speech, I would like to thank a number of those people.

I would like to thank Khaled Abu El Enian and Nicolas Michel, who contributed many new end-of-chapter configuration and troubleshooting exercises. Khaled also helped me out in a time crunch and wrote most sections in "Scaling BGP Functions" in Chapter 5, "Scaling BGP." I hope we can collaborate even closer on a future book or two.

I would also like to thank Pete Moyer, my longtime friend and associate, who has been a technical reviewer for every book I've written alone and has been a co-author on several other books. Pete has had a profound influence on my life beyond this and other book projects, and I will always be indebted to him.

Darien Hirotsu is the other technical reviewer on this book, and it's the first time we have worked together on a book project, although we have been associates across multiple companies and engineering projects. Darien is astoundingly detail-oriented and caught countless tiny errors throughout my manuscript.

My gratitude goes to Chris Cleveland for his expert guidance as development editor. We have collaborated on multiple books, and he has made each one a better book and me a better writer.

Thanks to Brett Bartow and all the folks at Cisco Press. Brett has shown superhuman patience with me as the book schedule constantly fell victim to "day job" priorities. He has continued to show me great kindness throughout the project when I'm sure he would have preferred to bash me on the head with a copy of Volume I.

I would like to thank my wife Sara, who has lived with me juggling multiple writing projects over many years. She long ago learned what it means when she notices me staring blankly at nothing, and says, "You're writing in your head again, aren't you?"

Finally, I would like to thank you, good reader, for making the two volumes of *Routing TCP/IP* such a success and for waiting so patiently for me to finish this new edition. I hope the book proves to be worth your wait.

Contents at a Glance

Contents

Command Syntax Conventions

The conventions used to present command syntax in this book are the same conventions used in the IOS Command Reference. The Command Reference describes these conventions as follows:

- **Boldface** indicates commands and keywords that are entered literally as shown. In actual configuration examples and output (not general command syntax), boldface indicates commands that are manually input by the user (such as a **show** command).

- *Italic* indicates arguments for which you supply actual values.

- Vertical bars (|) separate alternative, mutually exclusive elements.

- Square brackets ([ ]) indicate an optional element.

- Braces ({ }) indicate a required choice.

- Braces within brackets ([{ }]) indicate a required choice within an optional element.

Introduction

Since the publication of Volume I of *Routing TCP/IP*, many volumes have been added to the Cisco Press CCIE Professional Development series. And the CCIE program has expanded to include various areas of specialization. Yet the IP routing protocols remain the essential foundation on which CCIE candidates must build their expertise. If the foundation is weak, the house will tumble.

I stated in the introduction to Volume I that "...as internetworks grow in size and complexity, routing issues can become at once both large and subtle." Scalability and management of growth continues to be a central theme in this second volume, as we move beyond the interior gateway protocols to examine both inter-autonomous system routing and more exotic routing issues such as multicasting and IPv6.

My objective in this book is not only to help you walk away from the CCIE lab exam with one of those valued and valuable numbers after your name, but also to help you develop the knowledge and skills to live up to the CCIE title. As with the first volume, I want to make CCIEs, not people who can pass the CCIE lab. In this vein, you can find in this book more information than you need to pass the lab, but certainly all the material is important in your career as a recognized internetworking expert.

When I earned my CCIE, the lab still consisted mostly of AGS+ routers. Certainly, the lab and the nature of the exam has changed substantially since that ancient time. If anything, the lab is more difficult now. Another addition to the CCIE program has been the recertification requirement. Even before I took the recertification exam for the first time, people told me how much Volume I helped them prepare for the test—particularly for IS-IS, a protocol that few outside of service provider environments are exposed to. I have therefore written this second volume with not only CCIE candidates in mind, but also existing CCIEs who need to review for their recertification. The chapters on multicasting and IPv6 are directed to this audience.

I have endeavored to follow the same structure that I followed in Volume I, in which a protocol is introduced in generic terms, followed by examples of configuring the protocol using Cisco IOS, and finally by examples of IOS tools for troubleshooting the protocol. For BGP and IP multicast, this structure is far too lengthy for a single chapter and therefore spans multiple chapters.

I hope you learn as much from reading this book as I have writing it.

Introduction to the Second Edition

Almost from the moment the first edition of this volume went to print in 2001, I've wanted to add to it and, in some cases, change it. Some of that motivation came from my growing experience. Between 1998 and 2010, I worked almost exclusively with service providers and carriers, and I learned something new with almost every design project, technical discussion, and seminar I led or participated in. Certainly, some of this new knowledge just filled gaps in my own experience, but not all of it. I also learned along with the rest of the networking industry as BGP and multicast networks became more sophisticated, as new capabilities were added, and as best practices evolved.

What's Changed in the Industry?

The following sections outline what has changed in the industry since the first edition of this book was published.

BGP

All the core concepts of BGP were already around when the first edition of this book was released in 2001. It was the external gateway protocol—or inter-autonomous system routing protocol— used throughout the Internet. It had multiprotocol capabilities. Version 4 was the accepted version. Although a number of useful new features and capabilities have been added since then, the protocol itself actually hasn't changed that much.

What has changed is the industry experience with BGP. This has enhanced the way policies are used and has enhanced and in some cases changed accepted best practices. And multiprotocol BGP has become the workhorse of multiservice core networks, with quite a few new address families defined so that you can run a multitude of different services over a single shared core. I don't cover the other essential element of multiservice networks in this book—Multiprotocol Label Switching (MPLS)—because the subject can easily fill one or two volumes by itself. But you can learn enough about multiprotocol BGP here to understand how it supports the various MPLS-based address families. And you see plenty of examples in this book of multiprotocol BGP support for both unicast and multicast address families under both IPv4 and IPv6.

The first edition of this book had a chapter on EGP, the predecessor to BGP. Although obsolete even then, the protocol still existed in some obscure government networks. So I covered it both for that reason and just in case some devious lab proctor decided to throw a few EGP problems at you on the CCIE exam. The protocol is now most sincerely dead and is covered in this edition only from a historical context to introduce BGP.

Reflecting the expanded industry experience of BGP and many new features Cisco added to its support, the two chapters on BGP in the first edition is now six chapters in this edition.

IP Multicast

IP multicast networking has probably changed more than BGP networking has. Multicast and the associated routing protocols were complicated, and the networks were difficult to manage in 2001. To some degree that is still true, but also some changes make it not quite so difficult.

In 2001, the most common multicast routing protocols were DVMRP, PIM-DM, and PIM-SM. But I suspected that Core-Based Trees (CBT) and Multiprotocol OSPF

(MOSPF) might become mainstream, so I covered those protocols. However, CBT and MOSPF never found acceptance, and DVMRP has become the RIP of multicast routing protocol—obsolete but still encountered on rare occasions. As a result, CBT and MOSPF are dropped from this edition in all but passing mention, and DVMRP is covered in much less detail than it was in the first edition.

PIM is now the accepted multicast routing protocol for both IPv4 and IPv6, so PIM-DM and PIM-SM, along with PIM-SSM, are covered in more depth than they were in the first edition.

IPv6

I have been advocating IPv6 since the late 1990s; although by 2001, most interest in this new version of IP was limited to Japan, the People's Republic of China, and the Republic of Korea. Little interest was shown in the United States or Europe outside of a few military circles. IPv6 was for the most part out in the unforeseen future. Anyone predicting that the public IPv4 address pools would begin being depleted as soon as 2012 was considered a Chicken Little and probably more than a little ridiculous. So the first edition included a standalone chapter on IPv6 with little relation to the other topics in the book.

What a difference 15 years have made. IPv6 is now a mainstream protocol, and I predict that in not too many more years it will displace the now depleted IPv4. Reflecting this new reality, there is no standalone IPv6 chapter in this edition. Instead, IPv6 support is discussed in the context of BGP and IP multicast.

Network address translation in 2001 meant NAT-PT and always translation only between different IPv4 addresses. The technology has expanded since then, so now two chapters are included on NAT: one on IPv4-to-IPv4 translation and one on IPv6-to-IPv4 translation (NAT64).

What's Changed in This Edition?

The last chapter difference you'll find in this second edition is the elimination of the first-edition chapter on router management (Chapter 9 in the first edition). The subject of managing Cisco routers has expanded greatly since 2001, as have the number of routing platforms Cisco offers, and doing the topic justice would take more room than appropriate for this book. In addition, the book is titled *Routing TCP/IP* after all, not Managing Cisco *Routers*.

Following are other changes in this edition:

- **IOS:** IOS was the only Cisco router operating system in 2001. Now, in addition to IOS, we have IOS-XR, IOS-XE, and NX-OS. Trying to cover configuration examples and exercises under all these different systems would be confusing and complex, and would distract from the primary goal of the two volumes of *Routing TCP/IP*, which is to teach the protocols. So you'll find only IOS in this book. If you understand the topics covered here, you can easily make the jump to any of the other Cisco operating systems.

- **Cisco versus IOS:** Related to the previous bullet, in the first edition, I usually referred to "Cisco commands." Because of the multiple operating systems Cisco now offers, I try to be more specific in this edition and say "IOS commands."

- **Commands versus statements:** Again related to the previous bullet, I have endeavored in this edition to differentiate between an IOS command and an IOS statement. A command, in this edition, means something you enter and expect to get an immediate result, such as a **show** command. A statement, however, is a part of an IOS configuration that influences the router's operational state.

- **Command Reference:** The first edition included a tabular listing at the end of each chapter of the commands (and statements) covered in the chapter in their full syntax with a description of each. So many commands (and statements) are covered now, and in some cases with so many variations among different IOS versions, that the table became long and unwieldy. So there is no end-of-chapter Command Reference here. If you want the full syntax of a command (or...ahem...statement) you can easily look it up in the online *Cisco Command Reference Guide* for the IOS version you use. And speaking of versions....

- **IOS versions:** I used IOS 11.4 for most of the examples in the first edition. As you surely know, there have been many IOS releases since then. In a few cases, I have reused some outputs from the first edition, but in most cases I have used more recent 12.4 or 15.0. In all cases, I have ensured that the captured configurations or outputs include the information discussed; however, your outputs might look different in some cases depending on the version you use. You should focus on finding the relevant information in an output, not on whether it looks exactly the same as what I show you.

- **Integrated troubleshooting:** In Volume I of *Routing TCP/IP*, each chapter followed a set format of providing a generic technical overview of the chapter subject, a section on how to configure it in IOS, and then a section on troubleshooting it. The BGP and IP multicast chapters in this second volume are each complicated enough and cover so much ground that the better approach is to integrate troubleshooting examples into the general configuration examples.

- **Network versus internetwork:** This is a trivial change. In 2001, I tried to be precise in my definitions, so a network meant a common communications media such as Ethernet, whereas an internetwork was any number of networks connected by routers. That's now old-fashioned usage. Hardly anyone says *internetwork* any more, except in a few precise cases. As a result, I've tried to kill the word off in this edition. *Subnet* has a more logical and address-related meaning than shared communications medium, and *network* is understood from the context in which the word is used. So *network* might mean anything from two routers connected by a serial or Ethernet link to a massive inter-AS system such as the Internet. It might be less precise, but it's what people use in everyday router-nerd conversations. Speaking of trivial changes....

■ **Those weird zig-zag serial link icons:** Serial links have been represented with a zig-zag or "lightning-shaped" line since before I was teaching Cisco classes in the early 1990s. There was a reason for the distinction because serial links behaved differently than LAN links. But in the examples throughout this volume, the link type is irrelevant to the example. And I've found that the zig-zag icon often clutters an illustration. So I've tried to eliminate those icons throughout this book and just use a straight link for a connection between interfaces, regardless of what kind of connection it is.

Answers to Configuration and Troubleshooting Exercises

There are two appendixes you will need to download to review the answers to the configuration and troubleshooting exercises: Appendix B, "Answers to Configuration Exercises," and Appendix C, "Answers to Troubleshooting Exercises."

You can find these appendixes online by registering your book at www.ciscopress.com/ register. Simply log in to the site, enter the book ISBN on this page (9781587054709), and answer the security question presented to register the book. Once the book is registered, you will be able to download the files by going to your account page, opening the Registered Products tab, and selecting the Access Bonus Content link.

Chapter 1

Inter-Domain Routing Concepts

Imagine what today's Internet would be like if the whole thing was routed by a single routing protocol such as OSPF or IS-IS. The visibility of every subnet address would make stability almost impossible. Security would be a nightmare because an attack against the routing protocol—or even an innocent configuration error—could bring down the entire Internet. And who would administer it? How would we coordinate an upgrade or enhancement of the protocol among all the network administrators around the world?

As the ARPANET, the precursor to the modern Internet, began growing large in the late 1970s, these issues were quite real, and efforts were begun to create a scalable way to manage the network. The fundamental concepts that arose from this work were the ideas of administrative domains called *autonomous systems (AS)*, which define the boundaries of networks under a common administration, and a protocol that could route among these domains: a routing protocol that is *exterior* to the administrative domains.

The protocol now used for routing among autonomous systems is the Border Gateway Protocol (BGP). Chapters 2 through 6 describe the function, configuration, and troubleshooting of BGP and its associated routing policies. But before going there, this first chapter introduces you to the key concepts behind BGP and how they evolved. Said differently, Chapters 2 through 6 give you the *how* whereas this chapter gives you the *what* and the *why*.

Early Inter-Domain Routing: The Exterior Gateway Protocol (EGP)

The first edition of this book committed its entire first chapter to examining the Exterior Gateway Protocol (EGP), the precursor to BGP. Even at that time, the protocol was almost obsolete and was used only in a few quite old networks. In the intervening years, the protocol has completed its slide into obsolescence and is no longer supported in IOS.

Yet EGP still offers insights into the first steps made toward a workable inter-domain (or inter-AS) routing protocol. This section, then, takes a look at EGP as a technical history lesson to help you better understand the lessons learned from it that guided the development of BGP. You can skip this section if you like, but several essential concepts introduced here carry over to BGP, and several functions help you understand some of the concepts behind BGP's design.

Origins of EGP

In the early 1980s, the gateways (routers) that made up the ARPANET ran a distance vector routing protocol known as the *Gateway-to-Gateway Protocol (GGP)*. Every gateway knew a route to every reachable network, at a distance measured in gateway hops. As the ARPANET grew, its architects foresaw the same problem that administrators of many growing networks encounter today: Their routing protocol did not scale well.

Eric Rosen, in RFC 827, chronicles the scalability problems:

- With all gateways knowing all routes, "The overhead of the routing algorithm becomes excessively large." Whenever a topology change occurs, the frequency of which increases with the size of the network, all gateways have to exchange routing information and recalculate their forwarding tables. Even when the network is in a steady state, the size of the routing tables and routing updates becomes an increasing burden.

- As the number of GGP software implementations increases, and the hardware platforms on which they are implemented become more diverse, "It becomes impossible to regard the Internet as an integrated communications system." Specifically, maintenance and troubleshooting become "nearly impossible."

- As the number of gateways grows, so does the number of gateway administrators. As a result, resistance to software upgrades increases: "[A]ny proposed change must be made in too many different places by too many different people."

The solution Rosen proposed in RFC 827 was that the ARPANET be migrated from a single network to a system of interconnected, autonomously controlled networks. Within each network, known as an autonomous system (AS), the administrative authority for that AS is free to manage the network as it chooses. In effect, the concept of autonomous systems broadens the scope of internetworking and adds a new layer of hierarchy. Where there was a single internetwork—a network of networks—there is now a network of autonomous systems, each of which is itself an internetwork. And just as a network from the borders of the AS down to individual subnets is identified by an IP address, an AS is identified by an autonomous system number. An AS number is a 16-bit number assigned by the same addressing authority that assigns IP addresses.

Note   Also like IP addresses, some AS numbers are reserved for private use. These numbers range from 64512 to 65535. See RFC 6996 for more information.

And just as IPv6 is implemented to eliminate the problem of IPv4 address shortages, RFC 4893 (now obsoleted by RFC 6793) proposes 32-bit AS numbers to prevent a shortage of 16-bit AS numbers. The use of 32-bit AS numbers is discussed in Chapter 5, "Scaling BGP."

Chief among the choices the administrative authority of each AS is free to make is the routing protocol that its gateways run. Because the gateways are interior to the AS, their routing protocols are known as *interior gateway protocols (IGP)*. Because GGP was the routing protocol of the ARPANET, it became by default the first IGP. However, interest in the more modern (and simpler) *Routing Information Protocol (RIP)*[1] was building in 1982, and it was expected that this and other as-yet-unplanned protocols would be used in many autonomous systems. These days, GGP has been completely replaced by RIP, RIP-2, RIPng, Enhanced IGRP (EIGRP), Open Shortest Path First (OSPF) versions 2 and 3, and Integrated Intermediate System-to-Intermediate System (IS-IS).

Each AS is connected to other autonomous systems via one or more exterior gateways. RFC 827 proposes that the exterior gateways share routing information between each other by means of a protocol known as the EGP. Contrary to popular belief (well, popular when there were still people working with the protocol), although EGP is a distance vector protocol, it is not a routing protocol. It has no algorithm for choosing an optimal path between networks; rather, it is a common language that exterior gateways use to exchange *reachability information* with other exterior gateways. That reachability information is a simple list of major network addresses (no subnets) and the gateways by which they can be reached.

Operation of EGP

Version 1 of EGP was proposed in RFC 827. Version 2, slightly modified from version 1, was proposed in RFC 888, and the formal specification of EGPv2 is given in RFC 904.

EGP Topology Issues

EGP messages are exchanged between EGP neighbors, or *peers*.[2] If the neighbors are in the same AS, they are *interior neighbors*. If they are in different autonomous systems,

---

[1] As the 1982 date indicates, RIP is no longer modern and there is little or no reason you should be running it as your primary IGP. As one wit stated in a North American Network Operators Group meeting, "RIP now stands for Rest In Peace."

[2] Neighbor and peer are used interchangeably throughout this book, but they do have a subtle difference: Neighbors are two routers running a routing protocol session directly between them, whereas peers are two neighbors sharing reachability information over that session.

they are *exterior neighbors*. EGP has no function that automatically discovers its neighbors; the addresses of the neighbors are manually configured, and the messages they exchange are unicast to the configured addresses.

RFC 888 suggests that the Time-To-Live (TTL) of EGP messages be set to a low number because an EGP message should never travel farther than to a single neighbor. However, nothing in the EGP functionality requires EGP neighbors to share a common data link. For example, Figure 1-1 shows two EGP neighbors separated by a router that speaks only RIP. Because EGP messages are unicast to neighbors rather than broadcast or multicast, they can cross router boundaries. These concepts of interior and exterior peers and of unicast messages are essential to understand because they are also used by BGP.

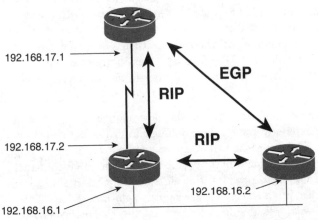

Figure 1-1   *EGP Neighbors Do Not Have to Be Connected to the Same Network*

EGP gateways are either *core* gateways or *stub* gateways. Both gateway types can accept information about networks in other autonomous systems, but a stub gateway is restricted to sending information about networks in its own AS. Only core gateways can send information they have learned about networks in autonomous systems other than their own.

To understand why EGP defines core and stub gateways, you need to understand the architectural limitations of EGP. As previously mentioned, EGP is not a routing protocol. Its updates list only reachable networks, without including enough information to determine shortest paths or to prevent routing loops. Therefore, the EGP topology must be built with no loops.

Figure 1-2 shows an EGP topology. There is a single core AS to which all other autonomous systems (stub autonomous systems) must attach. This two-level tree topology is similar to the two-level topology requirements of OSPF, and its purpose is the same. Recall from *Routing TCP/IP*, Volume I that inter-area OSPF routing is essentially a distance vector and therefore vulnerable to routing loops. Requiring all traffic between nonbackbone OSPF areas to traverse the backbone area reduces the potential for routing loops by forcing a loop-free inter-area topology. Likewise, requiring all EGP reachability information between stub autonomous systems to traverse the core, AS reduces the potential for routing loops in the EGP topology.

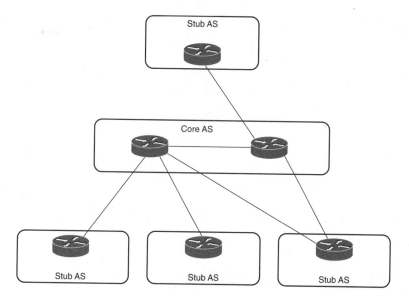

Figure 1-2 *To Prevent Routing Loops, Only Core Gateways Can Send Information Learned from One AS to Another AS*

EGP Functions

EGP consists of the following three mechanisms:

- Neighbor Acquisition Protocol
- Neighbor Reachability Protocol
- Network Reachability Protocol

These three mechanisms use ten message types to establish a neighbor relationship, maintain the neighbor relationship, exchange network reachability information with the neighbor, and notify the neighbor of procedural or formatting errors. Table 1-1 lists all the EGP message types and the mechanism that use each message type.

Table 1-1   *EGP Message Types*

Message Type	Mechanism
Neighbor Acquisition Request	Neighbor Acquisition
Neighbor Acquisition Confirm	Neighbor Acquisition
Neighbor Acquisition Refuse	Neighbor Acquisition
Neighbor Cease	Neighbor Acquisition
Neighbor Cease Acknowledgment	Neighbor Acquisition
Hello	Neighbor Reachability
I-Heard-You	Neighbor Reachability
Poll	Network Reachability
Update	Network Reachability
Error	All functions

The following sections provide an overview of each of the three EGP mechanisms.

Neighbor Acquisition Protocol

Before EGP neighbors can exchange reachability information, they must establish that they are compatible. This function is performed by a simple two-way handshake in which one neighbor sends a Neighbor Acquisition Request message, and the other neighbor responds with a Neighbor Acquisition Confirm message.

None of the RFCs specify how two EGP neighbors initially discover each other. In practice, an EGP gateway learns of its neighbor by manual configuration of the neighbor's IP address. The gateway then unicasts an Acquisition Request message to the configured neighbor. The message states a *Hello interval*, the minimum interval between Hello messages that the gateway is willing to accept from the neighbor, and a *Poll interval*, the minimum interval that the gateway is willing to be polled by the neighbor for routing updates. The neighbor's responding Acquisition Confirm message contains its own values for the same two intervals. If the neighbors agree on the values, they are ready to exchange network reachability information.

When a gateway first learns of a neighbor, it considers the neighbor to be in the *Idle* state. Before sending the first Acquisition Request, the gateway transitions the neighbor to the *Acquire* state; when the gateway receives an Acquisition Confirm, it transitions the neighbor to the *Down* state.

Note   See RFC 904 for a complete explanation of the EGP finite state machine.

A gateway can refuse to accept a neighbor by responding with a Neighbor Acquisition Refuse message rather than an Acquisition Confirm message. The Refuse message can include a reason for the refusal, such as a lack of table space, or it can refuse for an unspecified reason.

A gateway can also break an established neighbor relationship by sending a Neighbor Cease message. As with the Refuse message, the originating gateway has the option of including a reason for the Cease or leaving the reason unspecified. A neighbor receiving a Neighbor Cease message responds with a Neighbor Cease Acknowledgment.

The last case of a Neighbor Acquisition procedure is a case in which a gateway sends an Acquisition Request but the neighbor does not respond. RFC 888 suggests retransmitting the Acquisition message "at a reasonable rate, perhaps every 30 seconds or so." The Cisco now-defunct EGP implementation does not just repeat unacknowledged messages over a constant period. Rather, it retransmits an unacknowledged Acquisition message 30 seconds after the original transmission. It then waits 60 seconds before the next transmission. If no response is received within 30 seconds of the third transmission, the gateway transitions the neighbor state from Acquire to Idle (see Example 1-1). The gateway remains in the Idle state for 300 seconds (5 minutes) and then transitions to Acquire and starts the process all over.

Note   The EGP examples shown throughout these sections are from IOS 12.1.

Example 1-1   debug ip egp transactions *Command Output Displays EGP State Transitions*

```
Shemp#debug ip egp transactions
EGP debugging is on
Shemp#
EGP: 192.168.16.2 going from IDLE to ACQUIRE
EGP: from 192.168.16.1 to 192.168.16.2, version=2, asystem=1, sequence=0
    Type=ACQUIRE, Code=REQUEST, Status=0 (UNSPECIFIED), Hello=60, Poll=180
EGP: from 192.168.16.1 to 192.168.16.2, version=2, asystem=1, sequence=0
    Type=ACQUIRE, Code=REQUEST, Status=0 (UNSPECIFIED), Hello=60, Poll=180
EGP: from 192.168.16.1 to 192.168.16.2, version=2, asystem=1, sequence=0
    Type=ACQUIRE, Code=REQUEST, Status=0 (UNSPECIFIED), Hello=60, Poll=180
EGP: 192.168.16.2 going from ACQUIRE to IDLE
EGP: 192.168.16.2 going from IDLE to ACQUIRE
EGP: from 192.168.16.1 to 192.168.16.2, version=2, asystem=1, sequence=0
    Type=ACQUIRE, Code=REQUEST, Status=0 (UNSPECIFIED), Hello=60, Poll=180
EGP: from 192.168.16.1 to 192.168.16.2, version=2, asystem=1, sequence=0
    Type=ACQUIRE, Code=REQUEST, Status=0 (UNSPECIFIED), Hello=60, Poll=180
EGP: from 192.168.16.1 to 192.168.16.2, version=2, asystem=1, sequence=0
    Type=ACQUIRE, Code=REQUEST, Status=0 (UNSPECIFIED), Hello=60, Poll=180
EGP: 192.168.16.2 going from ACQUIRE to IDLE
```

Notice in Example 1-1 that each EGP message has a sequence number. The sequence number allows EGP message pairs (such as Neighbor Acquisition Request/Confirm, Request/Refusal, and Cease/Cease-Ack pairs) to be identified. The next section details how the sequence numbers are used.

When two EGP gateways become neighbors, one is the *active* neighbor and one is the *passive* neighbor. Active gateways always initiate the neighbor relationship by sending Neighbor Acquisition Requests. Passive gateways do not send Acquisition Requests; they only respond to them. The same is true for Hello/I-Heard-You message pairs, described in the following section: The active neighbor sends the Hello, and the passive neighbor responds with an I-Heard-You (I-H-U). A passive gateway can initiate a Neighbor Cease message, however, to which the active gateway must reply with a Cease Acknowledgment message.

A core gateway, which can be a neighbor of routers in several other autonomous systems, might be the active gateway of one neighbor adjacency and the passive gateway of another neighbor adjacency. The Cisco EGP implementation uses the AS numbers as the determining factor: The neighbor whose AS number is lower will be the active neighbor.

Neighbor Reachability Protocol

After a gateway has acquired a neighbor, it maintains the neighbor relationship by sending periodic Hello messages. The neighbor responds to each Hello with an I-H-U message. RFC 904 does not specify a standard period between Hellos; IOS uses a default period of 60 seconds, which can be changed with the command **timers egp**.

When three Hello/I-H-U message pairs have been exchanged, the neighbor state changes from Down to Up (see Example 1-2). The neighbors can then exchange network reachability information, as described in the next section.

Example 1-2 **debug ip egp transactions** *Command Output Displays a Two-Way Handshake Success and Resulting EGP State Transitions*

```
EGP: 192.168.16.2 going from IDLE to ACQUIRE
EGP: from 192.168.16.1 to 192.168.16.2, version=2, asystem=1, sequence=2
     Type=ACQUIRE, Code=REQUEST, Status=1 (ACTIVE-MODE), Hello=60, Poll=180
EGP: from 192.168.16.2 to 192.168.16.1, version=2, asystem=2, sequence=2
     Type=ACQUIRE, Code=CONFIRM, Status=2 (PASSIVE-MODE), Hello=60, Poll=180
EGP: 192.168.16.2 going from ACQUIRE to DOWN
EGP: from 192.168.16.1 to 192.168.16.2, version=2, asystem=1, sequence=2
     Type=REACH, Code=HELLO, Status=2 (DOWN)
EGP: from 192.168.16.2 to 192.168.16.1, version=2, asystem=2, sequence=2
     Type=REACH, Code=I-HEARD-YOU, Status=2 (DOWN)
EGP: from 192.168.16.1 to 192.168.16.2, version=2, asystem=1, sequence=2
     Type=REACH, Code=HELLO, Status=2 (DOWN)
EGP: from 192.168.16.2 to 192.168.16.1, version=2, asystem=2, sequence=2
```

```
    Type=REACH, Code=I-HEARD-YOU, Status=2 (DOWN)
EGP: from 192.168.16.1 to 192.168.16.2, version=2, asystem=1, sequence=2
    Type=REACH, Code=HELLO, Status=2 (DOWN)
EGP: from 192.168.16.2 to 192.168.16.1, version=2, asystem=2, sequence=2
    Type=REACH, Code=I-HEARD-YOU, Status=2 (DOWN)
EGP: 192.168.16.2 going from DOWN to UP
```

If an active neighbor sends three sequential messages without receiving a response, the neighbor state transitions to Down. The gateway sends three more Hellos at the normal Hello interval; if there is still no response, the state changes to Cease. The gateway sends three Neighbor Cease messages at 60-second intervals. If the neighbor responds to any of the messages with a Cease Acknowledgment, or does not respond at all, the gateway transitions the neighbor state to Idle and waits 5 minutes before transitioning back to Acquire and attempting to reacquire the neighbor. Example 1-3 shows this sequence of events.

Example 1-3   *The Neighbor at 192.168.16.2 Has Stopped Responding. The Interval Between Each of the Unacknowledged EGP Messages Is 60 Seconds*

```
Shemp#
EGP: from 192.168.16.1 to 192.168.16.2, version=2, asystem=1, sequence=2
    Type=REACH, Code=HELLO, Status=1 (UP)
EGP: from 192.168.16.2 to 192.168.16.1, version=2, asystem=2, sequence=2
    Type=REACH, Code=I-HEARD-YOU, Status=1 (UP)
EGP: from 192.168.16.1 to 192.168.16.2, version=2, asystem=1, sequence=2
    Type=REACH, Code=HELLO, Status=1 (UP)
EGP: from 192.168.16.1 to 192.168.16.2, version=2, asystem=1, sequence=2
    Type=POLL, Code=0, Status=1 (UP), Net=192.168.16.0
EGP: from 192.168.16.1 to 192.168.16.2, version=2, asystem=1, sequence=3
    Type=REACH, Code=HELLO, Status=1 (UP)
EGP: 192.168.16.2 going from UP to DOWN
EGP: from 192.168.16.1 to 192.168.16.2, version=2, asystem=1, sequence=3
    Type=REACH, Code=HELLO, Status=2 (DOWN)
EGP: from 192.168.16.1 to 192.168.16.2, version=2, asystem=1, sequence=3
    Type=REACH, Code=HELLO, Status=2 (DOWN)
EGP: from 192.168.16.1 to 192.168.16.2, version=2, asystem=1, sequence=3
    Type=REACH, Code=HELLO, Status=2 (DOWN)
EGP: 192.168.16.2 going from DOWN to CEASE
EGP: from 192.168.16.1 to 192.168.16.2, version=2, asystem=1, sequence=3
    Type=ACQUIRE, Code=CEASE, Status=5 (HALTING)
EGP: from 192.168.16.1 to 192.168.16.2, version=2, asystem=1, sequence=3
    Type=ACQUIRE, Code=CEASE, Status=1 (ACTIVE-MODE)
EGP: from 192.168.16.1 to 192.168.16.2, version=2, asystem=1, sequence=3
    Type=ACQUIRE, Code=CEASE, Status=1 (ACTIVE-MODE)
EGP: 192.168.16.2 going from CEASE to IDLE
```

Example 1-4 shows another example of a dead neighbor, except this time a core gateway (192.168.16.2) in the passive mode is discovering the dead neighbor (192.168.16.1).

Example 1-4   *Neighbor 192.168.16.1 Has Stopped Responding. The Debug Messages Are Taken from 192.168.16.2, a Gateway in Passive Mode*

```
Moe#
EGP: from 192.168.16.1 to 192.168.16.2, version=2, asystem=1, sequence=1
     Type=REACH, Code=HELLO, Status=1 (UP)
EGP: from 192.168.16.2 to 192.168.16.1, version=2, asystem=2, sequence=1
     Type=REACH, Code=I-HEARD-YOU, Status=1 (UP)
EGP: from 192.168.16.2 to 192.168.16.1, version=2, asystem=2, sequence=1
     Type=POLL, Code=0, Status=1 (UP), Net=192.168.16.0
EGP: from 192.168.16.2 to 192.168.16.1, version=2, asystem=2, sequence=2
     Type=POLL, Code=0, Status=1 (UP), Net=192.168.16.0
EGP: 192.168.16.1 going from UP to DOWN
EGP: 192.168.16.1 going from DOWN to CEASE
EGP: from 192.168.16.2 to 192.168.16.1, version=2, asystem=2, sequence=3
     Type=ACQUIRE, Code=CEASE, Status=5 (HALTING)
EGP: from 192.168.16.2 to 192.168.16.1, version=2, asystem=2, sequence=3
     Type=ACQUIRE, Code=CEASE, Status=2 (PASSIVE-MODE)
EGP: from 192.168.16.2 to 192.168.16.1, version=2, asystem=2, sequence=3
     Type=ACQUIRE, Code=CEASE, Status=2 (PASSIVE-MODE)
EGP: 192.168.16.1 going from CEASE to IDLE
```

When the gateway does not receive a Hello within the 60-second Hello interval, it tries to "wake up" its neighbor. Because a gateway in passive mode cannot send Hellos, it sends a Poll message. The gateway then waits for one Poll interval. (The IOS default Poll interval is 180 seconds, or 3 minutes.) If no response is received, it sends another Poll and waits another Poll interval. If there still is no response, the gateway changes the neighbor state to Down and then immediately to Cease. As in Example 1-3, three Cease messages are sent and the neighbor state is changed to Idle.

Network Reachability Protocol

When the neighbor state is Up, the EGP neighbors can begin exchanging reachability information. Each gateway periodically sends a Poll message to its neighbor, containing some sequence number. The neighbor responds with an Update message that contains the same sequence number and a list of reachable networks. Example 1-5 shows how IOS uses the sequence numbers.

Example 1-5 *EGP Neighbors Poll Each Other Periodically for Network Reachability Updates*

```
EGP: from 192.168.16.1 to 192.168.16.2, version=2, asystem=1, sequence=120
    Type=REACH, Code=HELLO, Status=1 (UP)
EGP: from 192.168.16.2 to 192.168.16.1, version=2, asystem=2, sequence=120
    Type=REACH, Code=I-HEARD-YOU, Status=1 (UP)
EGP: from 192.168.16.1 to 192.168.16.2, version=2, asystem=1, sequence=120
    Type=REACH, Code=HELLO, Status=1 (UP)
EGP: from 192.168.16.2 to 192.168.16.1, version=2, asystem=2, sequence=120
    Type=REACH, Code=I-HEARD-YOU, Status=1 (UP)
EGP: from 192.168.16.1 to 192.168.16.2, version=2, asystem=1, sequence=120
    Type=POLL, Code=0, Status=1 (UP), Net=192.168.16.0
EGP: from 192.168.16.2 to 192.168.16.1, version=2, asystem=2, sequence=120
    Type=UPDATE, Code=0, Status=1 (UP), IntGW=2, ExtGW=1, Net=192.168.16.0
    Network 172.17.0.0 via 192.168.16.2 in 0 hops
    Network 192.168.17.0 via 192.168.16.2 in 0 hops
    Network 10.0.0.0 via 192.168.16.2 in 3 hops
    Network 172.20.0.0 via 192.168.16.4 in 0 hops
    Network 192.168.18.0 via 192.168.16.3(e) in 3 hops
    Network 172.16.0.0 via 192.168.16.3(e) in 3 hops
    Network 172.18.0.0 via 192.168.16.3(e) in 3 hops
EGP: 192.168.16.2 updated 7 routes
EGP: from 192.168.16.2 to 192.168.16.1, version=2, asystem=2, sequence=3
    Type=POLL, Code=0, Status=1 (UP), Net=192.168.16.0
EGP: from 192.168.16.1 to 192.168.16.2, version=2, asystem=1, sequence=3
    Type=UPDATE, Code=0, Status=1 (UP), IntGW=1, ExtGW=0, Net=192.168.16.0
    Network 172.19.0.0 via 192.168.16.1 in 0 hops
EGP: from 192.168.16.1 to 192.168.16.2, version=2, asystem=1, sequence=121
    Type=REACH, Code=HELLO, Status=1 (UP)
EGP: from 192.168.16.2 to 192.168.16.1, version=2, asystem=2, sequence=121
    Type=REACH, Code=I-HEARD-YOU, Status=1 (UP)
```

Every Hello/I-H-U pair exchanged between neighbors contains the same sequence number until a Poll is sent. The Poll/Update pair also uses the same sequence number. After the Update has been received, the active neighbor increments the sequence number. In Example 1-5, the sequence number is 120 through the Poll/Update, and it then is incremented to 121. Notice that both neighbors send a Poll; in this example, the Poll from the passive neighbor (192.168.16.2) has an entirely different sequence number (3). A neighbor always responds with an Update containing the same sequence number as the Poll.

Normally, a gateway sends an Update only when it is polled; however, this means a topology change might go unannounced for up to 3 minutes. EGP provides for this eventuality by allowing a gateway to send one *unsolicited* Update—that is, an Update that is not in response to a Poll—each Poll interval. IOS, however, does not support unsolicited Updates.

Both the Poll and the Update messages include the address of a source network. For example, the Poll and Update messages in Example 1-5 show a source network of 192.168.16.0. The source network is the network from which all reachability information is measured—that is, all networks requested or advertised can be reached via a router attached to the source network. Although this network is usually the network to which the two neighbors are both attached, it is more accurately the network about which the Poll is requesting information, and the network about which the Update is supplying information. EGP is a purely classful protocol,[3] and the source network—as well as the network addresses listed in the Updates—are always major class network addresses and never subnets.

Following the source network address is a list of one or more routers and the networks that can be reached via those routers. The common characteristic of the routers on the list is that they are all attached to the source network. If a router on the list is not the EGP gateway that originated the Update, the router is an *indirect* or *third-party* neighbor.

Figure 1-3 illustrates the concept of indirect EGP neighbors. One router, Moe, is a core gateway and is peered with three other gateways.

The debug messages in Example 1-5 are taken from Shemp, the router in AS1. Notice in the Update originated by Moe (192.168.16.2) that three networks are listed as reachable via Moe, but also, four networks are listed as reachable via Larry (192.168.16.4) and Curly (192.168.16.3). These two routers are Shemp's indirect neighbors, via Moe. Joe, in AS3, is not an indirect neighbor because it is not attached to the source network. Its networks are merely advertised as being reachable via Moe.

The advertisement of indirect neighbors saves bandwidth on a common link, but more important, indirect neighbors increase efficiency by eliminating an unnecessary router hop. In Figure 1-3, for example, Shemp is not peered with any router other than Moe. In fact, Larry is not even speaking EGP but is advertising its networks to Moe via RIP. Moe is performing a sort of "preemptive redirect" by informing Shemp of better next-hop routers than itself.

It is possible for an EGP Update to contain indirect neighbors only—that is, the originator might not include itself as a next hop to any network. In this scenario, the originator is a *route server*. It has learned reachability information from an IGP or from static routes and advertises this information to EGP neighbors without performing any packet-forwarding functions.

---

[3] Classful and classless routing are explained later in this chapter in the section "Classless Inter-Domain Routing."

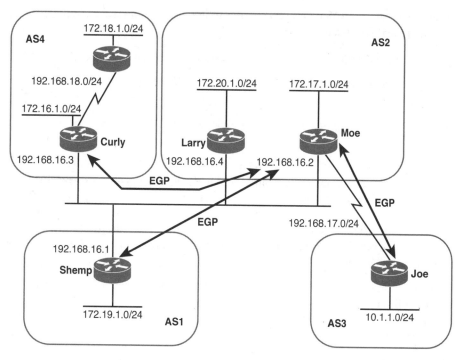

Figure 1-3 *Indirect EGP Neighbors*

From the perspective of an EGP gateway, a neighbor is either an *interior gateway* or an *exterior gateway*. A neighbor is an interior gateway if it is in the same AS, and it is an exterior gateway if it is in a different AS. In Figure 1-3, all the EGP gateways see all their neighbors as external gateways. If Larry were speaking EGP and peered with Moe, those two routers would see each other as interior gateways.

An EGP Update message includes two fields for describing whether the routers in its list are interior or exterior gateways. Looking at the first Update message in Example 1-5, you can see these fields just before the source network: IntGW=2 and ExtGW=1. The sum of these two fields tells how many routers are listed in the Update. All the interior gateways specified are listed first; therefore, if IntGW=2 and ExtGW=1, the first two routers listed are interior gateways and the last router listed is an exterior gateway. If you compare the Update message from 192.168.16.2 in Example 15 with Figure 1-3, you see that the three networks reachable via Curly are listed last in the Update and are marked as exterior—that is, they are reachable via a gateway exterior to Moe. Because stub gateways cannot advertise networks outside of their own AS, only Updates from core gateways can include exterior gateways.

The EGP Update message associates a distance with each network it lists. The distance field is 8 bits, so the distance can range from 0 to 255. RFC 904 does not specify how the distance is to be interpreted, however, other than that 255 is used to indicate unreachable networks. Nor does the RFC define an algorithm for using the distance to calculate shortest inter-AS paths. IOS chooses to interpret the distance as hops, as shown in Example 1-5. The default rules are basic:

- A gateway advertises all networks within its own AS having a distance of 0.

- A gateway advertises all networks within an AS other than its own as having a distance of 3.

- A gateway indicates that a network has become unreachable by giving it a distance of 255.

For example, you can see in Example 1-5 and Figure 1-3 that although network 172.20.0.0 is one router hop away from Moe, Moe is advertising the network with a distance of 0—the same distance as network 172.17.0.0, which is directly attached. Network 10.0.0.0 is also one router hop away, and network 172.18.0.0 is two hops away, but both are in different autonomous systems and are therefore advertised with a distance of 3. The point is that the distance used by EGP is virtually useless for determining the best path to a network.

Example 1-6 shows the routing table of Shemp and the route entries resulting from the Update in Example 1-5.

Example 1-6   *Shemp's Routing Table*

```
Shemp#show ip route
Codes: C - connected, S - static, I - IGRP, R - RIP, M - mobile, B - BGP
       D - EIGRP, EX - EIGRP external, O - OSPF, IA - OSPF inter area
       E1 - OSPF external type 1, E2 - OSPF external type 2, E - EGP
       i - IS-IS, L1 - IS-IS level-1, L2 - IS-IS level-2, * - candidate default

Gateway of last resort is not set

E    10.0.0.0 [140/4] via 192.168.16.2, 00:00:52, Ethernet0
C    192.168.16.0 is directly connected, Ethernet0
E    192.168.17.0 [140/1] via 192.168.16.2, 00:00:52, Ethernet0
E    192.168.18.0 [140/4] via 192.168.16.3, 00:00:52, Ethernet0
E    172.20.0.0 [140/1] via 192.168.16.4, 00:00:52, Ethernet0
E    172.16.0.0 [140/4] via 192.168.16.3, 00:00:52, Ethernet0
E    172.17.0.0 [140/1] via 192.168.16.2, 00:00:52, Ethernet0
E    172.18.0.0 [140/4] via 192.168.16.3, 00:00:52, Ethernet0
     172.19.0.0 255.255.255.0 is subnetted, 1 subnets
C       172.19.1.0 is directly connected, Loopback0
Shemp#
```

There are two points of interest in the routing table. First, notice that the EGP entries have an administrative distance of 140. This is higher than the administrative distance of any IGP (with the exception of External EIGRP), so a router always chooses an IGP route over an EGP advertisement of the same network.

Second, notice that the distances to each of the EGP-advertised networks are one higher than the distances shown in the Update of Example 1-5. The IOS EGP process increments the distance by one, just as a RIP routing algorithm does.

Shortcomings of EGP

The fundamental problem with EGP is its inability to detect routing loops. Because there is an upper boundary on the distance that EGP uses (255), you might be tempted to say that counting to infinity is at least a rudimentary loop-detection mechanism. It is, but the high limit combined with the typical Poll interval makes counting to infinity useless. Given a default Poll interval of 180 seconds, EGP peers could take almost 13 hours to count to infinity. As RFC 904 states, "If the topology does not obey the rules given for stubs...the Exterior Gateway Protocol does not provide enough topological information to prevent loops."

As a result, EGP must be run on an engineered loop-free topology. Although that was not a problem in 1983, when EGP was intended merely to connect stub gateways to the ARPANET backbone, the creators of EGP foresaw that such a limited topology would soon become inadequate. The autonomous systems making up the Internet would need to evolve into a less structured (or entirely unstructured) mesh, in which many autonomous systems could serve as transit systems for many other autonomous systems.

With the advent of the NSFnet, the limitations of EGP became more pronounced. Not only were there now multiple backbones, but also there were acceptable use policies concerning what traffic could traverse what backbone. Because EGP cannot support sophisticated policy-based routing, interim solutions had to be engineered (RFC 1092).

Another major problem with EGP is its inability to adequately interact with IGPs to determine a shortest route to a network in another AS. For example, EGP distances do not reliably translate into RIP hop counts. If the EGP distance causes the hop count to exceed 15, RIP declares the network unreachable. Other shortcomings of EGP include its susceptibility to failures when attempting to convey information on a large number of networks, and its vulnerability to intentionally or unintentionally inaccurate network information.

Last but certainly not least, EGP can be mind-numbingly slow to advertise a network change. The neighbor acquisition process is slow, and the advertisement of network changes is almost glacial. For example, EGP does not declare a route down until it has failed to receive six consecutive updates for the route. Couple this with a default update interval of 180 seconds, and you can see that an EGP router takes 18 minutes to declare a route down. Only then does it stop including the route in its own updates; 54 minutes pass before a router just three hops away from the failed network declares the route down! As a result, you might sometimes mistakenly assume there is a problem where none exists (except for the problematic nature of EGP itself).

Several attempts were made to create an EGPv3, but none were successful. In the end, EGP was abandoned in favor of an entirely new inter-AS protocol, BGP. Accordingly, Exterior Gateway Protocol is now not only the name of a protocol, but also the name of a class of protocols, giving rise to the notion of an EGP named EGP. Nonetheless, the legacy of EGP is still with us today in the form of autonomous systems and inter-AS routing.

The Advent of BGP

The attempts to enhance EGP failed because it was only a reachability protocol, not a true routing protocol. Turning it into a routing protocol would make it so different from its original versions that it could no longer be said to be an enhanced version; it would be something entirely different. And if that were the case, an entirely different inter-domain protocol—a true routing protocol capable of accurately differentiating multiple routes to the same destination, of avoiding loops, and of interacting with IGPs in calculating distances—might as well be designed from scratch.

That protocol, first introduced in 1989 in RFC 1105, is BGP. The first version of BGP was updated exactly 1 year later in RFC 1163. BGP was upgraded again in 1991 in RFC 1267, and with this third modification it became customary to refer to the three versions as BGP-1, BGP-2, and BGP-3, respectively.

The current version of BGP, BGP-4, was introduced in 1995 in RFC 1771 and has since been obsoleted by RFC 4271. BGP-4 differs significantly from the earlier versions; the most important difference is that BGP-4 is classless, whereas the earlier versions are classful. The motive for this fundamental change goes to the heart of the reason exterior gateway protocols exist: to keep routing within the Internet both manageable and reliable. Classless Inter-Domain Routing (CIDR)—originally introduced in RFCs 1517 in 1993, finalized in RFCs 1518 and 1519 in the same year as a standard proposal, and amended by RFC 1520—was created for this purpose, and BGP-4 was created to support CIDR. CIDR (pronounced "cider") is discussed in detail later in this chapter.

For almost a decade BGP-4 has been the production version of BGP, and for most of that time, it has been proper form to refer to the protocol with its version number. That practice was used in the first edition of this book, reflecting the times in which it was written. But the first three versions of BGP have long since faded into the mists, and all BGPs currently running (admittedly, there might still be one or two earlier versions creaking along out there somewhere) are BGP-4. It is therefore safe to drop the version number; when we speak of BGP here in the first part of the 21st century, we mean BGP-4. There is no other.

Note   Reflecting the universal nature of BGP-4, as of release 12.0(6)T IOS supports only version 4. Prior to that release, the BGP implementation would either automatically negotiate the version with each neighbor (the default) or allow you to manually set the version.

BGP Basics

Like EGP, BGP establishes a unique, unicast-based connection to each of its neighbors. To increase the reliability of the connection, BGP uses TCP (port 179) as its underlying delivery mechanism. The session maintenance and update mechanisms of BGP are also somewhat simplified by allowing the TCP layer to handle such duties as acknowledgment, retransmission, and sequencing. Because BGP rides on TCP—a point-to-point protocol—a separate point-to-point session to each neighbor must be established. MD5 authentication between neighbors is also handled by TCP, again simplifying BGP.

BGP is a vector protocol in that each BGP node relies on downstream neighbors to pass along routes from their routing table; the node makes its route calculations based on those advertised routes and passes the results to upstream neighbors. However, *distance vector* protocols quantify the distance with a single number, representing hop count or, in the case of EIGRP, a sum of total interface delays and lowest bandwidth. In contrast, BGP uses a list, by AS number, of the autonomous systems through which a packet must pass to reach the destination (see Figure 1-4). Because this list fully describes the path a packet must take, BGP is called a *path vector* routing protocol to contrast it with traditional distance vector protocols. The list of AS numbers associated with a BGP route is called the *AS_PATH* and is one of several *path attributes* associated with each route. Path attributes are described in Chapter 2, "Introduction to BGP," and various practical uses for them are described in Chapters 3 through 5.

> **Note**   Although BGP, like distance vector protocols, relies on its direct peers to share route information and becomes a part of a distributed calculation along the route, the view of the path to the destination provided by the AS_PATH list is more like a link state protocol than traditional distance vector protocols.

Recall that EGP is not a true routing protocol because it does not have a fully developed algorithm for calculating the shortest path and it cannot detect route loops. In contrast, the AS_PATH attribute qualifies BGP as a routing protocol on both counts. First, the shortest inter-AS path is simply determined by the least number of AS numbers. In Figure 1-4, AS7 is receiving two routes to 207.126.0.0/16. One of the routes has four AS hops, and the other has three hops. AS7 chooses the shortest path, (4,2,1).[4]

Route loops also are easily detected using the AS_PATH attribute. If a router receives an update containing its local AS number in the AS_PATH, it knows that a routing loop has occurred. In Figure 1-5, AS7 has advertised a route to AS8. AS8 advertises the route to AS9, which advertises it back to AS7. AS7 sees its own number in the AS_PATH and does not accept the update, thereby avoiding a potential routing loop.

---

[4] This is a simplified description of BGP path selection; the actual procedure considers many other factors than just the AS_PATH. Chapter 2 describes the complete BGP path selection procedure.

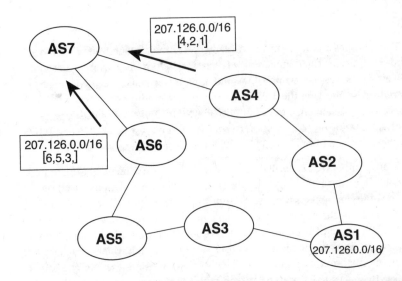

Figure 1-4   *BGP Determines the Shortest Loop-Free Inter-AS Path from a List of AS Numbers Known as the AS_PATH Attribute*

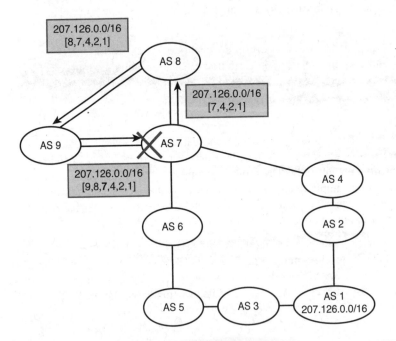

Figure 1-5   *If a BGP Router Sees Its Own AS Number in the AS_PATH Attribute of a Route Advertised from Another AS, It Rejects the Route*

Although the AS_PATH provides a view of the specific autonomous systems along the path to a destination, BGP does not show the details of the topologies within each AS. Because BGP sees only a tree of autonomous systems, it can be said that BGP takes a higher view of the entire internetwork than an IGP, which sees only the topology within an AS. And because this higher view is not actually compatible with the view seen by IGPs, IOS maintains a separate routing table—more accurately, a *route information database* or *RIB*—to hold BGP routes. Example 1-7 demonstrates a typical BGP routing table viewed with the **show ip bgp** command.[5]

Example 1-7   show ip bgp *Command Displays the BGP RIB*

```
route-views.oregon-ix.net>show ip bgp
BGP table version is 121115564, local router ID is 198.32.162.100
Status codes: s suppressed, d damped, h history, * valid, > best, i - internal,
              S Stale
Origin codes: i - IGP, e - EGP, ? - incomplete


   Network          Next Hop            Metric LocPrf Weight Path
*  3.0.0.0          217.75.96.60             0             0 16150 3549 701 703 80 i
*                   194.85.4.55                            0 3277 3216 3549 701 703 80 i
*                   64.125.0.137           124             0 6461 701 703 80 i
*                   213.200.87.254          10             0 3257 1239 701 703 80 i
*                   203.62.252.186                         0 1221 4637 703 80 i
*                   66.185.128.48          504             0 1668 701 703 80 i
*>                  4.68.1.166               0             0 3356 701 703 80 i
*                   154.11.11.113            0             0 852 1239 701 703 80 i
*                   144.228.241.81  4294967294             0 1239 701 703 80 i
*                   193.0.0.56                             0 3333 3356 701 703 80 i
*  4.0.0.0/9        217.75.96.60             0             0 16150 3549 3356 i
*                   194.85.4.55                            0 3277 3267 3343 25462 3356 3356 i
*>                  4.68.1.166               0             0 3356 i
*                   129.250.0.171            1             0 2914 3356 i
*                   144.228.241.81  4294967294             0 1239 3356 i
*                   208.51.134.254          53             0 3549 3356 i
*                   134.222.85.45                          0 286 3549 3356 i
*  4.0.0.0          217.75.96.60             0             0 16150 3549 3356 i
*                   194.85.4.55                            0 3277 3267 3343 25462 3356 3356 i
*                   64.125.0.137           124             0 6461 3356 i
*>                  4.68.1.166               0             0 3356 i
*  4.21.41.0/24     217.75.96.60             0             0 16150 3549 2914 16467 36806 i
```

---

[5] A number of publicly accessible routers enable you to observe the Internet routing tables, BGP tables, and such. This capture, edited so you can see entries from several prefixes, is taken from a router accessible at the University of Oregon Route Views Project (www.routeviews.org).

```
*                      194.85.4.55                          0 3277 3216 3549 2914 16467 36806 i

*                      64.125.0.137        124              0 6461 2914 16467 36806 i

*                      144.228.241.81  4294967294           0 1239 2914 16467 36806 i

*                      203.181.248.168                      0 7660 2516 209 2914 16467 36806 i

*>                     129.250.0.11        8                0 2914 16467 36806 i

*   4.23.112.0/24      217.75.96.60        0                0 16150 174 21889 i

*                      194.85.4.55                          0 3277 3267 3343 25462 174 21889 i

*                      64.125.0.137        120              0 6461 174 21889 i

*                      65.106.7.139        3                0 2828 174 21889 i

--More--
```

Although the BGP table in Example 1-7 looks somewhat different from the AS-internal routing table displayed with the **show ip route** command, the same elements exist. The table shows destination networks, next-hop routers, and a measure by which the shortest path can be selected. The **Metric**, **LocPrf**, and **Weight** columns are explained in Chapter 2, but what is of interest now is the **Path** column. This column lists the AS_PATH attributes for each network.

Notice also that for each destination network, multiple next hops are listed. Unlike the AS-internal routing table, which lists only the routes currently being used, the BGP RIB lists all known paths. A **>** following the * (valid) in the leftmost column indicates which path the router is currently using. This best path is the one with the shortest AS_PATH. When multiple routes have equivalent paths (refer to Example 1-7) the router must have some criteria for deciding which path to choose. That decision process is also covered in Chapter 2.

When there are parallel, equal-cost paths to a particular destination (refer to Example 1-7) the IOS implementation of BGP by default selects only one path—in contrast to other IP routing protocols, in which the default is to load balance across up to four paths. As with the other IP routing protocols, the **maximum-paths** command changes the default maximum number of parallel paths in the range from 1 to 16. Load balancing is discussed in more detail in Chapter 3, "BGP and NLRI."

When two neighbors first establish a BGP peer connection, they exchange their entire BGP routing tables. After that, they exchange incremental, partial updates; that is, they exchange routing information only when something changes, and only information about what changed. Because BGP does not use periodic routing updates, the peers must exchange keepalive messages to ensure that the connection is maintained. The IOS default keepalive interval is 60 seconds (RFC 4271 does not specify a standard keepalive time); if three intervals (180 seconds) pass without a peer receiving a keepalive message, the peer declares its neighbor down. You can change these intervals with the **timers bgp** command.

Autonomous System Types

The previous section mentioned that BGP takes a higher view of the overall internetwork than an IGP: Where an IGP route is concerned with hops through individual routers, a BGP route is concerned with hops through autonomous systems. There is another aspect to this "higher view" that has parallels to an IGP: Just as individual subnets are either stub or transit, autonomous systems are also either stub or transit.

- A *stub* AS is one in which all packets going out of the AS originated in the AS and all packets coming into the AS have a destination address within the AS.

- *transit* AS is one in which at least some packets entering the AS have a destination address that is outside of the AS and are forwarded to another AS en route to that destination.

You have already encountered this concept with EGP core and stub autonomous systems (refer to Figure 1-2); the EGP core AS is a transit AS, passing packets from one stub AS to another. The difference is that EGP can have only one core AS because of the loop avoidance issue. BGP can have a multitude of transit autonomous systems. In Figure 1-4, for example, autonomous systems 2, 3, 4, 5, and 6 are transit autonomous systems for packets originating in AS7 and destined for AS1. This does not necessarily mean that AS1 and AS7 in that illustration are stub autonomous systems, however. AS7 and AS1 might be transit autonomous systems for packets traveling from AS4 to AS6.

Routing into and out of a stub AS is usually quite simple, and the BGP configuration for a stub AS is straightforward. Actually, in many cases BGP is not even required. Chapter 2 discusses some alternatives to BGP for stub autonomous systems.

The real power of BGP is revealed when configuring transit autonomous systems. The protocol remains simple—much more so than EIGRP, OSPF, or IS-IS—but it associates with each route a number of *path attributes* that allow the routes to be manipulated in complex ways by a set of powerful policy tools. The path attributes and the tools for exploiting them enable the configuration of *route policies*. A route policy is a rule that imposes a preference on route handling that may override default behavior. Just a few examples are preferences related to

- The way packets move in and out of the AS

- Business relationships with neighboring autonomous systems

- Locally attached user networks (such as ISP customers)

- Both proactive and reactive security procedures

- Dynamic scaling properties

An overview of path attributes and routing policies is provided in Chapter 2, "Introduction to BGP"; the tools and procedures for creating routing policies are examined in Chapter 4, "BGP and Routing Policies," and the tools for scaling BGP are examined in Chapter 5.

By supporting multiple *address families*, BGP goes beyond mere unicast IP routing to become a foundation protocol for the enabling technologies behind many IP network services. Such services usually span transit autonomous systems but can also extend into stub autonomous systems. The concepts behind this enhancement to BGP, called *multi-protocol BGP (MP-BGP)*, are introduced in Chapter 6, "Multiprotocol BGP."

External and Internal BGP

Just as the concepts of stub and transit (core) autonomous systems were introduced in EGP, that pioneering protocol also introduced the concepts of interior and exterior neighbors. That is, if an EGP process peers with a neighbor in the same AS, the neighbor is interior; if the neighbor is in a different AS, the neighbor is exterior.

BGP uses the same concept: If a BGP session is established between two neighbors in different autonomous systems, the session is *external BGP (EBGP)*, and if the session is established between two neighbors in the same AS, the session is *internal BGP (IBGP)*. Figure 1-6 illustrates this concept.

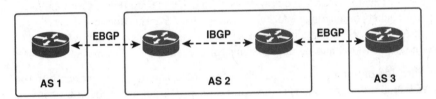

Figure 1-6   *Neighbors in Different Autonomous Systems Communicate Using EBGP, Whereas Neighbors in the Same AS Communicate Using IBGP*

Multiple routers usually exist within an AS, so IBGP is necessary whenever BGP-advertised information must be passed within a given AS. In Figure 1-6, for instance, the combination of EBGP and IBGP sessions makes it possible for the router in AS1 to advertise a route to the router in AS3. Traditionally, IBGP is associated with transit autonomous systems such as AS2 in Figure 1-6. A stub AS usually runs EBGP at one or more edge routers only, and routes packets to and from the edge routers via an IGP. However, with multiprotocol BGP being used more and more frequently for services, such as MPLS-based VPNs and IP multicast, IBGP is beginning to appear even in stub autonomous systems.

Recall that BGP routers use the AS_PATH not only as an AS hop count metric but also as a loop avoidance device: If a router sees its own AS number on the AS_PATH list, it drops the route. This presents some interesting problems for IBGP.

Consider, for example, a route being communicated from AS1 to AS3, through AS2, in Figure 1-7. The physical path across AS2 is through three routers, RTR1, RTR2, and RTR3. If each of these three routers adds its AS number to the AS_PATH list as it passes the route along, two problems arise:

- The AS_PATH list no longer is a true representation of the length of the inter-AS path. AS2 is a single AS hop and should be represented by one entry on the AS_PATH list. If each router makes an entry for AS2, the AS number would appear three times (Figure 1-8).

- The loop avoidance function of the AS_PATH stipulates that if a router sees its own AS number on the AS_PATH list, it assumes a loop has occurred and drops the route. So if RTR1 added AS number 2 to the list, RTR2, seeing that AS number and knowing it is in AS2, would drop the route (Figure 1-9).

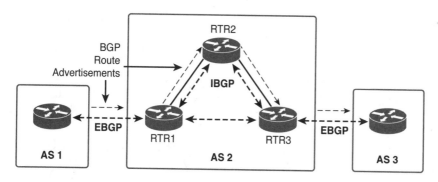

Figure 1-7 *A Route Advertisement from AS1 to AS3 Must Physically Pass Through Three Routers in AS2*

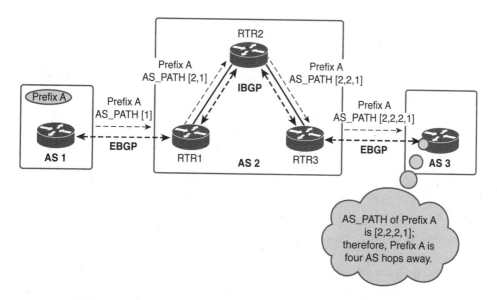

Figure 1-8 *If Each Router in AS2 Added Its AS number to the AS_PATH, the Router in AS3 Would Incorrectly Conclude That Prefix A Is Four AS Hops Away, Rather Than Two.*

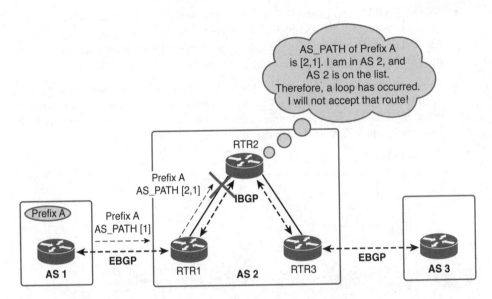

Figure 1-9 *If RTR1 Added Its AS Number to the AS_PATH, RTR2. Being in the Same AS, Would Incorrectly Conclude That a Loop Had Occurred and Drop the Route*

The solution to these problems is a special rule for IBGP:

> A router adds its AS number to a route's AS_PATH *only* when the route is sent to an EBGP neighbor. The AS number is not added to routes sent to an IBGP neighbor.

Figure 1-10 shows the effects of this rule: Routers within AS2 do not drop the route because they do not see their own AS number on the AS_PATH list, and the router in AS3 correctly determines the AS hop distance to prefix A.

This rule solves the problems represented in Figures 1-8 and 1-9 but introduces another problem. Detecting one's AS number on the AS_PATH list is BGP's method of detecting and avoiding routing loops; however, the AS_PATH is meaningless within the scope of a single AS. What if a routing loop does exist within the AS? How can you avoid it?

To answer this problem you must look again to EGP. That protocol had no loop avoidance mechanism, so the solution was to ensure a loop-free topology. This is also the rationale behind hierarchical area topologies in OSPF and IS-IS, as discussed in Volume I; SPF trees (the means by which link-state protocols "see" loops) do not span area boundaries, so a loop-free inter-area topology is imposed.

This, then, is also the solution to the IBGP routing loop vulnerability: Ensure that the IBGP peering sessions cannot loop by requiring a loop-free topology. One of the keys to this solution is that BGP sessions run over TCP, which is unicast point-to-point (avoiding at least some looping risks) and has no requirement that the two points of the session physically connect. So in the example network, even though the path through AS2 transits three routers, the IBGP session can be established directly between the edge routers, as shown in Figure 1-11. The IBGP session is following the physical path through RTR2 but logically exists only between RTR1 and RTR3.

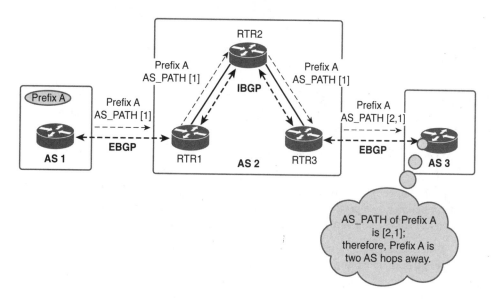

Figure 1-10   *The Problems of Figures 1-8 and 1-9 Are Prevented by Adding Only an AS Number to the AS_PATH When the Route Is Sent to an EBGP Neighbor*

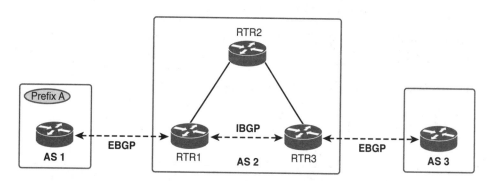

Figure 1-11   *Establishing an IBGP Session Only Between the Edge Routers Creates a Loop-Free IBGP Topology*

Our IBGP problems are still not completely solved, however. To understand the next problem, suppose the route to prefix A has been sent across the EBGP and IBGP sessions in Figure 1-11. The resulting route entry at RTR3 is shown in Figure 1-12. The entry is created from RTR1's advertisement, so RTR1 is indicated as the next hop toward the destination. And the next hop to reach RTR1 within AS2 is RTR2, so that entry is also shown.

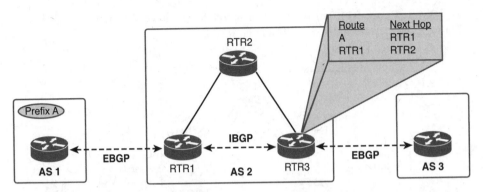

Figure 1-12   *RTR3's Route Table Shows RTR1 as the Next Hop to Prefix A, and RTR2 as the Next Hop to RTR1*

The problem becomes evident in Figure 1-13, in which a packet with a destination address belonging to prefix A is forwarded from AS3 to AS2. The sequence of events shown in Figure 1-13 follows:

1. When RTR3 receives the packet, it does a lookup of the destination address and sees that the next hop is RTR1.

2. Because RTR1 is not directly connected, RTR3 must do a second look up to find out how to forward the packet toward that next hop address.

3. The next hop of RTR1 is RTR2, so the packet is forwarded to that router.

4. RTR2 has no route entry to prefix A because the IBGP session communicating the route was directly from RTR1 to RTR3; therefore, RTR2 drops the packet.

So even though a loop-free route exchange is accomplished with the logical topology depicted in Figure 1-11, not enough information is shared across the actual path packets take for the packets to be forwarded successfully. This problem highlights two levels of information need to be considered when setting up IBGP:

1. Next-hop information about the advertised prefix

2. Next-hop information about the prefix next hop addresses

Figure 1-13 shows how a router performs a *recursive lookup*: It first looks up the route to the packet destination address; if the next hop address is not directly connected, it must perform a second look up to find the route to the next-hop address. IGPs normally route hop-by-hop, so recursive lookups are not a problem. This issue is typical for IBGP, though.

To prevent the problem depicted in Figure 1-13, every router along the path over which a packet will be forwarded must have enough information in its routing table to know what to do with the packet. One solution is to redistribute all the routes learned from

EBGP neighbors into the IGP.[6] In Figure 1-11, when RTR1 receives the route information about prefix A from AS1, it could, in addition to advertising the information to RTR3, redistribute the information into the local IGP. Now, when a packet is forwarded to RTR2, as shown in Figure 1-13, RTR2 has a route table entry for prefix A learned via the IGP from RTR1 and showing RTR1 as the next hop for the prefix.

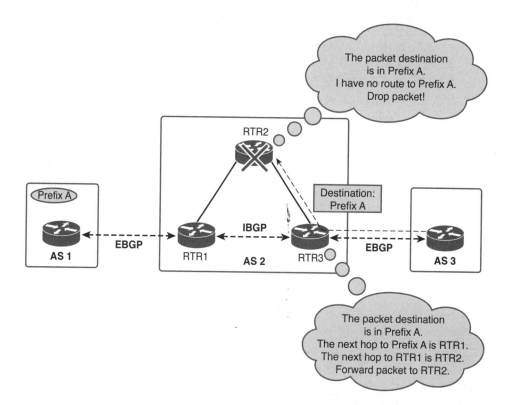

Figure 1-13 *Using the Route Entries Shown in Figure 1-12, RTR3 Forwards a Packet Destined for Prefix A to RTR2; RTR2 Does Not Have a Route to Prefix A, and Drops the Packet*

Although redistribution of BGP routes into the local IGP works just fine on paper, Chapter 3 explains in some detail why this is almost always a bad idea in practice. In short, there are two issues with redistributing BGP routes into the IGP:

■ One of the assumptions of BGP is that external peers are outside of your realm of trust, and therefore information received from those peers are subject to acceptance

---

[6] There is an IOS function related to the issues discussed here, called IGP synchronization. Chapter 3 provides a discussion of this function and an example of configuring properly for it.

under more cautious rules than information received from an IGP or IBGP peer. Promiscuously tossing external routes into your IGP database exposes you to security and stability threats.

■ The information received from an external BGP peer is usually either the full Internet routing table, a substantial subset of that table, or some other large set of routes. IGP performance degrades in inverse proportion to the size of its routing information databases. A large set of routes (the specific thresholds depend on the individual router's memory capacity, CPU speed, and efficiency of IGP coding) can cause the IGP to consume most or all the router's processing capacity, bringing the router's availability quickly down to 0 and in many cases causing a complete platform failure. Chapter 3 shows that it can get much worse than just a single router failure.

The best practice in the great majority of cases is to keep BGP-learned routes within BGP. If these routes must be distributed to routers within the AS to eliminate the problem, as shown in Figure 1-13, distribute them using IBGP, as shown in Figure 1-14. The practice for efficient routing across an IBGP infrastructure is that a full mesh of IBGP sessions should exist between all BGP routers within a single AS. Chapter 5 shows that this practice is subject to a few modifications in the interest of scaling, but until you get to that chapter, full IBGP meshes can confidently be written into your book of best practices.

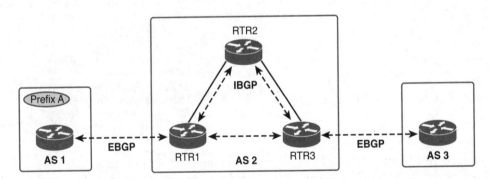

Figure 1-14   *IBGP Sessions Should Include Not Only AS Edge Routers, but Also All Routers That Might Forward Packets with Externally Learned Destination Addresses*

The logical topology of Figure 1-14 brings you back to the problem of loop avoidance. The physical topology you have been using up until now is easy to understand, but the reality is that the interior architecture of most autonomous systems is more complex. Figure 1-15, for instance, shows that the logical BGP topology is quite different from the autonomous system's physical topology. Although the EBGP sessions (represented by the arrows crossing the AS boundary) correspond with the external physical links, the fully meshed IBGP sessions are significantly more complex. It is essential to remember, however, that every IBGP session must travel over some physical link. The direct IBGP session between RTR5 and RTR6 in Figure 1-15, for instance, actually passes through RTR2 and RTR3.

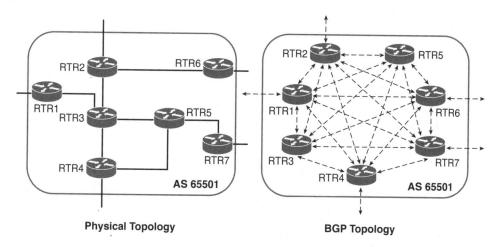

Physical Topology   **BGP Topology**

Figure 1-15   *The Requirement That IBGP Be Fully Meshed Can Result in a BGP Topology That Is Significantly Different from the Physical Topology*

How, then, are BGP routing loops avoided in a complex topology? By adding another special IBGP rule:

> Routes learned from an internal neighbor are never sent to another internal neighbor.

The objective of the full IBGP mesh is to ensure that all routers within the AS have the information they need to forward packets to the correct next hop. Suppose RTR6 in Figure 1-15 receives a packet on its AS-external link, and a route lookup shows RTR7 as the next hop. The path the packet must follow to get to that next hop is through RTR2, RTR3, and RTR5. The IBGP sessions ensure that whenever a router learns a route from an external neighbor, it passes the information directly to every router within the AS, without the need for any one of the routers to forward the information to any other router within the AS. And if no information learned from an internal neighbor is passed along to another internal neighbor, no routing loops can occur.

Multihoming

The AS depicted in Figure 1-15 has five external connections. Although no details are given in the illustration about where the connections go—they might all go to different autonomous systems, they might all go to just one AS, or something in between—the example of the packet entering the AS at RTR6 and leaving at RTR7 does tell you that this is a transit AS.

An AS with more than one external connection, such as the one in Figure 1-15, is *multi-homed*. A transit AS must, by definition, be multihomed for a packet to transit the AS. But a stub AS can also be multihomed. In this section, the drivers for and issues with multihoming in each AS type are examined.

Transit AS Multihoming

A transit AS is usually a service provider network, delivering services such as basic Internet connectivity or voice and video services to connected customers, or a carrier network, specializing in providing a geographically large backbone to smaller service provider networks. However, a transit AS might also be the backbone of a large commercial, government, or academic organization.

In general, three types of external connections from a transit network exist:

- **User (customer) peering:** Networks that originate or terminate traffic and use the transit AS to get to either other user networks connected to the AS or to get to user networks connected to some other AS.

- **Private peering:** When two or more service providers agree to share routes, they enter into a *peering agreement*. A peering agreement may be established directly between two providers (a *bilateral* peering agreement) or between a group of similar-sized providers (a *multilateral* peering agreement). Traffic patterns play a major role in determining the financial nature of the agreement. If the traffic between the peering partners is reasonably balanced in both directions, money usually does not exchange hands. (This is called *settlement-free* peering.) The peering is mutually beneficial for the two partners. But if the traffic is heavier in one direction than in the other across the peering point, as is the case when a small provider peers with a larger provider, the small provider usually must pay for the peering privilege. The rationale here is that the small provider benefits more from the peering, gaining access to the larger provider's larger customer base or more diverse connectivity. Typical of this is a regional (Tier II or III) ISP connecting to a national or global (Tier I) ISP.[7]

- **Public peering:** These connections take place at well-known *Internet exchange points (IXP)*[8] built specifically for allowing such peering. Public peering is usually free, beyond the cost of the equipment and connections at the IXP. Although Ethernet, FDDI, and occasionally ATM were used for interconnecting peers at an

---

[7] Tiers are defined by peering relationships. Tier 1 service providers peer with each other exclusively through settlement-free peering. Tier 2 service providers peer with some or, occasionally, all the Tier 1 providers (upstream peering), but with a combination of paid and settlement-free peering. Tier 3 service providers pay for all their upstream peering. The definition is not as clear as this sounds; depending on the list you consult, there may be from 13 to 46 Tier 1 providers.

[8] The term IXP has mostly replaced the older NSFnet-era term Network Access Point (NAP). A good list of IXPs around the world can be found at www.datacentermap.com/ixps.html.

IXP in the past, the vast majority of IXPs now use Ethernet switches or Virtual Private LAN Service (VPLS) for interconnection.

In a given transit AS, there are likely to be subsets of each of the three peering categories described here. For example, some customers might be paying for a more stringent service-level agreement (SLA) than other customers, obliging the service provider to be much more careful with those "premium" customers and giving preference to those customers' traffic in times of congestion or partial network outages. Similarly, it can be assumed that paid, private peering agreements are established due to some documented or assumed value to the peering. The routes through these peering points would accordingly be more valuable than the routes freely acquired from a public peering point. In both cases the network operator needs a set of tools and methodologies for arbitrarily imposing preferences and changing default routing behaviors within the AS.

Stub AS Multihoming

Although the need for multihoming is obvious in a transit AS—it cannot be a transit AS otherwise—multihoming is also common in stub autonomous systems. If a stub AS is small enough to not need multihoming—that is, it has only a single link to some higher-level AS—BGP probably is not needed. Static routes on each side of the connection are easy to configure and safer to manage. In Figure 1-16, for example, the stub AS has a single connection to the transit AS. Rather than running BGP between the peering routers, RTR1 in AS65501 has a default route configured statically, which is then advertised via the local IGP throughout the AS. Any router within the AS that cannot find a match for a packet's destination address matches the default route and forwards the packet to RTR1, which in turn forwards it to AS65510.

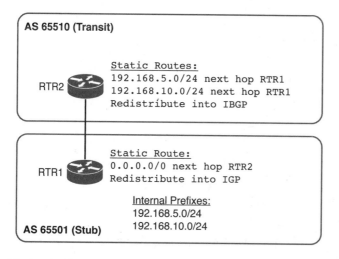

Figure 1-16 *Static Routes Are Usually a Better Choice Than BGP for a Single-Homed AS*

RTR2 has static routes configured for the prefixes in AS65501 and advertises the routes via IBGP throughout the AS. Other edge routers in the AS, learning the prefixes via IBGP, advertise them (or better, an aggregate that includes these prefixes) via EBGP to their respective external peers in other autonomous systems. The static routes of Figure 1-16 ensure strict control over what information is advertised in each AS about the other AS, with no risk of unwanted prefixes accidentally leaking across the administrative boundary.

Following are a number of good reasons for a stub AS to multihome:

- Redundancy against access loss because of link and interface failures

- Redundancy against access loss because of router failures

- Redundancy against access loss because of ISP failures

- Local connectivity for autonomous systems with wide geographical footprints

- Provider independence

- Corporate or external policies such as acceptable use policies or economic partnerships

- Load sharing

Figure 1-17 shows a simple multihoming setup for providing redundancy against a link or interface failure; two links, attached to separate interfaces at each of the externally linked neighbors, ensure that if any one link or interface fails AS65501 still has a path to its transit provider's AS.

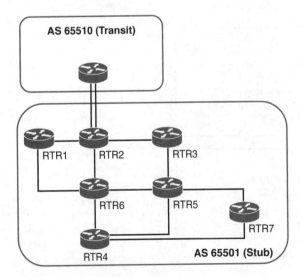

Figure 1-17 *Simple Multihoming Can Prevent Access Loss Due to a Link or Interface Failure at an Edge Router*

Redundancy against link or interface loss can be further improved simply by adding more links between the two edge routers. But access in that case can still be lost if the edge router in either AS fails. Another liability with this configuration is that the two links shown, if connected to the same physical router, are likely to be in the same cable or share a single conduit. A cut would take out both links.[9]

Figure 1-18 shows an improved topology: Now AS65501 cannot be isolated by the loss of any single link, interface, or router. The redundancy is further improved if the two routers are in separate and distant physical locations so that a disaster cannot take out both routers.

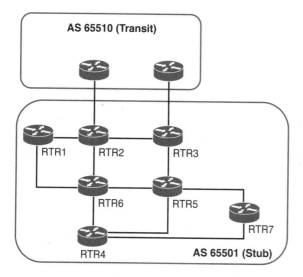

Figure 1-18 *Distributing the Redundant Links to Include Redundant Routers Further Reduces the Risk of Access Loss*

The stub AS in Figure 1-18 is still vulnerable to access loss if its single transit provider goes down. Failure of an entire service provider network can and does occasionally happen, almost always as the result of the misconfiguration of a BGP policy. (Chapter 4 discusses the dangers of careless policies.) Figure 1-19, then, shows a topology in which the stub AS is protected not just from link, interface, and router failures but also from the failure of an ISP. In this case, the AS is connected to three different transit providers. If one or even two of the transit autonomous systems fail, there is still a path into and out of the AS (assuming the transit providers all have upstream peering that provides them with full Internet routes).

A combination of redundant links, redundant routers, and redundant transit providers is shown in Figure 1-20. This topology provides tremendously robust access. However, as the level of access reliability increases, as shown in Figures 1-17 through 1-20, so does

---

[9] The problem of a single disruption breaking what should be redundant links is called fate sharing.

the capital, connection, and operational costs as well as operational complexity. So an ideal redundancy scheme similar to the one shown in Figure 1-20 is seldom practical in reality. Rather, redundancy is a compromise between acceptable risk and acceptable cost: something between the extremes of lowest cost/highest risk shown in Figure 1-16 and highest cost/lowest risk shown in Figure 1-20.

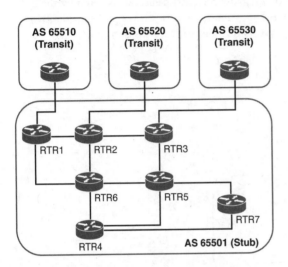

Figure 1-19 *Distributing the Redundant Links to Include Redundant Autonomous Systems Prevents Access Loss Due to the Failure of a Provider Network*

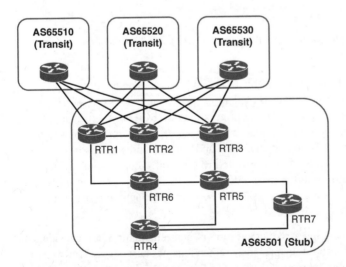

Figure 1-20 *Combining the Previously Illustrated Tactics of Redundant Links, Redundant Routers, and Redundant Transit Providers Reduces the Risk of Access Loss to Almost Zero*

Multihoming also provides local Internet connectivity across a geographically large AS, for example, an AS that spans most of the United States and peers with its ISP in New York City. Suppose a packet is originated in Los Angeles with an external destination in nearby San Diego. The packet has to travel across the internal network to its external peering point in New York and then travel all the way back across the country to the destination less than 100 miles from the originator. Return traffic to the originator has to again cross the entire country twice, San Diego to New York to Los Angeles. Such a traffic pattern not only is a poor use of network resources, it also causes unnecessary delay and unpredictable delay variation (jitter), which can be a serious problem for time-sensitive applications such as voice and video. The traffic pattern also reduces network reliability at least a little: The further a packet has to travel, the more likely it is to encounter a network problem and be lost.

Figure 1-21 shows a stub AS with an internal topology spanning most of the United States. Rather than a single ISP peering point, there are five distributed across the country. Packets originated anywhere in the country are then routed to the closest Internet peering point—the closest exit—to the originator. So the packet of the previous example, originated in Los Angeles for an external destination in San Diego, would exit the Los Angeles peering point. Return traffic would likely enter the AS at the same point, and session delay and jitter is sharply reduced.

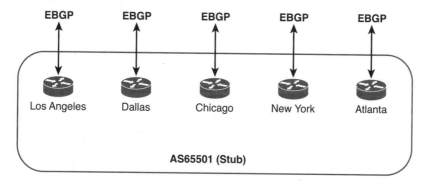

Figure 1-21   *Multihoming Can Be Used to Implement Local Connectivity over an AS with a Wide Geographic Footprint*

The EBGP peers in Figure 1-21 might all be in the same AS; that is, all going to the same ISP—or each might go to a different ISP to provide ISP redundancy (refer to Figure 1-19). Most real-life networks are likely to be a mix: For instance, Los Angeles, Chicago, and Atlanta might be peered with Level 3 Communications, whereas Dallas and New York are peered with Verizon.

Multihoming to multiple ISPs not only provides ISP redundancy, protecting your network from isolation due to a system-wide outage at a single provider, it also gives you provider independence. If you use a single ISP and want to change to another ISP—because of dissatisfaction with your ISP's reliability, performance, or price or because another ISP offers better service features or better connectivity to the destinations you use most often—the change can be complicated and expensive. If you are peered to multiple ISPs and want to change one of them, the change is less complex; you still have connectivity through the other providers while changing the one.

Peering with multiple ISPs can also have economic advantages. When the providers are first competing for your business, they are more likely to give you more attractive rates; and if you use two or more, none can afford to raise their rates higher than the others without the risk of losing your business. (And again, if you connect to multiple providers, dumping an overpriced one is much easier.)

Multihoming is also needed when you have acceptable use policies (AUP) or corporate policies that say certain traffic must always use one transit AS, and other traffic must use another transit network. For example, military or other government agencies can have strict policies requiring sensitive traffic to always use only certain transit providers that have passed strict security qualifications. Or an enterprise might have external peerings with several competing partners; no traffic to one partner should ever transit another partner's network.

Just as the transit AS operator needs a set of tools and methodologies for changing the default behavior of routing to serve his various types of peering, the operator of a multihomed stub AS also needs such tools and methodologies to, for instance, prevent her network from being inadvertently treated as a transit network by connected autonomous systems, or to reflect a preference for one connected ISP over another, or to implement acceptable use policies. This is the job of routing policies.

Multihoming and Routing Policies

You were introduced to the basic IOS tools for building routing policies in the later chapters of Volume I: route redistribution, default routes, route filters, and the most powerful of the IOS route policy tools, route maps. BGP is particularly suited for implementing routing policies—much more so than any IGP—by providing a set of characteristics called *path attributes* that can be added, changed, or removed with policy tools to impose various routing behaviors. You have already encountered one BGP path attribute: the AS_PATH. Chapter 2 introduces the other basic path attributes and explains how each is used. Chapter 4 then offers specific examples of configuring routing policies. A few specialized path attributes and their use are introduced in Chapters 5 and 6.

Multihoming Issues: Load Sharing and Load Balancing

The principal benefits of multihoming are redundancy, path diversity, and increased bandwidth to external peers. If increased bandwidth is a primary goal—which is usually the case when links are "bundled" between the same two routers (refer to Figure 1-17)—and if the individual link bandwidths are the same, the traffic load between the two peers can be shared reasonably equally across all links in the bundle.

When multihoming is primarily for redundancy, the load across any one link must never be more than a fraction of the total traffic across the redundant links. In Figure 1-18, for example, the normal traffic load across each of the two external links should always be below 50 percent of the link bandwidth. That way, if one of the links fails causing its normal traffic to be rerouted over the remaining link, that remaining link can handle the load. If under normal conditions the load on each link averages 75 percent of the link bandwidth, under a failure condition the traffic routed to the remaining link will be 150 percent of the link's bandwidth; one-third of the packets will be dropped.

Any time multiple links can carry the same packets, total incoming and outgoing traffic load is shared across the links. This can include topologies as simple as Figure 1-17 or as complex as Figures 1-20 and 1-21. In the latter cases, the load is shared not only across links but also through ISPs. And as the diversity of links and ISPs increases, so does the diversity of preferred routes. That is, not all links and ISPs carry the traffic with equal efficiency.

You should therefore not expect the traffic load to be balanced equally across all links; one of the ISPs will almost always be "better connected" than the others. One ISP or its upstream provider might have better routers, better physical links, or more peering connections than the other ISP, or one ISP might just be topologically closer to more of the destinations to which your users regularly connect.

The point is that *load sharing* is not the same as *load balancing*, in which an effort (usually misguided) is made to maintain equal load percentages on all external links in the name of efficient bandwidth usage.

That is not to say that you cannot, through the expenditure of considerable time and effort, manipulate route preferences to get a fairly even balance of your traffic across all external links. The problem is that you will probably degrade your Internet access performance by forcing some traffic to take a less-optimal route for the sake of load balancing. All you accomplish, in most cases, is an evening-out of the utilization numbers of your ISP links. In addition, because Internet destinations change constantly, the operational cost of constantly adjusting policies is high. Do not be too concerned if 75 percent of your traffic uses one link, whereas only 25 percent of your traffic uses the other link. Multihoming is for redundancy and increased routing efficiency, not load balancing.

Multihoming Issues: Traffic Control

Multihoming presents the possibility of traffic to the same destination and from the same source taking different, and hence less predictable, paths into and out of your AS. Such path diversity is usually not a concern when the external links are close to each other, but potential problems increase as the distance between the external links grows.

Figure 1-22 shows an AS that is peered to two ISPs, one in San Jose and one in Boston. The two ISPs are peered at an IXP in Chicago, and AS65501 has internal links that connect its east and west coast offices through Denver. The edge routers advertise a default route into the AS, which internal routers select when a more-specific route cannot be found.

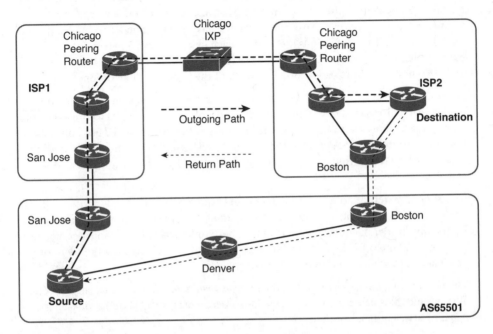

Figure 1-22   *A Multihomed AS with Geographically Distant External Peering Can Experience Asymmetric Traffic Flows*

In the illustration, a router on the west coast originates a packet with a destination that is connected to ISP2 on the east coast. The default route is chosen for this destination, and the San Jose edge router is selected as the nearest next hop for the default route; the Boston edge router is seen as the next-best route. The outgoing traffic then goes through ISP1, across the Chicago IXP to ISP2, and is delivered to the destination.

The destination router has two routes to AS65501, via ISP2's Boston router and via its Chicago peering router. It chooses the shortest route, through the Boston router, for packets responding to the source router. That path then traverses AS65501's internal links. As a result, the round-trip path between the source and destination routers is asymmetric.

Such traffic patterns are typical when default routes are used because the routers have no specifics about the destination outside of their domain or the actual distance to the destination; their only selection criteria is the nearest router advertising the default route.

Asymmetric traffic can be unwanted for several reasons:

■ Network traffic patterns become unpredictable, making baselining, capacity planning, and troubleshooting more problematic.

■ Link usage can become unbalanced. The bandwidth of some links can become saturated, whereas other links are underutilized. Although as the previous section explained, the remedies for this problem can be worse than the problem itself; severe imbalances can create unnecessary congestion.

■ A distinct variation can occur in the delay times of outgoing traffic and incoming traffic. This delay variation can be detrimental to some delay-sensitive applications such as voice and live video.

BGP can help solve the asymmetric routing (refer to Figure 1-22). If AS65501's edge routers in San Jose and Boston are speaking EBGP to their respective ISP peers, they can each learn a route to the depicted destination. If the source router then has access to those two routes, it can determine that the shortest path to the destination is through the Boston edge router rather than through San Jose. The traffic patterns between the source and destination are then symmetric, as shown in Figure 1-23.

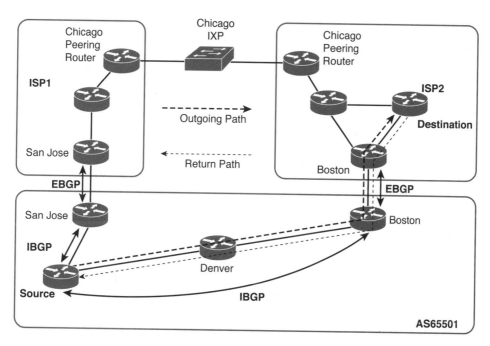

Figure 1-23 *BGP Can Help AS-Internal Routers Make Better Choices About Routes to External Destinations*

But BGP provides you with more than just the means for making better route choices. Its policy capabilities enable you to define a "better route," on your own terms, outside of what a routing protocol would define by default. For example, suppose you want to implement a policy of "hot potato routing," in which traffic to external destinations always goes to the nearest AS exit point, to conserve internal resources. But at the same time you want to avoid, whenever possible, asymmetric paths (refer to Figure 1-22).

With BGP, you can modify the way the prefixes associated with the source router are advertised by the Boston edge router so that the destination router sees the path into AS65501 through San Jose as the preferred route to the source router (see Figure 1-24). Chapter 4 demonstrates techniques for influencing how other autonomous systems choose the routes into your AS.

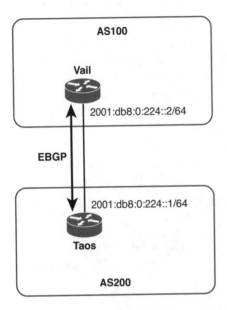

Figure 1-24 *BGP Policies Can Influence How Other Autonomous Systems Choose the Paths into the Local AS*

Multihoming Issues: Provider-Assigned Addressing

When smaller organizations connect to an ISP, they usually acquire their IP address space from the ISP. The addresses assigned are a part of a larger pool of addresses belonging to the ISP. Addresses assigned this way to the end user are called *provider-assigned* or *provider-aggregatable (PA)* addresses.

If the end-user organization is multihomed to more than one ISP, and the organization has a PA space assigned by one of the providers, advertising that address space in such a way that incoming packets are routed correctly can be a problem. Fully understanding the problem involves first understanding how ISPs are assigned, and in turn assign, blocks of addresses called CIDR blocks. The next section introduces CIDR and then revisits the issue of multihoming to multiple service providers.

Classless Inter-Domain Routing

The invention of autonomous systems and exterior gateway protocols solved the early scalability problems on the Internet in the 1980s. However, by the early 1990s the Internet was beginning to present a different set of scalability problems, including the following:

- Depletion of the Class B address space. In January 1993, 7133 of the 16,382 available Class B addresses had been assigned; at 1993 growth rates, the entire Class B address space would be depleted in less than 2 years (as cited in RFC 1519).

- Explosion of the Internet routing tables. The exponentially growing routing tables were becoming increasingly unmanageable both by the routers of the time and the people who managed them. The mere size of the tables was burden enough on Internet resources, but day-to-day topological changes and instabilities added heavily to the load.

- The eventual exhaustion of the entire 32-bit IPv4 address space.

Classless inter-domain routing (CIDR) was created to provide a short-term solution to these problems. Another short-term solution is *network address translation (NAT)*, discussed in Chapter 10, "IPv4 to IPv4 Network Address Translation (NAT44)." These solutions were intended to buy the Internet architects enough time to create a new version of IP with enough address space for the foreseeable future. That initiative, known as IP Next Generation (IPng), resulted in the creation of IPv6, with a 128-bit address format.[10] Interestingly, CIDR and NAT have been so successful that until recently few people placed as much urgency on the migration to IPv6 as they once did.

CIDR is merely a politically sanctioned address summarization scheme that takes advantage of the hierarchical structure of the Internet and does away with the artificial boundaries imposed by classful address assignments. So before discussing CIDR further, a review of summarization and classless routing is in order.

A Summarization Summary

Summarization or *route aggregation* (discussed extensively in Volume I) is the practice of advertising a contiguous set of addresses with a single, less-specific address. Basically, summarization/route aggregation is accomplished by reducing the length of the subnet mask until it masks only the bits common to all the addresses being summarized. Figure 1-25 shows the four subnets (172.16.100.192/28, 172.16.100.208/28, 172.16.100.224/28, and 172.16.100.240/28) are summarized with the single aggregate address 172.16.100.192/26.

---

[10] IPv6 is introduced in Chapter 2 of Volume I. This newer version of IP is discussed throughout this volume, with the assumption that you already understand its basics. If this is not the case, you are advised to read about the basics of IPv6 in Volume I or any other good introduction to the protocol.

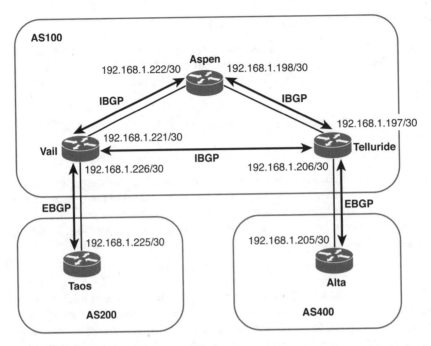

Figure 1-25   *Route Aggregation Combines Several Contiguous Addresses with a Common Prefix into a Single Address*

Many new networkers who view summarization as a difficult topic are surprised to learn that they use summarization daily. What is a subnet address, after all, other than a summarization of a contiguous group of host addresses? For example, the subnet address 192.168.5.224/27 is the aggregate of host addresses 192.168.5.224/32 through 192.168.5.255/32. (The "host address" 192.168.5.224/32 is, of course, the address of the data link itself.) The key characteristic of a summary address is that its mask is shorter than the masks of the addresses it is summarizing. The ultimate summary address is the default address, 0.0.0.0/0, often written as just 0/0. As the /0 indicates, the mask has shrunk until no network bits remain; the default address is the aggregate of *all* IP addresses.

Summarization can also cross class boundaries. For example, the four Class C networks (192.168.0.0, 192.168.1.0, 192.168.2.0, and 192.168.3.0) can all be summarized with the aggregate address 192.168.0.0/22. Notice that the aggregate, with its 22-bit mask, is no longer a legal Class C address. Therefore, to support the aggregation of major class network addresses, the routing environment must be classless.

Classless Routing

Following are two aspects of classless routing:

- Classlessness can be a characteristic of a routing protocol.

- Classlessness can be a characteristic of a router.

The "classful" IP routing protocols—RIPv1, IGRP, and BGP versions prior to BGP-4—are no longer used in modern networks.[11] And classful routing is no longer the default on most modern routers: IOS changed to classless routing as the default in 11.3, so all current versions of IOS are classless. Therefore, this section is to some extent of historical interest only. Nevertheless, you are encouraged read it because it is useful for understanding longest-match route lookups.

Classless routing protocols carry, as part of the routing information, a description of the network portion of each advertised address. The network portion of a network address is commonly referred to as the *address prefix*. An address prefix can be described by including an address mask, a length field that indicates how many leading bits of the address are prefix bits, or by including only the prefix bits in the update (see Figure 1-26). The classless IPv4 routing protocols are RIP-2, EIGRP, OSPF, Integrated IS-IS, and BGP-4.[12]

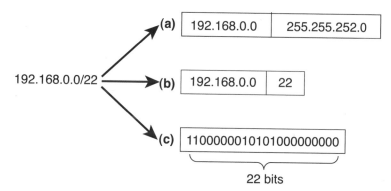

Figure 1-26 *Classless Routing Protocols Include Information About the Prefix Length in Their Route Advertisements*

A classful router records destination addresses in its routing table as major class networks and subnets of those networks. When it performs a route lookup, it first looks up the major class network address and then tries to find a match in its list of subnets under that major address. If no match exists, the packet is dropped—even if a route such as a

---

[11] RIPv1 is a possible exception. It might still be in use in some small networks where classful routing is not an issue.

[12] IPv6 has never had a concept of address classes, so this discussion is irrelevant to IPv6.

default route exists. Summarization and address aggregation, essential not only for CIDR but also for scalability in modern network design, become problematic in a classful environment.

A classless router ignores address classes and attempts a "longest match" of a destination address to all prefixes in its routing table. That is, for any given destination address, it chooses the route that matches the most bits of the address, reading left to right. The routing table in Example 1-8 shows several variably subnetted IP networks. If the router is classless, it attempts to find the longest match for each destination address.

Example 1-8   *This Routing Table Contains Several Variably Subnetted IP Networks*

```
Cleveland#show ip route
Codes: C - connected, S - static, I - IGRP, R - RIP, M - mobile, B - BGP
       D - EIGRP, EX - EIGRP external, O - OSPF, IA - OSPF inter area
       E1 - OSPF external type 1, E2 - OSPF external type 2, E - EGP
       i - IS-IS, L1 - IS-IS level-1, L2 - IS-IS level-2, * - candidate default


Gateway of last resort is 192.168.2.130 to network 0.0.0.0

O E2 192.168.125.0 [110/20] via 192.168.2.2, 00:11:19, Ethernet0
O    192.168.75.0 [110/74] via 192.168.2.130, 00:11:19, Serial0
O E2 192.168.8.0 [110/40] via 192.168.2.18, 00:11:19, Ethernet1
     192.168.1.0 is variably subnetted, 3 subnets, 3 masks
O E1    192.168.1.64 255.255.255.192
            [110/139] via 192.168.2.134, 00:11:20, Serial1
O E1    192.168.1.0 255.255.255.128
            [110/139] via 192.168.2.134, 00:00:34, Serial1
O E2    192.168.1.0 255.255.255.0
            [110/20] via 192.168.2.2, 00:11:20, Ethernet0
     192.168.2.0 is variably subnetted, 4 subnets, 2 masks
C       192.168.2.0 255.255.255.240 is directly connected, Ethernet0
C       192.168.2.16 255.255.255.240 is directly connected, Ethernet1
C       192.168.2.128 255.255.255.252 is directly connected, Serial0
C       192.168.2.132 255.255.255.252 is directly connected, Serial1
O E2 192.168.225.0 [110/20] via 192.168.2.2, 00:11:20, Ethernet0
O E2 192.168.230.0 [110/20] via 192.168.2.2, 00:11:21, Ethernet0
O E2 192.168.198.0 [110/20] via 192.168.2.2, 00:11:21, Ethernet0
O E2 192.168.215.0 [110/20] via 192.168.2.2, 00:11:21, Ethernet0
O E2 192.168.129.0 [110/20] via 192.168.2.2, 00:11:21, Ethernet0
O E2 192.168.131.0 [110/20] via 192.168.2.2, 00:11:21, Ethernet0
O E2 192.168.135.0 [110/20] via 192.168.2.2, 00:11:21, Ethernet0
O*E2 0.0.0.0 0.0.0.0 [110/1] via 192.168.2.130, 00:11:21, Serial0
O E2 192.168.0.0 255.255.0.0 [110/40] via 192.168.2.18, 00:11:22, Ethernet1
Cleveland#
```

If the router receives a packet with a destination address of 192.168.1.75, several entries in the routing table match the address: 192.168.0.0/16, 192.168.1.0/24, 192.168.1.0/25, and 192.168.1.64/26. The entry 192.168.1.64/26 is chosen (see Example 1-9) because it matches 26 bits of the destination address: the longest match.

Example 1-9   *A Packet with a Destination Address of 192.168.1.75 Is Forwarded Out Interface S1*

```
Cleveland#show ip route 192.168.1.75
Routing entry for 192.168.1.64 255.255.255.192
  Known via "ospf 1", distance 110, metric 139, type extern 1
  Redistributing via ospf 1
  Last update from 192.168.2.134 on Serial1, 06:46:52 ago
  Routing Descriptor Blocks:
  * 192.168.2.134, from 192.168.7.1, 06:46:52 ago, via Serial1
      Route metric is 139, traffic share count is 1
```

A packet with a destination address of 192.168.1.217 will not match 192.168.1.64/26, nor will it match 192.168.1.0/25. The longest match for this address is 192.168.1.0/24, as shown in Example 1-10.

Example 1-10   *Router Cannot Match 192.168.1.217 to a More Specific Subnet, So It Matches the Network Address 192.168.1.0/24*

```
Cleveland#show ip route 192.168.1.217
Routing entry for 192.168.1.0 255.255.255.0
  Known via "ospf 1", distance 110, metric 20, type extern 2, forward metric 10
  Redistributing via ospf 1
  Last update from 192.168.2.2 on Ethernet0, 06:48:18 ago
  Routing Descriptor Blocks:
  * 192.168.2.2, from 10.2.1.1, 06:48:18 ago, via Ethernet0
      Route metric is 20, traffic share count is 1
```

The longest match that can be made for destination address 192.168.5.3 is the aggregate address 192.168.0.0/16, as shown in Example 1-11.

Example 1-11   *Packets Destined for 192.168.5.3 Do Not Match a More Specific Subnet or Network and Therefore Match the Aggregate 192.168.0.0/16*

```
Cleveland#show ip route 192.168.5.3
Routing entry for 192.168.0.0 255.255.0.0, supernet
  Known via "ospf 1", distance 110, metric 139, type extern 1
  Redistributing via ospf 1
  Last update from 192.168.2.18 on Ethernet1, 06:49:26 ago
  Routing Descriptor Blocks:
  * 192.168.2.18, from 192.168.7.1, 06:49:26 ago, via Ethernet1
      Route metric is 139, traffic share count is 1
```

Finally, a destination address of 192.169.1.1 will not match any of the network entries in the routing table, as shown in Example 1-12. Packets with this destination address are not dropped, however, because the routing table of Example 1-8 contains a default route (represented as the "gateway of last resort" in the routing table). The packets are forwarded to next-hop router 192.168.2.130.

Example 1-12   *No Match Is Found in the Routing Table for 192.169.1.1; Packets Destined for This Address Are Forwarded to the Next Hop for the Default Route, 192.168.2.130, Out Interface S0, According to the Routing Table for Example 1-8*

```
Cleveland#show ip route 192.169.1.1
% Network not in table
```

The routing table in Example 1-8 and the associated examples demonstrates another characteristic of longest-match routing. Namely, a route to an aggregate address does not necessarily point to every member of the aggregate. Figure 1-27 shows the vectors of the routes in Examples 1-9 through 1-12.

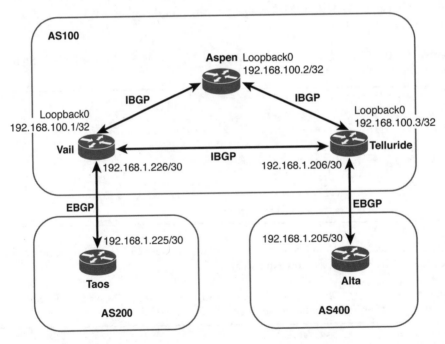

Figure 1-27   *Vectors of the Routes in the Routing table of Example 1-8*

You can consider network 192.168.1.0/24 an aggregate of all its subnets; Figure 1-27 shows that the route to this network address directs packets out interface E0. Yet routes to two of its subnets, 192.168.1.0/25 and 192.168.1.64/26, point out a different interface, S1.

Note   Actually, 192.168.1.64/26 is a member of 192.168.1.0/25. Distinct routes for these two addresses, both pointing out S1, hint that they are advertised by separate routers somewhere upstream.

Likewise, 192.168.1.0/24 is a member of the aggregate 192.168.0.0/16, but the route to that less-specific address is out E1. The least-specific route, 0.0.0.0/0, which is an aggregate of all other addresses, is out S0. Because of longest-match routing, packets to subnets 192.168.1.64/26 and 192.168.1.0/25 are forwarded out S1, whereas packets to other subnets of network 192.168.1.0/24 are forwarded out E0. Packets with destination addresses beginning with 192.168, other than 192.168.1, are forwarded out E1, and packets whose destination addresses do not begin with 192.168 are forwarded out S0.

Summarization: The Good, the Bad, and the Asymmetric

Summarization is a great tool for conserving network resources, from the amount of memory required to store the routing table to the amount of network bandwidth and router horsepower necessary to transmit and process routing information. Summarization also conserves network resources by "hiding" network instabilities.

For example, the network in Figure 1-28 has a flapping route—a route that, because of a bad physical connection or router interface, keeps transitioning down and up and down again.

Without summarization, every time subnet 192.168.1.176/28 goes up or down, the information must be conveyed to every router in the corporate network. Each of those routers, in turn, must process the information and adjust its routing table accordingly: a problem called *update churn*. If router Nashville advertises all the downstream routes with the single aggregate address 192.168.1.128/25, however, changes to any of the more-specific subnets—including 192.168.1.176/28—are not advertised past that router. Nashville is the aggregation point; the aggregate continues to be stable even if some of its members are not.

The price to be paid for summarization is a reduction in routing precision. In Example 1-13, interface S1 of the router in Figure 1-27 has failed, causing the routes learned from the neighbor on that interface to become invalid. Instead of dropping packets that would normally be forwarded out S1, however, such as a packet with a destination address of 192.168.1.75, the packet now matches the next-best route, 192.168.1.0/24, and is forwarded out interface E0. (Compare this to Example 1-9.)

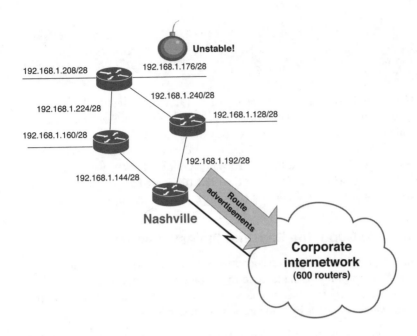

Figure 1-28   *A Flapping Route Can Destabilize the Entire Network*

Example 1-13   *A Failed Route Has Caused a Change in Forwarding Behavior*

```
Cleveland#
%LINEPROTO-5-UPDOWN: Line protocol on Interface Serial1, changed state to down
%LINK-3-UPDOWN: Interface Serial1, changed state to down
Cleveland#show ip route 192.168.1.75
Routing entry for 192.168.1.0 255.255.255.0
  Known via "ospf 1", distance 110, metric 20, type extern 2, forward metric 10
  Redistributing via ospf 1
  Last update from 192.168.2.2 on Ethernet0, 00:00:20 ago
  Routing Descriptor Blocks:
  * 192.168.2.2, from 10.2.1.1, 00:00:20 ago, via Ethernet0
      Route metric is 20, traffic share count is 1
```

This change in forwarding might be a problem, depending on what the rest of the network looks like. Continuing with the example, suppose the next-hop router 192.168.2.2
in Figure 1-27 still has a route entry to 192.168.1.64/26 via the router Cleveland in
Example 1-13, either because the routing protocol has not yet converged or because
the route was statically entered. In this case, a routing loop occurs. However, some
router reachable via Cleveland's E0 interface may have a "back door" route to subnet
192.168.1.64/26 that should be used only if the primary route, via Cleveland's S1,

becomes invalid. In this second case, the route to 192.168.1.0/24 has been designed as a backup route, and the behavior shown in Example 1-13 is intentional.

Figure 1-29 shows a network in which a loss of routing precision can cause a different sort of problem. Here, routing domain 1 is connected to routing domain 2 by routers in San Francisco and Atlanta. What defines these domains is unimportant for the example. What is important is that all the networks in domain 1 can be summarized with the address 172.16.192.0/18, and all the networks in domain 2 can be summarized with the address 172.16.128.0/18.

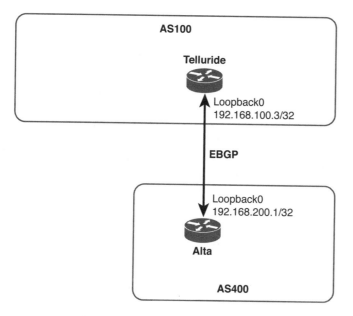

Figure 1-29 *When Multiple Routers Are Advertising the Same Aggregate Addresses, Loss of Routing Precision Can Become a Problem*

Rather than advertise individual subnets, Atlanta and San Francisco advertise the summary addresses into the two domains. If a host on Dallas' subnet 172.16.227.128/26 sends a packet to a host on Seattle's subnet 172.16.172.32/28, the packet most likely is routed to Atlanta because that is the closest router advertising domain 2's summary route. Atlanta forwards the packet into domain 2, and it arrives at Seattle. When the host on subnet 172.16.172.32/28 sends a reply, Seattle forwards that packet to San Francisco—the closest router advertising the summary route 172.16.192.0/18.

The problem here is that the traffic between the two subnets has become asymmetric: Packets from 172.16.227.128/26 to 172.16.172.32/28 take one path, whereas packets from 172.16.172.32/28 to 172.16.227.128/26 take a different path. Asymmetry occurs because the Dallas and Seattle routers do not have complete routes to each other's subnets. They have only routes to the routers advertising the summaries and must forward packets based on those routes. In other words, the summarization at San Francisco and Atlanta has hidden the details of the subnets behind those routers.

The scenario presented in the section "Multihoming Issues: Traffic Control," is the same issue described here because the default routes used in that example are just routes to summary addresses. The reasons asymmetric traffic might be undesirable were described in that section; however, you can now see that asymmetry might be a reasonable price to pay for the benefits of summarization. Like so many choices in network design, the positives of summarization versus the negatives of asymmetric traffic are a trade-off.

CIDR: Reducing Class B Address Space Depletion

The depletion of Class B addresses was due to an inherent flaw in the design of the IPv4 address classes. A Class C address provides 254 host addresses, whereas a Class B address provides 65,534 host addresses. That's a wide gap. Before CIDR, if your company needed 500 host addresses, a Class C address would not have served your needs. You probably would have requested a Class B address, even though you would be wasting 65,000 host addresses. With CIDR, your needs can be met with a /23 block. The host addresses that would have otherwise been wasted have been conserved.

CIDR does away with the original class concepts in IPv4. Although it is still occasionally easy to use some classful references, such as referring to the address space reserved for IPv4 multicast as the Class D space and the largely unused block of addresses set aside for experimental use as Class E, referring to Classes A, B, and C addresses is simply outdated terminology. In its place, CIDR terminology refers to the size of an address block by the length of its prefix: The shorter the prefix length, the larger the number of addresses the block contains. So in CIDR terminology, Classes A, B, and C address blocks are now /8, /16/ and /24 (pronounced "slash eight," "slash sixteen," and "slash twenty-four"), respectively. But more important, there are no artificial boundaries between prefix blocks. So CIDR also includes /23, /22, /21, and so on, all the way down to /0. Address blocks can, under CIDR, be far more efficiently allocated to meet actual needs without being wasteful.

CIDR: Reducing Routing Table Explosion

When CIDR was proposed in 1993, the route entries in the Internet routing tables were expanding far faster than had been anticipated when IPv4 was first adopted in the 1970s. As Figure 1-30 shows, in the 54 months between July 1988 and the end of 1992, the number of entries in the Internet routing tables was growing exponentially, approximately doubling every year:

- 173 entries July 1988

- 334 by the end of 1988

- 897 by the end of 1989

- 2190 by the end of 1990

- 4305 by the end of 1991

- 8561 by the end of 1992

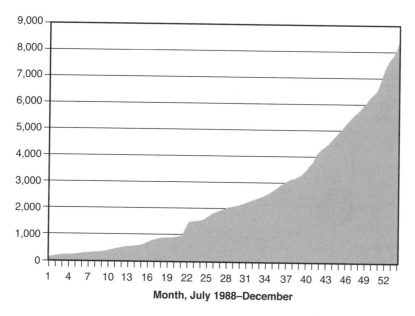

Figure 1-30   *The Internet Routing Table Was Growing Exponentially Between 1988 and the End of 1992*

When the Internet routing table is measured in the hundreds of thousands of routes, 8500 routes does not seem at all large these days, and even individual enterprises can have thousands of entries in their routing tables. But in the early 1990s, memory was far more expensive than it is today.

More important than the actual table size, however, was the instabilities that processing detailed route entries posed to core routers. This is the same update churn problem illustrated in Figure 1-28 and the associated discussion: The more "visibility" longer prefixes have in the Internet routing table, the more processing of BGP updates that is needed to keep track of relatively insignificant state changes.

Summarization is extremely effective at reducing the size of routing tables when the network topology is hierarchical, whether it is a hierarchy of OSPF areas or a hierarchy of autonomous systems. Figure 1-31 shows a typical OSPF design. The OSPF domain, AS1, has an assigned prefix of 198.133.180.0/22. The domain is divided into a backbone area and four nonbackbone areas, and the addresses assigned within each area are a contiguous subset of the AS prefix.[13] The ABRs for each area advertise the single summary address into the backbone area. The routers in each area, then, have just four Type 3 LSAs in their databases and four entries in their routing tables to represent all addresses outside of that area but within the OSPF domain.

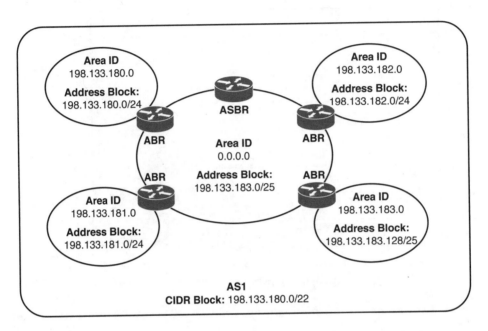

Figure 1-31 *Summarization Within an IGP Domain Can Sharply Reduce the Size of the Routing Tables Within the IGP Domain*

Figure 1-32 again shows AS1 with its assigned prefix of 198.133.180.0/22, but in a larger context of one of several autonomous systems. AS2 has a prefix of 198.133.176.0/22. Both AS1 and AS2 are attached to a service provider, AS6, that has assigned their prefixes from its larger CIDR block, 198.133.176.0/20. And that service provider, in turn, was assigned that block from its own service provider at AS8 from the block 198.133.0.0/16. AS8 also has another AS attached to it, AS7, and has assigned a different prefix to that AS. AS7 in turn is serving three autonomous systems, each with prefixes assigned out of AS7's prefix.

The important fact about the topology in Figure 1-32 is that the entire set of autonomous systems is addressed from a single CIDR prefix, 198.133.0.0/16. AS8 advertises only that prefix to the Internet, rather than the prefixes of each of the eight autonomous systems, helping to reduce the size of the Internet routing table. Actually, AS8 could

---

13 The design also shows a useful practice when efficient address summarization is used: Each Area ID corresponds to the address block used in that area.

assign six more /20s, or some other combination of longer prefixes, out of its /16, without having to advertise any more than the one /16 to the Internet.

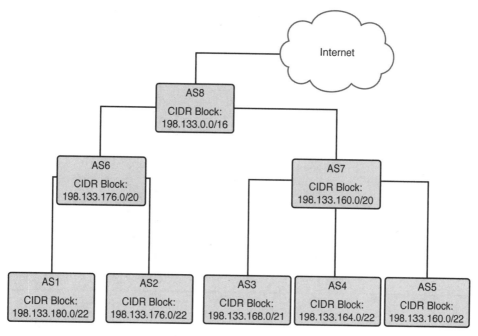

Figure 1-32 *Summarization in a Hierarchy of Autonomous Systems Helps Reduce the Size of the Internet Routing Table*

The advertisement of a single aggregate to the higher-level domain is obviously preferable to advertising possibly hundreds of individual addresses. But a more important benefit is the stability such a scheme adds to the Internet. If the state of a network in a low-level domain changes, that change is felt only up to the first aggregation point and no further.

Table 1-2 shows the different sizes of CIDR blocks down to /8, their equivalent size in Class C networks, and the number of hosts each block can represent.

Table 1-2 *CIDR Block Sizes*

CIDR Block Prefix Size	Number of Equivalent Class C Addresses	Number of Possible Host Addresses
/24	1	254
/23	2	510
/22	4	1022

CIDR Block Prefix Size	Number of Equivalent Class C Addresses	Number of Possible Host Addresses
/21	8	2046
/20	16	4094
/19	32	8190
/18	64	16,382
/17	128	32,766
/16	256	65,534
/15	512	131,070
/14	1024	262,142
/13	2048	524,286
/12	4096	1,048,574
/11	8192	2,097,150
/10	16,384	4,194,302
/9	32,768	8,388,606
/8	65,536	16,777,214

Managing and Assigning IPv4 Address Blocks

At the highest level, the *Internet Assigned Numbers Authority (IANA)* is responsible for allocating IP addresses under the management of the *Internet Corporation of Assigned Names and Numbers (ICANN)*. Originally IANA was the sole *Internet Registry (IR)*—that is, the body to which you apply for the registration and allocation of IP addresses, AS numbers, and the such—and for much of its early life was run by a single individual, the late Jon Postel.

Around the same time that CIDR came into being, a number of *Regional Internet Registries (RIR)* were established under the IANA to "be better able to serve the local community in terms of language and local customs" (RFC 1366). The current specification for Internet numbers management is RFC 7020. At press time, there are five RIRs:

- **African Network Information Centre (AfriNIC):** Established in 2005, serves Africa and portions of the Indian Ocean.

- **Asia-Pacific Network Information Centre (APNIC):** Established in 1993, serves the Asia Pacific region and portions of Oceana.

- **American Registry for Internet Numbers (ARIN):** Established in 1997, serves North America (United States and Canada), and many Caribbean and North Atlantic

Islands. Prior to the formation of ARIN by ICANN, the regional registry was the Internet Network Information Center (InterNIC), run privately by Network Solutions, Inc. InterNIC was established in 1993.

- **Latin American and Caribbean Network Information Centre (LACNIC):** Established in 2002, serves Latin (Central and South) America and portions of the Caribbean.

- **Réseaux IP Européens Network Coordination Centre (RIPE NCC):** Established in 1992, serves Europe, the Middle East, and central Asia.

The IANA allocates IPv4 addresses to the RIRs in /8 CIDR blocks, according to projected needs. The RIRs then allocate portions of those blocks to Local Internet Registries (LIRs), which are usually larger ISPs, and the LIRs allocate portions of their blocks to their customers.[14] Some organizations that can justify a need for large allocations, such as large enterprises, academic institutions, and government agencies, might get their CIDR blocks directly from the RIR.

The RIRs work under an assumption of a large enough pool of available IPv4 addresses to serve the needs of their LIRs for 18 months. Each RIR requests a new allocation from the IANA whenever

- The RIR's pool of available addresses falls below 50 percent.

- Or the RIR's pool of available addresses falls below the level necessary to serve the projected needs of its LIRs for another 9 months.

When either of those conditions occur, the IANA assigns one or more new /8 blocks to the RIR, enough to restore the RIR's pool for a further 18 months of allocations.

All five of the RIRs use a *slow start* policy when making initial allocations to LIRs. Slow start defines a minimum prefix size (and hence maximum address block size) for the initial allocation, to conserve IPv4 addresses as much as possible. The slow start size varies slightly among the RIRs:[15]

- AfriNIC starts with a /22.

- APNIC, LACNIC, and RIPE NCC start with a /21.

- ARIN starts with a /20.

All the RIRs require that a prior allocation is 80 percent utilized before they will make a subsequent allocation. For example, ARIN requires proof of address utilization by one

---

[14] In some cases National Internet Registries (NIRs) exist between the RIRs and the LIRs. With few exceptions NIRs exist only in Asia under APNIC.

[15] Although these numbers are accurate, they are not the entire story about how the RIRs allot prefixes. For specifics visit each RIR's website or for good comparative documents see the Internet Corporation for Assigned Names and Numbers (ICANN) and Numbers Research Organization (NRO) websites.

of two means: the use of the Shared WHOIS Project (SWIP) or the use of a Referral WHOIS Server (RWHOIS). SWIP, most commonly used, is the practice of adding WHOIS information to a SWIP template and e-mailing it to ARIN. To use RWHOIS, you establish an RWHOIS server on your premises that ARIN can access for WHOIS information. In both cases the WHOIS information establishes proof that the LIR has efficiently used, and is approaching exhaustion of, its present address space.

Note   The depletion of publicly available IPv4 address space is making all this discussion moot. As of this writing, AfriNIC is the only RIR that has not announced that its IPv4 address supply is depleted. However, similar address allocation policies are in place for IPv6 address blocks; although, because of the enormous size of the IPv6 address space, the IPv6 allocation policies are more generous.

LIRs are in turn encouraged to use the same documentation requirements when they allocate portions of their address blocks to their customers. The LIRs are also encouraged to use dynamic (DHCP) address allocations to their customers whenever possible to further conserve IPv4 addresses.

All the RIRs can make exceptions to their slow start sizes when clear justification is documented, but in no case do they assign prefixes shorter than /19. There are also cases in which longer prefixes can be assigned; these cases are discussed in the next three sections.

CIDR Issues: Multihoming and Provider-Assigned Addresses

Understanding the nature of CIDR and the way CIDR blocks are assigned now lets you clearly examine the issue of multihoming to multiple service providers, introduced in the earlier section "Multihoming Issues: Provider-Assigned Addresses."

Figure 1-33 shows an AS multihomed to two ISPs. ISP1 serves as the LIR for the AS1, in keeping with the address assignment policies described in the previous section, and has assigned the AS a prefix (198.133.180.0/22) out of its /20 CIDR block 198.133.176.0/20. Both ISPs advertise their prefixes upstream to the Internet; AS1's prefix is a part of ISP1's advertised aggregate.

The problem arises when any device beyond the ISPs wants to send packets to a destination in AS1. Internet routers match the destination address of the packets to the aggregate address 198.133.176.0/20 advertised by ISP1 and route all packets through that ISP, even if the better path from the source to the destination is through ISP2. All packets to any destination within AS1, originating from beyond the two ISPs, are routed through ISP1. The only incoming traffic to AS1 that arrives from ISP2 is traffic that has originated in ISP2 or one of its attached customers (assuming that a route to 198.133.180.0/22 exists within AS2).

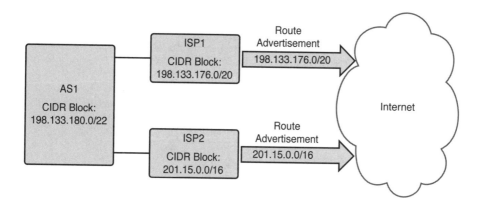

Figure 1-33 *AS1 Has Been Assigned Its Prefix from ISP1*

To have packets from the Internet use ISP2, it is necessary for that ISP to advertise AS1's prefix, as shown in Figure 1-34. But now the problem reverses: Packets destined for AS1 from the Internet will match the more-specific prefix 198.133.180.0/22 advertised by ISP2, and all traffic to AS1 is routed through that ISP.

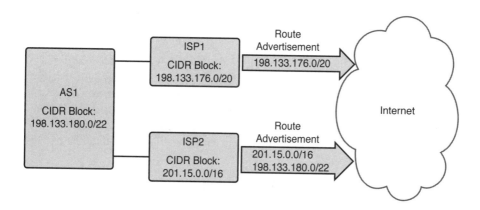

Figure 1-34 *Traffic from the Internet to AS1 Goes Through ISP2 Only if That ISP Advertises the Autonomous System's Prefix*

The solution to the problem is for ISP1 to "punch a hole" in its CIDR block (commonly called *prefix leaking, subdelegation,* or *de-aggregation*) and advertise the more-specific prefix 198.133.180.0/22, just as ISP2 is doing, along with its aggregate prefix (Figure 1-35). Traffic originating in the Internet now has two routes into AS1, and packets are routed over the best path, depending on the location of the source.

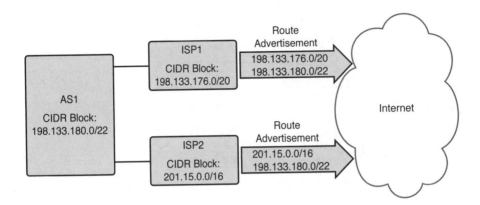

Figure 1-35 *ISP1 Must Punch a Hole in Its CIDR Block and Advertise the More Specific Prefix 198.133.180.0/22 in Addition to Its Aggregate Prefix for Packets to AS1 to Be Routed Through It*

The multihoming practice depicted in Figure 1-35 defeats the goals of CIDR, both in reducing routing table size and in hiding instabilities behind aggregation points. It also presents a few difficulties for both the providers and for the subscriber at AS1, as described in the following sections.

CIDR Issues: Address Portability

The first problem is one of portability. Suppose the ISP that has assigned your prefix is not living up to your expectations or contractual agreements, or you have just received a more attractive offer from another ISP. A change of ISPs most likely means you must re-address. It's unlikely that an ISP will allow a subscriber to keep its assigned block when the subscriber moves to a new provider. Aside from an ISP's unwillingness to give away a portion of its own address space, RIRs strongly encourage the return of address space when a subscriber changes ISPs.

For an end user, re-addressing carries varying degrees of difficulty. The process is probably the easiest for those who use private address space within their routing domain and network address translation (see Chapter 10) at the edges of the domain. In this case, only the "public-facing" addresses have to be changed, with minimal impact on the internal users. At the other extreme are end users who have statically assigned public addresses to all their internal network devices. These users have no choice but to visit every device in the network to re-address.

Even if the end user uses the CIDR block throughout the domain, the pain of re-addressing can be somewhat reduced by the use of DHCP. In this case, the DHCP scopes must be changed and users must reboot, but only some statically addressed network devices, such as servers and routers, must be individually re-addressed.

The most difficult readdressing challenge is changing security configurations. Firewalls and router access lists use IP addresses as a primary means of identifying packets, and reconfiguration can be time-consuming and risky.

The problem is increasingly amplified if you are an ISP, rather than an end user, and you want to change your upstream service provider. Not only must your own network be renumbered, but also so must any of your subscribers to whom you have assigned a portion of your CIDR block.

Although Figures 1-33 through 1-35 show ISP1 as having only a single connection to the Internet, in most cases an ISP has many connections to higher-level providers and at IXPs. At each of these connections, the provider must reconfigure its router to advertise the more-specific route in addition to the CIDR block. Administration is also complicated because the subscriber must closely coordinate IPP1's and ISP2's efforts to ensure that his /22 block is advertised correctly. Because ISP1 and ISP2 are competitors, either or both might be resistant to working so closely together.

Finally, the reconfiguration of router access lists, a challenge for end users, is almost prohibitively difficult for a service provider with a multitude of customer and upstream peering points, all of which will have complex access lists.

CIDR Issues: Provider-Independent Addresses

A possible solution for the multihomed subscriber in Figure 1-35 is to obtain a *provider-independent (PI)* address space. That is, the subscriber can apply directly to its RIR for a block that is not a part of either ISP1's or ISP2's CIDR block; both ISPs can advertise the subscriber's block without interference with their own address space. Although the RIRs encourage you to seek an address space first from your provider and second from your provider's provider, obtaining a provider-independent address space from your RIR is a last resort. However, you still face difficulties.

First, if you want to multihome, it is likely that your present address space was obtained from your original ISP. Changing to a provider-independent address space means renumbering, with all the difficulties already discussed.

Second, the registries assign address space based on justified need, not on long-term predicted need. This policy means that you probably will be allocated "just enough" space to fit your present needs and a 3-month predicted need. From there, you have to justify a further allocation by proving that you are efficiently using the original space. The bottom line is that CIDR allocation rules make multihoming a difficult problem for small subscribers and ISPs.

Although PI space is difficult to acquire, it is at least more reliably routed than it was just a few years ago. Some backbone providers, in a sincere attempt to enforce aggregation and thus control Internet routing table size and stability, set policies that dropped route updates of prefixes longer than /19; prefixes of that size or shorter were called "globally routable prefixes." So if you advertised, for example, a /23 prefix as a PI or as a result of a de-aggregated CIDR block, you could not be assured that the advertisement would reach all parts of the Internet—and thus you could not be assured that your network would be reachable from all parts of the Internet. This practice has since been abandoned in the face of customer complaints.

CIDR Issues: Traffic Engineering

The practice of engineering incoming traffic across multiple connections by manipulating prefix advertisements is also a strong contributor to CIDR de-aggregation. In Figure 1-36, AS1 has a /22 CIDR block but is advertising it as four separate /24 prefixes. The details of the paths the four advertisements take from AS1 to the Internet cloud are not shown, because they can vary. The advertisements might be across four links between the same two routers, across four links between four separate pairs of routers but to the same peering AS, or across four links to multiple autonomous systems. The point is that by advertising its one /22 prefix as four separate /24 prefixes, AS1 can manipulate incoming traffic; the destination addresses of packets to 198.133.180.0/22 match one of the four longer prefixes and are routed to AS1 over the path from which the matching /24 prefix was learned.

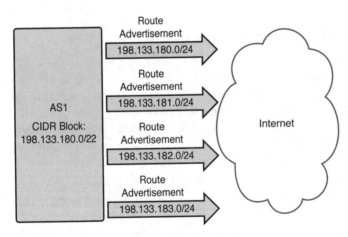

Figure 1-36 *AS1 Can Influence Its Incoming Traffic by De-Aggregating Its CIDR Block and Advertising It in Separate Updates*

Such traffic engineering practices are variously used to

- Balance traffic load across multiple links, entry points, or upstream providers.

- Draw incoming traffic to lower-cost or less-utilized internal links.

- Conserve internal resources by forcing incoming traffic to enter the AS at the peering point closest to the destination rather than the peering point closest to the originator.

Suppose AS1 has a global infrastructure, with Internet peering in Tokyo, Singapore, San Jose, and Frankfurt. The regions of this network are interconnected via transoceanic and intercontinental optical fiber. Such bandwidth is expensive, so the network operator wants to use the bandwidth primarily for intra-AS communications; externally originated packets should enter the AS as close to the internal destination as possible.

Figure 1-37 shows how this might be accomplished. The AS is divided into four regions, according to the nearest Internet peering point, and the subnets in each region are addressed from a designated /24 of the /22 CIDR block. The /24 for each region is advertised by the regional Internet access router.

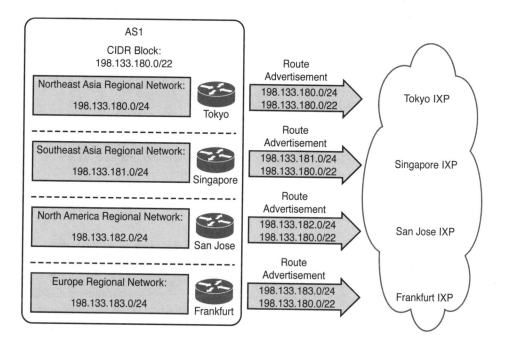

Figure 1-37   *Packets Originated Outside of AS1 Will Match the More Specific Prefixes and Be Routed Across the Internet to Enter the AS at the Peering Point Closest to the Destination, Rather Than Entering the AS at the Peering Point Closest to the Originator*

Suppose that a packet is originated from an external network in Tokyo with a destination address of 198.133.183.121, belonging to a device in AS1's Munich office. Rather than enter AS1 through the Tokyo IXP and then travel to Munich through the autonomous systems' expensive internal links, the Internet routers match the destination to the prefix 198.133.183.0/24, being advertised by AS1's Frankfurt peering router. The packet is then routed across networks external to AS1 until it reaches the Frankfurt IXP and only then enters AS1 a relatively short distance from its destination in Munich.

Although this practice is efficient for conserving AS1's internal bandwidth, it is selfish. The links that the external networks use to transport the packet through the Internet to the entry point AS1 designates as the most convenient are probably every bit as expensive as the internal links AS1 is trying to keep the traffic off of. Someone else is carrying the expense.

The practice is also selfish in that rather than advertise the one /22 at each peering point, it de-aggregates the block and advertises the four /24 constituent prefixes. But as Figure 1-37 shows, the proper /22 CIDR block must also be advertised at each peering point for insurance. If the external link from the Singapore router fails, for example, and updates carrying 198.133.182.0/24 stop, packets with a destination address belonging to that prefix will still match the shorter 198.133.180.0/22 and be routed into AS1 through one of the remaining three peering points. So AS1 is adding five prefixes to the Internet routing tables rather than one, making its own little contribution to Internet routing table bloating and instability.

CIDR Approaches Its Limits

As previously discussed, CIDR was invented (along with NAT and dynamic addressing) to slow the depletion of the available IPv4 addresses and to slow the growth of the Internet routing tables, buying time for IPv6 to be developed. Figure 1-38 shows the number of IPv4 /8 blocks assigned by the IANA from the inception of CIDR (and the corresponding inception of the RIRs) in 1993 through 2011. You can easily see that CIDR was quite effective in fulfilling its mission of slowing IPv4 address depletion through the 1990s.

Recall that when CIDR was implemented, rules were put into place requiring you to provide proof that you have efficiently used your existing allocation of IPv4 addresses before you can ask for more. Figure 1-38 shows that from 1994 to 1999 these rules were effective in keeping the allocation of IPv4 addresses low, as users with large pre-CIDR blocks of addresses used up what they had. But by 2000 the rate of allocations began to rise and on average continued to increase through the first decade of the 2000s. This reflects

- Many of the large blocks of IPv4 addresses assigned before 1993 have been used and the holders of those blocks have begun acquiring more.

- A tremendous number of new IP networks and IP services are being created, creating new and steadily increasing demands for new address space.

Note   Notice that the data in Figure 1-38 stops at 2011—well before you are reading this book. What has happened since that year? In short, nothing. In 2011, the IANA handed out the last of the assignable /8 address block in its inventory. There's nothing left to assign. At press time, all the RIRs except AfriNIC have announced that they are either out of assignable IPv4 addresses or are down to their last /8. Although many LIRs may still have some IPv4 addresses to assign, the IPv4 address space is effectively depleted.

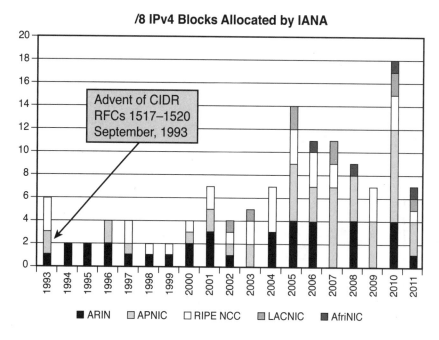

/8 IPv4 Blocks Allocated by IANA

Advent of CIDR
RFCs 1517–1520
September, 1993

■ ARIN   ☐ APNIC   ☐ RIPE NCC   ▨ LACNIC   ■ AfriNIC

Figure 1-38   *The Yearly IANA Allocation of IPv4 /8s Has Been Accelerating since 2000*[16]

The other goal of CIDR—slowing the growth of the Internet routing table—was also effectively accomplished in the 1990s. Figure 1-39 shows a graph of the entries in the BGP routing table between 1989 and 2015.[17] The curve shows an exponential increase in the number of entries between 1989 and the beginning of 1994. Notice that although the number of entries steadily increases between 1994 and 1999, the curve is linear rather than exponential: a reasonably consistent increase of approximately 10,000 entries per year. Between 1999 and mid-2001 the curve again becomes exponential; after that the increase is not as accelerated but is still exponential.

Figure 1-39 shows that although CIDR was effective from its inception through 1999 in slowing the growth of the Internet routing table, it has been less effective since then. The problem, as discussed in the previous sections, is the de-aggregation and leaking of long prefixes as a part of multihoming and traffic engineering practices. Just how severe an effect long prefixes are having can be seen in Table 1-3. Out of the 528,975 active

---

16   See www.iana.org/assignments/ipv4-address-space for a complete and up-to-date listing of the IPv4 blocks allocated by the IANA.

17   Up-to-date versions of this graph and graphs from other autonomous systems can be seen at http://bgp.potaroo.net/index-bgp.html. The number of BGP table entries varies somewhat from one AS to another, but the generalized trends are the same.

BGP entries in the table, only 18.73 percent are /20 or shorter and a whopping 53.27 percent are /24. So if just the /24 prefixes could be eliminated, the size of the Internet routing table could be halved.

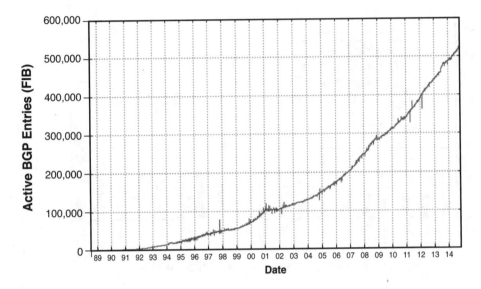

Figure 1-39 *The Number of Active IPv4 BGP Entries Between 1989 and 2015 Is Indicative of the Growth of the Internet Routing Table During That Time.*[18]

Table 1-3 *Number of BGP Table Entries by Prefix Length*[19]

Prefix Length	Entries	% of Total Entries
/8	16	0.00
/9	12	0.00
/10	31	0.01
/11	90	0.02
/12	262	0.05
/13	502	0.09
/14	1024	0.19
/15	1746	0.33

[18] Source: http://bgp.potaroo.net/as1221/bgp-active.html, used with the kind permission of Geoff Huston.

[19] The numbers in this table were taken on November 10, 2014.

Prefix Length	Entries	% of Total Entries
/16	13107	2.48
/17	7424	1.40
/18	12228	2.31
/19	25714	4.86
/20	36949	6.99
/21	38415	7.26
/22	56872	10.75
/23	49556	9.37
/24	281770	53.27
/25	1181	0.22
/26	1127	0.21
/27	761	0.14
/28	61	0.01
/29	51	0.01
/30	62	0.01
/31	1	0.00
/32	13	0.00

Note   Although multihoming and traffic engineering practices are commonly cited as the cause of the de-aggregation (highlighted in Table 1-3), some of the people who monitor the behavior of the Internet make the point that most de-aggregated prefixes wind up in the Internet tables not as the result of intentional practices but because of carelessness: Operators that could advertise only an aggregate nevertheless advertise their more-specifics.

A good view of what is happening regarding aggregation on a day-to-day basis is in the CIDR Report.[20] Among the useful information provided is a regularly updated list of the top 30 autonomous systems advertising de-aggregated prefixes and the how much the Internet routing table could be improved if these top autonomous systems were to aggregate. As this section is written, the 30 autonomous systems on the list together advertise 56,844 prefixes and, were they to aggregate properly, could reduce these to 15,046 prefixes, eliminating 41,798 entries from the Internet BGP table: An improvement of 73.5 percent.

---

[20] www.cidr-report.org, the source for the numbers in Table 1-3.

CIDR did the job it was supposed to do between 1993 and approximately 2000, and despite the factors that have undermined it since then, it continues to have a positive effect: Without the efficiency of CIDR, the increased IPv4 allocation rates and Internet routing table entries in the first decade of the 2000s would be far more severe.

Remember, though, that CIDR—along with NAT and dynamic IPv4 address assignment—was intended to buy some time for the development and deployment of IPv6. CIDR accomplished its mission; why, then, was IPv6 not deployed during the late 1990s?

IPv6 Comes of Age

The simple answer to the question at the end of the previous section is that IPv6 was not implemented in the mid-to-late 1990s because CIDR and the other stopgap measures were so successful in meeting their goals that concern for the continued supply of IPv4 addresses virtually vanished. Transitioning what had become a vast IPv4 infrastructure, encompassing everything from tiny home networks to the top-tier carrier backbones, would be a difficult, disruptive undertaking. As long as CIDR and NAT were extending the life of IPv4, there was little willingness to take on the job.

The talk was of a "chicken or egg" problem: Vendors and application developers did not want to invest the engineering resources into developing IPv6 because their customers were not asking for it; network operators were not implementing IPv6 because there were few products and applications supporting it. Other objections to IPv6 were that there was no business case (you can't make money with it, so there's no return on investment), and that there was no "killer application." (There's nothing to make IPv6 more attractive than IPv4 to paying customers.)

In the end, the driver for IPv6 remains what it was in the beginning: sufficient IP addresses. With CIDR rules becoming less effective and the accelerating allocation rate of IPv4 addresses shown in Figure 1-38, network operators are no longer thinking about business cases or killer apps; they are thinking about the ability to continue expanding their IP-based networks and services. And they are adding IPv6 support as a key factor in purchasing criteria, motivating vendors and applications developers to bring engineering resources to bear.

As this chapter is written, four of the five RIRs are out of IPv4 addresses, and users are widely creating IPv6 transition plans. By the time you read this chapter, IPv6 will be well into the early stages of replacing IPv4.

Routing Table Explosion, Again

Although IPv6 solves the IP address availability problem for the foreseeable future, it does nothing to improve the routing table explosion problem. Actually, it might make this problem much more severe. The limitation on IPv4 address availability and the necessity of using NAT has constrained the routing table size; IPv6 can lift this constraint. The IPv4 entries in the Internet routing table are not likely to go away, at least in the early stages of IPv6 deployment, so early widespread IPv6 deployment will at least double the table size. Take into account that key drivers for IPv6 are plentiful globally routable addresses, IP addresses on an immense array of end devices from household appliances to military and emergency services equipment to industrial and medical sensors, and an explosion of mobile IP devices, and the Internet routing table can be expected to grow to millions of entries.

As the Internet routing table continues to grow, performance will continue to decrease and the cost of core routing platforms will continue to increase. Although suppliers of core routing platforms, such as Cisco, have done a good job of regularly producing more powerful routers to stay ahead of this growth, questions are already being raised about the upper performance limits of silicon-based routers.

A few people have expressed the opinion that transition to IPv6 is a bad thing because it will exacerbate the scaling problems already seen in the IPv4-based Internet. This is, however, a misguided view for two reasons:

- IPv6 solves the problem of scarce IP addresses, which is the more immediate problem.

- By increasing the route scaling problem, IPv6 increases the incentive to solve a problem that exists anyway.

Given that the routing table explosion problem is accelerating, there must be both a long-term solution to effectively eliminate the problem and short-term solutions that can be quickly rolled out to mitigate the severity of the problem while the long-term solution is developed. As this chapter is written discussion of what those solutions should be is just beginning.

The long-term solution is, at present, entirely speculative. However, it will probably consist of a combination of router hardware based on new technologies such as optical switching and one or more protocols to replace BGP. An insight into the likely future of routing can be glimpsed from trends such as the physical separation of the control plane (intelligence) and the forwarding plane (performance), the adoption of technologies such as multiprotocol label switching (MPLS) that push intelligence to the edge of the networks, and Software Defined Networking (SDN) that breaks the one-to-one correspondence between the control and forwarding elements in the network.

At press time, the short-term solutions are also still in the discussion stage but may be apparent by the time you read this book. One solution suggested is administrative: that those benefiting from multihoming and traffic engineering bear more of the cost of leaking long prefixes into the Internet routing table. And if leaking a long prefix comes at a higher price, it could serve as an incentive for those who can aggregate to do so. But the practicalities of enforcing such an administrative solution are still debatable.

Another short-term solution discussed currently involves separating the *locator* function of IP addresses from the *identifier* function:

- A locator is used by routers to find the location of a device. As the device moves, its locator changes.

- An identifier names the device, and remains the same no matter where the device is located.

These two functions have overlapped in IP since its inception. When you query DNS for the name of a device, DNS returns an IP address that does not change. In this instance, the IP address is an identifier. But when a device moves to a new subnet, DHCP (or IPv6 stateless address autoconfiguration) assigns the device an address specific to that subnet. In this instance the IP address is a locator. Mobile IP exacerbates this problem by requiring that a device has a home IP address (its identifier) and a care-of IP address (its locator).

By separating these functions, the locator can be more flexible and more aggregatable, bringing more stability to the Internet routing table. Among the proposals for locator/identifier separation are

- Global, Site, and End System Address Elements (GSE), also known as 8+8

- Level 3 Multihoming Shim Protocol (Shim6)

- Host Identity Protocol (HIP)

- Locator/ID Separation Protocol (LISP)

Yet another short-term solution proposed is a means by which longer prefixes can be advertised to accomplish multihoming or traffic engineering, but a limit can be set on how many autonomous systems the route advertising the longer prefix can traverse before BGP rejects it. This AS_PATHLIMIT BGP route attribute is a trade-off, continuing to let longer prefix entries exist near the originating AS but preventing them from propagating beyond a distance where they have any influence on route selection. However, considering that most Internet routes are only five or six AS hops long, the benefit of this solution is also debatable.

For an up-to-date look at what proposals are current as you read this book, look at the Internet Research Task Force's Routing Research Group (RRG) webpage.[21]

Looking Ahead

This chapter has taken you from ancient history (EGP) to some speculative thoughts about the future of the Internet and the way it is routed. Along the way, you should have picked up a good understanding of the concepts behind BGP and inter-domain routing. Chapter 2 introduces you to the BGP protocol itself and its configuration and troubleshooting.

---

[21] www3.tools.ietf.org/group/irtf/trac/wiki/RoutingResearchGroup

Review Questions

1. What is an autonomous system?

2. What is the difference between an IGP and an EGP?

3. What is the difference between an internal and an external peer?

4. What is the transport protocol and port number used by BGP?

5. What are the two purposes of the BGP AS_PATH route attribute?

6. How does BGP use the AS_PATH attribute to detect routing loops?

7. What is the difference between a stub AS and a transit AS?

8. What is a BGP path attribute?

9. What is a recursive route lookup?

10. When BGP advertises a route among autonomous systems, when is an AS number added to the AS_PATH list? When is an AS number not added to the list, and why?

11. What is the purpose of a full IBGP mesh, and why is it considered best practice?

12. How does IBGP avoid routing loops?

13. What is a multihomed AS?

14. Name a few reasons why a stub AS might be multihomed.

15. What is CIDR, and what problems led to its creation?

16. What is an IP address prefix?

17. How does address summarization help stabilize a network?

18. What is the possible compromise made when summarization is implemented?

19. What does the CIDR notation /17 indicate?

20. What is an Internet Registry?

21. How have multihoming and traffic engineering practices reduced the effectiveness of CIDR?

Chapter 2

Introduction to BGP

Now that you have a firm understanding of the key issues surrounding inter-domain routing from Chapter 1, "Inter-Domain Routing Concepts," it is time to begin tackling BGP. This chapter covers the basic operation of BGP, including its message types, how the messages are used, and the format of the messages. You also learn about the various basic attributes BGP can associate with a route and how it uses these attributes to choose a best path. Finally, this chapter shows you how to configure and troubleshoot BGP peering sessions.

Who Needs BGP?

If you answer "yes" to all four of the following questions, you need BGP:

- Are you connecting to another routing domain?
- Are you connecting to a domain under a separate administrative authority?
- Is your domain multihomed?
- Is a routing policy required?

The answer to the first question—are you connecting to another routing domain?—is obvious; BGP is an inter-domain routing protocol. But as the subsequent sections explain, BGP is not the only means of routing between separate domains.

Connecting to Untrusted Domains

An underlying assumption of an IGP is that, by definition, its neighbors are all under the same administrative authority, and therefore the neighbors can be trusted: Trusted to not be malicious, trusted to be correctly configured, and trusted to not send bad route information. All these things can still happen occasionally within an IGP domain, but they are rare. An IGP is designed to freely exchange route information, focusing more on performance and easy configuration than on tight control of the information.

BGP, however, is designed to connect to neighbors in domains out of the control of its own administration. Those neighbors cannot be trusted, and the information you exchange with those neighbors is (if BGP is configured properly) carefully controlled with route policies.

But if connection to an external domain is your only requirement—particularly if there is only one connection—BGP is probably not called for. Static routes serve you better in this case; you don't have to worry about false information being exchanged because no information at all is being exchanged. Static routes are the ultimate means of controlling what packets are routed into and out of your network.

Figure 2-1 shows a subscriber attached by a single connection to an ISP. BGP, or any other type of routing protocol, is unnecessary in this topology. If the single link fails, no routing decision needs to be made because no alternative route exists. A routing protocol accomplishes nothing. In this topology, the subscriber adds a static default route to the border router and redistributes the route into his AS.

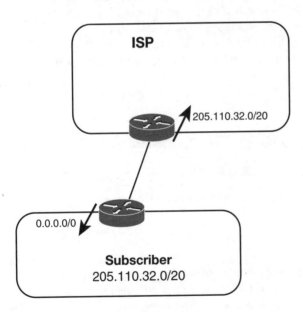

Figure 2-1   *Static Routes Are All That Is Needed in This Single-Homed Topology*

The ISP similarly adds a static route pointing to the subscriber's address range and advertises that route into its AS. Of course, if the subscriber's address space is a part of the ISP's larger address space, the route advertised by the ISP's router goes no farther than the ISP's own AS. "The rest of the world" can reach the subscriber by routing to the ISP's advertised address space, and the more-specific route to the subscriber can be picked up only within the ISP's AS.

An important principle to remember when working with inter-AS traffic is that each physical link actually represents two logical links: one for incoming traffic, and one for outgoing traffic, as shown in Figure 2-2.

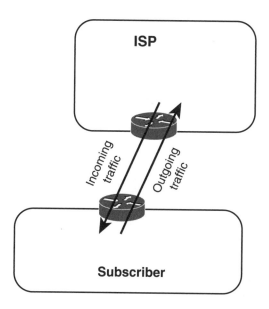

Figure 2-2 *Each Physical Link Between Autonomous Systems Represents Two Logical Links, Carrying Incoming and Outgoing Packets*

The routes you advertise in each direction influence the traffic separately. Avi Freedman, who has written many excellent articles on ISP issues, calls a route advertisement a promise to carry packets to the address space represented in the route. In Figure 2-1, the subscriber's router is advertising a default route into the local AS—a promise to deliver packets to any destination. And the ISP's router, advertising a route to 205.110.32.0/20, promises to deliver traffic to the subscriber's AS. The outgoing traffic from the subscriber's AS is the result of the default route, and the incoming traffic to the subscriber's AS is the result of the route advertised by the ISP's router. This concept may seem trivial and obvious at this point, but it is important to keep in mind as more complex topologies are examined and as we begin establishing policies for advertised and accepted routes.

The vulnerability of the topology in Figure 2-1 is that the entire connection consists of single points of failure. If the single data link fails, if a router or one of its interfaces fails, if the configuration of one of the routers fails, if a process within the router fails, or if one of the routers' all-too-human administrators makes a mistake, the subscriber's entire Internet connectivity can be lost. What is lacking in this picture is *redundancy*.

Connecting to Multiple External Neighbors

Figure 2-3 shows an improved topology, with redundant links to the same provider. How the incoming and outgoing traffic is manipulated across these links depends upon how the two links are used. For example, a frequent setup when multihoming to a single provider is for one of the links to be a primary, dedicated Internet access link and for the other link to be used only for backup.

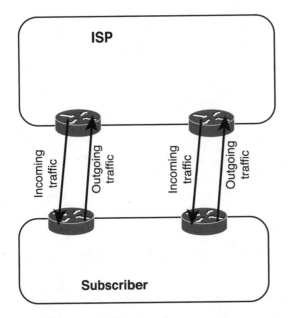

Figure 2-3   *When Multihoming You Must Consider the Incoming and Outgoing Advertisements and Resulting Traffic on Each Link*

When the redundant link is used only for backup, there is again no call for BGP. The routes can be advertised just as they were in the single-homed scenario, except that the routes associated with the backup link have the metrics set high so that they can be used only if the primary link fails.

Example 2-1 shows what the configurations of the routers carrying the primary and secondary links might look like.

Example 2-1   *Primary and Secondary Link Configurations for Multihoming to a Single Autonomous System*

```
Primary Router:
router ospf 100
 network 205.110.32.0 0.0.15.255 area 0
 default-information originate metric 10
!
```

```
ip route 0.0.0.0 0.0.0.0 205.110.168.108

Backup Router:
router ospf 100
 network 205.110.32.0 0.0.15.255 area 0
 default-information originate metric 100
!
ip route 0.0.0.0 0.0.0.0 205.110.168.113 150
```

In this configuration, the backup router has a default route whose administrative distance is set to 150 so that it will be only in the routing table if the default route from the primary router is unavailable. Also, the backup default is advertised with a higher metric than the primary default route to ensure that the other routers in the OSPF domain prefer the primary default route. The OSPF metric type of both routes is E2, so the advertised metrics remain the same throughout the OSPF domain. This ensures that the metric of the primary default route remains lower than the metric of the backup default route in every router, regardless of the internal cost to each border router. Example 2-2 shows the default routes in a router internal to the subscriber's OPSF domain.

Example 2-2 *The First Display Shows the Primary External Route; the Second Display Shows the Backup Route Being Used After the Primary Route Has Failed*

```
Phoenix#show ip route 0.0.0.0
Routing entry for 0.0.0.0 0.0.0.0, supernet
  Known via "ospf 1", distance 110, metric 10, candidate default path
  Tag 1, type extern 2, forward metric 64
  Redistributing via ospf 1
  Last update from 205.110.36.1 on Serial0, 00:01:24 ago
  Routing Descriptor Blocks:
  * 205.110.36.1, from 205.110.36.1, 00:01:24 ago, via Serial0
      Route metric is 10, traffic share count is 1

Phoenix#show ip route 0.0.0.0
Routing entry for 0.0.0.0 0.0.0.0, supernet
  Known via "ospf 1", distance 110, metric 100, candidate default path
  Tag 1, type extern 2, forward metric 64
  Redistributing via ospf 1
  Last update from 205.110.38.1 on Serial1, 00:00:15 ago
  Routing Descriptor Blocks:
  * 205.110.38.1, from 205.110.38.1, 00:00:15 ago, via Serial1
      Route metric is 100, traffic share count is 1
```

Although a primary/backup design satisfies the need for redundancy, it does not efficiently use the available bandwidth. A better design would be to use both paths, with each providing backup for the other if a link or router failure occurs. In this case, the configuration used in both routers is indicated in Example 2-3.

Example 2-3 *When Load Sharing to the Same AS, the Configuration of Both Routers Can Be the Same*

```
router ospf 100
 network 205.110.32.0 0.0.15.255 area 0
 default-information originate metric 10 metric-type 1
!
ip route 0.0.0.0 0.0.0.0 205.110.168.108
```

Note A key difference between building the simple peering of Figure 2-3 as a primary/backup configuration and as a load-sharing configuration is the consideration of bandwidth. If one link is a primary and one is a backup, the bandwidth of both links should be equal; if the primary fails, the load can be fully rerouted to the backup with no congestion. In some configurations, the backup link has considerably lower bandwidth, under the assumption that if the primary fails, the backup provides only enough bandwidth for critical applications to survive rather than full network functionality.

When a load-sharing configuration is used, the bandwidth of each of the two links should carry the total traffic load normally carried over both links. If one of the links fails, the other can then carry the full traffic load without packet loss.

The static routes in both routers have equal administrative distances, and the default routes are advertised with equal metrics (10). The default routes are now advertised with an OSPF metric type of E1. With this metric type, each of the routers in the OSPF domain takes into account the internal cost of the route to the border routers in addition to the cost of the default routes. As a result, every router chooses the closest exit point when choosing a default route, as shown by Figure 2-4.

In most cases advertising default routes into the AS from multiple exit points, and summarizing address space out of the AS at the same exit points, is sufficient for good internetwork performance. The one consideration is whether asymmetric traffic patterns will become a concern, as discussed in Chapter 1. If the geographical separation between the two (or more) exit points is large enough for delay variations to become significant, you might have a need for better control of the routing. BGP may now be a consideration.

For example, suppose the two exit routers in Figure 2-3 are located in Los Angeles and London. You might want all your exit traffic destined for the Eastern Hemisphere to use the London router, and all your exit traffic for the Western Hemisphere to use the Los Angeles router. Remember that the incoming route advertisements influence your outgoing traffic. If the provider advertises routes into your AS via BGP, your internal routers has more accurate information about external destinations.

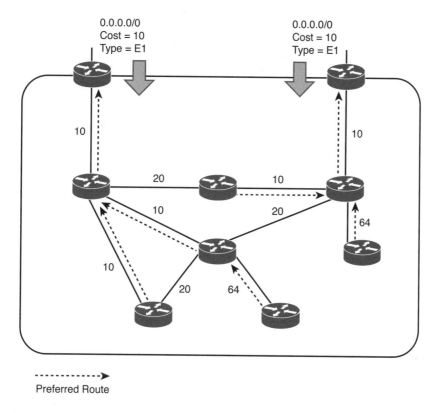

Figure 2-4   *The OSPF Border Routers Advertise a Default Route with a Metric of 10 and an OPSF Metric Type of E1*

Similarly, outgoing route advertisements influence your incoming traffic. If internal routes are advertised to the provider via BGP, you have influence over what routes are advertised at what exit point, and also tools for influencing (to some degree) the choices the provider makes when sending traffic into your AS.

When considering whether to use BGP, weigh the benefits gained against the cost of added routing complexity. BGP should be preferred over static routes only when an advantage in traffic control can be realized. Consider the incoming and outgoing traffic separately. If it is only important to control your incoming traffic, use BGP to advertise routes to your provider while still advertising only a default route into your AS.

However, if it is only important to control your outgoing traffic, use BGP just to receive routes from your provider. Consider the ramifications of accepting routes from your provider. "Taking full BGP routes" means that your provider advertises to you the entire Internet routing table. As of this writing, that is more than 500,000 IPv4 route entries, as shown in Example 2-4. The IPv6 Internet table is growing rapidly. You need a reasonably powerful router CPU to process the routes and enough router memory to store the entries. You also need sufficient TCAM or other forwarding plane memory to hold forwarding information. Example 2-4 shows that just the BGP routes require almost 155.7MB; the memory that BGP requires to process these routes, as shown in Example 2-5, is approximately 4.1GB. A simple default-routing scheme, however, can be implemented easily with a low-end router and a moderate amount of memory.

Example 2-4   *This Summary of the Full Internet Routing Table Shows 540,809 BGP Entries* [1]

```
route-views>show ip route summary
IP routing table name is default (0x0)
IP routing table maximum-paths is 32
Route Source    Networks     Subnets      Replicates   Overhead    Memory (bytes)
connected       0            2            0            192         576
static          1            57           0            5568        16704
application     0            0            0            0           0
bgp 6447        174172       366637       0            51917664    155752992
  External: 540809 Internal: 0 Local: 0
internal        7847                                               42922856
Total           182020       366696       0            51923424    198693128
route-views>
```

Example 2-5   *BGP Requires Approximately 4.1GB of Memory to Process the Routes Shown in Example 2-4*

```
route-views> show processes memory | include BGP
 117  0            0            232          41864       644         644 BGP Scheduler
 176  0 1505234352 262528       370120      14362638    14362638 BGP I/O
 299  0            0            10068312     41864       0           0 BGP Scanner
 314  0            0            0            29864       0           0 BGP HA SSO
 338  0 27589889144 2170064712 4102896864   3946        3946 BGP Router
 350  0            0            0            29864       0           0 XC BGP SIG RIB H
 383  0            0            0            41864       0           0 BGP Consistency
 415  0            0            0            41864       0           0 BGP Event
 445  0            0            0            29864       0           0 BGP VA
 450  0            3224         0            33160       1           0 BGP Open
 562  0            328104       262528       107440      0           0 BGP Task
 574  0            3248         0            33160       1           0 BGP Open
```

---

[1] This display was taken in 2014 from the public route server at University of Oregon (AS6447). The corresponding example in the first edition of this book, taken from an AT&T route server in 1999, showed 88,269 BGP entries.

```
 575   0       3120        0      33088      1         0 BGP Open
 577   0       3120        0      33040      1         0 BGP Open
 578   0       3120        0      33072      1         0 BGP Open
route-views>
```

Note The routing table summary in Example 2-4 and the related processes shown in Example 2-5 are taken from a route server at route-views.oregon-ix.net. By the time you read this chapter, the numbers shown in these two examples will have changed; telnet to the server, and see what they are now. There are a number of such publicly accessible route servers; for a good list, go to www.netdigix.com/servers.html.

Another consideration is that when running BGP, a subscriber's routing domain must be identified with an autonomous system (AS) number. Like IPv4 addresses, AS numbers are limited and are assigned only by the regional address registries when there is a justifiable need. And like IPv4 addresses, a range of AS numbers is reserved for private use: the AS numbers 64512 to 65534. As with private IPv4 addresses (RFC 1918), these AS numbers are not globally unique and must not be included in the AS_PATH of any route advertised into the public Internet. With few exceptions, subscribers that are connected to a single service provider (either single or multihomed) use an AS number out of the reserved range. The service provider filters the private AS number out of the advertised BGP path. Configuring and filtering private AS numbers is covered in Chapter 5, "Scaling BGP."

Although the topology in Figure 2-3 is an improvement over the topology in Figure 2-2 because redundant routers and data links have been added, it still entails a single point of failure. That point of failure is the ISP. If the ISP loses connectivity to the rest of the Internet, so does the subscriber. And if the ISP suffers a major internal outage, the single-homed subscriber also suffers.

Setting Routing Policy

Figure 2-5 shows a topology in which a subscriber has homed to more than one service provider. In addition to the advantages of multihoming already described, this subscriber is protected from losing Internet connectivity as the result of a single ISP failure. And with this topology BGP begins to become a better choice, in most cases, than static routes.

The subscriber in Figure 2-5 could still forego BGP. One option is to use one ISP as a primary Internet connection and the other as a backup only; another option is to default route to both providers and let the routing chips fall where they may. But if a subscriber has gone to the expense of multihoming and contracting with multiple providers, neither of these solutions is likely to be acceptable. BGP is the preferred option in this scenario.

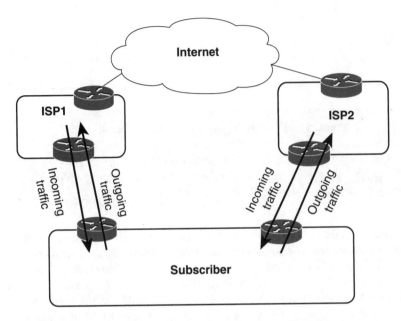

Figure 2-5   *Multihoming to Multiple Autonomous Systems*

Again, incoming and outgoing traffic should be considered separately. For incoming traffic, the most reliability is realized if all internal routes are advertised to both providers. This setup ensures that all destinations within the subscriber's AS are completely reachable via either ISP. Even though both providers are advertising the same routes, there are cases in which incoming traffic should prefer one path over another; such situations are discussed in the multihoming sections of Chapter 1. BGP provides the tools for communicating these preferences.

For outgoing traffic, the routes accepted from the providers should be carefully considered. If full routes are accepted from both providers, the best route for every Internet destination is chosen. In some cases, however, one provider might be preferred for full Internet connectivity, whereas the other provider is preferred for only some destinations. In this case, full routes can be taken from the preferred provider and partial routes can be taken from the other provider. For example, you might want to use the secondary provider only to reach its other subscribers and for backup to your primary Internet provider (see Figure 2-6). The secondary provider sends its customer routes, and the subscriber configures a default route to the secondary ISP to be used if the connection to the primary ISP fails.

The full routes sent by ISP1 probably include the customer routes of ISP2, learned from the Internet or perhaps from a direct peering connection. Because the same routes are received from ISP2, however, the subscriber's routers normally prefer the shorter path through ISP2. If the link to ISP2 fails, the subscriber uses the longer paths through ISP1 and the rest of the Internet to reach ISP2's customers.

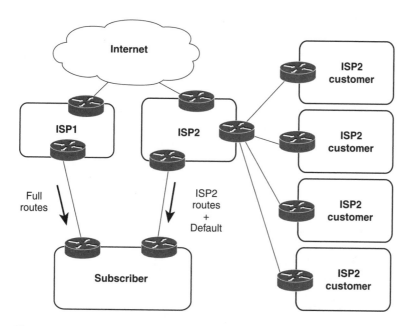

Figure 2-6 *ISP1 Is the Preferred Provider for Most Internet Connectivity; ISP2 Is Used Only to Reach Its Other Customers' Networks and for Backup Internet Connectivity*

Similarly, the subscriber normally uses ISP1 to reach all destinations other than ISP2's customers. If some or all of those more-specific routes from ISP1 are lost, however, the subscriber uses the default route through ISP2.

If router CPU and memory limitations prohibit taking full routes,[2] partial routes from both providers are an option. Each provider might send its own customer routes, and the subscriber points default routes to both providers. In this scenario, some routing accuracy is traded for a savings in router resources.

In yet another partial-routes scenario, each ISP might send its customer routes and also the customer routes of its upstream provider (which typically is a national or global backbone carrier such as Level 3 Communications, Sprint, NTT, or Deutsche Telekom). In Figure 2-7, for example, ISP1 is connected to Carrier1, and ISP2 is connected to Carrier2. The partial routes sent to the subscriber by ISP1 consist of all ISP1's customer routes and all Carrier1's customer routes. The partial routes sent by ISP2 consist of all ISP2's customer routes and all Carrier2's customer routes. The subscriber points to default routes at both providers. Because of the size of the two backbone carrier providers, the subscriber has enough routes to make efficient routing decisions on a large number of destinations. At the same time, the partial routes are still significantly smaller than a full Internet routing table.

---

[2] Taking full BGP routes from two sources doubles the number of BGP entries in all routers and consequently doubles the memory demand.

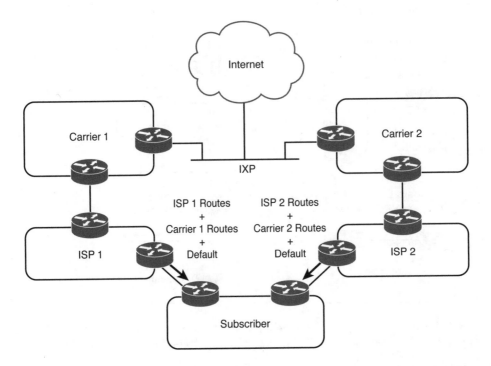

Figure 2-7   *The Subscriber Is Taking Partial Routes from Both ISPs, Consisting of All ISP's Customer Routes and the Customer Routes from Their Respective Upstream Providers*

All the examples here have shown a stub AS connected to one or more ISPs. Figures 2-5 through 2-7 begin introducing enough complexity that BGP and routing policy are probably called for. As the complexity of multihoming and its related policy issues grow, as illustrated in the transit AS examples in the previous chapter, the need for BGP becomes increasingly sure.

BGP Hazards

Creating a BGP peering relationship involves an interesting combination of trust and mistrust. The BGP peer is in another AS, so you must trust the network administrator on that end to know what she is doing. At the same time, if you are smart, you will take every practical measure to protect yourself if a mistake is made on the other end. When you implement a BGP peering connection, paranoia is your friend.

At the same time, you should be a good neighbor by taking practical measures to ensure that a mistake in your AS does not affect your BGP peers.

Recall the earlier description of a route advertisement as a promise to deliver packets to the advertised destination. The routes you advertise directly influence the packets you receive, and the routes you receive directly influence the packets you transmit. In a good

BGP peering arrangement, both parties should have a complete understanding of what routes are to be advertised in each direction. Again, incoming and outgoing traffic must be considered separately. Each peer should ensure that he is transmitting only the correct routes and should use route filters or other policy tools such as AS_PATH filters, described in Chapter 4, "BGP and Routing Policies," to ensure that he receives only the correct routes.

Your ISP might show little patience with you if you make mistakes in your BGP configuration, but the worst problems can be attributed to a failure on both sides of the peering arrangement. Suppose, for example, that through some misconfiguration you advertise 207.46.0.0/16 to your ISP. On the receiving side, the ISP does not filter out this incorrect route, allowing it to be advertised to the rest of the Internet. This particular CIDR block belongs to Microsoft, and you have just claimed to have a route to that destination. A significant portion of the Internet community could decide that the best path to Microsoft is through your domain. You will receive a flood of unwanted packets across your Internet connection and, more important, you will have black-holed traffic that should have gone to Microsoft. It will be neither amused nor understanding.

This kind of thing happens frequently: Not long ago, Yahoo experienced a brief outage due to a company in Seoul mistakenly advertising a /14 prefix that included addresses belonging to Yahoo.

Figure 2-8 shows another example of a BGP routing mistake. This same internetwork was shown in Figure 2-6, but here the customer routes that the subscriber learned from ISP2 have been inadvertently advertised to ISP1.

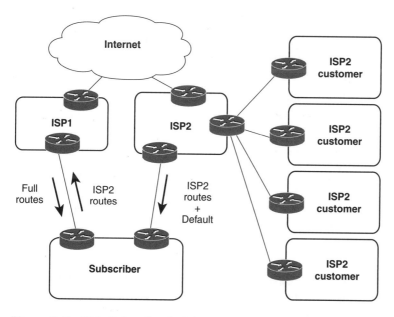

Figure 2-8 *This Subscriber Is Advertising Routes Learned from ISP2 into ISP1, Inviting Packets Destined for ISP2 and Its Customers to Transit His Domain*

Unless ISP1 and ISP2 have a direct peering connection, ISP1 and its customers probably see the subscriber's domain as the best path to ISP2 and its customers. In this case, the traffic is not black-holed because the subscriber does indeed have a route to ISP2. The subscriber has become a transit domain for packets from ISP1 to ISP2, to the detriment of its own traffic. And because the routes from ISP2 to ISP1 still point through the Internet, the subscriber has caused asymmetric routing for ISP2.

The point of this section is that BGP, by its nature, is designed to allow communication between autonomously controlled systems. A successful and reliable BGP peering arrangement requires an in-depth understanding of not only the routes to be advertised in each direction, but also the routing policies of each of the involved parties.

The remainder of this chapter introduces the technical basics of BGP and demonstrates how to configure and troubleshoot simple BGP sessions. With that foundation experience, you then get a good taste of configuring and troubleshooting policies in Chapter 4.

Operation of BGP

The section "BGP Basics" in Chapter 1 introduced you to the fundamental facts about BGP. To recap

- Unique among the common IP routing protocols, BGP sends only unicast messages and forms a separate point-to-point connection with each of its peers.

- BGP is an application layer protocol using TCP (port 179) for this point-to-point connection and relies on the inherent properties of TCP for session maintenance functions such as acknowledgment, retransmission, and sequencing.

- BGP is a vector protocol, although called a path vector rather than distance vector because it sees the route to a destination as a path through a series of autonomous systems rather than as a series of routers hops.

- A BGP route describes the path vector using a route attribute called the AS_PATH, which sequentially lists the autonomous system numbers comprising the path to the destination.

- The AS_PATH attribute is a shortest path determinant. Given multiple routes to the same destination, the route with an AS_PATH listing the fewest AS numbers is assumed to be the shortest path.

- The AS numbers on the AS_PATH list are used for loop detection; a router receiving a BGP route with its own AS number in the AS_PATH assumes a loop and discards the route.

- If a router has a BGP session to a neighbor with a different AS number, the session is called *external BGP (EBGP)*; if the neighbor has the same AS number as the router, the session is called *internal BGP (IBGP)*. The neighbors are called, respectively, *external* or *internal* neighbors.

This chapter builds on these basic facts to describe the operation of BGP.

BGP Message Types

Before establishing a BGP peer connection, the two neighbors must perform the standard TCP three-way handshake and open a TCP connection to port 179. TCP provides the fragmentation, retransmission, acknowledgment, and sequencing functions necessary for a reliable connection, relieving BGP of those duties. All BGP messages are unicast to the one neighbor over the TCP connection.

BGP uses four basic message types:

- Open

- Keepalive

- Update

- Notification

Note   There is a fifth BGP message type: Route Refresh. But unlike the four presented here, this fifth message type is not a part of basic BGP functionality and might not be supported by all BGP routers. The Route Refresh message and its use are described in Chapter 4.

This section describes how these messages are used; for a complete description of the message formats and the variables of each message field, see the section "BGP Message Formats."

Open Message

After the TCP session is established, both neighbors send Open messages. Each neighbor uses this message to identify itself and to specify its BGP operational parameters. The Open message includes the following information:

- **BGP version number:** This specifies the version (2, 3, or 4) of BGP that the originator is running; the IOS default is BGP-4. Prior to IOS 12.0(6)T, IOS would autonegotiate the version: If a neighbor is running an earlier version of BGP, it rejects the Open message specifying version 4; the BGP-4 router then changes to BGP-3 and sends another Open message specifying this version. If the neighbor rejects that message, an Open specifying version 2 is sent. BGP-4 has now become so prevalent that as of 12.0(6)T IOS no longer autonegotiates, but you can still configure a session to speak to a neighbor running version 2 or 3 with **neighbor version.**

- **Autonomous system number:** This is the AS number of the originating router. It determines whether the BGP session is EBGP (if the AS numbers of the neighbors differ) or IBGP (if the AS numbers are the same).

- **Hold time:** This is the maximum number of seconds that can elapse before the router must receive either a Keepalive or an Update message. The hold time must be either 0 seconds (in which case, keepalives must not be sent) or at least 3 seconds; the default IOS hold time is 180 seconds. If the neighbors' hold times differ, the smaller of the two times becomes the accepted hold time. The default hold time can be changed for the entire BGP process with the configuration statement **timers bgp or for a** specific neighbor or peer group with **neighbor timers.**

- **BGP identifier:** This is an IPv4 address that identifies the neighbor. IOS determines the BGP Identifier in exactly the same way as it determines the OSPF router ID: The numerically highest loopback address is used; if no loopback interface is configured with an IP address, the numerically highest IP address on a physical interface is selected. Or you can manually specify the BGP identifier with **bgp router-id.**

- **Optional parameters:** This field is used to advertise support for such optional capabilities as authentication, multiprotocol support, and route refresh.

Keepalive Message

If a router accepts the parameters specified in its neighbor's Open message, it responds with a Keepalive. Subsequent Keepalives are sent every 60 seconds by IOS default, or a period equal to one-third the agreed-upon holdtime. Like the holdtime, the keepalive interval can be changed for the entire BGP process with **timers bgp** or on a per-neighbor or per-peer-group basis with **neighbor timers.**

Note that although BGP offloads several reliability functions to the underlying TCP session, it does use its own keepalive rather than using the TCP keepalive.

Update Message

The Update message advertises feasible routes, withdrawn routes, or both. The Update message includes the following information:

- **Network Layer Reachability Information (NLRI):** This is one or more (Length, Prefix) tuples that advertise destination prefixes and their lengths. If 206.193.160.0/19 were advertised, for example, the Length portion would specify the /19 and the Prefix portion would specify 206.193.160. However, as discussed at the beginning of Chapter 3, "BGP and NLRI," and covered more extensively in Chapter 6, "Multiprotocol BGP," the NLRI can be more than just a unicast IPv4 prefix.

- **Path attributes:** The path attributes, described in a later section of the same name, are characteristics of the advertised NLRI. The attributes provide the information that allows BGP to choose a shortest path, detect routing loops, and determine routing policy.

- **Withdrawn routes:** These are (Length, Prefix) tuples describing destinations that have become unreachable and are being withdrawn from service.

Although multiple prefixes might be included in the NLRI field, each Update message describes only a single BGP path (because the path attributes describe only a single path, but that path might lead to multiple destinations). This, again, emphasizes that BGP takes a higher view of an internetwork than an IGP, whose routes always lead to a single destination IP address.

Notification Message

The Notification message is sent whenever an error is detected and always causes the BGP connection to close. The section "BGP Message Formats" includes a list of possible errors that can cause a Notification message to be sent.

An example of the use of a Notification message is the negotiation of a BGP version between neighbors. If, after establishing a TCP connection, a BGP-4 speaker receives an Open message specifying version 3, the router responds with a Notification message stating that the version is not supported, and the session is closed.

BGP Finite State Machine

The stages of a BGP neighbor connection establishment and maintenance can be described in terms of a finite state machine. Figure 2-9 and Table 2-1 show the complete BGP finite state machine and the input events that can cause a state transition.

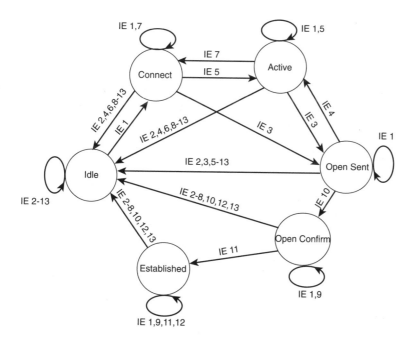

Figure 2-9   *BGP Finite State Machine*

Table 2-1   *Input Events (IE) of Figure 2-9*

IE	Description
1	BGP Start
2	BGP Stop
3	BGP Transport connection open
4	BGP Transport connection closed
5	BGP Transport connection open failed
6	BGP Transport fatal error
7	ConnectRetry timer expired
8	Hold timer expired
9	Keepalive timer expired
10	Receive Open message
11	Receive Keepalive message
12	Receive Update message
13	Receive Notification message

The following sections provide a brief description of each of the six neighbor states, as shown in Figure 2-9.

Idle State

BGP always begins in the Idle state, in which it refuses all incoming connections. When a Start event (IE 1) occurs, the BGP process initializes all BGP resources, starts the ConnectRetry timer, initializes a TCP connection to the neighbor, listens for a TCP initialization from the neighbor, and changes its state to Connect. The Start event is caused by an operator configuring a BGP process or resetting an existing process, or by the router software resetting the BGP process.

An error causes the BGP process to transition to the Idle state. From there, the router may automatically try to issue another Start event. However, limitations should be imposed on how the router does this—constantly trying to restart in the event of persistent error conditions causes flapping. Therefore, after the first transition back to the Idle state, the router sets the ConnectRetry timer and cannot attempt to restart BGP until the timer expires. IOS's initial ConnectRetry time is 120 seconds; this value cannot be changed. The ConnectRetry time for each subsequent attempt is twice the previous time, meaning that consecutive wait times increase exponentially.

Connect State

In this state, the BGP process is waiting for the TCP connection to the neighbor to be completed. If the TCP connection is successful, the BGP process clears the ConnectRetry timer, completes initialization, sends an Open message to the neighbor, and transitions to the OpenSent state. If the TCP connection is unsuccessful, the BGP process continues to listen for a connection to be initiated by the neighbor, resets the ConnectRetry timer, and transitions to the Active state.

If the ConnectRetry timer expires while in the Connect state, the timer is reset, another attempt is made to establish a TCP connection with the neighbor, and the process stays in the Connect state. Any other input event causes a transition to Idle.

Active State

In this state, the BGP process tries to initiate a TCP connection with the neighbor. If the TCP connection is successful, the BGP process clears the ConnectRetry timer, completes initialization, sends an Open message to the neighbor, and transitions to OpenSent. The IOS default Hold time is 180 seconds (3 minutes) and can be changed with the **timers bgp statement.**

If the ConnectRetry timer expires while BGP is in the Active state, the process transitions back to the Connect state and resets the ConnectRetry timer. It also initiates a TCP connection to the peer and continues to listen for connections from the peer. If the neighbor attempts to establish a TCP session with an unexpected IP address, the ConnectRetry timer is reset, the connection is refused, and the local process stays in the Active state. Any other input event (except a Start event, which is ignored in the Active state) causes a transition to Idle.

OpenSent State

In this state, an Open message has been sent, and BGP is waiting to hear an Open from its neighbor. When an Open message is received, all its fields are checked. If errors exist, a Notification message is sent and the state transitions to Idle.

If no errors exist in the received Open message, a Keepalive message is sent and the Keepalive timer is set. The Hold time is negotiated, and the smaller value is agreed upon. If the negotiated Hold time is zero, the Hold and Keepalive timers are not started. The peer connection is determined to be either internal or external, based on the peer's AS number, and the state is changed to OpenConfirm.

If a TCP disconnect is received, the local process closes the BGP connection, resets the ConnectRetry timer, begins listening for a new connection to be initiated by the neighbor, and transitions to Active. Any other input event (except a start event, which is ignored) causes a transition to Idle.

OpenConfirm State

In this state, the BGP process waits for a Keepalive or Notification message. If a Keepalive is received, the state transitions to Established. If a Notification is received, or a TCP disconnect is received, the state transitions to Idle.

If the Hold timer expires, an error is detected, or a Stop event occurs, a Notification is sent to the neighbor and the BGP connection is closed, changing the state to Idle.

Established State

In this state, the BGP peer connection is fully established and the peers can exchange Update, Keepalive, and Notification messages. If an Update or Keepalive message is received, the Hold timer is restarted (if the negotiated hold time is nonzero). If a Notification message is received, the state transitions to Idle. Any other event (again, except for the Start event, which is ignored) causes a Notification to be sent and the state to transition to Idle.

Path Attributes

A *path attribute* is a characteristic of an advertised BGP route. Although the term is specific to BGP, the concept is not unfamiliar to you: Every route advertisement, no matter what the originating routing protocol, has attributes. For example, every route advertisement has information (an address prefix) representing some destination, some quantification (metric) of the destination enabling comparison to other routes to the same destination, and some directional information about the destination, such as a next-hop address. BGP routes have the same attributes you are familiar with from other protocols but can also include a number of other attributes that are designed to be manipulated for the creation and communication of routing policies.

Each path attribute falls into one of four categories:

- Well-known mandatory
- Well-known discretionary
- Optional transitive
- Optional nontransitive

First, an attribute is either *well known*, meaning that it must be recognized by all BGP implementations, or it is *optional*, meaning that the BGP implementation is not required to support the attribute.

Well-known attributes are either *mandatory*, meaning that they must be included in all BGP Update messages, or they are *discretionary*, meaning that they may or may not be sent in a specific Update message.

An optional attribute is either *transitive*, meaning that a BGP process should accept the Update in which it is included—even if the process doesn't support the attribute—and should pass the attribute on to its peers, or it is *nontransitive*, meaning that a BGP process that does not recognize the attribute can quietly ignore the Update in which it is included and not advertise the path to its other peers. In simple terms, the attribute either can or cannot transit a router.

Table 2-2 lists the BGP path attributes. The three well-known mandatory attributes, because they are required to be in every BGP Update, are described in the following subsections. A Cisco-specific attribute called *weight* is also covered in this section. The other attributes are described within the context of their primary use as policy enablers (Chapter 4), for scaling (Chapter 5), or for carrying multiple NLRI types (Chapter 6).

Note   If you are already familiar with the Communities and Extended Community attribute, you might wonder why Table 2-2 lists them as scaling features rather than policy enablers. A policy enabler can directly influence the BGP decision process. Communities make it easier to apply policies to a group of routes but do not influence the BGP decision process.

Table 2-2   *BGP Path Attributes*

Attribute	Class	RFC	Application
ORIGIN	Well-known mandatory	4271	Policy
AS_PATH	Well-known mandatory	4271	Policy, loop detection
NEXT_HOP	Well-known mandatory	4271	Policy
LOCAL_PREF	Well-known discretionary	4271	Policy
ATOMIC_AGGREGATE	Well-known discretionary	4271	Address aggregation
AGGREGATOR	Optional transitive	4271	Address aggregation
COMMUNITIES	Optional transitive	1997	Scaling
EXTENDED COMMUNITY	Optional transitive	4360	Scaling
MULTI_EXIT_DISC (MED)	Optional nontransitive	4271	Policy
ORIGINATOR_ID	Optional nontransitive	4456	Scaling, loop detection, policy
CLUSTER_LIST	Optional nontransitive	4456	Scaling, loop detection, policy
AS4_PATH	Optional transitive	6793	Scaling, policy

Attribute	Class	RFC	Application
AS4_AGGREGATOR	Optional transitive	6793	Scaling, address aggregation
Multiprotocol Reachable NLRI	Optional nontransitive	4760	Multiprotocol BGP
Multiprotocol Unreachable NLRI	Optional nontransitive	4760	Multiprotocol BGP

ORIGIN Attribute

ORIGIN is a well-known mandatory attribute that specifies the origin of the routing update. When BGP has multiple routes to the same destination, it uses the ORIGIN as one factor in determining the preferred route. It specifies one of the following origins:

- **IGP:** The Network Layer Reachability Information (NLRI) was learned from a protocol internal to the originating AS. An IGP origin gets the highest preference of the ORIGIN values. IOS gives BGP routes an origin of IGP if they are learned from an IGP routing table via the BGP **network** statement, as described in Chapter 3.

- **EGP:** The NLRI was learned from the Exterior Gateway Protocol. EGP is preferred second to IGP. Because EGP is obsolete, you should never encounter this origin type; it's an artifact of the days when we transitioned from EGP to BGP.

- **Incomplete:** The NLRI was learned by some other means. Incomplete is the lowest-preferred ORIGIN value. Incomplete does not imply that the route is in any way faulty, only that the information for determining the origin of the route is incomplete. Routes that BGP learns through redistribution carry the incomplete origin attribute because there is no way to determine the original source of the route.

Although ORIGIN is still a mandatory part of the BGP standard, it was created to help—as the second of the three possible origins indicates—with the transition from EGP to BGP. It might have some limited use in a few "corner case" policy configurations but for the most part should be considered a legacy attribute.

AS_PATH Attribute

AS_PATH is a well-known mandatory attribute that uses a sequence of AS numbers to describe the inter-AS path, or AS-level route, to the destination specified by the NLRI. When an AS originates a route—when it advertises NLRI about a destination within its own AS to an external neighbor—it adds its AS number to the AS_PATH. As subsequent BGP speakers advertise the route to external peers, they *prepend* their own AS numbers to the AS_PATH (see Figure 210). The result is that the AS_PATH describes all the autonomous systems it has passed through, beginning with the most recent AS and ending with the originating AS.

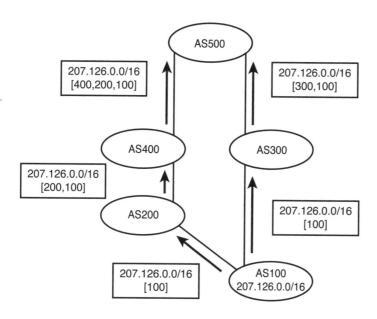

Figure 2-10 *AS Numbers Are Prepended (Added to the Front of) the AS_PATH List*

Note that a BGP router adds its AS number to the AS_PATH only when an Update is sent to a neighbor in another AS. That is, an AS number is prepended to the AS_PATH only when the route is advertised between EBGP peers. If the route is advertised between IBGP peers—peers within the same autonomous system—no AS number is added.

Usually, having multiple instances of the same AS number on the list would make no sense and would defeat the purpose of the AS_PATH attribute. In one case, however, adding multiple instances of a particular AS number to the AS_PATH proves useful. Remember that outgoing route advertisements directly influence incoming traffic. Normally, the route from AS500 to AS100 in Figure 2-10 passes through AS300 because the AS_PATH of that route is shorter (that is, lists fewer AS numbers). But what if the link to AS200 is AS100's preferred path for incoming traffic? The links along the (400,200,100) path might all be 10G, for example, whereas the links along the (300,100) path are only 1G. Or perhaps AS200 is the primary provider, and AS300 is only the backup provider. Outgoing traffic is sent to AS200, so it is desired that incoming traffic follow the same path.

AS100 can influence its incoming traffic by changing the AS_PATH of its advertised route (Figure 2-11). By adding multiple instances of its own AS number to the list sent to AS300, AS100 can make routers at AS500 think that the (400,200,100) path is the shorter path. This procedure of adding extra AS numbers to the AS_PATH is called *AS path prepending.*

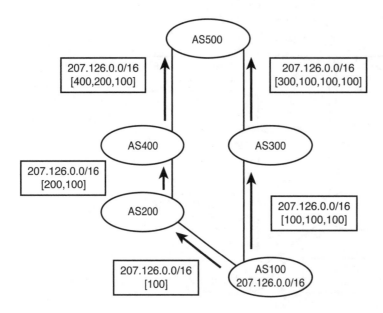

Figure 2-11 *AS100 Has Prepended Two Extra Instances of Its AS Number to the AS_ PATH Advertised to AS300, to Influence the Path Choice Made at AS500*

The AS_PATH attribute has been presented so far as consisting of an ordered sequence of AS numbers that describes the path to a particular destination. There are actually two types of AS_PATH:

- **AS_SEQUENCE:** This is the ordered list of AS numbers, as previously described.

- **AS_SET:** This is an *unordered* list of the AS numbers along a path to a destination.

These two types are distinguished in the AS_PATH attribute with a type code, as described in the section "BGP Message Formats."

> **Note** The AS_SEQUENCE and AS_SET types each have a modified version: AS_ CONFED_SEQUENCE and AS_CONFED_SET, respectively. They each perform the same functions as the AS_SEQUENCE and AS_SET but within the context of BGP Confederations (explained in Chapter 5).

Recall that the second function of the AS_PATH is loop prevention. If a BGP speaker sees its own AS number in a received route from an external peer, it knows that a loop has occurred and ignores the route. When aggregation is performed, however, some AS_PATH detail is lost. For example, AS3113 in Figure 2-12 is aggregating the prefixes advertised by AS225, AS237, and AS810. Because AS3113 originates the aggregate prefix, the AS_PATH associated with it contains only that AS number. As a result, the potential for a loop increases.

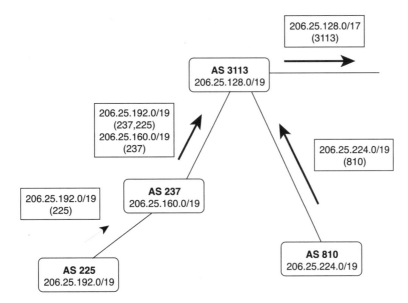

Figure 2-12 *The Aggregation at AS3113 Causes a Loss of the AS_PATH Information of the Aggregate's Constituent Prefixes*

Suppose, for example, AS810 has an alternative connection to another AS, as shown in Figure 2-13. The aggregate from AS3113 is advertised to AS6571 and from there back to AS810.

Because the AS numbers "behind" the aggregation point are not included in the AS_PATH, AS810 does not detect the potential loop. Next, suppose a network within AS810, such as 206.25.225.0/24, fails. The routers within that AS match the aggregate route from AS6571, and a loop occurs.

If you think about it, the loop-prevention function of the AS_PATH does not require that the AS numbers be included in any particular order. All that is necessary is that a receiving router recognize whether its AS number is a part of the AS_PATH. This is where AS_SET comes in.

When a BGP speaker creates an aggregate from NLRI learned from other autonomous systems, it can include all those AS numbers in the AS_PATH as an AS_SET. For example, Figure 2-14 shows the network of Figure 2-12 with an AS_SET added to the aggregate route.

The aggregating router still begins an AS_SEQUENCE, so receiving routers can trace the path back to the aggregator, but an AS_SET is included to prevent routing loops. In this example, you also can see why the AS_SET is an unordered list. Behind the aggregator in

AS3113 are branching paths to the autonomous systems in which the aggregated routes reside. There is no way for an ordered list to describe these separate paths.

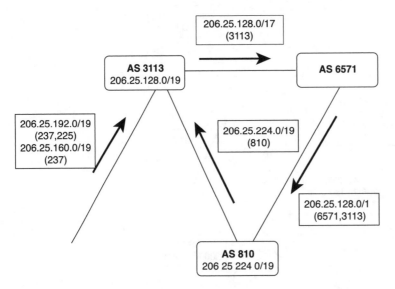

Figure 2-13   *The Loss of AS_PATH Information at Aggregation Points Weakens the AS_PATH Loop Avoidance Function*

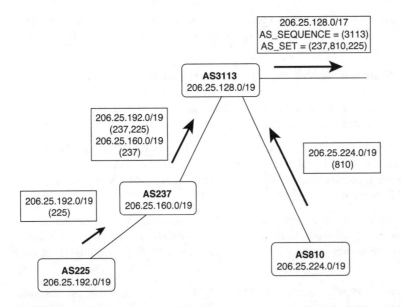

Figure 2-14   *Including an AS_SET in the AS_PATH of an Aggregate Route Restores the Loop Avoidance That Was Lost in the Aggregation*

AS_SET involves a trade-off. You already understand that one of the advantages of route summarization is route stability. If a network that belongs to the aggregate fails, the failure is not advertised beyond the aggregation point. But if an AS_SET is included with the aggregate's AS_PATH, this stability is reduced. If the link to AS225 in Figure 2-14 fails, for example, the AS_SET changes; this change must be advertised beyond the aggregation point. However, the visibility of constituent AS numbers associated with an aggregate route is much less of a concern that the visibility of many prefixes behind an aggregate.

As it turns out, AS_SET is seldom used in the public Internet at aggregation points. Given the potential instability discussed in the previous paragraph, plus the potential for accidentally including private AS numbers in the AS_SET, and other complexities, RFC 6472 recommends that AS_SET not be used except where a few "corner cases" might justify it. Although AS_SET is still supported by most Internet-grade BGP implementations, including Cisco IOS, RFC 6472 suggests that a future update of BGP might remove AS_SET support.

NEXT_HOP Attribute

As the name implies, this well-known mandatory attribute describes the IP address of the next-hop router on the path to the advertised destination. Unlike typical IGPs, however, the IP address described by the BGP NEXT_HOP attribute is not always the address of a neighboring router. The following rules apply:

- If the advertising router and receiving router are in different autonomous systems (external peers), the NEXT_HOP is the IP address of the advertising router's interface.

- If the advertising router and the receiving router are in the same AS (internal peers), and the Update's NLRI refers to a destination within the same AS, the NEXT_HOP is an IP address belonging to the neighbor that advertised the route.

- If the advertising router and the receiving router are internal peers and the Update's NLRI refers to a destination in a different AS, the NEXT_HOP is the IP address of the external peer from which the route was learned.

Figure 2-15 illustrates the first rule. Here, the advertising router and receiving router are in different autonomous systems. The NEXT_HOP is the interface address of the external peer. So far, this behavior is the same as would be expected of any routing protocol.

Figure 2-16 illustrates the second rule. This time, the advertising router and the receiving router are in the same AS, and the destination advertised is also in the AS. The NEXT_HOP associated with the NLRI is the IP address of the originating router.

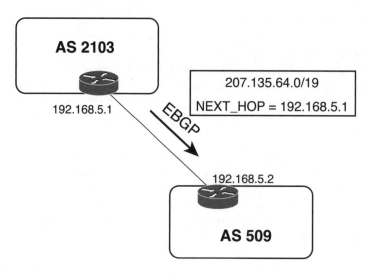

Figure 2-15 *If a BGP Update Is Advertised via EBGP, the NEXT_HOP Attribute Is the
IP Address of the External Peer*

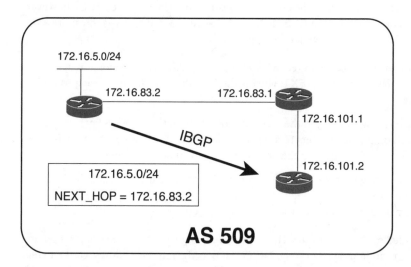

Figure 2-16 *If a BGP Update Is Advertised via IBGP and the Advertised Destination Is
in the Same AS, the NEXT_HOP Attribute Is the IP Address of the Originating Router*

The advertising router and the receiving router do not share a common data link, but the
IBGP TCP connection is passed through an IGP-speaking router. The receiving router
must perform a recursive route lookup (recursive lookups are discussed in *Routing
TCP/IP*, Volume I) to send a packet to the advertised destination. For example, suppose the router at 172.16.101.2 in Figure 2-16 must forward a packet with a destination
address of 172.16.5.30. It looks up the destination and matches the prefix 172.16.5.0/24;

that route indicates a next hop of 172.16.83.2. Because that IP address does not belong to one of the router's directly connected subnets, the router must then look up the route to 172.16.83.2. That route, learned via the IGP, indicates a next hop of 172.16.101.1. The packet can now be forwarded. This example is important for understanding the dependency of IBGP on the IGP.

Figure 2-17 illustrates the third rule. Here, a route has been learned via EBGP and is then passed to an internal peer. Because the destination is in a different AS, the NEXT_HOP of the route passed across the IBGP connection is the interface of the external router from which the route was learned.

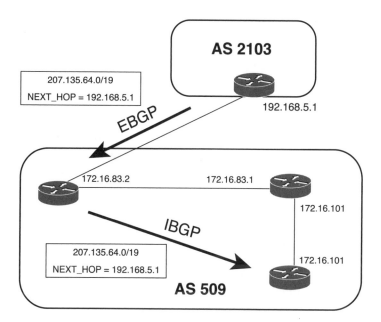

Figure 2-17 *If a BGP Update Is Advertised via IBGP and the Advertised Destination Is in a Different AS, the NEXT_HOP Attribute Is the IP Address of the External Peer from Which the Route Was Learned*

In Figure 2-17, the IBGP peer must perform a recursive route lookup to forward a packet to 207.135.64.0/19. However, a potential problem exists. The subnet 192.168.5.0, to which the next-hop address belongs, is not part of AS509. Unless the AS border router advertises it into AS509, the IGP—and hence the internal peers—will not know about this subnet. And if the subnet is not in the routing tables, the next-hop address for 207.135.64.0/19 is unreachable, and packets for that destination are dropped. Actually, although the route to 207.135.64.0/19 is installed in the internal peer's BGP table, it is not installed in the routing table because the next-hop address is invalid for that router.

One solution to the problem is, of course, to ensure that the external subnet linking the two autonomous systems is known to the internal routers. Although you could use static routes, the practical method is to run the IGP in passive mode on the external interfaces. In some cases, this might be undesirable. An alternative solution—and the solution that is considered best practice—is to use a configuration option called *next-hop-self* to cause the AS border router in AS509 to set its own IP address in the NEXT_HOP attribute, in place of the IP address of the external peer. The internal peers would then have a next-hop router address of 172.16.83.2, which is known to the IGP. The configuration of next-hop-self is covered in Chapter 3.

Weight

Weight[3] is a Cisco-specific BGP path attribute that applies only to routes within an individual router. It is not communicated to other routers. The weight is a number between 0 and 65,535 that can be assigned to a route; the higher the weight, the more preferable the route. When choosing a best path, the BGP decision process considers weight above all other route characteristics except specificity. By default, all routes learned from a peer have a weight of 0, and all routes generated by the local router have a weight of 32,768.

Weights can be set for individual routes, or for routes learned from a specific neighbor. For example, peer A and peer B might be advertising the same routes to a BGP speaker. By assigning a higher weight to the routes received from peer A, the BGP speaker prefers the routes through that peer. This preference is entirely local to the single router; weights are not included in the BGP updates or in any other way communicated to the BGP speaker's peers. Accordingly, weights are valuable for influencing the routing decisions of a single router without changing the routing decisions of any other router.

Weights are useful when you want one BGP router in an AS to treat some prefixes differently than the way other routers in the AS treat the same prefixes. But this can also be dangerous. Because weight affects only the BGP decision process in a single router, this tells you to carefully consider the implications of using it. Misuse can easily lead to unexpected or inconsistent routing results such as loops.

BGP Decision Process

The BGP Routing Information Base (RIB) consists of three parts:

- **Adj-RIBs-In:** Stores unprocessed routing information that has been learned from BGP Updates received from peers. The routes contained in Adj-RIBs-In are considered feasible routes.

- **Loc-RIB:** Contains the routes that the BGP speaker has selected by applying the decision process to the routes contained in Adj-RIBs-In. These routes populate the routing table (RIB) along with routes discovered by other routing protocols.

---

[3] Older IOS documentation calls this parameter Administrative Weight, but more recent documentation has moved away from that term in favor of just Weight. This is probably to avoid confusing it with Administrative Distance, an entirely different and protocol-independent parameter.

- **Adj-RIBs-Out:** Contains the routes that the BGP speaker advertises to its peers in BGP Updates. The outgoing routing policies determine what routes are placed in Adj-RIBs-Out.

These three parts of the RIB may be three distinct databases, or the RIB may be a single database with pointers to distinguish the three parts.

The BGP decision process selects routes by applying incoming routing policies to the routes in the Adj-RIBs-In and by entering the selected or modified routes into the Loc-RIB. The decision process entails three phases:

- Phase 1 calculates the degree of preference for each feasible route in the Adj-RIBs-In. It is invoked whenever a router receives a BGP Update from a peer in a neighboring AS containing a new route, a changed route, or a withdrawn route. Each route is considered separately, and a nonnegative integer is derived that indicates the degree of preference for that route.

- Phase 2 chooses the best route out of all the available routes to a particular destination and installs the route in the Loc-RIB. It is invoked only after phase 1 has been completed. Loops are also detected in Phase 2 by examining the AS_PATH. Any routes with the local AS number in the AS_PATH are dropped.

- Phase 3 adds the appropriate routes to the Adj-RIBs-Out for advertisement to peers. It is invoked after the Loc-RIB has changed, and only after phase 2 has been completed. Route aggregation, if it is to be performed, happens during this phase.

Barring a routing policy that dictates otherwise, phase 2 always selects the most specific route to a particular destination out of all feasible routes to that destination. It is important to note that if the address specified by the route's NEXT_HOP attribute is unreachable, the route is not selected. This has particular ramifications for IBGP: A route cannot be selected if it is not "synchronized" with the IGP (refer to Chapter 3).

You should have an appreciation by now of the multiple attributes that can be assigned to a BGP route to enforce routing policy within a single router, to internal peers, to adjacent autonomous systems, and beyond. A sequential set of rules is needed for considering these attributes as tie-breakers when a router must select among multiple, equally specific routes to the same destination. This set of rules is the BGP decision process. The decision process used by IOS is as follows:[4]

1. Prefer the route with the highest weight. This is an IOS-specific function, as described in the previous section.

2. If the weights are equal, prefer the route with the highest LOCAL_PREF value.

---

[4] The BGP decision processes can vary slightly among different vendors, so if you run a multivendor BGP network, you must understand the sequence of decision steps each of your vendors uses. Because the decision process is refined as newer features are added, it can even vary slightly between older and newer versions of IOS.

3. If the LOCAL_PREF values are the same, prefer the route that was originated locally on the router and injected into BGP with the **network** or **aggregate** statement or through redistribution. That is, prefer a route that was learned from an IGP or from a direct connection on the same router. Note that a route injected into BGP via the **network** statement or redistribution is preferred over a local aggregate injected by the **aggregate-address** statement. All these means of injecting prefixes are covered in Chapter 4.

4. If the LOCAL_PREF is the same and no route was locally originated, prefer the route with the shortest AS_PATH.

5. If the AS_PATH length is the same, prefer the path with the lowest ORIGIN code. IGP is lower than EGP, which is lower than Incomplete.

6. If the ORIGIN codes are the same, prefer the route with the lowest MED (MULTI_EXIT_DISC) value. By default, this comparison is done only if the AS number is the same for all the routes being considered.[5]

7. If the MED is the same, prefer EBGP routes over Confederation EBGP routes, and prefer Confederation EBGP routes over IBGP routes.

8. If the routes are still equal, prefer the route with the shortest path to the BGP NEXT_HOP. This is the route with the lowest IGP metric to the next-hop address.

9. If the routes are still equal, they are from the same neighboring AS, and BGP multipath is enabled with the **maximum-paths** statement; install all the equal-cost routes in the Loc-RIB.

10. If the routes are still equal and are external, prefer the path that was received first. This helps reduce flapping by allowing a newer route to take precedence over an older one. If the **bgp best path compare-routerid** statement is enabled, this step is skipped.

11. If multipath is not enabled, prefer the route with the lowest BGP router ID, or if route reflection (Chapter 5) is used, prefer the route with the lowest ORIGINATOR_ID.

12. If the routes are still equal and route reflection is used, prefer the route with the shortest CLUSTER_LIST.

13. If the routes are still equal, prefer the route advertised from the neighbor with the lowest IP address.

---

[5] IOS offers two alternatives to the default MED behavior, **bgp deterministic-med** and **bgp always-compare-med**; these alternatives are explained in Chapter 4.

BGP Message Formats

BGP messages are carried within TCP segments using TCP port 179. The maximum message size is 4096 octets, and the minimum size is 19 octets. All BGP messages have a common header (Figure 2-18). Depending on the message type, a data portion might or might not follow the header.

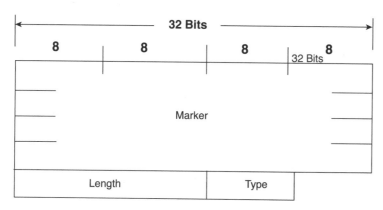

Figure 2-18 *BGP Message Header*

Marker is a 16-octet field that was intended to detect loss of synchronization between BGP peers and to authenticate messages when authentication is supported. However, its use is deprecated in RFC 4271, and modern BGP implementations set the field to all ones in all cases; it continues to exist in the message header for backward compatibility with older implementations.

Length is a 2-octet field that indicates the total length of the message, including the header, in octets.

Type is a 1-octet field specifying the message type. Table 2-3 indicates the possible type codes.

Table 2-3   *BGP Type Codes*

Code	Type
1	Open
2	Update
3	Notification
4	Keepalive
5	Route Refresh (covered in Chapter 4)

Open Message

The Open message, whose format is shown in Figure 2-19, is the first message sent after a TCP connection has been established. If a received Open message is acceptable, a Keepalive message is sent to confirm the Open. After the Open has been confirmed, the BGP connection is in the Established state and Update, Keepalive, and Notification messages can be sent.

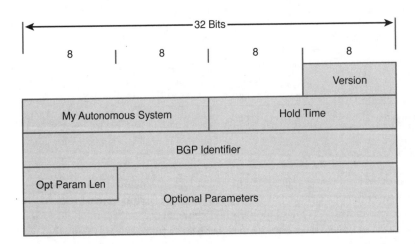

Figure 2-19   *BGP Open Message Format*

The minimum length of the Open message including the BGP message header is 29 octets.

The BGP Open message contains the following fields:

- **Version:** A 1-octet field specifying the BGP version running on the originator.

- **My Autonomous System:** A 2-octet field specifying the AS number of the originator.

- **Hold Time:** A 2-octet number indicating the number of seconds the sender proposes for the hold time. A receiver compares the value of the Hold Time field and the value of its configured hold time and accepts the smaller value or rejects the connection. The hold time must be either 0 or at least 3 seconds.

- **BGP Identifier:** The BGP router ID of the originator. Unless a router ID is specified in the BGP configuration, IOS sets its router ID as either the highest IP address of any of its loopback interfaces, or if no loopback interface is configured, the highest IP address of any of its physical interfaces.

- **Optional Parameters Length:** A 1-octet field indicating the total length of the following Optional Parameters field, in octets. If the value of this field is zero, no Optional Parameters field is included in the message.

- **Optional Parameters:** A variable-length field containing a list of optional parameters. Each parameter is specified by a 1-octet type field, a 1-octet length field, and a variable-length field containing the parameter value.

Update Message

The Update message, whose format is shown in Figure 2-20, advertises a single feasible route to a peer, or to withdraw multiple unfeasible routes, or both.

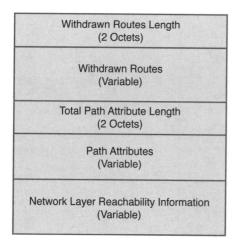

Figure 2-20   *BGP Update Message Format*

The BGP Update message contains the following fields:

- **Withdrawn Routes Length**[6]: A 2-octet field indicating the total length of the following Withdrawn Routes field, in octets. A value of zero indicates that no routes are being withdrawn and that no Withdrawn Routes field is included in the message.

- **Withdrawn Routes:** A variable-length field containing a list of routes to be withdrawn from service. Each route in the list is described with a (Length, Prefix) tuple in which the Length is the length of the prefix and the Prefix is the IP address prefix of the withdrawn route. If the Length part of the tuple is zero, the Prefix matches all routes.

- **Total Path Attribute Length:** A 2-octet field indicating the total length of the following Path Attribute field, in octets. A value of zero indicates that attributes and NLRI are not included in this message.

- **Path Attributes:** A variable-length field listing the attributes associated with the NLRI in the following field. Each path attribute is a variable-length triple of (Attribute Type, Attribute Length, Attribute Value). The Attribute Type part of the triple is a 2octet field consisting of four flag bits, four unused bits, and an Attribute Type code (see Figure 2-21). Table 2-4 shows the most common Attribute Type codes and the possible Attribute Values for each Attribute Type.

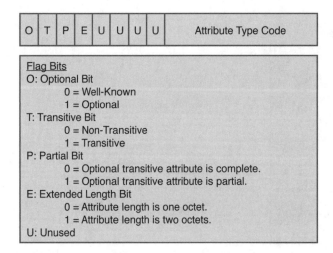

Figure 2-21   *Attribute Type Part of the Path Attributes Field in the Update Message*

---

[6] This field was called Unfeasible Routes Length in RFC 1771 and before. Although renamed Withdrawn Routes Length in RFC 4271, there is no difference in function.

■ **Network Layer Reachability Information:** A variable-length field containing a list of (Length, Prefix) tuples. The Length indicates the length in bits of the following prefix, and the Prefix is the IP address prefix of the NLRI. A Length value of zero indicates a prefix that matches all IP addresses.

Table 2-4 *Attribute Types and Associated Attribute Values[7]*

Attribute Type Code	Attribute Type	Attribute Value Code	Attribute Value
1	ORIGIN	0	IGP
		1	EGP
		2	Incomplete
2	AS_PATH	1	AS_SET
		2	AS_SEQUENCE
		3	AS_CONFED_SET
		4	AS_CONFED_SEQUENCE
3	NEXT_HOP	0	Next-hop IP address
4	MULTI_EXIT_DISC	0	4-octet MED
5	LOCAL_PREF	0	4-octet LOCAL_PREF
6	ATOMIC_AGGREGATE	0	None
7	AGGREGATOR	0	AS number and IP address of aggregator
8	COMMUNITY	0	4-octet community identifier
9	ORIGINATOR_ID	0	4-octet router ID of originator
10	CLUSTER_LIST	0	Variable-length list of cluster IDs
14	MP_REACH_NLRI	0	Variable-length Multiprotocol BGP NLRI
15	MP_UNREACH_NLRI	0	Variable-length Multiprotocol BGP NLRI

[7] Attributes are often added to BGP, so this list may not be complete.

Attribute Type Code	Attribute Type	Attribute Value Code	Attribute Value
16	EXTENDED COMMUNITIES	0	16-octet extended community identifier
17	AS4_PATH	0	AS path with 4-octet AS numbers
18	AS4_AGGREGATOR	0	4-octet AS number and IP address of aggregator

Keepalive Message

Keepalive messages are exchanged on a period one-third the hold time but not less than 1 second. If the negotiated hold time is 0, Keepalives are not sent.

The Keepalive message consists of only the 19-octet BGP message header, with no additional data.

Notification Message

Notification messages, whose format is shown in Figure 2-22, are sent when an error condition is detected. The BGP connection is closed immediately after the message is sent.

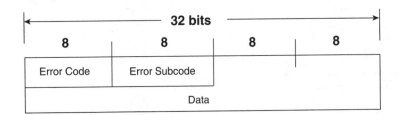

Figure 2-22   *BGP Notification Message Format*

The BGP Notification message contains the following fields:

- **Error Code:** A 1-octet field indicating the type of error.

- **Error Subcode:** A 1-octet field providing more-specific information about the error. Table 2-5 shows the possible error codes and associated error subcodes.

- **Data:** A variable-length field used to diagnose the reason for the error. The contents of the Data field depend on the error code and subcode.

Table 2-5 *BGP Notification Message Error Codes and Error Subcodes*

Error Code	Error	Error Subcode	Subcode Detail
1	Message Header Error	1	Connection not synchronized
		2	Bad message length
		3	Bad message type
2	Open Message Error	1	Unsupported version number
		2	Bad peer AS
		3	Bad BGP identifier
		4	Unsupported optional parameter
		5	Authentication failure (deprecated in RFC 4271)
		6	Unacceptable hold time
3	Update Message Error	1	Malformed attribute list
		2	Unrecognized well-known attribute
		3	Missing well-known attribute
		4	Attribute flags error
		5	Attribute length error
		6	Invalid ORIGIN attribute
		7	AS routing loop (deprecated in RFC 4271)
		8	Invalid NEXT_HOP attribute
		9	Optional attribute error
		10	Invalid network field
		11	Malformed AS_PATH
4	Hold Timer Expired	0	—
5	Finite State Machine Error	0	—
6	Cease	0	—

Configuring and Troubleshooting BGP Peering

Many newcomers to BGP approach the protocol with trepidation. The source of this sentiment is that BGP implementations are rarer than IGP implementations. Outside of ISPs, most network administrators deal with BGP far less than with IGPs, if at all. And even when BGP is used, the configurations in small ISPs and non-ISP subscribers are usually quite basic. Because most networking professionals lack in-depth experience with the protocol, it is often viewed as intimidating.

BGP configurations can unarguably be complex. But most of the complexity around BGP involves policy. BGP peering configuration, although still a little more involved than most IGP configurations, is not at all difficult. This section takes you step-by-step through the configuration of BGP peering, from the most basic elements to more refined setups.

Case Study: EBGP Peering

A BGP session between routers is configured in two steps:

Step 1.   Establish the BGP process and specify the local AS number with **router bgp.**

Step 2.   Specify a neighbor and the neighbor's AS number with **neighbor remote-as.**

Figure 2-23 shows two routers in different autonomous systems, and Example 2-6 shows their EBGP configurations.

Example 2-6   *EBGP Configurations for the Routers in Figure 2-23*

```
Taos
router bgp 200
 neighbor 192.168.1.226 remote-as 100


Vail
router bgp 100
 neighbor 192.168.1.225 remote-as 200
```

The BGP state changes at Vail can be seen, in Example 2-7, using **debug ip bgp.**[8] In the first few lines, Vail is attempting to open a connection to Taos (192.168.1.225); BGP is not yet enabled at Taos, so the attempts fail and Vail shows Taos in Active state. Then as BGP comes up at Taos, a TCP connection is accepted; its state transitions from Active to OpenSent as Vail sends an Open message to begin the BGP session. The two routers then

---

[8] Timestamps are turned off for the debug examples throughout this book unless time deltas are important to the example to simplify the output. However, in production networks timestamps are an important part of debug or any other logging function and should be enabled.

negotiate capabilities. (The multiprotocol and route refresh capabilities negotiated in this example are discussed in Chapters 6 and 4, respectively.) With capabilities agreed upon, Vail changes Taos' state from OpenSent to OpenConfirm and then to Established.

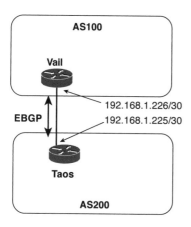

Figure 2-23   *An EBGP Session Is Established Between Taos and Vail*

Example 2-7   debug *Is Used to Observe Vail's BGP State Changes for Taos as the BGP Session Comes Up*

```
Vail#debug ip bgp
BGP debugging is on for address family: IPv4 Unicast
Vail#
BGP: 192.168.1.225 open active, local address 192.168.1.226
BGP: 192.168.1.225 open failed: Connection refused by remote host, open active d
elayed 34034ms (35000ms max, 28% jitter)
BGP: 192.168.1.225 open active, local address 192.168.1.226
BGP: 192.168.1.225 went from Active to OpenSent
BGP: 192.168.1.225 sending OPEN, version 4, my as: 100, holdtime 180 seconds
BGP: 192.168.1.225 send message type 1, length (incl. header) 45
BGP: 192.168.1.225 rcv message type 1, length (excl. header) 26
BGP: 192.168.1.225 rcv OPEN, version 4, holdtime 180 seconds
BGP: 192.168.1.225 rcv OPEN w/ OPTION parameter len: 16
BGP: 192.168.1.225 rcvd OPEN w/ optional parameter type 2 (Capability) len 6
BGP: 192.168.1.225 OPEN has CAPABILITY code: 1, length 4
BGP: 192.168.1.225 OPEN has MP_EXT CAP for afi/safi: 1/1
BGP: 192.168.1.225 rcvd OPEN w/ optional parameter type 2 (Capability) len 2
BGP: 192.168.1.225 OPEN has CAPABILITY code: 128, length 0
BGP: 192.168.1.225 OPEN has ROUTE-REFRESH capability(old) for all address-families
BGP: 192.168.1.225 rcvd OPEN w/ optional parameter type 2 (Capability) len 2
BGP: 192.168.1.225 OPEN has CAPABILITY code: 2, length 0
```

```
BGP: 192.168.1.225 OPEN has ROUTE-REFRESH capability(new) for all address-families
BGP: 192.168.1.225 rcvd OPEN w/ remote AS 200
BGP: 192.168.1.225 went from OpenSent to OpenConfirm
BGP: 192.168.1.225 went from OpenConfirm to Established
```

When you create a neighbor with the **neighbor remote-as** statement, an entry is created in the BGP neighbor database for the specified neighbor. The command **show ip bgp neighbor**[9] displays either the entire BGP neighbor database or a specified neighbor entry. In Example 2-8, the information Vail has recorded about Taos displays. The information in this display is particularly useful for troubleshooting.

The first line of output in Example 2-8 shows the address of Taos (192.168.1.225), its AS number (200), and the type of BGP connection to the router (external). The second line displays the BGP version used between Vail and Taos, and Taos' router ID. The third line begins by showing the state of the BGP finite state machine and then the time since the present peer connection was established. In this example, Taos has been peered continuously for 23 minutes and 25 seconds.

Also of interest are the details of the underlying TCP connection, the second set of highlighted lines in Example 2-8. They show that the TCP connection state is Established, that Vail is originating BGP messages from TCP port 13828, and that the destination port at Taos is 179. The source port can be especially important to note when you capture packets on a link carrying more than one BGP session.

Example 2-8   show ip bgp neighbors *Command Output Contains Essential Details About the Peer Connection to a Neighbor*

```
Vail#show ip bgp neighbors

BGP neighbor is 192.168.1.225,  remote AS 200, external link
  BGP version 4, remote router ID 192.168.1.225
  BGP state = Established, up for 00:23:25
  Last read 00:00:25, last write 00:00:25, hold time is 180, keepalive interval
is 60 seconds
  Neighbor capabilities:
    Route refresh: advertised and received(old & new)
    Address family IPv4 Unicast: advertised and received
  Message statistics:
    InQ depth is 0
```

---

[9] You can also use **show bgp neighbors** to display the same information; although, it is not documented in the IOS manuals and might not work with all IOS releases. The output of the show **ip bgp neighbors** command also varies depending on the IOS release you use.

```
    OutQ depth is 0
                      Sent      Rcvd
    Opens:             5          5
    Notifications:     0          0
    Updates:           0          0
    Keepalives:       51         52
    Route Refresh:     0          0
    Total:            56         57
  Default minimum time between advertisement runs is 30 seconds


 For address family: IPv4 Unicast
  BGP table version 1, neighbor version 1/0
  Output queue size: 0
  Index 1, Offset 0, Mask 0x2
  1 update-group member
                         Sent        Rcvd
  Prefix activity:       ----        ----
    Prefixes Current:      0           0
    Prefixes Total:        0           0
    Implicit Withdraw:     0           0
    Explicit Withdraw:     0           0
    Used as bestpath:    n/a           0
    Used as multipath:   n/a           0

                        Outbound    Inbound
  Local Policy Denied Prefixes:   --------    -------
    Total:                          0           0
  Number of NLRIs in the update sent: max 0, min 0


  Connections established 5; dropped 4
  Last reset 00:26:11, due to Peer closed the session
Connection state is ESTAB, I/O status: 1, unread input bytes: 0
Connection is ECN Disabled, Mininum incoming TTL 0, Outgoing TTL 1
Local host: 192.168.1.226, Local port: 13828
Foreign host: 192.168.1.225, Foreign port: 179
Connection tableid (VRF): 0


Enqueued packets for retransmit: 0, input: 0  mis-ordered: 0 (0 bytes)


Event Timers (current time is 0xA9F664):
Timer          Starts    Wakeups          Next
Retrans           26         0            0x0
TimeWait           0         0            0x0
```

```
AckHold              25           2          0x0
SendWnd               0           0          0x0
KeepAlive             0           0          0x0
GiveUp                0           0          0x0
PmtuAger              0           0          0x0
DeadWait              0           0          0x0
Linger                0           0          0x0
ProcessQ              0           0          0x0


iss:  842497347  snduna:  842497887  sndnxt:  842497887     sndwnd:   15845
irs: 2329656545  rcvnxt: 2329657085  rcvwnd:        15845 delrcvwnd:     539


SRTT: 435 ms, RTTO: 1159 ms, RTV: 724 ms, KRTT: 0 ms
minRTT: 212 ms, maxRTT: 992 ms, ACK hold: 200 ms
Status Flags: active open
Option Flags: nagle
IP Precedence value : 6


Datagrams (max data segment is 1460 bytes):
Rcvd: 50 (out of order: 0), with data: 25, total data bytes: 539
Sent: 31 (retransmit: 0, fastretransmit: 0, partialack: 0, Second Congestion: 0)
, with data: 26, total data bytes: 539
 Packets received in fast path: 0, fast processed: 0, slow path: 0
 fast lock acquisition failures: 0, slow path: 0
Vail#
```

Case Study: EBGP Peering over IPv6

The TCP connection between BGP routers can run over either IPv4 or IPv6. Keep in mind that the endpoint addresses of the TCP session have nothing to do with the address families supported by the BGP session running over the TCP connection or the types of prefixes exchanged by BGP. BGP peers can exchange both IPv4 and IPv6 prefixes regardless of whether the TCP session is between IPv4 addresses or IPv6 addresses.

Figure 2-24 shows the same two routers of Figure 2-23, except that in this case, the interfaces have IPv6 addresses. Example 2-9 shows the EBGP configurations for these two routers, and you can readily see that they are the same as the configurations in the previous case study except that the neighbor addresses are IPv6.

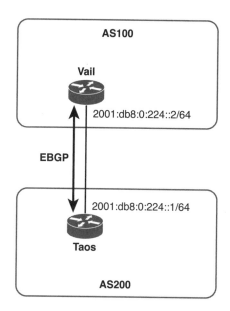

Figure 2-24 *An EBGP Session Is Established Between Taos and Vail, This Time with IPv6 Endpoints*

Example 2-9 *EBGP Configurations for the Routers in Figure 2-24*

```
Taos
router bgp 200
 neighbor 2001:db8:0:224::1 remote-as 100
```

```
Vail
router bgp 100
 neighbor 2001:db8:0:224::2 remote-as 200
```

Example 2-10 shows another output from **show ip bgp neighbors** at Vail, after the configurations of Example 2-9 have been implemented. The neighbor information looks almost identical to that of Example 2-8 (the same fields are highlighted) except the addresses are now IPv6 addresses. Notice, however, that Vail's BGP router ID remains 192.168.1.225; the BGP router ID is a 32-bit number so cannot be taken from an IPv6 address.

Example 2-10 *The Neighbor Database Looks Almost Identical to the One in Example 2-8, Except the Neighbor Addresses Are IPv6*

```
Vail#show ip bgp neighbors


BGP neighbor is 2001:DB8:0:224::1,  remote AS 200, external link
  BGP version 4, remote router ID 192.168.1.225
  BGP state = Established, up for 00:00:18
  Last read 00:00:18, last write 00:00:18, hold time is 180, keepalive interval
is 60 seconds
  Neighbor capabilities:
    Route refresh: advertised and received(old & new)
    Address family IPv4 Unicast: advertised and received
  Message statistics:
    InQ depth is 0
    OutQ depth is 0
                      Sent        Rcvd
    Opens:             6           6
    Notifications:     0           0
    Updates:           0           0
    Keepalives:        240         280
    Route Refresh:     0           0
    Total:             246         286
  Default minimum time between advertisement runs is 30 seconds


  For address family: IPv4 Unicast
  BGP table version 1, neighbor version 1/0
  Output queue size: 0
  Index 1, Offset 0, Mask 0x2
  1 update-group member
                          Sent        Rcvd
  Prefix activity:        ----        ----
    Prefixes Current:      0           0
    Prefixes Total:        0           0
    Implicit Withdraw:     0           0
    Explicit Withdraw:     0           0
    Used as bestpath:      n/a         0
    Used as multipath:     n/a         0

                          Outbound    Inbound
  Local Policy Denied Prefixes:    --------    -------
    Total:                 0           0
  Number of NLRIs in the update sent: max 0, min 0
```

```
    Connections established 6; dropped 5
    Last reset 00:00:39, due to Peer closed the session
Connection state is ESTAB, I/O status: 1, unread input bytes: 0
Connection is ECN Disabled, Mininum incoming TTL 0, Outgoing TTL 1
Local host: 2001:DB8:0:224::2, Local port: 179
Foreign host: 2001:DB8:0:224::1, Foreign port: 59051
Connection tableid (VRF): 0


Enqueued packets for retransmit: 0, input: 0  mis-ordered: 0 (0 bytes)


Event Timers (current time is 0x285A1B0):
Timer          Starts    Wakeups         Next
Retrans          3          0            0x0
TimeWait         0          0            0x0
AckHold          2          0            0x0
SendWnd          0          0            0x0
KeepAlive        0          0            0x0
GiveUp           0          0            0x0
PmtuAger         0          0            0x0
DeadWait         0          0            0x0
Linger           0          0            0x0
ProcessQ         0          0            0x0


iss: 1579724289  snduna: 1579724392  sndnxt: 1579724392     sndwnd:  16282
irs: 4090406841  rcvnxt: 4090406944  rcvwnd:        16282  delrcvwnd:    102


SRTT: 253 ms, RTTO: 2915 ms, RTV: 2662 ms, KRTT: 0 ms
minRTT: 40 ms, maxRTT: 1484 ms, ACK hold: 200 ms
Status Flags: passive open, gen tcbs
Option Flags: nagle
IP Precedence value : 6


Datagrams (max data segment is 1440 bytes):
Rcvd: 6 (out of order: 0), with data: 3, total data bytes: 102
Sent: 3 (retransmit: 0, fastretransmit: 0, partialack: 0, Second Congestion: 0),
 with data: 3, total data bytes: 230
 Packets received in fast path: 0, fast processed: 0, slow path: 0
 fast lock acquisition failures: 0, slow path: 0
```

Also highlighted in this neighbor data are the fields showing that the session supports only IPv4 unicast prefix advertisements; the routers' BGP sessions have not been configured to carry any other address families (as demonstrated in Chapter 6). So this EBGP session, although running between IPv6 endpoints, can carry only IPv4 prefixes—the default address family.

There is one small difference between the TCP sessions in Examples 2-8 and 2-10; it has nothing to do with IPv4 or IPv6 but is nevertheless worth noting. In Example 2-8, the local (Vail's) TCP port is ephemeral whereas the remote (Taos') TCP port is 179. Example 2-10 is just the opposite: Vail's local TCP port is 179 and the remote TCP port at Taos is ephemeral. What this indicates is that in the first case, Vail initiated the TCP connection (the TCP initiation is always directed at port 179 for BGP), whereas in the second case Taos initiated the TCP connection. This is consistent with the historical facts of the connections: In configuring the first example, Vail's BGP was configured before Taos (and you can observe in Example 2-7 Vail trying to connect to Taos before Taos is ready); in the second example, Taos' BGP was configured before Vail. Noticing small details such as this one can be useful when you troubleshoot or just try to fully understand a particular BGP session. Such details can also be important if you run an access list on a BGP interface. The ACL might be configured to permit TCP port 179, but depending on the direction of the session might inadvertently block the ephemeral port.

Case Study: IBGP Peering

Figure 2-25 shows another AS, AS400, connected to AS100. (The interfaces connecting Vail and Taos are again IPv4, for simplicity's sake.) Two more routers, Aspen and Telluride, are added within AS100 and Telluride connects to Alta, in AS400, via EBGP.

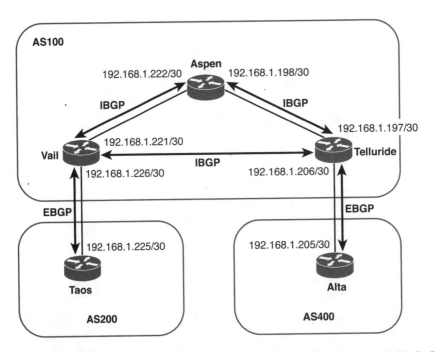

Figure 2-25 *Two Routers Are Added to AS100 and Are Peering via IBGP So That AS200 and AS400 Can Communicate Across AS100*

Each of the three routers in AS100 has an IBGP peering session with the other two routers in the same AS. Recall from the section "External and Internal BGP" in Chapter 1 that a full IBGP mesh—a direct IBGP connection between every BGP router within the same AS—is required for two reasons:

■ The AS_PATH attribute is meaningless within a single AS, so IBGP has no loop avoidance mechanism. A full IBGP mesh means every BGP router directly advertises its prefixes to every other BGP router in the same AS, removing any need for a router to advertise prefixes learned from one internal peer to another internal peer, which could lead to routing loops. A default BGP rule reinforces the full mesh requirement: BGP cannot advertise routes learned from an internal neighbor to another internal neighbor.[10]

■ Every BGP router along a forwarding path must know the BGP routes used at the routers with external peers so that packets forwarded to a purely internal BGP router on their way to an external next hop are not dropped by the internal router. For instance, in Figure 2-25 a packet traveling from AS400 to AS200 would be received by Telluride; Telluride's BGP route to the AS200 destination would have a next-hop address of 192.168.1.225 (Taos' external interface). Telluride would forward the packet to Aspen to get to that next hop, assuming Vail is advertising the subnet internally. But if Aspen does not also know the BGP route to the AS200 destination, it drops the packet. Therefore, in addition to the IBGP session between Vail and Telluride, each of those externally connected routers must tell Aspen about its external routes.

At a basic level, IBGP peering is configured exactly the same as EBGP peering; it is IBGP rather than EBGP only in that the AS number referenced by **neighbor remote-as** is the same as the local AS number referenced by **router bgp**. Example 2-11 shows the configurations for Vail, Aspen, and Telluride. The **router bgp** statements in all three configurations show that the routers are all in AS100; you can then easily see what **neighbor remote-as** statements in each configuration point to AS100, and from that you know that those sessions are IBGP.

Example 2-11 *Configurations for the Routers of AS100 in Figure 2-25*

```
Vail
router bgp 100
 neighbor 192.168.1.197 remote-as 100
 neighbor 192.168.1.222 remote-as 100
 neighbor 192.168.1.225 remote-as 200
```

[10] This rule is modified when route reflectors, examined in Chapter 5, are implemented.

```
Aspen
router bgp 100
 neighbor 192.168.1.197 remote-as 100
 neighbor 192.168.1.221 remote-as 100
```

```
Telluride
router bgp 100
 neighbor 192.168.1.198 remote-as 100
 neighbor 192.168.1.205 remote-as 400
 neighbor 192.168.1.221 remote-as 100
```

Example 2-12 introduces another command you can use regularly when maintaining and troubleshooting BGP networks: **show ip bgp summary**.[11] This command gives you an overview of the BGP peerings configured on the router and the state of each of those peerings. The output from this command first shows you the local router's BGP router ID and AS number, and the current version of the BGP table. (The table version is incremented when policies or other activities change the contents of the table.) After this information a table lists the following for each configured neighbor:

- The address configured in the **neighbor remote-as** statement

- The BGP version used for that neighbor

- The neighbor's AS number

- The number of BGP messages received from and sent to the neighbor

- The last version of the local BGP table sent to the neighbor

- The number of messages in queue from and to the neighbor

- The length of time the BGP session has been Established with the neighbor, or the status of the neighbor if not in Established state

- The state of the neighbor if not Established; or if the state is Established, the number of prefixes received from the neighbor

---

[11] You can also use **show bgp summary** to display the same information; although, it is not documented in the IOS manuals and might not work with all IOS releases. The output of the show ip bgp summary command also varies depending on the IOS release you use.

Example 2-12 *Although the Other BGP Sessions Are Established, the IBGP Peering Between Vail and Telluride Is Not; Its State Is Active*

```
! Vail
Vail#show ip bgp summary

BGP router identifier 192.168.1.226, local AS number 100
BGP table version is 1, main routing table version 1

Neighbor         V    AS MsgRcvd MsgSent   TblVer  InQ OutQ Up/Down  State/PfxRcd
192.168.1.197    4   100       0       0        0    0    0 never    Active
192.168.1.222    4   100      29      22        1    0    0 00:18:59            0
192.168.1.225    4   200      43      43        1    0    0 00:00:12            0


! Aspen
Aspen#show ip bgp summary
BGP router identifier 192.168.1.222, local AS number 100
BGP table version is 1, main routing table version 1
Neighbor         V    AS MsgRcvd MsgSent   TblVer  InQ OutQ Up/Down  State/PfxRcd
192.168.1.197    4   100      12      20        1    0    0 00:15:43            0
192.168.1.221    4   100      23      30        1    0    0 00:26:14            0


! Telluride
Telluride#show ip bgp summary
BGP router identifier 192.168.1.206, local AS number 100
BGP table version is 1, main routing table version 1

Neighbor         V    AS MsgRcvd MsgSent   TblVer  InQ OutQ Up/Down  State/PfxRcd
192.168.1.198    4   100      21      13        1    0    0 00:10:06            0
192.168.1.205    4   400       4       5        1    0    0 00:01:06            0
192.168.1.221    4   100       0       0        0    0    0 never    Active
```

The three displays in Example 2-12 show that all the EBGP and IBGP sessions are Established except for the IBGP session between Vail (192.168.1.221) and Telluride (192.168.1.197); Vail and Telluride each show the other in Active state. A quick look at Vail's routing table (Example 2-13) reveals the problem: Vail has no route to Telluride's interface 192.168.1.197. Although its routing table is not shown here, Telluride does not have a route to Vail's interface 192.168.1.221 either.

Example 2-13   *Vail Does Not Have a Route to 192.168.1.197 and Cannot Establish an IBGP Session with Telluride*

```
Vail#show ip route

Codes: C - connected, S - static, R - RIP, M - mobile, B - BGP
       D - EIGRP, EX - EIGRP external, O - OSPF, IA - OSPF inter area
       N1 - OSPF NSSA external type 1, N2 - OSPF NSSA external type 2
       E1 - OSPF external type 1, E2 - OSPF external type 2
       i - IS-IS, su - IS-IS summary, L1 - IS-IS level-1, L2 - IS-IS level-2
       ia - IS-IS inter area, * - candidate default, U - per-user static route
       o - ODR, P - periodic downloaded static route

Gateway of last resort is not set

     192.168.1.0/30 is subnetted, 2 subnets
C       192.168.1.224 is directly connected, Serial1/0
C       192.168.1.220 is directly connected, FastEthernet0/0
Vail#
```

This simple example demonstrates a problem commonly encountered when working with IBGP. Unlike IGPs, IBGP sessions often span multiple router hops; a router cannot establish an IBGP session unless it knows how to reach its peer. Therefore, one of the first steps in troubleshooting an IBGP session that stays in Active state (listening for a configured neighbor) is to look in the routing tables of both neighbors and see if they know how to find each other.

The problem with the IBGP session between Vail and Telluride is resolved by configuring an IGP within AS100—in this example, OSPF is used, but anything that gives the neighbors the reachability information they need in their routing tables can work. Example 2-14 shows that Vail's routing table now has a route to subnet 192.168.1.196 and to the neighbor address 192.168.1.197 configured for Telluride. Example 2-15 shows that with the three routers in AS100 now exchanging internal reachability information via OSPF, all IBGP sessions are Established.

Example 2-14   *After an IGP (OSPF in This Case) Is Configured, Vail Has a Route to Telluride*

```
Vail#show ip route

Codes: C - connected, S - static, R - RIP, M - mobile, B - BGP
       D - EIGRP, EX - EIGRP external, O - OSPF, IA - OSPF inter area
       N1 - OSPF NSSA external type 1, N2 - OSPF NSSA external type 2
       E1 - OSPF external type 1, E2 - OSPF external type 2
       i - IS-IS, su - IS-IS summary, L1 - IS-IS level-1, L2 - IS-IS level-2
```

```
        ia - IS-IS inter area, * - candidate default, U - per-user static route
        o - ODR, P - periodic downloaded static route

Gateway of last resort is not set



    192.168.1.0/30 is subnetted, 3 subnets
C       192.168.1.224 is directly connected, Serial1/0
O       192.168.1.196 [110/2] via 192.168.1.222, 00:00:07, FastEthernet0/0
C       192.168.1.220 is directly connected, FastEthernet0/0
Vail#
```

Example 2-15 *Vail and Telluride Now Know How to Find Each Other and Their IBGP Session Is Established*

```
Vail#show ip bgp summary
BGP router identifier 192.168.1.226, local AS number 100



BGP table version is 1, main routing table version 1

Neighbor        V    AS MsgRcvd MsgSent   TblVer  InQ OutQ Up/Down  State/PfxRcd
192.168.1.197   4   100       4       4        1    0    0 00:00:05           0
192.168.1.222   4   100      93      56        1    0    0 00:00:56           0
192.168.1.225   4   200     131     142        1    0    0 00:00:05           0
```

```
Aspen#show ip bgp summary
BGP router identifier 192.168.1.222, local AS number 100



BGP table version is 1, main routing table version 1

Neighbor        V    AS MsgRcvd MsgSent   TblVer  InQ OutQ Up/Down  State/PfxRcd
192.168.1.197   4   100      47      81        1    0    0 00:02:53           0
192.168.1.221   4   100      57      95        1    0    0 00:03:31           0
```

```
Telluride#show ip bgp summary
BGP router identifier 192.168.1.206, local AS number 100
BGP table version is 1, main routing table version 1

Neighbor        V    AS MsgRcvd MsgSent   TblVer  InQ OutQ Up/Down  State/PfxRcd
192.168.1.198   4   100      82      47        1    0    0 00:02:09           0
192.168.1.205   4   400      84      73        1    0    0 00:01:03           0
192.168.1.221   4   100       5       5        1    0    0 00:01:37           0
```

The IBGP configurations are now sufficient for the topology in Figure 2-25; however, the topology has a problem: If the link between Telluride and Aspen or the link between Aspen and Vail fails, AS100 and AS400 can no longer communicate. AS100 needs a more resilient topology both for packet forwarding and for BGP information exchange. A link added between Telluride and Vail, as shown in Figure 2-26, gives AS100 the redundancy to survive the failure of a single internal link.

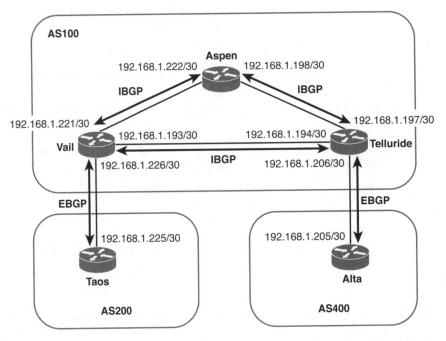

Figure 2-26 *A Link Between Vail and Telluride Gives AS100 Some Redundancy*

Although the added link does provide some redundancy, it raises a question about the IBGP configuration for AS100. If a link fails, you want the IBGP sessions that were using the link to be rerouted across the alternative path. With the IBGP sessions running between physical interfaces, you cannot be sure that this will happen. One remedy might be to configure redundant IBGP sessions. For example, Vail and Telluride might be configured for peering both between 192.168.1.193 and 192.168.1.194 and between 192.168.1.221 and 192.168.1.197. However, as the topology of an AS grows in complexity, this approach (configuring all routers with redundant IBGP connections to all physical interfaces) quickly escalates to undesirably long BGP configurations and to an undesirable number of IBGP sessions.

A better approach is to peer not between physical interfaces but between loopback interfaces, as shown in Figure 2-27. Note that the physical links have been removed from the drawing; when you peer between loopback addresses, you remove physical interface dependencies from the IBGP topology. Only a single IBGP session between each router within the AS is required, and that session is routed over the best available path. Should a link on that path fail, the session is rerouted—in most cases rerouted fast enough that the BGP session does not fail—over the next best path.

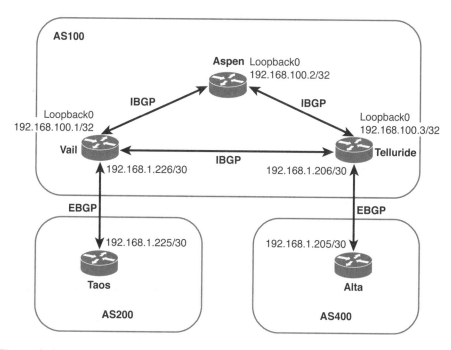

Figure 2-27 *Using Loopback Interfaces as the IBGP Endpoints Eliminates Any Dependencies on Physical Interfaces*

Configuring IBGP peering between loopback interfaces requires an extra configuration statement. You not only specify the neighbor's loopback address instead of a physical address for the remote end of the session, you must also specify the local router's loopback interface as the originating end of the session.

Example 2-16 shows an improved configuration for Vail. The EBGP configuration remains the same, but the **neighbor remote-as** statements for Aspen and Telluride now point to those routers' loopback interface addresses rather than physical interfaces as in the previous configuration examples. The IBGP configurations of Aspen and Telluride also now point to loopback interfaces instead of physical interfaces.

But that is not enough. By default, an outgoing TCP session is sourced from its outgoing physical interface address. If every router in Figure 2-27 tried to originate its IBGP TCP session from a physical interface and going to a loopback interface, although its peer also originates at a physical interface and terminates at the local router's loopback, the endpoints of the attempted TCP sessions never match and the sessions do not come up.

So **neighbor update-source** tells the router to originate the TCP session going to the specified neighbor from the specified local loopback interface.

Example 2-16   *Peering Between Loopback Addresses Requires the* **neighbor update-source** *Statement to Indicate That the Local End of the Session Should Be Sourced from the Local Loopback Interface, as Shown in Vail's Modified Configuration*

```
router bgp 100

 neighbor 192.168.1.225 remote-as 200
 neighbor 192.168.100.2 remote-as 100
 neighbor 192.168.100.2 update-source Loopback0
 neighbor 192.168.100.3 remote-as 100
 neighbor 192.168.100.3 update-source Loopback0
```

Example 2-17 shows the results of the three routers of AS100 in Figure 2-27. The IBGP sessions are all up (because of OSPF advertising the loopback addresses). You can also observe another difference from the earlier observed sessions. Recall from the discussion in the section on the Open message than BGP chooses its router ID the same way OSPF does: It prefers the loopback address and chooses the numerically highest physical interface address if the loopback is not available. With the new configuration we have made loopback addresses available, and you can see that the BGP router IDs in each of Example 2-17's three displays are the loopback address of that router. Because the same loopback address is probably used to identify the router in several other ways, such as the OSPF router ID and even as a DNS entry for telnetting to the router by name, using the loopback for the BGP router ID enforces consistency and makes the BGP ID easily recognizable.

The Case Study "Managing and Securing BGP Sessions" shows you an even better way to configure a predictable and consistent BGP router ID.

Example 2-17   *The IBGP Sessions Now Run Between Loopback Interfaces Instead of Physical Interfaces*

```
Vail#show ip bgp summary
BGP router identifier 192.168.100.1, local AS number 100
BGP table version is 1, main routing table version 1

Neighbor         V    AS MsgRcvd MsgSent   TblVer  InQ OutQ Up/Down   State/PfxRcd
192.168.1.225    4   200       5       5        1    0    0 00:01:09             0
192.168.100.2    4   100      15      14        1    0    0 00:11:26             0
192.168.100.3    4   100      12      13        1    0    0 00:09:00             0
```

```
Aspen#show ip bgp summary
BGP router identifier 192.168.100.2, local AS number 100
BGP table version is 1, main routing table version 1


Neighbor        V    AS MsgRcvd MsgSent   TblVer  InQ OutQ Up/Down  State/PfxRcd
192.168.100.1   4   100      14      14        1    0    0 00:11:42           0
192.168.100.3   4   100      11      13        1    0    0 00:08:59           0

Telluride#show ip bgp summary
BGP router identifier 192.168.100.3, local AS number 100
BGP table version is 1, main routing table version 1


Neighbor        V    AS MsgRcvd MsgSent   TblVer  InQ OutQ Up/Down  State/PfxRcd
192.168.1.205   4   400       8       7        1    0    0 00:03:02           0
192.168.100.1   4   100      20      20        1    0    0 00:17:09           0
192.168.100.2   4   100      21      19        1    0    0 00:16:51           0
```

Case Study: Connected Check and EBGP Multihop

Only the IBGP sessions in the previous example run between loopback addresses. The EBGP sessions still run between directly connected physical interfaces, and that is standard practice for the great majority of EBGP sessions. The IOS default settings ensure that external BGP peers are directly connected by two means:

- Setting a TTL value of 1 in packets containing BGP messages to external neighbors so that if the packet crosses a router hop the TTL is decremented to 0 and the packet is dropped

- Checking the IP address of the configured neighbor to ensure that it belongs to a directly connected subnet

However, there are cases in which running EBGP between loopback interfaces is useful. Consider Figure 2-28, in which Telluride and Alta are connected by four equal-cost links. Configuring four separate EBGP sessions, one for each link, is undesirable because you do not want the added configuration complexity. More important, such a configuration causes BGP to advertise four identical sets of prefixes between the routers, reducing network scalability.

At the same time, you do not want to choose just one of the four links to carry the EBGP session. If that link was to fail, EBGP would fail even though there are still three good links between the routers. You want to take advantage of the redundancy and load-sharing capabilities of the four parallel links. A solution for this case[12] is to run EBGP between the routers' loopback interfaces, as shown in Figure 2-29.

---

[12] Another solution is to "bundle" the links using a link aggregation protocol, which does not require you to configure EBGP Multihop or disable the connect check.

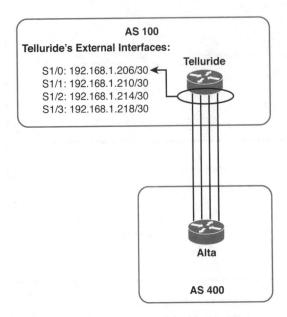

Figure 2-28 *Four Equal-Cost Links Connect Telluride and Alta*

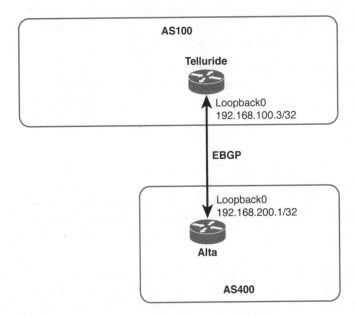

Figure 2-29 *Using Loopback Interfaces for the EBGP Endpoints Takes Advantage of the Redundancy and Load Sharing of Multiple Physical Links*

The configuration is similar to the configurations in the preceding IBGP example: You specify the neighbor's loopback address as the neighbor address, use the **neighbor update-source** statement to source the session from the local loopback interface, and give the routers on each side a means of finding the remote peering address. By definition an IGP is not run between routers in different autonomous systems, so in this case, static routes are used; for each physical link, a static route is configured pointing to the remote loopback address and specifying the address of the far end of the link as the next hop. Example 2-18 shows Alta's EBGP configuration; Telluride's configuration is similar.

Example 2-18   *Alta's EBGP Configuration Specifies That EBGP Messages It Originates to Neighbor 192.168.100.3 (Telluride) Are Originated from Its Loopback0 Interface, and Static Routes Are Configured to Find the Neighbor Address Across All Four of the Physical Links*

```
router bgp 400
 no synchronization
 bgp log-neighbor-changes
 neighbor 192.168.100.3 remote-as 100
 neighbor 192.168.100.3 disable-connected-check
 neighbor 192.168.100.3 update-source Loopback0
 no auto-summary
!
ip route 192.168.100.3 255.255.255.255 192.168.1.206
ip route 192.168.100.3 255.255.255.255 192.168.1.210
ip route 192.168.100.3 255.255.255.255 192.168.1.214
ip route 192.168.100.3 255.255.255.255 192.168.1.218
```

Example 2-19 shows that Alta's neighbor state to Telluride is Idle. A closer look shows, near the bottom of the display, that there is no active TCP session because the neighbor address 192.168.100.3 is not directly connected. This is the connected check that IOS does by default for EBGP neighbors.

Example 2-19   *The Neighbor State to Telluride Is Idle Because the IOS Default Connected Check Shows That the Address Is Not Directly Connected to a Local Subnet*

```
Alta#show ip bgp neighbor 192.168.100.3
BGP neighbor is 192.168.100.3,  remote AS 100, external link
  BGP version 4, remote router ID 0.0.0.0
  BGP state = Idle
  Last read 00:00:00, last write 00:00:00, hold time is 180, keepalive interval is
  60 seconds
  Message statistics:
    InQ depth is 0
    OutQ depth is 0
```

```
                        Sent          Rcvd
    Opens:                0             0
    Notifications:        0             0
    Updates:              0             0
    Keepalives:           0             0
    Route Refresh:        0             0
    Total:                0             0
  Default minimum time between advertisement runs is 30 seconds


 For address family: IPv4 Unicast
  BGP table version 1, neighbor version 0/0
  Output queue size: 0
  Index 1, Offset 0, Mask 0x2
  1 update-group member
                          Sent          Rcvd
  Prefix activity:        ----          ----
    Prefixes Current:       0             0
    Prefixes Total:         0             0
    Implicit Withdraw:      0             0
    Explicit Withdraw:      0             0
    Used as bestpath:     n/a             0
    Used as multipath:    n/a             0


                          Outbound    Inbound
  Local Policy Denied Prefixes:  --------    -------
    Total:                          0           0
  Number of NLRIs in the update sent: max 0, min 0


  Connections established 0; dropped 0
  Last reset never
  External BGP neighbor not directly connected.
  No active TCP connection
 Alta#
```

For situations in which an external BGP neighbor is directly connected but the neighbor address is not a part of a local subnet—the most common instance of which is EBGP peering between loopback interfaces—you can disable the IOS connected check with the statement **neighbor disable-connected-check**. Example 2-20 shows Alta's configuration with this statement added. The statement is also added to Telluride's configuration. Example 2-21 shows that the BGP session between the two loopback addresses is now established.

Example 2-20 *Alta's EBGP Configuration Now Includes the* **neighbor disable-connected-check** *Statement*

```
router bgp 400
 no synchronization
 bgp log-neighbor-changes
 neighbor 192.168.100.3 remote-as 100
 neighbor 192.168.100.3 disable-connected-check
 neighbor 192.168.100.3 update-source Loopback0
 no auto-summary
!
ip route 192.168.100.3 255.255.255.255 192.168.1.206
ip route 192.168.100.3 255.255.255.255 192.168.1.210
ip route 192.168.100.3 255.255.255.255 192.168.1.214
ip route 192.168.100.3 255.255.255.255 192.168.1.218
```

Example 2-21 *With the Connected Check Disabled, the EBGP Session Between Alta and Telluride Is Now Established*

```
Alta#show ip bgp neighbor 192.168.100.3
BGP neighbor is 192.168.100.3,  remote AS 100, external link
  BGP version 4, remote router ID 192.168.100.3
  BGP state = Established, up for 00:10:06
  Last read 00:00:05, last write 00:00:05, hold time is 180, keepalive interval is
  60 seconds
  Neighbor capabilities:

[Remaining output deleted]
```

Figure 2-30 depicts another EBGP peering scenario that is frequently encountered. An EBGP session is again running between the loopback interfaces of Alta and Telluride, but now the two routers are not directly connected. The session must pass through the router Copper, which is not running BGP at all. Copper might be a filtering router or some other security device that examines packets before they're allowed to enter AS100, or it might be one of many edge routers that aggregate EBGP sessions to one or a few routers interior to AS100. The point is that just disabling the IOS connected check is not sufficient to make this scenario work because by default EBGP messages are sent with a TTL of 1. Packets passing from Alta to Copper to Telluride must have a TTL of at least 2 to account for the TTL being decremented by 1 as it passes through Copper.

The **neighbor ebgp-multihop** statement changes the default TTL in EBGP messages to specified neighbors. Example 2-22 shows the configurations of the three routers in Figure 2-30. Simple reachability is configured with OSPF between Telluride and Copper, a static route at Copper for Alta's loopback address, and a static default route pointing to Copper at Alta. Most important, notice that there is no BGP running at Copper. The

neighbor ebgp-multihop statement is used at Telluride and Alta to change the default TTL of their EBGP messages to 2; when the messages transit Copper the TTL is decremented to 1, and the messages safely arrive at their destination. If the messages had retained their default TTL of 1 upon transmission, the TTL would be decremented to 0 at Copper, and the packets would be dropped.

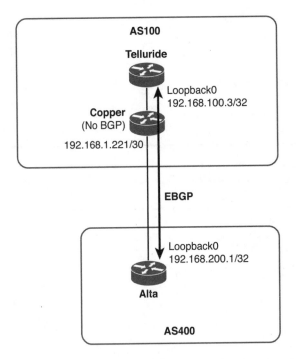

Figure 2-30 *EBGP Peering Scenario for Two Routers Not Directly Connected*

Example 2-22 *Routers Telluride and Alta in Figure 2-30 Are Configured to Establish an EBGP Session Across Two Router Hops*

```
Telluride
router ospf 1
 log-adjacency-changes
 network 0.0.0.0 255.255.255.255 area 0
!
router bgp 100
 no synchronization
 bgp log-neighbor-changes
 neighbor 192.168.200.1 remote-as 400
 neighbor 192.168.200.1 ebgp-multihop 2
```

```
  neighbor 192.168.200.1 update-source Loopback0
  no auto-summary
  !
```

```
Copper
router ospf 1
 log-adjacency-changes
 redistribute static
 network 0.0.0.0 255.255.255.255 area 0
!
ip route 192.168.200.0 255.255.255.0 192.168.1.222
!
```

```
Alta
router bgp 400
 no synchronization
 bgp log-neighbor-changes
 neighbor 192.168.100.3 remote-as 100
 neighbor 192.168.100.3 ebgp-multihop 2
 neighbor 192.168.100.3 update-source Loopback0
 no auto-summary
 !
ip route 0.0.0.0 0.0.0.0 192.168.1.221
```

Example 2-23 shows that Alta's neighbor state for Telluride is Established. Looking further down the display, you can also see that the outgoing TTL is 2, changed from the default outgoing TTL of 1.

Example 2-23 *Alta's Neighbor State to Telluride (192.168.100.3) Is Established*

```
Alta#show ip bgp neighbor 192.168.100.3
BGP neighbor is 192.168.100.3,  remote AS 100, external link
  BGP version 4, remote router ID 192.168.100.3
  BGP state = Established, up for 00:26:41
  Last read 00:00:41, last write 00:00:41, hold time is 180, keepalive interval is
  60 seconds
  Neighbor capabilities:
    Route refresh: advertised and received(old & new)
    Address family IPv4 Unicast: advertised and received
  Message statistics:
    InQ depth is 0
    OutQ depth is 0
                        Sent       Rcvd
    Opens:                 1          1
    Notifications:         0          0
```

```
  Updates:                    0          0
  Keepalives:                28         28
  Route Refresh:              0          0
  Total:                     29         29
 Default minimum time between advertisement runs is 30 seconds


For address family: IPv4 Unicast
 BGP table version 1, neighbor version 1/0
 Output queue size: 0
 Index 1, Offset 0, Mask 0x2
 1 update-group member
                            Sent       Rcvd
 Prefix activity:           ----       ----
   Prefixes Current:          0          0
   Prefixes Total:            0          0
   Implicit Withdraw:         0          0
   Explicit Withdraw:         0          0
   Used as bestpath:        n/a          0
   Used as multipath:       n/a          0

                          Outbound   Inbound
 Local Policy Denied Prefixes:   --------   -------
    Total:                      0          0
 Number of NLRIs in the update sent: max 0, min 0


 Connections established 1; dropped 0
 Last reset never
 External BGP neighbor may be up to 2 hops away.
Connection state is ESTAB, I/O status: 1, unread input bytes: 0
Connection is ECN Disabled, Mininum incoming TTL 0, Outgoing TTL 2
Local host: 192.168.200.1, Local port: 179
Foreign host: 192.168.100.3, Foreign port: 29761
Connection tableid (VRF): 0


Enqueued packets for retransmit: 0, input: 0  mis-ordered: 0 (0 bytes)


Event Timers (current time is 0x22885C):
Timer          Starts   Wakeups        Next
Retrans            29        0         0x0
TimeWait            0        0         0x0
AckHold            29        1         0x0
SendWnd             0        0         0x0
KeepAlive           0        0         0x0
GiveUp              0        0         0x0
```

```
PmtuAger            0           0           0x0
DeadWait            0           0           0x0
Linger              0           0           0x0
ProcessQ            0           0           0x0


iss: 3118002936  snduna: 3118003514  sndnxt: 3118003514     sndwnd:  16346
irs: 3626178200  rcvnxt: 3626178778  rcvwnd:      16346 .delrcvwnd:     38


SRTT: 294 ms, RTTO: 345 ms, RTV: 51 ms, KRTT: 0 ms
minRTT: 36 ms, maxRTT: 312 ms, ACK hold: 200 ms
Status Flags: passive open, gen tcbs
Option Flags: nagle
IP Precedence value : 6


Datagrams (max data segment is 536 bytes):
Rcvd: 58 (out of order: 0), with data: 29, total data bytes: 577
Sent: 31 (retransmit: 0, fastretransmit: 0, partialack: 0, Second Congestion: 0),
  with data: 28, total data bytes: 577
 Packets received in fast path: 0, fast processed: 0, slow path: 0
 fast lock acquisition failures: 0, slow path: 0
Alta#
```

You might ask why the **neighbor disable-connected-check** statement is not needed in this configuration. Alta and Telluride are obviously not directly connected, and the loopback addresses do not belong to the same subnet, yet just as obviously in Example 2-23 the EBGP session between their loopback interfaces works. The answer is that the connected check is automatically disabled when the neighbor e**bgp-multihop** statement increases the TTL

Using the **neighbor ebgp multihop** statement to change the TTL to 2 or more would make the scenario in Figure 2-29 work just as well as using the **neighbor disable-connected-check** statement did. This leads to a commonly held misconception that the TTL is decremented when a packet is sent to an IP address on a neighboring router when the destination address is not a part of a locally connected subnet. This is not the case. The TTL of any IP packet is decremented only when the packet leaves a router—a true router hop.

So if you want to establish an EBGP session to an IP address on a directly connected router that does not belong to a directly connected subnet, as shown in Figure 2-29, use the **neighbor disable-connected-check** statement. This enables you to establish the connection without sacrificing the default TTL behavior. If you must establish a EBGP session with a neighbor that is truly more than one router hop away, use the **neighbor ebgp-multihop** statement, but allow only the number of router hops necessary to reach the neighbor.

Case Study: Managing and Securing BGP Connections

The examples up to this point have given you everything you need to configure fully functional BGP sessions, and have given you an overview of the tools for observing and troubleshooting the sessions. But there are a few more configuration features that, although not necessary for getting a session up and running, are useful for making the session more manageable and that are essential for making the session secure.

> **Note**   In addition to the features demonstrated in this case study, BGP peer groups and peer templates make large BGP configurations more manageable. Peer groups and peer templates are covered in Chapter 5 as scaling features because as configuration complexity grows, these grouping tools become not just convenient but also almost essential for configuration control.

Example 2-24 shows the BGP configuration for Vail in Figure 2-27, with some added management and security features.

Example 2-24   *A Number of Management and Security Features Have Been Added to Vail's (Figure 2-27) BGP Configuration*

```
router bgp 100
 bgp router-id 192.168.100.1
 bgp log-neighbor-changes
 neighbor 192.168.1.225 remote-as 200
 neighbor 192.168.1.225 description Taos
 neighbor 192.168.1.225 password N0rdic
 neighbor 192.168.1.225 ttl-security hops 1
 neighbor 192.168.100.2 remote-as 100
 neighbor 192.168.100.2 description Aspen
 neighbor 192.168.100.2 password aLpine
 neighbor 192.168.100.2 update-source Loopback0
 neighbor 192.168.100.3 remote-as 100
 neighbor 192.168.100.3 description Telluride
 neighbor 192.168.100.3 password aLpine
 neighbor 192.168.100.3 update-source Loopback0
 neighbor 192.168.100.10 remote-as 100
 neighbor 192.168.100.10 description Whistler
 neighbor 192.168.100.10 password aLpine
 neighbor 192.168.100.10 shutdown
 neighbor 192.168.100.10 update-source Loopback0
 !
```

The first new statement in Vail's configuration is **bgp router-id.** As previously discussed, IOS uses the same procedure to acquire a BGP router ID as it does for the OSPF router

ID: It uses a loopback interface address if one exists, and if not it uses the numerically highest physical interface address. The **bgp router-id** statement overrides this automatic procedure and manually assigns a BGP router ID. You can use this statement if you want the BGP router ID to be something different from a loopback interface address, or—as in the example here—you can use the command to ensure that the BGP router ID remains stable and predictable even if the loopback address is added, changed, or deleted.

The next new statement shown in Example 2-24 is **bgp log-neighbor-changes**. In all recent IOS releases, this feature is enabled by default, so when you create a BGP configuration the statement is automatically entered. But it is worthwhile to check your configuration to ensure that the statement is there because it provides another key troubleshooting tool. When the status of a neighbor changes, this feature records the change and the cause of the change either in the router's logging buffer or, if syslog is configured, to an external syslog server.

The entries in the logging buffer display with the **show logging** command, as shown in Example 2-25. The log entries in this example (after some information about the logging buffer) reveal several neighbor events at Vail. The first entry records an adjacency establishment with neighbor 192.168.100.3 (Telluride in Figure 2-27). The second entry shows that a little less than 4 minutes later, the adjacency went down. The entry, also important, indicates the reason the adjacency went down: Telluride closed the session. You know from this information that the session was closed gracefully by BGP rather than suffering a "hard" failure. A minute later, according to the third entry, the adjacency to Telluride is re-established.

Example 2-25   bgp log-neighbor-changes *Statement Enables Logging of Changes in BGP Neighbor Status, Which Can Then Be Observed with the* show logging *Command*

```
Vail#show logging

Syslog logging: enabled (10 messages dropped, 0 messages rate-limited,
                0 flushes, 0 overruns, xml disabled, filtering disabled)

No Active Message Discriminator.



No Inactive Message Discriminator.


    Console logging: level debugging, 505 messages logged, xml disabled,
                    filtering disabled
    Monitor logging: level debugging, 0 messages logged, xml disabled,
                    filtering disabled
    Buffer logging:  level debugging, 505 messages logged, xml disabled,
```

```
                      filtering disabled
     Logging Exception size (8192 bytes)
     Count and timestamp logging messages: disabled


No active filter modules.


ESM: 0 messages dropped


    Trap logging: level informational, 509 message lines logged


Log Buffer (8192 bytes):

*Aug 21 07:11:38: %BGP-5-ADJCHANGE: neighbor 192.168.100.3 Up

*Aug 21 07:15:16: %BGP-5-ADJCHANGE: neighbor 192.168.100.3 Down Peer closed the
session

*Aug 21 07:16:17: %BGP-5-ADJCHANGE: neighbor 192.168.100.3 Up

*Aug 21 07:19:35: %LINEPROTO-5-UPDOWN: Line protocol on Interface Serial1/0, changed
  state to up

*Aug 21 07:21:03: %TCP-6-BADAUTH: No MD5 digest from 192.168.1.225(179) to
  192.168.1.226(20308)

*Aug 21 07:21:04: %TCP-6-BADAUTH: No MD5 digest from 192.168.1.225(179) to
  192.168.1.226(20308)

*Aug 21 07:21:04: %TCP-6-BADAUTH: No MD5 digest from 192.168.1.225(179) to
  192.168.1.226(20308)

*Aug 21 07:21:06: %TCP-6-BADAUTH: No MD5 digest from 192.168.1.225(179) to
  192.168.1.226(20308)

*Aug 21 07:21:09: %TCP-6-BADAUTH: No MD5 digest from 192.168.1.225(179) to
  192.168.1.226(20308)

*Aug 21 07:21:14: %TCP-6-BADAUTH: No MD5 digest from 192.168.1.225(179) to
  192.168.1.226(20308)

Vail#
```

The fourth entry shows that the state of interface S1/0—the interface connecting to Taos (192.168.1.225) referred to in Figure 2-27—has changed to Up. After the interface is up, the remaining entries show that Vail is making repeated attempts to open a TCP connection with Taos on port 179. The attempts are failing, according to the entries, because of an authentication problem.

The authentication problem leads to the next new feature in Vail's configuration: The **neighbor password** statement enables MD5 authentication and specifies a password for the neighbor.[13] The log entries in Example 2-25 tell you that while Vail is configured for MD5 authentication, Taos is not. If Taos were configured for authentication but its

---

[13] Normally, the passwords in the displayed configuration, like all other passwords, would be and should be encrypted. In this example, service password-encryption is disabled so that you can read the password.

password did not match Vail's, the entries would state "Invalid MD5 digest" rather than "No MD5 digest."

Each of Vail's neighbors in Example 2-24 is configured for authentication. As with any IGP, you must authenticate all your IBGP sessions; however, authenticating EBGP sessions is not merely important; it is also essential to the security of your network. The great majority of attempted attacks against routing protocols are against EBGP because that is the protocol exposed to the "outside world" and therefore the most accessible. Never run EBGP without authentication.

Example 2-24 shows that all the IBGP neighbors are configured with the same password (aLpine), whereas Taos, an external neighbor, has a different password (N0rdic). As with your IGP, it is acceptable and administratively easier to use the same password for all IBGP sessions; however, each EBGP session should have a unique password. Some network operators use the same password for multiple EBGP sessions to the same neighboring administrative domain, differing the passwords only for different domains, but the safest practice is to use a unique password for all EBGP sessions regardless of the domain.

Another EBGP security feature shown in Vail's configuration to Taos is **neighbor ttl-security**. To understand the effects of this statement, compare the highlighted lines in Example 2-26, taken with **neighbor ttl-security** enabled, with the corresponding lines in Example 2-8, taken for the same neighbor without the feature enabled. Vail's neighbor database for Taos in Example 2-8 shows the IOS default TTL behavior as discussed in the EBGP multihop case study: The TTL of incoming BGP message packets can be 0 or higher (this is after the local router has decremented the TTL value of the received packet), and the router sets the TTL of BGP message packets it originates to 1. Specifying **neighbor 192.168.1.225 ttl-security hops 1** in Vail's BGP configuration makes two changes to the default behavior, as shown in Example 2-26:

- The TTL of BGP message packets received from Taos must be 254 or higher (again, as measured after Vail has decremented the TTL value of the received packet) by subtracting the specified allowable hops from 255.

- The TTL of BGP message packets Vail sends to Taos is set to 255.

Example 2-26   neighbor ttl-security *Feature Changes the Acceptable TTL Value of Received EBGP Message Packets and the TTL Value of Transmitted BGP Message Packets*

```
Vail#show ip bgp neighbor 192.168.1.225

BGP neighbor is 192.168.1.225,  remote AS 200, external link
  BGP version 4, remote router ID 192.168.1.225
  BGP state = Established, up for 00:00:31
  Last read 00:00:30, last write 00:00:00, hold time is 180, keepalive interval
is 60 seconds
```

```
    Neighbor capabilities:
       Route refresh: advertised and received(old & new)
       Address family IPv4 Unicast: advertised and received
    Message statistics:
       InQ depth is 0
       OutQ depth is 0
                            Sent        Rcvd
       Opens:                 6           6
       Notifications:         0           0
       Updates:               0           0
       Keepalives:           75          77
       Route Refresh:         0           0
       Total:                81          83
    Default minimum time between advertisement runs is 30 seconds

  For address family: IPv4 Unicast
   BGP table version 1, neighbor version 0/0
   Output queue size: 0
   Index 2, Offset 0, Mask 0x4
   2 update-group member
                            Sent        Rcvd
    Prefix activity:        ----        ----
       Prefixes Current:      0           0
       Prefixes Total:        0           0
       Implicit Withdraw:     0           0
       Explicit Withdraw:     0           0
       Used as bestpath:     n/a          0
       Used as multipath:    n/a          0

                          Outbound    Inbound
    Local Policy Denied Prefixes:  --------    -------
       Total:                        0           0
    Number of NLRIs in the update sent: max 0, min 0

    Connections established 6; dropped 5
    Last reset 00:00:34, due to User reset
    External BGP neighbor may be up to 1 hop away.
Connection state is ESTAB, I/O status: 1, unread input bytes: 0
Connection is ECN Disabled, Mininum incoming TTL 254, Outgoing TTL 255
Local host: 192.168.1.226, Local port: 13408
Foreign host: 192.168.1.225, Foreign port: 179
Connection tableid (VRF): 0

Enqueued packets for retransmit: 0, input: 0   mis-ordered: 0 (0 bytes)
```

```
Event Timers (current time is 0x3D55F8):
Timer          Starts   Wakeups      Next
Retrans             4        0       0x0
TimeWait            0        0       0x0
AckHold             2        1       0x0
SendWnd             0        0       0x0
KeepAlive           0        0       0x0
GiveUp              0        0       0x0
PmtuAger            0        0       0x0
DeadWait            0        0       0x0
Linger              0        0       0x0
ProcessQ            0        0       0x0


iss:  379206806  snduna:  379206890  sndnxt:  379206890    sndwnd:  16301
irs: 3498356006  rcvnxt: 3498356109  rcvwnd:        16282  delrcvwnd:  102


SRTT: 206 ms, RTTO: 1891 ms, RTV: 1685 ms, KRTT: 0 ms
minRTT: 400 ms, maxRTT: 608 ms, ACK hold: 200 ms
Status Flags: active open
Option Flags: nagle, md5
IP Precedence value : 6


Datagrams (max data segment is 1440 bytes):
Rcvd: 4 (out of order: 0), with data: 2, total data bytes: 102
Sent: 6 (retransmit: 0, fastretransmit: 0, partialack: 0, Second Congestion: 0)
 with data: 3, total data bytes: 83
 Packets received in fast path: 0, fast processed: 0, slow path: 0
 fast lock acquisition failures: 0, slow path: 0
Vail#
```

The default behavior of setting the TTL value to 1 in originated packets ensures that the packets cannot travel beyond a directly connected router. But the default behavior of accepting packets with a TTL of 0 or higher means that a number of attacks can be launched remotely against EBGP; as long as the TTL of originated attack packets is high enough, the packets can traverse many routers and still be accepted by the local router. Authentication prevents BGP from accepting the packets internally, but a flood of invalid packets causing many authentication failures over short periods can break the EBGP session or spike the router's CPU, causing BGP to fail or even causing a router crash.

By setting the TTL of outbound packets to 255 and accepting only packets with a TTL of 254 or higher, packets cannot be sent to the local BGP process from routers that are not directly connected.[14] A maximum TTL of 255 is decremented to 254 when the packet transits a single router; arriving at the local router it is decremented to 253, which is below the acceptable minimum, and the packet is quietly discarded (that is, discarded without sending an ICMP error message) before reaching the local BGP process.

Of course, if you enable a minimum TTL value of 254 with **neighbor ttl-security**, the neighbor must send BGP message packets with a TTL of 255. So both neighbors must be configured with the feature, or if one of the neighbors is not an IOS router, it must support an equivalent feature. Another caveat is that **neighbor ttl-security** is incompatible with **neighbor ebgp-multihop**. But you can achieve the same results by adjusting the hops specification of the **neighbor ttl-security** statement.

Table 2-6 compares the use of EBGP-Multihop with that of TTL-Security.

Table 2-6   *Comparison of EBGP-Multihop and TTL-Security*

BGP Message Option	Minimum Acceptable TTL of Incoming BGP Messages	TTL of Outgoing BGP Messages
Default	0 or higher	1
neighbor ebgp-multihop	0 or higher	Specified TTL value
neighbor ttl-security hops	255 – (Specified hops value)	255

Another new statement in the configuration of Example 2-24 is **neighbor description**. This statement has no functional effect on BGP and merely provides a means of adding a textual description of up to 80 characters to the neighbor address, making the neighbor easier to identify in the configuration.

Finally, Example 2-24 includes a configuration for a new neighbor, Whistler, at 192.168.100.10. But Whistler has not yet been installed, so **neighbor shutdown** prevents Vail from attempting to connect to the non-existent neighbor. The **neighbor shutdown** statement is useful anytime you want to disable a neighbor connection without deleting its configuration.

Looking Ahead

This chapter provided you with a thorough grounding in the configuration and troubleshooting of BGP peering sessions and their underlying TCP sessions. But you surely have noticed that throughout the chapter, no routing information was actually passed over these sessions. The next chapter introduces you to the basic techniques of sending and receiving routing information over BGP sessions and the application of policies to change how the routing information is used.

---

[14] Securing against remote attacks by manipulating TTL values is called Generalized TTL Security Mechanism (GTSM) and is defined in RFC 3682.

Review Questions

1. What is an untrusted administrative domain, and why is it untrusted?

2. In what way does BGP require you to think differently about peering than an IGP does?

3. What AS numbers are reserved for private use?

4. What are the four BGP message types, and how is each one used?

5. What happens if two BGP neighbors advertise different hold times in their Open messages?

6. What does a negotiated hold time of 0 indicate?

7. What is the IOS default period for sending BGP Keepalive messages?

8. What is the BGP identifier, and how is it selected?

9. In what state or states can BGP peers exchange Update messages?

10. What is NLRI?

11. What is a path attribute?

12. What is a Withdrawn route?

13. What happens when a BGP Notification message is received?

14. What is the difference between the Connect state and the Active state?

15. What causes a transition to the OpenConfirm state, and what are the next steps when the BGP process shows a neighbor in this state?

16. What are the four categories of BGP path attributes?

17. What does well-known mandatory mean, and what are the three well-known mandatory path attributes?

18. What is the purpose of the ORIGIN attribute?

19. What is the purpose of the AS_PATH attribute?

20. When does a router add its AS number to the AS_PATH list of an Update?

21. What is AS path prepending?

22. What are AS_SEQUENCE and AS_SET, and what is the difference between them?

23. What is the purpose of the NEXT_HOP attribute?

24. What is a recursive route lookup, and why is it important to BGP?

25. What happens if a router receives a BGP route with a NEXT_HOP address that is unknown to the router?

26. What are the three parts of a BGP routing information database (RIB), and what is the function of each?

27. What do all the NLRI in a BGP Update message have in common?

28. Does BGP require a TCP connection between IPv6 addresses to advertise IPv6 prefixes?

29. What is the IOS default TTL value of BGP message packets sent to external peers?

Configuration Exercises

Table 2-7 lists the autonomous systems, routers, interfaces, and addresses used in Exercises 1 through 4. All interfaces of the routers are shown; physical interfaces may be changed for your solutions to fit your available resources. For each exercise, if the table indicates that the router has a loopback interface, that interface should be the source of all IBGP connections. EBGP connections should always be between physical interface addresses, unless otherwise specified in an exercise. Neighbor descriptions will always be configured to be the router names.

Table 2-7   *Details for Configuration Exercises 1–4*

AS	Router	Interface	IP Address/Mask
1	R1	G2/0	10.0.0.1/30
		G3/0	10.0.0.5/30
		S1/0	172.16.0.1/30
		Lo0	192.168.0.1/32
	R2	G2/0	10.0.0.2/30
		G3/0	10.0.0.9/30
		S1/0	172.16.0.5/30
		S1/1	172.16.0.9/30
		Lo0	192.168.0.2/32
	R3	G2/0	172.16.0.10/30
		G3/0	172.16.0.6/30
		S1/0	fc00::1/64
2	R4	Lo0	192.168.0.3/32
		S1/0	172.16.0.2/30
		Lo0	192.168.0.4/32
3	R5	Lo1	192.168.0.41/32
		S1/0	fc00::2/64

AS	Router	Interface	IP Address/Mask
4	R6	Lo0	192.168.0.5/32
		S1/0	172.16.0.6/30
		S1/1	172.16.0.10/30
		Lo0	192.168.0.6/32

1. Configure OSPF as the IGP for AS1. OSPF area 0 spans the whole AS. AS1 internal routes should not be advertised outside the AS. All point-to-point links over which EBGP is run should not be advertised into the AS. Then configure the IBGP full mesh for AS1. All IBGP connections will be MD5 authenticated using password Ch2_ExcerSizE1.

2. Configure an EBGP peering between R1 in AS1 and R4 in AS2. Authenticate the EBGP peering using password Ch2_ExcerSizE2. Set the router-id of R4 manually to be the IP address of Loopback 1. In addition, make sure both routers are secured against remote attacks that are based on manipulating TTL values.

3. Configure EBGP peering between R3 in AS1 and R5 in AS3 using the IPv6 point-to-point physical addresses configured on the routers. Make sure you configure both routers to log all neighbor state changes.

4. Configure EBGP peering between R2 in AS1 and R6 in AS4 such that load balancing is achieved over both physical links. Do not use link aggregation. Use static routing on R2 and R6.

Troubleshooting Exercises

1. Routers R1 and R3 in Figure 2-31 can ping each other's loopback 0 interfaces. The network operator configures an IBGP peering between both routers, as shown in Example 2-27. However, the IBGP session is not getting established. The command **bgp log-neighbor-changes** was configured on both routers, and the output from the **show logging** and the **show ip bgp neighbors** commands is shown in Example 2-28. What is likely to be preventing the IBGP peering from coming up?

Figure 2-31 *Topology for Troubleshooting Exercise 1*

Example 2-27   *Configuring an IBGP Peering Between R1 and R3*

```
! R1
!
router bgp 1
  bgp log-neighbor-changes
  neighbor 192.168.0.3 remote-as 1
  neighbor 192.168.0.3 update-source loopback 0
  neighbor 192.168.0.3 description R3
  neighbor 192.168.0.3 password Ch2_Troublesh00ting_ExcerSizE
!
```

```
! R3
!
router bgp 1
  bgp log-neighbor-changes
  neighbor 192.168.0.1 remote-as 1
  neighbor 192.168.0.1 update-source loopback 0
  neighbor 192.168.0.1 description R1
  neighbor 192.168.0.1 password Ch2_Troublesh00ting_ExcerSizE
!
```

Example 2-28   show logging *and* show ip bgp neighbors *Output*

```
R1
R1#show logging
Syslog logging: enabled (12 messages dropped, 9 messages rate-limited,
                0 flushes, 0 overruns, xml disabled, filtering disabled)


No Active Message Discriminator.




No Inactive Message Discriminator.


    Console logging: level debugging, 117 messages logged, xml disabled,
                    filtering disabled
    Monitor logging: level debugging, 0 messages logged, xml disabled,
                    filtering disabled
    Buffer logging:  level debugging, 126 messages logged, xml disabled,
                    filtering disabled
    Logging Exception size (8192 bytes)
    Count and timestamp logging messages: disabled
```

```
      Persistent logging: disabled

No active filter modules.

ESM: 0 messages dropped

      Trap logging: level informational, 59 message lines logged

Log Buffer (8192 bytes):

*Sep  4 01:21:00.311: %SYS-5-CONFIG_I: Configured from console by console
*Sep  4 01:21:20.835: BGP: 192.168.0.3 went from Idle to Active
*Sep  4 01:21:20.843: BGP: 192.168.0.3 open active delayed 30866ms (35000ms max, 28%
  jitter)
*Sep  4 01:21:51.711: BGP: 192.168.0.3 open active, local address 192.168.0.1
*Sep  4 01:21:51.891: BGP: 192.168.0.3 open failed: Destination unreachable; gateway
  or host down, open active delayed 31701ms (35000ms max, 28% jitter)
*Sep  4 01:22:23.595: BGP: 192.168.0.3 open active, local address 192.168.0.1


R1#show ip bgp neighbors
BGP neighbor is 192.168.0.3,  remote AS 1, internal link
  BGP version 4, remote router ID 0.0.0.0
  BGP state = Active
  Last read 00:03:33, last write 00:03:33, hold time is 180, keepalive interval is
  60 seconds
  Message statistics:
    InQ depth is 0
    OutQ depth is 0
                     Sent        Rcvd
    Opens:             0           0
    Notifications:     0           0
    Updates:           0           0
    Keepalives:        0           0
    Route Refresh:     0           0
    Total:             0           0
  Default minimum time between advertisement runs is 0 seconds

 For address family: IPv4 Unicast
  BGP table version 1, neighbor version 0/0
  Output queue size: 0
  Index 1, Offset 0, Mask 0x2
  1 update-group member
                          Sent        Rcvd
```

```
  Prefix activity:                       ----            ----
    Prefixes Current:                      0               0
    Prefixes Total:                        0               0
    Implicit Withdraw:                     0               0
    Explicit Withdraw:                     0               0
    Used as bestpath:                    n/a               0
    Used as multipath:                   n/a               0


                                     Outbound        Inbound
  Local Policy Denied Prefixes:      --------        -------
    Total:                                 0               0
  Number of NLRIs in the update sent: max 0, min 0


  Connections established 0; dropped 0
  Last reset never
  No active TCP connection
```

```
R3
R3#show logging
Syslog logging: enabled (12 messages dropped, 9 messages rate-limited,
                0 flushes, 0 overruns, xml disabled, filtering disabled)


No Active Message Discriminator.



No Inactive Message Discriminator.


    Console logging: level debugging, 115 messages logged, xml disabled,
                filtering disabled
    Monitor logging: level debugging, 0 messages logged, xml disabled,
                filtering disabled
    Buffer logging:  level debugging, 124 messages logged, xml disabled,
                filtering disabled
    Logging Exception size (8192 bytes)
    Count and timestamp logging messages: disabled
    Persistent logging: disabled

No active filter modules.

ESM: 0 messages dropped

    Trap logging: level informational, 55 message lines logged
```

```
Log Buffer (8192 bytes):


*Sep  4 01:20:55.003: %SYS-5-CONFIG_I: Configured from console by console

*Sep  4 01:21:28.723: BGP: 192.168.0.1 went from Idle to Active

*Sep  4 01:21:28.731: BGP: 192.168.0.1 open active delayed 34023ms (35000ms max, 28%
  jitter)

*Sep  4 01:22:02.755: BGP: 192.168.0.1 open active, local address 192.168.0.3

*Sep  4 01:22:02.811: BGP: 192.168.0.1 open failed: Destination unreachable; gateway
  or host down, open active delayed 25843ms (35000ms max, 28% jitter)

*Sep  4 01:22:28.655: BGP: 192.168.0.1 open active, local address 192.168.0.3

*Sep  4 01:22:28.831: BGP: 192.168.0.1 open failed: Destination unreachable; gateway
  or host down, open active delayed 27833ms (35000ms max, 28% jitter)

*Sep  4 01:22:56.667: BGP: 192.168.0.1 open active, local address 192.168.0.3

*Sep  4 01:22:56.859: BGP: 192.168.0.1 open failed: Destination unreachable; gateway
  or host down, open active delayed 33383ms (35000ms max, 28% jitter)


R3#show ip bgp neighbors
BGP neighbor is 192.168.0.1,  remote AS 1, internal link
  BGP version 4, remote router ID 0.0.0.0
  BGP state = Active
  Last read 00:03:57, last write 00:03:57, hold time is 180, keepalive interval is
  60 seconds
  Message statistics:
    InQ depth is 0
    OutQ depth is 0
                      Sent       Rcvd
    Opens:              0          0
    Notifications:      0          0
    Updates:            0          0
    Keepalives:         0          0
    Route Refresh:      0          0
    Total:              0          0
  Default minimum time between advertisement runs is 0 seconds


  For address family: IPv4 Unicast
  BGP table version 1, neighbor version 0/0
  Output queue size: 0
  Index 1, Offset 0, Mask 0x2
  1 update-group member
                        Sent       Rcvd
  Prefix activity:      ----       ----
    Prefixes Current:     0          0
    Prefixes Total:       0          0
    Implicit Withdraw:    0          0
    Explicit Withdraw:    0          0
```

```
    Used as bestpath:              n/a         0
    Used as multipath:             n/a        ·0

                               Outbound    Inbound
  Local Policy Denied Prefixes:  --------    -------
    Total:                          0          0
  Number of NLRIs in the update sent: max 0, min 0


  Connections established 0; dropped 0
  Last reset never
  No active TCP connection
```

2. Refer to Figure 2-32. R1 and R2 have been configured to establish an IBGP connection, but the connection is not coming up. Upon inspecting the logging buffer, the logs in Example 2-29 were found. Why is the IBGP session not coming up?

Figure 2-32   *Topology for Troubleshooting Exercise 2*

Example 2-29   *Logs Lack an IBGP Session*

```
R1#
*Sep  4 02:49:20.575: BGP: 192.168.0.2 open failed: Connection timed out; remote
  host not responding, open active delayed 457ms (1000ms max, 87% jitter)
*Sep  4 02:49:21.035: BGP: 192.168.0.2 open active, local address 192.168.0.1
R1#
*Sep  4 02:49:21.287: %TCP-6-BADAUTH: No MD5 digest from 192.168.0.2(179) to
  192.168.0.1(43661)
```

3. In an attempt to rectify the problem in Exercise 2, the network operator changed the BGP configuration on one of the routers. Now he receives the log messages shown in Example 2-30. Why is the IBGP session not coming up, and what is the difference between the log messages in this exercise and Exercise 2?

Example 2-30   *Logs Still Missing an IBGP Session*

```
R1#
*Sep  4 02:51:16.003: BGP: 192.168.0.2 open active, local address 192.168.0.1
R1#
```

```
*Sep  4 02:51:21.007: BGP: 192.168.0.2 open failed: Connection timed out; remote
  host not responding, open active delayed 30634ms (35000ms max, 28% jitter)
R1#
*Sep  4 02:51:21.739: %TCP-6-BADAUTH: Invalid MD5 digest from 192.168.0.2(28677) to
  192.168.0.1(179)
```

4. In Figure 2-33, routers R1 and R2 are in AS1. R3 is in AS2. OSPF is the IGP for
AS1 and area 0 spans the whole AS. Routers R1 and R2 have been configured
to peer over their loopback addresses. R1 peers with R3 over the physical link
addresses. The configurations for all three routers are listed in Example 2-31.
Interface Loopback0 of R3 (192.168.0.3) is shown in the output of **show ip bgp**
on router R2, but the route is not being installed in the IP routing table. What is
the reason for this? And what are two ways to fix this issue, and which method
is considered to be best practice configuration?

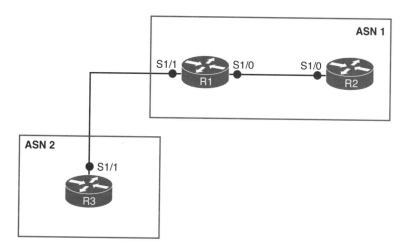

Figure 2-33 *Topology for Troubleshooting Exercise 4*

Example 2-31 *Router Configurations for Troubleshooting Exercise 4*

```
! R1
!
interface Serial1/0
 ip address 10.0.0.1 255.255.255.252
!
interface Serial1/1
 ip address 172.16.0.1 255.255.255.252
!
interface Loopback 0
 ip address 192.168.0.1 255.255.255.255
```

```
!
router ospf 1
 log-adjacency-changes
 network 10.0.0.1 0.0.0.0 area 0
 network 192.168.0.1 0.0.0.0 area 0
!
router bgp 1
 no synchronization
 bgp log-neighbor-changes
 neighbor 192.168.0.2 remote-as 1
 neighbor 192.168.0.2 update-source Loopback0
 neighbor 172.16.0.2 remote-as 2
 no auto-summary
!
```

```
! R2
!
interface Serial1/0
 ip address 10.0.0.2 255.255.255.252
!
interface Loopback 0
 ip address 192.168.0.2 255.255.255.255
!
router ospf 1
 log-adjacency-changes
 network 10.0.0.2 0.0.0.0 area 0
 network 192.168.0.2 0.0.0.0 area 0
!
router bgp 1
 no synchronization
 bgp log-neighbor-changes
 neighbor 192.168.0.1 remote-as 1
 neighbor 192.168.0.1 update-source Loopback0
 no auto-summary
!
```

```
! R3
!
interface Serial1/1
 ip address 172.16.0.2 255.255.255.252
!
interface Loopback 0
 ip address 192.168.0.3 255.255.255.255
!
```

```
router bgp 2
 no synchronization
 bgp log-neighbor-changes
 network 192.168.0.3 mask 255.255.255.255
 neighbor 172.16.0.1 remote-as 1
 no auto-summary
!
```

5. Reference Figure 2-33 in Exercise 4. The network operator fixed the problem that was stopping the bgp route from being installed in the IP routing table on R2. Now the route is in both the BGP table and the IP routing table. However, the ping from R2 to R3 is still not successful. What may be the reason for this and how would you fix it?

Chapter 3

BGP and NLRI

Chapter 2, "Introduction to BGP," showed you how to establish and maintain both EBGP and IBGP sessions. But unlike IGPs, BGP does not advertise any reachability information by default. This chapter demonstrates the techniques for configuring BGP to advertise Network Layer Reachability Information (NLRI) and demonstrates the use of a few simple routing policy tools as an introduction to the more in-depth routing policy discussion in the next chapter.

Note NLRI is self-defining, if you think about it. Reachability Information just means some kind of information about a reachable destination. And Network Layer means the network layer of the OSI model, meaning something that can be advertised in a routing table and reached through one or more router hops. Although IPv4 and IPv6 prefixes are the most readily understandable type of NLRI, the generalized term indicates that BGP can carry many other kinds of reachability information than just IP addresses. Chapter 6, "Multiprotocol BGP," details the multiprotocol capabilities of BGP.

Configuring and Troubleshooting NLRI in BGP

As Chapter 1, "Inter-Domain Routing Concepts," and Chapter 2 emphasize, BGP requires you to think differently about routing than the way you think about IGP routing. For instance, rather than the "holistic" view of the IGP domain, you must consider each EBGP session separately.

This conceptual shift also applies to the NLRI—in the context of this chapter, IPv4 address prefixes—that BGP advertises. IGPs are designed for the easy and efficient exchange of prefixes with trusted neighbors, so configuring the IGP typically involves specifying the interfaces or subnets on which the protocol runs; the IGP then advertises the subnets of those interfaces to its neighbors. BGP, however, does not "automatically" advertise any reachability information; its external neighbors are assumed to be untrusted, so it advertises only the information that you explicitly configure it to advertise.

For this reason, it is helpful to always think in terms of "injecting" prefixes into BGP. You can inject prefixes into an IGP, too, of course, using redistribution. The difference is that injection is the *only* way to get reachability information into BGP.

Injecting Prefixes with the network Statement

The most common, and usually the most reliable, means of injecting prefixes into BGP with IOS is the **network** statement. You must be careful not to confuse the BGP **network** statement with the IGP **network** statement; they do two different things. When you are configuring an IGP, you use a **network** statement to specify an address range, which might be as general as 0.0.0.0, which encompasses all possible addresses, or as specific as a single IP address. The IGP is then enabled on all interfaces whose addresses are included in the range given by the **network** statement.

The BGP **network** statement, however, has nothing to do with enabling the protocol on interfaces. Instead, it specifies a prefix to be injected into the local BGP process.

Routers Taos and Vail in Figure 3-1 reside in separate autonomous systems, and an EBGP session is configured between them. Taos is also connected to AngelFire in its local AS, and the IGP the two routers use to exchange intra-AS routes is EIGRP.

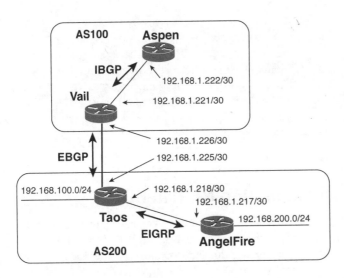

Figure 3-1   *Taos Is Advertising Prefixes 192.168.100.0 and 192.168.200.0 to Vail. AS200 Is Using EIGRP as Its IGP*

Subnet 192.168.100.0/24 is directly connected to Taos, and subnet 192.168.200.0/24 is directly connected to AngelFire; these two prefixes are to be advertised by Taos to Vail.

Example 3-1 shows the configuration of Taos, using two **network** statements to inject the two subnets into BGP. Taos' EIGRP configuration is also shown.[1]

Example 3-1 *Taos' Basic EIGRP and BGP Configuration*

```
router eigrp 200
 passive-interface Serial1/0
 network 192.168.1.0
 network 192.168.100.0
 auto-summary
!
router bgp 200
 no synchronization
 bgp log-neighbor-changes
 network 192.168.100.0
 network 192.168.200.0
 neighbor 192.168.1.226 remote-as 100
 no auto-summary
```

Examining Vail's routing table in Example 3-2, you can see that there are entries for 192.168.100.0 and 192.168.200.0 and that the entries are tagged with a "B" to indicate that they were learned from BGP. Simply showing the BGP configuration at Taos and the resulting routing table at Vail does not tell you the full story, however. With BGP a few things are going on "in the background" that are important to know both for troubleshooting and for setting route policies.

Example 3-2 *Two Prefixes Injected into BGP at Taos Can Be Seen in Vail's Routing Table*

```
Vail#show ip route
Codes: C - connected, S - static, R - RIP, M - mobile, B - BGP
       D - EIGRP, EX - EIGRP external, O - OSPF, IA - OSPF inter area
       N1 - OSPF NSSA external type 1, N2 - OSPF NSSA external type 2
       E1 - OSPF external type 1, E2 - OSPF external type 2
       i - IS-IS, su - IS-IS summary, L1 - IS-IS level-1, L2 - IS-IS level-2
       ia - IS-IS inter area, * - candidate default, U - per-user static route
       o - ODR, P - periodic downloaded static route

Gateway of last resort is not set
```

---

[1] The BGP configuration shown here is kept as simple as possible to make the statements of interest easier to observe. But remember that in a production BGP configuration, authentication should always be used.

```
B      192.168.200.0/24 [20/30720] via 192.168.1.225, 00:02:12
       192.168.1.0/30 is subnetted, 2 subnets
C         192.168.1.224 is directly connected, Serial1/0
C         192.168.1.220 is directly connected, FastEthernet0/0
B      192.168.100.0/24 [20/0] via 192.168.1.225, 01:03:35
```

The first detail to know about the way BGP advertises prefixes is that it maintains a table of prefixes separate from the routing table. The importance of the BGP table becomes more apparent in Chapter 4, "BGP and Routing Policies," but for now, it is enough to know that BGP records the prefixes it advertises and receives. You can observe the table with the **show ip bgp** command.

To begin the progression the injected prefixes take from Taos to Vail's routing table, notice in Taos' routing table (Example 3-3) that the two prefixes are in the table, but there are no BGP references associated with them. 192.168.100.0 is learned because it is directly connected; 192.168.200.0 is learned from EIGRP, as indicated by the "D" tag.

Example 3-3   *Two Prefixes Are Entered in Taos' Routing Table, but There Are No References to BGP Associated with the Prefixes*

```
Taos#show ip route
Codes: C - connected, S - static, R - RIP, M - mobile, B - BGP
       D - EIGRP, EX - EIGRP external, O - OSPF, IA - OSPF inter area
       N1 - OSPF NSSA external type 1, N2 - OSPF NSSA external type 2
       E1 - OSPF external type 1, E2 - OSPF external type 2
       i - IS-IS, su - IS-IS summary, L1 - IS-IS level-1, L2 - IS-IS level-2
       ia - IS-IS inter area, * - candidate default, U - per-user static route
       o - ODR, P - periodic downloaded static route


Gateway of last resort is not set

D      192.168.200.0/24 [90/30720] via 192.168.1.217, 00:00:17, FastEthernet0/0
       192.168.1.0/24 is variably subnetted, 3 subnets, 2 masks
D         192.168.1.0/24 is a summary, 02:13:01, Null0
C         192.168.1.224/30 is directly connected, Serial1/0
C         192.168.1.216/30 is directly connected, FastEthernet0/0
C      192.168.100.0/24 is directly connected, FastEthernet2/0
```

Using **show ip bgp** in Example 3-4, you can see the two prefixes in Taos' BGP table. There is a dependency between the two tables of Examples 3-3 and 3-4: When the prefixes were specified with the **network** statement, BGP looks into the IP routing table. If the specified prefix is not in that table, BGP does not enter it into the BGP table. That is, BGP does not inject a prefix unless the router has a valid path to the destination.

Example 3-4   *Two Prefixes Are Injected into Taos' BGP Table as a Result of the* network *Statements in Its Configuration*

```
Taos#show ip bgp
BGP table version is 121, local router ID is 192.168.100.1
Status codes: s suppressed, d damped, h history, * valid, > best, i - internal,
              r RIB-failure, S Stale
Origin codes: i - IGP, e - EGP, ? - incomplete


   Network          Next Hop          Metric LocPrf Weight Path
*> 192.168.100.0    0.0.0.0                0           32768 i
*> 192.168.200.0    192.168.1.217       30720         32768 i
```

Associated with the prefixes and next hops in Example 3-4 are metric values. Looking at the prefixes in the routing table of Figure 3-3, you can see where these metrics come from: They are the IGP metrics. 192.168.100.0 has a metric of 0 because it is directly connected, and 192.168.200.0 has a metric of 30720, which is its EIGRP metric. By default, the IGP metric of the injected prefix becomes the MULTI_EXIT_DISC (MED) attribute of the advertised BGP route, which displays in the BGP table as "Metric." The default MED value can be changed using the **default-metric** statement for redistributed routes or a route map for other routes; the use of the MED attribute is demonstrated in a case study in Chapter 4. There are no LOCAL_PREF attributes (also covered in Chapter 4) associated with the two prefixes.

Weight, as discussed in the previous chapter, is an IOS proprietary value that is useful for manipulating the selection of a BGP route in a single router. The weight value of the prefixes in Example 3-4, 32,768, is the default weight given to any prefix injected by the local router.

The last feature of interest in Example 3-4 is the "Path" column. This column shows both the AS_PATH and the ORIGIN attributes of the prefix. In our example, neither prefix has an AS_PATH attribute yet because the prefixes were injected at this router. (Remember, BGP does not add its local AS number until it advertises the prefix to an external neighbor.) They do, however, have ORIGIN attributes. Looking at the legend above the prefix entries, you can see that the "i" tag indicates that the ORIGIN is IGP. Prefixes injected with the **network** statement will always have an ORIGIN attribute of IGP.

Example 3-5 shows the BGP table at Vail. The next-hop address of 192.168.1.225 indicates that the prefixes were advertised by Taos. The MED values remain unchanged, but notice that the Weight values are now 0, the default value given to prefixes learned from a peer. Finally, the Path now shows the AS number of 200 prepended onto the AS_PATH and preceding the ORIGIN code.

Example 3-5 *Vail's BGP Table Shows the Prefixes Advertised by Taos (192.168.1.225)*

```
Vail#show ip bgp
BGP table version is 33, local router ID is 192.168.1.226
Status codes: s suppressed, d damped, h history, * valid, > best, i - internal,
             r RIB-failure, S Stale
Origin codes: i - IGP, e - EGP, ? - incomplete


  Network          Next Hop            Metric LocPrf Weight Path
*> 192.168.100.0   192.168.1.225            0           0 200 i
*> 192.168.200.0   192.168.1.225        30720           0 200 i
```

The BGP process at Vail checks each prefix in the BGP table and, if the next hop is valid (that is, the router knows how to reach the next hop) the prefix is added to the routing table. Configuring the BGP routing policy, the subject of Chapter 4, is primarily concerned with changing the default BGP decision process.

Using the network mask Statement

A new link has been added to router AngelFire in Figure 3-2. The link prefix, 192.168.172.0/22, is advertised to Taos via EIGRP, and we want to advertise the prefix from Taos to Vail. Notice, however, that there is a difference between the prefixes of the previous case study and this one: Although 192.168.100.0/24 and 192.169.200.0/24 are traditional "Class C" (24-bit) prefixes, 192.168.172.0/22 is not. Actually, this new prefix better reflects the modern CIDR environment in which the prefixes you need to advertise probably are not old-fashioned Class A, B, or C.

Recall from Chapter 2 that the Network Layer Reachability Information field of the BGP Update message consists of (Length, Prefix) tuples where the Length specifies the prefix length. When the prefix you want to advertise is a Class A, B, or C, you can specify just the prefix with the **network** statement and IOS's BGP implementation fills in the corresponding 8- 16- or 24-bit Length value (an artifact of the pre-CIDR days). But when the prefix length is anything else, you need to tell IOS what value to use in the Length part of the (Length, Prefix) tuple. For this, you use the **network mask** statement.

Example 3-6 shows Taos' BGP configuration, with the **network mask** statement to inject 192.168.172.0/22. The mask, 255.255.252.0, indicates the 22-bit prefix length to be used. Example 3-7 shows Vail's BGP table, and you can see that an entry has been created for the new prefix.

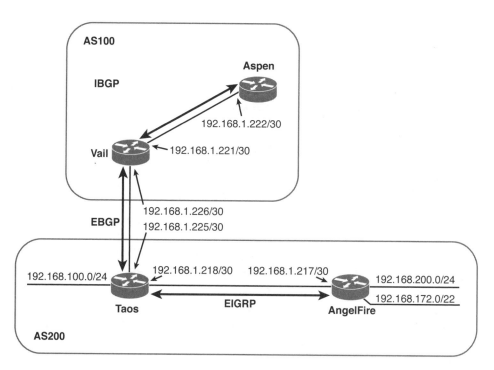

Figure 3-2   *AngelFire Is Advertising a New Prefix, 192.168.172.0/22, into EIGRP; Taos Must Advertise the Prefix via EBGP to Vail*

Example 3-6   **network mask** *Statement Is Used to Advertise Prefixes That Are Not Traditional Class A, B, or C Prefixes*

```
router bgp 200
 no synchronization
 bgp log-neighbor-changes
 network 192.168.100.0
 network 192.168.172.0 mask 255.255.252.0
 network 192.168.200.0
 neighbor 192.168.1.226 remote-as 100
 no auto-summary
```

Example 3-7   *Vail Has Received Taovs' Advertisement of 192.168.172.0/22 and Has Added It to the BGP Table*

```
Vail#show ip bgp
BGP table version is 10, local router ID is 192.168.1.226
Status codes: s suppressed, d damped, h history, * valid, > best, i - internal,
              r RIB-failure, S Stale
Origin codes: i - IGP, e - EGP, ? - incomplete
```

```
   Network              Next Hop         Metric LocPrf Weight Path
*> 192.168.100.0     192.168.1.225           0              0 200 i
*> 192.168.172.0/22 192.168.1.225        30720              0 200 i
*> 192.168.200.0     192.168.1.225        30720              0 200 i
```

Injecting Prefixes with Redistribution

Prefixes can also be injected into BGP by redistribution. Although this case study examines redistribution from an IGP to BGP, you need to know that this technique is almost always discouraged. Chapter 1 emphasized the importance of maintaining strict control over the sharing of information across AS boundaries. With **network** statements you can be specific about what prefixes are advertised to an EBGP peer; redistribution means that by default you tell the EBGP peer everything that your IGP knows.

Route filters are almost always necessary when redistributing an IGP's routes into BGP. By default, every route known by the IGP is redistributed. The administrator of the AS might want to advertise only a subset of the IGP routes, and must filter the others. Or perhaps a multihomed AS should not be a transit for any of its neighboring autonomous systems. Route filters must be used to prevent external routes learned from one AS from being advertised to other autonomous systems. Then there is the problem of route feedback, in which external routes received from EBGP are advertised into an IGP and then are redistributed from that IGP back into EBGP. At a minimum, best practice dictates that route filters should be used to ensure that only the correct routes are redistributed. In actual practice, redistribution of IGP prefixes into BGP is rarely used because of this lack of precise control.

There might, however, be corner cases in which redistribution is useful. For example, if a large number of prefixes originate in your AS and must be advertised externally, redistribution might be considered. But even here, you most likely need to implement route filters to block some of the IGP prefixes from being advertised. So where you might think you are simplifying your configuration by using redistribution rather than a long list of **network** statements, you might be merely trading complexity in one part of the configuration for complexity in another part.

Another example of where redistribution might be useful is a situation in which the prefixes in the local AS change frequently. But again, this is an unusual case and should not happen in a normal network.

Using **network** statements rather than redistribution is also preferred from a troubleshooting standpoint: A list of **network** statements tells you positively what prefixes you are injecting; redistribution coupled with a route filter tells you only what you are *not injecting*.

Bearing these warnings in mind, Example 3-8 shows Taos in Figure 3-2 reconfigured to use redistribution to advertise prefixes to Vail.

Example 3-8 *Router Taos (Figure 3-2) Is Reconfigured to Use Redistribution Instead of*
network *Statements to Inject Prefixes into BGP*

```
router eigrp 200
 passive-interface Serial1/0
 network 192.168.1.0
 network 192.168.100.0
 auto-summary
!
router bgp 200
 no synchronization
 bgp log-neighbor-changes
 redistribute eigrp 200
 neighbor 192.168.1.226 remote-as 100
 no auto-summary
```

Example 3-9 shows the resulting BGP table at Vail. Comparing this table with the one in
Example 3-7, you can see that the results are different. Although the three prefixes of
the previous table are present here, three more prefixes are also present—the result of
redistribution picking up every prefix Taos has learned via EIGRP.

Example 3-9 *Vail's BGP Table Shows What Prefixes Are Advertised by Taos as a Result*
of the Redistribution in Example 3-8

```
Vail#show ip bgp
BGP table version is 1129, local router ID is 192.168.1.226
Status codes: s suppressed, d damped, h history, * valid, > best, i - internal,
              r RIB-failure, S Stale
Origin codes: i - IGP, e - EGP, ? - incomplete

   Network          Next Hop          Metric LocPrf Weight Path
*> 192.168.1.0      192.168.1.225      28160            0 200 ?
*> 192.168.1.216/30 192.168.1.225          0            0 200 ?
r> 192.168.1.224/30 192.168.1.225          0            0 200 ?
*> 192.168.100.0    192.168.1.225          0            0 200 ?
*> 192.168.172.0/22 192.168.1.225      30720            0 200 ?
*> 192.168.200.0    192.168.1.225      30720            0 200 ?
```

Notice that 192.168.1.0 has been advertised in addition to two subnets
(192.168.1.216/30 and 192.168.1.224/30) of that prefix. A look at Taos' routing table, in
Example 3-10, shows why: Older versions of EIGRP, in which auto-summary is enabled
by default, automatically summarize subnets to the old class A, B, or C boundaries.
In this case, an EIGRP route for prefix 192.168.1.0 to Null 0 has been entered in the
routing table and subsequently picked up for redistribution into BGP. You can see the
default EIGRP **auto-summary** statement in Example 3-8.

Example 3-10 *EIGRP Automatically Entered a Summary Route for 192.168.1.0, Which Is Redistributed into BGP Along with the Other EIGRP Routes*

```
Taos#show ip route
Codes: C - connected, S - static, R - RIP, M - mobile, B - BGP
       D - EIGRP, EX - EIGRP external, O - OSPF, IA - OSPF inter area
       N1 - OSPF NSSA external type 1, N2 - OSPF NSSA external type 2
       E1 - OSPF external type 1, E2 - OSPF external type 2
       i - IS-IS, su - IS-IS summary, L1 - IS-IS level-1, L2 - IS-IS level-2
       ia - IS-IS inter area, * - candidate default, U - per-user static route
       o - ODR, P - periodic downloaded static route


Gateway of last resort is not set


D    192.168.200.0/24 [90/30720] via 192.168.1.217, 00:02:32, FastEthernet0/0
     192.168.1.0/24 is variably subnetted, 3 subnets, 2 masks
D       192.168.1.0/24 is a summary, 00:10:05, Null0
C       192.168.1.224/30 is directly connected, Serial1/0
C       192.168.1.216/30 is directly connected, FastEthernet0/0
C    192.168.100.0/24 is directly connected, FastEthernet2/0
D    192.168.172.0/22 [90/30720] via 192.168.1.217, 00:02:33, FastEthernet0/0
```

In some cases, this summary route might be okay; however, for the network used for this case study it is not: Subnets of 192.168.1.0 appear not only in AS200, but also AS100. (And subsequent case studies will make further use of subnets of this network in more than one AS.) You probably do not want a case in which a failure of one of these subnets causes packets to the unreachable subnet to match the summary and be routed to Taos.

Changing this behavior is a simple matter of turning EIGRP automatic summarization off at Taos, as shown in Example 3-11. In Example 3-12 you can see the result in Vail's BGP table: The entry for 192.168.1.0 is no longer there. As mentioned already, newer versions of EIGRP disable auto-summary by default. The point here, though, is that redistribution is a "broad net" that reduces your control over what is injected into BGP.

Example 3-11 *EIGRP Automatic Summarization Is Disabled at Taos*

```
router eigrp 200
 passive-interface Serial1/0
 network 192.168.1.0
 network 192.168.100.0
 no auto-summary
!
router bgp 200
 no synchronization
 bgp log-neighbor-changes
```

```
 redistribute eigrp 200
 neighbor 192.168.1.226 remote-as 100
 no auto-summary
!
```

Example 3-12 *Removing EIGRP Auto-summarization at Taos Prevents 192.168.1.0 from Being Redistributed into BGP, as Indicated in Vail's BGP Table*

```
Vail#show ip bgp
BGP table version is 1209, local router ID is 192.168.1.226
Status codes: s suppressed, d damped, h history, * valid, > best, i - internal,
              r RIB-failure, S Stale
Origin codes: i - IGP, e - EGP, ? - incomplete


   Network          Next Hop          Metric LocPrf Weight Path
*> 192.168.1.216/30 192.168.1.225          0             0 200 ?
r> 192.168.1.224/30 192.168.1.225          0             0 200 ?
*> 192.168.100.0    192.168.1.225          0             0 200 ?
*> 192.168.172.0/22 192.168.1.225      30720             0 200 ?
*> 192.168.200.0    192.168.1.225      30720             0 200 ?
```

Note Prior to IOS 12.2(8)T, auto-summarization was also the default for BGP. In earlier releases, BGP would create a classful summary entry in the local table when a subnet was redistributed into BGP. As you can see in Example 3-11 and the previous BGP configuration examples, the default now is for this function to be disabled (no auto-summary). You should be aware of this behavior when working with older releases of IOS; in most cases turning auto-summarization off is recommended.

Notice in Example 3-12 that 192.168.1.224/30 is marked with an "r," which according to the display key means "RIB-failure." This indicates that BGP could not enter a route for this prefix into the routing table (the Routing Information Base, or RIB). The **show ip bgp rib-failure** command provides you with more information about the cause of the RIB-failure: Example 3-13 indicates higher admin distance. That is, an entry for the prefix already exists in the routing table, learned from a source with a higher administrative distance than BGP, and therefore that existing entry cannot be replaced by the BGP route.

Example 3-13   *The Reason Given for the Failure to Add the BGP Entry for 192.168.1.224/30 into the Routing Table (RIB) Is That the RIB Already Has an Entry for the Prefix, with a Higher Administrative Distance*

```
Vail#show ip bgp rib-failure
Network          Next Hop              RIB-failure    RIB-NH Matches
192.168.1.224/30   192.168.1.225      Higher admin distance         n/a
```

Looking at the network diagram in Figure 3-2, you can readily see why this is happening: 192.168.1.224/30 is the subnet of the link connecting Taos and Vail. Therefore, Vail already has an entry in its routing table for the directly connected subnet (which you can verify in Vail's routing table shown in Example 3-1); directly connected subnets have an administrative distance of 0, overriding all other administrative distances including the EBGP admin distance of 20.

Even though 192.168.1.224/30 is not put into Vail's table, by default BGP still advertises it to other peers. You probably do not want this to happen because there is no reason for devices in other autonomous systems—or for that matter, devices in AS100 or 200 other than Taos and Vail—to reach that subnet.

One way of remedying this situation is to add the statement **bgp suppress-inactive** to Vail's BGP configuration. This statement tells the router that if an entry in the BGP table could not be entered into the local RIB, do not advertise the prefix to other BGP peers.

In this case study, however, there is a better solution. Notice in Example 3-12 that there is an entry in Vail's BGP table for subnet 192.168.1.216/30; this is the link between Taos and AngelFire in AS200, and like the link between Taos and Vail, you probably do not want to advertise it in BGP. Therefore, a route filter is called for to block both of these prefixes from being injected into BGP at Taos. (In the case of 192.168.1.224/30, it makes more sense to block it at Taos rather than to allow it to be injected into BGP, advertised to Vail, and then suppressed there.)

Example 3-14 shows Taos' BGP configuration with the route filter added. The filter is built by referencing a route map named ROUTES_IN in the redistribution statement. The route map has a single **permit** statement, and references access list 1. The access list then denies the two prefixes of interest and permits all other prefixes.

Example 3-14   *A Route Filter Is Added to the Redistribution Statement to Block the Injection of Prefixes 192.168.1.216/30 and 192.168.1.224/30 While Permitting All Others*

```
router bgp 200
 no synchronization
 bgp log-neighbor-changes
 redistribute eigrp 200 route-map ROUTES_IN
 neighbor 192.168.1.226 remote-as 100
 no auto-summary
!
```

```
access-list 1 deny    192.168.1.224
access-list 1 deny    192.168.1.216
access-list 1 permit any
!
route-map ROUTES_IN permit 10
 match ip address 1
!
```

The result of the route filter at Taos can be seen in Vail's BGP table (Example 3-15). Comparing this table to the one in Example 3-7, you can see that they are now almost the same. The only difference is that the Origin code is no longer an "i," but a "?" indicating incomplete. As the previous chapter discusses, this code means that the source of the routes is indeterminate. If all other route characteristics prior to the Origin code are the same in the BGP decision process, an IGP origin is preferred over an Incomplete origin. Specific to IOS, a route injected with the **network** statement is preferred over a route to the same destination injected by redistribution (assuming the Weight, LOCAL_PREF, and AS_PATH length of the two routes are the same).

Example 3-15 *Vail's BGP Table Now Shows Only the Wanted Prefixes*

```
Vail#show ip bgp
BGP table version is 1378, local router ID is 192.168.1.226
Status codes: s suppressed, d damped, h history, * valid, > best, i - internal,
              r RIB-failure, S Stale
Origin codes: i - IGP, e - EGP, ? - incomplete

   Network          Next Hop          Metric LocPrf Weight Path
*> 192.168.100.0    192.168.1.225          0             0 200 ?
*> 192.168.172.0/22 192.168.1.225      30720             0 200 ?
*> 192.168.200.0    192.168.1.225      30720             0 200 ?
```

You can change the logic of the route filter shown in Example 3-14 so that the routes you want to advertise are explicitly permitted for injection by access-list 1 and all other routes are denied. That would, however, simply give you the same results that are more easily obtained with the **network** statement.

Given the trouble taken to arrive at the BGP table of Example 3-15, and comparing it to the relative ease of arriving at the comparable BGP table of Example 3-7, you can see why the use of **network** statements is considered best practice for most networks.

NLRI and IBGP

The previous two chapters discuss the complications and amendments to basic BGP rules required to support IBGP. The section "External and Internal BGP" in Chapter 1 explains in a generic way why a full mesh of IBGP sessions is required in an autonomous system for prefixes to successfully transit. The case study "IBGP Peering" in Chapter 2 demonstrates how to reliably configure that full IBGP mesh. This section builds on what you learned in both of those sections, so a quick review of them is suggested.

Managing Prefixes in an IBGP Topology

Figure 3-3 shows the network used in this case study. It is similar to the network configured in Figure 2-26 of the previous chapter, except the loopback addresses are changed. The prefixes advertised by Taos to Vail are the same prefixes configured in Figure 3-1 of this chapter, so the configuration of Taos is the same as what has already been studied. Also shown is a set of prefixes advertised by Alta to Telluride via EBGP; Alta's configuration, although not shown here, is similar to that of Taos. For the purposes of this case study, what matters is the configuration of the routers in AS100 so that Taos can learn the prefixes advertised by Alta and Alta can see the prefixes advertised by Taos.

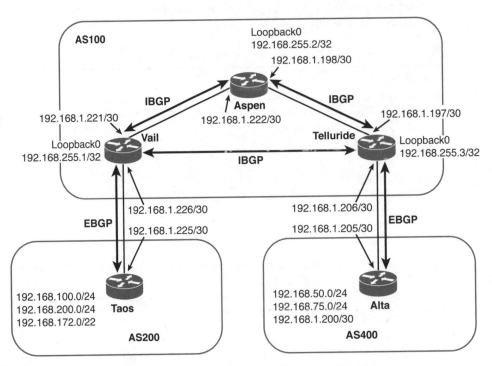

Figure 3-3 *AS200 and AS400 Advertise Prefixes to Each Other Through AS100*

Example 3-16 shows the beginning configuration of the three routers in AS100. OSPF is the IGP and runs on all interfaces internal to the AS—best practice dictates that your IGP should not run on any external links. A full IBGP mesh is configured between the three routers' loopback interfaces; Vail and Telluride run EBGP to Taos and Alta, respectively.

Example 3-16 *Configurations for the Routers in AS100 of Figure 3-3*

```
Vail
router ospf 100
 log-adjacency-changes
 network 192.168.1.221 0.0.0.0 area 0
 network 192.168.255.1 0.0.0.0 area 0
!
router bgp 100
 no synchronization
 bgp log-neighbor-changes
 neighbor 192.168.1.225 remote-as 200
 neighbor 192.168.255.2 remote-as 100
 neighbor 192.168.255.2 update-source Loopback0
 neighbor 192.168.255.3 remote-as 100
 neighbor 192.168.255.3 update-source Loopback0
 no auto-summary
!
```

```
Aspen
router ospf 100
 log-adjacency-changes
 network 192.168.1.198 0.0.0.0 area 0
 network 192.168.1.222 0.0.0.0 area 0
 network 192.168.255.2 0.0.0.0 area 0
!
router bgp 100
 no synchronization
 bgp log-neighbor-changes
 neighbor 192.168.255.1 remote-as 100
 neighbor 192.168.255.1 update-source Loopback0
 neighbor 192.168.255.3 remote-as 100
 neighbor 192.168.255.3 update-source Loopback0
 no auto-summary
!
```

```
Telluride
router ospf 100
 log-adjacency-changes
 network 192.168.1.197 0.0.0.0 area 0
 network 192.168.255.3 0.0.0.0 area 0
!
router bgp 100
 no synchronization
 bgp log-neighbor-changes
```

```
neighbor 192.168.1.205 remote-as 400
neighbor 192.168.255.1 remote-as 100
neighbor 192.168.255.1 update-source Loopback0
neighbor 192.168.255.2 remote-as 100
neighbor 192.168.255.2 update-source Loopback0
no auto-summary
!
```

Unfortunately, these configurations are not sufficient for the objectives of allowing prefixes to transit AS100. To start examining what else is needed, the BGP tables of Taos and Alta are shown in Example 3-17. You can see that each router has entries for the prefixes of their own AS but no external prefixes.

Example 3-17   *BGP at Taos Is Not Learning the Prefixes Advertised by AS400, and BGP at Alta Is Not Learning the Prefixes Advertised by AS200*

```
Taos#show ip bgp
BGP table version is 28, local router ID is 192.168.100.1
Status codes: s suppressed, d damped, h history, * valid, > best, i - internal,
              r RIB-failure, S Stale
Origin codes: i - IGP, e - EGP, ? - incomplete


   Network          Next Hop          Metric LocPrf Weight Path
*> 192.168.100.0    0.0.0.0                0         32768 i
*> 192.168.172.0/22 192.168.1.217      30720         32768 i
*> 192.168.200.0    192.168.1.217      30720         32768 i
```

```
Alta#show ip bgp
BGP table version is 4, local router ID is 192.168.1.205
Status codes: s suppressed, d damped, h history, * valid, > best, i - internal,
              r RIB-failure, S Stale
Origin codes: i - IGP, e - EGP, ? - incomplete


   Network          Next Hop          Metric LocPrf Weight Path
*> 192.168.1.200/30 0.0.0.0                0         32768 i
*> 192.168.50.0     0.0.0.0                0         32768 i
*> 192.168.75.0     0.0.0.0                0         32768 i
```

The obvious first step in troubleshooting is to look at what is happening at these two routers' EBGP neighbors, Vail and Telluride. Example 3-18 shows the BGP tables of those two routers, and you can clearly see the first hint of the problem. Both routers have learned the prefixes advertised by both AS200 and AS400; actually, the tables look almost identical. The only difference is the status codes to the left of each prefix. Vail shows an "i" with the prefixes advertised from AS400, and Telluride shows an "i" with the prefixes advertised from AS200. Checking the legend, it says that this code means the prefixes are `internal`. That is, they have been learned from an IBGP neighbor. From this it can be concluded that Vail and Telluride are correctly learning the prefixes advertised by their mutual EBGP peers and are successfully advertising the prefixes to each other.

Example 3-18   *Vail and Telluride Have the Prefixes of Both AS200 and AS400 in Their BGP Tables*

```
Vail#show ip bgp
BGP table version is 37, local router ID is 192.168.255.1
Status codes: s suppressed, d damped, h history, * valid, > best, i - internal,
              r RIB-failure, S Stale
Origin codes: i - IGP, e - EGP, ? - incomplete


   Network          Next Hop          Metric LocPrf Weight Path
* i192.168.1.200/30 192.168.1.205          0    100      0 400 i
* i192.168.50.0     192.168.1.205          0    100      0 400 i
* i192.168.75.0     192.168.1.205          0    100      0 400 i
*> 192.168.100.0    192.168.1.225          0             0 200 i
*> 192.168.172.0/22 192.168.1.225      30720             0 200 i
*> 192.168.200.0    192.168.1.225      30720             0 200 i
```

```
Telluride#show ip bgp
BGP table version is 4, local router ID is 192.168.255.3
Status codes: s suppressed, d damped, h history, * valid, > best, i - internal,
              r RIB-failure, S Stale
Origin codes: i - IGP, e - EGP, ? - incomplete


   Network          Next Hop          Metric LocPrf Weight Path
*> 192.168.1.200/30 192.168.1.205          0             0 400 i
*> 192.168.50.0     192.168.1.205          0             0 400 i
*> 192.168.75.0     192.168.1.205          0             0 400 i
* i192.168.100.0    192.168.1.225          0    100      0 200 i
* i192.168.172.0/22 192.168.1.225      30720    100      0 200 i
* i192.168.200.0    192.168.1.225      30720    100      0 200 i
```

The status codes provide a further hint to the problem: Vail tags the prefixes advertised from its EBGP neighbor with a ">", indicating `best`, but not the prefixes from AS400; Telluride does just the opposite, tagging the prefixes learned from its EBGP neighbor as `best` but not the ones from AS200.

Comparing a prefix with the `best` tag and one without in the same BGP table gets us even closer to an answer. (You have probably already figured it out.) In Example 3-19, prefix 192.168.100.0/24 from EBGP neighbor Taos and 192.168.50.0/24 from IBGP neighbor Telluride are examined at Vail.

Example 3-19   *Entries in Vail's BGP Table for 192.168.100.0/24, Advertised from an EBGP Peer, and 192.168.50.0/24, Advertised from an IBGP Peer, Are Examined in More Detail*

```
Vail#show ip bgp 192.168.100.0
BGP routing table entry for 192.168.100.0/24, version 7
Paths: (1 available, best #1, table Default-IP-Routing-Table)
  Advertised to update-groups:
        1
  200
    192.168.1.225 from 192.168.1.225 (192.168.100.1)
      Origin IGP, metric 0, localpref 100, valid, external, best
Vail#
Vail#show ip bgp 192.168.50.0
BGP routing table entry for 192.168.50.0/24, version 0
Paths: (1 available, no best path)
  Not advertised to any peer
  400
    192.168.1.205 (inaccessible) from 192.168.255.3 (192.168.255.3)
      Origin IGP, metric 0, localpref 100, valid, internal
```

First, the entry for 192.168.100.0/24 shows that it has been entered into the routing table (Default-IP-Routing-Table) and has been advertised to peers, indicated as update-group 1. As an aside, you can use the command **show ip bgp update-group**, as shown in Example 3-20, to see what neighbors belong to a specific update-group. 192.168.50.0/24, however, is not advertised to any peer. Further, the entry shows that the route's next hop, 192.168.1.205, is inaccessible. That brings us to the problem, although not yet the solution: Examining the next hops of all the entries in the two BGP tables of Example 3-17, you can see that all the routes advertised by Taos have a next hop of that router's external interface (192.168.1.225) and all the routes advertised by Alta have a next hop of that router's external interface (192.168.1.205). Checking the routing tables of Vail and Telluride in Example 3-21, you can see that Vail has no route to 192.168.1.205 and Telluride has no route to 192.168.1.225.

Example 3-20   *Vail Has Two BGP Update Groups: Group 1 Is Its IBGP Peers, and Group 2 Is Its Single EBGP Peer*

```
Vail#show ip bgp update-group
BGP version 4 update-group 1, internal, Address Family: IPv4 Unicast
  BGP Update version : 41/0, messages 0
  Update messages formatted 22, replicated 20
  Number of NLRIs in the update sent: max 2, min 1
```

```
    Minimum time between advertisement runs is 0 seconds
    Has 2 members (* indicates the members currently being sent updates):
      192.168.255.2    192.168.255.3

 BGP version 4 update-group 2, external, Address Family: IPv4 Unicast
    BGP Update version : 41/0, messages 0
    Update messages formatted 0, replicated 0
    Number of NLRIs in the update sent: max 0, min 0
    Minimum time between advertisement runs is 30 seconds
    Has 1 member (* indicates the members currently being sent updates):
      192.168.1.225
```

Example 3-21 *Vail Has No Route to Alta's Interface 192.168.1.205, and Telluride Has No Route to Taos' Interface 192.168.1.225. These Two Addresses Are the Next Hops for the Prefixes Alta and Taos Are Advertising*

```
Vail#show ip route
Codes: C - connected, S - static, R - RIP, M - mobile, B - BGP
       D - EIGRP, EX - EIGRP external, O - OSPF, IA - OSPF inter area
       N1 - OSPF NSSA external type 1, N2 - OSPF NSSA external type 2
       E1 - OSPF external type 1, E2 - OSPF external type 2
       i - IS-IS, su - IS-IS summary, L1 - IS-IS level-1, L2 - IS-IS level-2
       ia - IS-IS inter area, * - candidate default, U - per-user static route
       o - ODR, P - periodic downloaded static route

Gateway of last resort is not set

B    192.168.200.0/24 [20/30720] via 192.168.1.225, 00:22:32
     192.168.255.0/32 is subnetted, 3 subnets
O       192.168.255.3 [110/3] via 192.168.1.222, 02:27:39, FastEthernet0/0
O       192.168.255.2 [110/2] via 192.168.1.222, 02:27:39, FastEthernet0/0
C       192.168.255.1 is directly connected, Loopback0
     192.168.1.0/30 is subnetted, 3 subnets
C       192.168.1.224 is directly connected, Serial1/0
O       192.168.1.196 [110/2] via 192.168.1.222, 02:27:39, FastEthernet0/0
C       192.168.1.220 is directly connected, FastEthernet0/0
B    192.168.100.0/24 [20/0] via 192.168.1.225, 02:11:17
B    192.168.172.0/22 [20/30720] via 192.168.1.225, 00:22:32

Telluride#show ip route
Codes: C - connected, S - static, R - RIP, M - mobile, B - BGP
       D - EIGRP, EX - EIGRP external, O - OSPF, IA - OSPF inter area
       N1 - OSPF NSSA external type 1, N2 - OSPF NSSA external type 2
       E1 - OSPF external type 1, E2 - OSPF external type 2
```

```
        i - IS-IS, su - IS-IS summary, L1 - IS-IS level-1, L2 - IS-IS level-2
        ia - IS-IS inter area, * - candidate default, U - per-user static route
        o - ODR, P - periodic downloaded static route

Gateway of last resort is not set

B    192.168.75.0/24 [20/0] via 192.168.1.205, 02:21:09
     192.168.255.0/32 is subnetted, 3 subnets
C        192.168.255.3 is directly connected, Loopback0
O        192.168.255.2 [110/2] via 192.168.1.198, 02:27:48, FastEthernet2/0
O        192.168.255.1 [110/3] via 192.168.1.198, 02:27:48, FastEthernet2/0
B    192.168.50.0/24 [20/0] via 192.168.1.205, 02:21:40
     192.168.1.0/30 is subnetted, 4 subnets
B        192.168.1.200 [20/0] via 192.168.1.205, 02:21:09
C        192.168.1.204 is directly connected, Serial1/0
C        192.168.1.196 is directly connected, FastEthernet2/0
O        192.168.1.220 [110/2] via 192.168.1.198, 02:27:48, FastEthernet2/0
```

The problem is that when a router advertises a route to an EBGP peer, it adds the address of its outgoing interface as the NEXT_HOP attribute of the route. By default, when a router advertises a route to an IBGP peer, it does not change the NEXT_HOP attribute of the route.[2] So for prefix 192.168.100.0/24, for example, when Taos advertises the route to the prefix to Vail, the NEXT_HOP is set to the outgoing interface 192.168.1.225. When Vail receives this route, the NEXT_HOP is valid because 192.168.1.224/30 is a directly connected subnet as you can see in Vail's routing table. Vail knows how to reach the NEXT_HOP, so the route is added to the routing table.

Vail then advertises the route to its IBGP peer Telluride, and you can see an entry for the route in Telluride's BGP table. But obeying basic BGP rules, when Vail advertises the route to its IBGP peers, it does not change the NEXT_HOP. And because Telluride does not know how to reach that address, the route is considered invalid. It is not entered into Telluride's routing table, nor does Telluride advertise the route to its own EBGP peers.

There are two solutions to this problem:

- Make the default NEXT_HOP reachable within the AS.

- Change the default BGP NEXT_HOP behavior.

The first solution can be achieved by configuring static routes on the AS-internal routers for all EBGP neighbors, but this becomes unmanageable if there are a large number of EBGP neighbors to the AS, if there are a large number of AS_internal routers requiring the static routes, or both. The static routes could be configured only at the edge routers

---

[2] This behavior is also described in the section "The NEXT_HOP Attribute" in Chapter 2.

connecting to external peers and then redistributed into the IGP, or **redistribute connected** could be used at the edge routers, but these also can be problematic.

A better means of achieving this first solution is to run the IGP in passive mode on the interfaces linking to external peers. Example 3-22 shows Vail's configuration modified so that OSPF can run passively on the interface connecting to Taos. Example 3-23 shows the resulting BGP and routing tables at Telluride. OSPF is advertising the subnet 192.168.1.224/30 within AS100, so Telluride now has a route to the NEXT_HOP address 192.168.1.225. As a result, the prefixes advertised by Taos are marked as best in Telluride's BGP table and are added to the routing table. And because the routes are now valid at Telluride, they can be advertised to its EBGP neighbor Alta; Example 3-24 shows the prefixes in Alta's BGP table. Notice that the NEXT_HOP addresses of the prefixes are now Telluride's interface 192.168.1.206, again reflecting the BGP behavior of changing the NEXT_HOP attribute to the local outgoing interface when advertising a route to an EBGP peer.

Example 3-22 *Vail's OSPF Configuration Is Modified to Run Passively on the External Interface (Serial1/0, IP Address 192.168.1.226) Connecting to Taos*

```
router ospf 100
 log-adjacency-changes
 passive-interface Serial1/0
 network 192.168.1.221 0.0.0.0 area 0
 network 192.168.1.226 0.0.0.0 area 0
 network 192.168.255.1 0.0.0.0 area 0
!
router bgp 100
 no synchronization
 bgp log-neighbor-changes
 neighbor 192.168.1.225 remote-as 200
 neighbor 192.168.255.2 remote-as 100
 neighbor 192.168.255.2 update-source Loopback0
 neighbor 192.168.255.3 remote-as 100
 neighbor 192.168.255.3 update-source Loopback0
 no auto-summary
!
```

Example 3-23 *Because the OSPF Domain within AS100 Now Knows How to Reach the NEXT_HOP Address 192.168.1.225, the Prefixes Advertised by Taos Are Also Reachable*

```
Telluride#show ip bgp
BGP table version is 99, local router ID is 192.168.255.3
Status codes: s suppressed, d damped, h history, * valid, > best, i - internal,
              r RIB-failure, S Stale
Origin codes: i - IGP, e - EGP, ? - incomplete
```

```
    Network           Next Hop          Metric LocPrf Weight Path
*>  192.168.1.200/30 192.168.1.205          0           0 400 i
*>  192.168.50.0     192.168.1.205          0           0 400 i
*>  192.168.75.0     192.168.1.205          0           0 400 i
*>i192.168.100.0     192.168.1.225          0    100    0 200 i
*>i192.168.172.0/22 192.168.1.225      30720    100    0 200 i
*>i192.168.200.0     192.168.1.225      30720    100    0 200 i


Telluride#show ip route
Codes: C - connected, S - static, R - RIP, M - mobile, B - BGP
       D - EIGRP, EX - EIGRP external, O - OSPF, IA - OSPF inter area
       N1 - OSPF NSSA external type 1, N2 - OSPF NSSA external type 2
       E1 - OSPF external type 1, E2 - OSPF external type 2
       i - IS-IS, su - IS-IS summary, L1 - IS-IS level-1, L2 - IS-IS level-2
       ia - IS-IS inter area, * - candidate default, U - per-user static route
       o - ODR, P - periodic downloaded static route

Gateway of last resort is not set

B    192.168.75.0/24 [20/0] via 192.168.1.205, 07:55:18
B    192.168.200.0/24 [200/30720] via 192.168.1.225, 00:15:35
     192.168.255.0/32 is subnetted, 3 subnets
C       192.168.255.3 is directly connected, Loopback0
O       192.168.255.2 [110/2] via 192.168.1.198, 07:45:28, FastEthernet2/0
O       192.168.255.1 [110/3] via 192.168.1.198, 07:45:28, FastEthernet2/0
B    192.168.50.0/24 [20/0] via 192.168.1.205, 07:55:18
     192.168.1.0/30 is subnetted, 5 subnets
O       192.168.1.224 [110/66] via 192.168.1.198, 07:45:28, FastEthernet2/0
B       192.168.1.200 [20/0] via 192.168.1.205, 07:55:18
C       192.168.1.204 is directly connected, Serial1/0
C       192.168.1.196 is directly connected, FastEthernet2/0
O       192.168.1.220 [110/2] via 192.168.1.198, 07:45:28, FastEthernet2/0
B    192.168.100.0/24 [200/0] via 192.168.1.225, 07:45:24
B    192.168.172.0/22 [200/30720] via 192.168.1.225, 00:15:37
```

Example 3-24 *Telluride Advertises the Prefixes in AS200 to Its EBGP Peer Alta*

```
Alta#show ip bgp
BGP table version is 99, local router ID is 192.168.1.205
Status codes: s suppressed, d damped, h history, * valid, > best, i - internal,
              r RIB-failure, S Stale
Origin codes: i - IGP, e - EGP, ? - incomplete
```

```
     Network          Next Hop            Metric LocPrf Weight Path
*>  192.168.1.200/30 0.0.0.0                  0          32768 i
*>  192.168.50.0     0.0.0.0                  0          32768 i
*>  192.168.75.0     0.0.0.0                  0          32768 i
*>  192.168.100.0    192.168.1.206                       0 100 200 i
*>  192.168.172.0/22 192.168.1.206                       0 100 200 i
*>  192.168.200.0    192.168.1.206                       0 100 200 i
```

Note No Metric is associated with the three prefixes advertised from AS200, through AS100, to AS400 in Example 3-24. As mentioned previously, this metric is the MED attribute. Because Telluride removes the MED attribute from the routes before advertising them to Alta (compare the BGP tables in Examples 3-23 and 2-24) this reflects another BGP rule: MEDs advertised by an AS are seen only by their directly connected neighboring autonomous systems and are not passed on to other autonomous systems—that is, it's a nontransitive attribute. Chapter 4 discusses MEDs in detail.

The difficulty with this first solution is that your IGP should not run on a link external to your AS. Although running in passive mode is a compromise that eliminates the most serious liability—exposing your IGP to accidental or intentional connection from outside your administrative domain—it is still not considered good practice. If you are a service provider, for example, you might have thousands or tens of thousands of links to EBGP neighbors. Allowing all those subnets into your IGP can cause severe scaling and performance problems.

The second solution, changing the default BGP NEXT_HOP behavior, is therefore considered best practice: When a router advertises a route learned from an EBGP peer to an IBGP peer, the router changes the NEXT_HOP to one of its own addresses already known within the local AS. With few exceptions, the address used is the router's loopback interface address.

You can configure a routing policy to change the NEXT_HOP address, but IOS provides a much easier means of accomplishing the same goal. The **neighbor next-hop-self** statement causes the router to change the BGP NEXT_HOP attribute to its own loopback address in all routes advertised to the specified neighbor. Example 3-25 shows Telluride's BGP configuration changed to include this statement for its IBGP neighbors.

Example 3-25 neighbor next-hop-self *Statement Changes the NEXT_HOP Address of Routes Advertised to the Specified Neighbor to the Advertising Router's Loopback Address*

```
router ospf 100
 log-adjacency-changes
 network 192.168.1.197 0.0.0.0 area 0
 network 192.168.255.3 0.0.0.0 area 0
```

```
!
router bgp 100
 no synchronization
 bgp log-neighbor-changes
 neighbor 192.168.1.205 remote-as 400
 neighbor 192.168.255.1 remote-as 100
 neighbor 192.168.255.1 update-source Loopback0
 neighbor 192.168.255.1 next-hop-self
 neighbor 192.168.255.2 remote-as 100
 neighbor 192.168.255.2 update-source Loopback0
 neighbor 192.168.255.2 next-hop-self
 no auto-summary
```

Vail already knows how to reach Telluride's loopback address (192.168.255.3) (refer to the routing table in Example 3-21). So when Vail receives the AS400 routes from Telluride, with the modified NEXT_HOP, it marks the routes best in its BGP table (Example 3-26), enters them into its routing table, and advertises them to EBGP peer Taos. Example 3-27 shows the prefixes in Taos' BGP table.

Example 3-26   *Because the OSPF Domain Within AS100 Now Knows How to Reach the NEXT_HOP Address 192.168.225.3, the Prefixes Advertised by Alta Are Also Reachable*

```
Vail#show ip bgp
BGP table version is 178, local router ID is 192.168.255.1
Status codes: s suppressed, d damped, h history, * valid, > best, i - internal,
              r RIB-failure, S Stale
Origin codes: i - IGP, e - EGP, ? - incomplete

   Network          Next Hop          Metric LocPrf Weight Path
*>i192.168.1.200/30 192.168.255.3          0    100      0 400 i
*>i192.168.50.0     192.168.255.3          0    100      0 400 i
*>i192.168.75.0     192.168.255.3          0    100      0 400 i
*> 192.168.100.0    192.168.1.225          0             0 200 i
*> 192.168.172.0/22 192.168.1.225      30720             0 200 i
*> 192.168.200.0    192.168.1.225      30720             0 200 i
```

Example 3-27   *Vail Advertises the Prefixes in AS400 to Its EBGP Peer Taos*

```
Taos#show ip bgp
BGP table version is 205, local router ID is 192.168.100.1
Status codes: s suppressed, d damped, h history, * valid, > best, i - internal,
              r RIB-failure, S Stale
Origin codes: i - IGP, e - EGP, ? - incomplete
```

```
   Network          Next Hop         Metric LocPrf Weight Path
*> 192.168.1.200/30 192.168.1.226                      0 100 400 i
*> 192.168.50.0     192.168.1.226                      0 100 400 i
*> 192.168.75.0     192.168.1.226                      0 100 400 i
*> 192.168.100.0    0.0.0.0               0         32768 i
*> 192.168.172.0/22 192.168.1.217     30720         32768 i
*> 192.168.200.0    192.168.1.217     30720         32768 i
```

> **Note** This case study used passive-mode OSPF at Vail and next-hop-self at Telluride to demonstrate the effects of the two solutions to the IBGP NEXT_HOP problem. In a real network, of course, you would use one or the other solution, not both.

Example 3-28 shows two pings from Taos to a destination represented by one of the prefixes in AS400. Notice that to make the ping work, it must be sourced from an address that the destination knows how to reach. The first ping fails because by default it is sourced from Taos' interface to Vail, 192.168.1.225. AS400 does not know how to reach that address. The point of this example is that troubleshooting inter-AS routes sometimes takes a bit more thought about what is reachable and what is not than troubleshooting intra-AS routes.

Example 3-28 *When Pinging from AS200 to AS400, Care Must Be Taken to Ensure the ping Is Sourced from an Address the Destination Knows How to Reach*

```
Taos#ping 192.168.50.1

Type escape sequence to abort.
Sending 5, 100-byte ICMP Echos to 192.168.50.1, timeout is 2 seconds:
.....
Success rate is 0 percent (0/5)

Taos#ping 192.168.50.1 source 192.168.100.1

Type escape sequence to abort.
Sending 5, 100-byte ICMP Echos to 192.168.50.1, timeout is 2 seconds:
Packet sent with a source address of 192.168.100.1
!!!!!
Success rate is 100 percent (5/5), round-trip min/avg/max = 264/337/380 ms
```

IBGP and IGP Synchronization

Hopefully, you have noticed the **no synchronization** statement added by default to all the example BGP configurations in this chapter and the previous one. IGP synchronization is an artifact of an earlier networking era; it is almost never used anymore. As a result, synchronization is disabled by default in IOS release 12.2(8)T and later. Before that, synchronization was enabled by default, and in most cases you had to remember to turn it off. This section explains IGP synchronization so that

- If you work with an older version of IOS, you know why you probably need to disable it.

- If you come across the rare situation in which synchronization is useful, you understand its function.

- You can explain it should you be asked about it on some sort of networking certification exam.

- At the least, you know what the default **no synchronization** statement in your BGP configuration means.

The rule of synchronization states

> Before a route learned from an IBGP neighbor is entered into the local routing table, or advertised to an EBGP peer, the route must first be known via IGP.

To understand why the rule of synchronization exists, consider the network in Figure 3-4. In this case, IBGP is used only in a partial mesh, between Alshan and Huaibei. OSPF is the IGP within AS600. Alshan and Huaibei are connected to two separate autonomous systems and advertise the EBGP-learned routes with each other over an IBGP connection. The TCP session for this IBGP connection passes through PingTian and Nanshan, but no IBGP sessions are run to those two routers.

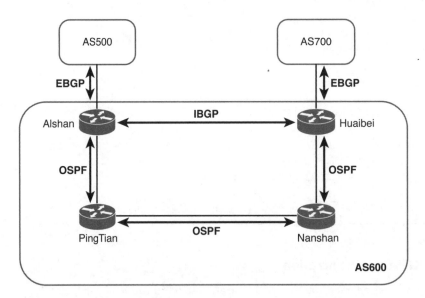

Figure 3-4 *This AS Uses a Single IBGP Session Between Edge Routers Alshan and Huaibei; OSPF Is Its IGP*

Next, suppose Alshan learns a route to 196.223.18.0/24 from AS500 and advertises the route over the IBGP connection to Huaibei, using a next-hop-self policy to change the NEXT_HOP attribute to its own router ID. Huaibei then advertises the route to AS700. Routers in AS700 now begin forwarding packets destined for 196.223.18.0/24 to Huaibei. (Remember, a route advertisement is a promise to deliver packets.) Here is where things go wrong. Huaibei does a route lookup for 196.223.18.0/24 and sees that the network is reachable via Alshan. It then does a lookup for Alshan's IP address and sees that it is reachable via the next-hop router Nanshan. So the packet destined for 196.223.18.0/24 is forwarded to Nanshan. But the external routes have been shared between Alshan and Huaibei via IBGP; the OSPF routers have no knowledge of the external routes. Therefore, when the packet is forwarded to Nanshan, that router does a route lookup and does not find an entry for 196.223.18.0/24. The router drops the packet and all subsequent packets for that address. Traffic for the network 196.223.18.0/24 has been black-holed.

Of course, if the OSPF routers referred to in Figure 3-4 know about the external routes, the situation just described will not happen. Nanshan will know that 196.223.18.0/24 is reachable via Alshan and will forward the packet correctly.

When Huaibei receives the advertisement for 196.223.18.0/24 from Alshan, it adds the route to its BGP table. It then checks its IGP routing table to see if an entry exists for the route. If not, Huaibei knows that the route is unknown to the IGP and cannot advertise the route. If and when the IGP makes an entry in the routing table for 196.223.18.0/24, (that is, when the IGP knows of the route), Huaibei's BGP route is *synchronized* with the IGP route, and the router is free to begin advertising the route to its BGP peers.

The basis for the synchronization rule is that the BGP routes are redistributed into the IGP so that the IGP has correct forwarding information. But this is rarely used and has not been used for a long time; best practice, instead, is to ensure that all transit routers have the forwarding information they need by using a full IBGP mesh. Keeping BGP routes in BGP makes a simpler logical architecture and prevents problems in which large numbers of BGP routes redistributed into an IGP cause performance degradation or even system meltdowns.

This author earned his CCIE in the early 1990s, and even then full IBGP meshes were standard practice. Forgetting to turn off synchronization was one of the best-known "gotchas" of the BGP portion of the lab, leaving CCIE candidates scratching their heads over why their full-mesh IBGP configurations looked right but their edge routers still would not advertise routes correctly.

Now that synchronization is off by default, that "gotcha" is gone. But now you know what it does if it is enabled and why. And should your properly configured full IBGP mesh stop working during the troubleshooting portion of your CCIE lab exam, you know to check and see if some sneaky lab proctor has enabled synchronization while you weren't looking.

Advertising BGP NLRI into the Local AS

The sections "Multihoming" in Chapter 1 and "Who Needs BGP?" in Chapter 2 explain that in most cases BGP routes do not need to be learned by routers other than the edge routers in a stub AS. If there is a single connection to an external AS, only a default route is required. A default route is sufficient even in most multihomed stub autonomous systems; each AS border router advertises a default route into the IGP, and internal routers select the default route to the closest border router.

However, in some cases you will want internal routers to have enough routing information to forward packets to the border router closest to the external destination. Default routes cannot do this; barring more detail about external routes, an internal router will forward all packets to all external destinations to the closest border router—a behavior called *hot-potato routing*, in which it is more important to get packets to the closest AS exit point than it is to get packets to the exit point closest to the destination.
Figure 3-5, a repeat of Figure 1-22 in Chapter 1, illustrates hot-potato routing. Packets from the source exit AS65501 use the closest border router (San Jose). Packets from the destination back to the source enter AS65501 at a different border router (Boston). Hot-potato routing is easily implemented with default routes. It saves internal bandwidth usage at the price of potentially longer delays and asymmetric traffic patterns.

Redistributing BGP NLRI into the IGP

One way of getting more route detail to the AS-internal routers is to use the **redistribute bgp** statement to redistribute BGP-learned routes into the IGP at AS-border routers. However, this is almost universally considered bad practice for two reasons.

As the section "Connecting to Untrusted Domains" in Chapter 2 explains, IGPs and BGP work under different design philosophies. By definition a neighboring AS is under someone else's administrative control, so BGP works under the assumption that its external neighbors cannot be trusted and that information accepted from them should be carefully regulated. An IGP, assuming its neighbors are under the same administrative control and therefore trusted, are liberal in what information they accept. Redistribution between BGP and an IGP breaks the "trust boundary," possibly exposing the IGP to bad information.

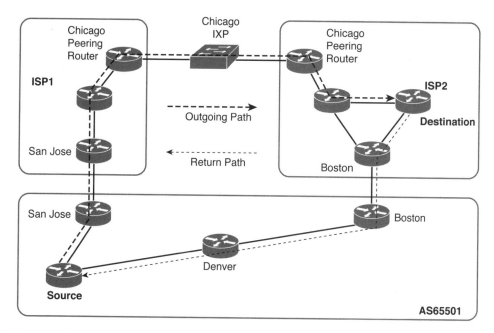

Figure 3-5 *Hot-Potato Routing Forwards Packets to the Nearest Exist Point of the Local Autonomous System*

More important, BGP is designed to handle Internet-scale routing tables; IGPs are not. As this chapter is being written, the Internet routing table has exceeded 600,000 entries. Redistributing this many entries into OSPF or IS-IS causes immense flooding, processing, and database overflow problems. Most OSPF and IS-IS implementations stop working under this load, and in many cases they cause the router to crash. Recovering from such a situation can take hours of systematically shutting down routers to flush the link state databases. Distance vector protocols such as EIGRP can better handle the large number of entries, but convergence times can increase to multiple minutes, damaging routing performance for destinations within the local AS.

Case Study: Distributing NLRI in a Stub AS with IBGP

The preferred way to get more routing detail into a multihomed stub AS is the same way you get the necessary routing detail into a transit AS: Using IBGP, as shown in Figure 3-6. Following are three advantages to using IBGP rather than redistributing into the IGP:

■ The external routes are kept separate from the IGP, preventing them from negatively impacting IGP performance.

■ You can selectively distribute the external route information. For example, you might create IBGP adjacencies from the border routers to designated routers in different regions of the AS and then use default routes to reach those local BGP routers, as shown in Figure 3-7.

■ Keeping the external routes in IBGP makes BGP's powerful policy tools available to you to express route preferences and prefix filtering.

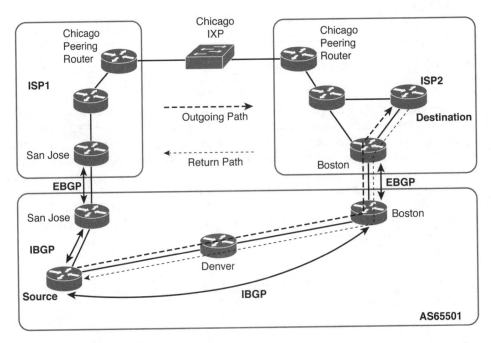

Figure 3-6   *IBGP Should Be Used in a Multihomed Stub AS When Better Route Detail About External Destinations Is Needed, Such as to Select the Border Router Closest to the Destination*

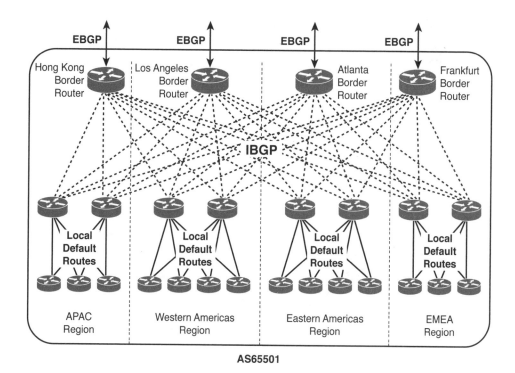

Figure 3-7 *IBGP Can Be Used to Distribute External Routes to Different Regions Within the AS, and Default Routes Can Be Used Within Those Regions*

Example 3-29 shows the configurations of Taos, Sandia, and AngelFire, adding IBGP sessions that allow the border routers to advertise external routes to AngelFire. The IBGP configurations are straightforward, peering between the loopback interfaces and using the **neighbor update-source** and **neighbor next-hop-self** statements as in the previous exercises in this chapter.

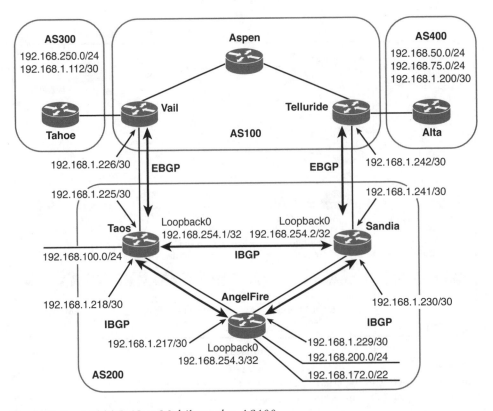

Figure 3-8   *AS200 Is Now Multihomed to AS100*

Example 3-29   *BGP Configurations for the Routers in AS200 of Figure 3-8.*

```
Taos
router bgp 200
 no synchronization
 bgp log-neighbor-changes
 network 192.168.100.0
 network 192.168.172.0 mask 255.255.252.0
 network 192.168.200.0
 neighbor 192.168.1.226 remote-as 100
 neighbor 192.168.254.2 remote-as 200
 neighbor 192.168.254.2 update-source Loopback0
 neighbor 192.168.254.2 next-hop-self
 neighbor 192.168.254.3 remote-as 200
 neighbor 192.168.254.3 update-source Loopback0
 neighbor 192.168.254.3 next-hop-self
 no auto-summary
!
```

```
Sandia
router bgp 200
 no synchronization
 bgp log-neighbor-changes
 network 192.168.100.0
 network 192.168.172.0 mask 255.255.252.0
 network 192.168.200.0
 neighbor 192.168.1.242 remote-as 100
 neighbor 192.168.254.1 remote-as 200
 neighbor 192.168.254.1 update-source Loopback0
 neighbor 192.168.254.1 next-hop-self
 neighbor 192.168.254.3 remote-as 200
 neighbor 192.168.254.3 update-source Loopback0
 neighbor 192.168.254.3 next-hop-self
 no auto-summary
!
```

```
AngelFire
router bgp 200
 no synchronization
 bgp log-neighbor-changes
 neighbor 192.168.254.1 remote-as 200
 neighbor 192.168.254.1 update-source Loopback0
 neighbor 192.168.254.2 remote-as 200
 neighbor 192.168.254.2 update-source Loopback0
 no auto-summary
!
```

AngelFire's routing table is shown in Example 3-30; you can see the BGP (B) entries for all the prefixes advertised by AS300 and AS400. There are also EIGRP (D) entries for all the prefixes internal to AS200, including the loopback addresses of the three routers. You might also notice something surprising: The entries for the three AS400 prefixes show Taos (192.168.254.1) as the next hop, even though (refer to Figure 3-8) the path through Sandia (192.168.254.2) has fewer router hops to AS400.

Example 3-30 *AngelFire's Routing Table Contains Entries for All the AS300 and AS400 Prefixes*

```
AngelFire#show ip route
Codes: C - connected, S - static, R - RIP, M - mobile, B - BGP
       D - EIGRP, EX - EIGRP external, O - OSPF, IA - OSPF inter area
       N1 - OSPF NSSA external type 1, N2 - OSPF NSSA external type 2
       E1 - OSPF external type 1, E2 - OSPF external type 2
       i - IS-IS, su - IS-IS summary, L1 - IS-IS level-1, L2 - IS-IS level-2
```

```
        ia - IS-IS inter area, * - candidate default, U - per-user static route
        o - ODR, P - periodic downloaded static route

Gateway of last resort is not set

B    192.168.75.0/24 [200/0] via 192.168.254.1, 03:39:20
C    192.168.200.0/24 is directly connected, FastEthernet1/0
B    192.168.250.0/24 [200/0] via 192.168.254.1, 03:39:20
     192.168.254.0/24 is variably subnetted, 4 subnets, 2 masks
D       192.168.254.2/32
            [90/156160] via 192.168.1.230, 03:48:40, FastEthernet3/0
C       192.168.254.3/32 is directly connected, Loopback0
D       192.168.254.0/24 is a summary, 05:09:13, Null0
D       192.168.254.1/32
            [90/156160] via 192.168.1.218, 04:25:44, FastEthernet0/0
B    192.168.50.0/24 [200/0] via 192.168.254.1, 03:39:20
     192.168.1.0/24 is variably subnetted, 7 subnets, 2 masks
D       192.168.1.0/24 is a summary, 05:29:53, Null0
D       192.168.1.224/30
            [90/2172416] via 192.168.1.218, 03:39:40, FastEthernet0/0
C       192.168.1.228/30 is directly connected, FastEthernet3/0
D       192.168.1.240/30
            [90/2172416] via 192.168.1.230, 03:48:41, FastEthernet3/0
B       192.168.1.200/30 [200/0] via 192.168.254.1, 03:39:22
C       192.168.1.216/30 is directly connected, FastEthernet0/0
B       192.168.1.212/30 [200/0] via 192.168.254.1, 03:39:22
D    192.168.100.0/24 [90/30720] via 192.168.1.218, 04:25:46, FastEthernet0/0
C    192.168.172.0/22 is directly connected, FastEthernet1/1
AngelFire#
```

A look at AngelFire's BGP table (Example 3-31) shows why Taos is the exit router for all the external prefixes. Remember that BGP looks at autonomous system hops rather than router hops. The BGP table shows entries for all the AS300 and AS400 prefixes advertised by both Taos (192.168.254.1) and Sandia (192.168.254.2), but the AS_PATH lengths of all the prefixes are the same: a hop through AS100 and then the destination AS. Running down the sequential steps of the BGP decision process as explained in Chapter 2, you find that for each pair of entries to the same destination

1. The weights are all equal (0).

2. The LOCAL_PREF values are the same (100).

3. The AS_PATH lengths are the same (2 ASNs).

4. The Origin codes are the same (IGP for the AS400 prefixes; Incomplete for the AS300 prefixes).

5. The MED values (Metric) are the same (0).

6. There are only IBGP routes (i) and no EBGP or Confederation EBGP routes to be preferred over them.

7. The paths to the two next hops, 192.168.254.1 and 192.168.254.2, are of equal length.

8. The prefixes are from the same AS, and BGP multipath is not enabled.

9. Finally, at this step, you find the decision point: Everything being equal up to this point, the route with the lowest BGP Router ID is chosen. Because next-hop-self is used, the Router IDs are the same as the loopback addresses, and 192.168.254.1 is lower than 192.168.254.2. So the Taos routes are deemed best (>) and are entered into the routing table.

Example 3-31 *AngelFire's BGP Table Shows That the Inter-AS Paths to AS400 Are Equal Through Both Taos and Sandia*

```
AngelFire#show ip bgp
BGP table version is 32, local router ID is 192.168.254.3
Status codes: s suppressed, d damped, h history, * valid, > best, i - internal,
              r RIB-failure, S Stale
Origin codes: i - IGP, e - EGP, ? - incomplete

   Network          Next Hop          Metric LocPrf Weight Path
*>i192.168.1.200/30 192.168.254.1          0    100      0 100 400 i
* i                 192.168.254.2          0    100      0 100 400 i
*>i192.168.1.212/30 192.168.254.1          0    100      0 100 300 ?
* i                 192.168.254.2          0    100      0 100 300 ?
*>i192.168.50.0     192.168.254.1          0    100      0 100 400 i
* i                 192.168.254.2          0    100      0 100 400 i
*>i192.168.75.0     192.168.254.1          0    100      0 100 400 i
* i                 192.168.254.2          0    100      0 100 400 i
r i192.168.100.0    192.168.254.2      33280    100      0 i
r>i                 192.168.254.1          0    100      0 i
r i192.168.172.0/22 192.168.254.2      30720    100      0 i
r>i                 192.168.254.1      30720    100      0 i
r i192.168.200.0    192.168.254.2      30720    100      0 i
r>i                 192.168.254.1      30720    100      0 i
*>i192.168.250.0    192.168.254.1          0    100      0 100 300 ?
* i                 192.168.254.2          0    100      0 100 300 ?
```

Make no mistake, though: The advertisements from Sandia are still good. Example 3-32 shows AngelFire's BGP table after the link between Vail and Taos has been disabled; you can see that the paths to all external destinations now use Sandia (192.168.254.2) after Taos no longer has an EBGP peer.

Example 3-32   *AngelFire's BGP Table After the Link between Taos and Vail Has Been Disabled Shows That the Path to the External Destinations Passes Through Sandia*

```
AngelFire#show ip bgp
BGP table version is 37, local router ID is 192.168.254.3
Status codes: s suppressed, d damped, h history, * valid, > best, i - internal,
              r RIB-failure, S Stale
Origin codes: i - IGP, e - EGP, ? - incomplete

   Network          Next Hop        Metric LocPrf Weight Path
*>i192.168.1.200/30 192.168.254.2        0    100      0 100 400 i
*>i192.168.1.212/30 192.168.254.2        0    100      0 100 300 ?
*>i192.168.50.0     192.168.254.2        0    100      0 100 400 i
*>i192.168.75.0     192.168.254.2        0    100      0 100 400 i
r i192.168.100.0    192.168.254.2    33280    100      0 i
r>i                 192.168.254.1        0    100      0 i
r i192.168.172.0/22 192.168.254.2    30720    100      0 i
r>i                 192.168.254.1    30720    100      0 i
r i192.168.200.0    192.168.254.2    30720    100      0 i
r>i                 192.168.254.1    30720    100      0 i
*>i192.168.250.0    192.168.254.2        0    100      0 100 300 ?
```

If AS200 were a real AS, there would probably be more internal routers, creating more unequal path lengths to the border routers and therefore more likelihood of selecting the exit router closer to the destination. But this example provides a good lead-in for routing policy in Chapter 4. By setting a policy that makes the weights, LOCAL_PREF, Origin codes, or MEDs uneven between any two routes to the same destination prefix, you can manipulate the results shown here to prefer one border router over another.

Another important detail in the BGP tables referred to in Examples 3-31 and 3-32 is that the prefixes that Taos and Sandia are configured to advertise to their EBGP peers (192.168.100.0/24, 192.168.172.0/22, and 192.168.200.0/24) are also in AngelFire's BGP table. This is because the **network** statements used to inject the prefixes at Taos and Sandia (refer to Example 3-29) are not specific to any BGP neighbor. At first glance this might be a problem because you want these internal prefixes to be known via the IGP, not BGP. However, all are tagged with an "r" indicating a RIB-failure that prevents them from being inserted into the routing table. Example 3-33, using the **show ip bgp rib-failures** command, gives the reason for the RIB-failure: The prefixes are also known by EIGRP, which has a lower administrative distance (90) than IBGP (200). So only the EIGRP routes make it into the routing table, which is the wanted result.

Example 3-33 *The AS200 Internal Prefixes Injected into BGP at Taos and Sandia*
Are Not Added to AngelFire's Routing Table Because They Have Higher Administrative
Distances Than the EIGRP Routes to the Same Prefixes

```
AngelFire#show ip bgp rib-failure
Network          Next Hop              RIB-failure     RIB-NH Matches
192.168.100.0    192.168.254.1    Higher admin distance          n/a
192.168.172.0/22 192.168.254.1    Higher admin distance          n/a
192.168.200.0    192.168.254.1    Higher admin distance          n/a
```

There is one more important observation to be made about the IBGP topology referred
to in Figure 3-8. In addition to AngelFire's IBGP sessions with Taos and Sandia, an IBGP
session exists directly between Taos and Sandia. This session is to add redundancy for
the border routers. For example, Sandia's BGP table at the top of Example 3-34 shows
the AS300 and AS400 routes received from both Taos (192.168.254.1) and Telluride
(192.168.1.242); the Telluride routes are preferred because according to Step 6 of the
BGP decision process, EBGP routes are preferred over IBGP routes to the same destination. But after the first display of Sandia's BGP table message referred to in Example
3-34, the link between Sandia and Telluride has failed. (That is, I disabled it.) When the
BGP table displays again, the routes that were advertised by Telluride are gone, but
Sandia can still reach the five external prefixes by sending packets through AngelFire
and then out to AS100 through Taos.

Example 3-34 *Sandia Prefers the Path Through Telluride (192.168.1.242) to Reach the*
Prefixes in AS300 and AS400, but After the Link to Telluride Fails Sandia Switches to the
Routes Through Taos (192.168.254.1)

```
Sandia#show ip bgp
BGP table version is 15, local router ID is 192.168.254.2
Status codes: s suppressed, d damped, h history, * valid, > best, i - internal,
              r RIB-failure, S Stale
Origin codes: i - IGP, e - EGP, ? - incomplete

   Network          Next Hop         Metric LocPrf Weight Path
* i192.168.1.200/30 192.168.254.1         0    100      0 100 400 i
*>                  192.168.1.242                       0 100 400 i
* i192.168.1.212/30 192.168.254.1         0    100      0 100 300 ?
*>                  192.168.1.242                       0 100 300 ?
* i192.168.50.0     192.168.254.1         0    100      0 100 400 i
*>                  192.168.1.242                       0 100 400 i
* i192.168.75.0     192.168.254.1         0    100      0 100 400 i
*>                  192.168.1.242                       0 100 400 i
* i192.168.100.0    192.168.254.1         0    100      0 i
*>                  192.168.1.229     33280          32768 i
* i192.168.172.0/22 192.168.254.1     30720    100      0 i
```

```
 *>                  192.168.1.229        30720             32768 i
 * i192.168.200.0    192.168.254.1        30720     100         0 i
 *>                  192.168.1.229        30720             32768 i
 * i192.168.250.0    192.168.254.1            0     100         0 100 300 ?
 *>                  192.168.1.242                              0 100 300 ?
Sandia#
*Jan  1 01:24:15.697: %LINEPROTO-5-UPDOWN: Line protocol on Interface Serial1/0,
  changed state to down
*Jan  1 01:24:15.757: %BGP-5-ADJCHANGE: neighbor 192.168.1.242 Down Interface flap
Sandia#show ip bgp
BGP table version is 20, local router ID is 192.168.254.2
Status codes: s suppressed, d damped, h history, * valid, > best, i - internal,
              r RIB-failure, S Stale
Origin codes: i - IGP, e - EGP, ? - incomplete

   Network          Next Hop         Metric LocPrf Weight Path
*>i192.168.1.200/30 192.168.254.1         0    100      0 100 400 i
*>i192.168.1.212/30 192.168.254.1         0    100      0 100 300 ?
*>i192.168.50.0     192.168.254.1         0    100      0 100 400 i
*>i192.168.75.0     192.168.254.1         0    100      0 100 400 i
* i192.168.100.0    192.168.254.1         0    100      0 i
 *>                 192.168.1.229     33280             32768 i
* i192.168.172.0/22 192.168.254.1     30720    100      0 i
 *>                 192.168.1.229     30720             32768 i
* i192.168.200.0    192.168.254.1     30720    100      0 i
 *>                 192.168.1.229     30720             32768 i
*>i192.168.250.0    192.168.254.1         0    100      0 100 300 ?
```

The IBGP session between Taos and Sandia might at first seem to be a risk because AS200 should be a stub AS. No prefixes, for example, advertised from Telluride to Sandia should then be advertised from Sandia to Taos and then from Taos to Vail. A link failure in AS100 might cause traffic to try to transit AS200 on the Vail-Taos-AngelFire-Sandia-Telluride path. But routes advertised to AngelFire cannot be advertised back to border routers because of the rule that a router cannot advertise a route learned from an internal neighbor to another internal neighbor. Therefore, AngelFire will not advertise routes learned from Sandia to Taos and vice versa.

Taos can, however, advertise routes learned from internal neighbor Sandia to external neighbor Vail; Sandia can advertise routes learned from internal neighbor Taos to external neighbor Telluride. But recall the BGP loop avoidance rule: When prefix 192.168.50.0/24 is advertised from Telluride to Sandia, Telluride adds its AS number 100 to the AS_PATH. Sandia advertises the prefix to Taos, which advertises it to Vail. Vail sees its own AS100 on the AS_PATH and drops the route. Therefore, the routes cannot be advertised in such a way that AS200 would be mistakenly used as a transit AS.

Distributing NLRI in a Stub AS with Static Routes

A compromise between redistributing BGP into the IGP and using IBGP within the AS is to create static routes for the external destinations you want to reach and redistribute the static routes into the IGP. This is a useful alternative when you need specific information about just a few external routes. Suppose, for instance, you want to impose the following rules on AS200 in Figure 3-8:

- AngelFire should prefer Taos when forwarding packets to 192.168.250.0/24 in AS300.

- AngelFire should prefer Sandia when forwarding packets to 192.168.50.0/24 and 192.168.75.0/24 in A 400.

- If either Taos or Sandia becomes unreachable or loses its external link, AngelFire should use the other border router for all packets, including packets to the preceding destinations.

- AngelFire should use a default route to reach all destinations other than the three prefixes named here, and either Taos or Sandia can be the default router.

Example 3-35 shows Taos and Sandia configured to comply to these rules. The previous IBGP configurations (refer to Example 3-29) have been removed (BGP has been removed completely from AngelFire) and static routes have been added. At each router static entries are made for the specific prefixes to be preferred through that router referencing the outgoing physical interface. Each router is also given a static default route (0.0.0.0/0) that points to interface Null0. The static routes are then redistributed into EIGRP. More important, the statics are redistributed into the IGP, not BGP, because you want them to have effect only in AS200. Redistributing them into BGP would, unless further routing policy were applied, cause the static routes to be advertised into AS100.

Example 3-35 *Taos and Sandia Are Configured to Redistribute Static Routes to Selected External Destinations into EIGRP*

```
Taos
router eigrp 200
 redistribute static metric 10000 100 255 1 1500
 passive-interface Serial1/0
 network 192.168.1.0
 network 192.168.100.0
 network 192.168.254.0
 no auto-summary
!
router bgp 200
 no synchronization
 bgp log-neighbor-changes
 network 192.168.100.0
 network 192.168.172.0 mask 255.255.252.0
```

```
 network 192.168.200.0
 neighbor 192.168.1.226 remote-as 100
 no auto-summary
!
ip route 0.0.0.0 0.0.0.0 Null0
ip route 192.168.250.0 255.255.255.0 Serial1/0
!
```

```
Sandia
router eigrp 200
 redistribute static metric 10000 100 255 1 1500
 network 192.168.1.0
 network 192.168.254.0
 no auto-summary
!
router bgp 200
 no synchronization
 bgp log-neighbor-changes
 network 192.168.100.0
 network 192.168.172.0 mask 255.255.252.0
 network 192.168.200.0
 neighbor 192.168.1.242 remote-as 100
 no auto-summary
!
ip route 0.0.0.0 0.0.0.0 Null0
ip route 192.168.50.0 255.255.255.0 Serial1/0
ip route 192.168.75.0 255.255.255.0 Serial1/0
!
```

Example 3-36 shows the resulting routing table at AngelFire. Referring to both this table and the physical interface addresses in Figure 3-8, you can see that Taos (192.168.1.218) is the next hop for prefix 192.168.250.0/24, and Sandia (192.168.1.230) is the next hop for prefixes 192.168.50.0/24 and 192.168.75.0/24. AngelFire also has default routes for both Taos and Sandia, and presently prefers Sandia as the default router. All packets that do not match a more specific route are forwarded to Sandia; there, they either match a more specific route that Sandia has learned via its EBGP neighbor, or they match the static default route to Null0 and are dropped.

Example 3-36 *AngelFire's Routing Table Shows the Results of the Redistributed Static Routes at Taos and Sandia*

```
AngelFire#show ip route
Codes: C - connected, S - static, R - RIP, M - mobile, B - BGP
       D - EIGRP, EX - EIGRP external, O - OSPF, IA - OSPF inter area
       N1 - OSPF NSSA external type 1, N2 - OSPF NSSA external type 2
```

```
         E1 - OSPF external type 1, E2 - OSPF external type 2
         i - IS-IS, su - IS-IS summary, L1 - IS-IS level-1, L2 - IS-IS level-2
         ia - IS-IS inter area, * - candidate default, U - per-user static route
         o - ODR, P - periodic downloaded static route

Gateway of last resort is 192.168.1.230 to network 0.0.0.0

D EX 192.168.75.0/24 [170/284160] via 192.168.1.230, 00:00:10, FastEthernet3/0
C    192.168.200.0/24 is directly connected, FastEthernet1/0
D EX 192.168.250.0/24
            [170/284160] via 192.168.1.218, 00:02:06, FastEthernet0/0
     192.168.254.0/24 is variably subnetted, 4 subnets, 2 masks
D       192.168.254.2/32
            [90/156160] via 192.168.1.230, 00:07:39, FastEthernet3/0
C       192.168.254.3/32 is directly connected, Loopback0
D       192.168.254.0/24 is a summary, 00:35:31, Null0
D       192.168.254.1/32
            [90/156160] via 192.168.1.218, 00:08:50, FastEthernet0/0
D EX 192.168.50.0/24 [170/284160] via 192.168.1.230, 00:00:27, FastEthernet3/0
     192.168.1.0/24 is variably subnetted, 5 subnets, 2 masks
D       192.168.1.0/24 is a summary, 00:35:32, Null0
D       192.168.1.224/30
            [90/2172416] via 192.168.1.218, 00:03:08, FastEthernet0/0
C       192.168.1.228/30 is directly connected, FastEthernet3/0
D       192.168.1.240/30
            [90/2172416] via 192.168.1.230, 00:07:40, FastEthernet3/0
C       192.168.1.216/30 is directly connected, FastEthernet0/0
D    192.168.100.0/24 [90/30720] via 192.168.1.218, 00:08:50, FastEthernet0/0
D*EX 0.0.0.0/0 [170/284160] via 192.168.1.230, 00:07:40, FastEthernet3/0
            [170/284160] via 192.168.1.218, 00:07:40, FastEthernet0/0
C    192.168.172.0/22 is directly connected, FastEthernet1/1
```

Some care must be taken when configuring the static routes. Because they have a much lower administrative distance, they replace the BGP routes to the specified destinations in Taos' and Sandia's routing tables. Therefore, the routes must point toward the EBGP neighbor, either by referencing the outgoing interface to the neighbor or the address of the neighbor's directly connected interface. Packets to the static destination are then forwarded to the external neighbor, where they match the neighbor's BGP route. A static route to a prefix more specific than the default route, and pointing to the Null0 interface rather than to a neighbor, will be dropped if it replaces a legitimate BGP route in the routing table.

Advertising a Default Route to a Neighboring AS

Although rare, at times an AS must advertise a default route to a neighboring AS. For example, some service provider networks might have control of the border routers in customer autonomous systems and want to originate a default route to those customer networks from their own border routers.

Example 3-37 shows Vail configured to send a default route to Taos, using the **neighbor default-originate** statement. Taos' BGP table (Example 3-38) has an entry for the default route from Vail. The previously configured static default route has been removed at Taos; if it remained, its administrative distance would override the default route entry in Taos' routing table and the BGP table would tag Vail's default route with a RIB failure.

Example 3-37   *Vail Is Configured to Send a Default Route to Taos (Neighbor 192.168.1.225)*

```
router bgp 100
 no synchronization
 bgp log-neighbor-changes
 neighbor 192.168.1.210 remote-as 300
 neighbor 192.168.1.225 remote-as 200
 neighbor 192.168.1.225 default-originate
 neighbor 192.168.255.2 remote-as 100
 neighbor 192.168.255.2 update-source Loopback0
 neighbor 192.168.255.2 next-hop-self
 neighbor 192.168.255.3 remote-as 100
 neighbor 192.168.255.3 update-source Loopback0
 neighbor 192.168.255.3 next-hop-self
 no auto-summary
!
```

Example 3-38   *Taos' BGP Table Shows the Default Route Advertised by Vail*

```
Taos#show ip bgp
BGP table version is 109, local router ID is 192.168.100.1
Status codes: s suppressed, d damped, h history, * valid, > best, i - internal,
              r RIB-failure, S Stale
Origin codes: i - IGP, e - EGP, ? - incomplete

   Network          Next Hop         Metric LocPrf Weight Path
*> 0.0.0.0          192.168.1.226         0           0 100 i
*> 192.168.1.200/30 192.168.1.226                     0 100 400 i
*> 192.168.1.212/30 192.168.1.226                     0 100 300 ?
*> 192.168.50.0     192.168.1.226                     0 100 400 i
*> 192.168.75.0     192.168.1.226                     0 100 400 i
*> 192.168.100.0    0.0.0.0               0         32768 i
```

```
*> 192.168.172.0/22 192.168.1.217      30720          32768 i
*> 192.168.200.0    192.168.1.217      30720          32768 i
*> 192.168.250.0    192.168.1.226                     0 100 300 ?
```

Although Vail (refer to Example 3-38) is now advertising a default route to Taos, it continues to advertise the prefixes from AS300 and AS400. The **neighbor default-originate** statement does not automatically block more specific routes from being advertised. This is useful when only a subset of prefixes must be advertised to the neighbor, and a default route is used to cover any prefixes not advertised. For the network referred to in Figure 3-8, for instance, perhaps the Sandia-Telluride link is to be used as the primary outgoing link from AS200, whereas the Taos-Vail link is used only as a link to the AS300 routes and a backup link for all other routes.

Of course, some policy must be set if only a subset of the known BGP routes are to be advertised with the default route. You saw a brief example of a policy for regulating what prefixes are redistributed into BGP, using a route map (refer to Example 3-14). An older tool for filtering prefixes is the **neighbor distribute-list** statement. Although route maps, prefix lists, and other policy tools tend to be preferred these days, the **neighbor distribute-list** can still be useful for simple filtering.

In Example 3-39, a distribute list is added to Vail's BGP configuration that permits prefix 192.168.1.112/30 and the default route, and blocks everything else from being advertised to Taos. The distribute list refers to access-list 1, in which the prefixes to be permitted and blocked are specified. Notice that the keyword **out** is used, to indicate that the filtering is applied to outgoing advertisements to the neighbor. As the keyword implies, you can also filter incoming advertisements from the neighbor with the in keyword.

Example 3-39 *Vail Is Configured to Block All Route Advertisements to Taos Except for 192.168.1.112/30 and the Default Route*

```
router bgp 100
 no synchronization
 bgp log-neighbor-changes
 neighbor 192.168.1.210 remote-as 300
 neighbor 192.168.1.225 remote-as 200
 neighbor 192.168.1.225 default-originate
 neighbor 192.168.1.225 distribute-list 1 out
 neighbor 192.168.255.2 remote-as 100
 neighbor 192.168.255.2 update-source Loopback0
 neighbor 192.168.255.2 next-hop-self
 neighbor 192.168.255.3 remote-as 100
 neighbor 192.168.255.3 update-source Loopback0
 neighbor 192.168.255.3 next-hop-self
 no auto-summary
!
```

```
access-list 1 permit 0.0.0.0
access-list 1 permit 192.168.1.212
access-list 1 deny    any
!
```

Example 3-40 shows the resulting BGP table at Taos. Comparing it to the BGP table referred to in Example 3-38, you can see that all the routes previously advertised to Taos by Vail, with the exception of the two permitted prefixes, are no longer in the table.

Example 3-40   *Taos' BGP Table Shows That the Distribute List at Vail Has Blocked All Advertisements from That Router Except the Default Route and 192.168.1.212/30*

```
Taos#show ip bgp
BGP table version is 125, local router ID is 192.168.100.1
Status codes: s suppressed, d damped, h history, * valid, > best, i - internal,
              r RIB-failure, S Stale
Origin codes: i - IGP, e - EGP, ? - incomplete

   Network          Next Hop        Metric LocPrf Weight Path
*> 0.0.0.0          192.168.1.226        0          0 100 i
*> 192.168.1.212/30 192.168.1.226                   0 100 300 ?
*> 192.168.100.0    0.0.0.0              0      32768 i
*> 192.168.172.0/22 192.168.1.217    30720      32768 i
*> 192.168.200.0    192.168.1.217    30720      32768 i
```

Advertising Aggregate Routes with BGP

Route aggregation—the representation of routes to multiple destination prefixes with a route to a single, shorter prefix—can be useful in many networks, but it is a particularly important technique for keeping large BGP networks under control. A website called The CIDR Report[3] is instructive of how much the lack of aggregation hurts the modern Internet. Updated regularly, the report lists the top (usually 30) autonomous systems "…who if they aggregated their announced prefixes could make a significant contribution to the reduction of the current size of the Internet routing table." As this chapter is being written, the CIDR Report shows that with better aggregation the current Internet IPv4 routing table could be reduced by more than 236,000 entries—a 45 percent reduction.[4]

The same poor practices are following the Internet's IPv6 routing table. As of this writing, the CIDR report shows that better aggregation could reduce the IPv6 table by 25 percent.

---

[3] www.cidr-report.org/as2.0/

[4] IPv4 address depletion is making the problem worse. Advertised IPv4 prefixes are becoming more and more fragmented as operators try to squeeze the last few addresses out of the public IPv4 space.

The CIDR Report also lists the autonomous systems that have added or withdrawn the most routes in the past 7 days. Each added or withdrawn route decreases the stability of the Internet by a tiny amount, and better aggregation could eliminate many of those destabilizing changes.

Note Before the advent of CIDR, the terms summarization and aggregation were used somewhat differently. *Summarization* usually referred to the grouping of more-specific routes to a class A, B, or C address block, whereas *aggregation* meant the grouping of two or more class A, B, or C blocks (a "supernet"). With the removal of IPv4 address classes, summarization and aggregation now mean the same thing although aggregation appears to be the more popular term.

Chapter 1 discusses the concepts of route aggregation and its benefits and trade-offs in the section "Classless Inter-Domain Routing"; you are encouraged to review those concepts if they are not fresh in your mind. In brief, the benefits follow:

■ Reduced routing table size, and the reduction of resources consumed in the advertisement, storage, and processing of the table

■ Increased network stability by "hiding" changes of specific prefixes behind an aggregation point

These days, with cheap memory, abundant bandwidth, powerful processors, and better route lookup algorithms, routing table reduction is not as important as it once was; network stability is the main benefit of aggregation.

The possible price you pay for the benefits of route aggregation is a reduction in network layer reachability information, which can lead to

■ Less optimal route selection

■ An increased risk of routing loops and blackholed packets

Case Study: Aggregation Using Static Routes

Autonomous system 100 in Figure 3-9 contains eight 24-bit prefixes, all of which can be summarized with the 21-bit aggregate address 192.168.192.0/21. Stowe is learning the internal networks via EIGRP and is advertising the aggregate to Sugarbush via EBGP.

There are two methods for creating an aggregate address under BGP. The first is to create a static entry in the routing table for the aggregate address and then advertise it with the **network** statement. The second method is to use the **aggregate-address** statement. The **aggregate-address** statement is demonstrated in the next case study, whereas this one demonstrates the static route approach.

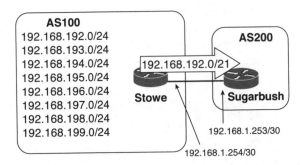

Figure 3-9 *All the Internal Prefixes of AS100 Can Be Aggregated into the Single Prefix 192.168.192.0/21*

Example 3-41 shows a configuration for Stowe using a static aggregate address advertised with the **network** statement.

Example 3-41 *A Static Aggregate Address Entry Is Created and Then Injected into BGP with the **network** Statement*

```
router eigrp 100
 network 192.168.199.0
!
router bgp 100
 network 192.168.192.0 mask 255.255.248.0
 neighbor 192.168.1.253 remote-as 200
!
ip classless
ip route 192.168.192.0 255.255.248.0 Null0
```

The static route is pointed at the null interface because the aggregate is not a legitimate end destination. It merely represents the more-specific routes in Stowe's routing table. Packets whose destination addresses belong to one of AS100's prefixes match the aggregate address in routers external to AS100 and are forwarded to Stowe. At that router, the packet is matched to the more-specific address and forwarded to the correct internal next-hop router. If for some reason the more-specific prefix is not in Stowe's routing table, the packet is forwarded to the null interface and dropped.

Example 3-42 shows the BGP tables of Stowe and Sugarbush. Only the aggregate address exists in Stowe's BGP table; that router's BGP configuration has not entered any of the more specific addresses.

Example 3-42   *BGP Tables of Both Stowe and Sugarbush Contain Only the Aggregate Route*

```
Stowe#show ip bgp
BGP table version is 2, local router ID is 192.168.199.2
Status codes: s suppressed, d damped, h history, * valid, > best, i - internal
Origin codes: i - IGP, e - EGP, ? - incomplete


   Network          Next Hop            Metric LocPrf Weight Path
*> 192.168.192.0/21 0.0.0.0                  0          32768 i
Stowe#
```

```
Sugarbush#show ip bgp
BGP table version is 18, local router ID is 172.17.3.1
Status codes: s suppressed, d damped, h history, * valid, > best, i - internal
Origin codes: i - IGP, e - EGP, ? - incomplete


   Network          Next Hop            Metric LocPrf Weight Path
*> 192.168.192.0/21 192.168.1.254            0            0 100 i
Sugarbush#
```

Aggregation Using the aggregate-address Statement

In a simple topology like the one in Figure 3-9, a statically configured aggregate is normally sufficient. But as the topology and the routing policies grow more complex, the options available with the **aggregate-address** statement make that method more useful. The remainder of the aggregation case studies use the **aggregate-address** statement and its options.

For the aggregate specified by the **aggregate-address** statement to be advertised, at least one of the more-specific addresses belonging to the aggregate must be entered into the BGP table either through redistribution or the **network** command. Example 3-43 demonstrates a configuration for Stowe using the **aggregate-address** command and redistribution.

Example 3-43   **aggregate-address** *Statement Injects an Aggregate at Stowe*

```
router eigrp 100
 network 192.168.199.0
!
router bgp 100
 aggregate-address 192.168.192.0 255.255.248.0 summary-only
 redistribute eigrp 100
 neighbor 192.168.1.253 remote-as 200
```

Example 3-44 shows the resulting BGP tables at Stowe and Sugarbush. Stowe's table looks quite different than it did in Example 3-42: All the more-specific routes are included. However, Sugarbush's table looks the same. Only the aggregate address is advertised.

Example 3-44 *Stowe's BGP Table Includes All the More Specific Routes of AS100, but Only the Aggregate Is Advertised to Sugarbush*

```
Stowe#show ip bgp
BGP table version is 23, local router ID is 192.168.199.2
Status codes: s suppressed, d damped, h history, * valid, > best, i - internal
Origin codes: i - IGP, e - EGP, ? - incomplete


   Network          Next Hop          Metric LocPrf Weight Path
s> 192.168.192.0    192.168.199.1     2297856          32768 ?
*> 192.168.192.0/21 0.0.0.0                             32768 i
s> 192.168.193.0    192.168.199.1     2297856          32768 ?
s> 192.168.194.0    192.168.199.1     2297856          32768 ?
s> 192.168.195.0    192.168.199.1     2297856          32768 ?
s> 192.168.196.0    192.168.199.1     2297856          32768 ?
s> 192.168.197.0    192.168.199.1     2297856          32768 ?
s> 192.168.198.0    192.168.199.1     2297856          32768 ?
s> 192.168.199.0    0.0.0.0                 0          32768 ?
Stowe#
```

```
Sugarbush#show ip bgp
BGP table version is 2, local router ID is 172.17.3.1
Status codes: s suppressed, d damped, h history, * valid, > best, i - internal
Origin codes: i - IGP, e - EGP, ? - incomplete


   Network          Next Hop          Metric LocPrf Weight Path
*> 192.168.192.0/21 192.168.1.254                      0 100 i
Sugarbush#
```

The keys to the left of the more-specific routes in Stowe's BGP table indicate that the routes have been suppressed. This is the result of the **summary-only** option used with the **aggregate-address** statement. Without that option, both the aggregate and the more-specific routes are advertised.

Although advertising both the aggregate and the more-specific routes makes no sense in the simple topology of Figure 3-9, Figure 3-10 shows a scenario in which such a scheme can be desirable. Here, AS100 is multihomed to AS200. AS200 needs the full routes from AS100 to set policy for the routes to AS100 but must send only the aggregate to AS300.

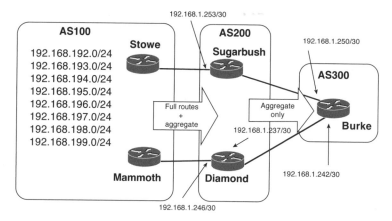

Figure 3-10 *AS100 Is Multihomed to AS200, and the More Specific Routes Are Required for Better Path Choices in That Neighboring AS. Only the Aggregate, However, Should Be Advertised Beyond ASS200*

An option of the COMMUNITY path attribute, called NO_EXPORT, is useful in this situation. (The COMMUNITY attribute is demonstrated more completely in Chapter 5, "Scaling BGP." This case study gives you just a brief example of one of its uses.) The NO_EXPORT community is a well-known option recognized by other routers; a router that receives routes with this attribute can advertise the routes to IBGP peers but not to EBGP peers. That is, the routes can be advertised throughout the local AS but cannot be advertised to other autonomous systems.

Example 3-45 shows the configuration for Stowe in Figure 3-10. The configuration for Mammoth is similar, and is shown later in this section. The **summary-only** keyword has been removed from the **aggregate-address** statement so that both the aggregate and the more-specific routes are advertised to AS200. The **neighbor 192.168.1.253 send-community** statement specifies that the COMMUNITY attribute be allowed in routes sent to Sugarbush. The **neighbor 192.168.1.253 route-map COMMUNITY out** command filters outgoing BGP routes through a route map named COMMUNITY. If the route map matches the update to access list 101, no COMMUNITY attribute is set, and the **set community none** statement removes any existing communities before the prefix is sent. If the route does not match access list 101, the route is given a COMMUNITY attribute of NO_EXPORT.

Example 3-45 *Stowe Is Configured to Advertise Both the Aggregate and the More-Specific Routes, and to Add the COMMUNITY NO_ADVERTISE Attribute to the More-specific Routes*

```
router eigrp 100
 network 192.168.199.0
!
router bgp 100
 aggregate-address 192.168.192.0 255.255.248.0
 redistribute eigrp 100
 neighbor 192.168.1.253 remote-as 200
 neighbor 192.168.1.253 send-community
 neighbor 192.168.1.253 route-map COMMUNITY out
!
ip classless
!
access-list 101 permit ip host 192.168.192.0 host 255.255.248.0
!
route-map COMMUNITY permit 10
 match ip address 101
 set community none
!
route-map COMMUNITY permit 20
 set community no-export
```

The usage of access list 101 in this example may be new to you. Normally, the first address specified in an extended IP access list is the source address, and the second address is the destination. But in this application, the first address is the route prefix and the second address is the prefix's mask. The reason such an odd access list is necessary is because the exact prefix must be identified. If **access-list 1 permit 192.168.192.0 0.0.7.255** were used, it would match both the aggregate 192.168.192.0/21 and the more-specific route 192.168.192.0/24.

Example 3-46 shows Sugarbush's BGP table, and you can see that it contains both the aggregate route and the more-specific routes. In addition, the command **show ip bgp community no-export** displays the routes with the NO_EXPORT COMMUNITY attribute. All routes from Stowe except for the aggregate are listed.

Example 3-46 *Sugarbush's BGP Table Contains Both the Aggregate Route and the More-specific Routes; All the Routes from Stowe Except for the Aggregate Have the* **COMMUNITY NO_EXPORT** *Attribute*

```
Sugarbush#show ip bgp
BGP table version is 30, local router ID is 172.17.3.1
Status codes: s suppressed, d damped, h history, * valid, > best, i - internal
Origin codes: i - IGP, e - EGP, ? - incomplete
```

```
   Network          Next Hop          Metric LocPrf Weight Path
 * i192.168.192.0    192.168.1.237     2297856   100     0 100 ?
 *>                  192.168.1.254     2297856           0 100 ?
 * i192.168.192.0/21 192.168.1.237               100     0 100 i
 *>                  192.168.1.254                       0 100 i
 * i192.168.193.0    192.168.1.237     2297856   100     0 100 ?
 *>                  192.168.1.254     2297856           0 100 ?
 * i192.168.194.0    192.168.1.237     2297856   100     0 100 ?
 *>                  192.168.1.254     2297856           0 100 ?
 * i192.168.195.0    192.168.1.237     2297856   100     0 100 ?
 *>                  192.168.1.254     2297856           0 100 ?
 * i192.168.196.0    192.168.1.237     2297856   100     0 100 ?
 *>                  192.168.1.254     2297856           0 100 ?
 * i192.168.197.0    192.168.1.237     2297856   100     0 100 ?
 *>                  192.168.1.254     2297856           0 100 ?
 *>i192.168.198.0    192.168.1.237           0   100     0 100 ?
 *                   192.168.1.254     2681856           0 100 ?
 * i192.168.199.0    192.168.1.237     2681856   100     0 100 ?
 *>                  192.168.1.254           0           0 100 ?


Sugarbush#show ip bgp community no-export
BGP table version is 10, local router ID is 172.17.3.1
Status codes: s suppressed, d damped, h history, * valid, > best, i - internal
Origin codes: i - IGP, e - EGP, ? - incomplete

   Network          Next Hop          Metric LocPrf Weight Path
 *> 192.168.192.0    192.168.1.254     2297856           0 100 ?
 *> 192.168.193.0    192.168.1.254     2297856           0 100 ?
 *> 192.168.194.0    192.168.1.254     2297856           0 100 ?
 *> 192.168.195.0    192.168.1.254     2297856           0 100 ?
 *> 192.168.196.0    192.168.1.254     2297856           0 100 ?
 *> 192.168.197.0    192.168.1.254     2297856           0 100 ?
 *  192.168.198.0    192.168.1.254     2681856           0 100 ?
 *> 192.168.199.0    192.168.1.254           0           0 100 ?
Sugarbush#
```

The access list usage in Stowe's configuration of Example 3-45 is dated, and as explained previously the access list configuration might be confusing. Luckily, there is another tool that you can use for the same end result: prefix lists. Example 3-47 shows Mammoth's configuration, using a prefix list to perform the same function as Stowe's access list in Example 3-45. You can readily see that with the CIDR notation, the prefix list is easier to interpret. Prefix lists are the preferred tool for matching a set of prefixes in BGP policies; they can be much more flexible than what is demonstrated in this example and are explained more fully in Chapter 4.

Example 3-47   *Configuration for Mammoth Uses a Prefix List Instead of an Access List to Identify Which Prefixes Should Have the COMMUNITY Attribute*

```
router eigrp 100
 network 192.168.198.0
!
router bgp 100
 aggregate-address 192.168.192.0 255.255.248.0
 redistribute eigrp 100
 neighbor 192.168.1.246 remote-as 200
 neighbor 192.168.1.246 send-community
 neighbor 192.168.1.246 route-map COMMUNITY out
!
ip classless
ip route 192.168.255.251 255.255.255.255 192.168.1.205
!
!
ip prefix-list AGGREGATE seq 5 permit 192.168.192.0/21
!
route-map COMMUNITY permit 10
 match ip address prefix-list AGGREGATE
 set community none
!
route-map COMMUNITY permit 20
 set community no-export
```

Like route maps, prefix lists are identified by a name, rather than by a number. In Example 3-47, the prefix list is named AGGREGATE. The lines of the list are distinguished by a sequence number (**seq**) that identifies each line's place in a multiple-line list and makes editing the list easier. If you do not type a sequence number when you enter a line, Cisco IOS enters it automatically in the order that you enter the lines. Following the **permit** | **deny** keyword, a prefix and the prefix length is specified.

Example 3-48 shows Burke's BGP table. No routes except the aggregate have been advertised because Sugarbush and Diamond have suppressed all routes that have the NO_EXPORT COMMUNITY attribute. Again, no configuration is required for those two routers to suppress the routes; they are following default behavior.

Example 3-48   *Burke's BGP Table Contains Only the Aggregate Route, Advertised by Sugarbush (192.168.1.249) and Diamond (192.168.1.241)*

```
Burke#show ip bgp
BGP table version is 15, local router ID is 172.21.1.1
Status codes: s suppressed, * valid, > best, i - internal
Origin codes: i - IGP, e - EGP, ? - incomplete
```

```
   Network          Next Hop         Metric LocPrf Weight Path
*> 192.168.192.0/21 192.168.1.249                    0 200 100 i
*                   192.168.1.241                    0 200 100 i
Burke#
```

ATOMIC_AGGREGATE and AGGREGATOR Attributes

By specifying a prefix in the **show ip bgp** command, you can observe more details about the BGP table entry. Example 3-49 shows the details of the entries in Diamond's BGP table for the default prefix 192.168.192.0/21 and one of the AS100 prefixes, 192.168.199.0/24. Relevant to the discussion in the previous section, you can see that the more-specific route has the COMMUNITY NO_EXPORT attribute, whereas the aggregate route does not.

Example 3-49 *Specifying a Prefix After the* **show ip bgp** *Command Displays the Complete Entry in the BGP Table for the Route to That Prefix*

```
Diamond#show ip bgp 192.168.192.0 255.255.248.0
BGP routing table entry for 192.168.192.0/21, version 59
Paths: (2 available, best #1)
  Advertised to non peer-group peers:
    192.168.1.238 192.168.1.242
  100, (aggregated by 100 192.168.198.2)
    192.168.1.245 from 192.168.1.245 (192.168.198.2)
      Origin IGP, localpref 100, valid, external, atomic-aggregate, best, ref 2
  100, (aggregated by 100 192.168.199.2)
    192.168.1.238 from 192.168.1.238 (192.168.1.253)
      Origin IGP, localpref 100, valid, internal, not synchronized,
  atomic-aggregate, ref 2
Diamond#
Diamond#show ip bgp 192.168.199.0
BGP routing table entry for 192.168.199.0/24, version 58
Paths: (2 available, best #1, not advertised to EBGP peer)
  Advertised to non peer-group peers:
    192.168.1.238
  100
    192.168.1.245 from 192.168.1.245 (192.168.198.2)
      Origin incomplete, metric 2681856, localpref 100, valid, external, best, ref 2
      Community: no-export
  100
    192.168.1.238 from 192.168.1.238 (192.168.1.253)
      Origin incomplete, metric 0, localpref 100, valid, internal, not synchronized,
  ref 2
Diamond#
```

Two other attributes of interest are attached to the aggregate route in Example 3-49: One is a simple entry stating `atomic-aggregate`, and the other is an entry stating `aggregated by 100 192.168.199.2`. These two entries indicate the `ATOMIC_AGGREGATE` and the `AGGREGATOR` path attributes, which are attached only to aggregate routes.

To understand what these two path attributes do, it is useful to think of what affects an aggregate route might have on the BGP decision process. 192.168.192.0/21 and 192.168.199.0/24 are *overlapping* routes, in that the second route is included in the first route, but the first route (the aggregate) points to other more-specific routes than just 192.168.199.0/24.

When making a best-path decision, a router always chooses the more-specific path. But when advertising routes, you have several BGP configuration options for dealing with overlapping routes:

- Advertise both the more-specific and the less-specific route.

- Advertise only the more-specific route.

- Advertise only the non-overlapping part of the route.

- Aggregate the two routes and advertise the aggregate.

- Advertise only the less-specific route.

- Advertise neither route.

Chapter 1 emphasized that when route aggregation is performed, some route information is lost and routing can become less precise. When aggregation is performed in a BGP-speaking router, the information that is lost is path detail. Figure 3-11[5] illustrates the loss of path detail.

AS3113 is advertising an aggregate address representing addresses in several autonomous systems. Because that AS is originating the aggregate, it includes only its own number in the AS_PATH. The path information to some of the more-specific prefixes represented by the aggregate is lost.

The ATOMIC_AGGREGATE is a well-known discretionary attribute that alerts downstream routers that a loss of path information has occurred. Any time a BGP speaker summarizes more-specific routes into a less-specific aggregate (the fifth option in the previous list), and path information is lost, the BGP speaker must attach the ATOMIC_AGGREGATE attribute to the aggregate route. Any downstream BGP speaker that receives a route with the ATOMIC_AGGREGATE attribute cannot make any NLRI information of that route more specific, and when advertising the route to other peers, the ATOMIC_AGGREGATE attribute must remain attached.

---

[5] This illustration is a repeat of Figure 2-12 in Chapter 2.

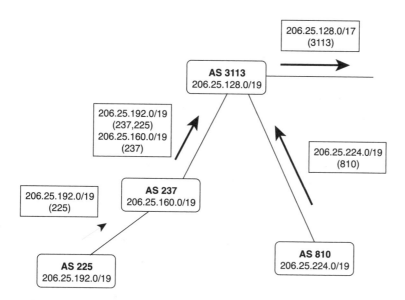

Figure 3-11 *Aggregation at AS3113 Causes a Loss of the AS_PATH Information of the Aggregate's Constituent Prefixes*

When the ATOMIC_AGGREGATE attribute is set, the BGP speaker has the option of also attaching the AGGREGATOR attribute. This optional transitive attribute provides information about where the aggregation was performed, by including the AS number and the IP address of the router that originated the aggregate route (see Figure 3-12). The IOS implementation of BGP inserts the BGP Router ID as the IP address in the attribute.

Referring to the entry for 192.168.192.0/21 in Diamond's BGP table in Example 3-48, you can see that there are two routes to the prefix: one advertised by Mammoth (192.168.1.245) and one advertised by Sugarbush (192.168.1.238). The second line of the display tells you that the first path—the one advertised by Mammoth—is the preferred path. The third and fourth lines tell you that this preferred path is advertised to Sugarbush (192.168.1.238) and Burke (192.168.1.242).

The AGGREGATOR attribute of the first route shows that the aggregation point is in AS100 and was aggregated by 192.168.198.2: That's the Router ID of Mammoth. The AGGREGATOR of the second route shows that it was also originated in AS100 but at 192.168.199.2, which is the Router ID of Stowe. Both routes have the ATOMIC_ AGGREGATE attribute.

Neither of these path attributes affects the BGP decision process and therefore are not policy tools. They can, however, provide useful references when troubleshooting an aggregate route. ATOMIC_AGGREGATE serves as a "tag" to remind you that the route is an aggregate; when examining a number of BGP routes, the ones that are aggregates might not be readily apparent to you, especially if you look at them far upstream of the aggregation point. AGGREGATOR, then, leads you back to the aggregation point.

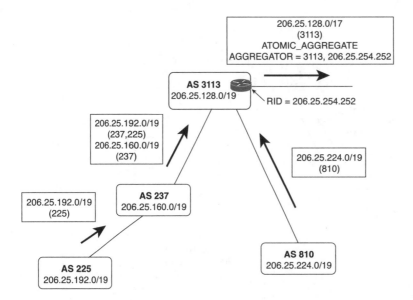

Figure 3-12   *ATOMIC_AGGREGATE Attribute Indicates That a Loss of Path Information Has Occurred, and the AGGREGATOR Attribute Indicates Where the Aggregation Occurred*

Using AS_SET with Aggregates

Recall from the discussion in Chapter 2, in the section "The AS_PATH Attribute," that one of the problems with loss of path detail beyond an aggregation point is that the BGP loop avoidance mechanism is weakened (refer to Figure 2-13 in Chapter 2). But the normal sequenced list of AS numbers in an AS_PATH attribute (AS_SEQUENCE) is not needed for loop avoidance; as long as the AS number is *somewhere* on the list, the path cannot loop back through that AS. To restore the loop avoidance information that would otherwise be lost at an aggregation point, an optional list called AS_SET can be added to the AS_PATH attribute (refer to Figure 2-14 in Chapter 2). The AS_SET is an unordered list of AS numbers and unlike AS_SEQUENCE can account for multiple paths to constituent prefixes behind an aggregation point.

Note   Although this section covers the use of AS_SET—because you need to understand how it works and what its intended use is—the IETF currently recommends not using it.[6] The reason for this recommendation has less to do with its effectiveness than that few ISPs and carriers actually use AS_SET for inter-AS aggregation, and those that do often use it incorrectly.

---

[6] W. Kumari and K. Sriram, "Recommendation for Not Using AS_SET and AS_CONFED_SET in BGP," RFC 6472, December 2011.

As you study this section, consider not just how AS_SET works, but also the relative likelihood of the kind of aggregation of routes from multiple other autonomous systems described here from a business standpoint. You'll probably correctly conclude that a single AS—representing a single provider or other business concern—is unlikely to aggregate routes from multiple downstream autonomous systems representing multiple other business concerns. You then understand why this tool is seldom used.

Figure 3-13 shows a modified version of the network referred to in Figure 3-10, including a change in the source of the aggregate address. Here, both AS100 and AS200 advertise the full routes of AS100 to AS300 and AS400 without an aggregate.

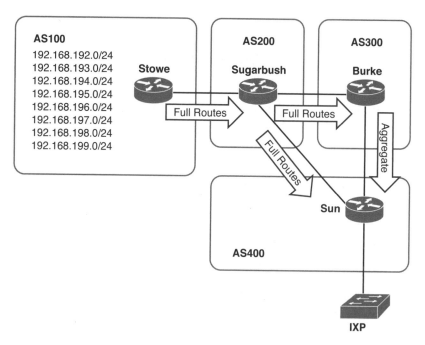

Figure 3-13   *Burke Is Creating an Aggregate and Advertising It to Sun*

Router Burke, in AS300, suppresses the more-specific addresses of AS100 and sends an aggregate to Sun in AS400. Burke's configuration is shown in Example 3-50. A filter implemented with the **neighbor distribute-list** statement prevents the aggregate from being advertised back to Sugarbush.

Example 3-50   *Burke Is Configured to Suppress Specific Addresses of AS100 and Send an Aggregate to Sun in AS400*

```
router bgp 300
 aggregate-address 192.168.192.0 255.255.248.0 summary-only
 neighbor 192.168.1.234 remote-as 400
 neighbor 192.168.1.234 next-hop-self
 neighbor 192.168.1.249 remote-as 200
 neighbor 192.168.1.249 distribute-list 1 out
!
access-list 1 deny    192.168.192.0
access-list 1 permit any
```

Example 3-51 shows the BGP table at Sun. As expected, the table includes the more-specific routes from Sugarbush and the aggregate route from Burke. Of interest to this case study is the AS_PATH associated with the aggregate. The AS_SEQUENCE of the AS_PATH attribute of an aggregate begins with the AS in which the aggregate was origi-nated. Burke originated the aggregate, so the AS_SEQUENCE includes only AS300. The aggregate actually points to destinations in AS100; like any summarization, the aggregate has caused a loss of routing information.

Example 3-51   *AS_PATH of the Aggregate from Burke Includes Only AS300, the AS in Which the Aggregate Was Originated*

```
Sun#show ip bgp
BGP table version is 20, local router ID is 192.168.1.234
Status codes: s suppressed, d damped, h history, * valid, > best, i - internal
Origin codes: i - IGP, e - EGP, ? - incomplete


   Network          Next Hop          Metric LocPrf Weight Path
*> 192.168.192.0    192.168.1.229                      0 200 100 ?
*> 192.168.192.0/21 192.168.1.233                      0 300 i
*> 192.168.193.0    192.168.1.229                      0 200 100 ?
*> 192.168.194.0    192.168.1.229                      0 200 100 ?
*> 192.168.195.0    192.168.1.229                      0 200 100 ?
*> 192.168.196.0    192.168.1.229                      0 200 100 ?
*> 192.168.197.0    192.168.1.229                      0 200 100 ?
*> 192.168.198.0    192.168.1.229                      0 200 100 ?
*> 192.168.199.0    192.168.1.229                      0 200 100 ?
Sun#
```

In Example 3-52, Burke sets the ATOMIC_AGGREGATE and AGGREGATOR attributes in the aggregate to indicate that a loss of information has occurred.

Example 3-52 *Aggregate from Burke Has the ATOMIC_AGGREGATE and AGGREGATOR (Aggregated by AS300, RID 192.168.1.250) Attributes Set to Indicate a Loss of Path Information*

```
Sun#show ip bgp 192.168.192.0 255.255.248.0
BGP routing table entry for 192.168.192.0/21, version 23
Paths: (1 available, best #1)
  Advertised to non peer-group peers:
    192.168.1.229
  300, (aggregated by 300 192.168.1.250)
    192.168.1.233 from 192.168.1.233 (192.168.1.250)
      Origin IGP, localpref 100, valid, external, atomic-aggregate, best, ref 2
Sun#
```

In the case of the topology referred to in Figure 3-13, the loss of path information causes a problem. Unlike Burke, Sun does not have a route filter in place to prevent the aggregate from being advertised to Sugarbush. Because Sugarbush does not see its own AS number in the AS_PATH of the aggregate from Sun, it enters the aggregate into its BGP table (Example 3-53).

Example 3-53 *Sugarbush Accepts the Aggregate Route from Sun Because It Does Not Find Its Own AS Number in the Route's AS_PATH*

```
Sugarbush#show ip bgp
BGP table version is 19, local router ID is 172.20.1.1
Status codes: s suppressed, d damped, h history, * valid, > best, i - internal
Origin codes: i - IGP, e - EGP, ? - incomplete

   Network          Next Hop         Metric LocPrf Weight Path
*> 192.168.192.0    192.168.1.254    2297856          0 100 ?
*> 192.168.192.0/21 192.168.1.230                     0 400 300 i
*> 192.168.193.0    192.168.1.254    2297856          0 100 ?
*> 192.168.194.0    192.168.1.254    2297856          0 100 ?
*> 192.168.195.0    192.168.1.254    2297856          0 100 ?
*> 192.168.196.0    192.168.1.254    2297856          0 100 ?
*> 192.168.197.0    192.168.1.254    2297856          0 100 ?
*> 192.168.198.0    192.168.1.254    2681856          0 100 ?
*> 192.168.199.0    192.168.1.254          0          0 100 ?
Sugarbush#
```

If one of the more-specific routes from AS100 becomes invalid, Sugarbush should drop any packets destined for that network. But with the aggregate in place, the packets instead are matched to the aggregate route. For example, suppose the interface to network 192.168.197.0/24 in AS100 fails. Stowe advertises the fact, and the route to that destination is removed from all BGP tables. Next, Sugarbush receives a packet with a destination address of 192.168.197.5. Not finding the more-specific address, the router matches the destination to the aggregate and forwards the packet to Sun. Sun again finds no more-specific address, matches the aggregate, and forwards the packet to Burke. Burke, as the originator of the aggregate, has no more-specific address and drops the packet. The packet to an invalid destination has been unnecessarily forwarded across two extra router hops before being correctly discarded. The problem would be even worse if Sugarbush was advertising an aggregate to Burke. In this case, instead of the packet being dropped later than necessary, it loops until its TTL expires.

To remedy the problem, Burke can advertise an AS_SET in addition to the AS_SEQUENCE as part of the AS_PATH attribute, by adding the **as-set** keyword to the **aggregate-address** statement, as shown in Example 3-54. As discussed in Chapter 2, the AS_SET is an unordered list of the AS numbers along the path to the more-specific addresses that make up the aggregate. Unlike the AS_SEQUENCE, the AS_SET is not used to determine a shortest path; rather, its only purpose is to restore the loop detection functionality lost in the aggregation.

Example 3-54 *Burke Is Configured to Add the AS_SET to the AS_PATH Attribute of the Aggregate Route*

```
router bgp 300
 aggregate-address 192.168.192.0 255.255.248.0 as-set summary-only
 neighbor 192.168.1.234 remote-as 400
 neighbor 192.168.1.234 next-hop-self
 neighbor 192.168.1.249 remote-as 200
 neighbor 192.168.1.249 distribute-list 1 out
!
access-list 1 deny   192.168.192.0
access-list 1 permit any
```

Example 3-55 shows the resulting BGP table at Sun. All the AS numbers on the path to the more-specific addresses are included in the AS_PATH of the aggregate. When the aggregate is advertised to Sugarbush, that router recognizes its AS number of 200 in the AS_PATH and does not accept the route.

Example 3-55 *When Burke Is Configured to Include the AS_SET in the AS_PATH Attribute, All the AS Numbers on the Path to the Constituent Prefixes of the Aggregate Are Included*

```
Sun#show ip bgp
BGP table version is 10, local router ID is 172.21.1.1
Status codes: s suppressed, d damped, h history, * valid, > best, i - internal
Origin codes: i - IGP, e - EGP, ? - incomplete
   Network          Next Hop          Metric LocPrf Weight Path
*> 192.168.192.0    192.168.1.229                      0 200 100 ?
*> 192.168.192.0/21 192.168.1.233                      0 300 200 100 ?
```

```
*> 192.168.193.0    192.168.1.229                    0 200 100 ?
*> 192.168.194.0    192.168.1.229                    0 200 100 ?
*> 192.168.195.0    192.168.1.229                    0 200 100 ?
*> 192.168.196.0    192.168.1.229                    0 200 100 ?
*> 192.168.197.0    192.168.1.229                    0 200 100 ?
*> 192.168.198.0    192.168.1.229                    0 200 100 ?
*> 192.168.199.0    192.168.1.229                    0 200 100 ?
Sun#
```

You need to know that when the AS_SET is advertised, the aggregate route inherits all
the attributes of the aggregated routes. Referring to Figure 3-13, the AS_PATH of all the
more-specific routes is (300,200,100). As a result, the AS_SET appears in Sun's BGP table
as an ordered sequence, indistinguishable from the AS_SEQUENCEs.

Figure 3-14 shows a different topology. A new AS is added, and network
192.168.197.0/24 has been moved from AS100 to the new AS500. Burke still receives
the same routes, but now not all AS_PATH attributes match. As a result, the AS_SET is
now advertised as an unordered sequence, as shown in Example 3-56.

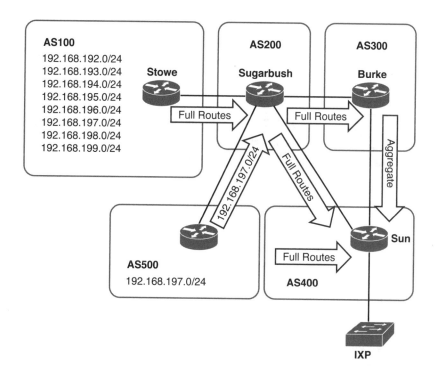

Figure 3-14 *Prefix 192.168.197.0/24 Is Moved from AS100 to AS500; Burke Can No
Longer Represent the AS_SET as an Ordered Set*

Example 3-56 *The AS_SET Now Displays in Sun's BGP Table as an Unordered Set, Distinguishable from the Ordered AS_SEQUENCE*

```
Sun#show ip bgp
BGP table version is 35, local router ID is 172.21.1.1
Status codes: s suppressed, d damped, h history, * valid, > best, i - internal
Origin codes: i - IGP, e - EGP, ? - incomplete

   Network          Next Hop           Metric LocPrf Weight Path
*> 192.168.192.0    192.168.1.229                      0 200 100 ?
*> 192.168.192.0/21 192.168.1.233                      0 300 {200,100,500} ?
*> 192.168.193.0    192.168.1.229                      0 200 100 ?
*> 192.168.194.0    192.168.1.229                      0 200 100 ?
*> 192.168.195.0    192.168.1.229                      0 200 100 ?
*> 192.168.196.0    192.168.1.229                      0 200 100 ?
*> 192.168.197.0    192.168.1.229                      0 200 500 i
*> 192.168.198.0    192.168.1.229                      0 200 100 ?
*> 192.168.199.0    192.168.1.229                      0 200 100 ?
Sun#
```

In some situations, you might want to advertise an aggregate with the AS_SET but do not want the aggregate to inherit all the attributes of all the aggregated routes. In Figure 3-15, Sugarbush receives all the routes from AS100 and AS500 and advertises an aggregate to Burke.

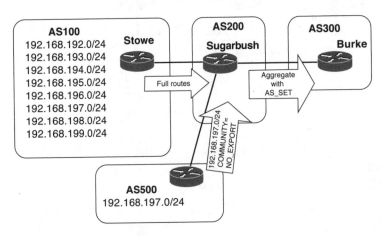

Figure 3-15 *For Sugarbush to Advertise the Aggregate with an AS_SET, the Aggregate Must Not Inherit the NO_EXPORT COMMUNITY Attribute of Prefix 192.168.197.0/24*

The problem with the setup in Figure 3-15 is that AS500 is advertising 192.168.197.0/24 with the COMMUNITY attribute of NO_EXPORT. When Sugarbush uses the AS_SET option, the aggregate inherits the NO_EXPORT attribute, as shown in Example 3-57.

Note that the NO_EXPORT attribute is given to the aggregate locally, not added to the advertisement of the aggregate. As a result, Sugarbush acts on the attribute and does not advertise the aggregate route.

Example 3-57 show ip bgp community no-export *Command Displays All Routes with the NO_EXPORT COMMUNITY Attribute; in This Case, the Aggregate Route Has Inherited the Attribute from One of the Aggregated Addresses, 192.168.197.0/24, and Is Suppressed as Indicated by the Status Code to the Left*

```
Sugarbush#show ip bgp community no-export
BGP table version is 19, local router ID is 172.20.1.1
Status codes: s suppressed, d damped, h history, * valid, > best, i - internal
Origin codes: i - IGP, e - EGP, ? - incomplete

   Network          Next Hop          Metric LocPrf Weight Path
*> 192.168.192.0/21 0.0.0.0                          32768 {100,500} ?
s> 192.168.197.0    192.168.1.1            0             0 500 i
Sugarbush#
```

The last option of the **aggregate-address** command to be discussed, **advertise-map**, enables you to choose the routes upon which to base the aggregate. Referring to the network in Figure 3-15, you can see that if Sugarbush does not consider 192.168.197.0/24 when forming the aggregate, the aggregate does not inherit that route's attributes. Example 3-58 shows the configuration for Sugarbush using the **advertise-map** option of the **aggregate-address** command.

Example 3-58 *Sugarbush Is Configured to Choose the Routes Upon Which to Base the Aggregates*

```
router bgp 200
 aggregate-address 192.168.192.0 255.255.248.0 as-set summary-only advertise-map
 ALLOW_ROUTE
 neighbor 192.168.1.1 remote-as 500
 neighbor 192.168.1.250 remote-as 300
 neighbor 192.168.1.254 remote-as 100
!
access-list 1 deny    192.168.197.0
access-list 1 permit any
!
route-map ALLOW_ROUTE permit 10
 match ip address 1
```

The **advertise-map** option in the configuration in Example 3-58 points to a route map named ALLOW_ROUTE, which identifies the more-specific routes on which the aggregate is based. The route map in turn points to access list 1, which rejects 192.168.197.0, and permits all other routes. Because Sugarbush now ignores 192.168.197.0/24 when forming the aggregate, the aggregate route does not inherit the NO_EXPORT attribute, as shown in Example 3-59.

Example 3-59   *After Sugarbush Is Reconfigured with the* **advertise-map** *Option, the Aggregate Route No Longer Has the NO-EXPORT Attribute*

```
Sugarbush#show ip bgp community no-export
BGP table version is 18, local router ID is 172.20.1.1
Status codes: s suppressed, d damped, h history, * valid, > best, i - internal
Origin codes: i - IGP, e - EGP, ? - incomplete

   Network          Next Hop          Metric LocPrf Weight Path
s> 192.168.197.0    192.168.1.1            0             0 500 i
Sugarbush#
```

Limiting the more-specific prefixes on which an aggregate is based can present some vulnerabilities. In the network referred to in Figure 3-15 and the associated configurations, suppose the link between Stowe and Sugarbush fails. The aggregate is based only on the prefixes from AS100 and is no longer advertised. As a result, the destinations within AS500 are no longer reachable from AS300 and beyond.

Looking Ahead

You should now have a good grasp of the various approaches to advertising prefixes over BGP adjacencies and most of the issues you might encounter when sending and receiving prefixes, such as interacting with the local IGP and advertising address aggregates. You have also seen several commands for observing and troubleshooting BGP prefixes. Finally, you have been introduced to a few IOS tools for configuring BGP routing polices. The next chapter delves further into the concepts of BGP routing policies, some of the attributes that are used for setting policy, and more IOS tools for creating and troubleshooting BGP policies.

Review Questions

1. What is a BGP NLRI?

2. How are prefixes added to BGP to be advertised? How is this different from the way prefixes are added to an IGP?

3. How does the BGP **network** statement differ in function from an IGP **network** statement?

4. What is the BGP table? How does it differ from the routing table, and how can it be observed?

5. When is the **mask** option of the **network** statement required?

6. Why is the **network** statement usually preferred over redistribution for injecting prefixes into BGP?

7. What is the RIB?

8. How is the Origin path attribute of a route injected into BGP with the **network** statement different from the Origin attribute of a route injected into BGP by redistribution?

9. What are the default rules for the NEXT_HOP path attribute when BGP advertises a route to an external peer and when BGP advertises a route to an internal peer?

10. How can the default BGP NEXT_HOP rules cause a problem within a single AS, and how can the problem be corrected?

11. How is the **neighbor next-hop-self** statement used?

12. What is the rule of IGP/BGP synchronization? Why is it seldom used in modern BGP networks?

13. Why is it generally considered bad practice to redistribute BGP into the IGP?

14. What is the preferred method of advertising AS-external routes through a multihomed stub AS, and why is it preferred?

15. What is route aggregation?

16. What are the main benefits and drawbacks of aggregation?

17. Why should the originator of an aggregate route point the next hop of the route to its Null0 interface?

18. What are the relative merits of using static aggregate routes and using the **aggregate-address** statement when injecting an aggregate route into BGP?

19. What does the **summary-only** option of the **aggregate-address** statement do?

20. What is the ATOMIC_AGGREGATE BGP path attribute?

21. What is the AGGRGATOR BGP path attribute?

22. What is the difference between AS_SEQUENCE and AS_SET?

23. What is the purpose of the **advertise-map** option of the **aggregate-address** configuration statement?

Configuration Exercises

Table 3-1 lists the autonomous systems, routers, interfaces, and addresses used in Exercises 1 through 12. All interfaces of the routers are shown as used in our solutions; you can use different physical interfaces depending on your available resources. For each exercise, if the table indicates that the router has a loopback interface, that interface should be the source of all IBGP connections. EBGP connections should always be between physical interface addresses, unless otherwise specified in an exercise. Neighbor descriptions are configured to be the router names.

Table 3-1   *Topology for Configuration Exercises*

AS	Router	Interface	IP Address/Mask
100	R1	Fa0/0	172.16.0.1/30
		G2/0	10.0.1.1/30
		G3/0	172.16.0.9/30
		Lo0	192.168.1.1/32
	R2	Fa0/0	172.16.0.5/30
		G2/0	10.0.1.10/30
		Lo0	192.168.1.2/32
	R3	Fa1/0	10.0.1.2/30
		Fa1/1	10.0.1.5/30
		Lo0	192.168.1.3/32
	R4	Fa1/0	10.0.1.9/30
		Fa1/1	10.0.1.6/30
		Lo0	192.168.1.4/32
200	R5	Fa0/0	172.16.0.2/30
		G2/0	10.0.2.1/30
		Lo0	192.168.2.1/32
	R6	Fa0/0	172.16.0.6/30
		G2/0	10.0.2.6/30
		Lo0	192.168.2.2/32
	R7	Fa1/0	10.0.2.2/30
		Fa1/1	10.0.2.5/30
		Lo0	192.168.2.3/32

AS	Router	Interface	IP Address/Mask
300	R8	Fa0/0	10.0.3.1/30
		G3/0	172.16.0.10/30
		Lo0	192.168.3.1/32
	R9	Fa0/0	10.0.3.2/30
		Lo0	192.168.3.2/32

1. Configure EIGRP as the IGP for AS100. AS100 internal routes should not be advertised outside the AS. All point-to-point links over which EBGP is run with routers in other autonomous systems should not be advertised into EIGRP. Inject the following prefixes into EIGRP at routers R3 and R4:

   10.100.64.0/20

   10.100.192.0/19

   192.168.100.0/24

   192.168.101.0/25

   192.168.102.128/25

   192.168.103.0/24

   192.168.104.0

   192.168.105.0/24

   The prefixes can be injected either by configuring them on a physical stub interface and running EIGRP on the interface or by configuring static routes to Null 0 and then redistributing static into EIGRP.

2. Configure OSPF as the IGP for AS200. OSPF area 0 spans the whole AS. AS200 internal routes should not be advertised outside the AS. All point-to-point links over which EBGP is run with routers in other autonomous systems should not be advertised into the AS. Inject the following prefixes into OSPF at router R7:

   192.168.198.0/23

   192.168.196.0/23

   192.168.200.0/26

   192.168.200.64/26

   192.168.200.128/26

   192.168.200.192/26

   192.168.201.0/24

The prefixes can be injected either by configuring them on a physical stub interface and running OSPF on the interface or by configuring static routes to Null 0 and then redistributing static into OSPF.

3. Establish EBGP peering between R1 in AS100 and R5 in AS200 and then another EBGP peering between R2 in AS100 and R6 in AS200.

4. Using the **network** command on routers R1 and R2, inject the following subnets into BGP:

10.100.64.0/20

10.100.192.0/19

192.168.100.0/24

192.168.101.0/25

192.168.102.128/25

192.168.103.0/24

192.168.104.0

192.168.105.0/24

Confirm that the injected routes are on routers R5 and R6 as expected.

5. Using IGP to BGP redistribution, configure routers R5 and R6 to inject the following subnets into BGP:

192.168.198.0/23

192.168.196.0/23

192.168.200.0/26

192.168.200.64/26

192.168.200.128/26

192.168.200.192/26

192.168.201.0/24

Use the necessary route filters to ensure that only the preceding subnets are injected into BGP and none other. When the configuration is completed, confirm that the routes are on routers R1 and R2 in AS100 as expected.

6. Configure a full mesh of IBGP peerings in AS100. Confirm that the routes injected into BGP by routers R5 and R6 in Questions 4 and 5 are in the BGP tables of all routers in AS100 as expected.

7. For internal next-hop reachbility for the routes learned over the EBGP sessions, use the recommended best practice method on routers R1 and R2 in AS100.

8. Provide next-hop reachbaility for the routes learned over the EBGP sessions for the routers in AS200 without amending the BGP configuration on routers R5 and R6 (that is, without using the **next-hop-self** statement). You may amend the IGP configuration, use static routes and use the **redistribute** command under the IGP configuration.

9. The network administrator of AS200 cannot run BGP on router R7 because of local policy restrictions. Configure routers R5 and and R6 to redistribute the EBGP learned routes into the IGP such that router R7 has reachability to all prefixes outside its own AS.

10. Configure OSPF as the IGP for AS300. OSPF area 0 spans the whole AS. AS300 internal routes should not be advertised outside the AS. All point-to-point links over which EBGP is run with routers in other autonomous systems should not be advertised into the AS. Configure router R8 to inject a default route into the IGP if it receives a default route from the ISP upstream router, R1.

11. Configure an EBGP session between router R8 in AS300 and router R1 in AS100. Configure router R1 to inject *only* a default route to router R8 while blocking all other prefixes. Confirm that router R9 is receiveing a default route from router R8 as a result of the injected default route over the EBGP session.

12. Using route aggregation, configure routers R5 and R6 such that AS100 routers use the link R1-R5 to reach subnets **192.168.200.0/26**, **192.168.200.64/26**, **192.168.200.128/26**, **192.168.200.192/26** and **192.168.201.0/24**, while providing a backup path for the rest of AS200's subnets and to prefer the link R2-R6 to reach subnets **192.168.196.0/23** and **192.168.198.0/23**, while providing a backup path for the rest of AS200's subnets, if the other link fails.

Troubleshooting Exercises

1. Figure 3-16 illustrates the topology for this exercise. Routers R1 and R2 are in AS100 and Routers R3 and R4 are in AS200. The IGP for AS100 is OSPF, and an EBGP peering is between R2 and R3. R2 is injecting the loopback addresses (192.168.255.1 and 192.168.255.2) into BGP and R3 is injecting the subnet 192.168.1.0/24 into BGP. However, when attempting to ping R3 to R1 or vice versa, the ping is not successful. Why? The relevant configurations and **show** outputs are illustrated in Examples 3-60 through 3-62.

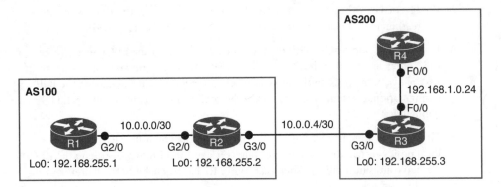

Figure 3-16 *Network Topology for Troubleshooting Exercise 1*

Example 3-60 *Failure of the ping Both Ways*

```
R1#ping 192.168.1.3 so 192.168.255.1

Type escape sequence to abort.
Sending 5, 100-byte ICMP Echos to 192.168.1.3, timeout is 2 seconds:
Packet sent with a source address of 192.168.255.1
.....
Success rate is 0 percent (0/5)
```
```
R3#ping 192.168.255.1 source 192.168.1.3

Type escape sequence to abort.
Sending 5, 100-byte ICMP Echos to 192.168.255.1, timeout is 2 seconds:
Packet sent with a source address of 192.168.1.3
.....
Success rate is 0 percent (0/5)
```

Example 3-61 *Configurations of R1, R2, and R3*

```
R1
!
interface Loopback0
 ip address 192.168.255.1 255.255.255.255
!
interface GigabitEthernet2/0
 ip address 10.0.0.1 255.255.255.252
 negotiation auto
!
router ospf 1
 log-adjacency-changes
```

```
 network 10.0.0.1 0.0.0.0 area 0
 network 192.168.255.1 0.0.0.0 area 0
 !
```

```
R2
 !
interface Loopback0
 ip address 192.168.255.2 255.255.255.255
 !
interface GigabitEthernet2/0
 ip address 10.0.0.2 255.255.255.252
 negotiation auto
 !
interface GigabitEthernet3/0
 ip address 10.0.0.5 255.255.255.252
 negotiation auto
 !
ip route 192.168.1.0 255.255.255.0 10.0.0.6
 !
router ospf 1
 log-adjacency-changes
 redistribute bgp 100 subnets
 network 10.0.0.2 0.0.0.0 area 0
 network 192.168.255.2 0.0.0.0 area 0
 !
router bgp 100
 no synchronization
 bgp log-neighbor-changes
 network 192.168.255.1 mask 255.255.255.255
 network 192.168.255.2 mask 255.255.255.255
 neighbor 10.0.0.6 remote-as 200
 no auto-summary
 !
```

```
R3
 !
interface Loopback0
 ip address 192.168.255.3 255.255.255.255
 !
interface FastEthernet0/0
 ip address 192.168.1.3 255.255.255.0
 duplex half
 !
interface GigabitEthernet3/0
```

```
 ip address 10.0.0.6 255.255.255.252
 negotiation auto
!
router bgp 200
 no synchronization
 bgp log-neighbor-changes
 network 192.168.1.0
 neighbor 10.0.0.5 remote-as 100
 no auto-summary
!
```

Example 3-62   show ip route *and* show ip bgp *of R1, R2, and R3*

```
R1#sh ip route
Codes: C - connected, S - static, R - RIP, M - mobile, B - BGP
       D - EIGRP, EX - EIGRP external, O - OSPF, IA - OSPF inter area
       N1 - OSPF NSSA external type 1, N2 - OSPF NSSA external type 2
       E1 - OSPF external type 1, E2 - OSPF external type 2
       i - IS-IS, su - IS-IS summary, L1 - IS-IS level-1, L2 - IS-IS level-2
       ia - IS-IS inter area, * - candidate default, U - per-user static route
       o - ODR, P - periodic downloaded static route

Gateway of last resort is not set

     10.0.0.0/30 is subnetted, 1 subnets
C       10.0.0.0 is directly connected, GigabitEthernet2/0
     192.168.255.0/32 is subnetted, 2 subnets
O       192.168.255.2 [110/2] via 10.0.0.2, 00:38:09, GigabitEthernet2/0
C       192.168.255.1 is directly connected, Loopback0
R1#
```

```
R2#sh ip route
Codes: C - connected, S - static, R - RIP, M - mobile, B - BGP
       D - EIGRP, EX - EIGRP external, O - OSPF, IA - OSPF inter area
       N1 - OSPF NSSA external type 1, N2 - OSPF NSSA external type 2
       E1 - OSPF external type 1, E2 - OSPF external type 2
       i - IS-IS, su - IS-IS summary, L1 - IS-IS level-1, L2 - IS-IS level-2
       ia - IS-IS inter area, * - candidate default, U - per-user static route
       o - ODR, P - periodic downloaded static route

Gateway of last resort is not set

     10.0.0.0/30 is subnetted, 2 subnets
C       10.0.0.0 is directly connected, GigabitEthernet2/0
```

```
C        10.0.0.4 is directly connected, GigabitEthernet3/0
     192.168.255.0/32 is subnetted, 2 subnets
C        192.168.255.2 is directly connected, Loopback0
O        192.168.255.1 [110/2] via 10.0.0.1, 00:38:06, GigabitEthernet2/0
S     192.168.1.0/24 [1/0] via 10.0.0.6
R2#

R2#sh ip bgp
BGP table version is 12, local router ID is 192.168.255.2
Status codes: s suppressed, d damped, h history, * valid, > best, i - internal,
              r RIB-failure, S Stale
Origin codes: i - IGP, e - EGP, ? - incomplete


   Network          Next Hop          Metric LocPrf Weight Path
r> 192.168.1.0      10.0.0.6               0            0 200 i
*> 192.168.255.1/32 10.0.0.1               2        32768 i
*> 192.168.255.2/32 0.0.0.0               0        32768 i
R2#
```

```
R3#sh ip route
Codes: C - connected, S - static, R - RIP, M - mobile, B - BGP
       D - EIGRP, EX - EIGRP external, O - OSPF, IA - OSPF inter area
       N1 - OSPF NSSA external type 1, N2 - OSPF NSSA external type 2
       E1 - OSPF external type 1, E2 - OSPF external type 2
       i - IS-IS, su - IS-IS summary, L1 - IS-IS level-1, L2 - IS-IS level-2
       ia - IS-IS inter area, * - candidate default, U - per-user static route
       o - ODR, P - periodic downloaded static route

Gateway of last resort is not set


     10.0.0.0/30 is subnetted, 1 subnets
C        10.0.0.4 is directly connected, GigabitEthernet3/0
     192.168.255.0/32 is subnetted, 3 subnets
C        192.168.255.3 is directly connected, Loopback0
B        192.168.255.2 [20/0] via 10.0.0.5, 00:33:00
B        192.168.255.1 [20/2] via 10.0.0.5, 00:32:30
C     192.168.1.0/24 is directly connected, FastEthernet0/0
R3#
R3#
R3#sh ip bgp
BGP table version is 4, local router ID is 192.168.255.3
Status codes: s suppressed, d damped, h history, * valid, > best, i - internal,
              r RIB-failure, S Stale
Origin codes: i - IGP, e - EGP, ? - incomplete
```

```
   Network              Next Hop          Metric LocPrf Weight Path
*> 192.168.1.0         0.0.0.0               0           32768 i
*> 192.168.255.1/32 10.0.0.5                 2               0 100 i
*> 192.168.255.2/32 10.0.0.5                 0               0 100 i
R3#
```

2. Refer to Figure 3-17. The AS numbers and IP subnets are indicated on the diagram.
    Router R1 in AS100 uses transit AS300 to access the subnet 192.168.200.0/24 behind
    router R2 in AS200. Although the subnet is installed in router R1's BGP and routing
    tables as it should be, the ping is failing. Why? The configurations of all five routers
    are listed in the examples following the figure. What other **show** commands may be
    helpful in this case?

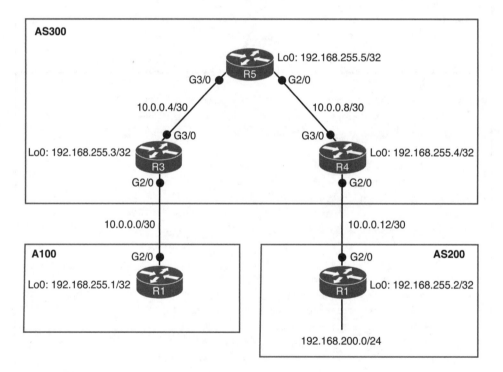

Figure 3-17   *Network Topology for Troubleshooting Exercise 2*

Example 3-63   *Failed ping*

```
R1#ping 192.168.200.2 so 192.168.255.1

Type escape sequence to abort.
Sending 5, 100-byte ICMP Echos to 192.168.200.2, timeout is 2 seconds:
```

```
Packet sent with a source address of 192.168.255.1
.....
Success rate is 0 percent (0/5)
R1#
```

Example 3-64 *Router Configurations*

```
R1
!
interface Loopback0
 ip address 192.168.255.1 255.255.255.255
!
interface GigabitEthernet2/0
 ip address 10.0.0.1 255.255.255.252
 negotiation auto
!
router bgp 100
 no synchronization
 bgp log-neighbor-changes
 network 192.168.255.1 mask 255.255.255.255
 neighbor 10.0.0.2 remote-as 300
 no auto-summary
!
```

```
R2
!
interface Loopback0
 ip address 192.168.255.2 255.255.255.255
!
interface FastEthernet0/0
 ip address 192.168.200.2 255.255.255.0
 duplex half
!
interface GigabitEthernet2/0
 ip address 10.0.0.14 255.255.255.252
 negotiation auto
!
router bgp 200
 no synchronization
 bgp log-neighbor-changes
 network 192.168.200.0
 network 192.168.255.2 mask 255.255.255.255
 neighbor 10.0.0.13 remote-as 300
 no auto-summary
```

```
!
```

R3

```
!
interface Loopback0
 ip address 192.168.255.3 255.255.255.255
!
interface GigabitEthernet2/0
 ip address 10.0.0.2 255.255.255.252
 negotiation auto
!
interface GigabitEthernet3/0
 ip address 10.0.0.5 255.255.255.252
 negotiation auto
!
router ospf 1
 log-adjacency-changes
 network 10.0.0.5 0.0.0.0 area 0
 network 192.168.255.3 0.0.0.0 area 0
!
router bgp 300
 no synchronization
 bgp log-neighbor-changes
 neighbor 10.0.0.1 remote-as 100
 neighbor 192.168.255.4 remote-as 300
 neighbor 192.168.255.4 update-source Loopback0
 neighbor 192.168.255.4 next-hop-self
 neighbor 192.168.255.5 remote-as 300
 neighbor 192.168.255.5 update-source Loopback0
 neighbor 192.168.255.5 next-hop-self
 no auto-summary
!
```

R4

```
!
interface Loopback0
 ip address 192.168.255.4 255.255.255.255
!
!
interface GigabitEthernet2/0
 ip address 10.0.0.13 255.255.255.252
 negotiation auto
!
interface GigabitEthernet3/0
```

```
 ip address 10.0.0.10 255.255.255.252
 negotiation auto
!
router ospf 1
 log-adjacency-changes
 network 10.0.0.10 0.0.0.0 area 0
 network 192.168.255.4 0.0.0.0 area 0
!
router bgp 300
 no synchronization
 bgp log-neighbor-changes
 neighbor 10.0.0.14 remote-as 200
 neighbor 192.168.255.3 remote-as 300
 neighbor 192.168.255.3 update-source Loopback0
 neighbor 192.168.255.3 next-hop-self
 neighbor 192.168.255.5 remote-as 300
 neighbor 192.168.255.5 update-source Loopback0
 neighbor 192.168.255.5 next-hop-self
 no auto-summary
!
```

R5
```
!
interface Loopback0
 ip address 192.168.255.5 255.255.255.255
!
interface GigabitEthernet2/0
 ip address 10.0.0.9 255.255.255.252
 negotiation auto
!
interface GigabitEthernet3/0
 ip address 10.0.0.6 255.255.255.252
 negotiation auto
!
router ospf 1
 log-adjacency-changes
 network 10.0.0.6 0.0.0.0 area 0
 network 10.0.0.9 0.0.0.0 area 0
 network 192.168.255.5 0.0.0.0 area 0
!
router bgp 300
 synchronization
 bgp log-neighbor-changes
 neighbor 192.168.255.3 remote-as 300
```

```
neighbor 192.168.255.3 update-source Loopback0
neighbor 192.168.255.4 remote-as 300
neighbor 192.168.255.4 update-source Loopback0
no auto-summary
!
```

Example 3-65   show ip route *and* show ip bgp

```
R1#sh ip route
Codes: C - connected, S - static, R - RIP, M - mobile, B - BGP
       D - EIGRP, EX - EIGRP external, O - OSPF, IA - OSPF inter area
       N1 - OSPF NSSA external type 1, N2 - OSPF NSSA external type 2
       E1 - OSPF external type 1, E2 - OSPF external type 2
       i - IS-IS, su - IS-IS summary, L1 - IS-IS level-1, L2 - IS-IS level-2
       ia - IS-IS inter area, * - candidate default, U - per-user static route
       o - ODR, P - periodic downloaded static route


Gateway of last resort is not set


B    192.168.200.0/24 [20/0] via 10.0.0.2, 00:09:51
     10.0.0.0/30 is subnetted, 1 subnets
C       10.0.0.0 is directly connected, GigabitEthernet2/0
     192.168.255.0/32 is subnetted, 2 subnets
B       192.168.255.2 [20/0] via 10.0.0.2, 00:09:51
C       192.168.255.1 is directly connected, Loopback0
R1#
R1#sh ip bgp
BGP table version is 4, local router ID is 192.168.255.1
Status codes: s suppressed, d damped, h history, * valid, > best, i - internal,
              r RIB-failure, S Stale
Origin codes: i - IGP, e - EGP, ? - incomplete


   Network          Next Hop          Metric LocPrf Weight Path
*> 192.168.200.0    10.0.0.2                            0 300 200 i
*> 192.168.255.1/32 0.0.0.0                0      32768 i
*> 192.168.255.2/32 10.0.0.2                            0 300 200 i
R1#
```

```
R2#sh ip route
Codes: C - connected, S - static, R - RIP, M - mobile, B - BGP
       D - EIGRP, EX - EIGRP external, O - OSPF, IA - OSPF inter area
       N1 - OSPF NSSA external type 1, N2 - OSPF NSSA external type 2
       E1 - OSPF external type 1, E2 - OSPF external type 2
       i - IS-IS, su - IS-IS summary, L1 - IS-IS level-1, L2 - IS-IS level-2
```

```
        ia - IS-IS inter area, * - candidate default, U - per-user static route
        o - ODR, P - periodic downloaded static route

Gateway of last resort is not set

C    192.168.200.0/24 is directly connected, FastEthernet0/0
     10.0.0.0/30 is subnetted, 1 subnets
C       10.0.0.12 is directly connected, GigabitEthernet2/0
     192.168.255.0/32 is subnetted, 2 subnets
C       192.168.255.2 is directly connected, Loopback0
B       192.168.255.1 [20/0] via 10.0.0.13, 00:10:26


R2#sh ip bgp
BGP table version is 4, local router ID is 192.168.255.2
Status codes: s suppressed, d damped, h history, * valid, > best, i - internal,
              r RIB-failure, S Stale
Origin codes: i - IGP, e - EGP, ? - incomplete

   Network          Next Hop          Metric LocPrf Weight Path
*> 192.168.200.0    0.0.0.0                0         32768 i
*> 192.168.255.1/32 10.0.0.13                            0 300 100 i
*> 192.168.255.2/32 0.0.0.0                0         32768 i
R2#
```

```
R3#sh ip route
Codes: C - connected, S - static, R - RIP, M - mobile, B - BGP
       D - EIGRP, EX - EIGRP external, O - OSPF, IA - OSPF inter area
       N1 - OSPF NSSA external type 1, N2 - OSPF NSSA external type 2
       E1 - OSPF external type 1, E2 - OSPF external type 2
       i - IS-IS, su - IS-IS summary, L1 - IS-IS level-1, L2 - IS-IS level-2
       ia - IS-IS inter area, * - candidate default, U - per-user static route
       o - ODR, P - periodic downloaded static route

Gateway of last resort is not set

B    192.168.200.0/24 [200/0] via 192.168.255.4, 00:11:01
     10.0.0.0/30 is subnetted, 3 subnets
O       10.0.0.8 [110/2] via 10.0.0.6, 00:15:01, GigabitEthernet3/0
C       10.0.0.0 is directly connected, GigabitEthernet2/0
C       10.0.0.4 is directly connected, GigabitEthernet3/0
     192.168.255.0/32 is subnetted, 5 subnets
O       192.168.255.5 [110/2] via 10.0.0.6, 00:15:01, GigabitEthernet3/0
O       192.168.255.4 [110/3] via 10.0.0.6, 00:15:01, GigabitEthernet3/0
C       192.168.255.3 is directly connected, Loopback0
```

```
B       192.168.255.2 [200/0] via 192.168.255.4, 00:11:01
B       192.168.255.1 [20/0] via 10.0.0.1, 00:22:31
R3#
R3#sh ip bgp
BGP table version is 4, local router ID is 192.168.255.2
Status codes: s suppressed, d damped, h history, * valid, > best, i - internal,
              r RIB-failure, S Stale
Origin codes: i - IGP, e - EGP, ? - incomplete


   Network          Next Hop         Metric LocPrf Weight Path
*>i192.168.200.0    192.168.255.4        0    100      0 200 i
*> 192.168.255.1/32 10.0.0.1             0             0 100 i
*>i192.168.255.2/32 192.168.255.4        0    100      0 200 i
R3#
```

```
R4#sh ip route
Codes: C - connected, S - static, R - RIP, M - mobile, B - BGP
       D - EIGRP, EX - EIGRP external, O - OSPF, IA - OSPF inter area
       N1 - OSPF NSSA external type 1, N2 - OSPF NSSA external type 2
       E1 - OSPF external type 1, E2 - OSPF external type 2
       i - IS-IS, su - IS-IS summary, L1 - IS-IS level-1, L2 - IS-IS level-2
       ia - IS-IS inter area, * - candidate default, U - per-user static route
       o - ODR, P - periodic downloaded static route


Gateway of last resort is not set


B    192.168.200.0/24 [20/0] via 10.0.0.14, 00:23:06
     10.0.0.0/30 is subnetted, 3 subnets
C       10.0.0.8 is directly connected, GigabitEthernet3/0
C       10.0.0.12 is directly connected, GigabitEthernet2/0
O       10.0.0.4 [110/2] via 10.0.0.9, 00:16:41, GigabitEthernet3/0
     192.168.255.0/32 is subnetted, 5 subnets
O       192.168.255.5 [110/2] via 10.0.0.9, 00:16:31, GigabitEthernet3/0
C       192.168.255.4 is directly connected, Loopback0
O       192.168.255.3 [110/3] via 10.0.0.9, 00:11:52, GigabitEthernet3/0
B       192.168.255.2 [20/0] via 10.0.0.14, 00:23:06
B       192.168.255.1 [200/0] via 192.168.255.3, 00:11:34
R4#
R4#sh ip bgp
BGP table version is 4, local router ID is 192.168.255.4
Status codes: s suppressed, d damped, h history, * valid, > best, i - internal,
              r RIB-failure, S Stale
Origin codes: i - IGP, e - EGP, ? - incomplete
```

```
      Network            Next Hop         Metric LocPrf Weight Path
*> 192.168.200.0      10.0.0.14              0           0 200 i
*>i192.168.255.1/32 192.168.255.3           0     100   0 100 i
*> 192.168.255.2/32 10.0.0.14               0           0 200 i
R4#
```

```
R5#sh ip route
Codes: C - connected, S - static, R - RIP, M - mobile, B - BGP
       D - EIGRP, EX - EIGRP external, O - OSPF, IA - OSPF inter area
       N1 - OSPF NSSA external type 1, N2 - OSPF NSSA external type 2
       E1 - OSPF external type 1, E2 - OSPF external type 2
       i - IS-IS, su - IS-IS summary, L1 - IS-IS level-1, L2 - IS-IS level-2
       ia - IS-IS inter area, * - candidate default, U - per-user static route
       o - ODR, P - periodic downloaded static route

Gateway of last resort is not set


     10.0.0.0/30 is subnetted, 2 subnets
C       10.0.0.8 is directly connected, GigabitEthernet2/0
C       10.0.0.4 is directly connected, GigabitEthernet3/0
     192.168.255.0/32 is subnetted, 3 subnets
C       192.168.255.5 is directly connected, Loopback0
O       192.168.255.4 [110/2] via 10.0.0.10, 00:18:03, GigabitEthernet2/0
O       192.168.255.3 [110/2] via 10.0.0.5, 00:12:25, GigabitEthernet3/0
R5#
R5#sh ip bgp
BGP table version is 1, local router ID is 192.168.255.5
Status codes: s suppressed, d damped, h history, * valid, > best, i - internal,
              r RIB-failure, S Stale
Origin codes: i - IGP, e - EGP, ? - incomplete


      Network            Next Hop         Metric LocPrf Weight Path
*  i192.168.200.0      192.168.255.4          0     100   0 200 i
*  i192.168.255.1/32 192.168.255.3           0     100   0 100 i
*  i192.168.255.2/32 192.168.255.4           0     100   0 200 i
R5#
```

Chapter 4

BGP and Routing Policies

No other IP routing protocol has the range of tools and attributes for imposing routing policies that BGP has. It is these policy capabilities that make BGP so powerful. You can also do great damage to your network, and even other peoples' networks, if you use these capabilities incorrectly. This chapter takes an in-depth tour of BGP policy tools, how to use them correctly, and how to troubleshoot them when things go wrong.

Webster's dictionary defines policy as a "...course or method of action selected from among alternatives and in light of given conditions to guide and determine present and future decisions." That general definition serves us well in defining routing policy. A routing policy is

- A set of rules for choosing a route to a destination
- When there are alternative routes to the destination
- Designed to comply with wider objectives for network behavior

Every routing protocol—not just BGP—has a defined set of rules for determining the "best path" among a set of alternate paths to a destination. So you might say that the first two bullets, taken alone, define the normal decision process for a routing protocol. It is the last bullet that differentiates routing policy: You define a set of rules that modifies the routing protocol's decision process in some way to ensure a desired network behavior.

A routing policy can almost always be verbally expressed: "I want router A," for example, "to always prefer paths through autonomous system 1 when forwarding packets to destinations X, Y, and Z."

Turning the expressed policy into something the routing protocol can understand requires a tool to identify some characteristic of a route and to specify an action to take when a positive identification is made. You're already familiar with these kinds of tools: Access lists specify a match condition, such as the destination address of a packet, and an action to take upon a match, such as permit or deny. Routing policy tools work in much the same way, except the matches and actions apply to routes rather than packets.

There are a number of such tools available for setting BGP policy, such as:

- Prefix lists and distribute lists, which filter on an individual NLRI

- AS_PATH lists, which filter on the AS_PATH attributes of routes rather than the NLRI

- Regular expressions, which enable flexible, powerful pattern matching for some tools

- Route maps, which enable complex policy combinations

Combined with this toolset is an array of characteristics called BGP *path attributes* that the BGP decision process evaluates when choosing a best path to a destination. Some path attributes are mandatory and are attached to every BGP route; others are optional and are attached to BGP routes only when they are needed.

The mandatory path attributes (AS_PATH, NEXT_HOP, and ORIGIN) have been examined in the previous chapters. Chapter 3, "BGP and NLRI," introduced a few optional attributes such as ATOMIC_AGGREGATE and AGGREGATOR, which associated with route aggregation, and it briefly touched on COMMUNITIES used for policy scaling.[1] The previous chapters, particularly Chapter 3, also introduced you to some simple routing policy configurations.

This chapter continues to use the mandatory attributes, particularly AS_PATH, as it demonstrates the many ways in which policy tools can be applied. It also introduces you to two optional attributes, LOCAL_PREF and MED, and a Cisco proprietary attribute, Weight. These are used for expressing the relative preference of one route over another.

Before getting to either tools or attributes, however, it is important to first look at how policy configurations are applied to the BGP reachability information within a router and how changes to policy configurations are managed between BGP neighbors.

Policy and the BGP Database

In Chapter 2, "Introduction to BGP," the section titled "The BGP Decision Process" begins by describing how the BGP Routing Information Base (RIB) is divided into three parts:

- **Adj-RIBs-In:** Stores unprocessed routing information that has been learned from BGP Updates received from peers. The routes contained in Adj-RIBs-In are considered feasible routes.

---

[1] Chapter 5 examines the COMMUNITES attribute in depth, in the context of BGP scaling.

- **Loc-RIB:** Contains the routes that the BGP speaker has selected by applying the decision process to the routes contained in Adj-RIBs-In.

- **Adj-RIBs-Out:** Contains the routes that the BGP speaker advertises to its peers in BGP Updates. The outgoing routing policies determine which routes are placed in Adj-RIBs-Out.

Figure 4-1 illustrates how these three databases relate to each other and to the BGP decision process. All "raw" BGP routes that are received in BGP Updates from neighbors go into the Adj-RIBs-In database. The BGP decision process is applied, and the results of that selection process are added to the Loc-RIB database.

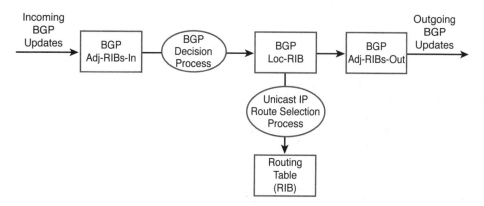

Figure 4-1   *Separation of the BGP Routing Information Base (RIB) into Three Parts Is Essential to the Application of Policy*

The information in Loc-RIB is used in two ways. First, it is evaluated by the local unicast IP route selection process. This process looks not only at the routes in the BGP Loc-RIB, but also at the routes learned by other unicast IP routing protocols, by locally configured static routes, and by local subnet connections. So, for example, if there is a route to a destination in the BGP Loc-RIB and a route to the same destination known by another routing protocol, the route selection process uses the administrative distance values assigned to different routing protocols to decide which route to select. The selected routes are added to the local router's routing table, more officially known as the Routing Information Base (RIB).

Example 4-1[2] shows a route in a BGP table that has been labeled as a "RIB-failure." This status indicates that the route is valid, but that the unicast IP route selection process has not installed it in the routing table. In Example 4-2, the command **show ip bgp rib-failure** is used to observe the reason for the RIB-failure. "Higher admin distance" indicates that this route has a higher administrative distance than another route to the same destination.

---

[2] Examples 4-1 and 4-2 are repeats of Examples 3-9 and 3-13 in Chapter 3.

Example 4-1   *A Route in the BGP Table Is Marked with a "RIB-failure" Status Code when the Route Is Valid, but the IP Unicast Route Selection Process Has Chosen a Route to the Destination from Some Other Process Tan BGP*

```
Vail#show ip bgp
BGP table version is 1129, local router ID is 192.168.1.226
Status codes: s suppressed, d damped, h history, * valid, > best, i - internal,
              r RIB-failure, S Stale
Origin codes: i - IGP, e - EGP, ? - incomplete

   Network          Next Hop          Metric LocPrf Weight Path
*> 192.168.1.0      192.168.1.225      28160          0 200 ?
*> 192.168.1.216/30 192.168.1.225          0          0 200 ?
r> 192.168.1.224/30 192.168.1.225          0          0 200 ?
*> 192.168.100.0    192.168.1.225          0          0 200 ?
*> 192.168.172.0/22 192.168.1.225      30720          0 200 ?
*> 192.168.200.0    192.168.1.225      30720          0 200 ?
```

Example 4-2   *The Reason Given for the Failure to Add the BGP Entry for 192.168.1.224/30 into the Routing Table (RIB) Is That Another Route to the Destination with a Lower Administrative Distance Was Chosen for the Routing Table (RIB)*

```
Vail#show ip bgp rib-failure
Network              Next Hop                    RIB-failure    RIB-NH Matches
192.168.1.224/30     192.168.1.225      Higher admin distance            n/a
```

In addition to providing information to the local routing table, the Loc-RIB sends its routes to the ADj-RIBs-Out database. The routes in this database are used to populate the BGP Updates that the router sends to its BGP peers. Looking just at Figure 4-1, the Adj-RIBs-Out appears to be unnecessary. Why not just use Loc-RIB to create the Updates to peers?

Figure 4-2 shows why Adj-RIBs-Out is needed. When an outgoing BGP routing policy is configured, it modifies the routes from Loc-RIB before they are added to Adj-RIBs-Out. Similarly, incoming BGP routing policy modifies the routes from Adj-RIBs-In before they are given to the BGP decision process.

A simple example will help clarify how incoming and outgoing policies relate to each other and how they effect BGP behavior. First, it is important to review the BGP decision process:[3]

---

[3] If you did not familiarize yourself with the IOS BGP decision process when it was introduced in Chapter 2, this is a good time to do so. Understanding the effects of most of the policy examples presented in this chapter requires an understanding of the BGP decision process.

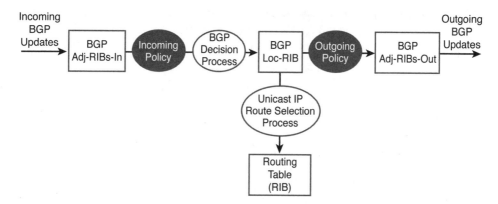

Figure 4-2 *Incoming BGP Policies Operate on the Routes in the Adj-RIBs-In Before They Go to the BGP Decision Process; Outgoing BGP Policies Operate on the Routes in Loc-RIB Before They Go to Adj-RIBs-Out to Be Advertised to Peers*

1. Prefer the route with the highest weight. This is an IOS-specific function, as described in the previous section.

2. If the weights are equal, prefer the route with the highest LOCAL_PREF value.

3. If the LOCAL_PREF values are the same, prefer the route that was originated locally on the router. That is, prefer a route that was learned from an IGP or from a direct connection on the same router.

4. If the LOCAL_PREF is the same, and no route was locally originated, prefer the route with the shortest AS_PATH.

5. If the AS_PATH length is the same, prefer the path with the lowest ORIGIN code. IGP is lower than EGP, which is lower than Incomplete.

6. If the ORIGIN codes are the same, prefer the route with the lowest MED (MULTI_EXIT_DISC) value. By default, this comparison is done only if the AS number is the same for all the routes being considered.[4]

7. If the MED is the same, prefer EBGP routes over Confederation EBGP routes, and prefer Confederation EBGP routes over IBGP routes.

8. If the routes are still equal, prefer the route with the shortest path to the BGP NEXT_HOP. This is the route with the lowest IGP metric to the next-hop address.

9. If the routes are still equal, they are from the same neighboring AS, and BGP multipath is enabled with the **maximum-paths** statement, install all the equal-cost routes in the Loc-RIB.

---

[4] IOS offers two alternatives to the default MED behavior, **bgp deterministic-med** and **bgp always-compare-med**; these alternatives are explained in Chapter 3.

10. If multipath is not enabled, prefer the route with the lowest BGP router ID or, if route reflection (Chapter 5) is being used, the route with the lowest ORIGINATOR_ID.

11. If the routes are still equal, and route reflection is being used, prefer the route with the shortest CLUSTER_LIST.

12. If the routes are still equal, prefer the route advertised from the neighbor with the lowest IP address.

AS500 in Figure 4-3 is advertising prefix 10.1.1.0/24 to peers in AS100 and AS200. Those two routers both advertise the prefix to Eldora in AS300, and Eldora enters both routes into its Adj-RIBs-In.[5] The decision process then evaluates the two routes. Everything about the two routes is equal until step 10 of the decision process is reached. The RID of the router in AS100 (Buttermilk) is 10.2.1.1 and the RID of the router in AS200 (Arapahoe) is 10.3.1.1, so the route through AS100 is selected as "best" (Example 4-3) and installed in the local routing table (Example 4-4).

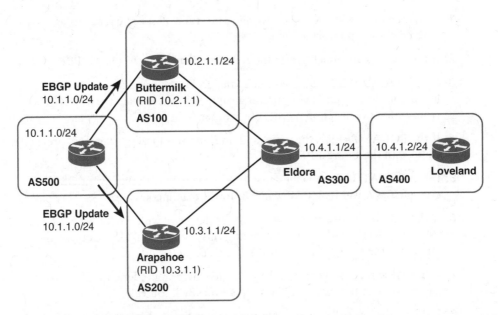

Figure 4-3 *Eldora Has Equal Paths to 10.1.1.0/24 Through AS100 and AS200*

---

[5] This description follows a generic model of BGP. As you will see in the next section, the actual IOS BGP implementation is slightly more abstract.

Example 4-3 *Eldora's BGP Decision Process Finds Everything About the Two Routes to 10.1.1.0 to Be Equal up to the Advertising Routers' Router IDs; the Route from the Peer with the Lower RID (10.2.1.1) Is Selected*

```
Eldora#show ip bgp 10.1.1.0
BGP routing table entry for 10.1.1.0/24, version 2
Paths: (2 available, best #2, table Default-IP-Routing-Table)
  Advertised to update-groups:
        1
  200 500
    10.3.1.1 from 10.3.1.1 (10.3.1.1)
      Origin IGP, metric 0, localpref 100, valid, external
  100 500
    10.2.1.1 from 10.2.1.1 (10.2.1.1)
      Origin IGP, metric 0, localpref 100, valid, external, best
Eldora#
```

Example 4-4 *No Protocol or Process with a Lower Administrative Distance Has a Route to 10.1.1.0/24, so the BGP Route Is Installed from the BGP Loc-RIBs to the Routing Table*

```
Eldora#show ip route
Codes: C - connected, S - static, R - RIP, M - mobile, B - BGP
       D - EIGRP, EX - EIGRP external, O - OSPF, IA - OSPF inter area
       N1 - OSPF NSSA external type 1, N2 - OSPF NSSA external type 2
       E1 - OSPF external type 1, E2 - OSPF external type 2
       i - IS-IS, su - IS-IS summary, L1 - IS-IS level-1, L2 - IS-IS level-2
       ia - IS-IS inter area, * - candidate default, U - per-user static route
       o - ODR, P - periodic downloaded static route

Gateway of last resort is not set

     10.0.0.0/24 is subnetted, 4 subnets
C       10.3.1.0 is directly connected, Serial1/1
C       10.2.1.0 is directly connected, Serial1/0
B       10.1.1.0 [20/0] via 10.2.1.1, 01:50:53
C       10.4.1.0 is directly connected, Serial1/2
Eldora#
```

Because the route through Buttermilk (10.2.1.1) has been chosen as the best route and marked as such in the loc-RIBs, that route is added to the Adj-RIBs-Out and advertised to Loveland, as shown in Example 4-5. Although the next hop of the route in Loveland's BGP table is Eldora (10.4.1.1) because of the EBGP NEXT_HOP rules, note that the AS_PATH passes through AS100 rather than AS200.

Example 4-5 *Eldora Advertises Only the Route from Buttermilk (AS_PATH 500, 100, 300) to Loveland*

```
Loveland#show ip bgp
BGP table version is 2, local router ID is 10.4.1.2
Status codes: s suppressed, d damped, h history, * valid, > best, i - internal,
              r RIB-failure, S Stale
Origin codes: i - IGP, e - EGP, ? - incomplete


  Network          Next Hop            Metric LocPrf Weight Path
*> 10.1.1.0/24     10.4.1.1                           0 300 100 500 i
Loveland#
```

Having established a baseline behavior for how BGP behaves by default, we can add a couple of policies and observe how they change the default behavior. Example 4-6 shows a very simple route map configured at Eldora that sets the ORIGIN attribute of any matching routes to "Incomplete." The route map is then applied to the session with Buttermilk (neighbor 10.2.1.1) as an incoming policy.

Example 4-6 *Eldora Is Configured to Set the ORIGIN Attribute of any Route Received from Neighbor 10.2.1.1 to "Incomplete"*

```
router bgp 300
 no synchronization
 bgp log-neighbor-changes
 neighbor 10.2.1.1 remote-as 100
 neighbor 10.2.1.1 route-map origin in
 neighbor 10.3.1.1 remote-as 200
 neighbor 10.4.1.2 remote-as 400
 no auto-summary
!
route-map origin permit 10
 set origin incomplete
!
```

According to step 5 of the BGP decision process, which compares the ORIGIN attributes, an ORIGIN code of "IGP" is preferable over an ORIGIN code of "Incomplete." By changing the ORIGIN of the route from Buttermilk to "Incomplete," the route from Arapahoe (neighbor 10.3.1.1)—which still has an ORIGIN code of "IGP"—is now the best route (Example 4-7). And because the route from Arapahoe is entered into the BGP table as the preferred route, that route is both entered into the routing table (Example 4-8) and advertised to Loveland (Example 4-9).

Example 4-7 *Eldora Chooses the Route from Neighbor 10.3.1.1 Because the ORIGIN Code Is More Preferable Than That of the Route from Neighbor 10.2.1.1.*

```
Eldora#show ip bgp
BGP table version is 2, local router ID is 10.4.1.1
Status codes: s suppressed, d damped, h history, * valid, > best, i - internal,
              r RIB-failure, S Stale
Origin codes: i - IGP, e - EGP, ? - incomplete


   Network          Next Hop           Metric LocPrf Weight Path
*> 10.1.1.0/24      10.3.1.1                0            0 200 500 i
*                   10.2.1.1                0            0 100 500 ?
Eldora#
```

Example 4-8 *Route from 10.3.1.1 Is Entered into Eldora's Routing Table*

```
Eldora#show ip route
Codes: C - connected, S - static, R - RIP, M - mobile, B - BGP
       D - EIGRP, EX - EIGRP external, O - OSPF, IA - OSPF inter area
       N1 - OSPF NSSA external type 1, N2 - OSPF NSSA external type 2
       E1 - OSPF external type 1, E2 - OSPF external type 2
       i - IS-IS, su - IS-IS summary, L1 - IS-IS level-1, L2 - IS-IS level-2
       ia - IS-IS inter area, * - candidate default, U - per-user static route
       o - ODR, P - periodic downloaded static route

Gateway of last resort is not set

     10.0.0.0/24 is subnetted, 4 subnets
C       10.3.1.0 is directly connected, Serial1/1
C       10.2.1.0 is directly connected, Serial1/0
B       10.1.1.0 [20/0] via 10.3.1.1, 02:32:45
C       10.4.1.0 is directly connected, Serial1/2
Eldora#
```

Example 4-9 *Route from 10.3.1.1 Is Entered into Eldora's Adj-RIBs-Out and Advertised to Loveland, as Indicated by the AS Path That Passes Through AS200*

```
Loveland#show ip bgp
BGP table version is 4, local router ID is 10.4.1.2
Status codes: s suppressed, d damped, h history, * valid, > best, i - internal,
              r RIB-failure, S Stale
Origin codes: i - IGP, e - EGP, ? - incomplete
```

```
    Network         Next Hop         Metric LocPrf Weight Path
*> 10.1.1.0/24      10.4.1.1                        0 300 200 500 i
Loveland#
```

The same route map is used in the configuration of Example 4-10, but now it is applied as an outgoing policy—indicated by the "out" keyword—to the Loveland adjacency. That is, the policy changes the ORIGIN attribute of routes taken from Loc-RIBs and added to Adj-RIBs-Out, but only the routes that are to be advertised to Loveland.

Example 4-10   *Eldora Is Configured to Set the ORIGIN Attribute of Any Route Advertised to Neighbor 10.4.1.2 to "Incomplete"*

```
router bgp 300
 no synchronization
 bgp log-neighbor-changes
 neighbor 10.2.1.



'Code of the Route to 10.1.1.0 is "IGP" in Eldora's BGP Table
```

Eldora's BGP table (Example 4-11) shows that the route from Buttermilk (10.2.1.1) is again the best route, because the outgoing policy does not effect the incoming routes. This route is also advertised to Loveland; but notice that while the ORIGIN attribute of the route in Eldora's BGP table is "IGP," in Loveland's BGP table (Example 4-12), it is "Incomplete." The **show ip bgp** command displays the contents of Loc-RIBs before any outgoing policy changes them.

Example 4-11   *ORIGIN Code of the Route to 10.1.1.0 is "IGP" in Eldora's BGP Table*

```
Eldora#show ip bgp
BGP table version is 2, local router ID is 10.4.1.1
Status codes: s suppressed, d damped, h history, * valid, > best, i - internal,
              r RIB-failure, S Stale
Origin codes: i - IGP, e - EGP, ? - incomplete

    Network         Next Hop         Metric LocPrf Weight Path
*  10.1.1.0/24      10.3.1.1              0           0 200 500 i
*>                  10.2.1.1              0           0 100 500 i
Eldora#
```

Example 4-12 *ORIGIN Code of the Route to 10.1.1.0 Is "Incomplete" in Loveland's BGP Table*

```
Loveland#show ip bgp
BGP table version is 7, local router ID is 10.4.1.2
Status codes: s suppressed, d damped, h history, * valid, > best, i - internal,
              r RIB-failure, S Stale
Origin codes: i - IGP, e - EGP, ? - incomplete


   Network          Next Hop          Metric LocPrf Weight Path
*> 10.1.1.0/24      10.4.1.1                            0 300 100 500 ?
Loveland#
```

Checking the result of an outgoing policy change at the BGP table of the receiving peer might not be the best approach. It worked in Example 4-12, but what if Loveland had an incoming routing policy configured that again modified the route from Eldora in some way before sending the route to its decision process? Or what if Loveland was receiving another route from another neighbor to the same destination, and its decision process chose that route rather than the one from Eldora? The resulting entry in Loveland's BGP table might be different from what is expected, or it might not be there at all.

If you just want to see what routes are being sent to a neighbor, you can use the command **show ip bgp neighbor advertised-routes**. Example 4-13 shows the command used at Eldora to observe the routes Eldora is advertising to Loveland (10.4.1.2). Notice, however, that the ORIGIN code is "IGP." You know from the display in Example 4-12 that the policy configured in Example 4-10 is working, so obviously this command shows the routes to the neighbor before the policy takes effect. Similarly, notice that the next hop is still 10.2.1.1; it has not yet been changed to Eldora's outgoing interface address.

Example 4-13 *Command* **show ip bgp neighbor advertised-routes** *Displays the Routes That Are to Be Advertised to the Specified Neighbor, but Does Not Show the Effects of Outgoing Policies. Here, the Policy Configuration of Example 4-10 Has Not Yet Changed the ORIGIN Code from "IGP" to "Incomplete"*

```
Eldora#show ip bgp neighbor 10.4.1.2 advertised-routes
BGP table version is 2, local router ID is 10.4.1.1
Status codes: s suppressed, d damped, h history, * valid, > best, i - internal,
              r RIB-failure, S Stale
Origin codes: i - IGP, e - EGP, ? - incomplete


   Network          Next Hop          Metric LocPrf Weight Path
*> 10.1.1.0/24      10.2.1.1               0            0 100 500 i

Total number of prefixes 1
```

The command **show ip bgp neighbor policy** (Example 4-14) can be helpful in determining what policies apply to a particular neighbor. In our simple exercise, it is easy enough to read the configuration and understand the routing policy; but, when an IOS BGP configuration includes many policies for many neighbors, the command can be instrumental in deciphering how the routes to and from a specific neighbor are being effected.

Example 4-14 *Command* **show ip bgp neighbor policy** *Shows What Incoming and Outgoing Policies Apply to the Specified Neighbor*

```
Eldora#show ip bgp neighbor 10.4.1.2 policy detail
 Neighbor: 10.4.1.2, Address-Family: IPv4 Unicast
 Locally configured policies:
  route-map origin out


 Neighbor: 10.4.1.2, Address-Family: IPv4 Unicast <detail>
 Locally configured policies:
  route-map origin out
route-map origin, permit, sequence 10
  Match clauses:
  Set clauses:
    origin incomplete
  Policy routing matches: 0 packets, 0 bytes

Eldora#
```

If **show ip bgp neighbor advertised-routes** displays the routes advertised *to* a neighbor, is there a command that shows the routes advertised *from* a neighbor? There is, although in Example 4-15 the command (**show ip bgp neighbor received-routes**) gives an unexpected response. Rather than display the routes from the specified neighbor, it says "inbound soft reconfiguration is not enabled" for that neighbor.

Example 4-15 *Command* **show ip bgp neighbor received-routes** *Displays Only Routes Received from a Neighbor if Inbound Soft Reconfiguration Is Enabled*

```
Eldora#show ip bgp neighbor 10.2.1.1 received-routes
% Inbound soft reconfiguration not enabled on 10.2.1.1
Eldora#
```

What the results of Examples 4-13 and 4-15 hint at is that while the theoretical structure of Figure 4-2 is useful for understanding how routing polices relate to the flow of information into and out of the BGP process, it is also important to understand how an individual router vendor implements BGP. The next section looks at the specifics of the IOS BGP implementation.

IOS BGP Implementation

The generic process flows depicted in Figures 4-1 and 4-2 help you to understand how incoming and outgoing policies relate to the flow, but they do not tell you anything about how those flows actually happen or how they are managed. It is up to an individual implementer to create software structures that not only adhere to the BGP standards but also interoperate with other BGP implementations and operate as efficiently as possible.

For example, the Adj-RIBs-In, Loc-RIB, and Adj-RIBs-Out are unlikely in a practical implementation to actually be three separate databases; instead, markers can be used in a single database to show where information in the database belongs. Adj-RIBs-In and Adj-RIBs-Out might, further, exist only as transient queues rather than permanent databases. This can sharply reduce the amount of memory BGP uses in a router.

InQ and OutQ

You have already seen, in numerous examples throughout Chapter 3, the IOS BGP table; this table is, for all practical purposes, the IOS implementation of Loc-RIB. Rather than Adj-RIBs-In and Adj-RIBs-Out, IOS uses queues called InQ and OutQ—one of each per neighbor—that hold routes only until they are advertised.[6] In Example 4-16, the InQ and OutQ for all three neighbors are empty; this is typical of IOS BGP in a steady state, where no routes are actively being sent or received. Although you will occasionally, by an accident of timing, see some prefixes displayed in the InQ or OutQ, consistent non-zero numbers in either of these columns are indicative of instability somewhere in the network. For instance, Example 4-17 displays the **show ip bgp summary** output from the Oregon Exchange route server,[7] connected to 43 neighbors and taking full Internet routes from most of them; yet even this router has no queued prefixes.

Example 4-16 *InQ and OutQ in an IOS BGP Implementation Serve as Transient Versions of the Adj-RIBs-In and Adj-RIBs-Out. That Is, Routes Being Received from or Sent to a Neighbor Are Temporarily Queued Rather Than Being Recorded in an Incoming or Outgoing Database*

```
Eldora#show ip bgp summary
BGP router identifier 10.4.1.1, local AS number 300
BGP table version is 2, main routing table version 2
1 network entries using 120 bytes of memory
2 path entries using 104 bytes of memory
3/1 BGP path/bestpath attribute entries using 372 bytes of memory
2 BGP AS-PATH entries using 48 bytes of memory
0 BGP route-map cache entries using 0 bytes of memory
```

---

[6] An exception to this is when **neighbor soft-reconfiguration inbound** is configured, in which case an IOS version of Adj-RIBs-In is enabled. The use of this option is discussed in the next section.

[7] Telnet to route-views.oregon-ix.net.

```
0 BGP filter-list cache entries using 0 bytes of memory
Bitfield cache entries: current 1 (at peak 1) using 32 bytes of memory
BGP using 676 total bytes of memory
BGP activity 1/0 prefixes, 2/0 paths, scan interval 60 secs


Neighbor       V    AS MsgRcvd MsgSent   TblVer  InQ OutQ Up/Down   State/PfxRcd
10.2.1.1       4   100       5       5        2    0    0 00:00:47            1
10.3.1.1       4   200       5       5        2    0    0 00:00:19            1
10.4.1.2       4   400       4       5        2    0    0 00:00:14            0
Eldora#
```

Example 4-17 *InQ and OutQ Should Normally Be Empty Unless There Is Instability in the Network. Here, a Router Receiving Full Internet Routes from 43 Neighbors Still Shows the Queues Empty*

```
route-views.oregon-ix.net>show ip bgp summary
BGP router identifier 198.32.162.100, local AS number 6447
BGP table version is 14911492, main routing table version 14911492
298165 network entries using 39357780 bytes of memory
8873171 path entries using 461404892 bytes of memory
1461075/54952 BGP path/bestpath attribute entries using 216239100 bytes of memory
1259136 BGP AS-PATH entries using 33839670 bytes of memory
24180 BGP community entries using 1717302 bytes of memory
26 BGP extended community entries using 882 bytes of memory
0 BGP route-map cache entries using 0 bytes of memory
0 BGP filter-list cache entries using 0 bytes of memory
BGP using 752559626 total bytes of memory
Dampening enabled. 2689 history paths, 13311 dampened paths
BGP activity 499245/195133 prefixes, 53977128/45082898 paths, scan interval 60 secs


Neighbor        V    AS MsgRcvd MsgSent    TblVer  InQ OutQ Up/Down   State/PfxRcd
4.69.184.193    4  3356 2026273   46235 14911493    0    0 1w6d        273991
12.0.1.63       4  7018 3606393   43403 14911493    0    0 4w5d        274811
64.71.255.61    4   812 4328756   71870 14911493    0    0 4d11h       275172
64.125.0.137    4  6461       0       0        0    0    0 never      Active
65.106.7.139    4  2828 2395239   71866 14911493    0    0 1w6d        277436
66.59.190.221   4  6539 2311776   71722 14911493    0    0 1w6d        275769
66.185.128.48   4  1668 2450491   68634 14911493    0    0 5d23h       276883
89.149.178.10   4  3257 3982094     449 14911493    0    0 5d22h       275085
114.31.199.1    4  4826  176045    4327 14911493    0    0 3d02h       278467
129.250.0.11    4  2914 6029121  141788 14911493    0    0 1w6d        275034
129.250.0.171   4  2914 6161875  141783 14911493    0    0 1d07h       275034
134.222.87.1    4   286 4665527     446 14911493    0    0 4w5d        275735
144.228.241.81  4  1239       0       0        0    0    0 never      Active
154.11.11.113   4   852 4194308   71820 14911493    0    0 5d23h       264445
```

```
154.11.98.225    4    852 3979914    71897 14911493     0    0 5d23h       264444
157.130.10.233   4    701 3488821   108254 14911493     0    0 1d07h       274310
164.128.32.11    4   3303 1445980    43403 14911493     0    0 4w5d        111574
192.203.116.253  4 22388  327289     43408 14911493     0    0 4w5d         12234
193.0.0.56       4   3333 7661277   141549 14911493     0    0 15:17:18    280499
193.251.245.6    4   5511 2799281    34566        0     0    0 1w3d        Active
194.85.4.55      4   3277 7214324    71914 14911493     0    0 15:17:20    279898
195.66.232.239   4   5459 2251224    43381 14911493     0    0 4w5d        184912
195.219.96.239   4   6453 3260525    43403 14911493     0    0 4w5d        274782
196.7.106.245    4   2905 2991282    71881 14911493     0    0 5d23h       274808
198.32.162.1     4   3582  147941   141794 14911493     0    0 4w5d             2
198.32.252.33    4 20080  130401     71868 14911493     0    0 11:29:54      5908
202.232.0.2      4   2497 3502275    43403 14911493     0    0 4w5d        275798
202.249.2.86     4   7500 2502215    71869 14911494     0    0 4d11h       280358
203.62.252.186   4   1221 2466972    43413 14911494     0    0 4w5d        279303
203.181.248.168  4   7660 2844825      450 14911494     0    0 2w5d        282005
205.189.32.44    4   6509  883836    21736 14911494     0    0 2w1d         12593
206.24.210.100   4   3561 3635923    43427 14911494     0    0 4w5d        274670
207.45.223.244   4   6453 3098773    43403 14911494     0    0 4w5d        274484
207.46.32.34     4   8075 3822700   141794 14911494     0    0 4d11h       277726
207.172.6.1      4   6079 2952579    71868 14911494     0    0 1w6d        275205
207.172.6.20     4   6079 2425627    71868 14911494     0    0 4d11h       275205
208.51.134.254   4   3549 8534043      464 14911494     0    0 4w5d        275442
209.10.12.125    4   4513       0        0        0     0    0 never       Active
209.10.12.156    4   4513       0        0        0     0    0 never       Active
209.10.12.160    4   4513       0        0        0     0    0 never       Active
213.140.32.146   4  12956 8075293    71883 14911494     0    0 5d23h       275709
216.218.252.164  4   6939 4436507    71885 14911494     0    0 4d11h       276068
217.75.96.60     4  16150 4127817    43416 14911494     0    0 2w2d        274682
route-views.oregon-ix.net>
```

IOS BGP Processes

There must also be processes that move information in and out of the databases and manage the information; just a hint of these processes is given in Figures 4-1 and 4-2, as the BGP Decision Process and the Unicast IP Route Selection Process.

Example 4-18 displays the actual steady-state processes of the IOS BGP implementation:

- I/O
- Router
- Scanner

Example 4-18   *Command* **show processes cpu** *Filtered to Display Anything Related to BGP Shows That There Are Four BGP Processes Running*

```
Eldora#show processes cpu | include BGP
  225        636        335     1898  0.08%  0.11%  0.12%   0 BGP Router
  226        120         75     1600  0.00%  0.04%  0.02%   0 BGP I/O
  227         92         10     9200  0.00%  0.07%  0.02%   0 BGP Scanner
  228          0          1        0  0.00%  0.00%  0.00%   0 BGP Event
Eldora#
```

The relationship among these processes is illustrated in Figure 4-4. The BGP Input/Output (I/O) process interfaces with the router's TCP socket. On the Input side, it assembles BGP messages received from TCP and puts the messages in the InQ. On the Output side, it takes BGP messages from OutQ and sends them to TCP.

> **Note**   Depending on the particular release of IOS that you're running, you might see more than these four processes running as a part of BGP. But the processes discussed in this section are the foundation processes and the most essential to understanding IOS BGP.

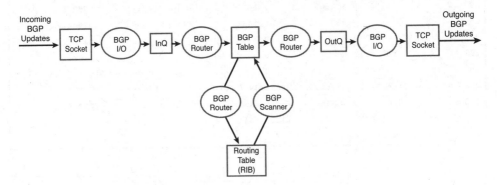

Figure 4-4   *IOS BGP Processes, Databases, and Queues Create a Practical Implementation of the Conceptual Components of Figure 4-2*

The BGP Router process performs the generic functions depicted in Figure 4-2. On the Input side, it takes BGP messages from InQ and processes them. When a message is an Update, it evaluates the routes with any configured incoming polices, runs the BGP decision process, and enters the appropriate information into the BGP table. On the Output side, the Router process takes routes from the BGP table, evaluates them with any configured outgoing policies, generates Update messages from the results, and adds the Update messages to the OutQ.

Locally, the BGP Router process takes routes that have been added, removed, or changed in the BGP table and tries to modify the information in the RIB accordingly. If the process tries to add a route to the RIB and cannot—for example because another route to the same destination exists in the RIB with a lower administrative distance—the process indicates a RIB-failure such as was shown in Example 4-2.

There must also be a process that can watch for any changes that might effect the information BGP has stored in its databases. For example, a change in the reachability of a next hop address in the RIB might make a previously valid BGP route invalid, or vice versa. Watching for such changes is the job of the BGP Scanner process.

The Scanner also evaluates prefixes in the RIB against configured **network**, **redistribute**, and **aggregate** statements, adds any default or configured path attributes to matching prefixes, and puts the resulting BGP routes into the BGP table.

Although keeping an eye on next hops and locally configured prefix injection is the most important job the Scanner does, it also performs a number of tasks such as managing the route dampening mechanism described in Chapter 5 and conditional route advertisements.[8]

Scanner activity is observed in Example 4-19 by enabling BGP event debugging. A quick read-through of the debugging messages shows that scans are run not only for unicast IPv4, but also for multicast IPv4, unicast and multicast IPv6, unicast VPNv4, and unicast ISO NSAP. Together, all these address types represent the routes that can be advertised by Multiprotocol BGP, discussed in Chapter 6, "Multiprotocol BGP." Highlighting is used in Example 4-19 to focus on just the unicast IPv4 scans.

Example 4-19   debug ip bgp events *Command Can Be Used to Observe BGP Scanner Activity*

```
Eldora#debug ip bgp events
BGP events debugging is on
Eldora#
*Mar  9 07:33:20.943: BGP: Performing BGP general scanning
*Mar  9 07:33:20.947: BGP(0): scanning IPv4 Unicast routing tables
*Mar  9 07:33:20.947: BGP(IPv4 Unicast): Performing BGP Nexthop scanning for general
  scan
*Mar  9 07:33:20.951: BGP(0): Future scanner version: 74, current scanner version: 73
*Mar  9 07:33:20.951: BGP(1): scanning IPv6 Unicast routing tables
*Mar  9 07:33:20.955: BGP(IPv6 Unicast): Performing BGP Nexthop scanning for general
  scan
*Mar  9 07:33:20.955: BGP(1): Future scanner version: 75, current scanner version: 74
*Mar  9 07:33:20.959: BGP(2): scanning VPNv4 Unicast routing tables
*Mar  9 07:33:20.959: BGP(VPNv4 Unicast): Performing BGP Nexthop scanning for general
  scan
*Mar  9 07:33:20.959: BGP(2): Future scanner version: 75, current scanner version: 74
*Mar  9 07:33:20.959: BGP(4): scanning IPv4 Multicast routing tables
```

---

[8] A conditional route is advertised or not advertised based on the status of another route; these are sometimes used in multihoming.

```
*Mar  9 07:33:20.959: BGP(IPv4 Multicast): Performing BGP Nexthop scanning for general
   scan
*Mar  9 07:33:20.959: BGP(4): Future scanner version: 75, current scanner version: 74
*Mar  9 07:33:20.959: BGP(5): scanning IPv6 Multicast routing tables
*Mar  9 07:33:20.959: BGP(IPv6 Multicast): Performing BGP Nexthop scanning for general
   scan
*Mar  9 07:33:20.959: BGP(5): Future scanner version: 75, current scanner version: 74
*Mar  9 07:33:20.959: BGP(6): scanning NSAP Unicast routing tables
*Mar  9 07:33:20.959: BGP(NSAP Unicast): Performing BGP Nexthop scanning for general
   scan
*Mar  9 07:33:20.959: BGP(6): Future scanner version: 75, current scanner version: 74
*Mar  9 07:33:35.959: BGP: Import timer expired. Walking from 1 to 1
*Mar  9 07:33:50.967: BGP: Import timer expired. Walking from 1 to 1
*Mar  9 07:34:05.979: BGP: Import timer expired. Walking from 1 to 1
*Mar  9 07:34:20.983: BGP: Performing BGP general scanning
*Mar  9 07:34:20.983: BGP(0): scanning IPv4 Unicast routing tables
*Mar  9 07:34:20.987: BGP(IPv4 Unicast): Performing BGP Nexthop scanning for general
   scan
*Mar  9 07:34:20.987: BGP(0): Future scanner version: 75, current scanner version: 74
*Mar  9 07:34:20.991: BGP(1): scanning IPv6 Unicast routing tables
*Mar  9 07:34:20.991: BGP(IPv6 Unicast): Performing BGP Nexthop scanning for general
   scan
*Mar  9 07:34:20.991: BGP(1): Future scanner version: 76, current scanner version: 75
*Mar  9 07:34:20.995: BGP(2): scanning VPNv4 Unicast routing tables
*Mar  9 07:34:20.995: BGP(VPNv4 Unicast): Performing BGP Nexthop scanning for general
   scan
*Mar  9 07:34:20.999: BGP(2): Future scanner version: 76, current scanner version: 75
*Mar  9 07:34:21.003: BGP(4): scanning IPv4 Multicast routing tables
*Mar  9 07:34:21.003: BGP(IPv4 Multicast): Performing BGP Nexthop scanning for general
   scan
*Mar  9 07:34:21.003: BGP(4): Future scanner version: 76, current scanner version: 75
*Mar  9 07:34:21.007: BGP(5): scanning IPv6 Multicast routing tables
*Mar  9 07:34:21.007: BGP(IPv6 Multicast): Performing BGP Nexthop scanning for general
   scan
*Mar  9 07:34:21.011: BGP(5): Future scanner version: 76, current scanner version: 75
*Mar  9 07:34:21.011: BGP(6): scanning NSAP Unicast routing tables
*Mar  9 07:34:21.015: BGP(NSAP Unicast): Performing BGP Nexthop scanning for general
   scan
*Mar  9 07:34:21.015: BGP(6): Future scanner version: 76, current scanner version: 75
*Mar  9 07:34:36.035: BGP: Import timer expired. Walking from 1 to 1
*Mar  9 07:34:51.043: BGP: Import timer expired. Walking from 1 to 1
*Mar  9 07:35:06.043: BGP: Import timer expired. Walking from 1 to 1
Eldora#
*Mar  9 07:35:21.047: BGP: Performing BGP general scanning
*Mar  9 07:35:21.051: BGP(0): scanning IPv4 Unicast routing tables
```

```
*Mar  9 07:35:21.051: BGP(IPv4 Unicast): Performing BGP Nexthop scanning for general
  scan
*Mar  9 07:35:21.055: BGP(0): Future scanner version: 76, current scanner version: 75
*Mar  9 07:35:21.055: BGP(1): scanning IPv6 Unicast routing tables
*Mar  9 07:35:21.059: BGP(IPv6 Unicast): Performing BGP Nexthop scanning for general
  scan
*Mar  9 07:35:21.059: BGP(1): Future scanner version: 77, current scanner version: 76
*Mar  9 07:35:21.063: BGP(2): scanning VPNv4 Unicast routing tables
*Mar  9 07:35:21.063: BGP(VPNv4 Unicast): Performing BGP Nexthop scanning for general
  scan
*Mar  9 07:35:21.067: BGP(2): Future scanner version: 77, current scanner version: 76
*Mar  9 07:35:21.067: BGP(4): scanning IPv4 Multicast routing tables
*Mar  9 07:35:21.071: BGP(IPv4 Multicast): Performing BGP Nexthop scanning for general
  scan
*Mar  9 07:35:21.071: BGP(4): Future scanner version: 77, current scanner version: 76
*Mar  9 07:35:21.075: BGP(5): scanning IPv6 Multicast routing tables
*Mar  9 07:35:21.075: BGP(IPv6 Multicast): Performing BGP Nexthop scanning for general
  scan
*Mar  9 07:35:21.075: BGP(5): Future scanner version: 77, current scanner version: 76
*Mar  9 07:35:21.079: BGP(6): scanning NSAP Unicast routing tables
*Mar  9 07:35:21.079: BGP(NSAP Unicast): Performing BGP Nexthop scanning for general
  scan
*Mar  9 07:35:21.083: BGP(6): Future scanner version: 77, current scanner version: 76
*Mar  9 07:35:36.083: BGP: Import timer expired. Walking from 1 to 1
*Mar  9 07:35:51.083: BGP: Import timer expired. Walking from 1 to 1
*Mar  9 07:36:06.087: BGP: Import timer expired. Walking from 1 to 1
*Mar  9 07:36:21.087: BGP: Performing BGP general scanning
*Mar  9 07:36:21.091: BGP(0): scanning IPv4 Unicast routing tables
*Mar  9 07:36:21.091: BGP(IPv4 Unicast): Performing BGP Nexthop scanning for general
  scan
*Mar  9 07:36:21.095: BGP(0): Future scanner version: 77, current scanner version: 76
*Mar  9 07:36:21.095: BGP(1): scanning IPv6 Unicast routing tables
*Mar  9 07:36:21.099: BGP(IPv6 Unicast): Performing BGP Nexthop scanning for general
  scan
*Mar  9 07:36:21.099: BGP(1): Future scanner version: 78, current scanner version: 77
*Mar  9 07:36:21.099: BGP(2): scanning VPNv4 Unicast routing tables
*Mar  9 07:36:21.099: BGP(VPNv4 Unicast): Performing BGP Nexthop scanning for general
  scan
*Mar  9 07:36:21.099: BGP(2): Future scanner version: 78, current scanner version: 77
*Mar  9 07:36:21.099: BGP(4): scanning IPv4 Multicast routing tables
*Mar  9 07:36:21.099: BGP(IPv4 Multicast): Performing BGP Nexthop scanning for general
  scan
*Mar  9 07:36:21.099: BGP(4): Future scanner version: 78, current scanner version: 77
*Mar  9 07:36:21.099: BGP(5): scanning IPv6 Multicast routing tables
*Mar  9 07:36:21.099: BGP(IPv6 Multicast): Performing BGP Nexthop scanning for general
  scan
```

```
*Mar  9 07:36:21.099: BGP(5): Future scanner version: 78, current scanner version: 77
*Mar  9 07:36:21.099: BGP(6): scanning NSAP Unicast routing tables
*Mar  9 07:36:21.099: BGP(NSAP Unicast): Performing BGP Nexthop scanning for general
  scan
*Mar  9 07:36:21.099: BGP(6): Future scanner version: 78, current scanner version: 77
*Mar  9 07:36:36.123: BGP: Import timer expired. Walking from 1 to 1
*Mar  9 07:36:51.127: BGP: Import timer expired. Walking from 1 to 1
```

Notice that at each of the highlighted scans, right after the general scan starts the IPv4 unicast routing table (the unicast IPv4 RIB) is scanned and then next hops are scanned. Also notice the time stamps: The Scanner runs every 60 seconds. This default time can be changed with the **bgp scan-time** statement, although it is a bad idea to change the default without a well-justified reason and without understanding what the effects will be on your network. The Scanner does cause the CPU utilization to increase—sometimes dramatically —every 60 seconds. So reducing the scan time might increase BGP performance at the cost of heavier CPU utilization, while decreasing the scan time eases the CPU load at the cost of BGP performance. In the little example network used in this section, with a single unicast IPv4 prefix, the complete scan over all address types is finished within a second. In a network with hundreds of thousands of routes, such as the one observed in Example 4-17, scanning might take 30 or 40 seconds. This is not as impacting on the CPU as it might first seem, however, for two reasons. First, the scan-time is the interval between scans; so even if a scan takes 30 seconds, there is still 60 seconds of quiet before the next one starts. Second, and more important, the Scanner is a low-priority process. So even if it causes spikes in CPU utilization, more important processes can still take CPU cycles away from the Scanner if needed.

NHT, Event, and the Open Processes

In addition, more recent versions of IOS include improvements that can reduce scan times by 75 pecent or more. One of the improvements is a lightweight scanner called the Next Hop Tracker (NHT). NHT is primarily intended to improve BGP performance, and is detailed in Chapter 5; but it also has the effect of removing next hop and best path validation duties from the Scanner reducing scan times. The other improvement is the addition of a process called BGP Event, which you can see in Example 4-18. This process makes **network** statements and redistribution event-driven—that is, the "event" of adding or removing a **network** or **redistribute** statement triggers the addition or removal of prefixes into the BGP table, removing the need to wait for the Scanner and removing the time it takes for the Scanner to perform that aspect of a scan.

Note   There is another aspect of Scanner called the Import Scanner, which is responsible for importing routes into the Virtual Routing and Forwarding (VRF) tables of MPLS-based unicast IPv4 Virtual Private Networks (VPNv4). MPLS VPNs are beyond the scope of this book, but it is interesting to note the activity of the Import Scanner in

Example 4-19. Unlike the regular scanning process, the Import Scanner runs every 15 seconds: Notice that in Example 4-19 every 15 seconds there is either an entry for a VPNv4 Unicast scan or an entry stating "Import timer expired."

There is another BGP process that is not shown in Example 4-18 because it is a transient process rather than a steady-state process. That is, the process is started as needed and stopped when it is finished. This is the BGP Open process, which runs whenever the router is trying to open a BGP session with a neighbor.

In Example 4-20, a **show ip bgp summary** command indicates that the state of all three of Eldora's neighbors is established. (The heading information normally displayed with this command has been deleted to help focus on the important information.) A **show processes cpu | include BGP** command is then issued; you can see that no Open process is running. Following these initial displays, a CLI message shows that Loveland (10.4.1.2) has closed the BGP session to Eldora; running **show ip bgp summary** again indicates that Eldora has changed the state of that neighbor to Active. A second look at the BGP processes shows that there is an Open process now running.

Example 4-20 *A Closure of the BGP Session to Loveland (10.4.1.2) Causes Eldora to Change the State of the Neighbor to Active and Start the BGP Open Process to Attempt to Open a New Session to the Neighbor*

```
Eldora#show ip bgp summary
Neighbor        V    AS MsgRcvd MsgSent   TblVer  InQ OutQ Up/Down  State/PfxRcd
10.2.1.1        4   100    446     446        2    0    0 07:16:31           1
10.3.1.1        4   200    446     446        2    0    0 07:16:31           1
10.4.1.2        4   400    382     387        2    0    0 00:00:44           0
Eldora#
Eldora#show processes cpu | include BGP
 225    10080    55200       182  0.00%  0.04%  0.02%   0 BGP Router
 226     7336     6116      1199  0.00%  0.27%  0.22%   0 BGP I/O
 227     9284     1757      5284  0.00%  0.04%  0.00%   0 BGP Scanner
 228        0        1         0  0.00%  0.00%  0.00%   0 BGP Event
Eldora#
Eldora#
*Mar  9 13:38:20.666: %BGP-5-ADJCHANGE: neighbor 10.4.1.2 Down Peer closed the session
Eldora#
Eldora#show ip bgp summary
Neighbor        V    AS MsgRcvd MsgSent   TblVer  InQ OutQ Up/Down  State/PfxRcd
10.2.1.1        4   100    447     447        2    0    0 07:17:08           1
10.3.1.1        4   200    447     447        2    0    0 07:17:08           1
10.4.1.2        4   400    383     388        0    0    0 00:00:13 Active
Eldora#
Eldora#
```

```
Eldora#show processes cpu | include BGP
 217          4        1      4000  0.00%  0.00%  0.00%   0 BGP Open
 225      10112    55280       182  0.00%  0.05%  0.02%   0 BGP Router
 226       7372     6139      1200  0.00%  0.19%  0.20%   0 BGP I/O
 227       9316     1760      5293  0.00%  0.07%  0.01%   0 BGP Scanner
 228          0        1         0  0.00%  0.00%  0.00%   0 BGP Event
Eldora#
```

If Eldora tried to open another session to another neighbor (either because an existing session has gone down or a new neighbor has been configured), a separate Open process would be started for that neighbor. That is, a separate Open process is started for each neighbor to which IOS attempts to open a BGP session.

Table Versions

With the various BGP processes updating the BGP table, the RIB, and perhaps many peers, there must be a means by which BGP can track what has been received, the latest version of a prefix, and what still needs to be updated with the latest version of a prefix. This is the job of the *table version* number. In Example 4-21, you can see several references to table versions: The display indicates that BGP has a table version 6, the main routing table (the RIB) has a table version number of 6, and each of the three neighbors—all of which are in Established state—has table version numbers of 6. There is one more place where the table version shows up: Each prefix in the BGP table has a table version. In Example 4-22, the prefix 10.1.1.1—shown here received from both Buttermilk (10.2.1.1) and Arapahoe (10.3.1.1) in Figure 4-3—has a table version number of, again, 6.

Example 4-21   *BGP Has a Table Version, the Main Routing Table (the RIB) Has a Table Version, and Each Established Neighbor Has a Table Version. In This Example, All Table Version Numbers Are 6*

```
Eldora#show ip bgp summary
BGP router identifier 10.4.1.1, local AS number 300
BGP table version is 6, main routing table version 6
1 network entries using 120 bytes of memory
2 path entries using 104 bytes of memory
3/1 BGP path/bestpath attribute entries using 372 bytes of memory
2 BGP AS-PATH entries using 48 bytes of memory
0 BGP route-map cache entries using 0 bytes of memory
0 BGP filter-list cache entries using 0 bytes of memory
Bitfield cache entries: current 1 (at peak 1) using 32 bytes of memory
BGP using 676 total bytes of memory
BGP activity 1/0 prefixes, 10/8 paths, scan interval 60 secs
```

Neighbor	V	AS	MsgRcvd	MsgSent	TblVer	InQ	OutQ	Up/Down	State/PfxRcd
10.2.1.1	4	100	44	46	6	0	0	00:08:57	1
10.3.1.1	4	200	38	37	6	0	0	00:12:05	1
10.4.1.2	4	400	35	43	6	0	0	00:03:16	0

Example 4-22 *The Prefix 10.1.1.0/24 in the BGP Table Has a Table Version Number of 6*

```
Eldora#show ip bgp 10.1.1.0
BGP routing table entry for 10.1.1.0/24, version 6
Paths: (2 available, best #2, table Default-IP-Routing-Table)
Flag: 0x820
  Advertised to update-groups:
        1
 200 500
    10.3.1.1 from 10.3.1.1 (10.3.1.1)
      Origin IGP, metric 0, localpref 100, valid, external
 100 500
    10.2.1.1 from 10.2.1.1 (10.2.1.1)
      Origin IGP, metric 0, localpref 100, valid, external, best
```

It is easy, based on the information in Examples 4-21 and 4-22, to assume all the citations of a table version refer to the same table version. After all, the number of each is 6. These are, it turns out, different table versions.

- Each neighbor has a table version.
- Each prefix has a table version.
- The RIB has a table version.
- The BGP process has a table version.

The reason all the table version numbers are the same in Examples 4-21 and 4-22 is that BGP is *converged*—that is, there is no changed information to be advertised to a neighbor or updated in the RIB.

The table version is a 32-bit number (notice that the table version numbers in Example 4-17 are much larger than in our simple example network). When BGP assigns a new table version number, it is always one higher than the last assigned number.

The table versions are assigned as follows:

1. When BGP starts up, the BGP initializes its table version to 1 and assigns this number to the RIB and to all established neighbors.

2. When a prefix is received, the BGP table version is increased by 1 and the prefix is assigned that number. So if prefixes A, B, and C are received in that order, their table versions will be 2, 3, and 4, respectively, and the BGP table version will be 4. The BGP table version, then, should always be the highest table version number of all the prefixes.

3. If a prefix that already exists in the BGP table changes in some way—for instance, there is more than one path to the destination and the preferred path changes—the prefix's table version is increased to the current BGP table version plus one and the BGP table version increments accordingly. Let's say that the best path of prefix A in step 2, which had a table version of 2, changes while the BGP table version is 4. Prefix A is given a new table version of 5; the BGP table version is also now 5, because that is the highest version number of any prefix in the BGP table.

4. If a prefix is withdrawn from the BGP table, the BGP table version is incremented. So if the BGP table version is 5 and prefixes B and C are withdrawn, the BGP table version becomes 7 (5 + 1 + 1).

5. As the BGP Router process updates the RIB from the prefixes in the BGP table, the RIB's table version becomes the highest table version of any prefix that has been added to, changed, or withdrawn from the RIB. If a prefix in the BGP table has a higher table version number than the RIB table version, the BGP Router knows that the prefix has not yet been added to the RIB.

6. Similarly, when prefixes are advertised to a neighbor, the neighbor's table version is increased to the highest version number of any prefix that has been advertised to that neighbor. Again this is a way to keep track of what has been advertised; if a prefix in the BGP table has a higher table version than the neighbor's table version, BGP knows that the prefix has not yet been advertised to the neighbor.

These steps can be confusing when you are trying to learn them; a step-by-step example will help. In Figure 4-5, AS500, AS100, and AS200 each advertise one prefix, as shown. This exercise observes how those three prefixes, plus the locally injected prefix 10.40.1.0/24, effects the table versions at Eldora. You will probably want to refer back to this diagram as the exercise progresses, so mark the page.

Eldora's BGP process has just started up in Example 4-23. You can see that all three neighbors are established, but none of them have advertised any prefixes to Eldora. BGP has a table version of 1, which it has assigned to the RIB (main routing table) and to each of the three neighbors.

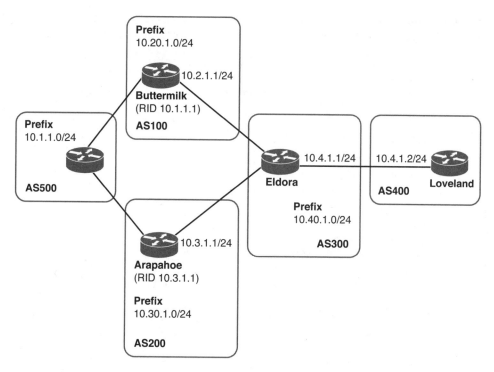

Figure 4-5 *Prefixes Advertised by Autonomous Systems 500, 100, and 200 Affect the Table Version Numbers at Eldora, as Does the Locally Injected Prefix in AS300*

Example 4-23 *BGP Has Started at Eldora, and No Prefixes Have Yet Been Advertised by Any Neighbor, Nor Has the Local Prefix Been Injected Yet. The BGP Table, RIB, and Neighbor Table Versions Are Initialized to 1*

```
Eldora#show ip bgp summary
BGP router identifier 10.4.1.1, local AS number 300
BGP table version is 1, main routing table version 1

Neighbor        V    AS MsgRcvd MsgSent   TblVer  InQ OutQ Up/Down  State/PfxRcd
10.2.1.1        4   100       4       4        1    0    0 00:00:12           0
10.3.1.1        4   200       4       4        1    0    0 00:00:12           0
10.4.1.2        4   400       4       4        1    0    0 00:00:16           0
Eldora#
```

Next, prefix 10.1.1.0 is advertised from Buttermilk to Eldora (Example 4-24). Arapahoe is not yet advertising any prefixes. The next available BGP table version is 2, so that number is assigned to the prefix. The prefix is added to the RIB, so the RIB table version becomes 2; the prefix is advertised to each of the three neighbors, so their table versions also become 2.

Example 4-24   *Eldora Receives an Advertisement of Prefix 10.1.1.0/24 from Buttermilk; the Prefix Is Assigned a Table Version of 2, and as the Prefix Is Added to the RIB and Advertised to Each Neighbor Those Table Versions Are Also Changed to 2*

```
Eldora#show ip bgp summary
BGP router identifier 10.4.1.1, local AS number 300
BGP table version is 2, main routing table version 2
1 network entries using 120 bytes of memory
1 path entries using 52 bytes of memory
2/1 BGP path/bestpath attribute entries using 248 bytes of memory
1 BGP AS-PATH entries using 24 bytes of memory
0 BGP route-map cache entries using 0 bytes of memory
0 BGP filter-list cache entries using 0 bytes of memory
Bitfield cache entries: current 1 (at peak 1) using 32 bytes of memory
BGP using 476 total bytes of memory
BGP activity 1/0 prefixes, 1/0 paths, scan interval 60 secs


Neighbor        V     AS MsgRcvd MsgSent   TblVer   InQ OutQ Up/Down   State/PfxRcd
10.2.1.1        4    100       7       7        2     0    0 00:02:02            1
10.3.1.1        4    200       6       7        2     0    0 00:02:03            0
10.4.1.2        4    400       6       7        2     0    0 00:02:06            0
Eldora#
```

Arapahoe then advertises 10.1.1.0/24 to Eldora. Notice in Example 4-25 that a prefix has been received from Arapahoe, but none of the table versions have changed. This is an important observation: A table version is assigned to a prefix, not to routes to the prefix. So even though both Buttermilk and Arapahoe are advertising routes to 10.1.1.0/24, the BGP increments the table version only when the first instance of the prefix is learned.

Example 4-25   *Eldora Receives an Advertisement of Prefix 10.1.1.0/24 from Arapahoe; Because the Prefix Was Already Learned from Buttermilk and Assigned a Table Version, BGP Does Not Increment the Table Version Again*

```
Eldora#show ip bgp summary
BGP router identifier 10.4.1.1, local AS number 300
BGP table version is 2, main routing table version 2
1 network entries using 120 bytes of memory
2 path entries using 104 bytes of memory
3/1 BGP path/bestpath attribute entries using 372 bytes of memory
2 BGP AS-PATH entries using 48 bytes of memory
0 BGP route-map cache entries using 0 bytes of memory
0 BGP filter-list cache entries using 0 bytes of memory
Bitfield cache entries: current 1 (at peak 1) using 32 bytes of memory
BGP using 676 total bytes of memory
BGP activity 1/0 prefixes, 2/0 paths, scan interval 60 secs
```

Neighbor	V	AS	MsgRcvd	MsgSent	TblVer	InQ	OutQ	Up/Down	State/PfxRcd
10.2.1.1	4	100	8	8	2	0	0	00:03:02	1
10.3.1.1	4	200	8	8	2	0	0	00:03:02	1
10.4.1.2	4	400	7	8	2	0	0	00:03:06	0
Eldora#									

Buttermilk advertises prefix 10.20.1.0/24 in Example 4-26, and Arapahoe advertises prefix 10.30.1.0/24 in Example 4-27. In Example 4-28, a **network** statement is configured at Eldora to inject the prefix 10.40.1.0/24. Notice that as each prefix is learned (through received advertisements in the first two examples and local configuration in the third) the BGP table version is incremented; the RIB table version is incremented as the prefix is added, and the neighbor table versions are incremented as the prefixes are advertised.

Example 4-26 *Eldora Receives an Advertisement of Prefix 10.20.1.0/24 from Buttermilk*

```
Eldora#show ip bgp summary
BGP router identifier 10.4.1.1, local AS number 300
BGP table version is 3, main routing table version 3
2 network entries using 240 bytes of memory
3 path entries using 156 bytes of memory
3/1 BGP path/bestpath attribute entries using 372 bytes of memory
2 BGP AS-PATH entries using 48 bytes of memory
0 BGP route-map cache entries using 0 bytes of memory
0 BGP filter-list cache entries using 0 bytes of memory
Bitfield cache entries: current 1 (at peak 1) using 32 bytes of memory
BGP using 848 total bytes of memory
BGP activity 2/0 prefixes, 3/0 paths, scan interval 60 secs
```

Neighbor	V	AS	MsgRcvd	MsgSent	TblVer	InQ	OutQ	Up/Down	State/PfxRcd
10.2.1.1	4	100	11	11	3	0	0	00:05:07	2
10.3.1.1	4	200	10	11	3	0	0	00:05:08	1
10.4.1.2	4	400	9	11	3	0	0	00:05:11	0
Eldora#									

Example 4-27 *Eldora Receives an Advertisement of Prefix 10.30.1.0/2v4 from Arapahoe*

```
Eldora#show ip bgp summary
BGP router identifier 10.4.1.1, local AS number 300
BGP table version is 4, main routing table version 4
3 network entries using 360 bytes of memory
4 path entries using 208 bytes of memory
```

```
3/2 BGP path/bestpath attribute entries using 372 bytes of memory

2 BGP AS-PATH entries using 48 bytes of memory

0 BGP route-map cache entries using 0 bytes of memory

0 BGP filter-list cache entries using 0 bytes of memory

Bitfield cache entries: current 1 (at peak 1) using 32 bytes of memory

BGP using 1020 total bytes of memory

BGP activity 3/0 prefixes, 4/0 paths, scan interval 60 secs


Neighbor        V    AS MsgRcvd MsgSent  TblVer  InQ OutQ Up/Down   State/PfxRcd
10.2.1.1        4    100      11      12       4    0    0 00:05:57          2
10.3.1.1        4    200      11      12       4    0    0 00:05:58          2
10.4.1.2        4    400      10      13       4    0    0 00:06:01          0
Eldora#
```

Example 4-28   *Prefix 10.40.1.0/24 Is Injected into BGP at Eldora*

```
Eldora#show ip bgp summary
BGP router identifier 10.4.1.1, local AS number 300
BGP table version is 5, main routing table version 5
4 network entries using 480 bytes of memory
5 path entries using 260 bytes of memory
4/3 BGP path/bestpath attribute entries using 496 bytes of memory
2 BGP AS-PATH entries using 48 bytes of memory
0 BGP route-map cache entries using 0 bytes of memory
0 BGP filter-list cache entries using 0 bytes of memory
Bitfield cache entries: current 1 (at peak 1) using 32 bytes of memory
BGP using 1316 total bytes of memory
BGP activity 4/0 prefixes, 5/0 paths, scan interval 60 secs


Neighbor        V    AS MsgRcvd MsgSent  TblVer  InQ OutQ Up/Down   State/PfxRcd
10.2.1.1        4    100      14      16       5    0    0 00:08:05          2
10.3.1.1        4    200      14      16       5    0    0 00:08:05          2
10.4.1.2        4    400      12      16       5    0    0 00:08:09          0
Eldora#
```

So far, the examples are consistent and not all that interesting. The table versions increment everywhere whenever a new prefix is received. Example 4-29 is a bit more infor-
mative. Each of the four prefixes in Eldora's BGP table is displayed, and each has a
different table version number. Compare these numbers with the preceding examples,
and you can see that each prefix retains the table version number BGP assigned to it
when it was first learned. The last prefix learned has the most recent table version number (5) as shown in Example 4-28.

Example 4-29 *Prefixes in Eldora's BGP Table Retain the Table Versions They Were Assigned When They Were First Learned*

```
Eldora#show ip bgp 10.1.1.0
BGP routing table entry for 10.1.1.0/24, version 2
Paths: (2 available, best #2, table Default-IP-Routing-Table)
  Advertised to update-groups:
        1
  200 500
    10.3.1.1 from 10.3.1.1 (10.3.1.1)
       Origin IGP, metric 0, localpref 100, valid, external
  100 500
    10.2.1.1 from 10.2.1.1 (10.2.1.1)
       Origin IGP, metric 0, localpref 100, valid, external, best
Eldora#
Eldora#show ip bgp 10.20.1.0
BGP routing table entry for 10.20.1.0/24, version 3
Paths: (1 available, best #1, table Default-IP-Routing-Table)
  Advertised to update-groups:
        1
  100 500
    10.2.1.1 from 10.2.1.1 (10.2.1.1)
       Origin IGP, metric 0, localpref 100, valid, external, best
Eldora#
Eldora#show ip bgp 10.30.1.0
BGP routing table entry for 10.30.1.0/24, version 4
Paths: (1 available, best #1, table Default-IP-Routing-Table)
  Advertised to update-groups:
        1
  200 500
    10.3.1.1 from 10.3.1.1 (10.3.1.1)
       Origin IGP, metric 0, localpref 100, valid, external, best
Eldora#
Eldora#show ip bgp 10.40.1.0
BGP routing table entry for 10.40.1.0/24, version 5
Paths: (1 available, best #1, table Default-IP-Routing-Table)
  Advertised to update-groups:
        1
  Local
    0.0.0.0 from 0.0.0.0 (10.4.1.1)
       Origin IGP, metric 0, localpref 100, weight 32768, valid, sourced, local, best
Eldora#
```

Notice also in Example 4-29 that of the two routes to 10.1.1.0/24, the path through Buttermilk (10.2.1.1) is preferred. This matches the case in Example 4-3, in which the

BGP decision process finds everything about the two routes to be equal until it reaches the router IDs of the advertising peers. What if the routes were changed, after they are learned, so that the BGP decision process prefers the route from Arapahoe (10.3.1.1) to the route from Buttermilk? One way to cause this change of best path preference is to configure a policy at Buttermilk, similar to the policies configured in the early examples of this chapter in the section "Policy and the BGP Database," that changes the ORIGIN attribute of 10.1.1.0/24 to "Incomplete."

Example 4-30 shows the results at Eldora. The ORIGIN attribute of the route from Buttermilk has changed, forcing Eldora's BGP decision process to change its preference to the route from Buttermilk (compare the entry with the previous entry for 10.1.1.0/24 in Example 4-29). The prefix has a new table version (6), and after the new route to the prefix is added to the RIB and advertised to the neighbors, those table versions are changed to this latest number.

Example 4-30   *A Change of the Best Path Selection for 10.1.1.0/24 Causes Eldora to Assign a New Table Version to the Prefix*

```
Eldora#show ip bgp 10.1.1.0
BGP routing table entry for 10.1.1.0/24, version 6
Paths: (2 available, best #1, table Default-IP-Routing-Table)
Flag: 0x820
  Advertised to update-groups:
        1
  200 500
    10.3.1.1 from 10.3.1.1 (10.3.1.1)
      Origin IGP, metric 0, localpref 100, valid, external, best
  100 500
    10.2.1.1 from 10.2.1.1 (10.2.1.1)
      Origin incomplete, metric 0, localpref 100, valid, external
Eldora#
Eldora#show ip bgp summary
BGP router identifier 10.4.1.1, local AS number 300
BGP table version is 6, main routing table version 6
4 network entries using 480 bytes of memory
5 path entries using 260 bytes of memory
5/3 BGP path/bestpath attribute entries using 620 bytes of memory
2 BGP AS-PATH entries using 48 bytes of memory
0 BGP route-map cache entries using 0 bytes of memory
0 BGP filter-list cache entries using 0 bytes of memory
Bitfield cache entries: current 1 (at peak 1) using 32 bytes of memory
BGP using 1440 total bytes of memory
BGP activity 4/0 prefixes, 5/0 paths, scan interval 60 secs
```

```
Neighbor        V     AS MsgRcvd MsgSent   TblVer   InQ OutQ Up/Down   State/PfxRcd
10.2.1.1        4    100      35      36        6     0    0 00:27:24             2
10.3.1.1        4    200      33      36        6     0    0 00:27:24             2
10.4.1.2        4    400      31      36        6     0    0 00:27:28             0
Eldora#
```

Table versions provide a quick reference for determining if BGP is converged on the router; if all the numbers are the same at the **show ip bgp summary** display, you know that the network is stable. Having such an easy reference can be important when the router has many BGP peers and is taking large routing tables such as full Internet routes. A rapidly increasing table version, along with high CPU utilization by the BGP Router and I/O processes, is a clear indicator that either the router is busy learning routes from a new peer or that (if the condition persists over a long period) there is an instability problem somewhere in the network.

Monitoring your table versions should also be a part of baselining your network. If a router is taking full Internet routes from many peers, such as the Oregon Internet Exchange router in Example 4-17, table version numbers that increment by 100 or so every minute might be normal. But that rate of increase on a router taking a few thousand routes from a few peers is probably indicative of instability in the network. You must first know what is normal for your network before you can know if the table versions are telling you that something is abnormal.

Managing Policy Changes

As the routing protocol of the Internet, BGP is designed to handle a much larger routing database than IGPs. One of the ways in which BGP manages hundreds of thousands of routes is that the protocol stays quiet when the network topology is stable. Distance vector IGPs send route updates to directly connected neighbors at some periodic interval, and link state IGPs periodically refresh their link state databases by flooding locally generated link state messages. In contrast, BGP never sends Update messages to its neighbors if nothing changes.

While this quietude helps BGP to scale, it introduces an issue for routing policies. Looking again at the generic diagram in Figure 4-2, incoming policies are applied to incoming routes before they are evaluated by the decision process. But what happens when you configure a new incoming policy? Until peers send new Updates, the policy has no effect. For example, suppose you configure the incoming policy at Eldora that changes the ORIGIN value of routes sent to it from Buttermilk, as was demonstrated in Example 4-6. The last time Buttermilk sent an Update message to Eldora was the last time the BGP session was established; Eldora's decision process was applied to the routes received at that time and the routes were entered into the Loc-RIB. Any incoming policy configured after that time will have no effect until Buttermilk again sends a BGP Update message, and if nothing changes, Buttermilk will not send a new Update.

Clearing BGP Sessions

One way of applying a newly configured policy, then, is to reset the BGP session to the neighbor using the **clear ip bgp** command, as shown in Example 4-31. When the command is issued, a Cease (Error Code 6, as shown in Table 2-5 of Chapter 2) Notification message is sent to the specified neighbor—or, depending on the implementation, a TCP packet with the FIN flag is sent—and the BGP session is then closed. One or the other neighbors then initiates a reestablishment of the session; when the session comes back up, the neighbors exchange new Update messages and the routes are evaluated by any policies that exist.

Example 4-31   clear ip bgp *Command Is Used to Reset the BGP Session to Buttermilk (10.2.1.1)*

```
Eldora#clear ip bgp 10.2.1.1
Eldora#
*Feb 27 09:38:43.355: %BGP-5-ADJCHANGE: neighbor 10.2.1.1 Down User reset
*Feb 27 09:38:44.247: %BGP-5-ADJCHANGE: neighbor 10.2.1.1 Up
Eldora#
```

Clearing the BGP session works for both incoming and outgoing policies, because new Update messages are sent by both neighbors when the session is reset. When the outgoing policy of Example 4-10 was configured, clearing the session to Loveland would cause the policy to be applied to the routes in Eldora's new Update message before it is sent to Loveland.

There are several options you can use when clearing a BGP session:

- You can specify an IPv4 or IPv6 neighbor address, as in Example 4-16, to clear only the session to that neighbor.

- You can specify an autonomous system number, to clear all sessions to all neighbors in that AS.

- You can use the keyword **external** to clear all sessions to all EBGP neighbors.

- You can use the **in** or **out** keuywords to only clear inbound or outbound sessions. If neither keyword is used, the sessions in both directions is reset.

You can use an asterisk (*) to clear all sessions to all neighbors.

- You can use the keyword **peer-group** to specify the name of a peer group, clearing all sessions to all neighbors belonging to the group (peer groups are discussed in Chapter 5).

- You can use the **prefix-filter** keyword to specify a prefix list associated with an outbound route filter. Outbound route filtering is discussed in Chapter 5.

■ You can use combinations of the keywords **ipv4**, **ipv6**, **unicast**, and **multicast** to clear all unicast or all multicast sessions of either IP version to all neighbors in a specific AS.

Clearing a BGP session has more uses than just ensuring that a new policy configuration takes effect; "bouncing" the BGP session can be a part of a troubleshooting procedure, for example, when you need to observe a message exchange between neighbors. But primarily it was used in older networks to force new policies into effect. Yet clearing a BGP session is obviously disruptive; it can take from several seconds to a few minutes, depending on the number of BGP routes to be updated, for a cleared BGP session to reestablish. During that time, effects of the reset can cascade throughout the network as news of first the withdrawn routes and then the readvertised routes spreads.

Note   The use of **clear ip bgp *** has particularly severe repercussions and should never be used on a production router unless you are confident that clearing every last one of the router's BGP sessions is what you want to do. The command is often used in labs, because it is quicker to type than a neighbor address and there is less concern about every session being cleared.

But even in the lab it can become dangerous if you become too casual about using it. This happened to this author; after working in a lab experimenting with different policy configurations and constantly resetting BGP sessions for a couple of days, typing **clear ip bgp *** became a habit. The first time the command was typed, without thinking, on a live network, the consequences were serious and embarrassing. It was a painful lesson to learn.

Soft Reconfiguraton

A better mechanism was needed that would make the prefixes sent from a peer available for evaluation or modification by a new policy without the disruption of the BGP session. Cisco created a solution called *soft reconfiguration*. This mechanism re-introduces the Adj-RIBs-In concept shown in Figure 4-1 and that was eliminated in the IOS BGP implementation in Figure 4-4. By storing the routes advertised from a neighbor before they have been applied to any incoming policy or to the decision process, the router has a way to apply new policies to the routes at any time without disrupting the session to the neighbor.

There are two steps to using soft reconfiguration:

Step 1.   Enable the Adj-RIBs-In for a neighbor using the **neighbor soft-reconfiguration inbound** statement.

Step 2.   When a new incoming policy is configured, apply it by invoking the **clear ip bgp soft** command.

Example 4-32 shows Eldora configured to support soft reconfiguration. If a BGP session to the neighbor is already established when soft reconfiguration is added, you must still use a hard reset of the session, with **clear ip bgp** *neighbor-address* so that the neighbor will resend its Updates and the Adj-RIBs-In can be populated with the neighbor's routes. This must be done only once; however, any time an inbound policy is changed after the ADJ-RIBs-In has recorded the neighbor's routes, you can use the **clear ip bgp soft in** command as demonstrated in Example 4-33. Compare the output in this example with the output in Example 4-31; notice that in this example, the command is not followed by messages, indicating that the BGP session has gone down and then comes back up.

Example 4-32   *Eldora Is Configured to Support Soft Reconfiguration on Each of Its Three BGP Neighbor Sessions*

```
router bgp 300
 no synchronization
 bgp log-neighbor-changes
 neighbor 10.2.1.1 remote-as 100
 neighbor 10.2.1.1 soft-reconfiguration inbound
 neighbor 10.2.1.1 route-map origin in
 neighbor 10.3.1.1 remote-as 200
 neighbor 10.3.1.1 soft-reconfiguration inbound
 neighbor 10.4.1.2 remote-as 400
 neighbor 10.4.1.2 soft-reconfiguration inbound
 no auto-summary
!
```

Example 4-33   clear ip bgp soft in *Command Uses the Locally Stored Routes from the Neighbor to Apply Any Inbound Policy, Rather Than Performing a Hard Reset of the BGP Session to Cause the Neighbor to Re-send Its Routes*

```
Eldora#clear ip bgp 10.2.1.1 soft in
Eldora#
```

The same options listed in the previous section for hard resets, such as specifying resets by IPv4 or IPv6 neighbor address, all sessions to an AS, EBGP sessions, or by IPv4 and IPv6 unicast or multicast, are available to you for soft resets.

Recall from Example 4-15 that you cannot observe routes advertised from a neighbor without soft reconfiguration enabled; the simple reason for this is that without soft reconfiguration, IOS has no record of the routes advertised from a neighbor before incoming policy and the decision process is applied. Example 4-34 shows that with soft reconfiguration enabled at Eldora, the routes advertised from Buttermilk can be observed because it is now stored locally in the Adj-RIBs-In.

Example 4-34   show ip bgp neighbor received-routes *Command Displays the Routes Advertised from the Specified Neighbor and Stored in the Adj-RIBs-In Database When Soft Reconfiguration Is Enabled*

```
Eldora#show ip bgp neighbor 10.2.1.1 received-routes
BGP table version is 4, local router ID is 10.3.1.2
Status codes: s suppressed, d damped, h history, * valid, > best, i - internal,
              r RIB-failure, S Stale
Origin codes: i - IGP, e - EGP, ? - incomplete

   Network          Next Hop          Metric LocPrf Weight Path
*> 10.1.1.0/24      10.2.1.1                         0 100 500 i
*> 10.20.1.0/24     10.2.1.1              0           0 100 i
*  10.30.1.0/24     10.2.1.1                         0 100 500 200 i

Total number of prefixes 3
Eldora#
```

You can also do a soft reset to apply outgoing policies, using the **clear ip bgp soft out** command. The router will generate new Update messages to all neighbors the command covers, without bouncing the session. There is no **neighbor soft-reconfiguration outbound** configuration statement corresponding to the **neighbor soft-reconfiguration inbound** statement demonstrated in Example 4-32 because no database must be created to support outbound soft resets. This can be used strategically in a network where a neighbor does not support soft reconfiguration or you do not want to configure soft reconfiguration on your routers. When you change an incoming policy, rather than doing a hard reset of the session to the neighbor you can connect to that neighbor and perform an outbound soft reset toward the neighbor on which you configured the incoming policy. The router then sends a new Update message to the neighbor with the new incoming policy, causing the policy to take effect.

This discussion of using outbound soft reconfiguration raises the question: Why would you not configure your routers to support inbound soft reconfiguration, if the option is available? The answer is that there is a price to be paid for inbound soft reconfiguration, because room in the router's memory must be made for the Adj-RIBs-In database. In a simple network such as the one we have been using—or any network in which the routers have no more than a few neighbors and each neighbor is sending a few tens or hundreds of routes—inbound soft reconfiguration does not require much memory. Example 4-35 shows the one prefix from Buttermilk, after policy is applied, requires 52 bytes to store. But if Buttermilk was sending full Internet routes to Eldora—612,000 prefixes as this chapter is being written—almost 32 megabytes would be required to store the prefixes (at 52 bytes per prefix). If a large number of neighbors are all sending full Internet routes—such as the case of Example 4-17, the amount of memory required to support inbound soft reconfiguration can run into the hundreds of megabytes. Another solution is needed that is neither as disruptive as hard resets nor as memory-expensive as soft reconfiguration. That solution is route refresh.

Example 4-35 *Neighbor Data for 10.2.1.1 Shows That Inbound Soft Reconfiguration Is Configured, That an Inbound Policy Is Configured, and That the Prefix Advertised by the Neighbor Has Been Saved*

```
Eldora#show ip bgp neighbors 10.2.1.1
BGP neighbor is 10.2.1.1,  remote AS 100, external link
  BGP version 4, remote router ID 10.2.1.1
  BGP state = Established, up for 00:02:22
  Last read 00:00:22, last write 00:00:22, hold time is 180, keepalive interval is
  60 seconds
  Neighbor capabilities:
    Route refresh: advertised and received(old & new)
    Address family IPv4 Unicast: advertised and received
  Message statistics:
    InQ depth is 0
    OutQ depth is 0
                      Sent        Rcvd
    Opens:              1           1
    Notifications:      0           0
    Updates:            2           1
    Keepalives:         4           4
    Route Refresh:      0           0
    Total:              7           6
  Default minimum time between advertisement runs is 30 seconds

  For address family: IPv4 Unicast
  BGP table version 3, neighbor version 3/0
  Output queue size: 0
  Index 1, Offset 0, Mask 0x2
  1 update-group member
  Inbound soft reconfiguration allowed
  Inbound path policy configured
  Route map for incoming advertisements is origin
                        Sent        Rcvd
  Prefix activity:      ----        ----
    Prefixes Current:     1           1 (Consumes 104 bytes)
    Prefixes Total:       2           1
    Implicit Withdraw:    1           0
    Explicit Withdraw:    0           0
    Used as bestpath:    n/a          0
    Used as multipath:   n/a          0
    Saved (soft-reconfig):  n/a       1 (Consumes 52 bytes)
```

```
                                    Outbound    Inbound
   Local Policy Denied Prefixes:    --------    -------
     Total:                            0            0
   Number of NLRIs in the update sent: max 1, min 1


   Connections established 1; dropped 0
   Last reset never
Connection state is ESTAB, I/O status: 1, unread input bytes: 0
Connection is ECN Disabled, Mininum incoming TTL 0, Outgoing TTL 1
Local host: 10.2.1.2, Local port: 179
Foreign host: 10.2.1.1, Foreign port: 63432
Connection tableid (VRF): 0


Enqueued packets for retransmit: 0, input: 0  mis-ordered: 0 (0 bytes)


Event Timers (current time is 0x2CD80):
Timer          Starts    Wakeups          Next
Retrans           6         0             0x0
TimeWait          0         0             0x0
AckHold           6         2             0x0
SendWnd           0         0             0x0
KeepAlive         0         0             0x0
GiveUp            0         0             0x0
PmtuAger          0         0             0x0
DeadWait          0         0             0x0
Linger            0         0             0x0
ProcessQ          0         0             0x0


iss: 3959681864  snduna: 3959682084  sndnxt: 3959682084     sndwnd: 16165
irs: 2000181844  rcvnxt: 2000182020  rcvwnd:      16209 delrcvwnd:    175


SRTT: 169 ms, RTTO: 1189 ms, RTV: 1020 ms, KRTT: 0 ms
minRTT: 12 ms, maxRTT: 336 ms, ACK hold: 200 ms
Status Flags: passive open, gen tcbs
Option Flags: nagle
IP Precedence value : 6


Datagrams (max data segment is 1460 bytes):
Rcvd: 11 (out of order: 0), with data: 6, total data bytes: 175
Sent: 9 (retransmit: 0, fastretransmit: 0, partialack: 0, Second Congestion: 0),
  with data: 6, total data bytes: 219
 Packets received in fast path: 0, fast processed: 0, slow path: 0
 fast lock acquisition failures: 0, slow path: 0
Eldora#
```

Route Refresh

The objective of both hard and soft resets is to acquire all the prefixes advertised by a neighbor to run them through a newly configured incoming policy. But the solutions discussed so far present significant problems. Hard resets are disruptive to the network, and soft reconfiguration can use an unacceptable amount of memory. A better solution, depicted in Figure 4-6, is to provide a means by which the router with the new incoming policy can *ask* a neighbor to resend its prefixes.

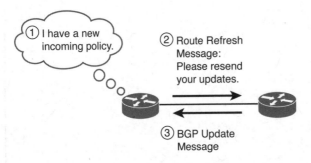

Figure 4-6 *Route Refresh Defines a New BGP Message Type That Asks a Neighbor to Resend Its Prefixes, Eliminating the Need to Store the Pre-Policy Prefixes Locally*

The procedure illustrated in Figure 4-6 is implemented with the *route refresh* mechanism. This mechanism sends a new BGP message—not surprisingly called the Route Refresh message (type code 5)—to a neighbor to tell the neighbor to retransmit its prefixes. The message is sent on command; that is, there is no automatic detection of a policy change that triggers the message. Instead, it is sent by the same **clear ip bgp soft in** command that is used with soft reconfiguration. The difference is that the **neighbor soft-reconfiguration inbound** statement is not included in the neighbor configuration.

Figure 4-7 shows the format of the Route Refresh message, which contains a simple set of codes after the BGP message header. The Address Family Identifier (AFI) and Subsequent Address Family Identifier (SAFI) allow the message to specify the type of prefixes to be sent, such as unicast or multicast IPv4 and unicast or multicast IPv6. Address families, which differentiate the various types of addresses that can be advertised by Multiprotocol BGP, are discussed in Chapter 6.

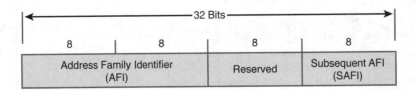

Figure 4-7 *BGP Route Refresh Message Format*

Of course, a router might have some neighbors that cannot support the route refresh capability. It is important to know who those neighbors are so that an alternative method of applying incoming policy changes—either hard resets or soft reconfiguration—can be used with that neighbor. Therefore, the route refresh capability is negotiated during the opening of the neighbor session; if the neighbor supports the capability, it is recorded in the neighbor table.

debug ip bgp in is enabled in Example 4-36 to observe a capabilities negotiation. The session to neighbor 10.2.1.1 is then cleared, and you can observe the capabilities negotiation as the session comes back up.

Example 4-36 *Route Refresh Capability Is Negotiated During the Opening of a BGP Session*

```
Eldora#debug ip bgp in
BGP debugging is on for address family: IPv4 Unicast
Eldora#clear ip bgp 10.2.1.1
Eldora#
*Mar 29 13:42:04.619: BGPNSF state: 10.2.1.1 went from nsf_not_active to
  nsf_not_active
*Mar 29 13:42:04.619: BGP: 10.2.1.1 went from Established to Idle
*Mar 29 13:42:04.623: %BGP-5-ADJCHANGE: neighbor 10.2.1.1 Down User reset
*Mar 29 13:42:04.623: BGP: 10.2.1.1 closing
*Mar 29 13:42:04.627: BGP: 10.2.1.1 went from Idle to Active
*Mar 29 13:42:04.647: BGP: 10.2.1.1 open active, local address 10.2.1.2
*Mar 29 13:42:06.419: BGP: 10.2.1.1 went from Active to OpenSent
*Mar 29 13:42:06.419: BGP: 10.2.1.1 sending OPEN, version 4, my as: 300, holdtime
  180 seconds
*Mar 29 13:42:06.639: BGP: 10.2.1.1 rcv message type 1, length (excl. header) 26
*Mar 29 13:42:06.643: BGP: 10.2.1.1 rcv OPEN, version 4, holdtime 180 seconds
*Mar 29 13:42:06.643: BGP: 10.2.1.1 rcv OPEN w/ OPTION parameter len: 16
*Mar 29 13:42:06.647: BGP: 10.2.1.1 rcvd OPEN w/ optional parameter type 2
  (Capability) len 6
*Mar 29 13:42:06.647: BGP: 10.2.1.1 OPEN has CAPABILITY code: 1, length 4
*Mar 29 13:42:06.647: BGP: 10.2.1.1 OPEN has MP_EXT CAP for afi/safi: 1/1
*Mar 29 13:42:06.647: BGP: 10.2.1.1 rcvd OPEN w/ optional parameter type 2
  (Capability) len 2
*Mar 29 13:42:06.647: BGP: 10.2.1.1 OPEN has CAPABILITY code: 128, length 0
*Mar 29 13:42:06.647: BGP: 10.2.1.1 OPEN has ROUTE-REFRESH capability(old) for all
  address-families
*Mar 29 13:42:06.647: BGP: 10.2.1.1 rcvd OPEN w/ optional parameter type 2
(Capability) len 2
*Mar 29 13:42:06.647: BGP: 10.2.1.1 OPEN has CAPABILITY code: 2, length 0
*Mar 29 13:42:06.647: BGP: 10.2.1.1 OPEN has ROUTE-REFRESH capability(new) for all
  address-families
BGP: 10.2.1.1 rcvd OPEN w/ remote AS 100
```

```
*Mar 29 13:42:06.647: BGP: 10.2.1.1 went from OpenSent to OpenConfirm
*Mar 29 13:42:06.647: BGP: 10.2.1.1 went from OpenConfirm to Established
*Mar 29 13:42:06.647: %BGP-5-ADJCHANGE: neighbor 10.2.1.1 Up
Eldora#
```

The neighbor table shown in Example 4-35 is shown again in Example 4-37, but with
a different part of the table highlighted. Notice that route refresh is indicated under
the neighbor capabilities. However, soft reconfiguration and route refresh are mutually
exclusive. If the **neighbor soft-reconfiguration inbound** statement is included in the
neighbor configuration, an Adj-RIBs-In is created even if the neighbor supports route
refresh; when the **clear ip bgp soft in** command is issued for that neighbor, the Adj-
RIBs-In database is used and no route refresh message is sent to the neighbor. To enable
route refresh for the neighbors in the configuration of Example 4-32, simply remove the
neighbor soft-reconfiguration inbound statements.

Example 4-37   *Neighbor Data for 10.2.1.1 Shows the Neighbor Supports the Route
Refresh Capability*

```
Eldora#show ip bgp neighbors 10.2.1.1
BGP neighbor is 10.2.1.1,  remote AS 100, external link
  BGP version 4, remote router ID 10.2.1.1
  BGP state = Established, up for 00:02:22
  Last read 00:00:22, last write 00:00:22, hold time is 180, keepalive interval is
  60 seconds
  Neighbor capabilities:
    Route refresh: advertised and received(old & new)
    Address family IPv4 Unicast: advertised and received
  Message statistics:
    InQ depth is 0
    OutQ depth is 0
                      Sent       Rcvd
    Opens:              1          1
    Notifications:      0          0
    Updates:            2          1
    Keepalives:         4          4
    Route Refresh:      0          0
    Total:              7          6
  Default minimum time between advertisement runs is 30 seconds

  For address family: IPv4 Unicast
  BGP table version 3, neighbor version 3/0
  Output queue size: 0
  Index 1, Offset 0, Mask 0x2
  1 update-group member
  Inbound soft reconfiguration allowed
```

```
   Inbound path policy configured
   Route map for incoming advertisements is origin
                                       Sent      Rcvd
   Prefix activity:                    ----      ----
     Prefixes Current:                   1         1 (Consumes 104 bytes)
     Prefixes Total:                     2         1
     Implicit Withdraw:                  1         0
     Explicit Withdraw:                  0         0
     Used as bestpath:                 n/a         0
     Used as multipath:                n/a         0
     Saved (soft-reconfig):            n/a         1 (Consumes 52 bytes)


                                     Outbound    Inbound
   Local Policy Denied Prefixes:     --------    -------
     Total:                              0          0
   Number of NLRIs in the update sent: max 1, min 1


   Connections established 1; dropped 0
   Last reset never
Connection state is ESTAB, I/O status: 1, unread input bytes: 0
Connection is ECN Disabled, Mininum incoming TTL 0, Outgoing TTL 1
Local host: 10.2.1.2, Local port: 179
Foreign host: 10.2.1.1, Foreign port: 63432
Connection tableid (VRF): 0


Enqueued packets for retransmit: 0, input: 0  mis-ordered: 0 (0 bytes)


Event Timers (current time is 0x2CD80):
Timer          Starts    Wakeups          Next
Retrans           6         0             0x0
TimeWait          0         0             0x0
AckHold           6         2             0x0
SendWnd           0         0             0x0
KeepAlive         0         0             0x0
GiveUp            0         0             0x0
PmtuAger          0         0             0x0
DeadWait          0         0             0x0
Linger            0         0             0x0
ProcessQ          0         0             0x0


iss: 3959681864  snduna: 3959682084  sndnxt: 3959682084    sndwnd:  16165
irs: 2000181844  rcvnxt: 2000182020  rcvwnd:       16209  delrcvwnd:    175


SRTT: 169 ms, RTTO: 1189 ms, RTV: 1020 ms, KRTT: 0 ms
minRTT: 12 ms, maxRTT: 336 ms, ACK hold: 200 ms
```

```
Status Flags: passive open, gen tcbs
Option Flags: nagle
IP Precedence value : 6

Datagrams (max data segment is 1460 bytes):
Rcvd: 11 (out of order: 0), with data: 6, total data bytes: 175
Sent: 9 (retransmit: 0, fastretransmit: 0, partialack: 0, Second Congestion: 0),
  with data: 6, total data bytes: 219
 Packets received in fast path: 0, fast processed: 0, slow path: 0
 fast lock acquisition failures: 0, slow path: 0
Eldora#
```

Example 4-38 contrasts soft reconfiguration with route refresh. At the beginning of the example, Eldora's configuration is that of Example 4-32. All neighbors are configured with the **neighbor soft-reconfiguration inbound** statement. **debug ip bgp in** and **debug ip bgp updates** are enabled to observe both incoming events and BGP update activity. The **clear ip bgp soft in** command is then issued for neighbor 10.2.1.1. Although no mention of the Adj-RIBs-In database is made, the debug messages clearly indicate that soft-reconfiguration has been run.

Next, the **neighbor soft-reconfiguration inbound** statement is removed from the configuration for neighbor 10.2.1.1. This disables soft reconfiguration and removes the Adj-RIBs-In. The **clear ip bgp soft in** command is again issued, and the debug messages show that now a Route Refresh (type 5) message is sent to the neighbor; the neighbor responds with a BGP Update message.

Example 4-38 *Debugging Is Used to Observe the Way Neighbor 10.2.1.1 Responds to the* **clear ip bgp soft in** *Command When Soft-reconfiguration Inbound Is Configured and When It Is Not; in the Latter Case, a BGP Route Refresh Message Is Sent to the Neighbor in Response to the Command and the Neighbor Sends an Update Message in Response to the Route Refresh Message*

```
Eldora#debug ip bgp in
BGP debugging is on for address family: IPv4 Unicast
Eldora#debug ip bgp updates
BGP updates debugging is on for address family: IPv4 Unicast
Eldora#
Eldora#clear ip bgp 10.2.1.1 soft in
Eldora#
*Mar 29 13:53:52.351: BGP(0): start inbound soft reconfiguration for 10.2.1.1
*Mar 29 13:53:52.355: BGP(0): process 10.1.1.0/24, next hop 10.2.1.1, metric 0 from
  10.2.1.1
```

```
*Mar 29 13:53:52.355: BGP(0): No inbound policy. Prefix 10.1.1.0/24 accepted
  unconditionally
*Mar 29 13:53:52.359: BGP(0): complete inbound soft reconfiguration, ran for 8ms
Eldora#
Eldora#conf t
Enter configuration commands, one per line.  End with CNTL/Z.
Eldora(config)#router bgp 300
Eldora(config-router)#no neighbor 10.2.1.1 soft-reconfiguration inbound
Eldora(config-router)#^Z
Eldora#
*Mar 29 13:54:36.811: %SYS-5-CONFIG_I: Configured from console by console
Eldora#
Eldora#clear ip bgp 10.2.1.1 soft in
Eldora#
*Mar 29 13:54:52.367: BGP: 10.2.1.1 sending REFRESH_REQ(5) for afi/safi: 1/1
*Mar 29 13:54:52.371: BGP: 10.2.1.1 send message type 5, length (incl. header) 23
*Mar 29 13:54:52.459: BGP(0): 10.2.1.1 rcvd UPDATE w/ attr: nexthop 10.2.1.1, origin
  i, metric 0, path 100 500
Eldora#
```

As these examples have demonstrated, there should never be a need in a modern BGP network to use a hard reset to assert a new inbound route policy. Route Refresh is the current preferred means of nondisruptively managing incoming policy changes. And while enabling an Adj-RIBs-In with6 **neighbor soft-reconfiguration inbound** is still useful when peering with older neighbors that do not support Route Refresh, even in that case you can get around using an Adj-RIBs-In if you have access to the neighboring router so that you can issue a **clear ip bgp soft out** command toward the router with the changed inbound policy.

Route Filtering Techniques

Access lists (ACL) came into use many years ago in the early days of Cisco routers— perhaps in the beginning—and were used, as their name infers, to permit or deny access of packets based on the source and/or destination addresses in their headers. Although we all still use the term "access list" to describe this indispensible tool, the name no longer sufficiently describes how it is used. "Packet identifier" might be a more descriptive term: Capabilities have been steadily added so that an ACL can now identify a packet with great precision based on any combination of header values and many values from upper-layer headers. More to the point, ACLs are now used for far more than just packet filters; a wide array of functions use them to identify packets on which some operation is to be performed from service classification to redistribution.

The same can be said for route filters. Although they can be used to permit or deny the advertisement or reception of a route, they can also be used to identify routes for a wide range of policy-setting functions. The key concept to remember is that route filters are used to identify routes rather than packets and are fundamental tools for configuring route polices.

This section introduces the various types of route filters available in IOS and demonstrates some basic applications of them. You will then see them used in further policy examples both later in this chapter and in the subsequent BGP chapters.

Filtering Routes by NLRI

Filtering routes by the destination prefixes of the routes—the routes' Network Layer Reachability Information—offers the most precision and is the best approach when there are just a few routes to identify or when there is no common characteristic by which to efficiently group the routes to be filtered. If the filter is used to simply permit or deny the advertisement (out) or reception (in) of a route, the filter is applied either to a neighbor or to a redistribution configuration.

IOS provides two tools for per-NLRI route filtering: Distribute lists and prefix lists. Prefix lists are the more recent and the more preferred tool; their configuration variables make them more versatile, and they can have less performance impact on the router. The following two case studies demonstrate each tool and show why prefix lists are preferred over distribute lists in modern BGP networks.

Case Study: Using Distribute Lists

The first and simplest of the route filters available to BGP are defined by the **distribute-list** command. This route filter is defined for each neighbor, and points to an access list that defines the prefixes, or NLRI, on which the filter will act.

The network in Figure 4-8 is used for this and the following two case studies.

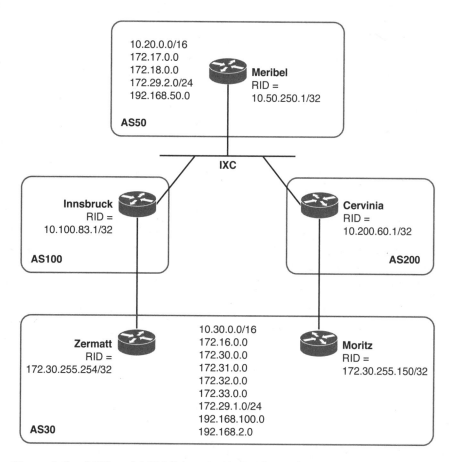

Figure 4-8 *AS30 and AS50 Advertise the Prefixes Shown; AS30 Is Physically Multihomed, Whereas AS50 Is Logically Multihomed by Separate BGP Sessions Through a Shared Internet Exchange (IXC)*

The preliminary configurations of the routers in Figure 4-8 are shown in Example 4-39.

Example 4-39 *Initial Configurations of the Routers in Figure 4-8*

```
Zermatt
interface Loopback0
 ip address 172.30.255.254 255.255.255.255
 ip router isis
!
router isis
 net 30.5678.1234.defa.00
 default-information originate
!
router bgp 30
```

```
  no synchronization
  bgp log-neighbor-changes
  network 10.30.0.0 mask 255.255.0.0
  network 172.16.0.0
  network 172.29.1.0 mask 255.255.255.0
  network 172.30.0.0
  network 172.31.0.0
  network 172.32.0.0
  network 172.33.0.0
  network 192.168.2.0
  network 192.168.100.0
  neighbor 10.100.83.1 remote-as 100
  neighbor 10.100.83.1 ebgp-multihop 2
  neighbor 10.100.83.1 update-source Loopback0
  neighbor 172.30.255.150 remote-as 30
  neighbor 172.30.255.150 update-source Loopback0
  neighbor 172.30.255.150 next-hop-self
  no auto-summary
 !
 ip route 10.100.83.1 255.255.255.255 Serial1/0
```

```
Moritz
interface Loopback0
 ip address 172.30.255.150 255.255.255.255
 ip router isis
 !
router isis
 net 30.1234.5678.abcd.00
 default-information originate
 !
router bgp 30
 no synchronization
 bgp log-neighbor-changes
 network 10.30.0.0 mask 255.255.0.0
 network 172.16.0.0
 network 172.29.1.0 mask 255.255.255.0
 network 172.30.0.0
 network 172.31.0.0
 network 172.32.0.0
 network 172.33.0.0
 network 192.168.2.0
 network 192.168.100.0
 neighbor 10.200.60.1 remote-as 200
 neighbor 10.200.60.1 ebgp-multihop 2
```

```
 neighbor 10.200.60.1 update-source Loopback0
 neighbor 172.30.255.254 remote-as 30
 neighbor 172.30.255.254 update-source Loopback0
 neighbor 172.30.255.254 next-hop-self
 no auto-summary
!
ip route 10.200.60.1 255.255.255.255 Serial1/0
```

Innsbruck
```
interface Loopback0
 ip address 10.100.83.1 255.255.255.255
!
!
router bgp 100
 no synchronization
 bgp log-neighbor-changes
 network 10.100.0.0 mask 255.255.0.0
 neighbor 10.50.250.1 remote-as 50
 neighbor 10.50.250.1 ebgp-multihop 2
 neighbor 10.50.250.1 update-source Loopback0
 neighbor 10.200.60.1 remote-as 200
 neighbor 10.200.60.1 ebgp-multihop 2
 neighbor 10.200.60.1 update-source Loopback0
 neighbor 172.30.255.254 remote-as 30
 neighbor 172.30.255.254 ebgp-multihop 2
 neighbor 172.30.255.254 update-source Loopback0
 no auto-summary
!
ip route 10.50.250.1 255.255.255.255 FastEthernet0/0
ip route 10.200.60.1 255.255.255.255 FastEthernet0/0
ip route 172.30.255.254 255.255.255.255 Serial1/0
```

Cervina
```
interface Loopback0
 ip address 10.200.60.1 255.255.255.255
!
router bgp 200
 no synchronization
 bgp log-neighbor-changes
 network 10.200.0.0 mask 255.255.0.0
 neighbor 10.50.250.1 remote-as 50
 neighbor 10.50.250.1 ebgp-multihop 2
 neighbor 10.50.250.1 update-source Loopback0
```

```
 neighbor 10.100.83.1 remote-as 100
 neighbor 10.100.83.1 ebgp-multihop 2
 neighbor 10.100.83.1 update-source Loopback0
 neighbor 172.30.255.150 remote-as 30
 neighbor 172.30.255.150 ebgp-multihop 2
 neighbor 172.30.255.150 update-source Loopback0
 no auto-summary
!
ip route 10.50.250.1 255.255.255.255 FastEthernet0/0
ip route 10.100.83.1 255.255.255.255 FastEthernet0/0
ip route 172.30.255.150 255.255.255.255 Serial1/0
```

```
Meribel
interface Loopback0
 ip address 10.50.250.1 255.255.255.255
!
router bgp 50
 no synchronization
 bgp log-neighbor-changes
 network 10.20.0.0 mask 255.255.0.0
 network 172.17.0.0
 network 172.18.0.0
 network 172.29.2.0 mask 255.255.255.0
 network 192.168.50.0
 neighbor 10.100.83.1 remote-as 100
 neighbor 10.100.83.1 ebgp-multihop 2
 neighbor 10.100.83.1 update-source Loopback0
 neighbor 10.200.60.1 remote-as 200
 neighbor 10.200.60.1 ebgp-multihop 2
 neighbor 10.200.60.1 update-source Loopback0
 no auto-summary
!
ip route 10.20.0.0 255.255.0.0 Null0
ip route 10.100.83.1 255.255.255.255 FastEthernet0/0
ip route 10.200.60.1 255.255.255.255 FastEthernet0/0
ip route 172.17.0.0 255.255.0.0 Null0
ip route 172.18.0.0 255.255.0.0 Null0
ip route 172.29.2.0 255.255.255.0 Null0
ip route 192.168.50.0 255.255.255.0 Null0
```

Notice in Figure 4-8 that no IP addresses are shown for any of the data links. All the EBGP sessions are configured between router IDs, defined by the loopback interfaces of the routers, so the data link addresses are irrelevant to this example. (IP addresses are configured for the broadcast Internet Exchange (IXC) link, and IP unnumbered is used on all serial links.) Also important in these configurations are the static routes, which tell the routers how to find their neighbors' router IDs. Without the static routes, the BGP sessions cannot be established. Notice that EBGP-multiphop is used because the EBGP endpoints are not directly connected subnets; the **neighbor update-source** command ensures that the local end of the EBGP sessions are originated on the loopback interfaces. Also recall from Chapter 2 that you can use **neighbor disable connected-check** instead of the neighbor ebgp-multihop statement in this scenario if you prefer.

Zermatt and Moritz each advertise a default route (via IS-IS) into AS30. The two routers run an IBGP session between them; this ensures that if one of the external links is lost, the external prefixes can be learned from the other router. For example, if the link between Moritz and Cervinia fails, Moritz will still learn the external routes from Zermatt. Then if a router internal to AS30 forwards a packet on the default route to Moritz, Moritz will forward the packet to Zermatt.

AS30 in Figure 4-8 is multihomed for redundancy but should not be a transit AS. That is, no traffic passing between AS100 and AS200 should cross AS30. Innsbruck's BGP table in Example 4-40 shows that this policy is in effect: Meribel (10.50.250.1) is shown as the best next hop to the prefixes in AS50, with Cervinia (10.200.60.1) as also a valid next hop. Zermatt (172.30.255.254) is not shown as a valid next-hop for any of the AS50 prefixes. That is, Innsbruck will not forward packets with a destination in AS50 to Meribel for transit across AS30. Cervinia's BGP table is similar.

Example 4-40 *Innsbruck Shows Meribel and Cervinia as Valid Next Hops to the Prefixes in AS50, with Meribel as the Best Path*

```
Innsbruck#show ip bgp
BGP table version is 27, local router ID is 10.100.83.1
Status codes: s suppressed, d damped, h history, * valid, > best, i - internal,
              r RIB-failure, S Stale
Origin codes: i - IGP, e - EGP, ? - incomplete

   Network          Next Hop          Metric LocPrf Weight Path
*> 10.20.0.0/16     10.50.250.1            0             0 50 i
*                   10.200.60.1                          0 200 50 i
*  10.30.0.0/16     10.50.250.1                          0 50 200 30 i
*                   10.200.60.1                          0 200 30 i
*>                  172.30.255.254        10             0 30 i
*> 10.100.0.0/16    0.0.0.0                0         32768 i
*  10.200.0.0/16    10.50.250.1                          0 50 200 i
*>                  10.200.60.1            0             0 200 i
*                   172.30.255.254                       0 30 200 i
*  172.16.0.0       10.50.250.1                          0 50 200 30 i
*                   10.200.60.1                          0 200 30 i
*>                  172.30.255.254        10             0 30 i
```

```
*> 172.17.0.0        10.50.250.1            0              0 50 i
*                    10.200.60.1                           0 200 50 i
*> 172.18.0.0        10.50.250.1            0              0 50 i
*                    10.200.60.1                           0 200 50 i
*  172.29.1.0/24     10.50.250.1                           0 50 200 30 i
*                    10.200.60.1                           0 200 30 i
*>                   172.30.255.254         10             0 30 i
*> 172.29.2.0/24     10.50.250.1            0              0 50 i
*                    10.200.60.1                           0 200 50 i
*  172.30.0.0        10.50.250.1                           0 50 200 30 i
*                    10.200.60.1                           0 200 30 i
*>                   172.30.255.254         0              0 30 i
*  172.31.0.0        10.50.250.1                           0 50 200 30 i
*                    10.200.60.1                           0 200 30 i
*>                   172.30.255.254         10             0 30 i
*  172.32.0.0        10.50.250.1                           0 50 200 30 i
*                    10.200.60.1                           0 200 30 i
*>                   172.30.255.254         20             0 30 i
*  172.33.0.0        10.50.250.1                           0 50 200 30 i
*                    10.200.60.1                           0 200 30 i
*>                   172.30.255.254         10             0 30 i
*  192.168.2.0       10.50.250.1                           0 50 200 30 i
*                    10.200.60.1                           0 200 30 i
*>                   172.30.255.254         10             0 30 i
*> 192.168.50.0      10.50.250.1            0              0 50 i
*                    10.200.60.1                           0 200 50 i
*  192.168.100.0     10.50.250.1                           0 50 200 30 i
*                    10.200.60.1                           0 200 30 i
*>                   172.30.255.254         10             0 30 i
Innsbruck#
```

Notice that the prefixes within AS30 are not only directly reachable through Zermatt, but that Meribel and Cervinia are also listed as valid next hops. This is fine: AS50 and AS200 can be used for transit paths to AS30 if the link between Innsbruck and Zermatt, or Zermatt itself, fails.

There is one hint in Innsbruck's BGP table, however, that the assumption that AS30 will not be used as a transit AS is wrong: Notice that the route to the AS200 prefix 10.200.0.0/16 has three valid next hops, one of which is Zermatt. More conclusive proof is provided in Example 4-41, in which Innsbruck's link to the IXC—and hence to both Meribel and Cervinia—is disabled. After waiting a moment for Innsbruck to stabilize its BGP table, the table then shows that the next hop to the prefixes in AS50 is Zermatt.

Example 4-41 *When Innsbruck's Interface to the IXC Is Shut Down, Its BGP Table Begins Showing Zermatt as the Next Hop to the Prefixes in AS50*

```
Innsbruck#
*May 13 15:35:43.411: %LINK-5-CHANGED: Interface FastEthernet0/0, changed state to
  administratively down
*May 13 15:35:43.411: %ENTITY_ALARM-6-INFO: ASSERT INFO Fa0/0 Physical Port
  Administrative State Down
*May 13 15:35:44.411: %LINEPROTO-5-UPDOWN: Line protocol on Interface
  FastEthernet0/0, changed state to down
Innsbruck#
Innsbruck#show ip bgp
BGP table version is 17, local router ID is 10.100.83.1
Status codes: s suppressed, d damped, h history, * valid, > best, i - internal,
              r RIB-failure, S Stale
Origin codes: i - IGP, e - EGP, ? - incomplete

   Network          Next Hop          Metric LocPrf Weight Path
*> 10.20.0.0/16     172.30.255.254                      0 30 200 50 i
*> 10.30.0.0/16     172.30.255.254        10            0 30 i
*> 10.100.0.0/16    0.0.0.0                0        32768 i
*> 10.200.0.0/16    172.30.255.254                      0 30 200 i
*> 172.16.0.0       172.30.255.254        10            0 30 i
*> 172.17.0.0       172.30.255.254                      0 30 200 50 i
*> 172.18.0.0       172.30.255.254                      0 30 200 50 i
*> 172.29.1.0/24    172.30.255.254        10            0 30 i
*> 172.29.2.0/24    172.30.255.254                      0 30 200 50 i
*> 172.30.0.0       172.30.255.254         0            0 30 i
*> 172.31.0.0       172.30.255.254        10            0 30 i
*> 172.32.0.0       172.30.255.254        20            0 30 i
*> 172.33.0.0       172.30.255.254        10            0 30 i
*> 192.168.2.0      172.30.255.254        10            0 30 i
*> 192.168.50.0     172.30.255.254                      0 30 200 50 i
*> 192.168.100.0    172.30.255.254        10            0 30 i
Innsbruck#
```

This might seem surprising at first. If Zermatt is a valid next hop in Example 4-41, why was it not listed as a valid next hop in Example 4-40? The answer is that it is a simple split horizon behavior. When Innsbruck's IXC connection is active, Innsbruck advertises the AS50 routes to Zermatt. So even though Zermatt is learning routes to the same prefixes from Moritz, it does not advertise the routes to Innsbruck. But when Innsbruck's IXC link goes down, that router sends a BGP Update to Zermatt withdrawing its routes to the AS50 prefixes. When that happens, Zermatt advertises the AS50 routes it learned from Moritz to Innsbruck.

With the BGP table of Example 4-41 in effect, Innsbruck will forward packets with AS50 destination addresses to Zermatt. What happens to the packets from there can be unpredictable. Zermatt shows Moritz as the next hop to the AS50 prefixes; if there is a direct connection between Zermatt and Moritz, the packets are forwarded to Moritz which in turns forwards them to Cervinia and AS30 has become a transit AS. If, on the other hand, the packets mush traverse internal routers between Zermatt and Moritz, those internal routers have no routes to the AS50 prefixes because there is neither an IBGP session to them or redistribution from BGP to the IGP. The internal routers do, however, have default routes advertised into IS-IS by Zermatt and Moritz. So if Zermatt forwards the packet to an internal router that has chosen the default route from Moritz, the router will forward the packet to Moritz and again the packet will successfully transit AS30. If, however, the internal router has chosen the default route from Zermatt, when Zermatt forwards the packet to the internal router, the router will forward the packet back to Zermatt and a routing loop will occur.

The bottom line for all this is that neither Innsbruck nor Cervinia in Figure 4-8 should ever forward a packet to AS30 unless the destination address of the packet belongs to one of the AS30 prefixes. Outgoing route filters should be used to ensure that Zermatt and Moritz advertise only the AS30 prefixes to their EBGP peers.

The configuration in Example 4-42 shows the **neighbor distribute-list** statement used to implement an outgoing route filter on Zermatt. The filter is applied to neighbor Innsbruck (10.100.83.1), ACL 1 is referenced to identify the prefixes to be filtered, and the **out** keyword makes it an outgoing filter.

Note   Do not forget to do a soft reset of the BGP session after applying the route filter.

Example 4-42   neighbor distribute-list *Statement Is Used to Create an Outgoing Route Filter on Zermatt Permits Advertisement of the AS30 Prefixes to Innsbruck and Denies All Other Prefixes*

```
router bgp 30
 no synchronization
 bgp log-neighbor-changes
 network 10.30.0.0 mask 255.255.0.0
 network 172.16.0.0
 network 172.29.1.0 mask 255.255.255.0
 network 172.30.0.0
 network 172.31.0.0
 network 172.32.0.0
 network 172.33.0.0
 network 192.168.2.0
 network 192.168.100.0
 neighbor 10.100.83.1 remote-as 100
 neighbor 10.100.83.1 ebgp-multihop 2
```

```
 neighbor 10.100.83.1 update-source Loopback0
 neighbor 10.100.83.1 distribute-list 1 out
 neighbor 172.30.255.150 remote-as 30
 neighbor 172.30.255.150 update-source Loopback0
 neighbor 172.30.255.150 next-hop-self
 no auto-summary
!
access-list 1 permit 192.168.100.0
access-list 1 permit 10.30.0.0
access-list 1 permit 192.168.2.0
access-list 1 permit 172.32.0.0
access-list 1 permit 172.33.0.0
access-list 1 permit 172.29.1.0
access-list 1 permit 172.31.0.0
access-list 1 permit 172.16.0.0
access-list 1 deny    any
!
```

Example 4-43 shows the effects of Zermatt's outgoing route filter in Innsbruck's BGP table. Innsbruck's IXC interface is still down, so it is not receiving routes from Meribel or Cervinia. You can see that the only entries now in the table, aside from its own AS100 prefix, are the routes permitted by Zermatt's route filter.

Example 4-43 *Innsbruck Is No Longer Receiving Routes to Prefixes Outside of AS30 from Zermatt*

```
Innsbruck#show ip bgp
BGP table version is 1, local router ID is 10.100.83.1
Status codes: s suppressed, d damped, h history, * valid, > best, i - internal,
              r RIB-failure, S Stale
Origin codes: i - IGP, e - EGP, ? - incomplete

   Network          Next Hop          Metric LocPrf Weight Path
*  10.30.0.0/16     172.30.255.254       10             0 30 i
*  10.100.0.0/16    0.0.0.0               0         32768 i
*  172.16.0.0       172.30.255.254       10             0 30 i
*  172.29.1.0/24    172.30.255.254       10             0 30 i
*  172.31.0.0       172.30.255.254       10             0 30 i
*  172.32.0.0       172.30.255.254       20             0 30 i
*  172.33.0.0       172.30.255.254       10             0 30 i
*  192.168.2.0      172.30.255.254       10             0 30 i
*  192.168.100.0    172.30.255.254       10             0 30 i
Innsbruck#
```

Of course, shutting down an interface to verify that a route filter is working correctly in a production network is hardly practical. A better approach is to use the **show ip bgp neighbors advertised-routes** command as shown in Example 4-44. But the information provided by this command may not be conclusive, either. Because of the split-horizon behavior, the command would not display the AS50 prefixes when Innsbruck is in a normal state and advertising the prefixes to Zermatt, even without the route filter. (A notable difference is that if the router filter were not configured you would see the AS200 prefix 10.200.0.0/16 included in the list of advertised routes.) There is no substitute for understanding how your network will behave both in normal circumstances and abnormal circumstances.

Example 4-44   show ip bgp neighbors advertised-routes *Command Displays What Prefixes Are Being Advertised to the Specified Neighbor*

```
Zermatt#show ip bgp neighbors 10.100.83.1 advertised-routes
BGP table version is 25, local router ID is 172.30.255.254
Status codes: s suppressed, d damped, h history, * valid, > best, i - internal,
              r RIB-failure, S Stale
Origin codes: i - IGP, e - EGP, ? - incomplete

   Network          Next Hop          Metric LocPrf Weight Path
*> 10.30.0.0/16     172.30.255.100       10           32768 i
*> 172.16.0.0       172.30.255.100       10           32768 i
*> 172.29.1.0/24    172.30.255.100       10           32768 i
*> 172.31.0.0       172.30.255.100       10           32768 i
*> 172.32.0.0       172.30.255.100       20           32768 i
*> 172.33.0.0       172.30.255.100       10           32768 i
*> 192.168.2.0      172.30.255.100       10           32768 i
*> 192.168.100.0    172.30.255.100       10           32768 i


Total number of prefixes 8
Zermatt#
```

Another problem shown in Example 4-40 is that Innsbruck lists not only Meribel (10.50.250.1) as a next hop for the destinations within AS50, but also Cervinia (10.200.60.1). The same double entry exists in the BGP table of Cervinia, which shows both Meribel and Innsbruck as next-hop routers for the AS50 addresses. The double entries are caused because Innsbruck and Cervinia are peered not only with Meribel, but also with each other: When Meribel advertises a route to its two EBGP peers, those peers in turn advertise the route to each other. Although those routes are marked as valid in the BGP tables, Cervinia is not a valid next hop from Innsbruck to Meribel and Innsbruck is not a valid next hop from Cervinia to Meribel because the shared IXC link is the only connection to Meribel.

If Meribel withdraws a route, Innsbruck and Cervinia will remove Meribel as a next hop to the destination and will advertise the withdrawal to each other. But during the short time between receiving the withdrawal from Meribel and receiving the withdrawal from Cervinia, Innsbruck will show Cervinia as the next hop to the route and Cervinia will show Innsbruck as the next hop to the route. A temporary routing loop will have occurred.

Example 4-45 shows an incoming route filter configured on Innsbruck to correct the problem (a similar filter is configured for Cervinia). ACL 1 denies the AS50 prefixes and permits everything else. The **distribute-list** is applied to Cervinia, and filters only the routes received from that neighbor. There is also an incoming filter applied to Meribel, using ACL 2 to ensure that the AS200 prefix is not accepted from that neighbor so that, similarly, a routing loop between Innsbruck and Meribel cannot occur should the route to 10.200.0.0/16 become unreachable through Cervinia.

Example 4-45 *Incoming Route Filters Are Configured on Innsbruck That Rejects Any AS50 Prefixes Received from Neighbor Cervinia (10.200.60.1) and the AS200 Prefix Received from Neighbor Meribel (10.50.250.1)*

```
router bgp 100
 no synchronization
 bgp log-neighbor-changes
 network 10.100.0.0 mask 255.255.0.0
 neighbor 10.50.250.1 remote-as 50
 neighbor 10.50.250.1 ebgp-multihop 2
 neighbor 10.50.250.1 update-source Loopback0
 neighbor 10.50.250.1 distribute-list 2 in
 neighbor 10.200.60.1 remote-as 200
 neighbor 10.200.60.1 ebgp-multihop 2
 neighbor 10.200.60.1 update-source Loopback0
 neighbor 10.200.60.1 distribute-list 1 in
 neighbor 172.30.255.254 remote-as 30
 neighbor 172.30.255.254 ebgp-multihop 2
 neighbor 172.30.255.254 update-source Loopback0
 no auto-summary
!
access-list 1 deny   10.20.0.0
access-list 1 deny   192.168.50.0
access-list 1 deny   172.29.2.0
access-list 1 deny   172.17.0.0
access-list 1 deny   172.18.0.0
access-list 1 permit any
access-list 2 deny 10.200.0.0
access-list 2 permit any
!
```

The results of the filter on Innsbruck's BGP table are shown in Example 4-46. Comparing this table to the one in Example 4-40, you can see that Moritz is now the only next hop to the AS50 destinations and Cervinia is now the only next hop to AS200 destinations. Although Zermatt is the preferred next hop to AS30 destinations, Cervinia is still available through the IXC link as a next hop to AS30 should Zermatt become unreachable.

Example 4-46   *Innsbruck's BGP Table No Longer Shows Cervinia as a Valid Next Hop for AS50 Destinations or Moritz as a Valid Next Hop for AS200 Destinations*

```
Innsbruck#show ip bgp
BGP table version is 16, local router ID is 10.100.83.1
Status codes: s suppressed, d damped, h history, * valid, > best, i - internal,
              r RIB-failure, S Stale
Origin codes: i - IGP, e - EGP, ? - incomplete


    Network          Next Hop          Metric LocPrf Weight Path
*>  10.20.0.0/16     10.50.250.1           0             0 50 i
*   10.30.0.0/16     10.200.60.1                         0 200 30 i
*>                   172.30.255.254       10             0 30 i
*>  10.100.0.0/16    0.0.0.0               0         32768 i
*>  10.200.0.0/16    10.200.60.1           0             0 200 i
*   172.16.0.0       10.200.60.1                         0 200 30 i
*>                   172.30.255.254       10             0 30 i
*>  172.17.0.0       10.50.250.1           0             0 50 i
*>  172.18.0.0       10.50.250.1           0             0 50 i
*   172.29.1.0/24    10.200.60.1                         0 200 30 i
*>                   172.30.255.254       10             0 30 i
*>  172.29.2.0/24    10.50.250.1           0             0 50 i
*   172.31.0.0       10.200.60.1                         0 200 30 i
*>                   172.30.255.254       10             0 30 i
*   172.32.0.0       10.200.60.1                         0 200 30 i
*>                   172.30.255.254       20             0 30 i
*   172.33.0.0       10.200.60.1                         0 200 30 i
*>                   172.30.255.254       10             0 30 i
*   192.168.2.0      10.200.60.1                         0 200 30 i
*>                   172.30.255.254       10             0 30 i
*>  192.168.50.0     10.50.250.1           0             0 50 i
*   192.168.100.0    10.200.60.1                         0 200 30 i
*>                   172.30.255.254       10             0 30 i
Innsbruck#
```

Route Filtering with Extended ACLs

As prefix filtering requirements become more complex, using ACLs to identify the prefixes to be filtered becomes more operationally challenging:

- Identifying groups of prefixes within class boundaries with netmasks are difficult and can be confusing.

- Identifying a contiguous range of prefixes with access lists is difficult.

- If the set of prefixes to be filtered changes frequently, editing the list can become operationally challenging.

The operational difficulty of using access lists as route filters comes from adapting a tool designed for packet identification to instead identify routes. The standard ACL in Example 4-45, identifying a simple list of single prefixes, was reasonably straightforward. But for more complex identification, extended access lists are required. Take, for example, an extended access list that can identify not just the single 16-bit prefix 10.20.0.0/16, but all longer prefixes whose first 16 bits are 10.20. The extended access list is:

```
access-list 100 permit ip 10.20.0.0 0.0.255.255 255.255.0.0 0.0.255.255
```

There are four 32-bit dotted-decimal components of this ACL:

- **10.20.0.0** specifies the meaningful numbers of the prefix.

- **0.0.255.255** is a wildcard mask specifying that the first 16 bits are invariable and the second 16 bits (marked by "don't care" bits in the wildcard) can be anything.

- **255.255.0.0** specifies the 16-bit mask of the prefix, as the minimum prefix length.

- **0.0.255.255** is a wildcard mask applied to the address mask, specifying that the first 16 bits of the mask must be all ones and the second 16 bits can be anything.

Suppose you want to reject all prefixes longer than 22 bits (a frequent practice to enforce a policy of not accepting long prefixes that should instead be a part of a shorter aggregate). The extended ACL is

```
access-list 101 deny ip any 255.255.252.0 0.0.3.255
```

- **any** matches any combination of digits in the masked portion of the prefix.

- **255.255.252.0** is the 22-bit address mask, meaning the **any** keyword apples to the first 22 bits of the prefix.

- **0.0.3.255** is the wildcard mask specifying that the first 22 bits of the address mask must be as shown in the preceding mask, and the remaining bits can be anything.

As these examples show, ACLs adapted for route filtering are far from intuitive. Fortunately, prefix lists provide a better and more easily interpreted tool for filtering NLRI.

Case Study: Using Prefix Lists

Example 4-47 shows a simple application of a prefix list that performs the exact same filtering function as the ACL configuration in Example 4-42. This example shows several advantageous features of the **ip prefix-list** statement:

- The prefix list uses a name rather that a number, making it easier to identify individual filters.[9]

- An **ip prefix-list description** statement can be added to the beginning of the list, with up to 80 characters of text to aid in interpreting the purpose of the list.

- Sequence numbers (seq) are added to aid in editing the list.

- CIDR notation, specifying the prefix bit length following a forward slash, is used instead of the prefix mask notation used with access lists. This notation is both easier to type and easier to interpret.

- The filter is applied to a BGP neighbor with the **neighbor prefix-list** statement. Like the **neighbor distribute-list** statement, the incoming (**in**) or outgoing (**out**) filer direction is specified. It should be noted that you can call a prefix-list using the **neighbor distribute-list prefix-list** statement, but using this statement rather than the simpler **neighbor prefix-list** statement usually makes little sense.

Example 4-47   **ip** prefix-list *Statements Are Used to Build an NLRI Filter Equivalent to the ACL-Based Filter in Example 4-42. The Filter Is Applied to a Neighbor with the* **neighbor prefix-list** *Statement*

```
router bgp 30
 no synchronization
 bgp log-neighbor-changes
 network 10.30.0.0 mask 255.255.0.0
 network 172.16.0.0
 network 172.29.1.0 mask 255.255.255.0
 network 172.30.0.0
 network 172.31.0.0
 network 172.32.0.0
 network 172.33.0.0
 network 192.168.2.0
 network 192.168.100.0
 neighbor 10.100.83.1 remote-as 100
 neighbor 10.100.83.1 ebgp-multihop 2
 neighbor 10.100.83.1 update-source Loopback0
 neighbor 10.100.83.1 prefix-list Innsbruck_Out out
 neighbor 172.30.255.150 remote-as 30
 neighbor 172.30.255.150 update-source Loopback0
 neighbor 172.30.255.150 next-hop-self
 no auto-summary
 !
```

---

[9] You can also use named access lists for route filtering.

```
ip prefix-list Innsbruck-Out description Filter outgoing routes to neighbor
 10.100.83.1
ip prefix-list Innsbruck_Out seq 5 permit 192.168.100.0/24
ip prefix-list Innsbruck_Out seq 10 permit 10.30.0.0/16
ip prefix-list Innsbruck_Out seq 15 permit 192.168.2.0/24
ip prefix-list Innsbruck_Out seq 20 permit 172.32.0.0/16
ip prefix-list Innsbruck_Out seq 25 permit 172.33.0.0/16
ip prefix-list Innsbruck_Out seq 30 permit 172.29.1.0/24
ip prefix-list Innsbruck_Out seq 35 permit 172.31.0.0/16
ip prefix-list Innsbruck_Out seq 40 permit 172.16.0.0/16
ip prefix-list Innsbruck_Out seq 45 deny 0.0.0.0/0 le 32
!
```

The results of the filter are observed in Example 4-48. Using the **show ip bgp neighbors advertised-routes** command, you can see that the only routes Zermatt advertises to Innsbruck are the ones permitted by the Innsbruck_Out filter.

Example 4-48   *Zermatt Advertises to Innsbruck Only the Routes Permitted by the Filter Configured in Example 4-47*

```
Zermatt#show ip bgp neighbors 10.100.83.1 advertised-routes
BGP table version is 17, local router ID is 172.30.255.254
Status codes: s suppressed, d damped, h history, * valid, > best, i - internal,
              r RIB-failure, S Stale
Origin codes: i - IGP, e - EGP, ? - incomplete

   Network          Next Hop          Metric LocPrf Weight Path
*> 10.30.0.0/16     172.30.255.100        10         32768 i
*> 172.16.0.0       172.30.255.100        10         32768 i
*> 172.29.1.0/24    172.30.255.100        10         32768 i
*> 172.31.0.0       172.30.255.100        10         32768 i
*> 172.32.0.0       172.30.255.100        20         32768 i
*> 172.33.0.0       172.30.255.100        10         32768 i
*> 192.168.2.0      172.30.255.100        10         32768 i
*> 192.168.100.0    172.30.255.100        10         32768 i

Total number of prefixes 8
Zermatt#
```

Note   In addition to the other advantages, prefix lists tend to use less CPU cycles and therefore have better performance on the router than an equivalent ACL-based route filter. On a router with an extensive policy configuration, this can make a significant difference.

Like access lists, prefix lists are executed sequentially from the top down. The sequence numbers are added by default—that is, you do not have to enter them—as you type the list entries. IOS sets the sequence number of the first entry to 5, and the sequence number of subsequent entries is added in increments of 5. Each new entry is added to the bottom of the list. If you need to add an entry somewhere other than the end of the list, specify a sequence number as you type the entry that will put the entry into the correct position in the list relative to the other sequence numbers.

In Example 4-49, a new entry is added to the prefix list without specifying the sequence number. The **show ip prefix-list** command, useful for observing a specified prefix-list configuration, shows that the new statement is added to the end of the list with a sequence number of 50—the next number in the automatic sequence. In that position, however, the entry has no effect because the line before it is a "deny all."

Example 4-49 *If a Sequence Number Is Not Specified When a New Entry Is Added to a Prefix List, the Entry Is Added to the End of the List with a Sequence Number Incremented by 5 from the Previously Ending Number*

```
Zermatt#conf t
Enter configuration commands, one per line.  End with CNTL/Z.
Zermatt(config)#ip prefix-list Innsbruck_Out permit 172.35.0.0/16
Zermatt(config)#^Z
Zermatt#
*May 24 16:01:33.279: %SYS-5-CONFIG_I: Configured from console by console
Zermatt#show ip prefix-list Innsbruck_Out
ip prefix-list Innsbruck_Out: 10 entries
   seq 5 permit 192.168.100.0/24
   seq 10 permit 10.30.0.0/16
   seq 15 permit 192.168.2.0/24
   seq 20 permit 172.32.0.0/16
   seq 25 permit 172.33.0.0/16
   seq 30 permit 172.29.1.0/24
   seq 35 permit 172.31.0.0/16
   seq 40 permit 172.16.0.0/16
   seq 45 deny 0.0.0.0/0 le 32
   seq 50 permit 172.35.0.0/16
Zermatt#
```

In Example 4-50, the incorrect entry is removed and then re-added but with a sequence number of 42. The **show ip prefix-list** command shows that the entry now appears before the ending "deny all" (sequence number 45), and routes with a matching prefix will now be permitted correctly.

Example 4-50 *Entry for 172.16.0.0/16 Is Removed from the Prefix List and Then Re-Entered with a Sequence Number of 42 to Place It Before the "deny all" at the End of the List*

```
Zermatt#conf t
Enter configuration commands, one per line.  End with CNTL/Z.
Zermatt(config)#no ip prefix-list Innsbruck_Out permit 172.35.0.0/16
Zermatt(config)#ip prefix-list Innsbruck_Out seq 42 permit 172.35.0.0/16
Zermatt(config)#^Z
Zermatt#
*May 24 16:07:03.815: %SYS-5-CONFIG_I: Configured from console by console
Zermatt#show ip prefix-list Innsbruck_Out
ip prefix-list Innsbruck_Out: 10 entries
   seq 5 permit 192.168.100.0/24
   seq 10 permit 10.30.0.0/16
   seq 15 permit 192.168.2.0/24
   seq 20 permit 172.32.0.0/16
   seq 25 permit 172.33.0.0/16
   seq 30 permit 172.29.1.0/24
   seq 35 permit 172.31.0.0/16
   seq 40 permit 172.16.0.0/16
   seq 42 permit 172.35.0.0/16
   seq 45 deny 0.0.0.0/0 le 32
Zermatt#
```

Of particular interest in the configuration of Example 4-47 is the last line, the "deny all." Notice that in addition to the prefix and prefix length of 0.0.0.0/0, there is a keyword **le** and a number, 32. The **le** keyword means "less than or equal to," and the number specifies a prefix length. Together the statement means "match any prefix with any length less than or equal to 32."

Note Like ACLs, prefix lists have an implicit "deny any;" if you send a prefix to a prefix list and there is not a match, the prefix is denied. And as with ACLs, it is good practice to explicitly configure the "deny any" at the end of a prefix list anyway, as a reminder to operators that the entry exists.

If you send a prefix to an undefined prefix list—that is, you enter a **neighbor prefix-list** statement referencing a prefix list that has not been configured—no action is taken.

One downside to the named prefix lists is the potential for misspelling a name. In the development of the examples in this chapter, this author several times mistyped "Insbruck_Out" or "Innsbruck_out." If your prefix list configuration does not have the expected result, a first troubleshooting step is to look carefully at your spelling.

Without the **le** keyword, the specified prefix and prefix length much match exactly. All of the entries before the last one in Example 4-50 require exact matches; for example, the only routes that will match the first entry on the list (seq 5) are those with a 24-bit prefix length and with those 24 bits being 192.168.100. A route to 192.168.100.0 with a prefix length of 25 or of 23 will not match.

For the last entry, if the **le** keyword were not present, the entry would match only the default route 0.0.0.0/0. With the keyword, the entry matches a range rather than an exact prefix and length: The 0.0.0.0 becomes merely a placeholder, and the prefix length of 0 becomes the beginning of the range of prefix lengths; the 32 after the **le** is the end of the range.

So with no prefix bits specified, and with a range of prefix lengths from 0 to 32, the entry matches all possible IPv4 prefixes.

There is another keyword that can specify a range of prefixes rather than an exact match: **ge**, which represents "greater than or equal to." When this keyword is used, it represents the beginning of a range of prefix lengths rather than the end as does **le**. Take, for instance, the following prefix list entry:

```
ip prefix-list Example-A seq 10 permit 192.168.5.0/24 ge 24
```

You can interpret the entry as "permit any prefix whose first 24 bits are 192.168.5, and whose length is 24 bits or longer." In other words, match any prefix whose first 24 bits are 192.168.5.

Given a second entry:

```
ip prefix-list Example-B seq 15 deny 172.16.0.0/16 ge 22
```

You can read this entry as "deny any prefix whose first 16 bits are 172.16, and whose length is 22 bits or longer." In this case, a prefix of 172.16.40.0/24 will match, but a prefix of 172.16.40.0/21 will not match.

In both of these cases, the end of the prefix length range is understood to be 32 because that is the longest possible IPv4 prefix length. You can use the **ge** and **le** keywords together to specify a range in which the prefix length is greater 0 but less than 32. For example:

```
ip prefix-list Example-C seq 20 permit 10.128.0.0/12 ge 16 le 24
```

This entry matches any prefix whose first 12 bits are 10.128, and whose length is at least 16 bits and no longer than 24 bits. So 10.143.0.0/16 will match, as will 10.131.15.0/24 and 10.128.252.0/22. But 10.128.0.0/14 and 10.131.15.0/26 will not match.

To demonstrate practical applications of prefix lists to filter on ranges, AS50 of the test network we have been using is reconfigured as shown in Figure 4-9. Meribel is now advertising a set of prefixes, of varying lengths, that all belong to the aggregate 10.20.0.0/16.

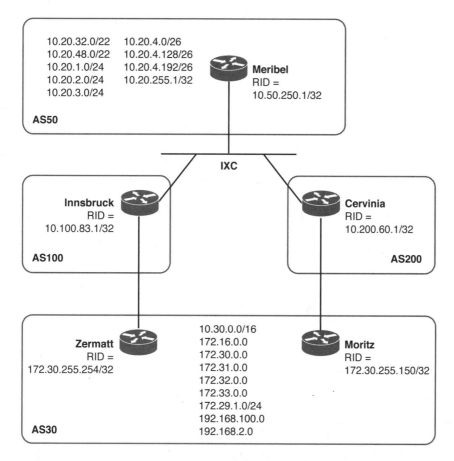

10.20.32.0/22   10.20.4.0/26
10.20.48.0/22   10.20.4.128/26
10.20.1.0/24   10.20.4.192/26
10.20.2.0/24   10.20.255.1/32
10.20.3.0/24

Meribel
RID =
10.50.250.1/32

AS50

IXC

Innsbruck
RID =
10.100.83.1/32

AS100

Cervinia
RID =
10.200.60.1/32

AS200

Zermatt
RID =
172.30.255.254/32

10.30.0.0/16
172.16.0.0
172.30.0.0
172.31.0.0
172.32.0.0
172.33.0.0
172.29.1.0/24
192.168.100.0
192.168.2.0

Moritz
RID =
172.30.255.150/32

AS30

Figure 4-9 *AS50 Is Reconfigured so That Meribel Is Advertising a Different Set of Prefixes, All of Which Belong to the Aggregate 10.20.0.0/16*

In Example 4-51, a prefix list named Innsbruck_In is configured on router Zermatt. The list permits routes to all the prefixes whose first 16 bits are 10.20 and whose prefix length is up to and including 32 bits; all other routes are denied. This prefix list is applied as an incoming filter on routes advertised from Innsbruck. The result of this filter is that the only packets Zermatt will forward to Innsbruck are those with a destination address belonging to one of the AS50 prefixes. Packets to AS100 or AS200, other than those matching Zermatt's static route to Innsbruck's loopback interface (necessary for the multihop EBGP session), will not be forwarded.

Example 4-51   *Prefix List Innsbruck_In Is Configured as an Incoming Filter on Zermatt's Interface to Innsbruck; This Filter Permits Routes to All the Prefixes in AS50 and Blocks Acceptance of Any Other Routes*

```
router bgp 30
 no synchronization
 bgp log-neighbor-changes
 network 10.30.0.0 mask 255.255.0.0
 network 172.16.0.0
 network 172.29.1.0 mask 255.255.255.0
 network 172.30.0.0
 network 172.31.0.0
 network 172.32.0.0
 network 172.33.0.0
 network 192.168.2.0
 network 192.168.100.0
 neighbor 10.100.83.1 remote-as 100
 neighbor 10.100.83.1 ebgp-multihop 2
 neighbor 10.100.83.1 update-source Loopback0
 neighbor 10.100.83.1 prefix-list Innsbruck_In in
 neighbor 10.100.83.1 prefix-list Innsbruck_Out out
 neighbor 172.30.255.150 remote-as 30
 neighbor 172.30.255.150 update-source Loopback0
 neighbor 172.30.255.150 next-hop-self
 no auto-summary
!
ip prefix-list Innsbruck_In description Incoming filter for neighbor 10.100.83.1
ip prefix-list Innsbruck_In seq 5 permit 10.20.0.0/16 le 32
ip prefix-list Innsbruck_In seq 10 deny 0.0.0.0/0 le 32
!
ip prefix-list Innsbruck-Out description Filter outgoing routes to neighbor
   10.100.83.1
ip prefix-list Innsbruck_Out seq 5 permit 192.168.100.0/24
ip prefix-list Innsbruck_Out seq 10 permit 10.30.0.0/16
ip prefix-list Innsbruck_Out seq 15 permit 192.168.2.0/24
ip prefix-list Innsbruck_Out seq 20 permit 172.32.0.0/16
ip prefix-list Innsbruck_Out seq 25 permit 172.33.0.0/16
ip prefix-list Innsbruck_Out seq 30 permit 172.29.1.0/24
ip prefix-list Innsbruck_Out seq 35 permit 172.31.0.0/16
ip prefix-list Innsbruck_Out seq 40 permit 172.16.0.0/16
ip prefix-list Innsbruck_Out seq 45 deny 0.0.0.0/0 le 32
```

The **show ip prefix-list** command displays the configuration of a prefix list named Cervinia, configured on router Moritz, in Example 4-52. This list permits routes to the AS50 prefixes whose lengths are 24 bits or longer; so 10.20.32.0/22 and 10.20.48.0/22 are not permitted, nor are any routes to prefixes in the other autonomous systems. Although not shown in the example, the filter is applied as an incoming filter for routes received from Cervinia.

Example 4-52 *Prefix List Cervinia Permits Only Routes to the AS50 Prefixes Whose Lengths Are 24 Bits or Longer*

```
Moritz#show ip prefix-list Cervinia
ip prefix-list Cervinia: 2 entries
   seq 5 permit 10.20.0.0/16 ge 24
   seq 10 deny 0.0.0.0/0 le 32
Moritz#
```

The configuration of Zermatt's prefix list Innsbruck_In is modified in Example 4-53. Like prefix list Cervinia in Example 4-52, this filter permits only routes to AS50 prefixes whose lengths are 24 bits or longer, but in this case, it also specifies that the lengths cannot be longer than 30 bits. Therefore, in addition to 10.20.32.0/22 and 10.20.48.0/22, routes to 10.20.255.1/32 are also rejected.

Example 4-53 *Zermatt's Prefix List Innsbruck_In Is Modified from the Configuration in Example 4-51 so That it Permits Only a Subset of the AS50 Routes*

```
ip prefix-list Innsbruck_In description Incoming filter for neighbor 10.100.83.1
ip prefix-list Innsbruck_In seq 5 permit 10.20.0.0/16 ge 24 le 30
ip prefix-list Innsbruck_In seq 10 deny 0.0.0.0/0 le 32
```

The results of the modified Innsbruck_In prefix list are shown in Example 4-54. The **show ip bgp prefix-list** command displays the subset of entries in Zermatt's BGP table that are effected by the Innsbruck_In list. Note that all the prefixes permitted by this filter are also permitted by the filter Cervinia at Moritz; therefore, Moritz is also shown as a valid next hop to each of the routes.

Example 4-54 show ip bgp prefix-list *Command Displays the BGP Table Entries Affected by a Specified Prefix List*

```
Zermatt#show ip bgp prefix-list Innsbruck_In
BGP table version is 106, local router ID is 172.30.255.254
Status codes: s suppressed, d damped, h history, * valid, > best, i - internal,
              r RIB-failure, S Stale
Origin codes: i - IGP, e - EGP, ? - incomplete

   Network          Next Hop          Metric LocPrf Weight Path
* i10.20.1.0/24     172.30.255.150         0   100      0 200 50 ?
*>                  10.100.83.1                          0 100 50 ?
* i10.20.2.0/24     172.30.255.150         0   100      0 200 50 ?
```

```
*>                      10.100.83.1                         0 100 50 ?
* i10.20.3.0/24        172.30.255.150      0      100       0 200 50 ?
*>                      10.100.83.1                         0 100 50 ?
* i10.20.4.0/26        172.30.255.150      0      100       0 200 50 ?
*>                      10.100.83.1                         0 100 50 ?
* i10.20.4.128/26      172.30.255.150      0      100       0 200 50 ?
*>                      10.100.83.1                         0 100 50 ?
* i10.20.4.192/26      172.30.255.150      0      100       0 200 50 ?
*>                      10.100.83.1                         0 100 50 ?
Zermatt#
```

BGP routers with extensive policy rules configured, such as those at peering points, can have many prefix lists and some of those prefix lists can be long. While the **show ip prefix-list** used in Example 4-52 allows you to view a single prefix list, the **show ip prefix-list summary** (Example 4-55) and **show ip prefix-list detail** (Example 4-56) commands give you information about all the prefix lists configured on the router. Both commands tell you the prefix lists configured on the router and some usage information about each one, with the detail option also displaying each entry of each prefix list.

Example 4-55   show ip prefix-list summary *Command Displays Information About All the Prefix Lists Configured on the Router*

```
Zermatt#show ip prefix-list summary
Prefix-list with the last deletion/insertion: Innsbruck_In
ip prefix-list Innsbruck_In:
   Description: Filter incoming routes from neighbor 10.100.83.1
   count: 2, range entries: 2, sequences: 5 - 10, refcount: 3
ip prefix-list Innsbruck_Out:
   Description: Filter outgoing routes to neighbor 10.100.83.1
   count: 9, range entries: 1, sequences: 5 - 45, refcount: 3
Zermatt#
```

The usage details displayed by the two commands, which help you with both management and troubleshooting of prefix lists, are

- An identification of the last prefix list to be modified

- The description of each prefix list, if configured

- The number of entries (count) comprising each list

- The number of entries in each list that specifies a range of prefixes (range count) using the **le** or **ge** keywords rather than an exact prefix match

- The range of sequence numbers (sequences) used in each list

- In the detail option, a count (hit count) of the number of prefixes that have matched each entry on the list; the hit count can be cleared (for example, after a prefix list has been reconfigured) with the command **clear ip prefix-list**

- An internal data structure counter (refcount) that provides a lock on prefix lists and list entries that are in use[10]

Example 4-56   show ip prefix-list detail *Command Displays the Same Information as* show ip prefix-list summary, *But Adds Information About the Individual Entries Comprising Each Prefix List*

```
Zermatt#show ip prefix-list detail
Prefix-list with the last deletion/insertion: Innsbruck_In
ip prefix-list Innsbruck_In:
   Description: Filter incoming routes from neighbor 10.100.83.1
   count: 2, range entries: 2, sequences: 5 - 10, refcount: 3
   seq 5 permit 10.20.0.0/16 ge 24 le 30 (hit count: 0, refcount: 1)
   seq 10 deny 0.0.0.0/0 le 32 (hit count: 9, refcount: 1)
ip prefix-list Innsbruck_Out:
   Description: Filter outgoing routes to neighbor 10.100.83.1
   count: 9, range entries: 1, sequences: 5 - 45, refcount: 3
   seq 5 permit 192.168.100.0/24 (hit count: 1, refcount: 3)
   seq 10 permit 10.30.0.0/16 (hit count: 1, refcount: 1)
   seq 15 permit 192.168.2.0/24 (hit count: 1, refcount: 1)
   seq 20 permit 172.32.0.0/16 (hit count: 1, refcount: 3)
   seq 25 permit 172.33.0.0/16 (hit count: 1, refcount: 1)
   seq 30 permit 172.29.1.0/24 (hit count: 1, refcount: 3)
   seq 35 permit 172.31.0.0/16 (hit count: 1, refcount: 1)
   seq 40 permit 172.16.0.0/16 (hit count: 1, refcount: 1)
   seq 45 deny 0.0.0.0/0 le 32 (hit count: 15, refcount: 1)
Zermatt#
```

Note   Although this section emphasizes the use of prefix lists instead of distribute lists to filter NLRI, you might have some reason for using both in a BGP configuration. For example, you might have an old configuration using distribute lists; you don't want to cause disruptions by changing the existing distribute list configurations, but you want to use prefix lists for any new filter configurations on the same router.

---

[10] The refcount has little troubleshooting use to the average user, and is mostly meaningful only to Cisco personnel working with the IOS code itself. You will, however, notice that the count changes when you add or delete references to the prefix list in the BGP configuration or clear the prefix list counters after a reconfiguration.

While you can do this, you cannot use both a prefix list and a distribute list for the same neighbor in the same direction. That is, you might have a distribute list for an incoming filter and a prefix list for an outgoing filter on a neighbor—or vice versa—but you cannot use both a prefix list and a distribute list for an incoming filer or an outgoing filter on the same neighbor.

Filtering Routes by AS_PATH

You learned from almost the beginning of this book that BGP takes a "higher" perspective of routes, tracking them according to paths through autonomous systems rather than paths through individual routers as IGPs do. The AS_PATH attribute is the primary mechanism BGP uses to track inter-AS paths.

It makes sense, then, that you will often want to apply policies to BGP routes based on the autonomous systems they have passed through rather than based on the individual prefix values themselves. For example, you might want to apply a policy to

- All routes originating in a certain AS
- All routes passing through a certain AS
- All routes advertised by a certain neighboring AS
- All routes passing through a certain sequence of autonomous systems

AS-path filters are powerful tools for identifying BGP routes according to their AS_PATH attributes rather than their NLRI. What makes AS-path filters so powerful is their use of a text-parsing tool called regular expressions to match on patterns within the AS_PATH attribute.

Regular Expressions

Regular expressions, or *regex* for short, are commonly used in such programming and scripting languages as Python, Perl, Expect, awk, and Tcl, in search engines, and in UNIX utilities such as *egrep*. Regular expressions use a string of characters, all of which are either *metacharacters* or *literals*, to find matches in text. In the case of AS_PATH access lists, they are used to find matches in the AS_PATH attributes of BGP updates.

Note   This section follows the excellent presentation made by Jeffrey E. F. Friedl in his book, *Mastering Regular Expressions*.[11] Almost everything you need to know about regular expressions to work with Cisco IOS is covered in the first chapter of the book; nonetheless, the book recommendation stands because you are very likely to find regular expressions useful in a wide variety of applications within the data communications

---

[11] Jeffrey E. F. Friedl, *Mastering Regular Expressions*, Third Edition, O'Reilly Media, Sebastopol, CA, 2006. ISBN 0-596-52812-4.

and data processing industry. If you work long with networks, you will eventually pick up some scripting skills with a language such as Python, Perl, or Tcl, and find regular expressions to be a big part of scripting. Friedl presents the subject clearly and with a liberal dose of humor.

Literals and Metacharacters

A typical AS-path filter entry might look like:

```
ip as-path access-list 83 permit ^1_701_(_5646_|_1240_).*
```

The first part is similar to an ACL, including the ACL number (the filter number can be any number between 1 and 500) and a **permit** or **deny** keyword. The string of characters following the **permit** keyword is a regular expression. The regex is composed of *literals* and *metacharacters*. Literals are just text characters that describe what the regex is going to try to match. In this example, "1," "701," "5646," and "1240" are literals describing autonomous system numbers.

Metacharacters are special regular expression characters that act as operators, telling the regex how to perform matches. Table 4-1 shows the metacharacters available for use with Cisco IOS; the remainder of this tutorial describes how each of the metacharacters is used.

Table 4-1 *Regular Expression Metacharacters Relevant to AS_PATH Access Lists*

Metacharacter	Matches
.	Any single character, including white space.
[]	Any character listed between the brackets.
[^]	Any character except those listed between the brackets. (The caret is placed before the sequence of literals.)
-	(Hyphen.) Any character in the range between the two literals separated by the hyphen.
?	0 or 1 instance of the character or pattern.
*	0 or more instances of the character or pattern.
+	1 or more instances of the character or pattern.
^	Start of a line.
$	End of a line.
|	Either of the literals separated by the metacharacter.
_	(Underscore.) A comma, the beginning of the line, the end of the line, or a space.

Delineation: Matching the Start and End of Lines

Consider the following AS-path filter:

```
ip as-path access-list 20 permit 850
```

This filter will match any AS_PATH that includes the string "850." Examples of matching AS_PATHs are [850], [23, 5, **850**, 155], and [3568, 5**850**, 310]. A match is found whether the string is alone in the attribute, one of several AS numbers in the attribute, or even a part of a larger AS number in the attribute.

But suppose you want to match only an AS_PATH that contains the single AS number 850. For this, you must be able to delineate the beginning and end of a line. A caret (^) matches the beginning of a line, and a dollar sign ($) matches the end of a line. So,

```
ip as-path access-list 20 permit ^850$
```

tells the regex to match the beginning of the line, followed immediately by the string "850," followed immediately by the end of the line. In a practical application this pattern is used to match all prefixes originating in the directly neighboring AS850; if the prefixes passed through any other AS, or an additional AS besides 850, the AS_PATH would not match.

The two metacharacters can also be used to match an empty AS_PATH:

```
ip as-path access-list 21 permit ^$
```

In this case, the regex matches the beginning of a line followed immediately by the end of the line; if any other characters exist between the beginning and end of the line, no match is made. The filter matches prefixes originated in the local AS, which have not yet had any ASN attached to the AS_PATH.

Bracketing: Matching a Set of Characters

Brackets allow you to specify a range of single characters. For example:

```
ip as-path access-list 22 permit ^85[0123459]$
```

This filter matches AS_PATHs with any singe AS number 850, 851, 852, 853, 854, 855, or 859.

If the range of characters is contiguous, you can specify just the beginning and end character in the sequence:

```
ip as-path access-list 23 permit ^85[0-5]$
```

This filter matches the same group of AS numbers as the previous filter, with the exception of 859.

Negating: Matching Everything Except a Set of Characters

When a caret (^) is used inside a bracket, it negates the range specified in the bracket. As a result, the regex will match on everything except the range. For example:

```
ip as-path access-list 24 permit ^85[^0-5]$
```

This filter looks like the previous filter, with the exception of the added caret inside the bracket, signifying "not 0-5." The regex will therefore match an AS_PATH with a single AS number in the range 856-859.

Wildcard: Matching Any Single Character

A dot (.) matches any single character. Interestingly, the single character may be a space. Consider the following filter:

```
ip as-path access-list 24 permit ^85.
```

This filter matches an AS_PATH that begins with an AS number in the range 850-859. And because the dot also matches whitespace, ASN 85 will match.

Alternation: Matching One of a Set of Characters

A bar (|) is used to specify an "or" operation. That is, a literal on one or the other side of the bar can be matched. For example:

```
ip as-path access-list 25 permit ^(851|852)$
```

This filter matches an AS_PATH in which there is a single AS number, which is either 851 or 852. The "or" function may be extended to check for more than two possible matches:

```
ip as-path access-list 26 permit ^(851|852|6341|53)$
```

Optional Characters: Matching a Character That May or May Not Be There

The question mark (?) matches 0 or 1 instances of a literal. For example:

```
ip as-path access-list 27 permit ^(850)?$
```

This filter matches an AS_PATH in which there is either a single AS number 850, or else there is an empty list. Note the use of parentheses here, to show that the metacharacter applies to the entire AS number. If the expression 850? is used, the metacharacter applies only to the last character. The expression would match 85 or 850.

Repetition: Matching a Number of Repeating Characters

Two metacharacters can be used to match repeating literals: The asterisk (*) matches 0 or more instances of a literal, and the plus (+) matches one or more instances. For example:

```
ip as-path access-list 28 permit ^(850)*$
```

This filter will match an AS_PATH in which there are no AS numbers, or in which one or more ASNs 850 exist. That is, the AS path could be [850], [850, 850], [850, 850, 850], and so on.[12]

---

[12] It might seem surprising to you that an AS number can appear in an AS_PATH more than once. This happens when AS Path Prepending is used, as described later in this chapter.

The following filter is similar, except that there must be at least one ASN 850 in the AS_PATH:

```
ip as-path access-list 29 permit ^(850)+$
```

Boundaries: Delineating Literals

The underscore (_) is used when you want to specify a string of literals, and must specify their separation. For example, suppose you want to match on the specific AS_PATH [5610, 148, 284, 13]. The filter is:

```
ip as-path access-list 30 permit ^5610_148_284_13$
```

The underscore matches a beginning of line, end of line, a comma, or a space. Notice the difference between the previous filter and this filter:

```
ip as-path access-list 31 permit _5610_148_284_13_
```

Because the first filter specified the beginning and end of the line, only AS_PATH [5610, 148, 284, 13] matches. In this second filter the specified sequence must be included in the AS_PATH, but is not necessarily the only AS numbers in the attribute. So, AS_PATHs [5610, 148, 284, 13], [23, 15, 5610, 148, 284, 13], and [5610, 148, 284, 13, 3005] all match. In other words, the first filter specifies a complete BGP route from source to destination, while the second specifies any route that includes that sequence of autonomous systems.

One of the most frequent uses of the underscore is to specify an AS number at the beginning or end of an AS_PATH of arbitrary length. Take the following two examples:

```
ip as-path access-list 32 permit ^850_
ip as-path access-list 33 permit _850$
```

The first matches any AS_PATH in which the first number on the list is 850. In other words, the routes can pass through any number of other autonomous systems, but the last AS they pass through before being received must be 850. This is obviously useful any time you need to match all prefixes advertised by a specific neighboring AS.

The second example is just the opposite. The routes can have passed through any number of ASs, but the last number on the path must be 850. In other words, this entry filters all prefixes originating in AS850. This is a highly useful filter for matching all prefixes originating in a particular AS, regardless of whether or not it is a neighboring AS.

Putting It All Together: A Complex Example

The real power of regular expressions comes into play when the metacharacters are used in combination to match some complex string of literals. Consider the following filter:

```
ip as-path access-list 10 permit ^(550)+_[880|2304]?_1805_.*
```

This filter looks for AS_PATHs in which the last AS before the route was received was 550. The caret preceding that number specifies that 550 is the first number in the list. The plus sign following the number means that there must be at least one instance of

550, but there can be more. By allowing for more than one instance of the number, the filter has allowed for the possibility that AS550 is practicing path prepending.

Immediately following the one or more instances of 550, there may or may not be a single instance of either 880 or 2304. Next, there must be a single instance of 1805. The last part of the expression specifies that after 1805, the AS_PATH can consist of any number of subsequent AS numbers, including none.

The result is a match on routes that can have originated anywhere but that must have passed through 1805 and then through neighboring AS550. The routes can pass either directly between AS1805 and AS550, or they can pass through either AS880 or AS2304 between AS1805 and AS550.

Case Study: Using AS-Path Filters

AS-path filters, consisting of one or more **ip as-path access-list** entries, are applied to a neighbor using the **neighbor filter-list** statement. As with distribute list and prefix list filters, an AS-path filter can be applied to either incoming or outgoing routes by using the **in** and **out** keywords.

In Examples 4-42 and 4-47, the routers Zermatt and Moritz were configured to advertise only routes to addresses interior to AS30. All other routes were filtered, to prevent AS100 or AS200 from attempting to use AS30 as a transit AS. To implement the filter, all of the AS30 addresses were individually listed in an access list (Example 4-42) or prefix list (Example 4-47). Example 4-57 shows the configuration for Zermatt using an AS_PATH access list to achieve the same results as in the previous case study.

Example 4-57 *Configuring Zermatt to Advertise Only Routes to Addresses Interior to AS30 Using an AS-path Access List*

```
router bgp 30
 no synchronization
 bgp log-neighbor-changes
 network 10.30.0.0 mask 255.255.0.0
 network 172.16.0.0
 network 172.29.1.0 mask 255.255.255.0
 network 172.30.0.0
 network 172.31.0.0
 network 172.32.0.0
 network 172.33.0.0
 network 192.168.2.0
 network 192.168.100.0
 neighbor 10.100.83.1 remote-as 100
 neighbor 10.100.83.1 ebgp-multihop 2
 neighbor 10.100.83.1 update-source Loopback0
 neighbor 10.100.83.1 prefix-list Innsbruck_In in
 neighbor 10.100.83.1 filter-list 1 out
```

```
neighbor 172.30.255.150 remote-as 30
neighbor 172.30.255.150 update-source Loopback0
neighbor 172.30.255.150 next-hop-self
no auto-summary
!
ip as-path access-list 1 permit ^$
!
```

Moritz's configuration has an identical AS-path access list. The regular expression here uses two metacharacters—the first matches the beginning of a line, and the second matches the end of a line. No literals are included. What the regex matches are AS_PATHs that include no AS numbers. The only routes in Zermatt's BGP table in Example 4-58 that have empty AS_PATHs are to the destinations interior to AS30—that is, routes that originate in AS30. They match the AS_PATH list statement and are permitted. Like other access lists, the AS_PATH list has an implicit "deny any" at the end; all the other routes in Example 3-74 match this implicit deny and are not advertised.

Example 4-58   *Only Empty AS_PATHs in Zermatt's BGP Table Are Those of Routes to Addresses Within AS30*

```
Zermatt#show ip bgp
BGP table version is 28, local router ID is 172.30.255.254
Status codes: s suppressed, d damped, h history, * valid, > best, i - internal,
              r RIB-failure, S Stale
Origin codes: i - IGP, e - EGP, ? - incomplete

   Network          Next Hop          Metric LocPrf Weight Path
*>i10.20.0.0/16     172.30.255.150         0    100      0 200 50 i
*  i10.30.0.0/16    172.30.255.150        10    100      0 i
*>                  172.30.255.100        10           32768 i
*>i10.100.0.0/16    172.30.255.150         0    100      0 200 100 i
*>i10.200.0.0/16    172.30.255.150         0    100      0 200 i
*  i172.16.0.0      172.30.255.150        10    100      0 i
*>                  172.30.255.100        10           32768 i
*>i172.17.0.0       172.30.255.150         0    100      0 200 50 i
*>i172.18.0.0       172.30.255.150         0    100      0 200 50 i
*  i172.29.1.0/24   172.30.255.150        10    100      0 i
*>                  172.30.255.100        10           32768 i
*>i172.29.2.0/24    172.30.255.150         0    100      0 200 50 i
*> 172.30.0.0       0.0.0.0                0           32768 i
*  i172.31.0.0      172.30.255.150        10    100      0 i
*>                  172.30.255.100        10           32768 i
*  i172.32.0.0      172.30.255.150        20    100      0 i
*>                  172.30.255.100        20           32768 i
*  i172.33.0.0      172.30.255.150        10    100      0 i
```

```
*>                      172.30.255.100        10              32768 i
* i192.168.2.0          172.30.255.150        10       100       0 i
*>                      172.30.255.100        10              32768 i
*>i192.168.50.0         172.30.255.150         0       100       0 200 50 i
* i192.168.100.0        172.30.255.150        10       100       0 i
*>                      172.30.255.100        10              32768 i
Zermatt#
```

Notice that the configuration of Example 4-57 still uses a prefix list for an incoming filter. In Example 4-53, the requirements for incoming filtering at Moritz was to allow some prefixes from AS50 but not others, so a prefix list is the appropriate tool for that filter.

In Example 4-45, Innsbruck was configured to reject AS50 prefixes advertised by Cervinia (neighbor 10.200.60.1) and to reject AS200 prefixes advertised by Meribel (10.50.250.1), in order to prevent temporary routing loops across the IXC during BGP reconvergence if either neighbor should become unreachable. Distribute lists were used to create the incoming filters.

Example 4-59 shows Innsbruck's configuration using AS_PATH access lists to accomplish similar goals. AS-path filter 1 is applied to incoming updates from Cervinia. The first statement of this list denies any update that includes the ASN50 anywhere in its AS_PATH. The metacharacters before and after the "50" ensure that this number alone is matched. If the metacharacters were left out, the statement would match not only "50," but also such numbers as "500," "5000," "350," and so on. The regex of the second statement says, "Match any character, and match 0 or more occurrences of that character." In other words, match anything. This is the AS-path access-list version of a "permit any." The result of these two lines is that Innsbruck does not accept any AS50 prefixes advertised by Cervinia, but accepts all other prefixes advertised by that router.

Example 4-59 *Configuring Innsbruck Using AS-path Access Lists to Accept Routes from Meribel Only if They Are Interior to AS50, and to Deny Any AS50 Prefixes Advertised by Cervinia*

```
router bgp 100
 no synchronization
 bgp log-neighbor-changes
 network 10.100.0.0 mask 255.255.0.0
 neighbor 10.50.250.1 remote-as 50
 neighbor 10.50.250.1 ebgp-multihop 2
 neighbor 10.50.250.1 update-source Loopback0
 neighbor 10.50.250.1 filter-list 2 in
 neighbor 10.200.60.1 remote-as 200
 neighbor 10.200.60.1 ebgp-multihop 2
 neighbor 10.200.60.1 update-source Loopback0
 neighbor 10.200.60.1 filter-list 1 in
```

```
neighbor 172.30.255.254 remote-as 30
neighbor 172.30.255.254 ebgp-multihop 2
neighbor 172.30.255.254 update-source Loopback0
no auto-summary
!
ip as-path access-list 1 deny _50_
ip as-path access-list 1 permit .*
ip as-path access-list 2 permit ^50$
ip as-path access-list 2 deny .*
!
```

Filter list 2 is applied to incoming updates from Meribel. The regex of the first ACL line reads, "Match the beginning of the line, followed by 50, followed by the end of the line." In other words, match AS_PATHs that include the AS number 50 and nothing else. Those routes are permitted. Any routes that Meribel advertises that it learned from another AS will have more than the number 50 in the AS_PATH. The second line denies all other routes.

Note   Like regular ACLs, AS-path ACLs have an implicit "deny any;" that is, if any route has not found a match by the end of the list, the default action is to deny it. And as with normal ACLs, it is good practice to explicitly configure a "deny any" or "permit any" at the end of an AS-path ACL to remove any doubts about the full behavior of the list.

Figure 4-10 shows an addition to the example topology: AS125 is added and serves as a backup transit AS between AS200 and AS50. If Meribel loses its link to the IXC, traffic into and out of AS50 should traverse AS125 and AS200. Under normal circumstances, BGP will only choose the path through AS125 if the path across the IXC is unavailable, because there is an extra AS hop.

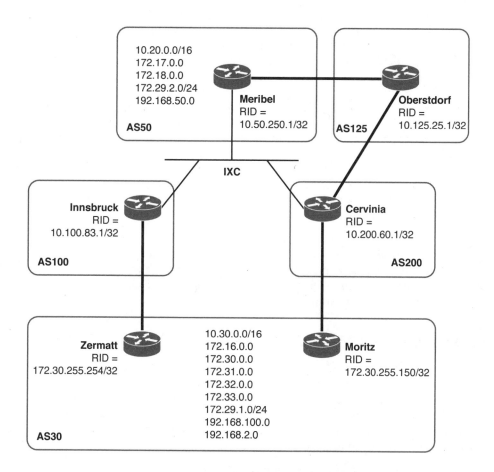

Figure 4-10 *AS125 Provides an Alternative Path to AS50*

Innsbruck's AS-path filter 1 in Example 4-59 does not work in this new topology, because it blocks all routes advertised from Cervinia that contain ASN50. Example 4-60 shows a modification of the AS-path ACL that will work for the new topology. Here, routes with the specific AS_PATH [200, 50]—that is, AS50 routes advertised directly from Meribel to Cervinia and then from Cervinia to Innsbruck—are blocked, again to prevent routing loops, while all other routes from Cervinia—including routes that pass through Oberstdorf—are accepted.

Example 4-60 *Innsbruck's Incoming Filter of Routes from Cervinia Is Modified to Accept the Transit Path Through AS125*

```
!
ip as-path access-list 1 deny ^200_50$
ip as-path access-list 1 permit .*
```

An alternative configuration is shown in Example 4-61. Here, routes with an AS_PATH of [200, 125, 50] are accepted, then all other routes containing ASN 50 are rejected, and then all other routes are accepted. This configuration works because, like normal ACLs, the lines of an AS-path ACL are processed in sequential order from top down.

Example 4-61 *An Alternative Configuration at Innsbruck That Also Accepts the Transit Path Through AS125 Advertised by Cervinia*

```
!
ip as-path access-list 1 permit ^200_125_50$
ip as-path access-list 1 deny _50_
ip as-path access-list 1 permit .*
```

Either configuration works in the simple topology of Figure 4-10. If the topology were expanded, the difference between the two configurations might matter. For example, if there are other alternative paths through Cervinia to AS50, the configuration in Example 4-60 would accept them whereas the configuration in Example 4-61 would reject all alternative paths except the one through AS125.

Case Study: Setting Policy with Route Maps

Route filters, by themselves, allow you to match on either the prefix (NLRI) of a route or the route's AS_PATH attribute. They perform a simple action on matching routes, which is to either accept (permit) or discard (deny) the route. And they allow you to apply the filter to routes received from a specific neighbor or to routes advertised to a specific neighbor. The resulting route policy works by regulating whether or not a router knows about a route through one of its neighbors.

As such, standalone route filters are the "big hammers" in your routing policy toolbox. Sometimes a big hammer is exactly the tool you need, and other times you need a more flexible or precise tool. For example, what if you want to match on both a specific prefix and a specific AS_PATH? What if you do not want to completely block a route, but want to change its attributes in some way?

Route maps give you both the flexibility and the precision to create more complicated route policies.

- Route maps allow you to match on a wide range of BGP route attributes.

- Route maps allow you to not only accept or discard routes, but also to set or change a route's attributes.

- Route maps allow you to combine multiple matching criteria, and set multiple attributes, to build complex route policies .

Route maps are introduced in Chapter 14, Volume I of this book. In that chapter, you learned how to use route maps for redistribution and for policy routing. Here, route maps are used for building complex BGP policies; the mechanics, however, are the same.

Route maps are named, like prefix lists, making their components and references easy to identify within an IOS configuration. They consist of one or more **route-map** statements, each of which has a sequence number to simplify editing the route map. Each statement also has a **permit** or **deny** keyword, just as ACLs and prefix lists do. So a basic route map statement named ASPEN might look like

```
route-map ASPEN deny 10
```

By itself, a route map statement matches every route that is referred to it. To moderate that matching behavior, one or more **match** clauses are added to the statement. For example:

```
route-map ASPEN deny 10
 match ip address prefix-list MILLER
```

This statement denies all routes with NLRI that match on the prefix list (not shown in the example) named MILLER. By itself, you could get the same results by applying the prefix list MILLER directly to a neighbor rather than referencing it through a route map. But route maps allow you to be precise about what routes you match by using multiple match clauses. For example:

```
route-map ASPEN deny 10
 match ip address prefix-list MILLER
 match local-preference 150
 match community WARREN
```

This route map statement only matches routes that have an NLRI matching the prefix list MILLER *and* that have a LOCAL_PREF value of 150 *and* that have a COMMUNITY attribute specified in the community list named WARREN.[13] In other words, if multiple **match** clauses are specified under a route map statement a route must match all the clauses in order for the **permit** or **deny** action of the statement to take effect.

---

[13] COMMUNITY attributes and their uses are covered in Chapter 5.

Table 4-2 lists the **match** conditions you can specify for a BGP policy.

Table 4-2   *BGP Route Attributes and Characteristics That Can Be Matched in a Route Map*

Match Keyword	Matches
as-path	AS_PATH attributes as specified in the associated AS-path ACL
ip address prefix-list	IPv4 NLRI as specified in the associated prefix list
ipv6 address prefix-list	IPv6 NLRI as specified in the associated prefix list
ip next-hop	IPv4 next-hop attributes as specified in the associated ACL or prefix list
ipv6 next-hop	IPv6 next-hop attributes as specified in the associated ACL or prefix list
local-preference	The specified value of the LOCAL_PREF attribute
Metric	The specified value of the MED attribute
route-type local	Locally generated routes (routes originated on the configured router)
source-protocol	The source protocil of routes locally redistribted into BGP
community	COMMUNITY attributes as specified in the associated community list name or number
ext-community	Extended COMMUNITY attributes as specified in the associated community number
tag	The specified route tag value
policy-list	The specified policy list name. The use of policy lists is described later in this chapter.

The **match** clauses can be used alone if you only want to permit or deny the identified routes. But using **set** clauses, you can change the characteristics of the route. As with **match** clauses, you can use one or more **set** clauses. For example:

```
route-map ASPEN permit 20
 match ip address prefix-list MILLER
 match local-preference 150
 match community WARREN
 set metric +50
 set local-preference 80
 set comm-list WARREN delete
```

This **route map** statement matches the same routes as the last example, but instead of just blocking the matching route this statement increases the route's metric by 50, changes the value of the LOCAL_PREF from 150 to 80, and removes the COMMUNITY attribute that matched the community list WARREN.

Notice also that this **route map** statement uses a **permit** action rather than the **deny** of the previous statements. It makes little sense to change the attributes of a route if you are going to then discard it.

Table 4-3 lists the changes you can make to a BGP route using **set** clauses.

Table 4-3 *BGP Route Attribtes and Characteristics That Can Be Set or Changed in a Route Map*

Set Keyword	Changes
as-path prepend	Adds one or more specified ASNs to the front of the AS_PATH. AS path prepending is covered later in this chapter.
as-path tag	Converts the tag of a route redistribted into BGP to the BGP route's AS_PATH attribute.
ip next-hop	Changes the NEXT_HOP route attribute to the specified IPv4 address. A list of addresses can be specified, and if the first address is unreachable the listed addresses are tried in order until a reachable address is found.
ipv6 next-hop	The same function as **ip next-hop**, but for IPv6 routes.
ip next-hop peer-address	When used with an inbound policy, the NEXT_HOP is changed to the IPv4 address of the advertising neighbor. When used with an outbound policy, the NEXT_HOP is changed to the IPv4 address of the local router. This usage is the same as the **neighbor next-hop-self** statement, but the match clauses allow a more granular application to selected routes rather than all routes advertised to a neighbor.
ipv6 next-hop peer-address	The same function as **ip next-hop peer-address**, but for IPv6 routes.
local-preference	Adds a LOCAL_PREF attribute with the specified value, or changes an existing LOCAL_PREF attribute to the specified value.
metric	Adds a MED attribute with the specified value, changes an existing MED attribute to the specified value, or increases/decreases an existing MED value by the specified amount.
metric-type internal	Adds a MED attribute to routes advertised to EBGP peers and sets its value to the metric of the IGP next hop.

Set Keyword	Changes
origin	Sets the ORIGIN attribute to **igp**, **egp**, or **incomplete**
community	Adds a COMMUNITY atribute by community number or well-known community name. Or, removes all COMMUNITY attributes when the **none** keyword is used.
comm-list delete	Removes the specified COMMUNITY attribute from the route, if it exists.
extcommunity	Adds the specified extended COMMUNITY attribute.
extmmunity cost	Adds a cost community attribute and sets its value as specified.
dampening	Applies the specified dampening factors to matching routes. Route dampening is covered in Chapter 5.
traffic-index	Specifies classification for BGP policy acconting, explained later in this chapter.
weight	Sets the route's weight to the specified value, as explained in the next section.

Route maps work sequentially from the top down, just like access lists. If a route matches all the **match** clauses of a **route map** statement, any configured **set** clauses are executed and the **permit** or **deny** action of the statement is taken. The processing of that route stops. If a route does not match all **match** clauses of a **route map** statement, it goes to the next statement. And as with access lists, there is an implicit "deny all" at the end of the route map's sequence of statements: A route not matching any statement in the route map is discarded.

The route map is applied to a specific neighbor with the **neighbor route-map** statement, and an **in** or **out** keyword is used to specify whether incoming or outgoing routes are processed by the route map.

Example 6-62 shows a route map named EXAMPLE configured on router Cervinia of Figure 4-10. The route map is applied as an incoming policy to all four of Cervinia's EBGP neighbors. The first statement (sequence number 10) matches on routes to 172.29.1.0/24 as identified by the prefix list ZERMATT, but there is also an AS path match clause that requires the route to have an AS_PATH of [100, 30]. That is, the route must have been advertised from Zermatt to Innsbruck and from Innsbruck directly to Cervinia. If a route matches these two clauses, its metric is set to 500 and its weight is set to 25.

Example 4-62 *Route Map EXAMPLE, Using Multiple Statements and Multiple Match and Set Clauses, Is Applied as an Incoming Policy on All of Cervinia's Neighbor Sessions*

```
router bgp 200
 no synchronization
 bgp log-neighbor-changes
 network 10.200.0.0 mask 255.255.0.0
 neighbor 10.50.250.1 remote-as 50
 neighbor 10.50.250.1 ebgp-multihop 2
 neighbor 10.50.250.1 update-source Loopback0
 neighbor 10.50.250.1 route-map EXAMPLE in
 neighbor 10.100.83.1 remote-as 100
 neighbor 10.100.83.1 ebgp-multihop 2
 neighbor 10.100.83.1 update-source Loopback0
 neighbor 10.100.83.1 route-map EXAMPLE in
 neighbor 10.125.25.1 remote-as 125
 neighbor 10.125.25.1 ebgp-multihop 2
 neighbor 10.125.25.1 update-source Loopback0
 neighbor 10.125.25.1 route-map EXAMPLE in
 neighbor 172.30.255.150 remote-as 30
 neighbor 172.30.255.150 ebgp-multihop 2
 neighbor 172.30.255.150 update-source Loopback0
 neighbor 172.30.255.150 route-map EXAMPLE in
 no auto-summary
!
ip as-path access-list 1 permit ^100_30$
!
ip prefix-list ZERMATT seq 5 permit 172.29.1.0/24
!
ip prefix-list ZERMATT-2 seq 5 permit 10.30.0.0/16
!
route-map EXAMPLE permit 10
 match ip address prefix-list ZERMATT
 match as-path 1
 set metric 500
 set weight 25
!
route-map EXAMPLE permit 20
 match ip address prefix-list ZERMATT-2
 match as-path 1
 set metric 250
 set weight 75
!
route-map EXAMPLE permit 30
!
```

Statement 20 of the route map matches on routes to 10.30.0.0/16, but again only if their AS_PATH is [100, 30]. (AS-path ACL 1 is used for both route map statements.) Matching routes have their metrics set to 250 and their weight set to 75.

Statement 30 is a simple "permit all." There are no match clauses, so it matches all routes that have not matched the first two statements. If this statement were not added to the route map, all routes not matching the first two statements would be discarded by the implicit "deny all."

Example 4-63 shows the resulting entries in Cervinia's BGP table. Notice that although there are three routes each to 172.29.1.0/24 and 10.30.0.0/16, only the routes with an AS_PATH of [100,30] have modified metric and weight values.

Example 4-63 *Results of Route Map EXAMPLE Can Be Observed in Cervinia's BGP Table*

```
Cervinia#show ip bgp
BGP table version is 75, local router ID is 10.200.60.1
Status codes: s suppressed, d damped, h history, * valid, > best, i - internal,
              r RIB-failure, S Stale
Origin codes: i - IGP, e - EGP, ? - incomplete

   Network          Next Hop          Metric LocPrf Weight Path
*> 10.20.0.0/16     10.50.250.1          0            0 50 i
*                   10.100.83.1                       0 100 50 i
*                   10.125.25.1                       0 125 50 i
*  10.30.0.0/16     10.50.250.1                       0 50 100 30 i
*>                  10.100.83.1          250         75 100 30 i
*                   172.30.255.150       10           0 30 i
*  10.100.0.0/16    10.50.250.1                       0 50 100 i
*>                  10.100.83.1          0            0 100 i
*> 10.200.0.0/16    0.0.0.0              0        32768 i
*  172.16.0.0       10.50.250.1                       0 50 100 30 i
*                   10.100.83.1                       0 100 30 i
*>                  172.30.255.150       10           0 30 i
*> 172.17.0.0       10.50.250.1          0            0 50 i
*                   10.100.83.1                       0 100 50 i
*                   10.125.25.1                       0 125 50 i
*> 172.18.0.0       10.50.250.1          0            0 50 i
*                   10.100.83.1                       0 100 50 i
*                   10.125.25.1                       0 125 50 i
*  172.29.1.0/24    10.50.250.1                       0 50 100 30 i
*>                  10.100.83.1          500         25 100 30 i
*                   172.30.255.150       10           0 30 i
*> 172.29.2.0/24    10.50.250.1          0            0 50 i
*                   10.100.83.1                       0 100 50 i
```

```
*                     10.125.25.1                        0 125 50 i
*   172.30.0.0        10.50.250.1                        0 50 100 30 i
*                     10.100.83.1                        0 100 30 i
*>                    172.30.255.150                     0 30 i
*   172.31.0.0        10.50.250.1                        0 50 100 30 i
*                     10.100.83.1                        0 100 30 i
*>                    172.30.255.150         10          0 30 i
*   172.32.0.0        10.50.250.1                        0 50 100 30 i
*                     10.100.83.1                        0 100 30 i
*>                    172.30.255.150         20          0 30 i
*   172.33.0.0        10.50.250.1                        0 50 100 30 i
*                     10.100.83.1                        0 100 30 i
*>                    172.30.255.150         10          0 30 i
*   192.168.2.0       10.50.250.1                        0 50 100 30 i
*                     10.100.83.1                        0 100 30 i
*>                    172.30.255.150         10          0 30 i
*> 192.168.50.0       10.50.250.1             0          0 50 i
*                     10.100.83.1                        0 100 50 i
*                     10.125.25.1                        0 125 50 i
*   192.168.100.0     10.50.250.1                        0 50 100 30 i
*                     10.100.83.1                        0 100 30 i
*>                    172.30.255.150         10          0 30 i
Cervinia#
```

You can observe an easy-to-read summary of a route map with the **show route-map**
command, as shown in Example 4-64. The display breaks the route map down into its
individual statements and each statement's match and set clauses.

Example 4-64   show route-map *Command Displays a Summary of a Route Map*

```
Cervinia#show route-map
route-map EXAMPLE, permit, sequence 10
  Match clauses:
    ip address prefix-lists: ZERMATT
    as-path (as-path filter): 1
  Set clauses:
    metric 500
    weight 25
  Policy routing matches: 0 packets, 0 bytes
route-map EXAMPLE, permit, sequence 20
  Match clauses:
    ip address prefix-lists: ZERMATT-2
    as-path (as-path filter): 1
```

```
    Set clauses:
      metric 250
      weight 75
    Policy routing matches: 0 packets, 0 bytes
route-map EXAMPLE, permit, sequence 30
  Match clauses:
  Set clauses:
  Policy routing matches: 0 packets, 0 bytes
Cervinia#
```

Filter Processing

You can, if necessary, configure one NLRI filter (either a prefix list or a distribute list, but not both), one AS path filter, and one route map for each neighbor in each direction, as shown in Example 4-65.

Example 4-65 *A Neighbor Session Can Have an NLRI Filter, an AS Path Filter, and a Route Map Configured Together in Each Direction*

```
Oberstdorf#show run | section bgp
router bgp 125
 no synchronization
 bgp log-neighbor-changes
 network 10.125.25.1
 neighbor 10.50.250.1 remote-as 50
 neighbor 10.50.250.1 ebgp-multihop 2
 neighbor 10.50.250.1 update-source Loopback0
 neighbor 10.50.250.1 prefix-list Meribel in
 neighbor 10.50.250.1 prefix-list Cervinia out
 neighbor 10.50.250.1 route-map EX1 in
 neighbor 10.50.250.1 route-map EX2 out
 neighbor 10.50.250.1 filter-list 1 in
 neighbor 10.50.250.1 filter-list 2 out
 neighbor 10.200.60.1 remote-as 200
 neighbor 10.200.60.1 ebgp-multihop 2
 neighbor 10.200.60.1 update-source Loopback0
 no auto-summary
Oberstdorf#
```

The ability to configure more than one type of filter in the same direction on a neighbor session often gives rise to the question, "When there are multiple filters, in what order are they processed?"

Is it prefix list, then route map, and then AS path filter? Is it AS path filter, then prefix list, and then route map? Or, is it some other order? And does the processing order change depending on whether the filters applied to incoming or outgoing routes?

Searching CCIE study groups, networking books, and even Cisco's IOS manuals, you will find almost as many different answers to this question as there are combinations of filter types. The processing order might change depending on what version of IOS is being used; even the order in which the filters appear in the configuration might change with IOS version.

There is a much simpler answer to all this, which is that the processing order does not matter. If there are multiple filters configured for the same direction for a single neighbor, a route must be permitted by all of the filters for it to be accepted (incoming) or advertised (outgoing). If a particular incoming route is matched in Example 4-65 by prefix list Meribel, route map EX1, or filter list 1, and if the accompanying action to any of those matches is a deny, the route will be discarded no matter which order the three filters evaluate the route. Most important, if the route is matched, modified, and permitted by the route map but denied by either the prefix list or AS path filter it will be discarded.

The confusion around processing sequences highlights why, unless you are sure that you will never need more than a single NLRI or AS path filter for a given neighbor, it is better to configure NLRI and AS path filters within route maps:

- The configured route policy for a neighbor is easier to understand.

- The sequenced route map statements make editing the policy easier, whenever the need arises.

- Because the route map statements are processed in sequence, you can control the order in which a route is evaluated by NLRI and AS path filters.

Influencing the BGP Decision Process

Now that you have examined all of the fundamental tools for creating BGP routing policy, we can begin looking at techniques for creating routing policies. BGP routing policies work by influencing the BGP decision process. Of course, NLRI and AS path filters on their own have a crude effect on the decision process by controlling what routes a router knows about—and hence, what routes the router can apply the decision process to. But more refined policies influence the decision process by changing the attributes of the route rather than just allowing or blocking the route.

Introduced in Chapter 2, the BGP decision process used by IOS is repeated here for your review:

1. Prefer the route with the highest weight. This is an IOS-specific function, as described in the previous section.

2. If the weights are equal, prefer the route with the highest LOCAL_PREF value.

3. If the LOCAL_PREF values are the same, prefer the route that was originated locally on the router. That is, prefer a route that was learned from an IGP or from a direct connection on the same router.

4. If the LOCAL_PREF is the same, and no route was locally originated, prefer the route with the shortest AS_PATH.

5. If the AS_PATH length is the same, prefer the path with the lowest ORIGIN code. IGP is lower than EGP, which is lower than Incomplete.

6. If the ORIGIN codes are the same, prefer the route with the lowest MED (MULTI_EXIT_DISC) value. By default, this comparison is done only if the AS number is the same for all the routes being considered.[14]

7. If the MED is the same, prefer EBGP routes over Confederation EBGP routes, and prefer Confederation EBGP routes over IBGP routes.

8. If the routes are still equal, prefer the route with the shortest path to the BGP NEXT_HOP. This is the route with the lowest IGP metric to the next-hop address.

9. If the routes are still equal, they are from the same neighboring AS, and BGP multipath is enabled with the **maximum-paths** statement, install all the equal-cost routes in the Loc-RIB.

10. If multipath is not enabled, prefer the route with the lowest BGP router ID or, if route reflection (Chapter 5) is being used, the route with the lowest ORIGINATOR_ID.

11. If the routes are still equal, and route reflection is being used, prefer the route with the shortest CLUSTER_LIST.

12. If the routes are still equal, prefer the route advertised from the neighbor with the lowest IP address.

The next five case studies demonstrate the use of route maps to implement more complex routing policies. Respectively, the five case studies demonstrate methods for influencing route preferences:

■ Within a single router (multiple BGP routes to the same destination)

■ Within the local autonomous system

■ Within neighboring autonomous systems

■ Within autonomous systems beyond the neighboring autonomous systems

■ Within a single router (multiple routes to the same destination from different routing protocols)

---

[14] IOS offers two alternatives to the default MED behavior, **bgp deterministic-med** and **bgp always-compare-med**; these alternatives are explained in Chapter 3.

Case Study: Administrative Weights

Administrative weight is not prescribed in any BGP standard; rather, it is a Cisco proprietary BGP path attribute. You can even argue that it is not a path attribute at all, because it is not attached to routes as they are advertised from one router to another. Instead, administrative weights are attached to a route only while it resides in the BGP table of a single router.

That description gives a clear hint at the weight's utility: The administrative weight is used when you want to influence the BGP Decision Process in a single router without causing that influence to carry over to any other router.

Each route is assigned a weight, which is a number between 0 and 65535. Given multiple routes to the same destination, the router will prefer the route with the highest weight. (Think heaviest weight wins.) By default, BGP routes originated by the router are given a weight of 32768, and routes learned from neighbors are given a weight of 0. You can observe that behavior in Example 4-63. Cervenia's locally generated route to its loopback interface, 10.200.0.0/16, has a weight of 32768. All other routes are learned from a BGP neighbor and therefore have a weight of 0 (except for the two that were assigned different weights by the example route map). Because higher (heavier) weights are preferred, this default behavior ensures that if multiple routes to the same destination exist and one of them is locally generated, the local router will prefer its own route to any one advertised by a neighbor. That makes sense: If a router is injecting a route into BGP, from a BGP viewpoint, this router is presumably the foremost authority on how to reach that destination.

Looking at the BGP decision process at the beginning of this section, you can see that weight is considered above all other path attributes. That means that administrative weight overrides all other factors in the BGP decision process.

In Figure 4-11, the connectivity of AS30 has been improved. Zermatt and Moritz are each multihomed to AS100 and AS200 for added redundancy. Each router receives routes to the addresses in AS50 from both Innsbruck and Cervinia. When selecting a preferred route from multiple same-destination routes, if all other attributes are equal the BGP decision process selects the route from the neighbor with the lowest router ID. This means that both Zermatt and Moritz in Figure 4-11 will use Innsbruck to reach the destinations in AS50, because its router ID is lower than Cervinia as demonstrated by the output in Example 4-66. Zermatt and Moritz show that the destinations within AS50 are reachable via either Innsbruck (10.100.83.1) or Cervinia (10.200.60.1). Both routers have marked the routes from Innsbruck as the best routes, because Innsbruck's router ID is lower.

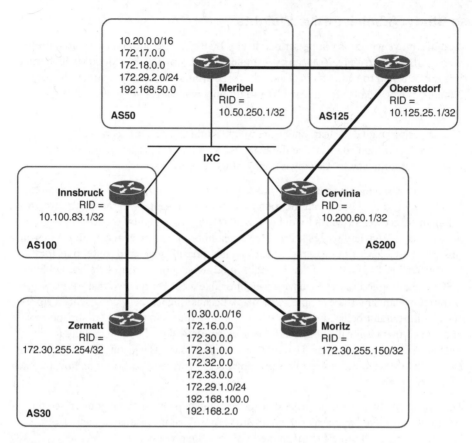

Figure 4-11 *Moritz and Zermatt Are Multihomed for Redundancy*

Example 4-66 *BGP Tables of Zermatt and Moritz Show That They Both Prefer the Paths Through Innsbruck (10.100.83.1) to Reach AS50 Routes*

```
Zermatt#show ip bgp
BGP table version is 54, local router ID is 172.30.255.254
Status codes: s suppressed, d damped, h history, * valid, > best, i - internal,
              r RIB-failure, S Stale
Origin codes: i - IGP, e - EGP, ? - incomplete


   Network          Next Hop          Metric LocPrf Weight Path
*> 10.20.0.0/16     10.100.83.1                        0 100 50 i
*                   10.200.60.1                        0 200 50 i
* i                 172.30.255.150         0    100    0 100 50 i
*> 10.30.0.0/16     172.30.255.100        10         32768 i
* i                 172.30.255.150        10    100    0 i
```

```
*    10.100.0.0/16    10.200.60.1                           0 200 100 i
*>                    10.100.83.1         0                 0 100 i
*  i                 172.30.255.150       0     100         0 100 i
*    10.125.0.0/16    10.100.83.1                           0 100 200 125 i
*>                    10.200.60.1         0                 0 200 125 i
*  i                 172.30.255.150       0     100         0 200 125 i
*    10.200.0.0/16    10.100.83.1                           0 100 200 i
*>                    10.200.60.1         0                 0 200 i
*  i                 172.30.255.150       0     100         0 200 i
*> 172.16.0.0        172.30.255.100      10             32768 i
*  i                 172.30.255.150      10     100         0 i
*> 172.17.0.0        10.100.83.1                           0 100 50 i
*                    10.200.60.1                           0 200 50 i
*  i                 172.30.255.150       0     100         0 100 50 i
*> 172.18.0.0        10.100.83.1                           0 100 50 i
*                    10.200.60.1                           0 200 50 i
*  i                 172.30.255.150       0     100         0 100 50 i
*> 172.29.1.0/24     172.30.255.100      10             32768 i
*  i                 172.30.255.150      10     100         0 i
*> 172.29.2.0/24     10.100.83.1                           0 100 50 i
*                    10.200.60.1                           0 200 50 i
*  i                 172.30.255.150       0     100         0 100 50 i
*> 172.30.0.0        0.0.0.0              0             32768 i
*> 172.31.0.0        172.30.255.100      10             32768 i
*  i                 172.30.255.150      10     100         0 i
*> 172.32.0.0        172.30.255.100      20             32768 i
*  i                 172.30.255.150      20     100         0 i
*> 172.33.0.0        172.30.255.100      10             32768 i
*  i                 172.30.255.150      10     100         0 i
*> 192.168.2.0       172.30.255.100      10             32768 i
*  i                 172.30.255.150      10     100         0 i
*> 192.168.50.0      10.100.83.1                           0 100 50 i
*                    10.200.60.1                           0 200 50 i
*  i                 172.30.255.150       0     100         0 100 50 i
*> 192.168.100.0     172.30.255.100      10             32768 i
*  i                 172.30.255.150      10     100         0 i
Zermatt#
```

```
Moritz#show ip bgp
BGP table version is 38, local router ID is 172.30.255.150
Status codes: s suppressed, d damped, h history, * valid, > best, i - internal,
              r RIB-failure, S Stale
Origin codes: i - IGP, e - EGP, ? - incomplete
```

```
    Network          Next Hop          Metric LocPrf Weight Path
 * i10.20.0.0/16     172.30.255.254        0    100      0 200 50 i
 *>                  10.100.83.1                         0 100 50 i
 *                   10.200.60.1                         0 200 50 i
 * i10.30.0.0/16     172.30.255.254       10    100      0 i
 *>                  172.30.255.100       10           32768 i
 *   10.100.0.0/16   10.200.60.1                         0 200 100 i
 *>                  10.100.83.1           0             0 100 i
 *   10.125.0.0/16   10.100.83.1                         0 100 200 125 i
 * i                 172.30.255.254        0    100      0 200 125 i
 *>                  10.200.60.1                         0 200 125 i
 *   10.200.0.0/16   10.100.83.1                         0 100 200 i
 * i                 172.30.255.254        0    100      0 200 i
 *>                  10.200.60.1           0             0 200 i
 * i172.16.0.0       172.30.255.254       10    100      0 i
 *>                  172.30.255.100       10           32768 i
 * i172.17.0.0       172.30.255.254        0    100      0 200 50 i
 *>                  10.100.83.1                         0 100 50 i
 *                   10.200.60.1                         0 200 50 i
 * i172.18.0.0       172.30.255.254        0    100      0 200 50 i
 *>                  10.100.83.1                         0 100 50 i
 *                   10.200.60.1                         0 200 50 i
 * i172.29.1.0/24    172.30.255.254       10    100      0 i
 *>                  172.30.255.100       10           32768 i
 * i172.29.2.0/24    172.30.255.254        0    100      0 200 50 i
 *>                  10.100.83.1                         0 100 50 i
 *                   10.200.60.1                         0 200 50 i
 *>i172.30.0.0       172.30.255.254        0    100      0 i
 * i172.31.0.0       172.30.255.254       10    100      0 i
 *>                  172.30.255.100       10           32768 i
 * i172.32.0.0       172.30.255.254       20    100      0 i
 *>                  172.30.255.100       20           32768 i
 * i172.33.0.0       172.30.255.254       10    100      0 i
 *>                  172.30.255.100       10           32768 i
 * i192.168.2.0      172.30.255.254       10    100      0 i
 *>                  172.30.255.100       10           32768 i
 * i192.168.50.0     172.30.255.254        0    100      0 200 50 i
 *>                  10.100.83.1                         0 100 50 i
 *                   10.200.60.1                         0 200 50 i
 * i192.168.100.0    172.30.255.254       10    100      0 i
 *>                  172.30.255.100       10           32768 i
Moritz#
```

To spread the traffic load out more evenly, Zermatt should use the link to Innsbruck to reach AS50, and use only the link to Cervinia as a backup. Likewise, Moritz should use the link to Cervinia, and use only Innsbruck as a backup. In Example 4-67, Moritz is configured with the **neighbor weight** statement to assign a weight of 50000 to all routes advertised from Cervinia (10.200.60.1) and a weight of 20000 to all routes advertised from Innsbruck (10.100.83.1). Zermatt is configured just the opposite.

Example 4-67 *Moritz Is Configured to Change the Weights of the Routes Received from Insbruck and Cervinia*

```
Moritz#show run | section bgp
router bgp 30
 no synchronization
 bgp log-neighbor-changes
 network 10.30.0.0 mask 255.255.0.0
 network 172.16.0.0
 network 172.29.1.0 mask 255.255.255.0
 network 172.30.0.0
 network 172.31.0.0
 network 172.32.0.0
 network 172.33.0.0
 network 192.168.2.0
 network 192.168.100.0
 neighbor 10.100.83.1 remote-as 100
 neighbor 10.100.83.1 ebgp-multihop 2
 neighbor 10.100.83.1 update-source Loopback0
 neighbor 10.100.83.1 weight 20000
 neighbor 10.100.83.1 filter-list 1 out
 neighbor 10.200.60.1 remote-as 200
 neighbor 10.200.60.1 ebgp-multihop 2
 neighbor 10.200.60.1 update-source Loopback0
 neighbor 10.200.60.1 weight 50000
 neighbor 10.200.60.1 filter-list 1 out
 neighbor 172.30.255.254 remote-as 30
 neighbor 172.30.255.254 update-source Loopback0
 neighbor 172.30.255.254 next-hop-self
 no auto-summary
Moritz#
```

The result is shown in Example 4-68 (after performing a soft reset of incoming routes). Comparing the routes to the AS50 prefixes in this table to the routes to the same prefixes in Moritz's BGP table in Example 4-66, you can see that Moritz now indicates Cervinia (10.200.60.1) as the best next hop because of their higher weights. You can also observe the assigned weight values of 20000 and 50000. Routes from neighbors not configured with the **neighbor weight** statement still use the default weight values.

Example 4-68   *Moritz Now Prefers the Routes Through Cervinia, with a Weight of 50000, over the Routes Through Innsbruck with a Lesser Weight of 20000*

```
Moritz#show ip bgp
BGP table version is 35, local router ID is 172.30.255.150
Status codes: s suppressed, d damped, h history, * valid, > best, i - internal,
              r RIB-failure, S Stale
Origin codes: i - IGP, e - EGP, ? - incomplete
```

	Network	Next Hop	Metric	LocPrf	Weight	Path
*	10.20.0.0/16	10.100.83.1			20000	100 50 i
*>		10.200.60.1			50000	200 50 i
* i		172.30.255.254	0	100	0	200 50 i
*>	10.30.0.0/16	172.30.255.100	10		32768	i
* i		172.30.255.254	10	100	0	i
*	10.100.0.0/16	10.100.83.1	0		20000	100 i
*>		10.200.60.1			50000	200 50 100 i
* i		172.30.255.254	0	100	0	100 i
*	10.125.0.0/16	10.100.83.1			20000	100 200 125 i
*>		10.200.60.1			50000	200 125 i
* i		172.30.255.254	0	100	0	200 125 i
*	10.200.0.0/16	10.100.83.1			20000	100 200 i
*>		10.200.60.1	0		50000	200 i
* i		172.30.255.254	0	100	0	200 i
*>	172.16.0.0	172.30.255.100	10		32768	i
* i		172.30.255.254	10	100	0	i
*	172.17.0.0	10.100.83.1			20000	100 50 i
*>		10.200.60.1			50000	200 50 i
* i		172.30.255.254	0	100	0	200 50 i
*	172.18.0.0	10.100.83.1			20000	100 50 i
*>		10.200.60.1			50000	200 50 i
* i		172.30.255.254	0	100	0	200 50 i
*>	172.29.1.0/24	172.30.255.100	10		32768	i
* i		172.30.255.254	10	100	0	i
*	172.29.2.0/24	10.100.83.1			20000	100 50 i
*>		10.200.60.1			50000	200 50 i
* i		172.30.255.254	0	100	0	200 50 i
*>i	172.30.0.0	172.30.255.254	0	100	0	i
*>	172.31.0.0	172.30.255.100	10		32768	i
* i		172.30.255.254	10	100	0	i
*>	172.32.0.0	172.30.255.100	20		32768	i
* i		172.30.255.254	20	100	0	i
*>	172.33.0.0	172.30.255.100	10		32768	i
* i		172.30.255.254	10	100	0	i
*>	192.168.2.0	172.30.255.100	10		32768	i

```
* i                     172.30.255.254       10    100      0 i
*   192.168.50.0        10.100.83.1                20000 100 50 i
*>                      10.200.60.1                50000 200 50 i
* i                     172.30.255.254        0    100      0 200 50 i
*> 192.168.100.0        172.30.255.100       10          32768 i
* i                     172.30.255.254       10    100      0 i
Moritz#
```

The **neighbor weight** command is useful if the weights for all routes learned from a particular neighbor are to be the same. But sometimes, different weights must be assigned to routes from the same neighbor. In this case a route map is needed to provide more specificity to the routes whose weights you are changing.

Notice in Example 4-68 that in addition to the AS50 routes advertised to Moritz from Cervinia, the routes to AS125 (10.125.0.0/16), AS200 (10.200.0.0/16), and AS100 (10.100.0.0/16) advertised from Cervinia have also been assigned a weight of 50000; the same routes advertised from Innsbruck have been assigned a weight of 20000. So the path through Cervinia is preferred over the path through Innsbruck. For the AS125 and AS200 routes, this is not a problem; Cervinia is the best next hop for those destinations anyway.

But for the AS100 route, assigning a higher weight value to the Cervinia route causes that path to be selected, even though there is a direct link from Moritz to Innsbruck. You can see the longer AS_PATH for the Cervinia route, but the high weight value overrides the preference for shorter AS_PATH lengths in the BGP decision process.

Example 4-69 shows Moritz reconfigured to use route maps to assign weights. Route map Inns_Weight is used for the connection to Innsbruck, and route map Cerv_Weight is used for the connection to Cervinia. Both route maps reference AS-path ACL 2 to identify routes that originate in AS50; the difference between them is that Ins_Weight assigns a weight of 20000 to matching routes while Cerv_Weight assigns a weight of 50000 to matching routes.

Example 4-69 *Moritz Is Reconfigured with Route Maps That Use an AS-path Access List to Assign Weights More Precisely*

```
router bgp 30
 no synchronization
 bgp log-neighbor-changes
 network 10.30.0.0 mask 255.255.0.0
 network 172.16.0.0
 network 172.29.1.0 mask 255.255.255.0
 network 172.30.0.0
 network 172.31.0.0
 network 172.32.0.0
 network 172.33.0.0
```

```
 network 192.168.2.0
 network 192.168.100.0
 neighbor 10.100.83.1 remote-as 100
 neighbor 10.100.83.1 ebgp-multihop 2
 neighbor 10.100.83.1 update-source Loopback0
 neighbor 10.100.83.1 route-map Inns_Weight in
 neighbor 10.100.83.1 filter-list 1 out
 neighbor 10.200.60.1 remote-as 200
 neighbor 10.200.60.1 ebgp-multihop 2
 neighbor 10.200.60.1 update-source Loopback0
 neighbor 10.200.60.1 route-map Cerv_Weight in
 neighbor 10.200.60.1 filter-list 1 out
 neighbor 172.30.255.254 remote-as 30
 neighbor 172.30.255.254 update-source Loopback0
 neighbor 172.30.255.254 next-hop-self
 no auto-summary
!
ip as-path access-list 2 permit _50$
!
route-map Inns_Weight permit 10
 match as-path 2
 set weight 20000
!
route-map Inns_Weight permit 100
!
route-map Cerv_Weight permit 10
 match as-path 2
 set weight 50000
!
route-map Cerv_Weight permit 100
!
```

The results are shown in Example 4-70. The AS50 prefixes advertised by Cervinia have a weight of 50000 and the prefixes advertised by Innsbruck have a weight of 20000; Moritz therefore designates the routes through Cervinia as best. But unlike Example 4-48, the routes to prefixes in AS125, AS100, and AS200 have not been assigned weights. The BGP decision process selects the best path to these prefixes based on the shortest AS_PATH.

Example 4-70 *Moritz Is Reconfigured with a Route Map That Uses an AS-path Access List to Assign Weights More Specifically*

```
Moritz#show ip bgp
BGP table version is 18, local router ID is 172.30.255.150
Status codes: s suppressed, d damped, h history, * valid, > best, i - internal,
```

```
                 r RIB-failure, S Stale
Origin codes: i - IGP, e - EGP, ? - incomplete

   Network          Next Hop          Metric LocPrf Weight Path
*  10.20.0.0/16     10.100.83.1                      20000 100 50 i
*>                  10.200.60.1                       50000 200 50 i
* i                 172.30.255.254        0    100       0 100 50 i
*> 10.30.0.0/16     172.30.255.100       10          32768 i
* i                 172.30.255.254       10    100       0 i
*> 10.100.0.0/16    10.100.83.1           0              0 100 i
*                   10.200.60.1                          0 200 100 i
* i                 172.30.255.254        0    100       0 100 i
*  10.125.0.0/16    10.100.83.1                          0 100 200 125 i
*>                  10.200.60.1                          0 200 125 i
* i                 172.30.255.254        0    100       0 200 125 i
*  10.200.0.0/16    10.100.83.1                          0 100 200 i
*>                  10.200.60.1           0              0 200 i
* i                 172.30.255.254        0    100       0 200 i
*> 172.16.0.0       172.30.255.100       10          32768 i
* i                 172.30.255.254       10    100       0 i
*  172.17.0.0       10.100.83.1                      20000 100 50 i
*>                  10.200.60.1                       50000 200 50 i
* i                 172.30.255.254        0    100       0 100 50 i
*  172.18.0.0       10.100.83.1                      20000 100 50 i
*>                  10.200.60.1                       50000 200 50 i
* i                 172.30.255.254        0    100       0 100 50 i
*> 172.29.1.0/24    172.30.255.100       10          32768 i
* i                 172.30.255.254       10    100       0 i
*  172.29.2.0/24    10.100.83.1                      20000 100 50 i
*>                  10.200.60.1                       50000 200 50 i
* i                 172.30.255.254        0    100       0 100 50 i
*>i172.30.0.0       172.30.255.254        0    100       0 i
*> 172.31.0.0       172.30.255.100       10          32768 i
* i                 172.30.255.254       10    100       0 i
*> 172.32.0.0       172.30.255.100       20          32768 i
* i                 172.30.255.254       20    100       0 i
*> 172.33.0.0       172.30.255.100       10          32768 i
* i                 172.30.255.254       10    100       0 i
*> 192.168.2.0      172.30.255.100       10          32768 i
* i                 172.30.255.254       10    100       0 i
*  192.168.50.0     10.100.83.1                      20000 100 50 i
*>                  10.200.60.1                       50000 200 50 i
* i                 172.30.255.254        0    100       0 100 50 i
*> 192.168.100.0    172.30.255.100       10          32768 i
* i                 172.30.255.254       10    100       0 i
Moritz#
```

Note   Earlier versions of IOS had another statement, **neighbor filter-list weight**, that was similar to the **neighbor weight** statement but referenced an AS-path ACL like route maps. That statement was demonstrated in the first edition of this book. Cisco deprecated it in IOS 12.1, so it is no longer available in current versions and is not discussed in this edition.

When route maps are used to set weights, only the AS_PATH can be matched; individual IP addresses cannot be matched with the **match ip address** clause. Weight-setting route maps also can be used in the same neighbor configuration as **neighbor weight** statements. If both are used, the route maps take precedence.

A word of warning is in order when using weights: Changing the decision process on a single router in an AS can lead to unexpected routing behavior if you don't fully understand the effects. While weight can have its uses, in the majority of cases the BGP decision process should be the same throughout an autonomous system.

Case Study: Using the LOCAL_PREF Attribute

Administrative weight is a useful attribute if, as the previous section shows, you want to influence the outgoing path selections of a single router without influencing any other router. But in most cases, when you set a policy to prefer one outgoing path over another you want that policy to apply throughout the autonomous system. The LOCAL_PREF attribute is used in this case. Unlike administrative weight, the LOCAL_PREF is not limited to a single router. Rather, it is attached to routes advertised to IBGP peers. The attribute is not communicated to EBGP peers—hence the name *local preference*. It applies only to its local autonomous system.

Of all the BGP path attributes manipulated for setting routing policy, LOCAL_PREF is probably the most commonly used.

A route's LOCAL_PREF attribute can be any number between 0 and 4294967295; the higher the number, the more preferable the route. By default, all routes advertised to IBGP peers have a LOCAL_PREF of 100. This default value can be changed with the **ip default local-preference** statement. The LOCAL_PREF attribute of individual routes is changed by using a route map and the statement **set local-preference**.

A new router, Davos, is added to the example network in Figure 4-12. IBGP sessions are established to both Moritz and Zermatt, and those two routers use the **neighbor next-hop-self** statement in their configurations to Davos.

The administrative weight configurations created in the previous section have been removed. All prefixes external to AS30 are advertised by both Moritz (172.30.255.150) and Zermatt (172.30.255.254) but the weights and AS_PATH lengths are equal in each case, as are the ORIGIN attributes and the length of the path to the next hops. Therefore, Davos chooses Moritz, as the neighbor with the lowest Router ID, as the preferred next hop for all AS-external routes.

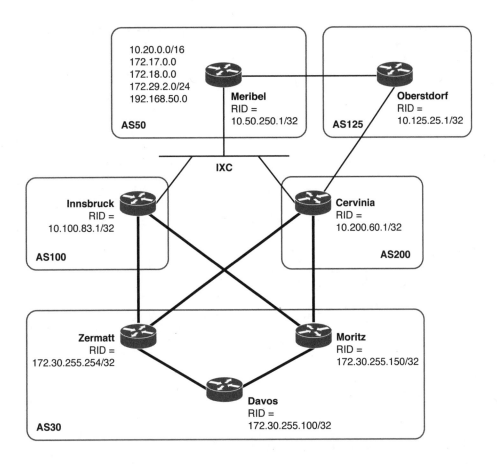

Figure 4-12 *Router Davos Is Added to AS30, with IBGP Sessions to Zermatt and Moritz*

Example 4-71 *Davos Prefers Moritz as the Best Next Hop for All Prefixes External to AS30 Based on Its Lower Router ID*

```
Davos# show ip bgp
BGP table version is 26, local router ID is 172.32.1.1
Status codes: s suppressed, d damped, h history, * valid, > best, i - internal,
              r RIB-failure, S Stale
Origin codes: i - IGP, e - EGP, ? - incomplete

   Network          Next Hop          Metric LocPrf Weight Path
* i10.20.0.0/16     172.30.255.254         0    100      0 200 50 i
*>i                 172.30.255.150         0    100      0 200 50 i
r i10.30.0.0/16     172.30.255.254        10    100      0 i
r>i                 172.30.255.150        10    100      0 i
```

```
* i10.100.0.0/16    172.30.255.254        0    100    0 100 i
*>i                 172.30.255.150        0    100    0 100 i
* i10.125.0.0/16    172.30.255.254        0    100    0 200 125 i
*>i                 172.30.255.150        0    100    0 200 125 i
* i10.200.0.0/16    172.30.255.254        0    100    0 200 i
*>i                 172.30.255.150        0    100    0 200 i
r i172.16.0.0       172.30.255.254       10    100    0 i
r>i                 172.30.255.150       10    100    0 i
* i172.17.0.0       172.30.255.254        0    100    0 200 50 i
*>i                 172.30.255.150        0    100    0 200 50 i
* i172.18.0.0       172.30.255.254        0    100    0 200 50 i
*>i                 172.30.255.150        0    100    0 200 50 i
r i172.29.1.0/24    172.30.255.254       10    100    0 i
r>i                 172.30.255.150       10    100    0 i
* i172.29.2.0/24    172.30.255.254        0    100    0 200 50 i
*>i                 172.30.255.150        0    100    0 200 50 i
*>i172.30.0.0       172.30.255.254        0    100    0 i
r i172.31.0.0       172.30.255.254       10    100    0 i
r>i                 172.30.255.150       10    100    0 i
r i172.32.0.0       172.30.255.254       20    100    0 i
r>i                 172.30.255.150       20    100    0 i
r i172.33.0.0       172.30.255.254       10    100    0 i
r>i                 172.30.255.150       10    100    0 i
r i192.168.2.0      172.30.255.254       10    100    0 i
r>i                 172.30.255.150       10    100    0 i
* i192.168.50.0     172.30.255.254        0    100    0 200 50 i
*>i                 172.30.255.150        0    100    0 200 50 i
r i192.168.100.0    172.30.255.254       10    100    0 i
r>i                 172.30.255.150       10    100    0 i
Davos#
```

Note   Notice that all the AS30 prefixes in Davos' BGP table are marked with a RIB-failure (r) status. These prefixes are picked up from the IGP tables at Zermatt and Moritz, and injected into BGP with **network** statements. Those two routers then advertise the prefixes to Davos via BGP. But because IGP routes to the prefixes already exist in Davos' RIB, the BGP routes to the prefixes are given a RIB-failure status and they are not added to the RIB.

In Example 4-72, Zermatt is configured to raise the LOCAL_PREF value of some of the routes it is learning from its EBGP peers. The goal is to balance the outgoing traffic from Davos (and any other routers internal to AS30) between Zermatt and Moritz, rather than forwarding all outgoing traffic to Moritz. Route map More-Pref refers to a prefix list named Set-Pref and sets the LOCAL_PREF of matching routes to 500. The policy is applied to incoming routes from neighbors Cervinia and Innsbruck.

Example 4-72 *Zermatt Is Configured to Set the LOCAL_PREF of Several Incoming Routes to 500*

```
router bgp 30
 no synchronization
 bgp log-neighbor-changes
 network 10.30.0.0 mask 255.255.0.0
 network 172.16.0.0
 network 172.29.1.0 mask 255.255.255.0
 network 172.30.0.0
 network 172.31.0.0
 network 172.32.0.0
 network 172.33.0.0
 network 192.168.2.0
 network 192.168.100.0
 neighbor 10.100.83.1 remote-as 100
 neighbor 10.100.83.1 ebgp-multihop 2
 neighbor 10.100.83.1 update-source Loopback0
 neighbor 10.100.83.1 route-map More-Pref in
 neighbor 10.100.83.1 filter-list 1 out
 neighbor 10.200.60.1 remote-as 200
 neighbor 10.200.60.1 ebgp-multihop 2
 neighbor 10.200.60.1 update-source Loopback0
 neighbor 10.200.60.1 route-map More-Pref in
 neighbor 172.30.255.100 remote-as 30
 neighbor 172.30.255.100 update-source Loopback0
 neighbor 172.30.255.100 next-hop-self
 neighbor 172.30.255.150 remote-as 30
 neighbor 172.30.255.150 update-source Loopback0
 neighbor 172.30.255.150 next-hop-self
 no auto-summary
!
ip prefix-list Set-Pref seq 5 permit 10.20.0.0/16
ip prefix-list Set-Pref seq 10 permit 172.17.0.0/16
ip prefix-list Set-Pref seq 15 permit 192.168.50.0/24
ip prefix-list Set-Pref seq 20 permit 10.100.0.0/16
!
route-map More-Pref permit 10
 match ip address prefix-list Set-Pref
 set local-preference 500
!
route-map More-Pref permit 100
!
```

Davos' BGP table in Example 4-73 shows the results: The routes through Zermatt (172.30.255.254) to the four prefixes specified in prefix list Set-Pref now have a LOCAL_PREF value of 500, and Davos has marked them as the preferred paths. Although this is the original objective, there is a problem. The alternative paths for these four routes through Moritz (172.30.255.150) are no longer in the BGP table. If the link to Zermatt fails, these four prefixes will become unreachable from Davos. Note that the other prefixes external to AS30 still have alternative routes; it is only the four modified prefixes that have lost their backup routes.

Example 4-73   *Four Routes Matching the Prefix List Set-Pref in Example 4-72 Have a LOCAL_PREF Value of 500, but the Alternative Paths to Those Prefixes Through Moritz (172.30.255.150) Have Disappeared*

```
Davos#show ip bgp
BGP table version is 135, local router ID is 172.32.1.1
Status codes: s suppressed, d damped, h history, * valid, > best, i - internal,
              r RIB-failure, S Stale
Origin codes: i - IGP, e - EGP, ? - incomplete

   Network          Next Hop          Metric LocPrf Weight Path
*>i10.20.0.0/16     172.30.255.254         0    500      0 100 50 i
*>  10.30.0.0/16    0.0.0.0                0          32768 i
*>i10.100.0.0/16    172.30.255.254         0    500      0 100 i
*  i10.125.0.0/16   172.30.255.254         0    100      0 200 125 i
*>i                 172.30.255.150         0    100      0 200 125 i
*  i10.200.0.0/16   172.30.255.254         0    100      0 200 i
*>i                 172.30.255.150         0    100      0 200 i
*>  172.16.0.0      0.0.0.0                0          32768 i
*>i172.17.0.0       172.30.255.254         0    500      0 100 50 i
*  i172.18.0.0      172.30.255.254         0    100      0 100 50 i
*>i                 172.30.255.150         0    100      0 100 50 i
*>  172.29.1.0/24   0.0.0.0                0          32768 i
*  i172.29.2.0/24   172.30.255.254         0    100      0 100 50 i
*>i                 172.30.255.150         0    100      0 100 50 i
*>i172.30.0.0       172.30.255.254         0    100      0 i
*>  172.31.0.0      0.0.0.0                0          32768 i
r  i172.32.0.0      172.30.255.254        20    100      0 i
r>i                 172.30.255.150        20    100      0 i
*>  172.33.0.0      0.0.0.0                0          32768 i
*>  192.168.2.0     0.0.0.0                0          32768 i
*>i192.168.50.0     172.30.255.254         0    500      0 100 50 i
*>  192.168.100.0   0.0.0.0                0          32768 i
Davos#
```

A look at Moritz' BGP table (Example 4-74) reveals the problem and also reveals another undesirable outcome of the policy configured in Example 4-72. Zermatt has IBGP sessions with both Moritz and Davos, and it advertises the routes with modified LOCAL_PREF values to both internal neighbors. Because LOCAL_PREF takes precedence over all other path attributes except weight, Moritz prefers the routes with the high LOCAL_PREF values. As a result, Moritz sends packets to those destinations back through Davos and Zermatt rather than through the more direct paths through Innsbruck or Cervinia.

Example 4-74 *Because of Their High LOCAL_PREF Value, Moritz Prefers the Routes Through Zermatt Rather Than the More Direct Routes Through Innsbruck or Cervinia*

```
Moritz#show ip bgp
BGP table version is 28, local router ID is 172.30.255.150
Status codes: s suppressed, d damped, h history, * valid, > best, i - internal,
              r RIB-failure, S Stale
Origin codes: i - IGP, e - EGP, ? - incomplete

   Network          Next Hop          Metric LocPrf Weight Path
*  10.20.0.0/16     10.100.83.1                       0 100 50 i
*                   10.200.60.1                       0 200 50 i
*>i                 172.30.255.254         0    500   0 100 50 i
*>i10.30.0.0/16     172.30.255.100         0    100   0 i
*  10.100.0.0/16    10.100.83.1            0          0 100 i
*                   10.200.60.1                       0 200 100 i
*>i                 172.30.255.254         0    500   0 100 i
*  10.125.0.0/16    10.100.83.1                       0 100 200 125 i
*>                  10.200.60.1                       0 200 125 i
*  i                172.30.255.254         0    100   0 200 125 i
*  10.200.0.0/16    10.100.83.1                       0 100 200 i
*>                  10.200.60.1            0          0 200 i
*  i                172.30.255.254         0    100   0 200 i
*>i172.16.0.0       172.30.255.100         0    100   0 i
*  172.17.0.0       10.100.83.1                       0 100 50 i
*                   10.200.60.1                       0 200 50 i
*>i                 172.30.255.254         0    500   0 100 50 i
*> 172.18.0.0       10.100.83.1                       0 100 50 i
*                   10.200.60.1                       0 200 50 i
*  i                172.30.255.254         0    100   0 100 50 i
*>i172.29.1.0/24    172.30.255.100         0    100   0 i
*> 172.29.2.0/24    10.100.83.1                       0 100 50 i
*                   10.200.60.1                       0 200 50 i
*  i                172.30.255.254         0    100   0 100 50 i
*>i172.30.0.0       172.30.255.254         0    100   0 i
*>i172.31.0.0       172.30.255.100         0    100   0 i
*> 172.32.0.0       172.30.255.100        20          32768 i
```

```
* i                    172.30.255.254      20    100      0 i
*>i172.33.0.0          172.30.255.100       0    100      0 i
*>i192.168.2.0         172.30.255.100       0    100      0 i
*  192.168.50.0        10.100.83.1                        0 100 50 i
*                      10.200.60.1                        0 200 50 i
*>i                    172.30.255.254       0    500      0 100 50 i
*>i192.168.100.0       172.30.255.100       0    100      0 i
Moritz#
```

Remember that a router does not advertise a route learned from an IBGP peer to another IBGP peer. In this example, because Moritz has chosen the routes advertised by Zermatt as its preferred paths to the four prefixes in question, it does not advertise the routes in question to Davos. Example 4-75 shows that Moritz is advertising to Davos all the prefixes external to AS30 except for the four prefixes with modified LOCAL_PREF values.

Example 4-75   show ip bgp neighbor advertised-routes *Command Shows That Moritz Is not Advertising to Davos (172.30.255.100) any of the Four Prefixes Modified by the Policy of Example 4-72*

```
Moritz#show ip bgp neighbor 172.30.255.100 advertised-routes
BGP table version is 27, local router ID is 172.30.255.150
Status codes: s suppressed, d damped, h history, * valid, > best, i - internal,
              r RIB-failure, S Stale
Origin codes: i - IGP, e - EGP, ? - incomplete

   Network          Next Hop            Metric LocPrf Weight Path
*> 10.125.0.0/16    10.200.60.1                        0 200 125 i
*> 10.200.0.0/16    10.200.60.1              0          0 200 i
*> 172.18.0.0       10.200.60.1                         0 200 50 i
*> 172.29.2.0/24    10.200.60.1                         0 200 50 i
*> 172.32.0.0       172.30.255.100          20      32768 i

Total number of prefixes 5
Moritz#
```

The solution to this problem is simple. Rather than configure route map More-Pref as an incoming policy for Zermatt's EBGP peers, in Example 4-76 it is configured as an outgoing policy only for Davos. Because routes learned from one IBGP peer are not advertised to other IBGP peers, setting the policy outbound to internal neighbors rather than inbound from external neighbors offers greater control over what routers are effected. In this case, the preferences of Davos are changed without changing the preferences of Moritz. And, as Example 4-77 shows, the routes in Moritz' BGP table are now unaffected by Zermatt's new LOCAL_PREF policy.

Example 4-76 *Route Map More-Pref Is Used as an Outgoing Policy Toward Davos Instead of an Incoming Policy from Innsbruck and Cervinia*

```
Zermatt#show run | section bgp
router bgp 30
 no synchronization
 bgp log-neighbor-changes
 network 10.30.0.0 mask 255.255.0.0
 network 172.16.0.0
 network 172.29.1.0 mask 255.255.255.0
 network 172.30.0.0
 network 172.31.0.0
 network 172.32.0.0
 network 172.33.0.0
 network 192.168.2.0
 network 192.168.100.0
 neighbor 10.100.83.1 remote-as 100
 neighbor 10.100.83.1 ebgp-multihop 2
 neighbor 10.100.83.1 update-source Loopback0
 neighbor 10.100.83.1 filter-list 1 out
 neighbor 10.200.60.1 remote-as 200
 neighbor 10.200.60.1 ebgp-multihop 2
 neighbor 10.200.60.1 update-source Loopback0
 neighbor 172.30.255.100 remote-as 30
 neighbor 172.30.255.100 update-source Loopback0
 neighbor 172.30.255.100 next-hop-self
 neighbor 172.30.255.100 route-map More-Pref out
 neighbor 172.30.255.150 remote-as 30
 neighbor 172.30.255.150 update-source Loopback0
 neighbor 172.30.255.150 next-hop-self
 no auto-summary
Zermatt#
```

Example 4-77 shows the new results in Davos' BGP table. The four prefixes specified in Zermatt's policy configuration have a LOCAL_PREF value of 500, and as a result the routes through Zermatt are preferred. But the alternative routes through Moritz are also in the table and will be used if Zermatt becomes unreachable.

Example 4-77 *Davos' BGP Table Now Shows the Desired Results with the Increased LOCAL_PREF Values Causing Zermatt (172.30.255.254) to Be Chosen as the Preferred Path of the Prefixes of Interest and Moritz (172.30.255.150) as a Backup Path*

```
Davos#show ip bgp
BGP table version is 149, local router ID is 172.32.1.1
Status codes: s suppressed, d damped, h history, * valid, > best, i - internal,
```

```
                    r RIB-failure, S Stale
Origin codes: i - IGP, e - EGP, ? - incomplete


   Network            Next Hop          Metric LocPrf Weight Path
*>i10.20.0.0/16       172.30.255.254         0    500      0 100 50 i
* i                   172.30.255.150         0    100      0 100 50 i
*> 10.30.0.0/16       0.0.0.0                0          32768 i
*>i10.100.0.0/16      172.30.255.254         0    500      0 100 i
* i                   172.30.255.150         0    100      0 100 i
* i10.125.0.0/16      172.30.255.254         0    100      0 200 125 i
*>i                   172.30.255.150         0    100      0 200 125 i
* i10.200.0.0/16      172.30.255.254         0    100      0 200 i
*>i                   172.30.255.150         0    100      0 200 i
*> 172.16.0.0         0.0.0.0                0          32768 i
*>i172.17.0.0         172.30.255.254         0    500      0 100 50 i
* i                   172.30.255.150         0    100      0 100 50 i
* i172.18.0.0         172.30.255.254         0    100      0 100 50 i
*>i                   172.30.255.150         0    100      0 100 50 i
*> 172.29.1.0/24      0.0.0.0                0          32768 i
* i172.29.2.0/24      172.30.255.254         0    100      0 100 50 i
*>i                   172.30.255.150         0    100      0 100 50 i
*>i172.30.0.0         172.30.255.254         0    100      0 i
*> 172.31.0.0         0.0.0.0                0          32768 i
r i172.32.0.0         172.30.255.254        20    100      0 i
r>i                   172.30.255.150        20    100      0 i
*> 172.33.0.0         0.0.0.0                0          32768 i
*> 192.168.2.0        0.0.0.0                0          32768 i
*>i192.168.50.0       172.30.255.254         0    500      0 100 50 i
* i                   172.30.255.150         0    100      0 100 50 i
*> 192.168.100.0      0.0.0.0                0          32768 i
Davos#
```

Example 4-78 *Routes in the BGP Table at Moritz Are Not Affected by the Newer Policy Configuration at Zermatt*

```
Moritz#show ip bgp
BGP table version is 28, local router ID is 172.30.255.150
Status codes: s suppressed, d damped, h history, * valid, > best, i - internal,
              r RIB-failure, S Stale
Origin codes: i - IGP, e - EGP, ? - incomplete


   Network            Next Hop          Metric LocPrf Weight Path
* i10.20.0.0/16       172.30.255.254         0    100      0 100 50 i
*>                    10.100.83.1                          0 100 50 i
```

```
*                       10.200.60.1                       0 200 50 i
*>i10.30.0.0/16         172.30.255.100      0    100      0 i
* i10.100.0.0/16        172.30.255.254      0    100      0 100 i
*                       10.200.60.1                       0 200 100 i
*>                      10.100.83.1         0             0 100 i
* i10.125.0.0/16        172.30.255.254      0    100      0 200 125 i
*                       10.100.83.1                       0 100 200 125 i
*>                      10.200.60.1                       0 200 125 i
* i10.200.0.0/16        172.30.255.254      0    100      0 200 i
*                       10.100.83.1                       0 100 200 i
*>                      10.200.60.1         0             0 200 i
*>i172.16.0.0           172.30.255.100      0    100      0 i
* i172.17.0.0           172.30.255.254      0    100      0 100 50 i
*>                      10.100.83.1                       0 100 50 i
*                       10.200.60.1                       0 200 50 i
* i172.18.0.0           172.30.255.254      0    100      0 100 50 i
*                       10.100.83.1                       0 100 50 i
*>                      10.200.60.1                       0 200 50 i
*>i172.29.1.0/24        172.30.255.100      0    100      0 i
* i172.29.2.0/24        172.30.255.254      0    100      0 100 50 i
*                       10.100.83.1                       0 100 50 i
*>                      10.200.60.1                       0 200 50 i
*>i172.30.0.0           172.30.255.254      0    100      0 i
*>i172.31.0.0           172.30.255.100      0    100      0 i
* i172.32.0.0           172.30.255.254      20   100      0 i
*>                      172.30.255.100      20        32768 i
*>i172.33.0.0           172.30.255.100      0    100      0 i
*>i192.168.2.0          172.30.255.100      0    100      0 i
* i192.168.50.0         172.30.255.254      0    100      0 100 50 i
*>                      10.100.83.1                       0 100 50 i
*                       10.200.60.1                       0 200 50 i
*>i192.168.100.0        172.30.255.100      0    100      0 i
Moritz#
```

Case Study: Using the MULTI_EXIT_DISC Attribute

What if, rather than influencing outgoing path selection, you want to influence incoming path selection? That is, when you advertise a prefix to multiple external peers in a neighboring AS, you want to "tell" the neighboring AS which route to prefer. One way of accomplishing this is to attach a MED attribute to the advertised prefixes.

The MULTI_EXIT_DISC attribute, or MED, is used to influence the routing decisions in neighboring autonomous systems. The MED is also known as the *external metric* and is labeled as "metric" in the BGP table. Like LOCAL_PREF, the MED is a 4-octet number and therefore can be any number from 0 to 4294967295.

The MED is a relatively weak attribute. In the BGP decision process, the Weights, LOCAL_PREFs, AS_PATH lengths, and ORIGINs of multiple routes to the same destination are all compared before MED. If all those variables are equal, however, the route with the lowest MED is chosen.

> **Note**   It can be a bit confusing to remember that the highest LOCAL_PREF is preferred, but the lowest MED is preferred. Another term for MED is *metric*, and another term for metric is *distance*. So remember "highest preference, shortest distance, heaviest weight." You can also remember that LOCAL_PREF and Weight are the only attributes where the higher value wins. With every other attriburte, the lower value wins.

Before exploring how MEDs are configured, it is important to examine MED rules and IOS's default treatment of this attribute.

MED is an optional, *nontransitive* attribute. When a BGP speaker learns a route from an external peer, it can pass the route's MED to any IBGP peers. But a router cannot advertise a MED that was originated in a neighboring AS to a peer in another AS. As a result, the MED has relevance only between neighboring autonomous systems. If router Innsbruck in Figure 4-12 advertises 172.17.0.0 with a certain MED to Zermatt, Zermatt can advertise the MED to Davos and Moritz. But if Moritz advertises the route to Cervinia in AS200, it cannot include the MED in the route—the MED attribute must be removed first.

This basic MED behavior can be observed by following a BGP route across the network of Figure 4-12. In Example 4-79, **show ip bgp 172.32.0.0** is used to observe the BGP table entries for the single prefix 172.32.0.0 at router Moritz. There are two entries, both of which show they were locally originated—that is, the prefix originates in AS30. The first of the routes was learned via IBGP from Zermatt (172.30.255.254) and the second is entered from Moritz's own routing table using the **network** statement (see Example 4-83). The BGP decision process chose the second entry because of the Weight value. (If Weight were not a factor, the second entry would be chosen because it is locally originated, whereas the first entry is learned from IBGP.)

Example 4-79   *Moritz Has Two Entries in Its BGP Table for Prefix 172.32.0.0, and Both Have a MED (Metric) of 20*

```
Moritz# show ip bgp 172.32.0.0
BGP routing table entry for 172.32.0.0/16, version 3
Paths: (2 available, best #2, table Default-IP-Routing-Table)
  Advertised to update-groups:
        1    2
```

```
  Local
    172.30.255.254 (metric 30) from 172.30.255.254 (172.30.255.254)
      Origin IGP, metric 20, localpref 100, valid, internal
  Local
    172.30.255.100 (metric 20) from 0.0.0.0 (172.30.255.150)
      Origin IGP, metric 20, localpref 100, weight 32768, valid, sourced, local,
  best
Moritz#
```

Next, Example 4-80 shows the same prefix in the BGP table of Cervinia, in neighboring AS200. There are four entries here, all of which were learned via EBGP as indicated by the AS_PATH values rather than the "local" keyword as in the previous example. In order, the four entries were learned from Meribel (10.50.250.1), Innsbruck (10.100.83.1), Moritz (172.30.255.150), and Zermatt (172.30.255.254). By the BGP decision process, the last two routes are preferred because they have the shortest AS_PATHs; and then out of these two entries, #3 is selected as best because of the lower Router ID (LOCAL_PREF, Origin IDs, and MEDs are the same). Notice that the two routes advertised from AS30 have a MED value of 20, whereas the routes advertised from AS50 and AS100 have no MED attached. Following the AS_PATHs of the two routes with no MED, you have the first indication that the attribute is nontransitive.

Example 4-80 *Cervinia Has Four Entries for 172.32.0.0, But Only the Entries from the Two Routers in AS30 Have a MED Value*

```
Cervinia#show ip bgp 172.32.0.0
BGP routing table entry for 172.32.0.0/16, version 13
Paths: (4 available, best #3, table Default-IP-Routing-Table)
  Advertised to update-groups:
        1
  50 100 30
    10.50.250.1 from 10.50.250.1 (172.18.1.1)
      Origin IGP, localpref 100, valid, external
  100 30
    10.100.83.1 from 10.100.83.1 (10.100.83.1)
      Origin IGP, localpref 100, valid, external
  30
    172.30.255.150 from 172.30.255.150 (172.30.255.150)
      Origin IGP, metric 20, localpref 100, valid, external, best
  30
    172.30.255.254 from 172.30.255.254 (172.30.255.254)
      Origin IGP, metric 20, localpref 100, valid, external
Cervinia#
```

The nontransitive nature of the MED is confirmed by observing the prefix in the BGP table of Meribel, in AS50 (Example 4-81). This table has three entries for 172.32.0.0, learned via EBGP from Cervinia (10.200.61.1), Innsbruck (10.100.83.1), and Oberstdorf (10.125.25.1). The second entry is chosen as the best, again with the lower Router ID being the determining factor.

Example 4-81   *Meribel Has Three Entries for 172.32.0.0, None of Which Have a MED Value*

```
Meribel#show ip bgp 172.32.0.0
BGP routing table entry for 172.32.0.0/16, version 119
Paths: (3 available, best #2, table Default-IP-Routing-Table)
Flag: 0x820
  Advertised to update-groups:
       1
  200 30
    10.200.60.1 from 10.200.60.1 (10.200.60.1)
      Origin IGP, localpref 100, valid, external
  100 30
    10.100.83.1 from 10.100.83.1 (10.100.83.1)
      Origin IGP, localpref 100, valid, external, best
  125 200 30
    10.125.25.1 from 10.125.25.1 (10.125.25.1)
      Origin IGP, localpref 100, valid, external
Meribel#
```

Notice in this case that none of the three entries have a MED value, including the route advertised from Cervinia, which has a MED attached to it in Example 4-80. Notice also that the AS_PATHS of all three routes have at least one ASN after the originating AS30. The MED does not transit AS30's neighboring autonomous systems.

Although the previous examples show how the MED attribute is nontransitive, they raise another question: How did the MED value of 20 become associated with prefix 172.32.0.0 in the first place? None of the routers in AS30 have yet been configured to add a MED. The questions multiply if you look at Moritz's complete BGP table in Example 4-82. Of all the prefixes in the table, the two entries for 172.32.0.0 are the only ones with a non-zero MED value. Some entries have MED values of 0, and and some entries have no MED at all. Of the three entries for 10.20.0.0/16, for example, one has a Med of 0 and the other two have no MED.

Example 4-82   *172.32.0.0 Is the Only Prefix in Moritz's BGP Table with a Non-Zero MED Value. Other Entries Either Have a MED of 0 or No MED at All*

```
Moritz#show ip bgp
BGP table version is 63, local router ID is 172.30.255.150
Status codes: s suppressed, d damped, h history, * valid, > best, i - internal,
              r RIB-failure, S Stale
Origin codes: i - IGP, e - EGP, ? - incomplete
```

```
      Network            Next Hop          Metric LocPrf Weight Path
*> 10.20.0.0/16        10.100.83.1                          0 100 50 i
*  i                   172.30.255.254        0    100       0 100 50 i
*                      10.200.60.1                .         0 200 50 i
*>i10.30.0.0/16        172.30.255.100        0    100       0 i
*  10.100.0.0/16       10.200.60.1                          0 200 100 i
*  i                   172.30.255.254        0    100       0 100 i
*>                     10.100.83.1           0              0 100 i
*  10.125.0.0/16       10.100.83.1                          0 100 200 125 i
*  i                   172.30.255.254        0    100       0 200 125 i
*>                     10.200.60.1                          0 200 125 i
*  10.200.0.0/16       10.100.83.1                          0 100 200 i
*  i                   172.30.255.254        0    100       0 200 i
*>                     10.200.60.1           0              0 200 i
*>i172.16.0.0          172.30.255.100        0    100       0 i
*> 172.17.0.0          10.100.83.1                          0 100 50 i
*  i                   172.30.255.254        0    100       0 100 50 i
*                      10.200.60.1                          0 200 50 i
*> 172.18.0.0          10.100.83.1                          0 100 50 i
*  i                   172.30.255.254        0    100       0 100 50 i
*                      10.200.60.1                          0 200 50 i
*>i172.29.1.0/24       172.30.255.100        0    100       0 i
*> 172.29.2.0/24       10.100.83.1                          0 100 50 i
*  i                   172.30.255.254        0    100       0 100 50 i
*                      10.200.60.1                          0 200 50 i
*>i172.30.0.0          172.30.255.254        0    100       0 i
*>i172.31.0.0          172.30.255.100        0    100       0 i
*  i172.32.0.0         172.30.255.254        20   100       0 i
*>                     172.30.255.100        20          32768 i
*>i172.33.0.0          172.30.255.100        0    100       0 i
*>i192.168.2.0         172.30.255.100        0    100       0 i
*> 192.168.50.0        10.100.83.1                          0 100 50 i
*  i                   172.30.255.254        0    100       0 100 50 i
*                      10.200.60.1                          0 200 50 i
*>i192.168.100.0       172.30.255.100        0    100       0 i
Moritz#
```

Finding the answer to these questions leads us to an understanding of default IOS treatment of MEDs.

First is the question of the MED value of 20 assigned to 172.32.0.0. Example 4-83 shows Moritz's BGP configuration, and you can see that the **network** statement is used to inject prefixes into BGP. You already know that for the **network** statement to pick up a prefix, it must be in the routing table. Looking at Moritz's routing table in Example 4-84, you can see that all of the prefixes specified with the **network** statement

are in the table. Notice that the next hop of all the prefixes except 172.30.0.0/16 is
Davos (172.30.255.100); the next hop of 172.30.0.0/16 is Zermatt (172.30.255.254).
More important, notice how the prefixes are learned: All of them, except 172.32.0.0,
are learned via IBGP. Specifically, the prefixes are added to the route tables in Davos or
Zermatt by configuring static routes to Null0 and are then injected into BGP with the
network statement (Example 4-85). Those routers then advertise the routes to Moritz
via IBGP. 172.32.0.0 is learned via IS-IS. Finally, notice the metrics of the routes. All the
IBGP-learned routes have a metric of 0, while the IS-IS route has a metric of 20. When
IOS injects a prefix into BGP with the **network** statement, it also adds a MED attribute
with a value corresponding to the IGP metric. The static routes at Davos and Zermatt
have a metric of 0, so those routes carry a corresponding MED value. The IS-IS route to
172.32.0.0 in Moritz's routing table has a metric of 20, so when it is injected into BGP, it
is given a MED with a value of 20.

Example 4-83   network *Statement Is Used in Moritz's BGP Configuration to Pick Up
Local Prefixes, Including 172.32.0.0, from the Routing Table*

```
Moritz#show running-config | section bgp
router bgp 30
 no synchronization
 bgp log-neighbor-changes
 network 10.30.0.0 mask 255.255.0.0
 network 172.16.0.0
 network 172.29.1.0 mask 255.255.255.0
 network 172.30.0.0
 network 172.31.0.0
 network 172.32.0.0
 network 172.33.0.0
 network 192.168.2.0
 network 192.168.100.0
 neighbor 10.100.83.1 remote-as 100
 neighbor 10.100.83.1 ebgp-multihop 2
 neighbor 10.100.83.1 update-source Loopback0
 neighbor 10.100.83.1 filter-list 1 out
 neighbor 10.200.60.1 remote-as 200
 neighbor 10.200.60.1 ebgp-multihop 2
 neighbor 10.200.60.1 update-source Loopback0
 neighbor 10.200.60.1 filter-list 1 out
 neighbor 172.30.255.100 remote-as 30
 neighbor 172.30.255.100 update-source Loopback0
 neighbor 172.30.255.100 next-hop-self
 neighbor 172.30.255.254 remote-as 30
 neighbor 172.30.255.254 update-source Loopback0
 neighbor 172.30.255.254 next-hop-self
 no auto-summary
Moritz#
```

Example 4-84 *All the Prefixes Specified by the* **network** *Statement in Moritz's BGP Configuration Are Learned via BGP, with a Metric of 0, with the Exception of 172.32.0.0. That Prefix Is Learned via IS-IS, with a Metric of 20*

```
Moritz#show ip route
Codes: C - connected, S - static, R - RIP, M - mobile, B - BGP
       D - EIGRP, EX - EIGRP external, O - OSPF, IA - OSPF inter area
       N1 - OSPF NSSA external type 1, N2 - OSPF NSSA external type 2
       E1 - OSPF external type 1, E2 - OSPF external type 2
       i - IS-IS, su - IS-IS summary, L1 - IS-IS level-1, L2 - IS-IS level-2
       ia - IS-IS inter area, * - candidate default, U - per-user static route
       o - ODR, P - periodic downloaded static route

Gateway of last resort is 172.30.255.100 to network 0.0.0.0

B    172.17.0.0/16 [20/0] via 10.200.60.1, 00:02:11
B    172.16.0.0/16 [200/0] via 172.30.255.100, 05:15:15
B    172.18.0.0/16 [20/0] via 10.200.60.1, 00:02:11
     172.29.0.0/24 is subnetted, 2 subnets
B       172.29.1.0 [200/0] via 172.30.255.100, 05:15:15
B       172.29.2.0 [20/0] via 10.200.60.1, 00:02:11
B    172.31.0.0/16 [200/0] via 172.30.255.100, 05:15:15
     172.30.0.0/16 is variably subnetted, 4 subnets, 2 masks
i L2    172.30.255.100/32 [115/20] via 172.30.255.100, Serial1/1
B       172.30.0.0/16 [200/0] via 172.30.255.254, 05:15:15
i L2    172.30.255.254/32 [115/30] via 172.30.255.100, Serial1/1
C       172.30.255.150/32 is directly connected, Loopback0
i L2 172.32.0.0/16 [115/20] via 172.30.255.100, Serial1/1
B    172.33.0.0/16 [200/0] via 172.30.255.100, 05:15:16
     10.0.0.0/8 is variably subnetted, 7 subnets, 2 masks
B       10.30.0.0/16 [200/0] via 172.30.255.100, 05:15:16
B       10.20.0.0/16 [20/0] via 10.200.60.1, 00:02:12
S       10.100.83.1/32 is directly connected, Serial1/3
B       10.100.0.0/16 [20/0] via 10.100.83.1, 05:15:12
B       10.125.0.0/16 [20/0] via 10.200.60.1, 05:15:12
B       10.200.0.0/16 [20/0] via 10.200.60.1, 05:15:12
S       10.200.60.1/32 is directly connected, Serial1/0
B    192.168.50.0/24 [20/0] via 10.200.60.1, 00:02:12
B    192.168.2.0/24 [200/0] via 172.30.255.100, 05:15:16
B    192.168.100.0/24 [200/0] via 172.30.255.100, 05:15:16
i*L2 0.0.0.0/0 [115/20] via 172.30.255.100, Serial1/1
Moritz#
```

Example 4-85   *Prefixes Specified by Moritz's **network** Statements, with the Exception of 172.30.0.0 and 172.32.0.0, Are Added to Davos' Routing Table Using Static Routes That Have a Metric of 0. These Routes Are Then Advertised Using IBGP. 172.32.0.0 Is Directly Connected from Interface Loopback1 and Is Advertised Using IS-IS*

```
Davos#show ip route
Codes: C - connected, S - static, R - RIP, M - mobile, B - BGP
       D - EIGRP, EX - EIGRP external, O - OSPF, IA - OSPF inter area
       N1 - OSPF NSSA external type 1, N2 - OSPF NSSA external type 2
       E1 - OSPF external type 1, E2 - OSPF external type 2
       i - IS-IS, su - IS-IS summary, L1 - IS-IS level-1, L2 - IS-IS level-2
       ia - IS-IS inter area, * - candidate default, U - per-user static route
       o - ODR, P - periodic downloaded static route

Gateway of last resort is 172.30.255.254 to network 0.0.0.0

B    172.17.0.0/16 [200/0] via 172.30.255.254, 01:17:40
S    172.16.0.0/16 is directly connected, Null0
B    172.18.0.0/16 [200/0] via 172.30.255.150, 01:17:40
     172.29.0.0/24 is subnetted, 2 subnets
S       172.29.1.0 is directly connected, Null0
B       172.29.2.0 [200/0] via 172.30.255.150, 01:17:40
S    172.31.0.0/16 is directly connected, Null0
     172.30.0.0/16 is variably subnetted, 4 subnets, 2 masks
C       172.30.255.100/32 is directly connected, Loopback0
B       172.30.0.0/16 [200/0] via 172.30.255.254, 06:30:45
i L2    172.30.255.254/32 [115/20] via 172.30.255.254, Serial1/1
i L2    172.30.255.150/32 [115/20] via 172.30.255.150, Serial1/0
C    172.32.0.0/16 is directly connected, Loopback1
S    172.33.0.0/16 is directly connected, Null0
     10.0.0.0/16 is subnetted, 5 subnets
S       10.30.0.0 is directly connected, Null0
B       10.20.0.0 [200/0] via 172.30.255.254, 01:17:41
B       10.100.0.0 [200/0] via 172.30.255.254, 06:30:41
B       10.125.0.0 [200/0] via 172.30.255.150, 06:30:41
B       10.200.0.0 [200/0] via 172.30.255.150, 06:30:41
B    192.168.50.0/24 [200/0] via 172.30.255.254, 01:17:41
S    192.168.2.0/24 is directly connected, Null0
S    192.168.100.0/24 is directly connected, Null0
i*L2 0.0.0.0/0 [115/10] via 172.30.255.254, Serial1/1
              [115/10] via 172.30.255.150, Serial1/0
Davos#
```

All this explains entry #2 in Example 4-79, and entry #1 can be deduced from this explanation. Just as Davos advertises 172.32.0.0 to Moritz via IS-IS, it also advertises the prefix to Zermatt via IS-IS. Zermatt injects the route into BGP, and uses the IS-IS metric of 20 to add a MED value. The route is then advertised via IBGP to Moritz; this is entry #1 in Example 4-79, showing a MED of 20.

The next challenge is to figure out why some entries in Moritz's BGP table in Example 4-82 have a MED and some do not. At first you might assume that this is the result of the basic rule that does not allow MEDs to pass more than one AS hop away from their originating AS. Moritz's BGP table shown in Example 4-82 is repeated in Example 4-86, to save you some page flipping. The first entry for 10.20.0.0/16 appears to bear out the rule. Looking at the AS_PATH, you can see that it originated in AS50 and passed through AS100 before being advertised by Innsbruck (10.100.83.1) to Moritz in AS30. So if the prefix was given a MED in AS50 before it was advertised to AS100, Innsbruck has to remove the MED before advetising the route to an EBGP neighbor.

Example 4-86 *Some of the Entries in Moritz's BGP Table Have a MED Value of 0, and Others Have No MED at All*

```
Moritz#show ip bgp
BGP table version is 63, local router ID is 172.30.255.150
Status codes: s suppressed, d damped, h history, * valid, > best, i - internal,
              r RIB-failure, S Stale
Origin codes: i - IGP, e - EGP, ? - incomplete

   Network          Next Hop           Metric LocPrf Weight Path
*> 10.20.0.0/16     10.100.83.1                          0 100 50 i
*  i                172.30.255.254          0    100     0 100 50 i
*                   10.200.60.1                          0 200 50 i
*>i10.30.0.0/16     172.30.255.100          0    100     0 i
*  10.100.0.0/16    10.200.60.1                          0 200 100 i
*  i                172.30.255.254          0    100     0 100 i
*>                  10.100.83.1             0            0 100 i
*  10.125.0.0/16    10.100.83.1                          0 100 200 125 i
*  i                172.30.255.254          0    100     0 200 125 i
*>                  10.200.60.1                          0 200 125 i
*  10.200.0.0/16    10.100.83.1                          0 100 200 i
*  i                172.30.255.254          0    100     0 200 i
*>                  10.200.60.1             0            0 200 i
*>i172.16.0.0       172.30.255.100          0    100     0 i
*> 172.17.0.0       10.100.83.1                          0 100 50 i
*  i                172.30.255.254          0    100     0 100 50 i
*                   10.200.60.1                          0 200 50 i
*> 172.18.0.0       10.100.83.1                          0 100 50 i
*  i                172.30.255.254          0    100     0 100 50 i
*                   10.200.60.1                          0 200 50 i
*>i172.29.1.0/24    172.30.255.100          0    100     0 i
*> 172.29.2.0/24    10.100.83.1                          0 100 50 i
```

```
*  i                172.30.255.254        0    100    0 100 50 i
*                   10.200.60.1                         0 200 50 i
*>i172.30.0.0       172.30.255.254        0    100    0 i
*>i172.31.0.0       172.30.255.100        0    100    0 i
*  i172.32.0.0      172.30.255.254       20    100    0 i
*>                  172.30.255.100       20         32768 i
*>i172.33.0.0       172.30.255.100        0    100    0 i
*>i192.168.2.0      172.30.255.100        0    100    0 i
*> 192.168.50.0     10.100.83.1                         0 100 50 i
*  i                172.30.255.254        0    100    0 100 50 i
*                   10.200.60.1                         0 200 50 i
*>i192.168.100.0    172.30.255.100        0    100    0 i
Moritz#
```

So far it makes sense, but then look at the second entry for 10.20.0.0/16. The AS_PATH is identical to the previous entry: It originates in AS50, and then passes through AS100. The route is then advertised into AS30 at Zermatt, which advertises the route to Moritz via IBGP. This last part is known because the next hop is 172.30.255.254 (Zermatt). Surprisingly, this route—even though it has passed more than one AS hop away from its originating AS—has a MED attached to it with a value of 0. The third entry for 10.20.0.0/16 originates in AS50, passes through AS200, and is advertised to Moritz by Cervinia (next hop 10.200.61.1). The entry has no MED, as we expect Cervinia to have removed it before advertising the route.

Entries #1 and #3 for 10.20.0.0/16 are behaving as expected; why, then, does entry #2 have a MED? The answer can be found by looking at Davos' BGP table, in Example 4-87. Notice that every route originating outside of AS30, as indicated by the AS_PATH, has a MED with a value of 0. This is true regardless of how many autonomous systems the path passes through before getting to AS30. Even, and this is most important, the routes in Moritz's BGP table that had no MED now have a MED in Davos' table. The conclusion to draw from this is that if an IOS router receives a prefix from an EBGP peer with no MED, it adds a MED with a default value of 0 before advertising the route to an IBGP peer. This explains why entry #2 for 10.20.0.0/16 in Example 4-86 has a MED: It is advertised by Zermatt (172.30.255.254), an IBGP peer. Zermatt added the MED before advertising it to Moritz.

Example 4-87 *All Externally Originated Routes Have a MED in Davos' BGP Table*

```
Davos#show ip bgp
BGP table version is 23, local router ID is 172.32.1.1
Status codes: s suppressed, d damped, h history, * valid, > best, i - internal,
              r RIB-failure, S Stale
Origin codes: i - IGP, e - EGP, ? - incomplete
```

```
   Network          Next Hop          Metric LocPrf Weight Path
*>i10.20.0.0/16     172.30.255.254         0    500      0 200 50 i
*  i                172.30.255.150         0    100      0 200 50 i
*>  10.30.0.0/16    0.0.0.0                0         32768 i
*>i10.100.0.0/16    172.30.255.254         0    500      0 100 i
*  i                172.30.255.150         0    100      0 100 i
*  i10.125.0.0/16   172.30.255.254         0    100      0 200 125 i
*>i                 172.30.255.150         0    100      0 200 125 i
*  i10.200.0.0/16   172.30.255.254         0    100      0 200 i
*>i                 172.30.255.150         0    100      0 200 i
*>  172.16.0.0      0.0.0.0                0         32768 i
*>i172.17.0.0       172.30.255.254         0    500      0 200 50 i
*  i                172.30.255.150         0    100      0 200 50 i
*  i172.18.0.0      172.30.255.254         0    100      0 200 50 i
*>i                 172.30.255.150         0    100      0 200 50 i
*>  172.29.1.0/24   0.0.0.0                0         32768 i
*  i172.29.2.0/24   172.30.255.254         0    100      0 200 50 i
*>i                 172.30.255.150         0    100      0 200 50 i
*>i172.30.0.0       172.30.255.254         0    100      0 i
*>  172.31.0.0      0.0.0.0                0         32768 i
r  i172.32.0.0      172.30.255.254        20    100      0 i
r>i                 172.30.255.150        20    100      0 i
*>  172.33.0.0      0.0.0.0                0         32768 i
*>  192.168.2.0     0.0.0.0                0         32768 i
*>i192.168.50.0     172.30.255.254         0    500      0 200 50 i
*  i                172.30.255.150         0    100      0 200 50 i
*>  192.168.100.0   0.0.0.0                0         32768 i
Davos#
```

You now have all the information you need to explain MED behavior on IOS:

- If a prefix is injected into BGP based on an IGP route in the routing table, the prefix is assigned a MED value equivalent to the IGP metric value.

- If a prefix is advdertised from its originating AS to a neighboring AS, the MED is preserved and is known by all IBGP routers within the neighboring AS.

- If the neighboring AS advertises the route to any of its own neighboring autonomous systems, it must remove the MED attribute before advertising.

- If a router receives a route with no MED from an EBGP peer, it records the route in its BGP table as-is, with no MED.

- If a router has a route in its BGP table with no MED and is going to advertise the route to an IBGP peer, it first adds a MED to the route with a default value of 0.

Using these rules, review each of the entries in Example 4-86 and you will find that you can completely explain why each entry does or does not have a MED, and why any MED has the value that it does.

Historically, the IETF BGP rules have been unclear about the default treatment of MEDs, and as a result, different vendors can have different defaults.[15] For example, while IOS assigns a MED value of 0 to all EBGP-learned routes before advertising them to IBGP peers, some other implementations assign a maximum MED value of 4294967295 ($2^{32} - 1$). This confusion stems directly from changes in the BGP specifications. Earlier specifications called for assignment of the maximum value to missing MEDs, whereas more recent specifications call for 0. This can cause inconsistent behavior in multi-vendor networks, because 0, as the lowest possible MED value, makes the MED the most preferable while some implementations interpret 4294967295 as "infinity" and indicative of an unfeasible metric. Therefore, when using MEDs in a multi-vendor network, it is important to understand the default behavior of all BGP implementations being used and adjust the defaults to be consistent.

IOS provides a statement, **bgp bestpath med missing-as-worst**, to help when adjusting default behaviors. When this statement is included in the BGP configuration, IOS will use a value of 4294967295 as the default value when adding a MED to routes with missing MEDs rather than 0. In Example 4-88, this statement is shown added to the BGP configuration of Moritz (the same modification is made at Zermatt), and the Moritz's resulting BGP table. Compare this table with the one in Exapmle 4-86, and you can see that routes with missing MEDs—whether incoming directly to Moritz from EBGP peers or incoming to Zermatt and then passed to Zermatt in IBGP —have a MED value of 4294967295. Note also that the routes injected into BGP by Davos and Zermatt still have the default MED value of 0; and 172.32.0.0, picked up by Moritz and Zermatt from IS-IS, still has the MED value of 20.

Example 4-88   *Results of Adding the* **bgp bestpath med missing-as-worst** *Statement to Moritz and Zermatt Are Shown in Moritz's BGP Table*

```
Moritz#show running-config | section bgp
router bgp 30
 no synchronization
 bgp log-neighbor-changes
 bgp bestpath med missing-as-worst
 network 10.30.0.0 mask 255.255.0.0
 network 172.16.0.0
 network 172.29.1.0 mask 255.255.255.0
 network 172.30.0.0
 network 172.31.0.0
 network 172.32.0.0
```

---

[15] RFC 4451 clears up much of the confusion around MEDs, and is recommended reading for anyone working with this attribute: Danny McPherson and Vijay Gill, "BGP MULTI_EXIT_DISC (MED) Considerations," RFC 4451, March 2006.

```
 network 172.33.0.0
 network 192.168.2.0
 network 192.168.100.0
 neighbor 10.100.83.1 remote-as 100
 neighbor 10.100.83.1 ebgp-multihop 2
 neighbor 10.100.83.1 update-source Loopback0
 neighbor 10.100.83.1 filter-list 1 out
 neighbor 10.200.60.1 remote-as 200
 neighbor 10.200.60.1 ebgp-multihop 2
 neighbor 10.200.60.1 update-source Loopback0
 neighbor 10.200.60.1 filter-list 1 out
 neighbor 172.30.255.100 remote-as 30
 neighbor 172.30.255.100 update-source Loopback0
 neighbor 172.30.255.100 next-hop-self
 neighbor 172.30.255.254 remote-as 30
 neighbor 172.30.255.254 update-source Loopback0
 neighbor 172.30.255.254 next-hop-self
 no auto-summary
Moritz#
Moritz#show ip bgp
BGP table version is 34, local router ID is 172.30.255.150
Status codes: s suppressed, d damped, h history, * valid, > best, i - internal,
              r RIB-failure, S Stale
Origin codes: i - IGP, e - EGP, ? - incomplete

   Network          Next Hop          Metric LocPrf Weight Path
*> 10.20.0.0/16     10.100.83.1      4294967295            0 100 50 i
*                   10.200.60.1      4294967295            0 200 50 i
* i                 172.30.255.254   4294967295    100     0 100 50 i
*>i10.30.0.0/16     172.30.255.100            0    100     0 i
*> 10.100.0.0/16    10.100.83.1               0            0 100 i
*                   10.200.60.1      4294967295            0 200 100 i
* i                 172.30.255.254            0    100     0 100 i
*   10.125.0.0/16   10.100.83.1      4294967295            0 100 200 125 i
*>                  10.200.60.1      4294967295            0 200 125 i
* i                 172.30.255.254   4294967295    100     0 200 125 i
*   10.200.0.0/16   10.100.83.1      4294967295            0 100 200 i
*>                  10.200.60.1               0            0 200 i
* i                 172.30.255.254            0    100     0 200 i
*>i172.16.0.0       172.30.255.100            0    100     0 i
*> 172.17.0.0       10.100.83.1      4294967295            0 100 50 i
*                   10.200.60.1      4294967295            0 200 50 i
* i                 172.30.255.254   4294967295    100     0 100 50 i
*> 172.18.0.0       10.100.83.1      4294967295            0 100 50 i
*                   10.200.60.1      4294967295            0 200 50 i
```

```
* i                       172.30.255.254  4294967295       100       0 100 50 i
*>i172.29.1.0/24          172.30.255.100           0       100       0 i
*> 172.29.2.0/24          10.100.83.1     4294967295                 0 100 50 i
*                         10.200.60.1     4294967295                 0 200 50 i
* i                       172.30.255.254  4294967295       100       0 100 50 i
*>i172.30.0.0             172.30.255.254           0       100       0 i
*>i172.31.0.0             172.30.255.100           0       100       0 i
*> 172.32.0.0             172.30.255.100          20             32768 i
* i                       172.30.255.254          20       100       0 i
*>i172.33.0.0             172.30.255.100           0       100       0 i
*>i192.168.2.0            172.30.255.100           0       100       0 i
*> 192.168.50.0           10.100.83.1     4294967295                 0 100 50 i
*                         10.200.60.1     4294967295                 0 200 50 i
* i                       172.30.255.254  4294967295       100       0 100 50 i
*>i192.168.100.0          172.30.255.100           0       100       0 i
Moritz#
```

You can add a MED attribute to a route using a route map and one of two **set** clauses:

- **set metric** is used when you want to arbitrarily set the metric to some value between 0 and 4294967295. Use this clause when you want to manually control the MED value.

- **set metric-type internal** is used when you want to link the MED to the IGP metric of the route's next hop. That is, rather than manually setting the MED value, the router automatically sets the MED to the same value as the IGP metric of the route to the prefix's next hop. When multiple routers are advertising a prefix to a neighboring AS, using this clause ensures that the router closest to the prefix's next hop advertises the lowest MED—and hence, the neighboring AS is asked to send packets to the AS border router closest to the destination. If the IGP metric to the prefix's next hop changes, the MED also changes—although BGP readvertises only the changed MED every 10 minutes, to help reduce destabilization when an IGP route to a next-hop is flapping.

You have seen an example of using a route map to set metric values on selected routes previously, in Example 4-62; however, that example was used just to demonstrate the use of **match** and **set** clauses, and it did not explain the results of the action. The following demonstration observes the results of the MED configuration.

Example 4-89 is a repeat of Example 4-80, in which the four entries for 172.32.0.0 are observed in router Cervinia's (Figure 4-12) BGP table. Of the two entries with the shortest AS_PATH, their LOCAL_PREF, Origin, and MED values are equivalent. Entry #3 is chosen as best because the Router ID of the next hop (Moritz, 172.30.255.150) is numerically lower than the Router ID in entry #4 (Zermatt, 172.30.255.254). We configure Zermatt in Figure 4-12 to attach a MED of 10 to its route to 172.32.0.0 before advertising it to Cervinia. Because MED is considered before Router ID in the BGP decision process and because 10 will be lower than entry #3's value of 20, Cervinia should change its determination of the best path to entry #4.

Example 4-89 *Cervinia Has Four Entries for 172.32.0.0. The Third Entry Is Selected as Best Because (a) It Is One of Two Entries with a Shortest AS_PATH and (b) Out of Those Two Entries, the Router ID of the Next Hop Is Numerically Lower*

```
Cervinia#show ip bgp 172.32.0.0
BGP routing table entry for 172.32.0.0/16, version 13
Paths: (4 available, best #3, table Default-IP-Routing-Table)
  Advertised to update-groups:
       1
  50 100 30
    10.50.250.1 from 10.50.250.1 (172.18.1.1)
      Origin IGP, localpref 100, valid, external
  100 30
    10.100.83.1 from 10.100.83.1 (10.100.83.1)
      Origin IGP, localpref 100, valid, external
  30
    172.30.255.150 from 172.30.255.150 (172.30.255.150)
      Origin IGP, metric 20, localpref 100, valid, external, best
  30
    172.30.255.254 from 172.30.255.254 (172.30.255.254)
      Origin IGP, metric 20, localpref 100, valid, external
Cervinia#
```

Example 4-90 shows the MED policy configured at Zermatt. A route map named Example 4-90 uses access-list 1 to match the single prefix 172.32.0.0 and to set its metric to 10. The route map is then configured as an outgoing policy on neighbor 10.200.60.1. After issuing a **clear ip bgp soft 10.200.60.1 out** command, the effects of the policy on the prefix entries in Cervinia's BGP table are observed in Example 4-91. Cervinia has changed its selection of the best route to entry #4, pointing to Zermatt, because it now has a lower MED value than entry #3 pointing to Moritz.

Example 4-90 *Route Map Example 4-90 Changes the MED of Prefix 172.32.0.0 and Is Applied as an Outgoing Policy for Neighbor Cervinia (10.200.60.1)*

```
router bgp 30
 no synchronization
 bgp log-neighbor-changes
 network 10.30.0.0 mask 255.255.0.0
 network 172.16.0.0
 network 172.29.1.0 mask 255.255.255.0
 network 172.30.0.0
 network 172.31.0.0
```

```
   network 172.32.0.0
   network 172.33.0.0
   network 192.168.2.0
   network 192.168.100.0
   neighbor 10.100.83.1 remote-as 100
   neighbor 10.100.83.1 ebgp-multihop 2
   neighbor 10.100.83.1 update-source Loopback0
   neighbor 10.100.83.1 filter-list 1 out
   neighbor 10.200.60.1 remote-as 200
   neighbor 10.200.60.1 ebgp-multihop 2
   neighbor 10.200.60.1 update-source Loopback0
   neighbor 10.200.60.1 route-map Example_4_90 out
   neighbor 172.30.255.100 remote-as 30
   neighbor 172.30.255.100 update-source Loopback0
   neighbor 172.30.255.100 next-hop-self
   neighbor 172.30.255.100 route-map More-Pref out
   neighbor 172.30.255.150 remote-as 30
   neighbor 172.30.255.150 update-source Loopback0
   neighbor 172.30.255.150 next-hop-self
   no auto-summary
   !
   access-list 1 permit 172.32.0.0
   access-list 1 deny    any
   !
   route-map Example_4_90 permit 10
    match ip address 1
    set metric 10
   !
```

Example 4-91   *Route to 172.32.0.0 to Zermatt, Entry #4, Is Now the Best Route at Cervinia Due to the Lowered MED Value*

```
Cervinia#show ip bgp 172.32.0
BGP routing table entry for 172.32.0.0/16, version 25
Paths: (4 available, best #4, table Default-IP-Routing-Table)
Flag: 0x4800
  Advertised to update-groups:
        1
  50 100 30
    10.50.250.1 from 10.50.250.1 (172.18.1.1)
      Origin IGP, localpref 100, valid, external
  100 30
    10.100.83.1 from 10.100.83.1 (10.100.83.1)
      Origin IGP, localpref 100, valid, external
```

```
    30
      172.30.255.150 from 172.30.255.150 (172.30.255.150)
        Origin IGP, metric 20, localpref 100, valid, external
    30
      172.30.255.254 from 172.30.255.254 (172.30.255.254)
        Origin IGP, metric 10, localpref 100, valid, external, best
Cervinia#
```

What happens when two routers in different neighboring autonomous systems advertise
routes to the same prefix to a local AS and the prefixes both carry MED attributes?
In the following example, both Innsbruck and Cervinia in the network of Figure 4-12
advertise prefix 10.20.0.0/16 (originated in AS50) to their peers in AS30. Innsbruck
sets the MED to 200, while Cervinia sets the MED to 100; both Zermatt and Moritz in
AS30, then, should select the route through Cervinia due to the lower MED value. The
MED policy configurations at Innsbruck and Cervinia are not shown, but their results
are shown in Example 4-92. You can see that the route from Cervinia (10.100.60.1) has a
MED value of 100 and the route from Innsbruck (10.100.83.1) has a MED value of 200.
But Example 4-92 also shows something that might be surprising at first examination:
Entry #2 from Innsbruck—even though it has a higher MED value than entry #1 from
Cervinia—is marked as the best route.

Example 4-92 *Zermatt Has Chosen the Route to 10.20.0.0 Through Innsbruck
(10.100.83.1) Even Though the Route Through Cervinia (10.200.60.1) Has a Lower MED*

```
Zermatt#show ip bgp 10.20.0.0
BGP routing table entry for 10.20.0.0/16, version 2
Paths: (3 available, best #2, table Default-IP-Routing-Table)
  Advertised to update-groups:
        1    2    3
  200 50
    10.200.60.1 from 10.200.60.1 (10.200.60.1)
      Origin IGP, metric 100, localpref 100, valid, external
  100 50
    10.100.83.1 from 10.100.83.1 (10.100.83.1)
      Origin IGP, metric 200, localpref 100, valid, external, best
  100 50
    172.30.255.150 (metric 30) from 172.30.255.150 (172.30.255.150)
      Origin IGP, metric 200, localpref 100, valid, internal
Zermatt#
```

The result in Example 4-92 is in fact default behavior. If the same route is advertised
from external peers in different autonomous systems, the MEDs of the routes are
ignored. So in this example, the decision process moves past the MED step and selects
the best route again based on the lowest Router ID of the next hop. (The third entry is

rejected earlier in the decision process; EBGP or external routes are preferred over IBGP or internal routes.)

Normally this is the right default behavior: You do not want to accept "competing" MED values from multiple administrative authorities outside of your (or each others') control. There are, however, occasional exceptions to the rule. For example, a service provider might have a single customer with multiple ASNs, and that customer might want to influence incoming path selection to those ASNs. The advertised prefix itself might belong to another ASN further downstream (such as 10.20.0.0/16 in our example) or it might be located in one of the single customer's autonomous systems but reachable across all of the ASNs through "backdoor routes."

IOS provides a configuration option for such a circumstance. The statement **bgp always-compare-med** causes the router to include MED values in the BGP decision process even if the prefixes are advertised by different ASNs. Example 4-93 shows the effects of this option. After the statement is added to Zermatt's BGP configuration and the sessions to AS100 and AS200 are reset, the entries for 10.20.0.0/16 are again observed in the router's BGP table. The entry from Cervinia, with the lower MED value, is now marked as the best path.

Example 4-93 *Zermatt Has Chosen the Route to 10.20.0.0 Through Innsbruck (10.100.83.1) Even Though the Route Through Cervinia (10.200.60.1) Has a Lower MED*

```
Zermatt(config-router)#bgp always-compare-med
Zermatt(config-router)#^Z
Zermatt#
*Mar  5 15:57:34.215: %SYS-5-CONFIG_I: Configured from console by console
Zermatt#
Zermatt#clear ip bgp 100
*Mar  5 15:57:51.583: %BGP-5-ADJCHANGE: neighbor 10.100.83.1 Down User reset
*Mar  5 15:57:53.171: %BGP-5-ADJCHANGE: neighbor 10.100.83.1 Up
Zermatt#clear ip bgp 200
*Mar  5 15:58:08.635: %BGP-5-ADJCHANGE: neighbor 10.200.60.1 Down User reset
*Mar  5 15:58:09.267: %BGP-5-ADJCHANGE: neighbor 10.200.60.1 Up
Zermatt#
Zermatt#show ip bgp 10.20.0.0
BGP routing table entry for 10.20.0.0/16, version 52
Paths: (3 available, best #1, table Default-IP-Routing-Table)
Flag: 0x820
  Advertised to update-groups:
        1    2
  200 50
    10.200.60.1 from 10.200.60.1 (10.200.60.1)
      Origin IGP, metric 100, localpref 100, valid, external, best
  100 50
    10.100.83.1 from 10.100.83.1 (10.100.83.1)
```

```
        Origin IGP, metric 200, localpref 100, valid, external
   100 50
     172.30.255.150 (metric 30) from 172.30.255.150 (172.30.255.150)
       Origin IGP, metric 200, localpref 100, valid, internal
Zermatt#
```

There are two more default IOS BGP behaviors to consider before leaving the topic of MEDs. The first is how multiple routes to the same destination are evaluated in the BGP table. IOS evaluates them "top down," two at a time. That is, if there are four entries, entries #1 and #2 are evaluated and the best route is chosen from the two based on the BGP decision process. That selected route is then evaluated against entry #3 and the best of the two is selected. That entry is evaluated against entry #4 and the best of those two is selected by the decision process. The "winner" of this final round then becomes the overall best route.

The other default IOS BGP behavior has to do with how received routes to the same prefix are recorded. As each route is received, an entry is added to the "top" of the list of entries for that prefix. For instance, in Example 4-93, there are three entries for prefix 10.20.0.0/16. Entry #1 from 10.200.60.1 is the newest, and entry #3 from 172.30.255.150 is the oldest. If another route to 10.20.0.0/16 was received, it would become entry #1 and the other entries would move down one increment. The oldest received route is always at the bottom of the list.

Together, these two default behaviors can cause some inconsistencies in the way BGP chooses a best path. To demonstrate, we again use the network in Figure 4-12. The **bgp always-compare-med** statement configured in the previous example is removed from router Zermatt; as discussed, there are only limited occasions when you want to compare MEDs between different autonomous systems. For this example, routers Innsbruck and Cervinia are configured to add a MED to the route to prefix 172.17.0.0 in AS50; but the values change depending on which neighbor they advertise the route to:

■ Innsbruck and Cervinia add a MED value of 50 when they advertise 172.17.0.0 to Zermatt.

■ Innsbruck adds a MED value of 100 when it advertises 172.17.0.0 to Moritz.

■ Cervinia adds a MED value of 200 when it advertises 172.17.0.0 to Moritz.

Example 4-94 shows the three entries for 172.17.0.0 in Moritz's BGP table:

■ Entry #1 is the route through Cervinia, with a MED value of 200. This is the most recent entry learned, because it is at the beginning of the list.

■ Entry #2 is the route through Innsbruck via Zermatt with a metric of 50.

■ Entry #3 is the route directly through Innsbruck, with a metric of 100.

Entry #3 is indicated as the best route. The selection process happened as follows:

- Running the list from top to bottom, Entry #1 is compared to Entry #2. The two routes are advertised by different autonomous systems, so the MEDs are not compared. Entry #1 is chosen as the better of the two because it is advertised by an external (EBGP) neighbor whereas Entry #2 is advertised by an internal (IBGP) neighbor.

- Entry #1 is then compared with entry #3. Again, the routes are not advertised by the same autonomous system and so their MEDs are not compared. This time both routes are advertised by external neighbors; Entry #3 is chosen as the better of the two because the Router ID of the next hop is numerically lower.

- There are no more entries to compare, so Entry #3 is selected as best.

Example 4-94 *Entries for 172.17.0.0 in Moritz' BGP Table Are Added in the Order They Are Received and Are Evaluated by the BGP Decision Process Sequentially from Top to Bottom*

```
Moritz#show ip bgp 172.17.0.0
BGP routing table entry for 172.17.0.0/16, version 8
Paths: (3 available, best #3, table Default-IP-Routing-Table)
Flag: 0x820
  Advertised to update-groups:
        1
  200 50
    10.200.60.1 from 10.200.60.1 (10.200.60.1)
      Origin IGP, metric 200, localpref 100, valid, external
  100 50
    172.30.255.254 (metric 30) from 172.30.255.254 (172.30.255.254)
      Origin IGP, metric 50, localpref 100, valid, internal
  100 50
    10.100.83.1 from 10.100.83.1 (10.100.83.1)
      Origin IGP, metric 100, localpref 100, valid, external, best
Moritz#
```

In Example 4-95, the session to Innsbruck is reset. The route through Innsbruck is lost when the session is lost, but acquired again when the session comes back up. But now, it is the newest route, so it appears as Entry #1. This change in the sequence of entries also changes which of the entries is chosen as best:

- Again, running the list from top to bottom, Entry #1 is compared to Entry #2. The two routes are advertised by different autonomous systems, so the MEDs are not compared. They are also advertised by external neighbors, so they are equivalent at that step of the decision process. Entry #1 is chosen as the better of the two because it has the lower Router ID of the two routes.

- Entry #1 is then compared with entry #3. This time the routes are advertised by the same AS, so the MEDs are compared. Entry #3 is chosen as the better of the two because it has a lower MED value.

- There are no more entries to compare, so Entry #3 is selected as best.

Example 4-95 *Resetting the BGP Session to Innsbruck Causes the Route Through Innsbruck to Be Lost and Then Re-Learned. When It Is Relearned It Is Added to the Top of the List, Which Changes the Selection of the Best Route*

```
Moritz#clear ip bgp 10.100.83.1
Moritz#
*Mar  6 13:26:36.335: %BGP-5-ADJCHANGE: neighbor 10.100.83.1 Down User reset
*Mar  6 13:26:37.267: %BGP-5-ADJCHANGE: neighbor 10.100.83.1 Up
Moritz#
Moritz#show ip bgp 172.17.0.0
BGP routing table entry for 172.17.0.0/16, version 29
Paths: (3 available, best #3, table Default-IP-Routing-Table)
Flag: 0x820
  Not advertised to any peer
  100 50
    10.100.83.1 from 10.100.83.1 (10.100.83.1)
      Origin IGP, metric 100, localpref 100, valid, external
  200 50
    10.200.60.1 from 10.200.60.1 (10.200.60.1)
      Origin IGP, metric 200, localpref 100, valid, external
  100 50
    172.30.255.254 (metric 30) from 172.30.255.254 (172.30.255.254)
      Origin IGP, metric 50, localpref 100, valid, internal, best
Moritz#
```

The selection of the best route changes according to the order of the entries, and the order of the entries depends on the order in which the routes are first received. The result is an inconsistent best path selection procedure. That is, the best path selection is *nondeterministic.*

IOS provides an option for making the best path selection deterministic. When the **bgp deterministic-med** statement is added to the BGP configuration, entries into the table are grouped by advertising ASN rather than simply listed newest to oldest. The best entry from each group is then compared. This grouping prevents a situation such as that of Example 4-95, an entry from AS100 and AS200 are compared, and then the winner is compared to another entry from AS100. Comparisons between entries from the same AS, in which the MEDs are a factor, are made before comparisons between entries from different autonomous systems, in which the MEDs are not considered.

Example 4-96 illustrates the use of this option. The **bgp deterministic-med** statement has been added to the BGP configuration of Moritz, and all BGP sessions have been reset with the **clear ip bgp *** command. Comparing the entries for 172.17.0.0 in Example 4-96 with those in Example 4-94, the order of the entries is the same but the results are different. This time, the selection process is as follows:

- Entries #2 and #3 are both from AS100, so they are compared. Entry #2 is selected as the better route because it has a lower MED value. In other words, the best entry from among the routes advertised from AS100 is selected first.

- Entry #1, from AS200, is compared with entry #2 (the AS100 best route). The MED values are not compared because the entries are advertised from different autonomous systems. Entry #1 is selected as better because it is learned from an external peer, whereas entry #2 is learned from an internal peer.

- There are no more AS groups to compare, so entry #1 is determined to the the best route.

Example 4-96   *After Adding the* **bgp deterministic-med** *Statement to Moritz's BGP Configuration and Resetting All Sessions, the Entries for 172.17.0.0 Look Similar to Example 4-94 But a Different Entry Is Chosen as Best*

```
Moritz#show ip bgp 172.17.0.0
BGP routing table entry for 172.17.0.0/16, version 4
Paths: (3 available, best #1, table Default-IP-Routing-Table)
  Advertised to update-groups:
       1
  200 50
    10.200.60.1 from 10.200.60.1 (10.200.60.1)
      Origin IGP, metric 200, localpref 100, valid, external, best
  100 50
    172.30.255.254 (metric 30) from 172.30.255.254 (172.30.255.254)
      Origin IGP, metric 50, localpref 100, valid, internal
  100 50
    10.100.83.1 from 10.100.83.1 (10.100.83.1)
      Origin IGP, metric 100, localpref 100, valid, external
```

In Example 4-97, the entry from 10.100.83.1 is again reset, as it was in Example 4-95, so that when the BGP session is reestablished, that entry becomes the newest. But unlike Example 4-95, the new entry is not added to the top of the list. Instead, it is added back to the AS100 group. As a result, the overall best route selection is not changed and entry #1 is again selected as the best route.

Example 4-97 *When the* **bgp deterministic-med** *Statement Is in Place, New Entries Are Added to the Appropriate ASN Group Rather Than Just Being Added to the Top of the List*

```
Moritz#clear ip bgp 10.100.83.1
Moritz#
*Mar  6 13:32:52.375: %BGP-5-ADJCHANGE: neighbor 10.100.83.1 Down User reset
*Mar  6 13:32:53.103: %BGP-5-ADJCHANGE: neighbor 10.100.83.1 Up
Moritz#show ip bgp 172.17.0.0
BGP routing table entry for 172.17.0.0/16, version 4
Paths: (3 available, best #1, table Default-IP-Routing-Table)
  Advertised to update-groups:
        1
  200 50
    10.200.60.1 from 10.200.60.1 (10.200.60.1)
      Origin IGP, metric 200, localpref 100, valid, external, best
  100 50
    172.30.255.254 (metric 30) from 172.30.255.254 (172.30.255.254)
      Origin IGP, metric 50, localpref 100, valid, internal
  100 50
    10.100.83.1 from 10.100.83.1 (10.100.83.1)
      Origin IGP, metric 100, localpref 100, valid, external
Moritz#
```

Although **bgp deterministic-med** is not enabled in IOS by default, modern best practice recommends using it to ensure consistent, predictable BGP path selection behavior when the same prefix is being learned from more than one AS. In most cases this circumstance will apply to service provider networks or to multihomed stub autonomous systems. However, if you use this option it is important that it be used on all BGP routers in your AS. Inconsistent use can cause unpredictable and possibly conflicting route selection.

Note that **bgp always-compare-med** also enforces deterministic behavior in the path selection. If you use this statement you do not need to also use the **bgp deterministic-med** statement. The difference between the two, of course, is that the former is only used when you want to compare the MEDs of routes from different autonomous systems.

The final point to be made about MEDs is that you might not want the MED settings sent to you by neighboring autonomous systems to influence the BGP decision process in your AS. You can manage this by configuring an incoming policy on all EBGP sessions that rewrites the MED values of received routes to the same value. If the MED values are equal on all routes, they will not influence the decision process. Typically the reset value is either 0 or 4294967295, although the latter is preferable in case you want to make some limited exceptions to your "no MED" rule. That is, resetting all MEDs to the highest value allows you to then accept and act on some MEDs at a lower value.

Case Study: Prepending the AS_PATH

The MULTI_EXIT_DISC attribute can influence the incoming traffic from neighboring autonomous systems, but it cannot influence the routing decisions of more remote autonomous systems.

Figure 4-13 repeats Figure 4-8, a topology used in an earlier case study. Looking at the BGP table of Meribel in Example 4-98, you can see that the router has duplicate, equal-cost paths to the destinations within AS30. Because all other values are equal, Meribel's BGP decision process has chosen Innsbruck as the next-hop router for all traffic to AS30 based on Innsbruck's lower Router ID. As a result, the Cervinia-Moritz link does not get used at all for traffic from AS50 to AS30; available bandwidth is poorly utilized.

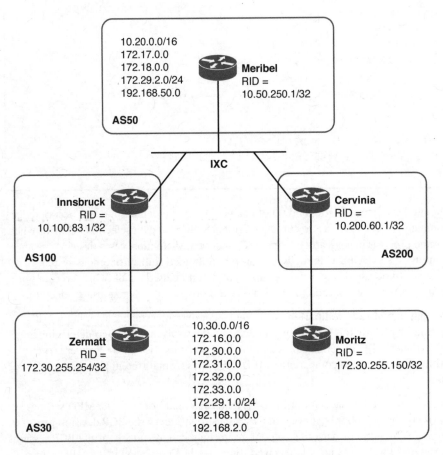

Figure 4-13   *Dual, Equal-Cost Paths Exist Between AS50 and AS30*

Example 4-98 *Meribel's BGP Table Shows the Dual Paths to the Destinations Within AS30. Innsbruck Is Chosen as the Best Path for All the Destinations Because Its Router ID (10.100.83.1) Is Lower Than Cervinia's (10.200.60.1)*

```
Meribel#show ip bgp
BGP table version is 52, local router ID is 172.18.1.1
Status codes: s suppressed, d damped, h history, * valid, > best, i - internal,
              r RIB-failure, S Stale
Origin codes: i - IGP, e - EGP, ? - incomplete

   Network          Next Hop        Metric LocPrf Weight Path
*> 10.20.0.0/16     0.0.0.0              0        32768 i
*> 10.30.0.0/16     10.100.83.1                      0 100 30 i
*                   10.200.60.1                      0 200 100 30 i
*> 10.100.0.0/16    10.100.83.1          0           0 100 i
*                   10.200.60.1                      0 200 100 i
*  10.200.0.0/16    10.100.83.1                      0 100 200 i
*>                  10.200.60.1          0           0 200 i
*  172.16.0.0       10.100.83.1                      0 100 30 i
*>                  10.200.60.1                      0 200 30 i
*> 172.17.0.0       0.0.0.0              0        32768 i
*> 172.18.0.0       0.0.0.0              0        32768 i
*> 172.29.1.0/24    10.100.83.1                      0 100 30 i
*                   10.200.60.1                      0 200 100 30 i
*> 172.29.2.0/24    0.0.0.0              0        32768 i
*> 172.30.0.0       10.100.83.1                      0 100 30 i
*                   10.200.60.1                      0 200 30 i
*> 172.31.0.0       10.100.83.1                      0 100 30 i
*                   10.200.60.1                      0 200 30 i
*> 172.32.0.0       10.100.83.1                      0 100 30 i
*                   10.200.60.1                      0 200 30 i
*> 172.33.0.0       10.100.83.1                      0 100 30 i
*                   10.200.60.1                      0 200 30 i
*> 192.168.2.0      10.100.83.1                      0 100 30 i
*                   10.200.60.1                      0 200 30 i
*> 192.168.50.0     0.0.0.0              0        32768 i
*> 192.168.100.0    10.100.83.1                      0 100 30 i
*                   10.200.60.1                      0 200 30 i
Meribel#
```

AS30 cannot influence the routing decisions of AS50 with MEDs, because the two autonomous systems are not directly connected neighbors. But AS30 can influence the routing decisions of AS50 by modifying the AS_PATH of the routes it advertises with a route map using the **set as-path prepend** clause. The clause allows you to prepend extra ASNs to the AS_PATH attribute of a route as it is advertised to an EBGP peer, making the path less preferable than another route to the same prefix advertised by another router in the same AS.

In this case study, AS_PATH prepending is used so that

- Meribel prefers the Innsbruck-Zermatt path to reach the following prefixes:

  - 10.30.0.0/16

  - 172.16.0.0

  - 172.30.0.0

  - 172.32.0.0

  - 192.168.100.0

- Meribel prefers the Cervinia-Moritz path to reach the following prefixes:

  - 172.31.0.0

  - 172.33.0.0

  - 172.29.1.0/24

  - 192.168.2.0

Example 4-99 shows a route map named PATH added to the configurations of Zermatt and Moritz. In each case, the route map uses access list 3 to identify the prefixes of the routes to be prepended. The route map adds an extra ASN 30 to the AS_PATH of the identified routes, so the outgoing AS_PATH is [30, 30] rather than [30]. The route map is then applied as an outgoing policy to the relevant EBGP neighbor configuration.

Example 4-99 *Zermatt and Moritz Are Configured to Prepend ASN 30 to Selected Routes Advertised to Their EBGP Peers*

```
Zermatt:
router bgp 30
 no synchronization
 bgp log-neighbor-changes
 network 10.30.0.0 mask 255.255.0.0
 network 172.16.0.0
 network 172.29.1.0 mask 255.255.255.0
 network 172.30.0.0
 network 172.31.0.0
 network 172.32.0.0
 network 172.33.0.0
 network 192.168.2.0
 network 192.168.100.0
 neighbor 10.100.83.1 remote-as 100
 neighbor 10.100.83.1 ebgp-multihop 2
```

```
 neighbor 10.100.83.1 update-source Loopback0
 neighbor 10.100.83.1 route-map PATH out
 neighbor 10.100.83.1 filter-list 1 out
 neighbor 172.30.255.100 remote-as 30
 neighbor 172.30.255.100 update-source Loopback0
 neighbor 172.30.255.100 next-hop-self
 neighbor 172.30.255.100 route-map More-Pref out
 neighbor 172.30.255.150 remote-as 30
 neighbor 172.30.255.150 update-source Loopback0
 neighbor 172.30.255.150 next-hop-self
 no auto-summary
!
access-list 3 permit 192.168.2.0
access-list 3 permit 172.33.0.0
access-list 3 permit 172.29.1.0
access-list 3 permit 172.31.0.0
!
route-map PATH permit 10
 match ip address 3
 set as-path prepend 30
!
route-map PATH permit 20
!
```

Moritz:

```
router bgp 30
 no synchronization
 bgp log-neighbor-changes
 network 10.30.0.0 mask 255.255.0.0
 network 172.16.0.0
 network 172.29.1.0 mask 255.255.255.0
 network 172.30.0.0
 network 172.31.0.0
 network 172.32.0.0
 network 172.33.0.0
 network 192.168.2.0
 network 192.168.100.0
 neighbor 10.200.60.1 remote-as 200
 neighbor 10.200.60.1 ebgp-multihop 2
 neighbor 10.200.60.1 update-source Loopback0
 neighbor 10.200.60.1 route-map PATH out
 neighbor 10.200.60.1 filter-list 1 out
 neighbor 172.30.255.100 remote-as 30
 neighbor 172.30.255.100 update-source Loopback0
 neighbor 172.30.255.100 next-hop-self
```

```
 neighbor 172.30.255.254 remote-as 30
 neighbor 172.30.255.254 update-source Loopback0
 neighbor 172.30.255.254 next-hop-self
 no auto-summary
!
access-list 3 permit 192.168.100.0
access-list 3 permit 10.30.0.0
access-list 3 permit 172.32.0.0
access-list 3 permit 172.30.0.0
access-list 3 permit 172.16.0.0
!
route-map PATH permit 10
 match ip address 3
 set as-path prepend 30
!
route-map PATH permit 20
!
```

Keep in mind that each router, Zermatt and Moritz, prepend the routes that they want to make less preferable to Meribel—that is, Zermatt prepends routes that should go through Moritz and Moritz prepends routes that should go through Zermatt.

Example 4-100 shows the resulting BGP table at Meribel. You can observe the pre-pended AS_PATHs, and you can observe that Meribel is selecting the routes into AS30 with the shorter AS_PATHs.

Example 4-100   *Meribel's BGP Table Shows the Prepended AS_PATHs from Zermatt and Moritz; the Router Chooses the Paths with the Shorter AS_PATH*

```
Meribel#show ip bgp
BGP table version is 17, local router ID is 172.18.1.1
Status codes: s suppressed, d damped, h history, * valid, > best, i - internal,
              r RIB-failure, S Stale
Origin codes: i - IGP, e - EGP, ? - incomplete

   Network          Next Hop         Metric LocPrf Weight Path
*> 10.20.0.0/16     0.0.0.0               0         32768 i
*> 10.30.0.0/16     10.100.83.1                         0 100 30 i
*                   10.200.60.1                         0 200 30 30 i
*> 10.100.0.0/16    10.100.83.1           0             0 100 i
*> 10.200.0.0/16    10.200.60.1           0             0 200 i
*> 172.16.0.0       10.100.83.1                         0 100 30 i
*                   10.200.60.1                         0 200 30 30 i
*> 172.17.0.0       0.0.0.0               0         32768 i
*> 172.18.0.0       0.0.0.0               0         32768 i
```

```
*   172.29.1.0/24    10.100.83.1                          0 100 30 30 i
*>                   10.200.60.1                          0 200 30 i
*> 172.29.2.0/24     0.0.0.0                   0     32768 i
*> 172.30.0.0        10.100.83.1                          0 100 30 i
*                    10.200.60.1                          0 200 30 30 i
*   172.31.0.0       10.100.83.1                          0 100 30 30 i
*>                   10.200.60.1                          0 200 30 i
*> 172.32.0.0        10.100.83.1                          0 100 30 i
*                    10.200.60.1                          0 200 30 30 i
*   172.33.0.0       10.100.83.1                          0 100 30 30 i
*>                   10.200.60.1                          0 200 30 i
*   192.168.2.0      10.100.83.1                          0 100 30 30 i
*>                   10.200.60.1                          0 200 30 i
*> 192.168.50.0      0.0.0.0                   0     32768 i
*> 192.168.100.0     10.100.83.1                          0 100 30 i
*                    10.200.60.1                          0 200 30 30 i
Meribel#
```

You should use AS_PATH prepending with great caution. If you do not fully understand the effects your configuration has, unexpected or broken routing can result. Suppose, for example, the clause **set as-path prepend 30 30** is used in Moritz's configuration. This command adds two instances of the ASN 30 to the AS_PATH rather than one. Examining the effects on the route to 10.30.0.0, Cervinia in Figure 4-13 receives the route from Moritz with an AS_PATH of [30,30,30] and a route from Meribel to the same destination with an AS_PATH of [50,100,30]. Because the routes have the same AS_PATH length, Cervinia chooses the route with the lowest Router ID: Meribel's. The original intention was to affect the routing at AS50 only, but this configuration would cause AS200 to choose a longer path to the destination.

It is also important when prepending to always use the AS number of the prepending router's AS. If another AS number is used, and an AS using that number is encountered by the advertised route, that AS will not accept the route. Although it appears to be common sense to use your own ASN when prepending, there are documented cases of autonomous systems using someone else's ASN. IOS has a configuration option, **bgp enforce-first-as**, that allows a network operator to create a rule whereby a route sent from a neighboring AS is not accepted unless the last ASN on the AS_PATH is that neighbor's ASN. For a neighbor using an ASN other than his own to prepend his advertised routes, this option causes those routes to be rejected. In newer IOS versions, **bgp enforce-first-as** is the default.

AS_PATH prepending is often a trial-and-error exercise. Prepending a route with different multiples of your ASN might have different results, and if an upstream AS filters prepended routes, it might have no effect at all. It is important to note, however, that the public Internet is seldom more than six or eight AS hops "deep"—that is, a path from any point on the Internet to any other point on the Internet is unlikely to traverse more than six or eight separate autonomous systems. Therefore, prepending a route with more than a few instances of your ASN is merely a waste of resources and an irritation to other operators on the Internet.

Yet if you go to a publicly accessible route server[16] and type a **show ip bgp paths** command, you can readily find routes in which an ASN is repeated 10 or more times: a result of poor understanding of the use of AS_PATH prepending, or of simple negligence. If your network is providing transit for other autonomous systems, you can use the IOS statement **bgp maxas-limit** to implement a policy that sets a maximum AS_PATH length.

Case Study: Administrative Distances and Backdoor Routes

An IOS-specific tool for manipulating preferences on a single router is *administrative distance*. Administrative weight influences preference among multiple routes to the same destination that have been learned from different BGP peers, whereas administrative distance influences preference among multiple routes to the same destination that have been learned from different routing protocols. This means that the effects of administrative weights are seen in the BGP table, whereas the effects of administrative distances are seen in the IP routing table.

Normally, an administrative distance is assigned to a route according to the protocol or source from which the route is learned. The lower the distance, the more preferable the route. Table 4-4 shows the default administrative distances for the various protocols. You can see that within an AS, if a router learns routes to the same destination from RIP and OSPF, the OSPF route is preferred because its distance (110) is lower than that of the RIP route (120).

EBGP has a default distance of 20, lower than any of the IGPs. At first, this might seem like a problem in networks such as the one in Figure 4-13. When Zermatt advertises one of the AS30 internal addresses to Innsbruck, the address is passed to Cervinia across the IXC, which can pass it back to Moritz. Moritz, hearing the route via EBGP, prefers it over the IGP route to the same destination within the AS, because the IGP route has a higher administrative distance. Actually, this doesn't happen, because of the basic BGP loop-avoidance mechanism. Moritz observes the 30 in the AS_PATH of the route from Cervinia and drops the route.

Table 4-4   *Cisco Default Administrative Distances*[17]

Route Source	Administrative Distance
Connected interface	0
Static route	1
EIGRP summary route	5

---

[16] A web search on "public route servers" or "looking glass" will reveal many lists of publicly accessible route servers.

[17] When a static route refers to an interface rather than a next-hop address, the destination is considered to be a directly connected network and gets an administrative distance of 0.

Route Source	Administrative Distance
External BGP	20
EIGRP	90
IGRP	100
OSPF	110
IS-IS	115
RIP	120
EGP	140
On Demand Routing (ODR)	160
External EIGRP	170
Internal BGP	200
Local BGP	200
Unknown	255

On the other hand, IBGP does not add an AS number to the AS_PATH. So a route learned from an IGP and then passed to an IBGP peer within a single AS could cause routing loops or black holes. For this reason, the distance of IBGP routes is 200, higher than that of any IGP. An IGP-learned route is always preferred over an IBGP route to the same destination.

Local BGP routes are those originated on the local router as the result of using the BGP **network** statement. Like IBGP routes, they have a default administrative distance of 200 so that they are not preferred over IGP routes.

Chapter 13, "Route Filtering," of Volume I includes a case study demonstrating how to manipulate the default distances of IGP routes. To change the default distances of BGP, you use the **distance bgp** statement. This statement sets the distances for EBGP, IBGP, and local BGP routes, respectively. The configuration in Example 4-101 changes the IBGP administrative distance to 95, making the IBGP routes preferred over all IGP routes to the same destination, except EIGRP routes.

Example 4-101 *Changing the IBGP Administrative Distance to 95 Makes IBGP Routes Preferred over All IGP Routes Except EIGRP*

```
router bgp 30
 neighbor 10.200.60.1 remote-as 200
 neighbor 10.200.60.1 ebgp-multihop 2
 neighbor 10.200.60.1 update-source Loopback0
 distance bgp 20 95 200
```

Unlike IGPs, there is seldom a good reason for changing the default BGP distances for all routes. (Manipulating administrative distances is the accepted way to migrate from one IGP to another.) However, there is a situation in which the distances of some BGP routes should be changed. The network in Figure 4-14 has a private link between routers Meribel and Lillehammer, and the routers speak RIP across the link. This link is used as a *back door*. That is, some traffic between AS50 and AS75 should be sent over the private backdoor route rather than across the public IXC. Perhaps AS50 and AS75 have a business partnership, and they want some of their communications to pass over their private link rather than the public Internet.

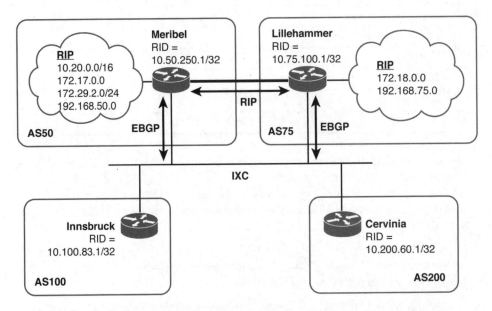

Figure 4-14   *AS50 and AS75 Have a Private Backdoor Link, Allowing the IGP Processes of Those Autonomous Systems to Communicate Directly Rather Than Across the IXC*

In this example, traffic between 172.17.0.0 in AS50 and 172.18.0.0 in AS75 should travel across the backdoor link and use the IXC route only if the backdoor route fails. The problem is the administrative distance. Lillehammer, for instance, learns the route to 172.17.0.0 from Meribel via both RIP across the backdoor link and EBGP across the IXC link. EBGP has a distance of 20 and RIP has a distance of 120, so the EBGP route is preferred, as indicated in the output in Example 4-102.

Example 4-102   *Lillehammer Learns the Route to 172.17.0.0 via Both RIP and EBGP; the EBGP Route, with an Administrative Distance of 20, Is Preferred*

```
Lillehammer#show ip route
Codes: C - connected, S - static, I - IGRP, R - RIP, M - mobile, B - BGP
       D - EIGRP, EX - EIGRP external, O - OSPF, IA - OSPF inter area
       N1 - OSPF NSSA external type 1, N2 - OSPF NSSA external type 2
```

```
          E1 - OSPF external type 1, E2 - OSPF external type 2, E - EGP
          i - IS-IS, L1 - IS-IS level-1, L2 - IS-IS level-2, * - candidate default
          U - per-user static route, o - ODR
          T - traffic engineered route

Gateway of last resort is not set

C    192.168.75.0/24 is directly connected, Ethernet2
B    172.17.0.0/16 [20/1] via 10.50.250.1, 00:01:24
B    172.16.0.0/16 [20/0] via 10.100.83.1, 00:01:22
C    172.18.0.0/16 is directly connected, Ethernet1
     172.29.0.0/16 is variably subnetted, 2 subnets, 2 masks
B       172.29.1.0/24 [20/0] via 10.100.83.1, 00:01:22
B       172.29.0.0/16 [20/1] via 10.50.250.1, 00:01:24
B    172.31.0.0/16 [20/0] via 10.100.83.1, 00:01:22
     192.168.4.0/29 is subnetted, 1 subnets
C       192.168.4.0 is directly connected, Ethernet0
     10.0.0.0/8 is variably subnetted, 7 subnets, 2 masks
B       10.30.0.0/16 [20/0] via 10.100.83.1, 00:01:22
B       10.20.0.0/16 [20/0] via 10.50.250.1, 00:01:24
C       10.21.0.0/16 is directly connected, Serial1.507
C       10.75.100.1/32 is directly connected, Loopback0
S       10.100.83.1/32 is directly connected, Ethernet0
S       10.50.250.1/32 is directly connected, Ethernet0
S       10.200.60.1/32 is directly connected, Ethernet0
B    192.168.50.0/24 [20/1] via 10.50.250.1, 00:01:27
B    192.168.100.0/24 [20/0] via 10.100.83.1, 00:01:25
Lillehammer#
```

One solution is to use the BGP **network** command, as demonstrated in Example 4-103.

Example 4-103 *Lillehammer and Meribel Use the* network *Command to Cause the EBGP-Discovered Routes to Be Treated as Local BGP Routes*

```
Lillehammer:
router rip
 redistribute bgp 75
 network 10.0.0.0
 network 172.18.0.0
 network 192.168.75.0
!
router bgp 75
 network 172.17.0.0
 network 172.18.0.0
 network 192.168.75.0
```

```
neighbor 10.50.250.1 remote-as 50
neighbor 10.50.250.1 ebgp-multihop 2
neighbor 10.50.250.1 update-source Loopback0
neighbor 10.100.83.1 remote-as 100
neighbor 10.100.83.1 ebgp-multihop 2
neighbor 10.100.83.1 update-source Loopback0
neighbor 10.200.60.1 remote-as 200
neighbor 10.200.60.1 ebgp-multihop 2
neighbor 10.200.60.1 update-source Loopback0
```

```
Meribel:
router rip
 redistribute bgp 50 metric 1
 network 10.0.0.0
!
router bgp 50
 network 172.18.0.0
 redistribute rip
 neighbor 10.75.100.1 remote-as 75
 neighbor 10.75.100.1 ebgp-multihop 2
 neighbor 10.75.100.1 update-source Loopback0
 neighbor 10.100.83.1 remote-as 100
 neighbor 10.100.83.1 ebgp-multihop 2
 neighbor 10.100.83.1 update-source Loopback0
 neighbor 10.200.60.1 remote-as 200
 neighbor 10.200.60.1 ebgp-multihop 2
 neighbor 10.200.60.1 update-source Loopback0
 no auto-summary
```

In the configurations in Example 4-103, the **network** statements cause the EBGP-discovered routes to be treated as local BGP routes. Network 172.17.0.0 is advertised to Lillehammer via EBGP, for instance, and is entered into the routing table. The configuration statement **network 172.17.0.0** is added to Lillehammer's BGP configuration, even though 172.17.0.0 is not a local route. Because the address is in the routing table, the **network** statement matches it and makes it a local route.

The logic sounds quite strange, but it works. By first being an EBGP route, 172.17.0.0 is changed into a local BGP route with the **network** statement. Because 172.17.0.0 is now considered a local route at Lillehammer, it is assigned an administrative distance of 200. The RIP route to 172.17.0.0 now has a lower distance and becomes the preferred route, as indicated in the output in Example 4-104.

Example 4-104 *By Causing Lillehammer to Treat the EBGP Route to 172.17.0.0 as a Local BGP Route with an Administrative Distance of 200, the RIP Route to That Network Becomes the Preferred Route*

```
Lillehammer#show ip route
Codes: C - connected, S - static, I - IGRP, R - RIP, M - mobile, B - BGP
       D - EIGRP, EX - EIGRP external, O - OSPF, IA - OSPF inter area
       N1 - OSPF NSSA external type 1, N2 - OSPF NSSA external type 2
       E1 - OSPF external type 1, E2 - OSPF external type 2, E - EGP
       i - IS-IS, L1 - IS-IS level-1, L2 - IS-IS level-2, * - candidate default
       U - per-user static route, o - ODR
       T - traffic engineered route


Gateway of last resort is not set

C    192.168.75.0/24 is directly connected, Ethernet2
R    172.17.0.0/16 [120/2] via 10.21.1.1, 00:00:06, Serial1.507
B    172.16.0.0/16 [20/0] via 10.200.60.1, 00:00:36
C    172.18.0.0/16 is directly connected, Ethernet1
     172.29.0.0/16 is variably subnetted, 2 subnets, 2 masks
B       172.29.1.0/24 [20/0] via 10.200.60.1, 00:00:36
B       172.29.0.0/16 [20/1] via 10.50.250.1, 00:00:24
B    172.31.0.0/16 [20/0] via 10.200.60.1, 00:00:36
     192.168.4.0/29 is subnetted, 1 subnets
C       192.168.4.0 is directly connected, Ethernet0
     10.0.0.0/8 is variably subnetted, 7 subnets, 2 masks
B       10.30.0.0/16 [20/0] via 10.200.60.1, 00:00:36
B       10.20.0.0/16 [20/0] via 10.50.250.1, 00:00:24
C       10.21.0.0/16 is directly connected, Serial1.507
C       10.75.100.1/32 is directly connected, Loopback0
S       10.100.83.1/32 is directly connected, Ethernet0
S       10.50.250.1/32 is directly connected, Ethernet0
S       10.200.60.1/32 is directly connected, Ethernet0
B    192.168.50.0/24 [20/1] via 10.50.250.1, 00:00:25
B    192.168.100.0/24 [20/0] via 10.200.60.1, 00:00:37
Lillehammer#
```

Although the administrative distances have been manipulated correctly, this configuration has a problem. By using the **network** statement to convert an EBGP route into a local route, the local BGP router now advertises the route in its own EBGP updates. Lillehammer, for example, now advertises 172.17.0.0 in its EBGP updates to its peers across the IXC. Because Meribel's BGP process learns the route to 172.17.0.0 from redistribution, it advertises the route with an ORIGIN of Incomplete. But Lillehammer, because of the **network** statement, advertises the route with an ORIGIN of IGP. As a result, Cervinia and Innsbruck choose Lillehammer as the best next hop to 172.17.0.0, as demonstrated in the output in Example 4-105. External traffic to 172.17.0.0 is forwarded to Lillehammer, which forwards the traffic across the backdoor link. Only traffic between 172.17.0.0 and 172.18.0.0 is supposed to use the backdoor link; all other traffic should use the IXC.

Example 4-105   *Cervinia's BGP Table Shows Lillehammer (10.75.100.1) as the Best Next Hop to Network 172.17.0.0, Causing the Backdoor Link Between Lillehammer and Meribel to Become a Transit Link for All External Traffic to 172.17.0.0*

```
Cervinia#show ip bgp 172.17.0.0
BGP routing table entry for 172.17.0.0/16, version 474
Paths: (3 available, best #2, advertised over EBGP)
  100 75
    10.100.83.1 from 10.100.83.1
      Origin IGP, localpref 100, valid, external
  75
    10.75.100.1 from 10.75.100.1 (192.168.75.1)
      Origin IGP, metric 2, localpref 100, valid, external, best
  50
    10.50.250.1 from 10.50.250.1
      Origin incomplete, metric 1, localpref 100, valid, external
Cervinia#
```

Example 4-106 shows a solution to this problem via the **network backdoor** statement, another IOS-specific tool.

Example 4-106   network backdoor *Statement Is Configured on Lillehammer and Meribel to Restrict External Traffic for Using the Backdoor Link*

```
Lillehammer:
router rip
 redistribute bgp 75
 network 10.0.0.0
 network 172.18.0.0
 network 192.168.75.0
!
router bgp 75
 network 172.17.0.0 backdoor
 network 172.18.0.0
 network 192.168.75.0
 neighbor 10.50.250.1 remote-as 50
 neighbor 10.50.250.1 ebgp-multihop 2
 neighbor 10.50.250.1 update-source Loopback0
 neighbor 10.100.83.1 remote-as 100
 neighbor 10.100.83.1 ebgp-multihop 2
```

```
neighbor 10.100.83.1 update-source Loopback0
neighbor 10.200.60.1 remote-as 200
neighbor 10.200.60.1 ebgp-multihop 2
neighbor 10.200.60.1 update-source Loopback0

Meribel:
router rip
 redistribute bgp 50 metric 1
 network 10.0.0.0
!
router bgp 50
 network 172.18.0.0 backdoor
 redistribute rip
 neighbor 10.75.100.1 remote-as 75
 neighbor 10.75.100.1 ebgp-multihop 2
 neighbor 10.75.100.1 update-source Loopback0
 neighbor 10.100.83.1 remote-as 100
 neighbor 10.100.83.1 ebgp-multihop 2
 neighbor 10.100.83.1 update-source Loopback0
 neighbor 10.200.60.1 remote-as 200
 neighbor 10.200.60.1 ebgp-multihop 2
 neighbor 10.200.60.1 update-source Loopback0
 no auto-summary
```

The **network backdoor** statement has the same effect as the **network** statement: The EBGP route is treated as a local BGP route, and the administrative distance is changed to 200. The difference is that the address specified by the **network backdoor** statement is not advertised to EBGP peers. In the case of network 172.17.0.0, the new configurations result in the same routing table at Lillehammer shown in Example 4-104. But Cervinia's BGP table no longer contains a route to that network from Lillehammer.

Controlling Complex Route Maps

The policy configurations we have been using in the examples of this chapter have been simple and designed for easy understanding by examining the available tools and individual building blocks of BGP routing policies. If you operate a stub network, your BGP configurations probably do not use even most of the simple configurations studied in this chapter. But if you operate a medium to large service provider network, your policy configurations are likely to be far more complex than the examples you have seen here.

As BGP routing policies do become more complex, one of the characteristics often encountered is that elements of the policies tend to repeat. IOS provides tools that allow you to pull such repeating or "reusable" sections of policy configuration out as separate objects, and tools that allow you to create conditional branches to other parts of the policy configuration. Combined with such "grouping" tools such as Community attributes and Peer Groups or Peer Templates, discussed in the next chapter, you have the ability to not only create complex BGP policies but also to efficiently organize and control them.

Continue Clauses

Continue clauses allow you to create conditional branches to other parts of a route map, a little like "if-then-else" constructs in programming languages. For example, a continue clause allows you to specify that at a certain sequence of a route map (as defined by the route map's sequence number), if certain match conditions are met, go to a different sequence of the route map and continue processing from there; otherwise, if the match conditions are not met, continue processing the route map normally.

Normally a route map is processed linearly from top to bottom. If a prefix is matched, any specified actions are taken and the processing stops. If a match is not made at a given sequence, the prefix drops to the next sequence and processing continues either until a match is found or until the default action at the end of the route map is taken.

Using a continue clause, you can match a prefix and perform an action, and then instead of stopping processing, you can send the prefix to a different part of the route map for further processing.

Continue clauses are particularly useful when you have many different match conditions specified, and possibly different set actions for each, but also want to execute the same actions on those different matched prefixes. Example 4-107 illustrates the use of continue clauses.

- Sequence 10 specifies that if a prefix matches ACL 1, jump to Sequence 100 in which a no-export commumity attribute is added to the route. If the prefix does not match ACL 1, go to Sequence 20.

- Sequence 20 uses a different ACL to match a different set of prefixes, but still sends positive matches to Sequence 100.

- Sequence 30 uses yet another ACL to send matching prefixes to Sequence 100, but in this case also sets a LOCAL_PREF value of 150 to the route.

- Sequence 40 uses AS-path filter 18 to find matches. Matching prefixes are given a MED of 200, an Origin type of Incomplete, and then sent to Sequence 150 where the route's AS_PATH is prepended three times with ASN 30.

- Sequence 50 has no match statement, so any routes that have not matched up to this point are prepended with a single ASN 30 and then sent to Sequence 200 where they are given a Community attribue of 1311135.

Example 4-107   *Continue Clauses Allow Branching from One Sequence of a Route Map to Another*

```
route-map Ex-4-107 permit 10
 match ip address 1
 continue 100
!
route-map Ex-4-107 permit 20
 match ip address 2
 continue 100
!
route-map Ex-4-107 permit 30
 match ip address 3
 continue 100
 set local-preference 150
!
route-map Ex-4-107 permit 40
 match as-path 18
 continue 150
 set metric 200
 set origin incomplete
!
route-map Ex-4-107 permit 50
 continue 200
 set as-path prepend 30
!
route-map Ex-4-107 permit 100
 set community no-export
!
route-map Ex-4-107 permit 150
 set as-path prepend 30 30 30
!
route-map Ex-4-107 permit 200
 set community 1311135
!
```

Although you can simply observe a configured route map as in Example 4-107, you can also observe it with the **show route-map** command as shown in Example 4-108. The advantage of this command is that the clauses making up each sequence of the route map are clearly defined in easily readable form, and the number of routes matching each sequence is shown. This helps to quickly decipher the route map for troubleshooting or for deciphering before modifiying it.

Example 4-108   *Output of the* **show route-map** *Command Is Useful for Observing the Structure and Function of a Longe Route Map, and Also for Observing Match Statistics at Each Sequence. These Statistics Can Be Useful for Troubleshooting Route Maps That Are Not Doing What You Expected*

```
Moritz#show route-map Ex-4-107
route-map Ex-4-107, permit, sequence 10
  Match clauses:
    ip address (access-lists): 1
  Continue: sequence 100
  Set clauses:
  Policy routing matches: 0 packets, 0 bytes
route-map Ex-4-107, permit, sequence 20
  Match clauses:
    ip address (access-lists): 2
  Continue: sequence 100
  Set clauses:
  Policy routing matches: 0 packets, 0 bytes
route-map Ex-4-107, permit, sequence 30
  Match clauses:
    ip address (access-lists): 3
  Continue: sequence 100
  Set clauses:
    local-preference 150
  Policy routing matches: 0 packets, 0 bytes
route-map Ex-4-107, permit, sequence 40
  Match clauses:
    as-path (as-path filter): 18
  Continue: sequence 150
  Set clauses:
    metric 200
    origin incomplete
  Policy routing matches: 0 packets, 0 bytes
route-map Ex-4-107, permit, sequence 50
  Match clauses:
  Continue: sequence 200
  Set clauses:
    as-path prepend 30
  Policy routing matches: 0 packets, 0 bytes
route-map Ex-4-107, permit, sequence 100
  Match clauses:
  Set clauses:
    community no-export
  Policy routing matches: 0 packets, 0 bytes
route-map Ex-4-107, permit, sequence 150
```

```
  Match clauses:
  Set clauses:
    as-path prepend 30 30 30
  Policy routing matches: 0 packets, 0 bytes
route-map Ex-4-107, permit, sequence 200
  Match clauses:
  Set clauses:
    community 1311135
  Policy routing matches: 0 packets, 0 bytes
Moritz#
```

Policy Lists

A single sequence in a route map is treated as an "if-then" statement: "If this match condition is met, then take this action."

A series of sequences within a route map can be thought of as being connected by "else" statements: "If sequence 10 matches, then take this action. Else, go to statement 20." Route maps are executed sequentinally unless, as the previous section showed, a continue clause was used to jump to a different part of the route map.

When there are multiple match or set clauses in a route map sequence, they are treated as a set of Boolean AND conditions: "If match A AND match B AND match C are true, then set X AND set Y AND set Z."

Often, one or more of the same match clauses are used in multiple sequences of a route map as a part of a string of match conditions. For example:

- **Sequence 10:** If A AND B AND C match, set X; else

- **Sequence 20:** If A AND B AND D match, set Y; else

- **Sequence 30:** If A AND B AND E match, set Z

To illustrate, the route map in Example 4-109 consists of four sequences, and the match conditions of each sequence specify a match to a community list 20 and an AS-path list 5. The third match condition is the LOCAL_PREF value, and is different in each sequence. A different community attribute is set in each sequence. So this route map looks at routes with the same AS_PATH and community attributes but different LOCAL_PREF attributes, and adds a different community attribute depending on the result.

Example 4-109 . *Route Maps Often Include Many of the Same Match Clauses in Multiple Sequences*

```
route-map Ex-4-109 permit 10
 match local-preference 50
 match as-path 5
```

```
  match community 20
  set community 2 additive
!
route-map Ex-4-109 permit 20
  match local-preference 100
  match as-path 5
  match community 20
  set community 4 additive
!
route-map Ex-4-109 permit 30
  match local-preference 150
  match as-path 5
  match community 20
  set community 6 additive
!
route-map Ex-4-109 permit 40
  match local-preference 200
  match as-path 5
  match community 20
  set community 8 additive
!
```

It is not unusual to find the same match statements appearing over and over as a portion of match conditions in a lengthy route map. Policy lists allow you to take those "reusable" match conditions and put them in one place. The route map can then refer to the policy list rather than repeating the specific match conditions. There are several advantages to using policy lists:

- If there are several shared match clauses, typing them once in a policy list—and then making a single reference to the policy list at each relevant route map sequence, rather than re-typing all the match clauses each time—saves configuration effort and reduces the chances of a typing error

- If some part of the set of match clauses must be changed, you can change it once in the policy list rather than searching through the route map to change every instance of the clause.

- Because the policy lists are named, it is easier to locate the sequences within a long route map that uses the shared set of match clauses.

A policy list is configured using the **ip policy-map** statement. Like route maps, it is identified by an arbitrary name and has a permit or deny stipulation; the policy list supports only match clauses, not set clauses.

Example 4-110 shows a route map referencing a policy map named PARTNER. The route map performs the same funtion as the one shown in Example 4-109, except the

AS-path and community match clauses are moved into the policy map. Each sequence still matches an individual LOCAL_PREF value AND the two clauses of the policy list.

Example 4-110   *A Policy List Specifies* **match** *Clauses That Are Used Multiple Times Within a Route Map*

```
ip policy-list PARTNER permit
 match as-path 5
 match community 20
!
route-map Ex-4-110 permit 10
 match local-preference 50
 match policy-list PARTNER
 set community 2 additive
!
route-map Ex-4-110 permit 20
 match local-preference 100
 match policy-list PARTNER
 set community 4 additive
!
route-map Ex-4-110 permit 30
 match local-preference 150
 match policy-list PARTNER
 set community 6 additive
!
route-map Ex-4-110 permit 40
 match local-preference 200
 match policy-list PARTNER
 set community 8 additive
!
```

A route map such as the one in Example 4-110 might be used to identify routes advertised from an IBGP peer (hence, the differing LOCAL_PREF values) but ultimately belonging to one special AS, such as a business partner (hence, the same AS-path and community attributes). Perhaps the community attributes added by the set clauses are used by yet another policy further downstream.

As noted, using a policy list makes it easier to change the parameters by which the routes are matched. For example, if the business partner changes the community attributes with which it is tagging the routes, the single reference to community list 20 can be changed within the policy list rather than having to find all the relevant references within the route map. It can be argued that it is just as easy to change the community list itself, or the referenced AS-path list, as it is to change the policy list. The difference, however, is that the policy list is relevant to all of its match clauses together. Community list 20 or AS-path list 5 in Example 4-110 might be individually referenced by other parts of the route map, outside of the context of the policy list. In such a case, you cannot change the community list or AS-path list without disrupting those other references to them.

Looking Ahead

This chapter has taken an extensive look at the many tools available to you for configuring routing policy in a BGP network. Although BGP itself is not a particularly complex protocol, the policies it supports can become quite complex and so can the BGP networks, particularly in large transit autonomous systems such as those of service providers.

As a BGP network becomes large, it is important to have tools at your disposal that can help you control and scale the network. These BGP scaling capabilities are the subject of Chapter 5.

Review Questions

1. What are the three parts of a BGP Routing Information Database (RIB), and how do they differ?

2. What does it mean when an entry in the BGP table is labeled "RIB-failure"?

3. What is the purpose of the BGP Decision Process?

4. What is the difference between the **in** and **out** keywords when a routing policy is applied to a neighbor configuration?

5. What are InQ and OutQ?

6. Name the steady state and transient IOS BGP processes, and describe what each process does.

7. If the command **show processes cpu | include BGP** is run on the router in Example 4-17, will any of the processes be BGP Open? If so, how many? Why?

8. What is a table version?

9. Refer to Figure 4-5, and assume the table versions are as shown in Example 4-30. If the command **clear ip bgp 10.4.1.1** is issued at Loveland, how will the table versions change, and why? If the command **clear ip bgp 10.2.1.2** is next issued at Buttermilk, how will the table versions change and why? If the command **clear ip bgp 10.3.1.2** is, after the other two, issued at Arapahoe how will the table versions change and why?

10. Look at the BGP, RIB, and neighbor table versions in Example 4-17. Can you explain why there is a difference between the BGP and neighbor table

versions, based on what you see in the display? It might be instructive in answering this question to telnet to the following public route servers running IOS and use **show ip bgp summary** at each two or three times:

- Oregon IX (route-views.orego-ix.net)

- Time Warner Telecom (route-server.twtelecom.net)

- AT&T (route-server.ip.att.net)

- Tiscali (route-server.ip.tiscali.net)

- SingTel/Optus (route-views.optus.net.au)

11. What is the advantage of using the **soft** keyword with the **clear ip bgp** command?

12. What is the purpose of the **neighbor soft-reconfiguration inbound** statement?

13. What is route refresh?

14. What two tools are used as NLRI-based route filters, and which is the more preferred?

15. When would you filter routes by AS_PATH rather than by NLRI?

16. When would you use a route map rather than a route filter?

17. When is an administrative weight used in a routing policy?

18. What are the default administrative weight values? How are weights evaluated?

19. When is LOCAL_PREF used in a routing policy?

20. What is the default LOCAL_PREF value? How is LOCAL_PREF evaluated?

21. When is MED used in a routing policy?

22. How is MED evaluated?

23. What does the **bgp bestpath med missing-as-worst** statement do, and when is it used?

24. How does the **set metric-type internal** statement differ from the **set metric** statement?

25. What is the purpose of the **bgp always-compare-med** statement?

26. What is the purpose of the **bgp deterministic-med** statement?

27. What is the purpose of AS_PATH prepending?

28. What is a continue clause?

29. What is a policy list?

Configuration Exercises

Table 4-5 lists the autonomous systems, routers, interfaces, and addresses used in Configuration Exercises 1 through 13. All interfaces of the routers are shown. For each exercise, if the table indicates that the router has a loopback interface, that interface should be the source of all IBGP connections. EBGP connections should always be between physical interface addresses, unless otherwise specified in an exercise.

Table 4-5 *Autonomous System, Router, Interface, and Address Information for Configuration Exercises*

AS	Router	Interface	IP Address/Mask
10	R1	Loopback 0	192.168.255.1/32
		Loopback 1	172.16.0.1/24
		FastEthernet 1/0	10.0.0.1/30
		FastEthernet 2/0	10.0.0.13/30
		FastEthernet 2/1	10.0.0.25/30
		GigabitEthernet 4/0	10.0.0.21/30
	R2	Loopback 0	192.168.255.2/32
		Loopback 1	172.16.4.129/25
		FastEthernet 1/0	10.0.0.2/30
		FastEthernet 2/0	10.0.0.17/30
		FastEthernet 2/1	10.0.0.38/30
		GigabitEthernet 4/0	10.0.0.5/30
	R3	Loopback 0	192.168.255.3/32
		Loopback 1	10.10.0.1/20
		FastEthernet 1/0	10.0.0.9/30
		FastEthernet 1/1	10.0.0.61/30
		FastEthernet 2/0	10.0.0.14/30
		GigabitEthernet 4/0	10.0.0.6/30
	R4	Loopback 0	192.168.255.4/32
		Loopback 1	10.10.64.1/18
		Loopback 2	10.11.0.1/16
		FastEthernet 1/0	10.0.0.10/30
		FastEthernet 1/1	10.0.0.57/30
		FastEthernet 2/0	10.0.0.18/30
		GigabitEthernet 4/0	10.0.0.22/30

AS	Router	Interface	IP Address/Mask
20	R5	Loopback 0	192.168.255.5/32
		Loopback 1	172.17.20.1/24
		FastEthernet 1/0	10.0.0.29/30
		FastEthernet 2/1	10.0.0.26/30
	R6	Loopback 0	192.168.255.6/32
		Loopback 1	172.17.21.65/26
		FastEthernet 1/1	10.0.0.34/30
		FastEthernet 2/1	10.0.0.37/30
	R7	Loopback 0	192.168.255.7/32
		Loopback 1	172.17.21.193/28
		Loopback 2	10.20.0.1/16
		Loopback 3	10.0.0.1/6
		FastEthernet 1/0	10.0.0.30/30
		FastEthernet 1/1	10.0.0.33/30
30	R12	Loopback 0	192.168.255.12/32
		Loopback 1	10.30.0.1/16
		FastEthernet 1/0	10.0.0.50/30
		FastEthernet 1/1	10.0.0.53/30
	R13	Loopback 0	192.168.255.13/32
		Loopback 1	10.31.128.1/17
		FastEthernet 2/0	10.0.0.45/30
		FastEthernet 2/1	10.0.0.42/30
	R14	Loopback 0	192.168.255.14/32
		Loopback 1	30.0.0.1/8
		Loopback 2	31.128.0.1/10
		FastEthernet 1/0	10.0.0.49/30
		FastEthernet 2/0	10.0.0.46/30
40	R8	Loopback 0	192.168.255.8/32
		Loopback 1	10.40.0.1/16
		Loopback 2	40.0.0.1/7
		FastEthernet 1/0	10.0.0.65/30
		FastEthernet 1/1	10.0.0.62/30
		FastEthernet 2/0	10.0.0.69/30

AS	Router	Interface	IP Address/Mask
50	R10	Loopback 0	192.168.255.10/32
		Loopback 1	10.50.0.1/16
		Loopback 2	50.0.0.1/11
		FastEthernet 1/0	10.0.0.73/30
		FastEthernet 2/0	10.0.0.70/30
60	R9	Loopback 0	192.168.255.9/32
		Loopback 1	10.60.0.1/16
		Loopback 2	60.0.0.1/9
		FastEthernet 1/0	10.0.0.66/30
		FastEthernet 1/1	10.0.0.58/30
		FastEthernet 2/0	10.0.0.77/30
70	R11	Loopback 0	192.168.255.11/32
		Loopback 1	10.70.0.0/16
		Loopback 2	70.0.0.1/14
		FastEthernet 1/0	10.0.0.74/30
		FastEthernet 1/1	10.0.0.54/30
		FastEthernet 2/0	10.0.0.78/30

Note   Loopback 0 used for IBGP session establishment is highlighted in dark gray. Subnets that will be injected into BGP for the subsequent exercises are Loopbacks 1 and above, highlighted in light gray.

1. Configure ISIS as the IGP for AS10. All routers will run Level-2 ISIS. The NET for all routers will be in the format 49.0001.0000.0000.000X.00 where X is the router number. AS10 internal routes should not be advertised outside the AS. All point-to-point links over which EBGP is run with routers in other autonomous systems should be advertised into ISIS for next-hop reachability.

2. Configure OSPF as the IGP for AS20. OSPF area 0 spans the whole AS. AS20 internal routes should not be advertised outside the AS. All point-to-point links over which EBGP is run with routers in other autonomous systems should be advertised into OSPF for next-hop reachability.

3. Configure EIGRP as the IGP for AS30. AS30 internal routes should not be advertised outside the AS. All point-to-point links over which EBGP is run with routers in other autonomous systems should be avertised into EIGRP for next-hop reachability.

4. Run an IBGP full mesh for all routers in autonomous systems 10, 20, and 30.

5. Run EBGP sessions between all edge routers in all autonomous systems as indicated in the figure. Then inject all subnets in Table 4-5 configured on Loopbacks 1, 2, or 3 on all the EBGP speakers in that AS.

6. AS20 is *not* a transit AS. Using only distribute lists and simple or extended ACLs on routers R5 and R6, filter outgoing BGP updates to limit these updates to subnets local to AS20 only. Using the relevant show commands on R5 and R6, confirm that the correct filtering has been applied. Use soft outbound reset to non-disruptively apply the new policies.

7. In order to load balance outgoing traffic in AS20, internal routers in the AS should prefer R5 as the exit point for the following subnets:

   10.50.0.0/16, 50.0.0.0/11, 10.70.0.0/16, 70.0.0.0/14, 10.30.0.0/16, 10.31.128.0/17

   R6 as the exit point for the following subnets:

   10.40.0.0/16, 40.0.0.0/7, 10.60.0.0/16, 60.0.0.0/9, 30.0.0.0/8, 31.128.0.0/10

   However, each router should provide an exit route from the AS for **all** subnets in case the other router fails. Configure both edge routers to implement this outgoing traffic policy.

8. AS20 is trying to influence AS10 to route traffic back to subnets **172.17.20.0/24**, **172.17.21.192/28**, and **10.20.0.0/16** via router R5, and to route traffic back to subnets **172.17.21.64/26** and **20.0.0.0/6** via router R6. *Without using AS prepending*, implement the aforementioned policy.

9. AS20 has a policy to not route any traffic *through* AS60. Configure a policy on R5 and R6 to exclude any route that includes AS60 in its AS_PATH. However, make sure that the subnets originating in AS60 are reachable. Do not amend the distribute lists and ACLs configured previously in Configuration Exercise 6.

10. Internal routers in AS10 should prefer R3 as the exit point for traffic to subnets originating in AS70. Configure R3 to implement this policy.

11. Configure R3 and R4 such that return traffic to AS10 subnets **172.16.0.0/24** and **10.10.0.0/20** should always prefer R3, whereas subnet **172.16.4.128/25**, **10.10.64.0/18**, and **10.11.0.0/16** prefer R4.

12. AS30 is a transit AS and has a policy not to accept prefixes with lengths shorter than 8 and longer than 24 bits. Use prefix lists on edge routers R12 and R13 to implement this policy.

13. AS70 policy states that:

    Traffic destined to subnets in AS10 should use the link to R12 in AS30 to transit to its destination.

    Traffic destined to subnets in AS20 should use either links to ASs 50 or 60 to transit to its destination.

    Configure R11 in AS70 to implement the previous policy.

Troubleshooting Exercises

1. In the simple network depicted in Figure 4-15, R1 and R2 have a basic EBGP peering between them. R2 announces a number of routes to R1. However, due to NLRI filtering applied on R1, only subnet 172.17.0.0/16 is allowed, as shown in the Example 4-111. The administrator needs to know to all subnets received from R2 and issues the command **show ip bgp neighbor 10.0.0.2 received-routes**. This does not work and returns the message shown in Example 4-112. Why is this message received and what command needs to be applied on which router to fix this issue?

Figure 4-15   *Network Topology for Troubleshooting Exercise 1*

Example 4-111   *NLRI Filtering Applied on R1 Allows Only Subnet 172.17.0.0/16*

```
R1#show run | sec bgp
router bgp 10
 bgp log-neighbor-changes
 neighbor 10.0.0.2 remote-as 20
 neighbor 10.0.0.2 route-map R2_Inbound in


R1#show route-map R2_Inbound
route-map R2_Inbound, permit, sequence 10
  Match clauses:
    ip address prefix-lists: allow_from_R2
  Set clauses:
  Policy routing matches: 0 packets, 0 bytes


R1#show ip prefix-list allow_from_R2
ip prefix-list allow_from_R2: 1 entries
   seq 5 permit 172.17.0.0/16


R1#sh ip bgp
BGP table version is 2, local router ID is 10.0.0.1
Status codes: s suppressed, d damped, h history, * valid, > best, i - internal,
              r RIB-failure, S Stale, m multipath, b backup-path, f RT-Filter,
              x best-external, a additional-path, c RIB-compressed,
Origin codes: i - IGP, e - EGP, ? - incomplete
RPKI validation codes: V valid, I invalid, N Not found
```

```
     Network         Next Hop           Metric LocPrf Weight Path
*>  172.17.0.0      10.0.0.2                0           0 20 i



R1#sh ip bgp summary
BGP router identifier 10.0.0.1, local AS number 10
BGP table version is 2, main routing table version 2
1 network entries using 148 bytes of memory
1 path entries using 64 bytes of memory
1/1 BGP path/bestpath attribute entries using 136 bytes of memory
1 BGP AS-PATH entries using 24 bytes of memory
0 BGP route-map cache entries using 0 bytes of memory
0 BGP filter-list cache entries using 0 bytes of memory
BGP using 372 total bytes of memory
BGP activity 3/2 prefixes, 3/2 paths, scan interval 60 secs


Neighbor        V        AS MsgRcvd MsgSent   TblVer  InQ OutQ Up/Down  State/
  PfxRcd
10.0.0.2        4        20    12      11        2     0    0 00:07:14        1
R1#
```

Example 4-112 show ip bgp neighbors 10.0.0.2 received-routes *Output*

```
R1#
R1#show ip bgp neighbors 10.0.0.2 received-routes
% Inbound soft reconfiguration not enabled on 10.0.0.2
R1#
```

2. R2 in AS20 and R3 in AS30, in Figure 4-16, belong to the same business entity, despite being in two different autonomous systems. R1 is in AS10 and is an upstream router, whereas R4 in AS 40 is a downstream router that is accessible only via either AS20 or AS30. This business entity has a rule that states that all upstream routers need to use the R1-R3 link for traffic going downstream and that the R1-R2 link is only for backup purposes. To implement this policy, the network administrator amends the MED of outgoing route updates on the R2 and R3 toward R1. However, this configuration does not work and traffic still uses the R1-R2 link, although the MED value of the route received from R2 is lower than the MED value of the same route received from R3. What is the problem with this configuration and what would be one possible solution to fix this scenario while still using different MED values to influence the traffic?

Example 4-113 shows the configuration on R2 and R3, as well as the relevant outputs on R1.

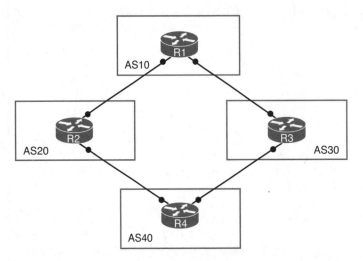

Figure 4-16   *Network Topology for Troubleshooting Exercise 2*

Example 4-113   *Before and After MED Configuration*

```
Before MED Configuration
R1#sh ip bgp
BGP table version is 2, local router ID is 10.0.0.5
Status codes: s suppressed, d damped, h history, * valid, > best, i - internal,
              r RIB-failure, S Stale, m multipath, b backup-path, f RT-Filter,
              x best-external, a additional-path, c RIB-compressed,
Origin codes: i - IGP, e - EGP, ? - incomplete
RPKI validation codes: V valid, I invalid, N Not found


     Network          Next Hop            Metric LocPrf Weight Path
 *   172.16.10.0/24   10.0.0.6                          0 30 40 i
 *>                   10.0.0.2                           0 20 40 i
R1#
```

```
After MED Configuration
R2#sh run | sec bgp
router bgp 20
 bgp log-neighbor-changes
 neighbor 10.0.0.1 remote-as 10
 neighbor 10.0.0.1 route-map SET_MED_UPSTREAM out
 neighbor 10.0.0.10 remote-as 40
R2#
R2#sh route-map SET_MED_UPSTREAM
```

```
route-map SET_MED_UPSTREAM, permit, sequence 10
  Match clauses:
  Set clauses:
    metric 100
  Policy routing matches: 0 packets, 0 bytes
R2#
```

```
R3#sh run | sec bgp
router bgp 30
 bgp log-neighbor-changes
 neighbor 10.0.0.5 remote-as 10
 neighbor 10.0.0.5 route-map SET_MED_UPSTREAM out
 neighbor 10.0.0.14 remote-as 40
R3#
R3#sh route-map SET_MED_UPSTREAM
route-map SET_MED_UPSTREAM, permit, sequence 10
  Match clauses:
  Set clauses:
    metric 50
  Policy routing matches: 0 packets, 0 bytes
R3#
```

```
R1#sh ip bgp
BGP table version is 3, local router ID is 10.0.0.5
Status codes: s suppressed, d damped, h history, * valid, > best, i - internal,
              r RIB-failure, S Stale, m multipath, b backup-path, f RT-Filter,
              x best-external, a additional-path, c RIB-compressed,
Origin codes: i - IGP, e - EGP, ? - incomplete
RPKI validation codes: V valid, I invalid, N Not found

     Network          Next Hop          Metric LocPrf Weight Path
 *   172.16.10.0/24   10.0.0.6              50            0 30 40 i
 *>                   10.0.0.2             100            0 20 40 i
R1#
```

3. Three ASs are interconnected as illustrated in Figure 4-17. The administrator of AS30 needs to enforce a policy to have all inbound traffic from AS20 to AS30 use the high bandwidth R3-R5 link and use only the R2-R4 link in case the primary link fails. To implement this policy, she decides to use AS prepending. However, after configuring the AS prepending on R2, traffic still prefers the R2-R4 link. Why is that?

BGP configurations on R2, R3, R4, and R5 are shown in Example 4-114.

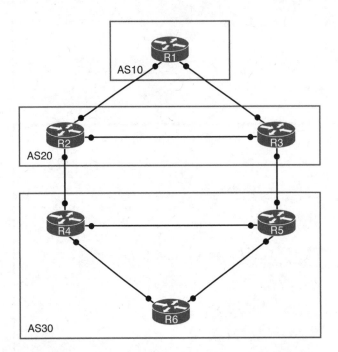

Figure 4-17   *Network Topology for Troubleshooting Exercise 2*

Example 4-114   *Before and After AS Prepending Configurations*

```
Before AS Prepending is Applied
R2#sh ip bgp
BGP table version is 10, local router ID is 192.168.255.2
Status codes: s suppressed, d damped, h history, * valid, > best, i - internal,
              r RIB-failure, S Stale, m multipath, b backup-path, f RT-Filter,
              x best-external, a additional-path, c RIB-compressed,
Origin codes: i - IGP, e - EGP, ? - incomplete
RPKI validation codes: V valid, I invalid, N Not found

     Network          Next Hop          Metric LocPrf Weight Path
 *>  172.16.60.0/24   10.0.0.14             11    200      0 30 i
 *>  172.17.0.0       10.0.0.14             11    200      0 30 i
 *  i 192.168.255.1/32 10.0.0.5              0    100      0 10 i
 *>                   10.0.0.1               0             0 10 i
 *>  192.168.255.2/32 0.0.0.0               0         32768 i
 r>i 192.168.255.3/32 192.168.255.3         0    100      0 i
 *>  192.168.255.4/32 10.0.0.14             0     200      0 30 i
 *>  192.168.255.5/32 10.0.0.14                   200      0 30 i
 *>  192.168.255.6/32 10.0.0.14                   200      0 30 i
```

```
R2#

R3#sh ip bgp
BGP table version is 9, local router ID is 192.168.255.3
Status codes: s suppressed, d damped, h history, * valid, > best, i - internal,
              r RIB-failure, S Stale, m multipath, b backup-path, f RT-Filter,
              x best-external, a additional-path, c RIB-compressed,
Origin codes: i - IGP, e - EGP, ? - incomplete
RPKI validation codes: V valid, I invalid, N Not found

     Network          Next Hop         Metric LocPrf Weight Path
 *>i 172.16.60.0/24   10.0.0.14            11    200      0 30 i
 *                    10.0.0.18            11             0 30 i
 *>i 172.17.0.0       10.0.0.14            11    200      0 30 i
 *                    10.0.0.18            11             0 30 i
 * i 192.168.255.1/32 10.0.0.1             0     100      0 10 i
 *>                   10.0.0.5             0              0 10 i
 r>i 192.168.255.2/32 192.168.255.2       0     100      0 i
 *>  192.168.255.3/32 0.0.0.0             0          32768 i
 *>i 192.168.255.4/32 10.0.0.14           0     200      0 30 i
 *                    10.0.0.18                         0 30 i
 *>i 192.168.255.5/32 10.0.0.14           0     200      0 30 i
 *                    10.0.0.18           0              0 30 i
 *>i 192.168.255.6/32 10.0.0.14           0     200      0 30 i
 *                    10.0.0.18                         0 30 i
R3#

R1#traceroute 172.16.60.6 so 192.168.255.1
Type escape sequence to abort.
Tracing the route to 172.16.60.6
VRF info: (vrf in name/id, vrf out name/id)
  1 10.0.0.2 6 msec 6 msec 5 msec
  2 10.0.0.14 6 msec 6 msec 5 msec
  3 10.0.0.26 6 msec 6 msec 6 msec
AS Prepending Configuration

AS Prepending Configuration
R4#sh run | sec bgp
router bgp 30
 bgp router-id 192.168.255.4
 bgp log-neighbor-changes
 network 172.16.60.0 mask 255.255.255.0
 network 172.17.0.0
 network 192.168.255.4 mask 255.255.255.255
 neighbor 10.0.0.13 remote-as 20
```

```
 neighbor 10.0.0.13 route-map AS_PREPENDING out
 neighbor 192.168.255.5 remote-as 30
 neighbor 192.168.255.5 update-source Loopback0
 neighbor 192.168.255.6 remote-as 30
 neighbor 192.168.255.6 update-source Loopback0
R4#
R4#sh route-map AS_PREPENDING
route-map AS_PREPENDING, permit, sequence 10
  Match clauses:
  Set clauses:
    as-path prepend 30 30
  Policy routing matches: 0 packets, 0 bytes
R4#
```

```
After AS Prepending Is Configured
R2#sh ip bgp
BGP table version is 10, local router ID is 192.168.255.2
Status codes: s suppressed, d damped, h history, * valid, > best, i - internal,
              r RIB-failure, S Stale, m multipath, b backup-path, f RT-Filter,
              x best-external, a additional-path, c RIB-compressed,
Origin codes: i - IGP, e - EGP, ? - incomplete
RPKI validation codes: V valid, I invalid, N Not found

     Network          Next Hop          Metric LocPrf Weight Path
 *>  172.16.60.0/24   10.0.0.14             11    200      0 30 i
 *>  172.17.0.0       10.0.0.14             11    200      0 30 i
 * i 192.168.255.1/32 10.0.0.5               0    100      0 10 i
 *>                   10.0.0.1               0             0 10 i
 *>  192.168.255.2/32 0.0.0.0                0         32768 i
 r>i 192.168.255.3/32 192.168.255.3          0    100      0 i
 *>  192.168.255.4/32 10.0.0.14              0    200      0 30 i
 *>  192.168.255.5/32 10.0.0.14                   200      0 30 i
 *>  192.168.255.6/32 10.0.0.14                   200      0 30 i
R2#
```

```
R3#sh ip bgp
BGP table version is 9, local router ID is 192.168.255.3
Status codes: s suppressed, d damped, h history, * valid, > best, i - internal,
              r RIB-failure, S Stale, m multipath, b backup-path, f RT-Filter,
              x best-external, a additional-path, c RIB-compressed,
Origin codes: i - IGP, e - EGP, ? - incomplete
RPKI validation codes: V valid, I invalid, N Not found

     Network          Next Hop          Metric LocPrf Weight Path
 *>i 172.16.60.0/24   10.0.0.14             11    200      0 30 i
 *                    10.0.0.18             11             0 30 i
```

```
 *>i 172.17.0.0        10.0.0.14              11    200      0 30 i
 *                     10.0.0.18              11             0 30 i
 * i 192.168.255.1/32 10.0.0.1                0    100      0 10 i
 *>                    10.0.0.5                0             0 10 i
 r>i 192.168.255.2/32 192.168.255.2           0    100      0 i
 *>  192.168.255.3/32 0.0.0.0                 0         32768 i
 *>i 192.168.255.4/32 10.0.0.14               0    200      0 30 i
 *                    10.0.0.18                             0 30 i
 *>i 192.168.255.5/32 10.0.0.14               0    200      0 30 i
 *                    10.0.0.18               0             0 30 i
 *>i 192.168.255.6/32 10.0.0.14               0    200      0 30 i
 *                    10.0.0.18                             0 30 i
R3#
```

BGP Configuration on R2 and R3

```
R2#sh run | sec bgp
router bgp 20
 bgp router-id 192.168.255.2
 bgp log-neighbor-changes
 network 192.168.255.2 mask 255.255.255.255
 neighbor 10.0.0.1 remote-as 10
 neighbor 10.0.0.14 remote-as 30
 neighbor 10.0.0.14 route-map SET_LOCAL_PREF in
 neighbor 192.168.255.3 remote-as 20
 neighbor 192.168.255.3 update-source Loopback0
R2#
R2#sh route-map SET_LOCAL_PREF
route-map SET_LOCAL_PREF, permit, sequence 10
  Match clauses:
  Set clauses:
    local-preference 200
  Policy routing matches: 0 packets, 0 bytes
R2#
```

```
R3#sh run | sec bgp
router bgp 20
 bgp router-id 192.168.255.3
 bgp log-neighbor-changes
 network 192.168.255.3 mask 255.255.255.255
 neighbor 10.0.0.5 remote-as 10
 neighbor 10.0.0.18 remote-as 30
 neighbor 192.168.255.2 remote-as 20
 neighbor 192.168.255.2 update-source Loopback0
R3#
```

Chapter 5

Scaling BGP

BGP is designed to support not only complex routing policies, as you learned in the previous chapter, but also large networks. The Internet is a mesh of autonomous systems interconnected by EBGP—in essence, one extremely large BGP network.

The problem with big networks is that, by their nature, they are supporting many reachable end systems, and hence a great many reachable addresses. As the network grows, the routine activity on the network also grows:

- End system addresses are added or removed.

- Links are added or removed.

- Routers are added or removed.

- Route attributes are changed.

- Routing policies are changed.

- Network components intermittently change due to routine maintenance activity.

- Network components intermittently change due to physical or software failures.

- Network links occasionally fail or flap.

All these activities impact the reachability information of at least some parts of the network, and it is the job of the routing protocol to calculate the effects of the changes, update the local RIB, and inform its neighbors of the changes. A network the size of the Internet, with tens of thousands of ASNs and hundreds of thousands of IP prefixes, experiences almost constant changes. That means BGP on an Internet-connected router—particularly a router in a transit AS—stays busy.

Inherent qualities in BGP help it handle the information in a large network: The protocol algorithms are simple, and its timer intervals allow information changes to "collect" at one router before being passed on to neighbors in bulk. The disadvantage is that BGP is slow; route changes can take minutes or even hours to permeate throughout the Internet.

The capability of a protocol, a device, or software to grow with a network is called its *scalability*. BGP can scale from a network of just a few routers, as most of the example networks in this book use, to an enormous network such as the Internet. Although the protocol gets slower as the Internet grows, we have not yet reached a size at which BGP stops working entirely.[1]

Just as a wide range of tools can help you define routing policies under BGP, as you learned in the Chapter 4, "BGP and Routing Policies," also you can use a range of tools and capabilities to help scale BGP to large networks. These tools can be roughly sorted into three categories:

- **Scaling the BGP configuration on a single router:** As the examples in the previous chapters have become more sophisticated, you have seen the BGP configurations and their associated policies grow large. And these are for small, simple example networks. The BGP and policy configurations of a large transit service provider can run for pages.

- **Scaling the BGP process on a single router:** As BGP handles growing RIBs and an increasing number of neighbors, these tools help make the protocol operate more efficiently.

- **Scaling the BGP network:** These are tools that help you build more manageable and more efficient BGP architectures.

These categories are "rough" because there can be some crossover in the advantages of some tools. Although route reflectors, for example, simplify BGP architectures, they also simplify BGP configurations.

This chapter is organized to discuss BGP scaling within these three categories. However, many scaling features have already been discussed. For example, route aggregation, discussed in Chapter 3, "BGP and NLRI," is an important means of scaling both the BGP process and the BGP network. The introduction of each of the three sections of this chapter recap scaling properties that you have already seen in earlier chapters.

Scaling the Configuration

You have already encountered a number of IOS features for controlling or more efficiently managing a BGP or BGP policy configuration:

- Regular expressions, which allow you to perform complex string matching within AS Path filters rather than having to write long lists of specific AS_PATHs to match

---

[1] The Routing Research Group (RRG) of the Internet Research Task Force (IRTF) is tasked with considering the eventuality of BGP reaching its upper limits and finding architectural and protocol solutions to the problem.

- **ge** and **le** keywords in prefix lists that allow specification of prefix ranges rather than long lists of individual prefixes

- Prefix lists, which are simpler to use than the older method of extended access lists connected to distribute lists

- Sequence numbers in prefix lists and route maps that allow easier editing

- Text descriptions within prefix lists and route maps

- Continue clauses within route maps to enable branching to other parts of the route map

- Policy lists that allow grouping of match parameters used in multiple parts of a route map

Other useful configuration scaling tools have been touched upon in previous chapters: Peer groups or peer templates, and Community attributes.

Peer Groups

The BGP examples you have seen in the previous chapters have generally involved two or three peers. But suppose a router has two or three hundred peers? Such can be the case on an access or border router in a service provider's network, or perhaps a router at a public peering point.

For example, say an access router has 200 EBGP peers. Each neighbor configuration will have, at a minimum

- **neighbor remote-as** statement
- **neighbor password** statement
- A statement specifying an incoming route policy
- A statement specifying an outgoing route policy

That means 800 statements in the configuration are required to configure 200 external peers. There are likely to be **network** statements and perhaps **neighbor ebgp multi-hop** statements, increasing the overall number of configuration statements.

As another example, suppose you have a router with 100 IBGP peers (not at all uncommon for route reflectors, discussed later in this chapter). Each neighbor configuration will have, at a minimum

- **neighbor remote-as** statement
- **neighbor update-source** statement
- **neighbor next-hop-self** statement (unless the router is a route reflector)
- **neighbor password** statement

These basic configuration statements multiply to 400 statements to support 100 IBGP neighbors.

When the same configuration parameters and routing policies are applied to many BGP peers, a router's BGP configuration can be greatly simplified by designating the peers as members of a single peer group. Most of the configuration options and routing policies that otherwise would be defined for each neighbor can instead be defined once, for the peer group. A peer group is relevant only to the router on which it is defined and is not communicated to the router's peers. Following are three steps to creating a peer group:

Step 1. Designate the peer group name.

Step 2. Designate the routing policies and configuration options common to all members of the peer group.

Step 3. Designate the neighbors that belong to the peer group.

The configuration in Example 5-1 creates a peer group named CLIENTS. The **neighbor CLIENTS peer-group** statement creates the peer group, and the next four statements define options and policies common to all members of the group. The EBGP neighbors are then designated as usual with **neighbor remote-as**, and a single statement is added designating the neighbor as a member of the peer group CLIENTS.

Example 5-1 *Creating a Peer Group Named CLIENTS and Adding Neighbors to the Group*

```
router bgp 100
 network 10.1.11.0 mask 255.255.255.0
 network 10.1.12.0 mask 255.255.255.0
 neighbor CLIENTS peer-group
 neighbor CLIENTS ebgp-multihop 2
 neighbor CLIENTS update-source Loopback2
 neighbor CLIENTS filter-list 2 in
 neighbor CLIENTS filter-list 1 out
 neighbor 10.1.255.2 remote-as 200
 neighbor 10.1.255.2 peer-group CLIENTS
 neighbor 10.1.255.3 remote-as 300
 neighbor 10.1.255.3 peer-group CLIENTS
 neighbor 10.1.255.4 remote-as 400
 neighbor 10.1.255.4 peer-group CLIENTS
 neighbor 10.1.255.5 remote-as 500
 neighbor 10.1.255.5 peer-group CLIENTS
 neighbor 10.1.255.6 remote-as 600
 neighbor 10.1.255.6 peer-group CLIENTS
 no auto-summary
 !
ip as-path access-list 1 permit ^$
ip as-path access-list 2 permit ^[2-6]00$
```

By consolidating shared options and policies, peer groups can significantly shorten a BGP configuration. The configuration also becomes much easier to interpret. All options are configured in one place, and all that is necessary is to know what neighbors are members of what peer group.

When all members of a peer group belong to the same AS, the configuration can be shortened even more by specifying the common AS under the peer group configuration. All the members could be EBGP peers in the same remote AS, but in most cases a large number of peers in the same AS will be IBGP peers.

In Example 5-2, two new routers are added to the configuration under the peer group LOCAL. Their common AS number is specified under the peer group configuration, as is a common outgoing routing policy.

Example 5-2   *A Peer Group Named LOCAL Has Been Added to the Previous Configuration, and Two IBGP Peers Are Added to the Group*

```
router bgp 100
 no synchronization
 network 10.1.11.0 mask 255.255.255.0
 network 10.1.12.0 mask 255.255.255.0
 neighbor CLIENTS peer-group
 neighbor CLIENTS ebgp-multihop 2
 neighbor CLIENTS update-source Loopback2
 neighbor CLIENTS filter-list 2 in
 neighbor CLIENTS filter-list 1 out
 neighbor LOCAL peer-group
 neighbor LOCAL remote-as 100
 neighbor LOCAL next-hop-self
 neighbor LOCAL filter-list 3 out
 neighbor 10.1.255.2 remote-as 200
 neighbor 10.1.255.2 peer-group CLIENTS
 neighbor 10.1.255.3 remote-as 300
 neighbor 10.1.255.3 peer-group CLIENTS
 neighbor 10.1.255.4 remote-as 400
 neighbor 10.1.255.4 peer-group CLIENTS
 neighbor 10.1.255.5 remote-as 500
 neighbor 10.1.255.5 peer-group CLIENTS
 neighbor 10.1.255.6 remote-as 600
 neighbor 10.1.255.6 peer-group CLIENTS
 neighbor 10.1.255.7 peer-group LOCAL
 neighbor 10.1.255.8 peer-group LOCAL
 no auto-summary
!
ip as-path access-list 1 permit ^$
ip as-path access-list 2 permit ^[2-6]00$
ip as-path access-list 3 permit ^[246]00$
```

If there is a conflict of configuration statements, the statements for a specific neighbor take precedence over the configuration statements of a peer group to which the neighbor belongs. For instance, incoming routing policies that are defined for a single peer group member take precedence over incoming routing policies defined for the peer group. Suppose the router referred to in Example 5-2 should accept only subnet 10.1.5.0/24 from EBGP peer neighbor 10.1.255.4, but all other peer group policies and options apply. Example 5-3 shows the new configuration.

Example 5-3   *Applying a Routing Policy to a Single Neighbor in a Peer Group*

```
router bgp 100
 no synchronization
 network 10.1.11.0 mask 255.255.255.0
 network 10.1.12.0 mask 255.255.255.0
 neighbor CLIENTS peer-group
 neighbor CLIENTS ebgp-multihop 2
 neighbor CLIENTS update-source Loopback2
 neighbor CLIENTS filter-list 2 in
 neighbor CLIENTS filter-list 1 out
 neighbor LOCAL peer-group
 neighbor LOCAL remote-as 100
 neighbor LOCAL next-hop-self
 neighbor LOCAL filter-list 3 out
 neighbor 10.1.255.2 remote-as 200
 neighbor 10.1.255.2 peer-group CLIENTS
 neighbor 10.1.255.3 remote-as 300
 neighbor 10.1.255.3 peer-group CLIENTS
 neighbor 10.1.255.4 remote-as 400
 neighbor 10.1.255.4 peer-group CLIENTS
 neighbor 10.1.255.4 distribute-list 10 in
 neighbor 10.1.255.5 remote-as 500
 neighbor 10.1.255.5 peer-group CLIENTS
 neighbor 10.1.255.6 remote-as 600
 neighbor 10.1.255.6 peer-group CLIENTS
 neighbor 10.1.255.7 peer-group LOCAL
 neighbor 10.1.255.8 peer-group LOCAL
 no auto-summary
!
ip as-path access-list 1 permit ^$
ip as-path access-list 2 permit ^[2-6]00$
ip as-path access-list 3 permit ^[246]00$
access-list 10 permit 10.1.5.0
```

Distribute list 10 has been added to the configuration for neighbor 10.1.255.4. Although the configuration defines that neighbor as a member of the CLIENTS peer group, the distribute list overrides the incoming filter list 2 for that peer—but only that peer.

Details about the peer groups defined on a router can be displayed with the command **show ip bgp peer-groups**, as shown by Example 5-4. The command also can be used to observe the details of a single peer group, by specifying the name of the group at the end of the command.

Example 5-4   show ip bgp peer-groups *Command Displays Details About a Router's Peer Groups*

```
Colorado#show ip bgp peer-group
BGP neighbor is CLIENTS, peer-group leader
 Index 1, Offset 0, Mask 0x2
  BGP version 4
  Minimum time between advertisement runs is 5 seconds
  Incoming update AS path filter list is 2
  Outgoing update AS path filter list is 1

BGP neighbor is LOCAL, peer-group leader,  remote AS 100
 Index 0, Offset 0, Mask 0x0
  NEXT_HOP is always this router
  BGP version 4
  Minimum time between advertisement runs is 5 seconds
  Outgoing update AS path filter list is 3
Colorado#
```

Reducing the number of configuration statements on routers with many BGP neighbors is only one of the benefits of peer groups. Another benefit is in the management of shared BGP session configurations. If a password or BGP timers must be changed, for example, it is much easier to change a statement once under a peer group than to change it under every neighbor using the same statement.

Another benefit of peer groups, and the reason they were originally created, applies to the scaling of the BGP process rather than the BGP configuration. When an outgoing policy is applied to a peer group, the members of the peer group are added to an *update group*. Updates are then generated for the group, rather than individual neighbors. Suppose a router has 150,000 prefixes to advertise as NLRI and 100 neighbors. If the updates are generated separately for each neighbor, 15,000,000 NLRI must be created as the router scans its routing table separately for each neighbor; but if the 100 neighbors are members of the same update group, only 100,000 NLRI are generated as the router scans its routing table once for the group.

As of IOS 12.0(24)S, Cisco has introduced a mechanism called *Dynamic Update Peer Groups*, which automatically groups peers using the same outbound policies for the purpose of controlling the number of routing table scans as described in the previous paragraph. Under traditional peer groups, all members of the group had to share the same outbound policies; so if some peers needed slightly different outbound policies, they had to belong to different peer groups. Although still helping to reduce the configuration size, a large BGP configuration tended to contain many small peer groups. Dynamic update peer groups automatically group updates for peers sharing the same outbound policies, with no configuration required.

When you observe the details of a neighbor session, the output tells you what dynamic update peer groups are associated with that session. In Example 5-5, the neighbor belongs to update-group 2.

Example 5-5   *BGP Session to Neighbor 172.30.255.100 Has Two Dynamic Update Peer Group Members*

```
Zermatt#show ip bgp nei 172.30.255.100
BGP neighbor is 172.30.255.100,  remote AS 30, internal link
  BGP version 4, remote router ID 172.32.1.1
  BGP state = Established, up for 00:05:19
  Last read 00:00:19, last write 00:00:19, hold time is 180, keepalive interval is
  60 seconds
  Neighbor capabilities:
    Route refresh: advertised and received(old & new)
    Address family IPv4 Unicast: advertised and received
  Message statistics:
    InQ depth is 0
    OutQ depth is 0
                       Sent       Rcvd
    Opens:               1          1
    Notifications:       0          0
    Updates:             4          1
    Keepalives:          7          7
    Route Refresh:       0          0
    Total:              12          9
  Default minimum time between advertisement runs is 0 seconds


 For address family: IPv4 Unicast
  BGP table version 12, neighbor version 12/0
  Output queue size: 0
  Index 2, Offset 0, Mask 0x4
  2 update-group member
  NEXT_HOP is always this router
  Outbound path policy configured
  Route map for outgoing advertisements is More-Pref
```

```
                              Sent        Rcvd
  Prefix activity:            ----        ----
    Prefixes Current:          3           7 (Consumes 364 bytes)
    Prefixes Total:            4           7
    Implicit Withdraw:         1           0
    Explicit Withdraw:         0           0
    Used as bestpath:         n/a          7
    Used as multipath:        n/a          0


                            Outbound    Inbound
  Local Policy Denied Prefixes:  --------    -------
    Bestpath from this peer:       7         n/a
    Total:                         7           0
  Number of NLRIs in the update sent: max 1, min 1


  Connections established 1; dropped 0
  Last reset never
Connection state is ESTAB, I/O status: 1, unread input bytes: 0
Connection is ECN Disabled, Mininum incoming TTL 0, Outgoing TTL 255
Local host: 172.30.255.254, Local port: 15538
Foreign host: 172.30.255.100, Foreign port: 179
Connection tableid (VRF): 0


Enqueued packets for retransmit: 0, input: 0  mis-ordered: 0 (0 bytes)


Event Timers (current time is 0x5FB3C):
Timer          Starts   Wakeups          Next
Retrans           12        0            0x0
TimeWait           0        0            0x0
AckHold            8        1            0x0
SendWnd            0        0            0x0
KeepAlive          0        0            0x0
GiveUp             0        0            0x0
PmtuAger           0        0            0x0
DeadWait           0        0            0x0
Linger             0        0            0x0
ProcessQ           0        0            0x0


iss: 2140615087  snduna: 2140615494  sndnxt: 2140615494   sndwnd:  15978
irs: 2160134940  rcvnxt: 2160135194  rcvwnd:      16131 delrcvwnd:    253


SRTT: 239 ms, RTTO: 712 ms, RTV: 473 ms, KRTT: 0 ms
minRTT: 20 ms, maxRTT: 300 ms, ACK hold: 200 ms
Status Flags: active open
```

```
Option Flags: nagle
IP Precedence value : 6


Datagrams (max data segment is 536 bytes):
Rcvd: 19 (out of order: 0), with data: 8, total data bytes: 253
Sent: 14 (retransmit: 0, fastretransmit: 0, partialack: 0, Second Congestion: 0),
  with data: 11, total data bytes: 406
 Packets received in fast path: 0, fast processed: 0, slow path: 0
 fast lock acquisition failures: 0, slow path: 0
Zermatt#
```

You can also observe what update groups a router has with the **show ip bgp update-group** command, as shown in Example 5-6. The output of this command shows how many update groups are on the router (four in this case) and the number of members of each group.

Example 5-6 show ip bgp update-group *Command Displays the Dynamic Update Peer Groups*

```
Zermatt#show ip bgp update-group
BGP version 4 update-group 1, internal, Address Family: IPv4 Unicast
  BGP Update version : 12/0, messages 0
  NEXT_HOP is always this router
  Update messages formatted 4, replicated 0
  Number of NLRIs in the update sent: max 1, min 1
  Minimum time between advertisement runs is 0 seconds
  Has 1 member (* indicates the members currently being sent updates):
   172.30.255.150


BGP version 4 update-group 2, internal, Address Family: IPv4 Unicast
  BGP Update version : 12/0, messages 0
  NEXT_HOP is always this router
  Route map for outgoing advertisements is More-Pref
  Update messages formatted 4, replicated 0
  Number of NLRIs in the update sent: max 1, min 1
  Minimum time between advertisement runs is 0 seconds
 Has 1 member (* indicates the members currently being sent updates):
   172.30.255.100


BGP version 4 update-group 3, external, Address Family: IPv4 Unicast
  BGP Update version : 12/0, messages 0
  Update messages formatted 5, replicated 0
  Number of NLRIs in the update sent: max 7, min 0
  Minimum time between advertisement runs is 30 seconds
```

```
    Has 1 member (* indicates the members currently being sent updates):
      10.200.60.1

BGP version 4 update-group 4, external, Address Family: IPv4 Unicast
    BGP Update version : 12/0, messages 0
    Outgoing update AS path filter list is 1
    Update messages formatted 3, replicated 0
    Number of NLRIs in the update sent: max 7, min 1
    Minimum time between advertisement runs is 30 seconds
    Has 1 member (* indicates the members currently being sent updates):
      10.100.83.1

Zermatt#
```

The command **show ip bgp update-group summary**, shown in Example 5-7, gives a different perspective on each update group, focusing more on the message activity of each group.

Example 5-7   show ip bgp update-group summary *Command Displays the Dynamic Update Peer Groups with a Focus on Messaging*

```
Zermatt#show ip bgp update-group summary
Summary for Update-group 1, Address Family IPv4 Unicast
BGP router identifier 172.30.255.254, local AS number 30
BGP table version is 14, main routing table version 14
10 network entries using 1200 bytes of memory
13 path entries using 676 bytes of memory
8/4 BGP path/bestpath attribute entries using 992 bytes of memory
2 BGP AS-PATH entries using 48 bytes of memory
0 BGP route-map cache entries using 0 bytes of memory
4 BGP filter-list cache entries using 48 bytes of memory
Bitfield cache entries: current 3 (at peak 4) using 96 bytes of memory
BGP using 3060 total bytes of memory
BGP activity 10/0 prefixes, 17/4 paths, scan interval 60 secs

Neighbor        V    AS MsgRcvd MsgSent   TblVer  InQ OutQ Up/Down  State/PfxRcd
172.30.255.150  4    30      43      42       14    0    0 00:33:53            2


Summary for Update-group 2, Address Family IPv4 Unicast
BGP router identifier 172.30.255.254, local AS number 30
BGP table version is 14, main routing table version 14
10 network entries using 1200 bytes of memory
13 path entries using 676 bytes of memory
8/4 BGP path/bestpath attribute entries using 992 bytes of memory
2 BGP AS-PATH entries using 48 bytes of memory
```

```
0 BGP route-map cache entries using 0 bytes of memory
4 BGP filter-list cache entries using 48 bytes of memory
Bitfield cache entries: current 3 (at peak 4) using 96 bytes of memory
BGP using 3060 total bytes of memory
BGP activity 10/0 prefixes, 17/4 paths, scan interval 60 secs


Neighbor          V    AS MsgRcvd MsgSent   TblVer  InQ OutQ Up/Down   State/PfxRcd
172.30.255.100  4     30      37       42      14   0    0 00:33:56        7


Summary for Update-group 3, Address Family IPv4 Unicast
BGP router identifier 172.30.255.254, local AS number 30
BGP table version is 14, main routing table version 14
10 network entries using 1200 bytes of memory
13 path entries using 676 bytes of memory
8/4 BGP path/bestpath attribute entries using 992 bytes of memory
2 BGP AS-PATH entries using 48 bytes of memory
0 BGP route-map cache entries using 0 bytes of memory
4 BGP filter-list cache entries using 48 bytes of memory
Bitfield cache entries: current 3 (at peak 4) using 96 bytes of memory
BGP using 3060 total bytes of memory
BGP activity 10/0 prefixes, 17/4 paths, scan interval 60 secs


Neighbor          V    AS MsgRcvd MsgSent   TblVer  InQ OutQ Up/Down   State/PfxRcd
10.200.60.1     4    200     39       43      14   0    0 00:33:55        1


Summary for Update-group 4, Address Family IPv4 Unicast
BGP router identifier 172.30.255.254, local AS number 30
BGP table version is 14, main routing table version 14
10 network entries using 1200 bytes of memory
13 path entries using 676 bytes of memory
8/4 BGP path/bestpath attribute entries using 992 bytes of memory
2 BGP AS-PATH entries using 48 bytes of memory
0 BGP route-map cache entries using 0 bytes of memory
4 BGP filter-list cache entries using 48 bytes of memory
Bitfield cache entries: current 3 (at peak 4) using 96 bytes of memory
BGP using 3060 total bytes of memory
BGP activity 10/0 prefixes, 17/4 paths, scan interval 60 secs


Neighbor          V    AS MsgRcvd MsgSent   TblVer  InQ OutQ Up/Down   State/PfxRcd
10.100.83.1     4    100     41       39      14   0    0 00:33:58        1


Zermatt#
```

Dynamic update peer groups remove the performance motivations for using peer groups—you now get that anyway—and leave only the reduced configuration size and improved configuration management as benefits. Although peer groups have been highly useful over the years, they were primarily created to apply shared policies to groups of neighbors. Peer groups are now replaced by more flexible *peer templates* that directly address the challenges of BGP configuration management.

Peer Templates

Peer templates were created specifically to simplify the configuration of BGP by grouping configuration options that are shared by multiple peers. Introduced at the same time as dynamic update peer groups in IOS 12.0(24)S, you can think of these two features as working together to replace the older peer groups feature: dynamic update peer groups to improve and automate the performance advantages of grouped updates, and peer templates to improve the flexibility of grouping peer configurations.

Note   Peer groups and peer templates are mutually exclusive. You can configure either, but a neighbor cannot belong to both a peer group and a peer template. Although peer groups are still supported, the newer peer templates should be used in modern IOS configurations.

One of the major improvements provided by peer templates is the concept of *inheritance*. Where members of a peer group had to all share the same group characteristics, a peer template could inherit characteristics from another template. For example, suppose you want all BGP sessions on a router to have 30-second keepalives and a 90-second holddown, and for all sessions to be sourced from interface loopback 0. But then you need to configure separate options for your EBGP and IBGP sessions. Under peer groups, you would have to configure the timers and update-source separately under your EBGP and IBGP groups, even though the values are the same in both cases. With peer templates, you can configure a high-level template with the options common to all BGP sessions and then have EBGP and IBGP templates inherit the high-level template.

An example of inheritance is illustrated in Figure 5-1. A template named BGP is configured with the timer and update-source statements that all BGP sessions on the router will use. Two templates, named EBGP and IBGP, both inherit the configurations of template BGP in addition to separate statements configured for those templates. Then there are two more templates, named IBGP1 and IBGP2, that inherit the configuration statements of IBGP; each of these templates configure separate passwords for their group members.

Templates IBGP1 and IBGP2 *directly* inherit the statements of template IBGP and *indirectly* inherit the statements of BGP through IBGP. If there is a conflict, directly inherited statements override indirectly inherited statements.

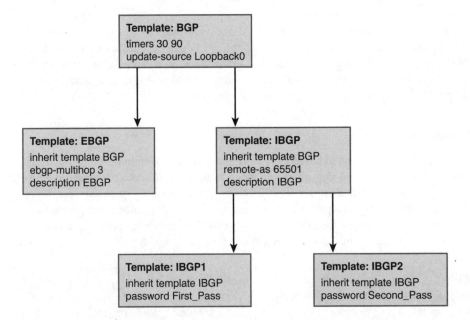

Figure 5-1 *Inheritance Allows a Peer Template to Inherit the Configurations Specified in Another Peer Template*

There are two types of peer templates:

- Session templates
- Policy templates

One session template and one policy template can be associated with each neighbor. This is an improvement over peer groups, in which session and policy configurations cannot be differentiated: If a group of neighbors all have the same session configurations but different policy configurations, they must be in different peer groups. Coupled with inheritance, peer templates give you much more flexibility in grouping a router's peers.

Session Templates

Session templates group statements configuring the BGP session. You start a session template with the statement **template peer-session**, giving the template a name of your choosing. You then add all the configuration statements you want to use in the template, which can be any of the following[2]:

allowas-in	description
bmp-activate	disable-connected-check
cluster-id	ebgp-multihop
default	fall-over

---

[2] As is true throughout this book, the options available to you can be dependent on the IOS version you are using.

local-as	translate-update
password	transport
path-attribute	ttl-security
remote-as	update-source
shutdown	version
timers	

When you have added all the statements you need in the session template, you end it with the statement **exit-peer-session**. Example 5-8 shows a simple session template being created.

Example 5-8 template peer-session statement *Creates a Session Template. When All Wanted Statements Have Been Added, the* **exit-peer-session** statement *Ends the Configuration*

```
Montana(config)#router bgp 600
Montana(config-router)#template peer-session Example_5_8
Montana(config-router-stmp)#password L00ky
Montana(config-router-stmp)#update-source lo0
Montana(config-router-stmp)#remote-as 400
Montana(config-router-stmp)#ebgp-multihop 3
Montana(config-router-stmp)#exit-peer-session
Montana(config-router)#
```

You then either apply the template to peers with the **neighbor inherit peer-session** statement, or you allow the template to be directly inherited by other templates with the **inherit peer-session** statement.

Example 5-9 shows a complete BGP configuration using session templates. In this example, a template named bgp_top is created, which specifies that BGP sessions are originated from the Loopback0 interface and that sessions have a keepalive of 30 seconds and a holddown of 90 seconds. A second template named ibgp specifies the parameters shared by all IBGP sessions: The remote AS is 100 (same as the local AS), a password used by all IBGP sessions, and the inherited parameters of template bgp_top. A third template, named ebgp, enables the TTL security hack with a hop count of 2 and also inherits the template bgp_top.

Example 5-9 *Three Session Templates Are Created in This Example. The Template* **bgp_top** *Defines Parameters That Are Then Inherited by Sessions Named* **ibgp** *and* **ebgp**. *One of Those Two Templates Are Then Applied to Neighbors*

```
router bgp 100
 template peer-session bgp_top
  update-source Loopback0
  timers 30 90
```

```
exit-peer-session
!
template peer-session ibgp
 remote-as 100
 password 7 1324243C345D547A
 inherit peer-session bgp_top
exit-peer-session
!
template peer-session ebgp
 ttl-security hops 2
 inherit peer-session bgp_top
exit-peer-session
!
no synchronization
bgp log-neighbor-changes
neighbor 192.168.255.2 inherit peer-session ibgp
neighbor 192.168.255.3 inherit peer-session ibgp
neighbor 192.168.255.4 remote-as 200
neighbor 192.168.255.4 inherit peer-session ebgp
neighbor 192.168.255.4 password 7 04695F393F205F5D
neighbor 192.168.255.5 remote-as 300
neighbor 192.168.255.5 inherit peer-session ebgp
neighbor 192.168.255.5 password 7 1337422D3B0D1739
neighbor 192.168.255.6 remote-as 400
neighbor 192.168.255.6 inherit peer-session ebgp
neighbor 192.168.255.6 password 7 142544343C053938
no auto-summary
!
```

Each neighbor is then configured to inherit either the **ibgp** or **ebgp** template. For IBGP neighbors, the template contains all the parameters the router needs to create the session. Each EBGP neighbor is in a different AS and uses a different password, so those parameters must be configured individually per neighbor in addition to the template parameters.

The command **show ip bgp template peer-session** is useful for understanding the interaction of your configured session templates. You can specify a template by name or, as shown in Example 5-10, leave the name unspecified to see all session templates. The display shows the three templates configured in Example 5-9, the parameters configured for each template (locally configured commands), and both the parameters the template has inherited and the parameters of the template inherited by other templates. The locally configured commands are, together, assigned a hexadecimal policy number; other templates then reference the number when showing what policies they have inherited. If a template has not inherited any policies, the hex number is 0x0.

Example 5-10 show ip bgp template peer-session *Command Displays Information About Session Templates*

```
Colorado#show ip bgp template peer-session
Template:bgp_top, index:1
Local policies:0xA0, Inherited polices:0x0
 *Inherited by Template ibgp, index= 2
 *Inherited by Template ebgp, index= 3
Locally configured session commands:  ;
 update-source Loopback0
 timers 30 90
Inherited session commands:


Template:ibgp, index:2
Local policies:0x11, Inherited polices:0xA0
This template inherits:
  bgp_top index:1 flags:0x0
Locally configured session commands:
 remote-as 100
Inherited session commands:
 update-source Loopback0
 timers 30 90


Template:ebgp, index:3
Local policies:0x800, Inherited polices:0xA0
This template inherits:
  bgp_top index:1 flags:0x0
Locally configured session commands:
 ttl-security hops 2
Inherited session commands:
 update-source Loopback0
 timers 30 90
```

Notice that each template referred to in Example 5-10 has an index. The indexes show the sequence in which the templates are processed, from lowest index number to highest. So if there is a conflict, the statement in the template with the higher index number overrides the same statement in the template with a lower index number. For example, if TemplateOne specifies a password and then TemplateTwo inherits TemplateOne and specifies a different password, the password of TemplateTwo overrides the password of TemplateOne.

Inheritance in session templates is linear. That is, only one session template can be applied to a neighbor, and a session template can directly inherit from only one other session template. By stringing together inherited templates, a neighbor can directly inherit from one session template and indirectly inherit from up to seven other session templates, as shown in Figure 5-2.

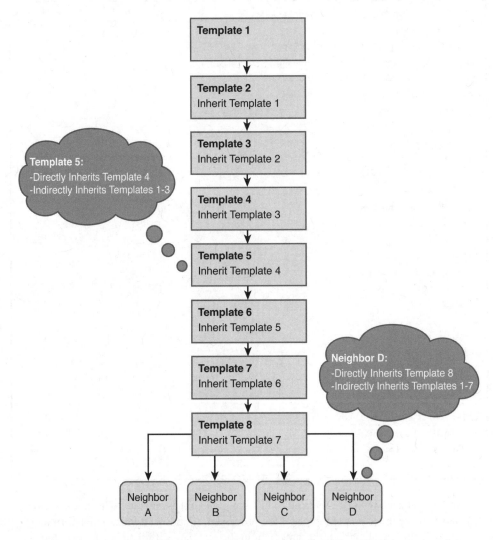

Figure 5-2   *A Neighbor Can Directly Inherit from One Session Template and Indirectly Inherit from up to Seven Templates, for a Total of Eight Session Templates. But No Neighbor and No One Session Template Can Directly Inherit from More Than One Session Template*

Policy Templates

Policy templates, as you might expect, are used to group policy configurations applied to multiple neighbors. You start a policy template with the statement **template peer-policy**, giving the template a name of your choosing. You then add all the configuration statements you want to use in the template, which can be any of the following:[3]

accept-route-policy-rt	maximum-prefix
additional-paths	next-hop-self
advertise	next-hop-unchanged
advertise-map	prefix-list
advertisement-interval	prefix-length-size
allowas-in	remove-private-as
allow-policy	route-map
as-override	route-reflector-client
capability	send-community
capability orf prefix-list	send-label
default	slow-peer
default-originate	soft-reconfiguration
distribute-list	soo
dmzlink-bw	transltate-topology
filter-list	unsuppress-map
inter-as-hybrid	validation
interval-vpn-client	weight

When you have added all the statements you need in the session template, you end it with the statement **exit-peer-policy**.

Unlike the linear inheritance of session templates, a policy template can either directly or indirectly inherit from up to seven other peer templates; like session templates, only one policy template can be applied to a neighbor. Figure 5-3 shows how these rules provide great flexibility for mixing and matching templates to create the right policy or combination of policies for each neighbor.

Example 5-11 shows the configuration of Example 5-9, with policy templates added. A number of policy templates are defined, but in two cases—EBGP_Standard and EBGP_Premium—the template inherits more than one template.

---

[3] Again, your options will depend on the IOS version you are using.

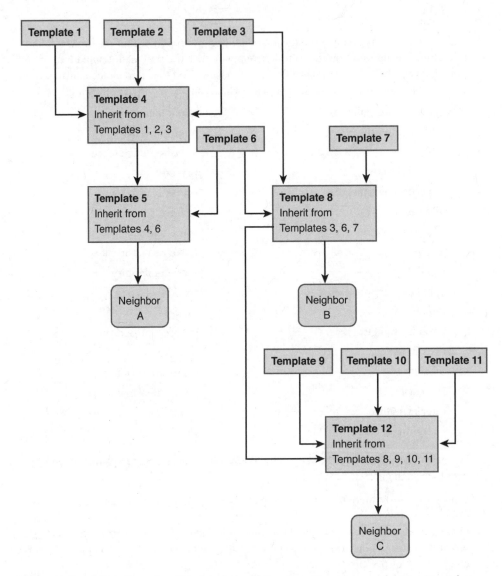

Figure 5-3 *A Neighbor Can Directly Inherit One Peer Template, and a Peer Template Can Directly or Indirectly Inherit from up to Seven Other Peer Templates*

Example 5-11 *Seven Policy Templates Are Created in This Example. Unlike Session Templates, a Policy Template Can Inherit from Multiple Policy Templates*

```
router bgp 100
 template peer-policy All_Peers
  soft-reconfiguration inbound
 exit-peer-policy
```

```
!
template peer-policy IBGP_Policy
 route-map internal_peers in
 route-map out_peers out
 route-reflector-client
 next-hop-self
 inherit peer-policy All_Peers 10
exit-peer-policy
!
template peer-policy EBGP_Out
 route-map external_peers out
 inherit peer-policy All_Peers 10
exit-peer-policy
!
template peer-policy EBGP_In
 prefix-list customers in
 remove-private-as
 maximum-prefix 30000
 inherit peer-policy All_Peers 10
exit-peer-policy
!
template peer-policy Premium
 route-map Premium_Customer in
exit-peer-policy
!
template peer-policy EBGP_Standard
 inherit peer-policy EBGP_In 20
 inherit peer-policy EBGP_Out 10
exit-peer-policy
!
template peer-policy EBGP_Premium
 inherit peer-policy Premium 30
 inherit peer-policy EBGP_In 20
 inherit peer-policy EBGP_Out 10
exit-peer-policy
!
template peer-session bgp_top
 update-source Loopback0
 timers 30 90
exit-peer-session
!
template peer-session ibgp
 remote-as 100
 password 7 1324243C345D547A
```

```
  inherit peer-session bgp_top
exit-peer-session
!
template peer-session ebgp
 ttl-security hops 2
 inherit peer-session bgp_top
exit-peer-session
!
no synchronization
bgp log-neighbor-changes
neighbor 192.168.255.2 inherit peer-session ibgp
neighbor 192.168.255.2 inherit peer-policy IBGP_Policy
neighbor 192.168.255.3 inherit peer-session ibgp
neighbor 192.168.255.3 inherit peer-policy IBGP_Policy
neighbor 192.168.255.4 remote-as 200
neighbor 192.168.255.4 inherit peer-session ebgp
neighbor 192.168.255.4 password 7 04695F393F205F5D
neighbor 192.168.255.4 inherit peer-policy EBGP_Standard
neighbor 192.168.255.5 remote-as 300
neighbor 192.168.255.5 inherit peer-session ebgp
neighbor 192.168.255.5 password 7 1337422D3B0D1739
neighbor 192.168.255.5 inherit peer-policy EBGP_Standard
neighbor 192.168.255.6 remote-as 400
neighbor 192.168.255.6 inherit peer-session ebgp
neighbor 192.168.255.6 password 7 142544343C053938
neighbor 192.168.255.6 inherit peer-policy EBGP_Premium
no auto-summary
!
```

Notice also that the inheritance statements have sequence numbers. This both specifies the sequence in which the statements are processed and helps edit the templates when a new inheritance statement needs to be added between two existing statements. As with session templates, when there are conflicting statements, the statement associated with the higher-numbered template overrides the statement associated with the lower-numbered template.

There is an important difference between the way sequenced inherited templates are processed and the way sequenced route map stanzas are processed: Where processing stops when a route matches a route map stanza and some action is taken, all inherited templates are processed. The sequence number specifies only the order in which they are processed.

The **show ip bgp template peer-policy** command, like its **session-policy** counterpart, displays information for analyzing and troubleshooting policy templates (Example 5-12). For each template, the locally configured policies are shown, as are the templates inherited by that template and the templates inheriting that template.

Example 5-12 show ip bgp template peer-policy *Command Displays Information About Session Templates*

```
Colorado#show ip bgp template peer-policy
Template:All_Peers, index:1.
Local policies:0x10000, Inherited polices:0x0
 *Inherited by Template IBGP_Policy, index:2
 *Inherited by Template EBGP_Out, index:3
 *Inherited by Template EBGP_In, index:4
Locally configured policies:
  soft-reconfiguration inbound
Inherited policies:


Template:IBGP_Policy, index:2.
Local policies:0x4203, Inherited polices:0x10000
This template inherits:
  All_Peers, index:1, seq_no:10, flags:0x4203
Locally configured policies:
  route-map internal_peers in
  route-map out_peers out
  route-reflector-client
  next-hop-self
Inherited policies:
  soft-reconfiguration inbound


Template:EBGP_Out, index:3.
Local policies:0x2, Inherited polices:0x10000
This template inherits:
  All_Peers, index:1, seq_no:10, flags:0x2
 *Inherited by Template EBGP_Standard, index:7
 *Inherited by Template EBGP_Premium, index:8
Locally configured policies:
  route-map external_peers out
Inherited policies:
  soft-reconfiguration inbound


Template:EBGP_In, index:4.
Local policies:0xA0040, Inherited polices:0x10000
This template inherits:
  All_Peers, index:1, seq_no:10, flags:0xA0040
 *Inherited by Template EBGP_Standard, index:7
 *Inherited by Template EBGP_Premium, index:8
Locally configured policies:
  prefix-list customers in
  maximum-prefix 30000
```

```
    remove-private-as
Inherited policies:
  soft-reconfiguration inbound


Template:Premium, index:5.
Local policies:0x1, Inherited polices:0x0
 *Inherited by Template EBGP_Premium, index:8
Locally configured policies:
  route-map Premium_Customer in
Inherited policies:


Template:EBGP_Standard, index:7.
Local policies:0x0, Inherited polices:0xB0042
This template inherits:
  EBGP_In, index:4, seq_no:20, flags:0x0
  EBGP_Out, index:3, seq_no:10, flags:0xB0040
Locally configured policies:
Inherited policies:
  prefix-list customers in
  route-map external_peers out
  soft-reconfiguration inbound
  maximum-prefix 30000
  remove-private-as


Template:EBGP_Premium, index:8.
Local policies:0x0, Inherited polices:0xB0043
This template inherits:
  Premium, index:5, seq_no:30, flags:0x0
  EBGP_In, index:4, seq_no:20, flags:0x1
  EBGP_Out, index:3, seq_no:10, flags:0xB0041
Locally configured policies:
Inherited policies:
  prefix-list customers in
  route-map Premium_Customer in
  route-map external_peers out
  soft-reconfiguration inbound
  maximum-prefix 30000
  remove-private-as


Colorado#
```

The long BGP configuration referred to in Example 5-11 might seem to be excessive for just five peers. But any time there are shared session parameters or shared policy elements, peer templates are extremely useful for managing your BGP configuration—both for interpreting policies and for easily changing policies when needed. And when routers have a large number of EBGP or IBGP peers, peer templates can appreciably consolidate repetitive configuration statements. Deciding when to use peer templates and when to just configure individual neighbors is a judgment call. If a router has only one or two neighbors and simple policies, and is unlikely to be changed, direct configuration of neighbors is probably good enough. But if a router has more than two or three BGP peers, has more than the simplest of policies, or has policies or session parameters that must be changed occasionally—or any combination of those three—then peer templates should be used. I highly recommend forming a habit of using them in your BGP configurations. Now that you have seen how peer templates are used, the subsequent BGP examples in this book make frequent use of them.

Communities

Whereas peer templates and the older peer groups enable you to apply common polices to a group of peers, communities enable you to apply policies to a group of routes. A community is a route attribute and therefore is attached to a route and passed from one BGP speaker to another when the route is advertised.

The advantage of communities is that, using a route map, you can assign one or more community attributes to a route at some point in the network—either in the local autonomous systems or even in another autonomous system—and then, at some other point in the network, apply a policy to all routes belonging to a given community. The most common use of communities is in autonomous systems with many BGP peers. By applying policies to community attributes rather than by routes, you do not have to change the policy configuration every time the routes advertised into the AS change.

A community is a 32-bit number, configured in the following steps:

Step 1. Use a route map to identify the routes to which a community attribute is to be set.

Step 2. Use the **set community** statement to set the community value.

Step 3. Use the **neighbor send-community** statement (or the **send-community** statement in a policy template) to specify the neighbors to which community attributes are to be sent. Note that without this statement, a router does not forward community attributes to the neighbor.

The value of a community attribute can be specified as

- A decimal number between 1 and 4294967200

- An AA:NN format, in which AA is a 16-bit decimal AS number between 1 and 65535 and NN is an arbitrary 16-bit decimal number between 1 and 65440

A community attribute value can also be specified in hexadecimal; although, that format is seldom used in modern networks.

Any of the following entries specify the community 400:50 (AS400, number 50):

set community 400:50

set community 26214450

set community 0x1900032

All these statements specify the same 32-bit number, and IOS accepts any of the three formats. However, by default when IOS displays a community value, it is in the decimal format. To display community values in the AA:NN format, you must change the default by adding the statement **ip bgp-community new-format** in global configuration mode. Your choice of which format to use depends on how you use communities. If you are tagging only routes to apply a few policies within your autonomous system, the decimal format—and using numerically low numbers—is probably sufficient. But if you work with routes from multiple autonomous systems or are sending community attributes to other autonomous systems, the AA:NN format is a better choice because of the easy identification of the originating AS.

Well-Known Communities

A few communities with reserved, well-known values can be specified in IOS by name rather than number, as listed in Table 5-1. Use of the well-known attributes is demonstrated in this section.

Table 5-1   *Well-Known Community Attributes*

Attribute Name	Hex Value	AA:NN Value	Description
INTERNET	0x0	0:0	Advertise this route to everyone (that is, to the Internet). This is used as a sort of "permit all" community; it's the default community for all prefixes. This community is Cisco-specific.
NO_EXPORT	0FFFFFF01	65535:65281	Do not advertise to any EBGP peer. That is, the prefix can be advertised throughout an AS (or confederation), but not to an external AS.
NO_ADVERTISE	0xFFFFFF02	65535:65282	Do not advertise to any EBGP or IBGP peer.

Attribute Name	Hex Value	AA:NN Value	Description
LOCAL_AS	0xFFFFFF03	65535:65283	Same as NO_EXPORT but applied to subconfederations as described later in this chapter. That is, the prefix can be advertised to any peer within the local AS or sub-AS but not to any EBGP or Confederation-EBGP peer. RFC 1997 calls this well-known community NO_EXPORT_SUBCONFED.

Figure 5-4 shows an example network to be used throughout this section. AS100 interconnects the other seven autonomous systems, and the illustration shows the three prefixes each AS advertises.

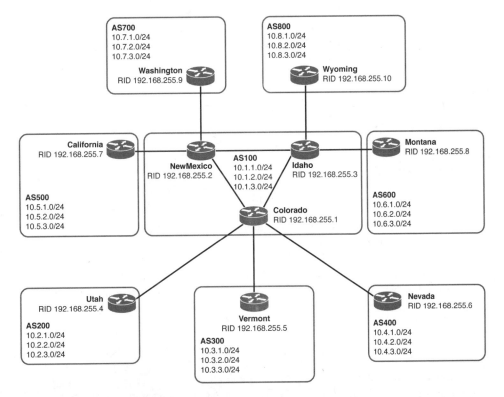

Figure 5-4 *Example Network for Demonstrating the Use of the Community Attribute*

A routing policy in AS500 states that prefix 10.5.2.0/24 should be advertised to AS100, but that AS100 should not advertise it to any other AS. To implement this policy, the NO_EXPORT community attribute is used. This attribute allows a route to be advertised throughout a neighboring AS but does not allow that AS to advertise the route to other autonomous systems. That is, the route can be advertised to IBGP peers but not EBGP peers. Example 5-13 shows router California's BGP and policy configurations.

Example 5-13 *Router California Is Configured to Add the NO_EXPORT Community to Prefix 10.5.2.0/24 Before Advertising It to Neighbor NewMexico*

```
router bgp 500
 no synchronization
 bgp log-neighbor-changes
 network 10.5.1.0 mask 255.255.255.0
 network 10.5.2.0 mask 255.255.255.0
 network 10.5.3.0 mask 255.255.255.0
 neighbor 10.0.0.37 remote-as 100
 neighbor 10.0.0.37 password 7 097E193629040401
 neighbor 10.0.0.37 send-community
 neighbor 10.0.0.37 route-map Exp-Policy out
 no auto-summary
!
ip prefix-list No-Exp seq 5 permit 10.5.2.0/24
!
route-map Exp-Policy permit 10
 match ip address prefix-list No-Exp
 set community no-export
!
route-map Exp-Policy permit 20
!
```

You can see that the **send-community** statement is used for neighbor NewMexico (10.0.0.37) to enable the forwarding of community attributes, and an outgoing policy named Exp-Policy is added. That policy sets the NO_EXPORT community for matched routes, and uses a prefix list to match 10.5.2.0/24 exactly. Example 5-14 shows the configuration of NewMexico, in which the **send-community** statement is added to IBGP peers; no other configuration is required here except specifying which neighbors to whom community attributes are to be sent.

> **Note** The **send-community** statement is added directly to the neighbor configuration at California because there is only the one neighbor, and a policy template probably does not provide any advantages. NewMexico has multiple neighbors, so using a policy template to add the **send-community** statement is the better choice here.

Example 5-14 *NewMexico Is Configured to Send Community Attributes to Its IBGP Peers*

```
router bgp 100
 template peer-policy IBGP
  next-hop-self
  send-community
 exit-peer-policy
 !
 template peer-session bgp_top
  update-source Loopback0
  timers 30 90
 exit-peer-session
 !
 template peer-session ibgp
  remote-as 100
  password 7 002520283B0A5B56
  inherit peer-session bgp_top
 exit-peer-session
 !
 no synchronization
 bgp log-neighbor-changes
 network 10.1.2.0 mask 255.255.255.0
 neighbor 10.0.0.34 remote-as 700
 neighbor 10.0.0.34 password 7 113B403A2713181F
 neighbor 10.0.0.38 remote-as 500
 neighbor 10.0.0.38 password 7 08131B7139181604
 neighbor 192.168.255.1 inherit peer-session ibgp
 neighbor 192.168.255.1 inherit peer-policy IBGP
 neighbor 192.168.255.3 inherit peer-session ibgp
 neighbor 192.168.255.3 inherit peer-policy IBGP
 no auto-summary
 !
```

Example 5-15 shows the results of California's configuration referred to in Example 5-13. Colorado's BGP table includes the route to 10.5.2.0/24, indicating that NewMexico has received the route from California and advertised it to its IBGP peers. But Vermont's BGP table does not contain the route; California has honored the NO_EXPORT attribute and has suppressed the route to its EBGP peers. The **send-community** statement does not need to be configured for California's EBGP neighbors; the community takes effect before route advertisement.

Example 5-15 *Route to 10.5.2.0/24 Has the NO_EXPORT Community Attribute Set, so Colorado Does Not Advertise the Route to Its EBGP Peers Such as Vermont*

```
Colorado#show ip bgp 10.5.2.0
BGP routing table entry for 10.5.2.0/24, version 14
Paths: (1 available, best #1, table Default-IP-Routing-Table, not advertised to EBGP
  peer)
Flag: 0x820
  Not advertised to any peer
  500
    192.168.255.2 (metric 65) from 192.168.255.2 (192.168.255.2)
      Origin IGP, metric 0, localpref 100, valid, internal, best
      Community: no-export
Colorado#
```

```
Vermont#show ip bgp 10.5.2.0
% Network not in table
Vermont#
```

Of course, an autonomous system would not be truly autonomous if another AS could tell it what to do. Suppose AS100 wants to override the NO_EXPORT attribute set by California and advertise 10.5.2.0/24 to its EBGP peers. Example 5-16 shows the configuration for NewMexico to implement such a policy. A policy template named EBGP is created, which references a route map named Clear-Comm as an incoming policy. The route map matches any prefixes whose first 8 bits match 10.0.0.0/8 and applies the **set community none** statement to those prefixes. The policy template is then applied to NewMexico's two EBGP peers.

Example 5-16 *NewMexico Is Configured to Delete the Communities Advertised by Its EBGP Peers*

```
router bgp 100
 template peer-policy IBGP
  next-hop-self
  send-community
 exit-peer-policy
 !
 template peer-policy EBGP
  route-map Clear-Comm in
 exit-peer-policy
 !
 template peer-session bgp_top
  update-source Loopback0
  timers 30 90
 exit-peer-session
 !
```

```
template peer-session ibgp
 remote-as 100
 password 7 002520283B0A5B56
 inherit peer-session bgp_top
exit-peer-session
!
no synchronization
bgp log-neighbor-changes
network 10.1.2.0 mask 255.255.255.0
neighbor 10.0.0.34 remote-as 700
neighbor 10.0.0.34 password 7 113B403A2713181F
neighbor 10.0.0.34 inherit peer-policy EBGP
neighbor 10.0.0.38 remote-as 500
neighbor 10.0.0.38 password 7 08131B7139181604
neighbor 10.0.0.38 inherit peer-policy EBGP
neighbor 192.168.255.1 inherit peer-session ibgp
neighbor 192.168.255.1 inherit peer-policy IBGP
neighbor 192.168.255.3 inherit peer-session ibgp
neighbor 192.168.255.3 inherit peer-policy IBGP
no auto-summary
!
ip prefix-list No-Comm seq 5 permit 10.0.0.0/8 le 32
!
route-map Clear-Comm permit 10
 match ip address prefix-list No-Comm
 set community none
!
route-map Clear-Comm permit 20
!
```

The **set community none** statement does not set any community attribute; rather, it
deletes existing community attributes. Example 5-17 shows the results at Colorado
and Vermont.

Example 5-17   *Route to 10.5.2.0/24 No Longer Has the NO_EXPORT Community
Attached to It, so Colorado Advertises the Route to Its EBGP Peers*

```
Colorado#show ip bgp 10.5.2.0
BGP routing table entry for 10.5.2.0/24, version 90
Paths: (1 available, best #1, table Default-IP-Routing-Table)
Flag: 0x820
  Not advertised to any peer
  500
    192.168.255.2 (metric 65) from 192.168.255.2 (192.168.255.2)
```

```
        Origin IGP, metric 0, localpref 100, valid, internal, best
Colorado#
```

```
Vermont#show ip bgp 10.5.2.0
BGP routing table entry for 10.5.2.0/24, version 200
Paths: (1 available, best #1, table Default-IP-Routing-Table)
Flag: 0x820
  Not advertised to any peer
  100 500
    10.0.0.6 from 10.0.0.6 (192.168.255.1)
      Origin IGP, localpref 100, valid, external, best
Vermont#
```

The NO_ADVERTISE community attribute triggers a similar action as NO_EXPORT,
except NO_ADVERTISE tells a receiving router to not advertise the route to either
EBGP or IBGP peers. Suppose that NewMexico in Figure 5-4 wants to advertise
AS500's prefixes 10.5.1.0/24 and 10.5.3.0/24 to its IBGP peers but does not want either
of those peers to advertise the routes to any of their own IBGP or EBGP peers.
Example 5-18 shows how NewMexico can be configured to do this. A route map named
No-Adv matches the two prefixes and adds the NO_ADVERTISE attribute to them; the
route map is then applied as an outgoing policy in the policy template IBGP.

Example 5-18 *NewMexico Is Configured to Add the NO_ADVERTISE Community to
Prefixes 10.5.1.0/24 and 10.5.3.0/24 Before They Are Advertised to Its IBGP Neighbors*

```
router bgp 100
 template peer-policy IBGP
  route-map No-Adv out
  next-hop-self
  send-community
 exit-peer-policy
 !
 template peer-policy EBGP
  route-map Clear-Comm in
 exit-peer-policy
 !
 template peer-session bgp_top
  update-source Loopback0
  timers 30 90
 exit-peer-session
 !
 template peer-session ibgp
  remote-as 100
  password 7 002520283B0A5B56
```

```
 inherit peer-session bgp_top
exit-peer-session
!
no synchronization
bgp log-neighbor-changes
network 10.1.2.0 mask 255.255.255.0
neighbor 10.0.0.34 remote-as 700
neighbor 10.0.0.34 password 7 113B403A2713181F
neighbor 10.0.0.34 inherit peer-policy EBGP
neighbor 10.0.0.38 remote-as 500
neighbor 10.0.0.38 password 7 08131B7139181604
neighbor 10.0.0.38 inherit peer-policy EBGP
neighbor 192.168.255.1 inherit peer-session ibgp
neighbor 192.168.255.1 inherit peer-policy IBGP
neighbor 192.168.255.3 inherit peer-session ibgp
neighbor 192.168.255.3 inherit peer-policy IBGP
no auto-summary
!
ip prefix-list No-Adv seq 5 permit 10.5.1.0/24
ip prefix-list No-Adv seq 10 permit 10.5.3.0/24
!
ip prefix-list No-Comm seq 5 permit 10.0.0.0/8 le 32
!
route-map Clear-Comm permit 10
 match ip address prefix-list No-Comm
 set community none
!
route-map Clear-Comm permit 20
!
route-map No-Adv permit 10
 match ip address prefix-list No-Adv
 set community no-advertise
!
route-map No-Adv permit 20
!
```

Recall that California is configured to advertise 10.5.2.0/24 with the NO_EXPORT community and the other two subnets of AS500 with no community attributes. NewMexico has now completely reversed that policy. Prefix 10.5.2.0/24 has no community attribute, and the prefixes 10.5.1.0/24 and 10.5.3.0/24 have the NO_ADVERTISE attribute, preventing them from being advertised outside of AS100. Example 5-19 shows the results of this configuration.

Example 5-19   *Colorado Has Knowledge of All Three Prefixes in AS500 but Advertises Only 10.5.2.0/24 to Vermont*

```
Colorado#show ip bgp regexp 500
BGP table version is 133, local router ID is 192.168.255.1
Status codes: s suppressed, d damped, h history, * valid, > best, i - internal,
              r RIB-failure, S Stale
Origin codes: i - IGP, e - EGP, ? - incomplete

   Network          Next Hop          Metric LocPrf Weight Path
*>i10.5.1.0/24      192.168.255.2          0    100      0 500 i
*>i10.5.2.0/24      192.168.255.2          0    100      0 500 i
*>i10.5.3.0/24      192.168.255.2          0    100      0 500 i
Colorado#
```

```
Vermont#show ip bgp regexp 500
BGP table version is 125, local router ID is 192.168.255.5
Status codes: s suppressed, d damped, h history, * valid, > best, i - internal,
              r RIB-failure, S Stale
Origin codes: i - IGP, e - EGP, ? - incomplete

   Network          Next Hop          Metric LocPrf Weight Path
*>  10.5.2.0/24     10.0.0.6                            0 100 500 i
Vermont#
```

Note   Example 5-19 also shows yet another way to use the **show ip bgp** command. Here, a regular expression displays all routes that have a 500 in their AS_PATH.

Arbitrary Communities

Although the well-known communities have their uses, the great majority of communities are defined within individual autonomous systems for the application and enforcement of their own policies. These locally defined, or arbitrary, communities are assigned the same way as well-known communities, with the **set community** statement, but rather than specifying a name, you specify a value—either as a simple decimal number or in the AA:NN format, as discussed in the beginning of this section.

In Figure 5-5, AS100 is a transit AS for its seven autonomous systems, which are designated as Customers A through G. As in the previous examples, each of the autonomous systems advertises three prefixes to AS100. In this exercise, you want a policy in which the prefixes whose third octet is 1 get a LOCAL_PREF of 50; those with a third octet of

2 get a LOCAL_PREF of 100; and those with a third octet of 3 get a LOCAL_PREF of 150.

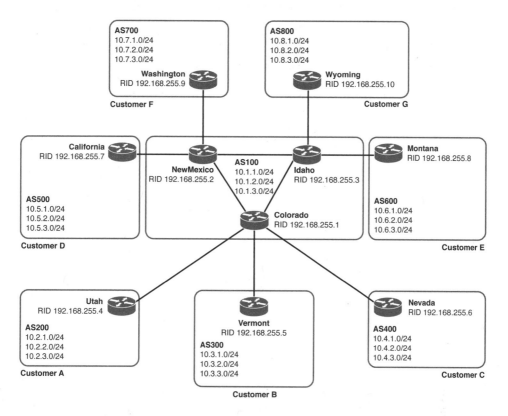

Figure 5-5 *Autonomous Systems Peered to AS100 Are Designated as Customers A Through G. Communities Will Be Used to Categorize the Prefixes Advertised by Each*

Example 5-20 shows the configuration of Utah referred to in Figure 5-5. A route map named pref-comm references prefix lists to identify the three local prefixes and assign a community value accordingly. Although any community values could be used, this example assigns the values 50, 100, and 150 to correspond to the LOCAL_PREF value that will eventually be assigned to the routes. The route map is then applied as an outgoing policy to the neighbor configuration. The **neighbor send-community** statement is also used to tell the router to attach community attributes to routes advertised to the neighbor. The routers in the other six customer autonomous systems are configured similarly; no policy templates are used in these configurations because there is only the one neighbor, and policy templates in this case do not gain us anything.

Note The community configurations and related policy configurations used in the previous examples have been deleted before beginning this example.

Example 5-20   *Router Utah in Figure 5-5 Is Configured to Add a Community Value of 50 to Prefix 10.2.1.0/24, 100 to 10.2.2.0/24, and 150 to 10.2.3.0/24*

```
router bgp 200
 no synchronization
 bgp log-neighbor-changes
 network 10.2.1.0 mask 255.255.255.0
 network 10.2.2.0 mask 255.255.255.0
 network 10.2.3.0 mask 255.255.255.0
 timers bgp 30 90
 neighbor 10.0.0.2 remote-as 100
 neighbor 10.0.0.2 password 7 107C5D2635160118
 neighbor 10.0.0.2 send-community
 neighbor 10.0.0.2 route-map pref-comm out
 no auto-summary
!
ip prefix-list 1 seq 5 permit 10.2.1.0/24
!
ip prefix-list 2 seq 5 permit 10.2.2.0/24
!
ip prefix-list 3 seq 5 permit 10.2.3.0/24
!
route-map pref-comm permit 5
 match ip address prefix-list 1
 set community 50
!
route-map pref-comm permit 10
 match ip address prefix-list 2
 set community 100
!
route-map pref-comm permit 15
 match ip address prefix-list 3
 set community 150
!
route-map pref-comm permit 20
!
```

The command **show ip bgp community** displays routes with the specified community. In Example 5-21 the command displays the routes at Colorado with community values 50, 100, and 150, respectively. You can see that seven prefixes display after each command—one for each of the seven customer autonomous systems—and that prefixes whose third octet is 1 belong to community 50; prefixes whose second octet is 2 belong to community 100; and prefixes whose third octet is 3 belong to community 150.

Example 5-21 show ip bgp community *Command Is Used to Observe Which Prefixes at Colorado Belong to Communities 50, 100, and 150*

```
Colorado#show ip bgp community 50
BGP table version is 85, local router ID is 192.168.255.1
Status codes: s suppressed, d damped, h history, * valid, > best, i - internal,
              r RIB-failure, S Stale
Origin codes: i - IGP, e - EGP, ? - incomplete


   Network          Next Hop          Metric LocPrf Weight Path
*> 10.2.1.0/24      10.0.0.1              0             0 200 i
*> 10.3.1.0/24      10.0.0.5              0             0 300 i
*> 10.4.1.0/24      10.0.0.9              0             0 400 i
*>i10.5.1.0/24      192.168.255.2         0    100      0 500 i
*>i10.6.1.0/24      192.168.255.3         0    100      0 600 i
*>i10.7.1.0/24      192.168.255.2         0    100      0 700 i
*>i10.8.1.0/24      192.168.255.3         0    100      0 800 i
Colorado#
Colorado#show ip bgp community 100
BGP table version is 85, local router ID is 192.168.255.1
Status codes: s suppressed, d damped, h history, * valid, > best, i - internal,
              r RIB-failure, S Stale
Origin codes: i - IGP, e - EGP, ? - incomplete


   Network          Next Hop          Metric LocPrf Weight Path
*> 10.2.2.0/24      10.0.0.1              0             0 200 i
*> 10.3.2.0/24      10.0.0.5              0             0 300 i
*> 10.4.2.0/24      10.0.0.9              0             0 400 i
*>i10.5.2.0/24      192.168.255.2         0    100      0 500 i
*>i10.6.2.0/24      192.168.255.3         0    100      0 600 i
*>i10.7.2.0/24      192.168.255.2         0    100      0 700 i
*>i10.8.2.0/24      192.168.255.3         0    100      0 800 i
Colorado#
Colorado#show ip bgp community 150
BGP table version is 85, local router ID is 192.168.255.1
Status codes: s suppressed, d damped, h history, * valid, > best, i - internal,
              r RIB-failure, S Stale
Origin codes: i - IGP, e - EGP, ? - incomplete


   Network          Next Hop          Metric LocPrf Weight Path
*> 10.2.3.0/24      10.0.0.1              0             0 200 i
*> 10.3.3.0/24      10.0.0.5              0             0 300 i
*> 10.4.3.0/24      10.0.0.9              0             0 400 i
*>i10.5.3.0/24      192.168.255.2         0    100      0 500 i
*>i10.6.3.0/24      192.168.255.3         0    100      0 600 i
```

```
*>i10.7.3.0/24      192.168.255.2          0    100      0 700 i
*>i10.8.3.0/24      192.168.255.3          0    100      0 800 i
Colorado#
```

The next step is to assign LOCAL_PREF values in AS100 according to the community to which a customer prefix belongs. Example 5-22 shows the configuration at Colorado; routers NewMexico and Idaho referred to in Figure 5-5 have similar configurations. Three *community lists* identify routes by their community attributes. Community lists, such as prefix lists and AS_PATH lists, are a special adaptation of access lists: There are possibly multiple lines in the list, each of which has a "permit" or "deny" action. The list is identified by a number between 1 and 99, and an implicit "deny any" is at the end. In the configuration referred to in Example 5-22, a route map named "pref-set" references three single-line community lists and assigns LOCAL_PREF values of 50, 100, or 150 to matching routes. A peer-template named EBGP uses the route map as an incoming policy, which is applied to Colorado's three external peers.

> **Note** The community lists demonstrated in this section are standard community lists. Standard lists are numbered in the range 1–99 or can be a named list with the keyword **standard** preceding the name. The subsequent section "Expanded Community Lists" demonstrates the use of expanded community lists, which are numbered in the range 100–500 or are named lists with the keyword **expanded** preceding the name. Although standard community lists enable you to specify one community number or well-known community name per entry, expanded community lists use regular expressions to specify a set of communities.

Example 5-22 *Standard Community Lists Are Used to Identify Routes with a Specified Community Value*

```
router bgp 100
 template peer-policy IBGP
  next-hop-self
  send-community
 exit-peer-policy
 !
 template peer-policy EBGP
  route-map pref-set in
 exit-peer-policy
 !
 template peer-session bgp_top
  update-source Loopback0
  timers 30 90
 exit-peer-session
 !
```

```
 template peer-session ibgp
  remote-as 100
  password 7 1324243C345D547A
  inherit peer-session bgp_top
 exit-peer-session
 !
 no synchronization
 bgp log-neighbor-changes
 network 10.1.1.0 mask 255.255.255.0
 neighbor 10.0.0.1 remote-as 200
 neighbor 10.0.0.1 password 7 073D75737E080A16
 neighbor 10.0.0.1 inherit peer-policy EBGP
 neighbor 10.0.0.5 remote-as 300
 neighbor 10.0.0.5 password 7 023451643B071C32
 neighbor 10.0.0.5 inherit peer-policy EBGP
 neighbor 10.0.0.9 remote-as 400
 neighbor 10.0.0.9 password 7 00364539345A1815
 neighbor 10.0.0.9 inherit peer-policy EBGP
 neighbor 192.168.255.2 inherit peer-session ibgp
 neighbor 192.168.255.2 inherit peer-policy IBGP
 neighbor 192.168.255.3 inherit peer-session ibgp
 neighbor 192.168.255.3 inherit peer-policy IBGP
 no auto-summary
!
ip community-list 1 permit 50
ip community-list 2 permit 100
ip community-list 3 permit 150
!
!
route-map pref-set permit 5
 match community 1
 set local-preference 50
!
route-map pref-set permit 10
 match community 2
 set local-preference 100
!
route-map pref-set permit 15
 match community 3
 set local-preference 150
!
route-map pref-set permit 20
!
```

Example 5-23 shows the results of the policy. The LOCAL_PREF values of the three 10.1.0.0/16 prefixes, local to AS100, remain at their default values because they did not match any of the community lists. The three prefixes of the seven customer autonomous systems have LOCAL_PREF values set according to the configured policy.

Example 5-23 *LOCAL_PREF Values of the Routes in Colorado's BGP Table Reflect the Effects of the Policy Configured in Example 5-22*

```
Colorado#show ip bgp
BGP table version is 53, local router ID is 192.168.255.1
Status codes: s suppressed, d damped, h history, * valid, > best, i - internal,
              r RIB-failure, S Stale
Origin codes: i - IGP, e - EGP, ? - incomplete


   Network          Next Hop          Metric LocPrf Weight Path
*> 10.1.1.0/24      0.0.0.0                0          32768 i
*>i10.1.2.0/24      192.168.255.2          0    100      0 i
*>i10.1.3.0/24      192.168.255.3          0    100      0 i
*> 10.2.1.0/24      10.0.0.1               0     50      0 200 i
*> 10.2.2.0/24      10.0.0.1               0    100      0 200 i
*> 10.2.3.0/24      10.0.0.1               0    150      0 200 i
*> 10.3.1.0/24      10.0.0.5               0     50      0 300 i
*> 10.3.2.0/24      10.0.0.5               0    100      0 300 i
*> 10.3.3.0/24      10.0.0.5               0    150      0 300 i
*> 10.4.1.0/24      10.0.0.9               0     50      0 400 i
*> 10.4.2.0/24      10.0.0.9               0    100      0 400 i
*> 10.4.3.0/24      10.0.0.9               0    150      0 400 i
*>i10.5.1.0/24      192.168.255.2          0     50      0 500 i
*>i10.5.2.0/24      192.168.255.2          0    100      0 500 i
*>i10.5.3.0/24      192.168.255.2          0    150      0 500 i
*>i10.6.1.0/24      192.168.255.3          0     50      0 600 i
*>i10.6.2.0/24      192.168.255.3          0    100      0 600 i
*>i10.6.3.0/24      192.168.255.3          0    150      0 600 i
*>i10.7.1.0/24      192.168.255.2          0     50      0 700 i
*>i10.7.2.0/24      192.168.255.2          0    100      0 700 i
*>i10.7.3.0/24      192.168.255.2          0    150      0 700 i
*>i10.8.1.0/24      192.168.255.3          0     50      0 800 i
*>i10.8.2.0/24      192.168.255.3          0    100      0 800 i
*>i10.8.3.0/24      192.168.255.3          0    150      0 800 i
Colorado#
```

Examples 5-24 and 5-25 also show the results of the policy. The displayed lists are the same in both cases, but the commands used are different according to what you want to observe. The **show ip bgp community** command displays prefixes with the specified community attribute (compare the LOCAL_PREF values in Example 5-24 with those in

Example 5-21), whereas the **show ip bgp community-list** command displays prefixes matching the specified community list.

Example 5-24 *Prefixes with the Community Values Specified in the* show ip bgp community *Command Show the LOCAL_PREF Values Set by the Policy in Example 5-22*

```
Colorado#show ip bgp community 50
BGP table version is 53, local router ID is 192.168.255.1
Status codes: s suppressed, d damped, h history, * valid, > best, i - internal,
              r RIB-failure, S Stale
Origin codes: i - IGP, e - EGP, ? - incomplete

   Network          Next Hop          Metric LocPrf Weight Path
*> 10.2.1.0/24      10.0.0.1               0     50      0 200 i
*> 10.3.1.0/24      10.0.0.5               0     50      0 300 i
*> 10.4.1.0/24      10.0.0.9               0     50      0 400 i
*>i10.5.1.0/24      192.168.255.2          0     50      0 500 i
*>i10.6.1.0/24      192.168.255.3          0     50      0 600 i
*>i10.7.1.0/24      192.168.255.2          0     50      0 700 i
*>i10.8.1.0/24      192.168.255.3          0     50      0 800 i
Colorado#
Colorado#show ip bgp community 100
BGP table version is 53, local router ID is 192.168.255.1
Status codes: s suppressed, d damped, h history, * valid, > best, i - internal,
              r RIB-failure, S Stale
Origin codes: i - IGP, e - EGP, ? - incomplete

   Network          Next Hop          Metric LocPrf Weight Path
*> 10.2.2.0/24      10.0.0.1               0    100      0 200 i
*> 10.3.2.0/24      10.0.0.5               0    100      0 300 i
*> 10.4.2.0/24      10.0.0.9               0    100      0 400 i
*>i10.5.2.0/24      192.168.255.2          0    100      0 500 i
*>i10.6.2.0/24      192.168.255.3          0    100      0 600 i
*>i10.7.2.0/24      192.168.255.2          0    100      0 700 i
*>i10.8.2.0/24      192.168.255.3          0    100      0 800 i
Colorado#
Colorado#show ip bgp community 150
BGP table version is 53, local router ID is 192.168.255.1
Status codes: s suppressed, d damped, h history, * valid, > best, i - internal,
              r RIB-failure, S Stale
Origin codes: i - IGP, e - EGP, ? - incomplete

   Network          Next Hop          Metric LocPrf Weight Path
*> 10.2.3.0/24      10.0.0.1               0    150      0 200 i
*> 10.3.3.0/24      10.0.0.5               0    150      0 300 i
```

```
*> 10.4.3.0/24        10.0.0.9                0   150     0 400 i
*>i10.5.3.0/24        192.168.255.2           0   150     0 500 i
*>i10.6.3.0/24        192.168.255.3           0   150     0 600 i
*>i10.7.3.0/24        192.168.255.2           0   150     0 700 i
*>i10.8.3.0/24        192.168.255.3           0   150     0 800 i
Colorado#
```

Example 5-25   show ip bgp community-list *Command Displays Routes Matching the Specified Community List. Again, the LOCAL_PREF Values Set in Example 5-22 Can Be Observed*

```
Colorado#show ip bgp community-list 1
BGP table version is 53, local router ID is 192.168.255.1
Status codes: s suppressed, d damped, h history, * valid, > best, i - internal,
              r RIB-failure, S Stale
Origin codes: i - IGP, e - EGP, ? - incomplete


   Network           Next Hop          Metric LocPrf Weight Path
*> 10.2.1.0/24        10.0.0.1               0    50     0 200 i
*> 10.3.1.0/24        10.0.0.5               0    50     0 300 i
*> 10.4.1.0/24        10.0.0.9               0    50     0 400 i
*>i10.5.1.0/24        192.168.255.2          0    50     0 500 i
*>i10.6.1.0/24        192.168.255.3          0    50     0 600 i
*>i10.7.1.0/24        192.168.255.2          0    50     0 700 i
*>i10.8.1.0/24        192.168.255.3          0    50     0 800 i
Colorado#
Colorado#show ip bgp community-list 2
BGP table version is 53, local router ID is 192.168.255.1
Status codes: s suppressed, d damped, h history, * valid, > best, i - internal,
              r RIB-failure, S Stale
Origin codes: i - IGP, e - EGP, ? - incomplete


   Network           Next Hop          Metric LocPrf Weight Path
*> 10.2.2.0/24        10.0.0.1               0   100     0 200 i
*> 10.3.2.0/24        10.0.0.5               0   100     0 300 i
*> 10.4.2.0/24        10.0.0.9               0   100     0 400 i
*>i10.5.2.0/24        192.168.255.2          0   100     0 500 i
*>i10.6.2.0/24        192.168.255.3          0   100     0 600 i
*>i10.7.2.0/24        192.168.255.2          0   100     0 700 i
*>i10.8.2.0/24        192.168.255.3          0   100     0 800 i
Colorado#
Colorado#show ip bgp community-list 3
BGP table version is 53, local router ID is 192.168.255.1
```

```
Status codes: s suppressed, d damped, h history, * valid, > best, i - internal,
              r RIB-failure, S Stale
Origin codes: i - IGP, e - EGP, ? - incomplete


   Network          Next Hop          Metric LocPrf Weight Path
*> 10.2.3.0/24      10.0.0.1               0    150      0 200 i
*> 10.3.3.0/24      10.0.0.5               0    150      0 300 i
*> 10.4.3.0/24      10.0.0.9               0    150      0 400 i
*>i10.5.3.0/24      192.168.255.2          0    150      0 500 i
*>i10.6.3.0/24      192.168.255.3          0    150      0 600 i
*>i10.7.3.0/24      192.168.255.2          0    150      0 700 i
*>i10.8.3.0/24      192.168.255.3          0    150      0 800 i
Colorado#
```

You already know that the LOCAL_PREF attribute sets preferences for outgoing traffic when there are multiple paths to the same destination. So you have likely been asking, during this example, why LOCAL_PREF is set when there is only one link into each of the seven customer autonomous systems. If the network of Figure 5-5 were all there is, setting LOCAL_PREFs would not make any sense at all.

But this example is focused on how to use community attributes to set policies, not on a practical LOCAL_PREF application. The example network is kept as simple as possible for that reason.

Figure 5-6 shows how the concepts of our exercise might be applied in a practical network. A customer AS is shown with three links to a service provider network and is advertising three prefixes to the provider over each of the links. Although incoming traffic to the customer network can reach any of the three prefixes through any of the three links, there should be a preference to use the link closest to each prefix. So a LOCAL_PREF attribute is assigned to each link according to its proximity to the prefix.

Now consider that the provider has 10,000 multihomed customers. By publishing a set of community values that the customers can attach to their advertised routes, the customers can easily indicate their preferences for incoming traffic from the provider, and the provider can easily implement the common policy for all their customers.

Using the AA:NN Format

The introduction to the communities section explained that the 32-bit community attribute can be specified and displayed in either simple decimal format or in an AA:NN format. Specifically,

- A decimal number between 1 and 4294967200

- An AA:NN format, in which AA is a 16-bit decimal AS number between 1 and 65535 and NN is an arbitrary 16-bit decimal number between 1 and 65440

By default, IOS displays community values in the decimal format. To change displays to the AA:NN format, you enter the statement **ip bgp new-format**.[4] In Example 5-26, the prefix 10.7.3.0/24 from our previous configuration example displays. You can see the community value of 150 in the last line. The **ip bgp new-format** is then entered, and the prefix displays again. This time, the same community displays as 0:150.

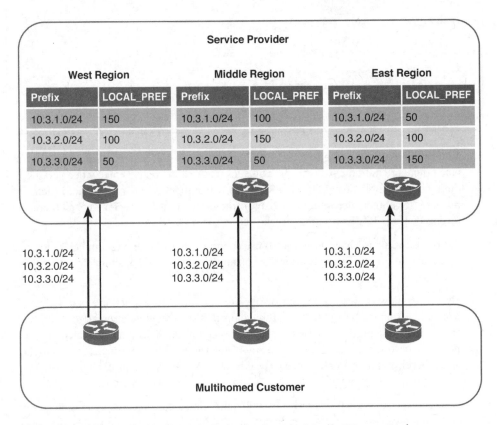

Figure 5-6   *A Service Provider with Multiple, Geographically Diverse Links to a Customer Might Use LOCAL_PREF to Specify the Preferred Paths to Each Customer Prefix. Communities Are Useful When Such a Policy Is Applied to Many Customers*

Example 5-26   *Entering the* ip bgp new-format *Command Tells IOS to Display Community Values in the AA:NN Format*

```
Colorado#show ip bgp 10.7.3.0
BGP routing table entry for 10.7.3.0/24, version 38
Paths: (1 available, best #1, table Default-IP-Routing-Table)
```

---

[4] The format is not actually new. The IOS command reflects a poor choice of words back when the format was new.

```
    Advertised to update-groups:
        2
    700
       192.168.255.2 (metric 65) from 192.168.255.2 (192.168.255.2)
          Origin IGP, metric 0, localpref 150, valid, internal, best
          Community: 150
Colorado#conf t
Enter configuration commands, one per line.  End with CNTL/Z.
Colorado(config)#ip bgp new-format
Colorado(config)#^Z
Colorado#
Colorado#show ip bgp 10.7.3.0
BGP routing table entry for 10.7.3.0/24, version 38
Paths: (1 available, best #1, table Default-IP-Routing-Table)
    Advertised to update-groups:
        2
    700
       192.168.255.2 (metric 65) from 192.168.255.2 (192.168.255.2)
          Origin IGP, metric 0, localpref 150, valid, internal, best
          Community: 0:150
Colorado#
```

The AA:NN format gives more flexibility when you set multiple policies for prefixes advertised from multiple autonomous systems. You can still define arbitrary meanings within the NN value, but now you can also set policies for selected autonomous systems using the AA value.

Expanded Community Lists

The example in the previous section "Arbitrary Communities" demonstrates how the community attribute might be used for an AS to convey certain routing preferences to another AS. This section demonstrates how an AS can use communities to enforce its own policies.

The community lists you've seen so far use standard community lists, which enable you to specify a single community—either by number or in the AA:NN format—per line. Standard community lists can be either numbered (1–99) or named, with the keyword **standard** preceding the name. Expanded community lists use regular expressions to give you more flexibility in matching a set of communities in a single line. They are either numbered in the range 100–500 or named with the keyword **expanded** preceding the name.

Figure 5-7 shows a variation of the autonomous systems referred to in Figure 5-5. There are no differences in the network itself, but the roles of some of the autonomous systems connected to AS100 are changed. The different types of peering relationships

AS100 has, and hence the policies configured, influence the policies applied to the route advertisements passing through the AS.

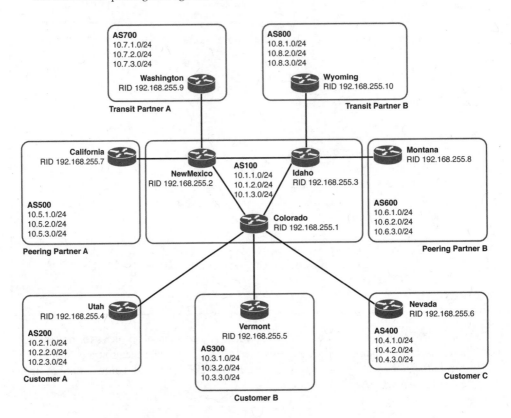

Figure 5-7   *Roles of Some of the Neighboring Autonomous Systems Referred to in Figure 5-5 Have Changed, Requiring a Different Set of Route Policies*

The roles referred to in Figure 5-7 and the policies that AS100 applies to them follows:

- A **Transit Partner** is an AS with which AS100 has a transit agreement, whereby traffic from one transit partner can pass through AS100 to reach another transit partner. But the prefixes internal to AS100 are not advertised to any transit partner. The traffic from a transit partner might originate from one of its internal prefixes or might originate from some other AS, not shown in Figure 5-7, which the transit partner is connected to.

- A **Customer** can reach AS100's internal prefixes. It can also transit AS100 to reach any prefix advertised by any transit partner. So customer prefixes are advertised to transit partners, and prefixes advertised by transit partners (whether internal to the transit partner or originated by some unshown upstream AS) are advertised to customers. A customer cannot, however, reach another customer or a peering partner through AS100.

- A **Peering Partner** can reach AS100's prefixes, and AS100 can reach the peering partner's prefixes. But a peering partner cannot reach a customer, a transit partner, or another peering partner through AS100. Nor can AS100 transit a peering partner to reach a destination in some other AS the peering partner might be connected to.

These rules are made up just for this case study, and no argument is made for whether they apply to any real-world scenario. The rules might also be a little difficult to follow in the descriptions you just read, but they can be broken down into some simple routing policies and configuration steps.

First, we decide how to assign communities. In this example, we use the AA:NN format. The NN part is assigned according to the following rules:

- Transit Partners = AA:1

- Peering Partners = AA:2

- Customers = AA:3

Example 5-27 shows the configurations of the three routers in AS100. Notice first that the **ip bgp new-format** statement is added to the configurations so that the AA:NN format displays. If this statement is not included, you can still configure the route maps to set a community in the AA:NN format, but when you observe the configuration, the community shows up as a decimal number.

Example 5-27   *Three Routers in AS100 Are Configured to Assign Communities to the Incoming Prefixes from Neighboring Autonomous Systems*

```
Colorado
router bgp 100
 template peer-policy IBGP
  next-hop-self
  send-community
 exit-peer-policy
 !
 template peer-session bgp_top
  update-source Loopback0
 exit-peer-session
 !
 template peer-session ibgp
  remote-as 100
  password 7 1324243C345D547A
  inherit peer-session bgp_top
 exit-peer-session
 !
 no synchronization
 bgp log-neighbor-changes
 network 10.1.1.0 mask 255.255.255.0
```

```
 neighbor 10.0.0.1 remote-as 200
 neighbor 10.0.0.1 password 7 073D75737E080A16
 neighbor 10.0.0.1 route-map comm-200 in
 neighbor 10.0.0.5 remote-as 300
 neighbor 10.0.0.5 password 7 023451643B071C32
 neighbor 10.0.0.5 route-map comm-300 in
 neighbor 10.0.0.9 remote-as 400
 neighbor 10.0.0.9 password 7 00364539345A1815
 neighbor 10.0.0.9 route-map comm-400 in
 neighbor 192.168.255.2 inherit peer-session ibgp
 neighbor 192.168.255.2 inherit peer-policy IBGP
 neighbor 192.168.255.3 inherit peer-session ibgp
 neighbor 192.168.255.3 inherit peer-policy IBGP
 no auto-summary
!
ip bgp-community new-format
!
route-map comm-300 permit 10
 set community 300:3
!
route-map comm-200 permit 10
 set community 200:3
!
route-map comm-400 permit 10
 set community 400:3
!
```

```
NewMexico
router bgp 100
 template peer-policy IBGP
  next-hop-self
  send-community
 exit-peer-policy
 !
 template peer-session bgp_top
  update-source Loopback0
  timers 30 90
 exit-peer-session
 !
 template peer-session ibgp
  remote-as 100
  password 7 002520283B0A5B56
  inherit peer-session bgp_top
 exit-peer-session
 !
```

```
 no synchronization
 bgp log-neighbor-changes
 network 10.1.2.0 mask 255.255.255.0
 neighbor 10.0.0.34 remote-as 700
 neighbor 10.0.0.34 password 7 113B403A2713181F
 neighbor 10.0.0.34 route-map comm-700 in
 neighbor 10.0.0.38 remote-as 500
 neighbor 10.0.0.38 password 7 08131B7139181604
 neighbor 10.0.0.38 route-map comm-500 in
 neighbor 192.168.255.1 inherit peer-session ibgp
 neighbor 192.168.255.1 inherit peer-policy IBGP
 neighbor 192.168.255.3 inherit peer-session ibgp
 neighbor 192.168.255.3 inherit peer-policy IBGP
 no auto-summary
!
ip bgp-community new-format
!
ip as-path access-list 1 permit ^500$
!
route-map comm-500 permit 10
match as-path 1
 set community 500:2
!
route-map comm-500 deny 20
!
route-map comm-700 permit 10
 set community 700:1
!
```

```
Idaho
router bgp 100
 template peer-policy IBGP
  next-hop-self
  send-community
 exit-peer-policy
 !
 template peer-session bgp_top
  update-source Loopback0
  timers 30 90
 exit-peer-session
 !
 template peer-session ibgp
  remote-as 100
  password 7 0132352A645A565F
  inherit peer-session bgp_top
```

```
exit-peer-session
!
no synchronization
bgp log-neighbor-changes
network 10.1.3.0 mask 255.255.255.0
neighbor 10.0.0.26 remote-as 600
neighbor 10.0.0.26 password 7 02345C643B071C32
neighbor 10.0.0.26 route-map comm-600 in
neighbor 10.0.0.30 remote-as 800
neighbor 10.0.0.30 password 7 06345E71737E080A16
neighbor 10.0.0.30 route-map comm-800 in
neighbor 192.168.255.1 inherit peer-session ibgp
neighbor 192.168.255.1 inherit peer-policy IBGP
neighbor 192.168.255.2 inherit peer-session ibgp
neighbor 192.168.255.2 inherit peer-policy IBGP
no auto-summary
!
ip bgp-community new-format
!
ip as-path access-list 1 permit ^600$
!
route-map comm-600 permit 10

 match as-path 1
 set community 600:2
!
route-map comm-600 deny 20
!
route-map comm-800 permit 10
 set community 800:1
!
```

For each external neighbor, there is a separate route map that is applied as an incoming policy for that neighbor and sets a community for all prefixes received from that neighbor. Although the route maps are simple—just tag everything the neighbor sends—the configuration still feels awkward, especially in a chapter that discusses scalable configurations. A more real-life configuration would probably use decimal community numbers so that the same route map could be used for each neighbor type. Router Colorado, for example, would have just a single "customer" route map, setting the same community value, for all three external neighbors instead of having a unique route map for each neighbor, as shown in Example 5-27.

But there is no way for a router to detect the AS number of a prefix advertised by an external peer and then somehow add it to an AA:NN formatted community value. And because the objective of this exercise is to demonstrate both expanded community lists and the AA:NN format, you can take a small step away from a realistic configuration.

The route maps for the peering partners at NewMexico and Idaho, in addition to setting the peering partner community value, use an AS-path access list to match routes that originate in the neighboring AS (that is, whose AS_PATHs contain only the neighboring AS number) and deny all other routes. This enforces the part of the policy that says AS100 can reach prefixes in the peering partner AS but cannot use the peering partner to reach any prefix beyond the partner's AS.

Example 5-28 shows the results, at Colorado, of the configurations in Example 5-27. Each of the expected community values is specified with the **ip bgp community** command, and the correct prefixes are verified for each.

Example 5-28   *Prefixes from Each of the Neighboring Autonomous Systems Are Verified to Have the Correct Community Values Attached*

```
Colorado#show ip bgp community 700:1
BGP table version is 53, local router ID is 192.168.255.1
Status codes: s suppressed, d damped, h history, * valid, > best, i - internal,
              r RIB-failure, S Stale
Origin codes: i - IGP, e - EGP, ? - incomplete


   Network          Next Hop          Metric LocPrf Weight Path
*>i10.7.1.0/24      192.168.255.2          0    100      0 700 i
*>i10.7.2.0/24      192.168.255.2          0    100      0 700 i
*>i10.7.3.0/24      192.168.255.2          0    100      0 700 i
Colorado#show ip bgp community 800:1
BGP table version is 53, local router ID is 192.168.255.1
Status codes: s suppressed, d damped, h history, * valid, > best, i - internal,
              r RIB-failure, S Stale
Origin codes: i - IGP, e - EGP, ? - incomplete


   Network          Next Hop          Metric LocPrf Weight Path
*>i10.8.1.0/24      192.168.255.3          0    100      0 800 i
*>i10.8.2.0/24      192.168.255.3          0    100      0 800 i
*>i10.8.3.0/24      192.168.255.3          0    100      0 800 i
Colorado#show ip bgp community 500:2
BGP table version is 53, local router ID is 192.168.255.1
Status codes: s suppressed, d damped, h history, * valid, > best, i - internal,
              r RIB-failure, S Stale
Origin codes: i - IGP, e - EGP, ? - incomplete


   Network          Next Hop          Metric LocPrf Weight Path
*>i10.5.1.0/24      192.168.255.2          0    100      0 500 i
*>i10.5.2.0/24      192.168.255.2          0    100      0 500 i
```

```
*>i10.5.3.0/24      192.168.255.2              0    100      0 500 i
Colorado#show ip bgp community 600:2
BGP table version is 53, local router ID is 192.168.255.1
Status codes: s suppressed, d damped, h history, * valid, > best, i - internal,
              r RIB-failure, S Stale
Origin codes: i - IGP, e - EGP, ? - incomplete


   Network          Next Hop          Metric LocPrf Weight Path
*>i10.6.1.0/24      192.168.255.3          0    100      0 600 i
*>i10.6.2.0/24      192.168.255.3          0    100      0 600 i
*>i10.6.3.0/24      192.168.255.3          0    100      0 600 i
Colorado#show ip bgp community 200:3
BGP table version is 53, local router ID is 192.168.255.1
Status codes: s suppressed, d damped, h history, * valid, > best, i - internal,
              r RIB-failure, S Stale
Origin codes: i - IGP, e - EGP, ? - incomplete


   Network          Next Hop          Metric LocPrf Weight Path
*>  10.2.1.0/24     10.0.0.1               0             0 200 i
*>  10.2.2.0/24     10.0.0.1               0             0 200 i
*>  10.2.3.0/24     10.0.0.1               0             0 200 i
Colorado#show ip bgp community 300:3
BGP table version is 53, local router ID is 192.168.255.1
Status codes: s suppressed, d damped, h history, * valid, > best, i - internal,
              r RIB-failure, S Stale
Origin codes: i - IGP, e - EGP, ? - incomplete


   Network          Next Hop          Metric LocPrf Weight Path
*>  10.3.1.0/24     10.0.0.5               0             0 300 i
*>  10.3.2.0/24     10.0.0.5               0             0 300 i
*>  10.3.3.0/24     10.0.0.5               0             0 300 i
Colorado#show ip bgp community 400:3
BGP table version is 53, local router ID is 192.168.255.1
Status codes: s suppressed, d damped, h history, * valid, > best, i - internal,
              r RIB-failure, S Stale
Origin codes: i - IGP, e - EGP, ? - incomplete


   Network          Next Hop          Metric LocPrf Weight Path
*>  10.4.1.0/24     10.0.0.9               0             0 400 i
*>  10.4.2.0/24     10.0.0.9               0             0 400 i
*>  10.4.3.0/24     10.0.0.9               0             0 400 i
Colorado#
```

The next step is to configure the outgoing policies. We'll configure the Customer policy. The requirements are that a customer can reach the prefixes internal to AS100 and any prefix advertised by a transit partner but cannot reach any peering partner. Example 5-29 shows Colorado's configuration. The route map "Customers," configured as an outgoing policy to Colorado's three external neighbors, first uses AS-path access list 1 to permit all routes with an empty AS_PATH list. This permits any prefix that originates internally to AS100. Next, it uses the expanded community list named Transit to permit any routes with a community with any autonomous system number in the AA part and 1 in the NN part. This permits any prefixes advertised by the Transit Partners. Last, the route map denies all other prefixes.

Example 5-29 *Colorado Is Configured with an Outgoing Policy Named Customers*

```
router bgp 100
 template peer-policy IBGP
  next-hop-self
  send-community
 exit-peer-policy
 !
 template peer-session bgp_top
  update-source Loopback0
  timers 30 90
 exit-peer-session
 !
 template peer-session ibgp
  remote-as 100
  password 7 1324243C345D547A
  inherit peer-session bgp_top
 exit-peer-session
 !
 no synchronization
 bgp log-neighbor-changes
 network 10.1.1.0 mask 255.255.255.0
 neighbor 10.0.0.1 remote-as 200
 neighbor 10.0.0.1 password 7 073D75737E080A16
 neighbor 10.0.0.1 route-map comm-200 in
 neighbor 10.0.0.1 route-map Customers out
 neighbor 10.0.0.5 remote-as 300
 neighbor 10.0.0.5 password 7 023451643B071C32
 neighbor 10.0.0.5 route-map comm-300 in
 neighbor 10.0.0.5 route-map Customers out
 neighbor 10.0.0.9 remote-as 400
 neighbor 10.0.0.9 password 7 00364539345A1815
 neighbor 10.0.0.9 route-map comm-400 in
 neighbor 10.0.0.9 route-map Customers out
```

```
 neighbor 192.168.255.2 inherit peer-session ibgp
 neighbor 192.168.255.2 inherit peer-policy IBGP
 neighbor 192.168.255.3 inherit peer-session ibgp
 neighbor 192.168.255.3 inherit peer-policy IBGP
 no auto-summary
!
ip bgp-community new-format
!
ip community-list expanded Transit permit .*:1
ip as-path access-list 1 permit ^$
!
route-map comm-300 permit 10
 set community 300:3
!
route-map comm-200 permit 10
 set community 200:3
!
route-map comm-400 permit 10
 set community 400:3
!
route-map Customers permit 10
 match as-path 1
!
route-map Customers permit 20
 match community Transit
!
route-map Cust°mers deny 30
```

Example 5-30 shows the results at router Vermont in AS300. You can verify that the prefixes of autonomous systems 100, 700, and 800 are in the BGP table but no prefixes from the Peering Partners at AS500 or 600.

Example 5-30 *BGP Table at Router Vermont in AS300 Shows the Effects of the Outgoing Policy Configuration of Example 5-29. The BGP Tables of Utah and Nevada (Not Shown) Include the Same External Prefixes*

```
Vermont#show ip bgp
BGP table version is 213, local router ID is 192.168.255.5
Status codes: s suppressed, d damped, h history, * valid, > best, i - internal,
              r RIB-failure, S Stale
Origin codes: i - IGP, e - EGP, ? - incomplete

   Network          Next Hop           Metric LocPrf Weight Path
*> 10.1.1.0/24      10.0.0.6                0            0 100 i
*> 10.1.2.0/24      10.0.0.6                             0 100 i
```

```
*>  10.1.3.0/24       10.0.0.6                                    0 100 i
*>  10.3.1.0/24       0.0.0.0                     0          32768 i
*>  10.3.2.0/24       0.0.0.0                     0          32768 i
*>  10.3.3.0/24       0.0.0.0                     0          32768 i
*>  10.7.1.0/24       10.0.0.6                                    0 100 700 i
*>  10.7.2.0/24       10.0.0.6                                    0 100 700 i
*>  10.7.3.0/24       10.0.0.6                                    0 100 700 i
*>  10.8.1.0/24       10.0.0.6                                    0 100 800 i
*>  10.8.2.0/24       10.0.0.6                                    0 100 800 i
*>  10.8.3.0/24       10.0.0.6                                    0 100 800 i
Vermont#
```

Example 5-31 shows the configurations of NewMexico and Idaho after the outgoing policies for peering and transit partners have been added. These configurations, like Colorado's, use expanded community lists. But here, for demonstration purposes, the lists are identified by being numbered in the 100–500 range, rather than using the **expanded** keyword and a name.

The "Peering_Partner" policy on both routers uses community list 200 to match any route with a community of the AA:NN format and with an NN value of 1, 2, or 3. The matching routes are denied, and all other routes are permitted. The results at the peering partner routers, shown in Example 5-32, is that no prefixes from any customer AS, transit AS, or the opposite peering partner AS are known. Only the prefixes local to AS 600 and the prefixes from AS100 are in the BGP table. This enables the rule that a peering partner should reach only the AS100 prefixes.

Example 5-31   *Peering_Partner and Transit_Partner Policy Configurations for NewMexico and Idaho Referred to in Figure 5-7*

```
NewMexico
router bgp 100
 template peer-policy IBGP
  next-hop-self
  send-community
 exit-peer-policy
 !
 template peer-session bgp_top
  update-source Loopback0
  timers 30 90
 exit-peer-session
 !
 template peer-session ibgp
  remote-as 100
  password 7 002520283B0A5B56
  inherit peer-session bgp_top
 exit-peer-session
```

```
!
no synchronization
bgp log-neighbor-changes
network 10.1.2.0 mask 255.255.255.0
neighbor 10.0.0.34 remote-as 700
neighbor 10.0.0.34 password 7 113B403A2713181F
neighbor 10.0.0.34 route-map comm-700 in
neighbor 10.0.0.34 route-map Transit_Partner out
neighbor 10.0.0.38 remote-as 500
neighbor 10.0.0.38 password 7 08131B7139181604
neighbor 10.0.0.38 route-map comm-500 in
neighbor 10.0.0.38 route-map Peering_Partner out
neighbor 192.168.255.1 inherit peer-session ibgp
neighbor 192.168.255.1 inherit peer-policy IBGP
neighbor 192.168.255.3 inherit peer-session ibgp
neighbor 192.168.255.3 inherit peer-policy IBGP
no auto-summary
!
ip bgp-community new-format
!
ip community-list 200 permit .*:1
ip community-list 200 permit .*:2
ip community-list 200 permit .*:3
ip community-list 250 permit .*:1
ip community-list 250 permit .*:3
ip as-path access-list 1 permit ^500$
!
!
route-map comm-500 permit 10
 match as-path 1
 set community 500:2
!
route-map comm-500 deny 20
!
route-map comm-700 permit 10
 set community 700:1
!
route-map Transit_Partner permit 10
 match community 250
!
route-map Transit_Partner deny 20
!
route-map Peering_Partner deny 10
 match community 200
!
```

```
route-map Peering_Partner permit 20
!
```

```
Idaho
router bgp 100
 template peer-policy IBGP
  next-hop-self
  send-community
 exit-peer-policy
 !
 template peer-session bgp_top
  update-source Loopback0
  timers 30 90
 exit-peer-session
 !
 template peer-session ibgp
  remote-as 100
  password 7 0132352A645A565F
  inherit peer-session bgp_top
 exit-peer-session
 !
 no synchronization
 bgp log-neighbor-changes
 network 10.1.3.0 mask 255.255.255.0
 neighbor 10.0.0.26 remote-as 600
 neighbor 10.0.0.26 password 7 02345C643B071C32
 neighbor 10.0.0.26 route-map comm-600 in
 neighbor 10.0.0.26 route-map Peering_Partner out
 neighbor 10.0.0.30 remote-as 800
 neighbor 10.0.0.30 password 7 06345E71737E080A16
 neighbor 10.0.0.30 route-map comm-800 in
 neighbor 10.0.0.30 route-map Transit_Partner out
 neighbor 192.168.255.1 inherit peer-session ibgp
 neighbor 192.168.255.1 inherit peer-policy IBGP
 neighbor 192.168.255.2 inherit peer-session ibgp
 neighbor 192.168.255.2 inherit peer-policy IBGP
 no auto-summary
!
ip bgp-community new-format
!
ip community-list 200 permit .*:1
ip community-list 200 permit .*:2
ip community-list 200 permit .*:3
ip community-list 250 permit .*:1
ip community-list 250 permit .*:3
```

```
ip as-path access-list 1 permit ^600$
!
route-map comm-600 permit 10
 match as-path 1
 set community 600:2
!
route-map comm-600 deny 20
!
route-map comm-800 permit 10
 set community 800:1
!
route-map Peering_Partner deny 10
 match community 200
!
route-map Peering_Partner permit 20
!
route-map Transit_Partner permit 10
 match community 250
!
route-map Transit_Partner deny 20
!
```

Example 5-32 *Results of the Peering_Partner Policy Configured on Routers New Mexico and Idaho Are Shown in the BGP Tables of California and Montana*

```
California#show ip bgp
BGP table version is 253, local router ID is 192.168.255.7
Status codes: s suppressed, d damped, h history, * valid, > best, i - internal,
              r RIB-failure, S Stale
Origin codes: i - IGP, e - EGP, ? - incomplete

   Network          Next Hop          Metric LocPrf Weight Path
*> 10.1.1.0/24      10.0.0.37                        0 100 i
*> 10.1.2.0/24      10.0.0.37              0          0 100 i
*> 10.1.3.0/24      10.0.0.37                         0 100 i
*> 10.5.1.0/24      0.0.0.0                0      32768 i
*> 10.5.2.0/24      0.0.0.0                0      32768 i
*> 10.5.3.0/24      0.0.0.0                0      32768 i
California#
```
```
Montana#show ip bgp
BGP table version is 233, local router ID is 192.168.255.8
Status codes: s suppressed, d damped, h history, * valid, > best, i - internal,
              r RIB-failure, S Stale
```

```
Origin codes: i - IGP, e - EGP, ? - incomplete

   Network          Next Hop          Metric LocPrf Weight Path
*> 10.1.1.0/24      10.0.0.25                          0 100 i
*> 10.1.2.0/24      10.0.0.25                          0 100 i
*> 10.1.3.0/24      10.0.0.25           0              0 100 i
*> 10.6.1.0/24      0.0.0.0             0          32768 i
*> 10.6.2.0/24      0.0.0.0             0          32768 i
*> 10.6.3.0/24      0.0.0.0             0          32768 i
Montana#
```

The policy Transit_Partner configured on NewMexico and Idaho referred to in Example 5-31 uses the expanded community list 250 to identify routes belonging to the customer (AA:3) and transit partner (AA:1) communities. The route map permits these routes and denies all other routes. The results, shown in Example 5-33, allow the transit partner routers to see all customer routes and the routes from the opposite transit peer, but no other routes. You can see that neither router knows about the prefixes from the peering partner autonomous systems or the prefixes internal to AS100.

Example 5-33 *Results of the Transit_Partner Policy Configured on Routers NewMexico and Idaho Are Shown in the BGP Tables of Washington and Wyoming*

```
Washington#show ip bgp
BGP table version is 250, local router ID is 192.168.255.9
Status codes: s suppressed, d damped, h history, * valid, > best, i - internal,
              r RIB-failure, S Stale
Origin codes: i - IGP, e - EGP, ? - incomplete

   Network          Next Hop          Metric LocPrf Weight Path
*> 10.2.1.0/24      10.0.0.33                          0 100 200 i
*> 10.2.2.0/24      10.0.0.33                          0 100 200 i
*> 10.2.3.0/24      10.0.0.33                          0 100 200 i
*> 10.3.1.0/24      10.0.0.33                          0 100 300 i
*> 10.3.2.0/24      10.0.0.33                          0 100 300 i
*> 10.3.3.0/24      10.0.0.33                          0 100 300 i
*> 10.4.1.0/24      10.0.0.33                          0 100 400 i
*> 10.4.2.0/24      10.0.0.33                          0 100 400 i
*> 10.4.3.0/24      10.0.0.33                          0 100 400 i
*> 10.7.1.0/24      0.0.0.0             0          32768 i
*> 10.7.2.0/24      0.0.0.0             0          32768 i
*> 10.7.3.0/24      0.0.0.0             0          32768 i
*> 10.8.1.0/24      10.0.0.33                          0 100 800 i
*> 10.8.2.0/24      10.0.0.33                          0 100 800 i
*> 10.8.3.0/24      10.0.0.33                          0 100 800 i
```

```
Washington#

Wyoming#show ip bgp
BGP table version is 254, local router ID is 192.168.255.10
Status codes: s suppressed, d damped, h history, * valid, > best, i - internal,
              r RIB-failure, S Stale
Origin codes: i - IGP, e - EGP, ? - incomplete

   Network          Next Hop          Metric LocPrf Weight Path
*> 10.2.1.0/24      10.0.0.29                         0 100 200 i
*> 10.2.2.0/24      10.0.0.29                         0 100 200 i
*> 10.2.3.0/24      10.0.0.29                         0 100 200 i
*> 10.3.1.0/24      10.0.0.29                         0 100 300 i
*> 10.3.2.0/24      10.0.0.29                         0 100 300 i
*> 10.3.3.0/24      10.0.0.29                         0 100 300 i
*> 10.4.1.0/24      10.0.0.29                         0 100 400 i
*> 10.4.2.0/24      10.0.0.29                         0 100 400 i
*> 10.4.3.0/24      10.0.0.29                         0 100 400 i
*> 10.7.1.0/24      10.0.0.29                         0 100 700 i
*> 10.7.2.0/24      10.0.0.29                         0 100 700 i
*> 10.7.3.0/24      10.0.0.29                         0 100 700 i
*> 10.8.1.0/24      0.0.0.0               0      32768 i
*> 10.8.2.0/24      0.0.0.0               0      32768 i
*> 10.8.3.0/24      0.0.0.0               0      32768 i
Wyoming#
```

Adding and Deleting Communities

As a next step in your community exercise, suppose the prefix 10.4.2.0/24 in AS400 has some special significance to the Transit Partners AS700 and AS800. AS700 wants the prefix to belong to community 1:1, and AS800 wants the prefix to belong to community 400:800, as shown in Figure 5-8. Assuming you are AS100, you have no need to know what policies are applied to the communities, only that you have agreed to ensure that those particular communities transit our AS. (Not to mention that I couldn't think of a good story for this scenario, and want to demonstrate only additions and deletions for the community attribute.)

Example 5-34 shows Nevada's configuration. A route map named "pass-through" is used to identify the prefix 10.4.2.0/24, using prefix list 5, and then set the community values 1:1 and 400:800 for that route. The only feature of this configuration that you haven't seen in previous examples is that the **set community** statement sets more than one community value.

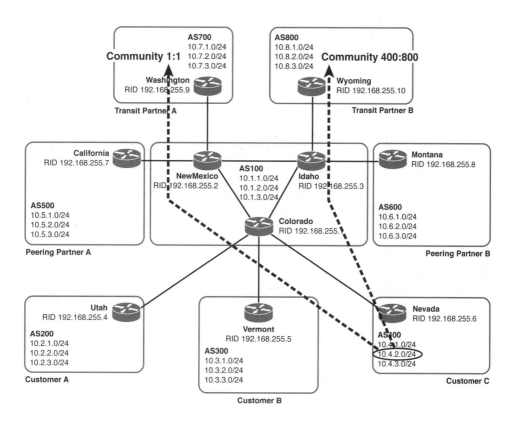

Figure 5-8   *Customer C Adds the Community Values 1:1 and 400:800 to Its Prefix 10.4.2.0/24 and Wants Transit Partner A to see 1:1 and Transit Partner B to See 400:800*

Example 5-34   *Router Nevada Is Configured to Add Community Values 1:1 and 400:800 to Prefix 10.4.2.0/24*

```
router bgp 400
 no synchronization
 bgp log-neighbor-changes
 network 10.4.1.0 mask 255.255.255.0
 network 10.4.2.0 mask 255.255.255.0
 network 10.4.3.0 mask 255.255.255.0
 timers bgp 30 90
 neighbor 10.0.0.10 remote-as 100
 neighbor 10.0.0.10 password 7 08131A7139181604
 neighbor 10.0.0.10 send-community
 neighbor 10.0.0.10 route-map pass-through out
 no auto-summary
!
ip bgp-community new-format
```

```
!
ip prefix-list 5 seq 5 permit 10.4.2.0/24
!
route-map pass-through permit 10
 match ip address prefix-list 5
 set community 1:1 400:800
!
route-map pass-through permit 20
!
```

Example 5-35 shows the results at Colorado, and they're not what you wanted. No prefixes are listed with either the community value of 1:1 or 400:800. And when the BGP entry for 10.4.2.0/24 is observed, only the community 400:3, configured previously in Example 5-27, is attached to the route.

Example 5-35   *Colorado Shows That There Are No Prefixes with Community Values of 1:1 or 400:800, and Prefix 10.4.2.0/24 Has Only the Community Value 400:3*

```
Colorado#show ip bgp community 1:1

Colorado#show ip bgp community 400:800

Colorado#show ip bgp 10.4.2.0/24
BGP routing table entry for 10.4.2.0/24, version 10
Paths: (1 available, best #1, table Default-IP-Routing-Table)
Flag: 0x820
  Advertised to update-groups:
        1
  400
    10.0.0.9 from 10.0.0.9 (192.168.255.6)
      Origin IGP, metric 0, localpref 100, valid, external, best
      Community: 400:3
Colorado#
```

This result, it turns out, is correct behavior. Looking back at Colorado's configuration referred to in Examples 5-27 or 5-29, the route map "comm-400" sets a community of 400:3 for all prefixes received from neighbor Nevada (10.0.0.9). But when the **set community** statement is used by itself, it deletes any community values that are carried by the matching BGP routes. Another way to look at this is that the default behavior of the **set community** statement is to change the community attributes of the matching route to whatever value the statement specifies.

In this example, you want the community attributes carried by the incoming prefix 10.4.2.0/24 to be preserved, and just add the community 400:3 so that AS100 can still apply the AS-internal policies defined in the earlier examples. For this to happen, you

need to use the keyword **additive** to tell the **set community** statement to add the specified community to any existing communities rather than replacing them.

Example 5-36 shows the route map "comm-400" changed to include the **additive** keyword. Nothing else about Colorado's configuration is changed, so only the route map
configuration is shown. If you want to remind yourself of the remainder of Colorado's
configuration, refer to Example 5-29.

Example 5-36 *Colorado's Route Map "comm-400" in Example 5-29 Is Changed to Use
the* **set community additive** *Statement so That Community 400:3 Is Added to Any Existing
Communities Rather Than Replacing Existing Communities*

```
!
route-map comm-400 permit 10
 set community 400:3 additive
 !
```

Example 5-37 shows the results. When the prefix 10.4.2.0/24 in Colorado's BGP table
displays now, communities 1:1, 400:3, and 400:800 are all present.

Example 5-37 *Prefix 10.4.2.0/24 Now Has All Three Communities Attached*

```
Colorado#show ip bgp 10.4.2.0
BGP routing table entry for 10.4.2.0/24, version 10
Paths: (1 available, best #1, table Default-IP-Routing-Table)
  Advertised to update-groups:
        1     2
  400
    10.0.0.9 from 10.0.0.9 (192.168.255.6)
      Origin IGP, metric 0, localpref 100, valid, external, best
      Community: 1:1 400:3 400:800
Colorado#
```

Now that you have verified that the two community attributes attached to 10.4.2.0/24
by router Nevada are retained in AS100, the next step is to ensure that AS700 receives
the route with only community 1:1, and AS800 receives the route with only community
400:800. The challenge at the AS100 border routers NewMexico and Idaho is that when
you add the **neighbor send-community** statement to the peer configurations for external neighbors Washington and Wyoming, all the prefixes advertised to those neighbors
would have all the community attributes configured in the previous exercises, meaningful only for the policies internal to AS100, attached. So NewMexico and Idaho need
additional policy configuration to remove the community attributes that you don't want
to send.

First, add the statements **neighbor 10.0.0.34 send-community** to NewMexico's BGP
configuration and **neighbor 10.0.0.30 send-community** to Idaho's BGP configuration.

You've seen those statements used multiple times so far, so there's no need to show the BGP configurations again. The statements, as you know, tell NewMexico and Idaho to allow community attributes to be attached to routes sent to Washington (10.0.0.34) and Wyoming (10.0.0.30). Example 5-38 verifies the results we expect at this point: All the prefixes that are sent to Washington and Wyoming have community attributes attached due to the policies previously implemented in AS100.

Example 5-38   *When the* **neighbor send-community** *Statement Is Added to the BGP Configurations at NewMexico and Idaho, All the Community Attributes Added to Prefixes in AS100 for Internal Routing Policies Remain Attached to the Routes When They Are Advertised to Washington and Wyoming*

```
Washington#show ip bgp community
BGP table version is 100, local router ID is 192.168.255.9
Status codes: s suppressed, d damped, h history, * valid, > best, i - internal,
              r RIB-failure, S Stale
Origin codes: i - IGP, e - EGP, ? - incomplete

   Network          Next Hop         Metric LocPrf Weight Path
*> 10.2.1.0/24      10.0.0.33                       0 100 200 i
*> 10.2.2.0/24      10.0.0.33                       0 100 200 i
*> 10.2.3.0/24      10.0.0.33                       0 100 200 i
*> 10.3.1.0/24      10.0.0.33                       0 100 300 i
*> 10.3.2.0/24      10.0.0.33                       0 100 300 i
*> 10.3.3.0/24      10.0.0.33                       0 100 300 i
*> 10.4.1.0/24      10.0.0.33                       0 100 400 i
*> 10.4.2.0/24      10.0.0.33                       0 100 400 i
*> 10.4.3.0/24      10.0.0.33                       0 100 400 i
*> 10.8.1.0/24      10.0.0.33                       0 100 800 i
*> 10.8.2.0/24      10.0.0.33                       0 100 800 i
*> 10.8.3.0/24      10.0.0.33                       0 100 800 i
Washington#
```

```
Wyoming#show ip bgp community
BGP table version is 100, local router ID is 192.168.255.10
Status codes: s suppressed, d damped, h history, * valid, > best, i - internal,
              r RIB-failure, S Stale
Origin codes: i - IGP, e - EGP, ? - incomplete

   Network          Next Hop         Metric LocPrf Weight Path
*> 10.2.1.0/24      10.0.0.29                       0 100 200 i
*> 10.2.2.0/24      10.0.0.29                       0 100 200 i
*> 10.2.3.0/24      10.0.0.29                       0 100 200 i
*> 10.3.1.0/24      10.0.0.29                       0 100 300 i
*> 10.3.2.0/24      10.0.0.29                       0 100 300 i
```

```
*> 10.3.3.0/24        10.0.0.29                                 0 100 300 i
*> 10.4.1.0/24        10.0.0.29                                 0 100 400 i
*> 10.4.2.0/24        10.0.0.29                                 0 100 400 i
*> 10.4.3.0/24        10.0.0.29                                 0 100 400 i
*> 10.7.1.0/24        10.0.0.29                                 0 100 700 i
*> 10.7.2.0/24        10.0.0.29                                 0 100 700 i
*> 10.7.3.0/24        10.0.0.29                                 0 100 700 i
Wyoming#
```

There are a couple ways to delete community attributes from routes. The first is to use the statement **set comm-list delete** within a route map, referencing a community list. Example 5-39 shows NewMexico's configuration, last seen in Example 5-31, modified to use this statement. The BGP configuration itself remains the same except for the previously added **neighbor 10.0.0.34 send-community** statement. The outbound policy Transit_Partner is still used so that the previously defined policies are still in effect but modified to add the necessary community attribute deletions.

Example 5-39 *NewMexico's Route Map Transit_Partner Is Modified to Use the* **set comm-list delete** *Statement to Eliminate Unwanted Community Attributes from Routes Before They're Advertised to Neighbor Washington (10.0.0.34)*

```
router bgp 100
 template peer-policy IBGP
  next-hop-self
  send-community
 exit-peer-policy
 !
 template peer-session bgp_top
  update-source Loopback0
  timers 30 90
 exit-peer-session
 !
 template peer-session ibgp
  remote-as 100
  password 7 002520283B0A5B56
  inherit peer-session bgp_top
 exit-peer-session
 !
 no synchronization
 bgp log-neighbor-changes
 network 10.1.2.0 mask 255.255.255.0
 neighbor 10.0.0.34 remote-as 700
 neighbor 10.0.0.34 send-community
 neighbor 10.0.0.34 password 7 113B403A2713181F
 neighbor 10.0.0.34 route-map comm-700 in
```

```
 neighbor 10.0.0.34 route-map Transit_Partner out
 neighbor 10.0.0.38 remote-as 500
 neighbor 10.0.0.38 password 7 08131B7139181604
 neighbor 10.0.0.38 route-map comm-500 in
 neighbor 10.0.0.38 route-map Peering_Partner out
 neighbor 192.168.255.1 inherit peer-session ibgp
 neighbor 192.168.255.1 inherit peer-policy IBGP
 neighbor 192.168.255.3 inherit peer-session ibgp
 neighbor 192.168.255.3 inherit peer-policy IBGP
 no auto-summary
!
ip bgp-community new-format
!
ip community-list 200 permit .*:1
ip community-list 200 permit .*:2
ip community-list 200 permit .*:3
ip community-list 250 permit .*:1
ip community-list 250 permit .*:3
ip community-list 275 permit 1:1
ip community-list 300 deny 1:1
ip community-list 300 permit .*:.*
ip community-list 350 permit .*:.*

ip as-path access-list 1 permit ^500$
!
!
route-map comm-500 permit 10
 match as-path 1
 set community 500:2
!
route-map comm-500 deny 20
!
route-map comm-700 permit 10
 set community 700:1
!
route-map Transit_Partner permit 5
 match community 275
 set comm-list 300 delete
!
route-map Transit_Partner permit 10
 match community 250
 set comm-list 350 delete
!
route-map Transit_Partner deny 20
!
```

```
route-map Peering_Partner deny 10
 match community 200
!
route-map Peering_Partner permit 20
!
```

A new stanza of the route map Transit_Partner is added with a sequence number of 5 to ensure that it appears before the other stanzas. This stanza matches any route with a community attribute of 1:1 as specified in community list 275. It then uses the **set comm-list delete** statement to reference expanded community list 300, which denies community 1:1—that is, this community is not deleted—and then permits all other communities to be deleted. The matching routes, after the specified community attributes have been deleted, are then sent on their way.

Stanza 10 of the route map is also modified. Where before this stanza just permitted all routes with community attributes matching those in expanded community list 250, those matching routes are now "scrubbed" of all community attributes, as specified in community list 350. Note that this is not the only approach for accomplishing the same results. Rather than referencing community list 350, the **set comm-list delete** statement could have instead referenced community list 250. In that case, a line would need to be added to that community list to permit community 400:800 to ensure that that attribute is also deleted. The deciding factor between these two options is whether you want to delete all community attributes—including any attributes that might show up in future configuration modifications—or delete a specific list of communities and only those communities.

Example 5-40 uses three commands to verify that your modified policy works. First, a **show ip bgp** verifies that Washington is still receiving the same prefixes specified by the policies of the earlier exercises. This output is the same as the one shown in Example 5-33, so you are assured that nothing in those polices has changed. Next, **show ip bgp community** shows that the only prefix in Washington's BGP table is 10.4.2.0/24. Compare this with the previous output of the same command in Example 5-38. Last, a **show ip bgp 10.4.2.0** verifies that the route still has community attribute 1:1, but 400:3 and 400:800 have been deleted. Compare this with the output in Example 5-37.

Example 5-40 *Washington's BGP Table Is Examined to Show That the Correct Prefixes Are Still Received from NewMexico, That 10.4.2.0/24 Is the Only Prefix with One or More Community Attributes Attached, and That 1:1 Is the Only Community Attribute Attached to That Prefix*

```
Washington#show ip bgp
BGP table version is 172, local router ID is 192.168.255.9
Status codes: s suppressed, d damped, h history, * valid, > best, i - internal,
              r RIB-failure, S Stale
Origin codes: i - IGP, e - EGP, ? - incomplete
```

```
     Network          Next Hop          Metric LocPrf Weight Path
*>  10.2.1.0/24       10.0.0.33                           0 100 200 i
*>  10.2.2.0/24       10.0.0.33                           0 100 200 i
*>  10.2.3.0/24       10.0.0.33                           0 100 200 i
*>  10.3.1.0/24       10.0.0.33                           0 100 300 i
*>  10.3.2.0/24       10.0.0.33                           0 100 300 i
*>  10.3.3.0/24       10.0.0.33                           0 100 300 i
*>  10.4.1.0/24       10.0.0.33                           0 100 400 i
*>  10.4.2.0/24       10.0.0.33                           0 100 400 i
*>  10.4.3.0/24       10.0.0.33                           0 100 400 i
*>  10.7.1.0/24       0.0.0.0               0             32768 i
*>  10.7.2.0/24       0.0.0.0               0             32768 i
*>  10.7.3.0/24       0.0.0.0               0             32768 i
*>  10.8.1.0/24       10.0.0.33                           0 100 800 i
*>  10.8.2.0/24       10.0.0.33                           0 100 800 i
*>  10.8.3.0/24       10.0.0.33                           0 100 800 i
Washington#
Washington#show ip bgp community
BGP table version is 172, local router ID is 192.168.255.9
Status codes: s suppressed, d damped, h history, * valid, > best, i - internal,
              r RIB-failure, S Stale
Origin codes: i - IGP, e - EGP, ? - incomplete


     Network          Next Hop          Metric LocPrf Weight Path
*>  10.4.2.0/24       10.0.0.33                           0 100 400 i
Washington#
Washington#show ip bgp 10.4.2.0
BGP routing table entry for 10.4.2.0/24, version 169
Paths: (1 available, best #1, table Default-IP-Routing-Table)
  Not advertised to any peer
  100 400
    10.0.0.33 from 10.0.0.33 (192.168.255.2)
      Origin IGP, localpref 100, valid, external, best
      Community: 1:1
Washington#
```

There is more than one way to delete community attributes from a route. In addition to the **set comm-list delete** statement, there is the **set community none** statement that deletes all community attributes connected to a matched route.

Example 5-41 shows Idaho's configuration, using this second statement. The first stanza of the route map Transit_Peer looks just like the one configured at NewMexico, other than matching on and allowing community 400:800 instead of 1:1. The real difference is in the second stanza, where instead of using the **set comm-list delete** to reference a community list with the specific community attributes you want to delete, **set community none** is used to simply delete all community attributes attached to all matching routes.

Example 5-41   *Peering_Partner and Transit_Partner Policy Configurations for NewMexico and Idaho in Figure 5-7*

```
router bgp 100
 template peer-policy IBGP
  next-hop-self
  send-community
 exit-peer-policy
 !
 template peer-session bgp_top
  update-source Loopback0
  timers 30 90
 exit-peer-session
 !
 template peer-session ibgp
  remote-as 100
  password 7 0132352A645A565F
  inherit peer-session bgp_top
 exit-peer-session
 !
 no synchronization
 bgp log-neighbor-changes
 network 10.1.3.0 mask 255.255.255.0
 neighbor 10.0.0.26 remote-as 600
 neighbor 10.0.0.26 password 7 02345C643B071C32
 neighbor 10.0.0.26 route-map comm-600 in
 neighbor 10.0.0.26 route-map Peering_Partner out
 neighbor 10.0.0.30 remote-as 800
 neighbor 10.0.0.30 password 7 06345E71737E080A16
 neighbor 10.0.0.30 send-community
 neighbor 10.0.0.30 route-map comm-800 in
 neighbor 10.0.0.30 route-map Transit_Partner out
 neighbor 192.168.255.1 inherit peer-session ibgp
 neighbor 192.168.255.1 inherit peer-policy IBGP
 neighbor 192.168.255.2 inherit peer-session ibgp
 neighbor 192.168.255.2 inherit peer-policy IBGP
 no auto-summary
 !
 ip bgp-community new-format
 !
 ip community-list 200 permit .*:1
```

```
ip community-list 200 permit .*:2
ip community-list 200 permit .*:3
ip community-list 250 permit .*:1
ip community-list 250 permit .*:3
ip community-list 275 permit 400:800
ip community-list 300 deny 400:800
ip community-list 300 permit .*:.*
ip as-path access-list 1 permit ^600$
!
route-map comm-600 permit 10
 match as-path 1
 set community 600:2
!
route-map comm-600 deny 20
!
route-map comm-800 permit 10
 set community 800:1
!
route-map Peering_Partner deny 10
 match community 200
!
route-map Peering_Partner permit 20
!
route-map Transit_Partner permit 5
 match community 275
 set comm-list 300 delete
!
route-map Transit_Partner permit 10
 match community 250
 set community none
!
route-map Transit_Partner deny 20
!
```

Whether you use the **set comm-list delete** statement or the set community none statement depends on whether you need to delete specific communities or delete all communities.

Example 5-42 verifies the results at router Wyoming by again showing that all expected routes are received, that prefix 10.4.2.0/24 is the only route with one or more communities, and that 400:800 is the only attached community for that route.

Example 5-42 *Wyoming's BGP Table Is Examined to Show That the Correct Prefixes Are Still Received from Idaho, That 10.4.2.0/24 Is the Only Prefix with One or More Community Attributes Attached, and That 400:800 Is the Only Community Attribute Attached to That Prefix*

```
Wyoming#show ip bgp
BGP table version is 142, local router ID is 192.168.255.10
Status codes: s suppressed, d damped, h history, * valid, > best, i - internal,
              r RIB-failure, S Stale
Origin codes: i - IGP, e - EGP, ? - incomplete

   Network          Next Hop          Metric LocPrf Weight Path
*> 10.2.1.0/24      10.0.0.29                            0 100 200 i
*> 10.2.2.0/24      10.0.0.29                            0 100 200 i
*> 10.2.3.0/24      10.0.0.29                            0 100 200 i
*> 10.3.1.0/24      10.0.0.29                            0 100 300 i
*> 10.3.2.0/24      10.0.0.29                            0 100 300 i
*> 10.3.3.0/24      10.0.0.29                            0 100 300 i
*> 10.4.1.0/24      10.0.0.29                            0 100 400 i
*> 10.4.2.0/24      10.0.0.29                            0 100 400 i
*> 10.4.3.0/24      10.0.0.29                            0 100 400 i
*> 10.7.1.0/24      10.0.0.29                            0 100 700 i
*> 10.7.2.0/24      10.0.0.29                            0 100 700 i
*> 10.7.3.0/24      10.0.0.29                            0 100 700 i
*> 10.8.1.0/24      0.0.0.0                0         32768 i
*> 10.8.2.0/24      0.0.0.0                0         32768 i
*> 10.8.3.0/24      0.0.0.0                0         32768 i
Wyoming#
Wyoming#show ip bgp community
BGP table version is 142, local router ID is 192.168.255.10
Status codes: s suppressed, d damped, h history, * valid, > best, i - internal,
              r RIB-failure, S Stale
Origin codes: i - IGP, e - EGP, ? - incomplete

   Network          Next Hop          Metric LocPrf Weight Path
*> 10.4.2.0/24      10.0.0.29                            0 100 400 i
Wyoming#
Wyoming#show ip bgp 10.4.2.0
BGP routing table entry for 10.4.2.0/24, version 139
Paths: (1 available, best #1, table Default-IP-Routing-Table)
  Not advertised to any peer
  100 400
    10.0.0.29 from 10.0.0.29 (192.168.255.3)
      Origin IGP, localpref 100, valid, external, best
    Community: 400:800
Wyoming#
```

Extended Community Lists

The 32-bit community attribute you have been studying so far seems like it would scale to any application, even when communities occasionally cross AS boundaries. However, newer network technologies raise concerns about the *standard* community attribute being neither scalable enough nor flexible enough for new applications. As a result, you now have, in addition to the standard community attribute, an *extended* community attribute that is either 64 bits (8 bytes) for IPv4 networks, specified in RFC 4360, or 160 bits (20 bytes) for IPv6, as specified in RFC 5701. Extended communities are designed to provide two improvements over standard communities:

- The larger size makes the community extendable over a larger range with less concern about overlapping other communities.

- The extended community attribute includes a type field that allows its format to be adaptable to different uses.

The extended community attribute is mainly driven by the MPLS-based multiservice networks that have arisen in service provider networks and some large enterprise networks. Although MPLS backbones are far beyond the scope of this book—a good treatment of the topic easily requires at least as many pages as this volume—a brief overview is called for to provide context for extended communities.

Multi-Protocol Label Switching (MPLS) was originally intended to provide high switching and forwarding speeds in routers (and other devices) comparable to ATM speeds. This was accomplished by encapsulating a frame or packet behind a 32-bit MPLS header, which includes a fixed-length nonhierarchical address called a label, conceptually similar to ATM VPI/VCI and Frame Relay DLCI addresses. The idea was that by eliminating longest-match IP route lookups, packets could be switched much faster within limited scales. However, the advent of vastly faster switching silicon, improved router architectures, and more sophisticated longest-match address algorithms resulted in a new generation of routers that were far faster than ATM switches without the need for MPLS.

The aspect of MPLS that stuck and that changed the service provider industry through the first decade of the 21st century, is the ability to encapsulate any kind of L2 or L3 data unit behind a common header and then switch the MPLS packets across a shared MPLS backbone. MPLS headers can even be "stacked"—that is, multiple headers can be added—to create scalable tunnels within tunnels. The result is a virtual circuit network such as ATM or Frame Relay but using routers rather than specialized switches.

As a result service providers could consolidate services that had required separate cores—usually IP data, telephony, and video—onto a single shared infrastructure, saving capital and operational expense, and could roll out new services to compete on multiple fronts. Suddenly, cable TV companies were offering telephone service and local telephone companies were offering entertainment services. And everyone was offering

Internet access. These same companies also began supplanting legacy business data communications companies with their own virtualized point-to-point and point-to-multipoint connection services, Virtual Private LAN Services (VPLS), and Layer 2 and Layer 3 virtual private networks (VPN).

It's these last services—VPLS, L2VPNs, and L3VPNs—that bring you to the need for extended communities. Figure 5-9 shows an MPLS network with three L3VPN customers attached, and each customer has three or four sites. The acronym VPN tells you its fundamental characteristics. Reading it backward

- **Network:** The VPN connects two or more devices or sites.

- **Private:** No customer can "see" any other customer. Customer A sites can see only other Customer A sites, Customer B sites can see only other Customer B sites, and so on. The separation also extends to addressing. As shown in Figure 5-9, multiple customers can use the same addresses.

- **Virtual:** There's no physical separation of customers within the cloud. The MPLS core is responsible for ensuring that reachability information and traffic is confined to the right customer.

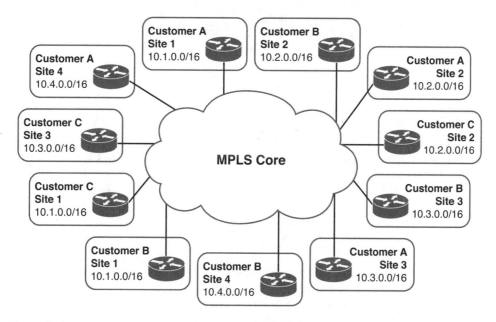

Figure 5-9 *An MPLS Network Can Virtualize Private Network Connectivity Across a Shared Infrastructure*

The key to keeping reachability information for each VPN separate and private is to maintain separate routing tables at each edge router, as shown in Figure 5-10. These L3VPN routing tables are called Virtual Routing and Forwarding tables, or VRFs. Next hops for the prefixes in each table are either MPLS tunnels, called Label Switched Paths (LSPs), or locally attached customer routers. (I'm generalizing much of the details of the VRFs because this discussion is more concerned with how the information gets into the tables than how the tables are structured.)

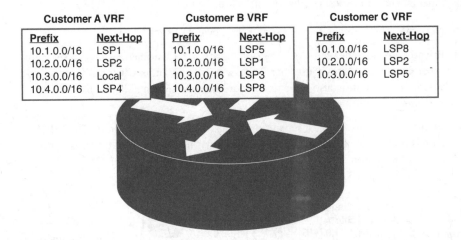

Customer A VRF

Prefix	Next-Hop
10.1.0.0/16	LSP1
10.2.0.0/16	LSP2
10.3.0.0/16	Local
10.4.0.0/16	LSP4

Customer B VRF

Prefix	Next-Hop
10.1.0.0/16	LSP5
10.2.0.0/16	LSP1
10.3.0.0/16	LSP3
10.4.0.0/16	LSP8

Customer C VRF

Prefix	Next-Hop
10.1.0.0/16	LSP8
10.2.0.0/16	LSP2
10.3.0.0/16	LSP5

Figure 5-10 *Separation of Reachability Information Is Maintained by Using VPN-Specific Routing Tables Called VRFs*

As Figure 5-11 shows, a single BGP instance advertises reachability across the core. But if all NLRI from all VRFs are advertised by the same BGP instance, two questions arise:

- If prefixes can overlap among different VPNs, as shown in Figure 5-9, how does BGP distinguish them? How, for example, does BGP distinguish 10.1.0.0/16 belonging to Customer A from 10.1.0.0/16 belonging to Customer B, and 10.1.0.0/16 belonging to Customer C?

- When NLRI are received in a BGP Update, how does the receiving router know which prefix belongs in which VRF?

The first question is answered by prepending an 8-byte VPN-specific *route distinguisher* to the prefixes of each VPN, turning the non-unique prefixes into unique prefixes. The concept is shown in Figure 5-12. The resulting 12-byte VPN-IPv4 or 24-byte VPN-IPv6 address belongs to a new address family, so multiprotocol BGP (see Chapter 6, "Multiprotocol BGP,") advertises the addresses.

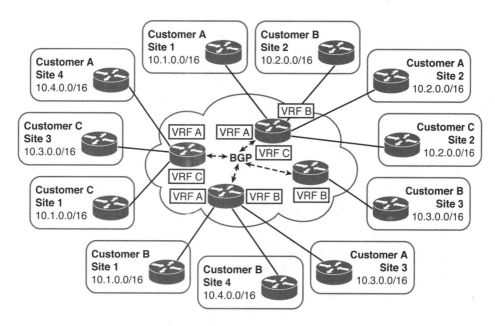

Figure 5-11 *Reachability Information in the Individual VRFs Are Advertised Across the MPLS Core by a Shared BGP Instance*

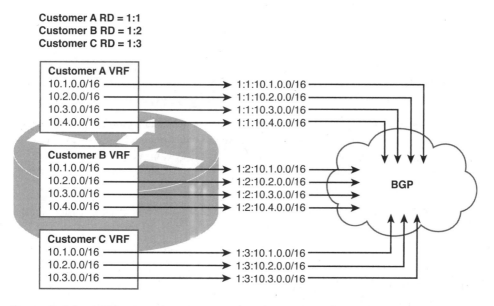

Figure 5-12 *A VPN-Specific Route Distinguisher (RD) Is Prepended onto IPv4 or IPv6 VPN Addresses Before They Are Advertised into BGP so That Overlapping Addresses in the VRFs Are Unique in the BGP Tables*

The second question is answered by attaching a special community attribute, called a route target, to the route that tells the receiving routers what VRF to put the route into, as shown in Figure 5-13. Perhaps the route distinguisher could have been used for the same purpose, but communities are better choices because they are designed for applying policies, and because you can apply more sophisticated policies to them than just sorting prefixes into VRFs, if necessary.

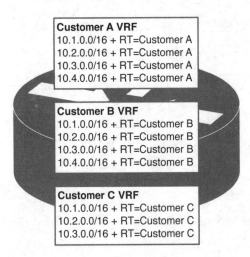

Customer A VRF
10.1.0.0/16 + RT=Customer A
10.2.0.0/16 + RT=Customer A
10.3.0.0/16 + RT=Customer A
10.4.0.0/16 + RT=Customer A

Customer B VRF
10.1.0.0/16 + RT=Customer B
10.2.0.0/16 + RT=Customer B
10.3.0.0/16 + RT=Customer B
10.4.0.0/16 + RT=Customer B

Customer C VRF
10.1.0.0/16 + RT=Customer C
10.2.0.0/16 + RT=Customer C
10.3.0.0/16 + RT=Customer C

Figure 5-13 *An Extended Community Attribute Called the Route Target (RT) Is Attached to VPN-IPv4 or VPN-IPv6 NLRI to Tell Receiving BGP Routers What VRF to Place the Prefix Into*

As mentioned previously, the larger size and flexible format of the extended community attribute makes in better suited for applications such as large MPLS VPN networks where there may be a tremendous number of prefixes advertised over the MPLS core.

Figure 5-14 shows the formats of the IPv4 and IPv6 extended community attribute. The key feature of the format that distinguishes extended communities for standard communities is the Type field, which specifies what the format of the Value field will be. There is also a Subtype field, the format of which can change depending on the type. Within the type field, there are two flags:

- **IANA Authority (I):** Designates whether the IANA-assignable type as either "first come first served (T=0) or part of the type field is reserved for IANA assignable types (T=1).

- **Transitive (T):** This flag designates whether the attribute is transitive (T=0) or non-transitive (T=1) across AS boundaries.

- **Remaining 6 bits:** Indicates the structure of the community attribute and is type-dependent.

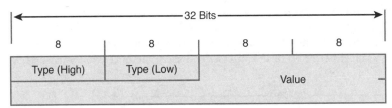

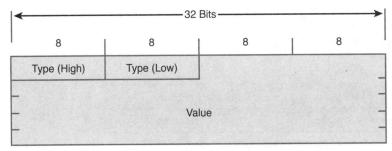

Figure 5-14   *Basic Format of the IPv4 and IPv6 Extended Community Attribute*

Current usage defines five formats of extended community.

- Two-Octet AS-Specific Extended Community
- Four-Octet AS-Specific Extended Community
- IPv4-Address-Specific Extended Community
- IPv6-Address-Specific Extended Community
- Opaque Extended Community

Figure 5-15 shows the three most basic of these formats. IPv6-Address-Specfic extended communities and Four-Octet AS-Specific extended communities match their IPv4 or two-octet AS counterparts except with the Global Administrator fields adjusted to the appropriate length.

The AS-specific and address-specific communities are used with L3VPNs, and provide designers with the flexibility to adapt to the scope of the VPN network. If the network spans multiple autonomous systems, the RT might use the AS-specific format to include a reference point to the originating AS. And example AS-specific RT might be 65501:23, and an example of an IPv4-address-specific extended community might be 192.168.15.20:65. In the first case the Global Administrator field is a 2-byte AS number and the Local Administrator field is any arbitrary 4-byte number the local AS chooses, which has meaning within that AS. In the second case the Global Administrator field is an IPv4 address and the Local Administrator field is a 2-byte arbitrary number chosen by the local administrative authority. In small-scale L3 VPN implementations the designers sometimes skip using either ASNs or IP addresses and use something simple such as 1:3.

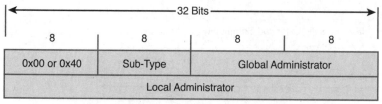

Two-Octet AS-Specific Extended Community

IPv4 Address Specific Extended Community

Opaque Extended Community

Figure 5-15 *Formats of Different Extended Community Types*

Four-Octet AS-Specific extended communities differ only in that newer 4-byte ASNs are used. Similarly, an IPv6-Address-Specific RT differs only in the use of an IPv6 address instead of an IPv4 address. The last format, the Opaque Extended community, is used when there is a need for a more generic structure in the Value field.

There is much more to know about extended communities, almost all of which is outside the scope of this book. The purpose of this section is just to give you a broad idea of how extended communities differ from standard communities and at least one context in which they are used. You can read the full listing of different extended community types in RFC 7153, and most any book on MPLS-based VPNs can give you a good perspective on how they are used.

Scaling BGP Functions

In addition to controlling complex BGP configurations, as discussed in the previous section, there must also be ways to scale and tune the BGP process running on an individual router. BGP is tasked with handling huge numbers of routes—far beyond the capabilities of OSPF or IS-IS—and to handle complex routing policies attached to those routes. Therefore, you need to ensure that a BGP process on a given router is well balanced to perform as well as it can without consuming all the available processing and memory resources on the router.

You've already encountered one mechanism for scaling the BGP process, dynamic update peer groups, earlier in this chapter. This section delves further into the tools available to you for scaling the BGP process.

Route Flap Dampening

You certainly know by now that BGP—the "language of the Internet"—is designed to handle hundreds of thousands of routes. The problem is that when there are that many routes, the chances are good that at least a few are unstable. That is, they "flap," going down and coming back up in short periods of time. Each time a route goes down, BGP has to withdraw the route and find an alternative path if one exists. And each time the route comes back up, BGP has to update its neighbors that the route is good again. The problem was discussed earlier in the context of aggregation, where misbehaving routes are hidden behind an aggregate route and flapping has only local effects. But there are still occasions in which an unstable route is visible on a wider, possibly Internet, scale.

Route Flap Dampening (RFD), specified in RFC 2439, is a process that can assign a penalty to a flapping. If the route accumulates enough penalties, the route is suppressed— that is, it is not advertised—for a certain period of time. By default, a route is assigned a penalty value of 1000 for each flap. If the value of the route's accumulated penalties exceeds 2000, the route is suppressed until the penalty value drops below 750. These upper and lower thresholds are the *suppress limit* and the *reuse limit*, as shown in Figure 5-16. The accumulated penalty is reduced every 5 seconds, at a rate such that the penalty is reduced by one-half every 15 minutes. You can see that this rate, known as the *half-life*, is exponential. If the penalty is 3000, it is reduced by 1500 over 15 minutes; if the penalty is 300, it is reduced by 150 over 15 minutes. There is also a maximum time the route can be suppressed, known as the *maximum suppress limit*. By default, this limit is four times the half-life, or 60 minutes. The maximum suppress limit ensures that a rapidly flapping route, accumulating many penalties over a short time, doesn't get a "life sentence" where it can never be advertised again.

Note   Depending on the document you are reading, the function covered in this section might be called "damping" or "dampening." IETF and RIR documentation usually uses damping, whereas Cisco documentation usually uses dampening. I tend to use the terms interchangeably, often with no conscious choice. Because this is a Cisco Press publication, "dampening" is used unless there is a reference to a specific document using the alternative term.

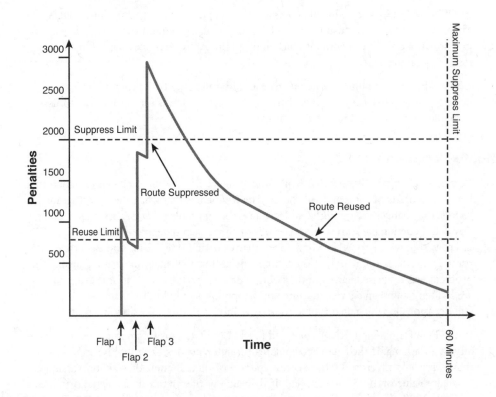

Figure 5-16 *Route Flap Dampening Assigns Penalties to an Unstable Route and Suppresses the Route if the Accumulated Penalties Exceed a Predetermined Threshold*

Route dampening is enabled under the BGP process configuration with the command **bgp dampening**. If you want to change the default values, the syntax is **bgp dampening** *half-life reuse suppress max-suppress*.

Figure 5-17 shows a topology in which one router, Colorado, is homed to five other autonomous systems. If the routes advertised by any of the remote autonomous systems flaps, Colorado must advertise the change to all other EBGP peers. Although this may not be much of a burden on the sample topology, imagine the effects if Colorado has 150 EBGP peers rather than the five shown. A regularly flapping route could cause a heavy processing burden on that hub router.

Example 5-43 provides the BGP configuration for Colorado.

Example 5-43 *Configuring Colorado to Send Updates to EBGP Peers to Advertise Changes When a Route Flaps*

```
router bgp 100
bgp dampening
network 10.1.11.0 mask 255.255.255.0
```

```
network 10.1.12.0 mask 255.255.255.0
neighbor 10.1.255.2 remote-as 200
neighbor 10.1.255.2 ebgp-multihop 2
neighbor 10.1.255.2 update-source Loopback2
neighbor 10.1.255.3 remote-as 300
neighbor 10.1.255.3 ebgp-multihop 2
neighbor 10.1.255.3 update-source Loopback2
neighbor 10.1.255.4 remote-as 400
neighbor 10.1.255.4 ebgp-multihop 2
neighbor 10.1.255.4 update-source Loopback2
neighbor 10.1.255.5 remote-as 500
neighbor 10.1.255.5 ebgp-multihop 2
neighbor 10.1.255.5 update-source Loopback2
neighbor 10.1.255.6 remote-as 600
neighbor 10.1.255.6 ebgp-multihop 2
neighbor 10.1.255.6 update-source Loopback2
no auto-summary
```

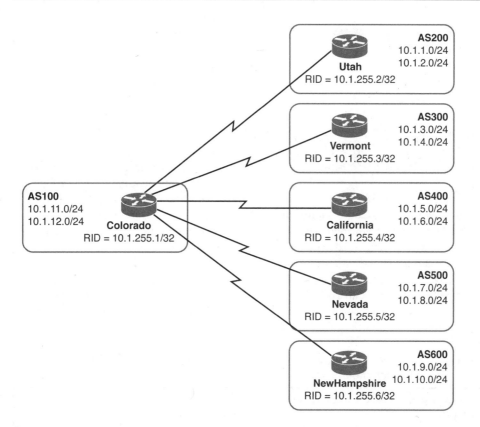

Figure 5-17 *If a Route in Any of the "Spoke" Autonomous Systems Flaps, the "Hub" Router, Colorado, Must Send an Update to All Its EBGP Peers Advertising the Change*

Example 5-44 shows Colorado's BGP table. Note that 10.1.4.0/24 is marked with a **d**, indicating that it has been damped, or suppressed. 10.1.7.0/24 has been marked with an **h**. This means that there is a history of flapping; that is, although the route has not accumulated a large-enough penalty to be suppressed, it does have a penalty.

Example 5-44 *Two Routes, 10.1.4.0/24 and 10.1.7.0/24, Have Accumulated Penalties; the First Has Accumulated More than 2000 and Has Been Dampened*

```
Colorado#show ip bgp
BGP table version is 756, local router ID is 10.1.255.1
Status codes: s suppressed, d damped, h history, * valid, > best, i - internal
Origin codes: i - IGP, e - EGP, ? - incomplete
   Network          Next Hop         Metric LocPrf Weight Path
*> 10.1.1.0/24      10.1.255.2            0             0 200 i
*> 10.1.2.0/24      10.1.255.2            0             0 200 i
*> 10.1.3.0/24      10.1.255.3            0             0 300 i
*d 10.1.4.0/24      10.1.255.3            0             0 300 i
*> 10.1.5.0/24      10.1.255.4            0             0 400 i
*> 10.1.6.0/24      10.1.255.4            0             0 400 i
 h 10.1.7.0/24      10.1.255.5            0             0 500 i
*> 10.1.8.0/24      10.1.255.5            0             0 500 i
*> 10.1.9.0/24      10.1.255.6            0             0 600 i
*> 10.1.10.0/24     10.1.255.6            0             0 600 i
*> 10.1.11.0/24     0.0.0.0               0         32768 i
*> 10.1.12.0/24     0.0.0.0               0         32768 i
```

The unstable routes are readily apparent in the BGP table of Example 5-44 because there are not many entries. What about a table with thousands of BGP entries, however? Finding unstable routes by looking for a **d** or **h** could be impractical. Two commands make finding these routes easier: **show ip bgp flap-statistics** and **show ip bgp damp-ened-paths**. As the names imply, the first command shows all routes that have flapped and how many times a route has flapped. The second command shows only those routes that have been suppressed. Example 5-45 shows these commands used at Colorado; notice that for suppressed routes, both outputs indicate when the route is expected to be advertised again. This time is contingent on the route's not being assigned further penalties. Note that flap statistics are recorded only if BGP dampening is configured. You cannot use the command **show ip bgp flap-statistics** to check for unstable routes on a router that is not running the dampening process.

Example 5-45 *You Can Display Only Those Routes in the BGP Table That Have Flapped or Only Those Routes That Have Been Suppressed*

```
Colorado#show ip bgp flap-statistics
BGP table version is 756, local router ID is 10.1.255.1
Status codes: s suppressed, d damped, h history, * valid, > best, i - internal
```

```
Origin codes: i - IGP, e - EGP, ? - incomplete


   Network          From           Flaps Duration Reuse    Path
*d 10.1.4.0/24      10.1.255.3      3     00:15:52 00:19:40 300
 h 10.1.7.0/24      10.1.255.5      2     00:20:49          500


Colorado#show ip bgp dampened-paths
BGP table version is 757, local router ID is 10.1.255.1
Status codes: s suppressed, d damped, h history, * valid, > best, i - internal
Origin codes: i - IGP, e - EGP, ? - incomplete


   Network          From           Reuse    Path
*d 10.1.4.0/24      10.1.255.3     00:19:2 300 i
```

Looking at the details of a route shows you not only the statistics displayed in
Example 5-45, but also the accumulated penalties. In Example 5-46, you can see that the
route to 10.1.4.0/24 has a penalty of 1815; the half-life decay process has reduced the
penalty below the suppress threshold of 2000, but not yet to the reuse threshold of 750.
That second threshold is expected to be reached in 19 minutes and 10 seconds.

Example 5-46 *If an Unstable Route Is Specified with the* show ip bgp *Command, the*
Route's Penalty Value Displays

```
Colorado#show ip bgp 10.1.4.0
BGP routing table entry for 10.1.4.0/24, version 755
Paths: (1 available, no best path, advertised over EBGP)
  300, (suppressed due to dampening)
    10.1.255.3 from 10.1.255.3
      Origin IGP, metric 0, localpref 100, valid, external
      Dampinfo: penalty 1815, flapped 3 times in 00:16:28, reuse in 00:19:10
Colorado#
```

In some cases, you might want to put a suppressed route back into service before the
reuse limit is reached. The administrator in AS300 might have assured you that the cause
of the flaps of subnet 10.1.4.0/24 has been identified and eliminated, for instance, and
now he wants traffic to resume. Two commands are available: **clear ip bgp flap-statistics**
and **clear ip bgp dampening**. These two commands have the same effect of clearing all
penalties for a route or for all routes (depending on whether a route is specified with
the command), but the second command clears only those routes that have been suppressed. The **clear ip bgp flap-statistics** also enables you to identify a group of routes
by their AS path, either by specifying a filter list or by using a regular expression. For
example, the command **clear ip bgp flap-statistics regexp _30_** clears the flap statistics
for all routes that have the AS number 30 in their AS_PATH attribute. This command
proves useful if AS30 is a transit AS, and a bad link has caused all destinations reachable
through that AS to accumulate penalties.

RFD was first created in 1992 and standardized in RFC 2439 in 1998. The typical flap scenario envisioned at the time was an unreliable copper or radio link causing routes to oscillate frequently. If you look at most protocols created in the early 1990s, most took this scenario into consideration. RFD appeared to be a common-sense remedy for what appeared to be an obvious source of BGP instability. By the late 1990s and early 2000s, RFD was considered a part of best practice for stabilizing and scaling BGP networks. The first edition of this volume reflected that understanding.

In August 2002, however, an important study was published[5] demonstrating that, counter-intuitively, RFD actually destabilized large BGP networks, including the public Internet. The study results were presented later that year to NANOG, RIPE, and other network operator groups.[6] Within a couple of years, BGP best practice evolved to concluding that RFD is harmful and recommending that RFD not be used.[7]

Recall from Networking 101—or perhaps from Volume I of this book—that a foundational characteristic of distance vector protocols is that they determine best paths by a distributed calculation of local information. That means that a topology change sets off a succession of calculations throughout a distance vector network as the protocol at each router attempts to update its routing information. BGP determines autonomous system paths rather than distances between routers, so it is called path vector, but the distributed calculation behavior is the same.

Unlike distance vector protocols such as RIP that depend on new updates from neighbors to find an alternative route after a route becomes invalid, BGP keeps track of all valid routes in the BGP table, selecting the best route through the BGP Selection Process.

Figure 5-18 shows how the routine operation of BGP can amplify the effects of a flap event in a well-meshed topology. At time t_0 AS5 has three valid routes to AS1: [5,2,1], [5,3,2,1], and [5,4,3,2,1]. It advertises the route with the shortest AS_PATH, [5,2,1].

At t_1, connection to AS1 is lost. AS2 sends a withdrawal to its neighbors AS5 and AS3. At t_2, AS5 selects the next-best path to AS1 from its BGP table and sends an update changing the route to AS_PATH [5,3,2,1]. During the same period AS3 sends a withdrawal to its two neighbors. At t_3, AS5 again sends an update, as a result of the withdrawal from AS3, changing the AS_PATH to [5,4,3,2,1]. In the same period AS4 sends a withdrawal. Finally, at t_4, as a result of the withdrawal from AS4, AS5 has no more valid route entries in its BGP table for AS1 and sends a withdrawal.

You can see in this example that a single event at AS1 resulted in multiple events—two updates and one withdrawal—at AS5. If the path to AS1 comes back up, routes associated with that AS will have accumulated so many penalties beyond AS5 that it remains

---

[5] Z.M. Mao, R. Govidan, G. Varghese, and R.H. Katz, "Route Flap Damping Exacerbates Internet Routing Convergence," Proceedings of SIGCOMM, August 2002.

[6] R. Bush, T. Griffin, and Z.M. Mao, "Route Flap Damping: Harmful?" Presentation to RIPE 43, September 2002 and NANOG 26, October 2002.

[7] For example: "RIPE Routing Working Group Recommendations on Route-Flap Damping," RIPE-378, May 2006.

suppressed when it should not be. The larger the BGP topology, the larger the search space in which this kind of effect amplification can take place. One study conducted by RIPE showed that in the public Internet, a single flap event resulted in 41 events just a few AS hops away.

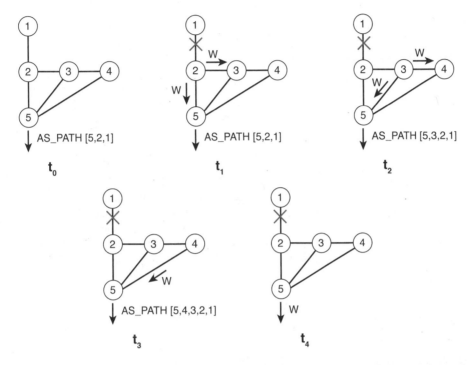

Figure 5-18 *BGP's Path Hunting Behavior Can Amplify the Downstream Effects of a Route Flap*

Following are multiple factors contributing to this effect:

- Normal propagation delay, as shown in Figure 5-18

- Varying Minimum Route Advertisement Intervals (MRAI) among different router vendors

- Differing router processing speeds

- Differing router loads

In addition to potentially suppressing routes that should not be suppressed, the original motivation for RFD—suppressing misbehaving routes that could destabilize networks by unnecessarily driving up CPU and buffer load—is far less compelling these days because of more powerful CPUs, improved BGP implementations, and better router design.

So, is route flap dampening advisable in modern networks? Even RIPE, which had advised against using RFD in 2006, has modified that recommendation to one in which

RFD might still be used, but with much less aggressive thresholds to punish the biggest offenders without suppressing routes that just flap now and then.[8] The specific RFD settings RIPE recommends follow:

■ Suppress Threshold = 6,000

■ Maximum Suppress Threshold = 50,000

Outbound Route Filters (ORF)

Although the route dampening feature helps scale BGP to cope with network instabilities, the Outbound Route Filtering (ORF) feature enhances BGP scalability by implementing a more efficient inbound route filtering mechanism.

ORF is a BGP capability specified in RFC 5291 that enables a BGP speaker to implement inbound filtering on the routes received from a BGP peer by implementing the filter as an outbound route filter on that peer.

To understand what ORF accomplishes, and what value the feature adds, consider the network in Figure 5-19. Routers Memphis and Alexandria are EBGP peers. Router Memphis is in AS100 and router Alexandria is in AS200. Alexandria sends three routes to Memphis: 10.1.0.0/16, 172.16.0.0/20, and 192.168.100.0/24. Memphis in turn implements a prefix-list that filters out the first two subnets and allows only the third subnet. Examples 5-47 and 5-48 show the BGP configurations and the BGP tables on both routers, respectively.

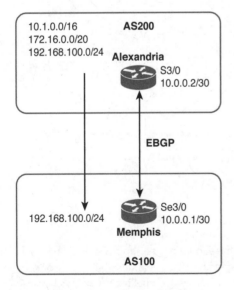

Figure 5-19 *BGP Configurations of Routers A and B*

---

[8] "RIPE Routing Working Group Recommendations on Route Flap Damping," RIPE-580, January 2013.

Example 5-47 *BGP Configurations of Routers Memphis and Alexandria in Figure 5-19*

```
Memphis
router bgp 100
 no bgp default ipv4-unicast
 bgp log-neighbor-changes
 neighbor 10.0.0.2 remote-as 200
 !
 address-family ipv4
  neighbor 10.0.0.2 activate
  neighbor 10.0.0.2 prefix-list INBOUND_FILTER in
  no auto-summary
  no synchronization
 exit-address-family
!
ip prefix-list INBOUND_FILTER seq 5 permit 192.168.100.0/24
```

```
Alexandria
router bgp 200
 no bgp default ipv4-unicast
 bgp log-neighbor-changes
 neighbor 10.0.0.1 remote-as 100
 !
 address-family ipv4
  neighbor 10.0.0.1 activate
  no auto-summary
  no synchronization
  network 10.1.0.0 mask 255.255.0.0
  network 172.16.0.0 mask 255.255.240.0
  network 192.168.100.0
 exit-address-family
```

Example 5-48 *BGP Tables at Routers Memphis and Alexandria*

```
Memphis#show ip bgp
BGP table version is 6, local router ID is 10.0.0.1
Status codes: s suppressed, d damped, h history, * valid, > best, i - internal,
              r RIB-failure, S Stale
Origin codes: i - IGP, e - EGP, ? - incomplete

   Network          Next Hop          Metric LocPrf Weight Path
*> 192.168.100.0    10.0.0.2               0          0 200 i
```

```
Alexandria#show ip bgp
BGP table version is 4, local router ID is 10.0.0.2
```

```
Status codes: s suppressed, d damped, h history, * valid, > best, i - internal,
              r RIB-failure, S Stale
Origin codes: i - IGP, e - EGP, ? - incomplete


   Network          Next Hop            Metric LocPrf Weight Path
*> 10.1.0.0/16      0.0.0.0                  0          32768 i
*> 172.16.0.0/20    0.0.0.0                  0          32768 i
*> 192.168.100.0    0.0.0.0                  0          32768 i
```

You may notice some configuration lines that do not look familiar in Example 5-27. The configuration starting with the line **address-family ipv4** on both routers is a Multi-Protocol BGP (MBGP) configuration that enables BGP to advertise routes for address families other than unicast IPv4, such as IPv6 and Multicast routes. For this section, only the IPv4 address family will be configured, however, this new configuration format is required for the ORF configuration. MBGP is covered in detail in Chapter 6.

In Example 5-49, the command **debug ip bgp updates** is issued on both routers to see the updates generated and sent from Alexandria, and then the filtering happens inbound at Memphis. Looking closely at the debug output, you find that Alexandria consumed processing power and memory to generate the update that included all three routes. Then an UPDATE message was sent over the WAN link to Memphis, including all three routes, consuming link bandwidth. Finally, Memphis consumed processing power and memory to pass all three routes through the incoming route filter (prefix-list INBOUND_FILTER) only to discard two routes and accept one. Imagine if Alexandria were sending the full Internet routing table to Memphis only to have Memphis discard the majority of routes and accept only a select few. Not an efficient filtering mechanism in terms of network resources utilization.

Example 5-49 *BGP Updates Sent from Alexandria and Filtered Inbound at Memphis*

```
Memphis#
*Sep 30 05:30:28.467: %BGP-5-ADJCHANGE: neighbor 10.0.0.2 Up
Memphis#
*Sep 30 05:30:28.651: BGP(0): 10.0.0.2 rcvd UPDATE w/ attr: nexthop 10.0.0.2, origin
  i, metric 0, path 200
*Sep 30 05:30:28.651: BGP(0): 10.0.0.2 rcvd 192.168.100.0/24
*Sep 30 05:30:28.655: BGP(0): 10.0.0.2 rcvd 172.16.0.0/20 -- DENIED due to:
  distribute/prefix-list;
*Sep 30 05:30:28.655: BGP(0): 10.0.0.2 rcvd 10.1.0.0/16 -- DENIED due to:
  distribute/prefix-list;
*Sep 30 05:30:28.663: BGP(0): Revise route installing 1 of 1 routes for
  192.168.100.0/24 -> 10.0.0.2(main) to main IP table
Memphis#

Alexandria#
*Sep 30 05:30:28.563: %BGP-5-ADJCHANGE: neighbor 10.0.0.1 Up
```

```
Alexandria#
*Sep 30 05:30:28.567: BGP(0): 10.0.0.1 send UPDATE (format) 192.168.100.0/24, next
   10.0.0.2, metric 0, path Local
*Sep 30 05:30:28.571: BGP(0): 10.0.0.1 send UPDATE (prepend, chgflags: 0x820)
   172.16.0.0/20, next 10.0.0.2, metric 0, path Local
*Sep 30 05:30:28.571: BGP(0): 10.0.0.1 send UPDATE (prepend, chgflags: 0x820)
   10.1.0.0/16, next 10.0.0.2, metric 0, path Local
Alexandria#
```

What if instead of Alexandria sending a bunch of routes that are just going to be discarded, Memphis has the capability to tell Alexandria, "I'm accepting only these routes, so don't bother sending any others." That's the purpose of ORF.

ORF provides the capability for Memphis to send the prefix-list it used as an *inbound* route filter over to Alexandria so that Alexandria implements this filter as an *outbound* route filter toward Memphis, thus filtering the routes at the source (Alexandria), by request from the destination (Memphis).

ORF configuration involves a single command on both routers:

neighbor {*IP_Address*} **capability orf** *prefix-list* [**both** | **receive** | **send**]

The statement is placed under the bgp address-family configuration and causes the router to advertise the ORF capability to the neighbor configured in the command. ORF can be enabled in either receive mode, where the BGP speaker announces its "willingness" to accept ORFs from the peer in send mode where the speaker announces that it will be sending ORFs to the peer, or both, which enables both send and receive modes.

Example 5-50 shows the BGP configuration after enabling ORF. Memphis is configured in send mode, whereas Alexandria is configured in receive mode because Memphis is the BGP speaker that will be sending the ORF to its peer.

Example 5-50 *BGP Configurations on Memphis and Alexandria After Applying the ORF Command*

```
Memphis
router bgp 100
 no bgp default ipv4-unicast
 bgp log-neighbor-changes
 neighbor 10.0.0.2 remote-as 200
 !
 address-family ipv4
  neighbor 10.0.0.2 activate
  neighbor 10.0.0.2 capability orf prefix-list send
  neighbor 10.0.0.2 prefix-list INBOUND_FILTER in
  no auto-summary
  no synchronization
 exit-address-family
```

```
Alexandria
router bgp 200
 no bgp default ipv4-unicast
 bgp log-neighbor-changes
 neighbor 10.0.0.1 remote-as 100
 !
 address-family ipv4
  neighbor 10.0.0.1 activate
  neighbor 10.0.0.1 capability orf prefix-list receive
  no auto-summary
  no synchronization
  network 10.1.0.0 mask 255.255.0.0
  network 172.16.0.0 mask 255.255.240.0
  network 192.168.100.0
 exit-address-family
```

Example 5-51 shows the debug output after issuing a soft reset at Memphis using the command **clear ip bgp 10.0.0.2 in prefix-filter.** You can see now that Alexandria is sending only the single route allowed by the route filter.

Example 5-51   *Debug Outputs After Configuring the ORF Capability*

```
Memphis#clear ip bgp 10.0.0.2 in prefix-filter
Memphis#
*Sep 30 06:47:50.515: BGP(0): 10.0.0.2 rcvd UPDATE w/ attr: nexthop 10.0.0.2, origin
 i, metric 0, path 200
*Sep 30 06:47:50.519: BGP(0): 10.0.0.2 rcvd 192.168.100.0/24...duplicate ignored
Memphis#
```

```
Alexandria#
*Sep 30 06:47:50.343: BGP(0): 10.0.0.1 send UPDATE (format) 192.168.100.0/24, next
 10.0.0.2, metric 0, path Local
```

To verify the new configuration, Example 5-52 illustrates the output of the **show ip bgp neighbor** command on both routers showing the ORF capability announcement. The command **show ip bgp neighbor 10.0.0.1 received prefix-filter** is then issued on Alexandria to show that R2 has received the ORF from Memphis.

Example 5-52   *ORF Configuration Verification*

```
Memphis#show ip bgp neighbors 10.0.0.2
BGP neighbor is 10.0.0.2,  remote AS 200, external link
  BGP version 4, remote router ID 192.168.100.1
  BGP state = Established, up for 00:13:22
  Last read 00:00:21, last write 00:00:21, hold time is 180, keepalive interval is
  60 seconds
```

```
   Neighbor capabilities:
     Route refresh: advertised and received(old & new)
     Address family IPv4 Unicast: advertised and received
   Message statistics:
     InQ depth is 0
     OutQ depth is 0
                         Sent          Rcvd
     Opens:                 6             6
     Notifications:         0             0
     Updates:               0            10
     Keepalives:          122           122
     Route Refresh:         3             0
     Total:               135           138
   Default minimum time between advertisement runs is 30 seconds


  For address family: IPv4 Unicast
   BGP table version 8, neighbor version 8/0
   Output queue size: 0
   Index 1, Offset 0, Mask 0x2
   1 update-group member
   AF-dependant capabilities:
     Outbound Route Filter (ORF) type (128) Prefix-list:
       Send-mode: advertised
       Receive-mode: received
   Outbound Route Filter (ORF): sent;
   Incoming update prefix filter list is INBOUND_FILTER
                         Sent          Rcvd
   Prefix activity:      ----          ----
     Prefixes Current:      0             1 (Consumes 52 bytes)
     Prefixes Total:        0             3
     Implicit Withdraw:     0             2
     Explicit Withdraw:     0             0
     Used as bestpath:    n/a             1
     Used as multipath:   n/a             0

                       Outbound      Inbound
   Local Policy Denied Prefixes:  --------      -------
     Suppressed duplicate:        0             2
     Bestpath from this peer:     1           n/a
     Total:                       1             2
   Number of NLRIs in the update sent: max 0; min 0


   Connections established 6; dropped 5
   Last reset 00:13:30, due to Peer closed the session
Connection state is ESTAB, I/O status: 1, unread input bytes: 0
```

```
Connection is ECN Disabled, Mininum incoming TTL 0, Outgoing TTL 1
Local host: 10.0.0.1, Local port: 179
Foreign host: 10.0.0.2, Foreign port: 15127
Connection tableid (VRF): 0

Enqueued packets for retransmit: 0, input: 0  mis-ordered: 0 (0 bytes)

Event Timers (current time is 0x6A4F6C):
Timer          Starts    Wakeups          Next
Retrans           17         0             0x0
TimeWait           0         0             0x0
AckHold           19         4             0x0
SendWnd            0         0             0x0
KeepAlive          0         0             0x0
GiveUp             0         0             0x0
PmtuAger           0         0             0x0
DeadWait           0         0             0x0
Linger             0         0             0x0
ProcessQ           0         0             0x0

iss: 2353748554  snduna: 2353749042  sndnxt: 2353749042    sndwnd:   15897
irs: 2372261415  rcvnxt: 2372261932  rcvwnd:       15868  delrcvwnd:    516

SRTT: 290 ms, RTTO: 564 ms, RTV: 274 ms, KRTT: 0 ms
minRTT: 172 ms, maxRTT: 348 ms, ACK hold: 200 ms
Status Flags: passive open, gen tcbs
Option Flags: nagle
IP Precedence value : 6

Datagrams (max data segment is 1460 bytes):
Rcvd: 34 (out of order: 0), with data: 20, total data bytes: 516
Sent: 25 (retransmit: 0, fastretransmit: 0, partialack: 0, Second Congestion: 0),
  with data: 20, total data bytes: 487
 Packets received in fast path: 0, fast processed: 0, slow path: 0
 Packets send in fast path: 0
 fast lock acquisition failures: 0, slow path: 0
Memphis#
```

```
Alexandria#show ip bgp neighbors 10.0.0.1
BGP neighbor is 10.0.0.1,  remote AS 100, external link
  BGP version 4, remote router ID 10.0.0.1
  BGP state = Established, up for 00:15:36
  Last read 00:00:36, last write 00:00:36, hold time is 180, keepalive interval is
    60 seconds
  Neighbor capabilities:
```

```
    Route refresh: advertised and received(old & new)
    Address family IPv4 Unicast: advertised and received
  Message statistics:
   InQ depth is 0
   OutQ depth is 0
                        Sent        Rcvd
   Opens:                 6           6
   Notifications:         0           0
   Updates:              10           0
   Keepalives:          124         124
   Route Refresh:         0           6
   Total:               140         137
  Default minimum time between advertisement runs is 30 seconds

 For address family: IPv4 Unicast
  BGP table version 4, neighbor version 4/0
  Output queue size: 0
  Index 1, Offset 0, Mask 0x2
  1 update-group member
  AF-dependant capabilities:
    Outbound Route Filter (ORF) type (128) Prefix-list:
      Send-mode: received
      Receive-mode: advertised
  Outbound Route Filter (ORF): received (1 entries)
                        Sent        Rcvd
  Prefix activity:      ----        ----
    Prefixes Current:     1           0
    Prefixes Total:       3           0
    Implicit Withdraw:    2           0
    Explicit Withdraw:    0           0
    Used as bestpath:    n/a          0
    Used as multipath:   n/a          0

                       Outbound   Inbound
  Local Policy Denied Prefixes:  --------   -------
    ORF prefix-list:              6        n/a
    Total:                        6         0
  Number of NLRIs in the update sent: max 3, min 1

  Connections established 6; dropped 5
  Last reset 00:15:43, due to User reset
Connection state is ESTAB, I/O status: 1, unread input bytes: 0
Connection is ECN Disabled, Mininum incoming TTL 0, Outgoing TTL 1
Local host: 10.0.0.2, Local port: 15127
Foreign host: 10.0.0.1, Foreign port: 179
```

```
Connection tableid (VRF): 0

Enqueued packets for retransmit: 0, input: 0  mis-ordered: 0 (0 bytes)

Event Timers (current time is 0x6C5664):
Timer          Starts   Wakeups          Next
Retrans          22         0            0x0
TimeWait          0         0            0x0
AckHold          18        14            0x0
SendWnd           0         0            0x0
KeepAlive         0         0            0x0
GiveUp            0         0            0x0
PmtuAger          0         0            0x0
DeadWait          0         0            0x0
Linger            0         0            0x0
ProcessQ          0         0            0x0

iss: 2372261415  snduna: 2372261970  sndnxt: 2372261970    sndwnd:  15830
irs: 2353748554  rcvnxt: 2353749080  rcvwnd:       15859  delrcvwnd:    525

SRTT: 297 ms, RTTO: 424 ms, RTV: 127 ms, KRTT: 0 ms
minRTT: 124 ms, maxRTT: 412 ms, ACK hold: 200 ms
Status Flags: active open
Option Flags: nagle
IP Precedence value : 6

Datagrams (max data segment is 1460 bytes):
Rcvd: 27 (out of order: 0), with data: 22, total data bytes: 525
Sent: 38 (retransmit: 0, fastretransmit: 0, partialack: 0, Second Congestion: 0),
  with data: 22, total data bytes: 554
 Packets received in fast path: 0, fast processed: 0, slow path: 0
 Packets send in fast path: 0
 fast lock acquisition failures: 0, slow path: 0
Alexandria#
Alexandria#show ip bgp neighbors 10.0.0.1 received prefix-filter
Address family: IPv4 Unicast
ip prefix-list 10.0.0.1: 1 entries
   seq 5 permit 192.168.100.0/24
Alexandria#
```

Now that we have demonstrated the ORF configuration and effects on the route updates, step back and look at some background information.

Cisco lists the following restrictions when configuring ORF feature:

- ORF supports IPv4 and IPv6 unicast routes. It does not support IP multicast routes.

- ORF can be used only with IP prefix-lists. Distribute-lists and ACLs are not supported.

- ORF has to be configured separately for every address family. It cannot be configured under the global BGP process.

- ORF is supported only over EBGP sessions. It is not supported over IBGP sessions.

A BGP speaker negotiates the ORF capability with its peers in the BGP OPEN Message using the Optional Parameters Field. If you recall the OPEN message format from Chapter 2, "Introduction to BGP," the Optional Parameters field consists of the following subfields:

- Parameter Type

- Parameter Length

- Parameter Value

For any capability, including the ORF capability, the Parameter Type field is always 2. The Length field specifies the length of the Value field that follows, in octets. Finally, the Value field is in turn split into three subfields, as follows:

- Capability Code

- Capability Length

- Capability Value

Figure 5-20 illustrates the Capabilities parameter. For the ORF capability in particular, the Capability Code is 3 and the capability Length is the length of the Value field that follows, in octets. The Capability Value consists of entries that indicate information such as the AFI/SAFI for which the ORF is enabled and which mode the BGP speaker has been configured for, that is, whether its mode is receive, send, or both, as explained earlier in this section.

After the capability is negotiated between the neighbors, the ORF entries are carried in the BGP ROUTE-REFRESH message. This is BGP message type 5 and is discussed in Chapter 4.

A ROUTE-REFRESH message that carries one or more ORF entries contains the following fields:

- Address Family Identifier (such as IPv4 or IPv6)

- Subsequent Address Family Identifier (such as Unicast or Multicast)

- When-to-refresh (Immediate, Defer)

- ORF Type (numerical value)

- Action (Add, Remove, Remove-all)

- Match (Permit, Deny)

- Type-specific field

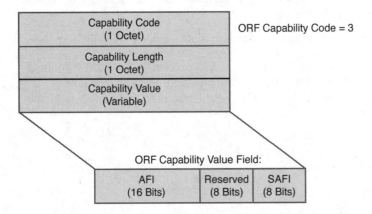

Figure 5-20   *ORF-Specific Capability Field in the BGP OPEN Message*

Next-Hop Tracking

This chapter illustrates the main strength of BGP that makes it a better choice for large-scale networks such as the Internet: scalability. As explained in the onset of this chapter, BGP is a stable routing protocol that can handle routing information for large networks supporting a large number of reachable end systems.

But this scalability comes at a cost. BGP is a "slow" protocol. BGP is slow detecting failures on a router and slow in converging to a steady state after a failure. This in turn means that BGP updates are slow to propagate through the network. Next-Hop Tracking (NHT) is one of several mechanisms that mitigate this slowness and contribute to speeding up both failure detection and convergence on the same router as well as through the network.

To illustrate how the NHT feature speeds up BGP failure detection and convergence, first look at how BGP accomplishes both, without NHT. Consider the topology in Figure 5-21. Routers Sharqia and Sinai are edge routers for AS100 that receive identical routes from their EBGP peers in other autonomous systems. There is a full IBGP mesh in AS100 using the routers' loopback addresses, and therefore, router Cairo receives the same external routes from both Sharqia and Sinai. Next-hop-self is configured on both Sharqia and Sinai for next-hop reachability. Eventually, at Cairo, the routes announced from Sharqia are preferred over the routes from Sinai because of Sharqia's lower BGP RID and are installed in both the BGP and the routing tables of Cairo.

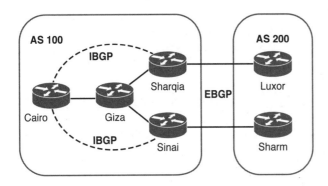

Figure 5-21 *Example Topology for Next-Hop Tracking*

Now what happens if Sharqia fails or its loopback becomes unreachable for some reason? There are two mechanisms that come into play here: the BGP keepalive and hold-time intervals, and the BGP Scanner process.

In the first scenario, the failure detection and convergence depends on the BGP timers. The default BGP keepalive timer is 60 seconds and the holdtime is 180 seconds. Cairo waits for 180 seconds without receiving a keepalive from Sharqia, after which it declares Sharqia dead, and tears down the IBGP session. After the IBGP session is brought down, all the corresponding routes learned from Sharqia are withdrawn from the BGP table on Cairo. The BGP best path algorithm is run, and the path via Sinai is installed as the new best path. The IP routing table is updated accordingly.

Before discussing the second scenario, recall from Chapter 4 that the IOS Scanner process periodically "walks" through all the prefixes in the BGP table to verify the reachability of the next hop of each route, among other things. If the next hop of a route is not reachable, this route is marked as invalid in the BGP table and does not participate in the BGP best path algorithm. The interval between BGP scanner process walks is 60 seconds. This is the time between one walk completing and the next starting, irrespective of how long the actual walk takes.

In the second scenario (which is the more likely one if the BGP timers are left at their default values), if the IGP in AS100 is properly tuned, IGP convergence is typically ranges from a fraction of a second to a few seconds. The IGP at Cairo becomes aware that Sharqia is no longer reachable long before BGP detects the same. Because the IBGP session has not been torn down yet, the routes received from Sharqia remain in the routing table. However, on the next BGP table walk by the BGP Scanner process, all routes using Sharqia as the next hop are marked as invalid. The BGP best path algorithm is run again and the routes via Sinai are installed. After the hold time expires and the session with Sharqia is torn down, the invalid routes via Sharqia are removed from the BGP table altogether.

In the first scenario, Cairo had to wait at least 180 seconds to detect the failure, and in the second scenario, Cairo had to wait at least 60 seconds to detect the failure. Considering the second, better scenario, instead of waiting for the Scanner interval to expire, and then for the Scanner process to do a walk through the full BGP table, validating the next-hop reachability of each route in the process, the Next-Hop Tracking makes this validation process *event-driven*. That is, any changes to the RIB that affect the next-hop reachability or metric of one or more BGP routes is reported to BGP within a tunable time-interval. This feature is enabled by default.

Here's how it works: BGP compiles a list of all next-hop IPs in the BGP table. This list is registered with the IP RIB Update IOS process. When a change happens to any of the registered next-hop IPs, the IP RIB Update process informs BGP that this next-hop IP address has changed. This happens after a default interval of 5 seconds and can be amended using the statement:

```
bgp nexthop trigger delay {sec}
```

The reason that BGP is informed of those changes after a finite time interval is for IGP to have reached a steady-state on all nodes in the network. When the trigger delay is set to 0 seconds, IGP changes are reported to BGP as they happen, without any delay. However, the best practice is to set this delay to a value slightly higher than the time required for full IGP convergence.

Although it's highly unlikely that you would need to, NHT can disabled using the **bgp router mode** command:

```
no bgp nexthop trigger enable
```

This may be required if the IGP in the network is not stable, and in turn affecting the BGP stability. However, if this is the case, the solution should be to investigate and resolve the IGP instability instead of disabling NHT.

Next-hop IPs can change in two ways: either the metric changes, or the next-hop becomes unreachable. In the first case, the BGP Router process is started and the BGP best path algorithm is run to calculate the new best paths (if any). In the second case, the BGP Scanner process marks the routes with unreachable next hops as not valid in the BGP table, and the BGP Router process runs the BGP best path algorithm to calculate the new best paths.

It is worth mentioning that NHT not only speeds up BGP convergence after an event affecting the next-hops takes place, but it also prevents black-holing of traffic in the time interval following the IGP convergence and before the BGP has completely converged. To elaborate on this point further, refer to Figure 5-20. As mentioned earlier, AS100 has a full mesh of IBGP sessions. Consequently, router Giza has full knowledge of all the external routes announced by both Sharqia and Sinai into the AS. Assume there is a failure on the link between Giza and Sharqia. Giza almost immediately learns that Sharqia is not reachable because it is directly connected, and the rest of routers (including Cairo) know of the failure as quickly as the IGP converges. However, until the BGP converges (either based on the timers or detected by the BGP Scanner process, whichever happens first), Cairo believes that Sharqia is still up and that the routes announced by Sharqia are still valid. Therefore, Cairo keeps sending packets to Sharqia's loopback address until the BGP converges. During the time in between the IGP convergence and the BGP convergence, all traffic sent from Cairo to Sharqia is dropped at Giza. This, of course, if the NHT feature is not present.

Recall that next-hop-self is used on Sharqia and Sinai to amend the next hop of routes learned over the EBGP sessions to their own loopback addresses. These loopback addresses are announced over the IGP. Therefore, any failure affecting these loopback addresses will be tracked and reported by the NHT feature. Now consider Figure 5-22. In this figure, Sharqia and Sinai are intact. However, the uplink to Sharqia's EBGP neighbor has failed. This link is not tracked by IGP and therefore the NHT feature does not affect the convergence in any way. In this case, Sharqia waits for the keepalive timer to expire, tears down the session with Luxor, and finally sends UPDATE messages down to its IBGP neighbors to withdraw the routes previously learned from Luxor.

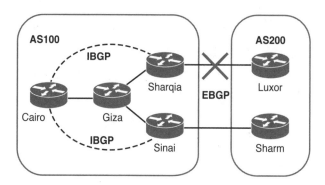

Figure 5-22   *Failure of the Link Between Sharqia and Luxor*

One solution to this problem is to run the IGP in passive mode on the interface connecting Sharqia and Luxor, as explained in Chapter 3, instead of using the next-hop-self statement on Sharqia and Sinai.

To display the value added by the NHT feature, test the convergence of the network referred to in Figure 5-22, first without and then with the NHT feature enabled. Example 5-53 shows the relevant configuration of the routers in Figure 5-22. For the sake of brevity, only the BGP configuration is shown. OSPF has been configured as the IGP for both AS100 and AS200. However, each AS is in a different OSPF domain. Both AS100 and AS200 have a full IBGP mesh. An EBGP session is established between routers Sharqia and Luxor and another EBGP peering is established between Sinai and Sharm. Networks 172.16.0.0/20, 10.10.10.0/24, and 10.20.20.0/25 are injected by an internal router in AS200 and announced by Luxor and Sharm over the EBGP sessions with AS100. As you can see in Cairo's configuration, Next Hop Tracking has been disabled using the command **no bgp nexthop trigger enable**. Example 5-54 shows Cairo's BGP and IP routing tables. Cairo has installed the three subnets internal to AS200 in its BGP and IP routing tables. The next hop for the three subnets is Sharqia (192.168.255.3).

Example 5-53 *BGP Configurations of the Routers in Figure 5-22*

```
Cairo
router bgp 100
 no synchronization
 bgp log-neighbor-changes
 no bgp nexthop trigger enable
 network 192.168.255.1 mask 255.255.255.255
 neighbor 192.168.255.2 remote-as 100
 neighbor 192.168.255.2 update-source Loopback0
 neighbor 192.168.255.3 remote-as 100
 neighbor 192.168.255.3 update-source Loopback0
 neighbor 192.168.255.4 remote-as 100
 neighbor 192.168.255.4 update-source Loopback0
 no auto-summary
```

```
Giza
router bgp 100
 no synchronization
 bgp log-neighbor-changes
 network 192.168.255.2 mask 255.255.255.255
 neighbor 192.168.255.1 remote-as 100
 neighbor 192.168.255.1 update-source Loopback0
 neighbor 192.168.255.3 remote-as 100
 neighbor 192.168.255.3 update-source Loopback0
 neighbor 192.168.255.4 remote-as 100
 neighbor 192.168.255.4 update-source Loopback0
 no auto-summary
```

```
Sharqia
router bgp 100
 no synchronization
 bgp log-neighbor-changes
 network 192.168.255.3 mask 255.255.255.255
 neighbor 10.0.0.14 remote-as 200
 neighbor 192.168.255.1 remote-as 100
 neighbor 192.168.255.1 update-source Loopback0
 neighbor 192.168.255.1 next-hop-self
 neighbor 192.168.255.2 remote-as 100
 neighbor 192.168.255.2 update-source Loopback0
 neighbor 192.168.255.2 next-hop-self
 neighbor 192.168.255.4 remote-as 100
 neighbor 192.168.255.4 update-source Loopback0
 neighbor 192.168.255.4 next-hop-self
 no auto-summary
```

```
Sinai
router bgp 100
 no synchronization
 bgp log-neighbor-changes
 network 192.168.255.4 mask 255.255.255.255
 neighbor 10.0.0.18 remote-as 200
 neighbor 192.168.255.1 remote-as 100
 neighbor 192.168.255.1 update-source Loopback0
 neighbor 192.168.255.1 next-hop-self
 neighbor 192.168.255.2 remote-as 100
 neighbor 192.168.255.2 update-source Loopback0
 neighbor 192.168.255.2 next-hop-self
 neighbor 192.168.255.3 remote-as 100
 neighbor 192.168.255.3 update-source Loopback0
 neighbor 192.168.255.3 next-hop-self
 no auto-summary
```

```
Luxor
router bgp 200
 no synchronization
 bgp log-neighbor-changes
 network 192.168.255.5 mask 255.255.255.255
 neighbor 10.0.0.13 remote-as 100
 neighbor 192.168.255.6 remote-as 200
 neighbor 192.168.255.6 update-source Loopback0
 neighbor 192.168.255.6 next-hop-self
 neighbor 192.168.255.7 remote-as 200
 neighbor 192.168.255.7 update-source Loopback0
 neighbor 192.168.255.7 next-hop-self
 no auto-summary
```

```
Sharm
router bgp 200
 no synchronization
 bgp log-neighbor-changes
 network 192.168.255.6 mask 255.255.255.255
 neighbor 10.0.0.17 remote-as 100
 neighbor 192.168.255.5 remote-as 200
 neighbor 192.168.255.5 update-source Loopback0
 neighbor 192.168.255.5 next-hop-self
 neighbor 192.168.255.7 remote-as 200
 neighbor 192.168.255.7 update-source Loopback0
 neighbor 192.168.255.7 next-hop-self
 no auto-summary
```

Example 5-54   *Cairo's BGP and IP Routing Tables*

```
Cairo#show ip bgp
BGP table version is 66, local router ID is 192.168.255.1
Status codes: s suppressed, d damped, h history, * valid, > best, i - internal,
              r RIB-failure, S Stale
Origin codes: i - IGP, e - EGP, ? - incomplete


   Network          Next Hop          Metric LocPrf Weight Path
*>i10.10.10.0/24    192.168.255.3          0    100      0 200 i
* i                 192.168.255.4          0    100      0 200 i
*>i10.20.20.0/25    192.168.255.3          0    100      0 200 i
* i                 192.168.255.4          0    100      0 200 i
*>i172.16.0.0/20    192.168.255.3          0    100      0 200 i
* i                 192.168.255.4          0    100      0 200 i
*> 192.168.255.1/32 0.0.0.0                0           32768 i
r>i192.168.255.2/32 192.168.255.2          0    100      0 i
r>i192.168.255.3/32 192.168.255.3          0    100      0 i
r>i192.168.255.4/32 192.168.255.4          0    100      0 i
*>i192.168.255.5/32 192.168.255.3          0    100      0 200 i
* i                 192.168.255.4          0    100      0 200 i
*>i192.168.255.6/32 192.168.255.3          0    100      0 200 i
* i                 192.168.255.4          0    100      0 200 i
*>i192.168.255.7/32 192.168.255.3          0    100      0 200 i
* i                 192.168.255.4          0    100      0 200 i
Cairo#


Cairo#show ip route
Codes: C - connected, S - static, R - RIP, M - mobile, B - BGP
       D - EIGRP, EX - EIGRP external, O - OSPF, IA - OSPF inter area
       N1 - OSPF NSSA external type 1, N2 - OSPF NSSA external type 2
       E1 - OSPF external type 1, E2 - OSPF external type 2
       i - IS-IS, su - IS-IS summary, L1 - IS-IS level-1, L2 - IS-IS level-2
       ia - IS-IS inter area, * - candidate default, U - per-user static route
       o - ODR, P - periodic downloaded static route


Gateway of last resort is not set

     172.16.0.0/20 is subnetted, 1 subnets
B       172.16.0.0 [200/0] via 192.168.255.3, 00:17:17
     10.0.0.0/8 is variably subnetted, 5 subnets, 3 masks
O       10.0.0.8/30 [110/2] via 10.0.0.2, 01:58:14, FastEthernet1/0
B       10.20.20.0/25 [200/0] via 192.168.255.3, 00:17:17
B       10.10.10.0/24 [200/0] via 192.168.255.3, 00:17:17
C       10.0.0.0/30 is directly connected, FastEthernet1/0
```

```
O       10.0.0.4/30 [110/2] via 10.0.0.2, 01:58:24, FastEthernet1/0
     192.168.255.0/32 is subnetted, 7 subnets
B       192.168.255.7 [200/0] via 192.168.255.3, 00:17:17
B       192.168.255.6 [200/0] via 192.168.255.3, 00:17:49
B       192.168.255.5 [200/0] via 192.168.255.3, 00:17:49
O       192.168.255.4 [110/3] via 10.0.0.2, 01:55:50, FastEthernet1/0
O       192.168.255.3 [110/3] via 10.0.0.2, 00:17:52, FastEthernet1/0
O       192.168.255.2 [110/2] via 10.0.0.2, 01:58:24, FastEthernet1/0
C       192.168.255.1 is directly connected, Loopback0
Cairo#
```

A failure is simulated by shutting down Sharqia's Loopback0 interface, which is the
interface that that router is using for its IBGP sessions. Because you are not looking at
failed BGP sessions, but rather at routes that will be marked as invalid in the BGP table,
the command **debug ip bgp rib-filter** has been entered on Cairo. Example 5-55 shows
the resulting log messages after shutting down the Loopback0 interface.

Example 5-55   *Intra-AS Failure Detection with NHT Disabled*

```
Sharqia#conf t
Enter configuration commands, one per line.  End with CNTL/Z.
Sharqia(config)#interface loopback 0
Sharqia(config-if)#shut
Sharqia(config-if)#
Oct  5 07:30:10.675: %LINK-5-CHANGED: Interface Loopback0, changed state to
  administratively down
Oct  5 07:30:11.675: %LINEPROTO-5-UPDOWN: Line protocol on Interface Loopback0,
  changed state to down
Sharqia(config-if)#
Oct  5 07:32:24.643: %BGP-5-ADJCHANGE: neighbor 192.168.255.2 Down BGP Notification
  sent
Sharqia(config-if)#
Oct  5 07:32:24.643: %BGP-3-NOTIFICATION: sent to neighbor 192.168.255.2 4/0 (hold
  time expired) 0 bytes
Sharqia(config-if)#
Oct  5 07:32:33.047: %BGP-5-ADJCHANGE: neighbor 192.168.255.4 Down BGP Notification
  sent
Sharqia(config-if)#
Oct  5 07:32:33.047: %BGP-3-NOTIFICATION: sent to neighbor 192.168.255.4 4/0 (hold
  time expired) 0 bytes
Sharqia(config-if)#
Oct  5 07:32:36.171: %BGP-5-ADJCHANGE: neighbor 192.168.255.1 Down BGP Notification
  sent
Sharqia(config-if)#
Oct  5 07:32:36.171: %BGP-3-NOTIFICATION: sent to neighbor 192.168.255.1 4/0 (hold
  time expired) 0 bytes
Sharqia(config-if)#
```

```
Cairo#debug ip bgp rib-filter
BGP Rib filter debugging is on
Cairo#
Oct   5 07:29:58.463: BGP- ATF: Debuging is OFF
Oct   5 07:29:58.467: BGP- ATF: Debuging is ON
Cairo#
Oct   5 07:30:14.279: BGP- ATF: EVENT 192.168.255.3/32 RIB update DOWN
Cairo#
Cairo#
Cairo#sh ip bgp summary
BGP router identifier 192.168.255.1, local AS number 100
BGP table version is 112, main routing table version 112
9 network entries using 1080 bytes of memory
15 path entries using 780 bytes of memory
4/3 BGP path/bestpath attribute entries using 496 bytes of memory
1 BGP AS-PATH entries using 24 bytes of memory
0 BGP route-map cache entries using 0 bytes of memory
0 BGP filter-list cache entries using 0 bytes of memory
Bitfield cache entries: current 1 (at peak 1) using 32 bytes of memory
BGP using 2412 total bytes of memory
BGP activity 32/23 prefixes, 76/61 paths, scan interval 60 secs


Neighbor        V    AS MsgRcvd MsgSent   TblVer  InQ OutQ Up/Down   State/PfxRcd
192.168.255.2   4   100     160     160      112    0    0 02:03:08            1
192.168.255.3   4   100     135     108      112    0    0 00:02:28            6
192.168.255.4   4   100     173     164      112    0    0 02:03:08            7
Cairo#
Cairo#
Cairo#sh ip bgp
BGP table version is 112, local router ID is 192.168.255.1
Status codes: s suppressed, d damped, h history, * valid, > best, i - internal,
              r RIB-failure, S Stale
Origin codes: i - IGP, e - EGP, ? - incomplete


   Network          Next Hop          Metric LocPrf Weight Path
*>i10.10.10.0/24    192.168.255.3          0    100      0 200 i
* i                 192.168.255.4          0    100      0 200 i
*>i10.20.20.0/25    192.168.255.3          0    100      0 200 i
* i                 192.168.255.4          0    100      0 200 i
*>i172.16.0.0/20    192.168.255.3          0    100      0 200 i
* i                 192.168.255.4          0    100      0 200 i
*> 192.168.255.1/32 0.0.0.0                0          32768 i
r>i192.168.255.2/32 192.168.255.2          0    100      0 i
r>i192.168.255.4/32 192.168.255.4          0    100      0 i
```

```
*>i192.168.255.5/32 192.168.255.3                 0    100    0 200 i
* i                  192.168.255.4                0    100    0 200 i
*>i192.168.255.6/32 192.168.255.3                 0    100    0 200 i
* i                  192.168.255.4                0    100    0 200 i
*>i192.168.255.7/32 192.168.255.3                 0    100    0 200 i
* i                  192.168.255.4                0    100    0 200 i
Cairo#
Oct  5 07:31:11.875: BGP- ATF: EVENT 10.10.10.0/24 RIB update MODIFY
Oct  5 07:31:11.879: BGP- ATF: EVENT 10.20.20.0/25 RIB update MODIFY
Oct  5 07:31:11.879: BGP- ATF: EVENT 172.16.0.0/20 RIB update MODIFY
Oct  5 07:31:11.883: BGP- ATF: EVENT 192.168.255.5/32 RIB update MODIFY
Oct  5 07:31:11.883: BGP- ATF: EVENT 192.168.255.6/32 RIB update MODIFY
Oct  5 07:31:11.887: BGP- ATF: EVENT 192.168.255.7/32 RIB update MODIFY
Cairo#


Cairo#
Oct  5 07:32:35.979: %BGP-3-NOTIFICATION: received from neighbor 192.168.255.3 4/0
  (hold time expired) 0 bytes
Cairo#
Oct  5 07:32:35.979: %BGP-5-ADJCHANGE: neighbor 192.168.255.3 Down BGP Notification
  received
Cairo#
Cairo#sh ip bgp summary
BGP router identifier 192.168.255.1, local AS number 100
BGP table version is 118, main routing table version 118
9 network entries using 1080 bytes of memory
9 path entries using 468 bytes of memory
4/3 BGP path/bestpath attribute entries using 496 bytes of memory
1 BGP AS-PATH entries using 24 bytes of memory
0 BGP route-map cache entries using 0 bytes of memory
0 BGP filter-list cache entries using 0 bytes of memory
Bitfield cache entries: current 1 (at peak 1) using 32 bytes of memory
BGP using 2100 total bytes of memory
BGP activity 32/23 prefixes, 76/67 paths, scan interval 60 secs

Neighbor        V    AS MsgRcvd MsgSent   TblVer  InQ OutQ Up/Down  State/PfxRcd
192.168.255.2   4   100    164     164      118    0    0 02:07:36            1
192.168.255.3   4   100    138     110        0    0    0 00:02:55 Active
192.168.255.4   4   100    177     168      118    0    0 02:07:36            7
Cairo#
Cairo#
Cairo#sh ip bgp
BGP table version is 118, local router ID is 192.168.255.1
Status codes: s suppressed, d damped, h history, * valid, > best, i - internal,
```

```
           r RIB-failure, S Stale
Origin codes: i - IGP, e - EGP, ? - incomplete


   Network           Next Hop          Metric LocPrf Weight Path
*>i10.10.10.0/24     192.168.255.4          0    100      0 200 i
*>i10.20.20.0/25     192.168.255.4          0    100      0 200 i
*>i172.16.0.0/20     192.168.255.4          0    100      0 200 i
*> 192.168.255.1/32 0.0.0.0                 0         32768 i
r>i192.168.255.2/32 192.168.255.2          0    100      0 i
r>i192.168.255.4/32 192.168.255.4          0    100      0 i
*>i192.168.255.5/32 192.168.255.4          0    100      0 200 i
*>i192.168.255.6/32 192.168.255.4          0    100      0 200 i
*>i192.168.255.7/32 192.168.255.4          0    100      0 200 i
Cairo#
```

The commands **show ip bgp summary** and **show ip bgp** were entered on Cairo after shutting down Loopback0 on Sharqia but before the holdtime expires. Both outputs show that Sharqia was still listed as a perfectly healthy neighbor at Cairo and the BGP, table was still showing the routes through Sharqia as valid and best routes. Approximately 3 minutes later, the holdtime expires, Sharqia is declared down, and the routes through that router are withdrawn from the BGP table.

Example 5-56 shows the BGP configuration on Cairo only. Note that the line **no bgp nexthop trigger enable** has disappeared. Because the feature is enabled by default, and the statement is not showing up in the configuration, and the negated form of the command is also not showing up, means that the feature is enabled. Also the trigger delay is decreased to 0 seconds using the command **bgp nexthop trigger delay 0** to make the failure detection immediate.

Example 5-56   *BGP Configuration on Cairo Showing the NHT Feature Enabled and the Trigger Delay Decreased to 0 Seconds*

```
Cairo
router bgp 100
 no synchronization
 bgp log-neighbor-changes
 bgp nexthop trigger delay 0
 network 192.168.255.1 mask 255.255.255.255
 neighbor 192.168.255.2 remote-as 100
 neighbor 192.168.255.2 update-source Loopback0
 neighbor 192.168.255.3 remote-as 100
 neighbor 192.168.255.3 update-source Loopback0
 neighbor 192.168.255.4 remote-as 100
 neighbor 192.168.255.4 update-source Loopback0
 no auto-summary
```

Now the same failure scenario is executed by shutting down interface Sharqia's Loopback0. Example 5-57 shows the commands and outputs on Sharqia and Cairo. Pay attention to the timestamps of the log messages to realize the speed by which the BGP table is updated after enabling the NHT feature. Moreover, before the hold timer expires and the routes are removed from the BGP table, the BGP best path algorithm has already been run, and the routes via Sinai are chosen as best.

Example 5-57 *Failure Scenario with the NHT Feature Enabled*

```
Sharqia(config)#interface loopback 0
Sharqia(config-if)#shut
Sharqia(config-if)#
Oct  5 07:39:03.019: %LINK-5-CHANGED: Interface Loopback0, changed state to
  administratively down
Oct  5 07:39:04.019: %LINEPROTO-5-UPDOWN: Line protocol on Interface Loopback0,
  changed state to down
Sharqia(config-if)#
```

```
Cairo#debug ip bgp rib-filter
BGP Rib filter debugging is on
Cairo#
Oct  5 07:38:55.595: BGP- ATF: Debuging is OFF
Oct  5 07:38:55.599: BGP- ATF: Debuging is ON
Cairo#
Oct  5 07:39:06.719: BGP- ATF: EVENT 192.168.255.3/32 RIB update DOWN
Oct  5 07:39:06.719: BGP- ATF: T 192.168.255.3/32 (0) c=0x6746C3A4 Query pending
Oct  5 07:39:06.723: BGP- ATF: R 192.168.255.3/32 (0) -> Fa1/0 10.0.0.2 Deleting
Oct  5 07:39:06.723: BGP- ATF: EVENT Query 192.168.255.3/32 (0) did not find route
Oct  5 07:39:06.727: BGP- ATF: Notifying 192.168.255.3/32 (0)
Oct  5 07:39:06.727: BGP- ATF: T 192.168.255.3/32 (0) c=0x6746C3A4 Adding to client
  notification queue
Oct  5 07:39:06.731: BGP- ATF: EVENT 192.168.255.4/32 (0) Track start
Oct  5 07:39:06.731: BGP- ATF: 192.168.255.4/32 (0) Adding track
Oct  5 07:39:06.735: BGP- ATF: EVENT Query 192.168.255.4/32 (0) found route
Oct  5 07:39:06.735: BGP- ATF: 192.168.255.4/32 (0) Adding route
Oct  5 07:39:06.735: BGP- ATF: R 192.168.255.4/32 (0) -> Updating route
Oct  5 07:39:06.739: BGP- ATF: R 192.168.255.4/32 (0) -> Fa1/0 10.0.0.2 Notifying
Oct  5 07:39:06.739: BGP- ATF: T 192.168.255.4/32 (0) c=0x6746C3CC Adding to client
  notification queue
Oct  5 07:39:06.743: BGP- ATF: EVENT 192.168.255.2/32 (0) Track start
Oct  5 07:39:06.743: BGP- ATF: 192.168.255.2/32 (0) Adding track
Oct  5 07:39:06.743: BGP- ATF: EVENT Query 192.168.255.2/32 (0) found route
Oct  5 07:39:06.747: BGP- ATF: 192.168.255.2/32 (0) Adding route
Oct  5 07:39:06.747: BGP- ATF: R 192.168.255.2/32 (0) -> Updating route
Oct  5 07:39:06.747: BGP- ATF: R 192.168.255.2/32 (0) -> Fa1/0 10.0.0.2 Notifying
Oct  5 07:39:06.751: BGP- ATF: T 192.168.255.2/32 (0) c=0x6746C3B8 Adding to client
  notification queue
```

```
Oct  5 07:39:06.767: BGP- ATF: EVENT 10.10.10.0/24 RIB update MODIFY
Oct  5 07:39:06.767: BGP- ATF: EVENT 10.20.20.0/25 RIB update MODIFY
Oct  5 07:39:06.771: BGP- ATF: EVENT 172.16.0.0/20 RIB update MODIFY
Oct  5 07:39:06.771: BGP- ATF: EVENT 192.168.255.5/32 RIB update MODIFY
Oct  5 07:39:06.775: BGP- ATF: EVENT 192.168.255.6/32 RIB update MODIFY
Oct  5 07:39:06.775: BGP- ATF: EVENT 192.168.255.7/32 RIB update MODIFY
Cairo#
Cairo#show ip bgp summary
BGP router identifier 192.168.255.1, local AS number 100
BGP table version is 133, main routing table version 133
9 network entries using 1080 bytes of memory
15 path entries using 780 bytes of memory
4/3 BGP path/bestpath attribute entries using 496 bytes of memory
1 BGP AS-PATH entries using 24 bytes of memory
0 BGP route-map cache entries using 0 bytes of memory
0 BGP filter-list cache entries using 0 bytes of memory
Bitfield cache entries: current 1 (at peak 1) using 32 bytes of memory
BGP using 2412 total bytes of memory
BGP activity 33/24 prefixes, 83/68 paths, scan interval 60 secs

Neighbor        V    AS MsgRcvd MsgSent   TblVer  InQ OutQ Up/Down  State/PfxRcd
192.168.255.2   4   100     169     169      133    0    0 02:12:50           1
192.168.255.3   4   100     148     117      133    0    0 00:02:28           6
192.168.255.4   4   100     182     173      133    0    0 02:12:50           7
Cairo#show ip bgp
BGP table version is 133, local router ID is 192.168.255.1
Status codes: s suppressed, d damped, h history, * valid, > best, i - internal,
              r RIB-failure, S Stale
Origin codes: i - IGP, e - EGP, ? - incomplete

   Network          Next Hop          Metric LocPrf Weight Path
* i10.10.10.0/24    192.168.255.3          0    100      0 200 i
*>i                 192.168.255.4          0    100      0 200 i
* i10.20.20.0/25    192.168.255.3          0    100      0 200 i
*>i                 192.168.255.4          0    100      0 200 i
* i172.16.0.0/20    192.168.255.3          0    100      0 200 i
*>i                 192.168.255.4          0    100      0 200 i
*> 192.168.255.1/32 0.0.0.0                0           32768 i
r>i192.168.255.2/32 192.168.255.2          0    100      0 i
r>i192.168.255.4/32 192.168.255.4          0    100      0 i
* i192.168.255.5/32 192.168.255.3          0    100      0 200 i
*>i                 192.168.255.4          0    100      0 200 i
* i192.168.255.6/32 192.168.255.3          0    100      0 200 i
*>i                 192.168.255.4          0    100      0 200 i
* i192.168.255.7/32 192.168.255.3          0    100      0 200 i
```

```
*>i                192.168.255.4          0    100      0 200 i
Cairo#
Cairo#
Oct  5 07:41:17.871: %BGP-3-NOTIFICATION: received from neighbor 192.168.255.3 4/0
  (hold time expired) 0 bytes
Cairo#
Oct  5 07:41:17.871: %BGP-5-ADJCHANGE: neighbor 192.168.255.3 Down BGP Notification
  received
Cairo#
```

You should have noticed by now that the NHT feature depends on the local RIB being updated by the IGP, which means that the feature works only for IBGP peers that have IGP running between them. Because EBGP peers do not run an IGP, this feature is not relevant, and other features are required for speeding up the detection of failures and the subsequent convergence. One of those features is the Fast External Fallover, also called Fast Session Deactivation, which is the subject of the following section.

Fast External Fallover

Fast External Fallover, also called *Fast Session Deactivation*, is an optimization for enhancing the detection of failures affecting EBGP sessions. Before the introduction of this feature, some context is required. If a link between two EBGP peers fails, the peers have to wait for the hold timer (default 180 seconds) to expire before declaring the peer dead and tearing down the EBGP session. Fast External Fallover eliminates the need to wait for the hold timer to expire by tracking the interface on which the peering is active. When the interface goes down, the EBGP peering is brought down immediately afterward. This feature is enabled by default in Cisco IOS.

In Figure 5-23, routers Memphis and Alexandria are EBGP peers. Memphis is in AS100 and Alexandria is in AS200. The EBGP session between them is up and the Fast External Fallover is enabled by default.

In Example 5-58, interface Serial3/0 is shut down on Cairo. The BGP session immediately goes down.

Example 5-58 *Interface Failure with the Default Fast External Fallover Enabled*

```
Cairo(config)#interface Serial 3/0
Cairo(config-if)#shut
Cairo(config-if)#
*Oct  3 07:21:16.322: %BGP-5-ADJCHANGE: neighbor 10.0.0.2 Down Interface flap
Cairo(config-if)#
*Oct  3 07:21:18.282: %LINK-5-CHANGED: Interface Serial3/0, changed state to
  administratively down
Cairo(config-if)#
*Oct  3 07:21:18.282: %ENTITY_ALARM-6-INFO: ASSERT INFO Se3/0 Physical Port
  Administrative State Down
```

```
*Oct  3 07:21:19.282: %LINEPROTO-5-UPDOWN: Line protocol on Interface Serial3/0,
  changed state to down
Cairo(config-if)#
```

```
Alexandria#
*Oct  3 07:21:47.270: %LINEPROTO-5-UPDOWN: Line protocol on Interface Serial3/0,
  changed state to down
*Oct  3 07:21:47.286: %BGP-5-ADJCHANGE: neighbor 10.0.0.1 Down Interface flap
Alexandria#
```

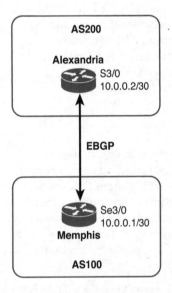

Figure 5-23 *Topology for the Fast External Fallover Example*

In Example 5-59, the command **no bgp fast-external-fallover** disables the feature under the BGP process.

Example 5-59 *Disabling Fast External Fallover*

```
Cairo
router bgp 100
 no bgp fast-external-fallover
 no bgp default ipv4-unicast
 bgp log-neighbor-changes
 neighbor 10.0.0.2 remote-as 200
 !
 address-family ipv4
  neighbor 10.0.0.2 activate
  no auto-summary
```

```
    no synchronization
  exit-address-family
```

```
Alexandria
router bgp 200
 no bgp fast-external-fallover
 no bgp default ipv4-unicast
 bgp log-neighbor-changes
 neighbor 10.0.0.1 remote-as 100
 !
 address-family ipv4
  neighbor 10.0.0.1 activate
  no auto-summary
  no synchronization
 exit-address-family
```

After disabling Fast External Fallover, the same failure scenario is repeated by shutting down interface Serial3/0 on Cairo (Example 5-60). Note that the EBGP session goes down approximately 3 minutes later, and the log message received explicitly states "hold time expired."

Example 5-60   *Failure After Disabling Fast External Fallover*

```
Cairo(config)#interface Serial 3/0
Cairo(config-if)#shut
Cairo(config-if)#
*Oct  3 07:27:31.874: %LINK-5-CHANGED: Interface Serial3/0, changed state to
  administratively down
Cairo(config-if)#
*Oct  3 07:27:31.874: %ENTITY_ALARM-6-INFO: ASSERT INFO Se3/0 Physical Port
  Administrative State Down
*Oct  3 07:27:32.874: %LINEPROTO-5-UPDOWN: Line protocol on Interface Serial3/0,
  changed state to down
Cairo(config-if)#
*Oct  3 07:29:49.026: %BGP-5-ADJCHANGE: neighbor 10.0.0.2 Down BGP Notification sent
Cairo(config-if)#
*Oct  3 07:29:49.026: %BGP-3-NOTIFICATION: sent to neighbor 10.0.0.2 4/0
  (hold time expired) 0 bytes

Alexandria#
*Oct  3 07:27:57.278: %LINEPROTO-5-UPDOWN: Line protocol on Interface Serial3/0,
  changed state to down
Alexandria#
*Oct  3 07:29:49.298: %BGP-5-ADJCHANGE: neighbor 10.0.0.1 Down BGP Notification sent
Alexandria#
*Oct  3 07:29:49.298: %BGP-3-NOTIFICATION: sent to neighbor 10.0.0.1 4/0
  (hold time expired) 0 bytes
```

Fast External Fallover may be configured under the general BGP process for all neighbors as detailed in the preceding example. It may also be configured per neighbor using the following statement:

```
neighbor {ip-address} fall-over
```

And finally, it may be configured per interface using the following statement:

```
ip bgp fast-external-fallover [permit | deny]
```

Bidirectional Forwarding Detection (BFD)

Before getting into how BFD is used by BGP to rapidly detect failures and thus significantly speed up convergence, review some background information on BFD.

BFD stands for Bidirectional Forwarding Detection and is a standard protocol defined in RFC 5880. The usage of BFD by IPv4 and IPv6 was standardized in RFC 5881.

BFD is a simple, independent[9] Hello protocol that detects failures between two systems. At a basic level, the operation of BFD constitutes two systems periodically transmitting BFD packets back and forth between them. The path is declared to be operational as long as there is two-way communication. If a system does not receive the BFD packets for a specific duration, the other system is declared to be down.

BFD is session-based and does not depend on neighbor discovery. The two systems using the BFD protocol do a three-way handshake and eventually become BFD neighbors. When the BFD neighbor relationship is established and the "liveness" of the peer is under the administration of the BFD protocol, another protocol, usually referred to as the "client" protocol, such as BGP, can then use this BFD service to determine whether a neighbor is up or down.

So far, BFD seems to be similar, if not identical, to most routing protocol Hello mechanisms. So what makes BFD different?

Following is a list of the characteristics of the BFD protocol that help differentiate it from other protocols:

- BFD provides failure detection within time intervals as low as 150 msec.

- BFD always runs in unicast mode.

- BFD always runs in point-to-point mode.

- BFD runs over any media.

- It operates over any data path, whether single-hop, multi-hop, physical, or virtual.

- It runs at any protocol layer, and BFD packets are carried as the payload of whatever encapsulating protocol is running over the network or path.

---

[9] That is, BFD can be leveraged by multiple routing and forwarding protocols on a given router.

- It has low overhead.

- Unlike routing protocol Hellos that are entirely implemented in the control plane, most components of BFD are implemented in the forwarding engine of a system, making it effective for use with graceful-restart and during other failures that directly affect the control engine of a system.

- BFD can run on unidirectional links, as long as there is some return path for BFD packets.

- One BFD session can be established per path between two systems when multiple paths exist between the two systems.

- BFD Control packets must be transmitted in UDP packets with destination port 3784 with a source port in the range 49152 through 65535.

- BFD Echo packets must be transmitted in UDP packets with destination UDP port 3784. (The Echo function is explained next.)

A BFD session is established upon request from the client protocol. The IP address of the system with which BFD is to establish a neighbor is also determined by the client protocol. As previously mentioned, BFD does not discover neighbors. However, it may establish a peering with a neighbor discovered by another protocol, such as via OSPF Hellos.

BFD operates in one of two modes: Asynchronous or Demand. In Asynchronous mode, the two systems continuously exchange BFD packets to establish liveness, whereas in Demand mode, BFD packets are sent only occasionally whenever the connectivity with the neighbor needs to be verified.

Finally, the BFD Echo function allows one system to send a series of BFD packets for the other system to loop back through the forwarding path back to the first system. This has an advantage in leveraging fast hardware-based switching of the packets on the far end system and removes all dependencies on the far-end system's CPU. The Echo function can be used with either Asynchronous or Demand modes.

Cisco has the following prerequisites published for BFD operations:

- Cisco CEF and IP routing must be enabled on routers running BFD.

- Before running BFD, at least one client routing protocol must be active on the router.

- Which routing protocols are supported as BFD client protocols, whether IPv6 networks are supported, whether the Demand mode and Echo function are supported, whether multihop BFD sessions are supported, are all dependent on the hardware platform and IOS version of the router running BFD.

To configure BFD on Cisco IOS, BFD is enabled per interface using the following interface-level command:

```
bfd interval {milliseconds} min_rx {milliseconds} multiplier {multiplier-value}
```

The following explanation clarifies what each value stands for

- **interval** {*milliseconds*}: This is the rate at which BFD control packets are sent to the BFD peer on this interface in milliseconds and could be any value between 50 to 999 msec inclusive.

- **min_rx** {*milliseconds*} This is the rate at which BFD control packets will be expected to be received from the BFD peer on this interface and could be any value between 50 to 999 msec inclusive.

- **multiplier** {*multiplier-value*}: This is the number of consecutive BFD control packets that if missed from the peer, that peer is declared dead. The number of packets can be between 3 and 50 inclusive.

The BFD Echo function is enabled by default. However, if it is not, or it has been disabled, the command to enable it under interface configuration mode is

```
bfd echo
```

Recall that the Echo function leverages the fast-switching path through hardware of the remote BFD peer, without causing any extra load on the CPU. For this reason, when it is used, the regular BFD control packets can be sent and received at much lower rates because now the Echo function is the primary mechanism for detecting failures rapidly. In this case, Cisco uses the following command to configure "Slow Timers":

```
bfd slow-timers [milliseconds]
```

When this statement is used, the BFD control packet transmit rate as well as the expected receive rate correspond to the value configured in this statement, whereas the faster rates configured earlier in the **bfd interval** statement are used for the Echo function. The value of the slow timers argument can be anything from 1,000 to 30,000 msec and when omitted takes the default value of 1000. What if the Echo function is enabled (as it is, by default) but the **bfd slow-timers** statement is not configured? In this case the BFD control packets are transmitted every 1000 msec, and the Echo packets are transmitted at the rate specified in the bfd interval command.

Now that you have established a baseline understanding of what BFD is, what it does, and how it is configured, examine how BGP uses BFD by becoming BFD's client to speed up failure detection.

The following router mode statement is used to enable BGP to track the status of a BFD session for a particular neighbor:

```
neighbor {ip-address} fall-over bfd
```

After the statement is entered, a BFD session is initiated with the neighbor IP address in the statement, and BFD control packets are exchanged between the BFD/BGP neighbors.

To verify your configuration and confirm that the BFD session is up, use the following command:

```
show bfd neighbors [details]
```

Figure 5-24 revisits our router friends Alexandria and Memphis to test the concepts and configurations studied so far. Routers Memphis and Alexandria are EBGP peers. The configuration on both routers is shown in Example 5-61.

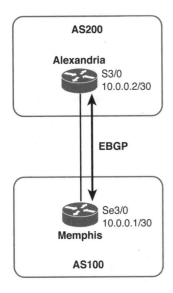

Figure 5-24   *Topology for the Bidirectional Forwarding Detection Example*

Example 5-61   *Basic EBGP Peering Configuration Between Routers Memphis and Alexandria*

```
Memphis
!
interface Serial2/0
 ip address 10.0.0.1 255.255.255.252
end
!
router bgp 100
 bgp log-neighbor-changes
 neighbor 10.0.0.2 remote-as 200
 !
```

```
Alexandria
!
interface Serial2/0
 ip address 10.0.0.2 255.255.255.252
end
!
router bgp 200
 bgp log-neighbor-changes
 neighbor 10.0.0.1 remote-as 100
 !
```

In Example 5-62, a basic BFD configuration is applied to interface Serial2/0 on both routers. The command **show bfd neighbors details** is used to check the status of the BFD neighborship between Memphis and Alexandria. As expected, there is no output. As previously mentioned, the BFD session is initiated only upon request from the client protocol, in this case, BGP.

Example 5-62   *Basic Interface-Level BFD Configuration*

```
Memphis
!
interface Serial2/0
 ip address 10.0.0.1 255.255.255.252
 bfd interval 500 min_rx 500 multiplier 5
end
!

Alexandria
!
interface Serial2/0
 ip address 10.0.0.2 255.255.255.252
 bfd interval 500 min_rx 500 multiplier 5
end
!

Memphis#show bfd neighbors details
Memphis#

Alexandria#show bfd neighbors details
Alexandria#
```

In Example 5-63 BGP is configured to request BFD to initiate a session between Memphis and Alexandria using the statement **neighbor** {*IP-Address*} **fall-over bfd**. That session will be tracked to confirm the neighbor liveness on both sides. When this configuration is in place, the command show bfd neighbors details is issued again, only this time, the bfd neighbor states show that the neighborship is up and active.

Example 5-63 *BGP Configured to Initiate a BFD Session*

```
Memphis
!
router bgp 100
 bgp log-neighbor-changes
 neighbor 10.0.0.2 remote-as 200
 neighbor 10.0.0.2 fall-over bfd
!
```

```
Alexandria
!
router bgp 200
 bgp log-neighbor-changes
 neighbor 10.0.0.1 remote-as 100
 neighbor 10.0.0.1 fall-over bfd
!
```

```
Memphis#show bfd neighbors details

IPv4 Sessions
NeighAddr                          LD/RD       RH/RS      State     Int
10.0.0.2                           1/1         Up         Up        Se2/0
Session state is UP and using echo function with 500 ms interval.
Session Host: Software
OurAddr: 10.0.0.1
Handle: 1
Local Diag: 0, Demand mode: 0, Poll bit: 0
MinTxInt: 1000000, MinRxInt: 1000000, Multiplier: 5
Received MinRxInt: 1000000, Received Multiplier: 5
Holddown (hits): 0(0), Hello (hits): 1000(254)
Rx Count: 237, Rx Interval (ms) min/max/avg: 1/2800/925 last: 321 ms ago
Tx Count: 255, Tx Interval (ms) min/max/avg: 4/2783/936 last: 17 ms ago
Elapsed time watermarks: 0 0 (last: 0)
Registered protocols: BGP
Uptime: 00:03:38
Last packet: Version: 1            - Diagnostic: 0
             State bit: Up         - Demand bit: 0
             Poll bit: 0           - Final bit: 0
             C bit: 0
             Multiplier: 5         - Length: 24
             My Discr.: 1          - Your Discr.: 1
```

```
                Min tx interval: 1000000      - Min rx interval: 1000000
                Min Echo interval: 500000
Memphis#


Alexandria#show bfd neighbors details


IPv4 Sessions
NeighAddr                          LD/RD      RH/RS     State    Int
10.0.0.1                           1/1        Up        Up       Se2/0
Session state is UP and using echo function with 500 ms interval.
Session Host: Software
OurAddr: 10.0.0.2
Handle: 1
Local Diag: 0, Demand mode: 0, Poll bit: 0
MinTxInt: 1000000, MinRxInt: 1000000, Multiplier: 5
Received MinRxInt: 1000000, Received Multiplier: 5
Holddown (hits): 0(0), Hello (hits): 1000(316)
Rx Count: 310, Rx Interval (ms) min/max/avg: 1/2906/941 last: 1655 ms ago
Tx Count: 318, Tx Interval (ms) min/max/avg: 4/2785/922 last: 13 ms ago
Elapsed time watermarks: 0 0 (last: 0)
Registered protocols: BGP
Uptime: 00:04:52
Last packet: Version: 1           - Diagnostic: 0
             State bit: Up         - Demand bit: 0
             Poll bit: 0           - Final bit: 0
             C bit: 0
             Multiplier: 5         - Length: 24
             My Discr.: 1          - Your Discr.: 1
             Min tx interval: 1000000   - Min rx interval: 1000000
             Min Echo interval: 500000
Alexandria#
```

Note a few things in the output of Example 5-63: the Echo function is enabled and uses the interval values configured in the interface-level command **bfd interval 500 min_rx 500 multiplier 5**. The second thing to notice is that the interval values for the BFD control packets, indicated in the outputs by MinTxInt and MinRxInt, are 1000 msec. (This version of IOS shows the intervals in micro-seconds.) Recall that when the Echo function is enabled (which is true by default) and the slow timers are not configured, the BFD control packets are exchanged at the default interval of 1000 msec. Furthermore, the line "Registered Protocols: BGP," indicating the protocols currently using the BFD protocol.

One interesting piece of information in the previous output is the field Demand bit: 0. When this bit is 0, the BFD runs in Asynchronous mode. When it is 1, then BFD runs in Demand mode. Although there is no statement to explicitly enable Demand mode in Cisco IOS, this bit still provides an indication to the BFD mode running on the router.

The slow timers are configured to be 20,000 msec in Example 5-64 using the command **bfd slow-timers** {*msec*}. Notice how the MinTxInt and MinRxInt values change to match the slow timers configured.

Example 5-64 *Configuring the BFD Slow Timers*

```
Memphis(config)#bfd slow-timers 20000
Memphis#
Memphis#show bfd neighbors details

IPv4 Sessions
NeighAddr                              LD/RD         RH/RS      State     Int
10.0.0.2                                1/1          Up         Up        Se2/0
Session state is UP and using echo function with 500 ms interval.
Session Host: Software
OurAddr: 10.0.0.1
Handle: 1
Local Diag: 0, Demand mode: 0, Poll bit: 0
MinTxInt: 20000000, MinRxInt: 20000000, Multiplier: 5
Received MinRxInt: 1000000, Received Multiplier: 5
Holddown (hits): 0(0), Hello (hits): 20000(869)
Rx Count: 853, Rx Interval (ms) min/max/avg: 1/21147/1595 last: 3268 ms ago
Tx Count: 872, Tx Interval (ms) min/max/avg: 4/19871/1583 last: 2162 ms ago
Elapsed time watermarks: 0 0 (last: 0)
Registered protocols: BGP
Uptime: 00:22:42
Last packet: Version: 1              - Diagnostic: 0
             State bit: Up           - Demand bit: 0
             Poll bit: 0             - Final bit: 0
             C bit: 0
             Multiplier: 5           - Length: 24
             My Discr.: 1            - Your Discr.: 1
             Min tx interval: 1000000 - Min rx interval: 1000000
             Min Echo interval: 500000
Memphis#

Alexandria(config)#bfd slow-timers 20000
Alexandria#
Alexandria#show bfd neighbors details

IPv4 Sessions
NeighAddr                              LD/RD         RH/RS      State     Int
10.0.0.1                                1/1          Up         Up        Se2/0
```

```
Session state is UP and using echo function with 500 ms interval.
Session Host: Software
OurAddr: 10.0.0.2
Handle: 1
Local Diag: 0, Demand mode: 0, Poll bit: 0
MinTxInt: 20000000, MinRxInt: 20000000, Multiplier: 5
Received MinRxInt: 20000000, Received Multiplier: 5
Holddown (hits): 0(0), Hello (hits): 20000(851)
Rx Count: 852, Rx Interval (ms) min/max/avg: 1/19869/1617 last: 14712 ms ago
Tx Count: 856, Tx Interval (ms) min/max/avg: 4/21121/1610 last: 14362 ms ago
Elapsed time watermarks: 0 0 (last: 0)
Registered protocols: BGP
Uptime: 00:23:11
Last packet: Version: 1          - Diagnostic: 0
            State bit: Up        - Demand bit: 0
            Poll bit: 0          - Final bit: 0
            C bit: 0
            Multiplier: 5        - Length: 24
            My Discr.: 1         - Your Discr.: 1
            Min tx interval: 20000000  - Min rx interval: 20000000
            Min Echo interval: 500000
Alexandria#
```

The statement for enabling BGP use of the BFD session is similar to the Fast External Fallover feature covered in the previous section. A question may arise as to the difference between them and why you would need BFD. Consider the topology in Figure 5-25. Here, routers Aswan and Suez are not directly connected. The EBGP session is established over an IXP. Connectivity over an IXP is similar to having a switch connect two routers. What happens if Suez fails or Suez's interface to the network fails? There is no IGP running between both routers, so NHT is irrelevant. Aswan's interface to the network is still up; therefore, Aswan does not detect any failures and Fast External Fallover does not function. In cases such as this, BFD is the best (sometimes only) solution for rapid failure detection. Without the use of BFD, Aswan must wait for the BGP hold time to expire, which is 180 seconds by default, before detecting a failure of its BGP peer.

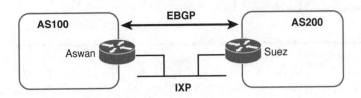

Figure 5-25 *BFD Is Needed for Aswan and Suez to Detect Power-Layer Failures if the IXP Is a Switch*

Testing the failure detection capabilities of BFD on the topology in Figure 5-25, interface Serial2/0 of router Aswan connected to the network is shut down in Example 5-65. From the timestamps, we can see that Suez waits for approximately 3 minutes to detect that Aswan is dead or unreachable. In Example 5-66, BFD is then configured on the BGP session between both routers and the same test is repeated again. Now, with an interval of 300 and a multiplier value of 3, the convergence is almost immediate.

Example 5-65 *Failure of Aswan's Interface to Suez Without BFD Configured*

```
Aswan(config)#interface e0/0
Aswan(config-if)#shut
Aswan(config-if)#
*Oct  4 11:48:47.764: %BGP-5-ADJCHANGE: neighbor 192.168.100.2 Down Interface flap
*Oct  4 11:48:47.771: %BGP_SESSION-5-ADJCHANGE: neighbor 192.168.100.2 IPv4 Unicast
  topology base removed from session  Interface flap
Aswan(config-if)#
*Oct  4 11:48:49.723: %LINK-5-CHANGED: Interface Ethernet0/0, changed state to
  administratively down
*Oct  4 11:48:50.792: %LINEPROTO-5-UPDOWN: Line protocol on Interface Ethernet0/0,
  changed state to down
Aswan(config-if)#
```

```
Suez#
*Oct  4 11:51:38.217: %BGP-5-ADJCHANGE: neighbor 192.168.100.1 Down BGP Notification
  sent
*Oct  4 11:51:38.217: %BGP-3-NOTIFICATION: sent to neighbor 192.168.100.1 4/0
  (hold time expired) 0 bytes
Suez#
*Oct  4 11:51:38.254: %BGP_SESSION-5-ADJCHANGE: neighbor 192.168.100.1 IPv4 Unicast
  topology base removed from session  BGP Notification sent
Suez#
```

Example 5-66 *Failure of Aswan's Interface After BFD Is Configured*

```
Aswan#sh bfd neighbors

IPv4 Sessions
NeighAddr                          LD/RD       RH/RS       State       Int
192.168.100.2                      1/1         Up          Up          Et0/0
Aswan#
```

```
Suez#show bfd neighbors

IPv4 Sessions
NeighAddr                          LD/RD       RH/RS       State       Int
192.168.100.1                      1/1         Up          Up          Et0/0
```

```
Suez#
```

```
Aswan(config)#interface Ethernet0/0
Aswan(config-if)#shut
Aswan(config-if)#
*Oct  4 11:58:21.484: %BGP-5-ADJCHANGE: neighbor 192.168.100.2 Down Interface flap
*Oct  4 11:58:21.485: %BGP_SESSION-5-ADJCHANGE: neighbor 192.168.100.2 IPv4 Unicast
  topology base removed from session  Interface flap
*Oct  4 11:58:23.619: %LINK-5-CHANGED: Interface Ethernet0/0, changed state to
  administratively down
*Oct  4 11:58:24.625: %LINEPROTO-5-UPDOWN: Line protocol on Interface Ethernet0/0,
  changed state to down
Aswan(config-if)#
```

```
Suez#
*Oct  4 11:58:22.361: %BGP-5-ADJCHANGE: neighbor 192.168.100.1 Down BFD adjacency
  down
*Oct  4 11:58:22.361: %BGP_SESSION-5-ADJCHANGE: neighbor 192.168.100.1 IPv4 Unicast
  topology base removed from session  BFD adjacency down
Suez#
```

An alternative method to apply the configuration commands covered so far in this section is to use a BFD template. This is similar in concept to session and policy templates discussed earlier in this chapter in that it groups all the commands under one template, which can then be applied to several interfaces (single-hop) or several BGP neighbors (multihop), keeping the configuration relatively compact and manageable. Beyond the compact and manageable configuration, some BFD configurations can be applied only under a BFD template, such as dampening and authentication. BFD templates could be used to configure single-hop or multi-hop BFD sessions. The configuration for each is different.

The following list identifies the tasks required to configure a single-hop BFD template:

■ Create a BFD template and enter the BFD configuration mode using the global configuration command **bfd-template single-hop** {template-name}.

■ Configure the BFD timers using the command **interval min-tx** {milliseconds} **min-rx** {milliseconds} **multiplier** {multiplier-value}.

■ Optionally, enable the Echo function using the command **echo**.

■ Optionally, configure BFD dampening using the command **dampening** [half-life-period reuse-threshold suppress-threshold max-suppress-time].

■ Optionally, configure BFD authentication. This requires the configuration of a key chain and then using the command **authentication** {authentication-type} **keychain** {keychain-name}.

- Apply the template to the interface using the interface mode command **bfd template** {template-name}.

- Use the command **neighbor** {IP-Address} **fall-over bfd** to enable BGP use of BFD for the corresponding neighbor session.

The following list identifies the tasks required to configure a multihop BFD template:

- Create a BFD template and enter the BFD configuration mode using the global configuration command **bfd-template multi-hop** {template-name}.

- Configure the BFD timers using the command **interval min-tx** {milliseconds} **min-rx** {milliseconds} **multiplier** {multiplier-value}.

- Optionally, configure BFD dampening using the command **dampening** [half-life-period reuse-threshold suppress-threshold max-suppress-time].

- Optionally, configure BFD authentication. This requires the configuration of a key chain and then using the command **authentication** {authentication-type} **keychain** {keychain-name}.

- Create a BFD map that associates the parameters configured in the template in step 1 with a unique address pair using the global configuration command **bfd map ipv4** {destination/length} {source/length} {template-name}.

- Use the command **neighbor** {IP-Address} **fall-over bfd multi-hop** to enable BGP use of BFD for the corresponding neighbor session.

Based on the two preceding lists, configuring BFD templates should be straightforward. When configured using a template, BFD and BGP both behave in the same way as displayed earlier in this section.

BGP Prefix Independent Convergence (PIC)

The previous sections discussing NHT, Fast External Fallover, and BFD have all covered techniques to speed up failure detection. However, when the failure is detected the following takes place:

- The failed routes are withdrawn from the BGP table, RIB, and FIB.

- Update messages are sent to the neighbors to withdraw the failed routes.

- The best path algorithm is run to choose new best paths.

- The new best paths are installed in the BGP table, RIB, and FIB.

- The new best paths are announced via Update messages to the BGP neighbors.

Therefore, BGP convergence primarily depends on the speed by which the router runs the best-path algorithm to find an alternative path to the destination. This, in turn, depends on the size of the BGP table, or in other words, the number of prefixes in the table.

Because the bottleneck in the convergence of BGP is in the number of prefixes in the BGP table, to speed up convergence, this dependency needs to be eliminated, and this is exactly what the BGP Prefix Independent Convergence (PIC) feature does. At press time, BGP PIC is still in the Internet-draft stage in the IETF.

This is how it works: In cases where more than one path to a prefix exists, when BGP runs the best path algorithm, instead of finding the best path only, it finds the best path and the second-best path and installs both in the BGP, RIB, and CEF tables. When a failure in the primary path is detected, the backup/alternative path immediately replaces the primary path in all three tables without the need to do any BGP table walks or running the best-path algorithm first. This is conceptually similar to the EIGRP Feasible Successor function. The dependency on the size of the BGP table is eliminated, and BGP convergence is dramatically enhanced. As you can see, BGP PIC is a purely data plane feature that operates at the RIB and CEF level.

The BGP PIC is complementary to the features listed at the start of this section, namely NHT, Fast External Fallover, and BFD. These features detect a failure, and the BGP PIC handles the convergence to the alternative path. However, the functionality of the BGP PIC does depend on the type of failure. If a link/node failure is internal to the AS, the failure is detected by the NHT feature, and the IGP updates the RIB which in turn updates the FIB. For a directly connected link or node failure, the failure is detected by the Fast External Fallover or BFD features that are directly monitored by CEF, which directly updates the FIB. The discussions so far imply that an alternative path needs to exist, and if only one path to a destination exists, the BGP PIC feature becomes irrelevant.

Consider the topology in Figure 5-26. The routers in AS100 form a full mesh of IBGP sessions and so do the routers in AS200. Subnet 10.20.30.0/24 is behind router Arish in AS200 and is announced to routers Luxor and Sharm via the AS IGP, and Luxor and Sharm in turn inject the subnet into BGP. The subnet is announced via EBGP to Sharqia and Sinai. Sharqia's best path to subnet 10.20.30.0/24 is via its EBGP peer Luxor. Similarly, Sinai's best path to the same subnet is via its EBGP peer Sharm. Because of the full mesh in AS100, Cairo receives two announcements for subnet 10.20.30.0/24, one from Sharqia and the other from Sinai.

When BGP PIC is enabled and the BGP best path algorithm is run, a best path is chosen as well as a second-best path, and both are installed in the BGP, RIB, and FIB tables in Cairo. After a failure happens affecting Sharqia or the path to Sharqia, the path via Sinai to 10.20.30.0/24 is installed in Cairo's RIB and FIB tables directly without the need to run the BGP best path algorithm first.

The BGP PIC feature is enabled using the command **bgp additional-paths install** under the BGP address-family configuration mode. Address-family configuration is covered in detail in Chapter 6. Example 5-67 shows Cairo's configuration. For the sake of brevity, the configurations of the other routers in Figure 5-26 are not because nothing new is in their BGP configurations.

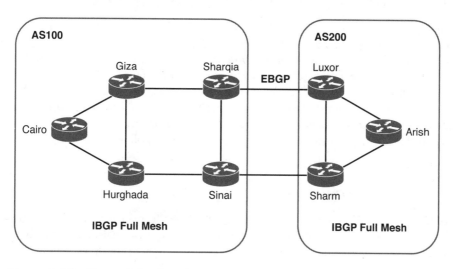

Figure 5-26 *Network for the BGP PIC Demonstration*

Example 5-67 *BGP Configuration on Cairo Showing the bgp additional-paths install Statement*

```
router bgp 100
 bgp log-neighbor-changes
 neighbor 192.168.255.2 remote-as 100
 neighbor 192.168.255.2 update-source Loopback0
 neighbor 192.168.255.3 remote-as 100
 neighbor 192.168.255.3 update-source Loopback0
 neighbor 192.168.255.4 remote-as 100
 neighbor 192.168.255.4 update-source Loopback0
 neighbor 192.168.255.5 remote-as 100
 neighbor 192.168.255.5 update-source Loopback0
 !
 address-family ipv4
  bgp additional-paths install
  neighbor 192.168.255.2 activate
  neighbor 192.168.255.3 activate
  neighbor 192.168.255.4 activate
  neighbor 192.168.255.5 activate
 exit-address-family
```

An important configuration statement related to BGP PIC is **no bgp recursion host** that is also configured under the bgp address-family section. This statement did not show up in the configuration in Example 5-66 because it's enabled by default.

To understand why bgp recursion needs to be disabled when using the BGP PIC feature, you need to understand what the default behavior of CEF is for BGP next hops. Now, by default, when a BGP prefix next hop fails, CEF "recurses" through the FIB to try to find the next longest matching path to a prefix (for example, 10.10.10.0/24 if 10.10.10.100/32 fails). When the BGP PIC feature is enabled, there is no requirement for CEF to do that because an alternative path for the prefix is already available. Not only is it not required, it actually slows down the BGP PIC. Therefore, when the BGP PIC feature is enabled, CEF recursion is disabled, by default, for the following next hops:

- Next hops with /32 masks

- Directly connected next hops

Disabling CEF recursion is not a prerequisite for the BGP PIC feature to work and it can be enabled by issuing the command **bgp recursion host** under the BGP address-family section. However, it is recommended to disable recursion to not slow down the BGP PIC functionality.

To verify that the backup/alternative/repair path has been installed in the BGP table, issue the command **show ip bgp** and its variants. To verify that the backup path has been installed in the RIB, issue the command **show ip route repair-paths** and its variants. Finally, to verify that the backup path has been installed in the FIB, issue to the command **show ip cef** {*ip-address*}{*mask*} **detail**. Example 5-68 shows the outputs for all three commands.

Example 5-68 *Verifying That the Backup Path Has Been Installed in the BGP, RIB, and FIB Tables*

```
Cairo#sh ip bgp
BGP table version is 12, local router ID is 192.168.255.1
Status codes: s suppressed, d damped, h history, * valid, > best, i - internal,
              r RIB-failure, S Stale, m multipath, b backup-path, f RT-Filter,
              x best-external, a additional-path, c RIB-compressed,
Origin codes: i - IGP, e - EGP, ? - incomplete
RPKI validation codes: V valid, I invalid, N Not found

     Network          Next Hop            Metric LocPrf Weight Path
 *>i 10.20.30.0/24    192.168.255.4           11    100      0 200 i
 *bi                  192.168.255.5           11    100      0 200 i
Cairo#
Cairo#sh ip bgp 10.20.30.0 255.255.255.0
BGP routing table entry for 10.20.30.0/24, version 12
Paths: (2 available, best #1, table default)
  Additional-path-install
```

```
   Not advertised to any peer
   Refresh Epoch 1
   200
     192.168.255.4 (metric 21) from 192.168.255.4 (192.168.255.4)
       Origin IGP, metric 11, localpref 100, valid, internal, best
   Refresh Epoch 1
   200
     192.168.255.5 (metric 21) from 192.168.255.5 (192.168.255.5)
       Origin IGP, metric 11, localpref 100, valid, internal, backup/repair
Cairo#
Cairo#sh ip route repair-paths
Codes: L - local, C - connected, S - static, R - RIP, M - mobile, B - BGP
       D - EIGRP, EX - EIGRP external, O - OSPF, IA - OSPF inter area
       N1 - OSPF NSSA external type 1, N2 - OSPF NSSA external type 2
       E1 - OSPF external type 1, E2 - OSPF external type 2
       i - IS-IS, su - IS-IS summary, L1 - IS-IS level-1, L2 - IS-IS level-2
       ia - IS-IS inter area, * - candidate default, U - per-user static route
       o - ODR, P - periodic downloaded static route, H - NHRP, l - LISP
       + - replicated route, % - next hop override


Gateway of last resort is not set

     10.0.0.0/8 is variably subnetted, 9 subnets, 3 masks
C       10.0.0.0/30 is directly connected, Ethernet0/0
L       10.0.0.1/32 is directly connected, Ethernet0/0
C       10.0.0.4/30 is directly connected, Ethernet0/1
L       10.0.0.5/32 is directly connected, Ethernet0/1
O       10.0.0.8/30 [110/20] via 10.0.0.6, 01:08:03, Ethernet0/1
                    [110/20] via 10.0.0.2, 01:08:03, Ethernet0/0
O       10.0.0.12/30 [110/20] via 10.0.0.2, 01:08:03, Ethernet0/0
O       10.0.0.16/30 [110/20] via 10.0.0.6, 01:08:03, Ethernet0/1
O       10.0.0.20/30 [110/30] via 10.0.0.6, 01:08:03, Ethernet0/1
                     [110/30] via 10.0.0.2, 01:08:03, Ethernet0/0
B       10.20.30.0/24 [200/11] via 192.168.255.4, 00:32:58
                      [RPR][200/11] via 192.168.255.5, 00:32:58
     192.168.255.0/32 is subnetted, 5 subnets
C       192.168.255.1 is directly connected, Loopback0
O       192.168.255.2 [110/11] via 10.0.0.2, 01:08:13, Ethernet0/0
O       192.168.255.3 [110/11] via 10.0.0.6, 01:08:03, Ethernet0/1
O       192.168.255.4 [110/21] via 10.0.0.2, 01:08:03, Ethernet0/0
O       192.168.255.5 [110/21] via 10.0.0.6, 01:08:03, Ethernet0/1
Cairo#
Cairo#sh ip route repair-paths 10.20.30.0 255.255.255.0
Routing entry for 10.20.30.0/24
  Known via "bgp 100", distance 200, metric 11
  Tag 200, type internal
```

```
   Last update from 192.168.255.4 00:33:19 ago
   Routing Descriptor Blocks:
 * 192.168.255.4, from 192.168.255.4, 00:33:19 ago
      Route metric is 11, traffic share count is 1
      AS Hops 1
      Route tag 200
      MPLS label: none
   [RPR]192.168.255.5, from 192.168.255.5, 00:33:19 ago
      Route metric is 11, traffic share count is 1
      AS Hops 1
      Route tag 200
      MPLS label: none
Cairo#
Cairo#sh ip cef 10.20.30.0 255.255.255.0 detail
10.20.30.0/24, epoch 0, flags rib only nolabel, rib defined all labels
  recursive via 192.168.255.4
    nexthop 10.0.0.2 Ethernet0/0
  recursive via 192.168.255.5, repair
    nexthop 10.0.0.6 Ethernet0/1
Cairo#
```

The alternative/backup entries in the BGP table is labeled in the output by either "b" or "backup/repair." The backup routes in the RIB are labeled "RPR." Finally the backup routes are labeled "repair" in the FIB (CEF) table.

ADD-PATHS Capability

The preceding does not conclude the discussion on BGP PIC. You need to consider several caveats. Recall that when a BGP speaker receives several alternative routes to a destination, all the routes are installed in the BGP table. However, after the BGP best-path algorithm is run and only one path is chosen as best, only that path is installed in the routing table, and only that path is announced in the outgoing BGP updates of that router. The BGP PIC feature changes this default behavior locally on the router that it is configured on, but it does not change the default behavior of the outgoing BGP updates. Even when the BGP PIC feature is enabled on a router, only the best path is announced to this router's BGP neighbors.

In Figure 5-27, a new link is added between Sharqia and Sharm, and EBGP peering is configured between both routers. In addition, the bgp additional-paths install is configured on router Sharqia, as shown in Example 5-69. Looking at Sharqia's BGP, RIB, and FIB tables in Example 5-70, you can see that the path through its EBGP neighbor Luxor is installed as the primary best path, whereas the path through its EBGP neighbor Sharm is installed as the backup/alternative path. The path through its IBGP peer Sinai is also installed in Sharqia's tables, but it is not marked as a backup/alternative path.

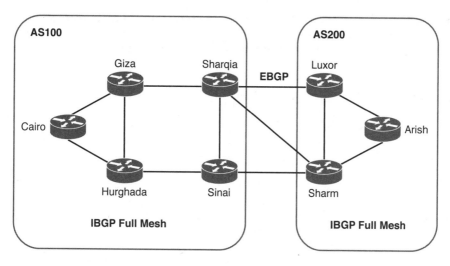

Figure 5-27 *A New Link Is Added Between Routers Sharqia and Sharm*

Example 5-69 *Sharqia's Configuration with the Added Link to Sharm and BGP PIC Enabled*

```
router bgp 100
 bgp log-neighbor-changes
 neighbor 10.0.0.26 remote-as 200
 neighbor 10.0.0.46 remote-as 200
 neighbor 192.168.255.1 remote-as 100
 neighbor 192.168.255.1 update-source Loopback0
 neighbor 192.168.255.2 remote-as 100
 neighbor 192.168.255.2 update-source Loopback0
 neighbor 192.168.255.3 remote-as 100
 neighbor 192.168.255.3 update-source Loopback0
 neighbor 192.168.255.5 remote-as 100
 neighbor 192.168.255.5 update-source Loopback0
 !
 address-family ipv4
  bgp additional-paths install
  neighbor 10.0.0.26 activate
  neighbor 10.0.0.46 activate
  neighbor 192.168.255.1 activate
  neighbor 192.168.255.1 next-hop-self
  neighbor 192.168.255.2 activate
  neighbor 192.168.255.2 next-hop-self
  neighbor 192.168.255.3 activate
  neighbor 192.168.255.3 next-hop-self
  neighbor 192.168.255.5 activate
  neighbor 192.168.255.5 next-hop-self
 exit-address-family
```

Example 5-70 *BGP, RIB, and FIB Tables on Sharqia Indicating That the Alternative/
Backup Path Has Been Installed in All Three Tables*

```
Sharqia#sh ip bgp
BGP table version is 5, local router ID is 192.168.255.4
Status codes: s suppressed, d damped, h history, * valid, > best, i - internal,
              r RIB-failure, S Stale, m multipath, b backup-path, f RT-Filter,
              x best-external, a additional-path, c RIB-compressed,
Origin codes: i - IGP, e - EGP, ? - incomplete
RPKI validation codes: V valid, I invalid, N Not found

     Network          Next Hop          Metric LocPrf Weight Path
 *b  10.20.30.0/24    10.0.0.46             11                0 200 i
 *  i                 192.168.255.5         11    100         0 200 i
 *>                   10.0.0.26             11                0 200 i
Sharqia#
Sharqia#sh ip route repair-paths 10.20.30.0 255.255.255.0
Routing entry for 10.20.30.0/24
  Known via "bgp 100", distance 20, metric 11
  Tag 200, type external
  Last update from 10.0.0.26 00:10:14 ago
  Routing Descriptor Blocks:
  * 10.0.0.26, from 10.0.0.26, 00:10:14 ago, recursive-via-conn
      Route metric is 11, traffic share count is 1
      AS Hops 1
      Route tag 200
      MPLS label: none
   [RPR]10.0.0.46, from 10.0.0.46, 00:10:14 ago, recursive-via-conn
      Route metric is 11, traffic share count is 1
      AS Hops 1
      Route tag 200
      MPLS label: none
Sharqia#
Sharqia#sh ip cef 10.20.30.0 255.255.255.0 detail
10.20.30.0/24, epoch 0, flags rib only nolabel, rib defined all labels
  recursive via 10.0.0.26
    attached to Ethernet1/1
  recursive via 10.0.0.46, repair
    attached to Ethernet1/2
Sharqia#
```

Now looking at what Sharqia announces to Cairo in Example 5-71 using the command **show ip bgp 192.168.255.1 neighbor advertised-routes**, you can see that even
though the path through Sharm is installed in Sharqia's tables as a backup path, it is
not announced to Cairo. Example 5-72 shows the BGP, RIB, and FIB tables on Cairo

showing that Cairo still uses the path through its IBGP peer Sinai as the backup path because it has not received the Sharqia-Sharm path.

Example 5-71 *Routes Advertised to Cairo by Sharqia Indicating Only Sharqia's Best Route Is Announced to Cairo*

```
Sharqia#sh ip bgp neighbors 192.168.255.1 advertised-routes
BGP table version is 5, local router ID is 192.168.255.4
Status codes: s suppressed, d damped, h history, * valid, > best, i - internal,
              r RIB-failure, S Stale, m multipath, b backup-path, f RT-Filter,
              x best-external, a additional-path, c RIB-compressed,
Origin codes: i - IGP, e - EGP, ? - incomplete
RPKI validation codes: V valid, I invalid, N Not found


     Network          Next Hop            Metric LocPrf Weight Path
 *>  10.20.30.0/24    10.0.0.26              11            0 200 i


Total number of prefixes 1
Sharqia#
```

Example 5-72 *BGP, RIB, and FIB Tables on Cairo Indicating That Sharqia Has Not Announced Its Alternative/Backup Sharqia-Sharm Path to Cairo*

```
Cairo#show ip bgp
BGP table version is 2, local router ID is 192.168.255.1
Status codes: s suppressed, d damped, h history, * valid, > best, i - internal,
              r RIB-failure, S Stale, m multipath, b backup-path, f RT-Filter,
              x best-external, a additional-path, c RIB-compressed,
Origin codes: i - IGP, e - EGP, ? - incomplete
RPKI validation codes: V valid, I invalid, N Not found


     Network          Next Hop            Metric LocPrf Weight Path
 *bi 10.20.30.0/24    192.168.255.5          11    100     0 200 i
 *>i                  192.168.255.4          11    100     0 200 i
Cairo#
Cairo#sh ip route repair-paths 10.20.30.0 255.255.255.0
Routing entry for 10.20.30.0/24
  Known via "bgp 100", distance 200, metric 11
  Tag 200, type internal
  Last update from 192.168.255.4 00:19:29 ago
  Routing Descriptor Blocks:
  * 192.168.255.4, from 192.168.255.4, 00:19:29 ago
      Route metric is 11, traffic share count is 1
      AS Hops 1
      Route tag 200
```

```
      MPLS label: none
    [RPR]192.168.255.5, from 192.168.255.5, 00:19:29 ago
      Route metric is 11, traffic share count is 1
      AS Hops 1
      Route tag 200
      MPLS label: none
Cairo#
Cairo#show ip cef 10.20.30.0 255.255.255.0 detail
10.20.30.0/24, epoch 0, flags rib only nolabel, rib defined all labels
  recursive via 192.168.255.4
    nexthop 10.0.0.2 Ethernet0/0
  recursive via 192.168.255.5, repair
    nexthop 10.0.0.6 Ethernet0/1
Cairo#
```

The preceding example has shown that the BGP PIC feature affects the behavior of the router on which it is configured, only locally, and that it does not affect the outgoing updates for that router. This has further implication on other topologies. Consider, for example, the topology in Figure 5-28. Similar to the previous topology in Figure 5-27, this topology consists of AS100 and AS200. Subnet 10.20.30.0/24 is behind router Arish. This subnet is announced to Luxor and Sharm via the AS IGP. Both routers then inject this subnet into BGP and announce it to Shaqia and Sinai in AS100 via EBGP. Now, the difference is that routers Giza and Hurghada are route reflectors. (Route reflectors are covered later in this chapter. You can read ahead to that section if this discussion confuses you.) Routers Sharqia and Sinai prefer their EBGP paths to subnet 10.20.30.0/24 via Luxor and Sharm, respectively. Sharqia and Sharm both announce their best path to the subnet to both route reflectors. Each RR now has two paths to the subnet, one via Sharqia and one via Sharm.

If all attributes are left at their default values, both RRs prefer the route via Sharqia because of its lower BGP RID. Consequently, only the path via Sharqia is installed in the RRs' routing tables and announced to Cairo. The route via Sinai is never known to Cairo, which renders the BGP PIC feature irrelevant in this case.

To take this one step further, consider Figure 5-29 in which routers Thebes, Gesa, and Hermopolis are border routers in AS100, whereas Amarna is a border router in AS200. Gesa receives an announcement for subnet 10.20.30.0/24 from its upstream EBGP peer (not shown in the figure) and also Hermopolis receives an announcement for the same subnet via its upstream EBGP peer. Both routers announce the two different routes to the same destination prefix to Thebes so that Thebes has two routes to subnet 10.20.30.0/24 in its BGP table. Thebes runs the BGP best path algorithm, chooses the best path to the subnet 10.20.30.0/24, and announces only that best path to its EBGP peer Amarna. Consequently, BGP PIC plays no role on Amarna if the current best path to 10.20.30.0/24 fails.

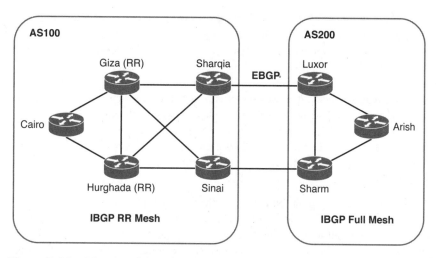

Figure 5-28   *The Topology of Figure 5-27 Is Changed, and Routers Giza and Hurghada Are Configured as Route Reflectors*

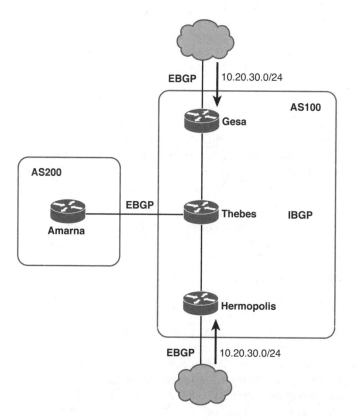

Figure 5-29   *AS100 Is Receiving Routes to the Same Destination Prefix from Two Different Neighboring Autonomous Systems*

Therefore, based on the previous case studies, the prerequisite of having multiple BGP paths to the same destination, for the BGP PIC to come into play, should be clear. Further, a BGP speaker announces only its best route to its BGP peers (rules related to IBGP versus EBGP sessions apply), normal BGP operations also dictate that: If a BGP speaker receives two consecutive announcements for the same prefix over the same session, and each announcement is via a different route/path, the newer one is maintained and the older one is withdrawn. This is called *implicit withdrawal*. For example, if Thebes and Gesa are BGP peers and Thebes sends an UPDATE message to Gesa for 10.0.0.0/8 via 1.1.1.1, and later sends an UPDATE message to Gesa again for 10.0.0.0/8, but this time via 2.2.2.2, Gesa withdraws the first route (10.0.0.0/8 via 1.1.1.1) from its BGP table and installs the newer route via 2.2.2.2.

To overcome the limitation of announcing only the best path as well as the function of implicit withdrawal, and hence allow a BGP speaker to announce more than just its best path to a prefix, and to allow a receiver to retain two or more different paths for the same destination prefix received over the same session, a new BGP capability called the ADD-PATH capability was introduced that has the Capability number 69. This capability allows a BGP speaker to indicate to its peer in the OPEN message whether it can send and receive more than one path per destination prefix. IETF draft draft-ietf-idr-add-paths-10 builds on this capability by defining a new 4-octet field in the BGP UPDATE message labeled Path Identifier. This Path ID is a value assigned by the announcing router that uniquely identifies a destination prefix along with the associated path/route. Therefore, two updates for two different paths to the same destination prefix can have two different Path Identifiers.

The ADD-PATH capability can be configured either per address-family using the statement **bgp additional-paths** {send[receive]|receive} or per neighbor (under the bgp address-family section) using the statement **neighbor** {*ip-address*} **additional-paths** {send[receive]|receive}, with the **neighbor-level** command having higher precedence over the **address-family** statement. The **send** and **receive** arguments indicate whether the BGP speaker can send only, receive only, or send and receive additional paths.

After the capability is configured, defining which routes qualify as "candidate" routes to be advertised is configured using either of the following statements:

- **bgp additional-paths select group-best**

- **bgp additional-paths select best** {number}

- **bgp additional-paths select all**

The first command selects only one best-path per AS so that the list of candidate routes is a list of each AS's best path. For example, for one particular prefix, a router receives paths P11 and P12 from AS1, paths P21 and P22 from AS2, and paths P31 and P32 from AS3. After running the best path algorithm per AS, it found that path P11 is the best path from AS1; path P21 is the best path from AS2; and finally, path P31 is the best path from AS3. Then the result of configuring this command will be that the list of candidate routes is P11, P12, and P13.

The second command simply selects the number of best paths that will be candidate paths for announcements. For example, if the {number} argument in the command is 3, the list of candidate paths include the best path, the second-best path, and the third-best path. The number argument can be either 2 or 3 only.

The third command includes all valid paths to a prefix into the list of candidate paths.

After the list of candidate paths is configured, the command **neighbor** {*ip-address*} **advertise additional-paths** [**best** *number*][**group-best**][**all**] advertises to a specific neighbor a subset of the candidate routes defined in the preceding step.

Referring to Figure 5-27, routers Cairo and Sharqia are configured to negotiate the ADD-PATH capability. Cairo is configured to receive additional paths, whereas Sharqia is configured to send additional paths. Sharqia is then configured to send to Cairo the best path in addition to the second-best path. Example 5-73 shows the relevant configurations.

Example 5-73 *Routers Cairo and Sharqia in Figure 5-26 Are Configured to Support the ADD-PATH Capability*

```
Cairo
router bgp 100
 bgp log-neighbor-changes
 neighbor 192.168.255.2 remote-as 100
 neighbor 192.168.255.2 update-source Loopback0
 neighbor 192.168.255.3 remote-as 100
 neighbor 192.168.255.3 update-source Loopback0
 neighbor 192.168.255.4 remote-as 100
 neighbor 192.168.255.4 update-source Loopback0
 neighbor 192.168.255.5 remote-as 100
 neighbor 192.168.255.5 update-source Loopback0
 !
 address-family ipv4
 bgp additional-paths receive
  bgp additional-paths install
  neighbor 192.168.255.2 activate
  neighbor 192.168.255.3 activate
  neighbor 192.168.255.4 activate
  neighbor 192.168.255.5 activate
 exit-address-family

Sharqia
router bgp 100
 bgp log-neighbor-changes
 neighbor 10.0.0.26 remote-as 200
 neighbor 10.0.0.46 remote-as 200
```

```
neighbor 192.168.255.1 remote-as 100
neighbor 192.168.255.1 update-source Loopback0
neighbor 192.168.255.2 remote-as 100
neighbor 192.168.255.2 update-source Loopback0
neighbor 192.168.255.3 remote-as 100
neighbor 192.168.255.3 update-source Loopback0
neighbor 192.168.255.5 remote-as 100
neighbor 192.168.255.5 update-source Loopback0
!
address-family ipv4
 bgp additional-paths select best 2
 bgp additional-paths send
 bgp additional-paths install
 neighbor 10.0.0.26 activate
 neighbor 10.0.0.46 activate
 neighbor 192.168.255.1 activate
 neighbor 192.168.255.1 next-hop-self
 neighbor 192.168.255.1 advertise additional-paths best 2
 neighbor 192.168.255.2 activate
 neighbor 192.168.255.2 next-hop-self
 neighbor 192.168.255.3 activate
 neighbor 192.168.255.3 next-hop-self
 neighbor 192.168.255.5 activate
 neighbor 192.168.255.5 next-hop-self
exit-address-family
```

Example 5-74 shows the output from the **show ip bgp neighbors 192.168.255.1 advertised-routes** on Sharqia and the **show ip bgp 10.20.30.0 255.255.255.0** output on Cairo. You can see that Sharqia now advertises to Cairo the two routes it learned from both its EBGP peers, whereas Cairo now has three routes to 10.20.30.0/24 in its BGP table.

Note   When the additional-paths capability is added to a neighbor, that session is reset so that the new capability can be negotiated. You should be aware of this disruption and only configure it on an existing neighbor during a maintenance window.

Example 5-74   *Outputs from Routers Cairo and Sharqia Showing the Effects of the* Additional-Paths *Configuration*

```
Cairo#show ip bgp
BGP table version is 11, local router ID is 192.168.255.1
Status codes: s suppressed, d damped, h history, * valid, > best, i - internal,
              r RIB-failure, S Stale, m multipath, b backup-path, f RT-Filter,
```

```
              x best-external, a additional-path, c RIB-compressed,
Origin codes: i - IGP, e - EGP, ? - incomplete
RPKI validation codes: V valid, I invalid, N Not found

      Network          Next Hop          Metric LocPrf Weight Path
 *bi 10.20.30.0/24     192.168.255.5         11    100     0 200 i
 *  i                  192.168.255.4         11    100     0 200 i
 *>i                   192.168.255.4         11    100     0 200 i
Cairo#
Cairo#show ip bgp 10.20.30.0 255.255.255.0
BGP routing table entry for 10.20.30.0/24, version 11
Paths: (3 available, best #3, table default)
  Additional-path-install
  Not advertised to any peer
  Refresh Epoch 2
  200
    192.168.255.5 (metric 21) from 192.168.255.5 (192.168.255.5)
      Origin IGP, metric 11, localpref 100, valid, internal, backup/repair
      rx pathid: 0, tx pathid: 0
  Refresh Epoch 1
  200
    192.168.255.4 (metric 21) from 192.168.255.4 (192.168.255.4)
      Origin IGP, metric 11, localpref 100, valid, internal
      rx pathid: 0x1, tx pathid: 0
  Refresh Epoch 1
  200
    192.168.255.4 (metric 21) from 192.168.255.4 (192.168.255.4)
      Origin IGP, metric 11, localpref 100, valid, internal, best
      rx pathid: 0x0, tx pathid: 0x0
Cairo#
Cairo#show ip route repair-paths 10.20.30.0
Routing entry for 10.20.30.0/24
  Known via "bgp 100", distance 200, metric 11
  Tag 200, type internal
  Last update from 192.168.255.4 00:04:49 ago
  Routing Descriptor Blocks:
  * 192.168.255.4, from 192.168.255.4, 00:04:49 ago
      Route metric is 11, traffic share count is 1
      AS Hops 1
      Route tag 200
      MPLS label: none
    [RPR]192.168.255.5, from 192.168.255.5, 00:04:49 ago
      Route metric is 11, traffic share count is 1
      AS Hops 1
      Route tag 200
```

```
        MPLS label: none
Cairo#
Cairo#sh ip cef 10.20.30.0 255.255.255.0 detail
10.20.30.0/24, epoch 0, flags rib only nolabel, rib defined all labels
  recursive via 192.168.255.4
    nexthop 10.0.0.2 Ethernet0/0
  recursive via 192.168.255.5, repair
    nexthop 10.0.0.6 Ethernet0/1
Cairo #



Sharqia#show ip bgp neighbors 192.168.255.1 advertised-routes
BGP table version is 8, local router ID is 192.168.255.4
Status codes: s suppressed, d damped, h history, * valid, > best, i - internal,
              r RIB-failure, S Stale, m multipath, b backup-path, f RT-Filter,
              x best-external, a additional-path, c RIB-compressed,
Origin codes: i - IGP, e - EGP, ? - incomplete
RPKI validation codes: V valid, I invalid, N Not found

    Network          Next Hop          Metric LocPrf Weight Path
 *>  10.20.30.0/24    10.0.0.46             11            0 200 i
 *b a10.20.30.0/24    10.0.0.26             11            0 200 i

Total number of prefixes 2
Sharqia#
```

There are two things to note in the output. First, the path id field in the **show ip bgp 10.20.30.0 255.255.255.0** output. Recall that this is a 4-byte value that is assigned by the advertising router that sends the additional paths to identify different routes for the same prefix. Second, note the "a" that was added to the output on Sharqia besides the entry for subnet 10.20.30.0/24 in the BGP table, identifying this route as an additional path to be advertised to the respective neighbors.

Graceful Restart

Another feature that enhances BGP scalability is Graceful Restart (GR). Similar to many features discussed so far, GR is a capability that is negotiated between two BGP speakers during the BGP session establishment by including this capability in the OPEN message. The Capability Code of GR is 64. BGP GR is defined in RFC4724 and is a key enabler of Non-Stop Forwarding (NSF).

To understand what GR accomplishes, recall what happens in normal cases in which a router running BGP fails or the BGP process goes down. Its BGP neighbors detect this failure. The speed of detecting this failure depends on whether the peer is directly connected, whether the session is IBGP or EBGP, and what features are enabled on the platforms. When the neighbor is declared dead, the routes received from this neighbor are withdrawn from the BGP, RIB, and FIB tables, followed by sending UPDATE messages to the other neighbors to withdraw these routes. Again, depending on which features are enabled and whether alternative routes exist, a neighbor may have to run the best path algorithm first, and install the new routes in the BGP, RIB, and FIB tables, before it resumes forwarding to the affected prefixes. All this can be destabilizing when a router is restarted as a part of a routine maintenance.

Graceful Restart gives a router that is intentionally restarted a way to tell its neighbors, "I'm going away, but I'll be right back." Neighbors can then, instead of declaring the router down and going through all the chaos that entails, wait a bit for the router to come back.

Because the GR feature is specific to systems with dual Route Processors (RP), first look at how dual RP routers deal with a failure on the primary RP, which is followed by a switchover to the standby RP. During normal operations, or right after a failure, a router receives BGP routes from neighbors, runs the best path algorithm, and then updates the Routing Information Base (RIB) with the best paths (assuming no other routing protocols with better admin distances have routes to the same prefixes). After the RIB is updated, CEF updates the Forwarding Information Base (FIB) and Adjacency tables. On dual RP routers, the CEF updates both the active RP as well as the standby RP, such that both RPs have replicas of the CEF forwarding tables. BGP runs on the primary RP only, not on the standby RP. Only the forwarding tables are updated on the standby RP.

Now when the primary RP fails, if the GR feature is not enabled, the BGP session on the failed RP is torn down, a switchover to the standby RP happens, the BGP session is re-established on the new primary RP, and the router goes through the same convergence process previously described.

How does the GR feature help mitigate the adverse effects on forwarding during the preceding sequence of events? The BGP GR feature identifies two types of routers: GR-capable and GR-aware routers. GR-capable routers are routers with dual Route Processors (RP) in which one acts as the primary RP and the other as the standby RP. If an RP switchover from the primary to the standby occurs, GR capable routers that have the feature enabled continue to forward traffic in the forwarding plane using CEF, even though the BGP process goes down and up again (flaps). GR-aware routers, however, are routers that are not necessarily dual RP routers but do understand and negotiate this capability and continue forwarding *to* a GR capable router that is experiencing an RP switchover.

How does GR accomplish this? As previously described, during normal operations, CEF updates both RPs such that the standby RP has the latest FIB and Adjacency tables up to the time that the primary RP fails. Moreover, routers that employ distributed CEF (dCEF) and perform the forwarding on the line cards also have their line cards updated with the latest forwarding tables up to the time that the failure happens. When a failure on the primary RP happens and a switchover to the standby RP is initiated, GR-aware neighbors (referred to as "Receiving Speaker" in the RFC) detect that the BGP with the GR-capable neighbor (referred to as the "Restarting Speaker" in the RFC) has gone down. A "restart timer" that is specified in the OPEN message during the capability negotiation defines how long the receiving speaker will wait for the restarting speaker to re-establish the BGP session. If this timer expires without the restarting speaker re-establishing the BGP session, it is assumed that this neighbor is not coming back up and the regular convergence process continues as normal. In the meantime, the restarting speaker maintains the forwarding capability, and the receiving speaker maintains the routes from the restarting speaker and keeps forwarding traffic to it. Despite using the old CEF tables for the forwarding, these entries are marked as "stale" in the RIB of the restarting speaker.

When the restart is complete and the BGP session is re-established on the new primary RP, the restarting speaker receives updates from its peers and deletes all the stale entries, replacing them with the newly received routes.

Graceful restart is configured as follows:

■ Globally using the router mode command **bgp graceful-restart [restart-time** *seconds* **| stalepath-time** *seconds*]**[all]**

■ per neighbor or peer group using the command **neighbor {***IP-Address***} ha-mode graceful-restart**

■ Inside a session template using the command **ha-mode graceful-restart**

The restart timer in the first command is 120 seconds by default and the stalepath-timer is 360 seconds by default. As mentioned earlier in this section, the restart timer defines how long the receiving speaker waits for the restarting speaker to re-establish the BGP session. As for the stalepath timer, it defines the maximum duration that the receiving speaker retains the stale routing entries before discarding them if it does not receive updated routes from the restarting speaker.

One feature that is usually referenced in the context of high availability is Non-Stop Routing (NSR). This feature is different than Non-Stop Forwarding (NSF) and it is, as the name implies, the capability of doing "uninterrupted" or "Non-Stop" routing (not forwarding) during an RP switchover. This feature is basically the capability of the router to keep the standby RP updated with the latest routing information, so it can "pick up" the BGP session as soon as the active RP goes down. The BGP peers to the NSR-capable router, and in this case, would be unaware of any failure events on the router that experienced the RP switchover. NSR is not standards-based, like GR/NSF because it does not need any interaction between the BGP peers. NSR is more convenient in cases in which BGP speakers are not GR/NSF-aware. However, NSR does consume significantly more system resources because both active and standby RPs maintain fully updated routing information.

Maximum Prefixes

As shown throughout this chapter, the main strength of BGP that makes it a better choice for large-scale networks such as the Internet is its scalability. Scalability, as you've already learned throughout this chapter, means that it functions in a stable, consistent, and predictive manner while locally maintaining a large number of routes as well as receiving a large number of routes from peers. However, there is always a limit for everything, including the number of routes that a router running BGP can receive, process, store, and maintain. If a router keeps receiving routes from a BGP neighbor nonstop, maybe because of some error at the sending peer, at some point, the receiving router will run out of resources and crash.

Therefore, some feature needs to maintain control of the number of routes received from any one BGP peer, and this feature needs to trigger some protective action if the number of received routes exceeds a specific threshold. This is exactly what the BGP Maximum-Prefixes feature does.

Another use for the BGP Maximum-Prefixes feature is in service provider edges. If part of an agreement with a customer is that they never send more than a given number of prefixes, Maximum-Prefixes can enforce that policy. Then, if through some configuration error, the customer tries to flood a large number of unauthorized prefixes to the service provider, he can be blocked or the SP can be warned.

To implement this feature effectively, a network operator first needs to have a baseline of the number of routes received per neighbor under normal operating conditions and the average change in the number of routes, due to normal operations, in a given time period. For example, a network operator should know that router R1 in his network receives a full Internet routing table from its EBGP neighbor R10. Therefore, the number of routes should not exceed 575,000 routes, whereas due to normal operations this number may increase or decrease by 2000 routes throughout 1 week. Then, it would be safe to assume that the maximum number of prefixes received from R10 will (or should) by no means exceed 580,000 routes.

The maximum-prefixes feature is a simple feature, both in concept and configuration. The number of routes received from a neighbor is monitored. As the number of received routes approaches a preconfigured maximum, one of three actions is taken:

- When the router receives a percentage of the configured maximum number of routes (referred to as the threshold) from the BGP neighbor, a warning log message is issued. Then, the BGP session is reset if the maximum number of routes received exceeds the configured maximum value.

- The exact same actions as previously discussed, except that the router re-establishes the BGP session with the violating BGP peer after a configured interval of time.

- The router issues a log message when a percentage of the maximum number of routes is received from the neighbor. Then another log message, per prefix is received after that. The routes are installed in the BGP table without any further action.

This feature is mostly useful with EBGP peers; however, it can be configured for any type of BGP neighbor.

The statement to enable this feature per neighbor follows:

```
neighbor {IP-Address} maximum-prefix {maximum} [threshold] [restart restart-
   interval] [warning-only]
```

The *maximum* argument specifies the maximum number of routes at which an action
will be taken, either to reset the peering session or to issue a log message. The optional
threshold argument is a percentage of the maximum number of routes at which the
router will issue a log message. If the optional keyword **warning-only** is used, the BGP
session is not reset if the maximum number of routes is reached. Instead, only a warning
log message is issued.

The optional *restart-interval* argument specifies a time interval in minutes, after which
the peering session with the violating peer is re-established. If this option is not used, a
clear ip bgp {*ip-address*} needs to be issued to re-establish the peering session with that
neighbor.

Figure 5-30 is a simple topology consisting of the same two routers we've seen before,
Memphis and Alexandria. A BGP session is established between them. As shown in
Example 5-75, Memphis is configured to accept a maximum number of 10 routes from
Alexandria and to log a warning message when 70 percent of this number of routes is
received (7 routes). Memphis is also configured to re-establish the peering session with
Alexandria after a time interval of 2 minutes, after the peering session is torn down
because of the violation.

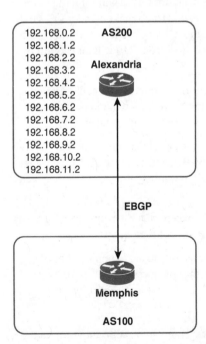

Figure 5-30   *Memphis Is Configured to Accept Only a Maximum of 10 Prefixes from
Alexandria*

Example 5-75 *BGP Configuration on R1 Showing the Maximum Prefix Feature Configuration*

```
Memphis
router bgp 100
 bgp log-neighbor-changes
 neighbor 10.0.0.2 remote-as 200
 neighbor 10.0.0.2 maximum-prefix 10 70 restart 2
```
```
Alexandria
router bgp 200
 bgp log-neighbor-changes
 neighbor 10.0.0.1 remote-as 100
```

The **show ip bgp neighbors** {*IP-Address*} command output on Memphis is shown in Example 5-76. Note the sections that show the specifics of the maximum-prefix feature configuration

Example 5-76 *Output from the* **show ip bgp neighbors** *Command on Both Memphis and Alexandria*

```
Memphis#show ip bgp neighbors
*Oct  5 00:44:41.888: %BGP-5-ADJCHANGE: neighbor 10.0.0.2 Up
R1#sh ip bgp neighbors 10.0.0.2
BGP neighbor is 10.0.0.2,  remote AS 200, external link
  BGP version 4, remote router ID 10.0.0.2
  BGP state = Established, up for 00:00:10
  Last read 00:00:10, last write 00:00:10, hold time is 180, keepalive interval is
  60 seconds
  Neighbor sessions:
    1 active, is not multisession capable (disabled)
  Neighbor capabilities:
    Route refresh: advertised and received(new)
    Four-octets ASN Capability: advertised and received
    Address family IPv4 Unicast: advertised and received
    Enhanced Refresh Capability: advertised and received
    Multisession Capability:
    Stateful switchover support enabled: NO for session 1
  Message statistics:
    InQ depth is 0
    OutQ depth is 0

                        Sent        Rcvd
    Opens:                 1           1
    Notifications:         0           0
```

```
     Updates:                  0          0
     Keepalives:               1          1
     Route Refresh:            0          0
     Total:                    2          2
   Default minimum time between advertisement runs is 30 seconds


For address family: IPv4 Unicast
 Session: 10.0.0.2
 BGP table version 1, neighbor version 1/0
 Output queue size : 0
 Index 1, Advertise bit 0
 1 update-group member
 Slow-peer detection is disabled
 Slow-peer split-update-group dynamic is disabled
                            Sent       Rcvd
 Prefix activity:           ----       ----
   Prefixes Current:           0          0
   Prefixes Total:             0          0
   Implicit Withdraw:          0          0
   Explicit Withdraw:          0          0
   Used as bestpath:         n/a          0
   Used as multipath:        n/a          0

                          Outbound    Inbound
 Local Policy Denied Prefixes:    --------    -------
   Total:                         0          0
 Maximum prefixes allowed 10
 Threshold for warning message 70%, restart interval 2 min
 Number of NLRIs in the update sent: max 0, min 0
 Last detected as dynamic slow peer: never
 Dynamic slow peer recovered: never
 Refresh Epoch: 1
 Last Sent Refresh Start-of-rib: never
 Last Sent Refresh End-of-rib: never
 Last Received Refresh Start-of-rib: never
 Last Received Refresh End-of-rib: never
                            Sent       Rcvd
     Refresh activity:      ----       ----
       Refresh Start-of-RIB    0          0
       Refresh End-of-RIB      0          0


 Address tracking is enabled, the RIB does have a route to 10.0.0.2
 Connections established 1; dropped 0
 Last reset never
```

```
   Transport(tcp) path-mtu-discovery is enabled
   Graceful-Restart is disabled
Connection state is ESTAB, I/O status: 1, unread input bytes: 0
Connection is ECN Disabled, Mininum incoming TTL 0, Outgoing TTL 1
Local host: 10.0.0.1, Local port: 179
Foreign host: 10.0.0.2, Foreign port: 53837
Connection tableid (VRF): 0
Maximum output segment queue size: 50


Enqueued packets for retransmit: 0, input: 0  mis-ordered: 0 (0 bytes)


Event Timers (current time is 0x2DE7EF):
Timer          Starts   Wakeups          Next
Retrans           2        0             0x0
TimeWait          0        0             0x0
AckHold           2        1             0x0
SendWnd           0        0             0x0
KeepAlive         0        0             0x0
GiveUp            0        0             0x0
PmtuAger          0        0             0x0
DeadWait          0        0             0x0
Linger            0        0             0x0
ProcessQ          0        0             0x0


iss: 3174016070  snduna: 3174016147  sndnxt: 3174016147
irs: 1483981710  rcvnxt: 1483981787


sndwnd:  16308  scale:     0  maxrcvwnd:  16384
rcvwnd:  16308  scale:     0  delrcvwnd:     76

SRTT: 234 ms, RTTO: 2984 ms, RTV: 2750 ms, KRTT: 0 ms
minRTT: 12 ms, maxRTT: 1000 ms, ACK hold: 200 ms
Status Flags: passive open, gen tcbs
Option Flags: nagle, path mtu capable
IP Precedence value : 6


Datagrams (max data segment is 1460 bytes):
Rcvd: 5 (out of order: 0), with data: 2, total data bytes: 76
Sent: 5 (retransmit: 0, fastretransmit: 0, partialack: 0, Second Congestion: 0),
  with data: 2, total data bytes: 76


 Packets received in fast path: 0, fast processed: 0, slow path: 0
 fast lock acquisition failures: 0, slow path: 0
TCP Semaphore      0xB2897C3C  FREE
Memphis#
```

To see the effects of the maximum prefixes feature configuration, **debug ip bgp updates** is configured on Memphis, as shown in Example 5-77. Then seven prefixes are injected by Alexandria into BGP, which is the exact configured threshold value. The updates are received by Memphis, and no errors are indicated by the log messages. Then one more prefix is injected by Alexandria to just exceed the threshold value. A log message appears on Memphis warning that eight prefixes have been received and that the maximum number of allowed prefixes is ten. Finally, three more prefixes are injected by Alexandria. As each prefix is added, a new log message appears with a warning indicating the number of prefixes received. After the eleventh prefix is received, which is one prefix more than the maximum configured value, Memphis sends a Notification message to Alexandria and resets the BGP sessions.

The output of the **show ip bgp neighbors** command is also shown on Memphis after it has reset the session with Alexandria. Note the highlighted line in the output stating that the reason for the BGP session reset was "due to Peer over prefix limit of session 1."

Example 5-77   *Log Messages on Memphis as Prefixes Are Injected by Alexandria into BGP*

```
Memphis#debug ip bgp updates
BGP updates debugging is on for address family: IPv4 Unicast


Oct 11 05:48:15.628: BGP(0): 10.0.0.2 rcvd UPDATE w/ attr: nexthop 10.0.0.2, origin
  i, metric 0, merged path 200, AS_PATH
Oct 11 05:48:15.629: BGP(0): 10.0.0.2 rcvd 192.168.0.2/32
Oct 11 05:48:15.630: BGP(0): 10.0.0.2 rcvd 192.168.1.2/32
Oct 11 05:48:15.632: BGP(0): 10.0.0.2 rcvd 192.168.2.2/32
Oct 11 05:48:15.632: BGP(0): 10.0.0.2 rcvd 192.168.3.2/32
Oct 11 05:48:15.632: BGP(0): Revise route installing 1 of 1 routes for
  192.168.0.2/32 -> 10.0.0.2(global) to main IP table
Oct 11 05:48:15.633: BGP(0): Revise route installing 1 of 1 routes for
  192.168.1.2/32 -> 10.0.0.2(global) to main IP table
Memphis#
Oct 11 05:48:15.633: BGP(0): Revise route installing 1 of 1 routes for
  192.168.2.2/32 -> 10.0.0.2(global) to main IP table
Oct 11 05:48:15.634: BGP(0): Revise route installing 1 of 1 routes for
  192.168.3.2/32 -> 10.0.0.2(global) to main IP table
Memphis#
Oct 11 05:48:45.560: BGP(0): 10.0.0.2 rcvd UPDATE w/ attr: nexthop 10.0.0.2, origin
  i, metric 0, merged path 200, AS_PATH
Oct 11 05:48:45.564: BGP(0): 10.0.0.2 rcvd 192.168.4.2/32
Oct 11 05:48:45.564: BGP(0): 10.0.0.2 rcvd 192.168.5.2/32
Oct 11 05:48:45.565: BGP(0): 10.0.0.2 rcvd 192.168.6.2/32
Oct 11 05:48:45.566: BGP(0): Revise route installing 1 of 1 routes for
  192.168.4.2/32 -> 10.0.0.2(global) to main IP table
Oct 11 05:48:45.567: BGP(0): Revise route installing 1 of 1 routes for
```

```
     192.168.5.2/32 -> 10.0.0.2(global) to main IP table
Oct 11 05:48:45.567: BGP(0): Revise route installing 1 of 1 routes for
     192.168.6.2/32 -> 10.0.0.2(global) to main IP table


-- Log messages after the eighth route is injected by R2 --


Memphis#
Oct 11 05:53:18.291: BGP(0): 10.0.0.2 rcvd UPDATE w/ attr: nexthop 10.0.0.2, origin
     i, metric 0, merged path 200, AS_PATH
Oct 11 05:53:18.291: BGP(0): 10.0.0.2 rcvd 192.168.7.2/32
Oct 11 05:53:18.292: %BGP-4-MAXPFX: Number of prefixes received from 10.0.0.2
(afi 0) reaches 8, max 10
Oct 11 05:53:18.293: BGP(0): Revise route installing 1 of 1 routes for
     192.168.7.2/32 -> 10.0.0.2(global) to main IP table


-- Log messages after three more routes are injected by R2 (total 11 routes to
     exceed maximum value) --


Memphis#
Oct 11 06:04:58.755: BGP(0): 10.0.0.2 rcvd UPDATE w/ attr: nexthop 10.0.0.2, origin
     i, metric 0, merged path 200, AS_PATH
Oct 11 06:04:58.761: BGP(0): 10.0.0.2 rcvd 192.168.8.2/32
Oct 11 06:04:58.761: %BGP-4-MAXPFX: Number of prefixes received from 10.0.0.2 (afi
     0) reaches 9, max 10
Oct 11 06:04:58.762: BGP(0): Revise route installing 1 of 1 routes for
     192.168.8.2/32 -> 10.0.0.2(global) to main IP table
Oct 11 06:05:30.219: BGP(0): 10.0.0.2 rcvd UPDATE w/ attr: nexthop 10.0.0.2, origin
     i, metric 0, merged path 200, AS_PATH
Oct 11 06:05:30.220: BGP(0): 10.0.0.2 rcvd 192.168.9.2/32
Oct 11 06:05:30.220: %BGP-4-MAXPFX: Number of prefixes received from 10.0.0.2 (afi
     0) reaches 10, max 10
Oct 11 06:05:30.225: BGP(0): Revise route installing 1 of 1 routes for
     192.168.9.2/32 -> 10.0.0.2(global) to main IP table
Oct 11 06:06:57.499: BGP(0): 10.0.0.2 rcvd UPDATE w/ attr: nexthop 10.0.0.2, origin
     i, metric 0, merged path 200, AS_PATH
Oct 11 06:06:57.499: BGP(0): 10.0.0.2 rcvd 192.168.10.2/32
Oct 11 06:06:57.499: %BGP-3-MAXPFXEXCEED: Number of prefixes received from 10.0.0.2
(afi 0): 11 exceeds limit 10
Oct 11 06:06:57.500: %BGP-5-NBR_RESET: Neighbor 10.0.0.2 reset (Peer over prefix
limit)
Oct 11 06:06:57.500: %BGP-3-NOTIFICATION: sent to neighbor 10.0.0.2 3/1 (update
malformed) 0 bytes
Oct 11 06:06:57.500: %BGP-4-MSGDUMP: unsupported or mal-formatted message received
from 10.0.0.2:
FFFF FFFF FFFF FFFF FFFF FFFF FFFF FFFF 0037 0200 0000 1B40 0101 0040 0206 0201
0000 00C8 4003 040A 0000 0280 0404 0000 0000 20C0 A80A 02
Oct 11 06:06:57.504: BGP(0): no valid path for 192.168.0.2/32
Oct 11 06:06:57.504: BGP(0): no valid path for 192.168.1.2/32
```

```
Oct 11 06:06:57.504: BGP(0): no valid path for 192.168.2.2/32
Oct 11 06:06:57.505: BGP(0): no valid path for 192.168.3.2/32
Oct 11 06:06:57.505: BGP(0): no valid path for 192.168.4.2/32
Oct 11 06:06:57.505: BGP(0): no valid path for 192.168.5.2/32
Oct 11 06:06:57.506: BGP(0): no valid path for 192.168.6.2/32
Oct 11 06:06:57.506: BGP(0): no valid path for 192.168.7.2/32
Oct 11 06:06:57.506: BGP(0): no valid path for 192.168.8.2/32
Oct 11 06:06:57.507: BGP(0): no valid path for 192.168.9.2/32
Oct 11 06:06:57.513: %BGP-5-ADJCHANGE: neighbor 10.0.0.2 Down BGP Notification sent
Oct 11 06:06:57.514: %BGP_SESSION-5-ADJCHANGE: neighbor 10.0.0.2 IPv4 Unicast
 topology base removed from session  BGP Notification sent


Memphis#show ip bgp neighbors 10.0.0.2
BGP neighbor is 10.0.0.2,  remote AS 200, external link
  BGP version 4, remote router ID 0.0.0.0
  BGP state = Idle
  Neighbor sessions:
    0 active, is not multisession capable (disabled)
    Stateful switchover support enabled: NO
  Default minimum time between advertisement runs is 30 seconds


 For address family: IPv4 Unicast
  BGP table version 21, neighbor version 1/21
  Output queue size : 0
  Index 0, Advertise bit 0
  Address family not supported notification sent
  Slow-peer detection is disabled
  Slow-peer split-update-group dynamic is disabled
  Peer had exceeded the max. no. of prefixes configured.
  Maximum prefixes allowed 10
  Threshold for warning message 70%, restart interval 2 min
  Reduce the no. of prefix from 10.0.0.2, will restart in 00:00:51
  Number of NLRIs in the update sent: max 0, min 0
  Last detected as dynamic slow peer: never
  Dynamic slow peer recovered: never
  Refresh Epoch: 1
  Last Sent Refresh Start-of-rib: never
  Last Sent Refresh End-of-rib: never
  Last Received Refresh Start-of-rib: never
  Last Received Refresh End-of-rib: never
                                 Sent       Rcvd
        Refresh activity:        ----       ----
          Refresh Start-of-RIB      0          0
          Refresh End-of-RIB        0          0
```

```
Address tracking is enabled, the RIB does have a route to 10.0.0.2
Connections established 1; dropped 1
Last reset 00:01:08, due to Peer over prefix limit of session 1
Transport(tcp) path-mtu-discovery is enabled
Graceful-Restart is disabled
No active TCP connection
Memphis#
```

The line in Example 5-77 advises the network operator to "Reduce the no. of prefix from 10.0.0.2" as Memphis "will restart in 00:00:51." The reason behind this message becomes clear through Example 5-78 that continues with the log messages on Memphis after it has reset the TCP session with Alexandria. It indicates that after the configured restart timer of 2 minutes, Memphis re-establishes the BGP session with Alexandria and starts receiving updates again. If the configuration is not amended on Alexandria to decrease the number of prefixes injected into BGP, Memphis again resets the session with Alexandria as soon as the number of prefixes received exceeds the configured maximum prefixes value. The session is then re-established after 2 minutes, and the cycle repeats until Alexandria's configuration is amended to decrease the number of prefixes.

Example 5-78 *Approximately 2 Minutes Later, Memphis Restarts the BGP Session with Alexandria*

```
Memphis#
Oct 11 06:09:06.035: %BGP-5-ADJCHANGE: neighbor 10.0.0.2 Up
Oct 11 06:09:06.840: BGP(0): 10.0.0.2 rcvd UPDATE w/ attr: nexthop 10.0.0.2,
  origin i, metric 0, merged path 200, AS_PATH
Oct 11 06:09:06.841: BGP(0): 10.0.0.2 rcvd 192.168.0.2/32
Oct 11 06:09:06.846: BGP(0): 10.0.0.2 rcvd 192.168.1.2/32
Oct 11 06:09:06.846: BGP(0): 10.0.0.2 rcvd 192.168.2.2/32
Oct 11 06:09:06.847: BGP(0): 10.0.0.2 rcvd 192.168.3.2/32
Oct 11 06:09:06.847: BGP(0): 10.0.0.2 rcvd 192.168.4.2/32
Oct 11 06:09:06.848: BGP(0): 10.0.0.2 rcvd 192.168.5.2/32
Oct 11 06:09:06.848: BGP(0): 10.0.0.2 rcvd 192.168.6.2/32
Oct 11 06:09:06.849: BGP(0): 10.0.0.2 rcvd 192.168.7.2/32
Oct 11 06:09:06.854: %BGP-4-MAXPFX: Number of prefixes received from 10.0.0.2
  (afi 0) reaches 8, max 10
Oct 11 06:09:06.855: BGP(0): 10.0.0.2 rcvd 192.168.8.2/32
Oct 11 06:09:06.856: BGP(0): 10.0.0.2 rcvd 192.168.9.2/32
Oct 11 06:09:06.856: BGP(0): 10.0.0.2 rcvd 192.168.10.2/32
Oct 11 06:09:06.856: %BGP-3-MAXPFXEXCEED: Number of prefixes received from 10.0.0.2
  (afi 0): 11 exceeds limit 10

-- Output truncated for brevity --
```

It is worth mentioning that the default value of the threshold is 75%, and this is the value at which a log message is generated if the threshold value is omitted from the command.

As mentioned earlier in this section, if the keyword warning-only were added to the maximum-prefixes command, a log message would be generated when the threshold value is exceeded and then generated once more for every prefix received after that. No other action is taken by Memphis. The BGP session remains up, and the prefixes are installed in the Memphis BGP table. Example 5-79 shows the configuration amended on Memphis to replace the restart {*interval*} keyword with the warning-only keyword. Example 5-80 then shows the log messages on Memphis as 12 prefixes are injected, one by one, by Alexandria. Finally, the BGP table in Example 5-81 shows all 12 prefixes installed in the Memphis BGP table, and all are valid and best.

Example 5-79 *Memphis Configuration After Replacing the* **restart** *Keyword with the* **warning-only** *Keyword*

```
router bgp 100
 bgp log-neighbor-changes
 neighbor 10.0.0.2 remote-as 200
 neighbor 10.0.0.2 maximum-prefix 10 70 warning-only
```

Example 5-80 *Log Messages on Memphis While Alexandria Injects the 11 Prefixes One by One*

```
Memphis#
Oct 11 07:46:25.474: BGP(0): 10.0.0.2 rcvd UPDATE w/ attr: nexthop 10.0.0.2, origin
   i, metric 0, merged path 200, AS_PATH
Oct 11 07:46:25.475: BGP(0): 10.0.0.2 rcvd 192.168.0.2/32
Oct 11 07:46:25.475: BGP(0): Revise route installing 1 of 1 routes for
   192.168.0.2/32 -> 10.0.0.2(global) to main IP table
Oct 11 07:46:55.774: BGP(0): 10.0.0.2 rcvd UPDATE w/ attr: nexthop 10.0.0.2, origin
   i, metric 0, merged path 200, AS_PATH
Oct 11 07:46:55.775: BGP(0): 10.0.0.2 rcvd 192.168.1.2/32
Oct 11 07:46:55.775: BGP(0): Revise route installing 1 of 1 routes for
   192.168.1.2/32 -> 10.0.0.2(global) to main IP table
Oct 11 07:47:26.842: BGP(0): 10.0.0.2 rcvd UPDATE w/ attr: nexthop 10.0.0.2, origin
   i, metric 0, merged path 200, AS_PATH
Oct 11 07:47:26.843: BGP(0): 10.0.0.2 rcvd 192.168.2.2/32
Oct 11 07:47:26.850: BGP(0): Revise route installing 1 of 1 routes for
   192.168.2.2/32 -> 10.0.0.2(global) to main IP table
Oct 11 07:47:58.421: BGP(0): 10.0.0.2 rcvd UPDATE w/ attr: nexthop 10.0.0.2, origin
   i, metric 0, merged path 200, AS_PATH
Oct 11 07:47:58.422: BGP(0): 10.0.0.2 rcvd 192.168.3.2/32
Oct 11 07:47:58.422: BGP(0): Revise route installing 1 of 1 routes for
   192.168.3.2/32 -> 10.0.0.2(global) to main IP table
Oct 11 07:48:29.540: BGP(0): 10.0.0.2 rcvd UPDATE w/ attr: nexthop 10.0.0.2, origin
   i, metric 0, merged path 200, AS_PATH
Oct 11 07:48:29.546: BGP(0): 10.0.0.2 rcvd 192.168.4.2/32
Oct 11 07:48:29.547: BGP(0): Revise route installing 1 of 1 routes for
   192.168.4.2/32 -> 10.0.0.2(global) to main IP table
```

```
Oct 11 07:49:00.086: BGP(0): 10.0.0.2 rcvd UPDATE w/ attr: nexthop 10.0.0.2, origin
   i, metric 0, merged path 200, AS_PATH

Oct 11 07:49:00.087: BGP(0): 10.0.0.2 rcvd 192.168.5.2/32

Oct 11 07:49:00.087: BGP(0): Revise route installing 1 of 1 routes for
   192.168.5.2/32 -> 10.0.0.2(global) to main IP table

Oct 11 07:49:31.623: BGP(0): 10.0.0.2 rcvd UPDATE w/ attr: nexthop 10.0.0.2, origin
   i, metric 0, merged path 200, AS_PATH

Oct 11 07:49:31.623: BGP(0): 10.0.0.2 rcvd 192.168.6.2/32

Oct 11 07:49:31.624: BGP(0): Revise route installing 1 of 1 routes for
   192.168.6.2/32 -> 10.0.0.2(global) to main IP table

Oct 11 07:50:01.828: BGP(0): 10.0.0.2 rcvd UPDATE w/ attr: nexthop 10.0.0.2, origin
   i, metric 0, merged path 200, AS_PATH

Oct 11 07:50:01.831: BGP(0): 10.0.0.2 rcvd 192.168.7.2/32

Oct 11 07:50:01.831: %BGP-4-MAXPFX: Number of prefixes received from 10.0.0.2
   (afi 0) reaches 8, max 10

Oct 11 07:50:01.832: BGP(0): Revise route installing 1 of 1 routes for
   192.168.7.2/32 -> 10.0.0.2(global) to main IP table

Oct 11 07:50:33.393: BGP(0): 10.0.0.2 rcvd UPDATE w/ attr: nexthop 10.0.0.2, origin
   i, metric 0, merged path 200, AS_PATH

Oct 11 07:50:33.393: BGP(0): 10.0.0.2 rcvd 192.168.8.2/32

Oct 11 07:50:33.393: %BGP-4-MAXPFX: Number of prefixes received from 10.0.0.2
   (afi 0) reaches 9, max 10

Oct 11 07:50:33.394: BGP(0): Revise route installing 1 of 1 routes for
   192.168.8.2/32 -> 10.0.0.2(global) to main IP table

Oct 11 07:51:04.338: BGP(0): 10.0.0.2 rcvd UPDATE w/ attr: nexthop 10.0.0.2, origin
   i, metric 0, merged path 200, AS_PATH

Oct 11 07:51:04.338: BGP(0): 10.0.0.2 rcvd 192.168.9.2/32

Oct 11 07:51:04.339: %BGP-4-MAXPFX: Number of prefixes received from 10.0.0.2
   (afi 0) reaches 10, max 10

Oct 11 07:51:04.339: BGP(0): Revise route installing 1 of 1 routes for
   192.168.9.2/32 -> 10.0.0.2(global) to main IP table

Oct 11 07:51:36.023: BGP(0): 10.0.0.2 rcvd UPDATE w/ attr: nexthop 10.0.0.2, origin
   i, metric 0, merged path 200, AS_PATH

Oct 11 07:51:36.023: BGP(0): 10.0.0.2 rcvd 192.168.10.2/32

Oct 11 07:51:36.024: %BGP-3-MAXPFXEXCEED: Number of prefixes received from 10.0.0.2
   (afi 0): 11 exceeds limit 10

Oct 11 07:51:36.025: BGP(0): Revise route installing 1 of 1 routes for
   192.168.10.2/32 -> 10.0.0.2(global) to main IP table

Oct 11 07:53:36.464: BGP(0): 10.0.0.2 rcvd UPDATE w/ attr: nexthop 10.0.0.2, origin
   i, metric 0, merged path 200, AS_PATH

Oct 11 07:53:36.465: BGP(0): 10.0.0.2 rcvd 192.168.11.2/32

Oct 11 07:53:36.465: %BGP-3-MAXPFXEXCEED: Number of prefixes received from 10.0.0.2
   (afi 0): 12 exceeds limit 10

Oct 11 07:53:36.466: BGP(0): Revise route installing 1 of 1 routes for
   192.168.11.2/32 -> 10.0.0.2(global) to main IP table
```

Example 5-81   *BGP Table on Memphis Showing All 12 Prefixes as Valid and Best*

```
Memphis#show ip bgp
BGP table version is 87, local router ID is 10.0.0.1
Status codes: s suppressed, d damped, h history, * valid, > best, i - internal,
              r RIB-failure, S Stale, m multipath, b backup-path, f RT-Filter,
              x best-external, a additional-path, c RIB-compressed,
Origin codes: i - IGP, e - EGP, ? - incomplete
RPKI validation codes: V valid, I invalid, N Not found

     Network          Next Hop          Metric LocPrf Weight Path
 *>  192.168.0.2/32   10.0.0.2               0             0 200 i
 *>  192.168.1.2/32   10.0.0.2               0             0 200 i
 *>  192.168.2.2/32   10.0.0.2               0             0 200 i
 *>  192.168.3.2/32   10.0.0.2               0             0 200 i
 *>  192.168.4.2/32   10.0.0.2               0             0 200 i
 *>  192.168.5.2/32   10.0.0.2               0             0 200 i
 *>  192.168.6.2/32   10.0.0.2               0             0 200 i
 *>  192.168.7.2/32   10.0.0.2               0             0 200 i
 *>  192.168.8.2/32   10.0.0.2               0             0 200 i
 *>  192.168.9.2/32   10.0.0.2               0             0 200 i
 *>  192.168.10.2/32  10.0.0.2               0             0 200 i
 *>  192.168.11.2/32  10.0.0.2               0             0 200 i
Memphis#
```

Tuning BGP CPU

Understanding the effects of BGP on CPU utilization is important because router or switch CPU is a shared resource. When this resource is fully utilized by one process, or a group of processes for one protocol, other processes are adversely affected. The CPU is used for both, running system and protocol processes, as well as for forwarding some classes of traffic that cannot be forwarded in hardware (traffic "punted" to the CPU). Therefore, the unavailability of CPU due to one process can adversely affect other processes, as well as traffic forwarding. In some cases, high CPU utilization causes the router to crash altogether. For BGP to be truly scalable, its processes and control traffic (that is handled by the CPU) should not "hog" the CPU, rendering the router incapable of performing any other tasks.

Before getting into BGP processes, their effects on CPU, and what can be done to tune BGP CPU utilization, quickly look at the IOS tools used to read CPU utilization.

The most important tool is the **show processes cpu** command. Several arguments can be used with this command and the output may differ significantly with each argument. Discussing each option of the command is out of scope of this book, so one commonly used format will be discussed, which uses the sorted argument. This argument sorts the

output in descending order by percentage CPU utilization. Example 5-82 shows a sample
output of this command.

Example 5-82   show processes cpu sorted *Output*

```
route-views.optus.net.au>show process cpu sorted
CPU utilization for five seconds: 14%/0%; one minute: 5%; five minutes: 4%
 PID Runtime(ms)     Invoked    uSecs   5Sec   1Min   5Min TTY Process
   4  518382764    28159777    18408 13.59%  1.77%  1.23%   0 Check heaps
 223    6104264      771384     7913  0.23%  0.02%  0.00%   0 Per-minute Jobs
  88   82283708  1174085919       70  0.23%  0.15%  0.16%   0 IP Input
 138     112024  2425182127        0  0.15%  0.10%  0.09%   0 HQF Input Shaper
  59       3740     9137110        0  0.07%  0.00%  0.00%   0 HC Counter Timer
 128      36668    95900968        0  0.07%  0.01%  0.00%   0 TCP Timer
 142    5265420   177121717       29  0.07%  0.01%  0.00%   0 BGP I/O
 137     124328  2425182041        0  0.07%  0.11%  0.10%   0 HQF Shaper Backg
 236   61650456   219313514      281  0.07%  0.05%  0.07%   0 BGP Router
```

Following are the fields in the output of the command:

- **CPU utilization for 5 seconds: 2%/0%; 1 minute: 2%; 5 minutes: 2%:** Average
  CPU utilization for all processes in the last 5 secs, 1 min, and 5 mins, respectively.
  The utilization for 5 seconds shows two values. The first is the utilization by all
  active processes. The second value is the CPU interrupt utilization.

- **PID:** Process ID

- **Runtime(ms):** Total CPU time in milliseconds used by this process since router
  bootup

- **Invoked:** The number of times this process was invoked

- **uSecs:** CPU time in microseconds used by the process each time it is invoked

- **5Sec/1Min/5Min:** Average CPU utilization in the last 5 Secs, 1 Min, and 5 Mins,
  respectively

- **Process:** Name of the Process

As mentioned, the first line of the command output shows the 5 seconds average CPU
utilization for both, all the processes added up, as well as the interrupt CPU utilization,
which is the CPU utilization for processing the traffic that cannot be processed in hardware and was punted to the CPU. This is an important piece of information because it
allows us to identify how much the CPU is utilized by the active processes versus how
much CPU is utilized due to forwarding traffic (that is not being switched in hardware
by CEF).

Now that we have understood the impact of high CPU utilization on the functioning of
a router as well as the output from the command **show processes cpu sorted**, go back

BGP. A study performed jointly by UCLA and Sprint researchers on CPU utilization by BGP processes, on routers in Sprint's tier-1 network, has concluded that BGP processes use up to 60% of total CPU resources. This value was measured by adding up the total number of CPU milliseconds consumed by each BGP process since router boot up (under the Runtime(ms) column in the **show processes cpu** command output), and calculating the percentage of this consumption out of the total CPU consumption.

Recall from Chapter 4 that in IOS, BGP has four foundation processes. (And depending on the IOS version, there may be more active BGP processes.) The following list is a refresher:

- **Open:** This is a transient BGP process that is responsible for neighbor establishment and is active only when new neighbors are coming up.

- **I/O:** Interfaces with the router's TCP socket, populating the InQ on the input side and taking the messages out of the OutQ for transmission. This process utilizes the CPU as long as BGP messages are sent or received.

- **Router:** This is the process that performs most of the core BGP functionality. On the input side, it reads the messages in the InQ, evaluates incoming routes against incoming policies, runs the best path algorithm, updates the BGP table and interfaces with the RIB update process to enter the routes into the routing table. On the output side, it evaluates routes in the BGP table against outgoing policies, generates the UPDATE messages, and adds them to the OutQ. It also processes route "churn" that is covered in more detail later in this section. This process runs once every second and whenever adding, removing, or soft-reconfiguring a neighbor.

- **Scanner:** This process scans the BGP table to make sure that the route next hops are reachable. It processes **network**, **redistribute** and **aggregate** statements and adds the resulting routes to the BGP table. It is also responsible for route dampening and conditional route advertisements. This scan happens once every 60 seconds.

Example 5-83 shows the output of **show processes cpu sorted** with the output filtered to show only the BGP processes.

Example 5-83   *BGP Processes*

```
route-views.optus.net.au>show processes cpu sorted | i utilization|Runtime|BGP
CPU utilization for five seconds: 31%/0%; one minute: 6%; five minutes: 5%
 PID Runtime(ms)      Invoked      uSecs    5Sec    1Min    5Min TTY Process
 172 1041018716      5620906      185210  28.63%   3.59%   2.53%   0 BGP Scanner
 236   61651656    219322619         281   0.23%   0.09%   0.08%   0 BGP Router
 142    5265568    177128939          29   0.07%   0.01%   0.00%   0 BGP I/O
   3          0            1           0   0.00%   0.00%   0.00%   0 BGP Open
 141       5648     44506740           0   0.00%   0.00%   0.00%   0 BGP Scheduler
 230    1674320     16109430         103   0.00%   0.00%   0.00%   0 BGP Task
 231       5988           33      181454   0.00%   0.00%   0.00%   0 BGP Event
```

During normal operations, the majority of CPU utilization is because of the BGP Scanner and Router processes, whereas the I/O, Open, and other processes do not consume a significant amount of CPU time. Therefore, the following discussion focuses on these two processes.

As discussed in the previous processes list, the BGP Scanner process runs once every 60 seconds, and when it runs it walks or scans the BGP and IP Routing tables. A scan starts 60 seconds after the previous scan is completed, irrespective of how long a scan takes. Therefore, the high CPU utilization condition because of the Scanner process occurs at 60 second intervals, and the duration depends on the size of the BGP and routing tables. Therefore, the bigger the BGP and IP routing tables, the longer the high CPU utilization condition persists, and the longer the Scanner process hogs the CPU and blocks lower-priority processes from running.

The BGP Router process runs once every second. In addition, it runs whenever a new peer is established, a peer is removed, or a peer is soft-reconfigured. The router process does the core functionality of the BGP protocol, which is to process updates and choose the best path and have this path installed in the IP routing table. During network stability periods, when no neighbors are changing states, the high CPU utilization caused by the Router process is not periodic, as is the case with the Scanner process. However, BGP convergence after a failure or when a new neighbor is established heavily depends on the performance of the Router process, Therefore, the Router process has a Medium priority, whereas the Scanner process has a Low priority. Example 5-84 shows the output of the **show processes** command, filtered to show only the BGP processes. Notice the column labeled "Q," which indicates the process priority. The process priority is "L" (Low) for the Scanner priority and "M" (Medium) for the rest of the processes, including the Router process.

Example 5-84 *BGP Process Priorities*

```
route-views.optus.net.au>show process | i utilization|Runtime|BGP
CPU utilization for five seconds: 0%/0%; one minute: 4%; five minutes: 5%
 PID QTy       PC Runtime (ms)     Invoked    uSecs    Stacks TTY Process
   3 ME  615299CC           0           1        0 4000/6000   0 BGP Open
 141 Mwe 609F82EC        5648    44511524        0 7236/9000   0 BGP Scheduler
 142 Mwe 60A03460     5265936   177146028       29 6892/9000   0 BGP I/O
 172 Lwe 609EEAF8  1041137460     5621562   185206 6832/9000   0 BGP Scanner
 230 Mwe 60A5892C     1674496    16111145      103 4444/6000   0 BGP Task
 231 Mwe 60A1A20C        5988          33   181454 4712/6000   0 BGP Event
 236 Mwe 60A06880    61655956   219344334      281 6044/9000   0 BGP Router
route-views.optus.net.au>
```

So, based on the preceding discussion, the CPU utilization of the Scanner and Router processes mainly depends on the number of BGP routes in the BGP table and the number of BGP peers. However, this would be true in steady state conditions, where BGP is converged and only minor changes are done on the network, such as adding a few routes. Tuning the CPU utilization of BGP processes in this case is achieved by the following mechanisms:

- **Update groups:** As discussed earlier in this chapter, update groups are automatically implemented in Cisco IOS without any further configuration by the operator. It basically eliminates the need for the BGP Scanner process to walk the BGP table once for each neighbor. Instead, all neighbors with the same outgoing policy are placed into one Update Group; one neighbor in the group is elected as the Group Leader, and the BGP table is walked once for each update group for the group leader only. After the updates are generated for the leader, those updates are replicated for each member of the group, without walking the BGP table and generating update messages again for each of those members. The efficiency of update groups can be checked using the commands **show bgp ipv4 unicast update-group** [*update-group-number*] and **show ip bgp replication** [*update-group-number*].

- **Optimizing the number of routes in the BGP table:** Because this issue directly and more severely affects router memory resources, this point is tackled in more detail in the next section, "Tuning BGP Memory."

- **Increasing the efficiency of the underlying transport layer of BGP, which is TCP:** This point is tackled in more detail in the section "Transport Optimization" later in this chapter.

Tuning BGP Memory

The subject of tuning (and hence optimizing) BGP usage of router memory is closely correlated with tuning CPU usage. Whatever is the cause of high CPU utilization probably also is a cause for high memory utilization. However, tuning memory is both, simpler in concept, but more complex in implementation. Tuning BGP usage of memory is a simple concept because the more BGP routes you have in the BGP table, the more memory you need on the platform. Nothing else about BGP significantly affects memory utilization as does the size of the BGP table. At the same time, the concepts involved in tuning BGP for better memory utilization are quite complicated because almost every decision you make while designing your BGP network, and almost every configuration line you enter, can positively or negatively impact memory utilization.

Following the same structure as the last section, first look at the tools that you can use to display the memory utilization of BGP on Cisco IOS. Example 5-85 illustrates the use of the commands **show ip bgp summary** to display the number of routes received per neighbor: **show ip route summary** to display the summary of the routes installed in the RIB, and the memory used by the RIB for those routes, and finally, **show processes memory** sorted to display the memory usage per BGP process. The primary focus is on the BGP Router process because this is the process responsible for installing routes in the RIB after running the best path algorithm on the routes in the BGP table.

Example 5-85 show *Commands for Monitoring Memory Utilization*

```
ns-route-server>show ip bgp summary
BGP router identifier 24.137.100.8, local AS number 11260
BGP table version is 1806994765, main routing table version 1806994765
552273 network entries using 66825033 bytes of memory
883996 path entries using 45967792 bytes of memory
157059/91213 BGP path/bestpath attribute entries using 11936484 bytes of memory
109427 BGP AS-PATH entries using 2822216 bytes of memory
1887 BGP community entries using 126342 bytes of memory
6 BGP extended community entries using 144 bytes of memory
0 BGP route-map cache entries using 0 bytes of memory
0 BGP filter-list cache entries using 0 bytes of memory
BGP using 127678011 total bytes of memory
Dampening enabled. 0 history paths, 0 dampened paths
BGP activity 46497518/45919837 prefixes, 643957540/643048108 paths, scan interval 60
  secs

Neighbor        V   AS MsgRcvd MsgSent   TblVer  InQ OutQ Up/Down  State/PfxRcd
24.137.100.1    4 11260 45522633  274190 1806994770    0    0 24w4d      489209
24.137.100.2    4 11260 77842109  263087 1806994770    0    0 23w4d      394333
24.137.100.3    4 11260  126361  137999 1806994770    0    0 12w2d         192
24.137.100.4    4 11260  237658  259964 1806994770    0    0 23w2d         226
ns-route-server>
ns-route-server>show ip route summary
IP routing table name is default (0x0)
IP routing table maximum-paths is 32
Route Source    Networks   Subnets    Replicates  Overhead   Memory (bytes)
connected       0          5          0           296        860
static          0          38         0           2048       6536
ospf 1          39         4874       0           261404     864688
   Intra-area: 60 Inter-area: 258 External-1: 4544 External-2: 51
   NSSA External-1: 0 NSSA External-2: 0
bgp 11260       172210     379891     0           28709252   94961372
   External: 0 Internal: 552101 Local: 0
internal        6366                                          22828740
Total           178615     384808     0           28973000   118662196
ns-route-server>
ns-route-server>show processes memory sorted | i PID|BGP
 PID TTY Allocated     Freed      Holding    Getbufs    Retbufs Process
 224   0 2045549580 3094957712  374062504     3120          0 BGP Router
 226   0     23864  399678964      33076        0          0 BGP Scanner
 225   0 1524686480   96218952       9988   369048        260 BGP I/O
 223   0  421781356       5520       9988        0          0 BGP Scheduler
 227   0         0      67432       6992        0          0 BGP Event
ns-route-server>
```

Notice the highlighted lines in the output of the **show ip bgp summary** command referred to in Example 5-84. You can see that the memory allocation is specified in bytes for three distinct components of BGP:

- **Prefixes:** Identified as "network entries" in the first highlighted line

- **Paths:** Identified as "path entries" in the second highlighted line

- **Attributes:** Identified by the following four highlighted lines in the output

And the total memory consumed by these three components is 127,678,011 bytes of memory, as shown on the last highlighted line of output, before the list of neighbors. Then comes the list of neighbors, with the number of prefixes received from each neighbor shown in the last column labeled State/PfxRcd.

Having identified the components of BGP that consume memory on the router, you need to look into what options are available to mitigate the adverse effects of each of them. Starting with the issue of having a large number of prefixes in the BGP table (such as a full Internet routing table), the following measures can be considered if deemed appropriate and feasible for the specific network that is being optimized:

- **Aggregation:** This would be easy to implement for greenfield implementations but may not be possible for networks already in production if their IP schema is not designed properly to start with.

- **Filtering:** To filter out routes that are not required or will not be used by this AS.

- Consider receiving partial routing tables and default routes from the upstream autonomous systems instead of a full Internet routing table.

The second component is the number of paths or routes. The following mitigations may be considered to decrease the number of paths in the BGP table, if found feasible and appropriate:

- Reduce the number of BGP neighbors/peerings. This may come at the expense of redundancy.

- Use Route Reflectors instead an IBGP full mesh. This may come at the expense of redundancy and the functionality of features such as BGP PIC (as discussed in an earlier section of this chapter) because by default an RR reflects only its best route.

Finally, the third component of BGP that consumes memory is the list of path attributes attached to the routes. This can be mitigated by simply reducing the number of attributes wherever possible:

- Filter (extended) communities from incoming updates that you will not be using in your AS or that do not have any significance to your network.

- Attempt to limit the communities that you assign inside your AS; use communities sparingly whenever possible.

Recall from Chapter 4 that some routers implement the soft-reconfiguration feature for one or more BGP neighbors. This feature maintains a copy of all incoming routes from that neighbor before the inbound policies are applied to these routes. If the inbound policy changes for this neighbor, the router would already have a copy of the routes from that neighbor, and there would be no need to reset the BGP session to apply the new policies. The router simply applies the new policies to the routes in store. This is handy and enables policy changes to be applied with no disruptions. However, maintaining two copies of the routes from a neighbor, one before applying inbound policies and another copy after the policies are applied (the BGP table), consumes at least twice the memory required without using this feature.

Using Route Refresh to replace the soft reconfiguration feature is always the recommended option. However, both routers involved in the BGP session need to support this capability for it to work. As of the writing of this edition, route refresh has been introduced for more than 15 years; therefore, the probability of having a router in your network that does not support this feature is minimal. Use the soft reconfiguration feature only if there is an explicit requirement to maintain a copy of the routes from a neighbor before the filtering. Otherwise, memory on the router will be severely impacted, especially if the router in question is peering with a large number of BGP neighbors, and it is receiving a full Internet routing table from some or all of them.

The final part of this section discusses different route reflector designs and their effects on memory consumption on routers, both on internal routers peering with the route reflectors and on the route reflectors themselves.

Route reflection is discussed in detail in a later section of this chapter. For now, you need to know that an RR relaxes the requirement for an IBGP full mesh inside an AS by having some or all routers peer with one or more RRs. Routers that peer only with the route reflectors are named RR clients. All other routers, that is, the route-reflectors and nonclient IBGP peers, still need to be fully meshed. The RRs relax the requirement for an IBGP full mesh by amending route forwarding rules inside the AS. When an RR receives a route from an RR client, that route is forwarded by the RR to another client, as well as other RRs and nonclient IBGP peers. Recall that this contradicts with the "classical" route forwarding rules that dictate that a route received from an IBGP peer should not be forwarded to another IBGP peer. This setup significantly decreases the number of BGP sessions required inside the AS.

Because this section does not discuss the foundations of route reflection or advanced RR network designs, consider the simple network in Figure 5-31. This is not a practical implementation of route reflection rather than a case study to illustrate the effects of route reflection network design on memory consumption on routers. R1 is an edge router connecting to route reflector RR1. R2 and R3 are AS internal routers connecting to RR1. Because of the presence of RR1, no IBGP full mesh is required. R1 receives Subnet S1 over its EBGP session; R2 and R3 inject subnets S2 and S3 into BGP, respectively. The RR reflects S1 to R2 and R3, S2 to R1 and R3 and finally S3 to R1 and R2. So far, so good.

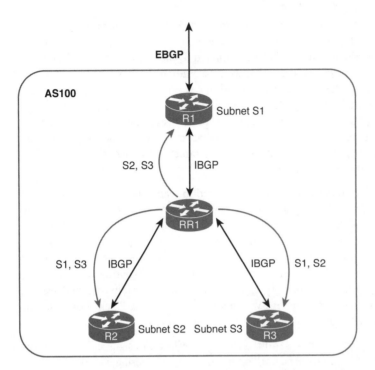

Figure 5-31 *Example Network for Tuning BGP Memory*

Now what happens if RR1 fails? R1 does not have reachability to the subnets inside
the AS and R2, and R3 will not have reachability to either internal or external subnets.
(Unless S2 and S3 are announced by the IGP, in this case R2 and R3 do not have reachability to the external subnets only.) For the sake of redundancy, RR2 was added to the
network in Figure 5-32. As per RR design rules, all RR clients need to peer with all route
reflectors; otherwise, they may not receive all routes. In this case, both RRs receive subnets S1, S2, and S3 from their clients. The routers R1, R2, and R3 now get a second copy
of the routes from the newly added route reflector: RR2. Each RR client now receives
double the number of BGP route that it received with a single RR. Assuming R1 is
receiving a full Internet routing table, R1 receives it only once over its EBGP session, so
R1 is not majorly affected by adding an extra RR for redundancy. However, R2 and R3
are now receiving two copies from the Internet routing table, requiring approximately
double the memory. As mentioned in earlier sections, such route redundancy may be
a good idea if features such as BGP PIC are going to be enabled. Otherwise, a second
route reflector does not add any value in steady state operations, that is, if no failure
occurs.

Now what could be a solution to highly available RR designs that employ only a single
RR? One of these solutions would be to implement the RR functionality on virtual routers, such as the CSR 1000v based on IOS XE or the XRv based on IOS XR. These routers are implemented in software on virtual machines. This would be practical only if the

RR is used in the control plane to reflect routes and is not involved in the forwarding of traffic in the data plane. These platforms provide huge processing power and an abundance of memory; however, they lack the complexity of forwarding hardware as well as port density, that is, needed in the forwarding plane of large ISP networks. Above and beyond the CPU and memory availability on these virtual platforms, redundancy can be easily provided for the physical chassis in a completely transparent manner to the network layer.

In some cases, designs involving multiple route reflectors would introduce loops in the network. Two new attributes were created to mitigate that. The first is the originator-id and the second is the Cluster-id.

When a route reflector receives a route from a client, it attaches the Originator-id attribute to the route if it is not already there. The value of the attribute is the BGP router-id of the RR client that sent the update to the RR. The second attribute is the cluster-id. This value is the BGP router-id of the route-reflector, by default. This new attribute enables the network designer to segment an AS into several smaller "clusters," each cluster having its own route reflector(s) and clients. Each standalone BGP speaker that is neither an RR nor an RR client becomes a one-router cluster. RRs of each cluster as well as standalone IBGP speakers have to be fully meshed.

When a BGP speaker receives an update for a route that has that speaker's BGP router-id in the Originator-id field, the update is discarded. And when an RR receives an update with its own Cluster-id (configured or default) in the Cluster-id field, that update is discarded.

Now, for a network such as the one shown in Figure 5-32 with four RRs, the question arises: Should all four RRs be in the same cluster, should each one be in a separate cluster, or should each two be grouped into one cluster? We will not answer this question from a "best design" perspective. We will rather study the impact on router memory of the same versus different Cluster-ids on RRs in the same AS.

First, look at the impact on router memory for the client routers. The primary purpose of clustering is to identify and group RRs along with their associated clients. Clients in a cluster need to have BGP sessions to all RRs in that cluster only and need not be connected to the RRs in other clusters. Based on the discussion in the previous paragraphs, the more RRs the client is connected to, the higher the redundancy, but the higher the memory required on each router. Therefore, the more RRs you have in a cluster, the higher the memory requirement on each client in that cluster.

Now what about the RRs themselves? As previously discussed, when an RR receives an update with its own Cluster-id, this update is discarded. Therefore, in the extreme case in which each of the RRs in Figure 5-33 has a different Cluster-id, each RR receives and retains an update from each of the other RRs. On the other extreme, if all four RRs have the same Cluster-id, each RR has only one copy of each route from each of its RR clients, and all updates from the other RRs will be discarded.

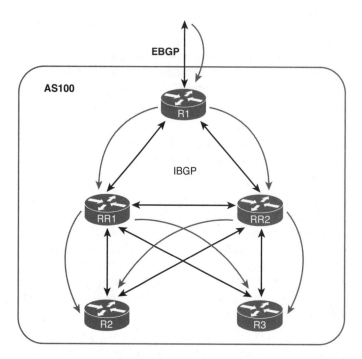

Figure 5-32   *A Second Route Reflector Is Added to the Topology*

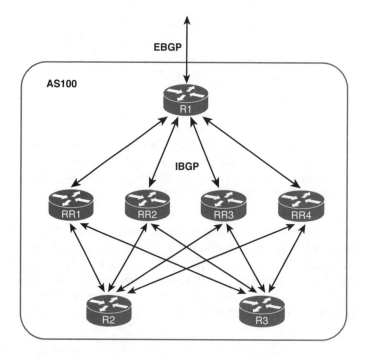

Figure 5-33   *Two More Route Reflectors Are Added to the Example Topology*

As mentioned in the previous section, wherever more memory is required, probably more CPU will also be required because the more the updates and the larger the BGP table, the more "walks" are required by the Scanner process and the more processing is required by the Router process.

One final technique to limit the memory (and CPU) requirements on RRs applies to RRs that are not forwarding any traffic in the data plane, and that is Selective RIB download. Because the RR is just functioning in the control plane and forwarding any traffic, the routes in the BGP table are not required to be installed in the RIB or FIB. Therefore, these routes are kept in the BGP table, and using the **table-map** command, the routes are not installed in the RIB and eventually not installed in the FIB as well.

BGP Transport Optimization

BGP's capability to scale means that BGP should deal, in a stable fashion, with a large number of BGP peers that send a large number of updates for a large number of routes, and eventually end up with a huge BGP table composed of prefixes, routes or paths to those prefixes, and their attached attributes. This leads to the need to optimize every aspect of BGP's operation, starting with BGP peer establishment, exchanging updates, all the way to convergence and steady state operations, and including failure detection and convergence after a failure. This section is primarily concerned with optimizing the transport layer on which BGP operates.

Transport optimization is basically composed of three factors:

- Optimizing TCP: Maximum Segment Size (MSS) and the TCP Window Size

- Optimizing the generation of BGP updates

- Optimizing the receipt of TCP ACK messages in response to those BGP updates

Optimizing TCP

BGP neighbors form a TCP client-server connection. To establish the session, the two routers go through the standard TCP negotiation process involving one BGP speaker acting as the TCP client initiating a TCP connection to the other BGP speaker, acting as a TCP server. The client attempts to open the session to TCP port 179 by sending a SYN message to the server. The server replies with a SYN ACK message. Finally, the client replies with an ACK message, at which point the TCP session is established and the BGP speakers start exchanging OPEN messages, all the way up to neighbor establishment where both peers, assuming the BGP speakers do not face any issues, settle in the established state.

TCP performance is tuned by two parameters: the Maximum Segment Size (MSS) and the TCP Window Size.

The MSS, which is "negotiated" during the exchange of the SYN messages, determines the maximum size of a TCP segment that is sent between two TCP endpoints. The reason this value is significant is because it determines how much data can be "packed" into a single TCP segment. The bigger the MSS, the more routes can be packed into one TCP segment, and therefore, the more routes can be sent into less UPDATE messages. The TCP MSS is closely associated with the Maximum Transmission Unit, which in turn determines how big an IP packet can be without being fragmented if it sent one IP node to the another IP node. The TCP MSS value is the value of the MTU minus 20 bytes for the IP header and minus another 20 bytes for the TCP header. For example, for the Ethernet MTU, which is 1500 bytes, the TCP MSS can be up to 1460 bytes.

RFC 1191 defines a feature called Path MTU Discovery, which provides a means to dynamically discover the MTU over a path between two IP nodes. This is how it works: A node with PMTUD enabled sends out a packet with the Don't Fragment (DF) bit set to a destination IP node. The size of this packet is the size of the next-hop interface's MTU. The packet traverses the L2 link to the next hop and is then switched to the exit interface on to the second hop. If the receiving interface of the second hop has a lower MTU than the size of the packet, the packet is discarded and an ICMP Destination Unreachable message (with a code meaning "fragmentation needed and DF set"—also called "Datagram Too Big" message) is sent back to the packet source. This ICMP message also contains the value of the lower MTU of the receiving interface of the router that discarded the packet. A new packet is then generated at the source router with a size equal to the newer, lower MTU and sent toward the destination IP node, again. This process is repeated until the source router that has the PMTUD feature enabled determines the smallest MTU along the path to the destination IP node and uses this as its MTU, and in the process, determines the TCP MSS.

But why go through all this hassle to discover the MTU? Because if the IP packet has the Don't Fragment (DF) bit set, and its size exceeds the link MTU, the packet is dropped. Alternatively, if the DF bit is not set and the packet size exceeds the link MTU, the packet is fragmented. Fragmenting IP packets into smaller packets that are MTU-compliant adds processing overhead both during fragmentation and reassembly. The newly formed fragmented packets each have new headers and therefore more overhead. Rearranging out-of-order fragments is a challenge. One fragment could be lost during transmission, which calls for re-sending the whole original packet. These are just a few of the downsides of fragmentation. Therefore, the PMTUD feature adds great efficiency to the transport over TCP.

PMTUD can be configured on Cisco IOS for the whole BGP process, or it can be configured per neighbor. PMTUD is enabled by default and no command shows in the configuration to indicate this, however, if it were disabled under the global BGP process, the following statement would appear:

```
no bgp transport path-mtu-discovery
```

To re-enable PMTUD, use the same statement without the no argument. Alternatively, PMTUD can be enabled or disabled for one specific neighbor using the following statement under the address-family configuration. (The address family configuration is discussed in more detail in Chapter 6.)

```
neighbor {ip-address} transport path-mtu-discovery {enable|disable}
```

Example 5-86 shows the output of the command **show ip bgp neighbor**. Note the highlighted line in the output indicating that the PMTUD feature is enabled.

Example 5-86 *Output of the* **show ip bgp neighbor** *Command Showing the PMTUD Feature Enabled*

```
route-views>sh ip bgp neighbor 12.0.1.63
BGP neighbor is 12.0.1.63,  remote AS 7018, external link
 Description: ATT
  BGP version 4, remote router ID 12.0.1.63
  BGP state = Established, up for 2w5d
  Last read 00:00:00, last write 00:00:19, hold time is 180, keepalive interval is
  60 seconds
  Neighbor sessions:
    1 active, is not multisession capable (disabled)
  Neighbor capabilities:
    Route refresh: advertised and received(new)
    Four-octets ASN Capability: advertised and received
    Address family IPv4 Unicast: advertised and received
    Graceful Restart Capability: received
      Remote Restart timer is 120 seconds
      Address families advertised by peer:
        none
    Enhanced Refresh Capability: advertised
    Multisession Capability:
    Stateful switchover support enabled: NO for session 1
  Message statistics:
    InQ depth is 0
    OutQ depth is 0

                    Sent        Rcvd
    Opens:              1           1
    Notifications:      0           0
    Updates:            1     6201206
    Keepalives:     31620       31919
    Route Refresh:      1           0
    Total:          31623     6233126
  Default minimum time between advertisement runs is 30 seconds
  BGP Monitoring(BMP) activated for servers: server 1

 For address family: IPv4 Unicast
  Session: 12.0.1.63
  BGP table version 98074172, neighbor version 98074033/98074172
  Output queue size : 0
  Index 1, Advertise bit 0
```

```
   1 update-group member
  Outbound path policy configured
  Route map for outgoing advertisements is nothing
  Slow-peer detection is disabled
  Slow-peer split-update-group dynamic is disabled
  Interface associated: (none)
                                   Sent       Rcvd
  Prefix activity:                 ----       ----
    Prefixes Current:                 0     550318 (Consumes 66038040 bytes)
    Prefixes Total:                   0    15071611
    Implicit Withdraw:                0    12382592
    Explicit Withdraw:                0     2138708
    Used as bestpath:               n/a       22847
    Used as multipath:              n/a           0

                                 Outbound   Inbound
  Local Policy Denied Prefixes:   --------   -------
    Other Policies:               424685515      n/a
    Total:                        424685515        0
  Number of NLRIs in the update sent: max 0, min 0
  Last detected as dynamic slow peer: never
  Dynamic slow peer recovered: never
  Refresh Epoch: 1
  Last Sent Refresh Start-of-rib: never
  Last Sent Refresh End-of-rib: never
  Last Received Refresh Start-of-rib: never
  Last Received Refresh End-of-rib: never
                                   Sent       Rcvd
        Refresh activity:          ----       ----
          Refresh Start-of-RIB       0          0
          Refresh End-of-RIB         0          0


  Address tracking is enabled, the RIB does have a route to 12.0.1.63
  Connections established 21; dropped 20
  Last reset 2w6d, due to Active open failed
  External BGP neighbor may be up to 255 hops away.
  Transport(tcp) path-mtu-discovery is enabled
  Graceful-Restart is disabled
  SSO is disabled
Connection state is ESTAB, I/O status: 1, unread input bytes: 0
Connection is ECN Disabled, Mininum incoming TTL 0, Outgoing TTL 255
Local host: 128.223.51.103, Local port: 54289
Foreign host: 12.0.1.63, Foreign port: 179
Connection tableid (VRF): 0
Maximum output segment queue size: 50
```

```
Enqueued packets for retransmit: 0, input: 0  mis-ordered: 0 (0 bytes)


Event Timers (current time is 0x2889CE7FA):
Timer          Starts    Wakeups        Next
Retrans        31673         50         0x0
TimeWait           0          0         0x0
AckHold      3299983    2992400         0x0
SendWnd            0          0         0x0
KeepAlive          0          0         0x0
GiveUp             0          0         0x0
PmtuAger           1          1         0x0
DeadWait           0          0         0x0
Linger             0          0         0x0
ProcessQ           0          0         0x0


iss:  668100903  snduna:  668701787  sndnxt:  668701787
irs: 3315518154  rcvnxt: 3788467185


sndwnd:  16384  scale:      0  maxrcvwnd:  16384
rcvwnd:  16230  scale:      0  delrcvwnd:    154


SRTT: 1000 ms, RTTO: 1003 ms, RTV: 3 ms, KRTT: 0 ms
minRTT: 82 ms, maxRTT: 7050 ms, ACK hold: 200 ms
uptime: 1724762752 ms, Sent idletime: 97 ms, Receive idletime: 339 ms
Status Flags: active open
Option Flags: nagle, path mtu capable
IP Precedence value : 6


Datagrams (max data segment is 1400 bytes):
Rcvd: 3354726 (out of order: 84), with data: 3333101, total data bytes: 472949030
Sent: 3363751 (retransmit: 50, fastretransmit: 0, partialack: 0, Second Congestion:
  0), with data: 31623, total data bytes: 600883


 Packets received in fast path: 0, fast processed: 0, slow path: 0
 fast lock acquisition failures: 0, slow path: 0
TCP Semaphore      0x7F63FD3D8C90   FREE
route-views>
```

The second parameter that dictates TCP performance is the TCP Window Size. This is
the amount of data that is sent by TCP before expecting an ACK message from the peer.
On Cisco IOS, this value is 16KB and is configurable for TCP. However, this does not
affect the TCP window size used by BGP. Even though this value is not configurable
on Cisco IOS, its value has significance because it directly affects the number of ACK

messages received back by a router sending out UPDATE messages to a large number of BGP peers. This is discussed in more detail later in this section.

Optimizing BGP Update Generation

Earlier in this chapter, the concept of dynamic update groups was discussed, which greatly increased the efficiency of update generation on a BGP speaker. Two more optimizations that add to the efficiency of transporting those UPDATE messages have been added to Cisco IOS:

- Each BGP Update Group has a "Message Cache" that stores the updates that are to be sent to this group of routers, instead of sending the updates as they are extracted from the BGP table, per combination of attributes. The size of this cache has become "adaptive," in the sense that its size changes per update group based on the number of peers in that update group. This allows update groups with a larger number of members to get equally large cache sizes. In addition, the cache size increases with the availability of memory resources on the platform, making use of available resources to speed up update message transmissions. This is a feature that needs no configuration from the operator.

- BGP routers now enter into a Read-Only Mode for a configurable interval of time as they receive UPDATE messages from their peers. When this interval is over, and not before, the best path algorithm is executed to choose the BGP best paths and hence announce those best paths in UPDATE messages to the BGP neighbors. Without this optimization, the best path algorithm would be run prematurely before all UPDATE messages are received, and several UPDATE messages would be sent that negate earlier updates for the same prefixes. This is called implicit withdrawal.

Optimizing TCP ACK Message Receipt

Now that TCP has been optimized and BGP update generation has also been optimized, what remains is the way the router reacts to the ACK messages that it receives from neighbors, to which it has sent UPDATE messages. This may not be a major concern for BGP speakers with two or three neighbors. However, it becomes a significant issue when the number of neighbors is large, as with route reflectors.

A TCP ACK message is received for every two UPDATE messages sent to a neighbor. If an ACK message is lost, the UPDATE messages that this ACK message was acknowledging have to be transmitted out again. This severely affects the efficiency of the update process and may cause some peers to be tagged as "slow peers" and eventually removed from an update group. To avoid losing any ACK messages, these messages are queued on the incoming interface on which they are received. Of course, this discussion applies to any TCP messages, whether sent or received, not just BGP messages. On Cisco routers, TCP messages encounter three queue types before reaching the router processor:

- **Input hold queue:** This is the first layer of input queuing on an interface and is set using the statement **hold-queue** {*value*} **in** and this value can be seen in the output of the **show interfaces** command. The number of ACK messages received in a worst-case scenario where all neighbors are sending ACKs simultaneously can be determined using the TCP window side, the MSS value, and the number of neighbors that this BGP speaker has.

■ **Selective Packet Discard Headroom:** This is not actually a separate queue but an extension to the hold queue described previously. This extension is used as a contingency for high priority packets (such BGP control packets) when the hold queue is full. The extra queuing is implemented via the statement **ip spd headroom** {*value*} and the value can be verified using the command **show ip spd.**

■ **System buffers:** These are the last level of queuing before the BGP control packets are sent to the processor, set using the statement **buffer small permanent** {*value*}, and can be viewed using the command **show buffers.**

Scaling the BGP Network

You examined features and techniques for scaling BGP configurations in a single router and the BGP process in a single router. The final topic of this chapter is how to make the entire BGP network more scalable.

Private AS Numbers

You were introduced to private AS numbers in Chapter 2 and have seen them used throughout this book. So this section just provides a brief recap of what you already know.

Private ASNs were introduced in RFC 1930 and consist of AS numbers 64512 through 65534. Their purpose is the same as the purpose of RFC 1918 private IPv4 addresses: to reserve a pool of ASNs that is not expected to be unique in the public domain and, therefore, can be used over and over in private networks, reducing the depletion of the pool of publicly assignable AS numbers.

The three most-common uses of private AS numbers follows:

■ A service provider may assign a private ASN to a "stub" customer—that is, a customer that is not connected to any other service provider. The SP filters private ASNs out of the AS_PATH of any routes received from these stub customers before advertising them to the public Internet.

■ Private ASNs number the sub-autonomous systems in confederations, described later in this section. Again, the private ASNs are removed from the AS_PATH of routes within a confederation before they are advertised outside of the confederation boundary.

■ Again, like private IPv4 addresses, private ASNs are frequently used in documentation as generic numbers to avoid the chance of using someone's actual assigned number and possibly causing objections. Although ASNs such as 1, 2, 3... or 100,

200, 300… are often used in examples in this book for simplicity, private ASNs are used in the examples in which they make sense.

Like private IPv4 addresses, it is important that private AS numbers not be advertised to the public Internet or into any network in a prefix's AS_PATH where they may no longer be unique. IOS does not remove private ASNs from an AS_PATH by default; to remove them, use the **neighbor remove-private-as** statement, as shown in the following example.

Figure 5-34 shows the same topology that was used for earlier examples in this chapter but with one difference: Five of the autonomous systems peering with AS100 now use private AS numbers. In this exercise we want AS100 to advertise the prefixes of its private autonomous system neighbors to AS700 and AS800. Think of a service provider and its customers.

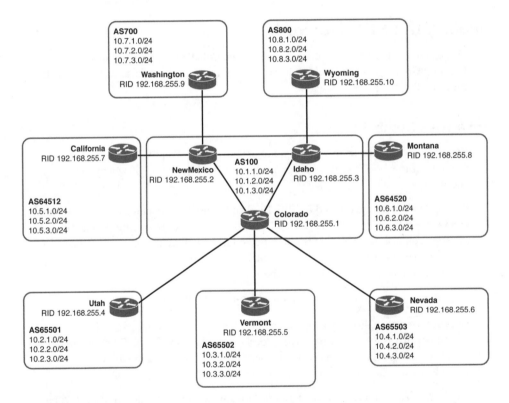

Figure 5-34 *Five of AS100's Peering Autonomous Systems Use Private AS Numbers. The Prefixes in These Autonomous Systems Must Be Advertised to AS700 and AS800, but the Private ASNs Must Not Be Advertised*

The BGP configuration of router NewMexico is shown in Example 5-87. The policy configurations used in previous exercises have been removed, and you can see that the configurations are straightforward. The same is true of the configuration of neighbor

California (not shown). The BGP statement there begins with **router bgp 64512**; nothing special has to be done to use private AS numbers.

Example 5-87   *BGP Configuration of Router NewMexico in Figure 5-33*

```
router bgp 100
 template peer-policy IBGP
  next-hop-self
  send-community
 exit-peer-policy
 !
 template peer-policy EBGP
  route-map pref-set in
 exit-peer-policy
 !
 template peer-session bgp_top
  update-source Loopback0
  timers 30 90
 exit-peer-session
 !
 template peer-session ibgp
  remote-as 100
  password 7 002520283B0A5B56
  inherit peer-session bgp_top
 exit-peer-session
 !
 no synchronization
 bgp log-neighbor-changes
 network 10.1.2.0 mask 255.255.255.0
 neighbor 10.0.0.34 remote-as 700
 neighbor 10.0.0.34 password 7 113B403A2713181F
 neighbor 10.0.0.38 remote-as 64512
 neighbor 10.0.0.38 password 7 08131B7139181604
 neighbor 192.168.255.1 inherit peer-session ibgp
 neighbor 192.168.255.1 inherit peer-policy IBGP
 neighbor 192.168.255.3 inherit peer-session ibgp
 neighbor 192.168.255.3 inherit peer-policy IBGP
 no auto-summary
 !
```

Example 5-88 shows the BGP table at router Washington. You can see that the AS_PATHs of the prefixes from the private autonomous systems still contain the private ASNs. If AS700 and AS800 in Figure 5-33 represent public neighbors such as a service provider's upstream Internet peers, the private ASNs must be removed.

Example 5-88   *When NewMexico Advertises the Prefixes of the Private Autonomous Systems to Washington, the Private ASNs Remain in the Prefixes' AS_PATHs*

```
Washington#show ip bgp
BGP table version is 55, local router ID is 192.168.255.9
Status codes: s suppressed, d damped, h history, * valid, > best, i - internal,
              r RIB-failure, S Stale
Origin codes: i - IGP, e - EGP, ? - incomplete

   Network          Next Hop          Metric LocPrf Weight Path
*> 10.1.1.0/24      10.0.0.33                          0 100 i
*> 10.1.2.0/24      10.0.0.33              0            0 100 i
*> 10.1.3.0/24      10.0.0.33                          0 100 i
*> 10.2.1.0/24      10.0.0.33                          0 100 65501 i
*> 10.2.2.0/24      10.0.0.33                          0 100 65501 i
*> 10.2.3.0/24      10.0.0.33                          0 100 65501 i
*> 10.3.1.0/24      10.0.0.33                          0 100 65502 i
*> 10.3.2.0/24      10.0.0.33                          0 100 65502 i
*> 10.3.3.0/24      10.0.0.33                          0 100 65502 i
*> 10.4.1.0/24      10.0.0.33                          0 100 65503 i
*> 10.4.2.0/24      10.0.0.33                          0 100 65503 i
*> 10.4.3.0/24      10.0.0.33                          0 100 65503 i
*> 10.5.1.0/24      10.0.0.33                          0 100 64512 i
*> 10.5.2.0/24      10.0.0.33                          0 100 64512 i
*> 10.5.3.0/24      10.0.0.33                          0 100 64512 i
*> 10.6.1.0/24      10.0.0.33                          0 100 64520 i
*> 10.6.2.0/24      10.0.0.33                          0 100 64520 i
*> 10.6.3.0/24      10.0.0.33                          0 100 64520 i
*> 10.7.1.0/24      0.0.0.0                0        32768 i
*> 10.7.2.0/24      0.0.0.0                0        32768 i
*> 10.7.3.0/24      0.0.0.0                0        32768 i
*> 10.8.1.0/24      10.0.0.33                          0 100 800 i
*> 10.8.2.0/24      10.0.0.33                          0 100 800 i
*> 10.8.3.0/24      10.0.0.33                          0 100 800 i
Washington#
```

In Example 5-89, the **neighbor remove-private-as** statement is added to NewMexico's neighbor configuration for Washington. In Example 5-90, you can see that the private ASNs are now removed from the prefixes in Washington's BGP table.

Example 5-89   neighbor remove-private-as statement *Is Added to NewMexico's Neighbor Configuration to Washington*

```
router bgp 100
 template peer-policy IBGP
  next-hop-self
  send-community
 exit-peer-policy
 !
 template peer-policy EBGP
  route-map pref-set in
 exit-peer-policy
 !
 template peer-session bgp_top
  update-source Loopback0
  timers 30 90
 exit-peer-session
 !
 template peer-session ibgp
  remote-as 100
  password 7 002520283B0A5B56
  inherit peer-session bgp_top
 exit-peer-session
 !
 no synchronization
 bgp log-neighbor-changes
 network 10.1.2.0 mask 255.255.255.0
 neighbor 10.0.0.34 remote-as 700
 neighbor 10.0.0.34 password 7 113B403A2713181F
 neighbor 10.0.0.34 remove-private-as
 neighbor 10.0.0.38 remote-as 64512
 neighbor 10.0.0.38 password 7 08131B7139181604
 neighbor 192.168.255.1 inherit peer-session ibgp
 neighbor 192.168.255.1 inherit peer-policy IBGP
 neighbor 192.168.255.3 inherit peer-session ibgp
 neighbor 192.168.255.3 inherit peer-policy IBGP
 no auto-summary
 !
```

Example 5-90   *Washington's BGP Table Shows That the Private ASNs Have Now Been Removed from the Prefixes Advertised by AS100*

```
Washington#show ip bgp
BGP table version is 97, local router ID is 192.168.255.9
Status codes: s suppressed, d damped, h history, * valid, > best, i - internal,
```

```
                    r RIB-failure, S Stale
Origin codes: i - IGP, e - EGP, ? - incomplete

   Network          Next Hop         Metric LocPrf Weight Path
*> 10.1.1.0/24      10.0.0.33                          0 100 i
*> 10.1.2.0/24      10.0.0.33            0             0 100 i
*> 10.1.3.0/24      10.0.0.33                          0 100 i
*> 10.2.1.0/24      10.0.0.33                          0 100 i
*> 10.2.2.0/24      10.0.0.33                          0 100 i
*> 10.2.3.0/24      10.0.0.33                          0 100 i
*> 10.3.1.0/24      10.0.0.33                          0 100 i
*> 10.3.2.0/24      10.0.0.33                          0 100 i
*> 10.3.3.0/24      10.0.0.33                          0 100 i
*> 10.4.1.0/24      10.0.0.33                          0 100 i
*> 10.4.2.0/24      10.0.0.33                          0 100 i
*> 10.4.3.0/24      10.0.0.33                          0 100 i
*> 10.5.1.0/24      10.0.0.33                          0 100 i
*> 10.5.2.0/24      10.0.0.33                          0 100 i
*> 10.5.3.0/24      10.0.0.33                          0 100 i
*> 10.6.1.0/24      10.0.0.33                          0 100 i
*> 10.6.2.0/24      10.0.0.33                          0 100 i
*> 10.6.3.0/24      10.0.0.33                          0 100 i
*> 10.7.1.0/24      0.0.0.0             0          32768 i
*> 10.7.2.0/24      0.0.0.0             0          32768 i
*> 10.7.3.0/24      0.0.0.0             0          32768 i
*> 10.8.1.0/24      10.0.0.33                          0 100 800 i
*> 10.8.2.0/24      10.0.0.33                          0 100 800 i
*> 10.8.3.0/24      10.0.0.33                          0 100 800 i
Washington#
```

The effects of removing private ASNs from an AS_PATH before advertising a prefix upstream is similar to the effects of route aggregation. Best path determination is made with AS100 as the last ASN on the AS_PATH list. When packets are forwarded to AS100, that AS has the further detail necessary to find the path to the connected private AS.

4-Byte AS Numbers

Another parallel between AS numbers and IP addresses is that even with the use of private ASNs the pool of publicly unique 2-byte ASNs is being depleted. The answer to this resource depletion also has its parallels to IP addresses: Just as IPv6, with its much larger address space, has been developed to augment and eventually replace IPv4, 4-byte (32-bit) autonomous system numbers were developed to provide a newer, larger pool of AS numbers. Where the 16-bit ASN pool is composed of 65,535 ASNs, the 4-byte ASN pool is composed of more than 4.3 billion ASNs. BGP support for 4-byte ASNs is specified in RFC 6793.

For IOS versions that support 4-byte ASNs, there is no special configuration needed other than just specifying the ASN in the **router bgp** statement. A router supporting 4-byte ASNs can also still support 2-byte ASNs.

Following are two formats for specifying ASNs in a 4-byte environment:

- **ASPlain format:** This is a simple number in a 32-bit range:
- **2-byte ASNs:** 1–65535
- **4-byte ASNs:** 65536–4294967295
- **ASDot format:** This format makes larger numbers easier to read by displaying the 4-byte ASN as two 16-bit numbers:
- **2-byte ASNs:** 1–65535
- **4-byte ASNs:** 1.0–65535.65535

If you want ASNs to display in the ASDot format, simply add the statement **bgp asnotation dot** to the BGP configuration.

There is also support for a private ASN range in 4-byte ASNs just as there is in 2-byte ASNs. Although the 2-byte private ASN range is 64512—65535, the 4-byte private ASN range is 4200000000–4294967294 (64086.59904–65535.65534 in ASDot notation).

IBGP and the N-Squared Problem

One of the most pressing scaling problems within an AS is the need to fully mesh IBGP to ensure that, unless EBGP routes are redistributed into the IGP, a bad practice in most cases, every BGP speaker has a direct session with every other BGP speaker within the AS. If there are only a few internal nodes, this isn't a problem. But as the number of IBGP speakers grows, they become a scaling challenge both for configuration size and management and router load as the router tries to maintain large numbers of IBGP peer relationships.

This is called the *n-squared* problem: As the number of fully meshed nodes' n increase, the number of connections between the nodes increases exponentially according to the formula:

$$\text{Connections} = .5(n^2 - n)$$

So If 6 IBGP nodes are in an AS, you need 15 IBGP sessions, as shown in Figure 5-35. 10 nodes exist, you need 45 IBGP sessions, and 20 nodes require 190 sessions. You can easily see that growth quickly becomes a problem for the configuration and for the BGP process.

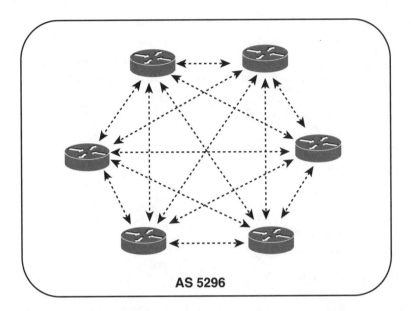

Figure 5-35   *Fully Meshed IBGP Peers*

You'll encounter the n-squared problem in any topology where every node is required to connect to every other node, such as a full mesh Frame Relay core, OSPF, or IS-IS routers sharing a multiaccess network.

The n-squared problem in IBGP topologies has two solutions: Confederations and Route Reflectors. They approach the problems in different ways. Confederations "subdivide" the AS into smaller sub-autonomous systems, allowing a special version of the simpler EBGP to be used between the sub-autonomous systems. Route Reflectors utilize a couple new route attributes that allow the IBGP full mesh rules to be relaxed. The remaining two subsections of this chapter cover confederations and route reflectors, the pros and cons of using each, and how they can even be used together to create a large single autonomous system, which is the subject of the last two sections in this chapter.

Confederations

A confederation is an AS that has been subdivided into a group of sub-autonomous systems, known as *member autonomous systems*, as shown in Figure 5-36. The BGP speakers within the confederation speak IBGP to peers in the same member AS, and a special version of EBGP called *confederation EBGP* to peers in other member autonomous systems. The confederation is assigned a *confederation ID*, which is represented to peers outside of the confederation as the AS number of the entire confederation. External peers do not see the internal structure of the confederation; rather, they see a single autonomous system. In Figure 5-36, AS 9184 is the confederation ID.

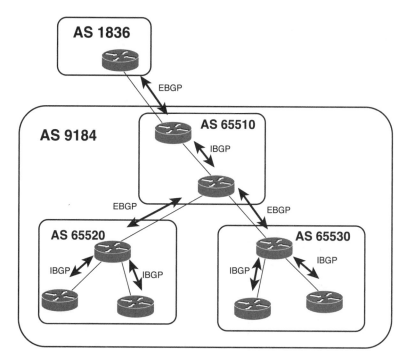

Figure 5-36 *A Typical Confederation*

You are familiar with the concept of subdividing entities for better manageability. IP subnets are subdivisions of IP networks, and VLSM subdivides subnets. Similarly, autonomous systems are subdivisions of large internetworks (such as the Internet). Confederations are subdivisions of autonomous systems.

The section "AS_SET," in Chapter 3, described two types of AS_PATH attributes: AS_SEQUENCE and AS_SET. Confederations add two more types to the AS_PATH:

- **AS_CONFED_SEQUENCE:** This is an ordered list of AS numbers along a path to a destination. It is used in exactly the same way as the AS_SEQUENCE, except that the AS numbers in the list belong to autonomous systems within the local confederation.

- **AS_CONFED_SET:** This is an unordered list of AS numbers along a path to a destination. It is used in exactly the same way as the AS_SET, except that the AS numbers in the list belong to autonomous systems within the local confederation.

Because the AS_PATH attribute is used in Updates between the member autonomous systems, loop avoidance is preserved. From the perspective of a BGP router within a member AS, all peers in other member autonomous systems are external neighbors.

When an Update is sent to a peer external to the confederation, the AS_CONFED_
SEQUENCE and AS_CONFED_SET information is stripped from the AS_PATH attribute, and the confederation ID is prepended to the AS_PATH. Because of this, external
peers see the confederation as a single AS rather than as a collection of autonomous
systems. As Figure 5-37 shows, it is common practice to use AS numbers from the
reserved range 64512 to 65535 to number the member autonomous systems within a
confederation.

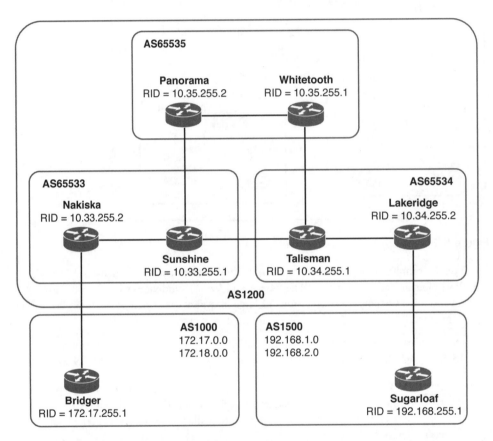

Figure 5-37 *AS1200 Is a BGP Confederation; Although It Consists of Several
Sub-Autonomous Systems, the Neighboring Autonomous Systems See the Confederation
Only as 1200*

When choosing a route, the BGP decision process remains the same, with one addition.
EBGP routes external to the confederation are preferred over EBGP routes to member
autonomous systems, which are preferred over IBGP routes. Another difference between
confederations and standard autonomous systems is the way in which some attributes
are handled. Attributes such as NEXT_HOP and MED can be advertised unchanged to
EBGP peers in another member AS within the confederation, and the LOCAL_PREF
attribute also can be sent.

All routers within a confederation must support the confederation functionality. This is because all routers must recognize the AS_CONFED_SEQUENCE and AS_CONFED_SET types in the AS_PATH attribute. However, because these AS_PATH types are removed from routes advertised out of the confederation, routers in other autonomous systems do not have to support confederations.

In large autonomous systems, confederations and route reflectors (discussed in the next section) can be used together. One or more RR clusters can be configured within one or more member autonomous systems for even more optimal control of IBGP peers.

Figure 5-37 shows an example of a confederation. AS1200 has been subdivided into three confederation autonomous systems: AS65533, AS65534, and AS65535. From the perspective of outside autonomous systems, such as 1000 and AS1500, the confederation is a single autonomous system: AS1200. These external autonomous systems have no knowledge of the confederation member autonomous systems.

Confederation EBGP is run between Panorama and Sunshine, between Sunshine and Talisman, and between Talisman and Whitetooth. Example 5-91 shows the configuration for Talisman.

Example 5-91 *Configuring Talisman as a Confederation Router*

```
router ospf 65534
 network 10.34.0.0 0.0.255.255 area 65534
 network 10.255.0.0 0.0.255.255 area 0
!
router bgp 65534
 no synchronization
 bgp confederation identifier 1200
 bgp confederation peers 65533 65535
 neighbor Confed peer-group
 neighbor Confed ebgp-multihop 2
 neighbor Confed update-source Loopback
 neighbor Confed next-hop-self
 neighbor MyGroup peer-group
 neighbor MyGroup remote-as 65534
 neighbor MyGroup update-source Loopback0
 neighbor 10.33.255.1 remote-as 65533
 neighbor 10.33.255.1 peer-group Confed
 neighbor 10.34.255.2 peer-group MyGroup
 neighbor 10.35.255.1 remote-as 65535
 neighbor 10.35.255.1 peer-group Confed
```

Talisman is configured so that its local AS is 65534. Its peer connections to Whitetooth and Sunshine are set up like any other EBGP session, and the connection to Lakeridge is IBGP. The **bgp confederation identifier** command tells the router that it is a member of a confederation and the confederation ID. The **bgp confederation peers** command lists the member autonomous systems to which Talisman is connected. This command tells the BGP process that the EBGP connection is confederation EBGP rather than normal EBGP.

A confederation may run BGP only, a common IGP throughout the entire confederation, or different IGPs within each member AS. In Figure 5-37, all the routers within AS1200 run OSPF. The OSPF permits local communication within the confederation and tells the BGP processes how to find their various neighbors. In the configuration in Example 5-90, no routes are redistributed between OSPF and BGP at any router. Subsequent configuration examples do not show the OSPF configuration.

Example 5-92 shows configurations of Lakeridge and Sugarloaf.

Example 5-92 *Configuring EBGP Between Confederation Router Lakeridge and External Router Sugarloaf*

```
Lakeridge
router bgp 65534
 no synchronization
 bgp confederation identifier 1200
 neighbor 10.34.255.1 remote-as 65534
 neighbor 10.34.255.1 update-source Loopback0
 neighbor 10.34.255.1 next-hop-self
 neighbor 192.168.255.1 remote-as 1500
 neighbor 192.168.255.1 ebgp-multihop 2
 neighbor 192.168.255.1 update-source Loopback0


Sugarloaf
router bgp 1500
 network 192.168.1.0
 network 192.168.2.0
 neighbor 10.34.255.2 remote-as 1200
 neighbor 10.34.255.2 ebgp-multihop 2
 neighbor 10.34.255.2 update-source Loopback0
```

At Lakeridge, the **bgp confederation peers** command is not used because Lakeridge is not running confederation EBGP. It does, however, have a normal EBGP connection to Sugarloaf. From the perspective of Sugarloaf, Lakeridge is in AS1200, not AS65534. Sugarloaf, being outside of the confederation, has no knowledge of the member autonomous systems.

Confederation EBGP is something of a hybrid between normal BGP and IBGP. Specifically, within a confederation, the following applies:

- The NEXT_HOP attribute of routes external to the confederation is preserved throughout the confederation.

- MULTI_EXIT_DISC attributes of routes advertised into a confederation are preserved throughout the confederation.

- LOCAL_PREF attributes of routes are preserved throughout the entire confederation, not just within the member AS in which they are assigned.

- The AS numbers of the member autonomous systems are added to the AS_PATH within the confederation but are not advertised outside of the confederation. By default, the member AS numbers are listed in the AS_PATH as AS_PATH attribute type 4, AS_CONFED_SEQUENCE. If the **aggregate-address** command is used within the confederation, the **as-set** keyword causes member AS numbers behind the aggregation point to be listed as AS_PATH attribute type 3, AS_CONFED_SET.

- The confederation AS numbers in an AS_PATH are used for loop avoidance but are not considered when choosing a shortest AS_PATH within the confederation.

Most of these characteristics are because from the outside, the confederation appears to be a single autonomous system. The following discussion provides examples of each of these characteristics.

In Figure 5-37, the routes in AS1000 are advertised from Bridger to Nakiska with a NEXT_HOP attribute of 172.17.255.1. This attribute is preserved when the routes are advertised via IBGP from Nakiska to Sunshine. If Sunshine were connected to Talisman with a normal EBGP connection, Sunshine would change the NEXT_HOP of the routes to 10.33.255.1 before advertising them to Talisman. Because the connection is confederation EBGP, however, the original NEXT_HOP attribute is preserved. As a result, Lakeridge could have route entries for 172.17.0.0 and 172.18.0.0 with a next-hop address of 172.17.255.1. Lakeridge's connection to Sugarloaf is normal EBGP, so the routes are advertised to Sugarloaf with a NEXT_HOP attribute of 10.34.255.2.

The **neighbor next-hop-self** command is used throughout the confederation of Figure 5-37 so that all next-hop addresses are known via the IGP. You can observe these commands in the configurations of Talisman and Lakeridge.

Bridger is configured to advertise its routes with a MED of 50, and Nakiska is configured to set the LOCAL_PREF of the same routes to 200. You can observe the results in Example 5-93. In a normal EBGP session, Sunshine would not advertise the MED that originated in AS1000, or the LOCAL_PREF that should have relevance only within AS65533. Because the confederation is seen from the outside as a single AS, however, these values must be consistent throughout the confederation.

Example 5-93 *Routes from AS1000 Have a MED of 50 and a LOCAL_PREF of 200 at Lakeridge; These Values Were Preserved Across the Confederation EBGP Connection from Sunshine*

```
Lakeridge#show ip bgp
BGP table version is 28, local router ID is 10.34.255.2
Status codes: s suppressed, * valid, > best, i - internal
Origin codes: i - IGP, e - EGP, ? - incomplete
```

```
    Network            Next Hop        Metric LocPrf Weight Path
*>i172.17.0.0         10.33.255.1         50    200      0 (65533) 1000 i
*>i172.18.0.0         10.33.255.1         50    200      0 (65533) 1000 i
*> 192.168.1.0        192.168.255.1        0             0 1500 i
*> 192.168.2.0        192.168.255.1        0             0 1500 i
Lakeridge#
```

You also can see in Example 5-93 that AS 65533 is included in the AS_PATH of the routes to the networks in AS1000. The AS_CONFED_SEQUENCE is shown in parentheses for two reasons. First, it is not advertised outside of the confederation, as demonstrated in Example 5-94. Second, it is used only for loop avoidance within the confederation, not for path selection.

Example 5-94 *Sugarloaf Sees the Confederation in Figure 5-37 as a Single Autonomous System and Does Not See the Member Autonomous Systems; the AS_CONFED_SEQUENCE, Shown in Parentheses in Example 92, Is Replaced with the Confederation ID 1200*

```
Sugarloaf#show ip bgp
BGP table version is 32, local router ID is 192.168.255.1
Status codes: s suppressed, d damped, h history, * valid, > best, i - internal
Origin codes: i - IGP, e - EGP, ? - incomplete

    Network            Next Hop        Metric LocPrf Weight Path
*> 172.17.0.0         10.34.255.2                        0 1200 1000 i
*> 172.18.0.0         10.34.255.2                        0 1200 1000 i
*> 192.168.1.0        0.0.0.0              0         32768 i
*> 192.168.2.0        0.0.0.0              0         32768 i
Sugarloaf#
```

In the BGP tables of Whitetooth and Panorama displayed in Example 5-94, you can observe a consequence because member AS numbers do not influence the path selection process. Both routers have two paths to each of the destinations in AS1000 and AS1500—one via its IBGP neighbor, and one via its confederation EBGP neighbor. Whitetooth, for instance, has two paths to network 172.17.0.0. The AS_PATH of one is (65534, 65533, 1000) and the other is (65533, 1000). Clearly the latter AS_PATH is shorter, but the member AS numbers are ignored. As a result, the two paths are seen as equivalent: (1000). All else being equal, the BGP decision process chooses normal EBGP routes over confederation EBGP routes and confederation EBGP routes over IBGP routes. In Example 5-95, the choice is between a confederation EBGP route and an IBGP route. Notice in the BGP tables of the two routers that the confederation EBGP path is chosen in every instance.

Example 5-95 *AS_CONFED_SEQUENCE, Shown in Parentheses in the Whitetooth and Panorama BGP Tables, Are Not Considered When Choosing a Shortest AS_PATH Within an AS Confederation*

```
Whitetooth#show ip bgp
BGP table version is 9, local router ID is 10.35.255.1
Status codes: s suppressed, d damped, h history, * valid, > best, i - internal
Origin codes: i - IGP, e - EGP, ? - incomplete


   Network          Next Hop          Metric LocPrf Weight Path
*> 172.17.0.0       10.34.255.1           50    200      0 (65534 65533) 1000 i
*  i                10.33.255.1           50    200      0 (65533) 1000 i
*> 172.18.0.0       10.34.255.1           50    200      0 (65534 65533) 1000 i
*  i                10.33.255.1           50    200      0 (65533) 1000 i
*> 192.168.1.0      10.34.255.1            0    100      0 (65534) 1500 i
*  i                10.33.255.1            0    100      0 (65533 65534) 1500 i
*> 192.168.2.0      10.34.255.1            0    100      0 (65534) 1500 i
*  i                10.33.255.1            0    100      0 (65533 65534) 1500 i
Whitetooth#
```

```
Panorama#show ip bgp
BGP table version is 5, local router ID is 10.35.255.2
Status codes: s suppressed, d damped, h history, * valid, > best, i - internal
Origin codes: i - IGP, e - EGP, ? - incomplete


   Network          Next Hop          Metric LocPrf Weight Path
*  i172.17.0.0       10.34.255.1          50    200      0 (65534 65533) 1000 i
*>                   10.33.255.1          50    200      0 (65533) 1000 i
*  i172.18.0.0       10.34.255.1          50    200      0 (65534 65533) 1000 i
*>                   10.33.255.1          50    200      0 (65533) 1000 i
*  i192.168.1.0      10.34.255.1           0    100      0 (65534) 1500 i
*>                   10.33.255.1           0    100      0 (65533 65534) 1500 i
*  i192.168.2.0      10.34.255.1           0    100      0 (65534) 1500 i
*>                   10.33.255.1           0    100      0 (65533 65534) 1500 i
Panorama#
```

In the topology of Figure 5-37, ignoring the member AS numbers presents no problem. Consider the topology in Figure 5-38, however, where everything is identical except the BGP router IDs in AS65534 and AS65535, which have been swapped. This change might seem innocent enough, but consider the effect that it has on the BGP decision process at Sunshine. The routes to the networks in AS1500 are advertised by both Talisman and Panorama. The AS_PATH lengths are the same because the member AS numbers are ignored, and both neighbors are confederation EBGP peers. Both Talisman and Panorama use the **neighbor next-hop-self** command, so the IGP path to the next-hop address of both routes is the same. The tiebreaker becomes the lowest neighboring

router ID, which is Panorama. Sunshine, therefore, chooses the path through
AS 65535 via Panorama rather than the more-direct path via Talisman, as shown in
Example 5-96.

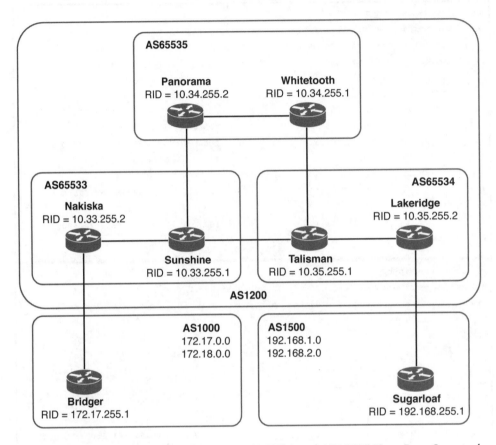

Figure 5-38   *Router IDs of the Routers in AS65534 and AS65535 Have Been Swapped*

Example 5-96   *Sunshine Has Chosen Suboptimal Paths to the Networks in AS1500
Based on Panorama's Lower Router ID*

```
Sunshine#show ip bgp
BGP table version is 17, local router ID is 10.33.255.1
Status codes: s suppressed, d damped, h history, * valid, > best, i - internal
Origin codes: i - IGP, e - EGP, ? - incomplete

   Network          Next Hop          Metric LocPrf Weight Path
*>i172.17.0.0       10.33.255.2           50    200      0 1000 i
*>i172.18.0.0       10.33.255.2           50    200      0 1000 i
*> 192.168.1.0      10.34.255.2            0    100      0 (65535 65534) 1500 i
```

```
*                   10.35.255.1          0    100     0 (65534) 1500 i
*> 192.168.2.0      10.34.255.2          0    100     0 (65535 65534) 1500 i
*                   10.35.255.1          0    100     0 (65534) 1500 i
Sunshine#
```

Little can be done to remedy the problems in the topology of Figure 5-38. Attempting to filter routes or manipulate administrative weights makes the configurations highly complex, defeating one of the reasons for creating a confederation in the first place. Attempting to manipulate the route choices with LOCAL_PREF or MED attributes is fraught with hazards because the attributes are advertised throughout the confederation; with the loops in the topology, the attributes can affect route choices in unintended locations.

You must design confederations so that problems such as those presented by the topology in Figure 5-38 do not arise. A common design technique takes its cue from OSPF, in which all areas must interconnect through a single backbone area, eliminating the possibility of inter-area loops.

Figure 5-39 shows the same routers as in the earlier illustrations, but the member autonomous systems have been redesigned. AS65000 is a backbone autonomous system, and all the other autonomous systems must interconnect through it. The result is that the path from any nonbackbone AS to any other nonbackbone AS is the same distance. The connections between AS65000 and AS65535 demonstrate that it is still possible to have redundant connections, but not between nonbackbone autonomous systems. BGP's loop-avoidance mechanism prevents the possibility of suboptimal inter-AS paths.

Another advantage of a loop-free topology, such as the one in Figure 5-39, is that the MED attribute can be used between member autonomous systems. To understand why MEDs are safe in this topology, look first at the topology in Figure 5-40. This is similar to the confederation in Figure 5-37, except that AS65534 has redundant connections to AS65535. Suppose MEDs are used so that AS65535 prefers the Whitetooth/Lakeridge link over the Panorama/Talisman link for traffic destined for AS1500. Correct results can be achieved between these two autonomous systems, but the problem is that the MEDs are also forwarded from AS65534 to AS65533. Depending on how the latter AS is configured to handle MEDs, and which MEDs are sent by Talisman, AS65533 could again choose a suboptimal route.

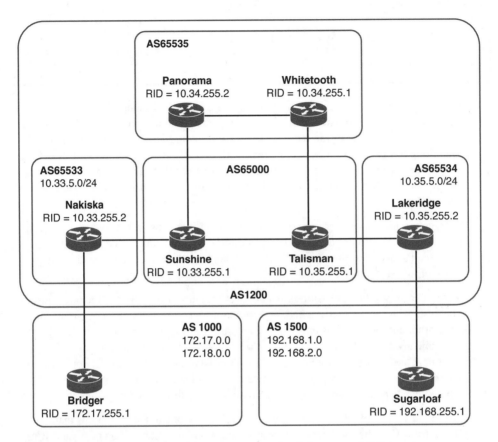

Figure 5-39   *AS65000 Is a Backbone AS in the Confederation; All Other Areas Interconnect Through It, Making the AS_PATHs Between All Nonbackbone Autonomous Systems the Same Length*

In Figure 5-39, AS65000 can safely send MEDs to AS65535. The only path AS65535 has to other nonbackbone autonomous systems is through the backbone. A route that includes 65000 in its AS_PATH is not accepted by Sunshine or Talisman, so MEDs sent from those routers to AS65535 are not seen by other member autonomous systems.

By default, Panorama and Whitetooth in Figure 5-40 prefer confederation EBGP routes over IBGP routes. So Panorama sends all traffic destined for the networks in AS1000 and AS1500 to Sunshine; Whitetooth sends all traffic for the same destinations to Talisman. MEDs can be used so that AS65535 sends all traffic destined for the networks in AS1000 across the Panorama/Sunshine link and all traffic destined for the networks in AS1500 across the Whitetooth/Talisman link. Example 5-97 shows the configurations of Sunshine and Talisman.

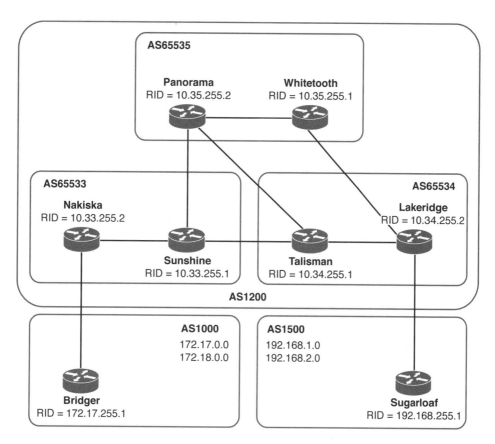

Figure 5-40 *MED Attributes Are Forwarded Throughout a Confederation; if AS65534 Uses MEDs to Influence the Preferences of AS65535, AS65533 Also Receives the MEDs*

Example 5-97 *Configuring Sunshine and Talisman to Send MEDs to AS 65535*

```
Sunshine
router bgp 65000
 no synchronization
 bgp confederation identifier 1200
 bgp confederation peers 65533 65535
 neighbor 10.33.255.2 remote-as 65533
 neighbor 10.33.255.2 ebgp-multihop 2
 neighbor 10.33.255.2 update-source Loopback0
 neighbor 10.34.255.2 remote-as 65534
 neighbor 10.34.255.2 ebgp-multihop 2
 neighbor 10.34.255.2 update-source Loopback0
 neighbor 10.34.255.2 next-hop-self
 neighbor 10.34.255.2 route-map SETMED out
```

```
 neighbor 10.35.255.1 remote-as 65000
 neighbor 10.35.255.1 update-source Loopback0
!
ip as-path access-list 1 permit _1000_
ip as-path access-list 2 permit _1500_
!
route-map SETMED permit 10
 match as-path 1
 set metric 100
!
route-map SETMED permit 20
 match as-path 2
 set metric 200
!
route-map SETMED permit 30

Talisman
router bgp 65000
 no synchronization
 bgp confederation identifier 1200
 bgp confederation peers 65534 65535
 neighbor 10.33.255.1 remote-as 65000
 neighbor 10.34.255.1 remote-as 65535
 neighbor 10.34.255.1 ebgp-multihop 2
 neighbor 10.34.255.1 update-source Loopback0
 neighbor 10.34.255.1 next-hop-self
 neighbor 10.34.255.1 route-map SETMED out
 neighbor 10.35.255.2 remote-as 65534
 neighbor 10.35.255.2 ebgp-multihop 2
 neighbor 10.35.255.2 update-source Loopback0
!
ip as-path access-list 1 permit _1500_
ip as-path access-list 2 permit _1000_
!
route-map SETMED permit 10
 match as-path 1
 set metric 100
!
route-map SETMED permit 20
 match as-path 2
 set metric 200
!
route-map SETMED permit 30
```

Sunshine sets to 100 the MED for all routes whose AS_PATH includes 1000; the MED for all routes whose AS_PATH includes 1500 is set to 200. Talisman does just the opposite. Example 5-98 shows before-and-after views of Panorama's BGP table. In the first table, the router prefers the confederation EBGP paths for all destinations. In the second table, the MEDs have been changed so that Panorama sends traffic destined for the networks of AS1500 across the IBGP link to Whitetooth, which forwards the traffic across its preferred confederation EBGP link.

Example 5-98   *Panorama's BGP Table Before and After the Routers in AS65000 Are Configured to Send MED Attributes*

```
Panorama#show ip bgp
BGP table version is 34, local router ID is 10.35.2.1
Status codes: s suppressed, d damped, h history, * valid, > best, i - internal
Origin codes: i - IGP, e - EGP, ? - incomplete

   Network          Next Hop          Metric LocPrf Weight Path
* i172.17.0.0       10.35.255.1            0    100      0 (65000 65533) 1000 i
*>                  10.33.255.1            0    100      0 (65000 65533) 1000 i
* i172.18.0.0       10.35.255.1            0    100      0 (65000 65533) 1000 i
*>                  10.33.255.1            0    100      0 (65000 65533) 1000 i
* i192.168.1.0      10.35.255.1            0    100      0 (65000 65534) 1500 i
*>                  10.33.255.1            0    100      0 (65000 65534) 1500 i
* i192.168.2.0      10.35.255.1            0    100      0 (65000 65534) 1500 i
*>                  10.33.255.1            0    100      0 (65000 65534) 1500 i
Panorama#


Panorama#show ip bgp
BGP table version is 47, local router ID is 10.35.2.1
Status codes: s suppressed, d damped, h history, * valid, > best, i - internal
Origin codes: i - IGP, e - EGP, ? - incomplete

   Network          Next Hop          Metric LocPrf Weight Path
* i172.17.0.0       10.35.255.1          200    100      0 (65000 65533) 1000 i
*>                  10.33.255.1          200    100      0 (65000 65533) 1000 i
* i172.18.0.0       10.35.255.1          200    100      0 (65000 65533) 1000 i
*>                  10.33.255.1          200    100      0 (65000 65533) 1000 i
*>i192.168.1.0      10.35.255.1          100    100      0 (65000 65534) 1500 i
*                   10.33.255.1          200    100      0 (65000 65534) 1500 i
*>i192.168.2.0      10.35.255.1          100    100      0 (65000 65534) 1500 i
*                   10.33.255.1          200    100      0 (65000 65534) 1500 i
Panorama#
```

In Figure 5-41, two subnets local to the confederation are added: 10.33.5.0/24 in AS65533, and 10.35.5.0/24 in AS65535. Sunshine and Talisman are reconfigured to apply the same routing policies to these two subnets as are applied to the external networks. That is, MEDs are set so that AS65535 sends traffic destined for 10.33.5.0/24 across the Panorama/Sunshine link and traffic destined for 10.35.5.0/24 across the Whitetooth/Talisman link.

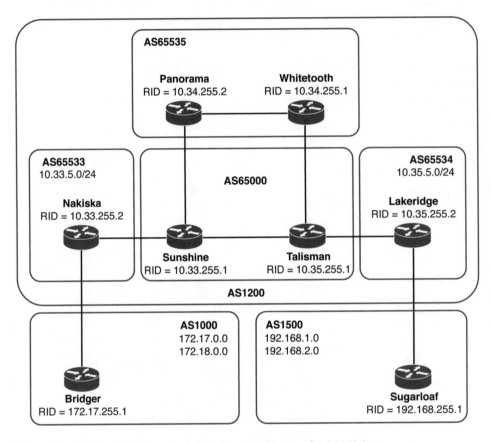

Figure 5-41 *Local Subnets Are Added to AS65533 and AS65535*

You can see in Panorama's BGP table in Example 5-99 that the policies are not having the wanted effect. The MEDs are correctly configured, but the router is still preferring its confederation EBGP path for both subnets rather than preferring the IBGP path, with its lower MED, for traffic to 10.35.5.0/24. The reason for this behavior is that by default, the MED of a confederation-interior route (signified by the absence of any exterior AS numbers in the AS_PATH) is not considered in the BGP decision process.

Example 5-99 *Panorama Is Choosing Paths to Confederation-Exterior Destinations Based on the Lowest MED, but the MED Is Not Considered When Choosing Confederation-Interior Paths*

```
Panorama#show ip bgp
BGP table version is 127, local router ID is 10.35.2.1
Status codes: s suppressed, d damped, h history, * valid, > best, i - internal
Origin codes: i - IGP, e - EGP, ? - incomplete

   Network          Next Hop          Metric LocPrf Weight Path
* i10.33.5.0/24     10.35.255.1          200    100      0 (65000 65533) i
*>                  10.33.255.1          100    100      0 (65000 65533) i
*> 10.35.5.0/24     10.33.255.1          200    100      0 (65000 65534) i
* i                 10.35.255.1          100    100      0 (65000 65534) i
*> 172.17.0.0       10.33.255.1          100    100      0 (65000 65533) 1000 i
*> 172.18.0.0       10.33.255.1          100    100      0 (65000 65533) 1000 i
*>i192.168.1.0      10.35.255.1          100    100      0 (65000 65534) 1500 i
*                   10.33.255.1          200    100      0 (65000 65534) 1500 i
*>i192.168.2.0      10.35.255.1          100    100      0 (65000 65534) 1500 i
*                   10.33.255.1          200    100      0 (65000 65534) 1500 i
Panorama#
```

The statement **bgp deterministic-med** tells the BGP process to compare MEDs when choosing paths to confederation-interior destinations. Example 5-100 shows the configuration for Panorama using **bgp deterministic-med**.

Example 5-100 *Configuring Panorama to Compare MEDs When Choosing Paths to Confederation-Interior Destinations*

```
router bgp 65535
 no synchronization
 bgp confederation identifier 1200
 bgp confederation peers 65000
 bgp deterministic-med
 neighbor 10.33.255.1 remote-as 65000
 neighbor 10.33.255.1 ebgp-multihop 2
 neighbor 10.33.255.1 update-source Loopback0
 neighbor 10.34.255.1 remote-as 65535
 neighbor 10.34.255.1 update-source Loopback0
```

Example 5-101 shows the results of configuring Panorama with the **bgp deterministic-med** statement. Panorama now uses the path with the lowest MED, whether the path is interior or exterior to the member AS. You can obtain similar results by using the **bgp always-compare-med** statement, discussed in an earlier case study. The difference is that this statement, unlike **bgp deterministic-med**, compares the MEDs of paths to the same destination regardless of whether the MEDs are advertised from the same AS.

In a backbone-based confederation such as the one in Figure 5-39, this is not an issue because no AS has a path to more than one neighboring AS.

Example 5-101   *Panorama Is Considering the MED When Choosing Both Confederation-Interior and Confederation-Exterior Routes*

```
Panorama#show ip bgp
BGP table version is 10, local router ID is 10.35.2.1
Status codes: s suppressed, d damped, h history, * valid, > best, i - internal
Origin codes: i - IGP, e - EGP, ? - incomplete

   Network          Next Hop          Metric LocPrf Weight Path
*> 10.33.5.0/24     10.33.255.1          100    100      0 (65000 65533) i
*  i                10.35.255.1          200    100      0 (65000 65533) i
*>i10.35.5.0/24     10.35.255.1          100    100      0 (65000 65534) i
*                   10.33.255.1          200    100      0 (65000 65534) i
*> 172.17.0.0       10.33.255.1          100    100      0 (65000 65533) 1000 i
*> 172.18.0.0       10.33.255.1          100    100      0 (65000 65533) 1000 i
*>i192.168.1.0      10.35.255.1          100    100      0 (65000 65534) 1500 i
*                   10.33.255.1          200    100      0 (65000 65534) 1500 i
*>i192.168.2.0      10.35.255.1          100    100      0 (65000 65534) 1500 i
*                   10.33.255.1          200    100      0 (65000 65534) 1500 i
Panorama#
```

You can use yet another statement to accomplish the same goals: **bgp bestpath med confed.** This statement has the same effect as **bgp deterministic-med,** with one difference. If a route has an external AS number in its AS_PATH, and other routes to the same destination have only confederation AS numbers in their AS_PATHs, the router picks the confederation-internal path with the lowest MED and ignores the path with the external AS number. However, such a situation should be rare. The existence of two routes to the same destination, one indicating that the destination is inside the confederation and another that the destination is outside, is probably evidence of a misconfiguration or a poor design.

Route Reflectors

Route reflectors are another way to reduce the number of IBGP peer connections in a large AS. The use of route reflectors has two advantages over confederations:

- All routers in a confederation must understand and support confederations. But only the route reflectors must understand route reflection; the client routers see their connection to the RR as just another IBGP connection.

- Route reflection is simpler to implement, both for the configuration statements needed and for topology issues.

However, you might want to take advantage of the sorts of controls available with EBGP to manage a large AS. In this case, confederations are a better choice. You can, fortunately, use both.

Route reflectors, specified in RFC 4456, work by relaxing the rule that IBGP peers cannot advertise routes learned from other IBGP peers. For example, in the network of Figure 5-42 the route reflector learns routes from each of its *clients*. Unlike other IBGP routers, the RR can advertise these routes to its other clients and to nonclient peers. In other words, the routes from one IBGP client are reflected from the RR to the other clients. To avoid possible routing loops or other routing errors, an IOS route reflector cannot change the attributes of the routes it receives from clients.

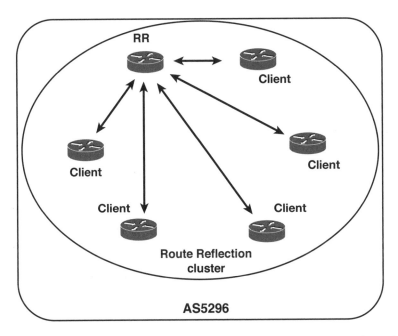

Figure 5-42 *IBGP Clients in a Route Reflection Cluster Peer Only with the Route Reflector, Reducing the Number of Necessary IBGP Connections*

A route reflector and its clients, or possibly multiple route reflectors sharing the same clients, is called a route reflection *cluster*. A client router in a route reflection cluster can peer with external neighbors, but the only internal neighbor it can peer with is a route reflector in its cluster or other clients in the cluster. However, the RR can peer with both internal and external neighbors outside of the cluster and reflect their routes to its clients, as shown by Figure 5-43.

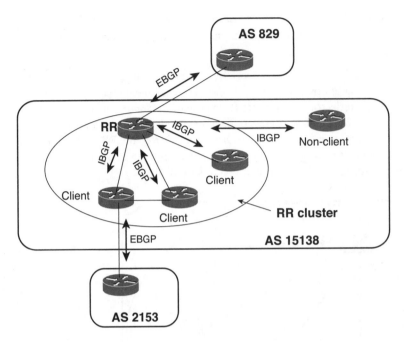

Figure 5-43   *Route Reflection Cluster Peering Relationships*

If an RR receives multiple routes to the same destination, it uses the normal BGP decision process to select the best path. RFC 4456 defines three rules that the RR uses to determine who the route is advertised to, depending upon how the route was learned:

■ If the route were learned from a non-client IBGP peer, it is reflected to clients only.

■ If the route were learned from a client, it is reflected to all nonclients and clients, except for the originating client.

■ If the route were learned from an EBGP peer, it is reflected to all clients and nonclients.

The route reflector functionality has to be supported only on the route reflector. From the clients' perspectives, they are merely peering with an internal neighbor. This is an attractive feature of route reflectors because routers with relatively basic BGP implementations can still be clients in a route reflection cluster. The client doesn't know that it's a client.

The concept of route reflectors is similar to that of route servers. The primary purpose of both devices is to reduce the number of required peering sessions by providing a single peering point for multiple neighbors. The neighbors then depend upon the one device to learn their routes. The difference between route reflectors and route servers is that route reflectors are also routers, whereas route servers are not.

Route reflectors also help scale the BGP tables on clients because only the best route from each RR is reflected to the client.

Because clients do not know they are clients, a route reflector can be a client of another route reflector. As a result, you can build "nested" route reflection clusters, as shown in Figure 5-44.

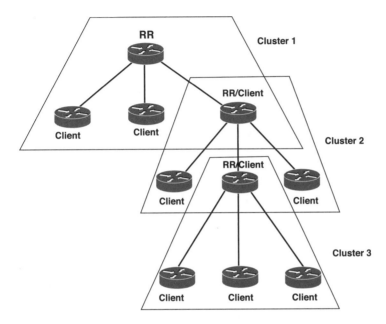

Figure 5-44 *A Route Reflector Can Be the Client of Another Route Reflector*

Although clients cannot peer with routers outside of their own cluster, they can peer with each other. As a result, a route reflection cluster can be fully meshed, as shown in Figure 5-45. When the clients are fully meshed, the route reflector is configured so that it does not reflect routes from one client to another. Instead, it reflects only routes from clients to its nonclient peers, and routes from nonclient peers to clients.

Recall from the discussion in the section "IBGP and IGP Synchronization" that BGP cannot forward a route learned from one internal peer to another internal peer because the AS_PATH attribute does not change within an AS and routing loops could result. Yet a route reflector is a BGP router in which this rule has been relaxed. To prevent routing loops, route reflectors use two BGP path attributes: ORIGINATOR_ID and CLUSTER_LIST.

ORIGINATOR_ID is an optional, nontransitive attribute (Type code 9) that is created by the route reflector. The ORIGINATOR_ID is the router ID of the originator of a route within the local autonomous system. A route reflector does not advertise a route back to the originator of the route; nonetheless, if the originator receives an update with its own

RID, the update is ignored. As a result, ORIGINATOR_ID prevents loops within a single RR cluster.

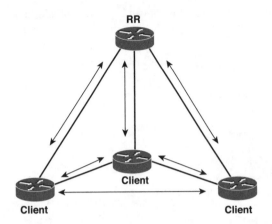

Figure 5-45   *A Route Reflection Cluster Can Be Fully Meshed*

Each cluster within an AS must be identified with a unique 4-octet *cluster ID*. If there is a single route reflector within the cluster, the cluster ID is the router ID of the route reflector. No configuration is necessary in this case; when a router is configured as an RR, it automatically uses its RID as the cluster ID unless configured to use a different number. If multiple route reflectors are in the cluster, each RR must be manually configured with a cluster ID.

CLUSTER_LIST is an optional, nontransitive attribute (Type code 10) that tracks cluster IDs the same way that the AS_PATH attribute tracks AS numbers. When a RR reflects a route from a client to a nonclient, it appends its cluster ID to the CLUSTER_LIST. If the CLUSTER_LIST is empty, the RR creates one. When an RR receives an update, it checks the CLUSTER_LIST. If it sees its own cluster ID in the list, it knows that a routing loop has occurred and ignores the update. It should be obvious to you that this is the same loop prevention function that AS_PATH performs. CLUSTER_LIST prevents loops between multiple RR clusters.

A single RR, like a single route server, introduces a single point of failure into a system. If the RR fails, the clients lose their only source of NLRI. Therefore, for redundancy a client can be connected to more than one RR. One way of doing this is to configure redundant RRs within a cluster, as shown in Figure 5-46. The clients have physical connections to each of the route reflectors, and peer to each. If one of the RRs fails, the clients still have a connection to the other RR and do not lose reachability information.

Note   Because IBGP sessions can traverse multiple router hops, it is possible for a client to have a physical link to only one RR and still peer to multiple RRs by having the redundant IBGP session pass through the first RR to the redundant RR. But this would defeat the purpose of having redundancy. The client would still be vulnerable to the failure of the single RR to which it is physically connected.

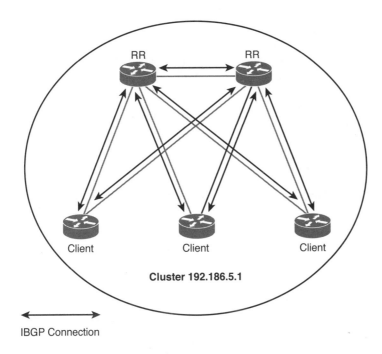

Figure 5-46   *A Cluster Can Have Multiple Route Reflectors for Redundancy*

There are situations, however, in which instability within a cluster can cause suboptimal routing or even routing loops when using redundant RRs within the cluster. An alternative approach is to let each RR define its own cluster, and peer the same clients to each RR, as shown in Figure 5-47. The key to this approach is, again, that clients don't know that they're clients, so they just see themselves as having two IBGP peers.

A single router can also serve as an RR for multiple clusters, as shown in Figure 5-48, by configuring per-neighbor cluster IDs.

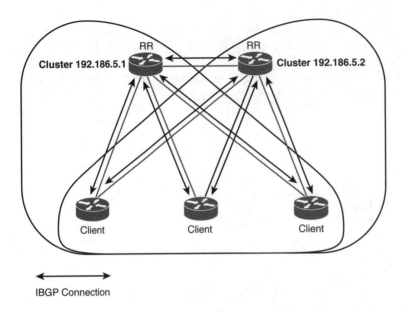

Figure 5-47   *Route Reflector Redundancy Can Be Achieved by Peering Clients to Multiple RRs*

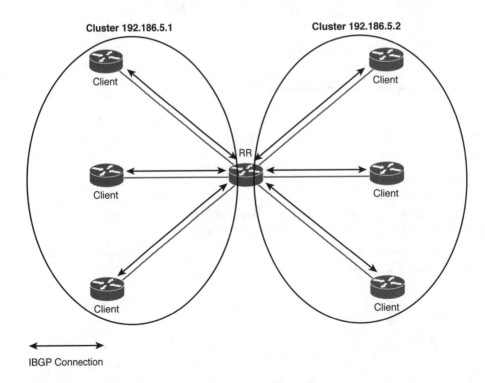

Figure 5-48   *A Single Router Can Serve as the RR for Multiple Clusters*

An autonomous system can have multiple clusters. Figure 5-49 shows an AS with two clusters. Each cluster has redundant route reflectors, and the clusters are interconnected redundantly.

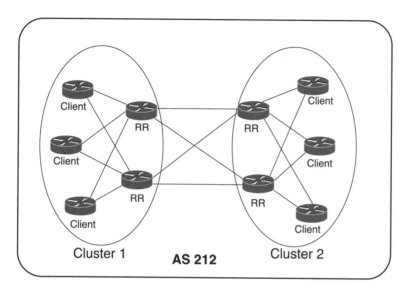

Figure 5-49 *Multiple Route Reflection Clusters Can Be Created Within a Single Autonomous System*

What all these examples show is that route reflectors provide you with great flexibility when designing scalable BGP topologies, a contributing factor to their popularity. Another contributing factor to the popularity of RRs is the simplicity of their configuration. Let's look at some examples.

Figure 5-50 shows a modification of AS 65533 in Figure 5-39. Fortress is a route reflector, and Nakiska and Marmot are the clients.

Example 5-102 shows the configuration of the three routers.

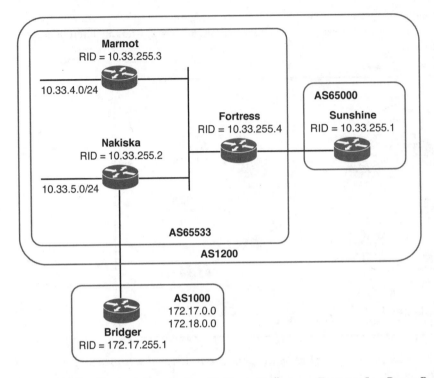

Figure 5-50   *Network Topology with Route Reflectors: Fortress Is a Route Reflector; Nakiska and Marmot Are Clients*

Example 5-102   *Configuring Fortress as the Route Reflector and Nakiska and Marmot as Clients*

```
Fortress
router bgp 65533
 no synchronization
 bgp confederation identifier 1200
 bgp confederation peers 65000
 neighbor 10.33.255.1 remote-as 65000
 neighbor 10.33.255.1 ebgp-multihop 2
 neighbor 10.33.255.1 update-source Loopback0
 neighbor 10.33.255.2 remote-as 65533
 neighbor 10.33.255.2 update-source Loopback0
 neighbor 10.33.255.2 route-reflector-client
 neighbor 10.33.255.2 next-hop-self
 neighbor 10.33.255.3 remote-as 65533
 neighbor 10.33.255.3 update-source Loopback0
 neighbor 10.33.255.3 route-reflector-client
 neighbor 10.33.255.3 next-hop-self
```

```
Nakiska
router bgp 65533
 no synchronization
 bgp confederation identifier 1200
 network 10.33.5.0 mask 255.255.255.0
 neighbor 10.33.255.4 remote-as 65533
 neighbor 10.33.255.4 update-source Loopback0
 neighbor 10.33.255.4 next-hop-self
 neighbor 172.17.255.1 remote-as 1000
 neighbor 172.17.255.1 ebgp-multihop 2
 neighbor 172.17.255.1 update-source Loopback0
```

```
Marmot
router bgp 65533
 no synchronization
 bgp confederation identifier 1200
 network 10.33.4.0 mask 255.255.255.0
 neighbor 10.33.255.4 remote-as 65533
 neighbor 10.33.255.4 update-source Loopback0
 neighbor 10.33.255.4 next-hop-self
```

Nakiska and Marmot have normal IBGP configurations, except that they peer only with the RR, not with each other. Nakiska also peers with Bridger, a router outside of the route reflection cluster. The only command added to Fortress, to make it a route reflector, is a **neighbor route-reflector-client** statement for each of its clients. This statement implements the relaxed IBGP rules necessary for route reflection; namely, that IBGP routes learned from one client are advertised to the other clients and to IBGP peers outside the cluster, and that IBGP routes learned from IBGP peers outside the cluster are advertised to clients.

Example 5-103 shows the entry for 10.33.5.0/24 in Marmot's BGP table. The ORIGINATOR_ID and CLUSTER_LIST attributes, added by the RR, are indicated on the last line. The ORIGINATOR_ID is added by the RR and indicates the client that advertises the route; the originator of the route to 10.33.5.0/24 is Nakiska (10.33.255.2). This attribute ensures that routes do not loop within the cluster. If Fortress receives this NLRI in an update, it recognizes Nakiska's router ID in the attribute and ignores the route. The attribute is optional nontransitive, so a router does not have to support or understand the attribute to participate in a route reflection cluster. Although some loop protection will be lost.

Example 5-103   *Marmot's BGP Entry for Subnet 10.33.5.0/24 Indicates the ORIGINATOR_ID and CLUSTER_LIST Attributes Added to the Route by the Route Reflector*

```
Marmot#show ip bgp 10.33.5.0
BGP routing table entry for 10.33.5.0 255.255.255.0, version 16
Paths: (1 available, best #1)
  Local
    10.33.255.2 (metric 11) from 10.33.255.4 (10.33.255.2)
      Origin IGP, metric 0, localpref 100, valid, internal, best
      Originator : 10.33.255.2, Cluster list: 10.33.255.4
Marmot#
```

Like the ORIGINATOR_ID, the CLUSTER_LIST is a loop-prevention measure. As already discussed, a 4-octet cluster ID identifies the cluster and the RR adds this number to the CLUSTER_LIST. If the RR receives an update with its own cluster ID in the CLUSTER_LIST, it knows a loop has occurred and it ignores the route. This function proves important when the path passes through multiple route reflection clusters. The CLUSTER_LIST of the route in Figure 5-50 is 10.33.255.4, Fortress' router ID. By default, the RR enters its own BGP RID in the CLUSTER_LIST. To specify a cluster ID other than the RR's RID, you use the **bgp cluster-id** command. You can specify a cluster ID as a number between 1 and 4294967295 or in dotted decimal format.

If you configure more than one route reflector in a cluster, you must use the **bgp cluster-id** command to ensure that all RRs are identifying themselves as members of the same cluster. You can specify the cluster ID either in decimal or dotted decimal format. In Figure 5-51, router Norquay is added and is configured as a second RR to add redundancy to the cluster.

Example 5-104 shows the configurations of Fortress and Norquay.

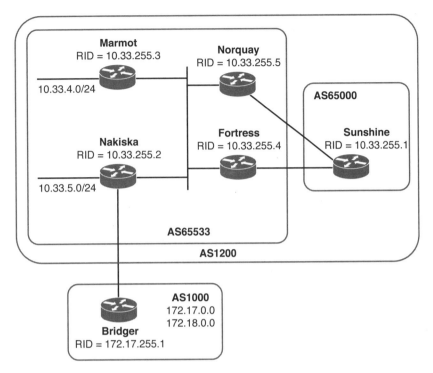

Figure 5-51 *Norquay Is Added to the Route Reflection Cluster for Redundancy*

Example 5-104 *Configuring Fortress and Norquay as Route Reflectors*

```
Fortress
router bgp 65533
 no synchronization
 bgp cluster-id 33
 bgp confederation identifier 1200
 bgp confederation peers 65000
 neighbor 10.33.255.1 remote-as 65000
 neighbor 10.33.255.1 ebgp-multihop 2
 neighbor 10.33.255.1 update-source Loopback0
 neighbor 10.33.255.2 remote-as 65533
 neighbor 10.33.255.2 update-source Loopback0
 neighbor 10.33.255.2 route-reflector-client
 neighbor 10.33.255.2 next-hop-self
 neighbor 10.33.255.3 remote-as 65533
 neighbor 10.33.255.3 update-source Loopback0
 neighbor 10.33.255.3 route-reflector-client
 neighbor 10.33.255.3 next-hop-self
 neighbor 10.33.255.5 remote-as 65533
```

```
 neighbor 10.33.255.5 update-source Loopback0
 neighbor 10.33.255.5 next-hop-self
Norquay
router bgp 65533
 no synchronization
 bgp cluster-id 33
 bgp confederation identifier 1200
 bgp confederation peers 65000
 neighbor 10.33.255.1 remote-as 65000
 neighbor 10.33.255.1 ebgp-multihop 2
 neighbor 10.33.255.1 update-source Loopback0
 neighbor 10.33.255.2 remote-as 65533
 neighbor 10.33.255.2 route-reflector-client
 neighbor 10.33.255.2 update-source Loopback0
 neighbor 10.33.255.2 next-hop-self
 neighbor 10.33.255.3 remote-as 65533
 neighbor 10.33.255.3 route-reflector-client
 neighbor 10.33.255.3 update-source Loopback0
 neighbor 10.33.255.3 next-hop-self
 neighbor 10.33.255.4 remote-as 65533
 neighbor 10.33.255.4 update-source Loopback0
 neighbor 10.33.255.4 next-hop-self
```

Both RRs are configured with a cluster ID of 33. They peer with each other via standard IBGP and then specify their route reflection clients using the **neighbor route-reflector-client** statement. As a result, the two RRs reflect routes to the clients, but IBGP rules prevent them from advertising the IBGP routes to each other.

The only change to the client configurations is the addition of an IBGP configuration for Norquay, as shown in Example 5-105.

Example 5-105   *Clients Nakiska and Marmot Peer to Both Fortress and Norquay*

```
Nakiska
router bgp 65533
 no synchronization
 bgp confederation identifier 1200
 network 10.33.5.0 mask 255.255.255.0
 neighbor 10.33.255.4 remote-as 65533
 neighbor 10.33.255.4 update-source Loopback0
 neighbor 10.33.255.4 next-hop-self
 neighbor 10.33.255.5 remote-as 65533
 neighbor 10.33.255.5 update-source Loopback0
 neighbor 10.33.255.5 next-hop-self
 neighbor 172.17.255.1 remote-as 1000
```

```
neighbor 172.17.255.1 ebgp-multihop 2
neighbor 172.17.255.1 update-source Loopback0
```

```
Marmot
router bgp 65533
 no synchronization
 bgp confederation identifier 1200
 network 10.33.4.0 mask 255.255.255.0
 neighbor 10.33.255.4 remote-as 65533
 neighbor 10.33.255.4 update-source Loopback0
 neighbor 10.33.255.4 next-hop-self
 neighbor 10.33.255.5 remote-as 65533
 neighbor 10.33.255.5 update-source Loopback0
 neighbor 10.33.255.5 next-hop-self
```

Example 5-106 shows the resulting entry in Marmot's BGP table for subnet 10.33.5.0/24. Where there was a single path to the destination in Example 5-103, there are now two. The paths are entirely equal; because the router is not configured to use both paths with the **maximum-paths** statement, the router chooses the route from 10.33.255.4, the lowest next-hop address.

Example 5-106   *Marmot Is Receiving Routes from RRs Fortress and Norquay*

```
Marmot#show ip bgp 10.33.5.0
BGP routing table entry for 10.33.5.0 255.255.255.0, version 2
Paths: (2 available, best #1)
  Local
    10.33.255.2 (metric 11) from 10.33.255.4 (10.33.255.2)
      Origin IGP, metric 0, localpref 100, valid, internal, best
      Originator : 10.33.255.2, Cluster list: 0.0.0.33
  Local
    10.33.255.2 (metric 11) from 10.33.255.5 (10.33.255.2)
      Origin IGP, metric 0, localpref 100, valid, internal
      Originator : 10.33.255.2, Cluster list: 0.0.0.33
Marmot#
```

The route reflectors referred to in Example 5-105 belong to the same cluster, as indicated by the shared cluster ID. However, the route reflectors could also belong to separate clusters, and the configurations of the clients referred to in Example 5-104, would not change. This approach, peering clients with redundant route reflectors in multiple clusters rather than in the same cluster, is used in many current route reflection designs.

Although route reflection clients can have EBGP connections, as Nakiska does in Figure 5-51, clients normally should not have any IBGP neighbors except the route reflector. This means that the connections between clusters must be made between the route reflectors, not between clients, because clients do not examine the CLUSTER_ LIST attribute of received routes. An intercluster loop would not be detected by a client. The RRs are peered via standard IBGP and obey all the IBGP rules. The only additional information passed between the RRs is the CLUSTER_LIST attribute, to prevent loops. The route reflectors within an AS must be fully meshed with all other route reflectors in the AS and with all other AS-interior routers that do not belong to a cluster, as shown in Figure 5-52.

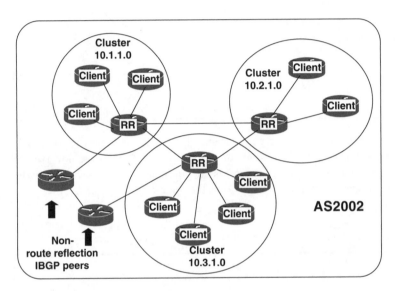

Figure 5-52 *Links Interconnecting Clusters Must Be Between Route Reflectors, Not Between Clients*

The rule that clients must peer only to their RRs has two exceptions. First, a client can be a route reflector for another cluster. This allows "nesting" of route reflection clusters, or the creation of a hierarchy of clusters, as shown previously in Figure 5-44.

The second exception is when there is a full IBGP mesh among the clients. Fully mesh-ing the clients, as shown previously in Figure 5-45, provides some increased robustness. When such a design is used, you should configure the route reflector with the command **no bgp client-to-client reflection**. Routes are then communicated between the fully meshed clients under normal IBGP rules, and the RR does not reflect routes from one client to another. It does, however, continue to reflect routes from clients to peers out-side of the cluster, and from peers outside of the cluster to clients.

Looking Ahead

As discussed in the first chapter, BGP is a simple protocol. It's the associated policy and scaling capabilities that make BGP configurations and networks complex. You now have a good grasp of the tools available to you to create policies and manage highly complex configurations and topologies, including scaling the BGP process. But you aren't done. In Chapter 6, you see how to configure BGP to carry multiple address families. That chapter focuses primarily on IPv6, but in later chapters you visit Multiprotocol BGP again in the context of multicast networks.

Review Questions

1. What is, in the context of networking, meant by scalability?

2. In what three general ways can BGP be scaled?

3. What is a peer group?

4. If a peer group is configured to use an update source of Loopback 0 and a neighbor belonging to that peer group is configured to use an update source of Loopback 3, what update source will the neighbor use?

5. What is a dynamic update peer group, and how does it change the traditional use of peer groups?

6. What are peer templates, and what are the two types of peer templates?

7. Can peer templates and peer groups be applied to the same neighbor.

8. What is meant by inheritance in the context of peer templates?

9. What is a BGP community?

10. How can a community be expressed (formatted) within an IOS configuration?

11. What is a well-known community?

12. What is the default action when a community is added to an identified route? Can this default be changed?

13. What is the difference between a standard community list and an expanded community list?

14. What is the difference between a standard community and an extended community attribute?

15. In route dampening, what is the half-life?

16. What is the IOS default penalty applied or a flap (a route going down or a route coming up):

17. Why is route flap dampening sometimes considered harmful in large, heavily meshed networks?

18. What is Outbound Route Filtering?

19. How does Next-Hop Tracking (NHT) help improve BGP convergence time?

20. How does Fast External Fallover improve BGP convergence time?

21. What is Bidirectional Forwarding Detection (BFD), and how does it help improve BGP performance?

22. What are the two BFD operational modes?

23. What is the BFD Echo function?

24. How does Prefix Independent Convergence (PIC) improve BGP performance?

25. What is Graceful Restart?

26. What major dependency must be met for a router to run Graceful Restart?

27. How can the Maximum Prefixes feature help stabilize and secure a BGP network?

28. What AS numbers are reserved for private use?

29. What two formats can 4-byte AS numbers be represented in?

30. What is a BGP confederation?

31. In what ways are Confederation EBGP rules different from regular EBGP rules?

32. What is the purpose of **bgp deterministic med**?

33. What is a route reflector? What is a route reflection client? What is a route reflection cluster?

34. What is the Cluster ID?

35. What is the purpose of the ORIGINATOR_ID and the CLUSTER_LIST path attributes?

36. Can route reflectors be used within confederations?

Configuration Exercises

Table 5-2 lists the autonomous systems, routers, interfaces, and addresses used in exercises 1 through 10. All interfaces of the routers are shown. For each exercise, if the table indicates that the router has a loopback interface, that interface should be the source of all EBGP and IBGP connections. Neighbor descriptions are always configured to be the router names. Password Chapter5_Exercises is used between for all BGP sessions. OSPF is the IGP for all autonomous systems. Initial configuration for basic reachability for all routers is listed in Example 5-106, at the end of the chapter.

Table 5-2 *AS, Router, Interface, and Address Information for Configuration Exercise 1-10*

AS	Confederation Member AS	Router	Interface	IPv4 Address/Mask
100	65000	RR1	Ethernet 0/0	10.0.0.1/30
			Ethernet 0/1	10.0.0.5/30
			Ethernet 0/2	10.0.0.9/30
			Ethernet 1/0	10.0.0.25/30
			Loopback 0	192.168.255.100/32
		RR2	Ethernet 0/0	10.0.0.2/30
			Ethernet 0/1	10.0.0.13/30
			Ethernet 0/2	10.0.0.17/30
			Loopback 0	192.168.255.200/32
			Loopback 1	172.10.10.0/24
			Loopback 2	172.10.20.0/24
			Loopback 3	172.10.30.0/24
			Loopback 4	172.10.40.0/24
		R1	Ethernet 0/0	10.0.0.6/30
			Ethernet 0/1	10.0.0.14/30
			Ethernet 1/0	10.0.0.21/30
			Loopback 0	192.168.255.1/32
		R2	Ethernet 0/0	10.0.0.10/30
			Ethernet 0/1	10.0.0.18/30
			Ethernet 0/2	10.0.0.29/30
			Ethernet 0/3	10.0.0.33/30
			Loopback 0	192.168.255.2/32
	65001	R3	Ethernet 0/2	10.0.0.30/30
			Ethernet 1/0	10.0.0.37/30
			Loopback 0	192.168.255.3/32
	65002	R4	Ethernet 0/3	10.0.0.34/30
			Ethernet 1/0	10.0.0.41/30
			Loopback 0	192.168.255.4/32

AS	Confederation Member AS	Router	Interface	IPv4 Address/Mask
200		R5	Ethernet 1/0	10.0.0.22/30
			Loopback 0	192.168.255.5/32
			Loopback 1	172.20.10.0/24
			Loopback 2	172.20.20.0/24
			Loopback 3	172.20.30.0/24
			Loopback 4	172.20.40.0/24
300		R6	Ethernet 1/0	10.0.0.26/30
			Loopback 0	192.168.255.6/32
			Loopback 1	172.30.10.0/24
			Loopback 2	172.30.20.0/24
			Loopback 3	172.30.30.0/24
			Loopback 4	172.30.40.0/24
400		R7	Ethernet 0/1	10.0.0.45/30
			Ethernet 1/0	10.0.0.38/30
			Loopback 0	192.168.255.7/32
		R8	Ethernet 0/0	10.0.0.49/30
			Ethernet 1/0	10.0.0.42/30
			Loopback 0	192.168.255.8/32
		R9	Ethernet 0/0	10.0.0.50/30
			Ethernet 0/1	10.0.0.46/30
			Loopback 0	192.168.255.9/32
			Loopback 1	172.40.10.0/24
			Loopback 2	172.40.20.0/24
			Loopback 3	172.40.30.0/24
			Loopback 4	172.40.40.0/24

1. AS 65000 has two route reflectors, RR1 and RR2. Routers R1 and R2 form iBGP sessions with the RRs only, and all four routers form a single RR cluster. Using Session and Policy templates on R1, R2, RR1, RR2, and Cluster-ID 1234, configure all routers in AS 65000 accordingly.

2. Autonomous systems 65000, 65001, and 65002 are confederation member autonomous systems inside of AS100. Configure all routers inside AS100 to

implement this design. Use peer session templates on R2 for the configuration related to routers R3 and R4.

3. Using session and policy templates where applicable, configure a full IBGP mesh in AS400.

4. Configure the following EBGP sessions between

   ■ R1 in AS100 and R5 in AS200

   ■ RR1 in AS100 and R6 in AS300

   ■ R3 in AS100 and R7 in AS400

   ■ R4 in AS100 and R8 in AS400

5. Inject subnets into BGP as follows:

   ■ Subnets 172.10.10.0/24, 172.10.20.0/24, 172.10.30.0/24, and 172.10.40.0/24 on RR2 in AS100

   ■ Subnets 172.20.10.0/24, 172.20.20.0/24, 172.20.30.0/24, and 172.20.40.0/24 on router R5 in AS200

   ■ Subnets 172.30.10.0/24, 172.30.20.0/24, 172.30.30.0/24, and 172.30.40.0/24 on router R6 in AS300

   ■ Subnets 172.40.10.0/24, 172.40.20.0/24, 172.40.30.0/24, and 172.40.40.0/24 on router R9 in AS

   Confirm that subnets S1 through S15 are reachable from all routers in all autonomous systems.

6. Using different MED values on routers R3 and R4, make sure that the R4-R8 link is used for all incoming traffic to AS100 from AS400. Then using different Local Preference values on routers R3 and R4, make sure that all outgoing traffic from AS100 to AS400 uses the R4-R8 link.

7. AS200 and AS300 are two customers to the transit AS100. These autonomous systems are allowed to reach AS400 as well as the internal subnets of AS100. However, the two customers are not allowed to speak to each other. AS400, however, is allowed to reach both customer autonomous systems, AS200 and AS300, but is not allowed to access the internal services provided by the ISP in AS100 or other transit autonomous systems. Using community tagging and filtering on the AS100 routers, implement this policy. The configuration should be scalable enough to allow the policies to take effect for new customers and transit autonomous systems with minimal configuration.

8. Configure Route Flap Dampening on RR1 for the subnet 172.30.40.0/24 only, using the following parameters:

   ■ Half-life = 20 minutes

   ■ Reuse limit = 1500

- Suppress limit = 10000

- Maximum suppress limit = 60 minutes

9. Configure BFD between R1 and R5 using the following values:

   - BFD interval for control packets: 2000 msec

   - BFD Echo function interval: 100 msec

   - BFD Echo receive rate: 100 msec

   - Number of BFD Echo packets missed from the neighbor before declaring it unreachable: 5 packets

   Configure BGP on both routers to use BFD for rapid link failure detection on those links.

10. Configure the trigger delay for Next-Hop Tracking on all routers internal to AS100 to zero for immediate route failure detection and reporting by the IGP.

Troubleshooting Exercises

1. AS100 needs to add community 123:123 to route 172.20.20.0/24 to implement a new policy for this route. To achieve this, the BGP configuration on R1 was amended, as shown in the following example. After this change, the customers in AS300 started having reachability to this route when they should not as per the policy described in question 7 in the Configuration Exercises section. Why has this happened? Correct the configuration to revert back to the reachability rules listed in Question 7.

```
R1
!
ip prefix-list ROUTE_172_20_20_0 seq 5 permit 172.20.20.0/24
!
route-map SET_COMM_CUST permit 10
 set community 200:2000
 continue 20
!
route-map SET_COMM_CUST permit 20
 match ip address prefix-list ROUTE_172_20_20_0
 set community 123:123
!
```

Resulting reachability on R6:

```
R6#sh ip bgp
BGP table version is 106, local router ID is 192.168.255.6
Status codes: s suppressed, d damped, h history, * valid, > best, i - internal,
              r RIB-failure, S Stale, m multipath, b backup-path, f RT-Filter,
              x best-external, a additional-path, c RIB-compressed,
Origin codes: i - IGP, e - EGP, ? - incomplete
RPKI validation codes: V valid, I invalid, N Not found

     Network          Next Hop          Metric LocPrf Weight Path
 *>  172.10.10.0/24   10.0.0.25                          0 100 i
 *>  172.10.20.0/24   10.0.0.25                          0 100 i
 *>  172.10.30.0/24   10.0.0.25                          0 100 i
 *>  172.10.40.0/24   10.0.0.25                          0 100 i
 *>  172.20.20.0/24   10.0.0.25                          0 100 200 i
 *>  172.30.10.0/24   0.0.0.0                0       32768 i
 *>  172.30.20.0/24   0.0.0.0                0       32768 i
 *>  172.30.30.0/24   0.0.0.0                0       32768 i
 *>  172.30.40.0/24   0.0.0.0                0       32768 i
 *>  172.40.10.0/24   10.0.0.25                          0 100 400 i
 *>  172.40.20.0/24   10.0.0.25                          0 100 400 i
 *>  172.40.30.0/24   10.0.0.25                          0 100 400 i
 *>  172.40.40.0/24   10.0.0.25                          0 100 400 i
R6#
```

2. R4 is continuously resetting the BGP session with R7 and then reestablishing the session again after exactly 3 minutes. R4's BGP configuration is listed in the following example. What is the root cause of this flapping BGP session?

```
R4
router bgp 65001
 bgp log-neighbor-changes
 bgp confederation identifier 100
 bgp confederation peers 65000 65002
 neighbor 10.0.0.42 remote-as 400
 neighbor 10.0.0.42 password Chapter5_Exercises
 neighbor 10.0.0.42 route-map SET_LOCAL_PREF in
 neighbor 10.0.0.42 route-map SET_MED out
 neighbor 10.0.0.42 maximum-prefix 3 restart 3
 neighbor 192.168.255.2 remote-as 65000
 neighbor 192.168.255.2 password Chapter5_Exercises
 neighbor 192.168.255.2 ebgp-multihop 2
 neighbor 192.168.255.2 update-source Loopback0
 neighbor 192.168.255.2 next-hop-self
 neighbor 192.168.255.2 send-community both
```

Chapter 6

Multiprotocol BGP

The previous chapters demonstrate how BGP, a simple protocol in its basic functionality, uses route attributes and various configuration options to support complex routing policies. You have also seen how the scaling features of BGP allow it to be the core routing protocol for many large networks including the Internet. All the examples you have seen so far are for routing IPv4. This chapter shows how BGP is extended to route for other protocols—specifically, how it is extended to carry the NLRI for *address families* other than IPv4.

The BGP extensions enabling it to carry additional address families make it *Multiprotocol BGP*, abbreviated as MBGP, M-BGP, or MP-BGP. (This book uses the acronym *MBGP* because it has the least characters and the author is lazy.) The IOS implementation of BGP is always multiprotocol-capable; although we tend to call it MBGP only when we actually configure it for additional address family support.

A large modern network is likely to need more than just unicast IPv4 to enable a wide range of services. It might support multicast IPv4, unicast and multicast IPv6, and several of the many virtual private network (VPN) options available over a Multiprotocol Label Switching (MPLS) infrastructure. The advantage of MBGP is that you can route for all these different protocols using a single integrated core routing protocol. You can even use MBGP to piggyback MPLS label mapping information over the same messages that carry route information (RFC 3107). Therefore, you can think of MBGP as yet another way to use BGP to scale your network.

This chapter introduces the concepts of MBGP and then demonstrates its use for interdomain IPv6 unicast routing. Chapter 9, "Scaling IP Multicast Routing," revisits MBGP for interdomain multicast routing.

Multiprotocol Extensions to BGP

RFC 4760 extends BGP for multiprotocol support by defining two new attributes:

- Multiprotocol Reachable NLRI or MP_REACH_NLRI (type 14)

- Multiprotocol Unreachable NLRIMP_UNREACH_NLRI (type 15)
  or MP_UNREACH_NLRI (type 15)

Both attributes are optional and nontransitive. Recall from Chapter 2, "Introduction to BGP," that this means BGP speakers are not required to support the attributes, and BGP speakers that do not support the attributes do not pass them to their peers.

The MP_REACH_NLRI, shown in Figure 6-1, is carried in BGP Update messages to advertise reachable routes. The attribute identifies the protocol advertised and the address type within the protocol, the next-hop of the route, and the NLRI itself.

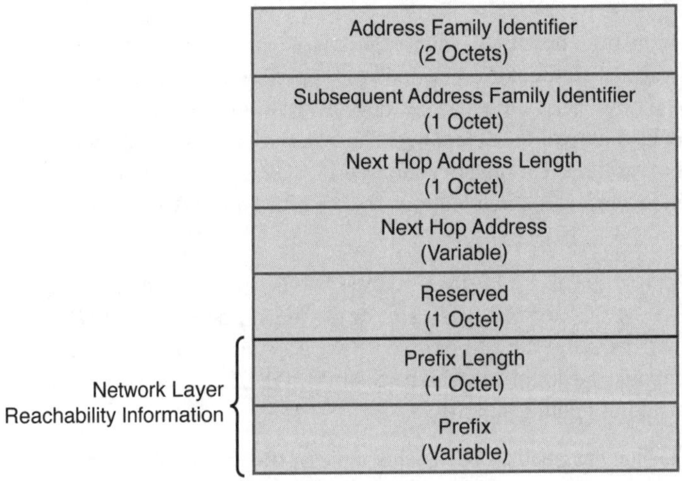

Figure 6-1   *Format of the MP_REACH_NLRI*

- **Address Family Identifier (AFI):** This field specifies the protocol to which the NLRI prefix belongs. There is a long list of AFI numbers including things such as IPX, AppleTalk, and Decnet IV but the only AFIs that matter to our discussions are IPv4 and IPv6. (This book is, after all, *Routing TCP/IP*.) IPv4 is AFI 1, and IPv6 is AFI 2.

- **Subsequent Address Family Identifier (SAFI):** This field specifies a functional address type under the major protocol. The SAFIs of interest to us in this book are unicast NLRI (SAFI 1) and multicast NLRI (SAFI 2).[1] However, many other IPv4 and

---

[1] The first edition of this book also listed a SAFI 3, which specified both unicast and multicast Reverse Path Forwarding. That SAFI has since been deprecated.

IPv6 SAFIs are beyond the scope of this book, such as MPLS-labeled NLRI, MPLS-based VPNs, and various tunnels.

■ **Next Hop Address Length:** Specifies the length, in octets, of the protocol next-hop address in the next field. Because this field is itself 1 octet, the maximum length next-hop address that can be specified is 256 bytes: This is far more than sufficient for any address. IPv4 addresses are 4 bytes and IPv6 addresses are 16 bytes. As described in the next section, there are circumstances in which the next-hop field contains both a global and a link-local IPv6 address. In this case, the Address Length value would indicate 32 bytes.

■ **Next Hop Address:** This is the network layer address, compliant with the address format of the specified AFI and SAFI, of the next hop of the advertised NLRI.

■ **Network Layer Reachability Information (NLRI):** This is the prefix and prefix length (in bits), compliant to the address format of the specified AFI/SAFI. In IP, the prefix/length taken together is interpreted as the CIDR notation for an IPv4 or IPv6 prefix. This includes a length of 0, specifying "all addresses" (a default route).

Figure 6-2 shows the format of the MP_UNREACH_NLRI. Note that the information is much the same as the information in the MP_REACH_NLRI, except there is no need to specify a next-hop address when a route is withdrawn.

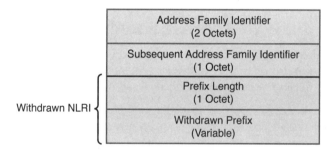

Figure 6-2 *Format of the MP_UNREACH_NLRI*

An important supporting function for MBGP is the BGP Capabilities option, specified in RFC 5492.[2] This option provides for the capability of a BGP speaker to include, in its Open messages, a description of the optional capabilities it supports. When a neighbor receives, during adjacency establishment, an Open message with the Capabilities parameter, it can either accept the described capabilities or send a Notification message with an Error Subcode 7 indicating that it does not support one or more of the capabilities. This Unsupported Capability notification is used only when the neighbor understands the capability but does not support it, and the session cannot be opened without it; a router never sends this notification if it does not understand the capability.

---

[2] J. Scudder and R. Chandra, "Capabilities Advertisement with BGP-4," RFC 5492, February 2009.

Figure 6-3 shows the format of the Capabilities parameter, and the settings used when the parameter is used to indicate MBGP support. The MBGP capabilities code is 1, and the Capability Length field is set to 4, indicating the length in octets of the Capability Value. The Capability Value itself, when indicating MBGP support, specifies the AFI and SAFI of the address family to be advertised.

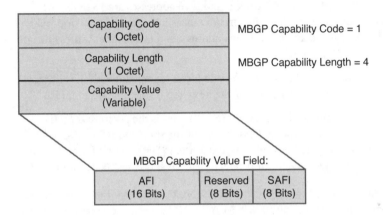

Figure 6-3   *BGP Capabilities Option and MBGP Specification*

MBGP Support for the IPv6 Address Family

The support of the IPv6 address family in MBGP is specified in RFC 2545.[3] This simple 5-page document—and most of that is just IETF boilerplate—is mostly concerned with resolving a few conflicts between some core concepts of IPv6 and BGP.

For example, IPv6 uses the concept of scoped unicast addresses more precisely than does IPv4. Both protocols define a globally unique unicast address scope, in which an address used on an interface cannot be used by any other interface anywhere in the world—and accordingly, require a hierarchy of address management authorities to ensure that uniqueness.

IPv4 also defines private-use addresses, commonly called RFC 1918 addresses (used in examples throughout this book). These addresses roughly correspond to a site-local scope; although, the scope itself is not defined in IPv4. IPv6 did define a site-local address scope, and the intention was to use these addresses in the same way IPv4 private addresses are used: The address must be unique within a single networking site but can be reused outside that scope. The problem with a site-local scope is that the definition of a "site" is fuzzy at best: What defines the boundaries of a site? This imprecise scoping led the IETF to deprecate the IPv6 site-local address scope and replace it with the

---

[3] P. Marques and F. Dupont, "Use of BGP-4 Multiprotocol Extensions for IPv6 Inter-Domain Routing," RFC 2545, March 1999.

Unique Local Address (ULA) format. Although the ULA format is intended to be used similarly to IPv4 RFC 1918 addresses—within a single site—it ducks the difficulties of defining "site" and instead provides a reasonable expectation that its addresses will be global in scope. The global uniqueness can be guaranteed by registering the ULA with an address registry or reasonably expected by using a pseudo-randomly generated prefix.

IPv6 also defines a link-local address scope. There is a link-local scope for IPv4 also (169.254.1.0–169.254.254.255), but it is not as integral to the functioning of the protocol as the IPv6 scope. As the name implies, link-local addresses are required to be unique only within the scope of a single link that might be a point-to-point link, a multiaccess broadcast link such as Ethernet, or a logical link such as a VLAN. The boundary of the scope, unless the link is unconnected to any larger network, is a set of one or more connected router interfaces that are not permitted to forward packets with link-local addresses. Link-local IPv6 unicast addresses always have a prefix of FE80::/64.

IPv6 assumes that interactions between devices connected to the same link use link-local addresses, and functions such as ICMPv6 Redirects and Neighbor Discovery Protocol require the use of link-local addresses. This conflicts with BGP, which needs global next-hop addresses when adjacencies traverse multiple links, such as multihop EBGP or many IBGP adjacencies. If a BGP speaker receives a route with a next-hop address that it cannot reach, it rejects the route.

MBGP for IPv6 adapts to these conflicts with two rules:

■ If the peer to which an IPv6 route is advertised is connected to the same subnet to which the route's global next-hop address belongs, the link-local address of the advertising interface is included in the Next Hop Address field of the MP_REACH_NLRI. The Next Hop Address Length field indicates 32 bytes (two 128-bit IPv6 addresses).

■ In all other cases, only the global next-hop address is included in the Next Hop Address field, and the Next Hop Address Length field indicates 16 bytes (a single 128-bit address).

The TCP session over which BGP advertises an IPv6 route can be either IPv4 or IPv6. The pros and cons of the different TCP connection options are discussed in the configuration examples that follow.

Configuring MBGP for IPv6

This section assumes that you are familiar with the basics of IPv6, in particular the IPv6 unicast address format and how to configure IPv6 addresses on IOS interfaces. The examples in this section show IPv6 address configurations but provide only cursory explanations of their format. If you are not already familiar with the basics of IPv6, you need to briefly read up on them in Volume I of this book or any reliable introductory material.

Figure 6-4 shows the topology used for the configuration examples in this section. It is familiar to you from Chapter 5, "Scaling BGP," Figure 5-4, except that IPv6 prefixes are now advertised from each of the nontransit autonomous systems.

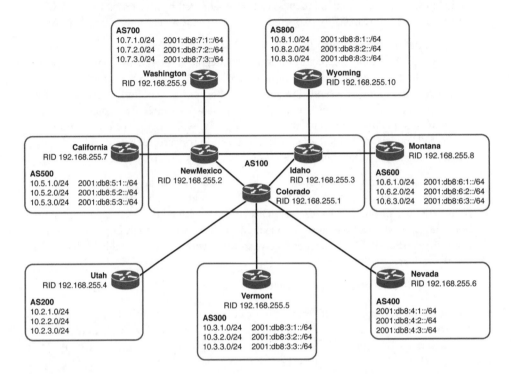

Figure 6-4   *Each of the Nontransit Autonomous Systems Advertise Three IPv4 Prefixes and Three IPv6 Prefixes to AS100*

IPv4 and IPv6 Prefixes over an IPv4 TCP Session

This first example configures MBGP between California in AS500 and NewMexico in AS100. Figure 6-5 shows more detail of the relationship between these two routers, including the interface addresses used for the connecting link.

Example 6-1 shows the starting configurations before the multiprotocol BGP configuration is added. The IPv4 interface addresses and BGP configuration is familiar to you already. New to the configuration is the **ipv6 unicast-routing** statement, which is required in any IOS configuration to enable IPv6 unicast routing. Next is the addition of IPv6 addresses to the serial interfaces connecting the two routers. The syntax is the same as an IPv4 address configuration except, of course, the **ipv6** keyword is used and an IPv6 address (with CIDR-style prefix length notation rather than an address mask) is specified. Note that California's configuration has three IPv6 static routes, pointing to Null 0, which are similar to the three IPv4 static routes. These six routes represent the prefixes to be injected into BGP to be advertised to NewMexico. The BGP configuration already uses a **neighbor remote-as** statement to establish an adjacency between the two IPv4 interface addresses, and **network** statements inject the three statically configured IPv4 prefixes into BGP.

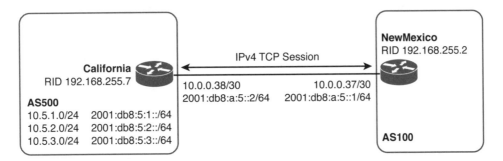

Figure 6-5 *A Closer Look at the Routers Connecting AS100 and AS500 in Figure 6-4, Including Interface Addresses and the Type of BGP Session to Be Established*

Example 6-1 *Configurations of Routers California and NewMexico in Figure 6-4*

```
! California
ipv6 unicast-routing
!
interface Loopback0
 ip address 192.168.255.7 255.255.255.255
!
interface Serial1/0
 ip address 10.0.0.38 255.255.255.252
 ipv6 address 2001:DB8:A:5::2/64
!
router bgp 500
 no synchronization
 bgp log-neighbor-changes
 network 10.5.1.0 mask 255.255.255.0
 network 10.5.2.0 mask 255.255.255.0
 network 10.5.3.0 mask 255.255.255.0
 neighbor 10.0.0.37 remote-as 100
 no auto-summary
!
ip route 10.5.1.0 255.255.255.0 Null0
ip route 10.5.2.0 255.255.255.0 Null0
ip route 10.5.3.0 255.255.255.0 Null0
!
```

```
ipv6 route 2001:DB8:5:1::/64 Null0
ipv6 route 2001:DB8:5:2::/64 Null0
ipv6 route 2001:DB8:5:3::/64 Null0
!
```

```
! NewMexico
ipv6 unicast-routing
!
interface Loopback0
 ip address 192.168.255.2 255.255.255.255
!
interface Serial1/2
 ip address 10.0.0.37 255.255.255.252
 ipv6 address 2001:DB8:A:5::1/64
!
router bgp 100
 no synchronization
 bgp log-neighbor-changes
 neighbor 10.0.0.38 remote-as 500
 no auto-summary
!
```

Note The use of static routes pointing to the Null interface is familiar to you from previous configuration exercises. The static routes represent the summary prefixes that BGP uses to find the local AS edge router; packets are then routed to more-specific destinations using IGP routes—although the IGP configurations within the autonomous systems are not shown in these examples. IPv6 static routes are configured and injected into BGP in the same way. This configuration approach provides a clean separation between BGP and the local IGP with no redistribution between the protocols.

Example 6-2 *IPv4 Prefixes Advertised from Router California Are Entered in NewMexico's IPv4 Unicast Routing Table*

```
NewMexico#show ip route 10.5.1.0
Routing entry for 10.5.1.0/24
  Known via "bgp 100", distance 20, metric 0
  Tag 500, type external
  Last update from 10.0.0.38 00:30:34 ago
  Routing Descriptor Blocks:
  * 10.0.0.38, from 10.0.0.38, 00:30:34 ago
      Route metric is 0, traffic share count is 1
      AS Hops 1
      Route tag 500
```

To add IPv6 support to these BGP configurations, the **address-family ipv6** statement
is used under the **router bgp** hierarchy. As Example 6-3 shows, this statement puts the
CLI into *(config-router-af)* mode, where statements specific to the IPv6 address family
can be added. The **neighbor activate** statement specifies that neighbor 10.0.0.37, already
established with the **neighbor remote-as** statement, is the active neighbor for exchanging
prefixes belonging to this address family. In this example, **network** statements inject the
three IPv6 prefixes into BGP. These statements are just like the **network** statements for
IPv4, except they specify IPv6 prefixes to inject. The **exit-address-family** statement then
takes the CLI out of that configuration mode. Example 6-3 shows the resulting addition
to the BGP configuration.

Example 6-3   *Adding IPv6 Address Family Support to California's BGP Configuration*

```
California(config)#router bgp 500
California(config-router)#address-family ipv6
California(config-router-af)#neighbor 10.0.0.37 activate
California(config-router-af)#network 2001:db8:5:1::/64
California(config-router-af)#network 2001:db8:5:2::/64
California(config-router-af)#network 2001:db8:5:3::/64
California(config-router-af)#exit-address-family
California(config-router)#^Z
California#
*Apr 28 23:04:46.182: %SYS-5-CONFIG_I: Configured from console by console
California#
California#show run | begin bgp
router bgp 500
 no synchronization
 bgp log-neighbor-changes
 network 10.5.1.0 mask 255.255.255.0
 network 10.5.2.0 mask 255.255.255.0
 network 10.5.3.0 mask 255.255.255.0
 neighbor 10.0.0.37 remote-as 100
 no auto-summary
 !
 address- ipv6
 neighbor 10.0.0.37 activate
 network 2001:DB8:5:1::/64
 network 2001:DB8:5:2::/64
 network 2001 family:DB8:5:3::/64
 exit-address-family
!
```

Example 6-4 shows the peering BGP configuration at NewMexico. The IPv6 address
family configuration is a bit simpler here because no prefixes are injected. Instead,

the address family is activated and the active BGP neighbor for the address family is specified.

Example 6-4   *MBGP Configuration at NewMexico*

```
router bgp 100
 no synchronization
 bgp log-neighbor-changes
 neighbor 10.0.0.38 remote-as 500
 no auto-summary
 !
 address-family ipv6
 neighbor 10.0.0.38 activate
 exit-address-family
 !
```

There is a problem, however. As Example 6-5 shows, the **show ipv6 route** command shows that NewMexico does not have the IPv6 routes in its IPv6 routing table. From what you already have learned about BGP, you probably know what is wrong, or at least have a good suspicion of what is wrong, but you need to do some troubleshooting to clearly identify the problem.

Example 6-5   *None of the Three IPv6 Prefixes in AS500 Appear in NewMexico's IPv6 Routing Table*

```
NewMexico#show ipv6 route 2001:db8:5:1::/64
% Route not found
NewMexico#show ipv6 route 2001:db8:5:2::/64
% Route not found
NewMexico#show ipv6 route 2001:db8:5:3::/64
% Route not found
NewMexico#
```

The first step is to determine whether NewMexico is receiving IPv6 route updates from California. In Example 6-6, the **debug bgp ipv6 unicast updates in** command is used to observe all IPv6 updates. A soft reconfiguration command is then used to send a Route Refresh message to California (in AS500), causing it to send an update.

Example 6-6   *Debugging Shows That California Is Sending IPv6 Updates with an Invalid Next-Hop Address*

```
NewMexico#debug bgp ipv6 unicast updates in
BGP updates debugging is on (inbound) for address family: IPv6 Unicast
NewMexico#
NewMexico#clear bgp ipv6 unicast 500 soft in
```

```
NewMexico#
*Apr 29 02:42:42.121: BGP: 10.0.0.38 Advertised Nexthop ::FFFF:10.0.0.38: Non-local
  or Nexthop and peer Not on same interface
*Apr 29 02:42:42.125: BGP(1): 10.0.0.38 rcv UPDATE w/ attr: nexthop ::FFFF:10.0.0.38
  (FE80::C806:16FF:FE8A:0), origin i, metric 0, originator 0.0.0.0, path 500,
  community , extended community
*Apr 29 02:42:42.137: BGP(1): 10.0.0.38 rcv UPDATE about 2001:DB8:5:3::/64 -- DENIED
  due to: non-connected MP_REACH NEXTHOP;
*Apr 29 02:42:42.137: BGP(1): 10.0.0.38 rcv UPDATE about 2001:DB8:5:2::/64 -- DENIED
  due to: non-connected MP_REACH NEXTHOP;
*Apr 29 02:42:42.141: BGP(1): 10.0.0.38 rcv UPDATE about 2001:DB8:5:1::/64 -- DENIED
  due to: non-connected MP_REACH NEXTHOP;
NewMexico#
```

The last three debug messages show that the updates for all three IPv6 prefixes were received but were rejected because of a nonconnected next-hop address. Looking at the message just before those three, you can see the update received from California (10.0.0.38) with an unusual next-hop address of ::ffff:10.0.0.38.[4] This address is an *IPv4-Mapped IPv6 Address*,[5] specifically intended to represent an IPv4 address within an IPv6 address format, and normally used for transition services such as NAT64, which is covered in Chapter 11, "IPv6 to IPv4 Network Address Translation (NAT64)." Because BGP is advertising over an IPv4 TCP session, it uses the IPv4 address of the advertising interface and uses the IPv4-mapped IPv6 address format to fit that address into the IPv6 Next Hop Address field. The receiving BGP process at NewMexico does not recognize the address as a valid next-hop address and rejects the routes.

We need a policy that changes the default next-hop address to the advertising interface's IPv6 address. Example 6-7 shows the creation of a route map named v6-Next-Hop, which uses an IPv6 prefix list named v6-Routes to identify the IPv6 prefixes belonging to AS500. Notice that the syntax of an IPv6 prefix list is the same as an IPv4 prefix list, other than obviously identifying IPv6 prefixes. The route map changes the next-hop address of routes whose prefixes match the prefix list to 2001:db8:a:5::2, the IPv6 address of California's interface to NewMexico. The route map is then applied as an outgoing policy to the **neighbor** statement under the BGP IPv6 address family configuration. It is applied only here and not to the default IPv4 address family configuration, as the route map has no relevance to the IPv4 prefixes California is advertising.

---

[4] Notice also that the Next Hop Address field also includes the link-local address fe80::c806:16ff:fe8a:0, in compliance with the rules discussed in the section "MBGP Support for the IPv6 Address Family."

[5] See RFC 4291, Section 2.5.5.2.

Example 6-7   *A Policy Is Configured That Sets the Next-Hop Address of the Local IPv6 Prefixes Advertised to NewMexico to the IPv6 Interface Address 2001:db8:a:5::2*

```
router bgp 500
 no synchronization
 bgp log-neighbor-changes
 network 10.5.1.0 mask 255.255.255.0
 network 10.5.2.0 mask 255.255.255.0
 network 10.5.3.0 mask 255.255.255.0
 neighbor 10.0.0.37 remote-as 100
 no auto-summary
 !
 address-family ipv6
 neighbor 10.0.0.37 activate
 neighbor 10.0.0.37 route-map v6-Next-Hop out
 network 2001:DB8:5:1::/64
 network 2001:DB8:5:2::/64
 network 2001:DB8:5:3::/64
 exit-address-family
!
ipv6 prefix-list v6-Routes seq 5 permit 2001:DB8:5::/48 le 64
!
route-map v6-Next-Hop permit 10
 match ipv6 address prefix-list v6-Routes
 set ipv6 next-hop 2001:DB8:A:5::2
!
```

The debug messages at NewMexico, shown in Example 6-8, indicate that the routes received from California now have the wanted next-hop address. However, the messages also show that the routes are still rejected. According to the messages, the next-hop address is not on the same interface. This might seem unusual because from the configuration of Example 6-1 and the illustration of Figure 6-5 the IPv6 address 2001:db8:a:5::2 obviously is on the interface from which the BGP updates are sent. But the IPv4 TCP session over which the BGP updates are sent is on IPv4 subnet 10.0.0.36/30, whereas the next-hop address is on IPv6 subnet 2001:db8:a:5::/64. The next-hop address is not on the same subnet on which the EBGP session is established.

Example 6-8   *California Is Now Advertising Its IPv6 Prefixes with a Next-Hop Address of 2001:db8:a:5::2, but the Routes Are Still Rejected*

```
NewMexico#
*Apr 29 03:31:46.281: BGP: 10.0.0.38 Advertised Nexthop 2001:DB8:A:5::2: Non-local
  or Nexthop and peer Not on same interface
*Apr 29 03:31:46.285: BGP(1): 10.0.0.38 rcv UPDATE w/ attr: nexthop 2001:DB8:A:5::2
  (FE80::C806:16FF:FE8A:0), origin i, metric 0, originator 0.0.0.0, path 500,
  community , extended community
```

```
*Apr 29 03:31:46.293: BGP(1): 10.0.0.38 rcv UPDATE about 2001:DB8:5:3::/64 -- DENIED
  due to: non-connected MP_REACH NEXTHOP;
*Apr 29 03:31:46.293: BGP(1): 10.0.0.38 rcv UPDATE about 2001:DB8:5:2::/64 -- DENIED
  due to: non-connected MP_REACH NEXTHOP;
*Apr 29 03:31:46.293: BGP(1): 10.0.0.38 rcv UPDATE about 2001:DB8:5:1::/64 -- DENIED
  due to: non-connected MP_REACH NEXTHOP;
```

You already know how to remedy this situation. EBGP by default expects the next-hop address to be directly connected (one hop away), but that default can be changed with the **neighbor ebgp multihop** statement. Example 6-9 extends NewMexico's EBGP configuration to accept next-hop addresses up to 2 hops away.

Example 6-9 *NewMexico Is Configured to Accept EBGP Next-Hops Up to Two Hops Away*

```
router bgp 100
 no synchronization
 bgp log-neighbor-changes
 neighbor 10.0.0.38 remote-as 500
 neighbor 10.0.0.38 ebgp-multihop 2
 no auto-summary
 !
 address-family ipv6
 neighbor 10.0.0.38 activate
 exit-address-family
!
```

Example 6-10 shows the results. The debug messages show that the three prefixes are now accepted and installed in NewMexico's IPv6 routing table, and one of the route entries is examined to verify the installation.

Example 6-10 *With the Correct Next-Hop Address and with the EBGP Multihop Configuration, the Three Prefixes from California Are Now Installed in NewMexico's IPv6 Routing Table*

```
NewMexico#clear bgp ipv6 uni 500 soft in
NewMexico#
*Apr 29 03:45:53.253: BGP(1): 10.0.0.38 rcvd UPDATE w/ attr: nexthop 2001:DB8:A:5::2
  (FE80::C806:16FF:FE8A:0), origin i, metric 0, path 500
*Apr 29 03:45:53.253: BGP(1): 10.0.0.38 rcvd 2001:DB8:5:3::/64
*Apr 29 03:45:53.257: BGP(1): 10.0.0.38 rcvd 2001:DB8:5:2::/64
*Apr 29 03:45:53.257: BGP(1): 10.0.0.38 rcvd 2001:DB8:5:1::/64
*Apr 29 03:45:53.257: BGP(1): Revise route installing 2001:DB8:5:1::/64 ->
  2001:DB8:A:5::2 (FE80::C806:16FF:FE8A:0) to main IPv6 table
*Apr 29 03:45:53.257: BGP(1): Revise route installing 2001:DB8:5:2::/64 ->
  2001:DB8:A:5::2 (FE80::C806:16FF:FE8A:0) to main IPv6 table
```

```
*Apr 29 03:45:53.257: BGP(1): Revise route installing 2001:DB8:5:3::/64 ->
  2001:DB8:A:5::2 (FE80::C806:16FF:FE8A:0) to main IPv6 table
NewMexico#
NewMexico#show ipv6 route 2001:db8:5:1::/64
IPv6 Routing Table - 6 entries
Codes: C - Connected, L - Local, S - Static, R - RIP, B - BGP
       U - Per-user Static route, M - MIPv6
       I1 - ISIS L1, I2 - ISIS L2, IA - ISIS interarea, IS - ISIS summary
       O - OSPF intra, OI - OSPF inter, OE1 - OSPF ext 1, OE2 - OSPF ext 2
       ON1 - OSPF NSSA ext 1, ON2 - OSPF NSSA ext 2
       D - EIGRP, EX - EIGRP external
B   2001:DB8:5:1::/64 [20/0]
     via FE80::C806:16FF:FE8A:0, Serial1/2
```

Although this first exercise does not cause any IPv6 routes to be sent from NewMexico to California, a look at the larger network topology in Figure 6-4 indicates that eventually NewMexico will be learning IPv6 routes from other autonomous systems and will be advertising them to California. So a policy similar to the one in Example 6-7 is required that sets the next-hop address of routes advertised to California to NewMexico's outgoing IPv6 address 2001:db8:a:5::1. California also must be configured with the **neighbor ebgp-multihop** statement to ensure that the changed next-hop address of the routes is accepted.

Example 6-11 shows the policy configured for NewMexico. The only functional change from the policy configured for California in Example 6-7 is the IPv6 prefix list, which matches any of the IPv6 prefixes in the topology of Figure 6-4.

Example 6-11 *A Policy Is Configured at NewMexico That Changes the Next-Hop Address of Any of the IPv6 Prefixes Shown in Figure 6-4 to 2001:db8:a:5::1 Before Sending Them to California*

```
router bgp 100
 no synchronization
 bgp log-neighbor-changes
 neighbor 10.0.0.38 remote-as 500
 neighbor 10.0.0.38 ebgp-multihop 2
 no auto-summary
 !
 address-family ipv6
 neighbor 10.0.0.38 activate
 neighbor 10.0.0.38 route-map v6-Routes-to-California out
 exit-address-family
 !
ipv6 prefix-list v6-Routes seq 5 permit 2001:DB8::/32 le 64
 !
```

```
route-map v6-Routes-to-California permit 10
 match ipv6 address prefix-list v6-Routes
 set ipv6 next-hop 2001:DB8:A:5::1
 !
```

Upgrading IPv4 BGP Configurations to the Address Family Format

The MBGP configurations of routers California and NewMexico in the previous section can be confusing to interpret. They support both IPv4 unicast and IPv6 unicast address families, but BGP configuration is IPv4 unicast by default, so although IPv6 had its own address family section, IPv4 remains as the default configuration syntax.

Although it works fine in that condition, an MBGP configuration should have an IPv4 address family section just like all the nondefault address families. Applying policies, neighbor and network statements, and other configuration variables are clearer if all address families are configured in the same way.

You can manually configure an **address-family ipv4** statement and add IPv4-specific statements under it. But IOS provides a command, **bgp upgrade-cli**, which easily converts the default syntax for you. Example 6-12 shows how it works. At router California, the BGP configuration as it was left in the previous section is shown. Then from the BGP configuration mode, the **bgp upgrade-cli** command is entered. You are prompted to be sure you want to enter the command—after you change the configuration format, you cannot back out—and the configuration format is changed. A second look at the BGP configuration shows that the IPv4 portion is now in the MBGP address family format like the IPv6 portion of the configuration.

Example 6-12   bgp upgrade-cli *Command Is Used in Router Configuration Mode to Change the IPv4 BGP Configuration from the Default Format to the Address Family Format*

```
California#show run | begin bgp
router bgp 500
 no synchronization
 bgp log-neighbor-changes
 network 10.5.1.0 mask 255.255.255.0
 network 10.5.2.0 mask 255.255.255.0
 network 10.5.3.0 mask 255.255.255.0
 neighbor 10.0.0.37 remote-as 100
 neighbor 10.0.0.37 ebgp-multihop 2
 no auto-summary
 !
 address-family ipv6
 neighbor 10.0.0.37 activate
 neighbor 10.0.0.37 route-map v6-Next-Hop out
```

```
 network 2001:DB8:5:1::/64
 network 2001:DB8:5:2::/64
 network 2001:DB8:5:3::/64
 exit-address-family
!


California#conf t
Enter configuration commands, one per line.  End with CNTL/Z.
California(config)#router bgp 500
California(config-router)#bgp upgrade-cli
You are about to upgrade to the AFI syntax of bgp commands

Are you sure ? [yes]: yes
California(config-router)#^Z
California#
*May  2 23:19:47.459: %SYS-5-CONFIG_I: Configured from console by console
California#
California#show run | begin bgp
router bgp 500
 bgp log-neighbor-changes
 neighbor 10.0.0.37 remote-as 100
 neighbor 10.0.0.37 ebgp-multihop 2
 !
 address-family ipv4
 neighbor 10.0.0.37 activate
 no auto-summary
 no synchronization
 network 10.5.1.0 mask 255.255.255.0
 network 10.5.2.0 mask 255.255.255.0
 network 10.5.3.0 mask 255.255.255.0
 exit-address-family
 !
 address-family ipv6
 neighbor 10.0.0.37 activate
 neighbor 10.0.0.37 route-map v6-Next-Hop out
 network 2001:DB8:5:1::/64
 network 2001:DB8:5:2::/64
 network 2001:DB8:5:3::/64
 exit-address-family
!
```

Even though **bgp upgrade-cli** is entered from (config-router) mode, it is a command, not
a configuration statement. It changes only the configuration format; it does not become
a part of the configuration. And the command does not change any functional part of

the BGP configuration, it just changes the configuration format. You can use the command on a running BGP router, and it does not disrupt the BGP session.

Example 6-13 shows NewMexico's BGP configuration after **bgp upgrade-cli** has been run on that router. You can compare this configuration with the one shown in Example 6-11. The parts of the configuration relevant only to IPv4 or IPv6 are much easier to distinguish and contrast now that the IPv4 portion is in the same address family format as the IPv6 portion.

Example 6-13 *NewMexico's MBGP Configuration, After the* **bgp upgrade-cli** *Command Is Run*

```
NewMexico#show run | begin bgp
router bgp 100
 bgp log-neighbor-changes
 neighbor 10.0.0.38 remote-as 500
 neighbor 10.0.0.38 ebgp-multihop 2
 !
 address-family ipv4
 neighbor 10.0.0.38 activate
 no auto-summary
 no synchronization
 exit-address-family
 !
 address-family ipv6
 neighbor 10.0.0.38 activate
 neighbor 10.0.0.38 route-map v6-Routes-to-California out
 exit-address-family
 !
```

The usual practice, when implementing a new address family on a running BGP router, is to use the **bgp upgrade-cli** command to change the default IPv4 configuration before adding the new address family configuration.

IPv4 and IPv6 over an IPv6 TCP Connection

Figure 6-6 details the connection from NewMexico to Washington of Figure 6-4. The IPv4 and IPv6 interface addresses are shown, and the MBGP adjacency this time is over IPv6, instead of IPv4.

Example 6-14 shows the initial configurations of Washington and NewMexico. The **bgp upgrade-cli** command was used to put Washington's BGP configuration into the address family format, and the static routes used to inject prefixes into BGP are shown. NewMexico's configuration shows the new statements for Washington added to the configuration created in the last section.

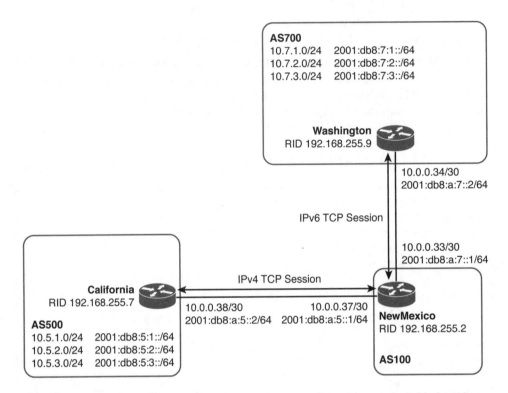

Figure 6-6 *MBGP Adjacency Between NewMexico and Washington Is Added, with a TCP over IPv6 Session*

> **Note**   Example 6-14 shows the **ipv6 unicast-routing** statement, the interface configurations, and the static routes used for prefix origination one more time. Subsequent examples assume you are familiar with these parts of the configuration and do not show them unless there is some relevance to the discussion.

In the configurations, you can see that the **neighbor remote-as** statements use the peering IPv6 address instead of the IPv4 address. The **neighbor activate** statement is used under each address family configuration to tell the router to use that session for advertising the address family.

Example 6-14   *Configurations of Routers Washington and NewMexico in Figure 6-6, Before Any BGP Policy Is Applied to the Session Between Them*

```
Washington:
ipv6 unicast-routing
!
interface Loopback0
 ip address 192.168.255.9 255.255.255.255
```

```
!
interface Serial1/0
 ip address 10.0.0.34 255.255.255.252
 ipv6 address 2001:DB8:A:7::2/64
 serial restart-delay 0
!
router bgp 700
 bgp log-neighbor-changes
 neighbor 2001:DB8:A:7::1 remote-as 100
 !
 address-family ipv4
 neighbor 2001:DB8:A:7::1 activate
 no auto-summary
 no synchronization
 network 10.7.1.0 mask 255.255.255.0
 network 10.7.2.0 mask 255.255.255.0
 network 10.7.3.0 mask 255.255.255.0
 exit-address-family
 !
 address-family ipv6
 neighbor 2001:DB8:A:7::1 activate
 network 2001:DB8:7:1::/64
 network 2001:DB8:7:2::/64
 network 2001:DB8:7:3::/64
 exit-address-family
!
ip route 10.7.1.0 255.255.255.0 Null0
ip route 10.7.2.0 255.255.255.0 Null0
ip route 10.7.3.0 255.255.255.0 Null0
!
ipv6 route 2001:DB8:7:1::/64 Null0
ipv6 route 2001:DB8:7:2::/64 Null0
ipv6 route 2001:DB8:7:3::/64 Null0
!
```

NewMexico:
```
ipv6 unicast-routing
!
interface Loopback0
 ip address 192.168.255.2 255.255.255.255
!
interface Serial1/2
 ip address 10.0.0.37 255.255.255.252
 ipv6 address 2001:DB8:A:5::1/64
```

```
!
interface Serial1/3
 ip address 10.0.0.33 255.255.255.252
 ipv6 address 2001:DB8:A:7::1/64
 serial restart-delay 0
!
router bgp 100
 bgp log-neighbor-changes
 neighbor 10.0.0.38 remote-as 500
 neighbor 10.0.0.38 ebgp-multihop 2
 neighbor 2001:DB8:A:7::2 remote-as 700
 !
 address-family ipv4
 neighbor 10.0.0.38 activate
 neighbor 2001:DB8:A:7::2 activate
 no auto-summary
 no synchronization
 exit-address-family
 !
 address-family ipv6
 neighbor 10.0.0.38 activate
 neighbor 10.0.0.38 route-map v6-Routes-to-California out
 neighbor 2001:DB8:A:7::2 activate
 exit-address-family
!
```

In the exercise of the previous section, where IPv6 routes were advertised over an IPv4
BGP session, it was necessary to configure a policy to change the next-hop address of
the IPv6 prefixes from the advertising interface's IPv4 address to the interface's IPv6
address. In this exercise, you can rightly assume that the opposite will be true: Because
IPv4 addresses are advertised over an IPv6 BGP session, their next-hop addresses will be
the advertising interface's IPv6 address instead of the IPv4 address. Instead of debugging, this exercise uses the **show bgp** command, with a specification of the address
family of interest, to verify the expected behavior.

First, Example 6-15 uses the **show bgp ipv6 unicast** command to display the IPv6
unicast prefixes in Washington's BGP table. You can see that the three prefixes from
AS500, advertised to NewMexico from California, have been received from NewMexico
and that their next-hop addresses are the IPv6 address of NewMexico's interface to
Washington (2001:db8:a:7::1). A **show ipv6 route** command specifying one of those prefixes verifies that it has been installed in the IPv6 routing table by BGP.

Example 6-15 *Washington Has Received Advertisements for the Three IPv6 Prefixes in AS500, with Legitimate IPv6 Next-Hop Addresses and Has Installed Them in the IPv6 Routing Table*

```
Washington#show bgp ipv6 unicast
BGP table version is 15, local router ID is 192.168.255.9
Status codes: s suppressed, d damped, h history, * valid, > best, i - internal,
              r RIB-failure, S Stale
Origin codes: i - IGP, e - EGP, ? - incomplete

   Network          Next Hop            Metric LocPrf Weight Path
*> 2001:DB8:5:1::/64
                    2001:DB8:A:7::1                      0 100 500 i
*> 2001:DB8:5:2::/64
                    2001:DB8:A:7::1                      0 100 500 i
*> 2001:DB8:5:3::/64
                    2001:DB8:A:7::1                      0 100 500 i
*> 2001:DB8:7:1::/64
                    ::                    0           32768 i
*> 2001:DB8:7:2::/64
                    ::                    0           32768 i
*> 2001:DB8:7:3::/64
                    ::                    0           32768 i
Washington#
Washington#show ipv6 route 2001:db8:5:1::
IPv6 Routing Table - 9 entries
Codes: C - Connected, L - Local, S - Static, R - RIP, B - BGP
       U - Per-user Static route, M - MIPv6
       I1 - ISIS L1, I2 - ISIS L2, IA - ISIS interarea, IS - ISIS summary
       O - OSPF intra, OI - OSPF inter, OE1 - OSPF ext 1, OE2 - OSPF ext 2
       ON1 - OSPF NSSA ext 1, ON2 - OSPF NSSA ext 2
       D - EIGRP, EX - EIGRP external
B   2001:DB8:5:1::/64 [20/0]
     via FE80::C801:23FF:FE07:0, Serial1/0
Washington#
```

Example 6-16 uses the **show bgp ipv4 unicast** command to display the IPv4 unicast prefixes in Washington's BGP table. You can see that the three IPv4 prefixes in AS500 have been received, but the IPv4 next-hop addresses are apparently not from NewMexico's interface. If the next-hop address is not reachable, BGP does not install the route in the routing table—a **show ip route** for one of the prefixes verifies that indeed the prefix is not in the IPv4 routing table.

Example 6-16 *Washington Has Received Advertisements for the Three IPv4 Prefixes in AS500, but the Next-Hop Addresses Are Not Reachable IPv4 Addresses, So BGP Does Not Install Them in the IPv4 Routing Table*

```
Washington#show bgp ipv4 unicast
BGP table version is 4, local router ID is 192.168.255.9
Status codes: s suppressed, d damped, h history, * valid, > best, i - internal,
              r RIB-failure, S Stale
Origin codes: i - IGP, e - EGP, ? - incomplete


   Network          Next Hop         Metric LocPrf Weight Path
*  10.5.1.0/24      32.1.13.184                       0 100 500 i
*  10.5.2.0/24      32.1.13.184                       0 100 500 i
*  10.5.3.0/24      32.1.13.184                       0 100 500 i
*> 10.7.1.0/24      0.0.0.0               0         32768 i
*> 10.7.2.0/24      0.0.0.0               0         32768 i
*> 10.7.3.0/24      0.0.0.0               0         32768 i
Washington#
Washington#show ip route 10.5.1.0
% Subnet not in table
Washington#
```

The IPv4 next-hop address that displays for the three AS500 routes—32.1.13.184—is surprising. Although it looks like a legitimate IPv4 address, it not only is not reachable from Washington, but also it does not appear anywhere in the network diagram of Figure 6-6. Where did that address come from?

Recall from the exercise in the previous section that when IPv6 addresses are advertised over an IPv4 session, the default behavior is to use the advertising interface's IPv4 address as the next-hop address, but the IPv6 update tries to interpret it as an IPv6 address. So, the IPv4 address appears as the last 32 bits of an IPv6 next-hop address. You might, knowing this, deduce that when an IPv4 prefix is advertised over an IPv6 session, the next-hop address will be the advertising interface's IPv6 address. You might further deduce that a BGP IPv4 route update will somehow try to interpret that IPv6 next-hop address as an IPv4 address.

Those two deductions give you enough information to figure out what that strange IPv4 next-hop address is. Look at what each of the four 8-bit decimal numbers in the IPv4 address is in hexadecimal:

32 = 0x20

1 = 0x01

13 = 0x0d

184 = 0xb8

32.1.13.184 is the dotted decimal representation of the first 32 bits (2001:db8::) of the IPv6 next-hop address 2001:db8:a:7::1.

A look at the prefixes in the BGP IPv4 table at NewMexico shows the same behavior (Example 6-17). The IPv4 routes received from AS500 have a legitimate IPv4 next-hop address, whereas the ones Washington has advertised from AS700 have that same odd IPv4 next-hop address—odd, that is, unless you know where it came from.

Example 6-17 *IPv4 Prefixes in NewMexico's BGP Table Show the Same Strange IPv4 Next-Hop Address as in California's BGP Table*

```
NewMexico#show bgp ipv4 unicast
BGP table version is 4, local router ID is 192.168.255.2
Status codes: s suppressed, d damped, h history, * valid, > best, i - internal,
              r RIB-failure, S Stale
Origin codes: i - IGP, e - EGP, ? - incomplete

   Network          Next Hop          Metric LocPrf Weight Path
*> 10.5.1.0/24      10.0.0.38              0           0 500 i
*> 10.5.2.0/24      10.0.0.38              0           0 500 i
*> 10.5.3.0/24      10.0.0.38              0           0 500 i
*  10.7.1.0/24      32.1.13.184            0           0 700 i
*  10.7.2.0/24      32.1.13.184            0           0 700 i
*  10.7.3.0/24      32.1.13.184            0           0 700 i
NewMexico#
```

As in the previous exercise, you need a policy to change default next-hop behavior. But this time, the policy changes the next-hop address of IPv4 routes advertised over IPv6 BGP sessions.

Example 6-18 shows an outgoing policy applied to Washington in which route-map v4-Next-Hop matches all IPv4 prefixes whose first 16 bits are 10.7.0.0/16 and whose prefix length is less than or equal to 24 bits—in other words, all the prefixes local to AS700. Matching prefixes have their next-hop address set to 10.0.0.34, Washington's outgoing interface toward NewMexico. Notice that the policy is applied only to the neighbor configuration under the IPv4 address family and not under the IPv6 address family.

Example 6-18 *A Policy Is Applied to All the Local IPv4 Prefixes Washington Advertises to NewMexico That Changes the Next-Hop Address to the IPv4 Address of Washington's Interface*

```
router bgp 700
 bgp log-neighbor-changes
 neighbor 2001:DB8:A:7::1 remote-as 100
 !
```

```
address-family ipv4
neighbor 2001:DB8:A:7::1 activate
neighbor 2001:DB8:A:7::1 route-map v4-Next-Hop out
no auto-summary
no synchronization
network 10.7.1.0 mask 255.255.255.0
network 10.7.2.0 mask 255.255.255.0
network 10.7.3.0 mask 255.255.255.0
exit-address-family
 !
address-family ipv6
neighbor 2001:DB8:A:7::1 activate
network 2001:DB8:7:1::/64
network 2001:DB8:7:2::/64
network 2001:DB8:7:3::/64
 exit-address-family
!
ip prefix-list v4-Routes seq 5 permit 10.7.0.0/16 le 24
!
route-map v4-Next-Hop permit 10
 match ip address prefix-list v4-Routes
 set ip next-hop 10.0.0.34
!
```

Example 6-19 shows the result of the policy at NewMexico: The IPv4 prefixes from AS700 now have a legitimate and reachable IPv4 next-hop address and are therefore installed in the IPv4 routing table.

Example 6-19   *IPv4 Prefixes in NewMexico's BGP Table Received from Washington Now Have the Correct Next-Hop Address and Are Installed in the IPv4 Routing Table*

```
NewMexico#show bgp ipv4 unicast
BGP table version is 13, local router ID is 192.168.255.2
Status codes: s suppressed, d damped, h history, * valid, > best, i - internal,
              r RIB-failure, S Stale
Origin codes: i - IGP, e - EGP, ? - incomplete

   Network          Next Hop          Metric LocPrf Weight Path
*> 10.5.1.0/24      10.0.0.38              0          0 500 i
*> 10.5.2.0/24      10.0.0.38              0          0 500 i
*> 10.5.3.0/24      10.0.0.38              0          0 500 i
*> 10.7.1.0/24      10.0.0.34              0          0 700 i
*> 10.7.2.0/24      10.0.0.34              0          0 700 i
*> 10.7.3.0/24      10.0.0.34              0          0 700 i
```

```
NewMexico#
NewMexico#show ip route 10.7.1.0
Routing entry for 10.7.1.0/24
  Known via "bgp 100", distance 20, metric 0
  Tag 700, type external
  Last update from 10.0.0.34 00:28:18 ago
  Routing Descriptor Blocks:
  * 10.0.0.34, from 32.1.13.184, 00:28:18 ago
      Route metric is 0, traffic share count is 1
      AS Hops 1
      Route tag 700
```

Of course, a policy must also be set at NewMexico for all IPv4 routes advertised to Washington over the IPv6 BGP session. Example 6-20 shows this policy. You can compare and contrast this policy with the policy previously configured for IPv6 routes advertised to California: In both cases, they match routes that NewMexico might learn from any of the autonomous systems in Figure 6-4, not just the prefixes of a single AS.

Example 6-21 shows the results of the policy at Washington. The IPv4 prefixes from AS500 now have a valid and reachable next-hop address and are installed in the IPv4 routing table.

Example 6-20 *A Policy Is Configured at NewMexico That Corrects the Next-Hop Address of All IPv4 Routes Sent to Washington*

```
router bgp 100
 bgp log-neighbor-changes
 neighbor 10.0.0.38 remote-as 500
 neighbor 10.0.0.38 ebgp-multihop 2
 neighbor 2001:DB8:A:7::2 remote-as 700
 !
 address-family ipv4
 neighbor 10.0.0.38 activate
 neighbor 2001:DB8:A:7::2 activate
 neighbor 2001:DB8:A:7::2 route-map v4-Routes-to-Washington out
 no auto-summary
 no synchronization
 exit-address-family
 !
 address-family ipv6
 neighbor 10.0.0.38 activate
 neighbor 10.0.0.38 route-map v6-Routes-to-California out
 neighbor 2001:DB8:A:7::2 activate
 exit-address-family
 !
```

```
ip prefix-list v4-Routes seq 5 permit 10.0.0.0/8 le 24
!
ipv6 prefix-list v6-Routes seq 5 permit 2001:DB8::/32 le 64
!
route-map v6-Routes-to-California permit 10
 match ipv6 address prefix-list v6-Routes
 set ipv6 next-hop 2001:DB8:A:5::1
!
route-map v4-Routes-to-Washington permit 10
 match ip address prefix-list v4-Routes
 set ip next-hop 10.0.0.33
!
```

Example 6-21   *IPv4 Prefixes in Washington's BGP Table Received from NewMexico Now Have the Correct Next-Hop Address and Are Installed in the IPv4 Routing Table*

```
Washington#show bgp ipv4 unicast
BGP table version is 127, local router ID is 192.168.255.9
Status codes: s suppressed, d damped, h history, * valid, > best, i - internal,
              r RIB-failure, S Stale
Origin codes: i - IGP, e - EGP, ? - incomplete

   Network          Next Hop            Metric LocPrf Weight Path
*> 10.5.1.0/24      10.0.0.33                            0 100 500 i
*> 10.5.2.0/24      10.0.0.33                            0 100 500 i
*> 10.5.3.0/24      10.0.0.33                            0 100 500 i
*> 10.7.1.0/24      0.0.0.0                   0         32768 i
*> 10.7.2.0/24      0.0.0.0                   0         32768 i
*> 10.7.3.0/24      0.0.0.0                   0         32768 i
Washington#
Washington#show ip route 10.5.1.0
Routing entry for 10.5.1.0/24
  Known via "bgp 700", distance 20, metric 0
  Tag 100, type external
  Last update from 10.0.0.33 07:44:20 ago
  Routing Descriptor Blocks:
  * 10.0.0.33, from 32.1.13.184, 07:44:20 ago
      Route metric is 0, traffic share count is 1
      AS Hops 2
      Route tag 100
Washington#
```

You have probably noticed a discrepancy between this configuration exercise and the previous exercise in which routes were advertised over an IPv4 session: Namely, in this exercise, it was unnecessary to configure Multihop EBGP for the IPv4 routes to be declared reachable and entered into the IPv4 routing table. The difference in behavior has nothing to do with MBGP rules. Rather, it is a remnant in IOS of the pre-address family days.

When you initialize a BGP process in IOS, it immediately builds the IPv4 data structures—a legacy of when BGP supported only unicast IPv4 routes. Even if you end up configuring peering exclusively between IPv6 neighbors and advertise only IPv6 routes, the IPv4 data structures still exist by default. No other address family is treated this way; their data structures are created only when you activate the address family.

So when, in the first configuration example, a unicast IPv6 address family is added to an existing IPv4 BGP peering, the IPv6 data structures do not automatically accept routes from an IPv4 peer when the next-hop address does not belong to the subnet the IPv4 peer is on. It doesn't matter that the IPv6 subnet to which the next hop belongs shares the same link with the IPv4 subnet; it is seen as not directly connected. Hence, multihop EBGP is needed to accept a "nonlocal" subnet.

In the second example, in which IPv4 routes are advertised over an IPv6 BGP session with an IPv4 next-hop address, unicast IPv4 data structures were already created, are aware of the local IPv4 interface address, and can accept routes with next hops belonging to that interface's subnet address. No multihop EBGP is needed.

The objective of these two introductory exercises is to introduce you not only to the basics of configuring multiple address families for BGP—and you will see multicast address families for BGP in Chapter 9—but also to get you to think a bit deeper about the behavior of EBGP route advertisements. You have also seen that although you can advertise both IPv4 and IPv6 routes over a BGP session that runs over either IPv4 or IPv6, you must put a little thought into next-hop addresses and simple policies to make them work correctly. In most cases, however, life is simpler when you advertise IPv4 over an IPv4 BGP session and IPv6 over an IPv6 BGP session. That is the topic of the next configuration exercise.

Note There are some cases in which you might want to consider using a single BGP session (either IPv4 or IPv6) for advertising both IP versions, but they should be rare. Best practice, based on operator experience, is to run separate BGP sessions for IPv4 and IPv6.

For example, suppose you must add IPv6 service to a router at the edge of a service provider network running EBGP to dozens or even hundreds of customers. Using separate sessions for IPv4 and IPv6 will, if you "dual stack" all customers, double the number of BGP adjacencies the router must maintain, and possibly introduce scaling problems. The extra policy configurations needed to advertise both address families over a single BGP session might in this case be a good trade-off of complexity for scalability.

Dual Stack MBGP Connection

This next exercise configures separate IPv4 and IPv6 BGP sessions for the IPv4 and IPv6 routes to be advertised. For this exercise, you use the connection between Idaho and Wyoming in Figure 6-4. Figure 6-7 details the interface addresses and the BGP sessions between the two routers, and Example 6-22 shows the MBGP configurations.

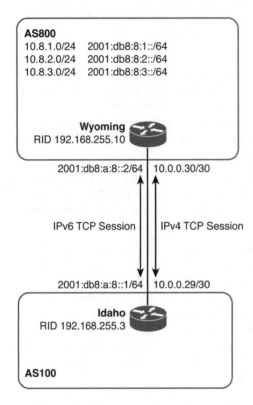

Figure 6-7 *Two MBGP Adjacencies Are Created Between Idaho and Wyoming, One over IPv4 and One over IPv6. IPv4 Prefixes Are Advertised over the IPv4 Adjacency, and IPv6 Prefixes Are Advertised over the IPv6 Adjacency*

The configurations, in address family format, should look familiar to you by now. The one point of interest is the **no neighbor 2001:db8:a:8::1 activate** statement under the IPv4 address family. This is, again, an artifact of the days when IPv4 was the only address family supported for BGP. When you configure the **neighbor remote-as** statements globally, IOS automatically enters the IPv4 **neighbor activate** statement under the IPv4 address family configuration and enters a **no neighbor activate** statement for any neighbors of other address families. This does not happen for any other address family. Under the IPv6 family, you must specify the active neighbor, and if you enter a **no neighbor activate** statement for IPv4 neighbors under the IPv6 address family, the statement does not show up in the configuration. As long as you understand this default behavior and what causes it, the appearance of the **no neighbor activate** statement should not cause you any confusion.

Example 6-22   *Configurations of Routers Wyoming and Idaho in Figure 6-7, with Separate IPv4 and IPv6 Peering Sessions*

```
Wyoming:
router bgp 800
 bgp log-neighbor-changes
 neighbor 10.0.0.29 remote-as 100
 neighbor 2001:DB8:A:8::1 remote-as 100
 !
 address-family ipv4
 neighbor 10.0.0.29 activate
 no neighbor 2001:DB8:A:8::1 activate
 no auto-summary
 no synchronization
 network 10.8.1.0 mask 255.255.255.0
 network 10.8.2.0 mask 255.255.255.0
 network 10.8.3.0 mask 255.255.255.0
 exit-address-family
 !
 address-family ipv6
 neighbor 2001:DB8:A:8::1 activate
 network 2001:DB8:8:1::/64
 network 2001:DB8:8:2::/64
 network 2001:DB8:8:3::/64
 exit-address-family
!
```

```
Idaho:
router bgp 100
 bgp log-neighbor-changes
 neighbor 10.0.0.30 remote-as 800
 neighbor 2001:DB8:A:8::2 remote-as 800
 !
 address-family ipv4
 neighbor 10.0.0.30 activate
 no neighbor 2001:DB8:A:8::2 activate
 no auto-summary
 no synchronization
 exit-address-family
 !
```

```
address-family ipv6
neighbor 2001:DB8:A:8::2 activate
exit-address-family
!
```

The most important point about this configuration is that it is straightforward. Simple **network** statements are the only requirement at Wyoming to inject IPv4 prefixes under the IPv4 family and IPv6 prefixes under the IPv6 family. No policy is needed to tinker with next-hop addresses.

Example 6-23 uses the **show bgp all summary** to display the important information about both the IPv4 and the IPv6 adjacencies created by the configuration. (If you want to look at the adjacency of a single address family, rather than all address families, with this command you can, by replacing the **all** keyword with the name of the address family.)

Example 6-23   show bgp all summary *Displays a Summary of the Important Information About All Address Family Adjacencies Formed Between Idaho and Wyoming*

```
Wyoming#show bgp all summary
For address family: IPv4 Unicast
BGP router identifier 192.168.255.10, local AS number 800
BGP table version is 4, main routing table version 4
3 network entries using 360 bytes of memory
3 path entries using 156 bytes of memory
2/1 BGP path/bestpath attribute entries using 248 bytes of memory
0 BGP route-map cache entries using 0 bytes of memory
0 BGP filter-list cache entries using 0 bytes of memory
Bitfield cache entries: current 1 (at peak 1) using 32 bytes of memory
BGP using 796 total bytes of memory
BGP activity 6/0 prefixes, 6/0 paths, scan interval 60 secs


Neighbor        V    AS MsgRcvd MsgSent   TblVer  InQ OutQ Up/Down  State/PfxRcd
10.0.0.29       4   100     705     706        4    0    0 11:41:29            0


For address family: IPv6 Unicast
BGP router identifier 192.168.255.10, local AS number 800
BGP table version is 4, main routing table version 4
3 network entries using 456 bytes of memory
3 path entries using 228 bytes of memory
2/1 BGP path/bestpath attribute entries using 248 bytes of memory
0 BGP route-map cache entries using 0 bytes of memory
0 BGP filter-list cache entries using 0 bytes of memory
Bitfield cache entries: current 1 (at peak 1) using 32 bytes of memory
BGP using 964 total bytes of memory
```

```
BGP activity 6/0 prefixes, 6/0 paths, scan interval 60 secs

Neighbor        V    AS MsgRcvd MsgSent   TblVer   InQ OutQ Up/Down  State/PfxRcd
2001:DB8:A:8::1 4    100    704    706        4     0    0 11:40:53            0
Wyoming#
```

Example 6-24 displays all prefixes for all address families received at Idaho. Here the
show bgp all command, without the **summary** keyword, is used. Again, if you are interested in the prefixes of only one address family, you can specify that in place of the **all**
keyword.

Example 6-24 *All Prefixes in Idaho's BGP Tables Display by Address Family Using the*
show bgp all *Command*

```
Idaho#show bgp all
For address family: IPv4 Unicast
BGP table version is 4, local router ID is 192.168.255.3
Status codes: s suppressed, d damped, h history, * valid, > best, i - internal,
              r RIB-failure, S Stale
Origin codes: i - IGP, e - EGP, ? - incomplete

   Network          Next Hop          Metric LocPrf Weight Path
*> 10.8.1.0/24      10.0.0.30              0             0 800 i
*> 10.8.2.0/24      10.0.0.30              0             0 800 i
*> 10.8.3.0/24      10.0.0.30              0             0 800 i


For address family: IPv6 Unicast
BGP table version is 4, local router ID is 192.168.255.3
Status codes: s suppressed, d damped, h history, * valid, > best, i - internal,
              r RIB-failure, S Stale
Origin codes: i - IGP, e - EGP, ? - incomplete

   Network          Next Hop          Metric LocPrf Weight Path
*> 2001:DB8:8:1::/64
                    2001:DB8:A:8::2        0             0 800 i
*> 2001:DB8:8:2::/64
                    2001:DB8:A:8::2        0             0 800 i
*> 2001:DB8:8:3::/64
                    2001:DB8:A:8::2        0             0 800 i
Idaho#
```

Finally, Example 6-25 shows the IPv4 and IPv6 routing tables at Idaho. You can see that
all three of the IPv4 prefixes and all three of the IPv6 prefixes received from Wyoming
have been installed in their appropriate address family routing table. The one feature of

note in these outputs is that the IPv6 routes are shown reachable via the link-local IPv6 address of Wyoming's peering interface (see Example 6-26) rather than the global IPv6 address. The BGP tables shown in Example 6-24 use the global IPv6 address as the next hop, but the routing tables reference the link-local address of the interface. Recall from the discussion earlier in this chapter that a BGP IPv6 update includes both the global address and the link-local address in its next-hop field.

Example 6-25   *Idaho's IPv4 and IPv6 Routing Tables Displayed*

```
Idaho#show ip route
Codes: C - connected, S - static, R - RIP, M - mobile, B - BGP
       D - EIGRP, EX - EIGRP external, O - OSPF, IA - OSPF inter area
       N1 - OSPF NSSA external type 1, N2 - OSPF NSSA external type 2
       E1 - OSPF external type 1, E2 - OSPF external type 2
       i - IS-IS, su - IS-IS summary, L1 - IS-IS level-1, L2 - IS-IS level-2
       ia - IS-IS inter area, * - candidate default, U - per-user static route
       o - ODR, P - periodic downloaded static route


Gateway of last resort is not set

     10.0.0.0/8 is variably subnetted, 7 subnets, 2 masks
B       10.8.2.0/24 [20/0] via 10.0.0.30, 00:03:48
B       10.8.3.0/24 [20/0] via 10.0.0.30, 00:03:48
B       10.8.1.0/24 [20/0] via 10.0.0.30, 00:03:48
C       10.0.0.28/30 is directly connected, Serial1/3
     192.168.255.0/32 is subnetted, 1 subnets
C       192.168.255.3 is directly connected, Loopback0
Idaho#
Idaho#show ipv6 route
IPv6 Routing Table - 6 entries
Codes: C - Connected, L - Local, S - Static, R - RIP, B - BGP
       U - Per-user Static route, M - MIPv6
       I1 - ISIS L1, I2 - ISIS L2, IA - ISIS interarea, IS - ISIS summary
       O - OSPF intra, OI - OSPF inter, OE1 - OSPF ext 1, OE2 - OSPF ext 2
       ON1 - OSPF NSSA ext 1, ON2 - OSPF NSSA ext 2
       D - EIGRP, EX - EIGRP external
B    2001:DB8:8:1::/64 [20/0]
      via FE80::C809:23FF:FE07:0, Serial1/3
B    2001:DB8:8:2::/64 [20/0]
      via FE80::C809:23FF:FE07:0, Serial1/3
B    2001:DB8:8:3::/64 [20/0]
      via FE80::C809:23FF:FE07:0, Serial1/3
C    2001:DB8:A:8::/64 [0/0]
      via ::, Serial1/3
L    2001:DB8:A:8::1/128 [0/0]
```

```
     via ::, Serial1/3
L   FF00::/8 [0/0]
     via ::, Null0
Idaho#
```

Example 6-26 show ipv6 interface *Command Displays Both the Link-Local Address and the Global Address of the Interface, Along with Other Important Information*

```
Wyoming#show ipv6 int s1/0
Serial1/0 is up, line protocol is up
  IPv6 is enabled, link-local address is FE80::C809:23FF:FE07:0
  No Virtual link-local address(es):
  Global unicast address(es):
    2001:DB8:A:8::2, subnet is 2001:DB8:A:8::/64
  Joined group address(es):
    FF02::1
    FF02::2
    FF02::1:FF00:2
    FF02::1:FF07:0
  MTU is 1500 bytes
  ICMP error messages limited to one every 100 milliseconds
  ICMP redirects are enabled
  ICMP unreachables are sent
  ND DAD is enabled, number of DAD attempts: 1
  ND reachable time is 30000 milliseconds
  Hosts use stateless autoconfig for addresses.
Wyoming#
```

The dual-session configuration demonstrated in this section is used in practice far more commonly than either the IPv4-only or IPv6-only sessions demonstrated previously. They are simpler and allow more separation of control between IPv4 and IPv6. The only potential drawback is that they double the number of BGP sessions maintained by the router. In most cases this does not matter, but in a case in which a router connects to large numbers of neighbors, this doubling could present a scaling problem.

Multihop Dual Stack MBGP Connection

Figure 6-8 details the connection between Idaho and Montana in Figure 6-4. A dual stack connection is again used, but in this example, the link between the routers is unnumbered for both IPv4 and IPv6.

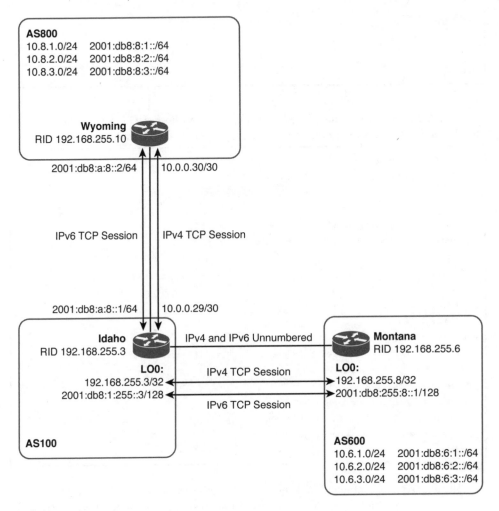

Figure 6-8 *Two MBGP Adjacencies Are Created Between the Loopback Interfaces of Idaho and Montana*

Example 6-27 shows Idaho's configuration, continued from the previous section, with Montana added. The IPv4 and IPv6 address configuration for Loopback0 is shown, as is the IPv4 and IPv6 unnumbered configuration for the Serial interface connecting Montana. Montana's configuration is easily deduced from this one.

Example 6-27 *Idaho's Configuration, Adding the Dual Stack MBGP Configuration to Montana in Figure 6-8*

```
interface Loopback0
 ip address 192.168.255.3 255.255.255.255
 ipv6 address 2001:DB8:1:255::3/128
!
```

```
interface Serial1/2
 ip unnumbered Loopback0
 ipv6 unnumbered Loopback0
!
router bgp 100
 bgp log-neighbor-changes
 neighbor 10.0.0.30 remote-as 800
 neighbor 2001:DB8:A:8::2 remote-as 800
 neighbor 2001:DB8:255:8::1 remote-as 600
 neighbor 2001:DB8:255:8::1 ebgp-multihop 2
 neighbor 2001:DB8:255:8::1 update-source Loopback0
 neighbor 192.168.255.8 remote-as 600
 neighbor 192.168.255.8 ebgp-multihop 2
 neighbor 192.168.255.8 update-source Loopback0
 !
 address-family ipv4
 neighbor 10.0.0.30 activate
 no neighbor 2001:DB8:A:8::2 activate
 no neighbor 2001:DB8:255:8::1 activate
 neighbor 192.168.255.8 activate
 no auto-summary
 no synchronization
 exit-address-family
 !
 address-family ipv6
 neighbor 2001:DB8:A:8::2 activate
 neighbor 2001:DB8:255:8::1 activate
 exit-address-family
!
ip route 192.168.255.8 255.255.255.255 Serial1/2
!
ipv6 route 2001:DB8:255:8::1/128 Serial1/2
!
```

You have seen a similar configuration before, in Chapter 2. In addition to the **neighbor ebgp-multihop** statement, a **neighbor update-source** statement is needed for both IPv4 and IPv6 to indicate that the BGP session originates from the loopback interface rather than from the physical outgoing interface. And notice the two static routes at the end of the configuration: Because the BGP endpoints are not directly connected, the router must have another way to find the neighbor addresses.

You can see from the example that configuring EBGP multihop requires all the same elements as IPv4. The more important aspect of this example is observing where the statements appear in an MBGP configuration. Statements having to do with the neighbor session itself—such as remote AS, multihop specification, and update source—appear globally in the BGP configuration. Whether the session is over IPv4 or IPv6 is a global specification because both address families can be advertised over any session. Statements having to do with a specific address family—such as the neighbor session to activate for advertising routes belonging to the address family, address family prefixes to inject into BGP, and incoming or outgoing policies applying to the family—are entered under the address family portion of the BGP configuration.

Mixed IPv4 and IPv6 Sessions

The use of Colorado's connections to three different autonomous systems (see Figure 6-9) emphasize the placement of MBGP configuration statements. AS200 has only IPv4 prefixes to advertise, so only an IPv4 BGP session will be configured there. AS300 has both IPv4 and IPv6 prefixes, so both an IPv4 and an IPv6 MBGP session are configured. AS400 has only IPv6 prefixes, so only an IPv6 MBGP session will be configured.

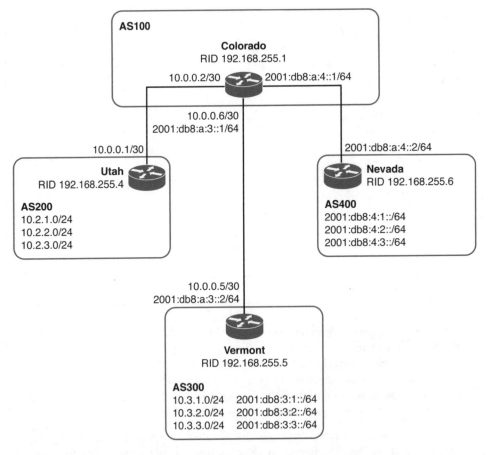

Figure 6-9 *Three Routers Connected to Colorado Have Mixed Requirements for MBGP Sessions*

The point of this exercise is to see how the various neighbor statements defining a session are distributed within the MBGP configuration. There's nothing in Vermont's configuration, in Example 6-28, that you haven't seen already in this chapter, except for the addition of password authentication. Session information for the neighbors goes in the global part of the BGP configuration, whereas what networks to advertise and what neighbor session to advertise them over goes in the address family specific part.

Example 6-28 *Vermont's Configuration in Figure 6-9*

```
router bgp 300
 bgp log-neighbor-changes
 neighbor 10.0.0.6 remote-as 100
 neighbor 10.0.0.6 password 7 0508050624
 neighbor 2001:DB8:A:3::1 remote-as 100
 neighbor 2001:DB8:A:3::1 password 7 0458080F0A
 !
 address-family ipv4
 neighbor 10.0.0.6 activate
 no neighbor 2001:DB8:A:3::1 activate
 no auto-summary
 no synchronization
 network 10.3.1.0 mask 255.255.255.0
 network 10.3.2.0 mask 255.255.255.0
 network 10.3.3.0 mask 255.255.255.0
 exit-address-family
 !
 address-family ipv6
 neighbor 2001:DB8:A:3::1 activate
 network 2001:DB8:3:1::/64
 network 2001:DB8:3:2::/64
 network 2001:DB8:3:3::/64
 exit-address-family
 !
```

Utah's configuration in Example 6-29 is also unremarkable. This router advertises only IPv4 routes and looks different from traditional IPv4 BGP configurations only in its newer address family format.

Example 6-29 *Utah's Configuration in Figure 6-9*

```
router bgp 200
 bgp log-neighbor-changes
 neighbor 10.0.0.2 remote-as 100
 neighbor 10.0.0.2 password 7 104D0A1000
 !
```

```
address-family ipv4
neighbor 10.0.0.2 activate
no auto-summary
no synchronization
network 10.2.1.0 mask 255.255.255.0
network 10.2.2.0 mask 255.255.255.0
network 10.2.3.0 mask 255.255.255.0
exit-address-family
!
```

Nevada's configuration in Example 6-30 does have an interesting part. Like Utah, Nevada is advertising only one address family, but this time it's IPv6. Notice, however, that a configuration for the IPv4 address family still appears in the configuration even though it is not used. Actually, you can issue a **no address-family ipv4** command, but that section still won't go away. This is, again, an artifact of legacy BGP in which only IPv4 was supported—when you enable BGP, the IPv4 address family is automatically enabled. Even though you don't use it, the configuration section is still there. There are no IPv4 prefixes to advertise in AS400, and there are no IPv4 addresses on the interfaces connecting Nevada and Colorado, so the address-family IPv4 configuration segment can be ignored.

Example 6-30 *Nevada's Configuration in Figure 6-9*

```
router bgp 400
 bgp log-neighbor-changes
 neighbor 2001:DB8:A:4::1 remote-as 100
 neighbor 2001:DB8:A:4::1 password 7 1511080501
 !
 address-family ipv4
 no neighbor 2001:DB8:A:4::1 activate
 no auto-summary
 no synchronization
 exit-address-family
 !
 address-family ipv6
 neighbor 2001:DB8:A:4::1 activate
 network 2001:DB8:4:1::/64
 network 2001:DB8:4:2::/64
 network 2001:DB8:4:3::/64
 exit-address-family
 !
```

The real point of interest in Figure 6-9 is the configuration of Colorado, as shown in Example 6-31. There are three connected neighbors and four peering sessions (two IPv4 and two IPv6) so a bit more attention must be paid to what neighbors are activated for which address family. The global portion is also getting lengthier as a password is configured for each of the four neighbors. By looking at the overall network topology in Figure 6-4, you know that IBGP needs to be added to connect the three core routers in AS100. Session and policy templates start becoming useful as the MBGP configuration grows more complex.

Example 6-31   *Colorado's Configuration in Figure 6-9*

```
router bgp 100
 bgp log-neighbor-changes
 neighbor 10.0.0.1 remote-as 200
 neighbor 10.0.0.1 password 7 1511080501
 neighbor 10.0.0.5 remote-as 300
 neighbor 10.0.0.5 password 7 1414110209
 neighbor 2001:DB8:A:3::2 remote-as 300
 neighbor 2001:DB8:A:3::2 password 7 0007100F01
 neighbor 2001:DB8:A:4::2 remote-as 400
 neighbor 2001:DB8:A:4::2 password 7 070C22454B
 !
 address-family ipv4
 neighbor 10.0.0.1 activate
 neighbor 10.0.0.5 activate
 no neighbor 2001:DB8:A:3::2 activate
 no neighbor 2001:DB8:A:4::2 activate
 no auto-summary
 no synchronization
 exit-address-family
 !
 address-family ipv6
 neighbor 2001:DB8:A:3::2 activate
 neighbor 2001:DB8:A:4::2 activate
 exit-address-family
 !
```

Before adding IBGP and templates for AS100, you need to verify that the EBGP configurations for Figure 6-9 work correctly. Example 6-32 uses the **show ip route bgp** and the **show ipv6 route bgp** commands to display only the BGP entries in the IPv4 and IPv6 routing tables. The displays show that Colorado has received all routes from AS200, AS300, and AS400 and has entered them into its routing tables.

Example 6-32   *BGP Entries in Colorado's IPv4 and IPv6 Routing Tables Show That the
EBGP Configurations Are Correct*

```
Colorado#show ip route bgp
     10.0.0.0/8 is variably subnetted, 12 subnets, 2 masks
B       10.3.1.0/24 [20/0] via 10.0.0.5, 09:36:44
B       10.2.1.0/24 [20/0] via 10.0.0.1, 09:37:26
B       10.3.3.0/24 [20/0] via 10.0.0.5, 09:36:44
B       10.2.2.0/24 [20/0] via 10.0.0.1, 09:37:26
B       10.3.2.0/24 [20/0] via 10.0.0.5, 09:36:44
B       10.2.3.0/24 [20/0] via 10.0.0.1, 09:37:26
Colorado#
Colorado#show ipv6 route bgp
IPv6 Routing Table - 11 entries
Codes: C - Connected, L - Local, S - Static, R - RIP, B - BGP
       U - Per-user Static route, M - MIPv6
       I1 - ISIS L1, I2 - ISIS L2, IA - ISIS interarea, IS - ISIS summary
       O - OSPF intra, OI - OSPF inter, OE1 - OSPF ext 1, OE2 - OSPF ext 2
       ON1 - OSPF NSSA ext 1, ON2 - OSPF NSSA ext 2
       D - EIGRP, EX - EIGRP external
B    2001:DB8:3:1::/64 [20/0]
     via FE80::C804:23FF:FE07:0, Serial1/1
B    2001:DB8:3:2::/64 [20/0]
     via FE80::C804:23FF:FE07:0, Serial1/1
B    2001:DB8:3:3::/64 [20/0]
     via FE80::C804:23FF:FE07:0, Serial1/1
B    2001:DB8:4:1::/64 [20/0]
     via FE80::C805:23FF:FE07:0, Serial1/2
B    2001:DB8:4:2::/64 [20/0]
     via FE80::C805:23FF:FE07:0, Serial1/2
B    2001:DB8:4:3::/64 [20/0]
     via FE80::C805:23FF:FE07:0, Serial1/2
Colorado#
```

Multiprotocol IBGP

The last step in fully configuring MBGP in the network of Figure 6-4 is to enable IBGP
in AS100. You have done this multiple times in previous chapters, and coupled with the
Multiprotocol EBGP configurations already enabled in this chapter, there should be
nothing unexpected about Multiprotocol IBGP.

Figure 6-10 details the links and addresses used in AS100. You have already seen that
separate IPv4 and IPv6 sessions are usually the best approach to EBGP, and the same
holds true for IBGP. You also know that when multiple paths exist between routers

within an AS, as in Figure 6-10, BGP sessions are best configured between loopback interfaces rather than physical interfaces. These practices are used in this example.

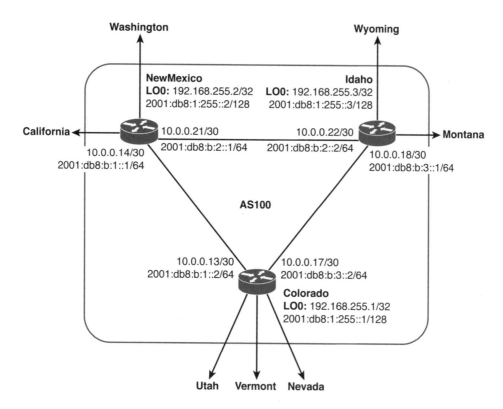

Figure 6-10   *Addresses Used Within AS100*

To begin, each router in AS100 must know how to reach all the IPv4 and IPv6 interface addresses internal to the autonomous system, including the loopback addresses. In this exercise, OSPF is used as the IGP to ensure that reachability. Because both IPv4 and IPv6 addresses must be advertised, both OSPFv2 and OSPFv3 are used. (Both OSPF versions are covered in Volume I.) Example 6-33 shows the interface and OSPF configurations at Colorado; the configurations of NewMexico and Idaho are similar.

Note   As of IOS 15.1 or 15.2 you can configure both IPv4 and IPv6 address families under OSPFv3, eliminating the need to run two versions of OSPF to support both versions of IP. The example here uses an IOS 12.4 release and must use both OSPFv2 and OSPFv3.

Example 6-33   *Interface and OSPF Configurations at Colorado for Support of MIBGP*

```
!
ipv6 unicast-routing
!
interface Loopback0
 ip address 192.168.255.1 255.255.255.255
 ipv6 address 2001:DB8:1:255::1/128
 ipv6 ospf 1 area 0
!
interface Serial1/3
 ip address 10.0.0.13 255.255.255.252
 ipv6 address 2001:DB8:B:1::2/64
 ipv6 ospf 1 area 0
!
interface Serial1/4
 ip address 10.0.0.17 255.255.255.252
 ipv6 address 2001:DB8:B:3::2/64
 ipv6 ospf 1 area 0
!
router ospf 1
 log-adjacency-changes
 network 10.0.0.13 0.0.0.0 area 0
 network 10.0.0.17 0.0.0.0 area 0
 network 192.168.255.1 0.0.0.0 area 0
!
ipv6 router ospf 1
 log-adjacency-changes
!
```

Example 6-34 shows that Colorado's OSPF adjacencies are up and that it has created entries in Colorado's IPv4 and IPv6 routing tables for the loopback addresses the router needs to reach to establish its IBGP sessions.

Example 6-34   *Colorado's Routing Tables Show That the Loopback Addresses Necessary for IPv4 and IPv6 IBGP Peering Are Reachable*

```
Colorado#show ip ospf neighbor

Neighbor ID     Pri   State        Dead Time   Address        Interface
192.168.255.3     0   FULL/  -     00:00:34    10.0.0.18      Serial1/4
192.168.255.2     0   FULL/  -     00:00:33    10.0.0.14      Serial1/3
Colorado#
Colorado#show ipv6 ospf neighbor
```

```
Neighbor ID      Pri   State         Dead Time   Interface ID    Interface
192.168.255.3     1    FULL/  -      00:00:34     6              Serial1/4
192.168.255.2     1    FULL/  -      00:00:34     5              Serial1/3
Colorado#
Colorado#show ip route ospf
     10.0.0.0/8 is variably subnetted, 12 subnets, 2 masks
O       10.0.0.20/30 [110/128] via 10.0.0.18, 02:48:52, Serial1/4
                     [110/128] via 10.0.0.14, 02:48:52, Serial1/3
     192.168.255.0/32 is subnetted, 5 subnets
O       192.168.255.3 [110/65] via 10.0.0.18, 02:48:52, Serial1/4
O       192.168.255.2 [110/65] via 10.0.0.14, 02:48:52, Serial1/3
Colorado#
Colorado#show ipv6 route ospf
IPv6 Routing Table - 20 entries
Codes: C - Connected, L - Local, S - Static, R - RIP, B - BGP
       U - Per-user Static route, M - MIPv6
       I1 - ISIS L1, I2 - ISIS L2, IA - ISIS interarea, IS - ISIS summary
       O - OSPF intra, OI - OSPF inter, OE1 - OSPF ext 1, OE2 - OSPF ext 2
       ON1 - OSPF NSSA ext 1, ON2 - OSPF NSSA ext 2
       D - EIGRP, EX - EIGRP external
O   2001:DB8:1:255::2/128 [110/64]
      via FE80::C801:23FF:FE07:0, Serial1/3
O   2001:DB8:1:255::3/128 [110/64]
      via FE80::C802:23FF:FE07:0, Serial1/4
O   2001:DB8:B:2::/64 [110/128]
      via FE80::C801:23FF:FE07:0, Serial1/3
      via FE80::C802:23FF:FE07:0, Serial1/4
O   2001:DB8:1:255::3/128 [110/64]
      via FE80::C802:23FF:FE07:0, Serial1/4
Colorado#
```

Example 6-35 shows Colorado's MBGP configuration with IBGP added. Other than the addresses themselves, each IPv4 and IPv6 IBGP adjacency is configured the same:

- The **neighbor remote-as** statement references the same ASN (AS100) as the local router, making the session IBGP. The referenced address is on the peer's loopback interface.

- The **neighbor update-source** statement tells the router to originate the TCP session from its loopback interface instead of the outgoing physical interface.

- The **neighbor password** statement increases the security of the adjacency.

- The **neighbor next-hop-self** statement tells the router to change the next-hop address of routes advertised to its own address. Recall that by default the next-hop address of a route learned from an external peer is not changed when the route is advertised to an internal peer. So AS-internal BGP routers must either know how to reach the external next-hop addresses (usually accomplished by running the IGP passively on the external links) or change the default behavior with a next-hop-self policy, as done here.

Example 6-35   *Colorado's MBGP Configuration, with the Added Statements to Enable IBGP within AS100*

```
router bgp 100
 bgp log-neighbor-changes
 neighbor 10.0.0.1 remote-as 200
 neighbor 10.0.0.1 password 7 1511080501
 neighbor 10.0.0.5 remote-as 300
 neighbor 10.0.0.5 password 7 1414110209
 neighbor 2001:DB8:1:255::2 remote-as 100
 neighbor 2001:DB8:1:255::2 password 7 06050C2849
 neighbor 2001:DB8:1:255::2 update-source Loopback0
 neighbor 2001:DB8:1:255::3 remote-as 100
 neighbor 2001:DB8:1:255::3 password 7 1511080501
 neighbor 2001:DB8:1:255::3 update-source Loopback0
 neighbor 2001:DB8:A:3::2 remote-as 300
 neighbor 2001:DB8:A:3::2 password 7 0007100F01
 neighbor 2001:DB8:A:4::2 remote-as 400
 neighbor 2001:DB8:A:4::2 password 7 070C22454B
 neighbor 192.168.255.2 remote-as 100
 neighbor 192.168.255.2 password 7 104D0A1000
 neighbor 192.168.255.2 update-source Loopback0
 neighbor 192.168.255.3 remote-as 100
 neighbor 192.168.255.3 password 7 06050C2849
 neighbor 192.168.255.3 update-source Loopback0
 !
 address-family ipv4
 neighbor 10.0.0.1 activate
 neighbor 10.0.0.5 activate
 no neighbor 2001:DB8:1:255::2 activate
 no neighbor 2001:DB8:1:255::3 activate
 no neighbor 2001:DB8:A:3::2 activate
 no neighbor 2001:DB8:A:4::2 activate
 neighbor 192.168.255.2 activate
 neighbor 192.168.255.2 next-hop-self
 neighbor 192.168.255.3 activate
 neighbor 192.168.255.3 next-hop-self
 no auto-summary
 no synchronization
 exit-address-family
```

```
!
address-family ipv6
neighbor 2001:DB8:1:255::2 activate
neighbor 2001:DB8:1:255::2 next-hop-self
neighbor 2001:DB8:1:255::3 activate
neighbor 2001:DB8:1:255::3 next-hop-self
neighbor 2001:DB8:A:3::2 activate
neighbor 2001:DB8:A:4::2 activate
exit-address-family
!
```

An interesting detail in Colorado's configuration is that although all the other statements enabling an IBGP peering session appear in the global portion of the BGP configuration, the **neighbor next-hop-self** statement appears under the address family. Why does this particular neighbor statement appear under the address family configuration section, when the other neighbor statements are global?

NewMexico's BGP configuration after IBGP has been added (Example 6-36) provides a hint. Remember that this router's EBGP sessions required policies to advertise both IPv4 and IPv6 routes to California over an IPv4 session and to Washington over an IPv6 session. Notice that the route maps defining the policies are applied under the address family to which the policy is relevant. The **neighbor next-hop-self** statement also defines a policy because it changes a characteristic of a route. Notice that all the statements under an address family define policy in some way; they specify what session to use for advertising and receiving prefixes belonging to that address family, what prefixes to inject, and any modifications to make to those prefixes. The global BGP statements, however, all specify some characteristic of a BGP session: what AS the neighbor is located in, what password to use to secure the session, where to source the session from, or how many routers can be traversed to find the external neighbor.

Example 6-36 *NewMexico's BGP Configuration Shows That BGP Session Configuration Statements Are Entered Globally, Whereas Policy Statements Are Entered Under the Address Family Sections to Which the Policy Applies*

```
router bgp 100
 bgp log-neighbor-changes
 neighbor 10.0.0.38 remote-as 500
 neighbor 10.0.0.38 ebgp-multihop 2
 neighbor 2001:DB8:1:255::1 remote-as 100
 neighbor 2001:DB8:1:255::1 password 7 0110050D5E
 neighbor 2001:DB8:1:255::1 update-source Loopback0
 neighbor 2001:DB8:1:255::3 remote-as 100
 neighbor 2001:DB8:1:255::3 password 7 121A061E17
 neighbor 2001:DB8:1:255::3 update-source Loopback0
 neighbor 2001:DB8:A:7::2 remote-as 700
```

```
neighbor 192.168.255.1 remote-as 100
neighbor 192.168.255.1 password 7 0110050D5E
neighbor 192.168.255.1 update-source Loopback0
neighbor 192.168.255.3 remote-as 100
neighbor 192.168.255.3 password 7 0007100F01
neighbor 192.168.255.3 update-source Loopback0
!
address-family ipv4
neighbor 10.0.0.38 activate
no neighbor 2001:DB8:1:255::1 activate
no neighbor 2001:DB8:1:255::3 activate
neighbor 2001:DB8:A:7::2 activate
neighbor 2001:DB8:A:7::2 route-map v4-Routes-to-Washington out
neighbor 192.168.255.1 activate
neighbor 192.168.255.1 next-hop-self
neighbor 192.168.255.3 activate
neighbor 192.168.255.3 next-hop-self
no auto-summary
no synchronization
exit-address-family
!
address-family ipv6
neighbor 10.0.0.38 activate
neighbor 10.0.0.38 route-map v6-Routes-to-California out
neighbor 2001:DB8:1:255::1 activate
neighbor 2001:DB8:1:255::1 next-hop-self
neighbor 2001:DB8:1:255::3 activate
neighbor 2001:DB8:1:255::3 next-hop-self
neighbor 2001:DB8:A:7::2 activate
exit-address-family
!
```

Two simple rules, then, help you understand where a statement belongs within an MBGP configuration:

- *Session* configuration statements appear globally in the BGP configuration.

- *Policy* configuration statements appear under the address family section to which the policy applies.

These two working guidelines should put you in mind of session templates and policy templates from Chapter 5. Looking at Colorado's configuration in Example 6-35 or NewMexico's configuration in Example 6-36, with their repetitive statements for different neighbors, should also put you in mind of how templates can simplify a large BGP configuration.

Example 6-37 shows Colorado's BGP configuration rewritten with session templates. Peer-session AS100 applies to all Colorado's IBGP peers, and peer-session Customers applies to all three of Colorado's EBGP peers. Both of these session templates inherit peer-session Password, which defines a single password for all peers both internal and external. Actually, inheritance of peer-session Password is the only session configuration that peer-session Customers contains. Although the wisdom of using a single password for all internal and external peers is debatable, the object of this example is that although peer-session Customers does not save any configuration steps over just applying the **neighbor password** statement for each neighbor, it saves administrative time if you regularly change passwords in your network (which you should). By changing the password in a single place, under peer-session Password, you change the password for all Colorado's neighbors.

Example 6-37   *Colorado's BGP Configuration Rewritten to Use Session Templates*

```
router bgp 100
 template peer-session AS100
  remote-as 100
  update-source Loopback0
  inherit peer-session Password
 exit-peer-session
 !
 template peer-session Password
  password 7 020507520E
 exit-peer-session
 !
 template peer-session Customers
  inherit peer-session Password
 exit-peer-session
 !
 bgp log-neighbor-changes
 neighbor 10.0.0.1 remote-as 200
 neighbor 10.0.0.1 inherit peer-session Customers
 neighbor 10.0.0.5 remote-as 300
 neighbor 10.0.0.5 inherit peer-session Customers
 neighbor 2001:DB8:1:255::2 inherit peer-session AS100
 neighbor 2001:DB8:1:255::3 inherit peer-session AS100
 neighbor 2001:DB8:A:3::2 remote-as 300
 neighbor 2001:DB8:A:3::2 inherit peer-session Customers
 neighbor 2001:DB8:A:4::2 remote-as 400
 neighbor 2001:DB8:A:4::2 inherit peer-session Customers
 neighbor 192.168.255.2 inherit peer-session AS100
 neighbor 192.168.255.3 inherit peer-session AS100
 !
 address-family ipv4
```

```
neighbor 10.0.0.1 activate
neighbor 10.0.0.5 activate
no neighbor 2001:DB8:1:255::2 activate
no neighbor 2001:DB8:1:255::3 activate
no neighbor 2001:DB8:A:3::2 activate
no neighbor 2001:DB8:A:4::2 activate
neighbor 192.168.255.2 activate
neighbor 192.168.255.2 next-hop-self
neighbor 192.168.255.3 activate
neighbor 192.168.255.3 next-hop-self
no auto-summary
no synchronization
exit-address-family
!
address-family ipv6
neighbor 2001:DB8:1:255::2 activate
neighbor 2001:DB8:1:255::2 next-hop-self
neighbor 2001:DB8:1:255::3 activate
neighbor 2001:DB8:1:255::3 next-hop-self
neighbor 2001:DB8:A:3::2 activate
neighbor 2001:DB8:A:4::2 activate
exit-address-family
!
```

Spend a few minutes comparing the configuration in Example 6-37 with the one in Example 6-35. You should see that the two configurations are identical in their configured functions. You can also see that all the peer-session templates are applied to neighbors in the global part of the BGP configuration, in keeping with that only policies are applied in the address family parts.

Example 6-38 shows that all Colorado's configured peering sessions are established. Consulting Figure 6-4 earlier in the chapter, you can see that the counts for prefixes received match the number of prefixes you would expect each of Colorado's peers to advertise to it. A look at the routing tables at Washington and Vermont (Example 6-39) shows that the prefixes listed in Figure 6-4 are distributed throughout the network.

Example 6-38 *All Colorado's EBGP and IBGP Sessions Are Established*

```
Colorado#show bgp all summary
For address family: IPv4 Unicast
BGP router identifier 192.168.255.1, local AS number 100
BGP table version is 43, main routing table version 43
18 network entries using 2160 bytes of memory
18 path entries using 936 bytes of memory
8/6 BGP path/bestpath attribute entries using 992 bytes of memory
```

```
7 BGP AS-PATH entries using 168 bytes of memory
0 BGP route-map cache entries using 0 bytes of memory
0 BGP filter-list cache entries using 0 bytes of memory
Bitfield cache entries: current 3 (at peak 4) using 96 bytes of memory
BGP using 4352 total bytes of memory
BGP activity 54/18 prefixes, 66/30 paths, scan interval 60 secs

Neighbor          V    AS MsgRcvd MsgSent   TblVer   InQ OutQ Up/Down  State/PfxRcd
10.0.0.1          4   200    4171    4181       43    0    0 2d21h              3
10.0.0.5          4   300    4170    4181       43    0    0 2d21h              3
192.168.255.2     4   100     436     438       43    0    0 07:10:12           6
192.168.255.3     4   100     435     438       43    0    0 07:09:32           6


For address family: IPv6 Unicast
BGP router identifier 192.168.255.1, local AS number 100
BGP table version is 55, main routing table version 55
18 network entries using 2736 bytes of memory
18 path entries using 1368 bytes of memory
8/6 BGP path/bestpath attribute entries using 992 bytes of memory
7 BGP AS-PATH entries using 168 bytes of memory
0 BGP route-map cache entries using 0 bytes of memory
0 BGP filter-list cache entries using 0 bytes of memory
Bitfield cache entries: current 3 (at peak 4) using 96 bytes of memory
BGP using 5360 total bytes of memory
BGP activity 54/18 prefixes, 66/30 paths, scan interval 60 secs

Neighbor          V    AS MsgRcvd MsgSent   TblVer   InQ OutQ Up/Down  State/PfxRcd
2001:DB8:1:255::2
                  4   100     433     436       55    0    0 07:07:48           6
2001:DB8:1:255::3
                  4   100     433     435       55    0    0 07:07:41           6
2001:DB8:A:3::2   4   300    4183    4194       55    0    0 2d21h              3
2001:DB8:A:4::2   4   400    4183    4196       55    0    0 2d21h              3
Colorado#
```

Example 6-39 *IPv4 and IPv6 Unicast Routing Tables of Washington and Vermont Include Entries for All the Prefixes of Figure 6-4, Confirming That with the Addition of IBGP in AS100 All Prefixes Are Advertised to All Routers*

```
Washington#show ip route bgp
     10.0.0.0/8 is variably subnetted, 19 subnets, 2 masks
B       10.8.2.0/24 [20/0] via 10.0.0.33, 1d19h
B       10.8.3.0/24 [20/0] via 10.0.0.33, 1d19h
B       10.8.1.0/24 [20/0] via 10.0.0.33, 1d19h
```

```
B       10.3.1.0/24 [20/0] via 10.0.0.33, 09:18:53
B       10.2.1.0/24 [20/0] via 10.0.0.33, 09:18:53
B       10.3.3.0/24 [20/0] via 10.0.0.33, 09:18:53
B       10.2.2.0/24 [20/0] via 10.0.0.33, 09:18:53
B       10.3.2.0/24 [20/0] via 10.0.0.33, 09:18:53
B       10.2.3.0/24 [20/0] via 10.0.0.33, 09:18:53
B       10.5.3.0/24 [20/0] via 10.0.0.33, 3d01h
B       10.6.1.0/24 [20/0] via 10.0.0.33, 1d19h
B       10.5.2.0/24 [20/0] via 10.0.0.33, 3d01h
B       10.6.2.0/24 [20/0] via 10.0.0.33, 1d19h
B       10.5.1.0/24 [20/0] via 10.0.0.33, 3d01h
B       10.6.3.0/24 [20/0] via 10.0.0.33, 1d19h
Washington#
Washington#show ipv6 route bgp
IPv6 Routing Table - 21 entries
Codes: C - Connected, L - Local, S - Static, R - RIP, B - BGP
       U - Per-user Static route, M - MIPv6
       I1 - ISIS L1, I2 - ISIS L2, IA - ISIS interarea, IS - ISIS summary
       O - OSPF intra, OI - OSPF inter, OE1 - OSPF ext 1, OE2 - OSPF ext 2
       ON1 - OSPF NSSA ext 1, ON2 - OSPF NSSA ext 2
       D - EIGRP, EX - EIGRP external
B    2001:DB8:3:1::/64 [20/0]
     via FE80::C801:23FF:FE07:0, Serial1/0
B    2001:DB8:3:2::/64 [20/0]
     via FE80::C801:23FF:FE07:0, Serial1/0
B    2001:DB8:3:3::/64 [20/0]
     via FE80::C801:23FF:FE07:0, Serial1/0
B    2001:DB8:4:1::/64 [20/0]
     via FE80::C801:23FF:FE07:0, Serial1/0
B    2001:DB8:4:2::/64 [20/0]
     via FE80::C801:23FF:FE07:0, Serial1/0
B    2001:DB8:4:3::/64 [20/0]
     via FE80::C801:23FF:FE07:0, Serial1/0
B    2001:DB8:5:1::/64 [20/0]
     via FE80::C801:23FF:FE07:0, Serial1/0
B    2001:DB8:5:2::/64 [20/0]
     via FE80::C801:23FF:FE07:0, Serial1/0
B    2001:DB8:5:3::/64 [20/0]
     via FE80::C801:23FF:FE07:0, Serial1/0
B    2001:DB8:6:1::/64 [20/0]
     via FE80::C801:23FF:FE07:0, Serial1/0
B    2001:DB8:6:2::/64 [20/0]
     via FE80::C801:23FF:FE07:0, Serial1/0
```

```
B   2001:DB8:6:3::/64 [20/0]
     via FE80::C801:23FF:FE07:0, Serial1/0
B   2001:DB8:8:1::/64 [20/0]
     via FE80::C801:23FF:FE07:0, Serial1/0
B   2001:DB8:8:2::/64 [20/0]
     via FE80::C801:23FF:FE07:0, Serial1/0
B   2001:DB8:8:3::/64 [20/0]
     via FE80::C801:23FF:FE07:0, Serial1/0
Washington#
```

```
Vermont#show ip route bgp
     10.0.0.0/8 is variably subnetted, 19 subnets, 2 masks
B       10.8.2.0/24 [20/0] via 10.0.0.6, 09:35:18
B       10.8.3.0/24 [20/0] via 10.0.0.6, 09:35:18
B       10.8.1.0/24 [20/0] via 10.0.0.6, 09:35:18
B       10.2.1.0/24 [20/0] via 10.0.0.6, 2d23h
B       10.2.2.0/24 [20/0] via 10.0.0.6, 2d23h
B       10.2.3.0/24 [20/0] via 10.0.0.6, 2d23h
B       10.7.1.0/24 [20/0] via 10.0.0.6, 09:36:20
B       10.5.3.0/24 [20/0] via 10.0.0.6, 09:36:20
B       10.6.1.0/24 [20/0] via 10.0.0.6, 09:35:18
B       10.5.2.0/24 [20/0] via 10.0.0.6, 09:36:20
B       10.7.3.0/24 [20/0] via 10.0.0.6, 09:36:20
B       10.6.2.0/24 [20/0] via 10.0.0.6, 09:35:18
B       10.5.1.0/24 [20/0] via 10.0.0.6, 09:36:20
B       10.7.2.0/24 [20/0] via 10.0.0.6, 09:36:20
B       10.6.3.0/24 [20/0] via 10.0.0.6, 09:35:18
Vermont#
Vermont#show ipv6 route bgp
IPv6 Routing Table - 21 entries
Codes: C - Connected, L - Local, S - Static, R - RIP, B - BGP
       U - Per-user Static route, M - MIPv6
       I1 - ISIS L1, I2 - ISIS L2, IA - ISIS interarea, IS - ISIS summary
       O - OSPF intra, OI - OSPF inter, OE1 - OSPF ext 1, OE2 - OSPF ext 2
       ON1 - OSPF NSSA ext 1, ON2 - OSPF NSSA ext 2
       D - EIGRP, EX - EIGRP external
B   2001:DB8:4:1::/64 [20/0]
     via FE80::C800:23FF:FE07:0, Serial1/0
B   2001:DB8:4:2::/64 [20/0]
     via FE80::C800:23FF:FE07:0, Serial1/0
B   2001:DB8:4:3::/64 [20/0]
     via FE80::C800:23FF:FE07:0, Serial1/0
B   2001:DB8:5:1::/64 [20/0]
     via FE80::C800:23FF:FE07:0, Serial1/0
```

```
B    2001:DB8:5:2::/64 [20/0]
       via FE80::C800:23FF:FE07:0, Serial1/0
B    2001:DB8:5:3::/64 [20/0]
       via FE80::C800:23FF:FE07:0, Serial1/0
B    2001:DB8:6:1::/64 [20/0]
       via FE80::C800:23FF:FE07:0, Serial1/0
B    2001:DB8:6:2::/64 [20/0]
       via FE80::C800:23FF:FE07:0, Serial1/0
B    2001:DB8:6:3::/64 [20/0]
       via FE80::C800:23FF:FE07:0, Serial1/0
B    2001:DB8:7:1::/64 [20/0]
       via FE80::C800:23FF:FE07:0, Serial1/0
B    2001:DB8:7:2::/64 [20/0]
       via FE80::C800:23FF:FE07:0, Serial1/0
B    2001:DB8:7:3::/64 [20/0]
       via FE80::C800:23FF:FE07:0, Serial1/0
B    2001:DB8:8:1::/64 [20/0]
       via FE80::C800:23FF:FE07:0, Serial1/0
B    2001:DB8:8:2::/64 [20/0]
       via FE80::C800:23FF:FE07:0, Serial1/0
B    2001:DB8:8:3::/64 [20/0]
       via FE80::C800:23FF:FE07:0, Serial1/0
Vermont#
```

Case Study: Multiprotocol Policy Configuration

With the network of Figure 6-4 fully functional, and peer-session templates configured, a good next step is to add some policy examples. The objective of this section is not to examine the many policy options available to BGP (you learned that in Chapter 4, "BGP and Routing Policies," and Chapter 5), but instead to provide an example of applying policy in an MBGP configuration. The same policy options (prefix filtering, communities, LOCAL_PREF and MEDs, and so on) that are available to IPv4 unicast routes are also available to IPv6 unicast routes.

You have already used polices twice in this chapter, to change the next-hop addresses of some of the routes advertised by California and Washington. In this section, you add a few more.

Figure 6-11 shows the context for the new policies. The autonomous systems in the example network you have been working with are grouped according to their relationship to AS100: Each is a Customer AS, a Partner AS, or a Service Provider AS. Policies are applied to enforce the following rules:

- Customer AS300 receives all Partner and Service Provider prefixes (a "Premium Customer").

- Customers AS200 and AS400 receive only a default route ("Standard Customers").

- Service Providers receive all Customer prefixes.

- Service Providers receive Partner prefixes, but with prepended AS_PATH attributes (making AS100 a less preferred path to the Partner networks).

- Partners receive Service Provider prefixes, but with a MED of 20. (The assumption here is that Partners have their own service provider connections, not shown in Figure 6-11, and use AS100 for backup Internet access only.)

- Partners receive prefixes from Customer AS300 but not from AS200 or AS400. (Standard Customers do not have direct access to Partner services.)

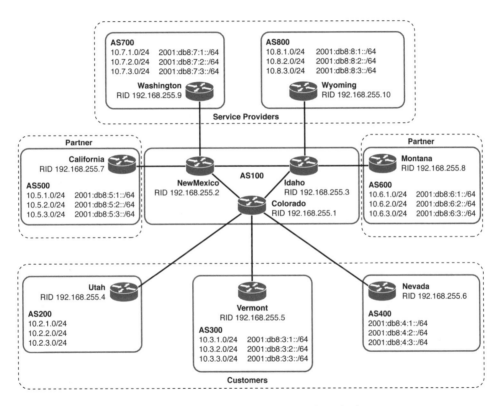

Figure 6-11 *AS100's Peer Autonomous Systems Are Classified as Customer, Partner, or Service Provider to Apply Policies to Their Routes*

The first step is to identify the prefixes to which each policy applies. Prefix filters can certainly be used; however, in this example, communities are a better approach for two reasons:

- The prefixes can be tagged with one or more community attributes at the point that they are advertised into AS100, preventing the repetitive configuration of lengthy prefix lists at every router where a policy must be applied.

- The policies defined here apply to all prefixes from an AS or group of autonomous systems. Assigning well-defined community attributes to all prefixes advertised from a given AS allows the autonomous systems to add or remove prefixes without AS100 having to modify its prefix lists.

Table 6-1 lists the community values to be used to enforce the inter-AS rules. The AA:NN format is used, with NN defining the customer type (10 for Standard Customer, 15 for Premium Customer, 20 for Partner, and 30 for Service Provider). The AA values are the ASNs that advertise the prefix. Although not used in the policies defined for this exercise, setting the AA value this way allows implementation of policies that distinguish prefixes by their originating AS, their peer type defined here, or a combination of both.

Table 6-1   *Community Values Used for This Exercise*

Peer AS	Type	Community
200	Standard Customer	200:10
400	Standard Customer	400:10
300	Premium Customer	300:15
500	Partner	500:20
600	Partner	600:20
700	Service Provider	700:30
800	Service Provider	800:30

Example 6-40 shows the addition of a policy at Colorado to add community attributes to the prefixes advertised by the three Customer autonomous systems. There appears to be quite a lot going on in this configuration, but it has been built step by step in previous exercises, and you should already be familiar with most of it. In keeping with the session templates used in Example 6-37, policy templates are used here. The **template peer-policy Customer** is defined at the top of the configuration and references **route-map Customers** as an incoming policy filter.

Notice where the Customers policy is applied: It is inherited by all neighbors belonging to a Customer AS, whether the neighbor address is IPv4 or IPv6. And because it is a policy, it is applied under the address-family sections rather than to the session-specific global section of the BGP configuration. Again, notice that the single call to a route-map could be applied to each neighbor instead of configuring it under a policy template and then adding a **neighbor inherit peer-policy Customer** for each relevant neighbor. But doing so is both consistent with the session template configuration already used and allows additional policies to be added to the same template later, if needed.

Example 6-40 *Colorado's Configuration Is Modified to Add Community Attributes to Prefixes Advertised from Customers*

```
router bgp 100
 template peer-policy Customer
  route-map Customers in
 exit-peer-policy
 !
 template peer-policy AS100
  next-hop-self
  send-community
 exit-peer-policy
 !
 template peer-session AS100
  remote-as 100
  update-source Loopback0
  inherit peer-session Password
 exit-peer-session
 !
 template peer-session Password
  password 7 020507520E
 exit-peer-session
 !
 template peer-session Customers
  inherit peer-session Password
 exit-peer-session
 !
 bgp log-neighbor-changes
 neighbor 10.0.0.1 remote-as 200
 neighbor 10.0.0.1 inherit peer-session Customers
 neighbor 10.0.0.5 remote-as 300
 neighbor 10.0.0.5 inherit peer-session Customers
 neighbor 2001:DB8:1:255::2 inherit peer-session AS100
 neighbor 2001:DB8:1:255::3 inherit peer-session AS100
 neighbor 2001:DB8:A:3::2 remote-as 300
 neighbor 2001:DB8:A:3::2 inherit peer-session Customers
 neighbor 2001:DB8:A:4::2 remote-as 400
 neighbor 2001:DB8:A:4::2 inherit peer-session Customers
 neighbor 192.168.255.2 inherit peer-session AS100
 neighbor 192.168.255.3 inherit peer-session AS100
 !
 address-family ipv4
 neighbor 10.0.0.1 activate
 neighbor 10.0.0.1 inherit peer-policy Customer
 neighbor 10.0.0.5 activate
```

```
 neighbor 10.0.0.5 inherit peer-policy Customer
 no neighbor 2001:DB8:1:255::2 activate
 no neighbor 2001:DB8:1:255::3 activate
 no neighbor 2001:DB8:A:3::2 activate
 no neighbor 2001:DB8:A:4::2 activate
 neighbor 192.168.255.2 activate
 neighbor 192.168.255.2 inherit peer-policy AS100
 neighbor 192.168.255.3 activate
 neighbor 192.168.255.3 inherit peer-policy AS100
 no auto-summary
 no synchronization
 exit-address-family
 !
 address-family ipv6
 neighbor 2001:DB8:1:255::2 activate
 neighbor 2001:DB8:1:255::2 inherit peer-policy AS100
 neighbor 2001:DB8:1:255::3 activate
 neighbor 2001:DB8:1:255::3 inherit peer-policy AS100
 neighbor 2001:DB8:A:3::2 activate
 neighbor 2001:DB8:A:3::2 inherit peer-policy Customer
 neighbor 2001:DB8:A:4::2 activate
 neighbor 2001:DB8:A:4::2 inherit peer-policy Customer
 exit-address-family
!
ip bgp-community new-format
!
ip prefix-list AS_200 seq 5 permit 10.2.0.0/16 le 24
!
ip prefix-list AS_300 seq 5 permit 10.3.0.0/16 le 24
!
ip prefix-list NULL seq 5 deny 0.0.0.0/0
!
ipv6 prefix-list AS_300 seq 5 permit 2001:DB8:3::/48 le 64
!
ipv6 prefix-list AS_400 seq 5 permit 2001:DB8:4::/48 le 64
!
ipv6 prefix-list NULL seq 5 deny ::/0
!
route-map Customers permit 10
 match ip address prefix-list
 match ipv6 address prefix-list NULL
 set community 200:10
!
```

```
route-map Customers permit 20
 match ip address prefix-list AS_300
 match ipv6 address prefix-list AS_300
 set community 300:15
!
route-map Customers permit 30
 match ip address prefix-list NULL
 match ipv6 address prefix-list AS_400
 set community 400:10
!
```

The route map referenced in the policy template is named Customers and can be observed at the end of Example 6-40's configuration. There are three sequences, corresponding to the three Customer Autonomous systems, and each sequence has an IPv4 match condition and an IPv6 match condition referencing a prefix-list. Community attributes are set for matching prefixes according to the values referred to in Table 6-1.

You must take care with the construction of this route-map because it is used on both IPv4 and IPv6 neighbors and uses match conditions for both IPv4 and IPv6 prefixes. It might seem unusual, for example, that there is an IPv6 match condition in sequence 10, when there are no IPv6 prefixes advertised by AS200. Further, the IPv6 prefix-list referenced (named NULL) merely denies all IPv6 prefixes. The opposite situation exists in sequence 30, which applies to AS400. There are no IPv4 prefixes in that AS, but the route map references a prefix list (again named NULL) that denies all IPv4 prefixes.

It makes sense, however, if you think about sequential processing of route maps. Because both IPv4 and IPv6 routes are filtered through the same sequence, you must be careful that each prefix hits the right match condition. In this configuration, the following happens:

- All the IPv4 prefixes in AS200 match the IPv4 prefix list in sequence 10 and are given a community value of 200:10.

- None of the IPv4 prefixes from AS300 match the IPv4 prefix list of sequence 10, so they drop to sequence 20 where they match the IPv4 prefix list there and are given community 300:15.

- The IPv6 prefixes from AS300 first go through sequence 10, where the NULL prefix list denies a match there. (Without this match condition the IPv6 routes would match a default permit any at this sequence.) The prefixes drop to sequence 20 where they match the IPv6 prefix list and are given a community of 300:15.

- The IPv6 prefixes of AS400 drop through sequence 10 because of the deny-all in IPv6 prefix-list NULL. They do not match the IPv6 prefix list of sequence 20, and drop to the IPv6 prefix list in sequence 30 where they are matched and given the community value of 400:10.

- The IPv4 prefix list NULL in sequence 30 has no effect on any route but is included for consistency of the configuration and aid for readers in understanding the actions of the IPv4 and IPv6 prefix lists at each sequence.

A last detail to notice is that a policy template named AS100 is created and is inherited by all IPv4 and IPv6 internal peers. Like policy Customer, it is applied in the address-family sections of the configuration. This policy adds the **send-community** statement to tell BGP to include the community attribute when advertising routes to the relevant neighbors. Comparing Example 6-40 with Colorado's previous MBGP configuration in Example 6-37, you can see that the **neighbor next-hop-self** statement has been removed from the IBGP neighbors under the address-family sections, and the **next-hop-self** statement has been added to policy template AS100. The effect is the same, we have just consolidated the policy statement into the template.

> **Note** An alternative configuration would be to use AS_PATH access lists to set incoming polices named, for example, Standard_Customer and Premium_Customer. These polices would match any prefix advertised from a given AS.
>
> There's a trade-off to consider in the two approaches. The AS_PATH filter access list would be a little easier to change, as standard and premium customers are added or removed. The policy used in Example 6-40 is a bit more trouble to change but gives you more exact control over what prefixes are accepted and tagged.

Example 6-41 shows the results of Colorado's configuration at router Idaho. A **show bgp all community** command displays all BGP routes that have attached community attributes. You can see that only the Customer prefixes display. Next, the **show bgp all community** command specifies the three different community values assigned in Example 6-40, and the display shows the correct prefixes under each value. Finally, the **show bgp ipv6 unicast 2001:db8:4:3::/64** command displays more detail about the route to that prefix in Idaho's BGP table. You can see not only the assigned community value, but also that the next-hop-self policy has correctly changed the next hop of the EBGP-learned route to Colorado's loopback address 2001:db8:1:255::1.

Example 6-41 *Results of Colorado's Communities Policy Can Be Observed in Idaho's BGP Table*

```
Idaho#show bgp all community
For address family: IPv4 Unicast
BGP table version is 103, local router ID is 192.168.255.3
Status codes: s suppressed, d damped, h history, * valid, > best, i - internal,
              r RIB-failure, S Stale
Origin codes: i - IGP, e - EGP, ? - incomplete

   Network          Next Hop          Metric LocPrf Weight Path
*>i10.2.1.0/24      192.168.255.1          0    100      0 200 i
*>i10.2.2.0/24      192.168.255.1          0    100      0 200 i
```

```
*>i10.2.3.0/24      192.168.255.1          0    100      0 200 i
*>i10.3.1.0/24      192.168.255.1          0    100      0 300 i
*>i10.3.2.0/24      192.168.255.1          0    100      0 300 i
*>i10.3.3.0/24      192.168.255.1          0    100      0 300 i


For address family: IPv6 Unicast
BGP table version is 103, local router ID is 192.168.255.3
Status codes: s suppressed, d damped, h history, * valid, > best, i - internal,
              r RIB-failure, S Stale
Origin codes: i - IGP, e - EGP, ? - incomplete


   Network          Next Hop          Metric LocPrf Weight Path
*>i2001:DB8:3:1::/64
                    2001:DB8:1:255::1
                                          0    100      0 300 i
*>i2001:DB8:3:2::/64
                    2001:DB8:1:255::1
                                          0    100      0 300 i
*>i2001:DB8:3:3::/64
                    2001:DB8:1:255::1
                                          0    100      0 300 i
*>i2001:DB8:4:1::/64
                    2001:DB8:1:255::1
                                          0    100      0 400 i
*>i2001:DB8:4:2::/64
                    2001:DB8:1:255::1
                                          0    100      0 400 i
*>i2001:DB8:4:3::/64
   Network          Next Hop          Metric LocPrf Weight Path
                    2001:DB8:1:255::1
                                          0    100      0 400 i
Idaho#
Idaho#show bgp all community 200:10
For address family: IPv4 Unicast
BGP table version is 103, local router ID is 192.168.255.3
Status codes: s suppressed, d damped, h history, * valid, > best, i - internal,
              r RIB-failure, S Stale
Origin codes: i - IGP, e - EGP, ? - incomplete


   Network          Next Hop          Metric LocPrf Weight Path
*>i10.2.1.0/24      192.168.255.1          0    100      0 200 i
*>i10.2.2.0/24      192.168.255.1          0    100      0 200 i
*>i10.2.3.0/24      192.168.255.1          0    100      0 200 i
```

```
For address family: IPv6 Unicast
Idaho#
Idaho#show bgp all community 300:15
For address family: IPv4 Unicast
BGP table version is 103, local router ID is 192.168.255.3
Status codes: s suppressed, d damped, h history, * valid, > best, i - internal,
              r RIB-failure, S Stale
Origin codes: i - IGP, e - EGP, ? - incomplete


   Network          Next Hop          Metric LocPrf Weight Path
*>i10.3.1.0/24      192.168.255.1          0    100     0 300 i
*>i10.3.2.0/24      192.168.255.1          0    100     0 300 i
*>i10.3.3.0/24      192.168.255.1          0    100     0 300 i


For address family: IPv6 Unicast
BGP table version is 103, local router ID is 192.168.255.3
Status codes: s suppressed, d damped, h history, * valid, > best, i - internal,
              r RIB-failure, S Stale
Origin codes: i - IGP, e - EGP, ? - incomplete


   Network          Next Hop          Metric LocPrf Weight Path
*>i2001:DB8:3:1::/64
                    2001:DB8:1:255::1
                                           0    100     0 300 i
*>i2001:DB8:3:2::/64
                    2001:DB8:1:255::1
                                           0    100     0 300 i
*>i2001:DB8:3:3::/64
                    2001:DB8:1:255::1
                                           0    100     0 300 i
Idaho#
Idaho#show bgp all community 400:10
For address family: IPv4 Unicast


For address family: IPv6 Unicast
BGP table version is 103, local router ID is 192.168.255.3
Status codes: s suppressed, d damped, h history, * valid, > best, i - internal,
              r RIB-failure, S Stale
Origin codes: i - IGP, e - EGP, ? - incomplete


   Network          Next Hop          Metric LocPrf Weight Path
*>i2001:DB8:4:1::/64
                    2001:DB8:1:255::1
                                           0    100     0 400 i
```

```
*>i2001:DB8:4:2::/64
                    2001:DB8:1:255::1
                                            0    100     0 400 i
*>i2001:DB8:4:3::/64
                    2001:DB8:1:255::1
                                            0    100     0 400 i
Idaho#
Idaho#show bgp ipv6 unicast 2001:db8:4:3::/64
BGP routing table entry for 2001:DB8:4:3::/64, version 101
Paths: (1 available, best #1, table Global-IPv6-Table)
  Advertised to update-groups:
        1
  400
    2001:DB8:1:255::1 (metric 64) from 2001:DB8:1:255::1 (192.168.255.1)
      Origin IGP, metric 0, localpref 100, valid, internal, best
      Community: 400:10
Idaho#
```

With Colorado's community assignments working correctly, you can move to the configuration of router NewMexico, as shown in Example 6-42. Recall that you configured NewMexico to peer with California over an IPv4 TCP session and with Washington over an IPv6 TCP session (Figure 6-6). Both IPv4 and IPv6 routes were received over each of these connections; although, some odd policies were required to get the route advertisements received correctly and installed in the unicast routing tables. That configuration is shown in Example 6-20. When you last left NewMexico, you had also configured it for separate IPv4 and IPv6 IBGP peering with Colorado and Idaho, in Example 6-36. Because Example 6-20 did not show the IBGP configuration, and Example 6-36 did not show the route maps and prefix-lists defining policies, the full configuration is repeated in Example 6-42 so that you do not have to flip pages back to those two previous examples. Take a minute to refresh your memory of what was configured at NewMexico because you need to make some changes.

Example 6-42 *NewMexico's BGP Configuration as It Was Left After Adding the IBGP Configuration in Example 6-36*

```
router bgp 100
 bgp log-neighbor-changes
 neighbor 10.0.0.38 remote-as 500
 neighbor 10.0.0.38 ebgp-multihop 2
 neighbor 2001:DB8:1:255::1 remote-as 100
 neighbor 2001:DB8:1:255::1 password 7 0110050D5E
 neighbor 2001:DB8:1:255::1 update-source Loopback0
 neighbor 2001:DB8:1:255::3 remote-as 100
 neighbor 2001:DB8:1:255::3 password 7 121A061E17
 neighbor 2001:DB8:1:255::3 update-source Loopback0
```

```
 neighbor 2001:DB8:A:7::2 remote-as 700
 neighbor 192.168.255.1 remote-as 100
 neighbor 192.168.255.1 password 7 0110050D5E
 neighbor 192.168.255.1 update-source Loopback0
 neighbor 192.168.255.3 remote-as 100
 neighbor 192.168.255.3 password 7 0007100F01
 neighbor 192.168.255.3 update-source Loopback0
 !
 address-family ipv4
 neighbor 10.0.0.38 activate
 no neighbor 2001:DB8:1:255::1 activate
 no neighbor 2001:DB8:1:255::3 activate
 neighbor 2001:DB8:A:7::2 activate
 neighbor 2001:DB8:A:7::2 route-map v4-Routes-to-Washington out
 neighbor 192.168.255.1 activate
 neighbor 192.168.255.1 next-hop-self
 neighbor 192.168.255.3 activate
 neighbor 192.168.255.3 next-hop-self
 no auto-summary
 no synchronization
 exit-address-family
 !
 address-family ipv6
 neighbor 10.0.0.38 activate
 neighbor 10.0.0.38 route-map v6-Routes-to-California out
 neighbor 2001:DB8:1:255::1 activate
 neighbor 2001:DB8:1:255::1 next-hop-self
 neighbor 2001:DB8:1:255::3 activate
 neighbor 2001:DB8:1:255::3 next-hop-self
 neighbor 2001:DB8:A:7::2 activate
 exit-address-family
!
ip prefix-list v4-Routes seq 5 permit 10.0.0.0/8 le 24
!
ipv6 prefix-list v6-Routes seq 5 permit 2001:DB8::/32 le 64
!
route-map v6-Routes-to-California permit 10
 match ipv6 address prefix-list v6-Routes
 set ipv6 next-hop 2001:DB8:A:5::1
!
route-map v4-Routes-to-Washington permit 10
 match ip address prefix-list v4-Routes
 set ip next-hop 10.0.0.33
 !
```

Example 6-43 shows MewMexico's configuration changed to use policy and session templates. All the polices that were defined in Example 6-42 are still there but are now in the template format. Specifically, the outbound policies referencing route maps **v6-Routes-to-California** and **v4-Routes-to-Washington** are still there and work the same way as before; they've just been moved to the policy templates AS500 and AS700, respectively, instead of being applied directly to the neighbors.

Inbound policies have been added to those same two policy templates, AS500 and AS700. The inbound policy **Partner** in template AS500 tags the IPv4 and IPv6 Partner prefixes received from California with community 500:20, in accordance with Table 6-1. Similarly, inbound policy **Service_Provider** in template AS700 tags all the IPv4 and IPv6 Service Provider prefixes received from Washington with community 700:30.

There is also a policy template named AS100 that applies the next-hop-self and send-community policies shared by all IBGP peers.

Example 6-43 *NewMexico's Configuration Is Modified to Add Community Attributes to Prefixes Advertised from the Partner in AS500 and the Service Provider in AS700*

```
router bgp 100
 template peer-policy AS500
  route-map Partner in
  route-map v6-Routes-to-California out
 exit-peer-policy
 !
 template peer-policy AS700
  route-map Service_Provider in
  route-map v4-Routes-to-Washington out
 exit-peer-policy
 !
 template peer-policy AS100
  next-hop-self
  send-community
 exit-peer-policy
 !
 template peer-session Password
  password 7 0508050624
 exit-peer-session
 !
 template peer-session AS500
  remote-as 500
  ebgp-multihop 2
  inherit peer-session Password
 exit-peer-session
 !
 template peer-session AS700
```

```
 remote-as 700
 inherit peer-session Password
exit-peer-session
!
template peer-session AS100
 remote-as 100
 update-source Loopback0
 inherit peer-session Password
exit-peer-session
!
bgp log-neighbor-changes
neighbor 10.0.0.38 inherit peer-session AS500
neighbor 2001:DB8:1:255::1 inherit peer-session AS100
neighbor 2001:DB8:1:255::3 inherit peer-session AS100
neighbor 2001:DB8:A:7::2 inherit peer-session AS700
neighbor 192.168.255.1 inherit peer-session AS100
neighbor 192.168.255.3 inherit peer-session AS100
 !
address-family ipv4
neighbor 10.0.0.38 activate
neighbor 10.0.0.38 inherit peer-policy AS500
no neighbor 2001:DB8:1:255::1 activate
no neighbor 2001:DB8:1:255::3 activate
neighbor 2001:DB8:A:7::2 activate
neighbor 2001:DB8:A:7::2 inherit peer-policy AS700
neighbor 192.168.255.1 activate
neighbor 192.168.255.1 inherit peer-policy AS100
neighbor 192.168.255.3 activate
neighbor 192.168.255.3 inherit peer-policy AS100
no auto-summary
no synchronization
exit-address-family
 !
address-family ipv6
neighbor 10.0.0.38 activate
neighbor 10.0.0.38 inherit peer-policy AS500
neighbor 2001:DB8:1:255::1 activate
neighbor 2001:DB8:1:255::1 inherit peer-policy AS100
neighbor 2001:DB8:1:255::3 activate
neighbor 2001:DB8:1:255::3 inherit peer-policy AS100
neighbor 2001:DB8:A:7::2 activate
neighbor 2001:DB8:A:7::2 inherit peer-policy AS700
exit-address-family
!
```

```
ip bgp-community new-format
!
ip as-path access-list 20 permit ^500_
ip as-path access-list 30 permit ^700_
!
ip prefix-list v4-Routes seq 5 permit 10.0.0.0/8 le 24
!
ipv6 prefix-list v6-Routes seq 5 permit 2001:DB8::/32 le 64
!
route-map Service_Provider permit 10
 match as-path 30
 set community 700:30
!
route-map Partner permit 10
 match as-path 20
 set community 500:20
!
route-map v6-Routes-to-California permit 10
 match ipv6 address prefix-list v6-Routes
 set ipv6 next-hop 2001:DB8:A:5::1
!
route-map v4-Routes-to-Washington permit 10
 match ip address prefix-list v4-Routes
 set ip next-hop 10.0.0.33
!
```

Looking to the bottom of the configuration, you see the two route maps that change the next-hop addresses of prefixes identified by prefix-lists. Nothing there has changed from the Example 6-42 configuration. What's of interest are the two route maps named **Partner** and **Service_Provider**, which are referenced from the policy templates AS500 and AS700, respectively. These two route maps reference AS_PATH access lists instead of prefix-lists. Route map **Service_Provider** uses access list 30 to identify routes whose AS_PATH list begins with ASN 700, meaning routes advertised by that AA 700, and adds community 700:30 to those routes. Likewise route map **Partner** uses access list 20 to identify routes whose AS_PATH begins with ASN 500 and tags adds community 500:20.

Note AS_PATH access lists are chosen in this example mostly just to give you an alternative configuration approach. In a real implementation, there are pros and cons to this choice. For a partner peering, prefix lists are probably a better choice for identifying incoming prefixes because like customer peering you probably wants the more fine-grained control over specific prefixes. But for a service provider, you almost certainly want to identify prefixes by AS_PATH; an SP will be advertising too many, too varied, and too changing a set of prefixes—more than one-half million, if you accept full Internet routes—to make prefix lists a practical means of identification.

Next, turn your attention to near the top of the configuration referred to in Example 6-43 to look at the session templates. There is a session template named **Password** that is inherited by all other session templates. Then session templates are defined for AS500, AS700, and AS100, each defining the session characteristics for the peers in those autonomous systems that were previously configured for each neighbor referred to in Example 6-42. Again, nothing has changed functionally; you've just gathered common configuration parameters into session templates.

Note   For the EBGP peers, the password is a partial change from the previous configuration in which no passwords were applied to external peers. Routers California and Washington have been reconfigured accordingly. I used the password configuration here to again emphasize inheritance within a template, but in a real network you almost certainly would not want to use the same password for your IBGP and EBGP peers. You would configure separate templates for one or more external passwords or just apply unique passwords directly to each external neighbor.

Notice that the policy templates and the session templates use the same names: AS100, AS500, and AS700. Does it make sense to you to use the same names for policy and session templates applied to the same neighbors, or do you feel that they could be confusing? Your naming choices should, of course, comply with whatever makes the most sense to you (or whatever naming convention your organization has specified). However, in this example, differentiating the names should be easy as long as you pay attention to whether, for example, the specific instance of the name AS100 is associated with a policy template or a session template.

And session and policy templates sharing the same name certainly are not confusing when they are applied in this configuration. Session templates are always applied in the global part of the configuration in which neighbors are specified, and policy templates are always applied under the address family sections.

There is a single IPv4 session to California (10.0.0.38), so that neighbor inherits session template AS500. There is a single IPv6 TCP session to Washington (2001:db8:a:7::2), so that neighbor inherits session template AS700. There are separate IPv4 and IPv6 sessions to internal peers Colorado and Idaho, and you can see in the configuration that two IPv4 neighbors and two IPv6 neighbors inherit the session template AS100.

One of the most important lessons to take away from this example is where individual neighbor addresses are specified and where policies are applied within the address family configurations. Some of this was emphasized in the previous MBGP configuration of NewMexico, but it's critical enough to your understanding of address family configuration to go over it again.

The easiest neighbor configurations are the ones for the IBGP neighbors Colorado (192.168.255.1 and 2001:db8:1:255::1) and Idaho (192.168.255.3 and 2001:db8:1:255::3). IPv4 routes are exchanged over an IPv4 TCP session, and IPv6 routes are exchanged over an Iv6 TCP session. So you can see these two routers' IPv4 addresses activated under the IPv4 address family and their IPv6 addresses activated under the IPv6 address family. The same policy template, AS100 applying next-hop-self and send-community, is inherited by all four of these sessions.

Both IPv4 and IPv6 routes are exchanged with router California over a single IPv4 TCP session; the California side of that connection is 10.0.0.38. That address is activated under the IPv4 address family, and even though it is an IPv4 address, it is also activated under the IPv6 address family. Without that second activation, IPv6 routes would not be exchanged over the connection. The peering session inherits policy template AS500, which specifies both the inbound policy that adds a community value to routes advertised by California, and the outbound policy that corrects the next-hop address of IPv6 routes advertised to California. It's important to note that the policy is applied to the peering session under both the IPv4 and IPv6 neighbor families. If this were not the case, communities would not be added to prefixes of both address types. And it's okay that the outbound policy changing the next-hop address of advertised IPv6 routes is applied under the IPv4 address family; the route map v6-Routes-to-California ignores IPv4 routes, so the outbound policy has no effect there.

Understanding how the IPv4 session to California is configured, it's easy to understand how the session to Washington is configured. Here IPv4 and IPv6 routes are exchanged over a single IPv6 session; the Washington end of that session is 2001:db8:a:7::2. The session is activated under both the IPv4 and IPv6 address families, and the policy template AS700 is applied under both families. The route map for the outbound policy that changes the next-hop address of advertised IPv4 routes, v4-Routes-to-Washington, ignores IPv6 routes, so it has no effect when applied under the IPv6 address family. And as with California, the policy template must be applied under both address families so that the inbound policy can add the appropriate community value to both IPv4 and Iv6 received routes.

The big question is, of course: Do the community policies work? According to Table 6-1, all prefixes advertised from Partner AS500 should belong to community 500:20, and all prefixes advertised by Service Provider AS700 should belong to community 700:30. Example 6-44 shows that this is the case.

Example 6-44 *Community Value 500:20 Has Been Added to IPv4 and IPv6 Routes from AS500, and Community Value 700:30 Has Been Added to IPv4 and IPv6 Routes from AS700*

```
NewMexico#show ip bgp all community 500:20
For address family: IPv4 Unicast
BGP table version is 19, local router ID is 192.168.255.2
Status codes: s suppressed, d damped, h history, * valid, > best, i - internal,
              r RIB-failure, S Stale
Origin codes: i - IGP, e - EGP, ? - incomplete

   Network          Next Hop          Metric LocPrf Weight Path
*> 10.5.1.0/24      10.0.0.38              0             0 500 i
*> 10.5.2.0/24      10.0.0.38              0             0 500 i
*> 10.5.3.0/24      10.0.0.38              0             0 500 i

For address family: IPv6 Unicast
BGP table version is 19, local router ID is 192.168.255.2
Status codes: s suppressed, d damped, h history, * valid, > best, i - internal,
              r RIB-failure, S Stale
Origin codes: i - IGP, e - EGP, ? - incomplete

   Network          Next Hop          Metric LocPrf Weight Path
*> 2001:DB8:5:1::/64
                    2001:DB8:A:5::2        0             0 500 i
*> 2001:DB8:5:2::/64
                    2001:DB8:A:5::2        0             0 500 i
*> 2001:DB8:5:3::/64
                    2001:DB8:A:5::2        0             0 500 i
NewMexico#
NewMexico#show ip bgp all community 700:30
For address family: IPv4 Unicast
BGP table version is 19, local router ID is 192.168.255.2
Status codes: s suppressed, d damped, h history, * valid, > best, i - internal,
              r RIB-failure, S Stale
Origin codes: i - IGP, e - EGP, ? - incomplete

   Network          Next Hop          Metric LocPrf Weight Path
*> 10.7.1.0/24      10.0.0.34              0             0 700 i
*> 10.7.2.0/24      10.0.0.34              0             0 700 i
*> 10.7.3.0/24      10.0.0.34              0             0 700 i

For address family: IPv6 Unicast
BGP table version is 19, local router ID is 192.168.255.2
Status codes: s suppressed, d damped, h history, * valid, > best, i - internal,
```

```
             r RIB-failure, S Stale
Origin codes: i - IGP, e - EGP, ? - incomplete


   Network          Next Hop          Metric LocPrf Weight Path
*> 2001:DB8:7:1::/64
                    2001:DB8:A:7::2        0            0 700 i
*> 2001:DB8:7:2::/64
                    2001:DB8:A:7::2        0            0 700 i
*> 2001:DB8:7:3::/64
                    2001:DB8:A:7::2        0            0 700 i
NewMexico#
```

Finally, we go to Idaho, the third router in AS100 (Figure 6-11). Remember that separate IPv4 and IPv6 sessions were configured to this router's external peers (Example 6-27), and that the IBGP sessions are also separate for IPv4 and IPv6, so the application of the community policies should be a little more straightforward than they were at NewMexico. Idaho peers to Wyoming (AS800) between the directly connected interface addresses. It peers with Montana (AS600) between the loopback interfaces, across an IP unnumbered link.

As with Colorado and NewMexico, Idaho is reconfigured to use session and policy templates and the community policies are added (Example 6-45). The more you become accustomed to using templates, the less cluttered the main neighbor session and address family configurations become. Given what you have already seen with the configurations at Colorado and NewMexico, you should now easily read and understand Idaho's configuration. Notice in particular that because all Idaho's peering sessions follow a rule of IPv4 routes over IPv4 sessions and IPv6 routes over IPv6 sessions, there is no confusion about what is happening in address family sections.

Example 6-45 *Idaho's Configuration Is Modified to Add Community Attributes to Prefixes Advertised from the Partner in AS600 and the Service Provider in AS800*

```
router bgp 100
 template peer-policy AS600
  route-map Partner in
 exit-peer-policy
 !
 template peer-policy AS800
  route-map Service_Provider in
 exit-peer-policy
 !
 template peer-policy AS100
  next-hop-self
  send-community
 exit-peer-policy
```

```
!
template peer-session Password
 password 7 08224F470C
exit-peer-session
!
template peer-session AS600
 remote-as 600
 ebgp-multihop 2
 update-source Loopback0
 inherit peer-session Password
exit-peer-session
!
template peer-session AS800
 remote-as 800
 inherit peer-session Password
exit-peer-session
!
template peer-session AS100
 remote-as 100
 update-source Loopback0
 inherit peer-session Password
exit-peer-session
!
bgp log-neighbor-changes
neighbor 10.0.0.30 inherit peer-session AS800
neighbor 2001:DB8:1:255::1 inherit peer-session AS100
neighbor 2001:DB8:1:255::2 inherit peer-session AS100
neighbor 2001:DB8:A:8::2 inherit peer-session AS800
neighbor 2001:DB8:255:8::1 inherit peer-session AS600
neighbor 192.168.255.1 inherit peer-session AS100
neighbor 192.168.255.2 inherit peer-session AS100
neighbor 192.168.255.8 inherit peer-session AS600
!
address-family ipv4
neighbor 10.0.0.30 activate
neighbor 10.0.0.30 inherit peer-policy AS800
no neighbor 2001:DB8:1:255::1 activate
no neighbor 2001:DB8:1:255::2 activate
no neighbor 2001:DB8:A:8::2 activate
no neighbor 2001:DB8:255:8::1 activate
neighbor 192.168.255.1 activate
neighbor 192.168.255.1 inherit peer-policy AS100
```

```
neighbor 192.168.255.2 activate
neighbor 192.168.255.2 inherit peer-policy AS100
neighbor 192.168.255.8 activate
neighbor 192.168.255.8 inherit peer-policy AS600
no auto-summary
no synchronization
exit-address-family
!
address-family ipv6
neighbor 2001:DB8:1:255::1 activate
neighbor 2001:DB8:1:255::1 inherit peer-policy AS100
neighbor 2001:DB8:1:255::2 activate
neighbor 2001:DB8:1:255::2 inherit peer-policy AS100
neighbor 2001:DB8:A:8::2 activate
neighbor 2001:DB8:A:8::2 inherit peer-policy AS800
neighbor 2001:DB8:255:8::1 activate
neighbor 2001:DB8:255:8::1 inherit peer-policy AS600
exit-address-family
!
ip bgp-community new-format
!
ip as-path access-list 20 permit ^600_
ip as-path access-list 30 permit ^800_
!
route-map Service_Provider permit 10
 match as-path 30
 set community 800:30
!
route-map Partner permit 10
 match as-path 20
 set community 600:20
!
```

Example 6-46 shows that the community policies at Idaho work correctly. Although
these commands do not display the specific communities, you can see that all prefixes
associated autonomous systems neighboring AS100 show up in these two lists. And in
Example 6-47, you can see that all the prefixes from all the autonomous systems neighboring AS100 in Figure 6-11 are listed at Idaho as belonging to at least one community.
It is reasonable to assume that all the same prefixes, with the same community values,
are also present at Colorado and NewMexico.

Example 6-46   *Community Value 600:20 Has Been Added to IPv4 and IPv6 Routes from AS600, and Community Value 800:30 Has Been Added to IPv4 and IPv6 Routes from AS800*

```
Idaho#show ip bgp all community 600:20
For address family: IPv4 Unicast
BGP table version is 19, local router ID is 192.168.255.3
Status codes: s suppressed, d damped, h history, * valid, > best, i - internal,
              r RIB-failure, S Stale
Origin codes: i - IGP, e - EGP, ? - incomplete


   Network          Next Hop          Metric LocPrf Weight Path
*> 10.6.1.0/24      192.168.255.8          0            0 600 i
*> 10.6.2.0/24      192.168.255.8          0            0 600 i
*> 10.6.3.0/24      192.168.255.8          0            0 600 i


For address family: IPv6 Unicast
BGP table version is 19, local router ID is 192.168.255.3
Status codes: s suppressed, d damped, h history, * valid, > best, i - internal,
              r RIB-failure, S Stale
Origin codes: i - IGP, e - EGP, ? - incomplete


   Network          Next Hop          Metric LocPrf Weight Path
*> 2001:DB8:6:1::/64
                    2001:DB8:255:8::1
                                           0            0 600 i
*> 2001:DB8:6:2::/64
                    2001:DB8:255:8::1
                                           0            0 600 i
*> 2001:DB8:6:3::/64
                    2001:DB8:255:8::1
                                           0            0 600 i
Idaho#
Idaho#show ip bgp all community 800:30
For address family: IPv4 Unicast
BGP table version is 19, local router ID is 192.168.255.3
Status codes: s suppressed, d damped, h history, * valid, > best, i - internal,
              r RIB-failure, S Stale
Origin codes: i - IGP, e - EGP, ? - incomplete


   Network          Next Hop          Metric LocPrf Weight Path
*> 10.8.1.0/24      10.0.0.30              0            0 800 i
*> 10.8.2.0/24      10.0.0.30              0            0 800 i
*> 10.8.3.0/24      10.0.0.30              0            0 800 i
```

```
For address family: IPv6 Unicast
BGP table version is 19, local router ID is 192.168.255.3
Status codes: s suppressed, d damped, h history, * valid, > best, i - internal,
            r RIB-failure, S Stale
Origin codes: i - IGP, e - EGP, ? - incomplete


   Network          Next Hop          Metric LocPrf Weight Path
*> 2001:DB8:8:1::/64
                    2001:DB8:A:8::2         0            0 800 i
*> 2001:DB8:8:2::/64
                    2001:DB8:A:8::2         0            0 800 i
*> 2001:DB8:8:3::/64
                    2001:DB8:A:8::2         0            0 800 i
Idaho#
```

Example 6-47   show ip bgp community *(Which Defaults to IPv4 Unicast) and* show ip bgp ipv6 unicast community *Commands Display All Prefixes at Idaho That Have at Least One Community Value Attached*

```
Idaho#show ip bgp community
BGP table version is 19, local router ID is 192.168.255.3
Status codes: s suppressed, d damped, h history, * valid, > best, i - internal,
            r RIB-failure, S Stale
Origin codes: i - IGP, e - EGP, ? - incomplete


   Network          Next Hop          Metric LocPrf Weight Path
*>i10.2.1.0/24      192.168.255.1          0    100     0 200 i
*>i10.2.2.0/24      192.168.255.1          0    100     0 200 i
*>i10.2.3.0/24      192.168.255.1          0    100     0 200 i
*>i10.3.1.0/24      192.168.255.1          0    100     0 300 i
*>i10.3.2.0/24      192.168.255.1          0    100     0 300 i
*>i10.3.3.0/24      192.168.255.1          0    100     0 300 i
*>i10.5.1.0/24      192.168.255.2          0    100     0 500 i
*>i10.5.2.0/24      192.168.255.2          0    100     0 500 i
*>i10.5.3.0/24      192.168.255.2          0    100     0 500 i
*> 10.6.1.0/24      192.168.255.8          0            0 600 i
*> 10.6.2.0/24      192.168.255.8          0            0 600 i
*> 10.6.3.0/24      192.168.255.8          0            0 600 i
*>i10.7.1.0/24      192.168.255.2          0    100     0 700 i
*>i10.7.2.0/24      192.168.255.2          0    100     0 700 i
*>i10.7.3.0/24      192.168.255.2          0    100     0 700 i
*> 10.8.1.0/24      10.0.0.30              0            0 800 i
*> 10.8.2.0/24      10.0.0.30              0            0 800 i
*> 10.8.3.0/24      10.0.0.30              0            0 800 i
```

```
Idaho#
Idaho#show ip bgp ipv6 unicast community
BGP table version is 19, local router ID is 192.168.255.3
Status codes: s suppressed, d damped, h history, * valid, > best, i - internal,
              r RIB-failure, S Stale
Origin codes: i - IGP, e - EGP, ? - incomplete


   Network           Next Hop            Metric LocPrf Weight Path
*>i2001:DB8:3:1::/64
                     2001:DB8:1:255::1
                                              0    100      0 300 i
*>i2001:DB8:3:2::/64
                     2001:DB8:1:255::1
                                              0    100      0 300 i
*>i2001:DB8:3:3::/64
                     2001:DB8:1:255::1
                                              0    100      0 300 i
*>i2001:DB8:4:1::/64
                     2001:DB8:1:255::1
                                              0    100      0 400 i
*>i2001:DB8:4:2::/64
                     2001:DB8:1:255::1
                                              0    100      0 400 i
*>i2001:DB8:4:3::/64
                     2001:DB8:1:255::1
                                              0    100      0 400 i
*>i2001:DB8:5:1::/64
                     2001:DB8:1:255::2
                                              0    100      0 500 i
*>i2001:DB8:5:2::/64
                     2001:DB8:1:255::2
                                              0    100      0 500 i
*>i2001:DB8:5:3::/64
                     2001:DB8:1:255::2
                                              0    100      0 500 i
*> 2001:DB8:6:1::/64
                     2001:DB8:255:8::1
                                              0             0 600 i
*> 2001:DB8:6:2::/64
                     2001:DB8:255:8::1
                                              0             0 600 i
*> 2001:DB8:6:3::/64
                     2001:DB8:255:8::1
                                              0             0 600 i
*>i2001:DB8:7:1::/64
```

```
                    2001:DB8:1:255::2
                                              0    100      0 700 i
*>i2001:DB8:7:2::/64
                    2001:DB8:1:255::2
                                              0    100      0 700 i
*>i2001:DB8:7:3::/64
                    2001:DB8:1:255::2
                                              0    100      0 700 i
*> 2001:DB8:8:1::/64
                    2001:DB8:A:8::2           0             0 800 i
*> 2001:DB8:8:2::/64
                    2001:DB8:A:8::2           0             0 800 i
*> 2001:DB8:8:3::/64
                    2001:DB8:A:8::2           0             0 800 i
Idaho#
```

Now that all the community values specified in Table 6-1 have been implemented, the second part of the case study is to apply the rules listed in the introduction. To recap

- Customer AS300 receives all Partner and Service Provider prefixes (a "Premium Customer").

- Customers AS200 and AS400 receive only a default route ("Standard Customers").

- Service Providers receive all Customer prefixes.

- Service Providers receive Partner prefixes, but with prepended AS_PATH attributes (making AS100 a less preferred path to the Partner networks).

- Partners receive Service Provider prefixes, but with a MED of 20. (The assumption here is that Partners have their own service provider connections not shown in Figure 6-11 and use AS100 for backup Internet access only.)

- Partners receive prefixes from Customer AS300, but not from AS200 or AS400 (Standard Customers do not have direct access to Partner services).

Note Anything not specifically permitted in the preceding rules should be denied. For example, a Service Provider should not receive any routes from another Service Provider. Otherwise, an SP might try to use AS100 as a transit AS to another SP.

Quite a bit of effort was put into reconfiguring the routers in AS100 to use session and policy templates. But with that done, modifying policies should be a relatively easy matter of modifying the relevant policy templates and route maps. We can use the same named community list (Example 6-48) on all three routers of AS100. Applying different actions at different points in the network is just a matter of referencing the right community list. As customers, partners, and service providers are added or removed in the future, the policies can be adapted simply by editing the appropriate community list.

Example 6-48 *Same Named Community Lists Can Be Used at All Routers in AS100. Specific Policies Can Be Applied at a Specific Router by Referencing the Appropriate Community*

```
Idaho#show ip community-list
Named Community expanded list CUSTOMERS
Named Community standard list STANDARD_CUSTOMERS
    permit 200:10
    permit 400:10
Named Community standard list PREMIUM_CUSTOMERS
    permit 300:15
Named Community standard list PARTNERS
    permit 500:20
    permit 600:20
Named Community standard list SERVICE_PROVIDERS
    permit 700:30
    permit 800:30
Idaho#
```

Because we left off with Idaho, let's start our policy changes there. According to the rules list, the following rules should be implemented for Idaho's peers:

- **Wyoming:** As a Service Provider, Wyoming should receive

    - All Customer prefixes (communities with :NN = :10 or :15)

    - All Partner prefixes (communities with :NN = :20) but with their AS_PATH prepended

- **Montana:** As a Partner, Montana should receive

    - All Service Provider prefixes (communities with :NN = :30), but with a MED of 20

    - Premium Customer prefixes (NN = :15) but not Standard Customer prefixes (NN = :10)

Example 6-49 shows the new policy configurations for Idaho. To save a little page space, only the community lists, policies, and policy templates are shown. The route maps of interest are named to_Partner and to_SP. The policy template AS600 is modified from the previous configuration to reference route map to_Partner as an outbound policy, and the policy template AS800 is modified to reference route map to_SP as an outbound policy. The sequences of the route maps reference the appropriate community list and permit the matching prefixes, either alone or with a set command; the last sequence in each route map denies everything else.

Example 6-49 *Parts of Idaho's Configuration That Influence the New Policies Are Shown*

```
router bgp 100
 template peer-policy AS600
  route-map Partner in
  route-map to_Partner out
 exit-peer-policy
 !
 template peer-policy AS800
  route-map Service_Provider in
  route-map to_SP out
 exit-peer-policy
 !
 template peer-policy AS100
  next-hop-self
  send-community
 exit-peer-policy
!
!
!
ip bgp-community new-format
!
ip community-list standard STANDARD_CUSTOMERS permit 200:10
ip community-list standard STANDARD_CUSTOMERS permit 400:10
ip community-list standard PREMIUM_CUSTOMERS permit 300:15
ip community-list standard PARTNERS permit 500:20
ip community-list standard PARTNERS permit 600:20
ip community-list standard SERVICE_PROVIDERS permit 700:30
ip community-list standard SERVICE_PROVIDERS permit 800:30
!
ip as-path access-list 20 permit ^600_
ip as-path access-list 30 permit ^800_
!
route-map to_Partner permit 10
 match community SERVICE_PROVIDERS
 set metric 20
!
route-map to_Partner permit 20
 match community PREMIUM_CUSTOMERS
!
route-map to_Partner deny 30
!
route-map Service_Provider permit 10
 match as-path 30
```

```
 set community 800:30
!
route-map to_SP permit 10
 match community STANDARD_CUSTOMERS
!
route-map to_SP permit 20
 match community PREMIUM_CUSTOMERS
!
route-map to_SP permit 30
 match community PARTNERS
 set as-path prepend 100 100
!
route-map to_SP deny 40
!
route-map Partner permit 10
 match as-path 20
 set community 600:20
!
```

Example 6-50 shows the results at Montana. The router sees the prefixes of premium customer AS300 but does not see the prefixes of the standard customers at AS200 and AS400 and does not see the prefixes of the other partner at AS500. It sees the prefixes of the service providers at AS700 and AS800, and those prefixes have a MED of 20. The local AS600 prefixes, of course, are also seen in the table.

Example 6-50 *Montana's BGP Prefixes After the New Polices of Example 6-49 Have Been Applied and a Soft Reset Issued at Idaho*

```
Montana#show ip bgp
BGP table version is 163, local router ID is 192.168.255.8
Status codes: s suppressed, d damped, h history, * valid, > best, i - internal,
              r RIB-failure, S Stale
Origin codes: i - IGP, e - EGP, ? - incomplete

   Network          Next Hop         Metric LocPrf Weight Path
*> 10.3.1.0/24      192.168.255.3                     0 100 300 i
*> 10.3.2.0/24      192.168.255.3                     0 100 300 i
*> 10.3.3.0/24      192.168.255.3                     0 100 300 i
*> 10.6.1.0/24      0.0.0.0               0        32768 i
*> 10.6.2.0/24      0.0.0.0               0        32768 i
*> 10.6.3.0/24      0.0.0.0               0        32768 i
*> 10.7.1.0/24      192.168.255.3       20            0 100 700 i
*> 10.7.2.0/24      192.168.255.3       20            0 100 700 i
*> 10.7.3.0/24      192.168.255.3       20            0 100 700 i
*> 10.8.1.0/24      192.168.255.3       20            0 100 800 i
```

```
*> 10.8.2.0/24       192.168.255.3         20            0 100 800 i
*> 10.8.3.0/24       192.168.255.3         20            0 100 800 i
Montana#
Montana#show ip bgp ipv6 unicast
BGP table version is 163, local router ID is 192.168.255.8
Status codes: s suppressed, d damped, h history, * valid, > best, i - internal,
            r RIB-failure, S Stale
Origin codes: i - IGP, e - EGP, ? - incomplete

   Network          Next Hop           Metric LocPrf Weight Path
*> 2001:DB8:3:1::/64
                    2001:DB8:1:255::3
                                                              0 100 300 i
*> 2001:DB8:3:2::/64
                    2001:DB8:1:255::3
                                                              0 100 300 i
*> 2001:DB8:3:3::/64
                    2001:DB8:1:255::3
                                                              0 100 300 i
*> 2001:DB8:6:1::/64
                    ::                     0          32768 i
*> 2001:DB8:6:2::/64
                    ::                     0          32768 i
*> 2001:DB8:6:3::/64
                    ::                     0          32768 i
*> 2001:DB8:7:1::/64
                    2001:DB8:1:255::3
                                           20            0 100 700 i
   Network          Next Hop           Metric LocPrf Weight Path
*> 2001:DB8:7:2::/64
                    2001:DB8:1:255::3
                                           20            0 100 700 i
*> 2001:DB8:7:3::/64
                    2001:DB8:1:255::3
                                           20            0 100 700 i
*> 2001:DB8:8:1::/64
                    2001:DB8:1:255::3
                                           20            0 100 800 i
*> 2001:DB8:8:2::/64
                    2001:DB8:1:255::3
                                           20            0 100 800 i
*> 2001:DB8:8:3::/64
                    2001:DB8:1:255::3
                                           20            0 100 800 i
Montana#
```

Example 6-51 shows the results at Wyoming. Standard and premium customer prefixes have been received, and partner prefixes with prepended AS_PATHs have been received. Notice that Wyoming does not see the prefixes from the other service provider at AS700.

Example 6-51   *Wyoming's BGP Prefixes After the New Polices of Example 6-49 Have Been Applied and a Soft Reset Issued at Idaho*

```
Wyoming#show ip bgp
BGP table version is 208, local router ID is 192.168.255.10
Status codes: s suppressed, d damped, h history, * valid, > best, i - internal,
              r RIB-failure, S Stale
Origin codes: i - IGP, e - EGP, ? - incomplete


   Network          Next Hop         Metric LocPrf Weight Path
*> 10.2.1.0/24      10.0.0.29                           0 100 200 i
*> 10.2.2.0/24      10.0.0.29                           0 100 200 i
*> 10.2.3.0/24      10.0.0.29                           0 100 200 i
*> 10.3.1.0/24      10.0.0.29                           0 100 300 i
*> 10.3.2.0/24      10.0.0.29                           0 100 300 i
*> 10.3.3.0/24      10.0.0.29                           0 100 300 i
*> 10.5.1.0/24      10.0.0.29                           0 100 100 100 500 i
*> 10.5.2.0/24      10.0.0.29                           0 100 100 100 500 i
*> 10.5.3.0/24      10.0.0.29                           0 100 100 100 500 i
*> 10.6.1.0/24      10.0.0.29                           0 100 100 100 600 i
*> 10.6.2.0/24      10.0.0.29                           0 100 100 100 600 i
*> 10.6.3.0/24      10.0.0.29                           0 100 100 100 600 i
*> 10.8.1.0/24      0.0.0.0               0          32768 i
*> 10.8.2.0/24      0.0.0.0               0          32768 i
*> 10.8.3.0/24      0.0.0.0               0          32768 i
Wyoming#
Wyoming#show ip bgp ipv6 unicast
BGP table version is 202, local router ID is 192.168.255.10
Status codes: s suppressed, d damped, h history, * valid, > best, i - internal,
              r RIB-failure, S Stale
Origin codes: i - IGP, e - EGP, ? - incomplete


   Network          Next Hop         Metric LocPrf Weight Path
*> 2001:DB8:3:1::/64
                    2001:DB8:A:8::1                     0 100 300 i
*> 2001:DB8:3:2::/64
                    2001:DB8:A:8::1                     0 100 300 i
*> 2001:DB8:3:3::/64
                    2001:DB8:A:8::1                     0 100 300 i
*> 2001:DB8:4:1::/64
```

```
                         2001:DB8:A:8::1                                 0 100 400 i
*> 2001:DB8:4:2::/64
                         2001:DB8:A:8::1                                 0 100 400 i
*> 2001:DB8:4:3::/64
                         2001:DB8:A:8::1                                 0 100 400 i
*> 2001:DB8:5:1::/64
                         2001:DB8:A:8::1                                 0 100 100 100 500 i
*> 2001:DB8:5:2::/64
                         2001:DB8:A:8::1                                 0 100 100 100 500 i
*> 2001:DB8:5:3::/64
                         2001:DB8:A:8::1                                 0 100 100 100 500 i
   Network        Next Hop          Metric LocPrf Weight Path
*> 2001:DB8:6:1::/64
                         2001:DB8:A:8::1                                 0 100 100 100 600 i
*> 2001:DB8:6:2::/64
                         2001:DB8:A:8::1                                 0 100 100 100 600 i
*> 2001:DB8:6:3::/64
                         2001:DB8:A:8::1                                 0 100 100 100 600 i
*> 2001:DB8:8:1::/64
                         ::                       0            32768 i
*> 2001:DB8:8:2::/64
                         ::                       0            32768 i
*> 2001:DB8:8:3::/64
                         ::                       0            32768 i
Wyoming#
```

Next, move to router NewMexico. According to the rules list, the following rules should be implemented for NewMexico's peers:

■ **Washington:** As a Service Provider, Washington should receive

  ■ All Customer prefixes (communities with :NN = :10 or :15)

  ■ All Partner prefixes (communities with :NN = :20) but with their AS_PATH prepended

■ **California:** As a Partner, California should receive

  ■ All Service Provider prefixes (communities with :NN = :30), but with a MED of 20

  ■ Premium Customer prefixes (NN = :15) but not Standard Customer prefixes (NN = :10)

These rules look just like the rules for Idaho; only the peers have been changed. So NewMexico's configuration should be almost identical to the one at Idaho, but there is one snag: Remember that because at this router all prefixes are advertised over a single

IPv4 or IPv6 session, some policies had to be created to modify next-hop addresses (Examples 6-11 and 6-20). Those polices were applied as outbound polices. Because only one inbound and one outbound policy per neighbor is allowed, and because you still need those original next-hop modifications, the next-hop policies must be moved.

This requires a little thought. The route maps **v6-Routes-to-California** and **v4-Routes-to-Washington** in Example 6-20 referenced an IPv6 or IPv4 prefix list and then set next-hop addresses on matching prefixes. You still want to differentiate between IPv4 and IPv6 prefixes for setting next hops, but you can't do that within the community lists. The communities you have established apply to both IPv4 and IPv6 routes. By default, a route map stops processing a prefix when it gets a match. So putting the address version matching in one sequence and the community matching in a different sequence will not work. Processing stops at the first match.

What you need is a way to match an address type, set the next hop, and then continue to process the matching prefixes so that you can take action on its community.

Remember Continue clauses from Chapter 4?

Example 6-52 shows the new configuration for NewMexico. The route maps **v6-Routes-to-California** and **v4-Routes-to-Washington** from Example 6-20 have been eliminated, but the components that match either IPv4 prefixes or IPv6 prefixes and then set the next-hop addresses are moved to the new route maps **to_Partner** and **to_SP** as the first sequences. A Continue clause (highlighted) is then used in those sequences to send matching prefixes to the community matching part of the route maps, beginning at sequence 50. The rest of the route maps are identical to the ones you configured at Idaho, and the route maps are applied as outbound policies in the peer templates AS500 and AS700.

Example 6-52   *Parts of NewMexico's Configuration That Influence the New Policies Are Shown*

```
router bgp 100
 template peer-policy AS500
  route-map Partner in
  route-map to_Partner out
 exit-peer-policy
 !
 template peer-policy AS700
  route-map Service_Provider in
  route-map to_SP out
 exit-peer-policy
 !
 template peer-policy AS100
  next-hop-self
  send-community
 exit-peer-policy
 !
```

```
!
!
ip bgp-community new-format
!
ip community-list standard STANDARD_CUSTOMERS permit 200:10
ip community-list standard STANDARD_CUSTOMERS permit 400:10
ip community-list standard PREMIUM_CUSTOMERS permit 300:15
ip community-list standard PARTNERS permit 500:20
ip community-list standard PARTNERS permit 600:20
ip community-list standard SERVICE_PROVIDERS permit 700:30
ip community-list standard SERVICE_PROVIDERS permit 800:30
!
ip as-path access-list 20 permit ^500_
ip as-path access-list 20 permit ^600_
ip as-path access-list 30 permit ^700_
ip as-path access-list 30 permit ^800_
!
ip prefix-list v4-Routes seq 5 permit 10.0.0.0/8 le 24
!
ipv6 prefix-list v6-Routes seq 5 permit 2001:DB8::/32 le 64
!
route-map to_Partner permit 10
 match ipv6 address prefix-list v6-Routes
 continue 50
 set ipv6 next-hop 2001:DB8:A:5::1
!
route-map to_Partner permit 50
 match community SERVICE_PROVIDERS
 set metric 20
!
route-map to_Partner permit 60
 match community PREMIUM_CUSTOMERS
!
route-map to_Partner deny 70
!
route-map Service_Provider permit 10
 match as-path 30
 set community 700:30
!
route-map v4-Next-Hop permit 10
 match ip address prefix-list v4-Routes
!
route-map to_SP permit 10
 match ip address prefix-list v4-Routes
```

```
continue 50
 set ip next-hop 10.0.0.33
 !
route-map to_SP permit 50
 match community STANDARD_CUSTOMERS
 !
route-map to_SP permit 60
 match community PREMIUM_CUSTOMERS
 !
route-map to_SP permit 70
 match community PARTNERS
 set as-path prepend 100 100
 !
route-map to_SP deny 80
 !
route-map Partner permit 10
 match as-path 20
 set community 500:20
 !
```

Examples 6-53 and 6-54 show the results after reconfiguration and a soft reset. Rather than explain the results again, you need to verify that the prefixes at California and Washington comply with the policy rules listed for those routers. Don't forget to check for MED values and prepended AS_PATHs.

Example 6-53 *California's BGP Prefixes After the New Polices of Example 6-52 Have Been Applied and a Soft Reset Issued at NewMexico*

```
California#show ip bgp
BGP table version is 265, local router ID is 192.168.255.7
Status codes: s suppressed, d damped, h history, * valid, > best, i - internal,
              r RIB-failure, S Stale
Origin codes: i - IGP, e - EGP, ? - incomplete

   Network          Next Hop         Metric LocPrf Weight Path
*> 10.3.1.0/24      10.0.0.37                        0 100 300 i
*> 10.3.2.0/24      10.0.0.37                        0 100 300 i
*> 10.3.3.0/24      10.0.0.37                        0 100 300 i
*> 10.5.1.0/24      0.0.0.0              0       32768 i
*> 10.5.2.0/24      0.0.0.0              0       32768 i
*> 10.5.3.0/24      0.0.0.0              0       32768 i
*> 10.7.1.0/24      10.0.0.37           20          0 100 700 i
*> 10.7.2.0/24      10.0.0.37           20          0 100 700 i
*> 10.7.3.0/24      10.0.0.37           20          0 100 700 i
*> 10.8.1.0/24      10.0.0.37           20          0 100 800 i
```

```
*> 10.8.2.0/24       10.0.0.37              20              0 100 800 i
*> 10.8.3.0/24       10.0.0.37              20              0 100 800 i
California#
California#show ip bgp ipv6 unicast
BGP table version is 229, local router ID is 192.168.255.7
Status codes: s suppressed, d damped, h history, * valid, > best, i - internal,
             r RIB-failure, S Stale
Origin codes: i - IGP, e - EGP, ? - incomplete


   Network          Next Hop         Metric LocPrf Weight Path
*> 2001:DB8:3:1::/64
                    2001:DB8:A:5::1                     0 100 300 i
*> 2001:DB8:3:2::/64
                    2001:DB8:A:5::1                     0 100 300 i
*> 2001:DB8:3:3::/64
                    2001:DB8:A:5::1                     0 100 300 i
*> 2001:DB8:5:1::/64
                    ::                   0          32768 i
*> 2001:DB8:5:2::/64
                    ::                   0          32768 i
*> 2001:DB8:5:3::/64
                    ::                   0          32768 i
*> 2001:DB8:7:1::/64
                    2001:DB8:A:5::1      20              0 100 700 i
*> 2001:DB8:7:2::/64
                    2001:DB8:A:5::1      20              0 100 700 i
*> 2001:DB8:7:3::/64
                    2001:DB8:A:5::1      20              0 100 700 i
*> 2001:DB8:8:1::/64
                    2001:DB8:A:5::1      20              0 100 800 i
*> 2001:DB8:8:2::/64
                    2001:DB8:A:5::1      20              0 100 800 i
*> 2001:DB8:8:3::/64
                    2001:DB8:A:5::1      20              0 100 800 i
California#
```

Example 6-54 *Washington's BGP Prefixes After the New Polices of Example 6-52 Have Been Applied and a Soft Reset Issued at NewMexico*

```
Washington#show ip bgp
BGP table version is 280, local router ID is 192.168.255.9
Status codes: s suppressed, d damped, h history, * valid, > best, i - internal,
             r RIB-failure, S Stale
Origin codes: i - IGP, e - EGP, ? - incomplete
```

```
   Network          Next Hop         Metric LocPrf Weight Path
*> 10.2.1.0/24      10.0.0.33                         0 100 200 i
*> 10.2.2.0/24      10.0.0.33                         0 100 200 i
*> 10.2.3.0/24      10.0.0.33                         0 100 200 i
*> 10.3.1.0/24      10.0.0.33                         0 100 300 i
*> 10.3.2.0/24      10.0.0.33                         0 100 300 i
*> 10.3.3.0/24      10.0.0.33                         0 100 300 i
*> 10.5.1.0/24      10.0.0.33                         0 100 100 100 500 i
*> 10.5.2.0/24      10.0.0.33                         0 100 100 100 500 i
*> 10.5.3.0/24      10.0.0.33                         0 100 100 100 500 i
*> 10.6.1.0/24      10.0.0.33                         0 100 100 100 600 i
*> 10.6.2.0/24      10.0.0.33                         0 100 100 100 600 i
*> 10.6.3.0/24      10.0.0.33                         0 100 100 100 600 i
*> 10.7.1.0/24      0.0.0.0              0         32768 i
*> 10.7.2.0/24      0.0.0.0              0         32768 i
*> 10.7.3.0/24      0.0.0.0              0         32768 i
Washington#
Washington#show ip bgp ipv6 unicast
BGP table version is 244, local router ID is 192.168.255.9
Status codes: s suppressed, d damped, h history, * valid, > best, i - internal,
              r RIB-failure, S Stale
Origin codes: i - IGP, e - EGP, ? - incomplete

   Network          Next Hop         Metric LocPrf Weight Path
*> 2001:DB8:3:1::/64
                    2001:DB8:A:7::1                   0 100 300 i
*> 2001:DB8:3:2::/64
                    2001:DB8:A:7::1                   0 100 300 i
*> 2001:DB8:3:3::/64
                    2001:DB8:A:7::1                   0 100 300 i
*> 2001:DB8:4:1::/64
                    2001:DB8:A:7::1                   0 100 400 i
*> 2001:DB8:4:2::/64
                    2001:DB8:A:7::1                   0 100 400 i
*> 2001:DB8:4:3::/64
                    2001:DB8:A:7::1                   0 100 400 i
*> 2001:DB8:5:1::/64
                    2001:DB8:A:7::1                   0 100 100 100 500 i
*> 2001:DB8:5:2::/64
                    2001:DB8:A:7::1                   0 100 100 100 500 i
*> 2001:DB8:5:3::/64
   Network          Next Hop         Metric LocPrf Weight Path
                    2001:DB8:A:7::1                   0 100 100 100 500 i
```

```
*> 2001:DB8:6:1::/64
                   2001:DB8:A:7::1                          0 100 100 100 600 i
*> 2001:DB8:6:2::/64
                   2001:DB8:A:7::1                          0 100 100 100 600 i
*> 2001:DB8:6:3::/64
                   2001:DB8:A:7::1                          0 100 100 100 600 i
*> 2001:DB8:7:1::/64
                   ::                        0         32768 i
*> 2001:DB8:7:2::/64
                   ::                        0         32768 i
*> 2001:DB8:7:3::/64
                   ::                        0         32768 i
Washington#
```

Finally, you come back to Colorado, the router where you started this case study long ago. The rules for Colorado follow:

- **Utah and Nevada:** As a Standard Customers, Utah and Nevada should receive a default route and nothing else.

- **Vermont:** As a Premium Customer, Vermont should receive

  - All Service Provider prefixes (communities with :NN = :30)

  - All Partner prefixes (:NN = :20)

  - No Standard Customer prefixes (:NN = :10)

Compared to Idaho and NewMexico, these rules should be easy to implement. And they are, but there's a difficulty that must be corrected first. When you configured the incoming policies that set the community values in Example 6-40, you used a single policy template, named **Customer**, to apply to both standard and premium customer neighbors. A single route map, named **Customers**, determined according to prefix lists whether a customer was standard and assigned to community X:10, or was premium and assigned to community X:15. Now you want to set different outbound policies: permit SP and Partner prefixes to Vermont, but deny all prefixes except a default to Utah and Nevada. You can't do both of those things within a single policy template.

Oops.

The fix is not much trouble, though. You get rid of the single policy template named **Customer** and create two new policy templates named **Standard_Customer** and **Premium_Customer** (see Example 6-55). For their inbound policies they can both still reference the single route map named **Customers**. It's only the outbound behavior that is different between the two new policies.

The outbound policy at **Premium_Customer** references a route map named **Prem_Cust**. This route map permits routes with community values in lists **PARTNERS** and **SERVICE_PROVIDERS** and denies everything else.

The outbound policy at **Standard_Customers** references a route-map named **NULL** that simply denies everything. It also has an additional policy statement, **default-originate**, that causes a default route to be sent.

Because different policy templates are applied to neighbors than the ones in Example 6-40, the entire BGP configuration is shown in Example 6-55. In addition to examining this new configuration, revisit Example 6-40 and observe what has changed.

Example 6-55 *Colorado's Configuration Shows the New Outbound Policies and the Changes to the Previous Configuration That Were Necessary to Accommodate the New Policies*

```
router bgp 100
template peer-policy AS100
  next-hop-self
  send-community
 exit-peer-policy
 !
template peer-policy Premium_Customer
  route-map Customers in
  route-map Prem_Cust out
 exit-peer-policy
 !
template peer-policy Standard_Customer
  route-map Customers in
  route-map NULL out
  default-originate
 exit-peer-policy
 !
template peer-session AS100
  remote-as 100
  update-source Loopback0
  inherit peer-session Password
 exit-peer-session
 !
template peer-session Password
  password 7 020507520E
 exit-peer-session
 !
template peer-session Customers
  inherit peer-session Password
 exit-peer-session
```

```
!
bgp log-neighbor-changes
neighbor 10.0.0.1 remote-as 200
neighbor 10.0.0.1 inherit peer-session Customers
neighbor 10.0.0.5 remote-as 300
neighbor 10.0.0.5 inherit peer-session Customers
neighbor 2001:DB8:1:255::2 inherit peer-session AS100
neighbor 2001:DB8:1:255::3 inherit peer-session AS100
neighbor 2001:DB8:A:3::2 remote-as 300
neighbor 2001:DB8:A:3::2 inherit peer-session Customers
neighbor 2001:DB8:A:4::2 remote-as 400
neighbor 2001:DB8:A:4::2 inherit peer-session Customers
neighbor 192.168.255.2 inherit peer-session AS100
neighbor 192.168.255.3 inherit peer-session AS100
!
address-family ipv4
neighbor 10.0.0.1 activate
neighbor 10.0.0.1 inherit peer-policy Standard_Customer
neighbor 10.0.0.5 activate
neighbor 10.0.0.5 inherit peer-policy Premium_Customer
no neighbor 2001:DB8:1:255::2 activate
no neighbor 2001:DB8:1:255::3 activate
no neighbor 2001:DB8:A:3::2 activate
no neighbor 2001:DB8:A:4::2 activate
neighbor 192.168.255.2 activate
neighbor 192.168.255.2 inherit peer-policy AS100
neighbor 192.168.255.3 activate
neighbor 192.168.255.3 inherit peer-policy AS100
no auto-summary
no synchronization
exit-address-family
!
address-family ipv6
neighbor 2001:DB8:1:255::2 activate
neighbor 2001:DB8:1:255::2 inherit peer-policy AS100
neighbor 2001:DB8:1:255::3 activate
neighbor 2001:DB8:1:255::3 inherit peer-policy AS100
neighbor 2001:DB8:A:3::2 activate
neighbor 2001:DB8:A:3::2 inherit peer-policy Premium_Customer
neighbor 2001:DB8:A:4::2 activate
neighbor 2001:DB8:A:4::2 inherit peer-policy Standard_Customer
exit-address-family
!
ip bgp-community new-format
```

```
!
ip community-list standard STANDARD_CUSTOMERS permit 200:10
ip community-list standard STANDARD_CUSTOMERS permit 400:10
ip community-list standard PREMIUM_CUSTOMERS permit 300:15
ip community-list standard PARTNERS permit 500:20
ip community-list standard PARTNERS permit 600:20
ip community-list standard SERVICE_PROVIDERS permit 700:30
ip community-list standard SERVICE_PROVIDERS permit 800:30
!
ip as-path access-list 10 permit ^200_
ip as-path access-list 10 permit ^400_
ip as-path access-list 15 permit ^300_
!
ip prefix-list AS_200 seq 5 permit 10.2.0.0/16 le 24
ip prefix-list AS_200 seq 10 deny 0.0.0.0/0
!
ip prefix-list AS_300 seq 5 permit 10.3.0.0/16 le 24
ip prefix-list AS_300 seq 10 deny 0.0.0.0/0
!
ip prefix-list NULL seq 5 deny 0.0.0.0/0
!
ipv6 prefix-list AS_300 seq 5 permit 2001:DB8:3::/48 le 64
ipv6 prefix-list AS_300 seq 10 deny ::/0
!
ipv6 prefix-list AS_400 seq 5 permit 2001:DB8:4::/48 le 64
ipv6 prefix-list AS_400 seq 10 deny ::/0
!
ipv6 prefix-list NULL seq 5 deny ::/0
route-map NULL deny 10
!
route-map Standard_Customers permit 10
 match as-path 10
!
route-map Prem_Cust permit 10
 match community PARTNERS
!
route-map Prem_Cust permit 15
 match community SERVICE_PROVIDERS
!
route-map Prem_Cust deny 20
!
route-map Customers permit 10
 match ip address prefix-list AS_200
 match ipv6 address prefix-list NULL
```

```
 set community 200:10
 !
route-map Customers permit 20
 match ip address prefix-list AS_300
 match ipv6 address prefix-list AS_300
 set community 300:15
 !
route-map Customers permit 30
 match ip address prefix-list NULL
 match ipv6 address prefix-list AS_400
 set community 400:10
 !
```

Looking Ahead

This is the last chapter on BGP. The following chapters study IP multicast. However, you have not gotten completely away from BGP—particularly MBGP. All the prefixes manipulated in the exercises in this chapter are unicast prefixes—whether IPv4 or IPv6. In the upcoming chapters you use MBGP to route multicast IPv4 and IPv6. But before getting there, you learn about multicast models, trees, groups, group management, and multicast routing.

Review Questions

1. What attributes enable multiprotocol extensions for BGP?

2. What are the Address Family Identifier and Subsequent Address Family Identifier?

3. BGP assumes that the neighbor's address used for peering is a globally routable address. IPv6 is designed to use link-local addresses for directly connected neighbors. How does MBGP reconcile this conflict when peering two IPv6 neighbors?

4. What does the **ipv6 unicast-routing** statement do?

5. How are address families differentiated in MBGP configurations?

6. What does the **neighbor activate** statement mean under an address-family configuration?

7. Where are session parameters for a neighbor specified in an MBGP configuration? Where are policies applied to neighbors in an MBGP configuration?

8. Can both IPv4 and IPv6 prefixes be advertised over a single IPv4 or IPv6 TCP session? Or is an IPv4 TCP session required for IPv4 prefixes and an IPv6 TCP session for IPv6 prefixes?

9. What does the **bgp upgrade-cli** command do? Where is it used? When this command is invoked, does it disrupt any BGP sessions?

Configuration Exercises

Table 6-2 lists the autonomous systems, routers, interfaces, and addresses used in Configuration Exercises 1 through 10. All interfaces of the routers are shown. For each exercise, if the table indicates that the router has a loopback interface, that interface should be the source of all IBGP connections. EBGP connections should always be between physical interface addresses, unless otherwise specified in an exercise. Neighbor descriptions are always configured to be the router names. Password Chapter6_Exercises is used between for all BGP sessions.

Table 6-2   *AS, Router, Interface, and Address Information for Configuration Exercises*

AS	Router	Interface	IPv4 Address/ Mask	IPv6 Address/Mask
100	R1	Ethernet 0/0	10.0.0.13/30	2001:db8:A:4::1/64
		Loopback 0	192.168.255.1/32	2001:db8:F:F::1/64
		Loopback 1	10.1.10.1/24	2001:db8:B:1::1/64
		Loopback 2	10.1.20.1/24	2001:db8:B:2::1/64
		Loopback 3	10.1.30.1/24	2001:db8:B:3::1/64
200	R2	Ethernet 0/0	10.0.0.14/30	2001:db8:A:4::2/64
		Ethernet 0/1	10.0.0.17/30	2001:db8:A:5::2/64
		Ethernet 0/2	10.0.0.1/30	2001:db8:A:1::2/64
		Ethernet 0/3	10.0.0.5/30	2001:db8:A:2::2/64
		Loopback 0	192.168.255.2/32	2001:db8:F:F::2/64
	R3	Ethernet 0/1	10.0.0.9/30	2001:db8:A:3::3/64
		Ethernet 0/2	10.0.0.21/30	2001:db8:A:6::3/64
		Ethernet 0/3	10.0.0.6/30	2001:db8:A:2::3/64
		Loopback 0	192.168.255.3/32	2001:db8:F:F::3/64
	R4	Ethernet 0/0	10.0.0.29/30	2001:db8:A:8::4/64
		Ethernet 0/1	10.0.0.10/30	2001:db8:A:3::4/64
		Ethernet 0/2	10.0.0.2/30	2001:db8:A:1::4/64
		Loopback 0	192.168.255.4/32	2001:db8:F:F::4/64

AS	Router	Interface	IPv4 Address/ Mask	IPv6 Address/Mask
300	R5	Ethernet 0/0	10.0.0.25/30	2001:db8:A:7::5/64
		Ethernet 0/1	10.0.0.18/30	2001:db8:A:5::5/64
		Ethernet 0/2	10.0.0.22/30	2001:db8:A:6::5/64
		Loopback 0	192.168.255.5/32	2001:db8:F:F::5/64
	R6	Ethernet 0/0	10.0.0.26/30	2001:db8:A:7::6/64
		Loopback 0	192.168.255.6/32	2001:db8:F:F::6/64
		Loopback 1	10.3.10.6/24	2001:db8:C:1::6/64
400	R7	Ethernet 0/0	10.0.0.30/30	2001:db8:A:8::7/64
		Loopback 0	192.168.255.7/32	2001:db8:F:F::7/64
		Loopback 1	10.4.10.7/24	2001:db8:D:1::7/64
		Loopback 2	10.4.20.7/24	2001:db8:D:2::7/64

Question 1:

1. An EBGP session is established between R1 in AS200 and R2 in AS100 using
the IPv4 addresses configured on the interfaces on both sides. R1 injects
the IPv4 subnets 10.1.10.0/24, 10.1.20.0/24, and 10.1.30.0/24 into BGP.
Example 6-56 shows the configurations on both routers. Using a single command on each router, convert the configurations to the Address-Family format.

Example 6-56 *R1 and R2 Configurations*

```
R1
router bgp 100
 bgp log-neighbor-changes
 network 10.1.10.0 mask 255.255.255.0
 network 10.1.20.0 mask 255.255.255.0
 network 10.1.30.0 mask 255.255.255.0
 neighbor 10.0.0.14 remote-as 200
```

```
R2
router bgp 200
 bgp log-neighbor-changes
 neighbor 10.0.0.13 remote-as 100
```

2. Configure R1 in AS200 to inject the IPv6 subnets 2001:DB8:B:1::/64, 2001:DB8:B:2::/64, and 2001:DB8:B:3::/64 into BGP. Confirm that all IPv4 and IPv6 subnets injected by R1 are reachable from R2.

3. Configure R4 in AS200 and R7 in AS400 to establish an EBGP session over IPv6 only. R7 injects the IPv4 subnets 10.4.10.7/24 and 10.4.20.7/24 and IPv6 subnets 2001:DB8:D:1::7/64 and 2001:DB8:D:2::7/64 into BGP. Confirm that all IPv4 and IPv6 subnets injected by R7 into BGP are reachable from R4.

4. AS200 uses OSPF as the IGP for the AS for both IPv4 and IPv6. Configure OSPF on all AS internal routers (R2, R3, and R4) to provide reachability for all loopback addresses inside the AS. Then configure the three routers for a full IBGP mesh using their loopback 0 addresses for peering. The BGP peering will be dual-stack, providing separate IPv4 and IPv6 sessions per router pair. Also, use session and policy templates to configure all neighbor parameters. Confirm that the subnets received from AS200 and AS300 are reachable from R3 now.

5. Configure OSPF in AS300 to provide reachability for all IPv4 and IPv6 addresses internal to the AS. Then configure a dual-stack IBGP session between R5 and R6 over their loopback 0 interfaces. Configure R6 to inject the IPv4 subnet 10.3.10.0/24 and the IPv6 subnet 2001:DB8:C:1::/64 into BGP.

6. Router R5 in AS300 is dual-homed to both routers, R2 and R3, in AS100. Using separate Session and Policy Templates on R5 for R2 and R3, configure dual-stack EBGP sessions between R5 and each of the routers R2 and R3. Confirm that all subnets injected by R6 into BGP are reachable from all routers in AS100 now.

7. Using prefix-lists on R4, make sure that subnets 10.1.10.0/24, 10.1.30.0/30, and 2001:DB8:B:2::/64 in AS100 are not reachable from R7.

8. Using as-path ACLs on R4, make sure that all AS300 subnets are not reachable from R7.

9. Using different weights for route updates from R2 and R3, configure R5 so that AS300 internal routers prefer R3 as the exit point for all traffic from AS300. Then using as-prepending, make sure that return traffic to AS300 also uses the R3–R5 link.

10. Tag subnets 10.1.10.0/24 and 2001:DB8:B:3::/64 from AS100 on R2 with community 200:1234. Using this community, filter out the updates for these routes on R2 and R3 to stop them from being announced to AS300.

Troubleshooting Exercises

1. What is the following output telling you?

```
*Jun  2 16:23:29.891: %BGP-3-NOTIFICATION: sent to neighbor 2001:DB8:A:3::1 2/7
 (unsupported/disjoint capability) 0 bytes  FFFF FFFF FFFF FFFF FFFF FFFF FFFF FFFF
 002D 0104 0064 00B4 C0A8 FF01 1002 0601 0400 0100 0102 0280 0002 0202 00
*Jun  2 16:23:57.227: %BGP-3-NOTIFICATION: received from neighbor 2001:DB8:A:3::1
 2/7 (unsupported/disjoint capability) 0 bytes
```

2. What would be the result if the following route map configuration was implemented with the configuration previously shown in Example 6-40 (everything else is the same)?

```
!
route-map Customers permit 10
 match ip address prefix-list AS_200
 set community 200:10
!
route-map Customers permit 20
 match ip address prefix-list AS_300
 set community 300:15
!
route-map Customers permit 30
 match ipv6 address prefix-list AS_300
 set community 300:15
!
route-map Customers permit 40
 match ipv6 address prefix-list AS_400
 set community 400:10
!
```

3. In the following output, you can see a list of IPv4 and IPv6 routes at router Idaho (refer to Figure 6-11) that have community values attached to them. Note that Example 6-47 is recorded before the remainder of that exercise, when policies restricting route advertisements by community have been configured. When you look at router Wyoming at that same time (in the output that follows), the commands **show ip bgp** and **show ip bgp ipv6 unicast** show that all the prefixes in Example 6-47 are advertised to Wyoming. But the command **show ip bgp all community** reveals that none of those prefixes have community values. Why do the prefixes at Idaho have community values, and the same prefixes at Wyoming do not? Refer to Idaho's configuration in Example 6-45 to help find your answer.

```
Wyoming#show ip bgp
BGP table version is 145, local router ID is 192.168.255.10
Status codes: s suppressed, d damped, h history, * valid, > best, i - internal,
              r RIB-failure, S Stale
Origin codes: i - IGP, e - EGP, ? - incomplete

   Network          Next Hop          Metric LocPrf Weight Path
*> 10.2.1.0/24      10.0.0.29                          0 100 200 i
*> 10.2.2.0/24      10.0.0.29                          0 100 200 i
*> 10.2.3.0/24      10.0.0.29                          0 100 200 i
*> 10.3.1.0/24      10.0.0.29                          0 100 300 i
*> 10.3.2.0/24      10.0.0.29                          0 100 300 i
*> 10.3.3.0/24      10.0.0.29                          0 100 300 i
*> 10.5.1.0/24      10.0.0.29                          0 100 500 i
*> 10.5.2.0/24      10.0.0.29                          0 100 500 i
*> 10.5.3.0/24      10.0.0.29                          0 100 500 i
*> 10.6.1.0/24      10.0.0.29                          0 100 600 i
*> 10.6.2.0/24      10.0.0.29                          0 100 600 i
*> 10.6.3.0/24      10.0.0.29                          0 100 600 i
*> 10.7.1.0/24      10.0.0.29                          0 100 700 i
*> 10.7.2.0/24      10.0.0.29                          0 100 700 i
*> 10.7.3.0/24      10.0.0.29                          0 100 700 i
*> 10.8.1.0/24      0.0.0.0                0          32768 i
*> 10.8.2.0/24      0.0.0.0                0          32768 i
*> 10.8.3.0/24      0.0.0.0                0          32768 i
Wyoming#show ip bgp ipv6 unicast
BGP table version is 139, local router ID is 192.168.255.10
Status codes: s suppressed, d damped, h history, * valid, > best, i - internal,
              r RIB-failure, S Stale
Origin codes: i - IGP, e - EGP, ? - incomplete

   Network          Next Hop          Metric LocPrf Weight Path
*> 2001:DB8:3:1::/64
                    2001:DB8:A:8::1                    0 100 300 i
*> 2001:DB8:3:2::/64
                    2001:DB8:A:8::1                    0 100 300 i
*> 2001:DB8:3:3::/64
                    2001:DB8:A:8::1                    0 100 300 i
*> 2001:DB8:4:1::/64
                    2001:DB8:A:8::1                    0 100 400 i
*> 2001:DB8:4:2::/64
                    2001:DB8:A:8::1                    0 100 400 i
*> 2001:DB8:4:3::/64
                    2001:DB8:A:8::1                    0 100 400 i
```

```
*> 2001:DB8:5:1::/64
                 2001:DB8:A:8::1                          0 100 500 i
*> 2001:DB8:5:2::/64
                 2001:DB8:A:8::1                          0 100 500 i
*> 2001:DB8:5:3::/64
                 2001:DB8:A:8::1                          0 100 500 i
*> 2001:DB8:6:1::/64
                 2001:DB8:A:8::1                          0 100 600 i
*> 2001:DB8:6:2::/64
                 2001:DB8:A:8::1                          0 100 600 i
*> 2001:DB8:6:3::/64
                 2001:DB8:A:8::1                          0 100 600 i
*> 2001:DB8:7:1::/64
                 2001:DB8:A:8::1                          0 100 700 i
*> 2001:DB8:7:2::/64
                 2001:DB8:A:8::1                          0 100 700 i
*> 2001:DB8:7:3::/64
                 2001:DB8:A:8::1                          0 100 700 i
*> 2001:DB8:8:1::/64
                 ::                       0        32768 i
*> 2001:DB8:8:2::/64
                 ::                       0        32768 i
*> 2001:DB8:8:3::/64
                 ::                       0        32768 i
Wyoming#
Wyoming#
Wyoming#show ip bgp all community
For address family: IPv4 Unicast


For address family: IPv6 Unicast
Wyoming#
```

Chapter 7

Introduction to IP Multicast Routing

Multicasting is the process of sending data to some *group* of receivers. It might be argued that unicasting and broadcasting are subsets of multicasting. For unicasting, there is only a single member of the group; for broadcasting, all possible receivers are members of the group. This chapter demonstrates why such an argument is only valid on a conceptual level; in networking, at least, distinct functional and protocol differences exist between multicasting and unicasting and broadcasting. That said, IPv6 does move a little closer to everything being a variant of multicast; instead of a broadcast address, it uses an all-nodes multicast address. The same results occur as broadcast but under the functional class of multicast.

The delivery of radio and television programming is commonly called *broadcasting*, but in reality it is multicasting. A transmitter sends data on a certain frequency, and some group of receivers acquires the data by tuning in to that frequency. The frequency is, in this sense, a multicast address. All receivers within the range of the transmission can receive the signal, but only those who listen to the correct frequency actually receive it.

The signal range brings up another important concept: Radio and television transmissions have *scope*—they are limited by the power of the transmitter. Receivers outside the scope of the transmission cannot receive the signal. You see in this chapter that IP multicast networks can also have scope.

You have already had some exposure to IP multicasting in Volume I. RIPv2, EIGRP, and OSPF all employ multicasting for efficiency in communicating routing information. Applications can use multicasting for exactly the same reason: to increase network efficiency and conserve network resources. Figure 7-1 shows a set of IP hosts. One of the hosts is a source (S) of data that must be delivered to a group (G) of receivers. There is more than one receiver, but the group does not contain all possible receivers.

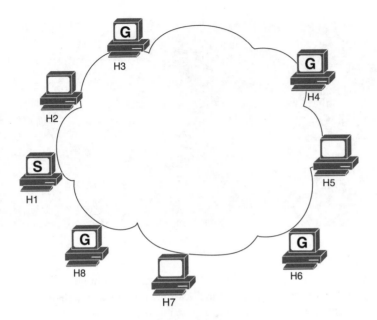

Figure 7-1   *The Source Must Deliver the Same Data to Multiple Receivers*

One approach is for the source to use replicated unicast. That is, the source creates a separate packet containing identical data for each destination host in the group. Each packet is then unicast to a specific host, as shown in Figure 7-2.

If only a few destinations exist, this scheme works fine. Actually, many "multicast" applications in use today actually use replicated unicast. But as the number of recipients grows into the hundreds or thousands, the burden on the host to create and send so many copies of the same data also increases. More important, the host's interface, directly connected medium, directly connected router, and slow WAN links all become potential bottlenecks. Problems also exist if the data is delay-sensitive and cannot be contained in a single packet. If all the copies of packet number 2 must wait for all the copies of packet number 1 to be queued and sent, the queuing delay can introduce unacceptable gaps in the data stream.

Another possible approach to multicasting is to broadcast the data, as shown in Figure 7-3. This removes the burden from the source and its local facilities, which now have to send only a single copy of each packet but can extend the burden to the other hosts in the network. Each host must accept a copy for the broadcasted packet and process the packet. It is only at the higher layers, or possibly within the application, that disinterested hosts recognize that the packet is to be discarded. If the number of hosts in the receiving group is small in relation to the total number of hosts in the network, this processing burden can again be unacceptable.

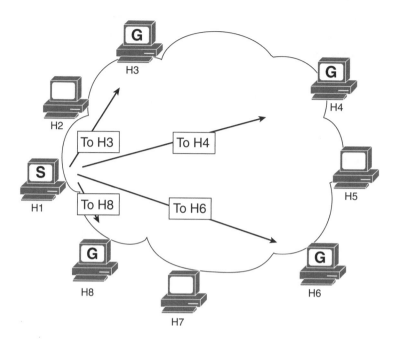

Figure 7-2 *Unicasting the Same Data to Multiple Receivers Places a Burden on the Source*

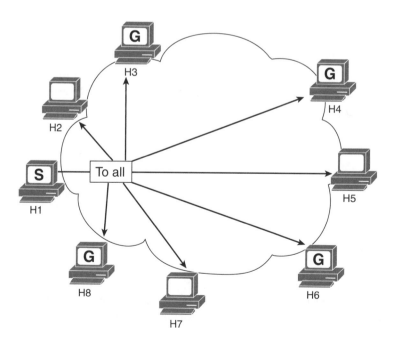

Figure 7-3 *Broadcasting Data Can Place a Burden on the Rest of the Network*

> **Note**   When there are relatively few group members in relation to the total number of hosts in a multicast domain, the domain is *sparsely populated*. You encounter this concept again later in this chapter.

Another difficulty with broadcasting is that IP routers do not forward packets to broadcast destinations. If the cloud in Figure 7-3 is a routed network rather than a single broadcast medium, broadcast packets cannot reach the remote hosts. Directed broadcasts could be used, but that may be the worst possible solution. Not only would all hosts receive the packet, but also the source would again be burdened with having to replicate packets.

Multicasting allows the source to send a single packet to a single multicast destination address, thus removing the processing burden of replicating packets from the host; the burden is distributed through the network. Any receiver that is listening for the multicast address can receive the packet, removing the need for disinterested hosts to process an unwanted packet. And unlike broadcast packets, multicast-aware routers can forward multicast packets.

Many aspects of IP multicasting are not covered in this chapter. This book is concerned only with IP routing, so the primary focus of the chapter is on IP multicast routing. Other topics are touched upon only as they pertain to routing; for a complete treatment of IP multicast, look at the references cited at the end of the chapter in the "Recommended Reading" section.

Requirements for IP Multicast

IP multicast is not a new concept; Steve Deering wrote the first RFC on multicast host requirements in 1986.[1] But it is only in the past few years that interest in multicasting has taken off as enterprises present increasing demands for one-to-many and many-to-many communications.

Examples of one-to-many applications include video and audio feeds for distance learning or company news, software distribution, network-based entertainment programs, news and stock updates, and database or website replication. The classic many-to-many application is conferencing, including video, audio, and shared whiteboards. Multiplayer games are another many-to-many application; although, most corporations would be loath to include them on a wish list. As the use of such group-based applications increases, the efficiency and performance advantages of multicast over broadcast and replicated unicast for packet delivery becomes attractive.

You must make a variety of protocol choices when implementing IP multicast. Because of this, multicast is found primarily in networks where a single administrative authority can make the design choices. This might range from a single building or campus environment to a nationwide provider such as Comcast or AT&T, but what they have in common is architectural control of the entire network.

An organization can also have multicast services covering geographically diverse offices or campuses by contracting with a backbone service provider that connects all locations via a native IP multicast network, multicast tunnels, or a multicast-enabled MPLS backbone. Even though the backbone provider is a separate administrative domain, the organization's IP multicast network is still privately contracted.

Multicast across the public Internet is problematic because every router from source to receiver must be multicast enabled. When I wrote the first edition of this volume in 2001, I predicted that entertainment services would be the likely driver for IP multicast across the Internet. Here we are 15 years later, with ubiquitous entertainment services available over the Internet from providers such as Netflix, Hulu, Amazon Instant Video, and Pandora; yet the movies, TV shows, and music are delivered to us over unicast streams. I am less sure that some use case will bring about a multicast-enabled public Internet than I was in 2001.

Multicast has been researched for some time on a subset of the Internet known as the Multicast Backbone, or MBone. But the MBone was never more than a research project, not a commercially viable public multicast service. Ubiquitous availability of multicast services across the entire Internet, if it ever happens, must await further research and development of inter-AS protocols, such as Multiprotocol BGP (MBGP) and Border Gateway Multicast Protocol (BGMP). Presently, no IP multicast routing protocols exist that support routing policies comparable to those supported by BGP. Until adequate tools for enforcing policy are introduced, it is unlikely that multicasting will find wide Internet acceptance. So this chapter and the subsequent two chapters focus primarily on multicast in single administrative domains or across a set of administrative domains with shared interests.

The three basic requirements for supporting multicast across a routed network follows:

- There must be a set of addresses by which multicast groups are identified.

- There must be a mechanism by which hosts can join and leave groups.

- There must be a routing protocol that allows routers to efficiently deliver multicast traffic to group members without over-taxing network resources.

This section examines the basics of each of these requirements; subsequent sections examine the various protocols that have been explored in the past to meet these requirements, and how experience with them has contributed to modern IP multicast networking.

IPv4 Multicast Addresses

The IANA set aside Class D IPv4 addresses for use as multicast addresses. Although CIDR techniques have mostly eliminated classful terminology when working with unicast IPv4 addresses, the group of addresses assigned for multicast has not changed, so it is still easy to refer to them as Class D. According to the First Octet rule, as described in Chapter 1 of Volume I, "TCP/IP Review," the first four bits of a Class D address are always 1110 (224.0.0.0/4), as shown in Figure 7-4. Finding the minimum and maximum 32-bit numbers within this constraint, the range of Class D addresses is 224.0.0.0–239.255.255.255.

Rule	Minimums and Maximums	Decimal Range
Class A: First bit is always 0.	**0**0000000 = 0 **0**1111111 = 127	1 - 126* * 0 and 127 are reserved.
Class B: First two bits are always 10.	**10**000000 = 128 **10**111111 = 191	128 - 191
Class C: First three bits are always 110.	**110**00000 = 192 **110**11111 = 223	192 - 223
Class D: First four bits are always 1110.	**1110**0000 = 224 **1110**1111 = 239	224 - 239

Figure 7-4   *IPv4 Class D Addresses Are in the Range 224.0.0.0–239.255.255.255*

Unlike the Class A, B, and C address ranges, the Class D range is "flat"—that is, subnetting is not used, as shown by Figure 7-5. Therefore, with 28 variable bits, 2^{28} (more than 268 million) multicast groups can be addressed out of the Class D IPv4 space.

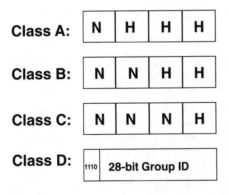

Figure 7-5   *Unlike Class A, B, and C IP Addresses, Class D Addresses Do Not Have a Network Portion and a Host Portion*

A multicast group is defined by its multicast IP address; groups may be permanent or transient. *Permanent* refers to the group that has a permanently assigned address; members are not permanently assigned to the group. Actually, hosts are free to join or leave any group. Transient groups are, as you might guess, groups that do not have a permanent existence—such as a video conference group. An unreserved address is assigned to the group and is relinquished when the group ceases to exist.

Table 7-1 shows some of the well-known addresses assigned to permanent groups by the IANA. You have encountered most of these addresses before when you studied the routing protocols to which they are assigned. For example, you know that on a multi-access network, OSPF DRothers send updates to the OSPF DR and BDR at 224.0.0.6; the DR sends packets to the DRothers at 224.0.0.5.

Table 7-1 *Some Well-Known IPv4 Multicast Addresses*

Address	Group
224.0.0.1	All systems on this subnet
224.0.0.2	All routers on this subnet
224.0.0.4	DVMRP routers
224.0.0.5	All OSPF routers
224.0.0.6	OSPF designated routers
224.0.0.9	RIP-2 routers
224.0.0.10	EIGRP routers
224.0.0.12	DHCP Server/Relay Agent
224.0.0.13	PIM routers
224.0.0.15	CBT routers
224.0.0.18	VRRP
224.0.0.22	IGMP
224.0.1.39	Cisco-RP-Announce
224.0.1.40	Cisco-RP-Discovery

The IANA reserves all the addresses in the range 224.0.0.0–224.0.0.255 for routing protocols and other network maintenance functions. Multicast routers do not forward packets with a destination address from this range. Also addresses outside of this range are reserved for open and commercial groups; for example, 224.0.1.1 is reserved for the Network Time Protocol (NTP), 224.0.1.8 is assigned to SUN NIS+, and 224.0.6.0–224.0.6.127 are assigned to the Cornell ISIS Project. You can also find a number of different multicast ranges assigned to stock exchanges such as the New York Stock Exchange and the London Stock Exchange, reflecting the widespread use of multicast in financial networks.

Yet another reserved range is 239.0.0.0–239.255.255.255. The use of this last group of addresses is discussed in the later section, "Multicast Scoping." For a complete list of reserved Class D addresses, see Appendix C ("Reserved Multicast Addresses"), RFC 1700 (now replaced by an online database), or the IANA's Assigned Numbers website at www.iana.org/assignments/multicast-addresses.

A group member's Network Interface Card (NIC) must also be multicast-aware. When a host joins a group, the NIC determines a predictable MAC address. To accomplish this, all multicast-aware Ethernet, Token Ring, and FDDI NICs use the reserved IEEE 802 address 0100.5E00.0000 to determine a unique multicast MAC. It is significant that the eighth bit of this address is 1; that bit, in the 802 format, is the Individual/Group (I/G) bit. When set, it indicates that the address is a multicast or broadcast address.

Note   The first edition of this volume included discussions of multicasting over Token Ring and FDDI, in addition to Ethernet. Those discussions have been eliminated in this edition, reflecting the obsolescence of TR and FDDI. If you want or need to know about the operation of those broadcast mediums, documentation is not hard to find.

Ethernet interfaces map the lower 23 bits of the group IPv4 address onto the lower 23 bits of the reserved MAC address to form a multicast MAC address, as shown in Figure 7-6. Here, the Class D IPv4 address 235.147.18.23 creates the MAC address 0100.5E13.1217.

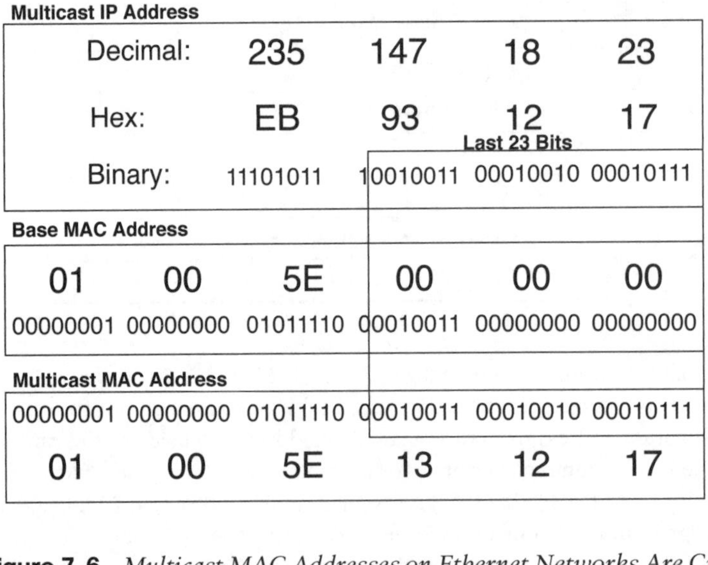

Multicast IP Address

Decimal:	235	147	18	23
Hex:	EB	93	12	17
			Last 23 Bits	
Binary:	11101011	10010011	00010010	00010111

Base MAC Address

01	00	5E	00	00	00
00000001	00000000	01011110	00010011	00000000	00000000

Multicast MAC Address

00000001	00000000	01011110	00010011	00010010	00010111
01	00	5E	13	12	17

Figure 7-6   *Multicast MAC Addresses on Ethernet Networks Are Created by Concatenating the Last 23 Bits of the IP Address with the First 25 Bits of the MAC Address 0100.5E00.0000v*

You have already encountered a couple of these addresses. Recall that in Chapter 8 of Volume I, "OSPFv2," it was briefly explained that the All OSPF routers address 224.0.0.5 uses a MAC address of 0100.5E00.0005, and the All OSPF Designated Routers address 224.0.0.6 uses the MAC address 0100.5E00.0006. Now you know why.

Because only the last 23 bits of the IPv4 address are mapped to the MAC address, the resulting multicast MAC address is not universally unique. For example, the IP address 225.19.18.23 produces the same MAC address, 0100.5E13.1217, as 235.147.18.23. Actually, calculating the ratio of the total number of Class D addresses (2^{28}) to the number of possible MAC addresses under the reserved prefix (223) reveals that 32 different Class D IP addresses can be mapped to every possible MAC address!

The IETF's position is that the odds of two or more group addresses existing on the same LAN producing the same MAC address are acceptably remote. On the rare occasion that such a conflict does arise, the members of the two groups on the LAN receive each other's traffic. In most of these cases, each group's packets are destined for different port numbers or possibly have different application layer authentication schemes; each group's members discard the other group's packets at the transport layer or above.

The hazards are not theoretical, however. One of the technical reviewers of this book relates a story in which he was rolling out new IPTV middleware for a "triple play" provider (voice video, Internet) and allocated 239.128.64.1 for an IPTV channel without checking for MAC overlap. It turned out that another channel was using 224.0.64.1. The result was a sustained outage for that channel because set top boxes were receiving traffic for both multicast groups and dropping packets due to rate limiting.

The benefits of this predictable MAC approach, however, are twofold:

- A multicast source or router on the local network has to deliver only a single frame to the multicast MAC address for all group members on the LAN to receive it.

- Because the MAC address is always known if the group address is known, there is no need for an ARP process.

IPv6 Multicast Addresses

IPv6 multicast addresses are a little easier to recognize than IPv4 multicast addresses. They have the single prefix of FF00::/8, or all ones in the first 8 bits, as shown in Figure 7-7, so there is no numerical range to remember. Any IPv6 address that starts with FF is a multicast address.

The flexibility comes from the next 8 bits. The 4 bits following the prefix are flags that indicate whether the address is a well-known multicast address or a transient address, whether the address has an embedded Rendezvous Point address (explained in Chapter 8. "Protocol Independent Multicast"), and whether the multicast address is based on an embedded unicast address (also explained in Chapter 8).

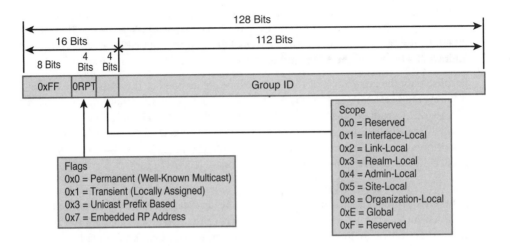

Figure 7-7   *IPv6 Multicast Address Format*

The next 4 bits define the scope of the address—that is, the boundaries within the network in which the address is relevant. The scope can range from interface-local all the way up to globally unique, as shown in Figure 7-7. Because there are 4 bits, up to 16 different scopes can be defined; although, not all possible values are defined. Multicast scoping is also explained Chapter 9, "Scaling IP Multicast Routing," but for now it's important to note that scoping IPv4 multicast is more complicated than scoping IPv6 multicast because IPv4 multicast addresses do not have this built-in scope field.

With the first 16 bits of the 128-bit IPv6 address used for prefix, flags, and scope, 112 bits remain to define specific multicast groups. That's an astronomically larger number of possible group addresses than are supported under the 24 available bits of the IPv4 multicast address format. IPv6 provides support for more uniquely identifiable multicast groups under any scope—including globally on the public Internet—than will ever realistically be used: some 74 trillion, trillion, trillion, trillion, multicast groups for every person currently living on planet Earth. And because we will never even scratch the surface of the number of available IPv6 multicast group addresses, we can use some of the 112 bits for a practical trick of using some of the bits to embed a Rendezvous Point address within a group address. As a result, a group's designated routers can identify the group's RP without static configuration or a protocol such as BSR. Don't worry if none of this explanation makes sense to you yet—it is explained in detail in Chapter 8. For now, it is enough to know that there are some significant practical advantages inherent in IPv6 multicast addresses that do not exist for Iv4 multicast.

Table 7-2 lists a few of the well-known IPv6 multicast addresses. There are a couple points to note in the table, when compared to the well-known IPv4 multicast addresses in Table 7-1. First, IPv6 does not have a broadcast address like IPv4's 255.255.255.255. Instead, it has an All-Nodes multicast group—a group in which all nodes are a member. Functionally, it's the same thing as a broadcast address, but because of the scope field, it can be defined for different network scopes. Address scopes are the second important comparison to make with Table 7-1: The All-Nodes and the All-Routers group can be either Local-Node or Link-Local scope. IGPs operate under Link-Local scope, just as they do in IPv4; although, IPv4 multicast addresses have no inherent scoping capabilities. Confining IPv4 routing protocol messages to direct links between neighbors must be enforced in the protocol.

Table 7-2   *Some Well-Known IPv6 Multicast Addresses*

Address	Group
Local-Node Scope	
FF01::1	All nodes
FF01::2	All routers
Link-Local Scope	
FF02::1	All nodes
FF02::2	All routers
FF02::4	DVMRP routers
FF02::5	All OSPFv3 routers
FF02::6	OSPFv3 designated routers
FF02::9	RIPng routers
FF02::A	EIGRP routers
FF02::C	SSDP
FF02::D	PIM routers
FF02::12	VRRP
FF02::16	MLDv2
Site-Local Scope	
FF05::2	All routers

The third point of interest is that an effort is made to keep IPv6 multicast groups similar to their IPv4 counterparts. For example, where OSPFv2 routers and OSPFv2 designated routers are 224.0.0.4 and 224.0.0.5, OSPFv3 routers and OSPFv3 designated routers are FF02::5 and FF02::6. Comparing Tables 7-1 and 7-2 you can see similar correspondences for DVMRP, RIP, EIGRP, PIM, and VRRP.

A type of IPv6 link-local multicast address is called *Solicited-Node* multicast, used by IPv6 Neighbor Discovery Protocol (NDP). As you should already know, NDP consolidates a number of link level functions that in IPv4 are performed by multiple protocols within a broadcast domain such as ARP and Redirect. Specifically, NDP uses Solicited-Node multicast addresses in its neighbor discovery function. When a node must solicit a neighbor or router at a particular IPv6 address for its MAC address, it takes the last 24 bits of the neighbor's IPv6 address and appends them to the link-local scoped multicast prefix FF02::1:FF00:0/104. For example, in Figure 7-8 the target IPv6 link-local unicast address FE80::BA8D:12FF:FE44:C7B6 creates the Solicited-Node multicast address FF02::1:FF44:C7B6. The ND solicitation is then sent to this address. All nodes on the link have previously computed the Solicited-Node multicast address for every one of the unicast IPv6 addresses on their links and are listening for packets sent to the computed addresses. That is, they have "joined" their respective solicited node multicast groups.

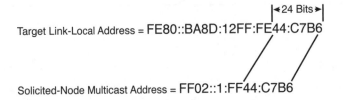

Figure 7-8   *The Solicited-Node Multicast Address Is Used by Neighbor Discovery Protocol to Reduce the Number of Local Nodes Impacted When a Device Must Query a Neighbor for Its MAC Address*

This procedure is more efficient than IPv4 ARP, which broadcasts its queries and therefore requires every node in the broadcast domain to process the query at least far enough to determine that they are not the target. IPv6 nodes listen only for multicast packets sent to their own computed solicited node groups.

In the rare case in which more than one node on the link has an interface address with the same last 24 bits, the soliciting node can examine the full IPv6 address of all responses to identify the response from the correct neighbor. This book is about routing IP, of course, rather than local neighbor maintenance functions. If you want to know more details about how IPv6 Neighbor Discovery works, look at RFC 4861.

IPv6 multicast addresses on Ethernet interfaces are mapped to multicast MAC addresses just as IPv4 multicast addresses are, but the procedure and the MAC addresses are different. An IPv6 multicast address is mapped to a MAC address by appending the last 32 bits of the multicast address to the 16-bit value 0x3333. For example, in Figure 7-9, the last 4 octets of the multicast address FF02::18:37B2:CA5D is prepended to 0x3333 to create the 48-bit MAC address 33:33:37:B2:CA:5D.

The Ethertype for frames carrying IPv6 addresses, including multicast addresses, is 0x86DD instead of the IPv4 0x0800.

Group Membership Concepts

Before a host can join a group, it (or its user) must know what groups are available to be joined and how to join them. There are various mechanisms available for advertising multicast groups, such as online "TV Guides," or web-based schedules.

|←—32 Bits—→|

IPv6 Multicast Address = FF02::18:37B2:CA5D

Mapped Ethernet MAC Address = 33:33:37:B2:CA:5D

Figure 7-9 *IPv6 Multicast Destination Addresses Are Mapped to Ethernet MAC Addresses by Prepending the 16-Bit Value 0x3333 onto the Last 32 Bits of the IPv6 Address to Create a 48-Bit MAC Address*

Also tools utilize such protocols as Session Description Protocol (SDR) and Session Advertisement Protocol (SAP) to describe multicast events and advertise those descriptions. Figure 7-10 shows an application that uses these protocols. A user may also learn of a multicast session by invitation, such as via a simple e-mail.

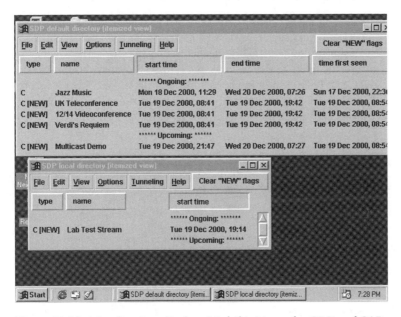

Figure 7-10 *Applications Such as Multikit Listen for SDR and SAP, and Display the Multicast Sessions Advertised by Those Protocols*

A detailed discussion of these mechanisms is beyond the scope of this book. This section presumes that hosts have somehow learned of a multicast group and examines the issues around joining and leaving the group. After examining these issues, you can see how they are handled by the Internet Group Management Protocol (IGMP) for IPv4 and Multicast Listener Discover (MLD) for IPv6, the *de facto* protocols for managing IP multicast groups on individual subnets.

Joining and Leaving a Group

Interestingly, the source of a multicast session does not have to be a member of the multicast group to which it sends traffic. The source typically does not even know what hosts, if any, are members of the group. Receivers are free to join and leave groups at any time. This again fits the earlier analogy of a radio or television signal; audience members can tune in or tune out at any time, and the originating station has no direct way of knowing who is listening.

If the source and all group members share a common LAN, no other protocols are required. The source sends packets to a multicast IP (and MAC) address, and the group members "tune in" to this address. But sending multicast traffic over a routed network becomes more complicated. Every router could merely forward all multicast packets onto every LAN, in case there are group members on the LAN, but this dramatically circumvents the goal of multicasting, which is to conserve network resources. If no group members are on the LAN, bandwidth and processing is wasted not only on that subnet, but also on all data links and routers connecting it to the source.

Therefore, a router must have some means to learn whether a connected network includes group members, and if so, members of what group. When a router becomes aware of a multicast session, it can query all its attached subnets for hosts that want to join the receiving group. The query might be addressed to the "all systems on this subnet" address of 224.0.0.1 or FF02::1, or it might be addressed to the specific address of the group for which it is querying. If one or more hosts respond, the router can then forward the session's packets onto the appropriate subnet, as shown in Figure 7-11.

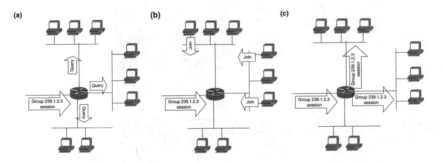

Figure 7-11 *Multicast Group Member Discovery*

The router can periodically re-send queries to the subnet. If there are still group members on the subnet, they respond to all queries to let the router know they are still active in the group. If no hosts respond, the router assumes that all hosts on the subnet have left the group and ceases forwarding the group's packets onto the subnet.

Join Latency

A problem with the scheme described so far is that if a host knows of a group it wants to join, it's not always practical for the host to wait for a router to query for the group. To reduce this wait time, a host could send a message to the router requesting a join, without waiting for a query. Upon receiving the join request, the router immediately forwards the multicast traffic onto the subnet.

This procedure has benefits for more than just the local subnet. In the later section "Multicast Routing Concepts," you see that having hosts initiate the join can help make multicast routing protocols more efficient. If a router has no group members on any of its attached subnets, and the subnets are not transit networks for multicast traffic to other routers, the router can request that upstream neighbors do not forward multicast traffic to it. The result is that the traffic streams do not enter parts of the network in which there are no group members. If the router then receives a join request on one of its attached subnets, it can send a request upstream to begin receiving the relevant data stream.

The trade-off of this scheme is that if a host sends a join request to its local router and then has to wait for the router to request the appropriate traffic from its upstream neighbors, the *join latency* is increased. Join latency is the period between the time a host sends a join request and the time the host actually begins receiving group traffic. Of course, if other group members are already on the subnet when the host decides to join, the join latency will be practically zero. The host has no reason to send a join request to the router; it can simply begin listening to the packets that are already being forwarded onto its subnet for the other group members.

Leave Latency

Allowing a host to explicitly notify its local router when it leaves a group can also increase efficiency. Rather than having to wait for no hosts to respond to its queries before it implicitly concludes that there are no group members on a subnet, the router can actively determine whether there are remaining members. Upon receiving a leave notification from a host, the router immediately sends a query onto the subnet asking if there are any remaining members. If no one responds, the router concludes that there are no more members and can cease forwarding packets for the group onto that subnet. The result is a decreased *leave latency*, which is the period between the time the last group member on a subnet leaves the group and the time the router stops forwarding group traffic onto the subnet.

Host-initiated group leaves also improve routing protocol efficiency. If a router knows that it no longer has any group members on any of its subnets, it can "prune" itself from the multicast tree. The sooner a router determines that there are no group members, the sooner it can prune itself.

Decreased join and leave latencies can also improve the overall quality of a multicast network. There could be a large lineup of multicast groups known to a host. Low join and leave latencies mean that the end user can easily "channel surf" through the available groups in the same way that users casually flip through radio and television channels.

Group Maintenance

The message that a host sends to a router to indicate that it wants to join a group is known as a *report*. A host could use several possible destination addresses when sending a report:

- The report could be unicast to the router that sent the query. The problem here is that there may be more than one router attached to the subnet that is tracking the group. All concerned routers must hear the report.

- The report could be sent to the "all routers on this subnet" address of 224.0.0.2 or FF02::2. However, you will see shortly that it is useful for other group members on the subnet to also hear the report.

- To ensure that other group members hear the report, it could be sent to the "all systems on this subnet" address of 224.0.0.1 or FF02::1. But this would reduce the efficiency of multicasting by forcing all multicast-capable hosts on the subnet, not just the group members, to process the report beyond Layer 2.

- The report could be sent to the group address. This ensures that all group members on the subnet, and any routers listening for members of the group, hear the report. The NICs of hosts that are not members of the group reject the reports based on their Layer 2 address.

As previously mentioned, the message a router sends on a subnet to look for group members is a *query*. If all group members on a subnet respond to a query, bandwidth is unnecessarily wasted. After all, the router needs to know only that there is at least one member of the group on the subnet; it does not need to know exactly how many there are, or who they are. Another problem with all group members responding to a query is the possibility of collisions if all members respond at once. Backing off and retransmitting consumes more network and host resources. If many group members are on the subnet, there is an increased probability that multiple collisions will occur before everyone sends their report.

Sending reports to the group address eliminates multiple reports on a subnet. When a query is received, each group member starts a timer based on a random value. The member does not send a report until the timer expires. Because the timers are random, it is much more likely that one member's timer will expire before the others. This member sends a report, and because the report is sent to the group address, all other members hear it. These other members, hearing the report, cancel their timers and do not send a report of their own. As a result, only one report is generally sent on the subnet. One report per subnet is all the router needs.

Multiple Routers on a Network

The possibility was raised in the last section that multiple routers might be attached to a subnet, all of which need to know whether there are group members present. Figure 7-12 shows an example. Two routers are attached to the subnet, both of which receive the same multicast stream from the same source, over different routes. If one router or route fails, the group members can continue to receive their multicast session from the other router. But under normal circumstances, it is inefficient for both routers to forward the same data stream onto the subnet.

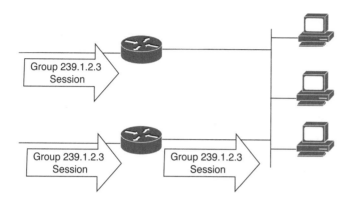

Figure 7-12 *Two Routers Receive the Same Multicast Session, but Only One Forwards It onto the Subnet*

The routers are aware of each other because of their routing protocols. So one way to ensure that only one router forwards the session onto the subnet is to add a designated router, or *Querier*, function to the multicast routing protocol. The Querier is responsible for forwarding the multicast stream. The other router or routers only listen and only begin forwarding the stream if the Querier fails. The problem with allowing the routing protocol to elect a Querier is that there are multiple IP multicast routing protocols available. If the two routers in Figure 7-12 are running incompatible protocols, their respective Querier election processes will not detect each other; each will decide that it is the Querier, and both will forward the data stream.

The local group management protocol, however, is independent of the routing protocols. The routers have to run this common protocol to query group members, so it makes sense to give the Querier function to the group management protocol. This guarantees that the routers are speaking a common language on the subnet and can agree on which is responsible for forwarding the session.

Internet Group Management Protocol (IGMP)

Regardless of which of the several routing protocols is used in a multicast network, IGMP is always the "language" spoken between hosts and routers.

Note Multicast Listener Discovery (MLD), described in the next section, is a subset of IGMP used for IPv6 multicast group management. Rather than use the clumsy acronym IGMP/MLD in this section, just be aware that most of the functional IGMP descriptions in this section also apply to MLD.

All hosts that want to join IPv4 multicast groups and all routers with interfaces on subnets containing multicast hosts must implement IGMP. It is a control protocol like ICMP, sharing some functional similarities. Like ICMP, it is responsible for managing higher-level data exchanges. IGMP messages are encapsulated in IP headers like ICMP (with a protocol number of 2), but unlike ICMP the messages are limited to the local data link. This is guaranteed both by the IGMP implementation rules, which require that a router never forward an IGMP message and by always setting the TTL in the IP header to 1.

There are three current versions of IGMP: IGMPv1 is described in RFC 1112, IGMPv2 is described in RFC 2236, and IGMPv3 is described in RFC 3376. Cisco IOS Software Release 11.1 and all later versions support IGMPv2 by default. However, some host TCP/IP implementations still support only version 1 (Windows NT 4.0 with service packs previous to SP4, for example) and newer hosts may support IGMPv3. For this reason, the default can be changed with the **ip igmp version** command. This section discusses IGMPv2 and then presents its differences with IGMPv1 and IGMPv3.

IGMPv2 Host Functions

Hosts running IGMPv2 use three types of messages:

- Membership Report messages

- Version 1 Membership Report messages

- Leave Group messages

Membership Report messages are sent to indicate that a host wants to join a group. The messages are sent when a host first joins a group and sometimes in response to a Membership Query from a local router.

When a host first learns of a group and wants to join, it does not wait for the local router to send a query. As you will learn in Chapter 8, the router may not (and most likely does not) have any knowledge of the particular group the host wants to join and therefore does not query for members. If the host had to wait for a query, it might never get the opportunity to join. Instead, when the host first joins a group, it sends an unsolicited Membership Report for the group.

Multicast sessions are identified in the routers by a (source, group) pair of addresses, where the source is the unicast address of the session's originator, and the group is the multicast group address. If the local multicast router does not already have knowledge of the multicast session the host wants to join, it sends a request upstream toward the source. The data stream is received, and the router begins forwarding the stream onto the subnet of the host that requested membership.

The destination address of the Membership Report message's IP header is the group address, and the message also contains the group address. To ensure that the local router receives the unsolicited Membership Report, the host sends one or two more duplicate reports separated by a short interval. RFC 2236 recommends an interval of 10 seconds.

IGMPv2 and IGMPv3 hosts support backward compatibility with older versions. The mechanisms that IGMPv2 and IGMPv3 use to detect and support previous versions on hosts and routers on its subnet are discussed later in this section.

The local router periodically polls the subnet with queries. Each query contains a value called the Max Response Time, which is normally 10 seconds (specified in units of tenths of a second). When a host receives a query, it sets a delay timer to a random value between 0 and the Max Response Time. If the timer expires, the host responds to the query with one Membership Report for each group to which it belongs.

Note   All multicast-enabled devices are members of the "all systems on this subnet" group, represented by the group addresses 224.0.0.1 and, if IPv6 is enabled, FF02::1. Because this is a default, hosts do not send Membership Reports for this group.

Because the destination of the Membership Report is the group address, other group members that might be on the subnet hear the report in addition to the router. If the host receives a Membership Report for a group before its delay timer expires, it does not send a Membership Report for that group. In this way, the router is informed of the presence of at least one group member on the subnet, without all members flooding the subnet with Reports.

When a host leaves a group, it notifies the local router with a Leave Group message. The message contains the address of the group being left, but unlike Membership Report messages, the Leave Group message is addressed to the "all routers on this subnet" address of 224.0.0.2. This is because only the multicast routers on the subnet need to know that the host is leaving; other group members do not.

RFC 2236 recommends that a Leave Group message be sent only if the leaving member was the last host to send a Membership Report in response to a query. As the next section explains, the local router always responds to a Leave Group message by querying for remaining group members. If group members other than the "last responder" leave quietly, the router continues forwarding the session and does not send a query. As a result, a little bandwidth is saved. However, this behavior is not required. If the designer of a multicast application does not want to include a state variable to remember whether this host was the last to respond to a query, the application can always send a Leave Group message when it leaves a group.

IGMPv2 Router Functions

The only type of IGMP message sent by routers is a query. Two subtypes of queries are within IGMPv2:

- General Query
- Group-Specific Query

The General Query is the message with which the router polls each of its subnets to discover if group members are present and to detect when there are no members of a group left on a subnet. By default, the queries are sent every 60 seconds; the default can be changed to any value between 0 and 65535 seconds with the statement **ip igmp query-interval**. As is usual for these kinds of timers, changing the default should be considered carefully. Decreasing the timer improves responsiveness but cost resources; increasing the timer saves resources at the cost of responsiveness.

As described in the last section, the query also contains a value called the Max Response Time. This value specifies the maximum amount of time the host has to respond to a query with a Membership Report. By default, the Max Response Time is 10 seconds; it can be changed with the statement **ip igmp query-max-response-time**. The value is carried in the message in an 8-bit field and is expressed in units of tenths of a second. (Although the value is specified with the **ip igmp query-max-response-time** in units of seconds. For example, the default 10 seconds is expressed within the message as 100 tenths of a second. Therefore, the range that can be specified is 0 to 255 tenths, or 0 to 25.5 seconds.

The General Query message is sent to the "all systems on this subnet" multicast address of 224.0.0.1 and does not contain a reference to any specific group. As a result, the single message polls for Reports from members of all groups that might be active on the subnet. The router tracks known groups and the interfaces attached to subnets with active members, as shown in the output in Example 7-1.

Example 7-1   show ip igmp groups *Command Displays the IP Multicast Groups of Which the Router Is Aware*

```
Gold#show ip igmp groups
IGMP Connected Group Membership
Group Address    Interface        Uptime    Expires   Last Reporter
224.0.1.40       Serial0/1.306    3d01h     never     0.0.0.0
228.0.5.3        Ethernet0/0      00:09:07  00:02:55  172.16.1.254
239.1.2.3        Ethernet0/0      1d08h     00:02:53  172.16.1.23

Gold#
```

If an IOS multicast router does not hear a Membership Report on a particular subnet for a group within three times the query interval (3 minutes by default), the router concludes that there are no active members of the group on the subnet. This covers the eventuality of a lone group member being disconnected or otherwise not following the IGMPv2 rules for leaving a group.

Note   This differs from RFC 2236, which specifies twice the query interval plus one Max Response Time interval.

The normal way that a host leaves a group is by sending a Leave Group message. When a router receives a Leave Group message, it must determine if there are any remaining members of that group on the subnet. To do this, the router issues a Group-Specific Query, which differs from a General Query in that it contains the group address, and it also uses the group address as its destination address.

If the Group-Specific Query were to become lost or corrupted, a remaining group member on the subnet might not send a Report. As a result, the router would incorrectly conclude that no group members are on the subnet and stop forwarding the session packets. To protect against this eventuality, the router sends two Group-Specific Queries, separated by a 1-second interval known as the Last Member Query interval.

When a multicast-enabled router first becomes active on a subnet, it assumes that it is the *Querier*—the router responsible for sending all General and Group-Specific Queries to the subnet—and immediately sends a General Query.

Note   RFC 2236 recommends sending multiple queries; however, IOS's IGMPv2 sends only one.

This action serves both to quickly discover the group members active on the subnet and also alerts other multicast routers that may be on the subnet. When there are multiple routers, the rule for electing the Querier is simple: The router whose connected interface has the lowest IP address is the Querier. So when the existing router on the subnet hears the General Query from the new router, it checks the source address. If the address is lower than its own IP address, it relinquishes the role of Querier to the new router. If its own IP address is lower, it continues sending queries. When the new router receives one of these queries, it sees that the old router has a lower IP address and becomes a Non-Querier.

If the Non-Querier does not hear queries from the Querier within a certain period of time known as the *Other Querier Present Interval*, it concludes that the Querier is no longer present and assumes that role. IOS has a default Other Querier Present Interval of twice the Query Interval, or 120 seconds, and can be changed with the statement **ip igmp querier-timeout**.

IGMPv1

The important differences between IGMPv1 and IGMPv2 follows:

- IGMPv1 has no Leave Group message, meaning that there is a longer period between the time the last host leaves a group and the time the router stops forwarding the group traffic.

- IGMPv1 has no Group-Specific Query because no Leave Group message exists.

- IGMPv1 does not specify a Max Response Time in its query messages. Instead, hosts have a fixed Max Response Time of 10 seconds.

■ IGMPv1 has no Querier election process. Instead, it relies on the IP multicast routing protocol to elect a designated router on the subnet. Because different protocols use different election mechanisms, it is possible under IGMPv1 to have more than one Querier on a subnet.

The section "IGMP Message Format" illustrates how these differences affect the fields in IGMPv1 and IGMPv2 messages.

There are cases in which IGMPv1 and IGMPv2 implementations might exist on the same subnet:

■ Some group members might run IGMPv1, whereas others run IGMPv2.

■ Some group members might run IGMPv2, whereas the router runs IGMPv1.

■ The router might run IGMPv2, whereas some group members run IGMPv1.

■ One router might run IGMPv1, whereas another router on the subnet runs IGMPv2.

RFC 2236 describes several mechanisms that allow IGMPv2 to adapt in these situations. If a mixture of Version 1 and Version 2 members are on the same subnet, the Version 2 members treat both Version 1 and Version 2 Membership reports the same when determining whether to suppress their own Membership Reports. That is, if a Version 2 member hears a Query from the router and subsequently hears a Version 1 Membership Report for its group before its own delay timer expires, it does not send a Membership Report. Version 1 hosts, however, ignore Version 2 messages. Therefore, if a Version 2 Membership Report is sent for a group first, the Version 1 member also sends a report when its delay timer expires. This does not cause problems for the Version 2 host and is important for the Version 2 router so that it is aware of the presence of Version 1 group members.

If a host is running Version 2 and the local router is running Version 1, the IGMPv1 router ignores the Version 2 messages. So when a Version 2 host receives a Version 1 query, it responds with Version 1 Membership Reports. The IGMPv1 query also does not specify a Max Response Time, so the IGMPv2 host uses the fixed Version 1 period of 10 seconds. The host may or may not send Leave Group messages in the presence of Version 1 routers; the IGMPv1 router does not recognize Leave Group messages and ignores them.

If a Version 2 router receives a Version 1 Membership Report, it treats all members of the group as if they are running Version 1. The router ignores Leave Group messages and hence does not send Group-Specific Queries that the Version 1 members would ignore. Instead it sets a timer, known as the *Old Host Present Timer*, as shown in Example 7-2. The period of the timer is the same value as the Group Membership Interval. Whenever a new Version 1 Membership Report is received, the timer is reset; if the timer expires, the router concludes that there are no more Version 1 members of the group on the subnet and reverts to Version 2 messages and procedures.

> **Note**   As described earlier, the Group Membership Interval is the period of time that the router waits to hear a Membership Report before declaring that there are no members on a subnet. The IOS default is three times the Query Interval.

Example 7-2   *This Multicast Router Is Receiving IGMPv2 Membership Reports for Group 239.1.2.3 and IGMPv1 Membership Reports for Group 228.0.5.3. The Version 1 Reports Cause the Router to Set an Old Host Present Timer for That Group*

```
Gold#debug ip igmp
IGMP debugging is on
Gold#
IGMP: Send v2 Query on Ethernet0/0 to 224.0.0.1
IGMP: Received v2 Report from 172.16.1.23 (Ethernet0/0) for 239.1.2.3
IGMP: Received v1 Report from 172.16.1.254 (Ethernet0/0) for 228.0.5.3
IGMP: Starting old host present timer for 228.0.5.3 on Ethernet0/0
IGMP: Send v2 Query on Ethernet0/0 to 224.0.0.1
IGMP: Received v2 Report from 172.16.1.23 (Ethernet0/0) for 239.1.2.3
IGMP: Received v1 Report from 172.16.1.254 (Ethernet0/0) for 228.0.5.3
IGMP: Starting old host present timer for 228.0.5.3 on Ethernet0/0
```

Notice in Example 7-2 that the router continues to send Version 2 General Queries. The only significant difference between these queries and Version 1 queries is that the Max Response Time is non-zero. The field in which this value is carried is unused in Version 1, and the Version 1 host ignores it. As a result, the host interprets Version 2 queries as Version 1 queries.

Another point of interest in Example 7-2 is that the Old Host Present timer is set only for group 228.0.5.3. The router treats only this group as an IGMPv1 group. Group 239.1.2.3, on the same interface, is treated as a Version 2 group.

If Version 1 and Version 2 routers exist on the same subnet, the Version 1 router does not participate in the Querier election process. Because of this, the Version 2 router must behave as a Version 1 router for consistency. There is no automatic conversion to Version 1; the Version 2 router must be manually configured with the **ip igmp version 1** statement.

IGMPv3

IGMPv3 officially obsoletes IGMPv2; however, version 2 is still widely used as of this writing and is still the IOS default, so you need to understand both versions.

The primary addition to IGMPv3 is the inclusion of a Group-and-Source-Specific Query. This allows a group to be identified not only by group address, but also by source address. The Membership Report and Group Leave messages are modified so that they also can make this identification.

When a group has many sources (a many-to-many group), the IGMPv3 router can perform source filtering based on the requests of group members. For example, a particular member may want to receive group traffic from only certain specified sources, or it may want to receive traffic from all sources except certain specified sources. The member can express these needs in a Membership Report with *Include* or *Exclude* filter requests. An Include filter specifies, "I want to receive from *only* these sources," whereas an Exclude filter specifies, "I want to receive from all sources *except* these." If no member on a particular subnet wants to receive traffic from a particular source, the router does not forward that source's traffic onto the subnet.

The filtering capabilities make ICMPv3 especially suited for Source-Specific Multicast (SSM) environments. The SSM model is introduced later in this chapter and then detailed in Chapter 8.

> **Note**   RFC 4604 updates the behavior of both IGMPv3 and MLDv2 when supporting SSM. Although the original specifications allow for backward compatibility with IGMPv1 and MLDv1 as described in the previous subsection, the backward compatibility can open a security vulnerability in SSM environments. The RFC 4604 modifications are described later in this chapter in the context of SSM.

Although source filtering is the most important difference between IGMPv2 and IGMPv3, following are a few more differences as listed in RFC 3376, Appendix B:

- Query messages include a Robustness Variable and Query Interval to allow synchronization between the Querier and Non-Queriers. These fields are described in the section "IGMP Message Format."

- The Max Response Time variable in Query messages has an exponential range, changing the maximum from 25.5 seconds to approximately 53 minutes.

- Report messages are sent to the well-known IGMP multicast address 224.0.0.22 to help with IGMP snooping (described later in this chapter).

- Report messages can contain multiple group records, as described in the next subsection, improving reporting efficiency.

- Query messages contain a Suppress Router-Side (S) flag, as described in the next subsection.

- Hosts no longer perform suppression, which simplifies functionality and permits explicit membership tracking.

IGMP Message Format

IGMPv2 uses a single message format, as shown in Figure 7-13. The IP header encapsulating the message indicates a protocol number of 2. Because the IGMP message must not leave the local subnet on which it was originated, the TTL is always set to 1.

In addition, IGMPv2 messages carry the IP Router Alert option that informs routers to "examine this packet more closely."

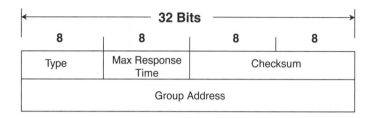

Figure 7-13   *IGMPv2 Message Format*

The fields for the IGMPv2 message are defined here:

- **Type** describes one of four message types:

  - Membership Query (0x11) is used by the multicast router to discover the presence of group members on a subnet. A General Membership Query message sets the Group Address field to 0.0.0.0, whereas a Group-Specific Query sets the field to the address of the group being queried.

  - Version 2 Membership Report (0x16) is sent by a group member to inform the router that there is at least one group member present on the subnet.

  - Version 1 Membership Report (0x12) is used by IGMPv2 hosts for backward compatibility with IGMPv1.

  - Leave Group (0x17) is sent by a group member, if it was the last member to send a Membership Report, to inform the router that it is leaving the group.

- **Max Response Time** is set only in Query messages. In all other message types, the field is set to 0x00. This field specifies a period, in units of 1/10 second, during which at least one group member must respond with a Membership Report message.

- **Checksum** is the 16-bit one's complement of the one's complement sum of the IGMP message. This is the standard checksum algorithm used by TCP/IP.

- **Group Address** is set to 0.0.0.0 in General Query messages and set to the group address in Group-Specific messages. Membership Report messages carry the address of the group reported in this field; Group Leave messages carry the address of the group left in this field.

Figure 7-14 shows the format of an IGMPv1 message.

The only differences in the IGMPv1 format from IGMPv2 follow:

- The first octet is split into a 4-bit Version field and a 4-bit Type field.

- The second octet, which is the Max Response Time in version 2, is unused. This field is set to 0x00.

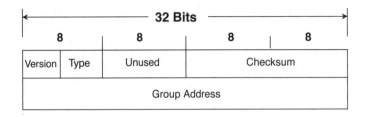

Figure 7-14 *IGMPv1 Message Format*

Another difference is that the Router Alert option is not set in the IP header of IGMPv1 messages.

IGMPv1 defines just two message types:

■ Host Membership Query (Type 1)

■ Host Membership Report (Type 2)

The Version field is always set to 1. As a result, you can see that the combined Version and Type field is 0x11 for a Host Membership Query message, which is the same value as the 8-bit Type field of a IGMPv2 Membership Query. The combined Version and Type fields of the Host Membership Report is 0x12, whereas the Type field of the IGMPv2 Membership Report is 0x16.

New features in IGMPv3—particularly the source filtering capability and the capability to carry multiple Group Records in one message—require separate formats for the IGMPv3 Membership Query message and the IGMPv3 Membership Report message. Figure 7-15 shows the IGMPv3 Membership Query message format.

The IGMPv3 Membership Query message can be one of three variants:

■ **General Query:** Sent by a multicast router to learn the multicast reception state of all interfaces on the subnet. The Group Address and Number of Sources fields in a Group Query message are 0.

■ **Group-Specific Query:** Sent by a multicast router to learn the reception state of interfaces on the subnet for a single multicast group address. In this variant, the Group Address field contains the IPv4 multicast group address of interest and the Number of Sources field is 0.

■ **Group-and-Source-Specific Query:** Sent by a multicast router to learn if any interfaces on the subnet want to join the specified IPv4 multicast group from any of the unicast source addresses listed. In this variant, the Group Address field contains the multicast IPv4 group address of interest and the message contains a list of one or more unicast IPv4 source addresses transmitting to the group.

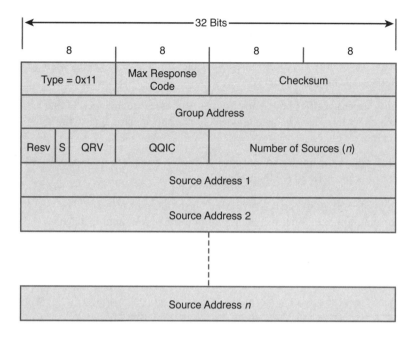

Figure 7-15 *IGMPv3 Membership Query Message Format*

Type (0x11), Checksum, and Group Address fields are the same as in the IGMPv2 Membership Query format. Notice that the field called *Max Response Time* in IGMPv2 is *Max Response Code* in version 3. This allows some added flexibility in function. If the value in the field is less than 128, the value is treated the same as in version 2 Max Response Time, with the value representing tenths of a second. But if the field value is equal to or greater than 128, it is interpreted as an exponential value with the second through fourth bits specifying the exponential and the fifth through eighth bits specifying the mantissa. Allowing these large exponential values can be useful when there are a large enough number of groups that IGMP traffic becomes bursty and needs to be controlled. The cost, of course, is in increased leave latency.

The new fields in the IGMPv3 Membership Query message follows:

- **Reserved (Resv)** is set to all zeroes at transmission and is ignored on reception.

- **S**, when set to 1, tells a receiving router to suppress the normal timer updates it performs upon reception of a query. The S flag is used with a variable called Last Member Query Time (LMQT) and the QRV field to improve IGMP robustness.

- **Querier's Robustness Variable (QRV)** tells the router the originator's Robustness Variable; the router adapts its own Robustness Variable, which by default is 2, to the received QRV for that Querier. Increasing the Robustness Variable can improve IGMPv3 behavior on lossy networks.

- **Querier's Query Interval Code (QQIC)** tells the receiver the Querier's query interval. The QI is specified in the same way as the Max Response Code; that is, if the value is less than 128, it's a flat number (although measured in seconds rather than tenths of seconds like the Max Response Time), and if equal to or greater than 128, the value represents an exponential.

- **Number of Sources** specifies how many Source Addresses are included in the query. If the query message is a general query or a group-specific query, the value of this field is 0.

- **Source Address** lists the unicast source IPv4 addresses, from 0 to n as specified in the Number of Sources field, for the Group.

Figure 7-16 shows the format of the ICMPv3 Membership Report message. The Type (0x22), the unused next 8 bits, and the Checksum are all the same as IGMPv2 Membership Report messages.

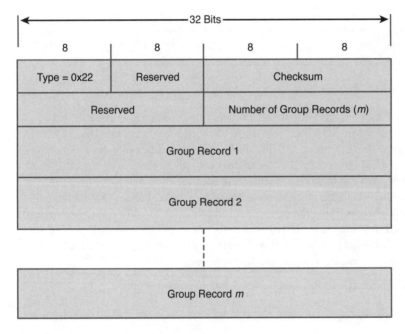

Figure 7-16   *IGMPv3 Membership Report Message Format*

The new fields in the IGMPv3 Membership Report message follow:

- **Reserved (Resv):** Set to all zeroes at transmission and is ignored on reception.

- **Number of Group Records:** Specifies how many Group Records are included in the report.

■ **Group Record:** Provides details of the multicast groups to which the originating host belongs, with one Group Record for each group. This is new to IGMPv3 and is the key to the capability for a single report to cover multiple groups.

The format of a group record is shown in Figure 7-17.

■ **Record Type:** Specifies (no surprise) the record type. There are six record types, divided into three categories.

■ **Current-State Record:** Sent in response to a query to report the interface's existing reception state of the group in question. There are two current-state record types, which specify whether the filter mode of the group and the listed source addresses (if any) is Include or Exclude:

  ■ MODE_IS_INCLUDE (Type 1)

  ■ MODE_IS_EXCLUDE (Type 2)

■ **Filter-Mode-Change Record:** Sent when the filter mode changes from Include to Exclude, or Exclude to Include:

  ■ CHANGE_TO_INCLUDE_MODE (Type 3)

  ■ CHANGE_TO_EXCLUDE_MODE (Type 4)

■ **Source-List-Change Record:** Sent when the source list changes within a filter mode; that is, a source is added or removed from the list without changing the filter mode:

  ■ ALLOW_NEW_SOURCES (Type 5)

  ■ BLOCK_OLD_SOURCES (Type 6)

■ **Auxiliary Data Length:** Specifies in units of 32-bit words the length of the Auxiliary Data field. If there is no Auxiliary Data, this field is zero. Currently, the default is zero.

■ **Number of Sources:** Specifies the number of unicast IPv4 source addresses are listed for this group record.

■ **Multicast Address:** Specifies the IPv4 multicast address for the group to which this record applies.

■ **Source Address:** Lists one or more IPv4 unicast source addresses transmitting to the specified multicast group.

■ **Auxiliary Data:** A future-use field for attaching additional data to the group record. The IGMPv3 specification current at this writing does not provide for any auxiliary data, so this field should not be included (and the Auxiliary Data Length field should be set to zero).

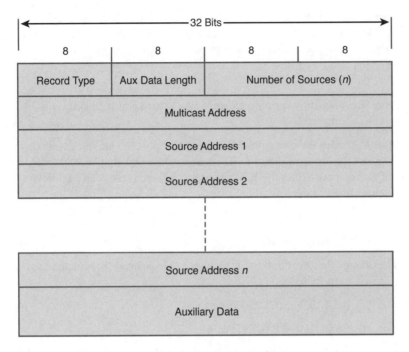

Figure 7-17 *IGMPv3 Membership Report Group Record Format*

Multicast Listener Discovery (MLD)

If you've come this far and are familiar with IGMP, here's some good news: You already know Multicast Listener Discovery (MLD). It's the same protocol but with a different name and, more significant, with the message formats adapted to carry IPv6 addresses. So MLD is just IGMP for IPv6 multicast. Functionally, there is no significant difference.

MLD comes in two versions, which correspond to the two current versions of IGMP:

- MLDv1 (RFC 2710) corresponds to IGMPv2.

- MLDv2 (RFC 3810) corresponds to IGMPv3.

MLDv2 is the IOS default.

And just as IGMPv3 is backward compatible with IGMPv2, MLDv2 is backward compatible with MLDv1. IGMP and MLD are not compatible with each other, however, because of the differing sizes of the address fields in the messages and, in a few cases, some variations in the message formats. If you want to run both IPv4 multicast and IPv6 multicast, you have to run both IGMP and MLD.

Figure 7-18 shows the MLDv1 message format. Comparing it to the IGMPv2 message format in Figure 7-13, you can see that there is a slight difference in the structure. The format difference comes is because MLD messages are a form of ICMPv6 message; therefore, the Type and Code fields in the first two octets. Keeping with the ICMPv6 format, the Types are specified in decimal rather than hex, as with IGMP.

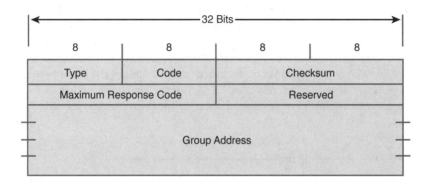

Figure 7-18   *MLDv1 Message Format*

- **Type** specifies the message type. However, the type codes differ from the corresponding IGMPv2 messages to differentiate the MLD message from an IGMP message:

  - Multicast Listener Query (type = decimal 130) corresponds to the IGMPv2 Membership Query. And like Membership Query, a Listener Query can be either a General Query or a Multicast Address (Group) Specific Query.

  - Multicast Listener Report (type = decimal 131) corresponds to the IGMPv2 Membership Report.

  - Multicast Listener Done (type = decimal 132) corresponds to the IGMPv2 Leave Group message.

- **Code** is currently unused. It's set to all zeroes by the originator and ignored by the receiver.

- **Checksum** is the same 16-bit one's complement of the one's complement sum of the IGMP message.

- **Maximum Response Delay** corresponds to the IGMPv2 Max Response Time and serves the same purpose. It is used only in Query messages and is otherwise set to 0. Unlike IGMPv2, however, where the Max Response Time value represents tenths of seconds, the Maximum Response Delay value represents milliseconds. The default value is 1000 (1 second).

■ **Group Address** is set to ::/128 in General Query messages and set to the IPv6 group multicast address in Multicast-Address-Specific messages. Multicast Listener Report messages carry the address of the group being reported in this field; Multicast Listener Done messages carry the address of the group being left.

Figure 7-19 shows the format of the MLDv2 Membership Query (type 130) message. Comparing it to its IGMPv2 counterpart in Figure 7-15, you can see that the fields are almost identical. The only difference is the inclusion (refer to Figure 7-18) of an unused Code field, and the Maximum Response Code field is expanded to 16 bits and in a different position within the message. The Maximum Response Code is used in the same way as the IGMPv2 Maximum Response Code, except that because of the larger field, the values can be larger. If the code is less than 32768, it represents milliseconds; if greater than or equal to 32768, it is an exponential value. The last 12 bits, in this case, are the mantissa.

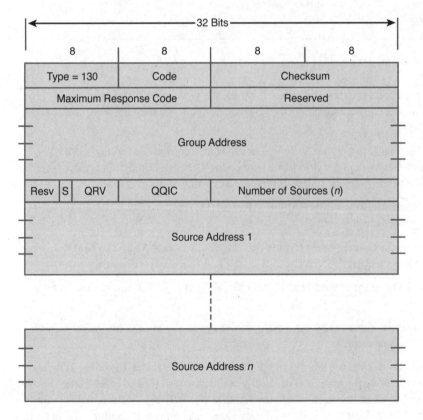

Figure 7-19   *MLDv2 Membership Query Format*

Figure 7-20 shows the format of the MLDv2 Membership Report (type 143) message, and Figure 7-21 shows the format of the individual Group Records within the report. Comparing these to their counterparts in Figures 7-15 and 7-16, you can see that the formats are identical other than the 128-bit address fields in the MLDv2 Group Record.

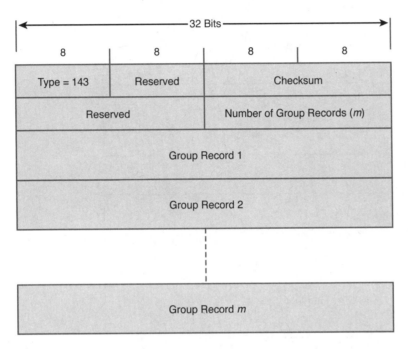

Figure 7-20 *MLDv2 Membership Report Message Format*

IGMP/MLD Snooping

A fundamental design principle of IP multicast is that traffic should be delivered only to destinations that want to receive the traffic. You have seen how IPv4/IPv6 multicast addresses and their associated MAC addresses help to meet this goal at the data link layer, and how IGMP/MLD allow routers to determine whether they should deliver sessions to particular subnets. You see in subsequent sections how IP multicast routing protocols extend this principle across networks, delivering multicast sessions only to those routers that have group members on their attached subnets.

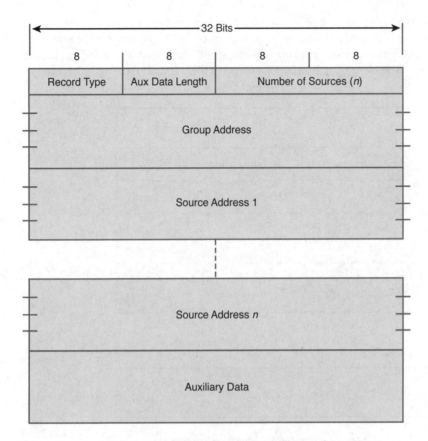

Figure 7-21   *MLDv2 Membership Report Group Record Format*

But what about a switched network, such as the one shown in Figure 7-22? Large office buildings and campuses abound with such networks. The Ethernet switches limit unicast traffic by learning what MAC addresses are associated with what ports. They can then filter and forward frames based on this information. But broadcast traffic is forwarded to every port of every switch. Such a large network (refer to Figure 7-22) is normally broken up into several virtual LANS (VLANs) to control the scope of the broadcast traffic. However, it is not unusual to find "flat" switched networks this large—one big subnet, or broadcast domain.

Just as broadcast frames are forwarded to every port within a broadcast domain, so too are frames carrying unknown IP unicast and IP multicast packets (often called BUM frames). After all, a broadcast domain is nothing more than a multicast group to which all hosts belong. Figure 7-23 illustrates the problem. Three group members are attached to a 24-port switch. An IGMP Membership Report is sent to the router, and the router begins forwarding the appropriate multicast session onto the subnet. Because IGMP is a Layer 3 protocol, the Ethernet switch has no easy way to determine what ports the group members are on. As a result, the multicast traffic is forwarded to all 23 ports (discounting the source port).

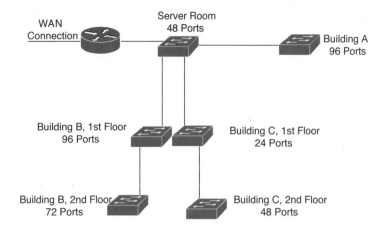

Figure 7-22 *Unless This Switched Campus Network Is Divided into Multiple VLANs, It Is Composed of a Single Broadcast Domain. That Is, the Router Port Defines a Layer 3 Subnet, and Any Broadcast Frame Is Transmitted Out All 384 Switch Ports*

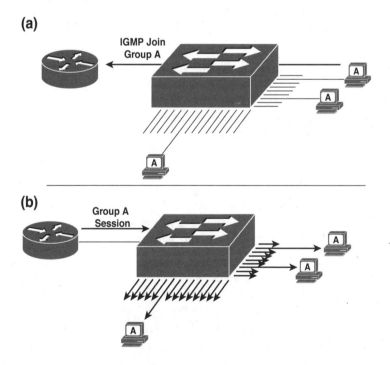

Figure 7-23 *One of the Three Group Members Sends an IGMP Membership Report, Joining Multicast Group A (a). When the Router Forwards the Multicast Session, the Switch Replicates the Frames to All Ports Except the Source Port (b)*

Obviously, the preferable behavior is for the switch to forward the multicast session only out those ports to which the group members are attached. If this can be accomplished, switching is not only more efficient, but is also the preferable way to implement LANs that carry multicast sessions. For example, a typical interactive multimedia application might use anywhere from 1 to 10 Mbps. If these sessions can be limited to the group members' ports, network and host resources are conserved.

IGMP/MLD Snooping, described in RFC 4541, is designed to do exactly that—distribute multicast sessions only to those switch ports on which group members are located. The "snooping" comes in because the switch (normally an L2 device) looks at the higher layer headers in multicast packets to identify IGMP/MLD messages. From these, it can identify which of its ports multicast routers are attached to, and which of its ports group members are attached to, and limit the relevant multicast traffic to those ports.

Note   The first edition of this book focused on a Cisco-proprietary predecessor to IGMP snooping called Cisco Group Management Protocol (CGMP) and only briefly discusses IGMP snooping. CGMP was supported in the now-discontinued CatOS on Catalyst switches and is rarely if ever used in modern networks. IGMP snooping, however, is now the accepted means of running IP multicast in a switched environment and is supported by many switch vendors. Therefore, coverage of CGMP is eliminated in this edition and IGMP snooping is covered in more detail.

A snooping switch can determine what ports multicast routers are on by listening to Membership Queries; it determines which ports group members are on by listening for Membership Reports. Queries, of course, must be sent to all active ports, so the querier can find group members. But when the switch learns what ports the routers are on, it sends Membership Reports only to those ports.

Under IGMPv1, IGMPv2, and MLDv1, hosts that hear a Membership Report from another host on the subnet suppress their own reports. With snooping, the switch does not forward reports from one member to other members. Each group member must respond to the query individually so that the switch can record the member port. The same applies to group leaves; each host, not being aware of other hosts on its subnet, sends a Leave Group (or MLD Listener Done) message when it leaves a group, and the switch removes the host from its port list for that group.

Note   The first edition of this book focused on CGMP as the widely accepted solution to multicast in switched environments and discussed IGMP snooping only in passing. Since that time, IGMP snooping has become the accepted standard and CGMP is outdated, if not entirely obsolete.

The influencing factors for IGMP snooping are that it is vendor neutral and therefore workable in multivendor switched networks as long as the switch supports snooping. CPUs have become powerful enough and snooping implementations efficient enough that early concerns about performance impact are allayed (although not entirely eliminated).

The largest influencing factor for CGMP becoming less used is that it is limited to Cisco and in particular the Catalyst line of switches. It isn't supported, for example, in the Cisco Nexus product line. The limited support is most likely due to limited user demand.

I debated whether to include coverage of CGMP in this edition. Polling many acquaintances in the industry, including many people within Cisco, the answer I invariably received is that no one has encountered CGMP in a production network in years.

Nevertheless, I decided to leave the CGMP section in this edition, on the off chance that you might encounter it. You can safely skip the following section if you want; although, it can be useful for gaining some historical background.

Cisco Group Management Protocol (CGMP)

A potential problem with IGMP/MLD snooping is that a switch must examine every multicast packet for IGMP/MLD information. Although higher performance switches should o do this with little performance impact, snooping might be CPU-intensive for lower-end switches.

Cisco addressed this problem early on with a proprietary solution called Cisco Group Management Protocol (CGMP). The key to this solution is that the switch does not have to snoop multicast packets. Instead, it relies on the attached multicast router to tell it which of its attached hosts belong to which groups and forwards or blocks multicast packets accordingly.

Although both Cisco routers and Cisco switches must be configured to run CGMP, only the routers produce CGMP packets. The CGMP process on switches reads only the packets. Following are two types of CGMP packets:

- **Join packets:** Sent by the router to tell the switch to add one or more members to a multicast group

- **Leave packets:** Sent by the router to tell the switch to remove one or more members from a multicast group, or to delete the group altogether

These two packet types have an identical format, and the destination of the packets is always the reserved MAC address 0100.0cdd.dddd. CGMP-enabled switches listen for this address.

The essential information in both packets is one or more pairs of MAC addresses:

- Group Destination Address (GDA)

- Unicast Source Address (USA)

When a CGMP router comes online, it makes itself known to the switch by sending a CGMP Join packet with the GDA set to zero (0000.0000.0000) and the USA set to its own MAC address. The CGMP-speaking switch now knows that a multicast router is attached to the port on which it received the packet. The router repeats the packet every 60 seconds as a keepalive.

When a host wants to join a group, it sends an IGMP Membership Report message, as shown in part a of Figure 7-24. The switch, following normal IEEE 802.1 procedures, enters the host's MAC address into its CAM table.

Note   The Catalyst's CAM table is a bridging table that records the MAC addresses it has heard and the ports on which they were heard.

When the router receives the IGMP Membership Report, it sends a CGMP Join packet with the GDA set to the group MAC address and the USA set to the host's MAC address (refer to part b of Figure 7-24). The switch is now aware of the multicast group; and because the switch knows the port on which the host is located, it can add that port to the group. When the router sends frames to the group MAC address, the switch forwards a copy of the frame out all ports (except the router port) associated with the group.

As long as group members remain on the switched network, the router sends IGMP Query messages every 60 seconds, which the switch forwards to the members. The switch forwards the IGMP Reports, sent in reply to the Queries, to the router.

When a host sends an IGMPv2 Leave message, the message is forwarded to the router as illustrated in part a of Figure 7-25. The router sends two IGMP Group-Specific Queries, which the switch forwards to all group ports. If another member responds to the Group-Specific Query, the router sends a CGMP Leave packet to the switch with the GDA set to the group MAC address, and the USA set to the leaving member's MAC address (refer to part b of Figure 7-25). This packet tells the switch to delete just the leaving member's port from the group. If no members respond to the Group-Specific Query, the router concludes that no members are left on the segment. In this case, it sends a CGMP Leave packet to the switch with the GDA set to the group MAC address, and the USA set to zero (refer to part c of Figure 7-25). This packet tells the switch to remove the group itself from the CAM table.

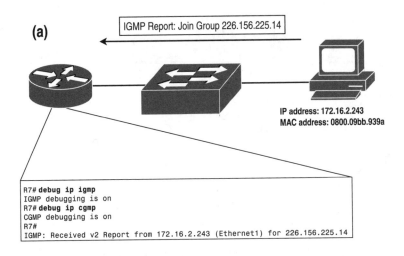

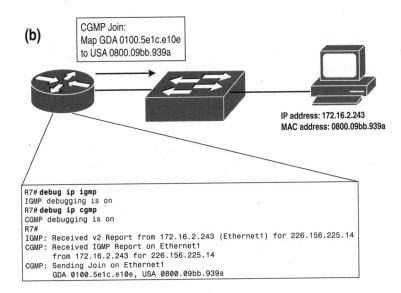

Figure 7-24 *When a Cisco Router Receives an IGMP Membership Report on a CGMP Interface (a), It Sends a CGMP Join Packet Telling the Switch to Map the Host MAC Address to the Group MAC Address (b)*

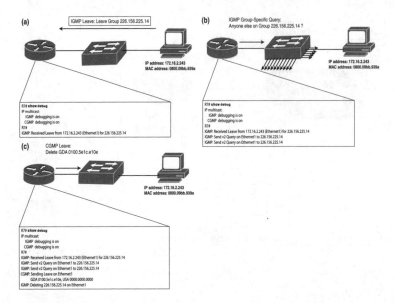

Figure 7-25 *When a Router Receives an IGMP Leave Message on a CGMP Interface (a), It Queries to Learn if There Are Other Members Left on the Subnet (b). If Other Members Respond, It Sends a CGMP Leave Packet to the Switch Removing Just the Leaving Member. If No Members Respond, the Router Sends a CGMP Leave Message to the Switch Removing the Entire Group (c)*

Table 7-3 summarizes the various possible values of the GDA and USA in CGMP packets, and the meaning of each. Only the last two Leave packets have not been discussed. A Leave with the GDA set to zero and the USA set to the router's MAC address signals the switch to remove all groups and ports associated with the router port from the CAM. This message is sent if the router's CGMP function has been disabled on that port. A Leave with both the GDA and the USA set to zero tells all switches receiving the message to delete all groups and associated ports from the CAM. This message is sent as the result of a **clear ip cgmp** command entered at the router.

Table 7-3 *CGMP Packets*

Type	GDA	USA	Function
Join	Zero	Router MAC	Identifies port as multicast router port
Join	Group MAC	Member MAC	Identifies multicast group, and adds member's port to the group
Leave	Group MAC	Member MAC	Removes member port from the specified group
Leave	Group MAC	Zero	Removes group from the CAM
Leave	Zero	Router MAC	Removes all groups and ports bound to the router's port from the CAM
Leave	Zero	Zero	Removes all groups from all switches

The source MAC address of frames carrying CGMP packets is the MAC address of the originating router, and the destination MAC address is the reserved multicast address 0100.0cdd.dddd. Only routers originate CGMP packets. Within the frame, the packet is encapsulated in a SNAP header. The OUI field of the SNAP header is 0x00000c, and the type field is 0x2001.

Figure 7-26 shows the format of the CGMP packet.

Figure 7-26 *CGMP Packet Format*

Following are the fields of the CGMP packet:

- **Version:** Is always set to 0x1 to signify version 1.

- **Type:** Specifies whether the packet is a Join (0x0) or Leave (0x1).

- **Reserved:** Always set to 0 (0x0000).

- **Count:** Specifies how many GDA/USA pairs the packet carries.

- **GDA:** The Group Destination Address; when the field is nonzero, it specifies the MAC address of a multicast group. When the field is set to zero (0000.0000.0000), it specifies all possible groups.

- **USA:** The Unicast Source Address; when the field is nonzero, it may specify the MAC address of the originating router or the MAC address of a group member. When it is zero, it specifies all group members and the originating router.

Multicast Routing Issues

When the first edition of this book was written, there were five IP multicast routing protocols in various stages of development:

- Distance Vector Multicast Routing Protocol (DVMRP)

- Multicast OSPF (MOSPF)

- Core-Based Trees (CBT)

- Protocol Independent Multicast, Dense Mode (PIM-DM)

- Protocol Independent Multicast, Sparse Mode (PIM-SM)

Although Cisco IOS at the time had full support of only PIM-DM and PIM-SM and just enough support for DVMRP to allow connection to DVMRP networks, there was enough anticipation of future deployments of MOSPF and CBT that I covered the operation and message formats of all five protocols.

It turns out that neither MOSPF nor CBT ever gained commercial acceptance, and DVMRP—already considered antiquated when the first edition was written—is now obsolete. There are currently four intra-AS IP multicast routing protocols (that is, multicast IGPs), all of which are variants of PIMv2:

- Protocol Independent Multicast, Dense Mode (PIM-DM)

- Protocol Independent Multicast, Sparse Mode (PIM-SM)

- Protocol Independent Multicast, Source-Specific Multicast (PIM-SSM)

- Bidirectional Protocol Independent Multicast (Bidir-PIM)

PIM-SSM and Bidir-PIM are actually subsets of PIM-SM but are treated independently in this book for clarity.

PIMv2 in all its variants is covered in Chapter 8, and inter-AS multicast routing is covered in Chapter 9. Multiprotocol BGP is used for inter-AS multicast routing. DVMRP, MOSPF, and CBT are not covered in this edition. But before we get to the protocol specifics, a number of multicast routing concepts need to be covered, which is the goal of the remainder of this chapter.

Multicast Forwarding

Like any other router, the two fundamental functions of a multicast router are route discovery and packet forwarding. This section addresses the unique requirements of multicast forwarding, and the next section looks at the requirements for multicast route discovery.

Unicast packet forwarding involves forwarding a packet toward a certain destination. Unless certain policies are configured, a unicast router is uninterested in the source of the packet. The packet is received, the destination IP address is examined, a longest-match route lookup is performed, and the packet is forwarded out a single interface toward the destination.

Rather than forwarding packets toward a destination, multicast routers forward packets away from a source. The distinction may sound trifling at first glance but is actually essential to correct multicast packet forwarding. A multicast packet is originated by a single source but is destined for a group of destinations. At a particular router, the packet arrives on some incoming interface, and copies of the packet may be forwarded out multiple outgoing interfaces.

If a loop exists so that one or more of the forwarded packets makes its way back to the incoming interface, the packet is again replicated and forwarded out the same outgoing interfaces. The result can be a *multicast storm*, in which packets continue to loop and be replicated until the TTL expires. It is the replication that makes a multicast storm potentially so much more severe than a simple unicast loop. Therefore, all multicast routers must be aware of the source of the packet and must forward packets only away from the source.

A useful and commonly used terminology is that of *upstream* and *downstream*. Multicast packets should always flow downstream from the source to the destinations, never upstream toward the source. To ensure this behavior, each multicast router maintains a multicast forwarding table in which (source, group) or *(S, G)* address pairs are recorded. Packets from a particular source and destined for particular group should always arrive on an upstream interface and be forwarded out one or more downstream interfaces. By definition, an upstream interface is closer to the source than any downstream interface, as shown in Figure 7-27. If a router receives a multicast packet on any interface other than the upstream interface for that packet's source, it quietly discards the packet.

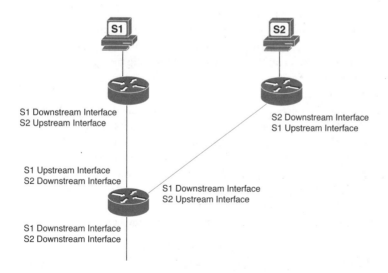

Figure 7-27 *By Identifying Upstream and Downstream Interfaces in Relation to Each Multicast Source, Routers Avoid Multicast Routing Loops*

Of course, the router needs some mechanism for determining the upstream and down-stream interfaces for a given (S,G). This is the job of the multicast routing protocol.

Multicast Routing

The function of a unicast routing protocol is to find the shortest path to a particular destination. This determination might be made from the advertisements of neighbor-ing routers (distance vector) or from a shortest path tree calculated from a topological database (link state). The end result in both cases is an entry in the routing or forward-ing table indicating the interface to forward packets out and possibly a next-hop router. From the perspective of the unicast routing protocol, the cited interface is the down-stream interface on the path to the destination—the closest interface to the destination.

In contrast, the function of a multicast routing protocol is to determine the upstream interface—the closest interface to the source. Because multicast routing protocols con-cern themselves with the shortest path to the source, rather than the shortest path to the destination, the procedure of forwarding multicast packets is known as *Reverse Path Forwarding (RPF)*.

The easiest way for a multicast routing protocol to determine the shortest path to a source is to consult the unicast forwarding table. However, as the last section pointed out, multicast packets are forwarded based on the information in a separate multi-cast forwarding table. The reason for this is that the router must record not only the upstream interface for the source S of a particular (S, G) pair, but also the downstream interfaces associated with the group G.

The simplest way to forward packets would be to merely declare all interfaces except the upstream interface to be downstream interfaces. This approach, known as *Reverse Path Broadcasting (RPB)*, has obvious shortcomings. As the name implies, packets are effectively broadcast to all subnets on the routed network. Group members probably exist on only a subset of the subnets—most likely a small subset. Flooding a copy of every multicast packet onto every subnet defeats not only the objective of multicast-ing to deliver packets only to interested receivers, but also actually defeats the purpose of routing itself. A slightly improved procedure is *Truncated Reverse Path Broadcast (TRPB)*. When a router discovers, via IGMP, that one of its attached subnets has no group members and no next-hop routers are on the subnet, the router stops sending mul-ticast traffic onto the subnet. In keeping with the arboreal terminology, such a nontransit subnet is a *leaf network*. Although TRPB helps conserve resources on leaf networks, it is little improvement over RPB. Inter-router links, on which bandwidth is more likely to be at a premium, continue to carry multicast traffic regardless if they need to.

So the second function of a multicast routing protocol is to determine the actual down-stream interfaces associated with an (S, G) pair. When all routers have determined their upstream and downstream interfaces for a particular source and group, a multicast tree has been established, as shown in Figure 7-28. The root of the tree is the source's directly connected router, and the branches lead to all subnets on which group mem-bers reside. No branches lead to "empty" subnets—subnets with no members of the associated group. The forwarding of packets only out interfaces leading to group members is called *Multicast Reverse Path Forwarding*, or simply *RPF*.

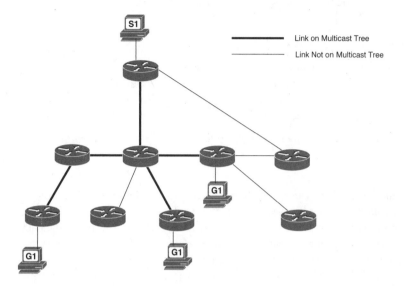

Figure 7-28   *Paths Leading from the Multicast Source to All Group Members' Subnets Form a Multicast Tree*

Note   Unicast Reverse Path Forwarding (uRPF) is related to Multicast RPF in that in both cases a router determines which interface is closest to a source. uRPF (RFC 3704) is used for avoiding certain types of network attacks that depend on spoofed source addresses, by blocking packets that arrive on interfaces other than the interface closest to the source.

Multicast trees last only for the duration of the multicast session. And because members can join and leave the group throughout the lifetime of the session, the structure of the tree is dynamic. The third function of a multicast routing protocol is to manage the tree, "grafting" branches as members join the group and "pruning" branches as members leave the group. The next three sections discuss issues surrounding this third function.

Sparse Versus Dense Topologies

A dense topology is one in which many multicast group members are relative to the total number of hosts in a network. Sparse topologies have few group members relative to the total number of hosts. Sparse does not mean few hosts exist. For example, a sparse topology might mean 2,000 members of a group, spread among 100,000 total hosts.

No specific numeric ratios delineate sparse and dense topologies. However, it is safe to say that dense topologies are usually found in switched LAN and campus environments, and sparse topologies usually involve WANs. What is important is that multicast routing protocols are designed to work best in one or the other topology and are designated as either *dense mode* protocols or *sparse mode* protocols.

Implicit Joins Versus Explicit Joins

As was previously observed, members may join or leave a group at any time during the lifetime of a multicast session, and as a result the multicast tree can change dynamically. It is the job of the multicast routing protocol to manage this changing tree, adding branches as members join and pruning branches as members leave.

The multicast routing protocol may accomplish this task by using either an *implicit* or *explicit* join strategy. Implicit joins are sender-initiated, whereas explicit joins are receiver-initiated.

Multicast routing protocols that maintain their trees by implicit joins are commonly called *broadcast-and-prune* or *flood-and-prune* protocols. When a sender first initiates a session, each router in the network uses reverse path broadcasting to forward the packets out every interface except the upstream interface. As a result, the multicast session initially reaches every router in the network. When a router receives the multicast traffic, it uses IGMP or MLD to determine if there are any group members on its directly connected subnets. If there are not, and there are no downstream routers to which the traffic must be forwarded, the router sends a poison-reverse message called a *prune message* to its upstream neighbor. That upstream neighbor then stops forwarding the session traffic to the pruned router. If the neighbor also has no group members on its subnets, and all downstream routers have pruned themselves from the tree, that router also sends a prune message upstream. The result is that the multicast tree is eventually pruned of all branches that do not lead to routers with attached group members. Figure 7-29 show the broadcast-and-prune technique.

For every (S, G) pair in its forwarding table, every router in the network maintains state for each of its downstream interfaces. The state is either *forward* or *prune*. The prune state has a timer associated with it, and when the timer expires, the session traffic is again forwarded to neighbors on that interface. Each neighbor again checks for group members and floods the traffic to its own downstream neighbors. If new group members are discovered, the traffic continues to be accepted. Otherwise, a new prune message is sent upstream.

The broadcast-and-prune technique is better-suited to dense topologies than to sparse ones. The initial flooding to all routers, the periodic reflooding as prune states expire, and the maintenance of prune states all contribute to a waste of network resources when many or most branches are pruned. There is also an element of illogic in the maintenance of prune state, requiring routers that are not participating in the multicast tree to remember that they are not a part of the tree.

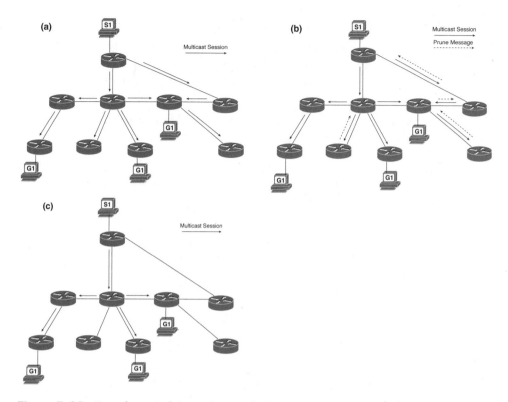

Figure 7-29 *Broadcast-and-Prune Protocols First Use RPB to Forward a Multicast Session to All Parts of the Network (a). Routers with No Connection to Group Members Then Prune Themselves from the Tree (b), So That the Resulting Tree Reaches Only Routers with Group Members (c)*

A better technique for sparse topologies is the explicit join, in which the routers with directly attached group members initiate the join. When a group member signals its router, via IGMP or MLD, that it wants to join a group, the router sends a message upstream toward the source indicating the join. In contrast to a prune message, this message can be thought of as a *graft* message; the router sending the message is grafting itself onto the tree. If all a router's group members leave, and the router has no downstream neighbors active on the group, the router prunes itself from the tree.

Because traffic is never forwarded to any router that does not explicitly request the traffic, network resources are conserved. And because prune state is not kept by nonparticipating routers, overall memory is conserved. As a result, explicit joins scale better in sparse topologies. The argument can be made, of course, that explicit joins always scale better, regardless of whether the topology is sparse or dense. DVMRP and PIM-DM use implicit joins, whereas PIM-SM uses explicit joins.

Source-Based Trees Versus Shared Trees

Some multicast routing protocols construct separate multicast trees for every multicast source. These trees are *source-based* trees because they are rooted at the source. The multicast trees that have been presented in previous sections have been source-based trees.

You have learned that multicast trees can change during the lifetime of a multicast session, as members join and leave the group, and that it is the responsibility of the multicast routing protocol to dynamically adapt the tree to these changes. However, some parts of the tree might not change. Figure 7-30 shows two multicast trees superimposed onto the same network. Notice that although the trees have different sources and different members, their paths pass through at least one common router.

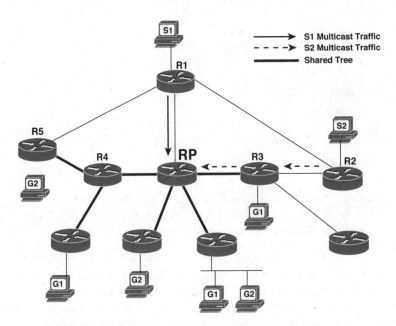

Figure 7-30 *These Two Multicast Trees Have Different Shapes, But They Both Pass Through the Single Router RP*

Shared trees take advantage that many multicast trees can share a single router within the network. Rather than root each tree at its source, the tree is rooted at a shared router called (depending upon the protocol) the *Rendezvous Point (RP)* or *core*. The RP is predetermined and strategically located in the network. When a source begins a multicast session, it registers with the RP. It may be up to the source's directly connected router to determine the shortest path to the RP, or it may be up to the RP to find the shortest path to each source. Explicit joins build trees from routers with attached group members to the RP. Rather than the (S, G) pair recorded for source-based trees, the shared trees use a (*, G) state. This state reflects that the RP is the root of the tree to the group, and many sources may be upstream of the RP. More important, a separate (S, G) pair must be recorded for each distinct source on a source-based tree. Shared trees, however, record only a single (*, G) for each group.

The impact of the (S, G) entries can be demonstrated with a few simple calculations. Suppose in some source-tree, flood-and-prune multicast domain, 200 multicast groups exist with an average of 30 sources per group. Each router must record 30 (S, G) entries for each group, or 30 * 200 = 6000 entries. If there are 150 sources in each of the 200 groups, the entries increase to 150 * 200 = 30,000.

Note   With interactive multicast applications, many group members (receivers) are also sources (senders).

In contrast, shared tree routers record a single (*, G) entry for each group. So, if 200 groups are in a shared-tree multicast domain, the RP records 200 (*, G) entries. Most significant, this number does not vary with the number of sources. Another way of stating these facts is that source-based trees scale on an order of (S_G * G_N), and shared trees scale on an order of (G_N), where G_N is the number of groups in the multicast domain and $S_{[G]}$ is the number of sources per group. Impact is greatly reduced on non-RP routers also because they do not keep state for groups for which they do not forward packets. These routers record a single (*, G) entry for each active downstream group.

This scalability means that shared trees are generally preferable in sparse topologies. But as usual, trade-offs exist. First, the path from the source through the RP may not be the optimum path to every group member for every group. Refer to Figure 7-30 where a member of group 2 is attached to router R5. The optimal path from the source S2 to this group member is R2-R1-R5. But the source traffic must reach the RP first, so the path taken is R2-R3-RP-R4-R5. RPs must be chosen carefully to minimize suboptimal paths. Another drawback is that the RP can become a bottleneck when there are multiple, high-bandwidth multicast sessions. Because of both suboptimal paths and RP congestion, latency can become a problem in poorly designed shared tree networks. The RP also represents a single point of failure, unless redundancy can be designed in. Finally, shared trees can be difficult to debug.

Source-Specific Multicast (SSM)

The (*, G) trees discussed so far represent an *Any-Source Multicast (ASM)* service model, where the * is a wildcard matching any unicast source address. That is, any source can send to the multicast group. You've read in the previous subsections how efficiencies have been introduced to IP multicast networks through explicit joins and shared trees. The problem, as the end of the previous section discussed, is that the RPs of shared trees can introduce some inefficiencies, complexities, and vulnerabilities of their own. RPs must be well placed in the network, they must be redundant, and there must be a means for the RPs to discover sources and for designated routers to discover RPs.

There's also a security concern with ASM. If any source can send to the group, there's the potential for a malicious source to launch a denial-of-service attack against the group.

Source-Specific Multicast (SSM) is a service model that returns to the (S, G) trees, while retaining the advantages of sparse mode protocol operation and explicit joins. The key to implementing SSM is the source filtering capabilities of IGMPv3 and MLDv2. These protocol versions are prerequisite; SSM is not supported with IGMPv1, IGMPv2, or MLDv1. On the routing protocol side, SSM is enabled by PIM-SSM, which is a variation of PIM-SM. The sparse-mode operations are retained but not the RPs.

The other prerequisite for SSM is that the group member must know, through the multicast application, which source it wants to receive the group traffic from. It specifies the (S, G)—called a *multicast channel*—to its designated router, which then grafts itself to an existing tree or initiates a new tree to the source.

The use of IGMPv3 and MLDv2 for SSM networks is specified in RFC 4604, and addressing is specified in RFC 4607. The IANA has reserved IPv4 group addresses in the range 232.0.0.0/8 and IPv6 group addresses in the range FF3x::/96 (with the assumption that this range will be expanded to FF3x::/32). Because not just any source can send to an SSM channel, the chances of a malicious source sending to the group is reduced—although it is still possible for a malicious source to spoof a legitimate source address.

The decision of whether to use ASM or SSM traditionally has been driven by the multicast application. A many-to-many application such as conferencing, in which many sources contribute to the group, calls for ASM. A one-to-many application, such as streaming video, calls for SSM.

However, in modern networks, many-to-many versus one-to-many is no longer a clear determinant. Many designers of multicast networks and multicast applications find "stacking" multiple SSM trees for many-to-many applications preferable to the problems of shared trees. So, for example, a videoconferencing application in which each group member is also a source might build a separate SSM tree for every source to every member. When a new participant joins, a new SSM tree is created, and when a participant leaves, that member's SSM tree is deleted.

The decision factors for determining whether to run an ASM model or an SSM model, then, are the following:

■ Are there enough multicast groups in your network that the efficiencies of RPs outweigh the potential management challenges?

- Do all the hosts in the network support IGMPv3/MLDv2, or do some support only IGMPv2/MLDv1 and can't initiate SSM?

- Are your multicast applications SSM-aware?

Even these determinants are not concrete. As Chapter 8 demonstrates, you can run both ASM (PIM-SM) and SSM (PIM-SSM) in the same network.

Multicast Scoping

You have seen in the preceding discussions of multicast routing issues that although multicast routing certainly uses less network resources than other strategies, such as replicated unicast or simple flooding, it can still be wasteful in some circumstances. This is particularly true of broadcast-and-prune protocols when used in sparse topologies. There are circumstances in which a multicast source and all group members can be found close together in relation to the size of the entire network. In such a case, a mechanism that limits the multicast traffic to the general area on the network in which the members are located helps to conserve resources. There may also be cases in which, for security or other policy reasons, the extent of the multicast traffic must be limited.

When multicast traffic is confined to "islands," the traffic is *scoped*. Put another way, multicast scoping is the practice of putting boundaries on the reach of multicast traffic.

TTL Scoping

One method for establishing boundaries to limit the scope of multicast traffic is to set a special filter on outgoing interfaces that checks the TTL value of all multicast packets. Only packets whose TTL value, after the normal decrement performed by the router, exceeds a configured threshold are forwarded. All other multicast packets are dropped.

Figure 7-31 shows an example. On this router, a multicast packet arrives on interface E2 with a TTL of 13. The router decrements the packet's TTL to 12. Interface E0 has a multicast TTL threshold of 0, which is the default; no multicast packets are blocked based on their TTL. Therefore, a copy of the packet is forwarded out E0. Likewise, a copy of the packet is forwarded out interface E1 because its TTL threshold is set to 5, which is less than the packet's TTL. However, the packet is not forwarded out E3. That interface's TTL threshold is 30, meaning that only packets whose TTL value is greater than 30 can be forwarded.

TTL scoping was regularly used on the now-defunct MBone. The MBone is constructed of regional multicast networks connected through the Internet by IP-over-IP tunnels. Table 7-4 shows typical TTL thresholds used to restrict multicast traffic in the MBone. If you want some traffic to stay within a single site—high-bandwidth real-time video, for example—you configure the source application to send packets with a TTL no higher than 15.

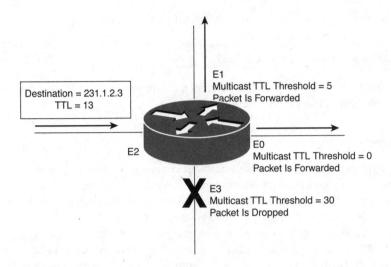

Figure 7-31 *Multicast Packets Are Forwarded Only Out Downstream Interfaces Whose TTL Threshold Is Less Than the Outgoing Packet's TTL*

Table 7-4 *MBone TTL Thresholds*

TTL Value	Restriction
TTL Value	Restriction
0	Restricted to same host
1	Restricted to same subnet
15	Restricted to same site
63	Restricted to same region
127	Worldwide
191	Worldwide, limited bandwidth
255	Unrestricted

TTL scoping has several shortcomings. First, it is inflexible. An interface's TTL threshold applies to all multicast packets. If you want some multicast sessions to pass the threshold, and others to be restricted by it, the separate applications sourcing the sessions must be manipulated. This leads to the second problem: Users must be trusted to set the TTLs in their multicast applications correctly. If a session is sourced with a too-high TTL, it passes outside the boundary you have set.

Another problem with TTL scoping is that it is difficult to implement in all but the simplest topologies. As your multicast network grows in both scale and complexity, predicting the correct thresholds to contain and pass the correct sessions becomes a challenge.

Finally, TTL scoping can cause inefficiencies with broadcast-and-prune protocols. Figure 7-32 shows the problem. The network is a multicast site, and the boundary router has a TTL threshold of 8 configured on the interfaces leading to other parts of the network. The multicast source is generating a session in which the TTL of all packets is set to 8, in keeping with local policy, to limit its traffic to the multicast site. No group members are anywhere along the left branch of the tree, so those routers should prune themselves all the way back to the source's directly connected router. Actually, you can see that one router has sent a prune message upstream to its neighbor.

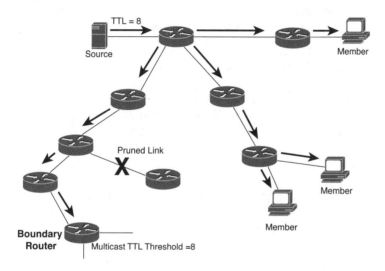

Figure 7-32 *TTL Multicast Filter at the Boundary Router Is Preventing It from Sending a Prune Message Upstream*

The problem is with the boundary router and its configured TTL filter. When the multicast packets reach this router, the packets are discarded at both downstream interfaces because the packets' TTL values are less than the TTL threshold. This is expected behavior. However, the packet discards also mean that no IGMP queries for group members take place. Without the queries, the router does not send a prune message back upstream. As a result, multicast traffic continues to be forwarded unnecessarily through all the routers leading to the boundary router.

Administrative Scoping

IPv4 administrative scoping, described in RFC 2365, takes a different approach to bounding multicast traffic. Rather than filter on TTL values, a range of IPv4 multicast addresses is reserved for scoping. Filtering on these group addresses can then set boundaries. The reserved range of multicast addresses is 239.0.0.0 to 239.255.255.255.

The administratively scoped address space can be further subdivided in a hierarchical manner. For example, RFC 2365 suggests using the range 239.255.0.0/16 for local or site scope and the range 239.192.0.0/14 for organization-wide scope. An enterprise is, however, free to utilize the address space in any way it sees fit. Therefore, the reserved IPv4 range is similar to the RFC 1918 addresses reserved for private use. And like those addresses, the administratively scoped multicast address space is non-unique. It is important to set filters for 239.0.0.0 to 239.255.255.255 so that none of the addresses in that range leak into the public Internet.

IPv6 multicast scoping is specified in RFC 7346. You have already learned that unlike IPv4, IPv6 multicast addresses have a built-in scope field; the scopes and corresponding scope field values (refer to Figure 7-7). So there is no need for a reserved range of IPv6 multicast addresses for scoping as there is with IPv4 multicast.

You have encountered both TTL scoping and address-based scoping already in this chapter and elsewhere in this book. Recall that the TTL for IGMP and OSPF packets is always set to 1, to prevent the packets from being forwarded by any receiving router. In this way, the scope is set to the local subnet. Similarly, routers do not to forward packets whose addresses are in the range 224.0.0.0 to 224.0.0.255. This range, which includes all the addresses shown in Table 7-1, is also scoped to the local subnet.

Looking Ahead

Of all the IP routing protocols examined in the two volumes of this book, the multicast protocols are the most unfamiliar to the most people. Although this chapter provides a reasonable overview of IP multicast routing principles, it is by no means exhaustive. There is much more to IP multicast that cannot be covered within the confines of this book; for more extensive coverage, refer to "Recommended Reading."

Now that you have some understanding of multicast issues, Chapter 8 examines the operation and configuration of the variants of PIMv2, which is the only intra-AS IP multicast routing protocol in production today. Chapter 9 examines scaling and inter-AS routing.

Recommended Reading

Williamson, Beau, *Developing IP Multicast Networks*, Indianapolis, IN, Cisco Press, 2000.

Review Questions

1. Give several reasons why replicated unicast is not a practical substitution for true multicast in a large network.

2. What range of addresses is reserved for IP multicast?

3. How many subnets can be created from a single class D prefix?

4. In what way do routers treat packets with destination addresses in the range 224.0.0.1–224.0.0.255 differently than other multicast addresses?

5. Write the Ethernet MAC addresses that correspond to the following IP addresses:

(a) 239.187.3.201

(b) 224.18.50.1

(c) 224.0.1.87

6. What multicast IP address or addresses are represented by the MAC address 0100.5E06.2D54?

7. Why is Token Ring a poor medium for delivering multicast packets?

8. What is join latency?

9. What is leave latency?

10. What is a multicast DR (or Querier)?

11. What device sends IGMP Query messages?

12. What device sends IGMP Membership Report messages?

13. How is an IGMP Membership Report message used?

14. What is the functional difference between a General IGMP Query and a Group-Specific IGMP Query?

15. Is IGMPv2 compatible with IGMPv1?

16. What IP protocol number signifies IGMP?

17. What is the purpose of the Cisco Group Membership Protocol (CGMP)?

18. What is the advantage of using IGMP Snooping instead of CGMP? What is the possible disadvantage?

19. What devices send CGMP messages: Routers, Ethernet switches, or both?

20. What is Reverse Path Forwarding?

21. How many hosts constitute a dense topology, and how many hosts constitute a sparse topology?

22. What is the primary advantage of explicit joins over implicit joins?

23. What is the primary structural difference between a source-based multicast tree and a shared multicast tree?

24. What is multicast scoping?

25. What are the two methods for IP multicast scoping?

26. From the perspective of a multicast router, what is meant by "upstream" and "downstream?"

27. What is an RPF check?

28. What is a prune? What is a graft?

29. What multicast group addresses are reserved for SSM?

Configuration Exercises

1. Your company is implementing two applications that are based on multicast. It has been decided to assign two multicast IP addresses for the project. Each application receives a specific class D IP address. The multicast traffic has to be restrained within the boundaries of the campus. (Other branches and core must not be transit.) The network engineers have chosen the following IP addresses: 239.65.10.10 and 239.193.10.10

  a. Can you explain how to restrain the multicast traffic dedicated for these two new applications from flowing all around the network?

  b. Explain why these two IP addresses are not the best choices for your network.

  Refer to the topology in Figure 7-33 for this exercise.

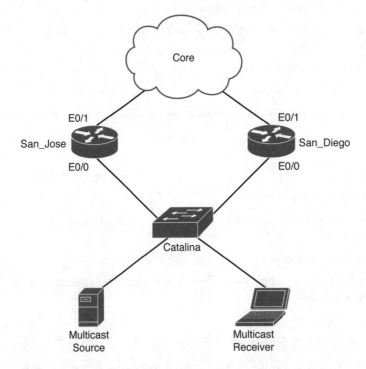

Figure 7-33   *Network Topology for Configuration Exercise 1*

2. Make sure that San_Jose is the multicast Querier on the broadcast domain shared by these hosts. Figure 7-34 shows the topology used for this question.

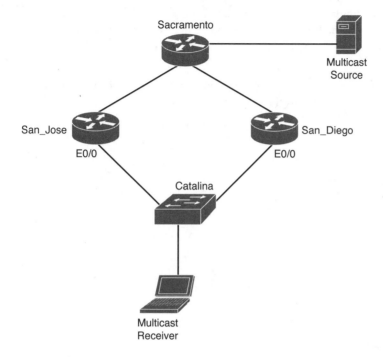

Figure 7-34   *Network Topology for Configuration Exercise 2*

Table 7-5 lists the routers, switches, multicast enabled hosts, interfaces, and addresses used in Configuration Exercises 2 and 3. All interfaces of the routers are shown.

Table 7-5   *Routers, Switches, Multicast Enabled Hosts, Interfaces, and Addresses Used in Configuration Exercises 2 and 3*

San Jose – Eth0/0	192.168.10.1/24
San Diego – Eth0/0	192.168.10.2/24
Multicast Receiver IP Address	192.168.10.20/24
Multicast IP Address used	239.1.1.1

3. Configure the multicast domain based on the following requirements:

a. Routers must send queries every 10 seconds.

b. If the Querier experiences an issue, failure must be detected within 80 seconds.

c. The maximum response time advertised in Internet Group Management Protocol (IGMP) queries must be 5 seconds.

d. Assume multiple receivers are on the subnet 192.168.10.0/24 subnet. Make sure the routers send only one IGMP group-specific query after it receives a group-specific leave. Otherwise, multicast traffic will be pruned from the subnet.

e. If some hosts are still interested by the multicast traffic, they should notify the routers within 1500 milliseconds.

f. Hosts must not join any other groups than 239.1.1.1 (from any sources).

Chapter 8

Protocol Independent Multicast

Although a number of unicast IGPs are available, Protocol Independent Multicast Version 2 (PIMv2) is currently the only multicast IGP deployed in production IP networks. However, a number of PIM modes and submodes exist:

- PIM Dense Mode (PIM-DM)

- PIM Sparse Mode (PIM-SM)

- PIM Source Specific Multicast (PIM-SSM)

- Bidirectional PIM (Bidir-PIM)

Although using the same base protocol, these modes are different enough that you can easily argue that there are, actually, four multicast IGPs.

This chapter examines the operation and application of each of these modes and demonstrates how to configure and troubleshoot them.

Introduction to Protocol Independent Multicast (PIM)

The first edition of this volume covered the operation of a number of multicast routing protocols other than PIM that were in various stages of proposal and experimentation at the time:

- Distance Vector Multicast Routing Protocol (DVMRP)

- Multicast OSPF (MOSPF)

- Core Based Trees (CBT)

None of these protocols gained industry acceptance, so the detailed coverage of their operation is removed from this edition; however, it's worth a few minutes of high-level review of what each of the protocols contributed to learning what is desirable about a multicast routing protocol.

DVMRP shares the characteristic of unicast distance vector protocols of being simple to implement—little more is required than to just turn it on. But this simplicity comes at the expense of high overhead, creating serious scaling problems in anything other than small, high-bandwidth networks densely populated with group members.

MOSPF brings the link-state advantages of OSPF to the table, but at the cost of increased design complexity. Its use of explicit joins eliminates DVMRP's topsy-turvy rule that routers not forwarding for a particular group must remember (hold state) that they are not forwarding packets for that group. The result is a reduced impact on network resources. Yet MOSPF's source-based trees still make the protocol unsuitable for topologies sparsely populated with group members. MOSPF never gained acceptance because given the limited increase in scalability, network designers were unwilling to pay the cost of MOSPF's more complex topological requirements.

DVMRP is "self-contained"; it uses its own built-in protocol to locate the unicast addresses necessary for the creation and maintenance of multicast trees. In this sense it is completely independent of any underlying unicast routing protocol, but the price of this independence is the consumption of network resources to gather information that probably already exists in the unicast routing table.

Note   This cost is not as high as it might seem. As the section "PIM-DM Basics" explains, costs are also associated with running a flood-and-prune protocol without a built-in unicast component.

MOSPF, however, is a multicast extension of a unicast protocol. So although MOSPF eliminates the redundancy of a separate unicast protocol, it cannot run independently of OSPF.

CBT introduces true protocol independence. It consults the existing unicast routing table for unicast destinations, without regard for what protocol is used to maintain that table. CBT also is scalable to sparse topologies; although, core placement must be carefully planned to minimize suboptimal paths and traffic bottlenecks. (A CBT core is conceptually the same thing as a PIM-SM Rendezvous Point.) So CBT was stuck in a Catch-22: The interest in the protocol for real-world applications was limited by its lack of maturity, and the protocol lacks maturity because of its limited use in the real world. CBT never moved into mainstream acceptance because it did not offer significant advantages over the currently favored and more versatile PIM-SM.

PIM is the only IP multicast routing protocol fully supported by Cisco IOS. (DVMRP is supported only to the degree that PIM can connect to a DVMRP network.)

Like CBT, and as its name asserts, PIM is protocol-independent. That is, it uses the unicast routing table to locate unicast addresses, without regard for how the table learned the addresses.

There is a standard list of PIM message formats. Some messages are used only by PIM-DM; some are used only by PIM-SM; and some are shared. All message formats, including those used only by PIM-DM, are described at the end of the section "Protocol Independent Multicast-Sparse Mode (PIM-SM)."

The current version of PIM is PIMv2. Version 1 of the protocol encapsulates its messages in IP packets with protocol number 2 (IGMP) and uses the multicast address 224.0.0.2. PIMv2, which is supported beginning with Cisco IOS Software Release 11.3(2)T, uses its own protocol number of 103 and the reserved multicast address 224.0.0.13. When a PIMv2 router peers with a PIMv1 router, it automatically sets that interface to PIMv1.

Operation of Protocol Independent Multicast-Dense Mode (PIM-DM)

PIM-DM is specified in RFC 3973. Beyond the common message formats, you are likely to find more similarities between PIM-DM and DVMRP than between PIM-DM and PIM-SM.

PIM-DM Basics

PIM-DM uses five PIMv2 messages:

- Hello
- Join/Prune
- Graft
- Graft-Ack
- State Refresh
- Assert

PIMv2 routers use Hello messages to discover neighbors. When a PIMv2 router (either PIM-DM or PIM-SM) becomes active, it periodically sends a Hello message on every interface on which PIM is configured. PIMv1 routers have the same functionality, except that they use Query messages. The Hello (or Query) messages contain a *holdtime*, that specifies the maximum time the neighbor should wait to hear a subsequent message before declaring the originating router dead. Both the PIMv2 Hello interval and the PIMv1 Query interval are 30 seconds in Cisco IOS Software by default and can be changed on a per-interface basis with the command **ip pim query-interval**. The holdtime is set automatically to 3.5 times the Hello/Query interval.

Example 8-1 shows a **debug** capture of PIM messages sent and received. The router has both PIMv1 and PIMv2 neighbors, as indicated by the **Hello** and **Router-Query** keywords.

The router sends Hellos on interface E0 but is receiving neither Hellos nor Queries on the interface, indicating that no PIM neighbors are on that subnet.

Example 8-1   *Router Steel Is Querying for Neighbors on Interfaces E0, E1, and S1.708. It Is Hearing from Neighbors on E1 and S1.708*

```
Steel#debug ip pim
PIM debugging is on
Steel#
PIM: Received v2 Hello on Ethernet1 from 172.16.6.3
PIM: Received Router-Query on Serial1.708 from 172.16.2.242
PIM: Send v2 Hello on Ethernet1
PIM: Send v2 Hello on Ethernet0
PIM: Send Router-Query on Serial1.708  (dual PIMv1v2)
PIM: Received v2 Hello on Ethernet1 from 172.16.6.3
PIM: Received Router-Query on Serial1.708 from 172.16.2.242
PIM: Send v2 Hello on Ethernet1
PIM: Send v2 Hello on Ethernet0
PIM: Send Router-Query on Serial1.708  (dual PIMv1v2)
PIM: Received v2 Hello on Ethernet1 from 172.16.6.3
```

Example 8-2 uses the **debug ip packet detail** command (linked to an access list to filter uninteresting packets) to get a closer look at the PIM messages. Here, you can see that the PIMv2 messages are sent to 224.0.0.13 and use protocol number 103, whereas the PIMv1 messages are sent to 224.0.0.2 and use protocol number 2.

Example 8-2   *This* **debug** *Capture Shows the Multicast Destination Addresses and the Protocol Numbers Used by PIMv1 and PIMv2*

```
Steel#debug ip packet detail 101
IP packet debugging is on (detailed) for access list 101
Steel#
IP: s=172.16.6.3 (Ethernet1), d=224.0.0.13, len 38, rcvd 0, proto=103
IP: s=172.16.2.241 (local), d=224.0.0.2 (Serial1.708), len 35, sending broad/
  multicast, proto=2
IP: s=172.16.2.242 (Serial1.708), d=224.0.0.2, len 32, rcvd 0, proto=2
IP: s=172.16.6.1 (local), d=224.0.0.13 (Ethernet1), len 30, sending broad/multicast,
  proto=103
IP: s=172.16.5.1 (local), d=224.0.0.13 (Ethernet0), len 30, sending broad/multicast,
  proto=103
IP: s=172.16.6.3 (Ethernet1), d=224.0.0.13, len 38, rcvd 0, proto=103
IP: s=172.16.2.241 (local), d=224.0.0.2 (Serial1.708), len 35, sending broad/
  multicast, proto=2
IP: s=172.16.2.242 (Serial1.708), d=224.0.0.2, len 32, rcvd 0, proto=2
```

```
IP: s=172.16.6.1 (local), d=224.0.0.13 (Ethernet1), len 30, sending broad/multicast,
   proto=103
IP: s=172.16.5.1 (local), d=224.0.0.13 (Ethernet0), len 30, sending broad/multicast,
   proto=103
```

In Example 8-3, the command **show ip pim neighbor** observes the resulting PIM neighbor table. .

Example 8-3   *PIM Neighbor Table Records the Neighbors Heard Referred to in Example 8-1*

```
Steel#show ip pim neighbor
PIM Neighbor Table
Neighbor Address  Interface       Uptime    Expires   Ver  Mode
172.16.6.3        Ethernet1       01:57:22  00:01:29  v2   Dense  (DR)
172.16.2.242      Serial1.708     04:55:56  00:01:05  v1   Dense
Steel#
```

When a source begins sending multicast packets, PIM-DM uses flood-and-prune to build the multicast tree. As each PIM-DM router receives a multicast packet, the router adds an entry to its multicast forwarding table. Ultimately, the packets are flooded to all leaf routers; that is, all routers that have no downstream PIM neighbors. If a leaf router receives a multicast packet for which it has no attached group members, the router must prune itself from the multicast tree. It does this by sending a Prune message to the upstream neighbor toward the source. The destination address of the Prune message is 224.0.0.13, and the address of the upstream router is encoded within the message. If that upstream neighbor has no attached members of the packet's group, and either has no other downstream neighbors or has received prunes from all its downstream neighbors, it sends a Prune message to its own upstream neighbor toward the source.

Referring to the bulleted list of PIMv2 message types earlier in this section, you can see that a "Prune" message type does not exist. Instead, you have a Join/Prune. This is a single message type that has separate fields for listing groups to be joined and groups to be pruned. This section continues to use "Prune message" and "Join message" for clarity, but you should be aware that a Prune message is actually a Join/Prune with a group address listed in the prune section. Likewise, a Join message is a Join/Prune message with a group address in the Join field.

Example 8-4 shows a forwarding table entry for multicast group 239.70.49.238. You can observe the (S,G) pair, showing the source to be 172.16.1.1. The router has consulted its unicast routing table for the upstream interface to the source, which is S1.708, and the upstream neighbor toward the source, which is 172.16.2.242. That information is entered into the multicast forwarding table and is used for the RPF check. As with DVMRP, if a packet with a source address of 172.16.1.1 and a destination address of 239.70.49.238 arrives on any interface other than S1.708, the RPF check fails and the packet is dropped.

Example 8-4   show ip mroute *Command Displays the Multicast Forwarding Table*

```
Steel#show ip mroute 239.70.49.238
IP Multicast Routing Table
Flags: D - Dense, S - Sparse, C - Connected, L - Local, P - Pruned
       R - RP-bit set, F - Register flag, T - SPT-bit set, J - Join SPT
Timers: Uptime/Expires
Interface state: Interface, Next-Hop or VCD, State/Mode

 (172.16.1.1, 239.70.49.238), 01:56:27/00:02:59, flags: CT
  Incoming interface: Serial1.708, RPF nbr 172.16.2.242
  Outgoing interface list:
    Ethernet1, Prune/Dense, 01:40:23/00:00:39
    Ethernet0, Forward/Dense, 00:00:46/00:00:00

Steel#
```

Note   Example 8-4 does not show all the information in the forwarding table pertaining to this group; some information has been deleted for clarity.

Associated with the (S,G) entry are two timers. The first timer indicates how long the entry has been in the table. The second timer indicates the expiration time of the entry. If a multicast packet is not forwarded for this (S,G) within 2 minutes and 59 seconds, the entry is deleted.

Two flags are also associated with the entry referred to in Example 8-4. The first flag (C) indicates that a group member is on a directly connected subnet of the router. The second flag (T) indicates that the router is an active member of the *shortest path tree (SPT)*.

Note   PIM calls source-based trees *shortest path trees (SPT)* and shared trees *rendezvous point trees (RPT)*. SPT is a descriptive name because as you will see in a subsequent section, these trees sometime traverse a shorter path to the source than do the RPTs.

Two interfaces are on the outgoing interface list in Example 8-4. The first interface, E1, is in prune state and dense mode. Therefore, you know that the downstream neighbor on this interface has sent a Prune message. The timers show that the entry has been in the multicast table for 1 hour, 40 minutes, and 23 seconds and that the prune state expires in 39 seconds. When a Prune message is received, a 210-second expiration timer starts. The prune state is maintained until the timer expires, at which time the state is changed to "forward," and packets are again forwarded downstream. It is up to the downstream router to again send a prune message to its upstream neighbor.

The second interface, E0, is in forward state. Recall from Example 8-1 that the router is sending Hellos on E0 but is receiving no Hellos from neighbors on that interface. Based on that information and the information in Example 8-4, you know that the router is forwarding on E0 because there is a group member on that subnet. Example 8-5 confirms this conclusion. Referring to Example 8-4 you can see an uptime associated with the interface but no expiration time. This is because there is no neighbor state to expire. Instead, the router deletes the interface from the forwarding table when IGMP tells it that there are no longer group members on the subnet or when the expiration timer shown in Example 8-5 reaches 0.

Example 8-5   **show ip igmp group** *Command Displays the Connected Group Members Recorded in the IGMP Membership Table*

```
Steel#show ip igmp group 239.70.49.238
IGMP Connected Group Membership
Group Address    Interface          Uptime     Expires    Last Reporter
239.70.49.238    Ethernet0          01:52:23   00:02:34   172.16.5.2
Steel#
```

Example 8-6 shows the forwarding table of the next router upstream toward the source. RPF checks are performed for (172.16.1.1, 239.70.49.238) against interface S1.803 and upstream neighbor 172.16.2.254, and there is only one downstream interface. Comparing the flag for this entry against the flags referred to in Example 8-4, you can see that this router is on the shortest path tree but that it has no directly connected group members.

Example 8-6   *Flags for This Entry Indicate That the Router Is on the SPT but That It Has No Directly Connected Group Members*

```
Nickel#show ip mroute 239.70.49.238
IP Multicast Routing Table
Flags: D - Dense, S - Sparse, C - Connected, L - Local, P - Pruned
       R - RP-bit set, F - Register flag, T - SPT-bit set
Timers: Uptime/Expires

 (172.16.1.1/32, 239.70.49.238), uptime 02:05:23, expires 0:02:58, flags: T
  Incoming interface: Serial1.803, RPF neighbor 172.16.2.254
  Outgoing interface list:
    Serial1.807, Forward state, Dense mode, uptime 02:05:24, expires 0:02:34

Nickel#
```

> **Note**   The output referred to in Example 8-6 is formatted slightly differently from the previous forwarding table. This is because of a different IOS. However, you can readily see that the information is the same.

Moving upstream again, Example 8-7 shows another forwarding table for the group. The flags again indicate "Connected," but what is connected in this instance is not a group member. The incoming interface, E0/0, shows an RPF neighbor address of 0.0.0.0, which indicates that the connected device is the source for the group.

Example 8-7   *This Router Connects to the Source 172.16.1.1, As Indicated by the RPF Neighbor Address of 0.0.0.0*

```
Bronze#show ip mroute 239.70.49.238
IP Multicast Routing Table
Flags: D - Dense, S - Sparse, C - Connected, L - Local, P - Pruned
       R - RP-bit set, F - Register flag, T - SPT-bit set, J - Join SPT
Timers: Uptime/Expires
Interface state: Interface, Next-Hop, State/Mode

 (172.16.1.1/32, 239.70.49.238), 02:10:43/00:02:59, flags: CT
  Incoming interface: Ethernet0/0, RPF nbr 0.0.0.0
  Outgoing interface list:
    Serial0/1.305, Prune/Dense, 02:10:43/00:01:28
    Serial0/1.308, Forward/Dense, 02:10:43/00:00:00

Bronze#
```

Example 8-7 also shows two outgoing interfaces (172.16.1.1, 239.70.49.238). One is in forwarding state, and the other is in prune state. Like all flood-and-prune protocols, PIM-DM must maintain prune state for all interfaces. The reason for this requirement is so that a router that has pruned itself from a multicast tree can graft itself back onto the tree when necessary.

For example, Example 8-8 shows a router's entry for (172.16.1.1, 239.70.49.238) in which there are no attached group members and no downstream neighbors. As a result, the outgoing interface list is null. The "P" flag indicates that the router has sent a Prune message to the upstream neighbor 172.16.2.246. If a connected host now sends an IGMP message requesting a join to the group, the router sends a PIM Graft message upstream toward the source. But the only way the router knows the address of the group's source is via the initial flood of multicast packets. Hence, prune state must be maintained, as shown in the example.

Example 8-8 *This Router Has a Null Outgoing Interface List for the (S,G) Pair (172.16.1.1, 239.70.49.238) and Has Pruned Itself from That Source Tree*

```
Lead#show ip mroute 239.70.49.238
IP Multicast Routing Table
Flags: D - Dense, S - Sparse, C - Connected, L - Local, P - Pruned
       R - RP-bit set, F - Register flag, T - SPT-bit set
Timers: Uptime/Expires
Interface state: Interface, Next-Hop, State/Mode

 (172.16.1.1/32, 239.70.49.238), 02:32:42/0:00:17, flags: PT
  Incoming interface: Serial1.605, RPF nbr 172.16.2.246
  Outgoing interface list: Null

Lead#
```

The Graft message is unicast to the upstream neighbor on the group tree. When the upstream router receives the Graft message, it adds the interface on which the message was received to its outgoing interface list. The interface is put into forward state, and a Graft Ack message is immediately unicast to the new downstream neighbor. If the router is already forwarding packets to other downstream neighbors, nothing else must be done. But if the router has also pruned itself from the tree, it too must send a Graft to its upstream neighbor. When a router sends a Graft message, it waits 3 seconds for a Graft Ack. If the acknowledgment is not received within that time, the router retransmits the Graft message.

This PIM-DM flood-and-prune mechanism is similar to that of DVMRP; however, there is one significant difference. DVMRP signals route dependencies to upstream neighbors using a poison reverse mechanism. The dependency tells an upstream DVMRP router that a particular downstream router depends on it to forward packets from a particular source. All this can happen even before the source begins forwarding packets because of DVMRP's built-in routing protocol. As a result, in some topologies, DVMRP can limit the scope of its flooding. PIM-DM does not have this capability because it does not have a built-in routing protocol. Therefore, PIM-DM always floods to the entire PIM domain. In the original Internet-draft for PIM-DM, the protocol designers stated:

> We choose to accept the additional overhead in favor of the simplification and flexibility gained by not depending on a specific type of topology discovery protocol.

Prune Overrides

Another advantage of DVMRP's downstream dependency mechanism is apparent during the prune process. In Figure 8-1, a single router has multiple downstream neighbors. The upstream router, Mercury, is flooding a group's multicast packets onto the LAN connecting the three routers. Copper has a null outgoing interface list and sends a prune to

Mercury. Silver, however, has an attached group member and wants to receive the multicast traffic.

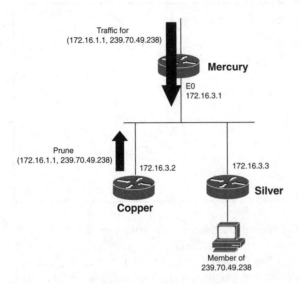

Figure 8-1   *Copper Has Sent a Prune Message for (172.16.1.1, 239.70.49.238) Because Its Outgoing Interface List for That (S, G) Pair Is Empty. But Silver Has a Member of the Group and Wants to Continue Receiving the Traffic*

If the three routers are running DVMRP, there is no problem. Mercury knows its downstream dependencies for the group's source, knows it has received a prune only from Copper, and therefore continues to forward traffic for Silver.

Suppose, though, that the routers referred to in Figure 8-1 run PIM-DM. Mercury certainly knows that it has two neighbors, based on the Hello messages, but nothing in the Hello messages describe dependencies. So when Copper sends a Prune message, Mercury does not know whether to prune the LAN interface.

PIM-DM circumvents this problem with a process called *prune override*. Copper sends the Prune message to Mercury, but Mercury's address is encoded in the message itself. The IP packet carrying the message is addressed to the *ALL PIM Routers* address 224.0.0.13. When Mercury receives the message, it does not immediately prune the interface. Instead, it sets a 3-second timer. At the same time, Silver has also received the Prune message because of the multicast destination address. It sees that the Prune is for a group it wants to continue receiving and that the message has been sent to its upstream neighbor forwarding the group traffic. Silver sends a Join message to Mercury, as shown in Figure 8-2. The result is that Silver overrides the Prune sent by Copper. As long as Mercury receives a Join before its 3-second timer expires, no interruption in traffic occurs.

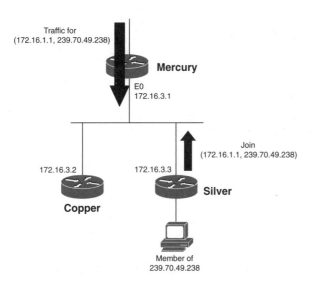

Figure 8-2 *Silver Overrides Copper's Prune with a Join Message*

Example 8-9 shows a prune override in action. Debugging captures PIM activity on Mercury, as referred to in Figures 8-1 and 8-2. The first message shows that a Prune (a Join/Prune message with 239.70.49.238 listed in its prune field) has been received on interface E0 from Copper (172.16.3.2) for the (S, G) pair (172.16.1.1, 239.70.49.238). Notice that the first line indicates that the message is "to us." This is an indicator that Mercury has recognized its own address encoded in the message.

Example 8-9 *Router Mercury in Figure 8-2 Has Received a Prune from Copper (172.16.3.2). Silver (172.16.3.3) Then Sends a Join, Overriding Copper's Prune*

```
Mercury#debug ip pim
PIM debugging is on
Mercury#
PIM: Received Join/Prune on Ethernet0 from 172.16.3.2, to us
PIM: Prune-list: (172.16.1.1/32, 239.70.49.238)
PIM: Schedule to prune Ethernet0 for (172.16.1.1/32, 239.70.49.238)
PIM: Received Join/Prune on Ethernet0 from 172.16.3.3, to us
PIM: Join-list: (172.16.1.1/32, 239.70.49.238)
PIM: Add Ethernet0/172.16.3.3 to (172.16.1.1/32, 239.70.49.238), Forward state
```

The second and third lines show that Mercury has scheduled the (S, G) entry to be pruned from interface E0. That is, the 3-second timer has started. On the fourth line, Mercury has received a Join from Silver (172.16.3.3). On lines 5 and 6, E0 has been put into forward state for the (S, G) pair. Copper's Prune has been overridden.

Unicast Route Changes

When a topology changes, the unicast routing table also changes. And if the unicast route changes affect the route to a source, PIM-DM must also change. An obvious case would be one in which a topology change results in a different previous-hop router on the path to a source.

When a source's RPF router changes, PIM-DM first sends a Prune message to the old router. A Graft message is then sent to the new RPF router to build the new tree.

PIM-DM Designated Routers

PIM-DM elects a designated router on multiaccess networks. The protocol does not need a DR, but recall that IGMPv1 does not have a Querier process and relies on the routing protocol to elect a DR to manage IGMP queries. This is the role of the PIM-DM (and PIM-SM) designated router.

The DR election process is quite simple. As you already know, every PIM-DM router sends a PIMv2 Hello message or a PIMv1 Query message every 30 seconds for neighbor discovery. On multiaccess networks, the PIM-DM router with the highest IP address becomes the DR, as shown by the output in Example 8-10. The other routers monitor the DR's Hello packets, and if none are heard within 105 seconds, the DR is declared dead and a new DR is elected.

Example 8-10   *PIM Neighbor Table of Mercury referred to in Example 8-9 Indicates That Silver, with the Highest Attached IP Address of 172.16.3.3, Is the Designated Router*

```
Mercury#show ip pim neighbor
PIM Neighbor Table
Neighbor Address   Interface        Uptime     Expires    Ver   Mode
172.16.3.3         Ethernet0        2d23h      00:01:17   v1v2  Dense     (DR)
172.16.3.2         Ethernet0        2d23h      00:01:21   v1    Dense
172.16.2.250       Serial1.503      09:15:11   00:01:17   v1    Dense
Mercury#
```

PIM Forwarder Election

In Figure 8-3, both Mercury and Copper have a route to source 172.16.1.1. They also have downstream interfaces to a member of group 239.70.49.238 that connect to a common multiaccess network. Both Mercury and Copper receive copies of the same multicast packets from the source, but it would be obviously inefficient for both routers to forward the packets onto the same network.

To prevent such a situation, PIM routers select a single *forwarder* on the shared network. DVMRP has a similar function, the designated forwarder. DVMRP designated forwarders are selected as part of the route exchange across the multiaccess network.

Because PIM does not have its own routing protocol, it instead uses Assert messages to select the forwarder.

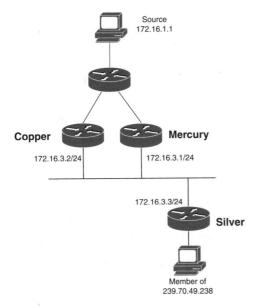

Figure 8-3 *Both Copper and Mercury Receive Copies of the Multicast Packets Sent by Source 172.16.1.1, but Only One Router Should Forward the Packets onto Subnet 172.16.3.0/24*

When a router receives a multicast packet on an outgoing multiaccess interface, it sends an Assert message on the network. The Assert message includes the source and group address, the metric of the unicast route to the source, and the metric preference (in IOS terms, the administrative distance) of the unicast protocol used to discover the route. The routers producing the duplicate packets compare the messages and determine the forwarder based on the following criteria:

- The router advertising the lowest metric preference (administrative distance) is the forwarder. The routers would advertise only different metric preferences if their routes to the source have been discovered via different unicast routing protocols.

- If the metric preferences are equal, the router advertising the lowest metric is the forwarder. In other words, if the routers run the same unicast routing protocol, the router metrically closest to the source becomes the forwarder.

- If both the metric preferences and the metrics are equal, the forwarder is the router with the highest IP address on the network.

The forwarder continues forwarding group traffic onto the multiaccess network. The other routers stop forwarding that group's traffic and remove the multiaccess interface from their outgoing interface list.

For example, when the multicast source referred to in Figure 8-3 first begins sending packets to group 239.70.49.238, both Copper and Mercury receive copies of the packets, and both routers forward the packets onto subnet 172.16.3.0/24, as shown in part (a) of Figure 8-4. When Copper receives a packet from Mercury for (172.16.1.1, 239.70.49.238) on its Ethernet interface, it sees that the interface is on the outgoing interface list for that (S, G) pair. As a result, it sends an Assert message on the subnet. When Mercury receives a multicast packet from Copper on the same interface, it takes the same action, as shown in part (b) of Figure 8-4.

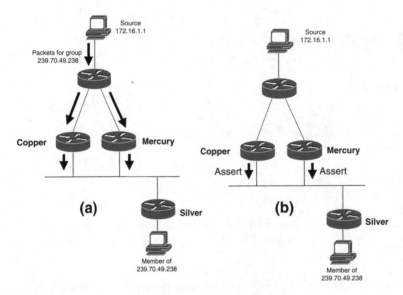

Figure 8-4   *When Copper and Mercury Detect Packets for (172.16.1.1, 239.70.49.238) on Their Downstream Multiaccess Interfaces, They Originate Assert Messages to Determine the Forwarder for the Group*

Example 8-11 shows Silver's unicast routing table and its multicast forwarding table. The unicast table indicates equal cost OSPF paths to the source 172.16.1.1 via either Copper (172.16.3.2) or Mercury (172.16.3.1). Because routes are OSPF, they have an equal administrative distance of 110. And because both routes have an OSPF cost of 74, the forwarder is the router with the highest IP address.

Example 8-11   *Silver's Unicast Routing Table Shows Two Next-Hop Routers to the Subnet of Source 172.16.1.1. The Multicast Routing Table Shows That the Next-Hop Router with the Highest IP Address Has Been Chosen as the Forwarder*

```
Silver#show ip route
Codes: C - connected, S - static, I - IGRP, R - RIP, M - mobile, B - BGP
       D - EIGRP, EX - EIGRP external, O - OSPF, IA - OSPF inter area
       N1 - OSPF NSSA external type 1, N2 - OSPF NSSA external type 2
       E1 - OSPF external type 1, E2 - OSPF external type 2, E - EGP
```

```
           i - IS-IS, L1 - IS-IS level-1, L2 - IS-IS level-2, * - candidate default
           U - per-user static route, o - ODR
           T - traffic engineered route
Gateway of last resort is not set
      172.16.0.0/16 is variably subnetted, 8 subnets, 2 masks
O        172.16.2.252/30 [110/138] via 172.16.3.1, 00:02:16, Ethernet1
                          [110/138] via 172.16.3.2, 00:02:16, Ethernet1
O        172.16.2.248/30 [110/74] via 172.16.3.1, 00:02:16, Ethernet1
O        172.16.2.244/30 [110/74] via 172.16.3.2, 00:02:16, Ethernet1
                          [110/74] via 172.16.3.1, 00:02:16, Ethernet1
O        172.16.2.240/30 [110/138] via 172.16.3.1, 00:02:16, Ethernet1
O        172.16.2.236/30 [110/74] via 172.16.3.1, 00:02:16, Ethernet1
C        172.16.5.0/24 is directly connected, Ethernet0
O        172.16.1.0/24 [110/84] via 172.16.3.1, 00:02:16, Ethernet1
                        [110/84] via 172.16.3.2, 00:02:16, Ethernet1
C        172.16.3.0/24 is directly connected, Ethernet1
Silver#
Silver#show ip mroute 172.16.1.1 239.70.49.238
IP Multicast Routing Table
Flags: D - Dense, S - Sparse, C - Connected, L - Local, P - Pruned
       R - RP-bit set, F - Register flag, T - SPT-bit set, J - Join SPT
Timers: Uptime/Expires
Interface state: Interface, Next-Hop or VCD, State/Mode

(172.16.1.1, 239.70.49.238), 00:02:02/00:02:59, flags: CT
  Incoming interface: Ethernet1, RPF nbr 172.16.3.2
  Outgoing interface list:
    Ethernet0, Forward/Dense, 00:01:50/00:00:00

Silver#
```

Operation of Protocol Independent Multicast-Sparse Mode (PIM-SM)

You learned in Chapter 7, "Introduction to IP Multicast Routing," how shared trees are more scalable in sparsely populated multicast networks, and how they can even be used in densely populated networks. The discussion may have left you with the impression that shared multicast trees are always preferable over source-based trees. Such is not the case.

Figure 8-5 shows a situation in which a source-based tree might be preferred over a shared tree. In this topology, the source and destination are closer to each other than they are to the rendezvous point router at which the shared tree is rooted. A source-based tree directly between the source and destination is preferable, if only the associated overhead could be reduced.

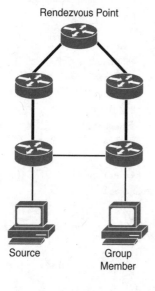

Figure 8-5   *A Source-Based Tree Might Be Preferable to the Shared Tree in This Network*

PIM-SM supports both shared and source-based trees, which is a key reason why it is the multicast routing protocol of choice in most modern networks.

PIM-SM is described in RFC 4601.

PIM-SM Basics

PIM-SM uses seven PIMv2 messages:

- Hello
- Bootstrap
- Candidate-RP-Advertisement
- Join/Prune
- Assert
- Register
- Register-Stop

Three of the messages (Hello, Join/Prune, and Assert) are also used by PIM-DM. Four messages are unique to PIM-SM, just as two messages (Graft and Graft-Ack) are used only by PIM-DM.

Several functions that are common to PIM-SM and PIM-DM follows:

- Neighbor discovery through exchange of Hello messages
- Recalculation of the RPF interface when the unicast routing table changes
- Election of a designated router on multiaccess networks
- Use of Prune Overrides on multiaccess networks
- Use of Assert messages to elect a designated forwarder on multiaccess networks

These functions are all described in the PIM-DM section and are not described again here.

Unlike PIM-DM, PIM-SM uses explicit joins, making the creation of both shared and source-based multicast trees more efficient.

Finding the Rendezvous Point

As you have already learned in Chapter 7, a shared tree is rooted at a router somewhere in the multicast network rather than at the source. CBT calls this router the *core*, and PIM-SM calls it the *Rendezvous Point (RP)*. Before a shared tree can be established, the joining routers must know how to find the RP. The router can learn the unicast IPv4 address of the RP in three ways:

- The RP address can be statically configured on all routers.
- An open-standard bootstrap protocol can designate and advertise the RP.
- The Cisco-proprietary Auto-RP protocol can designate and advertise the RP. Note that Auto-RP supports only IPv4 multicast; IPv6 multicast is not supported.

RPs with unicast IPv6 addresses have an additional and clever means of RP address discovery called *Embedded RP*. Because IPv6 group addresses are so large, a unicast IPv6 RP address can be compressed and embedded into an IPv6 group address. Any device knowing the group address can then find the RP without extra configuration or an extra protocol.

As with static routes, statically configuring RP addresses on all routers has the advantage of providing specific control of the network, but at the cost of high administrative overhead. Static RP configuration is generally only feasible on small multicast networks.

Bootstrap Protocol

The bootstrap protocol, specified in RFC 5059, is based on the protocol used by CBT to advertise core routers, with a few changes in message names and formats. To run the bootstrap protocol, *candidate bootstrap routers (C-BSR)* and *candidate rendezvous points (C-RP)* are administratively designated in the network. Typically, the same set of routers is configured as both C-BSRs and C-RPs. The C-BSRs and C-RPs identify themselves by means of an IPv4 or IPv6 address, which is typically configured to be the address of a loopback interface.

The first step is for a bootstrap router (BSR) to be elected from the C-BSRs. Each C-BSR is assigned a priority between 0 and 255 (the default is 0) and BSR IP address. When a router is configured as a candidate BSR, it sets a bootstrap timer to 130 seconds and listens for a Bootstrap message.

Bootstrap messages advertise the originator's priority and BSR IP address. When a C-BSR receives a Bootstrap message, it compares the originator's priority with its own priority. If the originator has a higher priority, the receiver resets its bootstrap timer and continues to listen. If the receiver's priority is higher, it declares itself the BSR and begins sending Bootstrap messages every 60 seconds. If the priorities are equal, the higher BSR IP address is the tie-breaker.

If a C-BSR's 130-second bootstrap timer expires, the router assumes that there is no BSR, declares itself the BSR, and begins sending Bootstrap messages every 60 seconds.

Bootstrap messages use the IPv4 All_PIM_Router's destination address of 224.0.0.13 or the IPv6 All_PIM_Router's destination address FF02::D, and have a TTL of 1. When a PIM router receives a Bootstrap message, it sends a copy out all interfaces except the one on which the message was received. This procedure not only ensures that the Bootstrap messages are flooded throughout the multicast domain, but it also ensures that every PIM router receives a copy and thus knows which router is the BSR.

A C-RP is configured with an RP IP address and a priority between 0 and 255. The router can be configured to be a candidate RP for only certain multicast groups, or it can be the C-RP for all groups. When the BSR is known by reception of Bootstrap messages, the C-RP begins unicasting Candidate-RP-Advertisement messages to the BSR. These messages contain the originator's RP address, the group addresses for which the originator is a candidate RP, and its priority.

The BSR compiles the C-RPs, their respective priorities, and their corresponding groups into an *RP-Set* and advertises the RP-Set throughout the PIM domain in Bootstrap messages. Also included in the Bootstrap message is an 8-bit hash-mask. Again, all PIM routers receive the Bootstrap messages because of the destination address 224.0.0.13 or FF02::D.

When a router must join a shared tree, as the result of receiving either an IGMP message or a PIM Join message, it examines the RP-Set learned from the BSR via Bootstrap messages.

- If there is only one C-RP for the group, that router is selected as the RP.

- If there are multiple C-RPs for the group, each with different priorities, the router with the lowest priority number is chosen as the RP.

- If there are multiple C-RPs for the group with equally low priorities, a hash function is run. The input of the function is the group prefix, the hash-mask, and the C-RP address, and the output is some numeric value. The C-RP with the highest resulting value becomes the RP.

- If the hash function returns the same value for more than one C-RP, the C-RP with the highest IP address becomes the RP.

Note   The hash function, if you must know, is

$\text{Value}(G,M,C) = (1103515245 * ((11035515245 * (G\&M) + 12345) \text{ XOR } C) + 12345) \bmod 2^{31}$

where

   G = Group prefix

   M = Hash-mask

   C = C-RP address

This set of procedures ensures that all routers in the domain select the same RP for the same group. The only reason the hash function is necessary is to incorporate the hash-mask, which allows some number of consecutive group addresses to be mapped to the same RP.

Auto-RP Protocol

Auto-RP was first supported in Cisco IOS Software Release 11.1(6) and was developed by Cisco to provide automatic discovery of the RP before the bootstrap protocol was specified for PIM-SM. It supports IPv4 RPs and although still occasionally found in multicast networks is mostly obsolete.

As with bootstrap, candidate RPs (C-RP) are designated in the PIM-SM domain and are identified by designated IP addresses, usually the address of a loopback interface. One or more *RP mapping agents*, routers that play a similar role to BSRs, are also designated. The four major differences from the bootstrap protocol follow:

- Auto-RP is Cisco-proprietary and usually cannot be used in multivendor topologies. However, some other vendors do support Auto-RP.

- RP mapping agents are designated, rather than elected from a set of candidates as BSRs are.

- RP mapping agents map groups to RPs, rather than advertising an RP-Set and distributing the selection process throughout the domain.

- Rather than the multicast address 224.0.0.13 used by bootstrap and understood by all PIM routers, Auto-RP uses two reserved multicast addresses, 224.0.1.39 and 224.0.1.40.

When a Cisco PIM-SM router is configured to be a candidate RP for one or more groups, it advertises itself and the groups for which it is a C-RP in *RP-Announce* messages. These messages are multicast every 60 seconds to the reserved Cisco-RP-Announce address 224.0.1.39. The configured mapping agents for the domain listen for this address. From all the received RP-Announce messages, the mapping agent selects an RP for a group based on the numerically highest IP address of all the group's C-RPs.

The RP mapping agent then advertises the complete list of group-to-RP mappings in *RP-Discovery* messages. These messages are sent every 60 seconds to the reserved Cisco-RP-Discovery address 224.0.1.40. All Cisco PIM-SM routers listen for this address and thus learn the correct RP to use for each known group.

A quality that more closely approaches a negative is that you cannot create redundant RPs using MSDP-based Anycast RP (discussed in Chapter 9, "Scaling IP Multicast Routing") because MSDP is IPv4-only. However, RFC 4610 specifies modifications to the PIM-SM Register and Register-Stop mechanisms so that Anycast RP can be used without MSDP.

Embedded RP Addresses

One of the downsides of PIM-SM networks, as you have seen in the preceding subsections, is the need to have either an extra protocol just for discovering the addresses of the RP, or using static RP address configurations with all their inflexibility and poor scalability. IPv6 PIM-SM networks have a clever workaround for this problem. Instead of needing a separate RP discovery protocol (although, BSR does support IPv6), the IPv6 address of the RP is embedded in the IPv6 group address. So if a PIM-SM router knows the group address, it also knows the RP address—assuming, of course, that the router knows to look for it.

This might seem strange at first. How can a 128-bit multicast group address contain a 128-bit RP address and still convey the specifics of the multicast group?

The answer has two parts. First, recall from Figure 7-7 in Chapter 7 that an IPv6 multicast group address has a 112-bit Group ID field. This field can identify many trillions of multicast groups, far more than needed in any closed multicast network—and probably more than needed for the entire public Internet should that ever become multicast-capable. So why not borrow some of those unused bits to indicate an RP address?

The second part of the answer—even if we use some of the 112 Group ID bits to embed an RP address, there still are not 128 bits available—is in the way we use address compression in IPv6. You're certainly aware of the use of the double colon notation (::) to indicate multiple 16-bit segments of all zeroes. You can use RP addresses with long strings of zeroes and then leave those zeroes out of a compressed form of the address that fits into the bits of the Group ID field you have designated as the RP address field.

Addressing the answers to the questions backward, Figure 8-6 shows how the second question is addressed (pun intended). Specifically, you use an IPv6 RP address that consists of a lot of zeroes without violating any IPv6 rule. IPv6 requires a 64-bit prefix, so you know you need that many bits. But a multicast network doesn't need that many

RPs. Say 16 RPs are enough for any one multicast network; 16 RPs can be represented by a 4-bit identifier, called the *RP Interface Identifier (RIID)*. If this is sufficient for identifying any RP (the RIID) in any network (the 64-bit prefix), you need only 70 bits. If you have a large IPv6 multicast network, you can use more than one 64-bit prefix. The remaining 58 bits are set to all zeroes, so as long as you can deal with that, you can squeeze a 128-bit address into a 70-bit space.

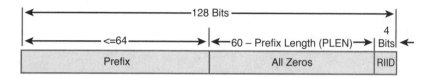

Figure 8-6 *An IPv6 RP Address Can Be Designed So That It Consists of Mostly Zeroes, Allowing It to Be Compressed Enough for Embedding in a Multicast Group Address*

Figure 8-7 shows how the RP address format referred to in Figure 8-6 fits into an IPv6 multicast group address. The trick is that you reduce the Group ID field in this IPv6 multicast address format from 112 bits to 32 bits—still a Group ID space as large as the entire IPv4 address space. That leaves you 80 bits to work with. Out of these 80 bits 64 bits are used as the RP Network Prefix, and another 8 bits are used to specify the Prefix Length (PLEN) in case the prefix is less than 64 bits. Then 4 bits are used for the RIID. The remaining 4 bits are not needed and are designated as reserved.

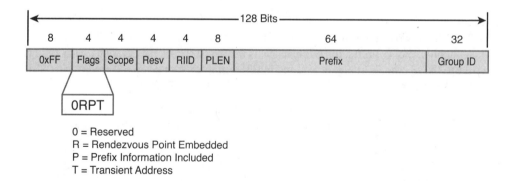

Figure 8-7 *IPv6 Multicast Group Address Format Is Modified to Accommodate an Embedded RP Address*

The last significant feature of the address format, as shown in Figure 8-7, is the settings of the Flags field. In this example

- R = 1 (Rendezvous Point embedded)

- P = 1 (Prefix information included)

- T = 1 (Address is transient)

So the state of the Flags fields, when the multicast group address has an embedded RP address, is binary 0111 or hex 0x7. Therefore, an IPv6 group address with an embedded RP address begins with the prefix ff:7x::/12, with the scope bits determining the value of x.

Figure 8-8 presents an example. The RP address 2001:db8:4e:f5::2 is designed so that the prefix is 64 bits (it can be shorter, but cannot be longer) and the RIID, ::2, is no more than 4 bits.

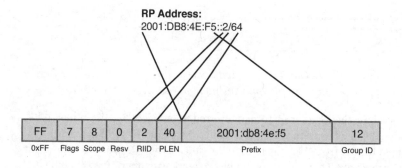

Figure 8-8 *An IPv6 RP Address Is Compressed and Embedded in an IPv6 Group Address*

The RIID is written into the RIID field of the group address, and the PLEN is set to 64 (0x40). The RP prefix 2001:db8:4e:f5:: is writing to the Prefix field. The Flags field is set to 0x7, as shown in Figure 8-7, and in this example we've given the group address an Organizational scope (0x8). Finally, the Group ID of 0x12 is used.

The resulting IPv6 multicast group address is ff78:240:2001:db8:4e:f5::12. The ff7:: at the beginning tells you that the multicast address has an embedded RP address.

It might appear strange to you that the RIID, the last part of the RP address, is the first of the significant fields in the Group address. When the RP address is extracted, the order makes more sense. As the group address is read left-to-right, the RIID is pulled first. Then, the PLEN is read so that the correct prefix length is known. The right number of zeroes are added and then the prefix. So the group address is read left-to-right, and the extracted information allows the embedded RP address to be built right-to-left.

There are several attractive qualities around embedded RP addresses. At the top of the list for most people is that there is not only no extra protocol to run to discover RP addresses, but also there's not even any extra configuration to be done or unique commands to be entered. As long as you choose the right RP and group addresses, and as long as the router software supports embedded RP addresses (IOS does), the routers know from the flags in the group address to extract the RP address from the group address.

> **Note** IOS does have a statement **ipv6 pim rp embedded**. However, because embedded RP addresses are supported by default, you should need only the "no" form of this statement if, for some reason, you want to disable embedded RP.

Embedded RP addresses may also prove to be useful in RP discovery across AS boundaries, as discussed in Chapter 9. However, as of this writing there is not enough experience with it to know how useful it may be.

Embedded RP addresses also have a couple of less ideal qualities, if not exactly negatives. First, they can be used only in IPv6 multicast networks. There's no way to do the same kinds of "packing" tricks to fit an IPv4 RP address into an IPv4 multicast group address. The reason this isn't a negative is that as of this writing IPv4 is depleted in four of the world's five RIRs, and IPv6 is quickly becoming established. Future large-scale multicast networks will most certainly be IPv6-based.

PIM-SM and Shared Trees

The major difference between a shared tree route entry and a source-based or shortest path tree (SPT) route entry is that the shared tree entry is not source-specific—in keeping with that many sources share the same tree. Therefore, the entry is a (*,G) pair, where the asterisk is a wildcard representing any and all source addresses sending to the group G.

When a PIM-SM DR receives an IGMP Membership Report from a host requesting a join to a multicast group, it first checks to see if there is already an entry in the multicast table for the group. If there is an entry for the group, the interface on which the IGMP message was received is added to the entry as an outgoing interface. No other action is necessary.

If no entry exists, a (*,G) entry is created for the group and the outgoing interface is added. The router then looks up the group-to-RP mapping for this group, as shown in Example 8-12, the unicast routing table is consulted for the route to the specified RP, and the upstream interface to the RP is added to the incoming (RPF) interface.

Example 8-12   show ip pim rp mapping *Command Displays a Router's Group-to-RP Mappings. Here, All Multicast Groups Are Mapped to the RP 172.16.224.1*

```
Iron#show ip pim rp mapping
PIM Group-to-RP Mappings

Group(s): 224.0.0.0/4, Static
    RP: 172.16.224.1 (?)
Iron#
```

Example 8-13 shows an example of a (*,G) route entry at router Iron in Figure 8-9.

Example 8-13   *This (*,G) Entry Indicates That the Upstream Neighbor on the Shared Tree for Group 236.82.134.23 is 172.16.2.242, Reachable Out Interface S1.708, and That the RP for the Group Is 172.16.224.1. The Flags Associated with the Entry Indicate Sparse Mode and That There Is a Connected Member (on Interface E0)*

```
Iron#show ip mroute 236.82.134.23
IP Multicast Routing Table
Flags: D - Dense, S - Sparse, C - Connected, L - Local, P - Pruned
       R - RP-bit set, F - Register flag, T - SPT-bit set, J - Join SPT
Timers: Uptime/Expires
Interface state: Interface, Next-Hop or VCD, State/Mode

(*, 236.82.134.23), 00:08:58/00:02:59, RP 172.16.224.1, flags: SC
  Incoming interface: Serial1.708, RPF nbr 172.16.2.242
  Outgoing interface list:
    Ethernet0, Forward/Sparse, 00:08:59/00:02:47

Iron#
```

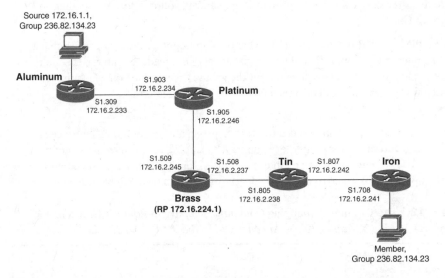

Figure 8-9   *Router Brass Is the RP for This PIM-SM Domain. Its RP Address, 172.16.224.1, Is Configured on Its Loopback Interface*

The router then sends a Join/Prune message out the upstream interface to 224.0.0.13, as shown by Figure 8-10. The message includes the address of the group to be joined and the address of the RP. The prune section of the message is empty. There are also two flags that are set, the wildcard bit (WC-bit) and the RP-tree bit (RPT-bit).

- The WC-bit = 1 indicates that the join address is an RP address rather than a source address.

- The RPT-bit = 1 indicates that the message is propagated along a shared tree to the RP.

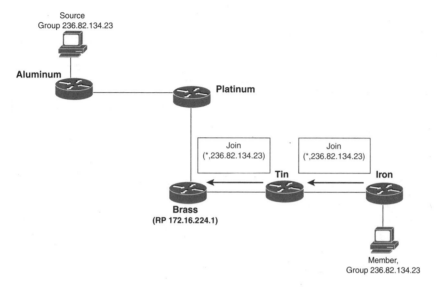

Figure 8-10 *A Join/Prune Message Is Multicast Hop-by-Hop to the RP*

When the upstream router receives the Join/Prune, one of four situations and associated actions holds true:

- The router is not the RP and is on the shared tree. The router adds the interface on which it received the Join/Prune to the outgoing interface list for the group.

- The router is not the RP and is not on the tree. The router creates a (*,G) entry and sends its own Join/Prune upstream toward the RP.

- The router is the RP and has an entry for the group. The router adds the interface on which it received the Join/Prune to the outgoing interface list for the group.

- The router is the RP and has no entry for the group. The router creates a (*,G) entry and adds the receiving interface to the outgoing interface list for the group.

The implication of the last bullet is that a group does not need a source for a tree to be built from members to the RP.

After the shared tree is established, routers periodically send Join/Prune messages to upstream neighbors as a keepalive. The Join/Prune lists all route entries for which the destination neighbor is the previous-hop router. The default period is 60 seconds and can be changed with the Cisco IOS Software command **ip pim message-interval**. The hold time is three times the Join/Prune interval, or 3 minutes by default, and is advertised in the Join/Prune message. If a PIM-SM router does not hear a Join/Prune for a known group from a downstream neighbor within the hold time, it prunes the downstream router from the outgoing interface list of the group entry. Example 8-14 shows the entry for group 236.82.134.23 in router Tin referred to in Figure 8-6. The outgoing interface to router Iron, S1.805, indicates that the interface will be pruned if a Join/Prune is not received from Iron within 2 minutes, 11 seconds.

Example 8-14   *Entry for Group 236.82.134.23 at Tin in Figure 8-6 Shows the Remaining Hold Time Associated with Downstream Router Iron. Notice That There Is No "C" Flag Set for This Entry Because Tin Has No Directly Connected Group Members*

```
Tin#show ip mroute 236.82.134.23
IP Multicast Routing Table
Flags: D - Dense, S - Sparse, C - Connected, L - Local, P - Pruned
       R - RP-bit set, F - Register flag, T - SPT-bit set
Timers: Uptime/Expires

(*, 236.82.134.23), 00:09:39/0:02:56, RP 172.16.224.1, flags: S
  Incoming interface: Serial1.805, RPF neighbor 172.16.2.237
  Outgoing interface list:
    Serial1.807, Forward state, Sparse mode, uptime 00:09:39, expires 0:02:11

Tin#
```

Pruning occurs in the same manner. When a router wants to prune itself from a shared tree, because it no longer has any directly connected group members or downstream neighbors, it sends a Join/Prune message out the RPF interface to the upstream neighbor. The group and RP address are listed in the Prune section, and the WC-bit and RPT-bit are set. The upstream router then removes the receiving interface from the outgoing interface list for the group. If that router has no more downstream neighbors and no connected group members, it also prunes itself.

Note   The Prune Override mechanism, as described in the PIM-DM section, ensures that downstream neighbors on multiaccess networks are not inadvertently pruned.

Source Registration

The fundamental concept of shared trees, mentioned several times already, is that the multicast tree is rooted at a core or rendezvous point rather than at the source. The question arises, then, of how the source delivers multicast packets to the RP for delivery over the branches of the tree. An earlier and now defunct multicast routing protocol, CBT, resolved the question by using bidirectional trees—packets can flow both down a branch from the core or up the branch toward the core. The source's directly connected router joins the shared tree to the core and then sends its traffic up the branch to the core. The problem with bidirectional trees is that it is hard to ensure a loop-free topology because RPF checks cannot be performed when there is no distinct "upstream" and "downstream."

Unlike CBT, PIM-SM uses RPF checks. Therefore, its trees must be unidirectional—that is, traffic can flow only down tree branches from the RP. The unidirectional traffic ensures a clearly defined incoming or RPF interface; however, if traffic flows only from the RP outward, how does a source deliver its multicast traffic to the RP?

When a PIM-SM router first receives a multicast packet from a directly connected source, it looks in its group-to-RP mappings to find the correct RP for the destination group, as shown in the output in Example 8-15. This step is the same as when a member signals a group join with an IGMP message.

Example 8-15 *Group-to-RP Mapping of Router Aluminum in Figure 8-11. Compare This to Example 8-12; Iron Has a Static RP Napping, Whereas Aluminum Has Learned the RP Address Dynamically*

```
Aluminum#show ip pim rp mapping
PIM Group-to-RP Mappings

Group(s) 224.0.0.0/4, uptime: 00:02:39, expires: 00:02:17
    RP 172.16.224.1 (?), PIMv2 v1
    Info source: 172.16.2.245 (?)
Aluminum#
```

After the group's RP is determined, the router encapsulates the multicast packet in a PIM Register message and sends the message to the RP. Rather than multicasting, the Register message is unicast to the RP address, as shown in Figure 8-11.

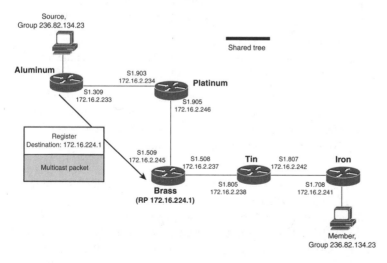

Figure 8-11 *First Multicast Packet Is Encapsulated in a PIM Register Message and Unicast to the RP*

When the RP receives the Register message, the multicast packet is decapsulated. If the multicast routing table already has an entry for the group, copies of the multicast packet are forwarded out all interfaces on the outgoing interface list, as shown in Figure 8-12.

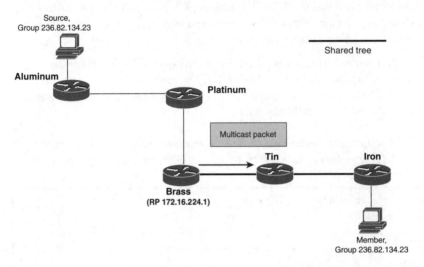

Figure 8-12   *Multicast Packet Is Removed from the Register Message and Forwarded Out All Interfaces on the Group's Outgoing Interface List*

If there is a significant amount of multicast traffic to be sent to the RP, it is inefficient to continue encapsulating the packets in Register messages to get them to the RP. Therefore, the RP creates a (S,G) entry in its multicast table and initiates a shortest-path tree (SPT) to the source DR by multicasting a Join/Prune message, as shown in Figure 8-13. In this message the source address is included, WC-bit = 0, and RPT-bit = 0 to indicate that the path is a source-based SPT rather than a shared RPT.

After the SPT is established and the RP receives the group traffic over that tree, it sends a Register Stop message to the source's DR to tell the router to stop sending the multicast packets in Register messages, as shown in Figure 8-14.

If there are no group members when the source begins sending multicast traffic to the RP, the RP does not build an SPT. Instead, it simply sends a Register Stop to the source's DR telling it to stop sending the encapsulated multicast packets in Register messages. The RP has a (*,G) entry for the group, and when a member joins, the RP can then initiate the SPT.

A mechanism known as *Register Suppression* helps to protect against the DR continuing to send packets to a failed RP. When a DR receives a Register Stop, it starts a 60-second *Register-Suppression* timer. When the timer expires, the router again sends its multicast packets to the RP in Register messages. However, 5 seconds before this occurs, the DR sends a Register message with a flag set, called the Null-Register bit, and with no encapsulated packets. If this message triggers a Register Stop from the RP, the Register-Suppression timer is reset.

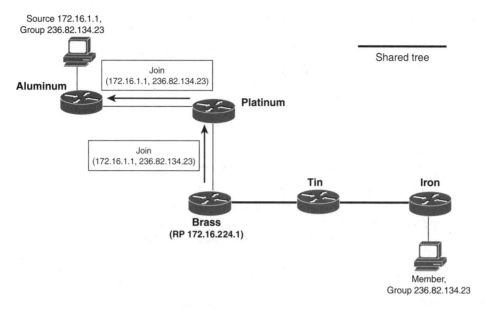

Figure 8-13   *RP Creates a Source-Based, Shortest-Path Tree to the Source's DR*

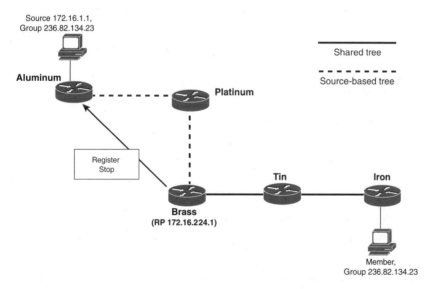

Figure 8-14   *RP Sends a Register Stop Message to Stop the Register Messages. The Source's Multicast Packets Are Now Sent to the RP Over the SPT*

The debug messages in Example 8-16 show the sequence of events that occurs when router Aluminum begins sending multicast traffic to group 236.82.134.23. In this particular case, no members have yet joined the group. As a result, the RP (Brass) immediately sends a Register Stop message to Aluminum in response to the Register.

Example 8-16   *This RP Has No Members for Group 236.82.134.23. As a Result, It Immediately Replies to the Register Message from Aluminum (172.16.2.233) with a Register Stop Message. Notice That Both Messages Are Unicast Rather than Multicast*

```
Brass#debug ip pim 236.82.134.23
PIM debugging is on
Brass#
PIM: Received Register on Serial1.509 from 172.16.2.233 for 172.16.1.1, group
  236.82.134.23
PIM: Send Register-Stop to 172.16.2.233 for 172.16.1.1, group 236.82.134.23
```

Example 8-17 shows the route entry for the group. There are both (*, G) and (S, G) entries for the group. The (*, G) entry shows a null incoming interface and an RPF neighbor of 0.0.0.0, indicating that this router is the root of the shared tree. The (S, G) entry shows that router Platinum (172.16.2.246), the upstream neighbor toward the source, is the RPF neighbor. There are no interfaces on the outgoing interface list, so the entry is pruned.

Example 8-17   *Routing Entry for Group 236.82.134.23 at the RP. No Members Have Joined the Group*

```
Brass#show ip mroute 236.82.134.23
IP Multicast Routing Table
Flags: D - Dense, S - Sparse, C - Connected, L - Local, P - Pruned
       R - RP-bit set, F - Register flag, T - SPT-bit set, J - Join SPT
Timers: Uptime/Expires
Interface state: Interface, Next-Hop or VCD, State/Mode

(*, 236.82.134.23), 00:07:38/00:02:59, RP 172.16.224.1, flags: S
  Incoming interface: Null, RPF nbr 0.0.0.0
  Outgoing interface list:
    Serial1.509, Forward/Sparse, 00:03:06/00:02:50

(172.16.1.1, 236.82.134.23), 00:07:38/00:01:21, flags: P
  Incoming interface: Serial1.509, RPF nbr 172.16.2.246
  Outgoing interface list: Null

Brass#
```

Example 8-18 shows the route entries for the group at Aluminum, the source's DR. Here, the (*, G) entry also exists, with the Ethernet interface connecting to the source in the outgoing interface list. The incoming interface list is null. The (S, G) entry shows the same Ethernet interface on the incoming interface list. There are two flags in common between the entries: One flag indicates that the source is directly connected, and the other (F) indicates that the router must send a Register message for the group traffic.

Example 8-18   *Corresponding Route Entry at the Source's DR Shows a Pruned SPT Entry*

```
Aluminum#show ip mroute 236.82.134.23
IP Multicast Routing Table
Flags: D - Dense, S - Sparse, C - Connected, L - Local, P - Pruned
       R - RP-bit set, F - Register flag, T - SPT-bit set, J - Join SPT
Timers: Uptime/Expires
Interface state: Interface, Next-Hop, State/Mode

(*, 236.82.134.23), 00:15:30/00:02:59, RP 172.16.224.1, flags: SJCF
  Incoming interface: Null, RPF nbr 0.0.0.0
  Outgoing interface list:
    Ethernet0/0, Forward/Sparse, 00:15:23/00:02:28

(172.16.1.1/32, 236.82.134.23), 00:00:29/00:02:30, flags: PCFT
  Incoming interface: Ethernet0/0, RPF nbr 0.0.0.0
  Outgoing interface list: Null

Aluminum#
```

The "T" flag on the (S, G) entry indicates that the entry represents a shortest-path tree, and the "P" entry indicates that there are no interfaces on the outgoing interface list. If there were an RPF neighbor, the router would send a Prune message to it for the group.

The final flag of interest is the "J" flag on the (*, G) entry. This flag indicates that the router will switch to the shortest-path tree when a packet is received on the shared tree. Just how PIM-SM routers switch from shared trees to SPTs is the subject of the following section.

The debug messages in Example 8-19 show the sequence of events that occurs when the host attached to router Iron joins the group. The Join/Prune message, which was generated by Iron and sent hop-by-hop to the RP, is received from Tin. The interface to Tin is added to the (*, G) entry; the interface is also added to the (S, G) entry because the SPT to Aluminum will be used. Next, an SPT Join is sent to Aluminum.

Example 8-19   *These* debug *Messages Show the Member Attached to Router Iron Joining Group 236.82.134.23*

```
Brass#debug ip pim 236.82.134.23
PIM debugging is on
Brass#
PIM: Received v2 Join/Prune on Serial1.508 from 172.16.2.238, to us
PIM: Join-list: (*, 236.82.134.23) RP 172.16.224.1, RPT-bit set, WC-bit set, S-bit
  set
PIM: Add Serial1.508/172.16.2.241 to (*, 236.82.134.23), Forward state
```

```
PIM: Add Serial1.508/172.16.2.241 to (172.16.1.1/32, 236.82.134.23)
PIM: Building Join/Prune message for 236.82.134.23
PIM: For 172.16.2.246, Join-list: 172.16.1.1/32
PIM: Send periodic Join/Prune to 172.16.2.246 (Serial1.509)
```

Example 8-20 shows the resulting route entries at the RP, and Example 8-21 shows the resulting route entries at the source's DR.

Example 8-20 *When a Group Member Joins, Its Interface Is Added to the (*, G) Entry. It Is Also Added to the (S, G) Entry Because of the SPT to Aluminum*

```
Brass#show ip mroute 236.82.134.23
IP Multicast Routing Table
Flags: D - Dense, S - Sparse, C - Connected, L - Local, P - Pruned
       R - RP-bit set, F - Register flag, T - SPT-bit set, J - Join SPT
Timers: Uptime/Expires
Interface state: Interface, Next-Hop or VCD, State/Mode

(*, 236.82.134.23), 00:29:58/00:03:05, RP 172.16.224.1, flags: S
  Incoming interface: Null, RPF nbr 0.0.0.0
  Outgoing interface list:
    Serial1.509, Forward/Sparse, 00:29:58/00:02:52
    Serial1.508, Forward/Sparse, 00:24:36/00:03:05

(172.16.1.1, 236.82.134.23), 00:24:54/00:02:59, flags: T
  Incoming interface: Serial1.503, RPF nbr 172.16.2.246
  Outgoing interface list:
    Serial1.508, Forward/Sparse, 00:24:36/00:02:35

Brass#
```

Example 8-21 *Interface Toward the RP Has Been Added to the Outgoing Interface List of Aluminum's (S, G) Entry, and the Entry Is No Longer in Prune State*

```
Aluminum#show ip mroute 236.82.134.23
IP Multicast Routing Table
Flags: D - Dense, S - Sparse, C - Connected, L - Local, P - Pruned
       R - RP-bit set, F - Register flag, T - SPT-bit set, J - Join SPT
Timers: Uptime/Expires
Interface state: Interface, Next-Hop, State/Mode

(*, 236.82.134.23), 00:00:47/00:02:59, RP 172.16.224.1, flags: SJCF
  Incoming interface: Serial0/1.309, RPF nbr 172.16.2.245
```

```
  Outgoing interface list:
    Ethernet0/0, Forward/Sparse, 00:00:01/00:02:58

(172.16.1.1/32, 236.82.134.23), 00:00:47/00:02:59, flags: CFT
  Incoming interface: Ethernet0/0, RPF nbr 0.0.0.0
  Outgoing interface list:
    Serial0/1.309, Forward/Sparse, 00:00:34/00:02:58

Aluminum#
```

PIM-SM and Shortest Path Trees

In Figure 8-15, router Lead has been added to the PIM-SM domain, and Lead has a group member attached. Under basic shared-tree rules, Lead would join the shared tree rooted at Brass. But it is obvious in the figure that the direct link to Aluminum is a more efficient path for the multicast packets from the source to Lead's group member.

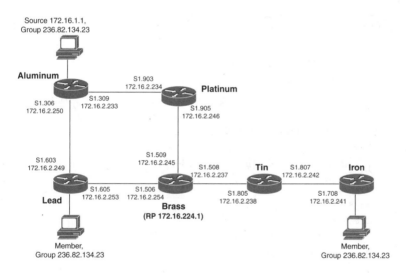

Figure 8-15 *Direct Link Between Lead and Aluminum Is a More Efficient Route for Multicast Packets to Lead's Attached Group Member Than the Aluminum-Platinum-Brass-Lead Path*

You have already seen how PIM-SM can build an SPT between the RP and the source DR. The protocol also allows SPTs to be built all the way from a router with attached group members to the source DR to alleviate inefficiencies in topologies, such as the one referred to in Figure 8-15.

Example 8-22 shows Lead building an SPT after its group member requests a join via IGMP. First, the router sends a Join to the RP (out S1.605), as expected. When the multicast packets begin arriving, the router can observe the IP address of the source. Consulting its unicast routing table, it sees that the source IP address is reachable via a different interface (S1.603) than the interface to the RP. Lead sends a Join to Aluminum, and an SPT is built directly between those two routers. When Lead begins receiving the multicast traffic for (172.16.1.1, 236.82.134.23) over the SPT, it sends a Prune message to the RP removing itself from the shared tree.

Example 8-22 *Lead Joins the Shared RPT. After It Begins Receiving the Multicast Traffic, It Joins the SPT Directly from the Source DR and Prunes Itself from the RPT*

```
Lead#debug ip pim 236.82.134.23
PIM debugging is on
Lead#
PIM: Check RP 172.16.224.1 into the (*, 236.82.134.23) entry
PIM: Send v2 Join on Serial1.605 to 172.16.2.254 for (172.16.224.1/32,
   236.82.134.23), WC-bit, RPT-bit, S-bit
PIM: Building batch join message for 236.82.134.23
PIM: Send Join on Serial1.603 to 172.16.2.250 for (172.16.1.1/32, 236.82.134.23),
   S-bit
PIM: Send v2 Prune on Serial1.605 to 172.16.2.254 for (172.16.1.1/32,
   236.82.134.23), RPT-bit, S-bit
Lead#
```

Example 8-23 shows the multicast route entries for group 236.82.134.23 at Lead. The (*, G) entry for the shared tree still exists and continues to exist as long as the router has members or downstream neighbors for the group. Notice, however, that the (S, G) entry indicates a different incoming interface and a different RPF neighbor.

Example 8-23 *Lead's Route Entries for Group 236.82.134.23 Show That the Router Has Switched from the RPT to the SPT*

```
Lead#show ip mroute 236.82.134.23
IP Multicast Routing Table
Flags: D - Dense, S - Sparse, C - Connected, L - Local, P - Pruned
       R - RP-bit set, F - Register flag, T - SPT-bit set, J - Join SPT
Timers: Uptime/Expires
Interface state: Interface, Next-Hop or VCD, State/Mode

(*, 236.82.134.23), 00:26:26/00:02:58, RP 172.16.224.1, flags: SJC
 ·Incoming interface: Serial1.605, RPF nbr 172.16.2.254
  Outgoing interface list:
    Ethernet0, Forward/Sparse, 00:26:26/00:02:12

(172.16.1.1, 236.82.134.23), 00:26:26/00:02:36, flags: CJT
```

```
    Incoming interface: Serial1.603, RPF nbr 172.16.2.250
    Outgoing interface list:
      Ethernet0, Forward/Sparse, 00:26:26/00:02:12


Lead#
```

Example 8-24 shows the route entries for Aluminum, and Example 8-25 shows the route entries for Brass. You can observe that Aluminum is forwarding on SPT trees to both Lead and Brass. At Brass, the interface to Lead is not in the outgoing interface list of the (S, G) entry because the RP is not forwarding to that router.

Example 8-24 *Aluminum's Multicast Route Entry for Group 236.82.134.23, Showing an SPT to Both Lead and Brass*

```
Aluminum#show ip mroute 236.82.134.23
IP Multicast Routing Table
Flags: D - Dense, S - Sparse, C - Connected, L - Local, P - Pruned
       R - RP-bit set, F - Register flag, T - SPT-bit set, J - Join SPT
Timers: Uptime/Expires
Interface state: Interface, Next-Hop, State/Mode

(*, 236.82.134.23), 00:08:17/00:02:59, RP 172.16.224.1, flags: SJCF
  Incoming interface: Serial0/1.309, RPF nbr 172.16.2.234
  Outgoing interface list:
    Ethernet0/0, Forward/Sparse, 00:07:33/00:02:30

(172.16.1.1/32, 236.82.134.23), 00:08:17/00:02:59, flags: CFT
  Incoming interface: Ethernet0/0, RPF nbr 0.0.0.0
  Outgoing interface list:
    Serial0/1.309, Forward/Sparse, 00:08:07/00:02:48
    Serial0/1.306, Forward/Sparse, 00:06:55/00:02:59

Aluminum#
```

Example 8-25 *Brass's Route Entries for Group 236.82.134.23. The Interface to Lead (S1.506) Remains on the Outgoing Interface List of the (*, G) Entry but Is Not on the Outgoing Interface List of the (S, G) Entry*

```
Brass#show ip mroute 236.82.134.23
IP Multicast Routing Table
Flags: D - Dense, S - Sparse, C - Connected, L - Local, P - Pruned
       R - RP-bit set, F - Register flag, T - SPT-bit set, J - Join SPT
Timers: Uptime/Expires
Interface state: Interface, Next-Hop or VCD, State/Mode
```

```
(*, 236.82.134.23), 00:13:13/00:03:20, RP 172.16.224.1, flags: S
  Incoming interface: Null, RPF nbr 0.0.0.0
  Outgoing interface list:
    Serial1.508, Forward/Sparse, 00:13:04/00:03:20
    Serial1.509, Forward/Sparse, 00:12:30/00:02:18
    Serial1.506, Forward/Sparse, 00:11:52/00:02:33

(172.16.1.1, 236.82.134.23), 00:13:14/00:02:59, flags: T
  Incoming interface: Serial1.509, RPF nbr 172.16.2.246
  Outgoing interface list:
    Serial1.508, Forward/Sparse, 00:13:05/00:02:49

Brass#
```

RFC 7761 specifies that a router should switch from the RPT to an SPT when "the data rate is high." What, then, constitutes a high data rate? The answer is rather arbitrary. It might depend on the cumulative available bandwidth across the route, the congestion along the route, the performance of the routers, or any number of other factors. You, as the network administrator, must make the determination based on the unique character-istics of your own network.

Cisco uses a simple default. Cisco routers join the SPT immediately after receiving the first packet on the shared tree for a given (S, G). This default can be changed with the command **ip pim spt-threshold**, in which the threshold for switching to the SPT is speci-fied in kilobits per second. (The default represents 0 kbps.) The router measures the arrival rate of packets once every second. If packets for either any group or some speci-fied group arrive at a rate exceeding the threshold, the router switches. When a router switches to the SPT, it monitors the arrival rate on the source tree. If the group's rate falls below the configured threshold for more than 60 seconds, the router attempts to switch back to the shared tree for that group.

The keyword **infinity** can also be used with the command to prevent a router from ever switching to the SPT.

Interestingly, a router switches to an SPT even if the shortest route to the source is through the RP. In the previous examples, router Iron stayed on the RPT. The reason is that, to simplify the introduction to PIM-SM tree behavior, the statement **ip pim spt-threshold infinity** was added to Iron's configuration. Example 8-26 displays Iron's route entry for group 236.82.134.23. The command is then removed from the router's configuration, and the route is observed again. You can see that the router, after the SPT threshold is set back to the default, immediately switched to the SPT. The route entries at the RP remain as they appear in Example 8-25 because the interface toward Iron is already on the outgoing interface list of the (S, G) entry.

Example 8-26 *Iron's Entries for Group 236.82.134.23, Before and After the SPT Switching Threshold Has Been Reset to the Default*

```
Iron#show ip mroute 236.82.134.23
IP Multicast Routing Table
Flags: D - Dense, S - Sparse, C - Connected, L - Local, P - Pruned
       R - RP-bit set, F - Register flag, T - SPT-bit set, J - Join SPT
Timers: Uptime/Expires
Interface state: Interface, Next-Hop or VCD, State/Mode
(*, 236.82.134.23), 00:00:57/00:02:59, RP 172.16.224.1, flags: SC
  Incoming interface: Serial1.708, RPF nbr 172.16.2.242
  Outgoing interface list:
    Ethernet0, Forward/Sparse, 00:00:57/00:02:02


Iron#conf t
Enter configuration commands, one per line.  End with CNTL/Z.
Iron(config)#no ip pim spt-threshold infinity
Iron(config)#^Z
Iron#
2d01h: %SYS-5-CONFIG_I: Configured from console by console


Iron#show ip mroute 236.82.134.23
IP Multicast Routing Table
Flags: D - Dense, S - Sparse, C - Connected, L - Local, P - Pruned
       R - RP-bit set, F - Register flag, T - SPT-bit set, J - Join SPT
Timers: Uptime/Expires
Interface state: Interface, Next-Hop or VCD, State/Mode

(*, 236.82.134.23), 00:01:23/00:02:59, RP 172.16.224.1, flags: SJC
  Incoming interface: Serial1.708, RPF nbr 172.16.2.242
  Outgoing interface list:
    Ethernet0, Forward/Sparse, 00:01:23/00:02:34

(172.16.1.1, 236.82.134.23), 00:00:11/00:02:59, flags: CJT
  Incoming interface: Serial1.708, RPF nbr 172.16.2.242
  Outgoing interface list:
    Ethernet0, Forward/Sparse, 00:00:12/00:02:47

Iron#
```

In Example 8-26 and in several previous figures, there is a "J" flag associated with either the (*, G) entry, the (S, G) entry, or both. This is the Join SPT flag. When associated with a (*, G) entry, it indicates that traffic flowing down the shared tree exceeds the SPT threshold. If the SPT has not already been joined, it will be following the next received group packet. When associated with an (S, G) entry, the J flag indicates that the SPT has been joined because the RPT traffic has exceeded the SPT threshold.

Table 8-1 lists and describes all the flags that may be associated with an **mroute**. This list is taken directly from the *Cisco IOS Software Command Reference*.

Table 8-1   Mroute *Flags*

Flag	Description
D-Dense	Entry is operating in dense mode.
S-Sparse	Entry is operating in sparse mode.
C-Connected	A member of the multicast group is present on the directly connected interface.
L-Local	The router itself is a member of the group.
P-Pruned	The route has been pruned.
R-RP-bit set	Indicates that the (S, G) entry is pointing toward the RP. This is typically prune state along the shared tree for a particular source.
F-Register flag	Indicates that the software is Registering for a multicast source.
T-SPT-bit set	Indicates that packets have been received on the shortest-path tree.

J-Join SPT	For (*, G) entries, indicates that the rate of traffic flowing down the shared tree is exceeding the SPT-Threshold set for the group. (The default SPT-Threshold setting is 0 kbps.) When the J-Join SPT flag is set, the next (S, G) packet received down the shared tree triggers an (S, G) join in the direction of the source thereby causing the router join the source tree.
	
	For (S, G) entries, indicates that the entry was created because the SPT-Threshold for the group was exceeded. When the J-Join SPT flag is set for (S, G) entries, the router monitors the traffic rate on the source tree and attempts to switch back to the shared tree for this source if the traffic rate on the source tree falls below the group's SPT-Threshold for more than one minute.

PIMv2 Message Formats

PIMv2 messages are encapsulated in IP packets with a protocol number of 103. Except for the cases in which the messages are unicast, the IP destination address is the reserved multicast address 224.0.0.13, and the TTL is set to 1. Both the multicast address and the TTL ensure that the messages are forwarded only to neighboring routers.

Version 2 is the current version as of this writing. PIMv1 might still be in use in some implementations but is mostly obsolete. That version uses an IP protocol number of 2, making it a subset of the IGMP protocol. Version 1 uses a multicast address of 224.0.0.2.

Cisco IOS supports PIMv2 beginning with 11.3(2)T. It provides backward compatibility with PIMv1 by automatically switching to that version on any interface on which a version neighbor is detected. An interface can also be manually set to PIMv1 or PIMv2 with the **ip pim version** command.

For the sake of space, only PIMv2 message formats are covered in this book. For PIMv1 formats, refer to the appropriate Internet drafts.

You can notice that several message types have field labels that refer to encoded addresses. For more information on the encoding formats and details of these fields, see section 4.9 of RFC 7761.

All *Reserved* fields in the following messages are set to all-zeroes and are ignored upon receipt.

PIMv2 Message Header Format

All PIM messages have a standard header, as shown in Figure 8-16.

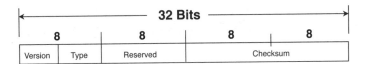

Figure 8-16 *PIMv2 Message Header*

The fields for the PIMv2 message header are defined as follows:

- *Version* specifies the version number. The current version number is 2; although, PIMv1 is still in limited usage.

- *Type* specifies the type of PIM message encapsulated behind the header. Table 8-2 lists the PIMv2 message types.

Table 8-2 *PIMv2 Message Types*

Type	Message
0	Hello
1	Register (used in PIM-SM only)
2	Register-Stop (used in PIM-SM only)
3	Join/Prune
4	Bootstrap (used in PIM-SM only)
5	Assert

Type	Message
6	Graft (used in PIM-DM only)
7	Graft-Ack (used in PIM-DM only)
8	Candidate-RP-Advertisement (used in PIM-SM only)

Checksum is a standard IP-style checksum, using a 16-bit one's complement of the one's complement of the PIM message, excluding the data portion of the Register message.

PIMv2 Hello Message Format

PIMv2 Hello messages, the format for which is shown in Figure 8-17, are used for neighbor discovery and for neighbor keepalives. The messages are sent every 30 seconds by default, and the period can be changed with the command **ip pim query-interval**.

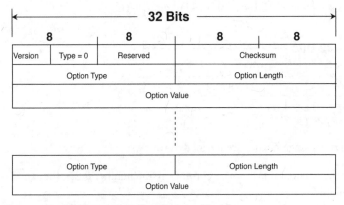

Figure 8-17   *PIMv2 Hello Message Format*

The fields for the PIMv2 Hello message are defined as follows:

- *Option Type* specifies the type of option in the Option Value field. The current Option Type values follow:

  - *Option Type 1:* Holdtime

  - *Option Type 2:* LAN Prune Delay

  - *Option Type 19:* DR Priority

  - *Option Type 20:* Generation ID

  - *Option Type 24:* Address List

- *Option Length* specifies the length, in bytes, of the Option Value field. When the Option Value is a holdtime (Option Type = 1), the Option Length is 2.

- *Option Value* is a variable length field carrying the value of whatever option is specified by the Option Type. Holdtime (Option Type = 1, Option Length =2) is the time that a router waits to hear a Hello message from a PIM neighbor before declaring the neighbor dead. The holdtime is 3.5 times the Hello interval.

The format shows that multiple option TLVs (type/length/value) can be carried in a single Hello message.

PIMv2 Register Message Format

Register messages, the format for which is shown in Figure 8-18, used only by PIM-SM, are unicast from the source's DR to the RP and carry the initial multicast packets from the source. That is, Register messages are used to tunnel multicast traffic from the source to the RP when a shortest-path tree has not yet been established from the source's DR to the RP.

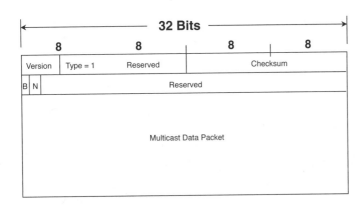

Figure 8-18 *PIMv2 Register Message Format*

The fields for the PIMv2 Register message are defined as follows:

- *Checksum*, in Register messages, is calculated only on the message header. The data packet portion is excluded.

- *B* is the Border bit. The bit is set to 0 if the originator is a DR with a directly connected source. The bit is set to 1 if the source is a PIM Multicast Border Router (PMBR). PMBRs, and other interdomain multicast issues, are discussed in Chapter 9, "Scaling IP Multicast Routing."

- *N* is the Null-Register bit. A DR that is probing the RP before expiring its local Register-Suppression timer sets this bit to 1.

- *Multicast Data Packet* is a single packet from the source that is being tunneled to the RP in the Register message.

PIMv2 Register Stop Message Format

The Register Stop message, the format for which is illustrated in Figure 8-19, is sent by an RP to a DR originating Register messages. The packet is used in one of two situations:

- The RP is receiving the sourced multicast packets over the SPT and no longer needs to receive them encapsulated in Register messages.

- There are no group members, either directly attached or over SPTs or RPTs, for the RP to forward the packets to.

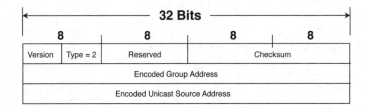

Figure 8-19 *PIMv2 Register Stop Message Format*

The fields for the PIMv2 Register Stop message are defined as follows:

- *Encoded Group Address* is the multicast group IP address for which the receiver should stop sending Register messages.

- *Encoded Unicast Source Address* is the IP address of the multicast source. This field can also specify the wildcard source for (*, G) entries by setting the address to all zeroes.

PIMv2 Join/Prune Message Format

Join/Prune messages, the format for which is shown in Figure 8-20, are sent upstream to either RPs or sources, and are used to join and prune both RPTs and SPTs. The message consists of a list of one more multicast groups. For each multicast address, there is a list of one or more source addresses. Together, these lists specify all (S, G) and (*, G) entries to be joined or pruned.

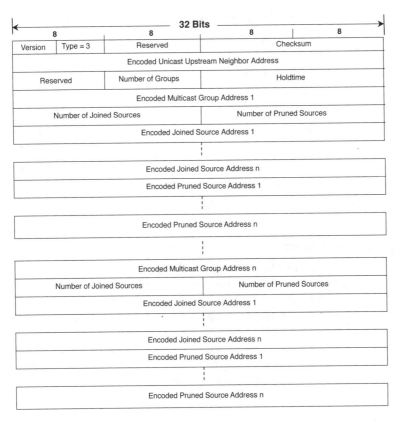

Figure 8-20 *PIMv2 Join/Prune Message Format*

The fields for the PIMv2 Join/Prune message are defined as follows:

- *Encoded Unicast Upstream Neighbor Address* is the IP address of the RPF or upstream neighbor to which the message is sent.

- *Number of Groups* specifies the number of multicast groups contained in the message.

- *Encoded Multicast Group Address* specifies an IP address of a multicast group.

- *Number of Joined Sources* specifies the number of Encoded Joined Source Addresses listed under this multicast group address.

- *Number of Pruned Sources* specifies the number of Encoded Pruned Source Addresses listed under this multicast group address.

- *Encoded Joined Source Address* specifies the source address for an (S, G) pair or a wildcard for a (*, G) pair. The two wildcards in a (*, *, RP) triple (described in Chapter 9) can also be specified in this field. In addition to the source address, there are three flags encoded into this field:

- *S* is the Sparse bit. The bit is set to 1 for PIM-SM and is used for version 1 compatibility.

- *W* is the wildcard (WC) bit. If set to 1, the Encoded Joined Source Address represents the wildcard in a (*, G) or (*, *, RP) entry. When set to 0, the Encoded Joined Source Address represents the source address in a (S, G) entry. When a join is sent to an RP, the W bit must be set to 1.

- *R* is the RPT bit. When the bit is set to 1, the join is sent to the RP. When the bit is set to 0, the join is sent to the source.

- *Encoded Pruned Source Address* specifies the address of a pruned source. The encoding is the same as for the Encoded Joined Source Address field, and the S, W, and R bits apply to the pruned address as they do to the joined address.

PIMv2 Bootstrap Message Format

Bootstrap messages, the format for which is shown in Figure 8-21, are originated by bootstrap routers (BSRs) every 60 seconds and are flooded throughout a PIM-SM domain to ensure that all routers determine the same RPs for the same groups. The message contains a list of one or more multicast group addresses. For each of these group addresses, there is a list of Candidate RPs (C-RPs) and their priorities. This list is the RP-Set for that group. Receiving routers use a common algorithm to determine, from the list of C-RPs, the RP for the group. The algorithm is designed to ensure that all routers in the PIM domain derive the same RP address. Bootstrap messages are also used to elect a BSR, as described in the section "The Bootstrap Protocol."

The fields for the PIMv2 Bootstrap message are defined as follows:

- *Fragment Tag* is used when a Bootstrap message must be divided into fragments because the message length exceeds the maximum packet size. The fragment tag is a randomly generated number that is assigned to all fragments of the same message. That is, all fragments of any unique Bootstrap message will have the same number in the Fragment Tag field.

- *Hash Mask Length* describes the mask to be used in the hash algorithm. The length of the mask is set using the **ip pim bsr-candidate** command.

- *BSR Priority* is a number between 0 and 255 that specifies the priority of the originating candidate BSR. The C-BSR with the highest priority becomes the BSR. This priority is set using the **ip pim bsr-candidate** command.

- *Encoded Unicast BSR Address* is the IP address of the domain's BSR.

- *Encoded Multicast Group Address* specifies an IP address of a multicast group.

- *RP Count* specifies the number of C-RPs listed for the given multicast group—that is, the size of the RP-Set. The description of the size of the RP-Set is important because if the Bootstrap message is fragmented and one of the fragments is lost, the determination of the RP may become inconsistent across the PIM domain.

Therefore, if the number of RPs in the received RP-Set does not match the RP count, the entire set is discarded.

■ *Fragment RP Count* specifies the number of C-RPs included in this fragment for this group.

■ *Encoded Unicast RP Address* is the IP address of a C-RP.

■ *RP Holdtime* is the time a BSR should wait to hear a Candidate-RP-Advertisement message from a C-RP before deleting the C-RP from the RP-Set. The holdtime is 150 seconds.

■ *RP Priority* is a number between 0 and 255 used in the RP selection algorithm. The "highest" priority is 0.

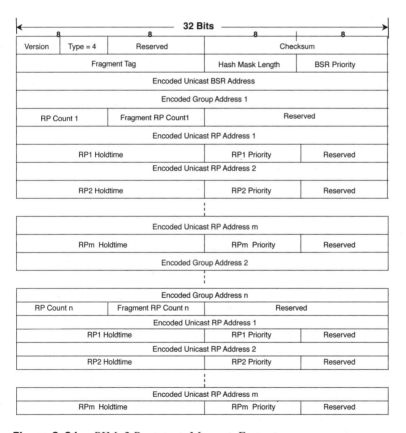

Figure 8-21 *PIMv2 Bootstrap Message Format*

PIMv2 Assert Message Format

The PIMv2 Assert message, the format for which is shown in Figure 8-22, is used to elect a designated forwarder on multiaccess networks. When a PIM router receives a multicast packet on an interface that is on the outgoing interface for the packet's group, the router assumes that there must be another router connected to that data link forwarding for the group. The router sends an Assert so that other routers sharing the multiaccess network can decide which of them will forward packets for the group.

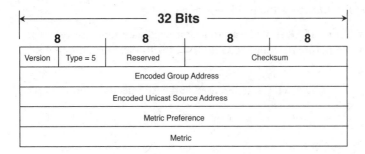

Figure 8-22   *PIMv2 Assert Message Format*

The fields for the PIMv2 Assert message are defined as follows:

- *Encoded Group Address* is the multicast IP destination address of the packet that triggered the Assert.

- *Encoded Unicast Source Address* is the IP source address of the multicast packet that triggered the Assert.

- *Metric Preference* is a preference value assigned to the unicast routing protocol that provided the route to the source. This value is used in the same way an administrative distance is used, to provide a consistent metric when comparing routes from diverse routing protocols.

- *Metric* is the metric associated with the route to the source in the originator's unicast routing table.

PIMv2 Graft Message Format

A PIM-DM router sends a PIMv2 Graft message to its upstream neighbor to request a rejoin to a previously pruned tree. The format of the message is the same as the Join/Prune message referred to in Figure 8-20, except that the Type = 6.

PIMv2 Graft-Ack Message Format

A PIM-DM router sends a Graft-Ack message to a downstream neighbor in response to a Graft message. The format of the Graft-Ack message is the same as the Join/Prune message referred to in Figure 8-20, except that the Type = 7.

Candidate-RP-Advertisement Message Format

Candidate RPs (C-RPs) periodically unicast Candidate-RP-Advertisement messages to BSRs. The BSR uses the information in the message to build its RP-Set, which is in turn advertised to all PIM-SM routers in the domain within Bootstrap Messages. Figure 8-23 shows the format for the Candidate-RP-Advertisement message.

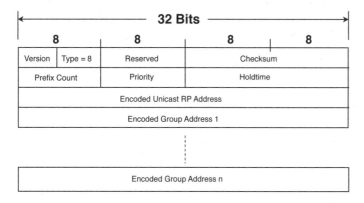

Figure 8-23   *Candidate-RP-Advertisement Message Format*

The fields for the Candidate-RP-Advertisement message are defined as follows:

- *Prefix Count* specifies the number of multicast group addresses included in the message. If the originator is a C-RP for all multicast groups in the domain, the Prefix Count is 0.

- *Priority* is a number between 0 and 255, specifying the priority of the originating C-RP. This number is used in the algorithm for selecting an RP. Priorities are represented inverse to the value of the priority number so that 0 is the highest priority and 255 is the lowest.

- *Holdtime* specifies the amount of time the message is valid.

- *Encoded Unicast RP Address* is the C-RP address. This address is the IP address of one of the routers interfaces; typically, the address of a loopback interface is used.

- *Encoded Group Address* specifies one or more multicast group addresses for which the originator is a candidate RP.

Configuring IP Multicast Routing

Before a particular IP multicast routing protocol can be configured, the router must be set up for general, protocol-neutral multicast routing.

> **Note**   "Protocol-independent" would be a better term than "protocol neutral," but for the confusion it would create in light of PIM.

Example 8-27 shows a configuration containing some of the commands you might use. Out of all the commands shown, **ip multicast-routing** is the only one that is required. Just as the default (and therefore hidden) **ip routing** enables unicast IP routing, this command enables the support of all IP multicast routing functions.

Example 8-27   *Command* **ip multicast-routing** *Is Required to Enable Multicast Routing Support. Other Commands in This Basic Configuration Might Be Required by Specific Implementations*

```
!
hostname Stovepipe
!
ip multicast-routing
!
interface Ethernet0
 ip address 172.17.1.1 255.255.255.0
 ip igmp version 2
!
interface Ethernet1
 ip address 172.17.2.1 255.255.255.0
 ip cgmp
!
interface Serial0
 ip address 172.18.1.254 255.255.255.252
 no ip mroute-cache
!
```

Of some interest in this configuration is that there are no commands evident enabling Internet Group Management Protocol (IGMP). When IP multicast routing is enabled on the router, IGMPv2 is automatically enabled on the LAN interfaces. The only IGMP command in this configuration is **ip igmp version** on interface E0, changing the default to IGMPv1. Table 8-3 lists all the IGMP commands that change the default values in a given interface. Other IGMP commands are demonstrated later in this chapter.

Table 8-3 *IGMP Interface Commands*

Command	Default Value	Description
ip igmp query-interval seconds	60	The frequency at which the router queries for group members on the interface.
ip igmp query-max-response-time seconds	10	The Max-Response-Time value advertised in IGMP query messages, telling hosts how long the router will wait before deleting the group. The command is only valid for IGMPv2.
ip igmp query-timeout seconds	2x query interval	The time the router waits to hear a query from another router before taking over as the querier.
ip igmp version {1	2}	2	Sets the interface to either IGMPv1 or IGMPv2.

The configuration of interface E1 in Example 8-27 includes the **ip cgmp** command, which causes Cisco Group Management Protocol (CGMP) messages to be originated for an attached Catalyst switch. Another option is **ip cgmp proxy**, which can be used when there are other routers on the subnet that are not CGMP-capable. This command tells the router to advertise those non-CGMP routers in its CGMP messages. If you configure a Cisco router as a CGMP proxy, you must ensure that router is elected as the IGMP Querier.

The next command of interest in Example 8-27 is **no ip mroute-cache** on S0. This command disables fast switching of IP multicast packets in the same way that **no ip route-cache** disables fast switching of unicast IP packets. You would disable the fast switching of multicast IP packets for the same reasons you would disable fast switching of unicast packets—for example, to enable per-packet load sharing across parallel paths rather than per-destination load sharing.

Case Study: Configuring Protocol Independent Multicast-Dense Mode (PIM-DM)

After you have enabled IP multicast routing on a Cisco router, you can enable PIM-DM by simply adding the **ip pim dense-mode** command to all the router's interfaces. Figure 8-24 shows a simple PIM-DM topology, and Example 8-28 shows the configuration of router Porkpie. The other router configurations are similar to that of Porkpie.

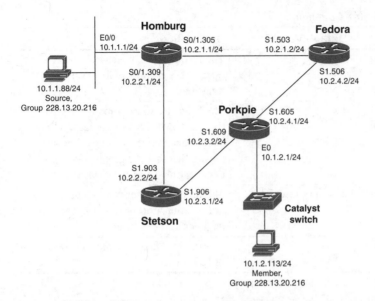

Figure 8-24   *This Topology Demonstrates Basic PIM-DM Functionality*

Example 8-28   ip pim dense-mode *Command Enables PIM-DM on an Interface*

```
hostname Porkpie
!
ip multicast-routing
!
interface Ethernet0
 ip address 10.1.2.1 255.255.255.0
 ip pim dense-mode
 ip cgmp
!
interface Serial1
 no ip address
 encapsulation frame-relay
 no ip mroute-cache
!
interface Serial1.605 point-to-point
 description PVC to Fedora
 ip address 10.2.4.1 255.255.255.0
 ip pim dense-mode
 no ip mroute-cache
 frame-relay interface-dlci 605
!
interface Serial1.609 point-to-point
 description PVC to Stetson
```

```
 ip address 10.2.3.2 255.255.255.0
 ip pim dense-mode
 no ip mroute-cache
 frame-relay interface-dlci 609
!
router ospf 1
 network 10.0.0.0 0.255.255.255 area 0
!
```

Two important considerations when configuring PIM-DM are reflected in Example 8-28. The first and most obvious is that a unicast routing protocol—in this case, OSPF—must be running. Without it, PIM has no mechanism for determining the Reverse Path Forwarding (RPF) interface. The second consideration can be observed by comparing the configuration in Example 8-28 with the topology diagram in Figure 8-24. When configuring PIM, the protocol should be enabled on every interface. Otherwise, you run the risk of inadvertent RPF failures.

Example 8-29 shows Porkpie's **mroute** entry for group 228.13.20.216 after source 10.1.1.88 has begun transmitting and after member 10.1.2.113 has joined. The PIM-DM section of Chapter 7 showed only the (S, G) mroute entry in its examples, for the sake of clarity. In reality, a (*, G) entry is created in addition to the (S, G). The (*, G) entry is not part of PIM-DM specification and is not used for packet forwarding. Rather, Cisco IOS Software creates the entry as a "parent" data structure of (S, G). All interfaces connected to PIM neighbors and all interfaces with directly connected group members are added to the outgoing interface list of the (*, G) entry. The incoming interface list of this entry, when only PIM-DM is running, is always empty. The incoming and outgoing interfaces in the (S, G) entry are then taken from this list.

Note Some differences exist in the field formats of commands such as **show ip mroute** and **show ip route** from earlier chapters because of differences in IOS versions used for examples.

Example 8-29 *Porkpie's* **mroute** *Entry for Group 228.13.20.216*

```
Porkpie#show ip mroute 228.13.20.216
IP Multicast Routing Table
Flags: D - Dense, S - Sparse, C - Connected, L - Local, P - Pruned
       R - RP-bit set, F - Register flag, T - SPT-bit set, J - Join SPT
       M - MSDP created entry, X - Proxy Join Timer Running
       A - Advertised via MSDP
Outgoing interface flags: H - Hardware switched
Timers: Uptime/Expires
Interface state: Interface, Next-Hop or VCD, State/Mode
```

```
(*, 228.13.20.216), 20:06:06/00:02:59, RP 0.0.0.0, flags: DJC
  Incoming interface: Null, RPF nbr 0.0.0.0
  Outgoing interface list:
   Ethernet0, Forward/Dense, 20:05:25/00:00:00
    Serial1.609, Forward/Dense, 00:03:32/00:00:00
    Serial1.605, Forward/Dense, 00:03:32/00:00:00

(10.1.1.88, 228.13.20.216), 00:03:21/00:02:59, flags: CT
  Incoming interface: Serial1.605, RPF nbr 10.2.4.2
  Outgoing interface list:
    Ethernet0, Forward/Dense, 00:03:21/00:00:00
    Serial1.609, Prune/Dense, 00:03:21/00:00:03

Porkpie#
```

In Example 8-29, you can see that E0, S1.609, and S1.605 are on the (*, G) outgoing
interface list. S1.605 is then entered as the RPF interface in the (S, G) entry, and packets
are forwarded out E0. S1.609 is also on the outgoing list but is pruned.

As discussed in Chapter 7, PIM (and any other multicast protocol that uses RPF checks)
can have only one incoming interface. Example 6-4 shows Porkpie's unicast routing
table. There are two equal-cost paths to source subnet 10.1.1.0/24, so PIM breaks the tie
by choosing the interface to the neighbor with the numerically highest IP address as the
RPF interface. In Example 8-30, this address is 10.2.4.2, on interface S1.605. A look back
at Example 8-29 verifies that this interface is on the incoming interface list.

Example 8-30   *Porkpie's Unicast Routing Table*

```
Porkpie#show ip route
Codes: C - connected, S - static, I - IGRP, R - RIP, M - mobile, B - BGP
       D - EIGRP, EX - EIGRP external, O - OSPF, IA - OSPF inter area
       N1 - OSPF NSSA external type 1, N2 - OSPF NSSA external type 2
       E1 - OSPF external type 1, E2 - OSPF external type 2, E - EGP
       i - IS-IS, L1 - IS-IS level-1, L2 - IS-IS level-2, ia - IS-IS inter area
       * - candidate default, U - per-user static route, o - ODR
       P - periodic downloaded static route


Gateway of last resort is not set

     10.0.0.0/24 is subnetted, 6 subnets
O       10.2.1.0 [110/128] via 10.2.4.2, 00:15:07, Serial1.605
C       10.1.2.0 is directly connected, Ethernet0
O       10.2.2.0 [110/128] via 10.2.3.1, 00:15:07, Serial1.609
```

```
O        10.1.1.0 [110/138] via 10.2.4.2, 00:15:07, Serial1.605
                  [110/138] via 10.2.3.1, 00:15:07, Serial1.609
C        10.2.3.0 is directly connected, Serial1.609
C        10.2.4.0 is directly connected, Serial1.605
Porkpie#
```

In Figure 8-25, another router has been added to the network. This router, Bowler, is connected to the Ethernet switch and is sharing a multiaccess link with Porkpie. The rules for IGMP Queriers, PIM designated routers, and PIM forwarders discussed in Chapter 7 all come into play here. To recap the rules:

- The router with the lowest IP address becomes the IGMPv2 Querier.

- The router with the highest IP address becomes the PIM designated router. The DR is only important when IGMPv1 is running on the subnet.

- The PIM forwarder is the router whose route to the source has the lowest administrative distance. If the administrative distances are equal, the router whose route to the source has the lowest metric is the forwarder. If both the administrative distances and the metrics are equal, the router with the highest IP address is the forwarder.

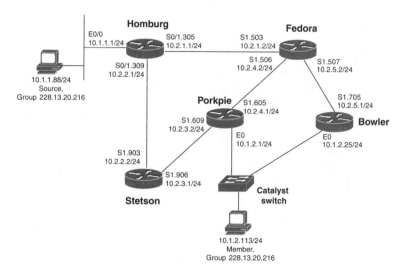

Figure 8-25 *Router Bowler Has Joined the Network of Figure 8-24. Bowler, Porkpie, and the Group Member Are Connected to a Multiaccess Network Through the Catalyst Switch*

Example 8-31 shows that the IGMPv2 Querier and PIM designated router rules have been applied. Porkpie (10.1.2.1) has the lower IP address on the subnet and is the IGMP

Querier. Bowler (10.2.1.25) has the higher IP address and is the designated router. Porkpie and Bowler are both running IGMPv2, so the DR has no importance here.

Example 8-31   *Porkpie (10.1.2.1) Is the IGMP Querier, but Bowler Is the PIM Designated Router*

```
Bowler#show ip igmp interface ethernet 0
Ethernet0 is up, line protocol is up
  Internet address is 10.1.2.25/24
  IGMP is enabled on interface
  Current IGMP version is 2
  CGMP is enabled on interface
  IGMP query interval is 60 seconds
  IGMP querier timeout is 120 seconds
  IGMP max query response time is 10 seconds
  Last member query response interval is 1000 ms
  Inbound IGMP access group is not set
  IGMP activity: 6 joins, 2 leaves
  Multicast routing is enabled on interface
  Multicast TTL threshold is 0
  Multicast designated router (DR) is 10.1.2.25 (this system)
  IGMP querying router is 10.1.2.1
  No multicast groups joined
Bowler#
```

Example 8-32 shows the unicast routes to source subnet 10.1.1.0/24 at both Porkpie and Bowler. Knowing that the network of Figure 8-22 runs OSPF exclusively, it comes as no surprise that both routes have an administrative distance of 110. You can also readily see that both routes have an OSPF cost of 138. Therefore, the PIM forwarder for (10.1.1.88, 228.13.20.216) on the attached subnet 10.1.2.0/24 is the router with the highest IP address: Bowler. Example 8-33 proves it. Comparing Porkpie's (S, G) entry with the one in Example 8-29, notice that interface E0 has now been pruned. Bowler's E0 interface is in forward mode, indicating that it is now forwarding the group traffic onto the subnet.

Example 8-32   *Unicast Routes to Source Subnet 10.1.1.0/24 in Porkpie and Bowler Have Equal Administrative Distances and Metrics. Therefore, the Router with the Highest IP Address Will Be the PIM Forwarder for Subnet 10.1.2.0/24*

```
Porkpie#show ip route 10.1.1.0
Routing entry for 10.1.1.0/24
  Known via "ospf 1", distance 110, metric 138, type intra area
  Redistributing via ospf 1
  Last update from 10.2.3.1 on Serial1.609, 01:01:30 ago
  Routing Descriptor Blocks:
  * 10.2.4.2, from 10.1.1.1, 01:01:30 ago, via Serial1.605
```

```
        Route metric is 138, traffic share count is 1
    10.2.3.1, from 10.1.1.1, 01:01:30 ago, via Serial1.609
        Route metric is 138, traffic share count is 1

Porkpie#
```

```
Bowler#show ip route 10.1.1.0
Routing entry for 10.1.1.0/24
  Known via "ospf 1", distance 110, metric 138, type intra area
  Redistributing via ospf 1
  Last update from 10.2.5.2 on Serial1.705, 01:02:22 ago
  Routing Descriptor Blocks:
  * 10.2.5.2, from 10.1.1.1, 01:02:22 ago, via Serial1.705
      Route metric is 138, traffic share count is 1

Bowler#
```

Example 8-33   *Comparing the* **mroutes** *for (10.1.1.88, 228.13.20.216) Shows That Bowler Is Now the Forwarder for the Group onto Subnet 10.1.2.0/24*

```
Porkpie#show ip mroute 228.13.20.216
IP Multicast Routing Table
Flags: D - Dense, S - Sparse, C - Connected, L - Local, P - Pruned
       R - RP-bit set, F - Register flag, T - SPT-bit set, J - Join SPT
       M - MSDP created entry, X - Proxy Join Timer Running
       A - Advertised via MSDP
Outgoing interface flags: H - Hardware switched
Timers: Uptime/Expires
Interface state: Interface, Next-Hop or VCD, State/Mode

(*, 228.13.20.216), 23:51:13/00:02:59, RP 0.0.0.0, flags: DJC
  Incoming interface: Null, RPF nbr 0.0.0.0
  Outgoing interface list:
    Serial1.609, Forward/Dense, 03:48:39/00:00:00
    Serial1.605, Forward/Dense, 03:48:39/00:00:00
    Ethernet0, Forward/Dense, 01:18:18/00:00:00

(10.1.1.88, 228.13.20.216), 00:03:06/00:02:53, flags: PCT
  Incoming interface: Serial1.605, RPF nbr 10.2.4.2
  Outgoing interface list:
    Serial1.609, Prune/Dense, 00:03:06/00:00:18
    Ethernet0, Prune/Dense, 00:03:06/00:02:53

Porkpie#
```

```
Bowler#show ip mroute 228.13.20.216
IP Multicast Routing Table
Flags: D - Dense, S - Sparse, C - Connected, L - Local, P - Pruned
       R - RP-bit set, F - Register flag, T - SPT-bit set, J - Join SPT
       M - MSDP created entry, X - Proxy Join Timer Running
       A - Advertised via MSDP
Outgoing interface flags: H - Hardware switched
Timers: Uptime/Expires
Interface state: Interface, Next-Hop or VCD, State/Mode

(*, 228.13.20.216), 01:47:12/00:02:59, RP 0.0.0.0, flags: DJC
  Incoming interface: Null, RPF nbr 0.0.0.0
  Outgoing interface list:
    Ethernet0, Forward/Dense, 01:26:34/00:00:00
    Serial1.705, Forward/Dense, 01:47:12/00:00:00

(10.1.1.88, 228.13.20.216), 01:27:43/00:02:59, flags: CTA
  Incoming interface: Serial1.705, RPF nbr 10.2.5.2
  Outgoing interface list:
    Ethernet0, Forward/Dense, 01:26:34/00:00:00

Bowler#
```

Interestingly, Porkpie is querying for group members on the subnet, whereas Bowler
is forwarding the multicast packets for group 228.13.20.216. Reviewing the rules
for IGMPv2 in Chapter 7, there is no conflict. Queries from Porkpie result in IGMP
Membership Reports from the group member, addressed to the group address. Bowler
hears the Membership Report and begins forwarding the group traffic. If the member
wants to leave the group, it sends IGMP Leave messages addressed to the All Multicast
Routers address 224.0.0.2, as shown by Example 8-34, which are also heard by Bowler.

Example 8-34 *Although Porkpie (10.1.2.1) Is the IGMP Querier, Bowler Still Hears
the IGMP Leave Message from the Attached Group Member. As the Forwarder for This
Group, It Deletes the Interface from the Outgoing Interface List for the Group*

```
Bowler#debug ip igmp
IGMP debugging is on
Bowler#
IGMP: Received Leave from 10.1.2.113 (Ethernet0) for 228.13.20.216
IGMP: Received v2 Query from 10.1.2.1 (Ethernet0)
IGMP: Received v2 Query from 10.1.2.1 (Ethernet0)
IGMP: Deleting 228.13.20.216 on Ethernet0
Bowler#
```

Referring back to Example 8-31, **show ip igmp interface** shows that Bowler's E0 uses the default IGMP query interval of 60 seconds and the default IGMP Querier timeout interval of 120 seconds. Porkpie uses the same defaults. The debugging messages with timestamps in Example 8-35 show these timers in action. The first three messages show Porkpie faithfully sending an IGMP query every 60 seconds. But then something happens and the queries stop. The fourth and fifth messages show that at 120 seconds, · Bowler takes over as Querier and immediately sends a query of its own. Subsequent queries are then sent at 60-second intervals. The last two messages show that Porkpie has returned and is again sending queries. Because that router has a lower IP address, Bowler recognizes Porkpie as the Querier and goes silent.

Example 8-35 *Debugging Shows What Happens When the IGMP Querier Fails and Then Returns*

```
Bowler#debug ip igmp
IGMP debugging is on
Bowler#
*Mar  5 23:41:36.318: IGMP: Received v2 Query from 10.1.2.1 (Ethernet0)
*Mar  5 23:42:36.370: IGMP: Received v2 Query from 10.1.2.1 (Ethernet0)
*Mar  5 23:43:36.422: IGMP: Received v2 Query from 10.1.2.1 (Ethernet0)
*Mar  5 23:45:36.566: IGMP: Previous querier timed out, v2 querier for Ethernet0 is
  this system
*Mar  5 23:45:36.570: IGMP: Send v2 Query on Ethernet0 to 224.0.0.1
*Mar  5 23:46:05.602: IGMP: Send v2 Query on Ethernet0 to 224.0.0.1
*Mar  5 23:47:05.654: IGMP: Send v2 Query on Ethernet0 to 224.0.0.1
*Mar  5 23:48:05.706: IGMP: Send v2 Query on Ethernet0 to 224.0.0.1
*Mar  5 23:48:36.698: IGMP: Received v2 Query from 10.1.2.1 (Ethernet0)
*Mar  5 23:49:36.742: IGMP: Received v2 Query from 10.1.2.1 (Ethernet0)
Bowler#
```

Remember from Chapter 7 that PIM sends hellos to its neighbors by default every 30 seconds, and the holdtime is 3.5 times the hello interval. If a hello is not heard from a neighbor within the holdtime, the neighbor is declared dead. This final example begins with both Bowler and Porkpie online and with Bowler forwarding packets onto the Ethernet for group 228.13.20.216. Example 8-36 shows what happens when Bowler fails.

Example 8-36 *Porkpie Takes over as PIM Forwarder for Group 228.13.20.216 After Failing to Hear Any PIM Hellos from Bowler for the Prescribed Holdtime*

```
Porkpie#debug ip pim 228.13.20.216
PIM debugging is on
Porkpie#
PIM: Neighbor 10.1.2.25 (Ethernet0) timed out
PIM: Changing DR for Ethernet0, from 10.1.2.25 to 10.1.2.1 (this system)
PIM: Building Graft message for 228.13.20.216, Serial1.609: no entries
```

```
PIM: Building Graft message for 228.13.20.216, Serial1.605: no entries
PIM: Building Graft message for 228.13.20.216, Ethernet0: no entries
Porkpie#
```

Porkpie has not heard a hello from Bowler within the holdtime and knows that it must take over the PIM forwarder duties. It assumes the role of the DR and sends PIM Graft messages to its neighbors. Comparing Porkpie's entry for (10.1.1.88, 228.13.20.216) in Example 8-37 with that at the top of Example 8-33, Porkpie is now forwarding the multicast packets onto the Ethernet, whereas it had pruned the interface before becoming the forwarder. Notice also that the Pruned flag, present in the entry in Example 8-33, is no longer in the entry in Example 8-37.

Example 8-37   *After the Failure of Bowler, Porkpie Is Forwarding Group Traffic onto the Ethernet*

```
Porkpie#show ip mroute 228.13.20.216
IP Multicast Routing Table
Flags: D - Dense, S - Sparse, C - Connected, L - Local, P - Pruned
       R - RP-bit set, F - Register flag, T - SPT-bit set, J - Join SPT
       M - MSDP created entry, X - Proxy Join Timer Running
       A - Advertised via MSDP
Outgoing interface flags: H - Hardware switched
Timers: Uptime/Expires
Interface state: Interface, Next-Hop or VCD, State/Mode

(*, 228.13.20.216), 1d01h/00:02:59, RP 0.0.0.0, flags: DJC
  Incoming interface: Null, RPF nbr 0.0.0.0
  Outgoing interface list:
    Serial1.609, Forward/Dense, 05:16:35/00:00:00
    Serial1.605, Forward/Dense, 05:16:35/00:00:00
    Ethernet0, Forward/Dense, 00:06:14/00:00:00

(10.1.1.88, 228.13.20.216), 00:23:10/00:02:59, flags: CT
  Incoming interface: Serial1.605, RPF nbr 10.2.4.2
  Outgoing interface list:
    Serial1.609, Prune/Dense, 00:23:10/00:01:44
    Ethernet0, Forward/Dense, 00:06:14/00:00:00

Porkpie#
```

Configuring Protocol Independent Multicast-Sparse Mode (PIM-SM)

It is probably obvious to you, after seeing the configuration statement for enabling PIM-DM on an interface how PIM-SM is enabled. It is accomplished, quite simply, by

using the **ip pim sparse-mode** command. This much of the configuration of PIM-SM is·
uninteresting and requires no stand-alone examples. The unique requirement of PIM-SM,
and the more interesting aspect of its configuration, is the identification of the rendezvous points. You learned in Chapter 7 that RPs can be statically configured, or they can
be dynamically discovered using either Cisco Auto-RP or the open-standard bootstrap
protocol. The following case studies demonstrate all three methods.

Case Study: Statically Configuring the RP

Figure 8-26 is the same network you have been observing previously in this chapter,
but now the routers are configured to run PIM-SM. Stetson has been chosen as the RP,
and all routers are statically configured with that information. The illustration shows
that Stetson's RP address is 10.224.1.1. This address can exist on any interface, as long
as it is advertised by the unicast routing protocol so that the other routers know how to
reach it. In practice, the loopback interface should be used. A minor reason for this is so
that the RP address can be more easily managed, but the major reason is so that the RP
address is not linked to any physical interface that might fail. This is the same reason that
the loopback interface is recommended for IBGP peering endpoints.

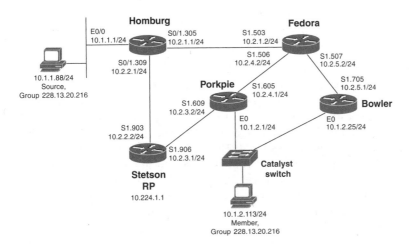

Figure 8-26 *Network Is Now Running PIM-SM with the RP Located at 10.224.1.1*

Example 8-38 shows Bowler's configuration. Notice that the interfaces that were configured for dense mode are now configured for sparse mode.

Example 8-38 *Configuration of Bowler in Figure 6-3*

```
hostname Bowler
!
ip multicast-routing
!
interface Ethernet0
```

```
 ip address 10.1.2.25 255.255.255.0
 ip pim sparse-mode
 ip cgmp
!
interface Serial1
 no ip address
 encapsulation frame-relay
!
interface Serial1.705 point-to-point
 description PVC to Fedora
 ip address 10.2.5.1 255.255.255.0
 ip pim sparse-mode
 no ip mroute-cache
 frame-relay interface-dlci 705
!
router ospf 1
 network 10.0.0.0 0.255.255.255 area 0
!
ip pim rp-address 10.224.1.1
!
```

The other point of interest in Example 8-38 is the command **ip pim rp-address 10.224.1.1**, which tells the router where to find the RP. When statically configuring the RP, all routers with attached group sources or members must have such a statement for them to know where the RP is. Note that Stetson's loopback interface does not need PIM running on it as indicated in Example 8-39. No PIM functionality is required of the interface, other than providing the RP address. That address is advertised to the network by OSPF. However, the **ip pim rp-address 10.224.1.1** statement is present in the con-figuration, even though there are no attached sources or group members. The reason for this statement on this router, of course, is so that the router knows that it is the RP. In practice, it is wise to statically configure the RP address on all routers in the network. It won't hurt if it isn't needed and prevents an accidentally missing statement where it is needed.

Example 8-39   *Configuration of Stetson, the RP, in Figure 6-3*

```
hostname Stetson
!
ip multicast-routing
!
interface Loopback0
 ip address 10.224.1.1 255.255.255.255
!
interface Serial1
 no ip address
```

```
 encapsulation frame-relay
!
interface Serial1.903 point-to-point
 description PVC to R3
 ip address 10.2.2.2 255.255.255.0
 ip pim sparse-mode
 frame-relay interface-dlci 903
!
interface Serial1.906 point-to-point
 description PVC to 906
 ip address 10.2.3.1 255.255.255.0
 ip pim sparse-mode
 frame-relay interface-dlci 906
!
router ospf 1
 network 10.0.0.0 0.255.255.255 area 0
!
ip pim rp-address 10.224.1.1
```

In the PIM-DM section, you compared the **mroute** entries for group 228.13.20.216 in
Porkpie and Bowler. The significance of the entries is that the routers share an Ethernet
subnet with a group member, and issues such as IGMP querying and PIM forwarding
arise. Example 8-40 again compares the two routers' mroute entries for the group. The
entries here appear a little more ambiguous than the dense mode entries in Example
8-33. For example, Porkpie's (*, G) entry shows E0 on the outgoing interface list and in
forwarding state. The outgoing interface list of its (S, G) entry is empty. But at Bowler,
E0 is on the incoming interface list of the (*, G) entry and the entry's outgoing interface
list is empty. And E0 is on the outgoing interface list of the (S, G) entry and in forwarding state. What router is actually forwarding the group packets?

Example 8-40 *Comparing the* mroute *Entries for Group 228.13.20.216 at Porkpie
and Bowler*

```
Porkpie#show ip mroute 228.13.20.216
IP Multicast Routing Table
Flags: D - Dense, S - Sparse, C - Connected, L - Local, P - Pruned
       R - RP-bit set, F - Register flag, T - SPT-bit set, J - Join SPT
       M - MSDP created entry, X - Proxy Join Timer Running
       A - Advertised via MSDP
Outgoing interface flags: H - Hardware switched
Timers: Uptime/Expires
Interface state: Interface, Next-Hop or VCD, State/Mode
```

```
(*, 228.13.20.216), 1d22h/00:02:59, RP 10.224.1.1, flags: SJC
  Incoming interface: Serial1.609, RPF nbr 10.2.3.1
  Outgoing interface list:
    Ethernet0, Forward/Sparse, 02:36:43/00:02:31

(10.1.1.88, 228.13.20.216), 03:08:42/00:02:02, flags: PCRT
  Incoming interface: Serial1.609, RPF nbr 10.2.3.1
  Outgoing interface list: Null

Porkpie#
```

```
Bowler#show ip mroute 228.13.20.216
IP Multicast Routing Table
Flags: D - Dense, S - Sparse, C - Connected, L - Local, P - Pruned
       R - RP-bit set, F - Register flag, T - SPT-bit set, J - Join SPT
       M - MSDP created entry, X - Proxy Join Timer Running
       A - Advertised via MSDP
Outgoing interface flags: H - Hardware switched
Timers: Uptime/Expires
Interface state: Interface, Next-Hop or VCD, State/Mode

(*, 228.13.20.216), 1d00h/00:02:59, RP 10.224.1.1, flags: SJPC
  Incoming interface: Ethernet0, RPF nbr 10.1.2.1
  Outgoing interface list: Null

(10.1.1.88, 228.13.20.216), 02:38:20/00:02:59, flags: CT
  Incoming interface: Serial1.705, RPF nbr 10.2.5.2
  Outgoing interface list:
    Ethernet0, Forward/Sparse, 02:37:36/00:02:12

Bowler#
```

You know what router is forwarding the group packets if you carefully studied PIM-SM procedures in Chapter 7. First, you know that Bowler is the DR because its IP address on subnet 10.1.2.0/24 is higher. You can verify the DR with the **show ip pim interface** command. as shown in Example 8-41.

Example 8-41   *PIM Designated Router on Subnet 10.1.2.0/24 Is Bowler (10.1.2.25)*

```
Porkpie#show ip pim interface

Address          Interface        Version/Mode     Nbr   Query   DR
                                                   Count Intvl
10.1.2.1         Ethernet0        v2/Sparse         1    30      10.1.2.25
10.2.4.1         Serial1.605      v2/Sparse         1    30      0.0.0.0
10.2.3.2         Serial1.609      v2/Sparse         1    30      0.0.0.0
Porkpie#
```

When a host first requests a join to a group, the DR joins the shared RP tree (RPT). Examining Bowler's unicast routing table in Example 8-42, the route from Bowler to the RP is through Porkpie, via subnet 10.1.2.0/24. You now know why Porkpie's E0 interface is on the outgoing interface list of the (*, G) entry. This entry represents the RPT linking Bowler to Stetson. Bowler's (*, G) entry has an empty outgoing interface list and a Pruned flag set because it is the endpoint of the RPT branch.

Example 8-42 *Shortest Route to the RP from Bowler Is Across Its Connected Ethernet to Porkpie*

```
Bowler#show ip route 10.224.1.1
Routing entry for 10.224.1.1/32
  Known via "ospf 1", distance 110, metric 75, type intra area
  Redistributing via ospf 1
  Last update from 10.1.2.1 on Ethernet0, 01:03:56 ago
  Routing Descriptor Blocks:
  * 10.1.2.1, from 10.224.1.1, 01:03:56 ago, via Ethernet0
      Route metric is 75, traffic share count is 1

Bowler#
```

Next, you know that by default after the first multicast packet is received, a PIM-SM router with an attached member will try to switch to the shortest path tree (SPT) to the source, whether that path leads through the RP or not. Bowler's unicast routing table shows that the shortest route to source subnet 10.1.1.0/24 is through Fedora, as indicated in Example 8-43. Looking again at the **mroutes** in Example 8-40, Bowler's (S, G) entry indicates that Fedora, at 10.2.5.2, is the upstream or RPF neighbor. E0 is on the entry's outgoing interface list and in forward state because packets are, of course, forwarded to the group member. Porkpie is not forwarding packets for this group, so its (S, G) entry has an empty outgoing interface list and a Pruned flag.

Example 8-43 *Bowler's Shortest Path to Source Subnet 10.1.1.0/24 Is Through Fedora, out Interface S1.705*

```
Bowler#show ip route 10.1.1.0
Routing entry for 10.1.1.0/24
  Known via "ospf 1", distance 110, metric 138, type intra area
  Redistributing via ospf 1
  Last update from 10.2.5.2 on Serial1.705, 01:17:30 ago
  Routing Descriptor Blocks:
  * 10.2.5.2, from 10.1.1.1, 01:17:30 ago, via Serial1.705
      Route metric is 138, traffic share count is 1

Bowler#
```

You also can use debugging to see how the multicast packets are forwarded. Example 8-44 shows that Bowler receives the multicast packets for group 228.13.20.216 from source 10.1.1.88, via Fedora on interface S1.705. The packets are forwarded out interface E0 to the connected group member.

Example 8-44   *Using Debugging to Capture IP Multicast Packets (**mpackets**), You Can Observe That Bowler Is Receiving Packets for (10.1.1.88, 228.13.20.216) on Interface S1.705 and Forwarding Them out Interface E0*

```
Bowler#debug ip mpacket 228.13.20.216
IP multicast packets debugging is on for group 228.13.20.216
Bowler#
IP: s=10.1.1.88 (Serial1.705) d=228.13.20.216 (Ethernet0) len 573, mforward
IP: s=10.1.1.88 (Serial1.705) d=228.13.20.216 (Ethernet0) len 573, mforward
IP: s=10.1.1.88 (Serial1.705) d=228.13.20.216 (Ethernet0) len 573, mforward
IP: s=10.1.1.88 (Serial1.705) d=228.13.20.216 (Ethernet0) len 573, mforward
IP: s=10.1.1.88 (Serial1.705) d=228.13.20.216 (Ethernet0) len 573, mforward
IP: s=10.1.1.88 (Serial1.705) d=228.13.20.216 (Ethernet0) len 573, mforward
IP: s=10.1.1.88 (Serial1.705) d=228.13.20.216 (Ethernet0) len 573, mforward
IP: s=10.1.1.88 (Serial1.705) d=228.13.20.216 (Ethernet0) len 573, mforward
IP: s=10.1.1.88 (Serial1.705) d=228.13.20.216 (Ethernet0) len 573, mforward
```

Using the same debugging command at Porkpie also presents interesting result, as shown in Example 8-45. The debug messages show that the router is not receiving packets for group 228.13.20.216 from either the RP or from Fedora. Rather, it receives the packets that Bowler is forwarding onto the Ethernet subnet 10.1.2.0/24. Porkpie's **mroute** entries in Example 8-40 show the RPF interface for the group to be S1.609. Because the packets are received on E0, the RPF check fails and the packets are dropped.

Example 8-45   *Porkpie Is Not Forwarding Any Packets for Group 228.13.20.216*

```
Porkpie#debug ip mpacket 228.13.20.216
IP multicast packets debugging is on for group 228.13.20.216
Porkpie#
IP: s=10.1.1.88 (Ethernet0) d=228.13.20.216 len 583, not RPF interface
IP: s=10.1.1.88 (Ethernet0) d=228.13.20.216 len 583, not RPF interface
IP: s=10.1.1.88 (Ethernet0) d=228.13.20.216 len 583, not RPF interface
IP: s=10.1.1.88 (Ethernet0) d=228.13.20.216 len 583, not RPF interface
IP: s=10.1.1.88 (Ethernet0) d=228.13.20.216 len 583, not RPF interface
IP: s=10.1.1.88 (Ethernet0) d=228.13.20.216 len 583, not RPF interface
IP: s=10.1.1.88 (Ethernet0) d=228.13.20.216 len 583, not RPF interface
IP: s=10.1.1.88 (Ethernet0) d=228.13.20.216 len 583, not RPF interface
IP: s=10.1.1.88 (Ethernet0) d=228.13.20.216 len 583, not RPF interface
```

So much of this example, as shown so far, depends upon that a Cisco router switches to the group's SPT after receiving the first multicast packet. You learned in Chapter 5, "Scaling BGP," that this default can be changed with the **ip pim spt-threshold** command. A threshold can be specified in kilobits per second, and the router will not switch to the SPT until the arrival rate of the group's packets exceeds the threshold. Alternatively, you can use the **infinity** keyword and the router never switches to the SPT. It is enlightening to see what happens when **ip pim spt-threshold infinity** is added to the configuration of Bowler in Figure 8-26.

Example 8-46 shows the resulting **mroute** entries at Porkpie and Bowler after Bowler's reconfiguration. Bowler's RPT passes out its E0 interface, across subnet 10.1.2.0/24, and through Porkpie. So Porkpie must now forward packets from the RP. But Bowler's E0 interface is also its RPF interface for the group, and a PIM router cannot forward a group's packets out that group's RPF interface. This is simply a multicast version of the split-horizon rule, which states that packets are not forwarded out the interface they arrived on. As a result, Bowler's (*, G) now sports a Pruned flag. Porkpie is now forwarding the packets to the group member. Interestingly, even though Porkpie has assumed the forwarding duties because Bowler must use the RPT, Porkpie is under no such constraints and has switched to an SPT through Fedora rather than through the RP.

Example 8-46 *After Bowler Is Configured to Never Switch to the SPT, the Forwarding Duties for Group 228.13.20.216 Passes to Porkpie*

```
Porkpie#show ip mroute 228.13.20.216
IP Multicast Routing Table
Flags: D - Dense, S - Sparse, C - Connected, L - Local, P - Pruned
       R - RP-bit set, F - Register flag, T - SPT-bit set, J - Join SPT
       M - MSDP created entry, X - Proxy Join Timer Running
       A - Advertised via MSDP
Outgoing interface flags: H - Hardware switched
Timers: Uptime/Expires
Interface state: Interface, Next-Hop or VCD, State/Mode

(*, 228.13.20.216), 00:45:09/00:02:59, RP 10.224.1.1, flags: SJC
  Incoming interface: Serial1.609, RPF nbr 10.2.3.1
  Outgoing interface list:
    Ethernet0, Forward/Sparse, 00:44:11/00:02:54

(10.1.1.88, 228.13.20.216), 00:44:30/00:02:59, flags: CT
  Incoming interface: Serial1.605, RPF nbr 10.2.4.2
  Outgoing interface list:
    Ethernet0, Forward/Sparse, 00:44:11/00:02:24


Porkpie#
```

```
Bowler#show ip mroute 228.13.20.216
IP Multicast Routing Table
Flags: D - Dense, S - Sparse, C - Connected, L - Local, P - Pruned
       R - RP-bit set, F - Register flag, T - SPT-bit set, J - Join SPT
       M - MSDP created entry, X - Proxy Join Timer Running
       A - Advertised via MSDP
Outgoing interface flags: H - Hardware switched
Timers: Uptime/Expires
Interface state: Interface, Next-Hop or VCD, State/Mode

(*, 228.13.20.216), 00:45:31/00:02:07, RP 10.224.1.1, flags: SPC
  Incoming interface: Ethernet0, RPF nbr 10.1.2.1
  Outgoing interface list: Null

Bowler#
```

At times, you might need to assign different groups to different RPs. Typically, this occurs as the number of groups in the multicast domain grows, and you need to divide the RP duties to decrease the memory and CPU demands placed on any one router. Figure 8-27 shows the same network you have been observing throughout this section, but now Fedora has also been designated as an RP, with an address of 10.244.1.2. With access lists, you can configure multiple RPs and specify what groups should use what RP.

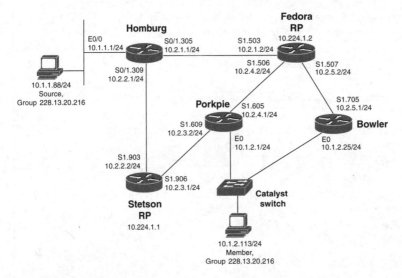

Figure 8-27   *Both Stetson and Fedora Are Rendezvous Points. Access Lists Are Used with the Static RP Addresses to Tell Each Router in the Domain Which RP to Use for a Particular Group*

For example, consider the configuration in Example 8-47.

Example 8-47 *Bowler's RP Filtering Configuration*

```
ip pim rp-address 10.224.1.1 10
ip pim rp-address 10.224.1.2 5
!
access-list 5 permit 239.0.0.0 0.255.255.255
access-list 5 permit 228.13.20.0 0.0.0.255
access-list 10 permit 224.2.127.254
access-list 10 permit 230.253.0.0 0.0.255.255
```

Access-list 5 specifies the groups that are permitted to use RP 10.224.1.2 (Fedora), and access-list 10 specifies the groups that are allowed to use RP 10.224.1.1 (Stetson). Any group whose address does not match one of these two access lists will not have an RP assigned and therefore cannot join either shared tree. This configuration is added to Bowler, and Example 6-48 shows the results. A quick examination shows that the groups listed (which are active groups on the router) have been mapped to an RP according to the constraints of access-list 5 and access-list 10.

Example 6-48 show ip pim rp *Command Displays the Groups Active on a Router, and the RP to Which They Are Mapped*

```
Bowler#show ip pim rp
Group: 239.255.255.254, RP: 10.224.1.2, v2, uptime 01:20:13, expires 00:02:08
Group: 228.13.20.216, RP: 10.224.1.2, v2, uptime 01:19:30, expires never
Group: 224.2.127.254, RP: 10.224.1.1, v2, uptime 01:20:05, expires never
Group: 230.253.84.168, RP: 10.224.1.1, v2, uptime 01:20:06, expires 00:01:48
Bowler#
```

Case Study: Configuring Auto-RP

In a stable PIM domain, static configuration of the RP is straightforward. As new routers are added, the routers are configured with the location of the RP or RPs. Static RP configuration becomes a problem under two circumstances:

- The address of the RP must be changed, either on the existing RP or because a new RP is installed. The network administrator must change the static configurations on all PIM routers, which in a large domain can involve significant down time.

- The RP fails. A statically configured PIM domain cannot easily handle a failover to an alternative RP.

Therefore, in all but the smallest PIM domains, the use of one of the two automatic RP discovery mechanisms, Auto-RP or bootstrap, is recommended both for ease of management and for better redundancy. This case study demonstrates Auto-RP, and a following case study demonstrates the bootstrap protocol.

As discussed in Chapter 7, Auto-RP is a Cisco-proprietary protocol developed before the bootstrap protocol was proposed as part of PIMv2. Auto-RP must be used with any Cisco IOS Software Release prior to Release 11.3, in which PIMv2 is first supported.

Two steps are required to configure basic Auto-RP:

Step 1. All candidate-RPs must be configured.

Step 2. All mapping agents must be configured.

Candidate RPs (C-RPs) are configured by the **ip pim send-rp-announce** command. When you enter this command, you specify the interface from which the router takes its RP address and a TTL value that is added to the advertisement messages. The TTL provides scoping so that packets do not travel outside the boundaries of the domain. When a router is configured as a candidate RP, it begins sending RP-Announce messages to the reserved address 224.0.1.39 every 60 seconds.

The mapping agent listens for RP-Announce messages from the C-RPs and selects the RPs. It then advertises the RPs to the rest of the PIM domain in RP-Discovery messages, sent to the reserved address 224.0.1.40 every 60 seconds.

Figure 8-28 shows an example topology. Here, routers Stetson and Fedora are candidate RPs with addresses 10.224.1.1 and 10.224.1.2, respectively. Porkpie is the mapping agent, with an identifying address of 10.224.1.3.

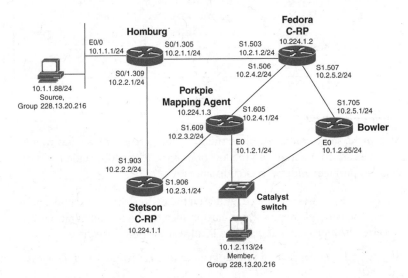

Figure 8-28 *Stetson and Fedora Are Candidate RPs, and Porkpie Is the Mapping Agent*

Example 8-49 shows the relevant parts of Fedora's configuration.

Example 8-49 *Configuring Fedora as a Candidate RP*

```
interface Loopback0
 ip address 10.224.1.2 255.255.255.255
!
ip pim send-rp-announce Loopback0 scope 5
```

Stetson's configuration is similar. The RP address is taken from interface L0, and the **scope** keyword sets the TTL of the originated RP-Announce messages.

Example 8-50 shows the configuration establishing Porkpie as a mapping agent.

Example 8-50 *Establishing Porkpie as a Mapping Agent*

```
interface Loopback0
 ip address 10.224.1.3 255.255.255.255
 ip pim sparse-mode
!
ip pim send-rp-discovery Loopback0 scope 5
```

Again, L0 is used to derive the mapping agent address, and the TTL is set to 5. In the configuration in Example 8-50, notice that PIM-SM must be configured on the loopback interface. This must be performed on the mapping agents; if you fail to enable PIM-SM on the interface first, you get an error message like the one in Example 8-51.

Example 8-51 *Failing to Enable PIM-SM on a Mapping Agent's Loopback Interface Results in an Error Message*

```
Porkpie(config)#ip pim send-rp-discovery Loopback0 scope 5
Non PIM interface ignored in accepted command.
Porkpie(config)#
```

The resulting configuration statement looks like the following:

```
ip pim send-rp-discovery scope 5
```

The interface specified was not accepted, and as a result the mapping agent does not work. Unlike mapping agents, PIM does not have to be configured on the loopback interface of a C-RP. Of course, on both mapping agents and C-RPs, PIM-SM must still be configured on all physical interfaces connected to PIM neighbors.

When a Cisco router is first configured with PIM-SM, it begins listening for the address 224.0.1.40. If changes have to be made to either the C-RPs or to the mapping agents, the changes are automatically advertised by the changed device and the routers throughout the domain learn of the change. Perhaps the most important feature, however, is that you can configure multiple RPs for any or all groups. The mapping agent chooses the RP for a group based on the highest RP address. If that RP fails, the mapping agent selects the next-highest qualifying RP and advertises that.

Example 8-52 shows an example of an RP failover. Here, **debug ip pim auto-rp** is used to display all Auto-RP activity. You can see that Porkpie, the mapping agent in Figure 8-25, receives RP-Announce messages from both Stetson (10.224.1.1) and Fedora (10.224.1.2). Because Fedora has the higher IP address, it is advertised to the domain as the RP for all multicast groups (224.0.0.0/4). After the first reception of RP-Announce messages from Fedora, that router fails. When Porkpie has not heard another RP-Announce message from Fedora within 180 seconds (three times the announcement interval), it declares the RP dead, selects Stetson as the new RP, and begins advertising the new RP. That sequence of events is highlighted at the bottom of the **debug** messages.

Example 8-52 *Debugging Observes an RP Failover at the Mapping Agent in Figure 6-5*

```
Porkpie#debug ip pim auto-rp
PIM Auto-RP debugging is on
Porkpie#
Auto-RP: Received RP-announce, from 10.224.1.1, RP_cnt 1, ht 181
Auto-RP: Update (224.0.0.0/4, RP:10.224.1.1), PIMv2 v1
Auto-RP: Received RP-announce, from 10.224.1.1, RP_cnt 1, ht 181
Auto-RP: Update (224.0.0.0/4, RP:10.224.1.1), PIMv2 v1
Auto-RP: Received RP-announce, from 10.224.1.2, RP_cnt 1, ht 181
Auto-RP: Update (224.0.0.0/4, RP:10.224.1.2), PIMv2 v1
Auto-RP: Received RP-announce, from 10.224.1.2, RP_cnt 1, ht 181
Auto-RP: Update (224.0.0.0/4, RP:10.224.1.2), PIMv2 v1
Auto-RP: Build RP-Discovery packet
Auto-RP:  Build mapping (224.0.0.0/4, RP:10.224.1.2), PIMv2 v1,
Auto-RP: Send RP-discovery packet on Loopback0 (1 RP entries)
Auto-RP: Send RP-discovery packet on Serial1.605 (1 RP entries)
Auto-RP: Send RP-discovery packet on Serial1.609 (1 RP entries)
Auto-RP: Send RP-discovery packet on Ethernet0 (1 RP entries)
Auto-RP: Received RP-announce, from 10.224.1.1, RP_cnt 1, ht 181
Auto-RP: Update (224.0.0.0/4, RP:10.224.1.1), PIMv2 v1
Auto-RP: Received RP-announce, from 10.224.1.1, RP_cnt 1, ht 181
Auto-RP: Update (224.0.0.0/4, RP:10.224.1.1), PIMv2 v1
Auto-RP: Build RP-Discovery packet
Auto-RP:  Build mapping (224.0.0.0/4, RP:10.224.1.2), PIMv2 v1,
Auto-RP: Send RP-discovery packet on Loopback0 (1 RP entries)
Auto-RP: Send RP-discovery packet on Serial1.609 (1 RP entries)
Auto-RP: Send RP-discovery packet on Ethernet0 (1 RP entries)
Auto-RP: Received RP-announce, from 10.224.1.1, RP_cnt 1, ht 181
Auto-RP: Update (224.0.0.0/4, RP:10.224.1.1), PIMv2 v1
Auto-RP: Received RP-announce, from 10.224.1.1, RP_cnt 1, ht 181
Auto-RP: Update (224.0.0.0/4, RP:10.224.1.1), PIMv2 v1
Auto-RP: Build RP-Discovery packet
```

```
Auto-RP:  Build mapping (224.0.0.0/4, RP:10.224.1.2), PIMv2 v1,
Auto-RP: Send RP-discovery packet on Loopback0 (1 RP entries)
Auto-RP: Send RP-discovery packet on Serial1.609 (1 RP entries)
Auto-RP: Send RP-discovery packet on Ethernet0 (1 RP entries)
Auto-RP: Received RP-announce, from 10.224.1.1, RP_cnt 1, ht 181
Auto-RP: Update (224.0.0.0/4, RP:10.224.1.1), PIMv2 v1
Auto-RP: Received RP-announce, from 10.224.1.1, RP_cnt 1, ht 181
Auto-RP: Update (224.0.0.0/4, RP:10.224.1.1), PIMv2 v1
Auto-RP: Mapping (224.0.0.0/4, RP:10.224.1.2) expired,
Auto-RP: Build RP-Discovery packet
Auto-RP:  Build mapping (224.0.0.0/4, RP:10.224.1.1), PIMv2 v1,
Auto-RP: Send RP-discovery packet on Loopback0 (1 RP entries)
Auto-RP: Send RP-discovery packet on Serial1.609 (1 RP entries)
Auto-RP: Send RP-discovery packet on Ethernet0 (1 RP entries)
Porkpie#
```

In Example 8-53, the **show ip pim rp** command is used at Bowler to display the groups that router is receiving for, and the RP that the group is mapped to. The first display is taken before Fedora fails and shows that all groups are mapped to its RP address. The second display, taken after Fedora fails and the mapping agent advertises the new RP, shows that all groups are now mapped to Stetson.

Example 8-53 *Before Fedora Fails, All Bowler's Groups Are Mapped to That RP (10.224.1.2). After the Failure, Bowler's Groups Are Remapped, Based on Information from the Mapping Agent, to Stetson (10.224.1.1).*

```
Bowler#show ip pim rp
Group: 239.255.255.254, RP: 10.224.1.2, v2, v1, uptime 00:08:07, expires 00:04:26
Group: 228.13.20.216, RP: 10.224.1.2, v2, v1, uptime 00:08:08, expires 00:04:26
Group: 224.2.127.254, RP: 10.224.1.2, v2, v1, uptime 00:08:07, expires 00:04:26
Group: 230.253.84.168, RP: 10.224.1.2, v2, v1, uptime 00:08:07, expires 00:04:26
Bowler#

Bowler#show ip pim rp
Group: 239.255.255.254, RP: 10.224.1.1, v2, v1, uptime 00:03:46, expires 00:02:56
Group: 228.13.20.216, RP: 10.224.1.1, v2, v1, uptime 00:03:46, expires 00:02:56
Group: 224.2.127.254, RP: 10.224.1.1, v2, v1, uptime 00:03:46, expires 00:02:56
Group: 230.253.84.168, RP: 10.224.1.1, v2, v1, uptime 00:03:46, expires 00:02:56
Bowler#
```

To change the 60-second default interval at which a C-RP sends RP-Announce messages, add the **interval** keyword to the **ip pim send-rp-announce** command. For example, the following causes Fedora to send RP-Announce messages every 10 seconds:

```
ip pim send-rp-announce Loopback0 scope 5 interval 10
```

The holdtime, the interval a mapping agent waits to hear an RP-Announce message from a C-RP, is always three times the announcement interval. So the result of the preceding command is to shorten the failover time of Fedora to 30 seconds, at the cost of six times as many RP-Announce messages originated by the router.

A C-RP advertises, in its RP-Announce messages, the groups for which it can act as the RP. The default is to announce 224.0.0.0/4, which represents all multicast groups. But as with static RPs in the last case study, you sometimes want to map different groups to different RPs. Suppose, for example, you want all groups 224.0.0.0 through 231.255.255.255 (224.0.0.0/5) to be mapped to Stetson, and all groups 232.0.0.0 through 239.255.255.255 (232.0.0.0/5) to be mapped to Fedora. The C-RP configurations of those two routers then looks like Example 8-54.

Example 8-54 *Configuring Stetson and Fedora as C-RPs*

```
Stetson
ip pim send-rp-announce Loopback0 scope 5 group-list 20
!
access-list 20 permit 224.0.0.0 7.255.255.255
```

```
Fedora
ip pim send-rp-announce Loopback0 scope 5 group-list 30
!
access-list 30 permit 232.0.0.0 7.255.255.255
```

The **group-list** keyword ties the **ip pim send-rp-announce** statement to an access list. The access list then describes what groups the router can become the RP for. Example 8-55 shows the results at Bowler, after mapping agent Porkpie has advertised the RPs according to the constraints in their RP-Announce messages. 239.255.255.254 is mapped to Fedora whereas the other three groups, all of whose addresses fall within the 224.0.0.0/5 range, are mapped to Stetson.

Example 8-55 *Bowler's Group-to-RP Mappings, Showing the Constraints Configured at Stetson and Fedora*

```
Bowler#show ip pim rp
Group: 239.255.255.254, RP: 10.224.1.2, v2, v1, uptime 00:04:25, expires 00:02:56
Group: 228.13.20.216, RP: 10.224.1.1, v2, v1, uptime 00:11:05, expires 00:03:57
Group: 224.2.127.254, RP: 10.224.1.1, v2, v1, uptime 00:11:05, expires 00:03:57
Group: 230.253.84.168, RP: 10.224.1.1, v2, v1, uptime 00:11:05, expires 00:03:57
Bowler#
```

Suppose you also want groups 228.13.0.0 through 228.13.255.255 to be mapped to Fedora. The configuration for router Fedora would then look like Example 8-56.

Example 8-56 *Configuring Fedora as the C-RP for Groups 228.13.0.0 Through 228.13.255.255*

```
ip pim send-rp-announce Loopback0 scope 5 group-list 30
!
access-list 30 permit 232.0.0.0 7.255.255.255
access-list 30 permit 228.13.0.0 0.0.255.255
```

Example 8-57 shows the result at Bowler. Note that Stetson's configuration has not changed. That C-RP is announcing 224.0.0.0/5 as its permitted group range, which includes 228.13.0.0/16. The mapping agent now has two C-RPs for groups in the 228.13.0.0/16 range and has chosen Fedora because its IP address is higher.

Example 8-57 *Multicast Group 228.13.20.216, Which Was Mapped to RP 10.224.1.1 in Example 8-55, Is Now Mapped to RP 10.224.1.2*

```
Bowler#show ip pim rp
Group: 239.255.255.254, RP: 10.224.1.2, v2, v1, uptime 00:01:43, expires 00:04:16
Group: 228.13.20.216, RP: 10.224.1.2, v2, v1, uptime 00:01:43, expires 00:04:16
Group: 224.2.127.254, RP: 10.224.1.1, v2, v1, uptime 00:36:05, expires 00:02:47
Group: 230.253.84.168, RP: 10.224.1.1, v2, v1, uptime 00:36:05, expires 00:02:47
Bowler#
```

Several variants of the **show ip pim rp** command allow you to observe group-to-RP mappings. The command in its basic form, as used in the previous few examples, shows you only the active groups on a router and the RP to which each group address is matched. To observe the full range of groups that may be matched to an RP, use **show ip pim rp mapping**, as shown in Example 8-58.

Example 8-58 *Through the Reception of RP-Discovery Messages from the Mapping Agent 10.224.1.3, Bowler Has Mapped Three Ranges of Multicast Group Addresses to Two Different RPs*

```
Bowler#show ip pim rp mapping
PIM Group-to-RP Mappings

Group(s) 224.0.0.0/5
  RP 10.224.1.1 (?), v2v1
    Info source: 10.224.1.3 (?), via Auto-RP
         Uptime: 01:14:37, expires: 00:02:42
Group(s) 228.13.0.0/16
  RP 10.224.1.2 (?), v2v1
    Info source: 10.224.1.3 (?), via Auto-RP
         Uptime: 00:43:15, expires: 00:02:37
```

```
Group(s) 232.0.0.0/5
  RP 10.224.1.2 (?), v2v1
    Info source: 10.224.1.3 (?), via Auto-RP
        Uptime: 00:43:15, expires: 00:02:41
Bowler#
```

A similar command is **show ip pim rp mapping in-use**, as demonstrated in
Example 8-59. In addition to the information displayed in Example 8-58, the group
ranges that are currently in use on the router display. Notice that the output in both
Examples 8-58 and 8-59 display the source of the mapping agent, 10.224.1.3. This
information is useful when there are multiple mapping agents.

Example 8-59   in-use *Keyword Displays the Group Address Ranges That Are Currently
in Use on the Router*

```
Bowler#show ip pim rp mapping in-use
PIM Group-to-RP Mappings

Group(s) 224.0.0.0/5
  RP 10.224.1.1 (?), v2v1
    Info source: 10.224.1.3 (?), via Auto-RP
        Uptime: 01:21:24, expires: 00:02:50
Group(s) 228.13.0.0/16
  RP 10.224.1.2 (?), v2v1
    Info source: 10.224.1.3 (?), via Auto-RP
        Uptime: 00:50:02, expires: 00:02:49
Group(s) 232.0.0.0/5
  RP 10.224.1.2 (?), v2v1
    Info source: 10.224.1.3 (?), via Auto-RP
        Uptime: 00:50:02, expires: 00:02:48

RPs in Auto-RP cache that are in use:
Group(s): 224.0.0.0/5,   RP: 10.224.1.1
Group(s): 232.0.0.0/5,   RP: 10.224.1.2
Group(s): 228.13.0.0/16,   RP: 10.224.1.2
Bowler#
```

On occasion, you might want to know what RP a particular group address will be
mapped to before that address is active on a router. For example, suppose you want to
know what RP the group 235.1.2.3 will be mapped to at Bowler. For this, you use the
command **show ip pim rp-hash** command, as demonstrated in Example 8-60. The result
shows that group 235.1.2.3 will be mapped to RP 10.224.1.2. The result is consistent
with the access list constraints configured previously.

Example 8-60   *Command* **show ip pim rp-hash** *Allows You to Determine to Which RP a Particular Group Will Be Mapped*

```
Bowler#show ip pim rp-hash 235.1.2.3
  RP 10.224.1.2 (?), v2v1
    Info source: 10.224.1.3 (?), via Auto-RP
        Uptime: 00:55:48, expires: 00:02:00
Bowler#
```

You can prevent your mapping agents from accepting unauthorized routers that may have been inadvertently or intentionally configured as C-RPs by setting up an RP announcement filter. Example 8-61 demonstrates an example configuration for Porkpie.

Example 8-61   *Configuring Porkpie with an RP Announcement Filter*

```
ip pim rp-announce-filter rp-list 1 group-list 11
ip pim send-rp-discovery Loopback0 scope 5
!
access-list 1 permit 10.224.1.2
access-list 1 permit 10.224.1.1
access-list 11 permit 224.0.0.0 15.255.255.255
```

The configuration referred to in Example 8-61 establishes an RP announcement filter to accept only the C-RPs specified in access list 1 and to accept only groups advertised by those C-RPs if they are specified in access list 11. In this configuration, access list 1 permits Stetson and Fedora, and permits those routers to be C-RPs for all multicast groups.

Throughout this case study, Stetson and Fedora in Figure 8-25 have been the C-RPs and Porkpie has been the mapping agent, for the sake of clarity. In practice, however, it makes little sense to configure multiple C-RPs for redundancy but configure only a single mapping agent. If the mapping agent fails, no RPs are advertised to the domain and PIM-SM fails. A more real-life approach would be to make Stetson and Fedora both C-RPs and mapping agents. The nature of Auto-RP ensures that both mapping agents derive and advertise the same RPs, and if one router fails, the other is still in service to advertise RPs to the domain.

Case Study: Configuring Sparse-Dense Mode

A slight "cheat" was used in the examples of the previous case study. Examining Figure 8-28, notice that the C-RPs are directly connected to the mapping agent and the mapping agent is directly connected to Bowler. In Figure 8-29, Homburg is now configured as the Auto-RP mapping agent. This topology gives rise to an interesting dilemma: Homburg advertises the RPs to all routers in RP-Discovery messages, using the reserved address 224.0.1.40. All PIM-SM routers listen for this address. But in a sparse mode environment, multicast packets must initially be forwarded on shared trees. That means the routers listening for 224.0.1.40 must notify their RP that they want to join that group, to receive the RP-Discovery messages. But how do the routers know where the RP is if they have not yet received the RP-Discovery messages?

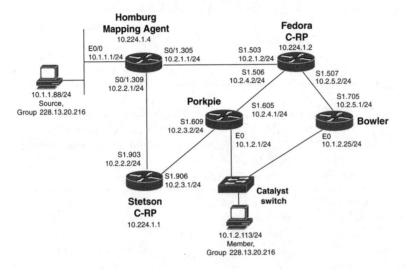

Figure 8-29   *Homburg Is Now the Mapping Agent*

The same Catch-22 would apply to the C-RPs, if they were not directly connected to the mapping agent. The mapping agent must receive RP-Announce messages from the C-RPs to select an RP, and to do this it must join group 224.0.1.39. But it can't join this group if it doesn't know where the RPs are, and it can't know where the RPs are unless it receives RP-Announce messages.

PIM sparse-dense mode was created to overcome this problem. When an interface is configured in this mode, it uses sparse mode if an RP is known for the group. If no RP is known, it uses dense mode. For 224.0.1.39 and 224.0.1.40, the groups are assumed to be in dense mode. Example 8-62 shows the sparse-dense mode configuration for Homburg.

Example 8-62   *PIM Sparse-Dense Mode Configuration for Router Homburg*

```
hostname Homburg
!
ip multicast-routing
!
interface Loopback0
 ip address 10.224.1.4 255.255.255.0
 ip pim sparse-mode
!
interface Ethernet0/0
 ip address 10.1.1.1 255.255.255.0
 ip pim sparse-dense-mode
 no ip mroute-cache
```

```
!
interface Serial0/1
 no ip address
 encapsulation frame-relay
 no ip mroute-cache
!
interface Serial0/1.305 point-to-point
 description PVC to R5
 ip address 10.2.1.1 255.255.255.0
 ip pim sparse-dense-mode
 no ip mroute-cache
 frame-relay interface-dlci 305
!
interface Serial0/1.309 point-to-point
 description PVC to R9
 ip address 10.2.2.1 255.255.255.0
 ip pim sparse-dense-mode
 no ip mroute-cache
 frame-relay interface-dlci 309
!
router ospf 1
 network 10.0.0.0 0.255.255.255 area 0
!
ip pim send-rp-discovery Loopback0 scope 5
!
```

The command **ip pim sparse-dense-mode** is used on all the physical interfaces and is configured similarly on all physical interfaces of all routers in the topology of Figure 8-29. The loopback interface is only in sparse mode because it is needed only as the mapping agent address and never must make any sparse/dense determinations. Interface E0/0 could also be put into sparse mode because it does not face any downstream routers and would not have to make sparse/dense decisions. However, it is good practice to place all interfaces in sparse-dense mode for consistency. Actually, it is commonly advised to use this mode in all modern PIM domains as long as all routers support the mode.

Example 8-63 shows the multicast routing table on Homburg after the reconfiguration. Notice that the entries for (*, 224.0.1.39) and (*, 224.0.1.40) have **D** flags, indicating that they operate in dense mode. All other (*, G) entries are flagged as sparse.

Example 8-63   *Flags Associated with (*,224.0.1.39) and (*,224.0.1.40) in Homburg's*
mroute *Table Show That Those Groups Are Operating in Dense Mode*

```
Homburg#show ip mroute
IP Multicast Routing Table
Flags: D - Dense, S - Sparse, C - Connected, L - Local, P - Pruned
       R - RP-bit set, F - Register flag, T - SPT-bit set, J - Join SPT
Timers: Uptime/Expires
Interface state: Interface, Next-Hop, State/Mode
(*, 228.13.20.216), 00:20:42/00:02:59, RP 10.224.1.2, flags: SJCF
  Incoming interface: Serial0/1.305, RPF nbr 10.2.1.2
  Outgoing interface list:
    Ethernet0/0, Forward/Sparse-Dense, 00:20:42/00:02:43
(10.1.1.88/32, 228.13.20.216), 00:20:42/00:02:59, flags: CFT
  Incoming interface: Ethernet0/0, RPF nbr 0.0.0.0
  Outgoing interface list:
    Serial0/1.305, Forward/Sparse-Dense, 00:20:04/00:02:47
(*, 224.2.127.254), 00:20:34/00:02:59, RP 10.224.1.2, flags: SJCF
  Incoming interface: Serial0/1.305, RPF nbr 10.2.1.2
  Outgoing interface list:
    Ethernet0/0, Forward/Sparse-Dense, 00:20:34/00:02:42
(10.1.1.88/32, 224.2.127.254), 00:20:34/00:02:56, flags: CFT
  Incoming interface: Ethernet0/0, RPF nbr 0.0.0.0
  Outgoing interface list:
    Serial0/1.305, Forward/Sparse-Dense, 00:20:06/00:02:44
(*, 224.0.1.39), 00:20:32/00:00:00, RP 0.0.0.0, flags: DJCL
  Incoming interface: Null, RPF nbr 0.0.0.0
  Outgoing interface list:
    Ethernet0/0, Forward/Sparse-Dense, 00:20:32/00:00:00
    Serial0/1.305, Forward/Sparse-Dense, 00:20:32/00:00:00
    Serial0/1.309, Forward/Sparse-Dense, 00:20:32/00:00:00
(10.224.1.1/32, 224.0.1.39), 00:20:32/00:02:27, flags: CLT
  Incoming interface: Serial0/1.309, RPF nbr 10.2.2.2
  Outgoing interface list:
    Ethernet0/0, Forward/Sparse-Dense, 00:20:32/00:00:00
    Serial0/1.305, Forward/Sparse-Dense, 00:20:32/00:00:00

(10.224.1.2/32, 224.0.1.39), 00:19:54/00:02:05, flags: CLT
  Incoming interface: Serial0/1.305, RPF nbr 10.2.1.2
  Outgoing interface list:
    Ethernet0/0, Forward/Sparse-Dense, 00:19:54/00:00:00
    Serial0/1.309, Forward/Sparse-Dense, 00:19:54/00:02:08
```

```
(*, 224.0.1.40), 00:20:13/00:00:00, RP 0.0.0.0, flags: DJCL
  Incoming interface: Null, RPF nbr 0.0.0.0
  Outgoing interface list:
    Ethernet0/0, Forward/Sparse-Dense, 00:20:14/00:00:00
    Serial0/1.305, Forward/Sparse-Dense, 00:20:14/00:00:00
    Serial0/1.309, Forward/Sparse-Dense, 00:20:14/00:00:00

(10.224.1.4/32, 224.0.1.40), 00:20:06/00:02:48, flags: CLT
  Incoming interface: Loopback0, RPF nbr 0.0.0.0
  Outgoing interface list:
    Ethernet0/0, Forward/Sparse-Dense, 00:20:06/00:00:00
    Serial0/1.305, Forward/Sparse-Dense, 00:20:06/00:00:00
    Serial0/1.309, Forward/Sparse-Dense, 00:20:06/00:00:00

Homburg#
```

In addition to the two Auto-RP groups, there may be times when you want to have some groups operating in sparse mode and others to be operating in dense mode. By using the **ip pim send-rp-announce group-list** command at the C-RPs, as shown in the last case study, you can regulate what groups are mapped to the RP and hence operate in sparse mode. Any groups not mapped to an RP operate in dense mode.

Case Study: Configuring the Bootstrap Protocol

When PIMv2 was first described in RFC 2117, the bootstrap protocol was specified as the mechanism for automatic RP discovery. Cisco first supported PIMv2 in Cisco IOS Software Release 11.3T, and the bootstrap protocol is included in that support.

The two steps to configure bootstrap are similar to the two steps for configuring Auto-RP:

Step 1. All candidate RPs must be configured.

Step 2. All candidate bootstrap routers (C-BSRs) must be configured.

Figure 8-30 shows the same PIM topology used in the last two case studies, but now it runs bootstrap instead of Auto-RP. Stetson and Fedora are again the C-RPs but now are also C-BSRs in keeping with a more robust design, providing failover of both the RP and the BSR function.

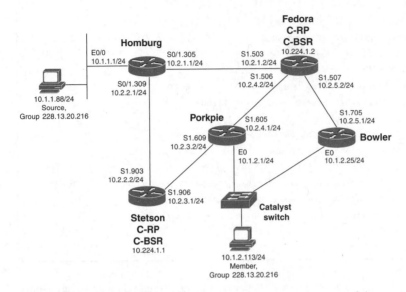

Figure 8-30   *Stetson and Fedora Serve as Both Candidate RPs and Candidate BSRs*

Example 8-64 shows the relevant configurations of Stetson and Fedora.

Example 8-64   *Configuring Routers Stetson and Fedora as Both Candidate RPs and Candidate BSRs*

```
Stetson
interface Loopback0
 ip address 10.224.1.1 255.255.255.255
!
ip pim bsr-candidate Loopback0 0
ip pim rp-candidate Loopback0
```
```
Fedora
interface Loopback0
 ip address 10.224.1.2 255.255.255.255
!
ip pim bsr-candidate Loopback0 0
ip pim rp-candidate Loopback0
```

The command **ip pim bsr-candidate** sets the router as a C-BSR and specifies that the BSR address is to be taken from interface L0. The **0** at the end of the command specifies the hash mask length, which is 0 by default on Cisco routers. Use of the hash mask is demonstrated later in this case study. The command **ip pim rp-candidate** sets the router as a C-RP and specifies that the RP address is also to be taken from interface L0.

First, a BSR must be elected from the available C-BSRs. The C-BSRs send bootstrap messages throughout the PIM domain, with the destination address 224.0.0.13, that contain the originator's BSR address and priority. In the configuration so far, the default priority of 0 and the default hash mask length of 0 remain unchanged, and therefore equal, on both C-BSRs. As a result, the highest BSR address is used as a tiebreaker. Fedora's BSR address (10.224.1.2) is higher than Stetson's (10.224.1.1), so Fedora is the BSR. Example 8-65 confirms the fact. By using **show ip pim bsr-router** on any router in the domain, you can observe not only the active BSR, but also the BSR's address, uptime, priority, hash mask length, and holdtime.

Example 8-65   show ip pim bsr-router *Command Displays the PIMv2 Domain's BSR*

```
Bowler#show ip pim bsr-router
PIMv2 Bootstrap information
  BSR address: 10.224.1.2 (?)
  Uptime:      00:17:35, BSR Priority: 0, Hash mask length: 0
  Expires:     00:01:56
Bowler#
```

After the C-RPs receive the bootstrap messages and determine the address of the BSR, they unicast their Candidate-RP-Advertisement messages to the BSR. These messages contain the C-RP's address and priority. The BSR collects the C-RPs into an RP-Set, which is then included in its bootstrap messages. This is where bootstrap diverges sharply from Auto-RP—Unlike the Auto-RP mapping agent, the BSR does not select RPs. The PIMv2 routers receive the bootstrap messages, and they select the RP. The algorithm used to make the selection ensures that all routers select the same RPs for the same groups.

Example 8-66 shows the group-to-RP mappings at Bowler. You can see that the RP is Stetson, which is the elected RP because of its lower RP address. (The C-RP priorities in this example are equal.)

Example 8-66   *Active Groups at Bowler Are All Mapped to Stetson. Unlike Auto-RP, the C-RP with the Lowest RP Address Is Elected as the RP*

```
Bowler#show ip pim rp
Group: 239.255.255.254, RP: 10.224.1.1, v2, uptime 00:25:16, expires 00:02:40
Group: 228.13.20.216, RP: 10.224.1.1, v2, uptime 00:25:16, expires 00:02:40
Group: 224.2.127.254, RP: 10.224.1.1, v2, uptime 00:25:16, expires 00:02:40
Group: 230.253.84.168, RP: 10.224.1.1, v2, uptime 00:25:16, expires 00:02:40
Bowler#
```

Example 8-67 shows the complete group address range that is mapped to the RP. Compare this display to that of Example 8-59; of particular interest here is that the mapping is shown to be derived from bootstrap and that the router knows all the C-RPs from the RP-Set.

Example 8-67 *Bowler Indicates That It Is Aware of Both Stetson and Fedora as C-RPs*

```
Bowler#show ip pim rp mapping
PIM Group-to-RP Mappings

Group(s) 224.0.0.0/4
  RP 10.224.1.1 (?), v2
    Info source: 10.224.1.2 (?), via bootstrap
        Uptime: 00:29:07, expires: 00:02:30
  RP 10.224.1.2 (?), v2
    Info source: 10.224.1.2 (?), via bootstrap
        Uptime: 00:29:07, expires: 00:02:17
Bowler#
```

The default behavior of both the BSR and the RP can be changed. For example, in Example 8-65 the BSR is Fedora because its IP address is higher. If you want Stetson to be the BSR, with Fedora acting only as a backup in case Stetson fails, you can change Stetson's priority to something higher than the default of 0. To change Stetson's priority to 100, you need to configure Stetson, as shown in Example 8-68.

Example 8-68 *Configuring Stetson with a Priority of 100 to Make It the BSR*

```
interface Loopback0
 ip address 10.224.1.1 255.255.255.255
!
ip pim bsr-candidate Loopback0 0 100
ip pim rp-candidate Loopback0
```

Example 8-69 shows the results of the new configuration. Bowler now shows Stetson as the BSR, with a priority of 100. Fedora assumes only that role should Stetson fail.

Example 8-69 *Stetson (10.224.1.1) with a Priority of 100 Has Become the BSR*

```
Bowler#show ip pim bsr-router
PIMv2 Bootstrap information
  BSR address: 10.224.1.1 (?)
  Uptime:      00:10:27, BSR Priority: 100, Hash mask length: 0
  Expires:     00:02:02
Bowler#
```

As with Auto-RP, access lists can distribute the RP duties among multiple RPs. Suppose, for example, that you want Fedora to be the RP for any groups whose addresses are in the 228.13.0.0/16 range and Stetson to be the RP for all other groups. You would use the configurations in Example 8-70.

Example 8-70 *Distributing RP Duties Between Fedora and Stetson*

```
Stetson
interface Loopback0
 ip address 10.224.1.1 255.255.255.255
!
ip pim bsr-candidate Loopback0 0 100
ip pim rp-candidate Loopback0 group-list 20
!
access-list 20 deny   228.13.0.0 0.0.255.255
access-list 20 permit any
```

```
Fedora
interface Loopback0
 ip address 10.224.1.2 255.255.255.255
!
ip pim bsr-candidate Loopback0 0
ip pim rp-candidate Loopback0 group-list 10
!
access-list 10 permit 228.13.0.0 0.0.255.255
```

Example 8-71 shows the results of these configurations. The BSR advertises the constraints in its bootstrap messages, and Bowler maps its groups to the RPs based on those constraints. Of course, these configurations are not advised in a real network. If one RP fails, the other can no longer assume a backup role. A more practical implementation would use access lists to distribute groups among multiple C-RPs, with at least two C-RPs for each group range created by the access lists.

Example 8-71 *After the Access Lists Are Added to Constrain the RP Mappings at Stetson and Fedora, Bowler Has Mapped Group 228.13.20.216 to Fedora, and the Other Groups to Stetson*

```
Bowler#show ip pim rp mapping
PIM Group-to-RP Mappings

Group(s) 224.0.0.0/4
  RP 10.224.1.1 (?), v2
    Info source: 10.224.1.1 (?), via bootstrap
        Uptime: 00:07:25, expires: 00:02:26
Group(s) 228.13.0.0/16
  RP 10.224.1.2 (?), v2
    Info source: 10.224.1.1 (?), via bootstrap
        Uptime: 00:07:25, expires: 00:02:54
```

```
Bowler#show ip pim rp
Group: 239.255.255.254, RP: 10.224.1.1, v2, uptime 00:07:30, expires 00:02:52
Group: 228.13.20.216, RP: 10.224.1.2, v2, uptime 00:07:30, expires 00:03:32
Group: 224.2.127.254, RP: 10.224.1.1, v2, uptime 00:07:30, expires 00:02:52
Group: 230.253.84.168, RP: 10.224.1.1, v2, uptime 00:07:30, expires 00:02:52
Bowler#
```

A better method of distributing the RP duties when using PIMv2 bootstrap is to use the hash mask. The hash mask is a 32-bit number assigned to the BSR and is used in a somewhat similar fashion to a standard IP address mask. The BSR advertises the hash mask in its bootstrap messages, and the receiving routers run a hash algorithm that assigns a consecutive number of group addresses to one C-RP and then assigns the next group of addresses to the next C-RP.

For example, if the hash mask is 30 bits, it masks the first 30 bits of all IP multicast addresses. The last 2 bits describe a range of four group addresses that will be assigned to an RP. So the addresses 225.1.1.0, 225.1.1.1, 225.1.1.2, and 225.1.1.3 are all part of one range and are assigned to one RP. The addresses 225.1.1.4, 225.1.1.5, 225.1.1.6, and 225.1.1.7 belong to the next range and are assigned to another RP. This "bundling" of group addresses continues throughout the entire IP multicast address range and across all available C-RPs. The result is that the IP multicast group addresses have been evenly distributed among the C-RPs. The mask gives you the flexibility to decide how many consecutive addresses are bundled into a single range so that related addresses are more likely to share the same RP. If the mask is 26 bits, for instance, 64 consecutive addresses are assigned to each range.

The hash mask length is specified as part of the **ip pim bsr-candidate** command. As you have observed in previous examples in this case study, the default mask length is 0, meaning that there is a single bundle of group addresses spanning the entire range of the IP multicast address space. Example 8-72 shows the configurations to assign a hash mask length of 30 for both Stetson and Fedora in Figure 8-26.

Example 8-72 *Assigning a Hash Mask Length of 30 to Routers Stetson and Fedora*

```
Stetson
interface Loopback0
 ip address 10.224.1.1 255.255.255.255
!
ip pim bsr-candidate Loopback0 30
ip pim rp-candidate Loopback0
```

```
Fedora
interface Loopback0
 ip address 10.224.1.2 255.255.255.255
!
ip pim bsr-candidate Loopback0 30
ip pim rp-candidate Loopback0
```

In Example 8-73, the **show ip pim rp-hash** command demonstrates the results. Beginning with 231.1.1.0, you can see that it and the next three consecutive group addresses are mapped to Fedora. Continuing the sequence, the next four addresses are mapped to Stetson. Across the entire range of IP multicast addresses, there should be a 50–50 distribution between the two RPs.

Example 8-73 *Hash Algorithm Distributes Group Addresses Evenly Among the Available C-RPs*

```
Bowler#show ip pim rp-hash 231.1.1.0
  RP 10.224.1.2 (?), v2
    Info source: 10.224.1.2 (?), via bootstrap
       Uptime: 07:22:14, expires: 00:02:29
Bowler#show ip pim rp-hash 231.1.1.1
  RP 10.224.1.2 (?), v2
    Info source: 10.224.1.2 (?), via bootstrap
       Uptime: 07:22:19, expires: 00:02:24
Bowler#show ip pim rp-hash 231.1.1.2
  RP 10.224.1.2 (?), v2
    Info source: 10.224.1.2 (?), via bootstrap
       Uptime: 07:22:22, expires: 00:02:21
Bowler#show ip pim rp-hash 231.1.1.3
  RP 10.224.1.2 (?), v2
    Info source: 10.224.1.2 (?), via bootstrap
       Uptime: 07:22:28, expires: 00:02:15
Bowler#show ip pim rp-hash 231.1.1.4
  RP 10.224.1.1 (?), v2
    Info source: 10.224.1.2 (?), via bootstrap
       Uptime: 07:22:31, expires: 00:02:13
Bowler#show ip pim rp-hash 231.1.1.5
  RP 10.224.1.1 (?), v2
    Info source: 10.224.1.2 (?), via bootstrap
       Uptime: 07:22:35, expires: 00:02:10
Bowler#show ip pim rp-hash 231.1.1.6
  RP 10.224.1.1 (?), v2
    Info source: 10.224.1.2 (?), via bootstrap
       Uptime: 07:22:38, expires: 00:02:06
Bowler#show ip pim rp-hash 231.1.1.7
  RP 10.224.1.1 (?), v2
    Info source: 10.224.1.2 (?), via bootstrap
       Uptime: 07:22:43, expires: 00:02:02
```

Case Study: Multicast Load Sharing

You may want to balance multicast traffic over parallel equal-cost paths, either to more fully utilize available bandwidth or to prevent a single path from becoming congested by heavy multicast traffic. But the RPF check prevents multicast load balancing directly over physical links.

The problem is shown in Figure 8-31 where the same PIM topology used in the previous case studies is repeated, except that Bowler is removed and Homburg is both the Auto-RP mapping agent and the RP.

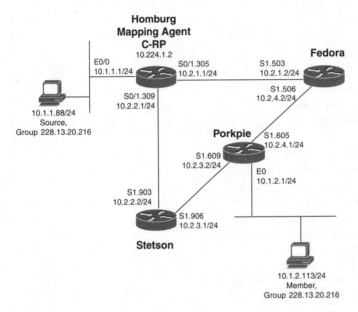

Figure 8-31 *Two Equal-Cost Paths Exist Between the Multicast Source and the Group Member*

Two equal-cost paths from the multicast source attach to Homburg and the group member attaches to Porkpie—One path transits Fedora, and the other transits Stetson. The problem exists because RPF must have only one incoming interface to work correctly. That means that if Fedora is chosen as the RPF neighbor and group traffic arrives from Stetson, that traffic does not arrive on the RPF interface and is dropped. Likewise, if Stetson is chosen as the RPF neighbor, traffic arriving from Fedora fails the RPF check and is dropped. RPF requires all traffic to arrive on the same upstream interface.

The way to get around this problem is to use a tunnel, as shown in Figure 8-32. The tunnel is built between the loopback interfaces of Homburg and Porkpie, and all multicast traffic from the source to the group member is sent to this virtual tunnel interface rather than to either physical link. The multicast packets are then encapsulated and forwarded as regular IP packets. At this point, the encapsulated packets can be balanced across the two links, using either the default per-destination balancing or the optional per-packet balancing as described in Volume I.

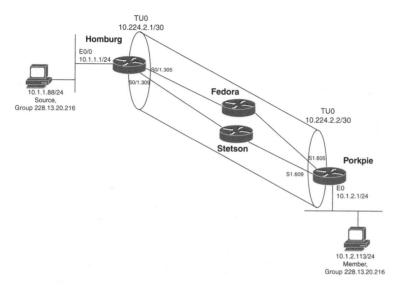

Figure 8-32 *To Load Balance over the Equal-Cost Paths, a Tunnel Is Created Between Homburg and Porkpie*

Note Per-packet load balancing is achieved by turning off fast switching, CEF, or its equivalent on the necessary interfaces. In the majority of cases this is not recommended because it is performance effecting.

When the packets arrive at Porkpie, it does not matter whether they were received from Fedora or from Stetson because their destination is the egress of the tunnel. At the virtual tunnel interface, the encapsulation is removed. From the perspective of the PIM process at Porkpie, the multicast packets appear to have all been received on the same interface, TU0, and to have been received from the same upstream neighbor, Homburg.

Example 8-74 shows the configurations of Homburg and Porkpie.

Example 8-74 *Configuring a Tunnel Between Homburg and Porkpie to Load Balance over Equal-Cost Paths*

```
Homburg
hostname Homburg
!
ip multicast-routing
!
interface Loopback0
```

```
 ip address 10.224.1.4 255.255.255.0
 ip pim sparse-mode
!
interface Tunnel0
 ip address 10.224.2.1 255.255.255.252
 ip pim sparse-dense-mode
 tunnel source Loopback0
 tunnel destination 10.224.1.3
!
interface Ethernet0/0
 ip address 10.1.1.1 255.255.255.0
 ip pim sparse-dense-mode
!
interface Serial0/1
 no ip address
 encapsulation frame-relay
!
interface Serial0/1.305 point-to-point
 description PVC to R5
 ip address 10.2.1.1 255.255.255.0
 frame-relay interface-dlci 305
!
interface Serial0/1.309 point-to-point
 description PVC to R9
 ip address 10.2.2.1 255.255.255.0
 frame-relay interface-dlci 309
!
router ospf 1
 passive-interface Tunnel0
 network 10.0.0.0 0.255.255.255 area 0
!
ip pim send-rp-announce Loopback0 scope 5
ip pim send-rp-discovery scope 5
```

```
Porkpie
hostname Porkpie
!
ip multicast-routing
!
interface Loopback0
 ip address 10.224.1.3 255.255.255.255
!
interface Tunnel0
 ip address 10.224.2.2 255.255.255.252
 ip pim sparse-dense-mode
```

```
 tunnel source Loopback0
 tunnel destination 10.224.1.4
!
interface Ethernet0
 ip address 10.1.2.1 255.255.255.0
 ip pim sparse-dense-mode
 ip cgmp
!
interface Serial1
 no ip address
 encapsulation frame-relay
!
interface Serial1.605 point-to-point
 description PVC to R5
 ip address 10.2.4.1 255.255.255.0
 frame-relay interface-dlci 605
!
interface Serial1.609 point-to-point
 description PVC to R9
 ip address 10.2.3.2 255.255.255.0
 frame-relay interface-dlci 609
!
router ospf 1
 passive-interface Tunnel0
 network 10.0.0.0 0.255.255.255 area 0
```

On both routers, the tunnel interface is configured with a source of the router's loopback interface and a destination of the other router's loopback interface. The tunnel uses Generic Route Encapsulation (GRE) and is given an IP address so that the virtual interface appears to the routing processes to be a physical IP interface. Finally, PIM is enabled on the tunnel interfaces. Notice that PIM is not enabled on any of the subinterfaces connecting to Stetson and Fedora. And on those two routers, multicasting is not enabled at all. Example 8-75 shows that, with these configurations, Porkpie has established a PIM adjacency with Homburg over the tunnel.

Example 8-75 *Porkpie Shows Homburg as a Neighbor Across the GRE Tunnel*

```
Porkpie#show ip pim neighbor
PIM Neighbor Table
Neighbor Address   Interface        Uptime     Expires   Ver  Mode
10.224.2.1         Tunnel0          04:09:21   00:01:11  v1   Sparse-Dense
Porkpie#
```

A further RPF problem needs be solved, however. When Porkpie receives packets from source 10.1.1.88, it checks the unicast routing table for the upstream neighbor. Example 8-76 shows what the router finds.

Example 8-76   *Unicast Routing Table Still Shows 10.2.3.1 or 10.2.4.2 as the Next-Hop Addresses to Reach 10.1.1.88*

```
Porkpie#show ip route 10.1.1.88
Routing entry for 10.1.1.0/24
  Known via "ospf 1", distance 110, metric 138, type intra area
  Redistributing via ospf 1
  Last update from 10.2.3.1 on Serial1.609, 01:13:30 ago
  Routing Descriptor Blocks:
  * 10.2.3.1, from 10.224.1.4, 01:13:30 ago, via Serial1.609
      Route metric is 138, traffic share count is 1
    10.2.4.2, from 10.224.1.4, 01:13:30 ago, via Serial1.605
      Route metric is 138, traffic share count is 1

Porkpie#
```

Porkpie's OSPF configuration has interface TU0 in passive mode to ensure that no unicast traffic crosses the tunnel—only multicast. Unfortunately, that means that OSPF still sees either Stetson (10.2.3.1) or Fedora (10.2.4.2) as the next hop toward 10.1.1.88. So when packets from 10.1.1.88 arrive on the tunnel interface, the RPF check fails, as shown in Example 8-77.

Example 8-77   *RPF Check Fails for Packets Arriving over the Tunnel from 10.1.1.88, Because the Unicast Routing Table Does Not Show TU0 as an Upstream Interface to That Address*

```
Porkpie#debug ip mpacket
IP multicast packets debugging is on
Porkpie#
IP: s=10.1.1.88 (Tunnel0) d=228.13.20.216 len 569, not RPF interface
IP: s=10.1.1.88 (Tunnel0) d=228.13.20.216 len 569, not RPF interface
IP: s=10.1.1.88 (Tunnel0) d=228.13.20.216 len 569, not RPF interface
IP: s=10.1.1.88 (Tunnel0) d=228.13.20.216 len 569, not RPF interface
IP: s=10.1.1.88 (Tunnel0) d=228.13.20.216 len 569, not RPF interface
IP: s=10.1.1.88 (Tunnel0) d=228.13.20.216 len 569, not RPF interface
IP: s=10.1.1.88 (Tunnel0) d=228.13.20.216 len 569, not RPF interface
IP: s=10.1.1.88 (Tunnel0) d=228.13.20.216 len 569, not RPF interface
IP: s=10.1.1.88 (Tunnel0) d=228.13.20.216 len 569, not RPF interface
IP: s=10.1.1.88 (Tunnel0) d=228.13.20.216 len 569, not RPF interface
```

To overcome this second RPF problem, a static multicast route is used. Static mroutes are similar to static unicast routes in that they override any dynamic route entries. The difference is that static mroutes are not used for any forwarding. Instead, they are used to statically configure the RPF interface for a source, overriding the information in the unicast routing table. The command **ip mroute** is used along with an IP address and mask to specify an address or range of addresses. An RPF interface or RPF neighbor address is also specified, just as a static unicast route specifies either an outgoing interface or a next-hop neighbor. Example 8-78 shows the configuration for Porkpie with the static **mroute**.

Example 8-78 *Configuring Porkpie with a Static* mroute

```
hostname Porkpie
!
ip multicast-routing
!
interface Loopback0
 ip address 10.224.1.3 255.255.255.255
!
interface Tunnel0
 ip address 10.224.2.2 255.255.255.252
 ip pim sparse-dense-mode
 tunnel source Loopback0
 tunnel destination 10.224.1.4
!
interface Ethernet0
 ip address 10.1.2.1 255.255.255.0
 ip pim sparse-dense-mode
 ip cgmp
!
interface Serial1
 no ip address
 encapsulation frame-relay
!
interface Serial1.605 point-to-point
 description PVC to R5
 ip address 10.2.4.1 255.255.255.0
 frame-relay interface-dlci 605
!
interface Serial1.609 point-to-point
 description PVC to R9
 ip address 10.2.3.2 255.255.255.0
 frame-relay interface-dlci 609
!
```

```
router ospf 1
 passive-interface Tunnel0
 network 10.0.0.0 0.255.255.255 area 0
!
ip mroute 10.1.1.88 255.255.255.255 Tunnel0
```

Example 8-79 again uses debugging to verify that the multicast packets are now passing the RPF check at Porkpie and are forwarded to the group member.

Example 8-79 *Packets from Source 10.1.1.88 Arriving on the Tunnel Interface Are Now Passing the RPF Check and Are Forwarded*

```
Porkpie#debug ip mpacket
IP multicast packets debugging is on
Porkpie#
IP: s=10.1.1.88 (Tunnel0) d=228.13.20.216 (Ethernet0) len 569, mforward
IP: s=10.1.1.88 (Tunnel0) d=228.13.20.216 (Ethernet0) len 569, mforward
IP: s=10.1.1.88 (Tunnel0) d=228.13.20.216 (Ethernet0) len 569, mforward
IP: s=10.1.1.88 (Tunnel0) d=228.13.20.216 (Ethernet0) len 569, mforward
IP: s=10.1.1.88 (Tunnel0) d=228.13.20.216 (Ethernet0) len 569, mforward
IP: s=10.1.1.88 (Tunnel0) d=228.13.20.216 (Ethernet0) len 569, mforward
IP: s=10.1.1.88 (Tunnel0) d=228.13.20.216 (Ethernet0) len 569, mforward
IP: s=10.1.1.88 (Tunnel0) d=228.13.20.216 (Ethernet0) len 569, mforward
IP: s=10.1.1.88 (Tunnel0) d=228.13.20.216 (Ethernet0) len 569, mforward
IP: s=10.1.1.88 (Tunnel0) d=228.13.20.216 (Ethernet0) len 569, mforward
```

Example 8-80 shows the **mroute** entries for group 228.13.20.216. You can readily observe that Homburg is receiving multicast traffic from 10.1.1.88 on its E0/0 interface and forwarding the traffic on the tunnel. Porkpie receives the traffic on the tunnel and forwards it to the group member on its E0 interface.

Example 8-80   mroute *Entries for (10.1.1.88, 228.13.20.216) Indicate That the Traffic for That Group Is Forwarded over the GRE Tunnel*

```
Homburg#show ip mroute 228.13.20.216
IP Multicast Routing Table
Flags: D - Dense, S - Sparse, C - Connected, L - Local, P - Pruned
       R - RP-bit set, F - Register flag, T - SPT-bit set, J - Join SPT
Timers: Uptime/Expires
Interface state: Interface, Next-Hop, State/Mode

(*, 228.13.20.216), 04:48:39/00:02:59, RP 10.224.1.4, flags: SJC
  Incoming interface: Null, RPF nbr 0.0.0.0
  Outgoing interface list:
    Tunnel0, Forward/Sparse-Dense, 01:35:18/00:02:01
```

```
      Ethernet0/0, Forward/Sparse-Dense, 04:48:39/00:02:59

(10.1.1.88/32, 228.13.20.216), 01:41:09/00:02:59, flags: CT
  Incoming interface: Ethernet0/0, RPF nbr 0.0.0.0
  Outgoing interface list:
    Tunnel0, Forward/Sparse-Dense, 01:35:19/00:02:01

Homburg#
```

```
Porkpie#show ip mroute 228.13.20.216
IP Multicast Routing Table
Flags: D - Dense, S - Sparse, C - Connected, L - Local, P - Pruned
       R - RP-bit set, F - Register flag, T - SPT-bit set, J - Join SPT
       M - MSDP created entry, X - Proxy Join Timer Running
       A - Advertised via MSDP
Outgoing interface flags: H - Hardware switched
Timers: Uptime/Expires
Interface state: Interface, Next-Hop or VCD, State/Mode

(*, 228.13.20.216), 00:56:23/00:02:59, RP 10.224.1.4, flags: SJC
  Incoming interface: Tunnel0, RPF nbr 10.224.2.1, Mroute
  Outgoing interface list:
    Ethernet0, Forward/Sparse-Dense, 00:56:23/00:02:58

(10.1.1.88, 228.13.20.216), 00:13:37/00:02:59, flags: CJT
  Incoming interface: Tunnel0, RPF nbr 10.224.2.1, Mroute
  Outgoing interface list:
    Ethernet0, Forward/Sparse-Dense, 00:13:37/00:02:58

Porkpie#
```

Troubleshooting IP Multicast Routing

Your primary weapon when attacking problems in IP multicast networks is a solid understanding of the IP multicast protocols. Without that, no number of troubleshooting tools is going to help you maneuver through the often confusing, sometimes complex behaviors of IP multicast to the root of a particular problem. And understanding a single protocol is not enough. You must also understand how PIM, IGMP, and unicast routing all interact.

If you have been closely following the troubleshooting sections of each chapter of both Volume I and this volume, you should by now have a well-developed grasp of the approaches and techniques necessary for resolving problems in routed networks. So rather than present further case studies illustrating troubleshooting techniques, this section demonstrates the use of the several specialized tools provided for analyzing multicast Internets.

Throughout this chapter, you have observed various **show** and **debug** commands useful for observing the behavior of IP multicast routing on Cisco routers. Table 8-4 lists the **show** commands available to you, and Table 8-5 lists the important multicast **debug** commands. Just as **show ip route** is the primary source of information when troubleshooting IP unicast routing, **show ip mroute** is the primary source of information when troubleshooting IP multicast routing.

Table 8-4   *Important* **show** *Commands for Troubleshooting IP Multicast*

Command	Description
show ip igmp groups [*group-name* / *group-address* / *type number*]	Displays the addresses of groups that have members on the router's interfaces
show ip igmp interface [*type number*]	Displays relevant details of IGMP-enabled the interface
show ip mcache [*group* [*source*]]	Displays the multicast contents of the fast switching cache
show ip mroute [*group-name* / *group-address*] [*source*] [**summary**] [**count**] [**active** *kbps*]	Displays the contents of the multicast routing table
show ip pim bsr	Displays information about PIM bootstrap routers
show ip pim interface [*type number*] [**count**]	Displays relevant details of PIM-enabled interfaces
show ip pim neighbor [*type number*]	Displays PIM neighbors
show ip pim rp [*group-name* / *group-address* / **mapping**]	Displays the known RPs and the groups mapped to the RPs
show ip pim rp-hash *group*	Displays the RP for the group specified
show ip rpf {*source-address* / *name*}	Displays details of how the router determines RPF information

Table 8-5   *Important* **debug** *Commands for Troubleshooting IP Multicast*

Command	Description
debug ip igmp [*hostname* / *group_address*]	Displays IGMP protocol activity
debug ip mcache [*hostname* / *group_address*]	Displays multicast caching operations

Command	Description
debug ip mpacket [*standard_access_list* | *extended_access_list*] [*hostname* | *group_address*][**detail**]	Displays multicast packets transiting the router
debug ip mrouting [*hostname* | *group_address*]	Displays multicast routing table activity
debug ip pim [*hostname* | *group_address*][**auto-rp**][**bsr**]	Displays PIM activity and events

Using mrinfo

Note   mrinfo is deprecated in the most recent releases of IOS. It's still covered here as a useful troubleshooting tool in versions previous to 15.x.

The **mrinfo** command enables you to observe a router's multicast connections and the details of those connections. The command is a part of the tools originally made available as part of *mrouted* for testing routers in the Mbone. Therefore, the command is useful in multivendor domains. Take, for example, the topology in Figure 8-33.

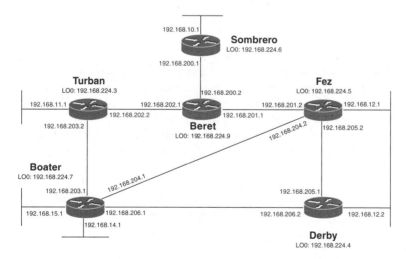

Figure 8-33   *This Topology Is Used Throughout the Troubleshooting Examples*

In Example 8-81, **mrinfo** is used at router Sombrero. The first line of the output shows the address used as the source of the query, the Cisco IOS Software version running on the router, and a number of flags. Table 8-6 lists the possible flags and their meaning. The next two lines of output show multicast interfaces on the router and any peers that the router may have. On the second line, Sombrero's interface 192.168.10.1 has no peers, indicated by the 0.0.0.0. The 1/0 indicates that the interface has a metric of 1 and that no TTL threshold set exists. PIM runs on the interface, the router is an IGMP Querier for the attached subnet, and the subnet is a leaf network. (That is, no multicast traffic transits the network to another multicast router.) The third line shows that Sombrero's interface 192.168.200.1 has a peer at address 192.168.200.2 (router Beret), the metric of the interface is 1, there is no TTL threshold, and PIM is running.

Example 8-81   *IP Multicast Connection Information for Sombrero in Figure 6-10*

```
Sombrero#mrinfo
192.168.10.1 [version  12.1] [flags: PMA]:
  192.168.10.1 -> 0.0.0.0 [1/0/pim/querier/leaf]
  192.168.200.1 -> 192.168.200.2 [1/0/pim]

Sombrero#
```

Table 8-6   *Flags Associated with the* **mrinfo** *Command*

Flag	Definition
P	Prune-capable
M	**mtrace**-capable
S	SNMP-capable
A	Auto-RP-capable

The true usefulness of **mrinfo**, however, is that you can use the command to query other routers in the domain. In Example 8-82, the command is used at Sombrero to query Boater by specifying one of Boater's IP addresses (here, its loopback address). Note that the flags indicate that SNMP is enabled on this router, whereas it is not on Sombrero. The router has five multicast-enabled interfaces, two of which are on leaf networks and three of which have PIM peers. A check of Figure 6-10 shows that this information is accurate.

Example 8-82   **mrinfo** *Is Used at Sombrero to Query Boater About Its Multicast Peers*

```
Sombrero#mrinfo 192.168.224.7
192.168.224.7 [version  12.1] [flags: PMSA]:
  192.168.14.1 -> 0.0.0.0 [1/0/pim/querier/leaf]
  192.168.15.1 -> 0.0.0.0 [1/0/pim/querier/leaf]
  192.168.203.1 -> 192.168.203.2 [1/0/pim]
  192.168.206.1 -> 192.168.206.2 [1/0/pim]
  192.168.204.1 -> 192.168.204.2 [1/0/pim]

Sombrero#
```

In Example 8-83, routers Derby and Fez are queried. These two routers share an Ethernet connection, and comparing the results of the queries shows that Derby (192.168.224.4) is the IGMP Querier on that subnet.

Example 8-83   *Derby (192.168.224.4) and Fez (192.168.224.5) Are Queried from Sombrero*

```
Sombrero#mrinfo 192.168.224.4
192.168.224.4 [version 12.1] [flags: PMA]:
  192.168.12.2 -> 192.168.12.1 [1/0/pim/querier]
  192.168.205.1 -> 192.168.205.2 [1/0/pim]
  192.168.206.2 -> 192.168.206.1 [1/0/pim]

Sombrero#mrinfo 192.168.224.5
192.168.224.5 [version 12.1] [flags: PMA]:
  192.168.12.1 -> 192.168.12.2 [1/0/pim]
  192.168.205.2 -> 192.168.205.1 [1/0/pim]
  192.168.204.2 -> 192.168.204.1 [1/0/pim]
  192.168.201.2 -> 192.168.201.1 [1/0/pim]

Sombrero#
```

Using mtrace and mstat

Another useful tool is the **mtrace** command, which enables you to trace the RPF path from a specified destination to a specified source. Like **mrinfo**, **mtrace** is a UNIX-based Mbone tool and can be used in multivendor domains. And again like **mrinfo**, you can issue the command from any router in the domain—you do not have to be on any router along the RPF path.

When the command is issued, you specify a source address and a destination address. A trace request is sent to the destination, which then uses a unicast trace to the source. The first-hop router on the path toward the source unicasts the results of the trace to the querying router.

Example 8-84 shows an example in which a request is issued at Sombrero to trace the RPF path from Derby's 192.168.12.2 interface to Turban's 192.168.11.1 interface. Remember, because this is a reverse-path trace, Turban's interface is the source and Derby's interface is the destination. The output begins at the destination address and displays each intermediate router until the source is reached. The number of hops from the source is indicated as is the multicast protocol used on that hop.

Example 8-84   mtrace *Examines the RPF Path from Destination 192.168.12.2 to Source 192.168.11.1*

```
Sombrero#mtrace 192.168.11.1 192.168.12.2
Type escape sequence to abort.
Mtrace from 192.168.11.1 to 192.168.12.2 via RPF
From source (?) to destination (?)
Querying full reverse path...
 0  192.168.12.2
-1  192.168.12.2 PIM  [192.168.11.0/24]
-2  192.168.206.1 PIM  [192.168.11.0/24]
-3  192.168.203.2 PIM  [192.168.11.0/24]
-4  192.168.11.1
Sombrero#
```

Aside from the obvious use of isolating multicast routing failures, **mtrace** has an additional use of enabling you to examine multicast behavior before you turn up live multicast traffic on your network. Notice in Figure 8-30 that there are no multicast sources or group members indicated. Suppose you are going to turn up a multicast source attached to Boater, with an address of 192.168.14.35. This source originates multicast traffic for group 235.100.20.18, and there will be group members at addresses 192.168.12.15, 192.168.10.8, and 192.168.11.102. Example 8-85 shows the results.

Example 8-85   mtrace *Can Test the RPF for Source, Destination, and Group Addresses That Do Not Yet Exist in the Multicast Domain*

```
Sombrero#mtrace 192.168.14.35 192.168.12.15 235.100.20.18
Type escape sequence to abort.
Mtrace from 192.168.14.35 to 192.168.12.15 via group 235.100.20.18
From source (?) to destination (?)
Querying full reverse path...
 0  192.168.12.15
-1  192.168.201.2 PIM  [192.168.14.0/24]
-2  192.168.204.1 PIM  [192.168.14.0/24]
-3  192.168.14.35

Sombrero#mtrace 192.168.14.35 192.168.10.8 235.100.20.18
Type escape sequence to abort.
Mtrace from 192.168.14.35 to 192.168.10.8 via group 235.100.20.18
From source (?) to destination (?)
Querying full reverse path...
 0  192.168.10.8
-1  192.168.10.1 PIM  [192.168.14.0/24]
-2  192.168.200.2 PIM  [192.168.14.0/24]
-3  192.168.202.2 PIM  [192.168.14.0/24]
```

```
-4   192.168.203.1 PIM   [192.168.14.0/24]
-5   192.168.14.35


Sombrero#mtrace 192.168.14.35 192.168.11.102 235.100.20.18
Type escape sequence to abort.
Mtrace from 192.168.14.35 to 192.168.11.102 via group 235.100.20.18
From source (?) to destination (?)
Querying full reverse path...
 0   192.168.11.102
-1   192.168.202.2 PIM   [192.168.14.0/24]
-2   192.168.203.1 PIM   [192.168.14.0/24]
-3   192.168.14.35
Sombrero#
```

The traces in Example 8-85 specify the multicast group along with the source and destination addresses. Although the RPF path would normally be the same for all groups, specifying the group can be useful in situations in which scoping or RP filtering affects the path taken. When no group is specified, as in the previous Example 8-84, the group address 224.2.0.1 (the Mbone audio group address) is used by default.

mstat is an adaptation of **mtrace** that provides not only a trace of the path from a source to a group destination, but also provides statistics about the path. Example 8-86 shows an example in which a trace is again requested from source 192.168.14.35 to destination 192.168.10.8 for group 235.100.20.18. Comparing the output in Example 8-86 to the output for the same trace in Example 8-85, you can see that **mstat** provides not only packet statistics, but also a more detailed view of the entire path.

Example 8-86   mstat *Provides a More Detailed Trace of Group Traffic from a Source to a Destination*

```
Sombrero#mstat 192.168.14.35 192.168.10.8 235.100.20.18
Type escape sequence to abort.
Mtrace from 192.168.14.35 to 192.168.10.8 via group 235.100.20.18
From source (?) to destination (?)
Waiting to accumulate statistics......
Results after 10 seconds:

  Source          Response Dest     Packet Statistics For     Only For Traffic
192.168.14.35     192.168.200.1      All Multicast Traffic      From 192.168.14.35
    |        __/  rtt 47   ms    Lost/Sent = Pct  Rate      To 235.100.20.18
    v       /     hop 27   ms    --------------------       --------------------
192.168.14.1
192.168.203.1    ?
    |       ^     ttl   0
    v       |     hop 5    ms    0/0 = --%      0 pps     0/0 = --%  0 pps
```

```
192.168.203.2
192.168.202.2    ?
      |    ^        ttl    1
      v    |        hop 7    ms    0/0 = --%       0 pps    0/0 = --%  0 pps
192.168.202.1
192.168.200.2    ?
      |    ^        ttl    2
      v    |        hop 4    ms    0/0 = --%       0 pps    0/0 = --%  0 pps
192.168.200.1
192.168.10.1     ?
      |    \__      ttl    3
      v     \ hop 0    ms        0            0 pps            0    0 pps
192.168.10.8     192.168.200.1
  Receiver        Query Source
```

Reading from bottom to top, the display in Example 8-86 shows the query source and response destination, which in this example are both 192.168.200.1 (Sombrero). Notice an ASCII representation of arrows showing that the Sombrero has sent the query to 192.168.10.1 (in this case, its own interface). The reverse path is then traced to the interface on Boater to which the source would be attached, and the response to the query is then sent to Sombrero. At the far left of the display, ASCII arrows also indicate the path multicast traffic takes from the source to the destination. At each hop, the **ttl** and **hop** statistics can be a little misleading. **ttl** actually shows the number of hops from that point to the source, whereas **hops** shows the delay (in milliseconds) between hops. Notice that the round-trip time (rtt) is indicated below the response destination. Statistics are then shown for all multicast traffic and for the (S, G) pair specified in the command. The first statistic compares the number of packets dropped to the number of packets sent. The second statistic shows the total traffic rate, in packets per second. In Example 8-85, all these statistics are 0, of course, because no traffic has passed from the source to the destination. Actually, the source and destination do not even exist yet.

In Example 8-87, the proposed hosts have been installed, the source is generating traffic, and the group member has joined. You can now observe the packet-per-second rates and the drop statistics. An important point to keep in mind when using **mstat** is that the delay times between routers is only valid if the routers' clocks are synchronized.

Example 8-87   *Same* mstat *Command Is Used After Multicast Traffic Is Begun Between the Source and Destination*

```
Sombrero#mstat 192.168.14.35 192.168.10.8 235.100.20.18
Type escape sequence to abort.
Mtrace from 192.168.14.35 to 192.168.10.8 via group 235.100.20.18
From source (?) to destination (?)
Waiting to accumulate statistics......
Results after 10 seconds:
```

```
   Source          Response Dest    Packet Statistics For    Only For Traffic
192.168.14.35     192.168.200.1     All Multicast Traffic     From 192.168.14.35
    |        __/  rtt 48    ms     Lost/Sent = Pct  Rate     To 235.100.20.18
    v       /     hop 48    ms     --------------------      --------------------
192.168.14.1
192.168.203.1   ?
    |      ^       ttl   0
    v      |      hop 10    ms      0/82 = 0%      8 pps     0/81 = --%  8 pps
192.168.203.2
192.168.202.2   ?
    |      ^       ttl   1
    v      |      hop 6     ms      0/82 = 0%      8 pps     0/81 = 0%  8 pps
192.168.202.1
192.168.200.2   ?
    |      ^       ttl   2
    v      |      hop 4     ms      0/82 = 0%      8 pps     0/81 = 0%  8 pps
192.168.200.1
192.168.10.1    ?
    |      \__     ttl   3
    v      \      hop 0     ms        82          8 pps       81      8 pps
192.168.10.8     192.168.200.1
  Receiver       Query Source

Sombrero#
```

Example 8-88 shows what the display migvht look like if the clocks are not in sync. The trace information and packet rates are still valid, but the delay times for the individual hops are obviously nonsensical. Also in Example 8-88, you can see that one packet has been lost on the hop between Turban and Beret. This may represent a problem; the only way to know is to run several iterations of **mstat** and observe whether the packet loss is consistent. If so, further investigation using debugging may be required.

Example 8-88 *If the Routers' Clocks Are Not Synchronized, the Delays Shown for the Router Hops Are Meaningless*

```
Sombrero#mstat 192.168.14.35 192.168.10.8 228.13.20.216
Type escape sequence to abort.
Mtrace from 192.168.14.35 to 192.168.10.8 via group 228.13.20.216
From source (?) to destination (?)
Waiting to accumulate statistics......
Results after 10 seconds:
   Source          Response Dest    Packet Statistics For    Only For Traffic
192.168.14.35     192.168.200.1     All Multicast Traffic     From 192.168.14.35
```

```
|         __/  rtt  44    ms    Lost/Sent = Pct   Rate     To 228.13.20.216
    v    /       hop  44    ms    --------------------      --------------------
192.168.14.1
192.168.203.1   ?
    |      ^       ttl   0
    v    |       hop -222 s    0/82 = 0%        8 pps    0/81 = 0%   8 pps
192.168.203.2
192.168.202.2   ?
    |      ^       ttl   1
    v    |       hop 113  s    1/82 = 1%        8 pps    1/81 = 1%   8 pps
192.168.202.1
192.168.200.2   ?
    |      ^       ttl   2
    v    |       hop 108  s    0/80 = 0%        8 pps    0/80 = 0%   8 pps
192.168.200.1
192.168.10.1    ?
    |     \__    ttl   3
    v      \  hop 0    ms         80            8 pps            80   8 pps
192.168.10.8    192.168.200.1
  Receiver      Query Source
```

Lastly, you may encounter a situation in which **mstat** shows a negative number of lost packets: For example, *-3/85*. The "negative packet loss" represents a packet gain. In other words, extra packets have been received. This may signify a loop and should warrant further investigation.

Looking Ahead

Of all the IP routing protocols examined in the two volumes of this book, the multicast protocols are the most unfamiliar (and most complex) to the most people. Although this chapter provides a reasonable overview of IP multicast routing principles, it is by no means exhaustive. There is much more to IP multicast that cannot be covered within the confines of this book; for more extensive coverage, refer to "Recommended Reading."

Now that you have some understanding of multicast issues and the operation and configuration of the variants of PIMv2, which is the only intra-AS IP multicast routing protocol in production today, Chapter 9 examines scaling and inter-AS routing.

Recommended Reading

Beau Williamson, *Developing IP Multicast Networks*, Indianapolis, IN, Cisco Press, 2000.

Review Questions

1. What is a PIM prune override?

2. What is a PIM forwarder? How is a forwarder selected?

3. What criteria does PIM use to select a DR?

4. What is a PIM SPT? What is a PIM RPT?

5. What two mechanisms are available for Cisco routers to automatically discover PIM-SM RPs?

6. Of the mechanisms in Question 43, which should be used in multivendor router topologies?

7. What is a C-RP?

8. What is a BSR?

9. What is an RP mapping agent?

10. What is the difference between a (S,G) **mroute entry and a (*,G) mroute entry?**

11. What is PIM-SM source registration?

12. When does a Cisco router switch from a PIM-SM RPT to an SPT?

13. What is PIM sparse-dense mode?

Configuration Exercises

Figure 8-34 shows the topology used for the configuration exercises.

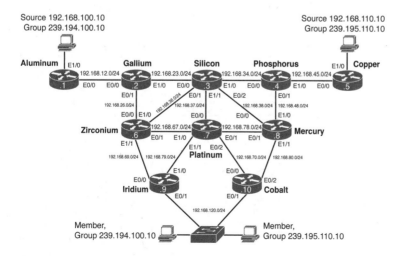

Figure 8-34 *Network Topology for Configuration Exercises*

Table 8-7 lists the routers, switches, multicast enabled hosts, interfaces, and addresses used in the exercises for this chapter. All interfaces of the routers are shown.

Table 8-7   *Router/Switch/Host Interfaces and IP Addresses for Configuration Exercises*

Network Device	Interface	IP Address
Aluminum	Eth0/0	192.168.12.1/24
	Eth1/0	192.168.100.1/24
	Loopback 0	10.224.1.1/32
Gallium	Eth0/0	192.168.12.2/24
	Eth0/1	192.168.26.2/24
	Eth1/0	192.168.23.2/24
	Loopback 0	10.224.1.2/32
Silicon	Eth0/0	192.168.23.3/24
	Eth0/1	192.168.36.3/24
	Eth0/2	192.168.38.3/24
	Eth1/0	192.168.34.3/24
	Eth1/1	192.168.37.3/24
	Loopback 0	10.224.1.3/32
Phosphorus	Eth0/0	192.168.34.4/24
	Eth0/1	192.168.48.4/24
	Eth1/0	192.168.45.4/24
	Loopback 0	10.224.1.4/32
Copper	Eth0/0	192.168.45.5/24
	Eth1/0	192.168.110.1/24
	Loopback 0	10.224.1.5/32
Zirconium	Eth0/0	192.168.26.6/24
	Eth0/1	192.168.67.6/24
	Eth1/0	192.168.36.6/24
	Eth1/1	192.168.69.6/24
	Loopback 0	10.224.1.6/32

Network Device	Interface	IP Address
Platinum	Eth0/0	192.168.37.7/24
	Eth0/1	192.168.78.7/24
	Eth0/2	192.168.70.7/24
	Eth1/0	192.168.67.7/24
	Eth1/1	192.168.79.7/24
	Loopback 0	10.224.1.7/32
Mercury	Eth0/0	192.168.38.8/24
	Eth0/1	192.168.78.8/24
	Eth1/0	192.168.48.8/24
	Eth1/1	192.168.80.8/24
	Loopback 0	10.224.1.8/32
Iridium	Eth0/0	192.168.69.9/24
	Eth0/1	192.168.120.1/24
	Eth1/0	192.168.79.9/24
	Loopback 0	10.224.1.9/32
Cobalt	Eth0/0	192.168.70.10/24
	Eth0/1	192.168.120.2/24
	Eth0/2	192.168.80.10/24
	Loopback 0	10.224.1.10/32

1. Application A relies on the Multicast IP Address 239.194.1.1 and application B relies on 239.195.1.1.

   Configure the network based on the following requirements:

   Sparse Mode is the multicast mode that must be configured in this question.

   Silicon must be the RP for all the multicast IP addresses in the range 239.195.0.0/16. Platinum must be the RP for all the multicast IP addresses in the range 239.194.0.0/16.

   If any interface fails on the RP, the router should still perform the wanted multicast function. In other words, choose the RP address wisely.

   The security IT department wants that Iridium and Cobalt should establish a PIM adjacency between them and with no one else.

Iridium must be the PIM Designated Router on the Ethernet segment toward the receivers. Make sure that Cobalt will failover within 3 seconds on that segment.

RP must be statically configured.

Verify that multicast flows are sent from the sources toward the receivers. Verify that the shared tree is sourced at the RP for the specified multicast flow. Verify that switchover for the shortest path tree has occurred.

2. Your Security IT team wants to make sure that only the legit source can be registered to the Silicon and Platinum RP. Use the Loopback0 IP addresses for this question

3. Make sure that Aluminum and Copper send unicast PIM register messages from their loopback.

4. The network team has decided to move forward and thinks that using static RP is deprecated (which is right). Their choice was evident and they decided to implement BSR.

Configure the network based on the following requirements:

Zirconium and Mercury should be candidates BSR and Zirconium would win the election. Both BSR candidates should accept Candidate-RP-Advertisement messages from Silicon and Platinum only.

Silicon and Platinum must use their loopback 0 interface to unicast their willingness to be the rendezvous point. Also, they must be RPs for the groups 239.194.0.0 and 239.195.0.0 only.

RP must be load balanced between the two candidate RPs. The hash must be 30.

Subnets in which the sources and receivers are not managed by your company and there are some other routers beyond. Your IT security department wants to prevent PIM BSR messages to be sent toward the sources and receivers.

Troubleshooting Exercises

1. What is the following output telling you?

```
R1#
Turban#debug ip mpacket
IP multicast packets debugging is on
R1#
IP: s=192.168.14.35 (Serial0/1.307) d=228.13.20.216 len 573, mrouting disabled
IP: s=192.168.14.35 (Serial0/1.307) d=228.13.20.216 len 573, mrouting disabled
IP: s=192.168.14.35 (Serial0/1.307) d=228.13.20.216 len 573, mrouting disabled
IP: s=192.168.14.35 (Serial0/1.307) d=228.13.20.216 len 573, mrouting disabled
IP: s=192.168.14.35 (Serial0/1.307) d=228.13.20.216 len 573, mrouting disabled
```

```
IP: s=192.168.14.35 (Serial0/1.307) d=228.13.20.216 len 573, mrouting disabled
IP: s=192.168.14.35 (Serial0/1.307) d=228.13.20.216 len 573, mrouting disabled
IP: s=192.168.14.35 (Serial0/1.307) d=228.13.20.216 len 573, mrouting disabled
IP: s=192.168.14.35 (Serial0/1.307) d=228.13.20.216 len 573, mrouting disabled
IP: s=192.168.14.35 (Serial0/1.307) d=228.13.20.216 len 573, mrouting disabled
IP: s=192.168.14.35 (Serial0/1.307) d=228.13.20.216 len 573, mrouting disabled
IP: s=192.168.14.35 (Serial0/1.307) d=228.13.20.216 len 573, mrouting disabled
IP: s=192.168.14.35 (Serial0/1.307) d=228.13.20.216 len 573, mrouting disabled
```

2. What is the following output telling you?

```
R2#

IP: s=192.168.13.5 (Ethernet0) d=227.134.14.26 len 583, not RPF interface
IP: s=192.168.13.5 (Ethernet0) d=227.134.14.26 len 583, not RPF interface
IP: s=192.168.13.5 (Ethernet0) d=227.134.14.26 len 583, not RPF interface
IP: s=192.168.13.5 (Ethernet0) d=227.134.14.26 len 583, not RPF interface
IP: s=192.168.13.5 (Ethernet0) d=227.134.14.26 len 583, not RPF interface
IP: s=192.168.13.5 (Ethernet0) d=227.134.14.26 len 583, not RPF interface
IP: s=192.168.13.5 (Ethernet0) d=227.134.14.26 len 583, not RPF interface
IP: s=192.168.13.5 (Ethernet0) d=227.134.14.26 len 583, not RPF interface
IP: s=192.168.13.5 (Ethernet0) d=227.134.14.26 len 583, not RPF interface
```

3. What is the following output telling you?

```
R3#debug ip mpacket
IP multicast packets debugging is on
R3#
IP: s=172.16.3.50 (Serial0.405) d=224.0.1.40 (Serial0.407) len 52, mforward
IP: s=172.16.3.50 (Ethernet0) d=224.0.1.40 len 62, not RPF interface
IP: s=172.16.3.50 (Ethernet0) d=224.0.1.39 len 62, not RPF interface
IP: s=172.16.3.50 (Serial0.405) d=224.0.1.39 (Serial0.407) len 52, mforward
```

4. In Figure 8-35, which of the four routers is the PIM designated router?

5. In Figure 8-35, which router is sending IGMPv2 queries to the group member?

6. Table 8-8 shows the unicast routes to source 172.16.12.18 in Figure 8-35. Which router is the PIM forwarder?

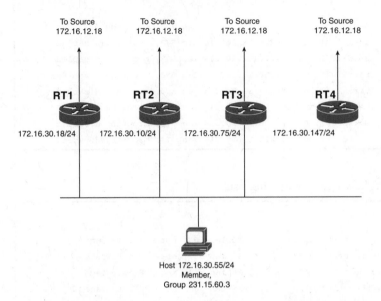

Figure 8-35   *Topology for Troubleshooting Exercises 4, 5, and 6*

Table 8-8   *Unicast Routes to 172.16.12.18 in Figure 6-12*

Router	Next Hop	Protocol	Metric
R1	172.16.50.5	OSPF	35
R2	172.16.51.80	EIGRP	307200
R3	172.16.13.200	EIGRP	2297856
R4	172.16.44.1	OSPF	83

7. The following output shows an RPF trace taken from the PIM domain in
    Figure 8-36, which runs RIP-2 as its unicast IGP. Does this trace indicate a
    possible problem?

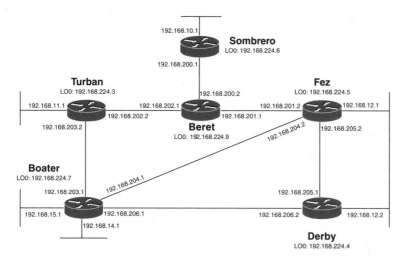

Figure 8-36 *Network Topology for Troubleshooting Exercise 7*

```
Sombrero#mtrace 192.168.14.35 192.168.10.8 235.1.2.3
Type escape sequence to abort.
Mtrace from 192.168.14.35 to 192.168.10.8 via group 235.1.2.3
From source (?) to destination (?)
Querying full reverse path...
 0  192.168.10.8
-1  192.168.10.1 PIM  [192.168.14.0/24]
-2  192.168.200.2 PIM  [192.168.14.0/24]
-3  192.168.201.2 PIM  [192.168.14.0/24]
-4  192.168.204.1 PIM  [192.168.14.0/24]
-5  192.168.14.35
Sombrero#
```

Chapter 9

Scaling IP Multicast Routing

The preceding two chapters explained the present state of IP multicast routing protocols and the basics of configuring Cisco IOS Software for multicast routing. As with unicast protocols, however, you must take additional measures as your multicast domain grows to maintain stability, scalability, and controllability. This chapter examines some of the techniques and protocols available to you to accomplish those objectives.

Multicast Scoping

A primary consideration when working with large-scale multicast domains is controlling the scope of the domain. You have read the discussion of the subject in Chapter 7, "Introduction to IP Multicast Routing," and you know that there are two methods of scoping multicast domains:

- TTL scoping
- Administrative scoping

With TTL scoping, the TTL value of multicast packets is set in such a way that the packets can travel only a certain distance before the TTL is decremented to 0 and the packet is discarded. You can add some granularity to this rough method by setting boundaries on interfaces with the **ip multicast ttl-threshold** command. For example, an interface might be configured with **ip multicast ttl-threshold 5**. Only packets with TTL values greater than 5 are forwarded out of this interface. Any packets with TTL values of 5 or below are dropped. Table 9-1 shows an example of TTL scoping values. The values in this table are a set of TTL values suggested for use with the now-obsolete MBone.

In Chapter 8, "Protocol Independent Multicast," you encountered several commands, such as the commands for enabling Auto-RP candidate RPs and mapping agents, that enable you to set the TTL values of the protocol messages for TTL scoping. You encounter more commands in this chapter with the same option. However, you saw in Chapter 7 that TTL scoping lacks flexibility—a TTL boundary at an interface applies to all multicast packets. This is fine for an absolute boundary, but at times you want some packets to be blocked and others to be forwarded.

Table 9-1 *MBone TTL Thresholds*

TTL Value	Restriction
0	Restricted to same host
1	Restricted to same subnet
15	Restricted to same site
63	Restricted to same region
127	Worldwide
191	Worldwide limited bandwidth
255	Unrestricted

For this purpose, administrative scoping provides more flexibility. IPv4 administrative scoping is just a procedure in which the multicast group address range 224.0.0.0–239.255.255.255 is partitioned in such a way that certain ranges of addresses are assigned certain scopes. Various domain boundaries can then be created by filtering on these address ranges. IPv4 administrative scoping is the subject of RFC 2365,[1] and Table 9-2 shows the partitions that RFC suggests. You have already seen how the link-local scope of 224.0.0.0/24 is used. Packets with multicast addresses in this range—such as IGMP (224.0.0.1 and 224.0.0.2), OSPF (224.0.0.5 and 224.0.0.6), EIGRP (224.0.0.10), and PIM (224.0.0.13)—are never forwarded by a router and thus are restricted to the scope of the data link on which they were originated.

Table 9-2 *RFC 2365 Administrative Partitions*

Prefix	Scope
224.0.0.0/24	Link-Local
224.0.1.0–238.255.255.255	Global
239.0.0.0/10	Unassigned
239.64.0.0/10	Unassigned
239.128.0.0/10	Unassigned
239.192.0.0/14	Organization-Local
239.255.0.0/16	Unassigned

Adding the **ip multicast boundary** command to an interface creates an administrative boundary. The command just references an IPv4 access list, which specifies the group address range to be permitted or denied at the interface, as demonstrated in Example 9-1.

---

[1] David Meyer, "RFC 2365: Administratively Scoped IP Multicast," July 1998.

Example 9-1 *Adding the* ip multicast boundary *Command to an Interface Creates an Administrative Boundary*

```
interface Ethernet0
 ip address 10.1.2.3 255.255.255.0
  ip multicast boundary 10
!
interface Ethernet1
 ip address 10.83.15.5 255.255.255.0
 ip multicast boundary 20
!
access-list 10 deny   239.192.0.0 0.3.255.255
access-list 10 permit 224.0.0.0 15.255.255.255
access-list 20 permit 239.135.0.0 0.0.255.255
access-list 20 deny   224.0.0.0 15.255.255.255
```

Interface E0 marks a boundary at which organization-local packets, as defined in Table 9-2, are blocked, whereas global-scoped packets are passed. The boundary at E1 permits packets whose destination addresses fall within the 239.135.0.0/16 range and denies all other multicast packets. This address range falls within an undefined range in Table 9-2 and therefore has been given some special meaning by the local network administrator.

Administrative scoping in IPv6 multicast networks is much simpler because the scope values are built in to the IPv6 address format, as shown in Figure 9-1. The scope values, listed in Table 9-3, are specified in RFC 7346. For example, an IPv6 group address with the prefix of FF02::/16 is link-local scoped (as are most protocol addresses, such as FF02::5 for all OSPFv3 routers or FF02::D for PIM routers), whereas the prefix FF08::/16 has organization-local scope.

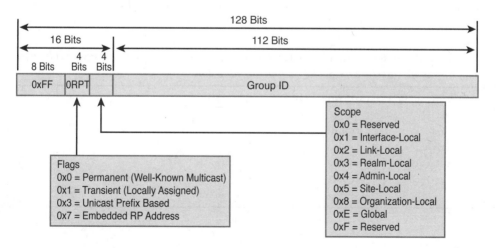

Figure 9-1 *IPv6 Multicast Address Format Has a Built-In Scope Specification*

Table 9-3   *IPv6 Multicast Scope Values*

Scope Field Value	Scope
0	Reserved
1	Interface-Local
2	Link-Local
3	Realm-Local
4	Admin-Local
5	Site-Local
6	Unassigned
7	Unassigned
8	Organization-Local
9	Unassigned
A	Unassigned
B	Unassigned
C	Unassigned
D	Unassigned
E	Global
F	Reserved

The built-in IPv6 scope field makes configuring IPv6 administrative scoping easy; you don't need an access list to define address scopes. Using the ipv6 multicast boundary scope statement, you can specify an IPv6 multicast boundary at an interface either by scope number or by name, as shown in Example 9-2. Note that if you use the scope number, you use decimal numbers (3–15) rather than the hexadecimal numbers (3–F) listed in Table 9-3.

Example 9-2   **ipv6 multicast boundary scope** *Statement Can Specify an IPv6 Multicast Boundary at an Interface by Scope Number or by Name*

```
Colorado(config-if)#ipv6 multicast boundary scope ?
  <3-15>              Scope identifier for this zone
  admin-local         Admin-local(4)
  organization-local  Organization-local(8)
  site-local          Site-local(5)
  subnet-local        Subnet-local(3)
  vpn                 Virtual Routing/Forwarding(14)
```

With IOS 15.0, you can also use the statement **ipv6 multicast boundary block source** to block the source of all incoming multicast traffic on an interface. Example 9-3 shows a configuration for IPv6 administrative scoping.

Example 9-3   *Interface Serial 1/1 Is Configured as an Administrative-Local Boundary, and Interface Serial 1/2 Is Configured as an Organization-Local Boundary*

```
!
interface Serial1/1
 ip address 10.0.0.6 255.255.255.252
 ipv6 address 2001:DB8:A:3::1/64
 ipv6 multicast boundary scope 4
 serial restart-delay 0
!
interface Serial1/2
 no ip address
 ipv6 address 2001:DB8:A:4::1/64
 ipv6 multicast boundary scope 8
 serial restart-delay 0
!
```

Case Study: Multicasting Across Non-Multicast Domains

One challenge you will face is connecting diverse multicast domains across domains in which multicast is not supported. This may certainly be the case when multicasting is required in only certain areas of a large routing domain. You would not want to enable multicast on every router in the unicast domain just to provide connectivity to a relatively small number of multicast routers. A second and common example is connecting multicast domains across the decidedly unicast Internet.

In Figure 9-2, two PIM domains are separated by a unicast-only IP domain. The unicast domain might be the backbone of an enterprise network, or it might be the Internet itself. The important point is that the two multicast domains must have connectivity across it. The solution is a simple one: Create a tunnel between the two routers that can carry the PIM traffic.

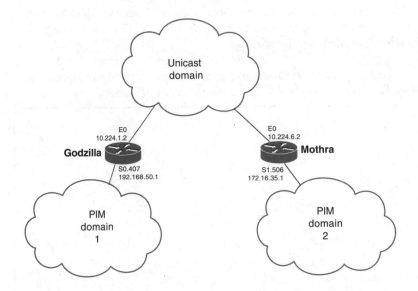

Figure 9-2   *PIM Domains Separated by a Unicast-Only IP Domain*

Example 9-4 shows the tunnel configurations of the two routers shown in Figure 9-2.

Example 9-4   *Configuring Godzilla and Mothra to Provide Connectivity Between the Multicast Domains Through the Unicast-Only Domain*

```
Godzilla
interface Tunnel0
 ip unnumbered Ethernet0
 ip pim sparse-dense-mode
 tunnel source Ethernet0
 tunnel destination 10.224.6.2
!
interface Ethernet0
 ip address 10.224.1.2 255.255.255.0
!
interface Serial0.407 point-to-point
 description PVC to R7
 ip address 192.168.50.1 255.255.255.0
 ip pim sparse-dense-mode
 frame-relay interface-dlci 407
!
router ospf 1
 passive-interface Tunnel0
 network 10.0.0.0 0.255.255.255 area 0
 network 192.168.0.0 0.0.255.255 area 0
```

```
!
ip mroute 172.16.0.0 255.255.0.0 Tunnel0
```

```
Mothra
interface Tunnel0
 ip unnumbered Ethernet0
 ip pim sparse-dense-mode
 tunnel source Ethernet0
 tunnel destination 10.224.1.2
!
interface Ethernet0
 ip address 10.224.6.2 255.255.255.0
!
interface Serial1.506 point-to-point
 description PVC to R6
 ip address 172.16.35.1 255.255.255.0
 ip pim sparse-dense-mode
 frame-relay interface-dlci 506
!
router ospf 1
 passive-interface Tunnel0
 network 0.0.0.0 255.255.255.255 area 0
!
ip mroute 192.168.0.0 255.255.0.0 Tunnel0
```

You already have seen a tunnel used in Chapter 8 to provide for load sharing across equal-cost paths. The configuration here is similar. The tunnel source is the Ethernet interface on each router, but PIM is not configured on that physical interface—only on the tunnel. GRE encapsulation, the default tunnel mode, is used. OSPF is configured to run passively on TU0 to ensure that no unicast traffic traverses the tunnel. Finally, static multicast routes are configured, referencing all possible source addresses from the opposite domain and showing their upstream interface as TU0. Recall from Chapter 8 that this route is necessary to prevent RPF failures. Without it, RPF checks would use the OSPF routes and determine the upstream interface to be the routers' E0 interfaces. As a result, all packets arriving on TU0 would fail the RPF check.

Example 9-5 shows the results of the configuration.

Example 9-5   *A PIM Adjacency Is Formed Across the GRE Tunnel*

```
Godzilla#show ip pim neighbor
PIM Neighbor Table
Neighbor Address  Interface      Uptime     Expires   Ver  Mode
192.168.50.2      Serial0.407    01:08:51   00:01:27  v2
172.16.35.1       Tunnel0        01:03:31   00:01:16  v2
Godzilla#
```

```
Mothra#show ip pim neighbor
PIM Neighbor Table
Neighbor Address  Interface        Uptime    Expires   Ver  Mode
172.16.35.2       Serial1.506      01:10:06  00:01:42  v2
192.168.50.1      Tunnel0          01:04:33  00:01:15  v2
Mothra#
```

Connecting to DVMRP Networks

You might, on rare occasion, have to connect your PIM router to a DVMRP router. This is not necessarily a large-scale multicast issue—routers that can speak only DVMRP can be encountered in a network of any size. You are most likely to encounter them during a migration of an old multicast network to a more up-to-date multicast network.

When you configure an interface on a Cisco router to run PIM, it listens for DVMRP Probe messages. When Probes are heard, as demonstrated in the output in Example 9-6, Cisco IOS Software automatically enables DVMRP on the interface. No special configuration is required. PIM routes are advertised to the DVMRP neighbor in DVMRP Report messages. DVMRP Report messages learned from the neighbor are kept in a separate DVMRP routing table shown in Example 9-7, but it is still PIM on the Cisco router that makes the multicast forwarding decisions. DVMRP Graft messages are sent and received normally, but it is the handling of Prunes and Probes that makes the Cisco IOS Software implementation of DVMRP different from a full implementation.

Example 9-6   *This Router Is Receiving DVMRP Probe Messages on Interface E0 from Neighbor 10.224.1.1*

```
Godzilla#debug ip dvmrp detail
DVMRP debugging is on
Godzilla#
DVMRP: Received Probe on Ethernet0 from 10.224.1.1
DVMRP: Aging routes, 0 entries expired
DVMRP: Received Probe on Ethernet0 from 10.224.1.1
DVMRP: Aging routes, 0 entries expired
DVMRP: Received Probe on Ethernet0 from 10.224.1.1
DVMRP: Aging routes, 0 entries expired
```

Example 9-7   show ip dvmrp route *Command Displays DVMRP-Specific Route Information*

```
Godzilla#show ip dvmrp route
DVMRP Routing Table - 7 entries
10.224.2.0/24 [0/1] uptime 00:04:21, expires 00:02:38
```

```
    via 10.224.1.1, Ethernet0, [version mrouted 3.255] [flags: GPM]
10.224.3.0/24 [0/1] uptime 00:04:21, expires 00:02:38
    via 10.224.1.1, Ethernet0, [version mrouted 3.255] [flags: GPM]
10.224.4.0/24 [0/1] uptime 00:04:21, expires 00:02:38
    via 10.224.1.1, Ethernet0, [version mrouted 3.255] [flags: GPM]
10.224.5.0/24 [0/1] uptime 00:04:21, expires 00:02:38
    via 10.224.1.1, Ethernet0, [version mrouted 3.255] [flags: GPM]
10.224.6.0/24 [0/1] uptime 00:04:21, expires 00:02:38
    via 10.224.1.1, Ethernet0, [version mrouted 3.255] [flags: GPM]
172.16.70.0/24 [0/1] uptime 00:04:21, expires 00:02:38
    via 10.224.1.1, Ethernet0, [version mrouted 3.255] [flags: GPM]
192.168.50.0/24 [0/1] uptime 00:04:21, expires 00:02:38
    via 10.224.1.1, Ethernet0, [version mrouted 3.255] [flags: GPM]
```

The first difference between a full implementation of DVMRP and a Cisco IOS
Software-based implementation of DVMRP is the handling of Probes. As already mentioned, the detection of Probe messages is how a Cisco router discovers DVMRP neighbors. Suppose, however, that the DVMRP neighbor is on a multiaccess network and
more than one Cisco router is attached to the same network. If one of the Cisco routers
were to originate a Probe, the neighboring Cisco routers would mistakenly assume the
originator is a DVMRP router rather than a PIM router, as illustrated by Figure 9-3.
Therefore, Cisco routers listen for Probe messages but do not originate them.

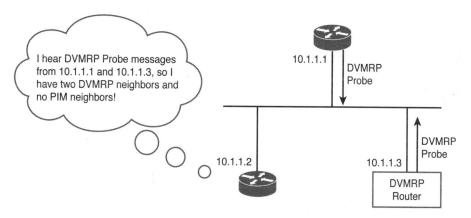

Figure 9-3 *If the Top Cisco Router Were to Generate a DVMRP Probe Message, the
Bottom Cisco Router Would Mistakenly Record the Originator as a DVMRP Neighbor;
Therefore, Cisco Routers Do Not Generate DVMRP Probes*

The second difference is the handling of Prune messages. Recall from the DVMRP discussion in Chapter 7 that a DVMRP router is required to maintain state for each downstream neighbor. If a downstream neighbor sends a Prune message, only that neighbor's
state is pruned. Traffic is still forwarded on the interface unless all DVMRP neighbors

send a Prune. This addresses the situation in which multiple downstream neighbors exist on a multiaccess network and prevents a Prune from one neighbor causing an unwanted Prune from another neighbor.

However, Cisco routers do not maintain DVMRP neighbor state. Therefore, to avoid the problem of one downstream neighbor's Prunes pruning traffic needed by another downstream neighbor, Cisco routers ignore DVMRP Prune messages received on multiaccess interfaces. On point-to-point interfaces, Prunes are received and processed normally because by definition there can be only one downstream neighbor. Cisco routers send Prune messages normally on both multiaccess and point-to-point interfaces on which DVMRP neighbors exist.

The difficulty, as this approach stands, should be apparent to you. If DVMRP routers connected across a multiaccess network to upstream Cisco routers cannot prune themselves, the Cisco routers forward unwanted multicast traffic into the DVMRP domain. The solution to the difficulty is, again, tunnels.

In Figure 9-4, a Cisco router is connected to two DVMRP routers across a multiaccess network. By creating tunnels to each of the DVMRP routers, Cisco IOS Software sees the DVMRP neighbors as connected via point-to-point links rather than a multiaccess link. The Cisco router then accepts prunes.

Example 9-8 shows the configuration for the Cisco router in Figure 9-4.

Example 9-8   *Configuring the Cisco Router in Figure 9-4 to Accept Prunes via Point-to-Point Links*

```
interface Tunnel0
 ip unnumbered Ethernet0
 ip pim sparse-dense-mode
 tunnel source Ethernet0
 tunnel destination 10.1.1.2
 tunnel mode dvmrp
!
interface Tunnel1
 no ip address
 ip pim sparse-dense-mode
 tunnel source Ethernet0
 tunnel destination 10.1.1.4
 tunnel mode dvmrp
!
interface Ethernet0
 ip address 10.1.1.1 255.255.255.0
```

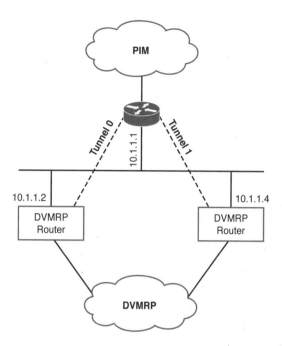

Figure 9-4 *Tunnels Are Used to Create Point-to-Point Connections to the DVMRP Routers Across the Multiaccess Network, so DVMRP Pruning Works Correctly*

The only significant difference from the earlier tunnel configurations you have seen is that the tunnel mode is set to DVMRP rather than the default GRE. As with the earlier tunnel configurations, PIM is configured on the tunnels but not on the physical interface. If there were also Cisco PIM routers on the multiaccess network, just configure PIM on the Ethernet interface so that the DVMRP routers connect over the tunnels and the PIM routers connect over the Ethernet.

Note   If multicast sources are reachable via the DVMRP routers, you must configure static mroutes to avoid RPF failures.

Inter-AS Multicasting

A challenge facing any multicast routing protocol (or any unicast routing protocol, for that matter) is scaling efficiently to the set of hosts requiring delivery of packets. You have seen how dense mode protocols such as PIM-DM and DVMRP do not scale well; by definition, the protocols assume that most hosts in the multicast domain are group members. PIM-SM, being a sparse mode protocol, scales better because it assumes most hosts in the multicast domain are not group members. Yet the assumption of both dense mode and sparse mode protocols is that they span a single domain. In other words, all the IP multicast routing protocols you have examined so far can be considered multicast IGPs.

How, then, can multicast packets be delivered across AS boundaries while maintaining the autonomy of each AS?

The PIM-SM Internet Draft begins to address the issue by defining a PIM Multicast Border Router (PMBR). The PMBR resides at the edge of a PIM domain and builds special branches to all RPs in the domain, as shown in Figure 9-5. Each branch is represented by a (*,*,RP) entry, where the two wildcard components represent all source and group addresses that map to that RP. When an RP receives traffic from a source, it forwards the traffic to the PMBR, which then forwards the traffic into the neighboring domain. The PMBR depends on the neighboring domain to send it prunes for any unwanted traffic, and the PMBR then sends prunes to the RP.

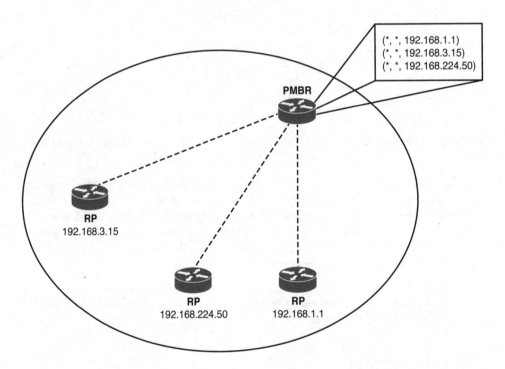

Figure 9-5 *A PIM Multicast Border Router Forms Multicast Branches to Each RP in Its Domain Called (*, *, RP) Branches. RPs Forward All Source Traffic to the PMBR Along These Branches*

The shortcoming of the PMBR concept is this flood-and-prune behavior. Actually, PMBRs were proposed primarily to connect PIM-SM domains to DVMRP domains. Because of the poor scalability inherent in the approach, Cisco IOS Software does not support PMBRs.

Accepting that PIM-SM is the de facto standard IP multicast routing protocol, the question of how to route multicast traffic between autonomous systems can be reduced to a question of how to route between PIM-SM domains. Two issues must be addressed:

- When a source is in one domain and group members are in other domains, RPF procedures must remain valid.

- To preserve autonomy, a domain cannot rely on an RP in another domain.

PIM-SM is protocol-independent, so the first issue seems easy to resolve. Just as PIM uses the unicast IGP routes to determine RPF interfaces within a domain, it can use BGP routes to determine RPF interfaces to sources in other autonomous systems. When moving traffic between domains, however, you may want your multicast traffic to use different links from your unicast traffic, as shown in Figure 9-6. If a multicast packet arrives on link A and BGP indicates that the unicast route to the packet's source is via link B, the RPF check fails. Static mroutes could prevent RPF problems, but they are obviously not practical on a large scale. Instead, BGP must be extended so that it can indicate whether an advertised prefix is to be used for unicast routing, multicast RPF checks, or both.

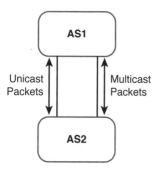

Figure 9-6 *Inter-AS Traffic Engineering Requirements May Dictate That Multicast Traffic Pass over a Link Separate from Unicast Traffic*

PIM can take advantage of existing extensions to BGP. The extended version of BGP is called *Multiprotocol BGP (MBGP)* as described in RFC 7606[2] and is introduced in Chapter 6, "Multiprotocol BGP."

Although the extensions were created to allow BGP to carry a diverse range of address families such as IPv6 and L3VPNs, the first widespread application of MBGP was to advertise multicast sources. As a result, the "M" in MBGP is frequently and inaccurately thought to represent "multicast" rather than "multiprotocol."

One common application of MBGP is for peer connections at NAPs or IXPs among service providers that have agreed to exchange multicast traffic. As Figure 9-7 shows, the autonomous systems may be peered for unicast traffic but must share a separate peering

---

[2] Tony Bates, Ravi Chandra, Dave Katz, and Yakov Rekhter, "RFC 7606: Multiprotocol Extensions for BGP-4," January 2007.

point for multicast traffic. Some prefixes will be advertised over both the unicast and multicast NAPs, so MBGP can differentiate multicast RPF paths from unicast paths.

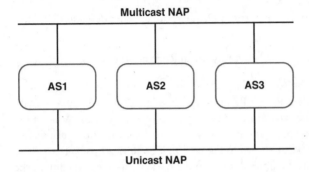

Figure 9-7 *MBGP Is Used When Separate Peering Points Are Required for Multicast and Unicast*

The second inter-AS PIM issue (to preserve autonomy, a domain cannot rely on an RP in another domain) stems from an AS not wanting to depend on an RP that it does not control. If each AS deploys its own RPs, however, there must be a protocol that each RP can use to share its source information with other RPs across AS boundaries and in turn discover sources known by other RPs, as shown in Figure 9-8. That protocol is the *Multicast Source Discovery Protocol (MSDP)*.[3]

The following two sections describe the MBGP extensions and the operation of MSDP.

Multiprotocol Extensions for BGP (MBGP)

RFC 2283 extends BGP for multiprotocol support by defining two new attributes:

- Multiprotocol Reachable NLRI, or MP_REACH_NLRI (type 14)
- Multiprotocol Unreachable NLRI, or MP_UNREACH_NLRI (type 15)

> **Note** See Chapter 2, "Introduction to Border Gateway Protocol 4," Table 2-7, for a more complete list of BGP attribute type codes.

Both attributes are optional, nontransitive. Recall from Chapter 2, that this means BGP speakers are not required to support the attributes, and BGP speakers that do not support the attributes do not pass them to their peers.

---

[3] Bill Fenner and David Meyer, "Multicast Source Discovery Protocol (MSDP)," RFC 3618, October 2003.

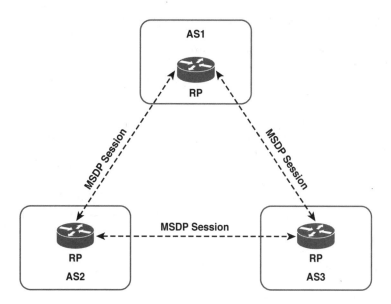

Figure 9-8 *Multicast Source Discovery Protocol Is Spoken Between RPs and Allows Each RP to Discover Sources Known by Other RPs*

The MP_REACH_NLRI attribute advertises feasible routes, and MP_UNREACH_NLRI withdraws feasible routes. The Network Layer Reachability Information (NLRI) contained in the attributes is the protocol-specific destination information. When MBGP is used for IP multicast, the NLRI is always an IPv4 prefix describing one or more multicast sources. Remember that PIM routers do not use this information for packet forwarding but only for determining the RPF interface toward a particular source. These two new attributes provide the capability of signaling to a BGP peer whether a particular prefix is to be used for unicast routing, multicast RPF, or both.

The MP_REACH_NLRI consists of one or more [Address Family Information, Next Hop Information, NLRI] triples. The MP_UNREACH_NLRI consists of one or more [Address Family Information, Unfeasible Routes Length, Withdrawn Routes] triples.

> **Note**   The complete format of the MP_REACH_NLRI is more complicated than is indicated here—some fields are irrelevant to IP multicast. For a complete description, see RFC 2283.

The Address Family Information consists of an Address Family Identifier (AFI) and a Subsequent AFI (Sub-AFI). The AFI for IPv4 is 1, and the AFI for IPv6 is 2, so it is always set to 1 for IPv4 multicast and 2 for IPv6 multicast. The sub-AFI describes whether the NLRI is to be used for unicast forwarding (1) or multicast forwarding (2).

Operation of Multicast Source Discovery Protocol (MSDP)

The purpose of MSDP is, as the name states, to discover multicast sources in other PIM domains. The advantage of running MSDP is that your own RPs exchange source information with RPs in other domains; your group members do not have to be directly dependent on another domain's RP.

> **Note**   You will see in some subsequent case studies how MSDP can prove useful for sharing source information within a single domain, too.

MSDP uses TCP (port 639) for its peering connections. As with BGP, using point-to-point TCP peering means that each peer must be explicitly configured. When a PIM DR registers a source with its RP, as shown in Figure 9-9, the RP sends a Source Active (SA) message to all its MSDP peers.

The SA contains the following:

- Address of the multicast source

- Group address to which the source is sending

- IP address of the originating RP

Each MSDP peer that receives the SA floods the SA to all its own peers downstream from the originator. In some cases, such as the RPs in AS6 and AS7 of Figure 9-9, an RP may receive a copy of an SA from more than one MSDP peer. To prevent looping, the RP consults the BGP next-hop database to determine the next hop toward the SA's originator. If both MBGP and unicast BGP are configured, MBGP is checked first, and then unicast BGP. That next-hop neighbor is the *RPF peer* for the originator, and SAs received from the originator on any interface other than the interface to the RPF peer are dropped. The SA flooding process is, therefore, called *peer RPF flooding*. Because of the peer RPF flooding mechanism, BGP or MBGP must be running with MSDP.

When an RP receives an SA, it checks to see whether there are any members of the SA's group in its domain by checking to see whether there are interfaces on the group's (*, G) outgoing interface list. If there are no group members, the RP does nothing. If there are group members, the RP sends an (S, G) join toward the source. As a result, a branch of the source tree is constructed across AS boundaries to the RP (a Rendezvous Point Tree or RPT). As multicast packets arrive at the RP, they are forwarded down its own shared tree to the group members in the RP's domain. The members' DRs then have the option of joining the RPT to the source using standard PIM-SM procedures.

The originating RP continues to send periodic SAs for the (S, G) every 60 seconds for as long as the source sends packets to the group. When an RP receives an SA, it has the option to cache the message. Suppose, for example, that an RP receives an SA for (172.16.5.4, 228.1.2.3) from originating RP 10.5.4.3. The RP consults its mroute table and finds no active members for group 228.1.2.3, so it passes the SA message to its peers downstream of 10.5.4.3 without caching the message. If a host in the domain then sends a join to the RP for group 228.1.2.3, the RP adds the interface toward the host to the outgoing interface list of its (*, 224.1.2.3) entry. Because the previous SA was not cached, however, the RP has no knowledge of the source. Therefore, the RP must wait until the next SA message is received before it can initiate a join to the source.

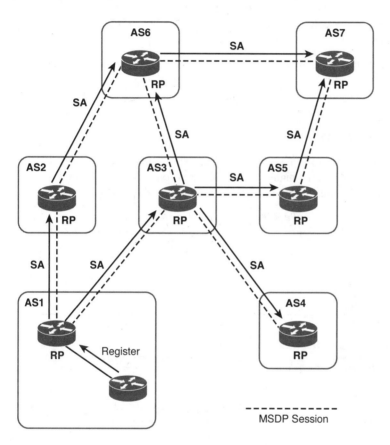

Figure 9-9   *RPs Advertise Sources to Their MSDP Neighbors with Source Active Messages*

If, however, the RP is caching SAs, the router has an entry for (172.16.5.4, 228.1.2.3) and can join the source tree as soon as a host requests a join. The trade-off here is that in exchange for reducing the join latency, memory is consumed caching SA messages that may or may not be needed. If the RP belongs to a large MSDP mesh, and there are large numbers of SAs, the memory consumption can be significant.

By default, Cisco IOS Software does not cache SAs. You can enable caching with the command **ip msdp cache-sa-state**. To help alleviate possible memory stress, you can link the command to an extended access list that specifies what (S, G) pairs to cache.

If an RP has an MSDP peer that is caching SAs, you can reduce the join latency at the RP without turning on caching by using *SA Request* and *SA Response* messages. When a host requests a join to a particular group, the RP sends an SA Request message to its caching peer(s). If a peer has cached source information for the group in question, it sends the information to the requesting RP with an SA Response message. The requesting RP uses the information in the SA Response but does not forward the message to any other peers. If a noncaching RP receives an SA Request, it sends an error message back to the requestor.

To enable a Cisco router to send SA Request messages, use the **ip msdp sa-request** command to specify the IP address or name of a caching peer. You can use the command multiple times to specify multiple caching peers.

MSDP Message Formats

MSDP messages are carried in TCP segments. When two routers are configured as MSDP peers, the router with the higher IP address listens on TCP port 639, and the router with the lower IP address attempts an active connect to port 639.

The MSDP messages use a TLV (Type/Length/Value) format and may be one of five types, as shown in Table 9-4. The following sections detail the format of each message type.

Table 9-4 *MSDP Message Types*

Type	Message
1	Source Active
2	Source Active Request
3	Source Active Response
4	Keepalive
5	Reserved (Notification in earlier MSDP implementations)

Source Active TLV

When an MSDP RP receives a PIM Register message from an IP multicast source, it sends a Source Active message to its peers. Figure 9-10 shows the MSDP Source Active TLV format. SA messages are subsequently sent every 60 seconds until the source is no longer active. Multiple (S, G) entries can be advertised by a single SA.

The fields for the MSDP Source Active TLV format are defined as follows:

- *Entry Count* specifies the number of (S, G) entries being advertised by the specified RP address.

- *RP Address* is the IP address of the originating RP.

- *Reserved* is set to all zeroes.

- *Sprefix Length* specifies the prefix length of the associated source address. This length is always 32.

- *Group Address* is the multicast IP address to which the associated source is sending multicast packets.

- *Source Address* is the IP address of the active source.

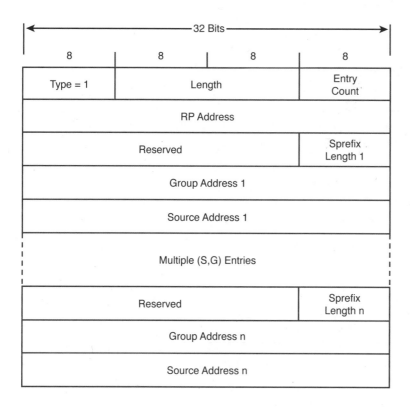

Figure 9-10 *MSDP Source Active TLV Format*

Source Active Request TLV

SA Request Messages, the format of which is shown in Figure 9-11, are used to request (S, G) information from MSPD peers that are caching SA state. SA Request messages should be sent only to caching peers (noncaching peers return an error notification) and are sent only by RPs that are explicitly configured to do so.

The fields for the MSDP Source Active Request TLV format are defined as follows:

- *Gprefix Length* specifies the length of the group address prefix.

- *Group Address Prefix* specifies the group address for which source information is requested.

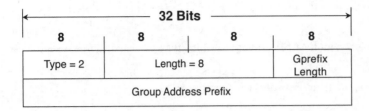

Figure 9-11   *MSDP Source Active Request TLV Format*

Source Active Response TLV

SA Response messages, the format of which is shown in Figure 9-12, are sent by a caching peer in response to an SA Request message. They provide the requesting peer the source address and RP address associated with the specified group address. The format is the same as the SA message.

```
|<------------------------- 32 Bits -------------------------->|
        8           8            8            8
  +-----------+------------------------+--------------+
  |  Type = 3 |        Length          | Entry        |
  |           |                        | Count        |
  +-----------+------------------------+--------------+
  |                RP Address                         |
  +-----------------------------------+--------------+
  |            Reserved                | Sprefix      |
  |                                    | Length       |
  +-----------------------------------+--------------+
  |                Group Address                     |
  +--------------------------------------------------+
  |                Source Address                    |
  +--------------------------------------------------+
```

Figure 9-12   *MSPD Source Active Response TLV Format*

Keepalive TLV

The active side (the peer with the lower IP address) of an MSDP connection tracks the passive side of the connection with a 75-second Keepalive timer. If no MSDP message is received from the passive side before the Keepalive timer expires, the active peer resets the TCP connection. If an MSDP message is received, the timer is reset. If the passive peer has no other MSDP messages to send, it sends a Keepalive message to prevent the active peer from resetting the connection. As Figure 9-13 shows, the Keepalive message is a simple 24bit TLV consisting of a type and length field.

Notification TLV

A Notification message, used in earlier versions of MSDP but now deprecated, is sent when an error is detected. Figure 9-14 shows the Notification message format.

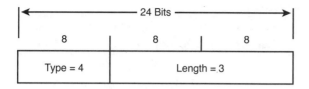

Figure 9-13   *MSDP Keepalive TLV Format*

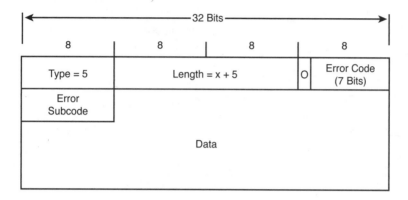

Figure 9-14   *(Now Deprecated) MSDP Notification TLV Format*

The fields for the MSDP Notification TLV format are defined as follows:

- *Length = x + 5* is the length of the TLV, where *x* is the length of the data field and 5 is the first 5 octets.

- *O* is the *open bit*. If this bit is cleared, the connection must be closed upon receipt of the Notification. Table 9-6 shows the states of the O bit for different error sub-codes. MC indicates *must close*; the O bit is always cleared. CC indicates *can close*; the O bit might be cleared.

- *Error code* is a 7-bit unsigned integer indicating the Notification type. Table 9-6 lists the error codes.

- *Error Subcode* is an 8-bit unsigned integer that may offer more details about the error code. If the error code has no subcode, this field is zero. Table 9-5 shows the possible error subcodes associated with the error codes.

- *Data* is a variable-length field containing information specific to the error code and error subcode. The various data fields are not covered in this chapter; see the MSDP Internet Draft for more information on the possible contents of this field.

Table 9-5 *MSDP Error Codes and Subcodes*

Error Code	Error Code Description	Error Subcode	Error Subcode Description	O-Bit State
1	Message header error	0	Unspecific	MC
		2	Bad message length	MC
		3	Bad message type	CC
2	SA Request error	0	Unspecific	MC
		1	Does not cache SA	MC
		2	Invalid group	MC
3	SA message/SA response error	0	Unspecific	MC
		1	Invalid entry count	CC
		2	Invalid RP address	MC
		3	Invalid group address	MC
		4	Invalid source address	MC
		5	Invalid sprefix length	MC
		6	Looping SA (self is RP)	MC
		7	Unknown encapsulation	MC
		8	Administrative scope boundary violated	MC
4	Hold timer expired	0	Unspecific	MC
5	Finite state machine error			
	0	Unspecific	MC	
		1	Unexpected message type FSM error	MC
6	Notification	0	Unspecific	MC
7	Cease	0	Unspecific	MC

Case Study: Configuring MBGP

Figure 9-15 depicts three autonomous systems. AS200 is advertising unicast prefixes 172.16.226.0/24 and 172.16.227.0/24 to transit AS100 and is used for normal inter-AS routing. AS200 also has several multicast sources. These are hosts at 172.16.224.1 and 172.16.225.50. In addition, several multicast sources are on subnet 172.16.227.0/24, and that prefix is advertised not only as a unicast prefix but also as a multicast source prefix.

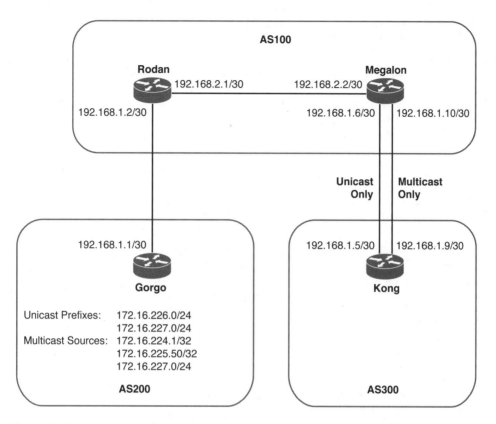

Figure 9-15 *AS200 Is Advertising Several Prefixes and Addresses; Some Are Unicast, Some Are Multicast, and One Is Both*

Example 9-9 shows the configurations of Gorgo and Rodan referred to in Figure 9-15. Remember from Chapter 6 that you must also enable IP multicast with the **ip multicast-routing** statement.

Example 9-9 *MBGP Configurations of Gorgo and Rodan Referred to in Figure 9-15*

```
Gorgo
router bgp 200
 no synchronization
 network 172.16.226.0 mask 255.255.255.0
 network 172.16.227.0 mask 255.255.255.0
 neighbor 192.168.1.2 remote-as 100
 no auto-summary
 !
 address-family ipv4 multicast
 neighbor 192.168.1.2 activate
 network 172.16.224.1 mask 255.255.255.255
```

```
network 172.16.225.50 mask 255.255.255.255
network 172.16.227.0 mask 255.255.255.0
exit-address-family
```

```
Rodan
router bgp 100
 no synchronization
 neighbor 192.168.1.1 remote-as 200
 neighbor 192.168.254.2 remote-as 100
 neighbor 192.168.254.2 update-source Loopback0
 neighbor 192.168.254.2 next-hop-self
 !
 address-family ipv4 multicast
 neighbor 192.168.1.1 activate
 neighbor 192.168.254.2 activate
 neighbor 192.168.254.2 next-hop-self
 exit-address-family
```

The unicast portion of both routers' BGP configurations is no different from the configurations you observed in Chapter 3, "BGP and NLRI." Neighbors and their AS numbers are identified, as are the two unicast prefixes that Gorgo is to advertise into AS100.

Note   This chapter assumes you are already familiar with unicast BGP configuration. If some of the IBGP tools such as next-hop-self and update-source are not clear to you, you are encouraged to review Chapter 3.

MBGP is activated with the **address-family ipv4 multicast** command. Recall from the section "Multiprotocol Extensions for BGP (MBGP)" that MBGP uses two new route attributes—MP_REACH_NLRI and MP_UNREACH_NLRI—and that the attributes' Address Family Indicator (AFI) code for IPv4 is 1. The **multicast** keyword sets the attributes' Sub-AFI to multicast. Following the **address-family** command, MBGP is configured similarly to unicast BGP. MBGP neighbors are identified, and the prefixes to be advertised as multicast are identified. The **activate** keyword shows that MBGP is to be activated for that neighbor. The peer's AS number is specified only under BGP, not MBGP. Notice that IBGP configurations, such as **next-hop-self**, are used under MBGP just as they are with BGP. You also can configure policies separately for MBGP neighbors. The final command, **exit-address-family**, is entered automatically by Cisco IOS Software to mark the end of the MBGP configuration stanzas.

Enabling **address-family ipv4 multicast** implicitly enables the **address-family ipv4 unicast** command. Although the command is never displayed in the configuration, it is applied to the unicast BGP configuration. Its result is that the prefixes specified under that configuration section are given the MP_REACH_NLRI attribute and are assigned a unicast Sub-AFI. Notice that the prefix 172.16.227.0/24 appears in Gorgo's configuration under both BGP and MBGP. This prefix is then advertised as both unicast and multicast (Sub-AFI = 3).

In Example 9-10, the **show ip bgp ipv4** command shows the results of the configurations. First, the **unicast** keyword is used, then the **multicast** keyword is used, and the prefixes whose Sub-AFI matches the keyword display. Notice again that 172.16.227.0/24 is included in both displays because it has been configured as both a unicast and a multicast prefix.

> **Note**   The output of **show ip bgp ipv4** unicast is the same as the output of **show ip bgp**.

Example 9-10   show ip bgp ipv4 *Command Displays Prefixes According to Their Sub-AFI Values*

```
Rodan#show ip bgp ipv4 unicast
BGP table version is 7, local router ID is 192.168.254.1
Status codes: s suppressed, d damped, h history, * valid, > best, i - internal
Origin codes: i - IGP, e - EGP, ? - incomplete

   Network          Next Hop          Metric LocPrf Weight Path
*> 172.16.226.0/24  192.168.1.1            0             0 200 i
*> 172.16.227.0/24  192.168.1.1            0             0 200 i


Rodan#show ip bgp ipv4 multicast
BGP table version is 10, local router ID is 192.168.254.1
Status codes: s suppressed, d damped, h history, * valid, > best, i - internal
Origin codes: i - IGP, e - EGP, ? - incomplete

   Network          Next Hop          Metric LocPrf Weight Path
*> 172.16.224.1/32  192.168.1.1            0             0 200 i
*> 172.16.225.50/32 192.168.1.1            0             0 200 i
*> 172.16.227.0/24  192.168.1.1            0             0 200 i
Rodan#
```

The configurations of Megalon and Kong referred to in Figure 9-15 are a bit more complicated because separate links are used for unicast BGP and for MBGP. Example 9-11 shows the configurations for these two routers.

Example 9-11 *Configuring Megalon and Kong to Use Separate Data Links for Multicast and Unicast*

```
Megalon
router bgp 100
 no synchronization
 no bgp default ipv4-unicast
 neighbor 192.168.1.5 remote-as 300
 neighbor 192.168.1.5 activate
 neighbor 192.168.1.9 remote-as 300
 neighbor 192.168.254.1 remote-as 100
 neighbor 192.168.254.1 update-source Loopback0
 neighbor 192.168.254.1 activate
 neighbor 192.168.254.1 next-hop-self
 no auto-summary
 !
 address-family ipv4 multicast
 neighbor 192.168.1.9 activate
 neighbor 192.168.254.1 activate
 exit-address-family
```

```
Kong
router bgp 300
 no synchronization
 no bgp default ipv4-unicast
 neighbor 192.168.1.6 remote-as 100
 neighbor 192.168.1.6 activate
 neighbor 192.168.1.10 remote-as 100
 no auto-summary
 !
 address-family ipv4 multicast
 neighbor 192.168.1.10 activate
 exit-address-family
```

The MBGP configurations show that only the 192.168.1.8/30 subnet is used for MBGP peering, and some new commands are under the unicast BGP section. Remember that when the **address-family ipv4 multicast** command is invoked, the **address-family ipv4 unicast** command is invoked automatically and implicitly. For subnet 192.168.1.8/30, unicast BGP traffic is unwanted. Therefore, the command **no ip default ipv4-unicast** prevents this automatic behavior. Then, the **neighbor activate** command explicitly enables unicast BGP on the wanted links. Notice that the 192.168.254.0/30 and 192.168.1.4/30 subnets are activated for unicast, but the 192.168.1.8/30 subnet is not. This link has only the AS number specified under BGP so that peering can occur.

Example 9-12 shows the results of the configurations in Example 9-11. The output here looks similar to that in Example 9-10, in that the unicast and multicast prefixes are correctly classified. In this case, however, the next-hop address of the unicast prefixes is 192.168.1.6, and the next-hop address (RPF neighbor) of the multicast prefixes is 192.168.1.10.

Example 9-12 *AS300 Received the Prefixes Advertised by AS200, Using the Correct Next-Hop Addresses for the Unicast-Only and Multicast-Only Links Between Kong and Megalon*

```
Kong#show ip bgp ipv4 unicast
BGP table version is 7, local router ID is 10.254.254.1
Status codes: s suppressed, d damped, h history, * valid, > best, i - internal
Origin codes: i - IGP, e - EGP, ? - incomplete


   Network          Next Hop          Metric LocPrf Weight Path
*> 172.16.226.0/24  192.168.1.6                         0 100 200 i
*> 172.16.227.0/24  192.168.1.6                         0 100 200 i


Kong#show ip bgp ipv4 multicast
BGP table version is 10, local router ID is 10.254.254.1
Status codes: s suppressed, d damped, h history, * valid, > best, i - internal
Origin codes: i - IGP, e - EGP, ? - incomplete


   Network          Next Hop          Metric LocPrf Weight Path
*> 172.16.224.1/32  192.168.1.10                        0 100 200 i
*> 172.16.225.50/32 192.168.1.10                        0 100 200 i
*> 172.16.227.0/24  192.168.1.10                        0 100 200 i
Kong#
```

Example 9-13 shows the practical application of BGP versus MBGP advertisements. Using the 172.16.227.0/24 prefix, which is advertised both as unicast and multicast, a route lookup is performed for 172.16.227.1. The display shows that the route carries a next-hop address of 192.168.1.6, which is the unicast-only link referred to in Figure 9-15. Next, an RPF lookup is performed on the same address. That lookup returns a next-hop address of 192.168.1.10, the multicast-only link. So the same address references two different links, depending on the function for which the address is used.

Example 9-13   *An IP Route Lookup for 172.16.227.1 Shows the Next Hop to Be 192.168.1.6, but an RPF Lookup of the Same Address Shows a Next Hop of 192.168.1.10*

```
Kong#show ip route 172.16.227.1
Routing entry for 172.16.227.0/24
  Known via "bgp 300", distance 20, metric 0
  Tag 100, type external
  Last update from 192.168.1.6 04:10:21 ago
  Routing Descriptor Blocks:
  * 192.168.1.6, from 192.168.1.6, 04:10:21 ago
      Route metric is 0, traffic share count is 1
      AS Hops 2

Kong#show ip rpf 172.16.227.1
RPF information for ? (172.16.227.1)
  RPF interface: Serial1
  RPF neighbor: ? (192.168.1.10)
  RPF route/mask: 172.16.227.0/24
  RPF type: mbgp
  RPF recursion count: 0
  Doing distance-preferred lookups across tables
Kong#
```

It is worth emphasizing one last time that MBGP does not affect the forwarding of multicast traffic. Further configuration is needed in a situation such as the parallel links referred to in Figure 9-15 to force multicast traffic over the multicast-only link. MBGP just allows the dissemination of RPF information across AS boundaries.

Case Study: Configuring MSDP

Figure 9-16 again shows the routers from the preceding case study. Here, the four routers are also RPs for their respective autonomous systems, and the illustration shows their RP addresses.

MSDP is enabled quite simply with the command **ip msdp peer**, specifying the peer's IP address. Example 9-14 shows the MSDP configurations for the four routers in Figure 9-16.

Example 9-14   *Configuring MSDP Sessions Between the Four RPs referred to in Figure 9-16*

```
Gorgo
ip msdp peer 192.168.1.2

Kong
ip msdp peer 192.168.1.10
```

```
Rodan

ip msdp peer 192.168.1.1

ip msdp peer 192.168.254.2 connect-source Loopback0
```

```
Megalon

ip msdp peer 192.168.254.1 connect-source Loopback0

ip msdp peer 192.168.1.9
```

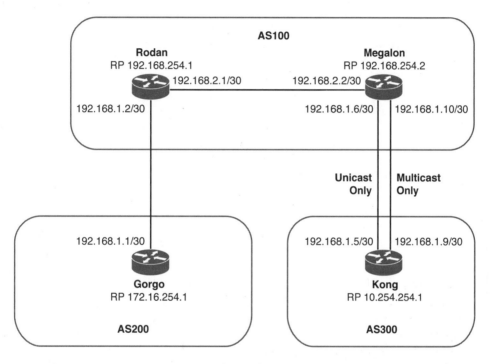

Figure 9-16 *MSDP Sessions Are Configured Between the Four RPs*

The peering between Gorgo and Rodan, and between Kong and Megalon, is quite straightforward. Each has only a single link over which to peer, so the session is configured between the two physical interface addresses. Between Rodan and Megalon, however, the peering is between loopback addresses. As with IBGP peering, MSDP sessions between loopback interfaces provide more resiliency. If the link shown between Rodan and Megalon referred to in Figure 7-15 should fail, and if there is another path between the routers (not shown in the illustration), the TCP session can be rerouted. By default, the source address of the TCP packets carrying the MSDP session is the address of the originating physical interface. For peering to an address that is not part of a directly connected subnet, the **connect-source** option changes the default source address.

Example 9-15 displays the status of Megalon's two MSDP sessions using the **show ip msdp peer** command. Such expected information as the state of the connection, uptime, and messages sent/received appears.

Example 9-15   show ip msdp peer *Command Displays the Status of MSDP Peering Sessions*

```
Megalon#show ip msdp peer
MSDP Peer 192.168.254.1 (?), AS 100
Description:
  Connection status:
    State: Up, Resets: 0, Connection source: Loopback0 (192.168.254.2)
    Uptime(Downtime): 3d22h, Messages sent/received: 5683/5677
    Output messages discarded: 0
    Connection and counters cleared 3d22h    ago
  SA Filtering:
    Input filter: none, route-map: none
    Output filter: none, route-map: none
  SA-Requests:
    Input filter: none
    Sending SA-Requests to peer: disabled
  Peer ttl threshold: 0
  Input queue size: 0, Output queue size: 0
MSDP Peer 192.168.1.9 (?), AS 300
Description:
  Connection status:
    State: Up, Resets: 0, Connection source: none configured
    Uptime(Downtime): 3d22h, Messages sent/received: 5674/5694
    Output messages discarded: 0
    Connection and counters cleared 3d22h    ago
  SA Filtering:
    Input filter: none, route-map: none
    Output filter: none, route-map: none
  SA-Requests:
    Input filter: none
    Sending SA-Requests to peer: disabled
  Peer ttl threshold: 0
  Input queue size: 0, Output queue size: 0
Megalon#
```

Example 9-14 also shows fields for displaying filters that might have been configured for SA and SA Request messages. You have several options for filtering at an MSDP router to control and scope MSDP activity. You can do the following:

Control the local sources that are allowed to register with the RP.

Control the SA messages the RP sends to and receives from its MSDP peers.

Control the SA Request messages the RP sends to and receives from its peers.

Other options for larger-scale MSDP environments are the addition of descriptions for each peer and configurable TTL values for the MSDP messages. Example 9-16 shows a more elaborate configuration for router Megalon referred to in Figure 9-16.

Note The configuration shown here is for demonstration purposes only. No argument is made as to the practicality of the configuration.

Example 9-16 *A More-Complex MSDP Configuration*

```
ip pim rp-address 192.168.254.2
ip msdp peer 192.168.254.1 connect-source Loopback0
ip msdp description 192.168.254.1 Rodan in AS 100
ip msdp sa-filter out 192.168.254.1 list 101
ip msdp filter-sa-request 192.168.254.1 list 1
ip msdp sa-request 192.168.254.1
ip msdp ttl-threshold 192.168.254.1 5
ip msdp peer 192.168.1.9
ip msdp description 192.168.1.9 Kong in AS 300
ip msdp sa-filter in 192.168.1.9 list 101
ip msdp sa-filter out 192.168.1.9 list 103
ip msdp sa-request 192.168.1.9
ip msdp ttl-threshold 192.168.1.9 2
ip msdp cache-sa-state list 101
ip msdp redistribute list 102
!
access-list 1 permit 229.50.0.0 0.0.255.255
access-list 101 permit ip 10.254.0.0 0.0.255.255 224.0.0.0 31.255.255.255
access-list 102 permit ip 192.168.224.0 0.0.0.255 224.0.0.0 31.255.255.255
access-list 103 permit ip 172.16.0.0 0.0.255.255 230.0.0.0 0.255.255.255
access-list 103 permit ip 192.168.224.0 0.0.0.255 224.0.0.0 31.255.255.255
```

The two statements enabling MSDP to Rodan and Kong, referred to in Example 9-14, remain. But added to the configuration is a text description for each peer, using the **ip msdp description** command. The description always appears directly after the **ip msdp peer** command for a specific peer, and it is obviously useful when there are large numbers of MSDP peers.

SA caching is enabled with **ip msdp cache-sa-state**, and in this configuration, an optional access list is referenced. Access list 101 specifies that Megalon will cache only SA messages for (S, G) pairs whose source address begins with 10.254.0.0/16. The group can be any multicast address (224.0.0.0/3).

An **ip msdp sa-request** statement is entered for each of the two peers to further reduce join latency. If the router receives a join message for a particular group, it sends an SA Request message to the two neighbors. The assumption here, as previously discussed, is that the two neighbors are configured to cache SA messages.

SA Requests to Rodan (192.168.254.1) are further restricted with the **ip msdp filter-sa-request** command. This filter references access list 1, which allows only 229.50.0.0/16. The result is that Megalon requests only source information from Rodan for groups whose addresses fall under prefix 229.50.0.0/16.

Next, Megalon is configured to send only SA messages for a subset of the possible sources that might send PIM-SM Register messages to it. The **ip msdp redistribute** statement references access list 102, which in turn permits source prefixes of 192.168.224.0/24 and group address prefixes of 224.0.0.0/3 (all multicast groups). Any source can still register with the RP, within the limits of the RP's PIM-SM configuration, but only those sources whose first 24 address bits are 192.168.224 are advertised in SA messages.

The forwarding of SA messages to MSDP peers is regulated with the **ip msdp sa-filter out** command. This filter applies to all SA messages, whether locally originated or received from another MSDP peer, whereas the **ip msdp redistribute** command applies only to locally originated SA messages. Megalon has two of these statements. For neighbor Rodan (192.168.254.1), only messages from source prefix 10.254.0.0/16 are forwarded, as specified by access list 101. Megalon sends to Kong (192.168.1.9) only SA messages that are permitted by access list 103. This access list permits messages whose source prefix is 172.16.0.0/16 and whose group addresses belong to 230.0.0.0/8, or sources whose prefix is 192.168.224.0/24 originating packets for any multicast group.

You can also filter incoming SA messages with the **ip msdp sa-filter in** command. Using this command, Megalon accepts SA messages from Kong only if the (S, G) pair is permitted by access list 101. Notice that this is the same constraint that is placed on outgoing SA messages to Rodan.

Finally, the TTL values of the MSDP messages are regulated with the **ip msdp ttl-threshold** command. The TTL of messages sent to Rodan is set to 5, whereas the TTL of messages sent to Kong is set to 2.

Example 9-17 shows the results of this configuration. Compare this display with the display in Example 9-15, and you can see the descriptions, filters, and TTL thresholds that have changed.

Example 9-17 *This Display Reflects the Changes Made to Megalon's MSDP Configuration*

```
Megalon#show ip msdp peer
MSDP Peer 192.168.254.1 (?), AS 100
Description: Rodan in AS 100
  Connection status:
    State: Up, Resets: 0, Connection source: Loopback0 (192.168.254.2)
    Uptime(Downtime): 4d14h, Messages sent/received: 6624/6617
    Output messages discarded: 0
    Connection and counters cleared 4d14h    ago
  SA Filtering:
    Input filter: none, route-map: none
    Output filter: 101, route-map: none
  SA-Requests:
    Input filter: 1
    Sending SA-Requests to peer: enabled
  Peer ttl threshold: 5
  Input queue size: 0, Output queue size: 0
MSDP Peer 192.168.1.9 (?), AS 300
Description: Kong in AS 300
  Connection status:
    State: Up, Resets: 0, Connection source: none configured
    Uptime(Downtime): 4d14h, Messages sent/received: 6614/6634
    Output messages discarded: 0
    Connection and counters cleared 4d14h    ago
  SA Filtering:
    Input filter: 101, route-map: none
    Output filter: 102, route-map: none
  SA-Requests:
    Input filter: none
    Sending SA-Requests to peer: enabled
  Peer ttl threshold: 2
  Input queue size: 0, Output queue size: 0
Megalon#
```

In addition to access lists, you can link incoming and outgoing SA filters to route maps for even better granularity of control and application of policy. You also can use route maps with MSDP redistribution, as well as path access lists.

Case Study: MSDP Mesh Groups

In the preceding case study, routers Rodan and Megalon are RPs in the same AS. Large multicast domains can frequently have many RPs to share the workload or to localize multicast trees. Although MSPD has been presented so far as a tool for sharing inter-AS source information, it also proves useful when there are multiple RPs in a single domain, and sources always register to certain RPs but members throughout the domain must find any source.

Every RP in the domain commonly has an MSDP peering session to every other RP in the domain, for redundancy and robustness. Figure 9-17 shows an example. The four RPs in the illustration are in the same AS, and each is peered to the other three. The four routers may or may not be directly connected and are probably physically remote from each other.

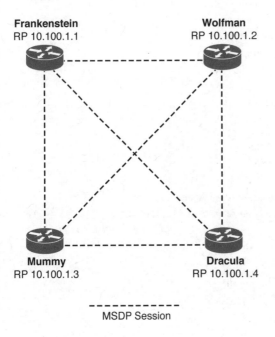

Figure 9-17 *A Full MSDP Mesh Exists Between These Four Routers*

Example 9-18 shows the configurations of the four routers in Figure 9-17.

Example 9-18 *Configuring MSDP on the Four Routers in Figure 9-17*

```
Frankenstein
ip pim rp-address 10.100.1.1
ip msdp peer 10.100.1.3 connect-source Loopback0
ip msdp description 10.100.1.3 to Mummy
ip msdp peer 10.100.1.2 connect-source Loopback0
ip msdp description 10.100.1.2 to Wolfman
ip msdp peer 10.100.1.4 connect-source Loopback0
ip msdp description 10.100.1.4 to Dracula
```

```
Wolfman
ip pim rp-address 10.100.1.2
ip msdp peer 10.100.1.1 connect-source Loopback0
ip msdp description 10.100.1.1 to Frankenstein
ip msdp peer 10.100.1.3 connect-source Loopback0
ip msdp description 10.100.1.3 to Mummy
ip msdp peer 10.100.1.4 connect-source Loopback0
ip msdp description 10.100.1.4 to Dracula
```

```
Mummy
ip pim rp-address 10.100.1.3
ip msdp peer 10.100.1.1 connect-source Loopback0
ip msdp description 10.100.1.1 to Frankenstein
ip msdp peer 10.100.1.2 connect-source Loopback0
ip msdp description 10.100.1.2 to Wolfman
ip msdp peer 10.100.1.4 connect-source Loopback0
ip msdp description 10.100.1.4 to Dracula
```

```
Dracula
ip pim rp-address 10.100.1.4
ip msdp peer 10.100.1.1 connect-source Loopback0
ip msdp description 10.100.1.1 to Frankenstein
ip msdp peer 10.100.1.2 connect-source Loopback0
ip msdp description 10.100.1.2 to Wolfman
ip msdp peer 10.100.1.3 connect-source Loopback0
ip msdp description 10.100.1.3 to Mummy
```

The problem with the configuration as it stands is that an SA message generated by one router is flooded by all the other routers, causing large numbers of peer RPF flooding failures and resulting MSDP notification messages. If every RP has an MSDP connection to every other RP, however, no flooding is necessary. Every RP receives a copy of every SA directly from the originator. To remedy the flooding problem, an MSDP mesh group is built.

An MSDP mesh group is a set of fully meshed MSDP peers such as the ones shown referred to in Figure 9-17, but no transiting of SA messages takes place. That is, when an RP receives an SA from a peer, it does not forward the message to any other peer.

Mesh groups are configured with the **ip msdp mesh-group** command. The group is given an arbitrary name (so that one RP can belong to more than one mesh group, if necessary), and the members of the mesh group are specified. The configurations in Example 9-19 add the RPs in Figure 9-17 to a mesh group named Boogeymen.

Example 9-19   *Adding the RPs Referred to in Figure 9-17 to Mesh Group Boogeymen*

```
Frankenstein
ip pim rp-address 10.100.1.1
ip msdp peer 10.100.1.3 connect-source Loopback0
ip msdp description 10.100.1.3 to Mummy
ip msdp peer 10.100.1.2 connect-source Loopback0
ip msdp description 10.100.1.2 to Wolfman
ip msdp peer 10.100.1.4 connect-source Loopback0
ip msdp description 10.100.1.4 to Dracula
ip msdp mesh-group Boogeymen 10.100.1.3
ip msdp mesh-group Boogeymen 10.100.1.2
ip msdp mesh-group Boogeymen 10.100.1.4
```

```
Wolfman
ip pim rp-address 10.100.1.2
ip msdp peer 10.100.1.1 connect-source Loopback0
ip msdp description 10.100.1.1 to Frankenstein
ip msdp peer 10.100.1.3 connect-source Loopback0
ip msdp description 10.100.1.3 to Mummy
ip msdp peer 10.100.1.4 connect-source Loopback0
ip msdp description 10.100.1.4 to Dracula
ip msdp mesh-group Boogeymen 10.100.1.1
ip msdp mesh-group Boogeymen 10.100.1.3
ip msdp mesh-group Boogeymen 10.100.1.4
```

```
Mummy
ip pim rp-address 10.100.1.3
ip msdp peer 10.100.1.1 connect-source Loopback0
ip msdp description 10.100.1.1 to Frankenstein
ip msdp peer 10.100.1.2 connect-source Loopback0
ip msdp description 10.100.1.2 to Wolfman
ip msdp peer 10.100.1.4 connect-source Loopback0
ip msdp description 10.100.1.4 to Dracula
ip msdp mesh-group Boogeymen 10.100.1.1
ip msdp mesh-group Boogeymen 10.100.1.2
ip msdp mesh-group Boogeymen 10.100.1.4
```

```
Dracula
ip pim rp-address 10.100.1.4
ip msdp peer 10.100.1.1 connect-source Loopback0
ip msdp description 10.100.1.1 to Frankenstein
ip msdp peer 10.100.1.2 connect-source Loopback0
ip msdp description 10.100.1.2 to Wolfman
ip msdp peer 10.100.1.3 connect-source Loopback0
```

```
ip msdp description 10.100.1.3 to Mummy
ip msdp mesh-group Boogeymen 10.100.1.1
ip msdp mesh-group Boogeymen 10.100.1.2
ip msdp mesh-group Boogeymen 10.100.1.3
```

Case Study: Anycast RP

Designers of large, geographically diverse PIM-SM domains must often wrestle with the dilemma of where to most efficiently place the RPs. PIM-SM allows only a single group-to-RP mapping, which presents several problems in large domains:[4]

- Possible traffic bottlenecks

- Lack of scalable register decapsulation (when using shared trees)

- Slow failover when an active RP fails

- Possible suboptimal forwarding of multicast packets

- Dependence on remote RPs

You read in Chapters 7 and 8 about different schemes for alleviating some of these problems, such as the hashing algorithm used with the PIMv2 bootstrap protocol and Auto-RP filtering. None of these tools offer a completely acceptable solution. Anycast RP is a method of allowing the mapping of a single group to multiple RPs. The RPs can be distributed throughout the domain, and all use the same RP address. As a result, a "virtual RP" is created. MSDP is fundamental to the creation of a virtual RP and redundant RPs.

> **Note** Generically, anycasting means that packets can be sent to a single address, and one of several devices can respond to the address. The response comes from the closest device as determined by the IGP.

Figure 9-18 shows the same routers from the preceding case study, but all four routers run Auto-RP and announce an RP address of 10.100.254.1. Source DRs within the domain know of just the one RP address and register with the closest physical RP. Normally, this causes partitioning of the PIM domain. Using an MSDP mesh group, however, the anycast RPs can exchange source information within the group.

The unicast routing protocol of each anycast RP advertises the common RP address. From the perspective of source and group DRs, there is just a single RP at this address, with several routes to it. A DR chooses the shortest route, which in reality leads to the

---

[4] Dorain Kim, David Meyer, Henry Kilmer, and Dino Farinacci, "Anycast RP Mechanism Using PIM and MSDP," RFC 3446, January 2003.

nearest anycast RP. If the anycast RP fails, the unicast protocol announces the route to the RP as unfeasible. The DR sees only the unfeasible route and chooses the next-best route, which in reality leads to the next-nearest anycast RP. As a result, RP failover is linked to and almost as fast as the unicast reconvergence time.

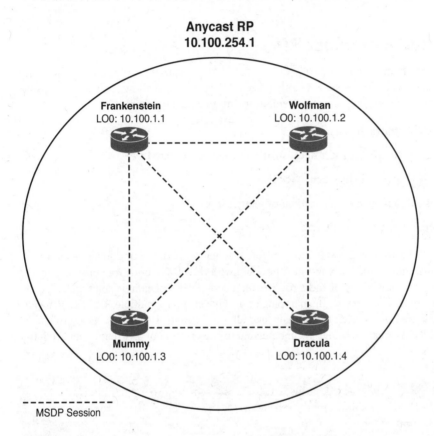

Figure 9-18 *Four Routers Form a Virtual RP, Announcing a Single RP Address of 10.100.254.1 and Using MSDP to Exchange Information About Sources That Have Registered to Each Router*

The MSDP peering takes place as before, between the LO0 interfaces; however, another loopback interface configures the RP address that the routers announce. Normally, MSDP uses the RP address in its SA messages. Because all four routers announce the same RP address, MSDP must be configured to use a unique address in its SA messages. The **ip msdp originator-id** command accomplishes this. Example 9-20 shows the relevant configurations of the four routers, using mesh groups and **ip msdp originator-id**.

Example 9-20 *Configuring Frankenstein, Wolfman, Mummy, and Dracula for Anycast RP*

```
Frankenstein
interface Loopback0
 ip address 10.100.1.1 255.255.255.255
!
interface Loopback5
 ip address 10.100.254.1 255.255.255.255
 ip pim sparse-dense-mode
!
router ospf 1
 router-id 10.100.1.1
 network 0.0.0.0 255.255.255.255 area 0
!
router bgp 6500
 bgp router-id 10.100.1.1
 neighbor Boogeymen peer-group
 neighbor Boogeymen remote-as 6500
 neighbor Boogeymen update-source Loopback0
 neighbor 10.100.1.2 peer-group Boogeymen
 neighbor 10.100.1.3 peer-group Boogeymen
 neighbor 10.100.1.4 peer-group Boogeymen
 !
 address-family ipv4 multicast
 neighbor 10.100.1.2 activate
 neighbor 10.100.1.3 activate
 neighbor 10.100.1.4 activate
 exit-address-family
!
ip pim send-rp-announce Loopback5 scope 20
ip pim send-rp-discovery Loopback5 scope 20
ip msdp peer 10.100.1.3 connect-source Loopback0
ip msdp description 10.100.1.3 to Mummy
ip msdp peer 10.100.1.2 connect-source Loopback0
ip msdp description 10.100.1.2 to Wolfman
ip msdp peer 10.100.1.4 connect-source Loopback0
ip msdp description 10.100.1.4 to Dracula
ip msdp mesh-group Boogeymen 10.100.1.3
ip msdp mesh-group Boogeymen 10.100.1.2
ip msdp mesh-group Boogeymen 10.100.1.4
ip msdp cache-sa-state
ip msdp originator-id Loopback0
```

```
Wolfman
interface Loopback0
 ip address 10.100.1.2 255.255.255.255
!
interface Loopback5
 ip address 10.100.254.1 255.255.255.255
 ip pim sparse-dense-mode
!
router ospf 1
 router-id 10.100.1.2
 network 0.0.0.0 255.255.255.255 area 0
!
router bgp 6500
 bgp router-id 10.100.1.2
 neighbor Boogeymen peer-group
 neighbor Boogeymen remote-as 6500
 neighbor Boogeymen update-source Loopback0
 neighbor 10.100.1.1 peer-group Boogeymen
 neighbor 10.100.1.3 peer-group Boogeymen
 neighbor 10.100.1.4 peer-group Boogeymen
 !
 address-family ipv4 multicast
 neighbor 10.100.1.1 activate
 neighbor 10.100.1.3 activate
 neighbor 10.100.1.4 activate
 exit-address-family
!
ip pim send-rp-announce Loopback5 scope 20
ip pim send-rp-discovery Loopback5 scope 20
ip msdp peer 10.100.1.1 connect-source Loopback0
ip msdp description 10.100.1.1 to Frankenstein
ip msdp peer 10.100.1.3 connect-source Loopback0
ip msdp description 10.100.1.3 to Mummy
ip msdp peer 10.100.1.4 connect-source Loopback0
ip msdp description 10.100.1.4 to Dracula
ip msdp mesh-group Boogeymen 10.100.1.1
ip msdp mesh-group Boogeymen 10.100.1.3
ip msdp mesh-group Boogeymen 10.100.1.4
ip msdp cache-sa-state
ip msdp originator-id Loopback0
```

```
Mummy
interface Loopback0
 ip address 10.100.1.3 255.255.255.255
!
```

```
interface Loopback5
 ip address 10.100.254.1 255.255.255.255
 ip pim sparse-dense-mode
!
router ospf 1
 router-id 10.100.1.3
 network 0.0.0.0 255.255.255.255 area 0
!
router bgp 6500
 bgp router-id 10.100.1.3
 neighbor Boogeymen peer-group
 neighbor Boogeymen remote-as 6500
 neighbor Boogeymen update-source Loopback0
 neighbor 10.100.1.1 peer-group Boogeymen
 neighbor 10.100.1.2 peer-group Boogeymen
 neighbor 10.100.1.4 peer-group Boogeymen
 !
 address-family ipv4 multicast
 neighbor 10.100.1.1 activate
 neighbor 10.100.1.2 activate
 neighbor 10.100.1.4 activate
 exit-address-family
ip pim send-rp-announce Loopback5 scope 20
ip pim send-rp-discovery Loopback5 scope 20
ip msdp peer 10.100.1.1 connect-source Loopback0
ip msdp description 10.100.1.1 to Frankenstein
ip msdp peer 10.100.1.2 connect-source Loopback0
ip msdp description 10.100.1.2 to Wolfman
ip msdp peer 10.100.1.4 connect-source Loopback0
ip msdp description 10.100.1.4 to Dracula
ip msdp mesh-group Boogeymen 10.100.1.1
ip msdp mesh-group Boogeymen 10.100.1.2
ip msdp mesh-group Boogeymen 10.100.1.4
ip msdp cache-sa-state
ip msdp originator-id Loopback0
```

```
Dracula
interface Loopback0
 ip address 10.100.1.4 255.255.255.255
!
interface Loopback5
 ip address 10.100.254.1 255.255.255.255
 ip pim sparse-dense-mode
!
router ospf 1
```

```
 router-id 10.100.1.4
 network 0.0.0.0 255.255.255.255 area 0
!
router bgp 6500
 bgp router-id 10.100.1.4
 neighbor Boogeymen peer-group
 neighbor Boogeymen remote-as 6500
 neighbor Boogeymen update-source Loopback0
 neighbor 10.100.1.1 peer-group Boogeymen
 neighbor 10.100.1.2 peer-group Boogeymen
 neighbor 10.100.1.3 peer-group Boogeymen
 !
 address-family ipv4 multicast
 neighbor 10.100.1.1 activate
 neighbor 10.100.1.2 activate
 neighbor 10.100.1.3 activate
 exit-address-family
!
ip pim send-rp-announce Loopback5 scope 20
ip pim send-rp-discovery Loopback5 scope 20
ip msdp peer 10.100.1.1 connect-source Loopback0
ip msdp description 10.100.1.1 to Frankenstein
ip msdp peer 10.100.1.2 connect-source Loopback0
ip msdp description 10.100.1.2 to Wolfman
ip msdp peer 10.100.1.3 connect-source Loopback0
ip msdp description 10.100.1.3 to Mummy
ip msdp mesh-group Boogeymen 10.100.1.1
ip msdp mesh-group Boogeymen 10.100.1.2
ip msdp mesh-group Boogeymen 10.100.1.3
ip msdp cache-sa-state
ip msdp originator-id Loopback0
```

In Example 9-20, each of the four routers is configured as both an Auto-RP candidate RP and a mapping agent. You also can use static mapping or PIMv2 bootstrap with any-cast RP. All four routers in this example are configured to cache SA messages.

Interface LO5 is used on each router to configure the virtual RP address, whereas LO0 is the endpoint of the MSDP sessions. Notice in the configurations that the Auto-RP commands reference LO5, whereas the **ip msdp originator-id** command references LO0. This is vital because MSDP must have unique IP addresses at the endpoints of its peering sessions.

The OSPF and BGP stanzas are shown for an important reason. Recall that OSPF and BGP use the highest IP address configured on any loopback interface as its router ID.

Unfortunately, the IP address on LO5 is higher on each router than the IP address on LO0. As a result, the OSPF and BGP processes on each router would by default use a router ID of 10.100.254.1. One of many undesirable results would be the thrashing of the OSPF databases as each router's LSAs try to override the other routers' LSAs. One solution is to always use a virtual RP address that is numerically lower than any other loopback address, but there are obvious impracticalities in this and some large vulnerabilities to inadvertent configuration mistakes. A better solution, used in this example, is to force each router to use its unique LO0 address with the **router-id** statement under the OSPF and BGP configurations.

Notice also that the LO0 interfaces are not running PIM. These interfaces are unnecessary to PIM functionality and serve only to provide router-specific IP addresses for MSDP peering.

Case Study: MSDP Default Peers

If an AS is a stub or nontransit AS, and particularly if the AS is not multihomed, there is little or no reason to run BGP to its transit AS. A static default route at the stub AS and a static route pointing to the stub prefixes at the transit AS is generally sufficient. But what if the stub AS is also a multicast domain and its RP must peer with an RP in the neighboring domain? The overview of the MSDP operation explained that MSDP depends on the BGP next-hop database for its peer RPF checks.

You can disable this dependency on BGP with the **ip msdp default-peer** command. MSDP just accepts all SA messages from default peers. Figure 9-19 shows a simple example. Here, the stub AS is peered to the transit AS by a single link. RPF checks are not necessary because there is only one path and therefore no possibility of loops.

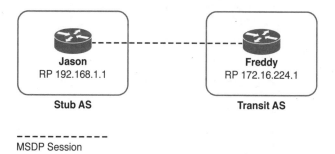

MSDP Session

Figure 9-19 *BGP Is Typically Not Run Between a Stub AS and Its Transit AS, but This Can Cause a Problem for MSDP*

Example 9-21 shows the MSDP configuration of the two routers.

Example 9-21   *MSDP Configurations for Routers Jason and Freddy*

```
Jason
ip msdp peer 172.16.224.1 connect-source Loopback0
ip msdp default-peer 172.16.224.1

Freddy
ip msdp peer 192.168.1.1 connect-source Loopback0
ip msdp default-peer 192.168.1.1
```

A stub AS also might want to have MSDP peering with more than one RP for the sake of redundancy, as shown in Figure 9-20. SA messages cannot just be accepted from both default peers because there is no RPF check mechanism. Instead, SA messages are accepted from only one peer. If that peer fails, messages are then accepted from the other peer. The underlying assumption here, of course, is that both default peers are sending the same SA messages.

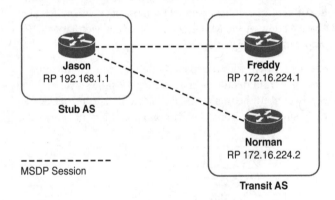

Figure 9-20   *Jason Is Connected to More Than One Default MSDP Peer*

Example 9-22 shows the configuration for Jason.

Example 9-22   *Configuring Jason to Have Redundant Peering with Both Freddy and Norman*

```
ip msdp peer 172.16.224.1 connect-source Loopback0
ip msdp peer 172.16.224.2 connect-source Loopback0
ip msdp default-peer 172.16.224.1
ip msdp default-peer 172.16.224.2
```

Under normal circumstances, the active default peer is the first peer in the configuration—in this case, 172.16.224.1. SAs are not accepted from 172.16.224.2 unless 172.16.224.1 fails.

The RP in a transit AS is likely to have more than one default MSDP peer, as shown in Figure 9-21. Just listing the default peers, as was shown in the preceding example, does not work because SAs would be accepted by only a single peer. To cause the RP to accept SA messages from multiple peers while still providing loop avoidance in the absence of a peer RPF check, BGP-style prefix lists are used. The RP then accepts SA messages from all its default peers but only for source prefixes allowed by each peer's associated prefix list. The underlying assumption here is that each AS uses distinct prefixes, so loop avoidance is ensured.

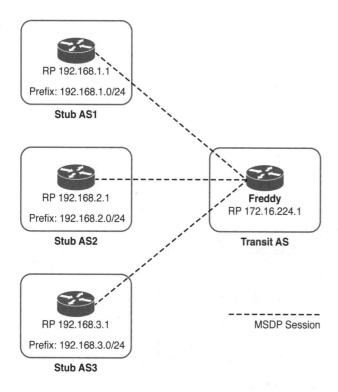

Figure 9-21 *RP in the Transit AS Has Three Default MSDP Peers*

Example 9-23 shows the configuration for Freddy.

Example 9-23 *Configuring an RP to Accept SA Messages from Multiple Peers*

```
ip msdp peer 192.168.1.1 connect-source Loopback0
ip msdp peer 192.168.2.1 connect-source Loopback0
ip msdp peer 192.168.3.1 connect-source Loopback0
ip msdp default-peer 192.168.1.1 prefix-list AS1
```

```
ip msdp default-peer 192.168.2.1 prefix-list AS2
ip msdp default-peer 192.168.3.1 prefix-list AS3
!
ip prefix-list AS1 seq 5 permit 192.168.1.0/24 le 32
ip prefix-list AS2 seq 5 permit 192.168.2.0/24 le 32
ip prefix-list AS3 seq 5 permit 192.168.3.0/24 le 32
```

Looking Ahead

The entirety of this volume up to now has been devoted to BGP and IP multicast. The last two chapters divert from routing but are still important topics within IP routing. Chapter 10, "IPv4 to IPv4 Network Address Translation (NAT44)," is devoted to using Network Address Translation (NAT) to scale IPv4 networks, and Chapter 11, "IPv6 to IPv4 Network Address Translation (NAT64)," discusses using NAT to translate between IPv4 and IPv6 addresses.

Review Questions

1. In the section "Multicast Scoping," a sample configuration is given for administrative scoping. The boundary at interface E0 blocks organization-local packets (destination addresses whose prefixes match 239.192.0.0/14) but passes packets with global scope. Will a packet with a group address 224.0.0.50 pass this boundary?

2. How does Cisco IOS Software handle DVMRP Prune messages on point-to-point and multiaccess interfaces that are configured to run PIM?

3. What is a PIM (*,*,RP) entry?

4. How does Multiprotocol BGP (MBGP) differ from normal BGP?

5. What is the MBGP AFI?

6. Is the following statement true or false? MSDP carries information about multicast sources and group members between RPs in different PIM domains.

7. What is the transport protocol for MSDP?

8. What is an MSDP SA message?

9. How does an MSDP RP determine whether an SA were received on an RPF interface?

10. What is SA caching?

11. Is there an alternative to reducing join latency without SA caching?

Configuration Exercise

Figure 9-22 shows the topology used for this configuration exercise.

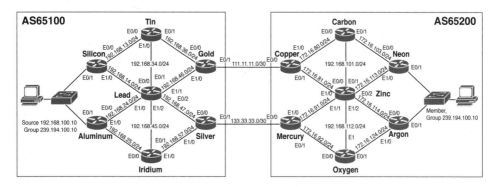

Figure 9-22   *Network Topology for Configuration Exercise*

Table 9-6 lists the routers, switches, multicast-enabled. hosts, interfaces, and addresses used in the exercises for this chapter. All interfaces of the routers are shown.

Table 9-6   *Router/Switch/Multicast-Enabled Host Interfaces and IP Addresses for Configuration Exercise*

Network Device	Interfaces	IP Addresses
Silicon	Eth0/0	192.168.13.1/24
	Eth1/1	192.168.100.9/24
	Eth1/0	192.168.14.1/24
	Loopback 0	10.224.1.1/32
Aluminum	Eth0/0	192.168.24.2/24
	Eth0/1	192.168.100.3/24
	Eth1/0	192.168.25.2/24
	Loopback 0	10.224.1.2/32
Tin	Eth0/0	192.168.13.3/24
	Eth0/1	192.168.36.3/24
	Eth1/0	192.168.34.3/24
	Loopback 0	10.224.1.3/32
Lead	Eth0/0	192.168.14.4/24
	Eth0/1	192.168.34.4/24
	Eth0/2	192.168.47.4/24
	Eth1/0	192.168.24.4/24
	Eth1/1	192.168.46.4/24

Network Device	Interfaces	IP Addresses
	Eth1/2	192.168.45.4/24
	Loopback 0	10.224.1.4/32
Iridium	Eth0/0	192.168.25.5/24
	Eth0/1	192.168.45.5/24
	Eth1/0	192.168.57.5/24
	Loopback 0	10.224.1.5/32
Gold	Eth0/0	192.168.36.6/24
	Eth0/1	111.11.11.1/30
	Eth1/0	192.168.46.6/24
	Loopback 0	10.224.1.6/32
Silver	Eth0/0	192.168.47.7/24
	Eth0/1	133.33.33.1/30
	Eth1/0	192.168.57.7/24
	Loopback 0	10.224.1.7/32
Copper	Eth0/0	111.11.11.2/30
	Eth0/1	172.16.81.8/24
	Eth1/0	172.16.80.8/24
	Loopback 0	10.224.1.8/32
Mercury	Eth0/0	133.33.33.2/30
	Eth0/1	172.16.92.9/24
	Eth1/0	172.16.91.9/24
	Loopback 0	10.224.1.9/32
Carbon	Eth0/0	172.16.80.10/24
	Eth0/1	172.16.103.10/24
	Eth1/0	172.16.101.10/24
	Loopback 0	10.224.1.10/32
Zinc	Eth0/0	172.16.81.11/24
	Eth0/1	172.16.101.11/24
	Eth0/2	172.16.113.11/24
	Eth1/0	172.16.91.11/24
	Eth1/1	172.16.112.11/24
	Eth1/2	172.16.114.11/24
	Loopback 0	10.224.1.11/32
Oxygen	Eth0/0	172.16.92.12/24
	Eth0/1	172.16.124.12/24

Network Device	Interfaces	IP Addresses
	Eth1/0	172.16.112.12/24
	Loopback 0	10.224.1.12/32
Neon	Eth0/0	172.16.103.13/24
	Eth0/1	192.168.110.9/24
	Eth1/0	172.16.113.13/24
	Loopback 0	10.224.1.13/32
Argon	Eth0/0	172.16.114.14/24
	Eth0/1	192.168.110.3/24
	Eth1/0	172.16.124.14/24
	Loopback 0	10.224.1.14/32

1. Your company shares an application with one of your customer. There is a direct IP connectivity between the two administrative domains (BGP AS 65100 for your company and BGP AS 65200 for your customer). The customer has agreed that you will lead the project and manage both networks. The multicast source 192.168.100.10 will send traffic that needs to be received by a host on the customer side that has an IP address of 192.168.110.10.

Assume that unicast routing is already set up and

- OSPF is the IGP of choice for each administrative domain.

- BGP AS 65100 will run on routers Silicon, Aluminum, Tin, Lead, Iridium, Gold, and Silver.

- BGP AS 65200 will run on routers Copper, Carbon, Zinc, Oxygen, Neon, and Argon.

- BGP Peering between both administrative domains will run as the following:

  - Gold will peer with Copper.

  - Silver will peer with Mercury.

Configure the network based on the following requirements:

- Sparse Mode is the multicast mode that must be configured in this question in each administrative domain.

- For AS 65100:

  - Tin and Iridium must be the BSR candidate using their loopback 0 interface.

  - Iridium must be the BSR router.

  - Lead must be the RP candidate using its loopback0 interface.

- No PIM BSR messages must be sent toward AS 65200.

- Inter-AS traffic must flow through Gold as the primary path, and the path between Silver and Mercury must be the backup path.

- HSRP election between Silicon and Aluminum must be run, and traffic from the multicast source must flow through Silicon, which must also be the PIM DR.

- Multicast traffic between the administrative domain is possible.

- Configure Lead to run MSDP with its peer in AS 65200: Zinc.

- For AS 65200:

  - Carbon and Oxygen must be the BSR candidate using their loopback 0 interface.

  - Oxygen must be the BSR router.

  - Zinc must be RP candidate using its loopback0 interface.

  - No PIM BSR messages must be sent toward AS 65100.

  - Inter-AS traffic must flow through Copper as the primary path, and the path between Mercury and Silver must be the backup path.

  - HSRP election between Neon and Argon must be run, and traffic from the multicast source must flow through Neon, which must also be the PIM DR.

  - Multicast traffic between the administrative domain is possible.

  - Configure Zinc to run MSDP with its peer in AS 65200: Lead.

Verify that multicast flows will be sent from the sources toward the receiver.

Chapter 10

IPv4 to IPv4 Network Address Translation (NAT44)

Network Address Translation (NAT) is a function by which IP addresses within a packet are replaced with different IP addresses. Routers, load balancers, and firewalls most commonly perform the function. This chapter and the next focus on NAT within routers.

Note The acronym NAT is used interchangeably to mean *network address translation* (the function itself) and *network address translator* (software that runs the NAT function).

When the first edition of this book was published, NAT was understood to mean IPv4-to-IPv4 translation. You might see funny acronym variations such as NAPT, but it remained an IPv4 thing. Now, of course, you have IPv6. And with it, you have a new kind of NAT that translates IPv4 addresses into IPv6 and vice versa. But that kind of translation involves much more than replacing addresses in a header. For IPv4/IPv6 translation, the entire header of one version must be replaced by a header of the other version. Quite a few adjustments to fields within the headers must also be made.

The point is, IPv4/IPv6 NAT is a different thing from IPv4/IPv4 NAT. It's even used differently within a network. To differentiate these two translation functions, the acronym has been expanded. These days, if you talk about translation between two IPv4 addresses, you use the term NAT44. If you translate between IPv6 and IPv4, use the term NAT64.

Note You'll often come across a further distinction between NAT64 and NAT46. They're used to distinguish direction of translation, either IPv6 to IPv4 or IPv4 to IPv6. In my opinion, this just muddies the waters unnecessarily. So in this book, you'll see only the acronym NAT64 when talking about interversion translators.

You'll also run across the acronym NAT444, which describes architecture rather than a technology. The NAT444 architecture is two levels of NAT44 that enables the IPv4 private address space to be used over and over. Some service providers use NAT444 to extend their dwindling IPv4 space while transitioning to IPv6.

In keeping with the differences in how the translators work and how they're used, each gets its own chapter. This chapter examines NAT44, and Chapter 11, "IPv6 to IPv4 Network Address Translation (NAT64)," examines NAT64. If the acronym "NAT" is used without the modifier in this chapter, it refers either to NAT44 or to a generic NAT function. Context is everything.

Operation of NAT44

NAT (what is now NAT44) is described in RFC 1631.[1] The original intention of NAT was, like classless inter-domain routing (CIDR), to slow the depletion of available IP address space by enabling many private IP addresses to be represented by some smaller number of public IP addresses. Since that time, users have found NAT to be a useful tool for network migrations and mergers, server load sharing, and creating "virtual servers." All these applications are examined in this section, but first the basics of NAT44 functionality and terminology are described.

Basic NAT Concepts

Figure 10-1 shows a simple NAT function. Device A has an IP address that belongs to the private range specified by RFC 1918, whereas device B has a public IP address. When device A sends a packet to device B, the packet passes through a router running NAT44. The NAT44 replaces device A's private address (192.168.2.23) in the source address field with a public address (203.10.5.23) that can be routed across the Internet and forwards the packet. When device B sends a reply to device A, the destination address of the packet is 203.10.5.23. This packet again passes through the NAT44 router, and the destination address is replaced with device A's private address.

NAT is transparent to the end systems involved in the translation. Referring to Figure 10-1, device A knows only that its IP address is 192.168.2.23; it is unaware of the 203.10.5.23 address. Device B, however, thinks the address of device A is 203.10.5.23; it knows nothing about the 192.168.2.23 address. That address is "hidden" from device B.

NAT can hide addresses in both directions. In Figure 10-2, NAT is performed on the addresses of both device A and device B. Device A thinks device B's address is 172.16.80.91, when actually device B's real address is 192.31.7.130. You can see that the

---

[1] K. Egevang, and P. Francis, "The Network Address Translator (NAT)," RFC1631, May 1994.

NAT router translate both the source and destination addresses in both directions to support this address scheme.

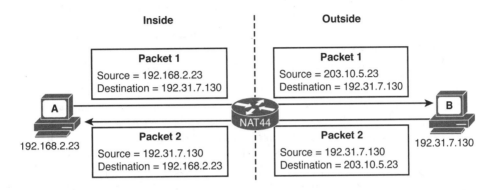

Figure 10-1 *NAT44 Replaces the Private Address of Device A (192.168.2.23) with a Publicly Routable Address (203.10.5.23)*

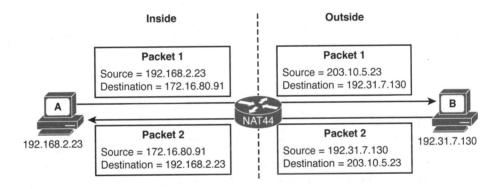

Figure 10-2 *This NAT44 Is Translating Both the Source and Destination Addresses in Both Directions*

IOS NAT44 devices divide their world into the *inside* and the *outside*. Typically, the inside is a private enterprise or ISP, and the outside is the public Internet or an Internet-facing service provider. In addition, an IOS NAT44 device classifies addresses as either *local* or *global*. A local address is an address that is seen by devices on the inside, and a global address is an address that is seen by devices on the outside. Given these four terms, an address may be one of four types:

- **Inside local (IL):** Addresses assigned to inside devices. These addresses are not advertised to the outside.

- **Inside global (IG):** Addresses by which inside devices are known to the outside.

■ **Outside global (OG):** Addresses assigned to outside devices. These addresses are not advertised to the inside.

■ **Outside local (OL):** Addresses by which outside devices are known to the inside.

Referring to Figure 10-2, device A is on the inside and device B is on the outside. 192.168.2.23 is an inside local address, and 203.10.5.23 is an inside global address. 172.16.80.91 is an outside local address, and 192.31.7.130 is an outside global address.

IG addresses are mapped to IL addresses, and OL addresses are mapped to OG addresses. The NAT device tracks these mappings in an *address translation table.* Example 10-1 shows the address translation table for the NAT router referred to in Figure 10-2. Three entries are in the table. Reading the entries from the bottom up, the first entry maps OL address 172.16.80.91 to the OG address 192.31.7.130. The next entry maps the IG address 203.10.5.23 to the IL address 192.168.2.23. These two entries are static, created when the router was configured to translate the specified addresses. The last (top) entry maps the inside addresses to the outside addresses. This entry is dynamic and was created when device A first sent a packet to device B.

Example 10-1 *Address Translation Table of the NAT44 Router Referred to in Figure 10-2 Indicates IG, IL, OL, and OG Address Mappings*

```
NATrouter#show ip nat translations
Pro Inside global     Inside local     Outside local     Outside global
--- 203.10.5.23       192.168.2.23     172.16.80.91      192.31.7.130
--- 203.10.5.23       192.168.2.23     ---               ---
--- ---               ---              172.16.80.91      192.31.7.130
NATrouter#
```

As the preceding paragraph demonstrates, a NAT44 entry may be *static* or *dynamic.* Static entries are one-to-one mappings of local addresses and global addresses. That is, a unique local address is mapped to a unique global address. Dynamic entries may be many-to-one or one-to-many. A many-to-one mapping means that many addresses can be mapped to a single address. In a one-to-many mapping, a single address can be mapped to one of several available addresses.

The following sections describe several common applications of NAT44 and demonstrate more clearly how static NAT and the various implementations of dynamic NAT operate.

NAT and IP Address Conservation

The original mission of NAT was to slow the depletion of IPv4 addresses, and this is the focus of RFC 1631. The core assumption of the concept is that only some of an enterprise's hosts will be connected to the Internet at any one time. Some devices (print servers, for example) never require connectivity outside of the enterprise. As a result, the enterprise can be addressed out of the private RFC 1918 address space, and a significantly smaller number of uniquely assigned public addresses are placed in a pool on a NAT at the edge of the enterprise, as shown in Figure 10-3. The non-unique private addresses are IL addresses, and the public addresses are IG addresses.

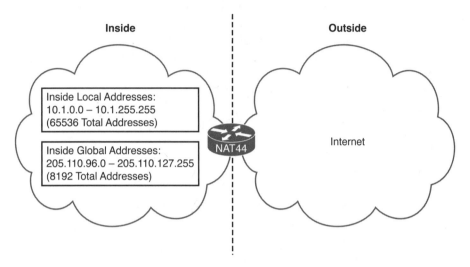

Figure 10-3 *In This NAT Design, a Pool of Public IPv4 Addresses Serves a Private Address Space Eight Times as Large*

When an inside device sends a packet to the Internet, the NAT dynamically selects a public address from the inside global address pool and maps it to the device's inside local address. This mapping is entered into the NAT table. For example, Example 10-2 shows that three inside devices referred to in the network in Figure 10-3—10.1.1.1.20, 10.1.197.64, and 10.1.63.148—have sent packets through the NAT. Three addresses from the IG pool—205.110.96.2, 205.110.96.3, and 205.110.96.1, respectively—have been mapped to the IL addresses.

Example 10-2 *Three Addresses from the Inside Local Address Space Referred to in Figure 4-3 Have Been Dynamically Mapped to Three Addresses from the Inside Global Address Pool*

```
NATrouter#show ip nat translations
Pro Inside global      Inside local      Outside local      Outside global
--- 205.110.96.2       10.1.1.20         ---                ---
--- 205.110.96.3       10.1.197.64       ---                ---
--- 205.110.96.1       10.1.63.148       ---                ---
NATrouter#
```

The destination address of any packet from an outside device responding to the inside device is the IG address. Therefore, the original mapping must be held in the NAT table for some length of time to ensure that all packets of a particular connection are translated consistently. Holding an entry in the NAT table for some period also reduces subsequent lookups when the same device regularly sends packets to the same or multiple outside destinations.

When an entry is first placed into the NAT table, a timer is started; the period of the timer is the *translation timeout*. Each time the entry translates the source or destination address of a subsequent packet, the timer is reset. If the timer expires, the entry is removed from the NAT table and the dynamically assigned address is returned to the pool. The IOS default translation timeout is 86400 seconds (24 hours) and can be changed with the command **ip nat translation timeout**.

Note   The default translation timeout varies according to protocol. These values are displayed later in the chapter in Table 10-3.

This particular NAT application is a many-to-one application because for each IG address in the pool, many IL addresses could be mapped to it. Referring to Figure 10-3, there is an 8:1 oversubscription. This is a familiar concept: Telcos use it when they design switches and trunks that can handle only a portion of their total subscribers, and airlines use it when they overbook flights. Much closer to home, network architects regularly oversubscribe bandwidth under the assumption that not everyone will be using available links at the same time. Think of it as statistically multiplexing IL addresses to IG addresses. The risk, as with telcos, airlines, and link bandwidth, is in underestimating peak usage periods and running out of capacity.

No restrictions apply to the ratio of the size of the local address space and the size of the address pool. Referring to Figure 10-3, the IL range and the IG range can be made larger or smaller to fit specific requirements. For example, the IL range 10.0.0.0/8, composed of more than 16 million addresses, can be mapped to a four-address pool of 205.110.96.1–205.110.96.4 or smaller. The real limitation is not the number of possible addresses in the specified IL range, but the number of actual devices using addresses in the range. If there are only four devices using addresses out of the 10.0.0.0/8 range at any one time, no more than four addresses are needed in the pool. If there are 500,000 devices on the inside, you need a bigger pool.

When an address from the dynamic pool is in the NAT table, it is not available to be mapped to any other address. If all the pool addresses are used up, subsequent inside packets attempting to pass through the NAT router cannot be translated and will be dropped. Therefore, it is important to ensure that the NAT pool is large enough and that the translation timeout is small enough so that the dynamic address pool never runs dry.

Almost all enterprises have some systems, such as mail, web, and FTP servers, which must be accessible from the outside. The addresses of these systems must remain the same, or outside hosts do not know from one time to the next how to reach them. That means dynamic NAT cannot be used with these systems; their IL addresses must be statically mapped to IG addresses. The IG addresses used for static mapping must not be included in the dynamic address pool; although, the IG address is permanently entered into the NAT table, the same address can still be chosen from the dynamic pool, creating an address ambiguity or address overlap.

The NAT technique described in this section can be useful for scaling a growing enterprise. Rather than repeatedly requesting more address space from the addressing authorities or the ISP, the existing public addresses can be moved into the NAT pool and the inside devices can be renumbered from a private address space. Depending upon the size of the organization and the structure of its existing address allocations, the renumbering can be done as a single project or as an incremental migration.

NAT and ISP Migration

One of the drawbacks of CIDR, as discussed in Chapter 1, "Inter-Domain Routing Concepts," is that it can increase the difficulty of changing Internet service providers. If you have been assigned an address block that belongs to ISP1 and want to change to ISP2, you are almost always required to return ISP1's addresses and acquire a new address range from ISP2. This can mean a painful and costly readdressing project within your enterprise.

> **Note** It cannot be overemphasized that the pain and expense of an address migration is sharply reduced when the addressing scheme is well designed originally.

Suppose you are a subscriber of ISP1, which has a CIDR block of 205.113.48.0/20, and the ISP has assigned you an address space of 205.113.50.0/23. You then decide to switch your Internet service to ISP2, which has a CIDR block of 207.36.64.0/19. ISP2 assigns you a new address space of 207.36.76.0/23. Rather than renumbering your inside systems, you can use NAT, as shown in Figure 10-4. The 205.113.50.0/23 address space has been returned to ISP1, but you continue to use this space for the IL addresses. Although the addresses are from the public address space, they no longer can be used to represent your network to the public Internet. You use the 207.36.76.0/23 space from ISP2 as the IG addresses and map (statically or dynamically) the IL addresses to these IG addresses.

The danger in using a scheme such as this is in the possibility that any of the inside local addresses might be leaked to the public Internet. If this were to happen, the leaked address would conflict with ISP1, which has legal possession of the addresses. If ISP2 uses appropriately paranoid route filtering, such a mistake should not cause leakage to the Internet. But as Chapter 1 emphasized, no assumption should ever be made that an AS-external peer filters properly. Therefore, extreme care must be taken to ensure that all of the IL addresses are translated before packets are allowed into ISP2.

Another problem arising from this scheme is that ISP1 probably re-assigns the 205.113.50.0/23 range to another customer. That customer is then unreachable to you. For example, suppose a host on your network wants to send a packet to newbie@ISP1. com. DNS translates the address of that destination as 205.113.50.100 so that is the address the host uses. Unfortunately, that address is interpreted as belonging to your local network and is either misrouted or is dropped as unreachable.

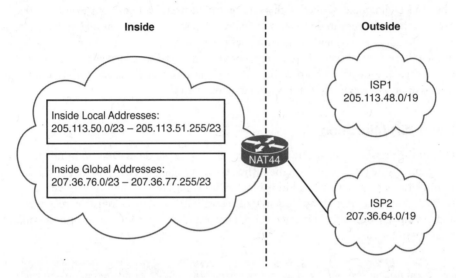

Figure 10-4   *This Enterprise Has an Inside Local Address Space That Belongs to ISP1 but Is a Subscriber of ISP2. It Uses NAT44 to Translate the IL Addresses to IG Addresses Assigned Out of ISP2's CIDR Block*

The moral of the story is that the migration scheme described in this section is useful on a temporary basis to reduce the complexity of the immediate move. But ultimately, you should still re-address your network with private addresses.

NAT and Multihomed Autonomous Systems

Another shortcoming of CIDR is that multihoming to different service providers becomes difficult. Figure 10-5 recaps the problem as discussed in Chapter 1. A subscriber is multihomed to ISP1 and ISP2 and has a CIDR block that is a subset of ISP1's block. To establish correct communication with the Internet, both ISP1 and ISP2 must advertise the subscriber's specific address space of 205.113.50.0/23. If ISP2 does not advertise this address, all the subscriber's incoming traffic passes through ISP1. And if ISP2 advertises 205.113.50.0/23 while ISP1 advertises only its own CIDR block, all the subscriber's incoming traffic matches the more-specific route and passes through ISP2. This poses several problems:

- ISP1 must "punch a hole" in its CIDR block, which probably means modifying the filters and policies on many routers.

- ISP2 must advertise part of a competitor's address space, an action that both ISPs are likely to find objectionable.

- Advertising the subscriber's more-specific address space represents a small reduction in the effectiveness of CIDR in controlling the size of Internet routing tables.

- Some large service providers do not accept prefixes longer than /19, meaning the subscriber's route through ISP2 is unknown to some portion of the Internet.

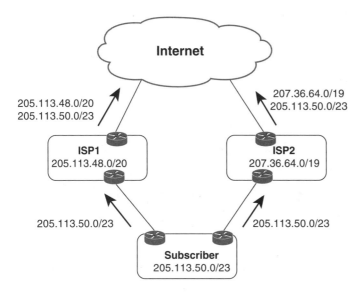

Figure 10-5 *Because the Multihomed Subscriber's Address Space Is a Subset of ISP1's Address Space, Both ISP1 and ISP2 Must Advertise the More-Specific Aggregate*

Figure 10-6 shows how NAT can help solve the problem of CIDR in a multihomed environment. Translation is configured on the router connecting to ISP2, and the IG address pool is a CIDR block assigned by ISP2. ISP2 no longer advertises an ISP1 address space, so it is no longer necessary for ISP1 to advertise the subscriber's more-specific aggregate. Hosts within the subscriber's network can access the Internet either by selecting the closest edge router or by some established policy. The IL address of the hosts' packets will be the same, no matter which router they pass through; but if packets are sent to ISP2, the address is translated. So from the perspective of the Internet, the source addresses of packets from the subscriber vary according to which ISP has forwarded the packets.

Figure 10-7 shows a more efficient design. NAT is implemented on both edge routers and the CIDR blocks from each ISP become the IG address pools of the respective
NATs. The IL addresses are from the private 10.0.0.0/8 address space. This network can
change ISPs with relative ease, needing to reconfigure only the IG address pools when
the ISP changes.

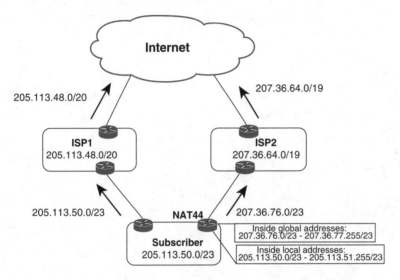

Figure 10-6   *NAT Resolves the Address Overlap Problem Referred to in Figure 10-5*

Port Address Translation (PAT)

The many-to-one applications of NAT44 discussed so far have involved a statistical
multiplexing of a large range of addresses into a smaller pool of addresses. However,
there is a one-to-one mapping of individual addresses. When an address from an inside
global pool is mapped to an inside local address, for instance, that IG address cannot be
mapped to any other address until the first mapping is cleared. However, a specialized
function of NAT enables many addresses to be mapped to a single address at the same
time. Cisco calls this function *Port Address Translation (PAT)* or *address overloading*.
The same function is known in other circles as *Network Address and Port Translation
(NAPT)* or *IP masquerading*.

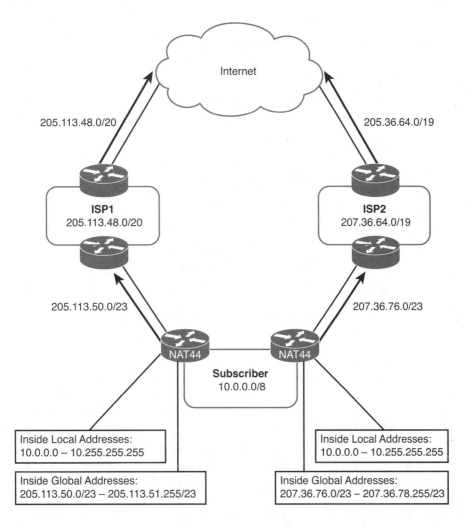

Figure 10-7 *This Subscriber's IL Addresses Have No Relationship to Any ISP. All ISP Address Blocks Are Assigned to NAT44 Inside Global Address Pools*

A TCP/IP session is not identified as a packet exchange between two IP addresses but as an exchange between two IP sockets. A socket is an (address, port) tuple. For example, a Telnet session might consist of a packet exchange between (192.168.5.2, 23) and 172.16.100.6, 1026). PAT translates both the IP address and the port. Packets from different addresses can be translated to a common address, but to different ports of that address, and therefore can share the same address. Figure 10-8 shows how PAT works.

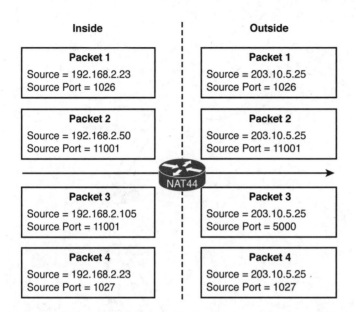

Figure 10-8   *By Translating Both the IPv4 Address and the Associated Port, PAT Enables Many Hosts to Simultaneously Use a Single Global Address*

Four packets with inside local addresses arrive at the NAT. Notice that packets 1 and 4 are from the same address but different source ports. Packets 2 and 3 are from different addresses but have the same source port. The source addresses of all four packets are translated to the same inside global address, but the packets remain unique because they each have a different source port.

TCP and UDP headers have 16-bit port fields, and at any given time, most of the 65,535 port numbers are unused. By translating ports, thousands of TCP and UDP sockets can be mapped to a single inside global address. As a result, PAT is a useful application for home and small office/home office (SOHO) installations, where several devices may share a single assigned address on a single connection to an ISP. Most home routers you install have a PAT function enabling all the networked devices in your home to share the single address your ISP gives you.

NAT and TCP Load Distribution

You can use NAT to represent multiple, identical servers as having a single address (a virtual IP address). In Figure 10-9, devices on the outside reach a server at address 206.35.91.10. In actuality, there are four mirrored servers on the inside, and the NAT distributes sessions among them in a round-robin fashion. Notice that the destination addresses of packets 1 through 4, each from a different source, are translated to servers 1 through 4. Packet 5, representing a session from yet another source, is translated to server 1.

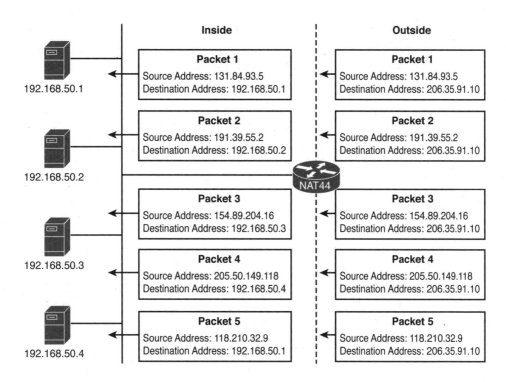

Figure 10-9 *TCP Packets Actual Sent to a Server Farm, Represented by the Single Address 206.35.91.10, Are Translated Round-Robin to the Addresses of the Four Identical Servers*

Obviously, the accessible contents of the four servers referred to in Figure 10-9 must be identical. A host accessing the server farm might hit server 2 at one time and server 4 another time. It must appear to the host that it has hit the same server on both occasions.

This scheme is similar to DNS-based load sharing, in which a single name is resolved round-robin to several IP addresses. The disadvantage of DNS-based load sharing is that when a host receives the name/address resolution, the host caches it. Future sessions are sent to the same address, reducing the effectiveness of the load sharing. NAT-based load sharing performs a translation only when a new TCP connection is opened from the outside, so the sessions are more likely to be distributed evenly. In NAT TCP load balancing, non-TCP packets pass through the NAT untranslated.

It is important to note that NAT-based load balancing, like DNS-based load balancing, is not robust. NAT has no way to know if one of the servers goes down and continues to translate packets to that address. As a result, a failed or offline server can cause some traffic to the server farm to be black-holed.

These days, server load balancing is much more likely to be implemented on a dedicated load balancer or as a virtualized network function, which can provide a more sophisticated translation at Layers 4 or 7 and can monitor server clusters.

NAT and Virtual Servers

NAT can also allow the distribution of services to different addresses, while giving the appearance that the services are all reachable at one address, as shown in Figure 10-10.

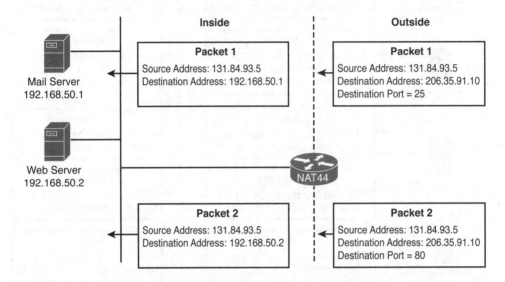

Figure 10-10 *NAT Can Be Configured to Translate Incoming Packets to Different Addresses Based on the Destination Port*

The enterprise has a mail server (TCP port 25) at the local address 192.168.50.1 and an HTTP server (TCP port 80) at the local address 192.168.50.2. Both servers have a global address of 206.35.91.10. When a host from the outside sends a packet to the inside, the NAT examines the destination port in addition to the destination address. Referring to Figure 10-10, a host has sent a packet to 206.35.91.10 with a destination port of 25, indicating mail. The NAT translates this packet's destination address to the mail server's 192.168.50.1. A second packet from the same host has a destination port of 80, indicating HTTP. The NAT translates this packet's destination address to the web server's 192.168.50.2.

NAT Issues

Although the general applications of NAT presented so far are straightforward, the underlying functions of NAT can be less so. This is due to two factors:

■ The general processing of IP and TCP headers

■ The nature of some specific protocols and applications

Changing the content of an IP address or TCP port can change the meaning of some of the other fields, especially the checksum. And many protocols and applications carry the IP address or information based on the IP address within their data fields. Changing an IP address in the header can change the meaning of the encapsulated data, possibly breaking the application. This section examines the most common issues surrounding the operation of NAT.

Header Checksums

The checksum of an IP packet is calculated over the entire header. If the source or destination IP address or both change, the checksum must be recalculated. The same is true of the checksum in the TCP header. This number is calculated over the TCP header and data and also over a pseudo header that includes the source and destination IP addresses. Therefore, if an IP address changes or a port number changes, the TCP checksum must also change. The Cisco NAT performs these checksum recalculations.

Fragmentation

Recall from the section "NAT and Virtual Servers" that NAT can translate to different local addresses based on the destination port. For example, a packet with a destination port of 25 can be translated to a particular IL address, whereas a packet with some other destination port numbers can be translated to other addresses. But what if the packet destined for port 25 becomes fragmented at some point in the network before it reaches the NAT? The TCP or UDP header, containing the source and destination port numbers, is only in the first fragment. If that fragment is merely translated and forwarded, the NAT has no way to tell if the subsequent fragments must be translated.

IP makes no guarantees that packets are delivered in order. The situation is quite real that the first fragment may not even arrive at the NAT before later fragments. NAT must be designed to handle such eventualities.

Cisco NAT keeps stateful information about fragments. If a first fragment is translated, information is kept so that subsequent fragments are translated the same way. If a fragment arrives before the first fragment, the NAT has no choice but to hold the fragment until the first fragment arrives and can be examined.

Encryption

Cisco NAT can change the IP address information carried within the data fields of many applications, as you see shortly. But if the data fields are encrypted, NAT has no way of reading the data. Therefore, for NAT to function, neither the IP addresses nor any information derived from the IP addresses (such as the TCP header checksum) can be encrypted.

Another concern is virtual private networks (VPN) using, for example, IPsec. If an IP address is changed in an IPsec packet, the IPsec becomes meaningless and the VPN will be broken. When any sort of encryption is used, the NAT must be placed on the secure side rather than in the encrypted path or a NAT Traversal (NAT-T) technique must be used.

Security

Some view NAT as a part of a security plan because it "hides" the details of the inside network. A translated host may appear on the Internet one day with one address and on another day with a different address. But this should be considered weak security, at best. Although NAT may slow an attacker that wants to hit a particular host, forcing him to play a sort of shell game with IP addresses, it does not stop any determined and knowledgeable aggressor. And worse, NAT does nothing to prevent such common attacks as denial of service, or attacks such as session hijacking. Actually, NAT can become an attractive target. An attacker might, for example, launch a DoS attack by causing a translator's mapping table to fill up.

Protocol-Specific Issues

NAT should be transparent to the end systems that send packets through it. For that matter, TCP/IP should be transparent to applications. But in reality, many applications—both commercial applications and applications that are part of the TCP/IP protocol suite—use IP addresses within their data. Information within the data field may be based on an IP address, or an IP address may be carried in the data field. If NAT translates an address in the IP header without being aware of the effects on the data, the application breaks.

Table 10-1 lists the applications that Cisco IOS NAT44 implementation supports. For the applications listed as carrying IP address information in the application data, NAT is aware of those applications and makes the appropriate corrections to the data. The table is current as of this writing. If you implement NAT, you should check the Cisco website or TAC for application support that might have been recently added.

Table 10-1   *IP Traffic Types/Applications Supported by IOS NAT*

Traffic Types/Applications Supported
Any TCP/UDP traffic that does not carry source and/or destination IP addresses in the application data stream.
HTTP (with some caveats)
TFTP
telnet
Archie
Finger
NTP
NFS
rlogin, rsh, rcp

Traffic Types/Applications Supported with IP Addresses in Their Data Stream
ICMP
FTP (including PORT and PASV)
NetBIOS over TCP/IP (datagram, name, and session services)
Progressive Networks' RealAudio
White Pines' CuSeeMe
Xing Technologies' StreamWorks
DNS "A" and "PTR" queries and responses
H.323/NetMeeting [12.0(1)/12.0(1)T and later]
VDOLive [11.3(4)/11.3(4)T and later]
Vxtreme [11.3(4)/11.3(4)T and later]
IP Multicast [12.0(1)T] (source address translation only)
Traffic Types/Applications Not Supported
Routing table updates
DNS zone transfers
BOOTP
talk, ntalk
SNMP
NetShow

Table 4-1 is taken directly from the Cisco whitepaper, "Cisco IOS Network Address Translation (NAT) Packaging Update," available at www.cisco.com.

ICMP

Some ICMP messages include the IP header of the packet that caused the message to be generated. Table 10-2 lists these message types. Cisco NAT44 checks the listed message types; if IPv4 information in the message matches a translated IPv4 address in the header, the NAT also translates the IP information. In addition, the checksum in the ICMP header is corrected in the same way it is corrected for TCP and UDP.

Table 10-2 *ICMP Message Types That Carry IP Header Information in the Message Body*

Message	Type Number
Destination Unreachable	3
Source Quench	4
Redirect	5
Time Exceeded	11
Parameter Problem	12

DNS

One of the core support functions of any TCP/IP network, and especially of the Internet, is the Domain Name System (DNS). If systems cannot get DNS queries and responses across a NAT, DNS can become complicated. Figure 10-11 shows how DNS servers might be implemented around a NAT that cannot translate DNS packets.

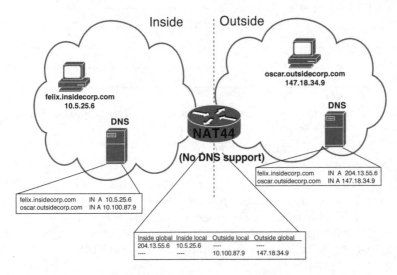

Figure 10-11 *If NAT Does Not Support DNS, Name Servers Must Be Implemented on Both Sides of the NAT Reflecting the Name-to-Address Mappings Appropriate for That Side of the NAT*

The NAT referred to in Figure 10-11 translates in both directions; outside hosts are made to appear to the inside as if they are on the 10.0.0.0 network, and inside hosts are made to appear to the outside as if they are on the 204.13.55.0 network. DNS servers reside on both the inside and the outside, and each contains resource records that map names to the addresses appropriate for their side of the NAT.

A problem with this approach is the difficulty of maintaining inconsistent resource records on the two DNS servers. A more serious problem is that the NAT mappings must be static to match the mappings in the DNS resource records. Pooled NAT does not work because the mappings change dynamically. A better approach, and one that is supported by Cisco implementation of NAT, is to have the NAT support translation of DNS queries.

Although a detailed examination of DNS operations is beyond the scope of this book, a short review of the key concepts can help you to understand where DNS can coexist with NAT. You are familiar with the structure of domain names; for example, the name *cisco.com* describes a second-level domain (*cisco*) under the top-level domain *com*. All the IP name space is organized in a tree structure with host names connected to increasingly higher-level domains until all domains meet at the root.

Note   An excellent text on DNS is by Paul Albitz and Cricket Liu, *DNS and BIND*, 5th Edition, O'Reilly and Associates, 2006.

Name servers store information about some part of the domain name space. The information in a particular name server may be for an entire domain, some portion of a domain, or even multiple domains. The portion of the name space for which a server contains information is the server's *zone*.

DNS servers are either *primary* or *secondary* servers. A primary DNS server acquires its zone information from files stored locally in the host on which the server runs and is said to be *authoritative* for its zone. A secondary DNS server acquires its zone information from a primary DNS server. It does this by downloading the zone files of the primary, in a process called a *zone transfer*.

Because a zone transfer is a file transfer, a NAT cannot parse the address information out of the file. Even if it could, zone files are often large, which would put a significant performance burden on the NAT device. Therefore, a primary and secondary DNS server for the same zone cannot be located on opposite sides of a NAT because the information in zone files will not be translated during a zone transfer.

The information within zone files consists of entries called *Resource Records (RR)*. Several types of resource records, such as Start-of-Authority (SOA) records, specify the authoritative server for the domain: Canonical Name (CNAME) records, for recording aliases; and Mail Exchange (MX) records specify mail servers for a domain. The three RRs of importance to NAT are Address (A) records, which map hostnames to IPv4 addresses, IPv6 Address (AAAA) records, which map host names to IPv6 addresses, and Pointer (PTR) records, which map IP addresses to names. When a host must find an IP address for a particular name, its DNS resolver queries a DNS server's A and AAAA records. If the host wants to find a name that goes with a particular IP address (a reverse lookup), it queries the server's PTR records.

Figure 10-12 shows the format of a DNS message, which carries both the queries from hosts and the responses from servers. The header, like most headers, is a group of fields carrying information for the management and processing of the message. The header information significant to NAT includes a bit specifying whether the message is a query or a response, and fields specifying the number of resource records contained in each of the other four sections.

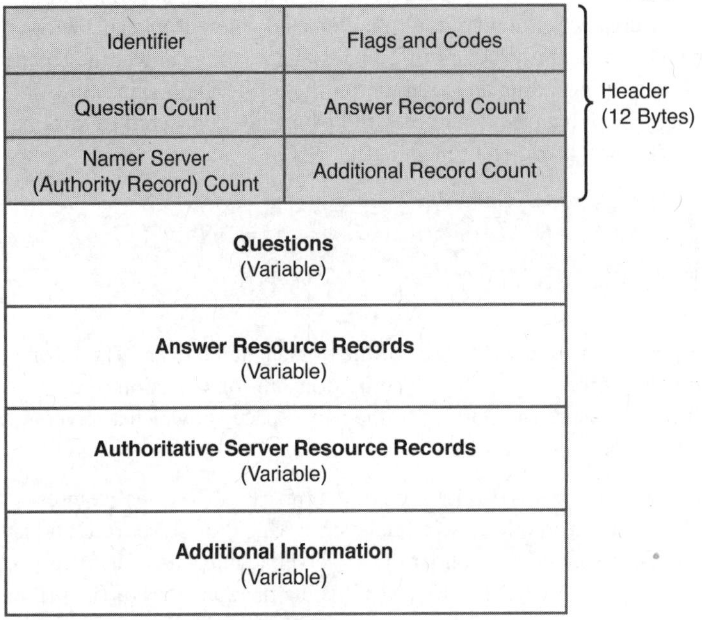

Identifier	Flags and Codes
Question Count	Answer Record Count
Namer Server (Authority Record) Count	Additional Record Count

Header (12 Bytes)

Questions (Variable)
Answer Resource Records (Variable)
Authoritative Server Resource Records (Variable)
Additional Information (Variable)

Figure 10-12 *DNS Message Format*

The Questions section is a group of fields that, as the name clearly describes, asks a question of the server. Among other things, the question may contain a name to which the server must try to match an address out of its A and AAAA records, or the question may contain an address to which the server must try to match a name from its PTR records. Every DNS message contains a question.

The Answers section contains resource records that, of course, answer the question. There may be one or many RRs listed in the answer, or there may be none at all. The Authority and Additional sections contain information that is supplemental to the answer and may also be empty.

When a DNS packet passes through IOS NAT44, the Questions, Answers, and Additional sections are examined. If the message is a query for an IP address to match a name, no addresses are yet included and the Answer and Additional sections are empty, so no translation takes place. The response to the query, however, contains one or more A RRs in the Answer section and possibly in the Additional section. NAT44 searches its table for a match to the address in these records, and translates the addresses in the message if a match is found. If a match is not found, the message is dropped.

If the DNS message is a query for a name to match a known IPv4 address (a reverse lookup), NAT examines its table for a match to the address in the Questions section. Again, either a match is found and the address is translated, or the message is dropped. The response to the query contains one or more PTR RRs in the Answers section and possibly in the Additional section, and the addresses in these records are also either translated or the message is dropped.

In summary, remember the following two facts when working with DNS and NAT44:

- DNS A and PTR queries can cross an IOS NAT, so a host on one side of a NAT can query a DNS server on the other side of the NAT.

- DNS zone transfers cannot cross an IOS NAT, so primary and secondary DNS servers for the same zone cannot reside on opposite sides of the NAT.

FTP

The File Transfer Protocol (FTP) is something of an unusual application protocol in that it uses two connections, as shown in Figure 10-13. The control connection is initiated by the host and is used to exchange FTP commands with the server. The data connection is initiated by the server and is used for the actual file transfer.

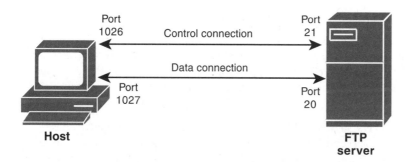

Figure 10-13 *An FTP Session Consists of Two Separate TCP Connections; the Host Initiates the Control Connection, and the Server Initiates the Data Connection*

The sequence of events for setting up an active FTP session and transferring a file follows:

1. The FTP server performs a passive open (that is, begins listening for a connection request) on TCP port 21, the control port.

2. The host selects ephemeral (temporary) ports for the control connection and for the data connection. Referring to Figure 10-13, these are ports 1026 and 1027, respectively.

3. The host performs a passive open on the data port.

4. The host performs an active open for the control connection, creating a TCP connection between its control port (refer to 1026 in Figure 10-13) and the server's port 21.

5. To transfer the file, the host sends a PORT command across the control connection, telling the server to open a data connection on the host's data port (refer to 1027 in Figure 10-13).

6. The server performs an active open for the data connection, creating a TCP connection between its port 20 and the host's data port.

7. The requested file is transferred across the data connection.

This sequence of events presents a problem for some secured networks. Specifically, it is a common security practice to configure a firewall or access list to disallow the initiation of connections from the outside to random ports. This is done by looking for a cleared ACK or RST bit in the TCP header, indicating a connection request. You can see that when the FTP server tries to establish a connection to the host's ephemeral port across such a firewall, the connection is denied.

Note   The **established** keyword tells an IOS access list to look for a cleared ACK or RST bit in the TCP header.

To overcome this difficulty, the host can issue a PASV command instead of a PORT command to open the data connection. This command asks the server to passively open a data port and inform the host of the port number. The host then performs the active open of the data connection to the server port. Because the connection request is outgoing through the firewall rather than incoming, the connection is not blocked.

The significance of all this to NAT44 is that the PORT and PASV commands carry not only the port numbers but also the IP addresses. If the messages cross a NAT, these addresses must be translated. To make matters worse, the IP address is encoded in ASCII in its dotted-decimal form. That means that the IP address in the FTP message is not of a fixed length, as it would be if it were a 32-bit binary representation. For example, the address 10.1.5.4 is 8 ASCII characters (including the dots), whereas 204.192.14.237 is 14 ASCII characters. So when the address is translated, the message size can change.

If the size of the translated FTP message remains the same, the IOS NAT44 recalculates only the TCP checksum (in addition to any operations performed on the IPv4 header). If the translation results in a smaller message, the NAT pads the message out with ACSII zeroes to make it the same size as the original message.

The problem becomes more complicated if the translated message is larger than the original message because the TCP sequence and acknowledgment numbers are based directly on the length of the TCP segments. IOS NAT44 keeps a table to track the changes in SEQ and ACK numbers. When an FTP message is translated, an entry is made into the table containing the source and destination IPv4 addresses and ports, the initial sequence number, the delta for the sequence numbers, and a timestamp. This information is used to correctly adjust the SEQ and ACK numbers in the FTP messages and can be deleted after the FTP connection is closed.

SMTP

Simple Mail Transfer Protocol (SMTP) messages normally contain domain names and not IP addresses. However, they can use IP addresses instead of names when requesting mail transfers. Therefore, IOS NAT44 does examine the appropriate fields within SMTP messages and makes translations when IPv4 addresses are found.

Unlike SMTP, which is used for uploading mail and for transferring mail between servers, the Post Office Protocol (POP) and the Internet Message Access Protocol (IMAP) are used only for downloading messages from a mail server to a client. Both protocols use only hostnames, never IP addresses, within the message bodies. Therefore, these protocols do not require special examination when crossing a NAT.

SNMP

Simple Network Management Protocol (SNMP) uses a rich and widely varying set of Management Information Bases (MIB) to manage a wide variety of networking devices. In addition to the many Internet-standard MIB groups, a vast number of private MIBs are created for the management of vendor-specific devices.

You can deduce from this basic description that many MIBs can contain one or more IPv4 addresses. Because of the many messages, formats, and variables possible with SNMP, NAT44 cannot easily examine the contents of an SNMP message for IP addresses. Therefore, NAT44 does not support the translation of IPv4 addresses within SNMP messages.

Routing Protocols

IPv4 routing protocols have a similar problem as presented by SNMP. Many IPv4 routing protocols exist, each with its own packet formats and each with its own operational characteristics. Therefore, NAT44 cannot translate IPv4 routing protocol packets. A NAT44 router can run a routing protocol on the inside interfaces and a routing protocol on the outside interfaces, but no routing protocol packets should transit a NAT44 boundary in which the advertised addresses change, either through a single protocol or by redistribution. This does not present much of a problem because NAT44 routers will be located on the edge of a routing domain and therefore can usually use a default address or a small set of summary addresses.

Traceroute

Route tracing utilities can vary somewhat. Some, such as the IOS **trace** command, use ICMP packets. Some older implementations from other vendors use UDP packets. But the basic functionality is the same: Packets are sent to a destination with an incrementally increasing TTL, and the addresses of the intermediate systems sending ICMP time exceeded error messages are recorded. You have already seen in the earlier section on ICMP that time exceeded messages are translated by IOS NAT44, so routes can be traced through NAT.

The NAT in Figure 10-14 is translating in both directions. The router jerry.insidenet.com has an IP address of 10.1.16.50, and is translated to an IG address of 204.13.55.6. The device berferd.outsidenet.com has an address of 147.18.34.9, and is translated to an OL address of 10.2.1.3. So, the OL address is the address by which jerry knows berferd.

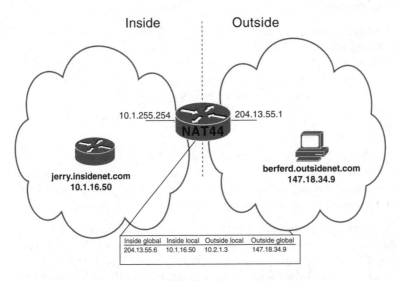

Figure 10-14   *This NAT Is Translating in Both Directions*

When jerry performs a trace to berferd, the destination is 10.2.1.3. Example 10-3 shows that the first hop is the NAT44 router. The NAT then translates the destination address to 147.18.34.9 and the source address to 204.13.55.6, and forwards the packet out its outside interface. When berferd receives the trace packet, which is sent to a bogus port, it responds with an ICMP port unreachable error packet. That packet has a destination of 204.13.55.6, and a source of 147.18.34.9. NAT translates these addresses to a destination of 10.1.16.50 and a source of 10.2.1.3, which is what jerry receives. Therefore, the trace is successful, but the inside device sees only the outside local address.

Example 10-3   *A Trace from jerry.insidenet.com to berferd.outsidenet.com Referred to in Figure 10-14 Shows That the Trace Is Successful, and NAT44 "Hides" the Outside Global Address from the Inside*

```
Jerry#trace berferd.outsidenet.com

Type escape sequence to abort.
```

```
Tracing the route to berferd.outsidenet.com (10.2.1.3)


  1 10.1.255.254 8 msec 8 msec 4 msec
  2 berferd.outsidenet.com (10.2.1.3) 12 msec *  8 msec
Jerry#
```

Configuring NAT44

The first step in configuring NAT44 is to designate the inside and outside interfaces. Beyond that, the configuration depends upon whether you configure static NAT or dynamic NAT. For static NAT, you simply create the appropriate mapping entries in the NAT table. For dynamic NAT, you create a pool of addresses to be used in the translation and create access lists to identify the addresses to be translated. A single command then ties the pool and the access list together.

This section demonstrates the most common configuration techniques for NAT44 in its most common uses.

Case Study: Static NAT

In Figure 10-15, the inside network is addressed out of the 10.0.0.0 address space. Two of the devices, hosts A and C, must communicate with the outside world. Those two devices are translated to the public addresses 204.15.87.1/24 and 204.15.87.2/24.

Example 10-4 shows the configuration to implement NAT at Mazatlan.

Example 10-4   *Static NAT Is Implemented at Router Mazatlan Referred to in Figure 10-15*

```
interface FastEthernet1/0
 ip address 10.1.1.1 255.255.255.0
 ip nat inside
 ip virtual-reassembly
 duplex auto
 speed auto
!
interface Serial2/0
 ip address 199.100.35.254 255.255.255.252
 ip nat outside
 ip virtual-reassembly
 serial restart-delay 0
!
router ospf 100
 log-adjacency-changes
 network 10.1.1.1 0.0.0.0 area 0
```

```
default-information originate
!
ip route 0.0.0.0 0.0.0.0 199.100.35.253
!
ip nat inside source static 10.1.1.3 204.15.87.1
ip nat inside source static 10.1.2.2 204.15.87.2
!
```

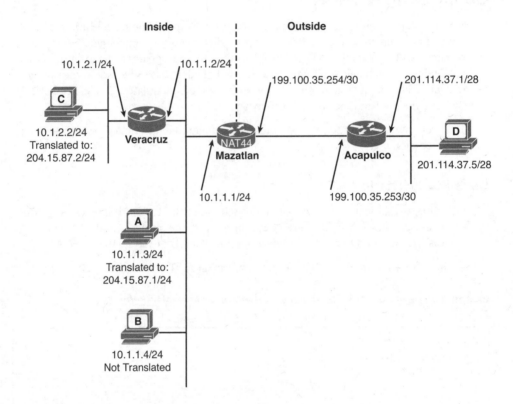

Figure 10-15   *Inside Local Addresses of Devices A and C Are Statically Translated to Inside Global Addresses by the NAT44 Process in Router Mazatlan*

The router's F1/0 interface is designated on the inside with the **ip nat inside** command, and the serial interface S2/0 is designated on the outside with the **ip nat outside** command.

Note   When you enable NAT on an interface, virtual fragment reassembly is automatically enabled, with the statement **ip virtual-reassembly**. This function collects all the parts of a fragmented packet, so it can examine the contents of the entire packet. It's virtual in that it doesn't actually reassemble the packet—after examination of the payload, it sends the fragments on to the destination. It merely delays forwarding any fragments until all fragments have arrived.

Virtual fragment reassembly has several uses, such as preventing fragmentation attacks against a firewall. In the case of NAT, it's used when an associated Application Layer Gateway (ALG) function needs to examine and possibly rewrite some of the upper-layer information in the packet payload.

Because it delays fragments, virtual fragment reassembly can affect performance. You can disable the feature if no ALGs need it.

Next, the inside local addresses are mapped to inside global addresses with the **ip nat inside source static** commands. Two of these commands include one for host C and one for host A. Example 10-5 shows the resulting NAT table.

Example 10-5 *IL Addresses of Hosts C and A Are Statically Mapped to IG Addresses*

```
Mazatlan#show ip nat translations
Pro Inside global      Inside local      Outside local      Outside global
--- 204.15.87.1        10.1.1.3          ---                ---
--- 204.15.87.2        10.1.2.2          ---                ---
Mazatlan#
```

When host A or C sends a packet to the outside, Mazatlan sees the source address in its NAT table and makes the appropriate translation. The router Acapulco has a route (in this case, a static route) to network 204.15.87.0 and has no knowledge of the 10.0.0.0 network. Therefore, Acapulco and host D can respond to packets from hosts A and C. If host B or router Veracruz sends a packet to host D, the packet is forwarded but without any translation; when D responds to the untranslated IL address, Acapulco has no route and drops the packet, as shown in Example 10-6.

Example 10-6 *When Host D Referred to in Figure 4-15 Responds to the Untranslated IL Address of Host B, Acapulco Has No Route to 10.0.0.0 and Drops the Packet*

```
Acapulco#debug ip icmp
ICMP packet debugging is on
Acapulco#
1d00h: ICMP: dst (10.1.1.4) host unreachable sent to 201.114.37.5
1d00h: ICMP: dst (10.1.1.4) host unreachable sent to 201.114.37.5
1d00h: ICMP: dst (10.1.1.4) host unreachable sent to 201.114.37.5
1d00h: ICMP: dst (10.1.1.4) host unreachable sent to 201.114.37.5
1d00h: ICMP: dst (10.1.1.4) host unreachable sent to 201.114.37.5
```

Outside global addresses can also be statically translated into outside local addresses. For example, suppose the administrator of the inside network in Figure 10-15 would like for host D to "appear" to be a part of the inside network—say, with an address of 10.1.3.1. Example 10-7 shows the NAT configuration for Mazatlan.

Example 10-7 *Mazatlan Is Configured to Statically Translate Outside Global Addresses to Outside Local Addresses*

```
ip nat inside source static 10.1.1.3 204.15.87.1
ip nat inside source static 10.1.2.2 204.15.87.2
ip nat outside source static 201.114.37.5 10.1.3.1
```

The router's NAT configuration remains the same except for the addition of the **ip nat outside source static** command, which in this case maps the OG address 201.114.37.5 to the OL address 10.1.3.1. Example 10-8 shows the resulting NAT table.

Example 10-8 *An OG-to-OL Mapping Is Added to the NAT Table by the Additional Command at Mazatlan*

```
Mazatlan#show ip nat translations
Pro Inside global     Inside local      Outside local      Outside global
--- 204.15.87.2       10.1.2.2          ---                ---
--- 204.15.87.1       10.1.1.3          ---                ---
--- ---               ---               10.1.3.1           201.114.37.5
Mazatlan#
```

Although this case study has involved only static mappings, some dynamic mapping occurs after traffic has passed between host A and host D and between host C and host D, as shown in Example 10-9. In each case, the inside mappings are automatically mapped to the outside mappings.

Example 10-9 *Inside Addresses of Hosts A and C Have Been Automatically Mapped to the Outside Addresses of Host D*

```
Mazatlan#show ip nat translations
Pro Inside global     Inside local      Outside local      Outside global
--- 204.15.87.2       10.1.2.2          ---                ---
--- 204.15.87.1       10.1.1.3          ---                ---
--- ---               ---               10.1.3.1           201.114.37.5
--- 204.15.87.1       10.1.1.3          10.1.3.1           201.114.37.5
--- 204.15.87.2       10.1.2.2          10.1.3.1           201.114.37.5
Mazatlan#
```

You need to understand that this configuration does nothing to prevent a host on the inside from sending packets to host D's OG address rather than the OL address. In

Example 10-10, host A can successfully ping host D at either its OL address (10.1.3.1) or its OG address (201.114.37.5).

Example 10-10 *Host A Can Send Packets to Either the OL or OG Address of Host D*

```
Host_A#ping 10.1.3.1

Type escape sequence to abort.
Sending 5, 100-byte ICMP Echos to 10.1.3.1, timeout is 2 seconds:
!!!!!
Success rate is 100 percent (5/5), round-trip min/avg/max = 8/43/52 ms
Host_A#
Host_A#ping 201.114.37.5

Type escape sequence to abort.
Sending 5, 100-byte ICMP Echos to 201.114.37.5, timeout is 2 seconds:
!!!!!
Success rate is 100 percent (5/5), round-trip min/avg/max = 12/47/68 ms
Host_A#
```

Debugging output from hosts C and D in Example 10-11 reveals a bit more detail about the behavior of this network. ICMP debugging is turned on both hosts, and echo replies—both sent and received—are recorded. The outputs from hosts C and D are captured at the same time, so you have to compare them carefully and refer to the mapping table in Example 10-9 to keep track of the addresses.

In step 1, host C pings host D on its OG address 201.114.37.5. Host D sends an echo reply to destination 204.15.87.2. This is host C's IG address, indicating that C's source address of 10.1.2.2 was translated as it passed through the NAT in Mazatlan.

Looking at the same echo reply received at C, you can see that although D sent the echo reply to C's IG address 204.15.87.2, the address of the received reply is translated to C's IL address 10.1.2.2.

Next, host D pings C at its IG address 204.15.87.2. The echo reply sent by C shows a source of C's IL address 10.1.2.2 and a destination of D's OG address 10.1.3.1. When the replies are received at D, the source is translated to C's IG address 204.15.87.2, and the destination is translated to D's OG address 201.114.37.5.

Example 10-11 *Simultaneous* **debug** *Outputs Are Recorded at Host C and Host D Referred to in Figure 10-15. First, Host C Pings Host D, and Then Host D Pings Host C*

```
Host_C#debug ip icmp
ICMP packet debugging is on
Host_C#                                    ##Step 1###
Host_C#ping 201.114.37.5
```

```
Type escape sequence to abort.
Sending 5, 100-byte ICMP Echos to 201.114.37.5, timeout is 2 seconds:
!!!!!
Success rate is 100 percent (5/5), round-trip min/avg/max = 48/60/84 ms
Host_C#
ICMP: echo reply rcvd, src 201.114.37.5, dst 10.1.2.2
ICMP: echo reply rcvd, src 201.114.37.5, dst 10.1.2.2
ICMP: echo reply rcvd, src 201.114.37.5, dst 10.1.2.2
ICMP: echo reply rcvd, src 201.114.37.5, dst 10.1.2.2
ICMP: echo reply rcvd, src 201.114.37.5, dst 10.1.2.2
Host_C#
Host_C#                                        ##Step 2##
ICMP: echo reply sent, src 10.1.2.2, dst 10.1.3.1
ICMP: echo reply sent, src 10.1.2.2, dst 10.1.3.1
ICMP: echo reply sent, src 10.1.2.2, dst 10.1.3.1
ICMP: echo reply sent, src 10.1.2.2, dst 10.1.3.1
ICMP: echo reply sent, src 10.1.2.2, dst 10.1.3.1
Host_C#
```

```
Host_D#debug ip icmp
ICMP packet debugging is on
Host_D#                                        ##Step 1##
ICMP: echo reply sent, src 201.114.37.5, dst 204.15.87.2
ICMP: echo reply sent, src 201.114.37.5, dst 204.15.87.2
ICMP: echo reply sent, src 201.114.37.5, dst 204.15.87.2
ICMP: echo reply sent, src 201.114.37.5, dst 204.15.87.2
ICMP: echo reply sent, src 201.114.37.5, dst 204.15.87.2
Host_D#
Host_D#                                        ##Step 2##
Host_D#ping 204.15.87.2

Type escape sequence to abort.
Sending 5, 100-byte ICMP Echos to 204.15.87.2, timeout is 2 seconds:
!!!!!
Success rate is 100 percent (5/5), round-trip min/avg/max = 16/56/96 ms
Host_D#
ICMP: echo reply rcvd, src 204.15.87.2, dst 201.114.37.5
ICMP: echo reply rcvd, src 204.15.87.2, dst 201.114.37.5
ICMP: echo reply rcvd, src 204.15.87.2, dst 201.114.37.5
ICMP: echo reply rcvd, src 204.15.87.2, dst 201.114.37.5
ICMP: echo reply rcvd, src 204.15.87.2, dst 201.114.37.5
Host_D#
```

Example 10-11 and the explanation of it might be difficult to follow at first. But when you get it, you have a good perspective on inside versus outside addresses, local versus global addresses, and what happens to source and destination addresses of packets flowing both directions through NAT44.

Tip If you re-create these examples in a lab or in a simulator, Examples 10-10 and 10-11 reveal a useful trick. The four hosts in Figure 10-15 are actually Cisco routers with IP routing disabled (**no ip routing**) and an **ip default-gateway** command pointing to their local router's attached interface. This enables you to use IOS's extensive debugging tools to observe network behavior from a host's perspective.

If the administrator of the inside network wants to prevent traffic from being sent to OG addresses, a filter must be implemented, as shown in Example 10-12.

Example 10-12 *A Filter Prevents Traffic of the Inside Network from Being Sent to OG Addresses*

```
interface FastEthernet1/0
 ip address 10.1.1.1 255.255.255.0
 ip access-group 101 in
 ip nat inside
 ip virtual-reassembly
 duplex auto
 speed auto
!
interface Serial2/0
 ip address 199.100.35.254 255.255.255.252
 ip nat outside
 ip virtual-reassembly
 serial restart-delay 0
!
router ospf 100
 log-adjacency-changes
 network 10.1.1.1 0.0.0.0 area 0
 default-information originate
!
ip route 0.0.0.0 0.0.0.0 199.100.35.253
!
ip nat inside source static 10.1.1.3 204.15.87.1
ip nat inside source static 10.1.2.2 204.15.87.2
ip nat outside source static 201.114.37.5 10.1.3.1
!
access-list 101 permit ip any host 10.1.3.1
access-list 101 permit ospf any any
!
```

Notice that an incoming filter is used on interface F1/0. The filtering must take place before the address translation; an outgoing filter on S2/0 would have no way to differentiate the already-translated destination address. Example 10-13 shows the results of the filter: Host C can still reach host D on its OL address, but packets to the OG address are blocked.

Example 10-13 *After the Filter Is Implemented on Mazatlan, Inside Hosts Can Reach Host D Only via Its OL Address*

```
Host_C#ping 10.1.3.1


Type escape sequence to abort.
Sending 5, 100-byte ICMP Echos to 10.1.3.1, timeout is 2 seconds:
!!!!!
Success rate is 100 percent (5/5), round-trip min/avg/max = 16/50/92 ms
Host_C#
Host_C#ping 201.114.37.5


Type escape sequence to abort.
Sending 5, 100-byte ICMP Echos to 201.114.37.5, timeout is 2 seconds:
U.U.U
Success rate is 0 percent (0/5)
Host_C#
```

Examples 10-10 and 10-11 emphasize that NAT does not, by itself, guarantee that private or illegal IP addresses do not leak into the public Internet. Wise administrators filter for the private classes A, B, and C addresses on interfaces connected to ISPs. Wise ISPs do the same on interfaces connected to their subscribers.

NAT44 and DNS

A difficulty with the various configurations shown in this case study so far is that very few "real-life" devices are going to use IP addresses to reach other devices. Names are almost always used. Therefore, DNS servers must have the correct IP addresses relevant to their side of the NAT. In Figure 10-16, DNS servers are placed on the inside and outside networks. DNS1 might have the following name-to-address mappings:

HostA.insidenet.com   IN A   10.1.1.3

HostB.insidenet.com   IN A   10.1.1.4

HostC.insidenet.com   IN A   10.1.2.2

Here, all hosts have local addresses (local to the inside network). DNS2 might have the following name-to-address mapping:

HostD.outsidenet.com   IN A   201.114.37.5

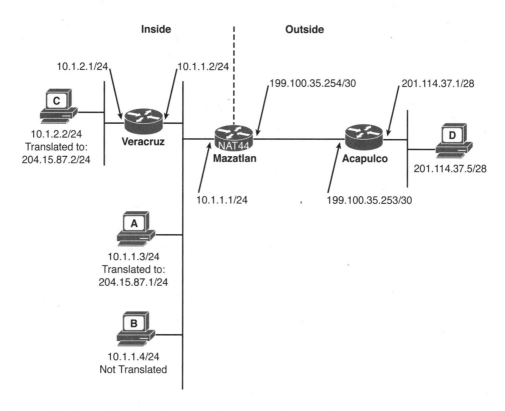

Figure 10-16 *DNS1 Is Authoritative for the Inside Network, and DNS2 Is Authoritative for the Outside Network*

These entries all map to global addresses. DNS1 is authoritative for inside.net, and DNS2 is authoritative for outside.net. Example 10-14 shows the NAT configuration for Mazatlan.

Example 10-14 *Mazatlan's NAT Configuration, Supporting DNS1 and DNS2 Referred to in Figure 10-16*

```
ip nat inside source static 10.1.1.3 204.15.87.1
ip nat inside source static 10.1.2.2 204.15.87.2
ip nat inside source static 10.1.1.4 204.15.87.3
ip nat inside source static 10.1.1.254 204.15.87.254
ip nat outside source static 201.114.37.5 10.1.3.1
ip nat outside source static 201.50.34.1 10.1.3.2
```

In addition to the three inside hosts and one outside host, the configuration referred to in Example 10-14 has entries for the two DNS servers. If host A wants to send a packet to host D, it sends a DNS query to DNS1 for the address of HostD.outsidenet.com. DNS1 then queries DNS2, which returns an address of 201.114.37.5. When this DNS message passes through the NAT, the address is translated to 10.1.3.1, and DNS1 passes this address on to host A. Host A then sends packets to this address, and the NAT translates the source and destination addresses of the packets.

If host D wants to speak to a host on the inside network, the opposite happens. Host D might query DNS2 for the address of HostC.insidenet.com, prompting DNS2 to query DNS1. DNS1 responds with an address of 10.1.2.2, which is translated to 204.15.87.2 by the NAT and passed to host D by DNS2. Again, when packets are exchanged between host D and host C, the NAT translates the source and destination addresses.

A setup such as the one referred to in Figure 10-16, with an inside DNS and an outside DNS, makes sense for an organization of some size but makes little sense for a smaller office. Actually, two DNS servers are not needed; a host on the inside can query a DNS server on the outside, and the responding A record can be translated by IOS.

The function within IOS that translates the address carried by the DNS A record itself is the DNS Application Level Gateway (ALG). It's one of several protocol-specific ALGs that are enabled with NAT44. Others include ICMP, FTP, H.323, SIP, SCCP, and ESP mode IPsec. What these protocols have in common is that they embed IPv4 addresses in the data payload; the ALGs examine the protocol packets and translate embedded addresses so that the protocol remains operable through the NAT.

The ALGs can be disabled, if needed. The DNS ALG, for example, is disabled with the global statements **no ip nat service alg udp dns** and **no ip nat service alg tcp dns**. It's also important to note that the DNS ALG does not work if overloading (described later in this chapter) is enabled, or if a route map is used with a static address mapping.

Case Study: Dynamic NAT

The problem with the configurations of the preceding case study is one of scalability. What if, instead of the four inside devices referred to in Figure 10-15, there are 60 or 6000? Maintaining static NAT mappings, such as maintaining static route entries, quickly becomes an administrative burden as the network grows.

The inside network in Figure 10-17 uses 10.1.1.0–10.1.2.255 for its IL address space and has been assigned the public address space 204.15.86.0/23 by its ISP. This public address space is used as a pool from which IG addresses are dynamically selected for mapping to the IL addresses. To make things more manageable and predictable, the space 10.1.1.0/24 is mapped to 204.15.86.0/24, and 10.1.2.0/24 is mapped to 204.15.87.0/24.

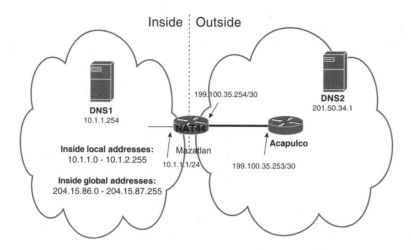

Figure 10-17 *Inside Network Has a Large Range of IL and IG Addresses*

The **ip nat pool** statement creates a pool of addresses and gives it a name. The pool is then designated as an IG pool and is linked to an IL address range with the statement **ip nat inside source list**. Example 10-15 shows the configuration for Mazatlan.

Example 10-15 *Mazatlan Is Configured to Dynamically Assign IG Addresses from an Address Pool*

```
interface FastEthernet1/0
 ip address 10.1.1.1 255.255.255.0
 ip nat inside
 ip virtual-reassembly
!
interface Serial2/0
 ip address 199.100.35.254 255.255.255.252
 ip nat outside
 ip virtual-reassembly
!
router ospf 100
 log-adjacency-changes
 network 10.1.1.1 0.0.0.0 area 0
 default-information originate
!
ip route 0.0.0.0 0.0.0.0 199.100.35.253
!
ip nat pool PoolOne 204.15.86.1 204.15.86.254 prefix-length 24
ip nat pool PoolTwo 204.15.87.1 204.15.87.253 prefix-length 24
```

```
ip nat inside source list 1 pool PoolOne
ip nat inside source list 2 pool PoolTwo
ip nat inside source static 10.1.1.254 204.15.87.254
!
access-list 1 permit 10.1.1.0 0.0.0.255
access-list 2 permit 10.1.2.0 0.0.0.255


!
```

Two pools are created, named PoolOne and PoolTwo. PoolOne is assigned an address range of 204.15.86.1–204.15.86.254. PoolTwo is assigned an address range of 204.15.87.1–204.15.87.253. Notice that the address ranges exclude the network addresses and the broadcast addresses; the **prefix-length** portion of the commands act as a sanity check, ensuring that such addresses as 204.15.87.255 are not mapped. An alternative to using the **prefix-length** keyword is the **netmask**. For example,

```
ip nat pool PoolTwo 204.15.87.1 204.15.87.253 netmask 255.255.255.0
```

has the same effect as the command with the **prefix-length 24** keyword. Because of these commands you could assign a range such as 204.15.86.0–204.15.86.255, and the "0" and "255" host addresses are not mapped. However, it is good practice to configure only the actual pool addresses to avoid confusion.

Notice also that PoolTwo does not include the address 204.15.87.254. This address is statically assigned to DNS1 so is left out of the pool. Any time an outside device must initiate a session to an inside device, as in the case of DNS1, there must be a statically assigned address. If its IG address were dynamic, outside devices would have no way of knowing what address to send packets to.

Next, access lists identify the addresses to be translated. In Mazatlan's configuration, access list 1 identifies the IL range 10.1.1.0–10.1.1.255, and access list 2 identifies the IL range 10.1.2.0–10.1.2.255.

Last, the IL addresses are linked to the correct IG address pool. For example, the statement **ip nat inside source list 1 pool PoolOne** says that an IP address sourced from the inside (that is, IL addresses) and matching the range specified in access list 1 are to be translated to an IG address taken from PoolOne.

Example 10-16 shows Mazatlan's NAT table just after the dynamic NAT configuration is added. You can see that the only mapping in the table is the static entry for DNS1.

Example 10-16 *When Mazatlan's Dynamic NAT Is First Configured, No Entries Reside in the NAT Table Except for the Single Static Entry*

```
Mazatlan#show ip nat translations
Pro Inside global      Inside local      Outside local      Outside global
--- 204.15.87.254      10.1.1.254        ---                ---
Mazatlan#
```

Example 10-17 shows the NAT table after several inside devices have originated traffic to the outside. The IG addresses are allocated from each pool numerically, beginning with the lowest available number, and with the newest allocation added to the top of the list.

Example 10-17   *Dynamic IL-to-IG Mappings Are Entered into the NAT Table as Inside Devices Send Packets to the Outside*

```
Mazatlan#show ip nat translations
Pro Inside global      Inside local      Outside local      Outside global
--- 204.15.86.4        10.1.1.3          ---                ---
--- 204.15.86.3        10.1.1.83         ---                ---
--- 204.15.86.2        10.1.1.239        ---                ---
--- 204.15.86.1        10.1.1.4          ---                ---
--- 204.15.87.3        10.1.2.164        ---                ---
--- 204.15.87.2        10.1.2.57         ---                ---
--- 204.15.87.1        10.1.2.2          ---                ---
--- 204.15.87.254      10.1.1.254        ---                ---
Mazatlan#
```

Occasionally, a network administrator may want the host portion of the IG address to match the host portion of the IL address to which it is mapped. To accomplish this, the keywords **type match-host** are added to the end of the statement defining the pool, as shown in Example 10-18. To change pool assignments back to sequential, replace the **match-host** keyword with the **rotary** keyword.

Example 10-18   **type match-host** *Option Matches the Host Portion of the IG Address to the Host Portion of the IL Address to Which It Is Mapped*

```
ip nat pool PoolOne 204.15.86.1 204.15.86.254 prefix-length 24 type match-host
ip nat pool PoolTwo 204.15.87.1 204.15.87.253 prefix-length 24 type match-host
ip nat inside source list 1 pool PoolOne
ip nat inside source list 2 pool PoolTwo
ip nat inside source static 10.1.1.254 204.15.87.254
!
ip route 0.0.0.0 0.0.0.0 199.100.35.253
!
access-list 1 permit 10.1.1.0 0.0.0.255
access-list 2 permit 10.1.2.0 0.0.0.255
!
```

Example 10-19 shows the resulting NAT table. Comparing it with the table in Example 10-17, you can see that all the same IL addresses have been translated. But rather than selecting IG addresses from their respective pools sequentially, IG addresses are selected with matching host portions.

Example 10-19 *Host Portions of the IG Addresses Match the Host Portions of the IL Addresses to Which They Are Mapped*

```
Mazatlan#show ip nat translations
Pro Inside global      Inside local      Outside local      Outside global
--- 204.15.86.4        10.1.1.4          ---                ---
--- 204.15.86.3        10.1.1.3          ---                ---
--- 204.15.86.83       10.1.1.83         ---                ---
--- 204.15.86.239      10.1.1.239        ---                ---
--- 204.15.87.2        10.1.2.2          ---                ---
--- 204.15.87.57       10.1.2.57         ---                ---
--- 204.15.87.164      10.1.2.164        ---                ---
--- 204.15.87.254      10.1.1.254        ---                ---
Mazatlan#
```

By default, the dynamic entries are held in the NAT table for 86400 seconds (24 hours). This time can be changed with the statement **ip nat translation timeout** to any time between 0 and 2147483647 seconds (approximately 68 years). The timeout period begins when a translation is first made and is reset each time a packet is translated by the mapping. Although a pool address is mapped to an address in the NAT table, it cannot be mapped to any other address. If the timeout period elapses with no new "hits" to the mapping, the entry is removed from the table, and the pool address is returned to the pool and becomes available. If 0 seconds or the keyword **never** is used with the **ip nat translation timeout** command, the mapping is never removed from the NAT table. The default timeouts are usually a good balance between maintaining address consistency to the outside and cleaning stale entries out of the NAT table to conserve memory.

You can also conserve memory by setting a threshold on how many entries are allowed in the NAT table at any one time, with the statement **ip nat translation max-entries**. On modern platforms, memory consumption should not be a problem, but this statement can still be useful if some policy limits the number of translations at any one time.

The translation timeout for each entry displays with the **show ip nat translations verbose** command, as shown in Example 10-20. The **ip nat translations verbose** command displays how long ago the mapping was entered into the NAT table, how long ago the mapping was last used to translate an address, and the time remaining before the end of the timeout period. The flags field can indicate translation types other than dynamic. For example, in Example 10-20 the last entry is shown to be a static translation.

Example 10-20 **show ip nat translations verbose** *Command Reveals Details About the Translation Timeout Periods for Each Mapping*

```
Mazatlan#show ip nat translations verbose
Pro Inside global      Inside local      Outside local      Outside global
--- 204.15.86.4         10.1.1.3         ---                ---
    create 00:31:55, use 00:31:55, left 23:28:04, flags: none
```

```
--- 204.15.86.3        10.1.1.83          ---             ---
    create 00:32:19, use 00:32:19, left 23:27:40, flags: none
--- 204.15.86.2        10.1.1.239         ---             ---
    create 00:33:38, use 00:33:38, left 23:26:21, flags: none
--- 204.15.86.1        10.1.1.4           ---             ---
    create 00:34:25, use 00:00:05, left 23:59:54, flags: none
--- 204.15.87.3        10.1.2.164         ---             ---
    create 00:31:02, use 00:31:02, left 23:28:57, flags: none
--- 204.15.87.2        10.1.2.57          ---             ---
    create 00:34:10, use 00:34:10, left 23:25:49, flags: none
--- 204.15.87.1        10.1.2.2           ---             ---
    create 00:35:04, use 00:35:04, left 23:24:55, flags: none
--- 204.15.87.254      10.1.1.254         ---             ---
    create 03:59:32, use 03:59:32, flags: static
Mazatlan#
```

The translation timeout period is important when the range of IL addresses is larger than the pool of IG addresses. Consider the configuration in Example 10-21.

Example 10-21 *1022 IL Addresses Share a Pool of 254 IG Addresses*

```
ip nat pool GlobalPool 204.15.86.1 204.15.86.254 prefix-length 24
ip nat inside source list 1 pool GlobalPool
!
access-list 1 permit 10.1.0.0 0.0.3.255
```

Here, 1022 possible IL addresses—10.1.0.1 through 10.1.3.254—are translated using a pool of 254 available IG addresses. That means that when 254 mapping entries are in the NAT table, no more IG addresses are available. Any packets with IL addresses that have not already been mapped will be dropped. The designer of such an addressing scheme is gambling that only a fraction of the total users in the network need outside access. But with each mapping remaining in the NAT table for 24 hours, the chances of using up all available IG addresses increase substantially. By reducing the translation timeout, the designer can reduce this likelihood.

Case Study: A Network Merger

NAT is useful for preventing possible address conflicts between networks. The previous two case studies demonstrated the connection of a network using private address space to a network using public addresses. The publicly addressed network may be some other enterprise, or it may be the Internet. The bottom line is that the private RFC 1918 addresses must be translated because they are not unique. Across the Internet, many enterprises use the same addresses in their networks and these addresses are "hidden" by NAT.

You could also use the configurations of the previous case studies in situations in which the inside network is addressed out of the public address space, but the addresses were not assigned by an addressing authority. For example, the inside network's address space might be 171.68.0.0/16. When connected to the Internet, NAT44 is required because this address space is assigned to another company. Allowing these untranslated packets onto the public Internet causes routing conflicts.

Another situation in which address conflicts may arise is the merger of two previously separate networks. In Figure 10-18, Surf Corporation and Sand, Inc., have formed a corporate merger to form Surf n' Sand Enterprises. Part of the merger is the connection of their two networks. Unfortunately, when the two networks were first constructed, the designers both chose to use the private 10.0.0.0 address space. As a result, many devices in Surf Corp.'s network have the same addresses as devices in Sand, Inc.'s network.

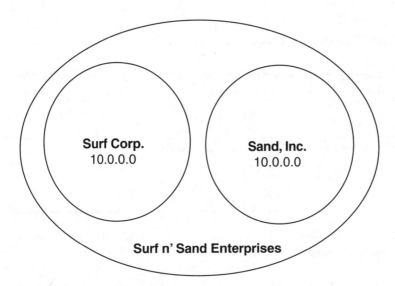

Figure 10-18 *Two Networks with Many Duplicate Addresses Must Be Connected*

The best solution is to re-address the new network. But address schemes are frequently designed poorly, making re-addressing a major project. In the Surf n' Sand network, for instance, all the devices have manually configured IPv4 addresses rather than having their addresses assigned by DHCP. NAT can be used as an interim solution to connect the networks until the re-addressing project can be completed.

Note In this application NAT should always be considered an interim solution. It is bad practice to allow address conflicts to exist within a network indefinitely.

The Surf n' Sand administrator first applies to his ISP or an addressing authority to acquire a public address space and is assigned the CIDR block 206.100.160.0/19. This block is then split in one-half. 206.100.160.0/20 is assigned to the former Sand network, and 206.100.176.0/20 is assigned to the former Surf network. An assumption is made here that although the 10.0.0.0 network can support more than 16 million host addresses, in reality there are not more hosts in either network than can be serviced out of the /20 address space.

The routers Cozumel and Guaymas in Figure 10-19 connect the two networks with the configurations in Example 10-22.

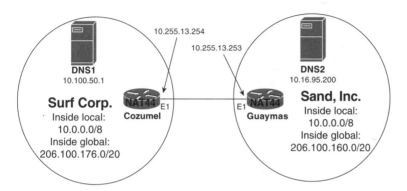

Figure 10-19 *NAT Is Used at the Boundaries of the Two Networks to Correct the Address Conflicts*

Example 10-22 *NAT Configurations for Routers Cozumel and Guaymas Referred to in Figure 10-19*

```
Cozumel
interface Ethernet0
 ip address 10.100.85.1 255.255.255.0
 ip nat inside
 ip virtual-reassembly
!
interface Ethernet1
 ip address 10.255.13.254 255.255.255.248
 ip nat outside
 ip virtual-reassembly
!
router ospf 1
 redistribute static
 network 10.100.85.1 0.0.0.0 area 18
!
ip nat pool Surf 206.100.176.2 206.100.191.254 prefix-length 20
ip nat inside source list 1 pool Surf
ip nat inside source static 10.100.50.1 206.100.176.1
!
```

```
ip route 206.100.160.0 255.255.240.0 10.255.13.253
!
access-list 1 deny    10.255.13.254
access-list 1 permit any
```

```
Guaymas
interface Ethernet0
 ip address 10.16.95.1 255.255.255.0
 ip nat inside
 ip virtual-reassembly
!
interface Ethernet1
 ip address 10.255.13.253 255.255.255.248
 ip nat outside
 ip virtual-reassembly
!
interface Serial1
 no ip address
 encapsulation frame-relay
!
interface Serial1.508 point-to-point
 ip address 10.18.3.253 255.255.255.0
 ip nat inside
 ip virtual-reassembly
 frame-relay interface-dlci 508
!
router eigrp 100
 redistribute static metric 1000 100 255 1 1500
 passive-interface Ethernet1
 network 10.0.0.0
 no auto-summary
!
ip nat pool Sand 206.100.160.2 206.100.175.254 prefix-length 20
ip nat inside source list 1 pool Sand
ip nat inside source static 10.16.95.200 206.100.160.1
!
ip route 206.100.176.0 255.255.240.0 10.255.13.254
!
access-list 1 deny    10.255.13.253
access-list 1 permit 10.0.0.0
!
```

The DNS servers are crucial to this design. In the NAT configurations, each server has a static IL-to-IG mapping. Suppose a device in the Sand network, Beachball.sand.com, wants to send a packet to Snorkel.surf.com in the Surf network. Suppose further that both devices have an IP address of 10.1.2.2. The following sequence of events occur:

1. Host Beachball queries DNS2 for the address of Snorkel.surf.com.

2. DNS2 queries DNS1, which is authoritative for the surf.com domain. The query has a source address of 10.16.95.200 and a destination address of 206.100.176.1. The query is forwarded to Guaymas, which is advertising a route into EIGRP for 206.100.176.0/20.

3. Guaymas translates the source address from 10.16.95.200 to 206.100.160.1, based on the static NAT entry, and forwards the packet to Cozumel.

4. Cozumel translates the destination address from 206.100.176.1 to 10.100.50.1, based on the static NAT entry, and forwards the query to DNS1.

5. DNS1 responds to the query, indicating that Snorkel.surf.com has an IP address of 10.1.2.2. The response message has a source address of 10.100.50.1 and a destination address of 206.100.160.1. The response is forwarded to Cozumel, which is advertising a route into OSPF for 206.100.160.0/20.

6. Cozumel translates the source address of the DNS response to 206.100.176.1. NAT also finds the address 10.1.2.2 in the Answer field of the message; the address matches access list 1 and is translated to an address from the pool named Surf. For this example, the address is 206.100.176.3. The mapping is entered into the NAT table, and the response is forwarded to Guaymas.

7. Guaymas translates the destination of the DNS response to 10.16.95.200 and forwards the message to DNS2.

8. DNS2 informs Beachball that the IP address of Snorkel.surf.com is 206.100.176.3.

9. Beachball sends a packet to Snorkel with a source address of 10.1.2.2 and a destination address of 206.100.176.3. Again, the packet is forwarded to Guaymas.

10. At Guaymas, the source address matches access list 1 and an address is selected from the pool named Sand. For this example, the address is 206.100.160.2. The source address is translated, the mapping is entered into the NAT table, and the packet is forwarded to Cozumel.

11. Cozumel finds that the destination address of 206.100.176.3 is mapped in its NAT table to 10.1.2.2 and makes the translation to that IL address. The packet is forwarded to Snorkel.

12. Snorkel sends a packet in response. The source address is 10.1.2.2 and the destination address is 206.100.160.2. The packet if forwarded to Cozumel.

13. Cozumel translates the packet's source address to 206.100.176.3 and forwards the packet to Guamas.

14. Guaymas translates the packet's destination address to 10.1.2.2 and forwards the packet to Beachball.

By following this example, you can see that although two devices have the same IP address, neither is aware of the other's true address. Key to making all this work is the routing configurations of Cozumel and Guaymas. Neither router leaks information about the 10.0.0.0 network to the other. Nothing in either configuration allows a packet with a destination address within the 10.0.0.0 network to be forwarded to the other router, with the exception of packets destined for the directly connected 10.255.13.248/29 subnet. Access list 1 is configured so that packets sourced from either router's E1 interface are not translated.

Note   The third Troubleshooting Exercise asks you to consider this access list configuration further.

Another detail of interest in Example 10-19 is that there is more than one inside interface at Guaymas. Multiple inside interfaces are quite acceptable.

One topic of importance, which is not readily evident in the configuration, concerns the coordination of the NAT translation timeout period and the DNS cache Time To Live (TTL) period. When a DNS server receives a resource record from another DNS server, it caches the record so that it can respond directly to subsequent queries for the same record. In this case study, DNS2 caches the A RR that maps Snorkel.surf.com to IP address 206.100.176.3. DNS2 can then respond to subsequent requests for Snorkel's IP address without again querying DNS1. This cached resource record has a TTL period associated with it and is flushed when the TTL expires. The DNS TTL period must be shorter than the NAT translation timeout period.

Suppose, for example, that the NAT translation timeout expires on the 10.1.2.2-to-206.100.176.3 mapping, and the IG address is returned to the pool. 206.100.176.3 is then mapped to a different IL address within the Surf network, but DNS2 still has an RR mapping Snorkel.surf.com to 206.100.176.3. If a device in the Sand network queries DNS2 for Snorkel's address, DNS2 responds with obsolete information and packets are sent to the wrong host.

A final note on this design concerns Internet access. This is easily accomplished by adding an access router to the subnet between Cozumel and Guaymas, as shown in Figure 10-20. The source addresses of packets from both the Surf and Sand networks are already translated to valid public addresses; all that is needed is for default routes to be added to Cozumel and Guaymas, pointing to the Internet access router.

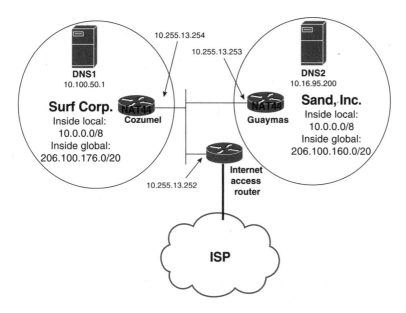

Figure 10-20   *Internet Access Router Does Not Have to Support NAT; Cozumel and Guaymas Perform All Translations for Internet Traffic*

Case Study: ISP Multihoming with NAT

The section "NAT and Multihomed Autonomous Systems" earlier in the chapter demonstrates how NAT can be employed to overcome the problem of multihoming to different ISPs with different CIDR blocks. The subscriber in Figure 10-7 is multihomed, and each ISP sees packets with source addresses belonging to its own address space. Neither ISP receives packets from the subscriber with source addresses belonging to the other ISP's block of addresses.

Based on the NAT case studies you have already seen, you can easily write configurations for the two NAT routers referred to in Figure 10-7. But what about a situation in which a single router is multihomed to both ISPs, as shown in Figure 10-21? Montego receives full BGP routes from both ISPs so that it can choose the best provider to any destination. When a packet is forwarded to ISP1, the packet must have a source address from the 205.113.50.0/23 block assigned by ISP1; when a packet is forwarded to ISP2, it must have a source address from the 207.36.76.0/23 block assigned by ISP2.

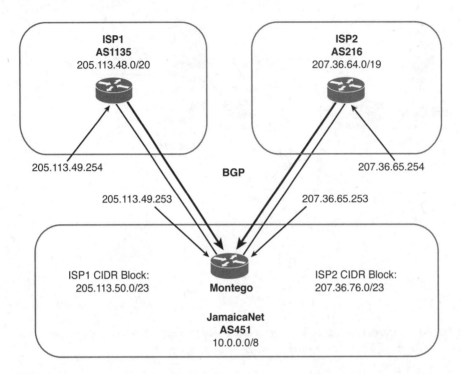

Figure 10-21　*ISP1 and ISP2 Have Each Assigned a CIDR Block to JamaicaNet. When Packets Are Forwarded to an ISP, They Must Have the Correct Source Address for That ISP*

Example 10-23 shows Montego's configuration for using different address pools on different interfaces.

Example 10-23　*Montego's Configuration Referred to in Figure 10-21 Enables the Use of ISP-Specific Address Pools as Source Addresses of Outgoing Packets*

```
interface Ethernet0
 ip address 10.1.1.1 255.255.255.0
 ip nat inside
!
interface Ethernet1
 ip address 10.5.1.1 255.255.255.0
 ip nat inside
!
interface Serial1
 no ip address
 encapsulation frame-relay
!
interface Serial1.708 point-to-point
```

```
 description PVC to ISP1
 ip address 205.113.49.253 255.255.255.252
 ip nat outside
 frame-relay interface-dlci 708
!
interface Serial1.709 point-to-point
 description PVC to ISP2
 ip address 207.36.65.253 255.255.255.252
 ip nat outside
 frame-relay interface-dlci 709
!
router ospf 10
 network 10.0.0.0 0.255.255.255 area 10
 default-information originate always
!
router bgp 451
 neighbor 205.113.49.254 remote-as 1135
 neighbor 207.36.65.254 remote-as 216
!
ip nat pool ISP1 205.113.50.1 205.113.51.254 prefix-length 23
ip nat pool ISP2 207.36.76.1 207.36.77.254 prefix-length 23
ip nat inside source route-map ISP1_MAP pool ISP1
ip nat inside source route-map ISP2_MAP pool ISP2
!
access-list 1 permit 10.0.0.0 0.255.255.255
access-list 2 permit 207.36.65.254
!
route-map ISP1_MAP permit 10
 match ip address 1
 match interface Serial1.708
!
route-map ISP2_MAP permit 10
 match ip address 1
 match ip next-hop 2
!
```

The address blocks assigned by the ISPs are specified in the pools ISP1 and ISP2. The
significant feature of this NAT configuration is that the **ip nat inside source** statements
make calls to route maps instead of access lists. By using route maps, you can specify not
only the IL address, but also the interface or the next-hop address to which the packet
is to be forwarded. ISP1_MAP specifies packets that have a source address belonging to
the 10.0.0.0 network (as identified by access list 1) and which are to be forwarded out
interface s1.708 to ISP1. ISP2_MAP also specifies packets from the 10.0.0.0 but which
are to be forwarded to the next-hop address 207.36.65.254 to ISP2.

Note   Normally, either the **match interface** or the **match ip next-hop** command would be used in both route maps for consistency. Both commands are used here for demonstration purposes.

For example, an inside device with an address of 10.1.2.2 sends a packet with a destination address of 137.19.1.1. The packet is forwarded to Montego because that router is advertising a default route into JamaicaNet via OSPF. Montego does a route lookup and determines that the best route to the destination is via ISP2 out S1.709 and with a next-hop address of 207.36.65.254. The first **ip nat inside source** statement checks this information against route map ISP1_MAP. Although the source address matches, the egress interface does not. The second **ip nat inside source** statement checks the information against route map ISP2_MAP. Here both the source address and the next-hop address match, so the source address is translated to an address out of the ISP2 pool.

Example 10-24 shows Montego's NAT table after some traffic has passed to the ISPs. Because an IL address can be mapped to an address from more than one pool, the address mappings are extended mappings, showing the protocol type and the port number. Extended mapping is discussed in more detail in the case study "Port Address Translation."

Example 10-24   *Montego's NAT Table Shows That the IG Address Chosen for Translation Depends Upon the ISP to Which the Packet Is to Be Forwarded*

```
Montego#show ip nat translations
Pro Inside global      Inside local     Outside local      Outside global
udp 207.36.76.2:4953   10.1.2.2:4953    137.19.1.1:69      137.19.1.1:69
udp 205.113.50.2:2716  10.1.1.2:2716    171.35.100.4:514   171.35.100.4:514
tcp 205.113.50.1:11009 10.5.1.2:11009   205.113.48.1:23    205.113.48.1:23
tcp 207.36.76.1:11002  10.1.1.2:11002   198.15.61.1:23     198.15.61.1:23
tcp 205.113.50.3:11007 10.1.2.2:11007   171.35.18.1:23     171.35.18.1:23
tcp 207.36.76.2:11008  10.1.2.2:11008   207.36.64.1:23     207.36.64.1:23
Montego#
```

Of interest in the NAT table referred to in Example 10-24 are the three entries for the IL address 10.1.2.2. The UDP traffic and one of the TCP sessions went to a destination via ISP2. The IG address to which the IL address is mapped is 207.36.76.2. The other TCP session was sent via ISP1, so was mapped to 205.113.50.3. These entries demonstrate that the pool from which the IG address is chosen changes, even for the same source address, depending upon where the packet is forwarded.

Figure 10-22 shows DNS servers for the three autonomous systems. The servers in ISP1 and ISP2 must access Ochee, the DNS server authoritative for JamaicaNet. This means that Ochee must have static NAT entries to addresses in both CIDR blocks. Statically mapping an IL address to more than one IG address is normally not allowed because the mappings are ambiguous. In this case, ambiguity is not a problem because the same NAT is doing both mappings. When Montego routes Ochee's DNS queries and responses to DNS1 or DNS2, the appropriate translations are made.

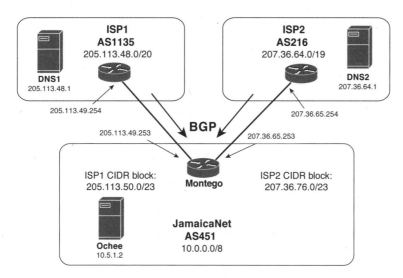

Figure 10-22 *DNS Server Ochee Must Have a Static IL-to-IG Mapping So That It Can Be Queried by DNS1 and DNS2*

To allow static NAT mappings of one IL address to multiple IG addresses, the keyword **extendable** is added to the end of the mapping statements. Example 10-25 shows the NAT configuration for Montego.

Example 10-25 *NAT Configuration for Montego Allows Static NAT Mappings of One IL Address to Multiple IG Addresses*

```
ip nat pool ISP1 205.113.50.2 205.113.51.254 prefix-length 23
ip nat pool ISP2 prefix-length 23
 address 207.36.76.1 207.36.76.99
 address 207.36.76.101 207.36.77.254
ip nat inside source route-map ISP1_MAP pool ISP1
ip nat inside source route-map ISP2_MAP pool ISP2
ip nat inside source static 10.5.1.2 207.36.76.100 extendable
ip nat inside source static 10.5.1.2 205.113.50.1 extendable
!
access-list 1 permit 10.0.0.0 0.255.255.255
access-list 2 permit 207.36.65.254
!
route-map ISP1_MAP permit 10
 match ip address 1
 match interface Serial1.708
!
```

```
route-map ISP2_MAP permit 10
 match ip address 1
 match ip next-hop 2
```

From the perspective of DNS1, Ochee's address is 205.113.50.1. Notice that NAT pool ISP1 is modified to exclude this address from the pool. From the perspective of DNS2, Ochee's address is 207.36.76.100. This address is taken from the middle of the 207.36.76.0/23 block rather than from one end or the other, making pool ISP2 discontiguous. The pool is modified in the configuration to specify two ranges of addresses: Those before Ochee's address and those after Ochee's address.

A discontiguous range of addresses is configured by first naming the pool and specifying the prefix length or netmask. The configuration prompt then enables you to enter a list of ranges. Example 10-26 shows the configuration steps for pool ISP2, including the prompts.

Example 10-26 *Configuring a NAT Pool for a Discontiguous Range of Addresses*

```
Montego(config)#ip nat pool ISP2 prefix-length 23
Montego(config-ipnat-pool)#address 207.36.76.1 207.36.76.99
Montego(config-ipnat-pool)#address 207.36.76.101 207.36.77.254
```

Port Address Translation

At the opposite extreme from the multihomed NAT router in the last case study is the Small Office/Home Office (SOHO) router connecting a few devices to the Internet. Rather than acquiring separate public addresses for each device, port address translation (PAT) enables all the SOHO devices to share a single IG address.

PAT allows *overloading*, or the mapping of more than one IL address to the same IG address. To accomplish this, the NAT entries in the routing table are *extended* entries; the entries track not only the relevant IP addresses, but also the protocol types and ports. By translating both the IP address and the port number of a packet, up to 65535 IL addresses could theoretically be mapped to a single IG address (based on the 16-bit port number).

> **Note** Each NAT entry uses approximately 312 bytes of DRAM, so 65535 entries would consume more than 20 MB of memory and large amounts of CPU power. Nowhere near this number of addresses are mapped in practical PAT configurations.

Cisco NAT attempts to preserve BSD semantics, mapping an IL port number to the same IG port number whenever possible. A different IG port number is used only when the port number associated with the IL address is already used in another mapping.

Figure 10-23 shows three devices connected to an ISP.

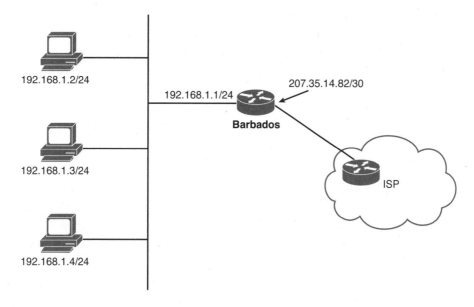

Figure 10-23 *Barbados Uses PAT to Map the Addresses of the Three Inside Hosts to the Single Serial Interface Address*

The access router has a single public IP address assigned by the ISP on its serial interface, as shown in Example 10-27.

Example 10-27 *Enabling PAT on Router Barbados Referred to in Figure 10-23*

```
interface Ethernet0
 ip address 192.168.1.1 255.255.255.0
 ip nat inside
!
interface Serial0
 ip address 207.35.14.82 255.255.255.252
 ip nat outside
!
ip nat inside source list 1 interface Serial0 overload
!
ip route 0.0.0.0 0.0.0.0 Serial0
!
access-list 1 permit 192.168.1.0 0.0.0.255
!
```

PAT is enabled with the **overload** keyword. Although the **ip nat inside source** command could reference an address pool, in this case it simply references the interface on which the IG address is configured. As usual, the access list identifies the IL addresses.

Example 10-28 shows the NAT table in the access router after a few packets have passed through it. Most of the IG ports match the IL ports, but notice that there are two instances in which an IL socket has a port number that has already been used (192.168.1.2:11000 and 192.168.1.2:11001). As a result, the NAT has chosen an unused port for these sockets that does not match the IL port.

Example 10-28 *Different IL Addresses Have Been Mapped to Different Ports of the Same IG Address*

```
Barbados#show ip nat translations
Pro Inside global      Inside local      Outside local       Outside global
tcp 207.35.14.82:11011 192.168.1.3:11011 191.115.37.2:23     191.115.37.2:23
tcp 207.35.14.82:5000  192.168.1.2:11000 191.115.37.2:23     191.115.37.2:23
udp 207.35.14.82:3749  192.168.1.2:3749  135.88.131.55:514   135.88.131.55:514
tcp 207.35.14.82:11000 192.168.1.4:11000 191.115.37.2:23     191.115.37.2:23
tcp 207.35.14.82:11002 192.168.1.2:11002 118.50.47.210:23    118.50.47.210:23
udp 207.35.14.82:9371  192.168.1.2:9371  135.88.131.55:514   135.88.131.55:514
icmp 207.35.14.82:7428 192.168.1.3:7428  135.88.131.55:7428 135.88.131.55:7428
tcp 207.35.14.82:5001  192.168.1.2:11001 135.88.131.55:23    135.88.131.55:23
tcp 207.35.14.82:11001 192.168.1.4:11001 135.88.131.55:23    135.88.131.55:23
Barbados#
```

Case Study: TCP Load Balancing

Figure 10-24 shows a topology similar to the one in the PAT case study. But here the three inside devices are not hosts but identical servers with mirrored content. The intent is to create a "virtual server" with an address of 199.198.5.1; that is, from the outside a single server at that IG address. In reality, the router Barbados is configured to perform round-robin translations to the three IL addresses.

Note These days, load balancing across multiple servers is more likely to be done by a dedicated load balancer, either as a physical appliance or as software, rather than configured on a router. The principles are the same, though.

Example 10-29 shows the configuration for Barbados.

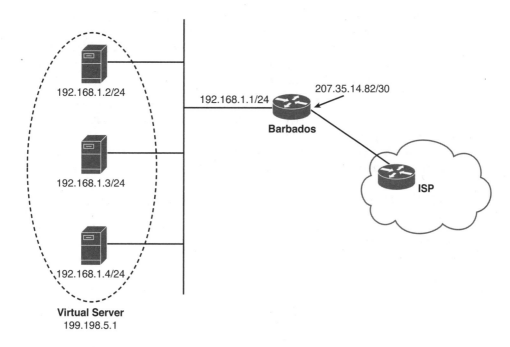

Figure 10-24   *Three Inside Devices Are Identical Servers with Mirrored Content, Which from the Outside Appear to Be a Single Server*

Example 10-29   *Barbados' NAT Configuration Evenly Distributes the TCP Load to the Three Identical Servers. Outside Devices See Only a Single Inside Global Address*

```
interface Ethernet0
 ip address 192.168.1.1 255.255.255.0
 ip nat inside
!
interface Serial0
 ip address 207.35.14.82 255.255.255.252
 ip nat outside
!
ip nat pool V-Server 192.168.1.2 192.168.1.4 prefix-length 24 type rotary
ip nat inside destination list 1 pool V-Server
!
ip route 0.0.0.0 0.0.0.0 Serial0
!
access-list 1 permit 199.198.5.1
!
```

Instead of translating an IL address as most of the previous case studies have demonstrated, this configuration translates the IG address. The address pool V-Server contains a list of the available IL addresses, and the keywords **type rotary** cause a round-robin assignment of the pool addresses. The access list, as usual, identifies the address to be translated—in this case, the single destination address 199.198.5.1.

Example 10-30 shows the resulting NAT table after four outside devices have sent TCP traffic to the virtual server. You can observe that the first three connections (reading from the bottom up) were allocated sequentially from the lowest IL address in the pool to the highest. There are only three addresses available in the pool, so the fourth connection is again mapped to the lowest IL address.

Example 10-30 *TCP Connections to the Virtual Server Address 199.198.5.1 Are Balanced Across the Three Real Server Addresses*

```
Barbados#show ip nat translations
Pro Inside global     Inside local      Outside local      Outside global
tcp 199.198.5.1:23    192.168.1.2:23    203.1.2.3:11003      203.1.2.3:11003
tcp 199.198.5.1:23    192.168.1.4:23    135.88.131.55:11002 135.88.131.55:11002
tcp 199.198.5.1:23    192.168.1.3:23    118.50.47.210:11001 118.50.47.210:11001
tcp 199.198.5.1:23    192.168.1.2:23    191.115.37.2:11000 191.115.37.2:11000
Barbados#
```

Case Study: Service Distribution

NAT can also create a virtual server in which connections are distributed by TCP or UDP services, rather than by TCP connection. The network in Figure 10-25 is similar to that referred to in Figure 10-24, except that the servers are not identical. Rather, different servers offer different services. From the outside, all three servers appear to be a single server with the address 199.198.5.1.

Example 10-31 shows the NAT configuration in Barbados.

Example 10-31 *NAT Configuration in Barbados Translates the Virtual IG Address According to the TCP or UDP Port Associated with the Address*

```
interface Ethernet0
 ip address 192.168.1.1 255.255.255.0
 ip nat inside
!
interface Serial0
 ip address 207.35.14.82 255.255.255.252
 ip nat outside
!
ip nat inside source static tcp 192.168.1.4 25 199.198.5.1 25 extendable
ip nat inside source static udp 192.168.1.3 514 199.198.5.1 514 extendable
```

```
ip nat inside source static udp 192.168.1.3 69 199.198.5.1 69 extendable
ip nat inside source static tcp 192.168.1.3 21 199.198.5.1 21 extendable
ip nat inside source static tcp 192.168.1.3 20 199.198.5.1 20 extendable
ip nat inside source static tcp 192.168.1.2 80 199.198.5.1 80 extendable
!
ip route 0.0.0.0 0.0.0.0 Serial0
!
```

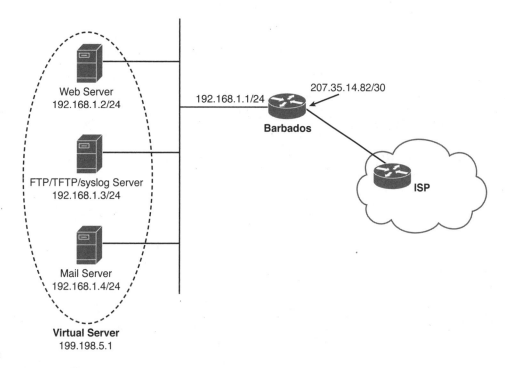

Figure 10-25 *Three Inside Devices That Offer Different Services Appear to Be a Single Server from the Outside*

You see that no address pools or access lists are used here; instead, the configuration is a series of simple IL-to-IG mappings. The difference between these statements and the static statements you have seen earlier is that TCP or UDP is specified, as are the source and destination ports. The **extendable** keyword is used because the same address—this time the IG address—appears in more than one statement. You do not have to type the keyword: Cisco IOS Software adds it automatically. In order, the statements map SMTP (TCP port 25), syslog (UDP port 514), TFTP (UDP port 69), FTP (TCP ports 20 and 21), and HTTP (TCP port 80).

Example 10-32 shows the NAT table just after Barbados is configured; the only entries are the static entries.

Example 10-32 *Before Any Dynamic Translations Occur, Barbados' NAT Table Contains Only the Static Mappings of IL Sockets to IG Sockets*

```
Barbados#show ip nat translations
Pro Inside global      Inside local      Outside local      Outside global
udp 199.198.5.1:514    192.168.1.3:514   ---                ---
udp 199.198.5.1:69     192.168.1.3:69    ---                ---
tcp 199.198.5.1:80     192.168.1.2:80    ---                ---
tcp 199.198.5.1:21     192.168.1.3:21    ---                ---
tcp 199.198.5.1:20     192.168.1.3:20    ---                ---
tcp 199.198.5.1:25     192.168.1.4:25    ---                ---
Barbados#
```

Example 10-33 shows the NAT table after some traffic has passed through Barbados. Notice that among all the dynamic mappings, only two OG addresses display. Yet the sessions have been mapped to different IL addresses, depending upon the port associated with the IG address.

Example 10-33 *UDP and TCP Packets Are Mapped to Different IL Addresses, Depending Upon Their Associated Port Numbers*

```
Barbados#show ip nat translations
Pro Inside global      Inside local      Outside local          Outside global
udp 199.198.5.1:514    192.168.1.3:514   ---                    ---
tcp 199.198.5.1:25     192.168.1.4:25    207.35.14.81:11003     207.35.14.81:11003
udp 199.198.5.1:69     192.168.1.3:69    ---                    ---
tcp 199.198.5.1:80     192.168.1.2:80    ---                    ---
tcp 199.198.5.1:21     192.168.1.3:21    ---                    ---
tcp 199.198.5.1:20     192.168.1.3:20    ---                    ---
tcp 199.198.5.1:25     192.168.1.4:25    ---                    ---
tcp 199.198.5.1:20     192.168.1.3:20    191.115.37.2:1027      191.115.37.2:1027
tcp 199.198.5.1:21     192.168.1.3:21    191.115.37.2:1026      191.115.37.2:1026
tcp 199.198.5.1:80     192.168.1.2:80    191.115.37.2:1030      191.115.37.2:1030
udp 199.198.5.1:69     192.168.1.3:69    191.115.37.2:1028      191.115.37.2:1028
udp 199.198.5.1:514    192.168.1.3:514   207.35.14.81:1029      207.35.14.81:1029
Barbados#
```

Troubleshooting NAT44

A lot can be done with IOS NAT44, and the configurations are straightforward. If it does not work, you can spot a few common causes by asking the following questions:

- Do the dynamic pools contain the correct range of addresses?

- Is there any overlap between dynamic pools?

- Is there any overlap between addresses used for static mapping and the addresses in the dynamic pools?

- Do the access lists specify the correct addresses to be translated? Are any addresses left out? Are there any addresses included that should not be included?

- Are the correct inside and outside interfaces specified?

One of the most common problems with a new NAT configuration is not NAT itself but routing. Remember that you are changing a source or destination address in a packet; after the translation, does the router know what to do with the new address?

Another problem can be timeouts. If a translated address is cached in some system after the dynamic entry has timed out of the NAT table, packets can be sent to the wrong address or the destination may seem to have disappeared. Besides the **ip nat translation timeout** command already discussed, several other default timeouts can be changed. Table 10-3 lists all the keywords that can be used with the **ip nat translation** command and the default values of the timeout periods. All the defaults can be changed within a range of 0–2147483647 seconds.

Table 10-3 *Dynamic NAT Table Timeout Values*

ip nat translation	Default Period (Seconds)	Description
timeout	86400 (24 hrs)	Timeout for all nonport-specific dynamic translations
dns-timeout	60	Timeout for DNS connections
finrst-timeout	60	Timeout after TCP FIN or RST flags are seen (closing a TCP session)
icmp-timeout	60	Timeout for ICMP translations
port-timeout tcp	60	Timeout for TCP port translations
port-timeout udp	60	Timeout for UDP port translations
syn-timeout	60	Timeout after TCP SYN flag is seen, and no further session packets
tcp-timeout	86400 (24 hrs)	Timeout for TCP translations (nonport-specific)
udp-port	300 (5 min)	Timeout for UDP translations (nonport-specific)

Theoretically, there is no limit on the number of mappings that the NAT table can hold. Practically, memory and CPU or the boundaries of the available addresses or ports place a limit on the number of entries. Each NAT mapping uses approximately 312 bytes of memory. In the rare case in which the entries must be limited either for performance or policy reasons, the **ip nat translation max-entries** command can be used.

Another useful command for troubleshooting is **show ip nat statistics**, as shown in Example 10-34. The command displays a summary of the NAT configuration, plus counts on active translation types, hits to an existing mapping, misses (causing an attempt to create a mapping), and expired translations. For dynamic pools, the type of pool, the total available addresses, the number of allocated addresses, the number of failed allocations, and the number of translations using the pool (refcount) display.

Example 10-34   show ip nat statistics *Displays Many Useful Details for Analyzing and Troubleshooting Your NAT Configuration*

```
StCroix#show ip nat statistics
Total active translations: 3 (2 static, 1 dynamic; 3 extended)
Outside interfaces:
  Serial0, Serial1.708, Serial1.709
Inside interfaces:
  Ethernet0, Ethernet1
Hits: 980  Misses: 43
Expired translations: 54
Dynamic mappings:
-- Inside Source
access-list 1 interface Serial0 refcount 0
StCroix#
```

Finally, dynamic NAT entries can be manually cleared from the NAT table. This action can be useful if you need to get rid of a particular offending entry without waiting for the timeout to expire, or if you need to clear the entire NAT table to reconfigure an address pool. Note that Cisco IOS Software does not enable you to change or delete an address pool while addresses from the pool are mapped in the NAT table. The **clear ip nat translations** command clears entries. You can specify a single entry by the global and local address or by TCP and UDP translations (including ports), or you can use an asterisk (*) to clear the entire table. Of course, only dynamic entries are cleared; the command does not remove static entries.

Looking Ahead

When the first edition of this book was written, NAT always meant translation from one IPv4 address to another IPv4 address. Things have changed since then, and a major use for address translation these days is translating between IPv4 and IPv6 addresses. As a result, NAT terminology has also changed. As this chapter reflects, NAT44 is traditional NAT, whereas NAT64 is translation between protocol versions—which involves not just replacing addresses but replacing entire headers. You also need to know the context in which the acronym "NAT" is used. It's used many times in this chapter, and in context it always meant NAT44. Chapter 11 examines NAT64 and the particular procedures needed for that translation. NAT is again frequently used there with no modifiers, but the context makes it clear that it is written about NAT64.

Review Questions

1. What is the difference between an inside address and an outside address?

2. What is the difference between a local address and a global address?

3. What is an address translation table?

4. What is the difference between static and dynamic translation?

5. What is the IOS default translation timeout period?

6. What is Port Address Translation, or PAT?

Configuration Exercises

Refer to Figure 10-26 for Configuration Exercises 1–5.

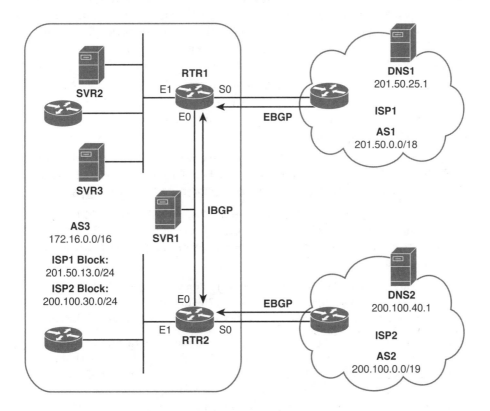

Figure 10-26   *Network for Configuration Exercises 1–5*

1. ISP1 in Figure 10-26 has assigned the address block 201.50.13.0/24 to AS3.
ISP2 has assigned the address block 200.100.30.0/24 to AS3. RTR1 and RTR2

accept full BGP routes from the ISP routers but do not transmit any routes to the ISPs. They run IBGP between them and OSPF on all Ethernet interfaces. No routes are redistributed between BGP and OSPF. The addresses of the router interfaces follow:

RTR1, E0: 172.16.3.1/24

RTR1, E1: 172.16.2.1/24

RTR1, S0: 201.50.26.13/30

RTR2, E0: 172.16.3.2/24

RTR2, E1: 172.16.1.1/24

RTR2, S0: 200.100.29.241/30

SVR1 is the DNS server authoritative for AS3; its address is 172.16.3.3. DNS1 reaches SVR1 at 201.50.13.1, whereas DNS2 reaches the same server at 200.100.30.254. Write routing and NAT configurations for RTR1 and RTR2, translating inside addresses appropriately for each ISP's assigned address block. Any inside device must reach either ISP, but no packets can leave AS3 with a private source address under any circumstance.

2. The address of SVR2 referred to in Figure 10-26 is 172.16.2.2, and the address of SVR3 is 172.16.2.3. Modify the configurations of Configuration Exercise 1 so that devices within ISP1's AS connect to the servers round-robin at the address 201.50.13.3.

3. HTTP packets sent to 200.100.30.50 from ISP2 are sent to SVR2, as referred to in Figure 10-26. SMTP packets sent to 200.100.30.50 from ISP2 are sent to SVR3. Modify the configurations of the previous exercises to implement these translations.

4. Five outside devices in referred to Figure 10-26, 201.50.12.67–201.50.12.71, must appear to devices within AS3 as having addresses 192.168.1.1–192.168.1.5, respectively. Add the appropriate NAT configurations to the previously created configurations.

5. Devices in AS3 referred to in Figure 10-26 with addresses in the 172.16.100.0/24 subnet should all appear to have the IG address 200.100.30.75 when sending packets to ISP2. Modify the configurations of the previous exercises to accommodate this.

6. Referring to Figure 10-27, redundant links have been added so that RTR1 and RTR2 each have connections to both ISPs, and each accept full BGP routes from both ISPs. The address of RTR1, S1 is 200.100.29.137/30, and the address of RTR2, S1 is 201.50.26.93/30. Write configurations for the two routers, ensuring that all features added in the previous exercises still work correctly.

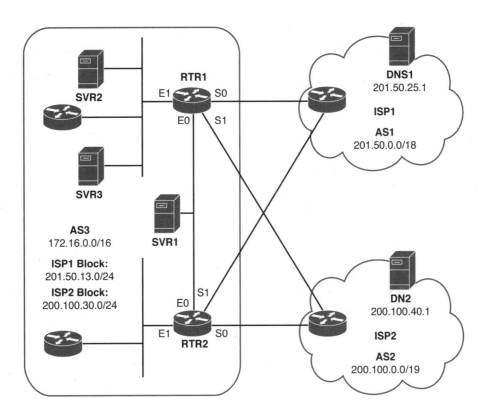

Figure 10-27   *Network for Configuration Exercise 6*

Troubleshooting Exercises

1. Identify the mistake in the configuration in Example 10-35.

Example 10-35   *Configuration for Troubleshooting Exercise 1*

```
ip nat pool EX1 192.168.1.1 192.168.1.254 netmask 255.255.255.0 type match-host
ip nat pool EX1A netmask 255.255.255.240
 address 172.21.1.33 172.21.1.38
 address 172.21.1.40 172.21.1.46
ip nat inside source list 1 pool EX1
ip nat inside source static 10.18.53.210 192.168.1.1
ip nat outside source list 2 pool EX1A
!
access-list 1 permit 10.0.0.0 0.255.255.255
access-list 2 permit 192.168.2.0 0.0.0.255
```

2. The router referred to in Figure 10-28 connects two internetworks with overlapping addresses.

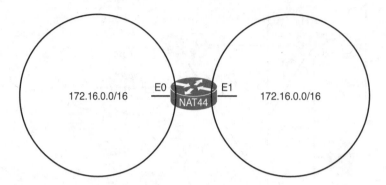

Figure 10-28   *Network for Troubleshooting Exercise 1*

NAT is implemented on the router as configured in Example 4-36, but devices cannot communicate across the router. What is wrong?

Example 4-36   *Configuration for Troubleshooting Exercise 2*

```
interface Ethernet0
 ip address 172.16.10.1 255.255.255.0
 ip nat inside
!
interface Ethernet1
 ip address 172.16.255.254 255.255.255.0
 ip nat outside
!
router ospf 1
 redistribute static metric 10 metric-type 1 subnets
 network 10.0.0.0 0.255.255.255 area 0
!
ip nat translation timeout 500
ip nat pool NET1 10.1.1.1 10.1.255.254 netmask 255.255.0.0
ip nat pool NET2 192.168.1.1 192.168.255.254 netmask 255.255.0.0
ip nat inside source list 1 pool NET1
ip nat outside source list 1 pool NET2
!
ip classless
!
ip route 10.1.0.0 255.255.0.0 Ethernet0
ip route 192.168.0.0 255.255.0.0 Ethernet1
!
access-list 1 permit 172.16.0.0 0.0.255.255
```

3. Refer to the configurations of Cozumel and Guaymas in Example 10-22. If the first line of access list 1 in both configurations is removed, what is the result? Can Guaymas and Cozumel still ping each other?

Chapter 11

IPv6 to IPv4 Network Address Translation (NAT64)

The last chapter covered NAT44, in which the source or destination or both IPv4 address fields in a packet are rewritten to a different address. This chapter continues the concept of packet translation but takes it to a higher level of complexity. Instead of just changing an IP address in a packet's source or destination address field, the mechanisms discussed in this chapter also remove the entire header of an IP packet and replace it with a different header—an IPv4 header is replaced with an IPv6 header, or vice versa. The purpose is to provide a translation service between IPv4 and IPv6 devices.

As this book is being written, we are in the early transitional phase from IPv4 to IPv6. You certainly know the story: IPv4 was created in the 1970s, before the Internet as you know it now; before the World Wide Web; before always-on broadband services available almost anywhere; before smartphones; and certainly before the so-called Internet of Things (IoT) (that is, device-to-device communication over the Internet with no human involved). When it was created, IPv4's 4.3 billion addresses were more than enough for the tiny experimental network TCP/IP was meant to support. But presently there are more than 3.2 billion people connected to the Internet and many more "things." Cisco estimated that there were 12.5 billion devices connected to the Internet in 2010 and predicts 50 billion Internet-connected devices by 2020.[1] The Cisco prediction is mid-range of some wildly varying prognostications: Gartner predicts 25 billion "things" by 2020, whereas Morgan Stanley says 75 billion. Whatever size the IoT grows to in the near future, it is already far larger than anything that can be served by a paltry 4.3 billion addresses.

The reality, however, is not that we are currently running out of IPv4 addresses or that we recently ran out. The reality is that from a capacity standpoint, we ran out of IPv4 addresses in the mid-1990s. We just stretched the available IPv4 addresses through a

---

[1] As this edition goes to press, the IANA and four of the five Regional Internet Registries (RIR) have announced that their supply of public IPv4 addresses is depleted—only AfriNIC still has a supply; although, that one will be depleted before 2020, too. IPv4 addresses are still available at many Local Internet Registries (LIR) , but those too are quickly running dry.

number of "tricks" such as dynamically assignable address pools, private IPv4 addresses, NAT44, and efficiency measures like CIDR, to serve what was already an Internet of devices far exceeding the address capacity of IPv4. Those tricks are losing their effectiveness, and we're now dealing with a creaky, poorly performing, poorly secured Internet that is less and less capable of supporting the flood of new devices and services attaching to it.

So IPv6 is essential and inevitable. However, several big speedbumps are on the road to an IPv6-only Internet:

- The Internet has no centralized management; it's a confederation of independently managed autonomous systems. So there is no way to mandate or coordinate a "flash cut" from IPv4 to IPv6.

- Making a network fully IPv6-capable carries a cost in money, man-hours, and technical headaches. Few network operators in the world have willingly deployed IPv6 without first concluding that they have no other choice.

- IPv6 is not backward compatible with IPv4. When IPv6 was planned in the 1990s, the designers assumed operators would be motivated to adopt it, and that dual-stacked interfaces would be sufficient for transition. Few planned for the resistance to IPv6 and, in many cases, downright denial of the need for it, until IPv4 depletion has rendered dual stacking impractical in many cases.

Because of these unfortunate factors, we're left with an awkward transition that will last many years before we settle down to a clean, IPv6-only Internet. In this early phase of transition, the biggest challenges stem from version interoperability:

- Almost all modern IP devices are IPv6-capable, but still many older devices are IPv4-only. We need a way to connect these devices across an IPv6 network.

- Some older applications that incorporate IPv4 addresses into the upper layers can be expected to still be around for a while and must be adapted to IPv6.

- As IPv4 addresses become unavailable, IPv6 addresses are assigned to new devices; however, the majority of reachable content on the Internet is still IPv4. These new devices must reach that content. (In the later stages of the transition, the opposite will apply: The majority of content will be IPv6, but the few remaining IPv4-only devices must still reach it.)

- IPv4-only devices must speak to IPv6-only devices with minimal or no user awareness.

Without backward compatibility in IPv6, we're left with the necessity of transition mechanisms, which fall into one of three classes:

- **Dual-stacked interfaces:** The simplest solution to IPv4 and IPv6 co-existence (not interoperability) is to make interfaces "bilingual," so they can speak IPv4 to IPv4 devices and IPv6 to IPv6 devices. Which version they use depends either on the version of packets they receive from a device or the type of address DNS gives them when they query for a device address. Dual stack was the intended means of transitioning from IPv4 to IPv6, but the assumption was that the transition would be complete before IPv4 was depleted. That has happened, so dual stacking becomes more complex: How do you give every interface both an IPv4 address and an IPv6 address when not enough IPv4 addresses are available to go around?

- **Tunnels:** Tunnels are also about co-existence, not interoperability. They allow devices or sites of one version to communicate across a network segment—including the Internet—of the other version. So two IPv4 devices or sites can exchange IPv4 packets across an IPv6 network, or two IPv6 devices or sites can exchange IPv6 packets across an IPv4 network.

- **Translators:** Translators create interoperability between an IPv4 device and an IPv6 device by changing the header of a packet of one version to the header of the other version.

You have seen examples of dual-stack interface configurations throughout this volume and in Volume I of this book, so you should be comfortable with them and with configuring IOS to route both IPv4 and IPv6. Tunnels as transition mechanisms are not covered in this book because they don't apply to routing—they are just encapsulation mechanisms. A tunnel interface might or might not exist on the router.

You can make the same argument about translators. They're a service, not a means of routing TCP/IP. But the service directly impacts routing by enabling packets from a device of one IP version to be routed to a device of the other IP version. As you see in this chapter, rules require an inter-version translator to behave as a router for things such as IPv4 fragmentation. The service usually appears on a router (less often on a firewall or a stand-alone appliance), and it can affect the way a packet is handled. And, the topic makes sense as a follow-up topic to NAT44.

Stateless IP/ICMP Translation (SIIT)

Translation between IPv4 and IPv6 involves more than just changing address formats. The packet headers have significant differences, including fields that exist in one version but not the other. Figure 11-1 gives a simple perspective on what a translator must address in replacing headers on an IP packet. In this illustration, the header fields are all drawn the same size, with the actual size of the field in bits indicated separately. Immediately evident in this illustration is that the IPv6 header has fewer fields than the IPv4 header—either because of some functions moved to extension headers or because of the improved efficiency of the IPv6 header.

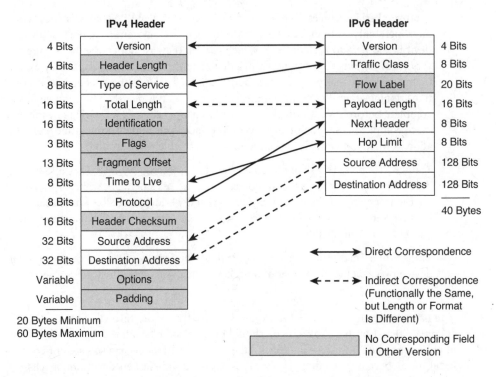

Figure 11-1 *Translating Between IPv4 and IPv6 Requires a Set of Rules to Compensate for the Many Differences in the Two Headers*

And although swapping headers is complicated, there is more a translator must do to maintain a routable path between an IPv4 device and an IPv6 device, such as the following:

- ICMP/ICMPv6 messages must be translated to maintain management and error detection across the entire route.

- Upper layer headers must be adjusted for changing checksums.

- Differences in how fragmentation is handled must be accounted for. IPv4 routers fragment packets, and IPv6 routers do not. This also has a direct bearing on Path MTU Discovery (PMTU). Because IPv6 routers do not fragment packets, PMTU is mandatory with IPv6; PMTU is optional in IPv4, where a source can count on routers to fragment packets along the path if needed.

The base algorithm for IPv4/IPv6 translation is called Stateless IP/ICMP Translation (SIIT). Originally specified in RFC 2765, the latest specification is RFC 6145. Although RFC 6145 does update some aspects of the algorithm, the main difference is that many details of translation included in RFC 2765 are now broken out into separate RFCs, as listed in Table 11-1. The reason for this separation is that there was a single type of IPv4/IPv6 translator (NAT-PT) when RFC 2765 was created, but now NAT-PT has been deprecated and several new translation mechanisms have taken its place. This chapter details the translation mechanisms supported by IOS, including the now-deprecated NAT-PT.

Table 11-1 *RFCs Relevant to IPv4/IPv6 Translation*

RFC	Description
2765	Stateless IP/ICMP Translation Algorithm (Obsolete)
6145	IP/ICMP Translation Mechanism
6144	Framework for IPv4/IPv6 Translation
6052	IPv6 Addressing of IPv4/IPv6 Translators
2766	Network Address Translation[md]Protocol Translation (NAT-PT) (Obsolete)
4966	Reasons to Move NAT-PT to Historical Status
6146	Stateful NAT64
6147	DNS64: DNS Extensions for NAT
5382	NAT Behavioral Requirements for TCP
4787	NAT Behavioral Requirements for Unicast UDP
6791	Stateless Source Address Mapping for ICMPv6 Packets
7269	NAT64 Deployment Options and Experience

IPv4/IPv6 Header Translation

SIIT translates IPv4 packets into IPv6 and IPv6 packets into IPv4, by reading the header of the incoming packet, removing the header from the packet, and then adding a new header of the opposite type to the packet. Figure 11-1 illustrates what fields are translated between the two header types. Table 11-2 describes the actions taken for translating an IPv4 header into an IPv6 header, and Table 11-3 shows the actions taken for translating an IPv6 header into an IPv4 header.

Table 11-2 *SIIT Actions for Translating an IPv4 Header into an IPv6 Header*

Incoming IPv4 Header Field	Action	Resulting IPv6 Header Field
Version	Change version number from 4 to 6.	Version
Header Length	Discard.	
Type of Service	Copy IPv4 ToS bits to IPv6 Traffic Class field. If the older IPv4 ToS/Precedence format is used, Traffic Class can be administratively set to 0.	Traffic Class
N/A	Set IPv6 Flow Label field to 0.	Flow Label

Incoming IPv4 Header Field	Action	Resulting IPv6 Header Field
Total Length	Subtract IPv4 Header Length from Total Length, and set IPv6 Payload Length to resulting value.	Payload Length
Identification	Discard.	
Flags	Discard.	
Fragment Offset	Discard.	
Time To Live	Decrement TTL by 1 (because the translator counts as a router) and add resulting value to Hop Limit field. If decrement results in a value of 0, drop packet and send ICMP TTL Exceeded message to source.	Hop Limit
Protocol	Copy value from IPv4 Protocol field to IPv6 Next Header field. Exception: If Protocol = 1 (ICMP), change to Next Header = 58 (ICMPv6).	Next Header
Header Checksum	Discard.	
Source Address	IPv4 to IPv6 address translation is dependent on whether translator is NAT-PT, Stateless NAT64, Stateful NAT64, or MAP-T. See the relevant section in this chapter.	Source Address
Destination Address	IPv4 to IPv6 address translation is dependent on whether translator is NAT-PT, Stateless NAT64, Stateful NAT64, or MAP-T. See the relevant section in this chapter.	Destination Address
Options and Padding	Discard.	

Table 11-3 *SIIT Actions for Translating an IPv6 Header into an IPv4 Header*

Incoming IPv6 Header Field	Action	Resulting IPv4 Header Field
Version	Change version number from 6 to 4.	Version
	Set Header Length = 5.	Header Length
Traffic Class	Copy IPv6 Traffic Class bits to IPv4 ToS field.	Type of Service
Flow Label	Discard.	N/A

Incoming IPv6 Header Field	Action	Resulting IPv4 Header Field
Payload Length	Add IPv4 Header Length (5) to IPv6 Payload Length and set IPv4 Total Length to resulting value.	Total Length
	Set Identification to 0.	Identification
	Set More Fragments flag to 0. Set Don't Fragment (DF) flag to 1.	Flags
	Set Fragment Offset to 0.	Fragment Offset
Hop Limit	Decrement Hop Limit by 1 (because the translator counts as a router) and add resulting value to Time To Live field. If decrement results in a value of 0, drop packet and send ICMPv6 Hop Limit Exceeded message to source.	Time To Live
Next Header	Copy value from IPv6 Next Header field to IPv4 Protocol field. Exceptions: If Next Header = 58 (ICMPv6), change to Protocol = 1 (ICMP) If Next Header = 44 (Fragment extension header) handle as described in the section "Fragmentation and PMTU." If Next Header = 0, 43, or 60, skip to next relevant Next Header value in extension headers as these three extension headers are meaningless to IPv4.	Protocol
	Compute IPv4 Header Checksum after IPv4 header is created.	Header Checksum
Source Address	IPv6 to IPv4 address translation is dependent on whether translator is NAT-PT, Stateless NAT64, Stateful NAT64, or MAP-T. See the relevant section in this chapter.	Source Address
Destination Address	IPv6 to IPv4 address translation is dependent on whether translator is NAT-PT, Stateless NAT64, Stateful NAT64, or MAP-T. See the relevant section in this chapter.	Destination Address
	Do not add an Options field.	Options and Padding

ICMP/ICMPv6 Translation

ICMP and ICMPv6 messages have quite a few differences, starting with ICMP that is Protocol #1, whereas ICMPv6 is Next Header #58, which is translated in the header. SIIT must also translate types and codes between ICMP and ICMPv6, adjust checksums, and depending on the message type may need to adjust internal message parameters, which can in turn require changes to Length fields in the IPv4 or IPv6 header.

Detailing the many changes that SIIT must adjust between ICMP and ICMPv6 is beyond the scope of this chapter (see RFC 6145 and 6791 for details), but Tables 11-4 and 11-5 provide a comparison of ICMP (Table 11-4) and ICMPv6 (Table 11-5) messages, type values, and codes. Table 11-6 shows how SIIT translates type and code values between the two protocols. Notice that a number of ICMP messages do not have an ICMPv6 counterpart. When these ICMP messages are encountered by SIIT, they are quietly dropped. There are also several cases in which multiple ICMP codes translate to a single ICMPv6 code.

Table 11-4   *ICMP Messages and Codes*

ICMP Type	ICMP Code	ICMP Message
0	0	ECHO REPLY
3		DESTINATION UNREACHABLE
	0	Network Unreachable
	1	Host Unreachable
	2	Protocol Unreachable
	3	Port Unreachable
	4	Fragmentation Needed and DF Flag Set
	5	Source Route Failed
	6	Destination Network Unknown
	7	Destination Host Unknown
	8	Source Host Isolated
	9	Destination Network Administratively Prohibited
	10	Destination Host Administratively Prohibited
	11	Destination Network Unreachable for Type of Service
	12	Destination Host Unreachable for Type of Service
	13	Communication Administratively Prohibited
	14	Host Precedence Violation
	15	Precedence Cutoff in Effect
4	0	SOURCE QUENCH (Deprecated)

ICMP Type	ICMP Code	ICMP Message
5	5	REDIRECT
	0	Redirect Datagram for the Network (or Subnet)
	1	Redirect Datagram for the Host
	2	Redirect Datagram for the Network and Type of Service
	3	Redirect Datagram for the Host and Type of Service
6	0	ALTERNATE HOST ADDRESS (Deprecated)
8	0	ECHO
9	0	ROUTER ADVERTISEMENT
10	0	ROUTER SOLICITATION
11		TIME EXCEEDED
	0	TTL Exceeded in Transit
	1	Fragment Reassembly Time Exceeded
12		PARAMETER PROBLEM
	0	Pointer Indicates the Error
	1	Missing a Required Option
	2	Bad Length
13	0	TIMESTAMP
14	0	TIEMSTAMP REPLY
15	0	INFORMATION REQUEST (Obsolete)
16	0	INFORMATION REPLY (Obsolete)
17	0	ADDRESS MASK REQUEST (Obsolete)
18	0	ADDRESS MASK REPLY (Obsolete)

Table 11-5   ICMPv6 Messages and Codes

ICMPv6 Type	ICMPv6 Code	ICMPv6 Message
1		DESTINATION UNREACHABLE
	0	No route to destination
	1	Communication with destination administratively prohibited
	2	Not a neighbor
	3	Address unreachable
	4	Port unreachable
2	0	PACKET TOO BIG

ICMPv6 Type	ICMPv6 Code	ICMPv6 Message
3		TIME EXCEEDED
	0	Hop limit exceeded in transit
	1	Fragment reassembly time exceeded
4		PARAMETER PROBLEM
	0	Erroneous header field encountered
	1	Unrecognized Next Header type encountered
	2	Unrecognized IPv6 option encountered
128	0	ECHO REQUEST
129	0	ECHO REPLY
130	0	MULTICAST LISTENER QUERY
131	0	MULTICAST LISTENER REPORT
132	0	MULTICAST LISTENER DONE
133	0	ROUTER SOLICITATION
134	0	ROUTER ADVERTISEMENT
135	0	NEIGHBOR SOLICITATION
136	0	NEIGHBOR ADVERTISEMENT
137	0	REDIRECT
138		ROUTER RENUMBERING
	0	Router renumbering command
	1	Router renumbering result
	255	Sequence number reset

Table 11-6 *SIIT Translation of ICMP/ICMPv6 Type and Code Values*

ICMP Type	ICMP Code	ICMPv6 Type	ICMPv6 Code
0	0	128	0
3		1	
	0	1	0
	1	1	0
	2	4	1
	3	1	4
	4	2	0
	5	1	0
	6	1	0
	7	1	0
	8	1	0

ICMP Type	ICMP Code	ICMPv6 Type	ICMPv6 Code
3	9	1	1
	10	1	1
	11	1	0
	12	1	0
4	0	Silently Drop	
5			
	0	Silently Drop	
	1	Silently Drop	
	2	Silently Drop	
	3	Silently Drop	
6	0	Silently Drop	
8	0	129	0
9	0	Silently Drop	
10	0	Silently Drop	
11		3	
	0	3	0
	1	3	1
12		4	
	0	4	0
	1	Silently Drop	
	2	4	0
13	0	Silently Drop	
14	0	Silently Drop	
15	0	Silently Drop	
16	0	Silently Drop	
17	0	Silently Drop	
18	0	Silently Drop	

Fragmentation and PMTU

Fragmentation poses a challenge to a translator because of the fundamental difference between IPv4 and IPv6 routers. If an IPv4 router receives a packet that is larger than the MTU of the next-hop interface, it fragments the packet. An IPv6 router never fragments a packet, so an arriving packet is dropped if it is too big for the next hop. IPv6 hosts are responsible for fragmenting packets, if necessary, before sending them. This, in turn, means that IPv6 hosts must either use Path MTU Discovery (PMTU) or fragment any packets that are larger than 1,280 bytes.[2] ICMP/ICMPv6 translation is essential for supporting PMTU from an IPv6 source to an IPv4 destination.

Fragmentation also poses a complexity for translators because while the information necessary for reassembly is included in the IPv4 header, IPv6 puts fragment reassembly information in a Fragment extension header.

When a fragmented IPv6 packet arrives at a SIIT translator, the procedure is straightforward. The translator uses the information in the IPv6 Fragment extension header to populate the corresponding Information and Fragment Offset fields in the IPv4 header. The DF bit is set in the IPv4 Flags field and the resulting fragmented IPv4 packets are sent on their way.

In the opposite case, when an IPv4 packet larger than the IPv6 minimum MTU of 1280 bytes is received, the translator first checks the DF bit in the IPv4 header. If set, the packet is dropped. If the DF bit is clear, the IPv4 packet is fragmented before it is translated. The resulting fragment reassembly information is then transferred from the IPv4 headers of the fragments to Fragment extension headers in the IPv6 fragments. In no case does the translator perform PMTU Discovery, which would violate the rules of an IPv6 router. IPv4 packets exceeding 1280 bytes are always fragmented on the IPv4 side, where the translator behaves as an IPv4 router before they are translated.

Translation in both the IPv4-to-IPv6 direction and the IPv6-to-IPv4 direction must, when fragmentation is involved, copy the Identification value precisely between the Identification field in the IPv6 Fragment extension header and the Identification field in the IPv4 header to ensure consistent information end-to-end and thus accurate packet reassembly at the destination. Note that the Information field in the IPv4 header is 16 bits, whereas it is 32 bits in the IPv6 Fragment extension header (Figure 11-2). Consistency is maintained when translating an IPv6 fragment to an IPv4 fragment by using only the last 16 bits of the Information field in the Fragment extension header for the IPv4 Information field.

Upper-Layer Header Translation

Transport Layer headers that contain checksums must have the checksums recalculated when their packets are translated. SIIT must support this for TCP and ICMP headers, and for UDP headers that contain a nonzero checksum field.

Other upper-layer header support is implementation optional.

---

[2] IPv6 interfaces are required to support MTUs of at least 1,280 bytes, whereas the fragmentation behavior of IPv4 allows the MTU of IPv4 interfaces to be as small as 68 bytes.

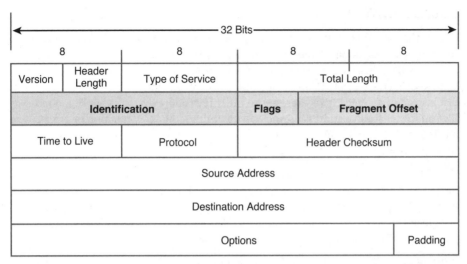

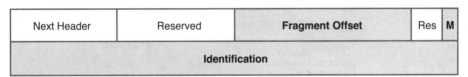

Figure 11-2 *When Translating Fragments, the Information in the Corresponding Fields of the IPv4 Header and the IPv6 Fragment Extension Header Are Used*

Network Address Translation with Port Translation (NAT-PT)

NAT-PT was the original IPv4/IPv6 translator mechanism. Specified in RFC 2766, it uses the older RFC 2765 flavor of SIIT for its translation algorithm but is stateful in nature. The IETF has now obsoleted NAT-PT in favor of NAT64. The reasons for deprecating NAT-PT are discussed at the end of this subsection, but because it is still supported in IOS (and can still have applications in some corner cases), first, we examine how the translator works and how it is configured. If nothing else, this section provides a good introduction as to why more modern translators are designed the way they are.

Operation of NAT-PT

The "NAT" part of NAT-PT is similar in operation to the Network Address Translation functions you read about in the previous chapter: The translator maintains a pool of assignable IP addresses and swaps the addresses from packets passing through the translator, keeping track of the address bindings in a mapping table. The difference here is that instead of mapping IPv4 addresses to other IPv4 addresses, as in NAT44, it maps IPv4 addresses to IPv6 addresses. And as with NAT44, the NAT function of NAT-PT can use TCP and UDP port numbers to multiplex multiple IPv6 addresses to one or a few IPv4 addresses.

The "PT" part of NAT-PT is the SIIT protocol translation you read about in the previous section, in which headers of one version are swapped for headers of the other version. Although SIIT is stateless, NAT-PT is stateful because of the address mapping table it must maintain. The restrictions that apply to NAT44, such as ensuring that session traffic passing one direction through a NAT returns through the same NAT, also apply here.

If the v4/v6 NAT part and the PT part work together properly, the result should be a translation that is entirely transparent to the devices using it, as shown in Figure 11-3. An IPv6 device is talking to an IPv4 device, but because of the NAT-PT, the IPv6 device thinks it's talking to another IPv6 device, and the IPv4 device thinks its talking to another IPv4 device.

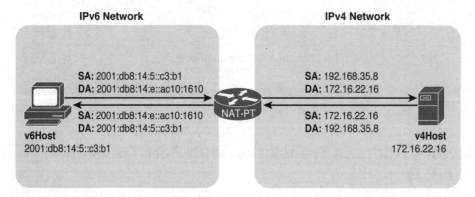

Figure 11-3 *NAT-PT Should Be Transparent So That Two Devices of Different IP Versions Communicating with Each Other Think They Are Speaking to a Device of the Same Version*

In this example, v6Host sends an IPv6 packet to v4Host, using an IPv6 destination address of 2001:db8:14:e::ac10:1610. The packet passes through the NAT-PT, where the IPv6 header and IPv6 addresses are replaced with an IPv4 header and IPv4 addresses. NAT-PT then forwards the resulting IPv4 packet to v4Host. When v4Host responds, the opposite actions occur: NAT-PT replaces the IPv4 header and addresses with an IPv6 header and addresses, and forwards the packet to v6Host.

A few questions should be immediately occurring to you at this point:

- How does NAT-PT know how to map the IPv4 and IPv6 addresses?

- How does v6Host discover the IPv6 address to use for v4Host when v4Host is not an IPv6 device?

- How do the packets from the host get to the translator?

Regarding the first question, there's something about the IPv6 destination address v6Host is using that isn't readily evident in Figure 11-3. The last 32 bits of the IPv6 destination address—::ac10:1610—is, in dotted decimal, 172.16.22.16. NAT-PT knows what IPv4 destination address to map because it is embedded in the IPv6 destination address.

NAT-PT knows to look for an embedded IPv4 address because the first 96 bits of the IPv6 destination address is a designated prefix known to the translator. Referring to Figure 11-3, the prefix is 2001:db8:14:5::/96, and the NAT-PT is configured to recognize this prefix in the local IPv6 network. There's nothing special about the prefix you choose to designate as the IPv6 NAT-PT prefix, other than that it belongs to the local IPv6 network to which the translator is attached. Therefore, in Figure 11-3, the prefix of the local IPv6 network is 2001:db8:14::/48.

On the IPv4 side referred to in Figure 11-3, NAT-PT represents v6Host with the IPv4 address 192.168.35.8. The translator takes this address from a configured pool of IPv4 addresses, just as NAT44 does. And to conserve IPv4 addresses NAT-PT can, optionally, multiplex many inside IPv6 addresses to one or a few outside IPv4 addresses by using the upper layer port addresses—again, just as NAT44 can. This optional variant of NAT-PT is called *Network Address and Port Translation with Protocol Translation*, or *NAPT-PT*.

The second question is, How does v6Host know to use the address 2001:db8:14:e::ac10:1610 to reach v4Host? The answer is a separate translation algorithm within NAT-PT called the *DNS Application Layer Gateway*, or DNS-ALG. Figure 11-4 shows how the DNS-ALG works to make v6Host think it is sending a packet to an IPv6 destination and at the same time embed the IPv4 destination address in the IPv6 destination address.

When v6Host wants to reach v4Host, it sends a DNS Query for the IP address bound to that name. Because v6Host is on an IPv6 network, the query is sent as an IPv6 packet. The host is configured with an IPv6 DNS server address that takes the query to the NAT-PT. NAT-PT, which knows the IPv4 address of the DNS server, translates the packet header to IPv4 and forwards it to the server. The server returns an A Record containing v4Host's IPv4 address to the NAT-PT. The DNS-ALG translates the A Record into a AAAA Record containing the IPv4 address from the A Record embedded behind the configured 96-bit NAT prefix. The resulting AAAA Record is sent to v6Host, and v6Host now has an IPv6 address for v4Host. The communication referred to in Figure 11-3 can now take place.

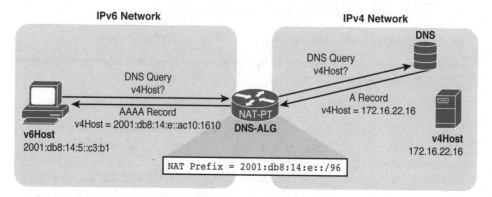

Figure 11-4 *NAT-PT Uses a DNS Translator Called a DNS Application Layer Gateway, or DNS-ALG, to Translate DNS A Records into AAAA Records*

The third question asks how packets from the IPv6 host get to the NAT-PT for translation. This part is simple. The configured NAT prefix is advertised into the local IGP. This is another reason why NAT-PT is considered a router; it must run whatever IPv4 and IPv6 routing protocols are used in its connected networks and must forward packets—with TTL or Hop Limit decremented properly—just like any other router.

Configuring NAT-PT

Figure 11-5 shows the NAT-PT example topology. Router Wagner is connecting the IPv6 domain on the left and the IPv4 domain on the right, so this is the router on which NAT-PT is enabled. The IPv6 NAT prefix to be used, taken from the IPv6 domain prefix 2001:db8:14::/48, is 2001:db8:14:ef:a:b::/96. Wagner embeds the IPv4 source address of any incoming IPv4 packets as the last 32 bits of this prefix, and it knows that any incoming IPv6 packets with a destination address belonging to this prefix has an IPv4 address embedded as the last 32 bits.

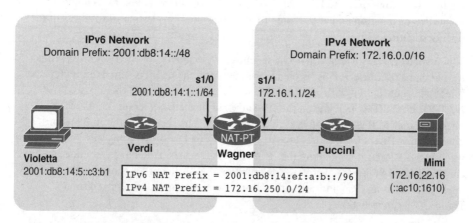

Figure 11-5 *Example Topology for Demonstrating NAT-PT*

The IPv4 prefix that will be used for translated IPv6 addresses is 172.16.250.0/24. Any host in the IPv6 domain will be represented in the IPv4 domain by an IPv4 address belonging to this prefix.

The goal, of course, is to enable communication between hosts Violetta and Mimi. Routers Verdi and Puccini are added to the mix just so you can observe any additional steps that might be needed in a routed environment behind the translator.

The initial setup of NAT-PT requires two steps:

1. The 96-bit NAT-PT prefix is configured globally on the router with the statement **ipv6 nat prefix**.

2. Interfaces connect to NAT-PT with the statement **ipv6 nat**. Note that this same statement is used on both the IPv6 and the IPv4 interfaces.

Example 11-1 shows the initial configuration of router Wagner.

Example 11-1 *NAT-PT Is Enabled on Wagner by Specifying the NAT Prefix with the* **ipv6 nat prefix** *Statement and Connecting the Relevant Interfaces to NAT-PT with the* **ipv6 nat** *Statement*

```
ipv6 unicast-routing
!
interface Loopback0
 ip address 172.16.255.1 255.255.255.255
!
interface Serial1/0
 no ip address
 ipv6 address 2001:DB8:14:1::1/64
 ipv6 nat
 ipv6 ospf 1 area 0
!
interface Serial1/1
 ip address 172.16.1.1 255.255.255.0
 ipv6 nat
!
router ospf 1
 log-adjacency-changes
 network 172.16.0.0 0.0.255.255 area 0
 default-information originate always
!
ipv6 router ospf 1
 log-adjacency-changes
 default-information originate always
!
ipv6 nat prefix 2001:DB8:14:EF:A:B::/96
!
```

In addition to the basic NAT-PT configuration statements highlighted, there are a few other features to point out. First, IPv6 routing is enabled with the **ipv6 unicast-routing** statement. You have seen this statement in several previous chapters both in this volume and in Volume I, so you should be thoroughly familiar by now with it. Second, OSPF is running in both domains: OSPFv2 in the IPv4 domain and OSPFv3 in the IPv6 domain. Again, these configurations should be familiar to you from previous chapters.

The last feature of interest referred to Example 11-1 comes from the question of how, when host Violetta sends a packet with a destination prefix of 2001:db8:14:ef:a:b::/96 to its local router Verdi, Verdi knows where to forward the packet. Similarly, when host Mimi sends an IPv4 packet to a destination with a prefix of 172.16.250.0/24, how does router Puccini know to forward the packet to Wagner? There's nothing NAT-PT-specific about this; it's just a simple routing problem. There are a number of ways to solve it, such as configuring Verdi and Puccini with static routes. In Example 11-1, the problem is addressed by configuring OSPFv2 and OSPFv3 to advertise default routes. This might or might not be a good solution for every network, but it serves the purposes of the network in Figure 11-5.

A few options are available for finishing the configuration of NAT-PT. One is to statically map IPv6 host addresses to addresses belonging to the IPv4 NAT prefix, using the statement **ipv6 nat v6v4 source**. In Example 11-2, this statement is used to map host Violetta's IPv6 address 2001:db8:14:5::c3:b1 to the IPv4 address 172.16.250.1. Notice that there is no statement reserving 172.16.250.0/24 as the IPv4 prefix to be used for IPv6-to-IPv4 address mapping; that's just the prefix we have decided to use. Any IPv4 address could be used—even an IPv4 address not belonging to the IPv4 domain of Figure 11-5—as long as the IPv4 domain knows to send packets with that destination address to Wagner.

Example 11-2   **ipv6 nat v6v4 source** *Statement Maps Violetta's Host Address to the IPv4 Address 172.16.250.1*

```
ipv6 unicast-routing
!
interface Loopback0
 ip address 172.16.255.1 255.255.255.255
!
interface Serial1/0
 no ip address
 ipv6 address 2001:DB8:14:1::1/64
 ipv6 nat
 ipv6 ospf 1 area 0
!
interface Serial1/1
 ip address 172.16.1.1 255.255.255.0
 ipv6 nat
!
```

```
router ospf 1
 log-adjacency-changes
 network 172.16.0.0 0.0.255.255 area 0
 default-information originate always
!
ipv6 router ospf 1
 log-adjacency-changes
 default-information originate always
!
ipv6 nat v6v4 source 2001:DB8:14:5::C3:B1 172.16.250.1
ipv6 nat prefix 2001:DB8:14:EF:A:B::/96
!
```

Example 11-3 shows the resulting NAT-PT address mapping table with 172.16.250.1 mapped to 2001:db8:14:5::c3:b1. The question now is, is this enough? If host Violetta sends an IPv6 packet to 2001:db8:14:ef:a:b:ac10:1610, the IPv6 default route at Verdi should forward the packet to Wagner. Because of the **ipv6 nat prefix** statement, Wagner should recognize the 96-bit prefix and extract host Mimi's IPv4 address 172.16.22.16 from the last 32 bits ::ac10:1610 and map 2001:db8:14:ef:a:b:ac10:1610 to 172.16.22.16 in the address mapping table. The **ipv6 nat v6v4 source** statement has already mapped the packet's source address to an IPv4 address, so Wagner should have everything it needs to preform SIIT translation of the header and forward the packet on to Puccini.

Example 11-3   *Command* **show ipv6 nat translations** *Displays the NAT-PT Address Mapping Table*

```
Wagner#show ipv6 nat translations
Prot   IPv4 source           IPv6 source
       IPv4 destination      IPv6 destination
---    172.16.250.1          2001:DB8:14:5::C3:B1
       ---                   ---

Wagner#
```

Example 11-4 shows that a ping from Violetta to Mimi fails.

Example 11-4   *Host Violetta Referred to in Figure 11-5 Cannot Successfully Ping Host Mimi, Using the IPv6 Address 2001:db8:14:ef:a:b:ac10:1610.*

```
Violetta#ping 2001:db8:14:ef:a:b:ac10:1610

Type escape sequence to abort.
Sending 5, 100-byte ICMP Echos to 2001:DB8:14:EF:A:B:AC10:1610, timeout is 2
  seconds:
```

```
.....
Success rate is 0 percent (0/5)
Violetta#
```

The failed ping does not indicate an ICMPv6 destination unreachable message. Instead, the pings just time out. Turning on debugging at Wagner and then repeating the ping from Violetta shows us what is going on. When Wagner receives the ping, it consults its address mapping table and cannot find an IPv4-to-IPv6 address mapping for the return path, so it drops the packets.

Example 11-5 *Debugging NAT-PT Wagner, Using the* **debug ipv6 nat detail** *Command, Shows Why Violetta Cannot Ping Mimi*

```
Wagner#debug ipv6 nat detail
IPv6 NAT-PT detailed debugging is on
Wagner#
*Oct  3 07:24:13.461: IPv6 NAT: ipv6nat_find_entry_v4tov6:
   ref_count = 1,
                              usecount = 0, flags = 257, rt_flags = 0,
                              more_flags = 0

*Oct  3 07:24:13.465: IPv6 NAT: Dropping v6tov4 packet
*Oct  3 07:24:15.437: IPv6 NAT: ipv6nat_find_entry_v4tov6:
   ref_count = 1,
                              usecount = 0, flags = 257, rt_flags = 0,
                              more_flags = 0

*Oct  3 07:24:15.441: IPv6 NAT: Dropping v6tov4 packet
*Oct  3 07:24:17.449: IPv6 NAT: ipv6nat_find_entry_v4tov6:
   ref_count = 1,
                              usecount = 0, flags = 257, rt_flags = 0,
                              more_flags = 0

*Oct  3 07:24:17.453: IPv6 NAT: Dropping v6tov4 packet
*Oct  3 07:24:19.461: IPv6 NAT: ipv6nat_find_entry_v4tov6:
   ref_count = 1,
                              usecount = 0, flags = 257, rt_flags = 0,
                              more_flags = 0

*Oct  3 07:24:19.461: IPv6 NAT: Dropping v6tov4 packet
*Oct  3 07:24:21.441: IPv6 NAT: ipv6nat_find_entry_v4tov6:
   ref_count = 1,
                              usecount = 0, flags = 257, rt_flags = 0,
                              more_flags = 0
```

> **Note** As I've done a few other times in this book, the hosts referred to in Figure 11-5 are actually just IOS routers with no routing protocol running. This is useful in a test environment because you have **show** and **debug** capabilities available to you on your "hosts" if something isn't working as you expected.

In Example 11-6, an interesting thing happens when Mimi tries to ping Violetta using the IPv4 address 172.16.250.1 by which Mimi knows Violetta. The ping is successful. And now, when Violetta again tries to ping Mimi in Example 11-7, that ping too is successful.

Example 11-6 *Host Mimi in Figure 11-5 Successfully Pings Host Mimi, Using the IPv4 Address 172.16.250.1*

```
Mimi#ping 172.16.250.1

Type escape sequence to abort.
Sending 5, 100-byte ICMP Echos to 172.16.250.1, timeout is 2 seconds:
!!!!!
Success rate is 100 percent (5/5), round-trip min/avg/max = 8/23/52 ms
Mimi#
```

Example 11-7 *Violetta Can Now Successfully Ping Mimi*

```
Violetta#ping 2001:db8:14:ef:a:b:ac10:1610

Type escape sequence to abort.
Sending 5, 100-byte ICMP Echos to 2001:DB8:14:EF:A:B:AC10:1610, timeout is 2
  seconds:
!!!!!
Success rate is 100 percent (5/5), round-trip min/avg/max = 20/39/108 ms
Violetta#
```

The debugging output at Wagner, in Example 11-8, shows what happened. When the ping packet arrived from Mimi, Wagner has enough configuration information to map the source IPv4 address to an IPv6 address using the configured NAT-PT prefix and embedding the IPv4 source address as the last 32 bits. That IPv4 to IPv6 address mapping is then entered in the NAT-PT address mapping table, as you can see in Example 11-9.

> **Note** It is worthwhile to carefully read the debugging outputs in Examples 11-5 and 11-8. In particular, notice when the entries refer to "v4tov6" and when they refer to "v6tov4." These can help you understand what the NAT-PT is looking at as it tries to perform translations.

Example 11-8 *Host Violetta in Figure 11-5 Cannot Successfully Ping Host Mimi, Using the IPv6 Address 2001:db8:14:ef:a:b:ac10:1610*

```
Wagner#
*Oct  3 07:43:24.089: IPv6 NAT: ipv6nat_find_entry_v4tov6:
       ref_count = 1,
                                usecount = 0, flags = 257, rt_flags = 0,
                                more_flags = 0


*Oct  3 07:43:24.093: IPv6 NAT: ipv6nat_find_entry_v4tov6:
       ref_count = 1,
                                usecount = 0, flags = 257, rt_flags = 0,
                                more_flags = 0


*Oct  3 07:43:24.101: IPv6 NAT: ipv6nat_find_entry_v4tov6:
       ref_count = 1,
                                usecount = 0, flags = 257, rt_flags = 0,
                                more_flags = 0


*Oct  3 07:43:24.105: IPv6 NAT: addr allocated 2001:DB8:14:EF:A:B:AC10:1610
*Oct  3 07:43:24.105: IPv6 NAT: icmp src (172.16.22.16) ->
  (2001:DB8:14:EF:A:B:AC10:1610), dst (172.16.250.1) -> (2001:DB8:14:5::C3:B1)
*Oct  3 07:43:24.113: IPv6 NAT: ipv6nat_find_entry_v4tov6:
       ref_count = 1,
                                usecount = 0, flags = 64, rt_flags = 0,
                                more_flags = 0


*Oct  3 07:43:24.113: IPv6 NAT: icmp src (2001:DB8:14:5::C3:B1) -> (172.16.250.1),
  dst (2001:DB8:14:EF:A:B:AC10:1610) -> (172.16.22.16)
*Oct  3 07:43:24.121: IPv6 NAT: ipv6nat_find_entry_v4tov6:
       ref_count = 1,
                                usecount = 0, flags = 64, rt_flags = 0,
                                more_flags = 0


[REMAINING OUTPUT IS THE SAME]

Wagner#
```

Example 11-9 *Wagner's Address Mapping Table Now Has All the Information It Needs to Map IPv4 and IPv6 Addresses for Packets Passing Either Direction Through the NAT-PT*

```
Wagner#show ipv6 nat translations
Prot  IPv4 source            IPv6 source
      IPv4 destination        IPv6 destination
```

```
   ---    ---                    ---
          172.16.22.16           2001:DB8:14:EF:A:B:AC10:1610

   ---    172.16.250.1           2001:DB8:14:5::C3:B1
          172.16.22.16           2001:DB8:14:EF:A:B:AC10:1610

   ---    172.16.250.1           2001:DB8:14:5::C3:B1
          ---                    ---


Wagner#
```

Of course, this isn't an acceptable solution, for two reasons. First, you don't want communication between Violetta and Mimi to be dependent on Mimi initiating communications first—at least, under most circumstances. And second, the mapping that results when Mimi initiates communications is transient. It times out eventually, and Violetta again cannot reach Mimi until Mimi initiates a new mapping. Example 11-10 illustrates this problem. The command **clear ipv6 nat translation** clears all transient entries out of the mapping table, and you can see that the result is that only the static mapping resulting from the **ipv6 nat v6v4 source** statement remains.

Example 11-10 *After Wagner's Address Mapping Table Is Cleared—Either Manually as Shown Here or by the Transient Entries Timing Out—Only the Static Entries Remain, Meaning Violetta Again Cannot Reach Mimi*

```
Wagner#clear ipv6 nat translation *
Wagner#
Wagner#
Wagner#show ipv6 nat translation
Prot   IPv4 source            IPv6 source
       IPv4 destination       IPv6 destination
---    172.16.250.1           2001:DB8:14:5::C3:B1
       ---                    ---


Wagner#
```

The solution to this problem is to add a static address mapping for Mimi's address, using the **ipv6 nat v4v6 source** statement. Example 11-11 shows Wagner's configuration with this statement added, mapping Mimi's IPv4 address 172.16.22.16 to the IPv6 address 2001:db8:14:ef:1:b:ac10:1610. Keep in mind that while **ipv6 nat v6v4 source** maps IPv6-to-IPv4 for packets traveling from the IPv6 side to the IPv4 side of the NAT-PT, **ipv6 nat v4v6 source** maps IPv4-to-IPv6 for packets traveling from the IPv4 side to the IPv6 side.

Example 11-11 *Mimi's IPv4 Address Is Mapped to an IPv6 Address Using the* **ipv6 nat v4v6 source** *Statement*

```
ipv6 unicast-routing
!
interface Loopback0
 ip address 172.16.255.1 255.255.255.255
!
interface Serial1/0
 no ip address
 ipv6 address 2001:DB8:14:1::1/64
 ipv6 nat
 ipv6 ospf 1 area 0
!
interface Serial1/1
 ip address 172.16.1.1 255.255.255.0
 ipv6 nat
!
router ospf 1
 log-adjacency-changes
 network 172.16.0.0 0.0.255.255 area 0
 default-information originate always
!
ipv6 router ospf 1
 log-adjacency-changes
 default-information originate always
!
ipv6 nat v4v6 source 172.16.22.16 2001:DB8:14:EF:A:B:AC10:1610
ipv6 nat v6v4 source 2001:DB8:14:5::C3:B1 172.16.250.1
ipv6 nat prefix 2001:DB8:14:EF:A:B::/96
!
```

Example 11-12 shows the results. Static entries now reside in the address mapping table for both Violetta and Mimi, and Violetta (Example 11-13) can successfully ping Mimi without waiting for Mimi to initiate a mapping entry.

Example 11-12 *Wagner's NAT-PT Address Mapping Table Now Has Static Entries for Packets Forwarded from Violetta to Mimi and for Packets Forwarded from Mimi to Violetta*

```
Wagner#show ipv6 nat translations
Prot   IPv4 source              IPv6 source
       IPv4 destination         IPv6 destination
---    ---                      ---
       172.16.22.16             2001:DB8:14:EF:A:B:AC10:1610
```

```
--- 172.16.250.1              2001:DB8:14:5::C3:B1
    172.16.22.16             2001:DB8:14:EF:A:B:AC10:1610


--- 172.16.250.1              2001:DB8:14:5::C3:B1
    ---                      ---


Wagner#
```

Example 11-13 *With the Addition of the* **ipv6 nat v4v6 source** *Statement in Wagner's Configuration, Violetta Can Now Successfully Ping Mimi*

```
Violetta#ping 2001:db8:14:ef:a:b:ac10:1610

Type escape sequence to abort.
Sending 5, 100-byte ICMP Echos to 2001:DB8:14:EF:A:B:AC10:1610, timeout is 2
  seconds:
!!!!!
Success rate is 100 percent (5/5), round-trip min/avg/max = 20/52/72 ms
Violetta#
```

The static NAT-PT configuration you have seen so far has the same pros and cons as static routes. They give you precise control over what entries go into the address mapping table, and hence precise control over what devices can communicate across an IPv4/IPv6 border. As with static routes, there are many scenarios in which this level of control is desirable—such as restricting cross-border communication to just one or a few devices. But again like static routes, manual configuration of address mapping does not scale well.

Suppose that instead of setting up communication between the two hosts referred to in Figure 11-5, you want to ensure that any host in either domain can communicate with any host in the other domain. This is certainly a reasonable objective, and if more than a few hosts are in the two domains, you need a means of dynamically mapping addresses.

Figure 11-6 shows the addition of two more hosts, one in each domain. These represent what in a practical network would be many hosts in each domain—actually, it could represent an IPv6-only network connected to the IPv4 public Internet. The goal of the next exercise is to allow either of the hosts in one domain to communicate with either of the hosts in the other domain.

For packets flowing in the IPv6-to-IPv4 direction, use the **ipv6 nat v6v4 source** statement, but instead of directly mapping an IPv4 address to an IPv6 address, use the **list** keyword to specify an IPv6 access list to control what IPv6 addresses are permitted to the translator, and a **pool** keyword that references by name an **ipv6 nat v6v4 pool** statement. Example 11-14 shows Wagner's configuration using this dynamic translation pool.

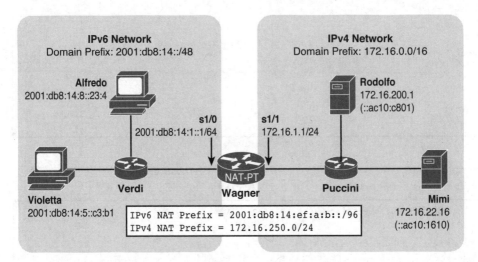

Figure 11-6 *Two New Hosts Are Added to the Example Topology, with the Expectation That Any Host Can Communicate with Any Other Host*

Example 11-14 *Wagner Is Configured for Dynamic Translation of Packets Flowing from the IPv6 Domain to the IPv4 Domain*

```
ipv6 unicast-routing
 !
interface Loopback0
 ip address 172.16.255.1 255.255.255.255
 !
interface Serial1/0
 no ip address
 ipv6 address 2001:DB8:14:1::1/64
 ipv6 nat
 ipv6 ospf 1 area 0
 !
interface Serial1/1
 ip address 172.16.1.1 255.255.255.0
 ipv6 nat
 !
router ospf 1
 log-adjacency-changes
 network 172.16.0.0 0.0.255.255 area 0
 default-information originate always
 !
ipv6 router ospf 1
 log-adjacency-changes
 default-information originate always
```

```
!
ipv6 nat v6v4 source list v6Domain pool v4Pool
ipv6 nat v6v4 pool v4Pool 172.16.250.1 172.16.250.200 prefix-length 24
ipv6 nat prefix 2001:DB8:14:EF:A:B::/96
!
ipv6 access-list v6Domain
 permit ipv6 2001:DB8:14::/48 any
!
```

The statement **ipv6 nat v6v4 source list v6Domain pool v4Pool** first points to a named IPv6 access list named "v6Domain." This access list permits any address with the prefix 2001:db8:14::/48, which covers any address in the IPv6 domain referred to in Figure 11-6. The next part of the statement references an IPv4 address pool named "v4Pool." That pool, created with the statement **ipv6 nat v6v4 pool v4Pool**, specifies IPv4 addresses in the range 172.16.250.1 through 172.16.250.200, with a prefix length of 24. The source address of the arriving IPv6 packet is mapped to a selected IPv4 address from the specified pool.

An example of where a configuration like this would apply is connecting an IPv6-only office or campus to the public Internet, enabling users in the network to still access IPv4 destinations. You can also use a dynamic address pool for IPv4-to-IPv6 traffic, using an **ipv6 nat v4v6 source list** statement to reference an **ipv6 nat v4v6 pool** statement. An example of where this second configuration might be useful would be in a router connecting an IPv4-only data center to the public Internet, allowing IPv6 users to access the relatively limited number of IPv4 destinations within the data center.

The configuration referred to in Example 11-14 addresses only how the translator maps the IPv6 source address of a packet to an IPv4 source address. We also have to configure the translation of the IPv6 destination address to an IPv4 destination address. The aforementioned **ipv6 nat v4v6 list** statement could be used, but there is another approach for dynamically mapping IPv4 addresses into IPv6 addresses, using the 96-bit prefix you used in earlier examples but with an explicit mapping keyword: **v4-mapped**. Example 11-15 shows Wagner's configuration with this statement added.

Example 11-15   *Configuration of Example 11-14 Is Expanded for Dynamic Translation of Packets Flowing from the IPv4 Domain to the IPv6 Domain*

```
ipv6 unicast-routing
 !
interface Loopback0
 ip address 172.16.255.1 255.255.255.255
 !
interface Serial1/0
 no ip address
 ipv6 address 2001:DB8:14:1::1/64
 ipv6 nat
```

```
  ipv6 ospf 1 area 0
 !
 interface Serial1/1
  ip address 172.16.1.1 255.255.255.0
  ipv6 nat
 !
 router ospf 1
  log-adjacency-changes
  network 172.16.0.0 0.0.255.255 area 0
  default-information originate always
 !
 ipv6 router ospf 1
  log-adjacency-changes
  default-information originate always
 !
ipv6 nat translation icmp-timeout 1200
ipv6 nat v6v4 source list v6Domain pool v4Pool
ipv6 nat v6v4 pool v4Pool 172.16.250.1 172.16.250.200 prefix-length 24
ipv6 nat prefix 2001:DB8:14:EF:A:B::/96 v4-mapped LocalDomain
 !
ipv6 access-list v6Domain
 permit ipv6 2001:DB8:14::/48 any
 !
ipv6 access-list LocalDomain
 permit ipv6 2001:DB8:14::/48 2001:DB8:14:EF:A:B::/96
 !
```

The statement **ipv6 nat prefix 2001:db8:14:ef:a:b::/96 v4-mapped LocalDomain** specifies the same 96-bit prefix you've been using all along but adds the **v4-mapped** keyword referencing an IPv6 access list named LocalDomain. How all this works together
bears some attention, as it is not obvious. If an IPv6 packet arrives with a destination
address whose prefix is 2001:db8:ef:a:b::/96, NAT-PT uses the access list LocalDomain
to verify first that the source address belongs to the prefix 2001:db8:14::/48, the prefix
of the IPv6 domain. If so, the IPv6 destination address is mapped to the embedded IPv4
address. With this mapping in the address mapping table, IPv4 packets passing from the
IPv4 domain to the IPv6 domain can also be successfully translated.

Example 11-16 shows the results. Pings can be successfully sent among all the four hosts
referred to in Figure 11-6. Admittedly there is a little hand-waving going on in Example
11-16. Hosts Rodolfo and Mimi in the IPv4 domain "know" only the IPv4 addresses
to ping for Alfredo (172.16.250.1) and Violetta (172.16.250.2) because I looked
at Wagner's address mapping table beforehand. And those mappings existed only
because Violetta and Alfredo first sent packets to the IPv4 domain. Similarly, Violetta
and Alfredo "know" what IPv6 addresses to ping because I worked out ahead of time
what the hex equivalent of Rodolfo's and Mimi's IPv4 addresses would be—shown in

parentheses in Figure 11-6—and then appended those to the configured IPv6 NAT prefix 2001:db8:14:ef:a:b::/96. In a real network Violetta and Rodolfo would discover the destination addresses by querying a DNS server in the IPv4 domain, and then receiving the responses after the DNS-ALG at Wagner translated the resulting IPv4 A records into IPv6 AAAA records using the IPv6 NAT prefix.

Example 11-16 *All the Hosts in Figure 11-6 Can Ping All the Other Hosts*

```
Violetta#ping 2001:db8:14:ef:a:b:ac10:c801

Type escape sequence to abort.
Sending 5, 100-byte ICMP Echos to 2001:DB8:14:EF:A:B:AC10:C801, timeout is 2
  seconds:
!!!!!
Success rate is 100 percent (5/5), round-trip min/avg/max = 20/27/52 ms
Violetta#
Violetta#ping 2001:db8:14:ef:a:b:ac10:1610

Type escape sequence to abort.
Sending 5, 100-byte ICMP Echos to 2001:DB8:14:EF:A:B:AC10:1610, timeout is 2
  seconds:
!!!!.
Success rate is 80 percent (4/5), round-trip min/avg/max = 20/57/92 ms
Violetta#
Violetta#ping 2001:db8:14:8::23:4

Type escape sequence to abort.
Sending 5, 100-byte ICMP Echos to 2001:DB8:14:8::23:4, timeout is 2 seconds:
!!!!!
Success rate is 100 percent (5/5), round-trip min/avg/max = 4/14/44 ms
Violetta#
```

```
Rodolfo#ping 172.16.250.1

Type escape sequence to abort.
Sending 5, 100-byte ICMP Echos to 172.16.250.1, timeout is 2 seconds:
!!!!!
Success rate is 100 percent (5/5), round-trip min/avg/max = 12/42/88 ms
Rodolfo#
Rodolfo#ping 172.16.250.2

Type escape sequence to abort.
Sending 5, 100-byte ICMP Echos to 172.16.250.2, timeout is 2 seconds:
!!!!!
Success rate is 100 percent (5/5), round-trip min/avg/max = 12/24/56 ms
```

```
Rodolfo#
Rodolfo#ping 172.16.22.16

Type escape sequence to abort.
Sending 5, 100-byte ICMP Echos to 172.16.22.16, timeout is 2 seconds:
!!!!!
Success rate is 100 percent (5/5), round-trip min/avg/max = 4/31/60 ms
Rodolfo#
```

```
Alfredo#ping 2001:db8:14:ef:a:b:ac10:c801

Type escape sequence to abort.
Sending 5, 100-byte ICMP Echos to 2001:DB8:14:EF:A:B:AC10:C801, timeout is 2
  seconds:
!!!!!
Success rate is 100 percent (5/5), round-trip min/avg/max = 8/44/84 ms
Alfredo#
Alfredo#ping 2001:db8:14:ef:a:b:ac10:1610

Type escape sequence to abort.
Sending 5, 100-byte ICMP Echos to 2001:DB8:14:EF:A:B:AC10:1610, timeout is 2
  seconds:
!!!!!
Success rate is 100 percent (5/5), round-trip min/avg/max = 4/22/80 ms
Alfredo#
Alfredo#ping 2001:db8:14:5::c3:b1

Type escape sequence to abort.
Sending 5, 100-byte ICMP Echos to 2001:DB8:14:5::C3:B1, timeout is 2 seconds:
!!!!!
Success rate is 100 percent (5/5), round-trip min/avg/max = 8/36/68 ms
Alfredo#
```

```
Mimi#ping 172.16.250.1

Type escape sequence to abort.
Sending 5, 100-byte ICMP Echos to 172.16.250.1, timeout is 2 seconds:
!!!!!
Success rate is 100 percent (5/5), round-trip min/avg/max = 4/20/48 ms
Mimi#
Mimi#ping 172.16.250.2

Type escape sequence to abort.
Sending 5, 100-byte ICMP Echos to 172.16.250.2, timeout is 2 seconds:
```

```
!!!!!
Success rate is 100 percent (5/5), round-trip min/avg/max = 4/57/96 ms
Mimi#
Mimi#ping 172.16.200.1

Type escape sequence to abort.
Sending 5, 100-byte ICMP Echos to 172.16.200.1, timeout is 2 seconds:
!!!!!
Success rate is 100 percent (5/5), round-trip min/avg/max = 8/39/56 ms
Mimi#
```

In spite of taking some shortcuts such as not including a DNS server in the example and peeking at the address mapping table, the example network referred to in Figure 11-6 and the corresponding configuration does represent a practical translation setup for a small IPv6-only network connected to an IPv4 network. Hosts in the IPv6 domain have to initiate communication to IPv4 hosts to create an entry in the address mapping table, and IPv4 hosts can respond only as long as those mappings still exist in the table. That corresponds to many IPv4-to-IPv4 setups, too, where devices outside a firewall or access list can respond only to "established" connections initiated from devices inside the firewall or access list. If a server or other device is within the IPv6 domain that outside IPv4 devices must reach at any time, a static address mapping is entered in the NAT-PT and a corresponding A record for the server's mapped IPv4 address is added to the DNS server on the IPv4 side.

Dynamic entries in the address mapping table do time out, and the timeout periods vary according to the protocols. The timeout defaults, as shown in Table 11-7, can be changed with the statement **ipv6 nat translation**. The keywords used with this statement for the different timeout defaults are also shown in the table.

Table 11-7 *Default Timeout Values for Entries in the NAT-PT Address Mapping Table (86400 seconds = 24 hours, 300 seconds = 5 minutes)*

Keyword	Default (Seconds)	Description
timeout	86,400	Timeout of nonport-specific dynamic entries
udp-timeout	300	UDP port entries
dns-timeout	60	DNS record translation entries
tcp-timeout	86,400	TCP port entries
finrst-timeout	60	TCP FIN and RST entries
icmp-timeout	60	ICMP protocol entries
syn-timeout	None	Timeout when TCP SYN flag is received but no session data is received
never	N/A	Dynamic entries never expire

You can see an example of changing a timeout value in Wagner's configuration referred to in Example 11-15. Here, **ipv6 nat translation icmp-timeout 1200** changes the timeout of ICMP entries from the default of 60 seconds to 1200 seconds (20 minutes). This was entered to ensure that ICMP entries would stay in Wagner's mapping table long enough to run all the pings referred to in Example 11-16 and still display all of the resulting mappings. Example 11-17 shows the results. In addition to the pings, I performed a Telnet and a traceroute to generate some TCP and UDP mappings.

Example 11-17 *Wagner's Address Mapping Table Shows the ICMP Entries Resulting from the Pings in Example 11-16, Plus a TCP Entry for a Telnet Session and UDP Entries for a **traceroute** from Violetta to Mimi*

```
Wagner#show ipv6 nat translations
Prot   IPv4 source              IPv6 source
       IPv4 destination         IPv6 destination
---    ---                      ---
       172.16.22.16             2001:DB8:14:EF:A:B:AC10:1610

---    ---                      ---
       172.16.200.1             2001:DB8:14:EF:A:B:AC10:C801

icmp   172.16.250.3,4072        2001:DB8:14:1::2,4072
       172.16.22.16,4072        2001:DB8:14:EF:A:B:AC10:1610,4072

icmp   172.16.250.3,0           2001:DB8:14:1::2,0
       172.16.200.1,36          2001:DB8:14:EF:A:B:AC10:C801,36

icmp   172.16.250.3,1714        2001:DB8:14:1::2,1714
       172.16.200.1,1714        2001:DB8:14:EF:A:B:AC10:C801,1714

---    172.16.250.3             2001:DB8:14:1::2
       ---                      ---

tcp    172.16.250.2,0           2001:DB8:14:5::C3:B1,0
       172.16.22.16,31620       2001:DB8:14:EF:A:B:AC10:1610,31620

---    172.16.250.2             2001:DB8:14:5::C3:B1
       172.16.22.16             2001:DB8:14:EF:A:B:AC10:1610

tcp    172.16.250.2,31876       2001:DB8:14:5::C3:B1,31876
       172.16.200.1,23          2001:DB8:14:EF:A:B:AC10:C801,23

udp    172.16.250.2,33440       2001:DB8:14:5::C3:B1,33440
       172.16.200.1,49160       2001:DB8:14:EF:A:B:AC10:C801,49160
```

```
udp   172.16.250.2,33441    2001:DB8:14:5::C3:B1,33441
      172.16.200.1,49161    2001:DB8:14:EF:A:B:AC10:C801,49161

udp   172.16.250.2,33442    2001:DB8:14:5::C3:B1,33442
      172.16.200.1,49162    2001:DB8:14:EF:A:B:AC10:C801,49162

udp   172.16.250.2,33443    2001:DB8:14:5::C3:B1,33443
      172.16.200.1,49163    2001:DB8:14:EF:A:B:AC10:C801,49163

udp   172.16.250.2,33444    2001:DB8:14:5::C3:B1,33444
      172.16.200.1,49164    2001:DB8:14:EF:A:B:AC10:C801,49164

udp   172.16.250.2,33445    2001:DB8:14:5::C3:B1,33445
      172.16.200.1,49165    2001:DB8:14:EF:A:B:AC10:C801,49165

---   172.16.250.2          2001:DB8:14:5::C3:B1
      172.16.200.1          2001:DB8:14:EF:A:B:AC10:C801

---   172.16.250.2          2001:DB8:14:5::C3:B1
      ---                   ---

---   172.16.250.1          2001:DB8:14:8::23:4
      172.16.22.16          2001:DB8:14:EF:A:B:AC10:1610

---   172.16.250.1          2001:DB8:14:8::23:4
      172.16.200.1          2001:DB8:14:EF:A:B:AC10:C801

---   172.16.250.1          2001:DB8:14:8::23:4
      ---                   ---

Wagner#
```

When NAT-PT is used with small office or home access, there might be only a single IPv4 address available for the "outside" interface. This is a similar situation to NAT44 used in the same scenarios, and you can use the same solution: Map multiple inside addresses to a single outside address by exploiting port mapping. With NAT44 this is sometimes called Network Address and Port Translation (NAPT), so it comes as no surprise that the NAT-PT version of it is sometimes called NAPT-PT or overloading. Example 11-18 shows Wagner reconfigured to use NAPT-PT. Instead of referring to a dynamic pool, the **ipv6 nat v6v4 source list** statement references the IPv4-side interface Serial 1/1 and uses the keyword **overload**. Wagner now maps the source address of IPv6 packets to interface S1/1's IPv4 address 172.16.1.1 and a usable port of that address.

Example 11-18 *Wagner Referred to in Figure 11-6 Is Configured to Use the Single IPv4 Address of Serial 1/1 (172.16.1.1) for Mapping the Source Addresses of IPv6 Packets*

```
ipv6 unicast-routing
 !
interface Loopback0
  ip address 172.16.255.1 255.255.255.255
 !
interface Serial1/0
  no ip address
  ipv6 address 2001:DB8:14:1::1/64
  ipv6 nat
  ipv6 ospf 1 area 0
 !
interface Serial1/1
  ip address 172.16.1.1 255.255.255.0
  ipv6 nat
 !
router ospf 1
  log-adjacency-changes
  network 172.16.0.0 0.0.255.255 area 0
  default-information originate always
 !
ipv6 router ospf 1
  log-adjacency-changes
  default-information originate always
 !
ipv6 nat translation icmp-timeout 1200
ipv6 nat v6v4 source list v6Domain interface Serial1/1 overload
ipv6 nat prefix 2001:DB8:14:EF:A:B::/96 v4-mapped LocalDomain
 !
ipv6 access-list v6Domain
 permit ipv6 2001:DB8:14::/48 any
 !
ipv6 access-list LocalDomain
 permit ipv6 2001:DB8:14::/48 2001:DB8:14:EF:A:B::/96
 !
```

Example 11-19 shows the entries in Wagner's mapping table after three hosts in the IPv6 domain ping the two hosts in the IPv4 domain. You can easily see that all IPv6 source addresses are mapped to the single IPv4 address 172.16.1.1, using random port numbers to differentiate the mappings. This should look familiar to you from Chapter 10.

Example 11-19 *Multiple IPv6 Source Addresses Are Mapped to the Single IPv4 Address 172.16.1.1*

```
Wagner#show ipv6 nat translations
Prot   IPv4 source          IPv6 source
       IPv4 destination     IPv6 destination
---    ---                  ---
       172.16.22.16         2001:DB8:14:EF:A:B:AC10:1610

---    ---                  ---
       172.16.200.1         2001:DB8:14:EF:A:B:AC10:C801

icmp   172.16.1.1,6493      2001:DB8:14:1::2,6493
       172.16.22.16,6493    2001:DB8:14:EF:A:B:AC10:1610,6493

icmp   172.16.1.1,2742      2001:DB8:14:1::2,2742
       172.16.200.1,2742    2001:DB8:14:EF:A:B:AC10:C801,2742

icmp   172.16.1.1,8343      2001:DB8:14:5::C3:B1,8343
       172.16.22.16,8343    2001:DB8:14:EF:A:B:AC10:1610,8343

icmp   172.16.1.1,4316      2001:DB8:14:5::C3:B1,4316
       172.16.200.1,4316    2001:DB8:14:EF:A:B:AC10:C801,4316

icmp   172.16.1.1,4791    -  2001:DB8:14:8::23:4,4791
       172.16.22.16,4791    2001:DB8:14:EF:A:B:AC10:1610,4791

icmp   172.16.1.1,5594      2001:DB8:14:8::23:4,5594
       172.16.200.1,5594    2001:DB8:14:EF:A:B:AC10:C801,5594

Wagner#
```

Why Is NAT-PT Obsolete?

As mentioned at the beginning of this section, the IETF has obsoleted NAT-PT by moving it to Historic status. The reasons for making this move are defined in RFC 4966, which summarizes problems cited in other RFCs, Internet-drafts, and other sources.

A major source of problems found through operational experience with NAT-PT have to do with the integrated DNS-ALG, detailed in RFC 2766. Specifically:

■ If an IPv6 host queries for the address of a dual-stacked host, it is likely to receive two different AAAA RRs, one from an authoritative DNS server containing the correct IPv6 address of the target and one from the DNS-ALG containing a translated IPv6 address. Choosing the translated address—which is likely in many or most cases—can cause problems. There are a few proposed solutions, but none completely solve the problem.

■ Some applications pass the address received in a DNS record to other applications. There is an assumption here that the address is universally valid. But if the other application is on a separate node outside the realm of the NAT-PT and its DNS-ALG, the address might be unusable, causing the application to fail.

■ If a dual-stack host queries for the A Record of a host and the query passes through the DNS-ALG, the stateless nature of the ALG causes it to inappropriately translate the resulting A Record into a AAAA Record using a translated IPv6 address.

■ If a host uses multiple addresses, such as in a multihomed scenario, the DNS-ALG has no way of knowing what address will be used by a querying application and therefore must translate and respond with all of them, potentially causing a strain on resources.

■ Secure DNS (DNSSEC) does not work through NAT-PT and its DNS-ALG as specified. Although workarounds have been proposed, they have been determined prohibitively complex.

RFC 4966 also cites a number of NAT-PT problems that, although not directly caused by DNS-ALG, are exacerbated by it:

■ Because the DNS-ALG is a part of the NAT-PT and because all traffic flow initiators are dependent on the DNS-ALG, the NAT-PT must be the default router for the translated site. This can cause scaling concerns as a site grows.

■ Related to the previous bullet, requiring all traffic to flow in and out of the site through the same NAT-PT not only presents scaling concerns, the NAT-PT becomes a potential bottleneck and a single point of failure. This also exposes the NAT-PT and its DNS-ALG as a Denial of Service target by flooding bogus queries that overwhelm the device's mapping table or address bindings.

■ Address timeouts either in the NAT-PT mapping tables or the DNS-ALGs can cause address persistence problems with applications that expect consistent addresses across multiple sessions.

Finally, there are a few problems with NAT-PT that do not involve the DNS-ALG:

■ Applications that embed numeric IP addresses in their payloads break when passing through NAT-PT, because the inside and outside addresses change. This is a problem shared with NAT44 but is exacerbated because the addresses on the two sides of the translator are of different lengths. It's easy to argue that any application level reference to a network layer address violates the principles of layering, but that doesn't help in the real world.

■ NAT-PT necessarily maintains a timeout mechanism on its address mapping to prevent address resource depletion. However, this presents an address persistence problem for applications that are silent for long periods of time. Unless the application is designed with a keepalive mechanism or to periodically send some sort of activity, the address mappings can time out, breaking the application session.

■ A number of incompatible headers between IPv4 and IPv6 such as the IPv6 Flow Label field, and ICMP messages that are not equally supported in both versions— such as the ICMP Parameter Problem message that is not supported in ICMPv6— can lead to information loss across the translation boundary.

■ Port translation (NAPT-PT) cannot translate fragmented packets because only the first fragment contains the port number.

■ Fragmented IPv4 UDP packets must be reassembled before a checksum can be calculated for the IPv6 UDP packet, potentially causing transmission delays and bottlenecks.

■ SIIT cannot translate multicast packets.

NAT64, which replaces NAT-PT, does not solve all these problems. But it does represent an improvement, particularly by separating the translation and DNS functions.

Stateless NAT64

Stateless NAT64 uses the newer IP/ICMP Translation Algorithm specified in RFC 6145. Unlike SIIT specified in RFC 2765 and used by NAT-PT, this mechanism has both a stateless and a stateful mode. It doesn't take too great a stretch to figure out that stateless NAT64 uses the stateless mode, and stateful NAT64 uses the stateful mode.

Another shared characteristic of stateless and stateful NAT64 is that unlike NAT-PT, they do not support a DNS-ALG. Instead, the DNS translation is completely separated into a DNS64 function, as shown in Figure 11-7. This separation eliminates some, although not all, of the problems associated with an integrated DNS-ALG listed in the previous section.

Operation of Stateless NAT64

Stateless translation by definition means that there is no address pool and no stateful mapping table in the translator. But that does not mean that there is no binding of IPv4 addresses to IPv6 addresses. The key to stateless NAT64 is that an IPv4 address is embedded in an IPv6 address. These *IPv4-embedded IPv6 addresses* are maintained in DNS64 and must be assigned to IPv6 hosts either manually or by DHCPv6.

The format of IPv4-embedded IPv6 addresses is specified in RFC 6052 and is based on work done by the now-concluded IETF Behavior Engineering for Hindrance Avoidance (BEHAVE) Working Group. Stateless NAT64 translators recognize these address formats and hence know how to extract the IPv4 addresses from IPv6 addresses by one of two means:

- The IPv6 address can use the Well-Known Prefix, reserved in RFC 6052, of 64:ff9b::/96. The translator knows that the next 32 bits after the 96-bit prefix is the embedded IPv4 address.

- The address uses a prefix reserved within the organization for use with the deployed translator. The translator must be configured to recognize a locally designated prefix.

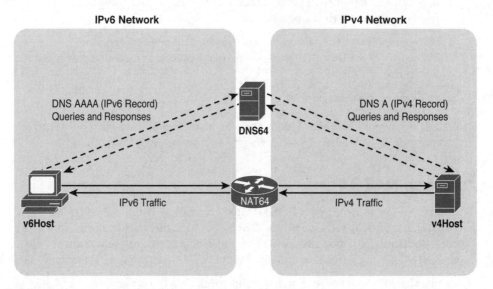

Figure 11-7 *Instead of Using an Integrated DNS-ALG, NAT64 and DNS64 Are Separate Entities*

Prefix Length				Bits 64-71				
32	Prefix		IPv4 (32)	Null	Suffix (56)			
40	Prefix		IPv4 (24)	Null	IPv4 (8)	Suffix (48)		
48	Prefix		IPv4 (16)	Null	IPv4 (16)	Suffix (40)		
56	Prefix		IPv4 (8)	Null	IPv4 (24)		Suffix (32)	
64	Prefix			Null	IPv4 (32)		Suffix (24)	
96	Prefix						IPv4 (32)	

Figure 11-8 *Format of the RFC 6052 IPv4-Embedded IPv6 Address*

The format of the IPv4-embedded IPv6 address, referred to in Figure 11-8, has the following components:

- The IPv6 prefix, which can be 32, 40, 48, 56, 64, or 96 bits in length. No other prefix length can be used. If the RFC 6052-reserved Well-Known Prefix is used, it is always 96 bits.

- The 32-bit embedded IPv4 address, which always begins immediately following the IPv6 prefix. So if a 32-bit prefix is used, the IPv4 address begins at the 33rd bit; if a 56-bit prefix is used, the IPv4 address begins at the 57th bit. and so on.

- A null octet (sometimes designated the "U" octet), bits 64 through 71, which is always set to all zeroes. This octet is reserved for compatibility with the host octet format defined in the IPv6 addressing architecture of RFC 4291. Note that this modifies the rule in the previous bullet for the 64-bit prefix length. In this prefix, the IPv4 address does not start immediately after the prefix but instead starts immediately after the null octet at the 72nd bit. The null octet also "splits" the embedded IPv4 address in the 40-, 48-, and 56-bit prefix lengths. And there is no null octet for the 96-bit prefix.

- A suffix whose length varies according to the prefix length, except for the 96-bit prefix, which has no suffix. The suffix must be set to all zeroes.

Tables 11-8 and 11-9 show examples of how an IPv4 address, 172.16.30.5, would be encoded into the various prefix lengths. Note how the null octet influences the encoding of the IPv4 address in different prefix lengths. Note that it is assumed you already understand the rules for IPv6 address representation, particularly the rule for compression of leading zeroes. Also note that when the 96-bit prefix is used, so that the embedded IPv4 address is the last 32 bits, the address can be represented in dotted decimal rather than hex.

Table 11-8 *IPv4 Address 172.16.30.5 Embedded into Organization-Specific IPv6 Prefixes*

Prefix	IPv4 Address	IPv4-Embedded IPv6 Address
2001:db8::/32	172.16.30.5 (0x ac10:1e05)	2001:db8:ac10:1e05::
2001:db8:aa00::/40	172.16.30.5 (0x ac10:1e05)	2001:db8:aaac:100e:5::
2001:db8:aabb::/48	172.16.30.5 (0x ac10:1e05)	2001:db8:aabb:ac10:1e:5::
2001:db8:aabb:1200::/56	172.16.30.5 (0x ac10:1e05)	2001:db8:aabb:1200:ac00:101e:5::
2001:db8:aabb:1234::/64	172.16.30.5 (0x ac10:1e05)	2001:db8:aabb:1234:ac:101e:5::
2001:db8:aabb:1234::/96	172.16.30.5	2001:db8:aabb:1234::172.16.30.5

Table 11-9 *IPv4 Address 172.16.30.5 Embedded Using the Well-Known Prefix*

Prefix	IPv4 Address	IPv4-Embedded IPv6 Address
64:ff9b::/96	172.16.30.5	64:ff9b::172.16.30.5

In Figure 11-9, v6Host wants to communicate with v4Host. It has already been configured with an IPv4-embedded IPv6 address, either manually or via DHCPv6. It uses a
96-bit prefix, and you can see that its embedded IPv4 address is 192.168.10.20. NAT64
has also been configured to recognize the prefix 2001:db8:14:e::/96 as indicating an
IPv4-embedded address.

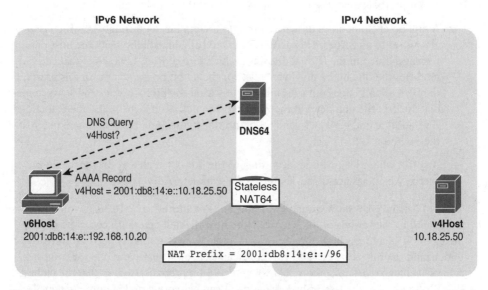

Figure 11-9 *v6Host Queries DNS64 for the Address of v4Host and Is Given an AAAA
Record Containing an IPv4-Embedded IPv6 Address*

v6Host queries the DNS64 server for the address of v4Host. The server, knowing the
IPv4 address of v4Host, 10.18.25.50, and the local IPv4-embedded address prefix,
returns the AAAA Record 2001:db8:14:e::10:18:25:50. V6Host now has everything
it needs to send packets to v4Host through the stateless NAT64, and the NAT64 has
everything it needs to translate the traffic in both directions statelessly, as shown in
Figure 11-10.

If v4Host wants to initiate communication with v6Host, it also queries the DNS64 server,
as shown in Figure 11-11. In this case, DNS64 returns an A Record with v6Host's embedded IPv4 address 192.168.10.20. Again, all devices have the information they need to
communicate, referred to in Figure 11-10. There is an assumption here, of course, that
routing is set up correctly throughout this example domain and internally in the NAT64
router.

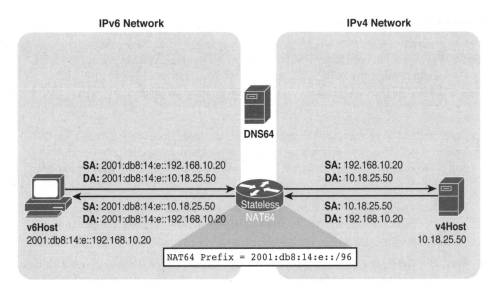

Figure 11-10 *All Devices Have the Information Needed for v6Host to Initiate Communication with v4Host and for v4Host to Respond*

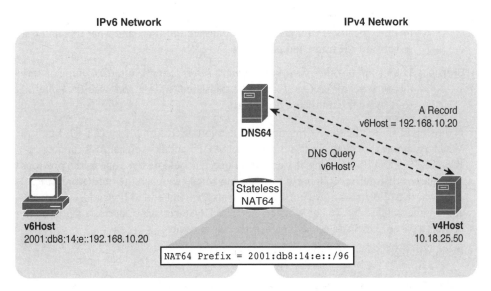

Figure 11-11 *v4Host Queries DNS64 for the Address of v6Host and Is Given an A Record Containing v6Host's Embedded IPv4 Address*

Configuration of Stateless NAT64

> **Note**   This book has used IOS exclusively. As of this writing, both Stateless and Stateful NAT64 are available only on IOS-XE. Although both are expected to eventually be supported in IOS, the configuration examples in this book are limited.

Stateless NAT64 is configured in just a few simple steps. These steps assume that IPv6 unicast routing has been enabled and that interfaces have been configured with IPv4 and IPv6 addresses as appropriate. It also assumes that IPv4 and IPv6 routing has been configured.

Step 1.   Enable NAT64 on *both* the IPv6-facing interfaces and the IPv4-facing interfaces through which translatable traffic will flow, with the statement **nat64 enable**.

Step 2.   Define the prefix to be used for the IPv4-embedded IPv6 addresses with the statement **nat64 prefix stateless** ipv6-prefix/length. The prefix specified by this statement is used both to identify IPv4-embedded IPv6 addresses on the IPv6 side of the translator, and to embed IPv4 addresses of packets arriving on the IPv4 side of the translator, so they can be forwarded to IPv6 destinations.

Step 3.   Use the **nat64 route** *ipv4-prefix/mask interface-type interface-number* statement to specify IPv4 prefixes to be translated to IPv6, and what IPv6 interface to forward the translated packets to.

Step 4.   Use the **ipv6 route** *ipv6-prefix/length interface-type interface-number* statement to specify IPv6 prefixes to be translated to IPv4, and what IPv4 interface to forward the translated packets to.

Figure 11-12 shows the same demonstration network used earlier for NAT-PT, but now Wagner supports Stateless NAT64 instead of NAT-PT and is likely an ASR running IOS-XE. IPv4 and IPv6 routing at Verdi and Puccini should be the same as the previous examples so that traffic from hosts Violetta and Mimi can reach the translator. Note, however, that Violetta is now configured with an IPv4-embedded IPv6 address recognizable by the stateless NAT64 at Wagner. Also, no DNS64 is shown because that is configured as a part of DNS and not as a part of the Cisco devices.

Example 11-20 shows Wagner's configuration.

Example 11-20   *Wagner Is Configured for Dynamic Translation of Packets Flowing from the IPv6 Domain to the IPv4 Domain*

```
ipv6 unicast-routing
 !
interface Loopback0
 ip address 172.16.255.1 255.255.255.255
 !
```

```
interface GigabitEthernet0/0/0
 no ip address
 ipv6 address 2001:DB8:14:1::1/64
 nat64 enable
 ipv6 ospf 1 area 0
!
interface GigabitEthernet0/0/1
 ip address 172.16.1.1 255.255.255.0
 nat64 enable
!
router ospf 1
 log-adjacency-changes
 network 172.16.0.0 0.0.255.255 area 0
 default-information originate always
!
ipv6 router ospf 1
 log-adjacency-changes
 default-information originate always
!
nat64 prefix stateless 2001:DB8:14:5::/96
!
ipv6 route 2001:db8:14:5::/96 GigabitEthernet0/0/1
!
nat64 route 172.16.22.0/24 GigabitEthernet0/0/0
!
```

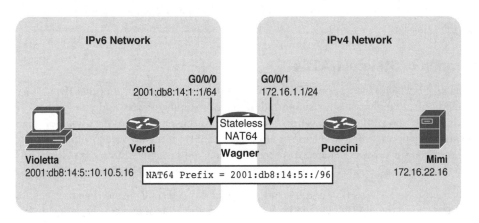

Figure 11-12   *Example Network for Stateless NAT64 Configuration*

Limitations of NAT64

It should be apparent to you that stateless NAT64 is simpler to configure and operate than NAT-PT. And "stateless" anything seems attractive for scaling. Its stateless nature also means that there are no concerns about asynchronous traffic—traffic can leave through one translator and return through another. However, stateless NAT64 has a few limitations that leave it impractical for some IPv4/IPv6 translation applications:

- A 1:1 mapping between IPv4 and IPv6 addresses is required. That is, every IPv6 device must have an IPv4 address for its IPv4-embedded IPv6 address. Because of this, there is no IPv4 address conservation.

- The requirement of IPv4-embedded IPv6 addresses can become a hindrance to good IPv6 address design in many networks.

- Although there is end-to-end address transparency, a good translator should not place any requirements on end systems. The need for specialized addresses, assigned either manually or via DHCPv6, violates this.

Stateful NAT64

Stateful NAT64, like its stateless counterpart, uses the more recent IP/ICMP Translation Algorithm specified in RFC 6145 rather than the older SIIT specified in RFC 2765 and used by NAT-PT. And also like stateless NAT64, it uses a separate DNS64 rather than an integrated DNS-ALG, referred to in Figure 11-7.

The difference from stateless NAT64, obviously, is that stateful NAT64 takes a step back toward NAT-PT because it maintains an IPv4-to-IPv6 address mapping table and can support mapping many IPv6 addresses to one IPv4 address, providing IPv4 address conservation.

Operation of Stateful NAT64

Stateful NAT64 translates only TCP, UDP, and ICMP packets. As with other IPv4/IPv6 translators, IP multicast is not supported. Dynamic mapping of IPv6 addresses to IPv4 addresses from an IPv4 address pool—either one-to-one or many-to-one using port mapping—is supported only when the session is initiated from the IPv6 side. Static mapping is required for sessions initiated from the IPv4 side, unless there is already a mapping in the table from a previous IPv6-initiated session that has not yet timed out.

Similar to NAT-PT, an IPv4 and IPv6 address pool defined by IPv4 and IPv6 prefixes is assigned to the NAT64. On the IPv6 side, this can be an administratively designated prefix different from the prefixes used by the local IPv6 devices, or it can be the Well-Known Prefix 64:ff9b::/96. The prefix must also be known by DNS64 so that it can create AAAA Records with embedded IPv4 addresses.

On the IPv4 side, the address pool can be a range of IPv4 addresses or can be a single IPv4 address for port-based mapping. The NAT64 can also use the IPv4 address assigned to its IPv4 interface for port mapping, similar to the behavior of NAT44.

In Figure 11-13, v6Host wants to initiate a session with v4Host. As in previous examples, it starts by querying DNS64. The IPv6 prefix 2001:db8:14:e::/96 has been designated for NAT64 translation and configured both at DNS64 and on the NAT64. DNS64 finds an A Record for v4Host, and because the query comes from the IPv6 side, it creates an AAAA Record using the designated NAT64 prefix and embedding the IPv4 address as the last 32 bits, and returns that record to v6Host.

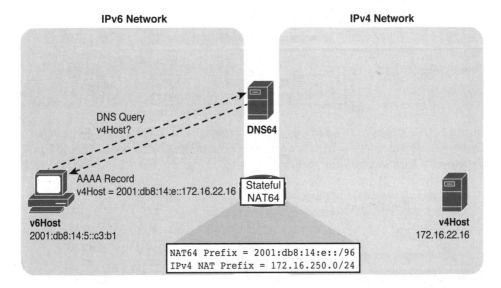

Figure 11-13 *v6Host Queries DNS64 for the Address of v4Host and Receives an AAAA Record with v4Host's IPv4 Address Embedded*

v6Host then sends an IPv6 packet to the NAT64, as shown in Figure 11-14. NAT64 recognizes the designated prefix in the destination address and extracts the IPv4 destination address. It then selects an IPv4 address from its IPv4 pool and creates an entry in its mapping table, mapping the IPv6 source address to an IPv4 address. In this example, port translation is used, so the address 2001:db8:14:5::c3:b1 is mapped to IPv4 address 172.16.250.1, port 2015.

NAT64 can then perform the translation of the IPv6 header to an IPv4 header and forward the packet to v4Host, as shown in Figure 11-15. When v4Host responds, the existing mapping allows NAT64 to perform an IPv4-to-IPv6 translation and send the responding packets back to v6Host.

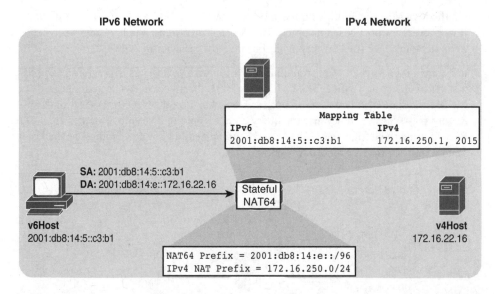

Figure 11-14 *When NAT64 Receives a Packet from v6Host, It Creates an Entry in Its Mapping Table, Mapping the IPv6 Source Address to an IPv4 Address and (if NAPT Is Configured) a Port Selected from the IPv4 Pool*

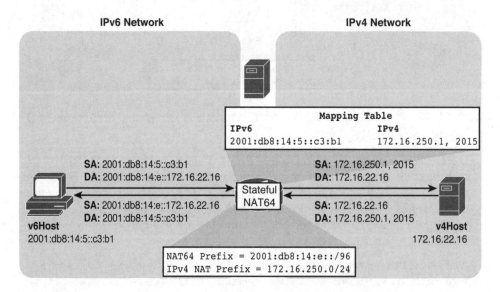

Figure 11-15 *With the Address Mapping Complete, NAT64 Can Translate Between IPv6 and IPv4 in Both Directions*

Configuration of Stateful NAT64

Stateful NAT64 is configured similarly to stateless NAT64; the only difference is in the configuration of the address pools.

These steps assume that IPv6 unicast routing has been enabled and that interfaces have been configured with IPv4 and IPv6 addresses as appropriate. It also assumes that IPv4 and IPv6 routing has been configured.

Step 1. Enable NAT64 on *both* the IPv6-facing interfaces and the IPv4-facing inter-faces through which translatable traffic will flow, with the statement **nat64 enable**.

Step 2. Define the IPv6 translation prefix with the **nat64 prefix stateful** *ipv6-prefix/ length*. The prefix specified by this statement creates IPv6 addresses with embedded IPv4 addresses.

The last step depends on whether you want to create static one-to-one mappings between IPv4 and IPv6 addresses, dynamic one-to one address mappings from a pool of IPv4 addresses, or dynamic port mappings to one or more IPv4 addresses from a pool.

■ **Static one-to-one mapping:** Use the **nat64 v6v4 static** *ipv6-address ipv4-address* statement.

■ **Dynamic one-to-one mapping:** Use the **nat64 v4 pool** *pool-name start-ip-address end-ip-address* statement toUse the **nat64 v4 pool** create the pool, and then enable mapping with the **nat64 v6v4 list** *access-list-name* **pool** *pool-name* statement. The referenced access list permits the IPv6 prefix created in the **nat64 prefix stateful** statement.

■ **Dynamic port mapping:** This is the same configuration procedure as the previous one except the **overload** keyword enables port mapping. Use the **nat64 v4 pool** *pool-name start-ip-address end-ip-address* statement to create the pool, and then enable mapping with the **nat64 v6v4 list** *access-list-name* **pool** *pool-name* **overload** statement. The referenced access list permits the IPv6 prefix created in the **nat64 prefix stateful** statement.

Figure 11-16 shows the same demonstration network used in previous examples. IPv4 and IPv6 routing at Verdi and Puccini should be the same as the previous examples so that traffic from hosts Violetta and Mimi can reach the translator. No DNS64 is shown because that is configured as a part of DNS and not as a part of Cisco devices. Also note that unlike the stateless NAT64 example, IPv4-embedded IPv6 addresses are not used.

Example 11-21 shows Wagner's configuration. In this example, dynamic port configuration is used.

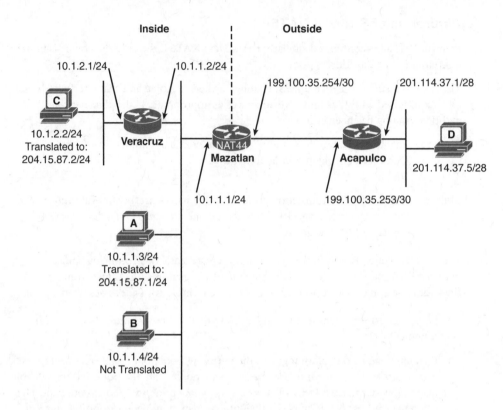

Figure 11-16   *Example Network for Stateful NAT64 Configuration*

Example 11-21   *Wagner Is Configured for Dynamic Port Translation of Packets Flowing from the IPv6 Domain to the IPv4 Domain*

```
ipv6 unicast-routing
 !
 interface Loopback0
  ip address 172.16.255.1 255.255.255.255
 !
 interface GigabitEthernet0/0/0
  no ip address
  ipv6 address 2001:DB8:14:1::1/64
  nat64 enable
  ipv6 ospf 1 area 0
 !
 interface GigabitEthernet0/0/1
  ip address 172.16.1.1 255.255.255.0
  nat64 enable
 !
 router ospf 1
```

```
 log-adjacency-changes
 network 172.16.0.0 0.0.255.255 area 0
 default-information originate always
!
ipv6 router ospf 1
 log-adjacency-changes
 default-information originate always
!
nat64 prefix stateful 2001:DB8:14:e::/96
!
ipv6 access-list nat64-example
 permit ipv6 2001:db8:14:e::/96 any
!
nat64 v4 pool examplepool 172.16.250.1 172.16.250.254
!
nat64 v6v4 list nat64-example pool examplepool overload
!
ipv6 route 2001:db8:14:5::/96 GigabitEthernet0/0/1
!
nat64 route 172.16.22.0/24 GigabitEthernet0/0/0
!
```

Limitations of Stateful NAT64

NAT64 is still not a perfect solution; no translator is. There are just too many variables, and the more variables you address, the more complex the solution becomes. Current specific limitations of NAT64 follow:

- It doesn't allow IPv4 devices to initiate a session to an IPv6 device without a static address mapping.

- Specific to Cisco, NAT64 (both stateful and stateless) has limited support in software.

- As with all translators, IP multicast is not supported.

- Many applications are not supported without separate ALGs.

Looking Ahead

It seems odd to have a "Looking Ahead" section in the final chapter of what is so far the final volume of this series on Routing TCP/IP. But for you, there is plenty to look ahead to. These two volumes have given you a grounding in the basics of both unicast and multicast routing, both within an autonomous system and between autonomous systems, and for both IPv4 and IPv6. But many topics aren't covered because of a lack of time and space, so there's plenty more for you to study.

And what about next steps? For routing, MPLS and MPSL-based multiservice networks are an excellent next step. You can find a number of excellent books from Cisco Press on the topic. You should also look into network virtualization, which is moving out of the data center and into the service provider and WAN environments. These are all topics that as a network expert you will be expected to be conversant about.

I hope these two volumes have helped to further your knowledge and your career, and I hope you have enjoyed the journey through these topics as much as I have enjoyed leading you through them.

Review Questions

1. What is SIIT?

2. What are some examples of header fields than cannot be translated between IPv4 and IPv6?

3. How does SIIT handle an ICMP message that has no corresponding message in ICMPv6?

4. What is the difference between NAT44 and NAT-PT?

5. What is the major difference between NAT-PT and NAT64 (either stateful or stateless)?

6. If IPv4 address conservation is important, would you choose stateless or stateful NAT64?

7. What is an IPv4-embedded IPv6 address?

Configuration Exercise

Refer to Figure 11-17 for the Configuration Exercise.

Table 11-10 lists the routers, interfaces, and addresses used in the exercises for this chapter. All interfaces of the routers are shown.

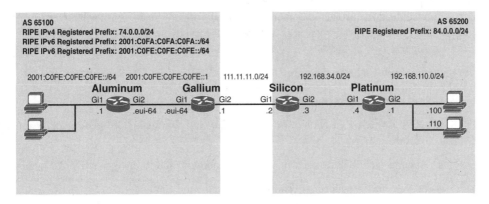

Figure 11-17   *Network Topology for Configuration Exercise*

Table 11-10   *Router Interfaces and IP Addresses for Configuration Exercise*

Network Device	Interface	IP Address
Aluminum	Gi1	2001:C0FE:C0FE:C0FE::1/64
	Gi2	2001:C0FA:C0FA:C0FA::/64 eui-64
	2001:C0FA:C0FA:C0FA:5200:FF:FE01:1	
	Loopback 0	74.0.0.1/24
Gallium	Gi1	2001:C0FA:C0FA:C0FA::/64 eui-64 2001:C0FA:C0FA:C0FA:5200:FF:FE02:0
	Gi2	111.11.11.1/24
Silicon	Gi1	111.11.11.2/24
	Gi2	192.168.34.3/24
Platinum	Gi1	192.168.34.4/24
	Gi2	192.168.110.1/24
	Loopback 0	84.0.0.1/24

Configuration Exercise Premise

The company you work for has a greenfield IPv6 network infrastructure. As a network engineer, you need to allow communications between your new IPv6 infrastructure and the "legacy" IPv4 Internet.

Because you are knowledgeable in IPv6, you want to use the best solution for your network address translation conceptual design.

There is a direct IP connectivity between the two administrative domains (BGP AS 65100 for your company and BGP AS 65200 for your customer). The customer has agreed that you will lead the project and manage both networks. Your network will advertise 74.0.0.0/24 to the customer network and you will receive the 84.0.0.0/24 prefix from the customer.

Assume the following statements:

- Unicast routing is already set up:

  - OSPF is the IGP of choice for each administrative domain (OSPFv3 for BGP AS 65100).

  - Assume each BGP router will advertise a default route to its respective IGP peers.

  - BGP AS 65100 will run on routers Aluminum and Gallium.

  - BGP AS 65200 will run on routers Silicon and Platinum.

  - NAT will be performed by the following devices: Aluminum for AS65100 and Silicon for AS65200.

Configure the network based on the following requirements:

For AS 65100:

- Create a loopback interface on Aluminum and make sure it is advertised into OSPF.

- Advertise the 74.0.0.0/24 prefix into BGP.

- Make sure that inside local IPv6 address 2001:c0fe:c0fe:c0fe:ed72:bacc:b8fb:e06e can reach 84.0.0.0/24.

- Make sure that inside local IP address 2001:c0fe:c0fe:c0fe:653a:cf2b:b88d:f639 can reach 84.0.0.0/24.

- The requirements follow:

  - The NAT translations should conserve IPv4 addresses.

  - You are not providing any services to the legacy IPv4 Internet, so the connectivity request should be initiated by your IPv6 infrastructure.

  - You still have registered the 74.0.0.0/24 IPv4 Prefix and must use a single IPv4 to map all your IPv6 to IPv4 network address translation.

For AS 65200:

- Create a loopback interface on Platinum and make sure it is advertised into OSPF.

- Advertise the 84.0.0.0/24 prefix into BGP.

- Assume the BGP configurations are finished and are the same as in the previous exercises chapter.

Verify that any IP traffic is translated to the right IP address and that IP traffic can be exchanged.

Appendix A

Answers to Review Questions

Chapter 1

1. What is an autonomous system?

   Answer: An autonomous system is an administrative domain in which all the networks are under a single administrative authority.

2. What is the difference between an IGP and an EGP?

   Answer: An Interior Gateway Protocol is a routing protocol that runs interior to an autonomous system; an Exterior Gateway Protocol is a routing protocol that routes between autonomous systems.

3. What is the difference between an internal and an external peer?

   Answer: An internal peer is in the same AS; an external peer is in a different AS.

4. What is the transport protocol and port number used by BGP?

   Answer: BGP sessions are transported over TCP, using port 179.

5. What are the two purposes of the BGP AS_PATH route attribute?

   Answer: The AS_PATH list is used to detect routing loops and to help BGP determine the shortest number of AS hops to a destination.

6. How does BGP use the AS_PATH attribute to detect routing loops?

   Answer: If a router receives a BGP route with the router's own AS number on the list, it discards the route.

7. What is the difference between a stub AS and a transit AS?

   Answer: All packets entering a stub AS have a destination address within the AS, and all packets leaving a stub AS have a source address originating in the AS. At least some packets entering a transit AS have a destination in a different AS, and at least some packets leaving a transit AS have a source address that originated in a different AS.

8. What is a BGP path attribute?

Answer: A path attribute is a characteristic or value attached to a route that can help in best-path selection and enable routing policies.

9. What is a recursive route lookup?

Answer: A recursive lookup is one in which the router must perform multiple route lookups to get all the information it needs to forward a packet. For example, the result of a route lookup might return a next-hop address that is not directly attached to the router. A second lookup is then required to find the route to the next-hop address.

10. When BGP advertises a route among autonomous systems, when is an AS number added to the AS_PATH list? When is an AS number not added to the list, and why?

Answer: A BGP router adds its AS number to the AS_PATH list of a route only when the route is advertised to an EBGP peer. It does not add its AS number to the list if the route is advertised to an IBGP peer, both because doing so would distort the number of AS hops represented by the list and because the IBGP peer, following BGP loop avoidance rules, would drop the route when it saw its own AS number on the AS_PATH list.

11. What is the purpose of a full IBGP mesh, and why is it considered best practice?

Answer: A full IBGP mesh ensures that all routers have all the information necessary to forward transit packets. It is considered best practice because the alternative, redistributing BGP information into the IGP, is neither secure nor scalable.

12. How does IBGP avoid routing loops?

Answer: A BGP router does not advertise routes learned from an IBGP peer to another IBGP peer. (This is another reason why a full IBGP mesh is necessary.)

13. What is a multihomed AS?

Answer: A multihomed AS has more than one external link.

14. Name a few reasons why a stub AS might be multihomed.

Answer: A stub AS might use multihoming to provide redundancy, local connectivity across a geographically large AS, provider independence, corporate or external policies, or load sharing.

15. What is CIDR, and what problems led to its creation?

Answer: Classless Inter-Domain Routing changed the rules of IPv4 address assignment, doing away with the older Classes A, B, and C boundaries, so prefixes could be more efficiently assigned and aggregated according to need. CIDR was created to slow the depletion of IPv4 addresses (particularly class B addresses) and the exponentially increasing size of the Internet routing table.

16. What is an IP address prefix?

Answer: The prefix of an IP address is the bits of the address representing the network portion (as opposed to the host portion) of the address. The prefix is the portion of the address that routers are interested in, and what routers enter into their routing tables.

17. How does address summarization help stabilize a network?

Answer: Summarization helps stabilize a network by "hiding" changes in more-specific addresses that belong to the summary. That is, a change to a prefix is not advertised beyond an upstream aggregation point.

18. What is the possible compromise made when summarization is implemented?

Answer: The main compromise made for the benefits of summarization is a loss of more specific routing information, possibly causing less than optimal forwarding choices.

19. What does the CIDR notation /17 indicate?

Answer: In general, the CIDR notation of a forward slash followed by a number indicates an address prefix or the number of leading bits in an address composed of a prefix. So /17 indicates a 17-bit prefix.

20. What is an Internet Registry?

Answer: An IR is an organization that manages and allocates IP addresses and AS numbers, among other things. Originally the IANA was the only IR, but Regional Internet Registries were formed under the management of IANA in 1993 to provide more regional management of these resources. As of this writing there are five RIRs. Local Internet Registries operate under the RIRs and are usually service providers.

21. How have multihoming and traffic engineering practices reduced the effectiveness of CIDR?

Answer: Multihoming and traffic engineering practices have reduced the effectiveness of CIDR by de-aggregating CIDR blocks, advertising more specific prefixes of the blocks to the Internet routing tables in attempts to manipulate incoming traffic behavior.

Chapter 2

1. What is an untrusted administrative domain, and why is it untrusted?

Answer: An untrusted administrative domain is a routing domain under someone else's administrative authority. Usually, this means another autonomous system, but not necessarily. The domain is untrusted because you have no control over security, policy, or routing decisions (and possibly mistakes) made in that domain.

2. In what way does BGP require you to think differently about peering than an IGP does?

Answer: Whereas you normally think of an IGP peering session as "exchanging routes," you must think of the incoming and outgoing advertisements across a BGP peering session separately. In most cases you do not allow a free two-way exchange of information across a BGP session like you do across an IGP session; you manipulate them separately, with the understanding that outgoing advertisements influence incoming traffic and incoming advertisements influence outgoing traffic.

3. What AS numbers are reserved for private use?

Answer: The AS numbers 64512 through 65534 are private-use AS numbers. Like RFC 1918 private IPv4 addresses, these AS numbers are not globally unique and must not appear in AS_PATH lists of routes advertised to the public Internet.

4. What are the four BGP message types, and how is each one used?

Answer: The four BGP message types are Open, Keepalive, Update, and Notification. Open messages are used to initially identify a BGP speaker to its neighbor, advertise capabilities, and begin a peering session. Keepalives maintain the peer connection. Updates advertise routes, and Notification messages advise peers of errors.

5. What happens if two BGP neighbors advertise different hold times in their Open messages?

Answer: The neighbors agree to use the lower of the two hold time values.

6. What does a negotiated hold time of 0 indicate?

Answer: If the agreed-upon hold time between neighbors is 0, no Keepalives are sent between the neighbors.

7. What is the IOS default period for sending BGP Keepalive messages?

Answer: The IOS default BGP Keepalive interval is 60 seconds.

8. What is the BGP identifier, and how is it selected?

Answer: The BGP identifier identifies a specific BGP speaker. It is used similarly to the way an OSPF router ID is used and is selected in the same way: If a BGP identifier is manually specified with the **bgp router-id** statement, that identifier is used; if the identifier is not specified, the numerically highest loopback interface address is used; if no loopback addresses are available, the numerically highest physical interface address is used.

9. In what state or states can BGP peers exchange Update messages?

Answer: BGP peers can exchange Update messages only when both are in the Established state.

10. What is NLRI?

Answer: Network Layer Reachability Information is the IP address prefix or prefixes advertised in a BGP Update.

11. What is a path attribute?

Answer: A path attribute is a characteristic of a BGP route.

12. What is a Withdrawn route?

Answer: A Withdrawn route is a prefix indicated in a BGP Update as no longer reachable and therefore withdrawn from service.

13. What happens when a BGP Notification message is received?

Answer: The reception of a Notification message always causes the session to close.

14. What is the difference between the Connect state and the Active state?

Answer: In Connect state the BGP process is waiting for a TCP connection to a neighbor to be completed. In Active state the process is actively trying to initiate a TCP connection.

15. What causes a transition to the OpenConfirm state, and what are the next steps when the BGP process shows a neighbor in this state?

Answer: A neighbor is transitioned from OpenSent (in which an Open message has been sent to the neighbor) to OpenConfirmed with an error-free Open message received from the neighbor and capabilities are agreed upon. From OpenConfirm the neighbor is transitioned to Established if a Keepalive is received from the neighbor or is transitioned to Idle if a Notification or TCP disconnect is received.

16. What are the four categories of BGP path attributes?

Answer: The four categories of BGP path attributes are

Well-known Mandatory
Well-known Discretionary
Optional Transitive
Optional Nontransitive

17. What does well-known mandatory mean, and what are the three well-known mandatory path attributes?

Answer: Well-known mandatory means every BGP process must recognize the attribute (well-known) and every BGP Update must include the attribute (mandatory). The three well-known mandatory attributes are ORIGIN, AS_PATH, and NEXT_HOP.

18. What is the purpose of the ORIGIN attribute?

Answer: The ORIGIN attribute indicates the origin (IGP, EGP, or Incomplete) of the NLRI in the Update. The attribute was created to help transition from EGP to BGP, and has limited usefulness in modern BGP networks.

19. What is the purpose of the AS_PATH attribute?

Answer: The AS_PATH attribute describes the AS numbers that a received Update has crossed after it left the originating router. This information can determine the shortest inter-AS path, and can also detect routing loops.

20. When does a router add its AS number to the AS_PATH list of an Update?

Answer: A router adds its AS number to the AS_PATH only when it sends an Update to an external peer.

21. What is AS path prepending?

Answer: AS path prepending means an AS number is added as the first AS number on the AS_PATH, which is the default behavior for Updates sent to an external peer. AS path prepending also refers to the policy practice of adding multiple instances of the local AS number to the list to manipulate remote routing of incoming packets.

22. What are AS_SEQUENCE and AS_SET, and what is the difference between them?

Answer: Both are subsets of the AS_PATH attribute. AS_SEQUENCE is an ordered list of AS numbers, whereas AS_SET can be unordered. AS_SET maintains loop avoidance when aggregation has obscured the information normally carried in AS_SEQUENCE.

23. What is the purpose of the NEXT_HOP attribute?

Answer: The NEXT_HOP attribute describes the IP address of the next-hop router that packets should be forwarded to in order to reach the destination advertised as the NLRI in a BGP Update.

24. What is a recursive route lookup, and why is it important to BGP?

Answer: A recursive route lookup occurs when a router looks up a route to a destination address and then must look up the route to the next-hop address associated with the destination route. It is a fundamental function for BGP because the IBGP sessions (and multihop EBGP sessions) are not always run between directly connected neighbors. Recursive lookups are also important for finding the next hops of externally learned routes because the NEXT_HOP of routes learned from external neighbors is not changed by default as the route is passed to internal neighbors.

25. What happens if a router receives a BGP route with a NEXT_HOP address that is unknown to the router?

Answer: The router adds the route to its BGP table but does not add the route to its routing table.

26. What are the three parts of a BGP routing information database (RIB), and what is the function of each?

Answer: The BGP RIB includes Adj-RIBs-In, which stores routes exactly as learned from neighbors before the application of incoming policies; Loc-RIB

contains the routes modified by incoming policy and selected by the BGP decision process; and Adj-RIBs-Out contains the routes selected and modified by
outgoing routing policies that are advertised to neighbors.

27. What do all the NLRI in a BGP Update message have in common?

Answer: All path attributes in a BGP Update message apply to all NLRI listed
in the Update. If an NLRI has a different set of attributes associated with it, it
must be advertised in a separate Update.

28. Does BGP require a TCP connection between IPv6 addresses to advertise IPv6
prefixes?

Answer: There is no relationship between the addresses of the TCP endpoints
and the address families of the prefixes advertised over the BGP session. The
TCP endpoints can be either IPv4 or IPv6, and the types of prefixes advertised
by the BGP session running over the TCP connection are dependent only on
the address families BGP is configured to advertise.

29. What is the IOS default TTL value of BGP message packets sent to external
peers?

Answer: The default TTL value IOS sets for EBGP packets to external peers
is 1.

Chapter 3

1. What is a BGP NLRI?

Answer: Network Layer Reachability Information is the destination of a BGP
route. As the name implies it is always a network layer address; in the context
of this chapter the NLRI is always an IP prefix.

2. How are prefixes added to BGP to be advertised? How is this different from the
way prefixes are added to an IGP?

Answer: The prefixes to be "injected" into BGP must be either individually
specified with the **network** statement or redistributed into BGP from some
other protocol from a directly connected interface or from a static route. No
prefixes are automatically injected into BGP. This differs from an IGP, which
picks up the subnet address of any interface on which it is running. (Although,
redistribution can also be used with IGPs).

3. How does the BGP **network** statement differ in function from an IGP **network**
statement?

Answer: The BGP **network** statement specifies a prefix to be injected from the
routing table into BGP, whereas the IGP **network** statement specifies the address
of one or more local interfaces on which the IGP should run.

4. What is the BGP table? How does it differ from the routing table, and how can it be observed?

Answer: The BGP table is a database of the prefixes (NLRI) that BGP advertises and receives. The prefixes in the BGP table might or might not be entered into the routing table, depending on default or configured policy. Routing decisions are made based on the routing table, not the entries in the BGP table. The BGP table can be observed with the **show ip bgp** command; specifying an individual prefix in the **show ip bgp** command displays all the information about the entry in the BGP table for that prefix, such as the associated path attributes.

5. When is the **mask** option of the **network** statement required?

Answer: The **mask** option is used whenever the prefix specified with the **network** statement is something other than a traditional Class A, B, or C prefix. That is, the **mask** specifies the prefix length.

6. Why is the **network** statement usually preferred over redistribution for injecting prefixes into BGP?

Answer: The **network** statement is precise in the prefixes it injects into BGP, whereas redistribution injects everything the IGP knows into BGP unless filters are used.

7. What is the RIB?

Answer: The Routing Information Base is the "official" name of the routing table.

8. How is the Origin path attribute of a route injected into BGP with the **network** statement different from the Origin attribute of a route injected into BGP by redistribution?

Answer: A route injected into BGP with the **network** statement has an ORIGIN code of IGP, whereas a route injected by redistribution has an Origin code of Incomplete.

9. What are the default rules for the NEXT_HOP path attribute when BGP advertises a route to an external peer and when BGP advertises a route to an internal peer?

Answer: By default, when BGP advertises a route to an external peer, it sets the NEXT_HOP attribute of the route to the IP address of the outgoing interface toward the peer; when BGP advertises a route to an internal peer, it does not change the NEXT_HOP attribute.

10. How can the default BGP NEXT_HOP rules cause a problem within a single AS, and how can the problem be corrected?

Answer: When a BGP speaker advertises a route learned from an external peer to an internal peer, the internal peer declares the route unreachable if it does not know how to reach the NEXT_HOP address. This problem can be remedied by either making the NEXT_HOP address reachable (by using a static route, the **redistribute connected** statement, or running the IGP in passive mode on the external interface) or by changing the default NEXT_HOP rules with the **neighbor next-hop-self** statement.

11. How is the **neighbor next-hop-self** statement used?

Answer: The **neighbor next-hop-self** statement sets the NEXT_HOP attribute of routes advertised to the specified neighbor to the address of the local loopback interface. This ensures that internal neighbors know how to reach the routes' next hop (assuming that the loopback address is advertised by the IGP).

12. What is the rule of IGP/BGP synchronization? Why is it seldom used in modern BGP networks?

Answer: The IGP/BGP synchronization rule requires that a route learned from an internal BGP neighbor must be known by the IGP before it can be advertised to an EBGP peer. The rule was built on the assumption that the IGP must have knowledge of the route for packets to transit an AS. Modern BGP networks use a full IBGP mesh, eliminating the need for the IGP to know the external routes.

13. Why is it generally considered bad practice to redistribute BGP into the IGP?

Answer: Internet-connected BGP is assumed to carry hundreds of thousands of routes. Although BGP is designed to handle this capacity, IGPs are not. Redistribution of more than a few thousand routes into an IGP can cause performance and conversion problems; Internet-scale routing tables can cause network-side system failures, especially with link state IGPs. In addition, redistribution of BGP into the IGP allows the direct connection of an untrusted domain to your trusted domain.

14. What is the preferred method of advertising AS-external routes through a multihomed stub AS, and why is it preferred?

Answer: Advertising the routes via IBGP, without redistribution into the IGP, is the preferred method of getting routes into a multihomed stub AS where granular route detail is needed, such as for selecting exit points nearest the external destination. Keeping the routes separate from the IGP protects IGP performance and security enables control over how the prefixes are distributed within the AS and enables better control over the routes through BGP policy tools.

15. What is route aggregation?

Answer: Route aggregation is the advertisement of a single, short prefix that represents routes to multiple, longer prefixes. A router can find a best match of the destination address of a packet to the aggregate prefix and forward to the packet to the originator of the aggregate, where the destination address is then matched to a longer, more-specific prefix and forwarded on to the destination.

16. What are the main benefits and drawbacks of aggregation?

Answer: The main benefits of aggregation are reduced network resource usage (bandwidth used for carrying updates, CPU, and router memory) and increased network stability. The drawbacks to aggregation are reduction of route information leading to possible suboptimal route selection and an increased chance of routing loops and black-holed traffic.

17. Why should the originator of an aggregate route point the next hop of the route to its Null0 interface?

Answer: A packet for which the aggregate prefix is the longest match to its destination address will be forwarded to the aggregate originator. If that router does not then have a more specific route on which to forward the packet (either because the route has failed or because it does not exist), the router should drop the packet by "sending" it to Null0.

18. What are the relative merits of using static aggregate routes and using the **aggregate-address** statement when injecting an aggregate route into BGP?

Answer: Static aggregate routes are simple and can be precisely injected into BGP using the **network** statement. The **aggregate-address** statement can be useful in more complex topologies or when more complex aggregate behavior is required.

19. What does the **summary-only** option of the **aggregate-address** statement do?

Answer: The **summary-only** option suppresses all the more-specific routes belonging to the aggregate so that only the aggregate is advertised. Without the option, the aggregate and the more-specific routes are all advertised.

20. What is the ATOMIC_AGGREGATE BGP path attribute?

Answer: The ATOMIC_AGGREGATE attribute is a simple indicator that the route is an aggregate.

21. What is the AGGRGATOR BGP path attribute?

Answer: The AGGREGATOR attribute indicates the RID and AS number of the router that created the aggregate. Coupled with the ATOMIC_AGGREGATE, the two attributes are useful for identifying aggregates and tracing them back to their origin when troubleshooting.

22. What is the difference between AS_SEQUENCE and AS_SET?

Answer: AS_SEQUENCE is the normal ordered list of AS numbers in the AS_PATH attribute. The sequence is a step-by-step description of the inter-AS path from the point where the route is observed back to the route's origin. AS_SET is an optional unordered list of all AS numbers on all paths to destinations represented by an aggregate route. The AS_SET is useful for retaining BGP loop avoidance when the aggregate represents destinations that are reachable over more than a single path.

23. What is the purpose of the **advertise-map** option of the **aggregate-address** configuration statement?

Answer: Aggregate routes inherit the path attributes of their constituent routes by default; this might not always be desirable because some routes might have attributes that should not be added to the aggregate. The **advertise-map** option enables the specification of which constituent routes can and cannot add attributes to the aggregate.

Chapter 4

1. What are the three parts of a BGP Routing Information Database (RIB), and how do they differ?

Answer:

Adj-RIBs-In—Stores unprocessed routing information that has been learned from BGP Updates received from peers. The routes contained in Adj-RIBs-In are considered feasible routes.

Loc-RIB—Contains the routes that the BGP speaker has selected by applying the decision process to the routes contained in Adj-RIBs-In.

Adj-RIBs-Out—Contains the routes that the BGP speaker advertises to its peers in BGP Updates. The outgoing routing policies determine what routes are placed in Adj-RIBs-Out.

2. What does it mean when an entry in the BGP table is labeled "RIB-failure"?

Answer: "RIB-failure" means the route is valid, but it has not been installed in the unicast routing table; usually because another routing protocol's route to the destination has been selected over the BGP route.

3. What is the purpose of the BGP Decision Process?

Answer: The BGP Decision Process compares the characteristics of two or more routes to the same destination to determine which of them is the "best" route.

4. What is the difference between the in and out keywords when a routing policy is applied to a neighbor configuration?

Answer: In applies the policy to routes received from the neighbor (incoming) and out applies the policy to routes being advertised to the neighbor (outgoing).

5. What are InQ and OutQ?

Answer: InQ and OutQ are transient queues that serve, in IOS, as Adj-RIBs-In and Adj-RIBs-Out. IOS creates an InQ and OutQ for each BGP neighbor configured.

6. Name the steady state and transient IOS BGP processes, and describe what each process does.

Answer: I/O interfaces with the router's TCP socket. It controls BGP messages going into and out of InQ and OutQ.

Router is responsible for the processing of BGP messages (including the BGP Decision Process), applying policies, and creating entries in the BGP table. It interacts between InQ, OutQ, and the routing table.

Scanner monitors and interacts with non-BGP functions on the router that might effect BGP.

Next Hop Tracker performs next hop and best path validation, reducing the workload of the Scanner process in some IOS versions.

Event adds or removes prefixes in the BGP table based on network or redistribution statements.

Open is the only transient process listed here; it manages the opening of a BGP session with a neighbor and runs only during the open attempts.

7. If the command show processes cpu | include BGP is run on the router in Example 4-17, will any of the processes be BGP Open? If so, how many? Why?

Answer: Six instances of the BGP Open process will be running if show processes cpu |include BGP is issued soon after the display in Example 4-17, because there are six neighbors in Active state. There will be a separate Open process for each neighbor to which the router is trying to open a BGP session:

```
route-views.oregon-ix.net>sh proc cpu | include BGP
 149   204638952    4582172     44660  0.00%   6.25%  5.51%   0 BGP Scheduler
 163     2105380   38103772        55  0.08%   0.06%  0.07%   0 BGP I/O
 185   176824084    1126241    157008 43.10%   7.26%  4.90%   0 BGP Scanner
 187    31644560   40453977       782  0.80%   1.07%  0.89%   0 BGP Router
 249         516      60824         8  0.00%   0.00%  0.00%   0 BGP Open
 251       20340        105    193714  0.00%   0.00%  0.00%   0 BGP Event
 264        3284     300850        10  0.00%   0.00%  0.00%   0 BGP Open
 265       10420     359468        28  0.00%   0.00%  0.00%   0 BGP Open
 266        3208     300734        10  0.00%   0.00%  0.00%   0 BGP Open
 275        3272     300650        10  0.00%   0.00%  0.00%   0 BGP Open
 285        3368     300780        11  0.00%   0.00%  0.00%   0 BGP Open
route-views.oregon-ix.net>
```

8. What is a table version?

Answer: Table version is a 32-bit number by which IOS tracks prefixes through the various processes and databases. Table versions are assigned to

- Each neighbor
- Each prefix
- The BGP RIB
- The BGP process

9. Refer to Figure 4-5, and assume the table versions are as shown in Example 4-30. If the command clear ip bgp 10.4.1.1 is issued at Loveland, how will the table versions change, and why? If the command clear ip bgp 10.2.1.2 is next issued at Buttermilk, how will the table versions change and why? If the command clear ip bgp 10.3.1.2 is, after the other two, issued at Arapahoe how will the table versions change and why?

Answer: When the **clear ip bgp** command is issued the session to the specified neighbor is closed and then is re-established. In the case of Loveland, when the session is re-established Eldora sends a new Update to Loveland. However, nothing about the prefixes changes at Eldora, so no table versions change in that router.

When the session from Buttermilk is closed, the two prefixes advertised by that router to Eldora are withdrawn. When 10.20.1.0/24 is withdrawn the loss of the route must be entered in the RIB and advertised to neighbors, so the BGP, RIB, and neighbor table versions increment to 7. However, 10.1.1.0/24 is still advertised by Arapahoe and the route through Arapahoe is preferred (as shown in Example 4-30); therefore, the prefix is still known and the best path does not change, so the table version for that prefix does not change. When the session is re-established Buttermilk advertises 10.20.1.0/24 and 10.1.1.0/24. The reception of 10.20.1.0/24 causes Eldora to increment the table version to 8, but the reception of 10.1.1.0/24 does not cause a table version change because the prefix is already known and the new route does not cause a change of best path preference.

When the session from Arapahoe is closed, the two prefixes advertised by that router are withdrawn. The withdrawal of 10.30.1.0/24 causes a table version increment; the withdrawal of 10.1.1.0/24 causes Eldora to select the path through Buttermilk. Therefore, the table versions increment twice, to 10 (assuming it was 8 before the session was reset). When the session is re-established, the two prefixes are advertised again. The reception of 10.30.1.0/24 causes the table versions to increment, and the reception of 10.1.1.0/24 causes a change of best path preference back to the route through Arapahoe, which also causes the table versions to increment. Therefore, the table versions after the session is back up and the prefixes advertised from Eldora is 12.

10. Look at the BGP, RIB, and neighbor table versions in Example 4-17. Can you explain why there is a difference between the BGP and neighbor table versions, based on what you see in the display? It might be instructive in Answering this

question to telnet to the following public route servers running IOS and use
show ip bgp summary at each two or three times:

- Oregon IX (route-views.orego-ix.net)
- Time Warner Telecom (route-server.twtelecom.net)
- AT&T (route-server.ip.att.net)
- Tiscali (route-server.ip.tiscali.net)
- SingTel/Optus (route-views.optus.net.au)

Answer: Notice that the routers on which the neighbor table versions differ
the most—and the most often—from the BGP and RIB table versions are
routers with a large number of peers. Notice also that when the neighbor table
versions differ from the BGP table version, the neighbor number is always
higher. Finally, notice that if the neighbor table versions differ from each other
the numbers almost always increase from the top to the bottom of the neighbor list.

The number differences are not a result of the BGP process but of the low
priority of the show command. If BGP is increasing the table version rapidly
as it sends large Updates to its peers, the number can increment several times
as the show ip bgp summary command finds and returns the table versions of
the neighbors. That is why the neighbor numbers, if they differ from the BGP
table version, are usually larger and why, if they differ from each other, increase
as the neighbor list is built. He more peers a router has, and the more prefixes
that must be advertised to the peers, the more likely you are to observe this
phenomenon.

11. What is the advantage of using the soft keyword with the **clear ip bgp**
command?

    Answer: Soft reconfiguration causes a re-application of policies to inbound
    routes or the retransmission of routes (depending on the in or out keywords)
    without resetting—and hence disrupting—the BGP session.

12. What is the purpose of the neighbor soft-reconfiguration inbound statement?

    Answer: The neighbor soft-reconfiguration inbound statement is used with
    older BGP implementations, and tells the router to save copies incoming routes
    from the specified neighbor before applying incoming policies. The stored
    routes can then be referenced whenever the clear ip bgp soft in command is
    used to new or changed inbound policies.

13. What is route refresh?

    Answer: Route refresh is a function supported in newer BGP implementations
    that can send a message (the BGP Route Refresh message) to a neighbor when
    the **clear ip bgp soft in** command is issued, telling the neighbor to re-send its
    routes. This eliminates the need for the neighbor soft-reconfiguration inbound
    statement and its associated memory consumption to store the neighbor's

routes locally. Route refresh capability is negotiated during a BGP session opening, and the neighbor's route refresh capability is recorded in the neighbor table.

14. What two tools are used as NLRI-based route filters, and which is the more preferred?

Answer: Distribute lists and prefix lists are used for NLRI-based route filtering. Prefix lists are the more preferred (and more modern) tool, because they are more flexible, easier to work with, and have less performance impact on the router. Distribute lists require Extended ACLs for all but the simplest filtering, and Extended ACLs when applied to NLRI are difficult to interpret.

15. When would you filter routes by AS_PATH rather than by NLRI?

Answer: AS-path filters are used whenever you want to filter all routes originating in or advertised by a particular AS, or all routes belonging to a particular path. NLRI route filters are more precise, but AS-path filters allow you to filter more routes without specifying individual prefixes.

16. When would you use a route map rather than a route filter?

Answer: Route maps are used when a more complex routing policy is required than simply permitting or denying a route. This includes

- Matching on multiple route attributes
- Changing one or more route attributes, rather than just permitting or denying the routs
- Creating a sequence of route match conditions and set actions
- Creating policy configurations that are expected to change occasionally

17. When is an administrative weight used in a routing policy?

Answer: Weight is used when you want to influence the preference of a route within a single router but do not want that preference to be communicated to any other router.

18. What are the default administrative weight values? How are weights evaluated?

Answer: The default administrative weights are 32768 for routes originated locally and 0 for routes learned from neighbors. Weight takes preference over all other attributes in the BGP decision process, and the higher weight value is more preferable.

19. When is LOCAL_PREF used in a routing policy?

Answer: LOCAL_PREF is used when you want to influence the preference of a route within the local AS. A LOCAL_PREF attribute is not carried across AS boundaries (that is, over EBGP sessions).

20. What is the default LOCAL_PREF value? How is LOCAL_PREF evaluated?

Answer: The default LOCAL_PREF value is 100. LOCAL_PREF is evaluated before any other attribute except weight, and the higher value is preferred.

21. When is MED used in a routing policy?

Answer: The MED attribute is used to express a preference to a neighboring AS about what path to send incoming packets across. In other words, it is used to try to influence the BGP decision process in a neighboring AS and hence influence incoming traffic.

22. How is MED evaluated?

Answer: The MED is a 4-byte number, and is evaluated after the AS_PATH length and the Origin code; the lowest MED value is preferred. This relatively low position within the BGP decision process makes the MED a weak attribute.

23. What does the **bgp bestpath med missing-as-worst** statement do, and when is it used?

Answer: **bgp bestpath med missing-as-worst** changes the default IOS MED behavior, which normally adds the lowest MED value (0) to any route learned from an EBGP neighbor and advertised to an IBGP neighbor, to instead add the maximum MED value (4294967295). The statement is used when you want IOS to adapt to the default behavior of some other vendors' BGP implementations that add the maximum MED value instead of the lowest MED value.

24. How does the set metric-type internal statement differ from the set metric statement?

Answer: Set metric is used to set the MED value of a route to any value you want, between 0 and 4294967295. Set metric-type internal automatically sets the MED value of a route to the IGP metric to the route's internal next hop. This is used when you want a neighboring autonomous system to route packets to the local edge router closest to the internal destination.

25. What is the purpose of the **bgp always-compare-med** statement?

Answer: The **bgp always-compare-med** statement compares the MEDs of routes to the same destination, even when they are advertised from different autonomous systems. Normally, only MEDs from the same AS are compared. This is useful when multiple neighboring autonomous systems are under the same administrative control or otherwise coordinate the management of their MEDs.

26. What is the purpose of the **bgp deterministic-med statement**?

Answer: The b**gp deterministic-med statement** causes routes to the same destination to be grouped by ASN. Routes from the same AS are compared first (including MEDs) and the best chosen. The best route from each AS is then compared (without comparing MEDs) and the overall best route is chosen.

This prevents inconsistent route choices from occurring as can happen with routes are entered simply in the order they are received.

27. What is the purpose of AS_PATH prepending?

Answer: AS_PATH prepending is the act of adding one or more instances of your own ASN to the front of the AS_PATH of a route being advertised to an external neighbor (in addition to the one ASN added automatically). The purpose of prepending is to intentionally make the AS_PATH longer, and thus make the route less preferable to the BGP decision processes in other autonomous systems. Unlike MEDs, which are limited to a directly neighboring AS, AS_PATH prepending can affect the choices of distant autonomous systems.

28. What is a continue clause?

Answer: A continue clause allows a nonlinear "jump" from one route map sequence to another after a successful match. It is similar to a "go-to" statement in a program.

29. What is a policy list?

Answer: A policy list is a collection of two or more match clauses. Rather than repeatedly configuring the same match clauses within a route map (if such a pattern is reused within the route map), the route map can reference the policy list whenever the set of match clauses are needed. This allows for easier changes of the match clauses and easier identification of the locations within the route map where the combination of match clauses is used.

Chapter 5

1. What is, in the context of networking, meant by scalability?

Answer: Scalability means the capability of a protocol, device, or software to grow with a network without significantly changing its capability to perform its network function.

2. In what three general ways can BGP be scaled?

Answer: (a) The BGP configuration in a single router can be scaled for more efficient management; (b) the BGP process in a single router can be scaled for improved performance; and (c) the BGP network can be scaled for more efficient management and performance.

3. What is a peer group?

Answer: A peer group is an older IOS configuration technique in which BGP neighbors sharing the same policies can be groups to share similar configuration parameters.

4. If a peer group is configured to use an update source of Loopback 0 and a neighbor belonging to that peer group is configured to use an update source of Loopback 3, what update source will the neighbor use?

Answer: If there is a parameter configuration conflict between the peer group and a specific neighbor, the neighbor configuration takes precedence. So in this example, the neighbor uses Loopback 3 as its update source.

5. What is a dynamic update peer group, and how does it change the traditional use of peer groups?

Answer: Dynamic update peer groups automatically group neighbors sharing the same outbound policies, reducing the number of scans of the BGP table when building a BGP Update. This was the original motivation for creating peer groups, so with Dynamic update peer groups, the only utility of configured peer groups is to control the size of a large BGP configuration.

6. What are peer templates, and what are the two types of peer templates?

Answer: Peer templates are a more modern way of grouping neighbors sharing the same configuration parameters. The two types of peer templates are policy templates, for applying to neighbors sharing the same policies, and session templates, for neighbors sharing the same session parameters.

7. Can peer templates and peer groups be applied to the same neighbor.

Answer: Peer templates and peer groups are mutually exclusive, and a neighbor cannot belong to a peer group and have peer templates applied to it.

8. What is meant by inheritance in the context of peer templates?

Answer: Inheritance is the capability of a session template to inherit the parameters of another session template, and a policy template to inherit the parameters of another policy template. The advantage of inheritance is the capability to scale peer templates and, in the case of policy templates, to create a branching structure of policies.

9. What is a BGP community?

Answer: A community is a BGP attribute that can be attached to a BGP route, either by itself or as one of several communities, that allow policies to be applied to a set of routes belonging to the same community, instead of having to identify all individual routes to apply a shared policy.

10. How can a community be expressed (formatted) within an IOS configuration?

Answer: A community can be expressed as a decimal number, a hexadecimal number, or as AA:NN, where AA is an autonomous system number and NN is a 16-bit number having some designated meaning within the AS.

11. What is a well-known community?

Answer: A well-known community is a community value that is reserved, always results in some well-understood policy action, and can be expressed by name instead of number. Examples of well-known communities in IOS are INTERNET, NO_EXPORT, NO_ADVERTISE, and LOCAL_AS.

12. What is the default action when a community is added to an identified route? Can this default be changed?

Answer: The default action when setting a community is to delete any other community attributes that route might have. This default action can be changed with the additive keyword, which adds the new community without deleting other attributes.

13. What is the difference between a standard community list and an expanded community list?

Answer: A standard community list, numbered 1–99 or named with the keyword standard specifies a single community per line. An expanded community list, numbered 100–500 or named with the keyword expanded can use regular expressions to specify a set of communities per line.

14. What is the difference between a standard community and an extended community attribute?

Answer: A standard community is a 32-bit attribute expressed either as a single decimal or hex number or in an AA:NN format. An extended community attribute is either 64 bits for IPv4 networks or 160 bits for IPv6 networks and has variable formats specified by a type field.

15. In route dampening, what is the half-life?

Answer: The half-life is a period of time used by route dampening, 15 minutes by default, over which the penalties accumulated by a route are decreased by one-half.

16. What is the IOS default penalty applied or a flap (a route going down or a route coming up):

Answer: The default RFD penalty in IOS is 1000.

17. Why is route flap dampening sometimes considered harmful in large, heavily meshed networks?

Answer: RFD can sometimes be harmful because a single flap event can cause many events further into the network, causing a route to accumulate enough penalties that the route is suppressed when it shouldn't be.

18. What is Outbound Route Filtering?

Answer: ORF is the capability for a router to inform a neighbor of its inbound policies so that the neighbor suppresses advertisement of routes that will be dropped on reception.

19. How does Next-Hop Tracking (NHT) help improve BGP convergence time?

Answer: NHT improves BGP convergence time by linking next hops within an AS to the much faster IGP. So when the IGP detects the loss of a next hop, BGP is immediately triggered instead of waiting for the BGP keepalive to declare the neighbor dead.

20. How does Fast External Fallover improve BGP convergence time?

Answer: Fast External Fallover informs BGP immediately of a detected link failure so that BGP does not have to wait for the 180-second hold timer to expire before declaring a neighbor unreachable.

21. What is Bidirectional Forwarding Detection (BFD), and how does it help improve BGP performance?

Answer: BFD is a lightweight, protocol-independent hello protocol that can detect link failures in time periods as low as 50 milliseconds. It can improve BGP responsiveness to link failures by quickly informing BGP of failures of links to neighbors.

22. What are the two BFD operational modes?

Answer: BFD can operate in Asynchronous mode or Demand mode. In Asynchronous mode BFD neighbors continuously exchange hellos. In Demand mode hellos are sent occasionally only to verify liveness.

23. What is the BFD Echo function?

Answer: The BFD Echo function allows one system to send a series of BFD hellos, and the neighboring system loops the packets back to the originator, leveraging fast hardware switching without impacting the looping system's CPU.

24. How does Prefix Independent Convergence (PIC) improve BGP performance?

Answer: PIC improves BGP performance by identifying a second-best path (if one exists) in the BGP table so that if the best path is lost, the second-best path can be immediately used without having to run the BGP Path Determination process. It thus speeds reconvergence after a path failure.

25. What is Graceful Restart?

Answer: Graceful Restart is a BGP capability by which a router that is about to be rebooted or about to switch to its standby route processor can inform its neighbors that it is going down but will come back up within a certain time.

26. What major dependency must be met for a router to run Graceful Restart?

Answer: A router must have dual Route Processors to support GR.

27. How can the Maximum Prefixes feature help stabilize and secure a BGP network?

Answer: The Maximum Prefixes feature can help stabilize and secure a BGP network by setting a limit on the number of prefixes a router accepts from a neighbor, based on the number of prefixes normally expected from the neighbor. If the limit is exceeded, either because of a neighbor's misconfiguration or because of a security or software problem, the session to the neighbor can be closed or a warning can be generated, protecting the BGP network from being flooded with presumably illegitimate routes.

28. What AS numbers are reserved for private use?

Answer: The AS numbers 64512 through 65535 are private-use AS numbers. Like RFC 1918 private IPv4 addresses, these AS numbers are not globally unique and must not appear in AS_PATH lists of routes advertised to the public Internet.

29. What two formats can 4-byte AS numbers be represented in?

Answer: 4-Byte AS numbers can be represented in ASPlain format, which is just a simple number in the range 65536–4294967295, or in ASDot format which is in the range 1.0–65535.65535.

30. What is a BGP confederation?

Answer: A BGP confederation is a large AS that has been subdivided into a group of smaller autonomous systems for easier manageability.

31. In what ways are Confederation EBGP rules different from regular EBGP rules?

Answer: Confederation EBGP rulers modify regular EBGP rules in the following ways:

- The NEXT_HOP attribute of routes external to the confederation is preserved throughout the confederation.
- MULTI_EXIT_DISC attributes of routes advertised into a confederation are preserved throughout the confederation.
- LOCAL_PREF attributes of routes are preserved throughout the entire confederation, not just within the member AS in which they are assigned.
- The AS numbers of the member autonomous systems are added to the AS_PATH within the confederation but are not advertised outside of the confederation. By default, the member AS numbers are listed in the AS_PATH as AS_PATH attribute type 4, AS_CONFED_SEQUENCE. If the aggregate-address command is used within the confederation, the as-set keyword causes member AS numbers behind the aggregation point to be listed as AS_PATH attribute type 3, AS_CONFED_SET.
- The confederation AS numbers in an AS_PATH are used for loop avoidance but are not considered when choosing a shortest AS_PATH within the confederation.

32. What is the purpose of bgp deterministic med?

Answer: The **bgp deterministic med** statement tells the BGP process to compare MEDs when choosing paths to confederation-interior destinations.

33. What is a route reflector? What is a route reflection client? What is a route reflection cluster?

Answer: A route reflector is similar to a route server; it permits IBGP routers to peer with it rather than with each other. Routes from one peer are advertised, or reflected, to the other peers. As a result, the number of peering sessions is reduced from what would be required if the IBGP peers were fully meshed.

Route reflectors differ from route servers; the route reflector is also a router. A route reflection client is an IBGP router that has peered with a route reflector. A route reflection cluster is a route reflector and its clients. A cluster can have more than one route reflector, but all the clients in the cluster must be peered with all the route reflectors in the cluster.

34. What is the Cluster ID?

Answer: The Cluster ID is a 32-bit identifier used to differentiate one route reflection cluster from another. When there is a single RR within the cluster, the RID of the RR is automatically used as the Cluster ID. If multiple RRs exist within the same cluster, a configured cluster is required.

35. What is the purpose of the ORIGINATOR_ID and the CLUSTER_LIST path attributes?

Answer: The ORIGINATOR_ID and CLUSTER_LIST attributes prevent routing loops when route reflectors are used. ORIGINATOR_ID is the RID of a route originator advertising via IBGP to a RR and prevents loops within the cluster. CLUSTER_LIST is a list of Cluster IDs used similarly to the AS_PATH to prevent loops between different RR clusters.

36. Can route reflectors be used within confederations?

Answer: Yes, route reflectors can be used within confederations. Combining the two scaling methodologies can scale BGP to large networks.

Chapter 6

1. What attributes enable multiprotocol extensions for BGP?

Answer: Multiprotocol Reachable NLRI and Multiprotocol Unreachable NLRI.

2. What are the Address Family Identifier and Subsequent Address Family Identifier?

Answer: AFI identifies the protocol to which the NLRI in the Multiprotocol Reachable and Multiprotocol Unreachable NLRI attributes belong, such as IPv4 or IPv6. The SAFI identifies a functional address type within that protocol, such as unicast or multicast.

3. BGP assumes that the neighbor's address used for peering is a globally routable address. IPv6 is designed to use link-local addresses for directly connected neighbors. How does MBGP reconcile this conflict when peering two IPv6 neighbors?

Answer: If the peer to which an IPv6 route is advertised is connected to the same subnet to which the route's global next-hop address belongs, the link-local address of the advertising interface is included in the Next Hop Address field of the MP_REACH_NLRI. The Next Hop Address Length field indicates 32 bytes (two 128 bit IPv6 addresses). In all other cases, only the global next-hop address is included in the Next Hop Address field, and the Next Hop Address Length field indicates 16 bytes (a single 128-bit address).

4. What does the **ipv6 unicast-routing** statement do?

   Answer: The **ipv6 unicast-routing** statement enables IPv6 unicast routing globally on the router.

5. How are address families differentiated in MBGP configurations?

   Answer: Address families are differentiated by **address-family** configurations. So, for example, **address-family ipv6** designates all statements having to do with IPv6 unicast prefixes advertised and received.

6. What does the **neighbor activate** statement mean under an address-family configuration?

   Answer: The **neighbor activate** statement under the address-family configuration makes the specified neighbor active for advertising prefixes belonging to the relevant address family and advertises the address-family capability to the neighbor. It does not influence the peering session.

7. Where are session parameters for a neighbor specified in an MBGP configuration? Where are policies applied to neighbors in an MBGP configuration?

   Answer: Session parameters are specified for neighbors under the main body of the BGP configuration, outside of the address family sections. Policies are applied to neighbors within the individual address family sections.

8. Can both IPv4 and IPv6 prefixes be advertised over a single IPv4 or IPv6 TCP session? Or is an IPv4 TCP session required for IPv4 prefixes and an IPv6 TCP session for IPv6 prefixes?

   Answer: Both address versions can be advertised over a single IPv4 or IPv6 session. However, often extra policy steps are required to make that work. Usual practice is to configure separate TCP sessions to the same neighbor, an IPv4 session for IPv4 routes and an IPv6 session for IPv6 routes.

9. What does the **bgp upgrade-cli** command do? Where is it used? When this command is invoked, does it disrupt any BGP sessions?

   Answer: The **bgp upgrade-cli** command causes a change of the default IPv4 BGP configuration to the address-family format. It is issued within the BGP configuration mode, but it is a transient command; a copy of it is not entered into the configuration. And because it changes only the appearance of the configuration, not any functional aspect of the configuration, it does not disrupt BGP sessions.

Chapter 7

1. Give several reasons why replicated unicast is not a practical substitution for true multicast in a large network.

   Answer: unicast places a processing burden on the source and can cause severe bottlenecks at the source interface, data link, and connected router. The source must also hold state to remember what addresses to send the replicated packets, and there must be some potentially complex mechanism for members to signal joins and leaves to the source. Finally, replicated unicast can cause queuing problems and unacceptable latency between packets.

2. What range of addresses is reserved for IP multicast?

Answer: The Class D addresses, in which the first 4 bits are 1110. This address range is 224.0.0.0 through 239.255.255.255.

3. How many subnets can be created from a single class D prefix?

Answer: No subnets are created from a Class D prefix. IP multicast uses only single addresses, not subnets.

4. In what way do routers treat packets with destination addresses in the range 224.0.0.1–224.0.0.255 differently than other multicast addresses?

Answer: Routers do not forward packets with destination addresses in the range 224.0.0.1 through 224.0.0.255.

5. Write the Ethernet MAC addresses that correspond to the following IP addresses:

(a) 239.187.3.201

(b) 224.18.50.1

(c) 224.0.1.87

Answer:

(a) 0100.5E3B.03C9

(b) 0100.5E12.3201

(c) 0100.5E00.0157

6. What multicast IP address or addresses are represented by the MAC address 0100.5E06.2D54?

Answer: The MAC address 0100.5E06.2D54 can represent any of 32 IP addresses, in which the first octet is one of 15 numbers in the range 224–239, the second octet is either 134 or 6, the third octet is always 45, and the last octet is always 84.

7. Why is Token Ring a poor medium for delivering multicast packets?

Answer: Token Ring is a poor medium for delivery of IP multicast packets because of the Token Ring frame's little endian format, which prevents an easy encoding of the multicast IP address into the MAC address. Instead, either a reserved functional MAC address or a broadcast MAC address must be used, either of which can sharply reduce efficiency on the data link.

8. What is join latency?

Answer: Join latency is the time between when a host first signals it wants to join a group and the time the host begins receiving group traffic.

9. What is leave latency?

   Answer: Leave latency is the time between when a host first leaves a group and the time the host is removed from the group.

10. What is a multicast DR (or Querier)?

   Answer: A multicast Querier is the router on a subnet responsible for querying the attached hosts for group membership.

11. What device sends IGMP Query messages?

   Answer: IGMP Query messages are sent by routers. If more than one router is attached to the subnet, the router with the lowest IP address is the Querier.

12. What device sends IGMP Membership Report messages?

   Answer: Hosts send IGMP Membership Report messages.

13. How is an IGMP Membership Report message used?

   Answer: An IGMP Membership Report is sent by a host to inform the local router that it wants to join a group.

14. What is the functional difference between a General IGMP Query and a Group-Specific IGMP Query?

   Answer: A router sends a General IGMP Query to discover members of any and all groups. A Group-Specific IGMP Query is sent to discover a query for members of a specific group, usually after the reception of a Leave Group message.

15. Is IGMPv2 compatible with IGMPv1?

   Answer: IGMPv2 is mostly compatible with IGMPv1; although, if there is an IGMPv1 router on a subnet, all routers should be set to IGMPv1.

16. What IP protocol number signifies IGMP?

   Answer: IGMP uses protocol number 2.

17. What is the purpose of the Cisco Group Membership Protocol (CGMP)?

   Answer: CGMP is a protocol by which Ethernet switches can discover what ports group members are connected to and thereby avoid having to forward IP multicast frames out all ports.

18. What is the advantage of using IGMP Snooping instead of CGMP? What is the possible disadvantage?

   Answer: Unlike CGMP, IGMP Snooping is not proprietary and therefore may be preferable in a mixed-vendor environment. Its potential disadvantage is that if IGMP Snooping is supported on a switch only in software, it can be performance affecting.

19. What devices send CGMP messages: Routers, Ethernet switches, or both?

Answer: Only routers send CGMP messages. Switches listen for CGMP messages.

20. What is Reverse Path Forwarding?

Answer: RPF is the basic forwarding mechanism of IP multicast routing. Because the routers find shortest paths to the source rather than the destination, when multicast packets are forwarded toward the destination (or more accurately, away from the source) they are forwarded in the reverse direction along the shortest path.

21. How many hosts constitute a dense topology, and how many hosts constitute a sparse topology?

Answer: There is no set number differentiating sparse and dense topologies.

22. What is the primary advantage of explicit joins over implicit joins?

Answer: The primary advantage of explicit joins over implicit joins is that routers do not have to hold state for interfaces that are not upstream from any group members.

23. What is the primary structural difference between a source-based multicast tree and a shared multicast tree?

Answer: A source-based tree is rooted at the source subnet or source router, whereas a shared tree is rooted at some common rendezvous point or core and can be, by definition, shared by multiple sources.

24. What is multicast scoping?

Answer: Multicast scoping is the practice of limiting the range of certain multicast packets to a determined topological area.

25. What are the two methods for IP multicast scoping?

Answer: The two methods of IP multicast scoping are TTL scoping and administrative scoping.

26. From the perspective of a multicast router, what is meant by "upstream" and "downstream?"

Answer: "Upstream" is the direction toward a multicast source, and "downstream" is the direction away from the source.

27. What is an RPF check?

Answer: An RPF check is a verification that a multicast packet from a particular source has arrived on the upstream interface closest to that source and no other interface.

28. What is a prune? What is a graft?

Answer: A prune is the action of removing a router from a multicast tree. A graft is the action of adding a router to a multicast tree.

29. What multicast group addresses are reserved for SSM?

Answer: IPv4 group addresses belonging to 232.0.0.0/8 and IPv6 group addresses belonging to FF3x::/96 are reserved for SSM.

Chapter 8

1. What is a PIM prune override?

Answer: A prune override is a Join message sent to an upstream router on a multiaccess network to cancel a prune requested by another router on the same network.

2. What is a PIM forwarder? How is a forwarder selected?

Answer: When there are multiple upstream routers connected to the same multiaccess network and receiving packets for the same group, the PIM forwarder is the router that forwards the packets onto the network. The forwarder is elected by the lowest administrative distance advertised in an Assert message. If the administrative distances are equal, the lowest route metric is used. If the metrics are the same, the lowest IP address is the tie-breaker.

3. What criteria does PIM use to select a DR?

Answer: The PIM router with the highest IP address (according to the PIM Hello messages) is the DR.

4. What is a PIM SPT? What is a PIM RPT?

Answer: A Shortest Path Tree is a source-based tree, and a Rendezvous Point Tree is a shared tree rooted at a rendezvous point.

5. What two mechanisms are available for Cisco routers to automatically discover PIM-SM RPs?

Answer: PIM-SM RPs can be automatically discovered using either Auto-RP or the Bootstrap protocol.

6. Of the mechanisms in Question 43, which should be used in multivendor router topologies?

Answer: Auto-RP may not be supported by other vendors, so Bootstrap protocol should be used.

7. What is a C-RP?

Answer: A C-RP is a Candidate RP, or a router that is eligible to become an RP for either all groups or a specified set of groups.

8. What is a BSR?

Answer: When the Bootstrap protocol is used, a Bootstrap Router advertises C-RPs throughout the PIM-SM domain in an RP-Set.

9. What is an RP mapping agent?

Answer: When Auto-RP is used, an RP mapping agent advertises group-to-RP mappings.

10. What is the difference between a (S,G) **mroute** entry and a (*,G) **mroute** entry?

Answer: A (S,G) entry refers to an SPT, whereas a (*,G) entry refers to an RPT.

11. What is PIM-SM source registration?

Answer: Source registration is a mechanism whereby a router forwards packets from a multicast source to an RP in unicast PIM Register Messages. If there is significant traffic from the source, the RP builds an SPT and then sends a Register Stop.

12. When does a Cisco router switch from a PIM-SM RPT to an SPT?

Answer: Cisco routers switch from an RPT to an SPT immediately after receiving the first packet for a particular (S,G) on the RPT, or when the arrival rate of the packets for the (S,G) exceed a threshold specified with the command **ip pim spt-threshold.**

13. What is PIM sparse-dense mode?

Answer: PIM sparse-dense mode tells an interface to use sparse mode if an RP is known and dense mode if an RP is not known.

Chapter 9

1. In the section "Multicast Scoping," a sample configuration is given for administrative scoping. The boundary at interface E0 blocks organization-local packets (destination addresses whose prefixes match 239.192.0.0/14) but passes packets with global scope. Will a packet with a group address 224.0.0.50 pass this boundary?

Answer: Packets with a destination address of 224.0.0.50 pass this boundary only if the local router originates them. Although 224.0.0.50 is permitted by access list 10, it is in the link-local range and is not forwarded by any next-hop router.

2. How does Cisco IOS Software handle DVMRP Prune messages on point-to-point and multiaccess interfaces that are configured to run PIM?

Answer: DVMRP Prunes are ignored on multiaccess interfaces and are processed normally on point-to-point interfaces.

3. What is a PIM (*,*,RP) entry?

Answer: A (*,*,RP) entry is a PIM Multicast Border Router. MBRs are not supported by Cisco IOS Software.

4. How does Multiprotocol BGP (MBGP) differ from normal BGP?

Answer: MBGP is extended with two route attributes: MP_REACH_NLRI and MP_UNREACH_NLRI.

5. What is the MBGP AFI?

Answer: The AFI is the Address Family Identifier. When MBGP is used for multicasting, the AFI is always set to 1 (for IPv4) or 2 (for IPv6), and the sub-AFI indicates whether the related NLRI is to be used for multicast, unicast, or both.

6. Is the following statement true or false? MSDP carries information about multicast sources and group members between RPs in different PIM domains.

Answer: False. MSDP communicates information only about multicast sources, not group members, and can carry that information both within the same PIM domain or between different PIM domains.

7. What is the transport protocol for MSDP?

Answer: MSDP uses TCP port 639.

8. What is an MSDP SA message?

Answer: An SA is a Source Active message. When a source's DR registers with an RP, if the RP runs MSDP, it advertises the (S,G) pair to its peers in SA messages.

9. How does an MSDP RP determine whether an SA were received on an RPF interface?

Answer: It checks the BGP next-hop database (MBGP first and then unicast BGP) for the correct upstream interface.

10. What is SA caching?

Answer: SA caching is the storage of (S,G) state information learned from SA messages. SA caching trades some memory in the router for reduced join latency.

11. Is there an alternative to reducing join latency without SA caching?

Answer: Yes. If an MSDP peer is caching, you can configure an RP to use SA Request messages to request (S,G) information from the peer as soon as a join is received.

Chapter 10

1. What is the difference between an inside address and an outside address?

Answer: Inside and outside are defined relative to the NAT. Typically, although not always, the inside is a bounded local network domain whereas the outside is the rest of the world. But inside and outside could also be two private domains, defined only by the NAT configuration. Inside and outside addresses are the addresses of devices on the defined inside or outside of the NAT.

2. What is the difference between a local address and a global address?

Answer: Local addresses are addresses Known to the inside domain, as defined by the NAT. They may be Inside Local (IL), which are the addresses of inside devices unknown to the outside, or Outside Local (OL), which are the addresses by which outside devices are known to inside devices. Global addresses are addresses known by the outside, again as defined by the NAT. They may be Outside Global (OG), which are the addresses of outside devices unknown to the inside, or Inside Global (IG), which are the addresses by which outside devices are known to the inside.

3. What is an address translation table?

Answer: An address translation table keeps track of the mappings between IG, IL, OL, and OG addresses.

4. What is the difference between static and dynamic translation?

Answer: Static translation is a manual configuration of the address mappings in the address translation table. Dynamic translation provides temporary mappings of addresses to a range or pool of addresses.

5. What is the IOS default translation timeout period?

Answer: The translation timeout period is the period a dynamic mapping remains in the translation table. The default period is 86400 seconds (24 hours).

6. What is Port Address Translation, or PAT?

Answer: Also known as address overloading or NAPT, PAT maps not only IPv4 addresses but also the ports. The advantage is that many inside addresses can be mapped to a much smaller pool of outside addresses—including a single outside address.

Chapter 11

1. What is SIIT?

Answer: SIIT (Stateless IP/ICMP Translation) is an algorithm for translating between IPv4 and IPv6 packet headers.

2. What are some examples of header fields than cannot be translated between IPv4 and IPv6?

Answer: IPv4 Header Checksum, Options and Padding, and IPv6 Flow Label Fields have no corresponding fields in the opposite version. IPv4 Identification, Flags, and Fragment Offset fields do not have counterparts in the default IPv6 header; although, they are supported in the IPv6 Fragmentation Extension Header.

3. How does SIIT handle an ICMP message that has no corresponding message in ICMPv6?

Answer: When SIIT cannot translate an ICMP message to a matching or similar ICMPv6 message, the message is silently dropped.

4. What is the difference between NAT44 and NAT-PT?

   Answer: NAT44 translates between different IPv4 addresses. NAT-PT translates between IPv4 and IPv6. The "PT" part stands for Protocol Translation.

5. What is the major difference between NAT-PT and NAT64 (either stateful or stateless)?

   Answer: NAT-PT usually includes a DNS Application Layer Gateway (ALG), whereas NAT64 does not.

6. If IPv4 address conservation is important, would you choose stateless or stateful NAT64?

   Answer: Stateful NAT64 is better for IPv4 address conservation because it supports dynamic port mapping. Stateless NAT64 supports only one-to-one address mapping, so does not conserve IPv4 addresses.

7. What is an IPv4-embedded IPv6 address?

   Answer: An IPv4-enbedded IPv6 address used by stateless NAT64 is an IPv6 address with a specially reserved IPv6 prefix and an embedded IPv4 address.

Index

Symbols

A

B

I

J

M

N

O

P

T

CISCO

Connect, Engage, Collaborate

The Award Winning Cisco Support Community

Attend and Participate in Events

Ask the Experts
Live Webcasts

Knowledge Sharing

Documents
Blogs
Videos

Top Contributor Programs

Cisco Designated VIP
Hall of Fame
Spotlight Awards

Multi-Language Support

https://supportforums.cisco.com